Art Song in the United States, 1759–1999

An Annotated Bibliography
Third Edition

Judith E. Carman
William K. Gaeddert
Rita M. Resch
with Gordon Myers

Third Edition edited by Judith E. Carman

The Scarecrow Press, Inc.
Lanham, Maryland, and London
2001

SCARECROW PRESS, INC.

Published in the United States of America
by Scarecrow Press, Inc.
4720 Boston Way, Lanham, Maryland 20706
www.scarecrowpress.com

4 Pleydell Gardens, Folkestone
Kent CT20 2DN, England

Copyright © 2001 by Judith E. Carman, William K. Gaeddert, Rita M. Resch, and Gordon Myers
First edition (1976), Supplement (1978), and Second Edition (1987) all published by the National Association of Teachers of Singing.

British Library Cataloguing-in-Publication Information Available

Library of Congress Cataloging-in-Publication Data

Carman, Judith E.
    Art song in the United States, 1759–1999 : an annotated bibliography / Judith E. Carman, William K. Gaeddert, Rita M. Resch ; with Gordon
    Myers. — 3rd ed./ edited by Judith E. Carman.
      p. cm.
    Rev. ed. of: Art-song in the United States, 1801–1987. 2nd ed. 1987.
    Includes a special section, Art song in the United States, 1759–1810, by Gordon Myers.
    Includes discography, bibliographical references, and index.
    ISBN: 0-8108-4137-1 (alk. paper)
    1. Songs—United States—Bibliography. 2. Songs—United States—Indexes. I. Gaeddert, William K. II. Resch, Rita M. III. Carman, Judith E.
Art-song in the United States, 1801–1987. IV. Myers, Gordon. Art-song in the United States, 1759–1810. V. Title.

ML128.S3 C37 2001
016. 78242168'0973—dc21   2001042636

To all students of American song. . .

and to Pangur,
the scholar's companion

CONTENTS

FOREWORD

For countless teachers and singers, students and, yes, professionals, here is a guide to a wide repertory of American song. There is little problem in finding one's way to the vast established European repertory our musical culture and study have made essential, but knowledge of American song literature has been relatively rare. With the third edition of *Art Song in the United States, 1759–1999: An Annotated Bibliography*, singers and teachers will find a canny guide to excellent repertory, acquainting the reader with composers, publishers, specific works, their subject matter, particular musical and vocal demands, and even programming suggestions. Having become acquainted with this splendid resource, the reader and user will be well equipped to search out American works and sing from this wonderful body of music, past and present.

Phyllis Curtin
Great Barrington, Mass.
September 2000

PREFACE

In 1976 the National Association of Teachers of Singing was to hold its national convention in Philadelphia in honor of the nation's Bicentennial year. In 1975 Gean Greenwell, then the national president, proposed that a compilation of art songs by American composers be included as a part of the convention program materials. Accordingly, he asked me in September of that year to take on this task. A "Committee on American Song" was formed, including William K. Gaeddert, Rita M. Resch, Gordon Myers, and myself. What was to have been "a list of about 300 songs" grew into an annotated bibliography of 1,439 entries, several appendixes, and subject-poet, composer, and title indexes. *Art-Song in the United States: An Annotated Bibliography* turned out to be the first compilation of its kind on the subject of American art song. In his foreword to the first edition, the new president of NATS, Bruce Lunkley, made the following statement: "This publication is intended to assist teachers and students in the selection and performance of American song so that recitals and programs in our country will contain a better balance of repertoire produced by the composers whose heritage and musical roots are shared by today's performers." It was a clear statement of the purpose of our work, and that purpose remains the same for this edition.

The original research investigated various private collections of American art song, inventories of music stores, holdings of several university libraries, the American art song collection of the Library of Congress, various books that included chapters on American art song, and much music supplied directly by music publishers. In the following years, the authors collected new publications of American art song and brought out a first supplement in 1978, and a second edition (William K. Gaeddert, editor) in 1987. Since that time the bibliography has served as a primary source for other researchers and writers on the subject. The idea of a teaching tool for studio voice teachers, therefore, has taken on a second life as a research tool for various facets of American art song, including, in this edition, both current and historical discography.

Any annotated bibliography of a large subject area must, of course, be selective. Most of the original limitations for inclusion of a work remain in effect: (1) composed art songs by American composers for one solo voice; (2) piano accompaniment only; (3) English text or singable English version of a foreign language text (exceptions are included in the foreign-language appendix); and (4) published and currently or at one time available for sale through normal retail music outlets, including numerous small presses.

The first item for consideration is the question of just who is American. Given the large number of immigrant musicians who have contributed to the richness of our musical culture, we made the decision to include as American not only native-born composers, but also those composers who immigrated to this country before age thirty-three, and who subsequently either became American citizens, or who participated so completely in our musical culture as to have been adopted as Americans. The limitation of "composed art song" eliminates folk song settings, concert and operatic arias, and most songs composed for occasional use, such as church solos. There are, however, numerous Psalm settings and a few songs with religious texts that seem particularly suitable for recital use. In cases where the work may have been composed for chamber ensemble or orchestral accompaniment, but is published in a usable piano reduction, it seems natural to include the work.

There are many songs listed that have long been out of print. We have included these songs because of their musical or historical value in order to present as complete a view of our American song heritage as possible. Many of these songs can still be found in libraries or in private collections. Beyond these basic limitations, space alone serves as a limitation to what can be included. To this end, the authors have included as many works of major composers as possible and have selected, according to their best judgment, individual works by dozens of other composers that would seem to be effective for teaching and performance. In some cases, songs have been deleted if it seems unlikely that they would be used by today's student, due to dated texts or various musical considerations.

The number of classical solo vocal compositions by American composers published or reprinted since 1986 is quite large and expands the number of entries considerably. In addition, the number of anthologies and single composer collections has increased by more than two-thirds. New features of the third edition include a discography; the title index now containing both entry numbers and a discography indication (where applicable); an appendix listing selected songs by American composers to foreign language texts; a composer index; a chronological list of composers; and a revised and restructured special characteristics index, including songs especially suitable for elementary school audiences. The special section, *Art Song in the United States:1759–1810* by Gordon Myers, remains a separate section for ease in finding songs from the eighteenth and early-nineteenth centuries.

The authors hope that this revised and enlarged third edition of *Art Song in the United States 1759–1999: An Annotated Bibliography* will stimulate every facet of American art song: composition, publishing, purchasing, teaching, and performance, and that we as singers and teachers will increasingly turn to our own American heritage for a larger part of our repertoire.

Judith E. Carman, editor

ACKNOWLEDGMENTS

Since this third edition of *Art Song in the United States 1759–1999: An Annotated Bibliography* is the first printing to be widely available to teachers of singing, researchers in American music, and performers of American song, the authors wish to acknowledge those individuals and institutions that were instrumental in the original research for the first and second editions of the book. Four past presidents of the National Association of Teachers of Singing have actively supported our work. Gean Greenwell, Bruce Lunkley, and Edward Baird made possible the publication of the first two editions. The fourth, Jean Westerman Gregg, requested that we undertake a third edition and provided support in finding a publisher. We are grateful for the sponsorship of the National Association of Teachers of Singing in the first and second editions. It was this initial support and encouragement that gave incentive to our research.

The gathering together of a large amount of information into a single source always rests on the previous work and knowledge of other people who have already distinguished quality work from a large amount of material. Our major source for the period 1880–1930 was the extensive song collection and the personal knowledge of Professor Louis Nicholas of Peabody College, Nashville, Tennessee. A champion of American song as both performer and teacher, and a singer to whom several composers dedicated songs, Prof. Nicholas graciously made his song collection available for research. We were also fortunate to have access to the large personal song collections of Professor Gean Greenwell and Pauline Greenwell (Michigan State University, East Lansing), Professor Herald I. Stark (University of Iowa), Professor Conan Castle and Professor Ralph Hart (Central Missouri State University, Warrensburg).

In addition to personal song collections, we had access to and were helped by the staffs of the following libraries: Library of Congress, Music Division (for eighteenth- and early nineteenth-century literature); Benton Music Library of the University of Iowa; Thomas Gorton Music Library of the University of Kansas; Ward Edwards Library (now James C. Kirkpatrick Library) of Central Missouri State University; Peabody College Music Library (now Vanderbilt University) in Nashville, Tennessee; and Baker University Music Department Library. A major source for all three editions, both of music and of assistance by a gracious staff, has been Luyben Music of Kansas City, Missouri.

Many publishers have supplied review copies of countless songs for all three editions, as well as biographical information about the composers whose music they publish. Our chief supporter in this respect for the third edition has been Glendower Jones of Classical Vocal Reprints. He has provided review copies of his entire catalog of American song and, equally as important, his interest, encouragement, knowledge of the music publishing industry, and his time to review our publishers' list for accuracy and current addresses. We cannot thank him enough for his help. We also wish to thank the following publishers for providing us with biographical information about the composers they publish: Boosey & Hawkes, Boston Music Company, Carl Fischer Music, ECS Publishing, Hildegard Publishing, Leyerle Publishing, C. F. Peters Corporation, Theodore Presser Company, and Recital Publications. Organizations that were also helpful in this respect were the American Music Center and ASCAP. Publishers who furnished review copies of music for annotation for this edition are the following: Arsis Press, Boosey & Hawkes, Carl Fischer Music, C. F. Peters Corporation, Classical Vocal Reprints, E. C. Schirmer Music (ECS Publishing), Filpat Publishing, G. Schirmer, Glouchester Press (Heilman Music), Hal Leonard Corporation, Hildegard Publishing, Howlet Press~Music, Leyerle Publishing, Oxford University Press, Recital Publications, Sisra Publications, Southern Music Company (San Antonio), (Peer)Southern

Music Publishing Co., Theodore Presser Company, Voice of the Rockies, and The Willis Music Company.

Our thanks also to Carol Kimball (Profssor of Music, University of Las Vegas, Nevada) and Judith Nicosia (Associate Professor of Music, Rutgers University, New Brunswick, New Jersey) for assistance in finding music we needed, and to Ruth Doyle (Professor of Modern Languages, Central Missouri State University) and Christian Girardet (Houston Grand Opera Chorus) for providing translations of French and Spanish texts. Special thanks is due Barbara Gaeddert, Librarian *extraordinaire* (Music and Science/Technology Cataloger, University of Kansas Libraries, retired), for her continued research support and gracious hospitality beginning with the original work in 1976.

To Kathleen Fisher Hardin we owe a large debt of gratitude for her selfless service in formatting this edition of the bibliography. An accomplished singer herself, her interest and expertise has been invaluable.

And finally, we wish to thank Phyllis Curtin, American soprano, teacher of singing, distinguished interpreter and lifelong champion of American song, for her positive and enthusiastic foreword.

INTRODUCTION

The main body of the bibliography is arranged alphabetically on two levels: (1) by composer, and (2) by title under the specific composer. Sets and cycles are listed alphabetically by the collective title of the group, and the individual songs in each group are listed in the order indicated by the composer or publisher. Each title entry has a number and each individual song of a set or cycle has a letter that indicates it is a subdivision of the main entry. For each composer entry, birth and death place and date are given where known and applicable. All composers included have been accepted as American, even where complete information is not known.

The annotations consist of the following information:

TITLE
POET (a question mark (?) following poet's name indicates probable authorship)
PUBLICATION DATA (publisher and copyright date, or anthology/collection
    number [#])
DATE OF COMPOSITION, if known (as distinct from copyright date)
DEDICATION, if to a specific singer (or other person of particular interest)
KEY (tonality, or lack of tonality)
RANGE of vocal line
TESSITURA of vocal line
METER SIGNATURE
TEMPO INDICATION (as given by the composer)
LENGTH in minutes, pages, or measures
DIFFICULTY LEVELS for
    (1) Vocal line
    (2) Piano score
VOICE TYPE(s) suitable for performance (most suitable type listed first)
MOOD (and/or subject) of the song
VOCAL LINE (description and character)
PIANO SCORE (description and character)
SPECIAL DIFFICULTIES, if any
USES often includes suggestions for teaching and programming and/or an
    evaluation of quality
RECORDING, if commercially recorded

In general, each song has a complete set of annotations. There are, however, some variations on the format. For example, song cycles carry a complete annotation for the work as a whole, and partial annotations appear for the individual songs following their title entries, which are designated by a *lower case* letter. Information given here usually includes tonality, range, tessitura, meter and tempo indications, and length. The same is true for sets of songs intended to be sung together. Those sets listed under a collective title that is merely a publisher's set, or that are listed as a complete opus number, generally have complete annotations for each individual song title, which carries an *upper case* letter. Only the publication data and the poet, if the same for all songs in the set, are given in the main title entry.

Following this explanation is a sample bibliographic entry with explanatory material in the entry format and two actual entries for comparison. There are, of course, four different styles of verbal description, corresponding to the four different approaches of the individual annotators. The final general style is intended to be as clear and readable as possible. Standard abbreviations have been used for certain items or words that recur regularly throughout the bibliography. (For these special terms see the *List of Abbreviations*.) The information is generally given in short phrases, single words when possible, separated by semicolons. Following the sample entries is the *Key to Song Anthologies and Collections*, the numbers of which correspond to the collection numbers given in brackets [ ] in the actual entries. Collection numbers in the special section, *Art Song in the United States: 1759–1810*, by Gordon Myers, are preceded by the letters **MC**, entry numbers by the letter **M.** Entry numbers in the foreign-language appendix are preceded by the letter **A**.

In order to facilitate finding songs for specific singers and specific occasions, the bibliography is indexed by *Composer* (by page number), *Poet* (by entry number), *Special Characteristics* (by entry number), and *Title* (by entry number). Preceding these indexes, there is an *Appendix* containing songs with foreign language texts, the *Special Section:Art Song in the United States:1759–1810,* a *Discography*, a *Chronological List of Composers*, *Publishers Represented*, and *References*.

LIST OF ABBREVIATIONS

accomp.	=	accompani(ment)(ed)
anon.	=	anonymous
aug.	=	augmented
©	=	copyright
ca.	=	circa
cf.	=	compare to
cmp	=	composed
comp.	=	compiled
cresc.	=	crescendo
decresc.	=	decrescendo
Diff	=	difficulty
V	=	voice (V/d)
P	=	piano (P/d)
dim.	=	diminished
ed.	=	edition/editor
esp.	=	especially
8ve(s)	=	octave(s)
incl.	=	including
m	=	minor interval
M	=	Major interval
maj	=	major key
meas.	=	measure
min	=	minor key
MS	=	reproduced composer's manuscript
opt.	=	optional
orig.	=	original/originally
pub.	=	published/publisher
recit.	=	recitative
rev.	=	revised/ revisor
sig.(s)	=	signature(s)
Tess	=	tessitura
trans.	=	translated/translator
X	=	not clearly in a key or mode
[ ]	=	collection no. indication (Key to Collections, p. xix)
▲	=	CD recording
◆	=	Recording(s)

Tessitura & Key Indications:

HH	=	very high
H	=	high
mH	=	moderately high
M	=	medium
mL	=	moderately low
L	=	low
LL	=	very low

Difficulty Level Indications:

ee	=	very easy
e	=	easy
me	=	moderately easy
m	=	medium
md	=	moderately difficult
d	=	difficult
dd	=	very difficult

Octave Placement Indications:

C–B	=	(great octave, bass clef)
c–b	=	(small octave, bass clef)
c'–b'	=	(first octave, treble clef)
c"–b"	=	(second octave, treble clef)
c'''–b'''	=	(third octave, treble clef)

NOTE: c' is middle c

SAMPLE ENTRY

COMPOSER
(Birth place and date; death place and date)

1. **TITLE (Poet). Publisher, Copyright Date, Reprints**
    (if any), or **[ ]** [Collection # (see *Key to Song Anthologies
    and Collections*, p. xix)]; **Composition Date**, where
    known. **Dedication**, if to a well-known singer. **Tonality**
    [specific key, tonal center, X, or a general description
    if a cycle or set; Cmaj-Cmin, for example, indicates
    that the song begins in one key and ends in another;
    songs published in more than one key are listed in order
    from the highest to the lowest]; **Range** of voice part
    [ex.: c'–f ", b–a", or B–f '; optional notes given in
    parentheses; if song is listed as published in more than
    one key, range of each key is given, from highest to
    lowest]; **Tessitura** [Tess-M-mH indicates medium to
    medium-high; Tess-M, L indicates that both medium
    and low tessituras occur in the song; Tess-cs indicates
    that the tessitura covers the staff; Tess-wide indicates
    that the tessitura covers more than an octave]; **Meter**
    [common time (C) has been indicated as 4/4, and "alla
    breve" as 2/2 to avoid confusion]; **Tempo** [initial tempo
    indication has been given as it appears in the score;
    metronome markings are usually provided when given;
    in some cases other tempo markings are given if
    important changes occur in the course of the song];
    Length is given in minutes (if provided in the score),
    pages, or measures; **Difficulty Level** [vocal line
    (V/md, for example) and piano score (P/md, for
    example) are indicated together (Diff-V/md, P/md);
    difficulty estimations necessarily reflect the judgment
    of the individual annotator].

For: most suitable voice type listed first, or general type
suitable for performance
Mood: general mood of song; subject often also given
Voice: description of the vocal line with reference to pitch,
rhythm, word-setting, and other pertinent information;
any special effects are also given here
Piano: general description of the piano score with reference to
texture [linear, chordal, or a combination]; rhythmic
structure; harmonic structure; patterns; special pedal,
dynamic, and articulation instructions; any special
difficulties; any doubling of the vocal line
Diff: the most difficult aspects of the song, or special
difficulties to be considered
Uses: specific uses for developing vocal technique, or for
programming, if any; often a general evaluation of the
song given here
Rec: Discography numbers [D#(s)] given here

    a. *Titles* and annotations of individual songs in set or
cycle given here

ACTUAL ENTRIES

ROREM, NED
(b. Richmond, IN, 1923)

1903. **SNAKE** (Theodore Roethke). [156]. cmp1959. "To
Alice Estey." Fmin; e'–f "; Tess-M; 4/4, Presto; 1+min;
Diff-V/m, P/d.
For: soprano; tenor
Mood: intense; sensuous; compelling; theme of regeneration
Voice: stepwise and chromatic; small skips; direction is snake-
like; some dotted notes; repetitive; 2–5-note slurs; two
longer melismas
Piano: rapid triplets in serpentine pattern, sometimes in both
hands; various registers; dynamic contrasts very
important; some doubling of vocal line with octave
displacement
Diff: needs very smooth legato lines; voice must glide;
ensemble difficult; easy for piano to cover voice in low
range
Uses: good song; can end group or recital
Rec: D#s 288, 289, 291

BASSETT, LESLIE
(b. Hanford, CA, 1923)

197. **TO MUSIC.** Three Songs for High Voice and Piano.
Cycle. Galaxy, 1966. Atonal; b–a"; Tess-M-mH; mostly
regular but changing meters with various divisions of
the beat; slow–moderate–fast; 8min (16pp); Diff-V/d,
P/d.
For: tenor; soprano
Mood: subject of cycle is the divine power of music; atonal
idiom gives sense of mysticism
Voice: sustained phrases; melismatic passages; difficult pitches
in atonal idiom; words hard to project; ensemble
problems
Piano: virtuoso solo techniques required; solo passages; many
accidentals
Diff: difficulties abound for any but the most advanced
students; perfect pitch helpful
Uses: interesting atonal group

    a. *Slow, Slow, Fresh Fount* (Ben Jonson). b–f♯';
Tess-M; 4/4, 9/8, 6/4, 2/4, Slow; 3pp.
    b. *To Music* (Robert Herrick). f♯–f "; Tess-M; 4/4,
5/4, 3/4, Moderately slow; 5pp.
    c. *Great Art Thou, O Music* (William Billings).
c♯'–a"; Tess-mH; 4/4, 3/4, Rather fast and with
strong pulse; 8pp.

KEY TO SONG ANTHOLOGIES AND COLLECTIONS

(Numbers given in brackets [ ] in entries correspond to this key)

ANTHOLOGIES

[1].   **AN ALBUM OF NEW SONGS BY AMERICAN COMPOSERS.** New York: Breitkopf & Härtel, 1898.

[2].   **ALL TIME FAVORITE ART SONGS FROM THE MODERN REPERTOIRE.** New York: G. Schirmer, Inc., 1984; distributed by Hal Leonard Corp.

[3].   **AMERICAN ARTSONG ANTHOLOGY,** Vol. 1: Contemporary American Songs for High Voice and Piano. Ed. by John Belisle. New York: Galaxy Music Corporation, 1982.

[4].   **AMERICAN ART SONGS:** A Collection of 20th Century Songs by American Composers from Charles Ives to Elliott Carter for Medium Voice & Piano. Comp. by Barry O'Neal. New York: Associated Music Publishers, Inc., 1980.

[5].   **AMERICAN ART SONGS OF THE TURN OF THE CENTURY.** Ed. by Paul Sperry. New York: Dover Publications, Inc., 1991.

[6].   **ANTHOLOGY OF ART SONGS BY BLACK AMERICAN COMPOSERS.** Comp. by Willis C. Patterson. New York: Edward B. Marks Music Corporation, 1977; distributed by Hal Leonard Corp.

[7].   **THE ART SONG:** Four Centuries of Select Vocal Repertoire. Comp. & ed. by Alice Howland & Poldi Zeitlin. *Music for Millions* Series, Vol. 25. New York: Consolidated Music Publishers, Inc., 1960.

[8].   **ART-SONG ARGOSY.** Comp. & ed. by William Breach. Medium high & Medium low voice eds. New York: G. Schirmer, Inc., 1937.

[9].   **THE ART SONG COLLECTION:** Winners of the 1995 Young Americans' Art Song Competition. Medium-high Voice and Piano. New York: G. Schirmer, Inc., 1996; distributed by Hal Leonard Corp.

[10]. **ART SONGS AND SPIRITUALS BY AFRICAN-AMERICAN WOMEN COMPOSERS.** Ed. by Vivian Taylor. Bryn Mawr, PA: Hildegard Publishing Co., 1995.

[11]. **ART SONGS BY AMERICAN WOMEN COMPOSERS.** Ed. by Ruth C. Friedberg. 11 vols. San Antonio, TX: Southern Music Co., 1994–1996.

Vol. 1: **FIVE SONGS ON FRENCH AND GERMAN TEXTS** by Mrs. H. H. A. Beach.
Vol. 2: **TWO SONGS** by Florence Price.
Vol. 3: **THREE SONGS FOR HIGH VOICE** by Edith Borroff.
Vol. 4: **TWO SONGS** by Emma Lou Diemer.
Vol. 5: **TWO SONGS FROM "MEN I HAVE KNOWN"** by Elizabeth Raum.
Vol. 6: **TWO SONGS FROM "LEOPARD FLOWERS"** by Deena Grossman.
Vol. 7: **THREE SONGS** by Mary Howe.
Vol. 8: **FOUR SONGS ON WALLACE STEVENS** by Claire Brook.
Vol. 9: **FOUR SONGS** by Ruth Schonthal.
Vol. 10: **TWO SONGS ON AMY LOWELL** by Flicka Rahn.
Vol. 11: **EARLY SONGS WITH TEXTS BY RAINER MARIA RILKE** by Ruth Schonthal.

[12]. **ART SONGS BY CONTEMPORARY TEXAS COMPOSERS.** San Antonio, TX: Southern Music Co., 1987.

[13]. **ART SONGS FOR SCHOOL AND STUDIO.** Ed. by Mabelle Glenn & Alfred Spouse. First Year & Second Year vols.; Medium high & Medium low voice eds. Boston: Oliver Ditson Company, 1930.

[14]. **BASICS OF SINGING.** 4th ed. Comp. & ed. by Jan Schmidt. New York: Schirmer Books, 1998.

[15]. **THE CLIPPINGER CLASS-METHOD OF VOICE CULTURE.** D. A. Clippinger. Boston: Oliver Ditson Company, 1932.

[16]. **CONTEMPORARY AMERICAN ART SONGS.** Comp. & ed. by Bernard Taylor. Bryn Mawr, PA: Oliver Ditson Company (Theodore Presser Co.), 1977.

[17]. **CONTEMPORARY AMERICAN SONGS.** Comp. & ed. by Bernard Taylor. High voice & Low voice eds. Evanston, IL: Summy-Birchard Publishing Company, 1960. Reprint, Bloomington, IN: Frangipani Press, n.d.

[18]. **CONTEMPORARY ART SONG ALBUM FOR HIGH VOICE.** Cleveland Composers Guild Series. New York: Galaxy Music Corp., 1969.

[19]. **CONTEMPORARY ART SONG ALBUM FOR**

MEDIUM VOICE. Cleveland Composers Guild Publication Series. New York: Galaxy Music Corp., 1972.

[20].   CONTEMPORARY ART SONGS: 28 Songs by American and British Composers. New York: G. Schirmer, Inc., 1970.

[21].   CONTEMPORARY SONGS IN ENGLISH: Songs by American and English Composers for Recital, Concert, and Studio Use. Ed. by Bernard Taylor. Medium high & Medium low voice eds. New York: Carl Fischer, Inc., 1956.

[22].   COS COB SONG VOLUME. Cos Cob Press, Inc., 1935; reissued under auspices of Arrow Music Press, Inc., New York, NY.

[23].   DEAR OLDE SONGS. Boston: Chapple Publishing Co., n.d.

[24].   15 AMERICAN ART SONGS. Comp. by Gary Arvin. High voice & Low voice eds. New York: G. Schirmer, Inc., 1993; distributed by Hal Leonard Corp.

[25].   FIFTY ART SONGS FROM THE MODERN REPERTOIRE. New York: G. Schirmer, Inc., 1939.

[26].   FIFTY SHAKSPERE [sic] SONGS. Ed. by Charles Vincent. *The Musicians Library* Series. High & Low voice eds. Boston: Oliver Ditson Co., 1906.

[27].   55 ART SONGS. Comp. & ed. by Sigmund Spaeth & Carl O. Thompson. Boston: C. C. Birchard & Company, 1943.

THE FIRST and SECOND BOOK[] OF SOPRANO, MEZZO-SOPRANO / ALTO, TENOR, and BARITONE / BASS SOLOS. Comp. by Joan Frey Boytim. New York: G. Schirmer, Inc., 1991–1994; distributed by Hal Leonard Corp.

[28].   THE FIRST BOOK OF SOPRANO SOLOS. 1991.

[29].   THE FIRST BOOK OF SOPRANO SOLOS: Part II. 1993.

[30].   THE SECOND BOOK OF SOPRANO SOLOS. 1994.

[31].   THE FIRST BOOK OF MEZZO-SOPRANO / ALTO SOLOS. 1991.

[32].   THE FIRST BOOK OF MEZZO-SOPRANO / ALTO SOLOS: Part II. 1993.

[33].   THE SECOND BOOK OF MEZZO-SOPRANO / ALTO SOLOS. 1994.

[34].   THE FIRST BOOK OF TENOR SOLOS. 1991.

[35].   THE FIRST BOOK OF TENOR SOLOS: Part II. 1993.

[36].   THE SECOND BOOK OF TENOR SOLOS. 1994.

[37].   THE FIRST BOOK OF BARITONE / BASS SOLOS. 1991.

[38].   THE FIRST BOOK OF BARITONE / BASS SOLOS: Part II. 1993.

[39].   THE SECOND BOOK OF BARITONE / BASS SOLOS. 1994.

[40].   FRENCH DICTION SONGS from the 17th to the 20th Centuries. Ed. by Anne L. & William D. Leyerle. Geneseo, NY: Leyerle Publications, 1983.

[41].   FUNCTIONAL LESSONS IN SINGING. 2nd ed. Ed. by Ivan Trusler & Walter Ehret. Englewood Cliffs, NJ: Prentice-Hall, Inc., 1972.

[42].   GEMS OF ENGLISH SONG. Boston: Oliver Ditson & Company, 1875.

[43].   HUMOROUS ART SONGS for Solo Voice. Comp; & ed. by Barbara Meister. New York: G. Schirmer, Inc., 1985; distributed by Hal Leonard Corp.

[44].   THE INTERNATIONAL LIBRARY OF MUSIC, VOCAL SERIES, Vol. III: SONGS. New York: The University Society, 1935.

[45].   LYRIC FANCIES: A Selection of Songs by American Composers. 2 vols. Schmidt's Educational Series. High, Medium, & Low voice eds. Boston: Arthur P. Schmidt & Company, 1919. Reprint (Vol. 1, 15 SONGS BY AMERICAN COMPOSERS) Riverdale, NY: Classical Vocal Reprints, n.d.

[46].   MARIAN ANDERSON ALBUM OF SONGS AND SPIRITUALS. Ed. by Franz Rupp. New York: G. Schirmer, Inc., 1948.

[47].   NEGRO ART SONGS: Album by Contemporary Composers. Ed. by Edgar Rogie Clark. New York: Edward B. Marks Music Corp., 1946.

[48].   A NEW ANTHOLOGY OF AMERICAN SONG: 25 Songs by Native American Composers. High voice & Low voice eds. New York: G. Schirmer, Inc., 1942.

[49].   NEW VISTAS IN SONG. New York: Marks Music Corporation, 1964.

[50].   A PROGRAM OF EARLY AND MID-NINETEENTH CENTURY AMERICAN SONGS. Collected, ed. & arr. by John Tasker Howard. New York: J. Fischer & Bro., 1931.

[51].   ROMANTIC AMERICAN ART SONGS: 50 Songs by 14 Composers. Compiled by Richard Walters. New York: G. Schirmer, Inc., 1990; distributed by Hal Leonard Corp.

THE SECOND BOOK OF SOPRANO, MEZZO-SOPRANO / ALTO, TENOR, and BARITONE / BASS SOLOS. see THE FIRST BOOK . . .

[52]. **SEVEN CENTURIES OF SOLO SONG** (13th to 20th Centuries), Vol. VI. Comp. & arr. by James Woodside. High voice & Low voice eds. Boston: The Boston Music Company, 1943.

[53]. **SINGABLE SONGS FOR STUDIO AND RECITAL.** Comp. by Martin Mason. High voice & Medium voice eds. Boston: Oliver Ditson Company, 1936.

[54]. **THE SINGING ROAD,** Vol. I. Comp. & ed. by Arthur E. Ward. New York: Carl Fischer, 1939.

[55]. **SONG ANTHOLOGY ONE.** Ed. by Anne L. Leyerle & William D. Leyerle. 3rd rev. ed. Geneseo, NY: Leyerle Publications, 1985.

[56]. **SONG ANTHOLOGY TWO.** Ed. by Anne L. Leyerle & William D. Leyerle. 2nd rev. ed. Geneseo, NY: Leyerle Publications, 1998.

[57]. **SONG LITERATURE:** A Singer's Guide. Ed. by Helen B. Grossman. Plainview, NY: Harold Branch Publishing, Inc., 1979. (This collection includes notes on the performance of each song by the composer.)

[58]. **SONGS BY THIRTY AMERICANS.** Ed. by Rupert Hughes. *The Musicians Library*. Boston: Oliver Ditson Company, 1904.

[59]. **SONGS BY 22 AMERICANS.** Comp. by Bernard Taylor. High voice & Low voice eds. New York: G. Schirmer, Inc., 1960.

[60]. **SONGS IN ENGLISH:** 19 Contemporary Settings by American and English Composers. Ed. by Bernard Taylor. High voice & Low voice eds. New York: Carl Fischer, Inc., 1970.

[61]. **SONGS OF AN INNOCENT AGE.** Comp. & ed. by Paul Sperry. New York: G. Schirmer, Inc., 1984.

[62]. **SONGS OF LOVE AND AFFECTION.** New York: Boosey & Hawkes, 1985.

[63]. **SONGS THROUGH THE CENTURIES:** 41 Vocal Repertoire Pieces from the 17th through the 20th Centuries. High / Low Voice. Comp. & ed. by Bernard Taylor. New York: Carl Fischer, Inc., 1987.

[64]. **20TH CENTURY ART SONGS.** New York: G. Schirmer, Inc., 1967.

[65]. **VOTE FOR NAMES!** The Peer-Southern 20th Century American Songbook. Comp. by Paul Sperry. New York: Peer Southern Music, n.d.

[66]. **THE WA-WAN PRESS: 1901–1911.** Ed. by Vera Brodsky Lawrence. 5 vols. Reprint, New York: Arno Press & the *New York Times*, 1970.

[67]. **THE WORLD'S BEST MUSIC:** Famous Songs and Those Who Made Them. Ed. by Helen K. Johnson, Frederic Dean, Reginald deKoven, and Gerrit Smith. 4 vols. New York: The University Society, 1904.

[68]. **THE YOUNG SINGER.** Comp. & ed. by Richard D. Row. 4 vols. Book One: Soprano; Book Two: Contralto (Mezzo-soprano); Book Three: Tenor; Book Four: Baritone (Bass). New York: R. D. Row Music Company, Inc., 1965.

SINGLE COMPOSER COLLECTIONS

[69]. **ADLER, Samuel. COLLECTED SONGS.** San Antonio, TX: Southern Music Company, 1991.

[70]. **AVSHALOMOV, Aaron & Jacob. SONGS IN SHADOW.** High voice ed. Portland, OR: Howlet Press–Music, 1994.

[71]. **AVSHALOMOV, Jacob. SONGS ~ PENSIVE & AGILE.** Medium voice ed. Portland, OR: Howlet Press–Music, 1994.

[72]. **BACON, Ernst. FIFTY SONGS.** Georgetown, CA: Dragon's Teeth Press, 1974.

[73]. **BACON, Ernst. QUIET AIRS.** New York: Mercury Music Corporation, 1952. Reprint, Riverdale, NY: Classical Vocal Reprints, 1998.

[74]. **BACON, Ernst. SIX SONGS.** Riverdale, NY: Classical Vocal Reprints, 1994.

[75]. **BACON, Ernst. SONGS AT PARTING:** A Selection of Walt Whitman's Poems Set to Music. Riverdale, NY: Classical Vocal Reprints, 1994.

[76]. **BACON, Ernst. SONGS FROM EMILY DICKINSON.** Medium / High voice ed. Riverdale, NY: Classical Vocal Reprints, 1998.

[77]. **BACON, Ernst. TEN SONGS** (English & German Songs). Riverdale, NY: Classical Vocal Reprints, 1998.

[78]. **BACON, Ernst. TRIBUTARIES.** Limited ed.; MS reproduction, 1978. Reprint, Riverdale, NY: Classical Vocal Reprints, 1991.

[79]. **BARBER, Samuel. COLLECTED SONGS.** High voice & Low voice eds. New York: G. Schirmer, Inc., 1955; rev. eds., 1971 & 1980.

[80]. BARBER, Samuel. TEN EARLY SONGS. Middle voice ed. New York: G. Schirmer, Inc., 1994; distributed by Hal Leonard Corp.

[81]. BEACH, Amy Marcy Cheney. TWELVE SONGS. Medium to High Voice. Ed. by Deborah Cook. Hildegard Publishing Company, 1994.

[82]. BEACH, Amy Marcy (Mrs. H. H. A.). 28 SONGS in Four Volumes. Reprint, Huntsville, TX: Recital Publications, 1985.

[83]. BERNSTEIN, Leonard. AN ALBUM OF SONGS. New York: G. Schirmer, Inc. (Amberson Enterprises, Inc.), 1974.

[84]. BINKERD, Gordon. FOUR SONGS FOR HIGH SOPRANO. New York: Boosey & Hawkes, 1976.

[85]. BOOTT, Francis. BOOTT'S ALBUM OF SONGS. 4 vols. Boston: Oliver Ditson Company, 1892–1904.

[86]. BOWLES, Paul. SELECTED SONGS. Santa Fe, NM: Soundings Press, 1984.

[87]. CADMAN, Charles W. ALBUM OF SONGS. Medium voice & High voice eds. Riverdale, NY: Classical Vocal Reprints, n.d.

[88]. CARPENTER, John Alden. EIGHT SONGS. Medium voice ed. Masters Music Publications, 1991.

[89]. CARPENTER, John Alden. FOUR SONGS FOR A MEDIUM VOICE. Riverdale, NY: Classical Vocal Reprints, n.d.

[90]. CHADWICK, George W. SONG ALBUM: 15 Songs for Soprano or Tenor. High voice ed. Arthur P. Schmidt, Edition Schmidt No. 13. Reprint, Riverdale, NY: Classical Vocal Reprints, n.d.

[91]. CHADWICK, George W. SONG ALBUM: 17 Songs for Alto or Baritone. Medium voice ed. Arthur P. Schmidt, Edition Schmidt No. 38. Reprint, Riverdale, NY: Classical Vocal Reprints, n.d.

[92]. CHANLER, Theodore. THE COLLECTED SONGS OF THEODORE CHANLER. Medium / High voice ed. New York: G. Schirmer, Inc., 1994; distributed by Hal Leonard Corp.

[93]. CHARLES, Ernest. SONGS OF ERNEST CHARLES. High voice & Low voice eds. New York: G. Schirmer, 1990; distributed by Hal Leonard Corp.

[94]. COPLAND, Aaron. FOUR EARLY SONGS. New York: Boosey & Hawkes, 1989.

[95]. COPLAND, Aaron. SONG ALBUM. High voice ed. New York: Boosey & Hawkes, 1980.

[96]. DUKE, John. THE JOHN DUKE COLLECTION. New York: Boosey & Hawkes, 1994.

[97]. DUKE, John. SONGS BY JOHN DUKE, Vol. 1: High voice. Published in Collaboration with The Society of the Friends of John Duke. San Antonio, TX: Southern Music Co., 1985.

[98]. DUKE, John. SONGS BY JOHN DUKE, Vol. 2: Medium voice. Published in Collaboration with The Society of the Friends of John Duke. San Antonio, TX: Southern Music Co., 1985.

[99]. DUKE, John. SONGS BY JOHN DUKE, Vol. 3. Published in Collaboration with The Society of the Friends of John Duke. San Antonio, TX: Southern Music Co., 1987.

[100]. DUKE, John. SONGS OF JOHN DUKE. High voice & Low voice eds. 2nd ed. New York: G. Schirmer, Inc. n.d.; distributed by Hal Leonard Corp.

[101]. EDMUNDS, John. HESPERIDES: Fifty Songs. Georgetown, CA: Dragon's Teeth Press, 1975. Reprint, Riverdale, NY: Classical Vocal Reprints, n.d.

[102]. FAITH, Richard. THE SONGS OF RICHARD FAITH. Vol. I, High voice & Low voice eds. Geneseo, NY: Leyerle Publications, 1993.

[103]. FAITH, Richard. THE SONGS OF RICHARD FAITH. Vol. II, High voice & Low voice eds. Geneseo, NY: Leyerle Publications, 1997.

[104]. FOOTE, Arthur. ALBUM OF SELECTED SONGS BY ARTHUR FOOTE. Boston: Arthur P. Schmidt, 1907.

[105]. FOOTE, Arthur. SONGS, Op. 26. Boston: Arthur P. Schmidt, 1892. Reprint, Riverdale, NY: Classical Vocal Reprints, n.d.

[106]. FOSTER, Stephen Collins. SONGS, COMPOSITIONS AND ARRANGEMENTS. Indianapolis, IN: Foster Hall Reproductions, 1933.

[107]. FOSTER, Stephen Collins. STEPHEN FOSTER SONG BOOK. Selected by Richard Jackson. New York: Dover Publications, Inc., 1974.

[108]. FOSTER, Stephen Collins. A TREASURY OF STEPHEN FOSTER. Arr. by Ray Lev & Dorothy Berliner Commins. New York: Random House, Publishers, 1946.

[109]. FOSTER, Walter. COLLECTED SONGS. High voice ed. Huntsville, TX: Recital Publications, 1984.

[110]. GIANNINI, Vittorio. TWENTY-FOUR SONGS by Vittorio Giannini and Karl Flaster. Compiled & ed. by Jeffrey W. Price, D.M. Dubuque, IA: Kendall/Hunt Publishing Co., 1995.

[111]. GORDON, Ricky Ian. A HORSE WITH WINGS. Williamson Music, 1995; distributed by Hal Leonard Corp.

[112]. GRIFFES, Charles Tomlinson. SEVEN SONGS. Medium to High voice ed. Ed. by Donna K. Anderson. New York: Henmar Press, Inc. (C. F. Peters Corporation), 1986.

[113]. GRIFFES, Charles Tomlinson. SIX SONGS. Medium voice ed. Ed. & trans. by Donna K. Anderson. New York: Henmar Press, Inc. (C. F. Peters Corporation), 1986.

[114]. GRIFFES, Charles Tomlinson. THE SONGS OF CHARLES GRIFFES. Vol. I: High voice. Ed. by Paul Sperry. New York: G. Schirmer, Inc., 1989; distributed by Hal Leonard Corp.

[115]. GRIFFES, Charles Tomlinson. THE SONGS OF CHARLES GRIFFES. Vol. II: Medium voice. Ed. by Paul Sperry. New York: G. Schirmer, Inc., 1989; distributed by Hal Leonard Corp.

[116]. HARRIS, Roy. FOUR SONGS BY ROY HARRIS. Melville, NY: Belwin-Mills Publishing Corp., 1981.

[117]. HOIBY, Lee. ELEVEN SONGS. Middle voice ed. New York: G. Schirmer, Inc., 1995; distributed by Hal Leonard Corp.

[118]. HOIBY, Lee. SONGS AND ARIAS BY LEE HOIBY, Vol. II (High voice) and Vol. III (Middle voice). Long Eddy, NY: Aquarius Music Company (now Rock Valley Music Company), n.d. (songs & arias individually dated & copyrighted).

[119]. HOIBY, Lee. SONGS FOR LEONTYNE. Six Songs. High voice ed. New York: Southern Music Publishing Co., Inc., 1985.

[120]. HOIBY, Lee. THIRTEEN SONGS. High voice ed. New York: G. Schirmer, Inc., 1990; distributed by Hal Leonard Corp.

[121]. HOMER, Sidney. SEVENTEEN SONGS. Comp. by Samuel Barber. High voice & Low voice eds. New York: G. Schirmer, Inc., 1943.

[122]. HOMER, Sidney. THREE SONGS. Medium voice ed. Boca Raton, FL: Masters Music Publications, Inc., n.d.

[123]. HOPKINSON, Francis. SIX SONGS. High voice ed. Riverdale, NY: Classical Vocal Reprints, n.d.

[124]. HOWE, Mary. SONGS BY MARY HOWE, Vol. II: English Songs: Part I. New York: Galaxy Music Corporation, 1959.

[125]. HOWE, Mary. SONGS BY MARY HOWE, Vol. VI: English Songs: Part II. New York: Galaxy Music Corporation, 1959.

[126]. HOWE, Mary. SONGS BY MARY HOWE, Vol. VII: English Songs: Part III. New York: Galaxy Music Corporation, 1959.

[127]. HUNDLEY, Richard. EIGHT SONGS. New York: Boosey & Hawkes, 1981.

[128]. HUNDLEY, Richard. FOUR SONGS. New York: Boosey & Hawkes, 1989.

[129]. HUNDLEY, Richard. OCTAVES AND SWEET SOUNDS. High voice & Medium voice eds. New York: Boosey & Hawkes, 1993.

[130]. IVES, Charles. ELEVEN SONGS & TWO HARMONIZATIONS. Ed. by John Kirkpatrick. New York: Associated Music Pub., Inc., 1968; distributed by Hal Leonard Corp.

[131]. IVES, Charles. FOUR SONGS. Bryn Mawr, PA: Mercury Music Corporation (Theodore Presser), 1950.

[132]. IVES, Charles. FOURTEEN SONGS. New York: Peer International Corporation, 1955.

[133]. IVES, Charles. NINETEEN SONGS. Bryn Mawr, PA: Merion Music, Inc. (Theodore Presser), 1935.

[134]. IVES, Charles. 114 SONGS. Reprint, New York: Associated Music Publishers and Peer International Corporation; Bryn Mawr, PA: Theodore Presser Company, 1975.

[135]. IVES, Charles. SEVEN SONGS. New York: Associated Music Publishers, Inc., 1957.

[136]. IVES, Charles. THIRTY-FOUR SONGS BY CHARLES IVES. New Music Edition. Bryn Mawr, PA: Merion Music, Inc. (Theodore Presser), 1933.

[137]. IVES, Charles. THREE SONGS. New York: Associated Music Publishers, Inc., 1968.

[138]. IVES, Charles. TWELVE SONGS. New York: Peer International Corporation, 1954.

[139]. LANG, Margaret Ruthven. [10] SONGS. Reprint, Huntsville, TX: Recital Publications, 1985.

[140]. MacDOWELL, Edward. FIVE SONGS, Op. 11 & 12. Medium high voice ed. Riverdale, NY: Classical Vocal Reprints, n.d.

[141]. MacDOWELL, Edward. SIX SELECTED SONGS BY EDWARD MacDOWELL. High voice & Low voice eds. Boston: Arthur P. Schmidt, 1912. Reprint, Riverdale, NY: Classical Vocal Reprints, n.d.

[142]. MacDOWELL, Edward. SONGS (Opus 40, 47, 56, 58, & 60). Vol. VII of Earlier American Music, ed. by H. Wiley Hitchcock. New York: Da Capo Press, 1972.

[143]. MENOTTI, Gian Carlo. FIVE SONGS. New York: G. Schirmer, Inc., 1983; distributed by Hal Leonard Corp.

[144]. MILLARD, Harrison. HARRISON MILLARD'S SONGS. New York: R. A. Saalfield, 1884.

[145]. MUSTO, John. SELECTED SONGS. High voice ed. New York: Southern Music Publishing Co., Inc., 1995.

[146]. NELHYBEL, Vaclav. PSALM SETTINGS. Carol Stream, IL: Agape (Hope Publishing Company), 1981.

[147]. NEVIN, Ethelbert. ALBUM OF SONGS BY ETHELBERT NEVIN. Boston: Oliver Ditson Company, 1899.

[148]. NILES, John Jacob. THE SONGS OF JOHN JACOB NILES. New edition containing eight additional songs. High and Low voice eds. New York: G. Schirmer, Inc., 1990; distributed by Hal Leonard Corp.

[149]. PASATIERI, Thomas. SELECTED SONGS. New York: Southern Music Publishing Co., Inc., 1971, 1985.

[150]. PASATIERI, Thomas. SONGS, Vol. One. Melville, NY: Belwin-Mills Publishing Corp., 1977.

[151]. PASATIERI, Thomas. SONGS, Vol. Two. Melville, NY: Belwin-Mills Publishing Corp., 1980.

[152]. PENHORWOOD, Edwin. SONGS. Bloomington, IN: T.I.S. Publications, 2000.

[153]. PFAUTSCH, Lloyd. SIX SONGS. High voice ed. New York: Lawson-Gould Music Publishers, Inc., n.d.

[154]. PRESSER, William. SEVEN SECULAR SONGS. Bass voice. Bryn Mawr, PA: Tenuto Publications (Theodore Presser), 1979.

[155]. ROREM, Ned. FOUR SONGS. Boston: E. C. Schirmer Music Co., Inc., 1986.

[156]. ROREM, Ned. 14 SONGS ON AMERICAN POETRY. New York: Henmar Press (C. F. Peters Corporation), n.d.

[157]. ROREM, Ned. SONG ALBUM. [Vol. 1]. New York: Boosey & Hawkes, Foreword, 1980.

[158]. ROREM, Ned. SONG ALBUM, Vol. 2. New York: Boosey & Hawkes, 1982.

[159]. ROREM, Ned. SONG ALBUM. Vol. 3. New York: Boosey & Hawkes, 1990.

[160]. SIEGMEISTER, Elie. SONGS OF ELIE SIEGMEISTER. Sherman Oaks, CA: Alfred Publishing Co., Inc., 1978.

[161]. SINGER, Jeanne. SELECTED SONGS to Texts by American Poets. Georgetown, CA: Dragon's Teeth Press, 1976.

[162]. WALKER, George. NINE SONGS. Revised 1994. St. Louis, MO: MMB Music, Inc., 1994.

[163]. WALKER, George. THREE SONGS. St. Louis, MO: MMB Music, Inc., 1992.

[164]. WARING, Tom. SONGS BY TOM WARING (For Medium Solo Voice). Delaware Water Gap, PA: Shawnee Press, Inc., 1964.

[165]. WARREN, Elinor Remick. SELECTED SONGS BY ELINOR REMICK WARREN. New York: Carl Fischer, Inc., 1982.

[166]. WILSON, Richard. EIGHT COMIC SONGS. High voice ed. New York: Southern Music Publishing Co., Inc., 1988, 1994.

ADDENDA

[167]. BACON, Ernst. SIX SONGS (Transposed into Higher Keys). High Voice and Piano. Riverdale, NY: Classical Vocal Reprints, 2000.

[168]. GRIFFES, Charles Tomlinson. Songs of Charles Griffes. Vol. III. Medium Voice and Piano. Ed. by Donna K. Anderson. G. Schirmer, Inc.; distributed by Hal Leonard Corporation.

[169]. HEGGIE, Jake. THE FACES OF LOVE. The Songs of Jake Heggie. Vols. I, II, & III. Associated, 2000; distributed by Hal Leonard Corp.

[170]. LAITMAN, Lori. THE METROPOLITAN TOWER and other songs for Soprano and Piano. Merion Music, 1997; distributed by Theodore Presser Co.

[171]. PASATIERI, Thomas. WINDSONGS. A Collection of Songs by Thomas Pasatieri for Soprano. G. Schirmer, Inc., 1989; distributed by Hal Leonard.

[172]. WARREN, Elinor Remick. CENTENNIAL ALBUM. Sixteen Songs for High Voice and Piano. Boca Raton, FL: Masters Music Publications, Inc., 1999.

ADAMS, LESLIE
(b. Cleveland, OH, 1933)

1. **FOR YOU THERE IS NO SONG** (Edna St. Vincent Millay). [6]; 1st©1976. B♭min; b♭–f"; Tess-M; 9/8, Adagio espressivo; 3pp; Diff-V/m, P/m.
For: mezzo-soprano; baritone
Mood: sadly lyrical and philosophical
Voice: long, flowing phrases, often beginning low and rising; many duplets in compound meter
Piano: arpeggiated chord figures under r.h. melody; independent of vocal line; some duplets
Uses: good recital possibilities
Rec: D#12

ADLER, SAMUEL
(b. Mannheim, Germany, 1928)

2. **FOUR POEMS OF JAMES STEPHENS.** For High Voice and Piano. Oxford Univ. Press, 1963. Pub. separately. Traditional harmonies with some altered chords; c♯'–b♭"; Tess-H, M, L; regular meters; varied tempos; 14pp; Diff-V/md-d, P/md-d.
For: high lyric soprano
Mood: varied moods of autumn and approaching winter–agitated, lonely, pastoral, stormy
Voice: vocal line demanding in high tessitura; much singing at top of staff
Piano: mostly linear texture; nimble fingers and secure rhythmic sense needed
Diff: high tessitura; some rhythmic intricacies; fast declamation
Uses: excellent set of songs–well composed, exciting; good program ender
Rec: D#72

    a. *The Wind.* B♭min; f'–b"; Tess-H; 4/4, Moderately fast, but very agitated; 3pp.
    b. *Chill of the Eve.* Bmin-Emin; c♯'–f♯"; Tess-M, L; 4/4, Rather slow; 3pp.
    c. *The Piper.* Cmin-Cmaj; d'–a"; Tess-M; 6/8 with changes, Very slowly–Faster and resolute–Gaily, and fast; 4pp.
    d. *And It Was Stormy Weather.* Amin-Dmaj; e'–a"; Tess-H; 4/4, Very fast; 4pp.

3. **IN THINE OWN IMAGE** (Fania Kruger). Oxford Univ. Press, 1960. "To Mack Harrell." E♭-centered; b♭–f"; Tess-M; 3/4, 4/4, Slowly; 2+min; Diff-V/d, P/md.
For: mezzo-soprano; baritone; some sopranos
Mood: questioning: "What color is Thy face, Lord?"
Voice: rather disjunct; many accidentals; rhythms fairly complicated
Piano: countermelody independent of vocal line; fluid rhythms; many accidentals
Diff: singer needs good sense of pitch; rather dramatic at climaxes; ensemble problems
Uses: strengthening ability in modern idiom; recital use
Rec: D#72

4. **PSALM 23.** [69]. E-centered; c♯'–f♯"; Tess-M; 3/4, 6/8, 5/8, Gently Flowing ♩ = 108; 4pp; Diff-V/md, P/md.
For: medium voices
Mood: faith; reassurance
Voice: scalar and skips along chord lines; predominantly syllabic with expressive melismas; many chromatic alterations; word and phrase repetitions; vocal line part of contrapuntal texture
Piano: predominantly linear, 3 & 4 voices; mostly 8th-note motion; many accidentals
Diff: some rhythms; breath management; a few phrases encompass range of 8ve or 10th
Uses: effective setting for recital or religious service; can be grouped with Psalm 92 (in Hebrew) and Psalm 96 (English) from this collection; composer says piano or organ; would need adaptation by organist

5. **PSALM 96.** [69]. Cmaj-Fmaj; c'–g"; Tess-mH; 3/4, 4/4, Triumphantly ♩ = 124; 6pp; Diff-V/md, P/m.
For: medium or high voices
Mood: praise of God
Voice: stepwise and chordal skips; dramatic; some melismas; unaccomp. phrase; accidentals
Piano: many double and triple sustained tones in center of texture, with alternating 8th notes above and quarters below; 2-voice linear passages often in 10ths or 3rds
Diff: little doubling of vocal line by piano
Uses: recital material–pair with Psalm 23; religious service; for organ accomp. some adaptation would be required

6. **THREE SONGS ABOUT LOVE.** [69]. No key sigs.; b(d')–a"; Tess-M-mH; changing meters predominate; 8pp; Diff-V/md, P/m.
For: high voice; soprano most suitable
Mood: love songs
Voice: mostly stepwise and small skips; many accidentals; changing meters in first two songs accommodate poetic rhythm; rhythms not difficult; syllabic
Piano: block chords in (a.) with 3–4-voice textures; (b.) mostly linear; (c.) in afterbeat style with scale passages in contrary motion as prelude and postlude; many accidentals
Diff: high tessitura in (a.) for some singers; some pitch patterns; some rhythms in second song
Uses: set for soprano; text of (b.) is for a woman; tenor could use (a.) & (c.)
Rec: D#72

    a. *Go Lovely Rose* (Edmund Waller). Polytonality; b(d')–g♯"; 3/4, 4/4, 2/4, 5/4, etc., Moderately fast; 2+min.
    b. *A Ditto* (Sir Philip Sidney). E-centered; e'–a"; 3/4, 2/4, 4/4, Gently flowing; 2min.
    c. *Song* (Oliver Goldsmith). Dmaj with excursions; d'–g♯"; 2/4, Fast; 30sec.

7. **THREE SONGS FOR MEDIUM VOICE AND PIANO.** [69]. (b.) cmp1954. Set of 3 songs, not necessarily for the same voice.

A. **TIME YOU OLD GYPSY MAN** (Ralph Hodgson).

G-centered; b♭–g"; Tess-mH; mostly 6/8, Excitedly rushing; 6pp; Diff-V/d, P/md.

For: mezzo-soprano
Mood: excited; somewhat dramatic; perpetual motion
Voice: much syncopation; stepwise and small skips; long f", f♯" & g"; also long c'; short quasi recit. section; dynamics *pp–ff*
Piano: mostly linear; syncopation; many accidentals
Diff: rhythms; emphasis on high notes for some singers
Uses: exciting song to end a group; see also setting by Elinor Remick Warren
Rec: D#s 58, 72

B. **OLD AGE** (Judith Stampfer). A-centered; a–e"; Tess-M; 2/4, 6/8, Slowly, but do not drag; 3pp; Diff-V/m, P/me.

For: mezzo-soprano; baritone
Mood: somber
Voice: stepwise and small skips; one 8ve leap; syncopation; accidentals
Piano: block chords; 6/8 section linear; many accidentals
Diff: chromatic alterations in melody
Uses: mature subject–probably not for young students
Rec: D#72

C. **BUT I WAS YOUNG AND FOOLISH** (William Butler Yeats). E-centered; b–f♯"; Tess-M, wide; 2/2, Quite fast, and very crisp throughout; 4pp; Diff-V/m, P/m.

For: baritone
Mood: lost love
Voice: stepwise and small skips; accidentals; several phrases have large range
Piano: linear; 2-voice texture; accidentals; prelude, interlude, and postlude
Diff: achieving proper mood at this tempo; min./maj. juxtaposition; some intervals
Uses: recital song; contrasts other settings of this text with slower tempos (e.g., Britten, "Down by the Salley Gardens")
Rec: D#72

8. **TWO SONGS FOR THREE YEARS.** Boosey & Hawkes, 1974. Tonal centers; a–f"; Tess-M; regular meters, some changes; 5min; Diff-V/m-md, P/md.

For: (a.), mezzo-soprano; baritone; (b.), baritone
Mood: (a.), quiet lullaby; (b.), lighthearted
Voice: mostly stepwise and small skips; accidentals; syncopation; triplets
Piano: chordal and linear; many accidentals; large reaches; arpeggios; passages in 3rds & 6ths; solo passages; no doubling of vocal line
Diff: some intervals; irregular rhythms; long passages with no rests
Uses: possible use in group concerning children; (b.) effective for singer with comic flair

    a. *My Daughter the Cypress* (Ruth Whitman). F♯-centered; c♯'–f"; Tess-M; 6/8, Gently rocking; 3pp.
    b. *Song to Be Sung by the Father of Infant Female Children* (Ogden Nash). C-centered (bitonal); a–e"; Tess-M; 6/8 with changes, With verve; 3min.

9. **TWO SONGS FROM THE PORTUGUESE** (Gil Vincente; trans. Henry Wadsworth Longfellow). [69]. No key sigs.; b♭–f♯"; Tess-mH; changing meters; quick tempos; 2+min; Diff-V/m,P/m.

For: high baritone; tenor; man's texts
Mood: lighthearted
Voice: mostly stepwise and small skips; larger skips within harmonic structure; changing meters in (a.); (b.), all sung measures in 6/8; syllabic with 2- or 3-note slurs
Piano: afterbeats and block chords in (a.); (b.) has block chords and linear writing; Spanish flavor in interludes
Diff: possibly changing meters (a.); changing modes (b.)
Uses: good student songs; light songs to end a recital
Rec: D#72

    a. *Simple Song.* G-centered; d'–f♯"; 2/4, 3/4, 4/4; 2pp.
    b. *Ballad.* Begins and ends Aeolian on A; b♭–f"; 7/8, 6/8, With much verve; 3pp.

10. **TWO SONNETS FOR DELORES** (Gilmore D. Clarke). [69]. Tonal; d♯'–a♯"; Tess-mH; 3/4, 6/8, Fairly slow; 6pp; Diff-V/md, P/md-d.

For: soprano; tenor
Mood: praising love; eternal love
Voice: mostly syllabic; some chant-like passages; some melismas; some wide leaps; many different subdivisions of the beat, depending on word rhythms; both songs end on long high notes (f♯", g♯")
Piano: some block chord texture; some broken chord and arpeggiated; polyrhythms; some apparently quintal harmonies; passages in parallel 6ths, 8ves, & 10ths
Diff: speech-like rhythms; finding pitches in these textures, e.g. dim.8ve; many modulations
Uses: as a pair or singly; recital material for a sizeable voice

    a. *Without You . . .* G♯min, unsettled; d♯'–a♯"; Tess-mH; 3/4, Gently moving, but with great fervor ♩ = 69; 3pp.
    b. *Forever Is Not Measured in the Lives of Men . . .* Unsettled, some bitonality; d♯'–a"; Tess-mH; 6/8, Restless ♩. = 56; 3pp.

11. **UNHOLY SONNETS** (John Donne). Five Love Songs for Tenor and Piano. [69]. "Commissioned for Joseph Evans." Tonal and bitonal; c♯'–b"(c♭'''falsetto); Tess-mH; regular and mixed meters; varied tempos; 31pp; Diff-V/md-d, P/m-d.

For: tenor
Mood: dramatic and impassioned: awakening of love; broken heart; changing love; defending promiscuity; writing poetry allays love's pain
Voice: mostly syllabic; some chant-like passages on a single pitch; some dramatic recit.; much stepwise, small-skip motion; some more angular lines; many accidentals; various subdivisions of the beat suit word stress and moods; needs good range of dynamics
Piano: broken and block chords, sometimes with a moving line; staccato passages; bitonality; some tone clusters; some widely spaced chords; polyrhythms; (c.), 10-meas. slow interlude for piano and a boisterous ending; prelude for (e.) sets up double-dotted accomp. figure used throughout the song

Diff: vocabulary and spelling of Donne's era; sustaining intensity of the drama; length of set; pitch and rhythm patterns that usually differ from the accomp.; phrases encompassing a wide range
Uses: good group for mature tenor (cf. Britten's *Holy Sonnets of John Donne*)
Rec: D#72

   a. *The Good-Morrow.* d#'–b"; Tess-mH; 3/4, Fast and excited ♩ = 126-132; 8+pp.
   b. *The Broken Heart.* c#'–a"; Tess-M; 4/4, Fast and wild ♩ = 136; 8pp.
   c. *Woman's Constancy.* e'–c♭"; Tess-wide; 3/4, 4/4, With a great deal of pathos ♩ = 60; 5+pp.
   d. *The Indifferent.* d♭'–a"; Tess-mH; 9/8, 6/8, With abandon ♩. = 120; 6pp.
   e. *The Triple Foole.* d♭'–b♭"; Tess-mH; 3/4, Gently moving ♩ = 72-76; 5pp.

ADOLPHE, BRUCE
(b. New York, NY, 1955)

12. **TO HIS IMAGINARY MISTRESS** (Robert Herrick). Solo Tenor and Piano. Cycle. Ione, 1982. "For John Aler." Tertian harmony without clearly defined tonal centers; e'–b"; Tess-M-mH; regular meters with changes; moderate to slow tempos; 8+pp; Diff-V/md, P/md.
For: tenor specified (lyric)
Mood: love songs; philosophical; nature imagery
Voice: stepwise and small skips, most often of a 3rd; a few large leaps for dramatic emphasis; chromatic; lyrical and flowing; syllabic with 2–4-note slurs
Piano: chordal with prominent use of harp-like arpeggiations; counterpoint in first song and in 11-meas. postlude after last song; chromatic; independent of vocal line
Diff: requires tenor with easy top capable of delicate phrasing
Uses: excellent recital material

   a. *Upon My Julia's Clothes.* X; f#'–b"; Tess-mH; unmetered , 3/4, 2/4, With graceful movement; 2pp.
   b. *To the River.* X; e'–g"; Tess-M; 2/2 , 3/4, 2/4, 4/4, Recit.–Slow waltz–Maestoso; 2+pp.
   c. *The Amber Bead.* X; b♭'–a"; Tess-mH; 3/4, 4/4, 2/4, 1/4, Slowly; 1p.
   d. *A Willow Garland.* X; g'–b"; Tess-M; 5/4, 3/4, 4/4, 2/4, 7/4, 6/4, Sadly; 2+pp.
   e. *Postlude.* 4/4, 3/4, Flowing; 11meas.

AGAY, DENES
(b. Kiskunfelegyhaza, Hungary, 1911)

13. **OLD IRISH BLESSING** (Traditional). WB [Warner Bros.], 1970. Bmin; c#'–e"(f#"); Tess-M; 4/4; 4pp; Diff-V/me, P/m.
For: any medium voice
Mood: familiar text: "May the road rise to meet you . . ."
Voice: lyrical and flowing; somewhat popular in style; a few chromatic tones

Piano: chordal texture; r.h. doubles vocal line; l.h. plays repeated notes and broken chords
Uses: appealing student song

14. **THE YANKEE PEDDLER** (Sydney Lief). Weintraub, 1950. Cmaj-Fmaj; c'–f "(g"); Tess-M; 3/4, 4/4, 2/4, Lively (with several changes); 8pp; Diff-V/m, P/d.
For: soprano; tenor
Mood: descriptive; humorous
Voice: partly recit.-like, imitating peddler's calls; refrain suggests joyous singing of peddler in lyrical melody
Piano: dancing melody in r.h. 8ths, 16ths, & triplets with broken-chord figures in l.h.; rolled chords, afterbeats, tremolos, grace notes, etc.
Diff: needs good vocal actor and pianist
Uses: good for contrast; group or recital ender

THE AIDS QUILT SONGBOOK (No. 15A–R; songs listed in published order; various composers)

15. **THE AIDS QUILT SONGBOOK.** [A song cycle created by eighteen different composers] Boosey & Hawkes, 1993. First performed June 4, 1992; dedicated to William Parker. Originally performed by Mr. Parker and three other baritones; some could be performed by women singers. "Several of these songs deal only metaphorically with AIDS, but most confront the painful details of the disease and its attendant havoc. They are variously mordant and bitter, jazzy and plaintive, tonal and atonal. Some offer hope and even humor." (Jeffrey Stock, Nov., 1993) Each song is by a different composer, and many could be excerpted from the cycle. Songs listed in order of complete cycle.

WHEELOCK, DONALD
(b. Stamford, CT, 1940)

A. **FURY** (Susan Snively) [no.1 of *Shadows*, a cycle of 4 songs on texts by Susan Snively] F-centered; g#–f "; Tess-M; 2/4, Con moto (♩ = ca.80); 10pp; Diff-V/md, P/d.
For: baritone; bass-baritone; possibly alto
Mood: facing death; calling on others to acknowledge the situation; a very strong and personal text
Voice: repeated notes and dotted rhythms; intervals of 6th, 7th, & 8ve; numerous accidentals; dramatic–*fff* with strong accents at climax
Piano: chordal, with insistent rhythm in triplet 16ths; character somewhat reminiscent of Schubert's "Der Erlkönig"; many accidentals; does not double vocal line
Diff: singer with secure sense of pitch and ability to handle the text needed
Uses: a powerful song for the appropriate occasion
Rec: D#1

HERSCH, FRED
(b. Cincinnati, OH, 1955)

B. **BLUES FOR AN IMAGINARY VALENTINE** (Fred Hersch). E-centered; a–e♭"; Tess-mL; 4/4, ♩ = 60; 4pp;

Diff-V/md, P/me.

For: baritone; bass-baritone; possibly alto

Mood: "how ironic that I should be the one to go before you"; somewhat in a blues style

Voice: mostly conjunct motion and small intervals; triplets and dotted rhythms; many accidentals; many nuances of tempo and dynamics; glissandos

Piano: chordal, with syncopated afterbeat feeling; many accidentals; supports but does not double vocal line

Diff: singer with secure sense of pitch and rhythm needed

Uses: could be very effective in the appropriate situation

Rec: D#1

MUSTO, JOHN
(b. Brooklyn, NY, 1954)

C.   HEARTBEATS (Melvin Dixon) X; c'–g"; Tess-M; 5/8, with changes, ♪ = 232 with changes; 12pp; Diff-V/dd, P/dd.

For: baritone; possibly mezzo-soprano

Mood: highly agitated recital of symptoms and healthy lifestyle of person with AIDS

Voice: quite disjunct, both melodically and rhythmically, reflecting increased agitation as song progresses, with overall pitch level becoming higher; numerous accidentals; extremely fast tempo

Piano: highly disjunct in both pitch and rhythm; agitated 8ths, moving toward 16ths as song progresses; harmonized quotation from *Stabat mater* chant incorporated into an interlude; many accidentals; does not double vocal line

Diff: singer with secure sense of pitch and ability to handle the text needed; technical difficulties for pianist at tempo indicated

Uses: best in context of cycle

For: D#s 1, 29

ROREM, NED
(b. Richmond, IN, 1923)

D.   A DREAM OF NIGHTINGALES (David Bergman). cmp1992. A-centered; a–e"; Tess-M; 3/4, Limpid (♩ = 76, 112); 4pp; Diff-V/md, P/m.

For: baritone; bass-baritone; possibly alto

Mood: lyrical, contemplative poem on the beauty of life and death

Voice: mostly conjunct motion with repeated notes and a few large intervals; numerous accidentals

Piano: chordal; many accidentals; grace notes; supports vocal line; some incidental doubling

Diff: singer will need a secure sense of pitch

Uses: effective recital song in almost any context

Rec: D#1

DeBLASIO, CHRIS
(b. 1959; d. New York, NY, 1993)

E.   WALT WHITMAN IN 1989 (Perry Brass). X-B♭maj; a–f"; Tess-mL; 4/4, 4/2, Recitativo, Moderato (♩ = 76), Largo (♩ = ♩ = 54); 5pp; Diff-V/md, P/m.

For: baritone; bass-baritone; possibly alto

Mood: relating the Civil War poems of Walt Whitman to the AIDS epidemic, though not in a direct or obvious way

Voice: somewhat recit.-like with repeated notes and small intervals in opening section; second section a broadly flowing melody using longer note values; some accidentals

Piano: chordal, with downward flourishes in septuplets in first section and block quarter notes in second section; numerous accidentals; supports but does not double vocal line

Diff: pitches and rhythms, esp. in first section

Uses: effective recital song in almost any context

Rec: D#s 1, 29

KRAKAUER, DAVID
(b. New York, NY, 1956)

F.   THE 80's MIRACLE DIET (Melvin Dixon). [original version for clarinet and baritone] cmp1992. X; a–f"; Tess-M; unmetered, ♩ = 100, 72, 60; 5pp; Diff-V/dd, P/dd.

For: baritone specified

Mood: bitter; parodying a weight-loss advertisement

Voice: speaking, falsetto, "like Tom Jones/Vegas Singer," glissando, and other special instructions; calls for little or no conventional singing tone; sung portions conjunct; numerous accidentals; completely independent of piano

Piano: detailed instructions for preparing piano and special playing techniques; many accidentals; provides little pitch or rhythmic assistance to singer

Diff: singer and pianist must have an affinity for this style of music; singer needs strong sense of pitch and rhythm and excellent vocal acting skills; pianist needs a high level of technical security

Uses: an effective song in context of cycle

Rec: D#1

LOCKWOOD, ANNEA
(b. Christchurch, New Zealand, 1939)

G.   FOR RICHARD (Eve Ensler). X; E♭-centered; a–e♭"; Tess-M; 5/4, with frequent changes, ♩ = approx. 56; 2pp; Diff-V/dd, P/e.

For: baritone; bass-baritone

Mood: bitter and sarcastic

Voice: rather disjunct with leaps of 7th & 8ve; irregular rhythms; grace notes; *Sprechstimme*; speaking; "tongue to palate"

Piano: consists almost entirely of irregular short punctuations of e♭, two of which are pizzicato on the strings inside the piano

Diff: secure pitch and ability to handle the text needed

Uses: best in context of cycle

Rec: D#1

ST. PIERRE, DONALD
(b. Madison, WI, 1951)

H.   FAIRY BOOK LINES (Charles Barber). X; c'–g♭"; Tess-M; 2/2, with changes, Andante (♩ = 69); 9pp; Diff-V/d, P/md.

For: baritone; possibly mezzo-soprano

Mood: twisted quotations from nursery rhymes, etc., lead into decriptions of ravages of AIDS, and finally to death

Voice: a mixture of conjunct and disjunct motion; frequent large intervals, some more than an 8ve; many accidentals; generally regular rhythms within changing time sigs.

Piano: chordal sections with countermelodies alternate with somewhat contrapuntal sections; generally regular rhythms; does not double vocal line

Diff: singer needs secure sense of pitch and possibly rhythm, as well as the ability to handle this text

Uses: best in context of cycle

Rec: D#1

BOLCOM, WILLIAM
(b. Seattle, WA, 1938)

I. **VASLAV'S SONG** (Ethyl Eichelberger). cmp1991. E-centered; g–f"; Tess-M; 4/4, Not too slow; 3pp; Diff-V/d, P/d.

For: baritone; possibly mezzo-soprano or alto

Mood: false cheerfulness at the end of life; "Da svedanya [good-bye] Mama." used several times

Voice: rather disjunct; numerous large intervals; many accidentals; "lightly as possible, like a jazzy folk-song"; syncopation and dotted rhythms

Piano: chordal; many accidentals; syncopation and dotted rhythms; does not double vocal line

Diff: singer needs secure sense of pitch and rhythm; pianist needs secure rhythm; both need to understand jazz style

Uses: could be an effective recital song in various settings

Rec: D#s 1, 29

THOMAS, RICHARD PEARSON
(b. Great Falls, MT, 1957)

J. **AIDS ANXIETY** (Richard Pearson Thomas). Traditional tonal centers with numerous changes; bb'–f♯"; Tess-M; changing regular meters; generally quick tempos; 19pp; Diff-V/md, P/md.

For: baritone (an extended scene for three baritones)

Mood: three different characters worried about various possible ways in which they might have contracted the AIDS virus; situations given intentionally humorous treatment

Voice: vocal lines vary in style–recit.-like, waltz-like, patter song, etc.; motion generally conjunct with small intervals; numerous accidentals within a tonal framework; three singers together in close harmony in final section; regular rhythms; some syncopation

Piano: chordal with melodic and countermelodic material; regular rhythms; some syncopation; supports and sometimes doubles vocal line

Diff: excellent vocal actors needed to make this effective

Uses: best in context of cycle

Rec: D#1

HARBISON, JOHN
(b. Orange, NJ, 1938)

K. **THE FLUTE OF INTERIOR TIME** (Kabir; English version by Robert Bly). cmp1991. A minor; b–e"; Tess-mL; 4/4 with changes, ♩ = 60; 3pp; Diff-V/me, P/m.

For: baritone; any medium or low voice

Mood: lyrical and philosophical with an Eastern flavor

Voice: mostly stepwise motion with a few small intervals; some triplets, irregular note groupings, and syncopation

Piano: unison 8ves doubling the vocal line, with chords and contrapuntal motion; a few accidentals

Diff: possibly rhythms

Uses: effective recital song in almost any setting

Rec: D#s 1, 29

BYRON, CARL
(b. 20th Century)

L. **THE BIRDS OF SORROW** (Ron Schreiber). cmp1992. X; a–a"; Tess-mL; 4/4, ♩ = 56; 7pp; Diff-V/dd, P/dd.

For: baritone implied; could be sung by a mezzo-soprano

Mood: grief expressed through nature and winter imagery

Voice: somewhat disjunct, although few large intervals; some accidentals; final leap of 9th to a" marked "falsetto"

Piano: block chords, with 16th- & 32nd-note flourishes, often in irregular rhythmic groupings; triplets; often independent of vocal line; incidental doubling

Diff: singer needs secure sense of pitch and rhythm; skillful pianist needed

Uses: could be an effective recital song in many settings

Rec: D#1

HOIBY, LEE
(b. Madison, WI, 1926)

M. **INVESTITURE AT CECCONI'S** (James Merrill). cmp1991. X; a–b"; Tess-mL; 4/4, with frequent changes, Moderato (♩ = 84, 92, 138); 7pp; Diff-V/d, P/dd.

For: baritone

Mood: a man dreams of visiting the tailor and receiving a new robe

Voice: much conjunct motion but also large intervals, incl. several larger than an 8ve; numerous accidentals; varied rhythms and meters; 8ve leap to b" "falsetto," with portamento downward

Piano: chordal and contrapuntal; block- and broken-chord patterns, regular and irregular groupings, unison melodies; many accidentals; doubles vocal line in first part of song, then becomes largely independent

Diff: singer needs secure sense of pitch and rhythm; must be good vocal actor; highly skilled pianist needed

Uses: an interesting recital song in many settings

Rec: D#s 1, 218

BROWN, ELIZABETH C.
(b. 20th Century)

N. **A CERTAIN LIGHT** (Marie Howe). cmp1992. X; a–db'''(f"); Tess-M; 2/4, with frequent changes, ♩ = 60 (elastic); 9pp; Diff-V/dd, P/dd.

For: baritone

Mood: dramatic and graphic description of illness

Voice: much conjunct motion, but also large intervals, incl. several larger than an 8ve; many accidentals; somewhat recit.-like; many irregular note groupings; falsetto phrases to c'" and d♭'" have alternatives an 8ve lower

Piano: chordal; block chords and broken-chord figures in irregular groupings; many accidentals; sometimes supports but often dissonant to vocal line

Diff: singer needs very secure sense of pitch and rhythm, as well as the ability to handle this text; highly skilled pianist needed

Uses: best in context of cycle

Rec: D#1

GORDON, RICKY IAN
(b. Long Island, NY, 1956)

O.   I NEVER KNEW (Ricky Ian Gordon). Cmin; b♭–g♭"; Tess-mL; 4/4, Slow (♩ = 63); 5pp; Diff-V/m, P/m.

For: baritone; possibly mezzo-soprano

Mood: lyrical reflection on death of loved one

Voice: legato phrases, often short, with stepwise motion and small intervals; few accidentals

Piano: chordal with contrasting contrapuntal sections; some accidentals; much doubling of vocal line

Diff: modal flavor and shifts in tonal center may be difficult for some singers

Uses: could be an effective song in a variety of settings

Rec: D#1

WILSON, RICHARD
(b. Cleveland, OH, 1941)

P.   THE SECOND LAW (Stephen Sandy). cmp1991. X; a–f"; Tess-M; 3/4, with some changes, ♩ = 66; 6pp; Diff-V/dd, P/dd.

For: baritone; possibly mezzo-soprano

Mood: sad; at the bedside of a dying patient

Voice: rather disjunct; many intervals of a 7th; many accidentals; wide-ranging phrases, incl. a slow melisma covering the range of the song

Piano: mostly chordal with some contrapuntal interpolations; many accidentals; some irregular groupings and 32nd-note passages; quite independent of vocal line

Diff: singer with secure sense of pitch and rhythm and skillful pianist are needed

Uses: probably best in context of cycle, although possible in a group of songs relating to death

Rec: D#1

LARSEN, LIBBY
(b. Wilmington, DE, 1950)

Q.   PERINEO (Roberto Echavarren). cmp1992. X; b–f"; Tess-M; 4/4 with frequent changes, Freely (alternating with ♩ = 120); 11pp; Diff-V/d, P/d.

For: baritone; possibly mezzo-soprano

Mood: text partly in Spanish, partly in English; no trans. provided; poet is conscious of his body

Voice: recit.-like passages with many repeated notes alternate with somewhat disjunct melodic passages; some accidentals; changing meters and rhythms; portamento, hiss, and specific breathing instructions indicated

Piano: chordal with afterbeat patterns; some melodic material; triplets; numerous accidentals; glissandos; independent of vocal line

Diff: singer will need good sense of pitch and rhythm, as well as the ability to handle this text

Uses: could be effective in the appropriate situation

Rec: D#29

HOUTZ, STEVEN
(b. 1956)

R.   THE ENTICING LANE (Christopher Hewitt). X; b♭–f"; Tess-M; 4/4, Moderately, freely (♩ = 69-80); 10pp; Diff-V/d, P/d.

For: baritone; mezzo-soprano

Mood: reflecting on one's life

Voice: much conjunct motion; also intervals of 7th & 9th; many accidentals; regular rhythms with some triplets

Piano: chordal–block chords, broken-chord patterns, some in triplets; many accidentals; independent of vocal line

Diff: singer will need secure sense of pitch

Uses: could be effective in a variety of settings

Rec: D#29

[End of AIDS Quilt Songbook]

AIKMAN, JAMES
(b. Indianapolis, IN, 1959)

16.   SPRING IS PURPLE JEWELRY (Anonymous). [9]. X; a♭–b♭"; Tess-cs; changing regular and irregular meters; ♩ = 44-56; 3+min; Diff- V/d, P/d.

For: soprano

Mood: a reverie of color and sound; spring

Voice: opening passage hummed over fairly wide intervals into vocal sounds with glissandos; syllabic setting; one melisma; several large intervals; detailed dynamic markings; much *messa di voce*; irregular meters; ends with humming and "ah"

Piano: pointillistic texture of single 8th- & 16th-note patterns high on the keyboard; birdcall patterns; liberal use of damper pedal gives impressionistic aura

Diff: rhythms in irregular meters; wide range for singer

Uses: unusual and excellent song for light lyric soprano with good ear and clear chest tones

ALBERT, STEPHEN
(b. New York, NY, 1941; d. Truro, MA, 1992)

17.   SUN'S HEAT (from *Distant Hills*) (James Joyce). G. Schirmer, 1992 (Hal Leonard). cmp1989. "Commissioned by the Chamber Music Society of Lincoln Center," and first performed in 1990 by David Gordon, to whom the work is dedicated. Versions for both chamber and full orchestra exist, in addition to the piano reduction. This work is the first of the two movements of *Distant Hills*, on texts from James Joyce's *Ulysses*; the second, "Flower of the Mountain" is written for soprano with chamber or full orchestra. X; c♯'–b"; Tess-cs; 6/8, with changes, (♩. = 80, with changes); 15min; Diff-V/dd, P/dd.

For: tenor specified; not suitable for very light voices

Mood: poetic and abstract; relationship between a man and a woman

Voice: both conjunct and disjunct motion; intervals larger than a 5th are usually not difficult ones; many accidentals; irregular meters and rhythms; generally short phrases; b" occurs twice, but only a third of the way through the lengthy work–can be touched rather lightly and not sustained; many instructions for shadings of tempo, dynamics, and expression

Piano: originally for tenor and orchestra, although an excellent piano reduction; quite pianistically written, with a few instrumental cues on a third staff not practical to perform; chordal–block and broken; contrapuntal sections; many meter changes with irregular meters; beat unit remains consistent at the 8th note in the first part of the work and the quarter note in the last; many accidentals; wide-ranging broken-chord figures in l.h.; rapid repeated-note and repeated-chord figures; some special notation; supports at crucial points but does not double vocal line

Diff: secure sense of pitch needed for singer, as well as vocal stamina; good interpreter needed to make the meaning clear to an audience; secure sense of rhythm and high level of musicianship needed in both singer and pianist; highly skillful pianist required

Uses: can be very effectively performed with piano; a *tour de force* for a tenor recital

ALETTE, CARL
(b. Philadelphia, PA, 1922)

18. GOD'S WORLD (Edna St. Vincent Millay). Theodore Presser, 1963. Dmaj; c♯'–a"; Tess-M; 4/4, Allegro; 6pp; Diff-V/md, P/md.

For: soprano
Mood: lyrical; ecstatic song of beauty
Voice: soaring line; some melismas; sustained a" and a♭"; quiet ending
Piano: arpeggiated throughout with short chordal section
Diff: sustained high tones and soaring lines aria-like
Uses: good song for soaring lyric voice; suitable for recital

19. THREE SECULAR SONGS. Theodore Presser, 1963. Traditional keys; c'–g"; Tess-M; regular meters; slow to moderate tempos; 10min; Diff-V/m, P/m.

For: soprano; mezzo-soprano
Mood: lyrical night songs; loneliness and sorrow
Voice: conjunct motion with skips along chord lines; some small divisions of the beat
Piano: mostly patterned with 8th-note motion predominating; some accidentals
Uses: nice group for an intermediate student

    a. *The Moon Has Gone* (Carolyn Brandt). Fmin; c'–e♭"; Tess-mL-M; 4/4, ♩ = 60; 2min.
    b. *Ashes of Life* (Edna St. Vincent Millay). Dmin; d'–e♭"; Tess-M; 4/4, ♩ = 76; 3+min.
    c. *What Lips My Lips Have Kissed* (Edna St. Vincent Millay). Fmin-E♭min; d♭'–g"; Tess-M; 4/4, ♩ = 50; 4+min.

ALEXANDER, JOSEF
(b. Boston, MA, 1907; d. Seattle, WA, 1989)

20. SONGS FOR EVE (Archibald MacLeish). Cycle. General, 1972. 2 vols. Dissonant (much quartal harmony and occasional major tonal resolutions); b♯–c'''; Tess-wide, L-M-mH-H; regular and irregular meters with many changes; very fluid movement; variety of tempos–begins fast, ends slow; 53pp; Diff-V/d, P/d.

For: soprano with easy top and good b" and c'''
Mood: lyrical with some dramatic sections; Eve's celebration of the fall "from earth to God"; awakened humanity; sense of eternity
Voice: many skips and large leaps; two-8ve range; repeated high tones; some melismas; some rhythmic complexity; climactic high tones
Piano: mostly linear texture; no key sigs., many accidentals; patterned but not consistently so; trills; some polyrhythms; flowing movement in 8ths & 16ths; needs excellent pianist
Diff: range; tessitura; endurance; text projection; ensemble; advanced singers only, with special affinity for metaphysical poetry
Uses: could be an attractive and effective cycle for the right singer; cf. Ezra Laderman cycle of same title, with some different poems and different overall concept
Rec: D#73

    a. *What Eve Sang.* c'–g♯"; Tess-M; 5/4 with changes, Allegro non troppo; 5pp.
    b. *What Eve Said.* c'–a"; Tess-M; 3/4, Lento; 3pp.
    c. *Eve's Exile.* b♯–a"; Tess-L & H; 6/4 with changes, Allegro molto, quasi presto; 5pp.
    d. *Eve Answers the Burdock.* c'–a"; Tess-mH; 3/4, Andantino; 2pp.
    e. *The Fall.* c'–a♭"; Tess-M; 4/4, Allegro moderato–Maestoso; 3pp.
    f. *Eve's Now-I-Lay-Me.* d'–g♯"; Tess-M; 3/4, 3/8, Andante semplice; 1p.
    g. *Eve in the Dawn.* c'–a"; Tess-M; 4/4, Allegro energico; 6pp.
    h. *Eve's Child.* c'–g♯"; Tess-M; 3/4, 4/4, Andante sostenuto; 5pp.
    i. *Adam's Riddle.* c'–e"; Tess-mL; 3/8, 2/4, Presto; 2pp.
    j. *The Serpent's Riddle.* b♯–g♯"; Tess-M; 3/8, 3/4, Presto; 2pp.
    k. *Eve's Riddle.* c♯'–g♯"; Tess-M; 3/8, 5/8, 2/4, Allegro; 2pp.
    l. *The Babe's Riddle.* c'–a"; Tess-M & H; 3/8, Allegretto; 2pp.
    m. *Eve's Rebuke to Her Child.* c♯'–c''' (a"); Tess-M & H; 4/4, 5/4, 3/4, Maestoso; 5pp.
    n. *Eve to the Storm of Thunder.* c'–a"; Tess-M; 3/4, 4/4, Allegro moderato; 5pp.
    o. *Eve Old.* c'–b"; Tess-M; 2/4, 3/4, Andantino; 5pp.

ALLEN, ROBERT E.
(b. Minneapolis, MN, 1920)

21.   **AWAY,** Op. 2, No. 2 (Walter de la Mare). Galleon, 1948. Dmaj; d'–e♭"; Tess-mL; 2/2, Moderato; 3pp; Diff-V/m, P/me.
For: any medium voice
Mood: philosophical; sad; somewhat sentimental
Voice: lyrical; short phrases separated by rests; some chromaticism
Piano: chordal texture with whole notes in the bass; somewhat chromatic
Diff: pitches require care
Uses: likely to have popular appeal

22.   **THE FLIGHT,** Op. 7, No. 2 (Sara Teasdale). Galleon, 1950 & 1962. Fmaj; f'–a"; Tess-mH; 6/8, Allegro moderato; 1+min; Diff-V/m, P/m.
For: soprano
Mood: sentimental love song
Voice: duplets against piano triplets; duplets and triplets juxtaposed; many small skips
Piano: does not double vocal line; some 2 vs. 3; almost constant 3rds in r.h.; many accidentals
Diff: two sustained a"s
Uses: good training song for young soprano

23.   **VOCALISE,** Op. 2, No. 3. Galleon, 1949. X-Cmin-Bmaj; e♭'–g"; Tess-M; 4/4, Andante cantando; 2+min; Diff-V/me-m; P/me.
For: soprano
Mood: lyrical; meditative; pleasant
Voice: much use of sequence and imitation; many small skips; uncomplicated but varied rhythms
Piano: l.h. repeated chords under r.h. melody; harmonic interest in manner of Chopin's E Minor Prelude; many accidentals
Diff: composer suggests doing entire vocalise on "ah," but may be modified if desired; dynamic control needed
Uses: relatively easy vocalise; could be used to teach modification on "ah" vowel

AMES, WILLIAM T.
(b. Cambridge, MA, 1901; d. 1987)

24.   **A DREAM PANG** (Robert Frost). Associated, 1946. X-B♭maj; e'–g"; Tess-mH; 4/4 with several changes, Andante; 5pp; Diff-V/m, P/m.
For: tenor; soprano
Mood: lyric; quiet; narrative
Voice: many skips; duplets against piano triplets
Piano: syncopated repeated chords; broken chords in triplet pattern; wide-spread registers; no vocal line doubling
Diff: some long, sustained phrases; speech rhythms
Uses: atmospheric piece

25.   **DUST OF SNOW** (Robert Frost). Seesaw, 1945. Dmin; d'–g"; Tess-M; 3/4, Andante; 2pp; Diff-V/m, P/m.
For: soprano; tenor
Mood: descriptive; lyric; quiet

Voice: some large skips; several long tones; legato
Piano: r.h. block 7th chords in repetitive rhythm; l.h. staccato arpeggio; many accidentals; no vocal line doubling
Diff: needs good register control
Uses: effective atmospheric song; quiet ending

26.   **FIRE AND ICE** (Robert Frost). Associated, 1944. [4]. Bmin; c♯'–f♯"; Tess-mH; 2/2, 3/2, Moderato; 4pp; Diff-V/md, P/md.
For: tenor
Mood: dramatic; philosophical
Voice: many leaps; many long tones; some triplet syncopation and dotted-rhythm subdivisions
Piano: chordal; much 8ve parallel motion; syncopation; large reaches; varied registers; long postlude; does not double vocal line
Diff: long tones at phrase ends; ensemble
Uses: an intense setting; suitable for recital

27.   **JUDGEMENT** (William Rose Benét). Associated, 1947. cmp1945. B♭min-maj; b♭–a♭"(g"); Tess-mH; 4/4, Moderato; 50meas; Diff-V/md, P/me.
For: dramatic soprano; mezzo-soprano; some tenors
Mood: dramatic; intense; foreboding
Voice: dramatic; some difficult skips; difficult rhythms; many accidentals
Piano: built entirely over B♭ pedal tone; texture builds to end; not difficult to transpose
Diff: high sustained climax; little piano support for singer; difficult poem
Uses: powerful song for mature singer; could end a group

28.   **NOTHING GOLD CAN STAY** (Robert Frost). Associated, 1944. D♭maj; d♭'–f"; Tess-M; 4/4, Andante ben moderato; 5pp; Diff-V/m, P/d.
For: all voices except extremely low
Mood: serene; quiet; all things change
Voice: stepwise and easy skips; syncopation; long tones
Piano: chords and chordal figuration in 16ths awkward; many accidentals; much motion; 15 meas. solo material
Diff: long phrases; irregular phrase length could cause ensemble problems

29.   **SPRING POOLS** (Robert Frost). Associated, 1946. Bmaj; c♯'–g♯"; Tess-mH; 2/4 (voice) and 6/8 (piano) with some changes, Allegretto piacevole; 5pp; Diff-V/md, P/m.
For: tenor; soprano
Mood: philosophical; nature poem
Voice: triplet and duplet subdivisions juxtaposed; skips of up to 8ve
Piano: syncopated repeated chords; high register counter-melody; some cross-hands; no doubling of vocal line
Diff: polymeters and piano syncopation make ensemble difficult; needs secure register control

30.   **TWO SONGS** (Robert Frost). Associated, 1966. X; c'–g"; Tess-M-mH; regular meters with changes; moderate tempos; 3+min; Diff-V/d-dd, P/md-d.
For: composer says medium voice; better for soprano or tenor
Mood: lyrical; wistful; narrative; introspective

Voice: many skips; dissonant intervals; many accidentals; fluid rhythms
Piano: quarter note divided many different ways; fluid; many accidentals; dissonant harmonies; mostly high range
Diff: voice and piano independent; singer needs secure pitch and rhythmic sense
Uses: most effective as a pair

    a. *A Minor Bird.* e♭'–g"; Tess-mH-H; 4/4 with changes, Fairly slow; 2min; Diff-V/dd, P/d; for simpler setting see Celius Dougherty.
    b. *A Patch of Old Snow.* [4]. c'–g"; Tess-M–mH; 4/4 with changes, Moderato; 1+min; Diff-V/d, P/md.

AMRAM, DAVID
(b. Philadelphia, PA, 1930)

31. **THREE SHAKESPEARE SONGS.** Bass (Baritone) Voice and Piano. C. F. Peters, 1986. Separate entries below.

A. **MALVOLIO'S ARIA** ("Tis But Fortune," from the Opera: *Twelfth Night*). A-centered; F♯–e'; Tess-wide; 4/4 with changes, ♩ = 88 with changes; 13pp; Diff-V/d, P/md.
For: bass; bass-baritone
Mood: dramatic and humorous
Voice: monologue; somewhat angular with speech-like rhythms; some long-ranged phrases (F♯–c♯', B♭–e♭'); many accidentals; some staccato; one trill; dynamics *pp–fff*
Piano: predominantly linear; many accidentals; uses wide keyboard range; trills and tremolo; grace notes; some rolled chords; various subdivisions of the beat; does not double vocal line
Diff: characterization; range
Uses: probably should stand alone

B. **BLOW, BLOW THOU WINTER WIND.** Ends Fmaj; B♭–d♭'; Tess-M; 4/4, ♩ = 76–80; 3pp (with repeats); Diff-V/m, P/me.
For: bass; bass-baritone
Mood: hearty; ironic
Voice: stepwise motion and small skips; several accidentals; easy rhythms; a few dotted notes; syllabic
Piano: contrapuntal, 3-voice texture; many accidentals; some doubling of vocal line
Uses: in a group of songs from Shakespeare's plays or pair with "Fool's Song" (see below)

C. **FOOL'S SONG** (*King Lear*). E-centered; B–e'; Tess-M; 6/8, Allegretto moderato; 2pp; Diff-V/me, P/m.
For: bass; bass-baritone
Mood: ironic loyalty; lyric
Voice: stepwise and skips outlining chords; easy rhythms; syllabic
Piano: contrapuntal, 4-voice texture; many accidentals; some dotted rhythms; vocal line doubled 8ve higher
Diff: high notes (e', d♯') for some young singers
Uses: in a group of songs from Shakespeare's plays or pair

with "Blow, Blow Thou Winter Wind" (see above)

32. **THREE SONGS FOR AMERICA** (for bass voice, woodwind quintet, and string quartet; piano reduction by composer). C. F. Peters, 1974. cmp1969. X and tonal; F–e'; Tess-M; regular meters; moderate tempos; 8+min; Diff-V/d-dd, P/dd.
For: bass specified; some bass-baritones
Mood: patriotic and humanitarian
Voice: some disjunct sections; speech rhythms; many accidentals; wide tessitura
Piano: orchestral–most pianists will have to edit; some 3-stave notation; very complex; does not double vocal line; more effective with chamber orchestra
Diff: in every area
Uses: very effective for the mature singer; powerful texts and powerful settings
Rec: D#74

    a. *I (John F. Kennedy).* X, E♭-centered; F♯–e♭'; Tess-M; 4/4, ♩ = 60–63.
    b. *II (Martin Luther King, Jr.).* X, B♭-centered; F–e'; Tess-M; 6/8, ♪ = 66.
    c. *III (Robert F. Kennedy).* X, G-centered; (E)F♯–d'; Tess-M; 4/4, Animato, ♩ = 100.

ANDERSEN, ARTHUR OLAF
(b. Newport, RI, 1880; d. Tucson, AZ, 1958)

33. **GUARDED.** A Slumber Song ("Kinderwacht"). [66, vol.5]; 1st©1909. Cmaj; c'–g"; Tess-M; 2/4, Slowly and simply; 27meas; Diff-V/m, P/m.
For: soprano
Mood: lullaby; sustained; gentle
Voice: some stepwise motion; several leaps
Piano: sustained 4-part chords with countermelody
Diff: smooth, soft singing, even at high climax
Uses: a very nice song for a young singer or any soprano

ANDREWS, MARK
(b. Gainsborough, England, 1875; d. Montclair, NJ, 1939)

34. **IN FLANDERS FIELDS** (Lieut.-Col. John McRae). Huntzinger & Dilworth, 1919. H & L keys: E♭maj & D♭maj; e♭'–g" & d♭'–f "; Tess-M–mH; 4/4, Andante; 5pp; Diff-V/m, P/m.
For: tenor; baritone; some basses;
Mood: lyric-dramatic; World War I song
Voice: mostly conjunct motion; alternate high notes at climax; serious text
Piano: chordal and broken-chord patterns; tremolo; some ornamental scale passages; trills
Diff: establishing mood of nobility
Uses: period piece; a good and durable song

35. **SEA-FEVER** (John Masefield). [8, 38]; 1st©1920. H & L keys: Fmaj & Dmaj; c'–f " & a–d"; Tess-M; 6/8, With a hearty swing; 4pp; Diff-V/m, P/m.
For: any male voice
Mood: vigorous sea song

Voice: short phrases; strong accents; sturdy, swinging rhythm; some chromaticism
Piano: chordal, basically 4-voice; often doubles vocal line
Uses: good teaching song

36.   **WHEN TO SLEEP I MUST** (Richard W. Gilder). H. W. Gray, 1914. D♭maj; b♭–d♭"(g♭"); Tess-M; 4/4, With breadth and sincerity; 2pp; Diff-V/e, P/m.
For: baritone; bass
Mood: lyrical; prayer-like
Voice: sustained but short phrases; short range; simple rhythmic pattern repeated; thoughtful text
Piano: chordal; quiet ending
Uses: good for young baritone or bass

ANTES, JOHN (See Special Section)

ANTHEIL, GEORGE
(b. Trenton, NJ, 1900; d. New York, NY, 1959)

37.   **FIVE SONGS, 1919–1920,** for Soprano and Piano (Adelaide Crapsey). Boosey & Hawkes, 1934 & 1961. Blurred harmonies; c'–a♯"; Tess-M-H; changing meters predominate; 7min; Diff-V/md-d, P/m-d.
For: lyric soprano
Mood: lyrical; atmospheric short settings with some intense points; most concern death or symbolic death
Voice: chromatic lines; speech rhythms
Piano: repeated and arpeggiated chord patterns, often using 7ths or cluster chords; large reaches; atmospheric; does not double vocal line
Diff: singer must be good musician; mature poetic interpretation needed
Uses: effective short set

    a. *November Night.* B-centered; d"–a♯"; Tess-H; 3/2, ♩ = 72-80 with a frosty, nebulous accompaniment, senza arpeggiare; 1min.
    b. *Triad.* Amin; a'–g"; Tess-mH; 3/4 with changes, ♪ = 80-88; 1+min.
    c. *Susanna and the Elders.* X; f♯'–g"; Tess-M; 3/4, ♩ = 69; 1+min.
    d. *Fate Defied.* X; e'–e"(g"); Tess-M; changing meters, 2/4 predominates, ♩ = 58; 1+min.
    e. *The Warning.* A-centered; c'–e"; Tess-M, L; changing meters, ♪ = 92; 2min.

APPLEBAUM, EDWARD
(b. Los Angeles, CA, 1937)

38.   **PORTRAITS.** Soprano and Piano. MMB Music, n.d. cmp1991; also published for soprano and chamber ensemble. X; sop. c'–b", pianist d♯'–b♭'; Tess-wide; unmetered; 20pp; Diff-V/dd, P/dd.
For: soprano
Mood: beginning, middle, and end are haiku about "Rain," framing poems about a newborn and a famous painting
Voice: angular; many accidentals; wide intervals; complex rhythms, sometimes speech-like; some whistling and

humming; some spoken lines; many dynamic markings; long high notes
Piano: thin, colorful score; covers the keyboard with many register changes; bell-like passages; many pedaling instructions; trills, tremolo; many ostinato passages; piano often has to "fit in" while voice sings in rhythm; very complex rhythms and polyrhythms; syncopation; many tempo fluctuations; pianist sings in two places; many dynamic markings; special instructions in piano score, and special notation explained in front material; only incidental doubling of vocal line
Diff: ensemble, as well as pitches, rhythms, tessitura, tempo changes, and high ending on b" and a♯"
Uses: for two ambitious performers who enjoy performing in this idiom and want something different (successive songs are done without pause, or with a short pause)

    a. *Three Haiku: Light Rain i* (Andrew Lansdown). X; f♯'–f♯"; unmetered, ♩ = 56; 1p.
    b. *Song for the New Born* (Andrew Burke). X; c'–b♭"; unmetered, ♩ = 42–138; 7+pp.
    c. *Three Haiku: Light Rain iii* (Andrew Lansdown). X; d♯'–g♯"; unmetered, ♩ = 56; 2pp.
    d. *Nude Descending a Staircase* (Alex Choate). X; c'–g♯"; unmetered, ♩ = 63-112; 9pp.
    e. *Three Haiku: Light Rain ii* (Andrew Lansdown). X; e'–b"; unmetered, ♩ = 56; 1p.

ARGENTO, DOMINICK
(b. York, PA, 1927)

39.   **THE ANDRÉE EXPEDITION.** Song-cycle for Baritone and Piano (Texts from the diaries and notebooks of S. S. Andrée and Nils Strindberg, Arctic adventurers). Boosey & Hawkes, 1987. cmp1982(?). "for Håkan Hagegård." Tonal; A♯–g'; Tess-mH-H-HH; simple and compound regular meters; varied tempos; 40min; Diff-V/d, P/d.
For: baritone (with easy top); dramatic tenor
Mood: fatal polar adventure romanticized; excerpts from 1897 diaries of balloonists' flight to the North Pole set to music that evokes icy backdrop for the fatal adventure
Voice: lyric and dramatic recit.; sections of straightforward melody; many accidentals; many different rhythmic groupings that follow word stress; numerous sustained high tones at all dynamic levels; some portamento; unusually high tessitura frequent; some large leaps; predominantly conjunct lines; many dynamic and expressive markings; one phrase in French and three in Swedish; long texts
Piano: motivic structure; repeated patterns; many accidentals; many rhythmic groupings; some three-stave scoring; chordal and linear sections; rich harmonic content; piano part highly descriptive of mood of text and natural setting of snow and ice
Diff: not really as difficult musically as it looks on the page; facsimile clearly readable, but somewhat intimidating at first glance; high tessitura; ability to tell a dramatic story; ensemble; endurance
Uses: for professional or advanced graduate level singers only; a wonderful and effective work for a mature voice

of considerable size; program with perhaps two much lighter groups

Rec: D#s 75, 76

PART ONE: IN THE AIR

    a. *Prologue* (Fraenkel). Quartal on A; [ranges in 𝄢] c♯–e♯'; Tess-H; unmeasured, 3/4, 2/4, 9/8, Recitativo a piacere–Con moto (♩ = 76ca.); 4+pp.

    b. *The Balloon Rises* (Strindberg: Letter to Anna). Dmaj; c♯–f♯'; Tess-mH-H; 6/4, 9/4, Allegro con slancio (♩.= 66ca.); 6+pp.

    c. *Pride and Ambition* (Andrée: First Journal). G; B–f'; Tess-H; 4/2, 2/2, Tranquillissimo (♩ = 45ca.) Mezza voce e molto contento; 4+pp.

    d. *Dinner Aloft* (Strindberg: Letter to Anna). Cmaj; c♯–f♯'; Tess- H; 2/2, 3/2, Allegro con spirito (♩ = 72); 3+pp.

    e. *The Unforseen Problem* (Fraenkel). F; B♭–f'; Tess-H; 2/2, 3/2, Larghetto (♩ = 48ca.); 4+pp.

    f. *The Flight Aborted* (Andrée: First Journal). B♭; A–f♯'; Tess-cs, HH; 4/4, 3/4, Agitato misterioso, mosso (♩ = 96ca.); 6+pp.

PART TWO: ON THE ICE

    g. *Mishap with a Sledge* (Strindberg: Letter to Anna). E♭; B♭–f'; Tess-cs, H, HH; unmeasured, quasi 4/8, A piacere–Moderato e rubato (♪ = 76ca.) (Alla canzona); 5pp.

    h. *The King's Jubilee* (Andrée: First Journal). Polytonal; d–f'; Tess-H; 4/8, Adagio assai (♪= 50ca.); 4+pp.

    i. *Illness and Drugs* (Fraenkel). F♯min; A♯–e'; Tess-mH; unmeasured, 4/4, Recitativo, lento (♩ = 46ca.); 2+pp.

    j. *Hallucinations* (Andrée: First Journal). F♯min; c♯–g'; Tess-mH-H; 6/8, 9/8, 4/8, 7/8, Scorrevole con moto (♩. = 69); 6pp.

    k. *Anna's Birthday* (Strindberg: Letter to Anna). C♭maj; B♭–g♭'; Tess-mH-H; 4/4, Andantino pesante (♩ = 60)–Adagietto dolce (♩ = 56ca.); 5pp.

    l. *Epilogue* (Fraenkel). E- & C♯-centered; B–g'; Tess-mH-H; unmeasured, 4/4, 2/4, 5/4, 3/4, Recitativo a piacere–Largo assai e rubato (♩ = 40ca.); 7pp.

    m. *Final Words* (Andrée: Second Journal). A; e–e'; Tess-M; 4/8, Lento, quasi senza tempo (♪ = 40ca.); 2pp.

40.   **CASA GUIDI** (Elizabeth Barrett Browning). A Cycle of Five Songs for Mezzo-soprano and Piano. Boosey & Hawkes, 1984. cmp1983. "For Frederica von Stade." Version for voice and orchestra first performed in 1983 by von Stade and the Minnesota Orchestra. Some traditional keys and harmonies, but many alterations; a♭–a"(a♭"); Tess-wide; traditional meters with changes; many tempo changes within each song; 20min (31pp); Diff-V/dd, P/dd.

For: mezzo-soprano

Mood: texts are letters written from Florence, Italy, by E.B.B. to her sister in England, 1846–1859; describe scenes from her life–her home, her servants, her happiness in marriage, her feelings at death of her father, and an

evening at home in November

Voice: mostly disjunct; chromatic; rhythmically complex; some humming; some staccato; portamentos; some recit.-like sections; several melismas; many changes in dynamics, some sudden

Piano: mixture of linear and chordal sections; many accidentals, rapid scales, and arpeggios for occasional color; (b.), many repeated notes; passages in 8ves in (b.) & (c.); passages in 3rds (one hand) in (b.); (e.), mostly in arpeggiated patterning; complex rhythms; doubling of vocal line rare and incidental

Diff: in every aspect, incl. ensemble

Uses: for mature performers and excellent musicians; interesting cycle in every way

    a. *Casa Guidi.* B♭-centered; b–a"(g"); 4/4 with changes, Andante mosso e semplice (8 changes); 5pp.

    b. *The Italian Cook and the English Maid.* E-centered; b–g♯"; 6/4 with changes, Allegro scherzoso (13 new tempo designations); 8pp.

    c. *Robert Browning.* D♭-centered; a♭–a♭"; 4/8 with changes, Adagietto (12 new tempo designations); 6pp.

    d. *The Death of Mr. Barrett.* Amin-maj; c'–g"; 4/4 with changes, Mesto con moto ma molto calmo (4 changes); 3pp.

    e. *Domesticity.* Dmaj-B♭maj; c'–g"; 9/8 with changes, Allegro moderato (6 changes); 10pp.

41.   **FROM THE DIARY OF VIRGINIA WOOLF.** Medium Voice and Piano. Cycle. Boosey & Hawkes, 1975. cmp1974. "For Janet Baker." Some traditional keys (much alteration within basically romantic harmonies); a–g♯"; Tess-cs; regular and irregular changing meters; varied tempos, much rubato; 42pp; Diff-V/dd, P/dd.

For: dramatic mezzo-soprano

Mood: moods range from lyrical reflection to dramatic anxiety about events in the poet's life and her gradual descent into fatal depression

Voice: much dramatic recit.; repeated notes and many skips and leaps; a few melismas along chord lines; chromatic; rhythmically complicated with prose speech rhythms; many different divisions of the beat and many tempo changes; wide-ranged; some humming; numerous unaccomp. passages; detailed dynamic and expressive markings; high notes have a variety of dynamic markings *ppp–ff*; staccato and legato singing; many accidentals

Piano: linear and chordal with many different figurations: repeated chords, triplet broken chords, rolled chords, melodic and countermelodic material, tremolo, fast repeated notes in high register; motivic construction; rhythmically complex with many tempo changes; many accidentals; wide-spread over keyboard; large reach helpful; virtuoso technique required; some 3-stave notation; highly programmatic

Diff: in every area; for mature virtuoso performers who understand the texts and have good dramatic instincts

Uses: rich score; dramatic and powerful for the right singer

Rec: D#s 81, 82, 83, 84

a. *The Diary* (April, 1919). B♭-centered; b–g♭"; Tess-M; 4/4, Mosso e pensieroso; 4pp.

b. *Anxiety* (October, 1920). Bmin; b♭–f♯"; Tess-cs; 6/8 with changes, Presto ed inquieto; 6pp.

c. *Fancy* (February, 1927). X-A♭maj; c'–g♭"; Tess-cs; 4/8 with many changes, Allegretto capriccioso (with many tempo changes); 2pp.

d. *Hardy's Funeral* (January, 1928). c♯'–g♭"; Tess-cs; unmeasured sections alternate with 2/4, Solenne e meditativo (many tempo changes); 7pp.

e. *Rome* (May, 1935). Cmin; c'–f"; Tess-M; 2/4, Lento e languido; 5pp.

f. *War* (June, 1940). C♯- & G♯-centered (note absence of key sig.in treble clef of piano score); a–g♯"; Tess-cs; unmeasured, Rubato e grave, quasi improvvisato; 6pp.

g. *Parents* (December, 1940). Emaj; b–g"; Tess-M; 4/8, 12/16, Largo ed affettuoso; 5pp.

h. *Last Entry* (March, 1941). C♯maj-B♭; c♯'–g♭"; Tess-mH; 12/8 with many changes, Risoluto ed appassionato; 7pp.

42. SIX ELIZABETHAN SONGS. Song Cycle for High Voice and Piano. Boosey & Hawkes, 1970. "For Nicholas Di Virgilio." No key sigs. but generally traditional keys with many altered-chord structures; d♯'–a"; Tess-mH; regular meters; varied tempos; 12+min; Diff-V/m-d, P/md.

For: lyric tenor; soprano

Mood: playful, lyrical, boisterous, melancholy, ecstatic, and lyrical

Voice: both conjunct and disjunct: stepwise phrases, chord outlining phrases, large skips and leaps; numerous sustained tones in all registers; mostly syllabic; some soft slow melismas in (e.); sustained f", a♭", and a" in (c.); mostly regular meters and rhythms with numerous different divisions of beat; polyrhythms with piano

Piano: supports voice and creates moods; patterned construction mostly chordal in various figurations; much staccato in the few linear sections; polyrhythms; some very fast tempos; numerous accidentals; nimble fingers as well as smooth, warm playing needed; wide reach helpful

Diff: sustained high tones; fast articulation; poetic imagery

Uses: excellent work for teaching many different techniques; frequent occurrence of "oo" vowel on high tones good for head voice; fine recital group for advanced singer

Rec: D#s 77, 78, 79, 80, 85

a. *Spring* (Thomas Nash). Fmaj; e♭–f"; Tess-M; 2/4, Allegretto piacevole; 1+min.

b. *Sleep* (Samuel Daniel). B♭; d♯'–f"; Tess-M; 8/8 with changes, Lentamente; 3min.

c. *Winter* (William Shakespeare). Amaj; e'–a"; Tess-M; 6/8, 2/4, 3/4, Allegro vivace con slancio; 1+min.

d. *Dirge* (William Shakespeare). Gmaj-Cmaj; e'–e"; Tess-mL; 4/8, Largo e semplice; 3min.

e. *Diaphenia* (Henry Constable). Gmaj-C♯maj; f♯'–g"; Tess-M; 9/8, Allegro brillante; 1+min.

f. *Hymn* (Ben Jonson). Dmaj; d♯'–g"; Tess-M-mH; 6/8, 9/8, Andante maestoso; 2+min.

43. SONGS ABOUT SPRING (e. e. cummings). Cycle. Boosey & Hawkes, 1980. First performance 1951. "For Carolyn Bailey." No key sigs, moderately dissonant; c♯'–c'''; Tess-H, wide; regular meters with some changes; varied tempos, ends fast and brilliant; 12min; Diff-V/d, P/d-dd.

For: soprano

Mood: light, fanciful, joyous, innocent, and spring-like

Voice: wide range in many phrases; wide leaps; (a.) has many scale passages and some staccato; several long, sustained tones; unexpected intervals; (c.) has both duple and triple division of the measure

Piano: fits hands reasonably well, but l.h. needs wide reach; many accidentals; some solo interludes; (d.) is canon between voice and single-line piano part; (e.) contains passages for r.h. in rapid 3rds; balance between linear and chordal writing; metronome markings

Diff: ensemble; some entrances for singer; wide range and leaps; rapid diction in (c.) & (e.); polyrhythms in (c.); low tessitura in (d.); high tessitura in (e.)

Uses: ends recital or first half of recital well; good work; rewarding for both performers

Rec: D#s 86, 87

a. *who knows if the moon's a balloon.* e'–a"; 6/8 with changes, Allegretto piacevole; 4pp.

b. *spring is like a perhaps hand.* d♯'–g"; 4/8 with changes, Larghetto semplice; 2pp.

c. *in just-spring.* d'–c'''(a♭); 3/8, Leggero e giojoso; 3pp.

d. *in spring comes.* c♯'–f♯"; 2/4, Adagietto innocentamente; 1p.

e. *when faces called flowers float out of the ground.* d'–b♭"; 3/4, Tempo di valse; 5pp; same text as "the mountains are dancing," set by John Duke.

ASIA, DANIEL
(b. Seattle, WA, 1953)

44. BREATH IN A RAM'S HORN (Paul Pines) (Songs for My Father) for Tenor (or Soprano) and Piano. Merion Music, 1998 (Theodore Presser). cmp1995. "for Paul Sperry." Tonal; b–g♯"; Tess-L-M; mostly regular meters with changes; ♩ = 66–120; 13min; Diff-V/me-md, P/me-m.

For: tenor; soprano

Mood: distant memories; fragile relationships; a son's search for his father's faith

Voice: declamation, chant-like melody, lyric melody, folk-like narrative; frequent syncopation in rhythmic line; frequent large ascending intervals; sustained tones on f" and g"; syllabic

Piano: mostly thin textures and muted colors; many moving 8th- & 16th-note patterns; numerous accidentals; some polyrhythms; expressive of the mood of each text

Diff: large ascending leaps; long sustained tones at top of staff; *ppp* to *f* dynamics on g"

Uses: good material for graduate level tenor; effective work

a. *What Do We Know.* B♭min; c'–g"; Tess-M; 2/4, 3/4, ♩ = 72; 2pp.

b. *Old Medals, Prayer Shawls.* X; d'–g♯"; Tess-M; 3/4, 3/8, 5/8, ♩ = 72; 3pp.

c. *Job Longed for the Grave.* Dmaj; a'–g"; Tess-M; 3/8, 5/4, 0, 4/4, 2/4, ♩ = 120, drammático; 4pp.

d. *Yom Kippur.* Lydian on D; e♭'–g"; Tess-M; 2/4, 3/4, ♩ = 96 (tentatively) ♩ = 104, Lightly, but with a nostalgic quality; 5pp.

e. *My Father's Name Was . . .* Bmin; b–g"; Tess-L, M; 2/4, ♩ = 66 (very casual, matter of fact); 4pp.

ATOR, JAMES
(b. Kansas City, MO, 1938)

45. **HAIKU,** for Mezzo-soprano. Seesaw, 1973. cmp1971. X; c♯'–g"; Tess-M; regular and irregular meters; varied tempos; 4pp; Diff-V/dd, P/d.

For: mezzo-soprano

Mood: lyrical; Oriental in style; somewhat humorous and risqué

Voice: chromatic and disjunct; pitches very difficult; vocal glissandos and semi-spoken tones; difficult rhythms; fragmented phrases

Piano: highly chromatic and dissonant; tone clusters; pointillistic style, fragmented by rests

Diff: perfect pitch desirable; good rhythmic sense necessary; command of special vocal effects

Uses: effective recital songs for a fine musician

a. *Oh, Moon! . . .* (Koyo). 7/8, ♪ = 96.

b. *Oh, You Bawdy Breeze!* (Issa). 5/4, ♩ = 72.

c. *No Wonder Today All the Men Need Mid-Day Naps . . .* (Teitok). 4/4, 3/4, ♩ = 60.

d. *Such a Fine First Dream . . .* (Basho). 3/4, ♩ = 48.

AVSHALOMOV, JACOB
(b. Tsingtao, China, 1919)

46. **BIBLICAL SONGS.** [71]. cmp1944-1945. Mostly tonal; g–f"; Tess-mL, M, wide; changing regular and irregular meters; slow and moderate tempos; 12pp; Diff-V/m-md, P/m-d.

For: low voices: bass; contralto

Mood: devotion; a cry against violence; faith

Voice: (a.) lyrical lines; some large intervals; short melismas; (b.) dramatic lines; speech rhythms; sustained f"; many accidentals; (c.) lyrical; some large intervals; some tone painting; low phrases; ends on low a

Piano: (a.) chordal introduction; arpeggiated figuration; some polyrhythms; three interludes; accidentals; wide spacing; (b.) 32nd-note triplet ornaments; trills; 8ves and broken-chord patterns; 8ve displacement in r.h.; one interlude; long postlude; many accidentals; broad dynamic range; (c.) mostly linear; many 8ves; two interludes; some wide spacing

Diff: some rhythmic groupings; many accidentals; ensemble in (b.)

Uses: beautiful settings of "Entreat me not to leave thee" and Psalm XXIII; powerful setting of "How long, Oh Lord"; use as group in concert or separately for appropriate occasions

Rec: D#88

a. *Ruth's Song* (Ruth 1:16, 17). Amin; a♭–e"; Tess-mL; 4/4, 5/4, 3/4, Lento ♩ = 84; 3pp.

b. *How Long, Oh Lord* (Isaiah). X; a–f"; Tess-M; 3/4, 5/4, 4/4, 9/8, 5/8, Lento ♩ = 60; 5pp.

c. *Psalm XXIII.* Tonal; g–e"; Tess-wide; 3/4, 4/4, 3/2, Semplice ♩ = 84; 4pp.

47. **DORIS SONGS.** Twelve Lyric Poems (Doris Avshalomov). Set for Medium Voice. Piano or Harp. Howlet Press–Music, 1999 (Facsimile). cmp1996. Tonal and X; g♯–a"; Tess-L, mL, M, cs; mostly regular meters with changes; varied tempos; 20min (1–7pp. each); Diff-V/m-d, P/me-d.

For: mezzo-soprano

Mood: a collection of short poems about various everyday experiences, all with nature images; ordinary things seen through imaginative eyes

Voice: mostly conjunct lines with some skips and larger leaps; tone-painting melismas occur within generally syllabic settings; numerous phrases below c'; some phrases at top of staff; various rhythmic groupings; polyrhythms; numerous accidentals; one song in 7/8

Piano: originally composed for guitar and here transcribed for piano (or harp); mostly linear; fairly thin textures; numerous accidentals; some irregular meters

Diff: some rhythms; melodic direction sometimes unclear; ensemble; facsimile score

Uses: composer says each group of four songs may be performed separately; songs can be done with guitar, harp, or piano; best for more mature singer to whom the poetry is meaningful

a. *Fog Gentles Distance.* Aeolian on A; c'–e"; Tess-M; 6/8, 9/8, Tranquil ♪ = 96; 1+p.

b. *Folding Away My Summer Dresses.* Tonal; c♯'–d"; Tess-mL; 3/4, 4/4, Pensive ♩ = 69; 1+p.

c. *Scars on Two Fir Trees.* Tonal; g♯–f♯"; Tess-mL; 3/4, 4/4, 5/4, Pensive ♩ = 76; 3+pp.

d. *Winds Toss Down Red and Gold.* C♯min; a–e"; Tess-wide; 3/4, 4/4, Bracing ♩ = 120; 3+pp.

e. *On Being Laid Up.* Tonal; a–f♯"; Tess-mL-M; 3/4, 4/4, Fevered ♩ = 104; 4+pp.

f. *While I Was Listening for Owls.* X; g♯–e"; Tess-L; 4/4, 3/4, Nocturne ♩ = 96; 2+pp.

g. *The Station.* X; a♭–e"; Tess-M; 3/4, 4/4, Longing ♩ = 126; 4+pp.

h. *More about Stars.* X; c♯'–a"; Tess-cs; 6/8, 9/8, Teasing ♩. = 120; 7pp.

i. *The Scarlet Antherium.* Cmaj; c♯'–g"; Tess-cs; 6/8, 2/4, 3/4, 5/8, Ironic ♩. = 100; 3+pp.

j. *The Carpet.* X; b–g♯"; Tess-cs; 7/8, Orientale ♩ = 92; 4+pp.

k. *The Tribute.* X; b–d♯"; Tess-M; 3/4, 4/4, Inquiry ♩ = 66; 3+pp.

l. *A Sea Text.* X; b–g♭"; Tess-cs; 9/8, 6/8, Fluid ♩. = 69; 3+pp.

48. **FED BY MY LABORS** (Gordon Newell). [71]. cmp1940; rev1994. X; b♭–e♭"; Tess-mL; 3/4, 2/4, 6/8, 3/8, 5/8, 9/8, Vigoroso ♩ = 78; 5pp; Diff-V/md, P/md.

For: baritone
Mood: philosophical; a look at what life has become
Voice: mostly conjunct, some small skips, one 8ve; chromatic; speech rhythms; middle section lyrical with longer notes; syllabic
Piano: dissonant; many 8ves and open chords; arpeggiated middle section in 16th-note groups of 6 & 5; accidentals; powerful chordal ending; no doubling of vocal line
Diff: pitches against dissonance in piano; changing meters; understanding poem
Uses: a rather stark song, grouped by the composer with three other dark songs; could be powerful for a mature singer
Rec: D#88

49. **THE GLASS TOWN** (Alastair Reid). Galaxy, 1959. cmp1955. Cmin; b–g"; Tess-M; 4/4, 5/4, Andante calmato; 3min; Diff-V/m, P/m.
For: soprano; tenor
Mood: lyrical; glassy; description of reflections in water
Voice: many skips; speech rhythms; meter changes; wide-ranged phrases; some chromaticism
Piano: linear; 8ves; bell-like figures; 8th-note motion; glassy texture
Diff: some difficult pitches; voice needs smooth sound
Uses: interesting song; attractive for performance

50. **LULLABY** (without words). [71]. cmp1941. Emin; b–e"; Tess-wide; 4/4, Lento; 2pp; Diff-V/e, P/e.
For: any voice
Mood: tender; quiet
Voice: melody without words; falling phrases
Piano: chordal; rocking motion; some countermelody
Diff: singer must be able to hum freely throughout range
Uses: lovely song in lullaby group; good for teaching the hum

51. **O TIME** (Anne Bradstreet). [71]. cmp1966. X; c#'–f#"; Tess-M; 4/4, 6/4, 5/4, Larghetto ♩ = 72; 3pp; Diff-V/md, P/md.
For: medium voice
Mood: stark; the impermanence of all worldly things; only the soul shall last
Voice: speech rhythms and sustained phrases; mostly conjunct; a few large intervals; lyrical
Piano: chordal; dissonant (many 2nds); many accidentals; parallel chords; sostenuto pedal used
Diff: dissonant harmonic structure
Uses: use with other Avshalomov songs or in a group of songs about time; effective song
Rec: D#88

52. **SONGS FOR ALYCE.** Howlet Press–Music, 1994. cmp1975–1976. "For Alyce Rogers." X; a–g"; Tess-wide; regular meters with changes; very slow to very fast tempos; 23pp; Diff-V/m-d, P/md-d.
For: mezzo-soprano
Mood: sense of awe; playful; calm of evening; mock serious
Voice: (a.) sustained vocal line with very wide range and large intervals; (b.) angular lines; short phrases; speech rhythms; (c.) both conjunct lines and large intervals; entire melodic line paints the text; (d) strict meter; short phrases in speech rhythms, and long phrases over

activity in the piano
Piano: (a.) dissonant chords three 8ves apart create sense of great size, space, and age; some 32nd-note ornamental figurations; some 3-stave scoring; (b.) ostinato figuration high in the treble in triplets and quadruplets; some punctuating, commenting, and illustrative passages; (c.) chordal; many accidentals; (d.) tick-tock figures in strict rhythm; chromatic; polyrhythms; chiming figures; familiar melody quoted
Diff: wide-ranged phrases; many accidentals; singer will need excellent ear for pitch
Uses: excellent and interesting group with much variety for advanced singer; should be attractive to audiences
Rec: D#88

a. *The Mountain Sat upon the Plain* (Emily Dickinson). Pentatonic and quartal; a–f#"; Tess-wide; 2/2, 3/2, Grave ♩ = 52; 4pp.
b. *Answer July* (Emily Dickinson). E-centered; b–e"; Tess-M; 3/4, 2/4, Allegro scherzando ♩ = 138–144; 7pp.
c. *A Day Is Laid By* (May Swenson). Bitonal-Bmaj; bb–g"; Tess-wide; 3/4, 2/4, Lento ♩ = 69; 3pp.
d. *The Watch* (May Swenson). E-centered; a–g"; Tess-wide; 2/4, 5/8, 3/4, 2/2; 9pp.

53. **THREE CHINESE SONGS.** [71]. cmp1937, 1940, 1941. Pentatonic; g–f"; Tess-M; regular meters with changes; slow-fast-slow; 6pp; Diff-V/e-m, P/e-m.
For: medium voices
Mood: nocturnal love song; humorous; meditative
Voice: short phrases; pentatonic melodic patterns
Piano: mostly chordal; some broken chord patterns; some wide spacing and parallel 8ves; some decorative figurations
Uses: interesting group of short songs; contrast with other Oriental subject songs
Rec: D#88

a. *On the T'ung T'ing Lake* (Li-Po). Pentatonic; g–e"; Tess-wide; 4/4, 3/4, 5/4, 6/8, Tranquillo (♩ = 60); 2pp.
b. *Moon in the Yellow River* (Denis Johnston). Pentatonic; d'–f"; Tess-M; 2/4, 4/4, 3/4, Allegretto ♩ = 132; 2pp.
c. *The Ch'ing T'ing Mountain* (Li-Po). Pentatonic; bb–c"; Tess-M; 3/4, 4/4; 2pp.

54. **THRENOS - I** (Ezra Pound). [70, 71]. cmp1974. Two different keys: [70] G minorish; a#–g" & [71] F minorish; g#–f"; Tess-mL, M; 4/4, Calmato ♩ = 50–54; 2pp; Diff-V/m, P/m.
For: high voice [70]; medium voice [71]
Mood: song of lamentation
Voice: most phrases narrow in compass; chromatic; some larger intervals; syllabic; speech rhythms
Piano: wide spacing; chromatic
Diff: pitches
Uses: pair with "Threnos - ii"; good in elegiac group
Rec: D#88

55. **THRENOS - II** (Ezra Pound). [70 & 71]. cmp1974. Two different keys: [70] Gmin; bb–g"; [71] Fmin;

a♭–f"; Tess-M; 4/4, 3/4, Calmato ♩ = 50–54; 2pp; Diff-V/m, P/me.

For: high voice [70]; medium voice [71]
Mood: true self remains; one loves his true heritage
Voice: lyrical; speech rhythms; ends on d'; delicately dissonant
Piano: accidentals; some doubling of vocal line
Diff: one low phrase; clear diction needed for unusual words
Uses: pair with "Threnos - i"
Rec: D#88

56. WHIMSIES. [71]. cmp1955; rev.1974. Tonal; g–g"; Tess-wide; regular and irregular changing meters; fast-slow-fast; 6pp; Diff-V/m-d, P/m-md.

For: medium voice (good low notes)
Mood: humorous; autumnal and bittersweet; driving and frantic
Voice: (a.) fast rhythms; rapid diction; angular lines; ends very low; (b.) lyrical; many repeated notes; (c.) dotted rhythms; mostly conjunct lines with some large leaps
Piano: (a.) doubles vocal line much of the time; mostly chordal; (b.) chordal; some broken chords; syncopation; somewhat thick texture at soft dynamic levels; (c.) unison both hands two 8ves apart; some punctuating chords; conversational with voice (imitation)
Diff: (a.) fast diction; low ending; (b.) making the repeated material different in expression; (c.) fast diction; rhythms; ensemble
Uses: very interesting group for a good musician
Rec: D#88

a. *Tweedledee and Tweedledoom* (Ogden Nash). Amin; g–f♯"; Tess-wide; 2/4, 3/4, 5/8, 6/8, Capriccioso ♩ = 116; 2pp.
b. *Raker* (Philip Booth). E-centered; e'–e"; Tess-M; 5/4, 4/4, Sostenuto ♩ = 52; 2pp.
c. *Central Park Tourney* (Mildred Weston). A-centered; b–g"; Tess-wide; 4/4, 2/4, Veloce ♩ = 132; 2pp.

57. WHO IS MY SHEPHERD (John Malcolm Brinnin). [70]. cmp1949. Two different keys: [70] Amin; c'–a"; [71] Gmin; b♭–f"; Tess-M; 3/4, 6/8, 4/4, 2/4, Andante ♩ = 58; 5pp; Diff-V/m, P/m.

For: tenor
Mood: dark; troubled; questioning; original title of poem: "Oedipus' Cradle Song"
Voice: mostly conjunct; a few large intervals; speech rhythms; accidentals
Piano: uneasy mood created by syncopated figure underlying much of the music; dissonance; linear; many r.h. 8ves
Diff: meaning of poem; some pitches; speech rhythms
Uses: for a mature singer
Rec: D#88

58. WONDERS (William Blake). [71]. rev.1974. X; g–a♭"; Tess-wide; regular and irregular changing meters; moderate and fast tempos; 12pp; Diff-V/md-d, P/md.

For: dramatic medium voices (low a♭ and g required)
Mood: mystical
Voice: some conjunct lines; many wide intervals; sustained phrases; many accidentals; various rhythmic groupings

staccato fragmented phrases; very fast tempos; much word repetition; vocal lines instrumentally conceived–one line in the whole texture
Piano: contrapuntal; many altered chords; many accidentals; doubles vocal line frequently; looks like string quartet writing (actually exists in a string quartet version)
Diff: poetry; instrumental texture; ensemble
Uses: interesting songs; would be effective with string quartet
Rec: D#88

a. *The Smile.* X (E-centered); g–g"; Tess-wide; 4/4, 3/4, 5/4, 3/2, Andante semplice ♩ = 72; 3+pp.
b. *The Grain of Sand.* X; b–a♭"; Tess-wide; 4/4, 6/8, 3/4, 3/2, 5/4, 2/2, Allegro scherzando ♩ = 144; 9pp.

AYRES, FREDERIC
(b. Binghamton, NY, 1876; d. Colorado Springs, CO, 1926)

59. SEA DIRGE (William Shakespeare). [66, vol.5]; 1st©1907. X-Emaj; b♭–c"; Tess-mH; 4/4, Largo misterioso; 49meas; Diff-V/e, P/me.

For: baritone; bass; mezzo-soprano; contralto
Mood: mysterious, but peaceful; enchanted
Voice: stepwise and easy skips; chromaticism, but supported by accomp.
Piano: bell-like sounds, high and low; also sea-wave motion
Diff: features b' and c"; poem needs explanation
Uses: effective song for a singer with a short range; useful in a Shakespeare group

60. THREE SONGS, Op. 3 (William Shakespeare). [5]. Separate entries below.

A. TAKE, O, TAKE THOSE LIPS AWAY, Op. 3, No. 1. [66, vol.5]; 1st©1906. D♭maj; a♭(c')–f"; Tess-M; 2/4, Andante; 18meas; Diff-V/m, P/m.

For: baritone
Mood: tender; disappointed love song
Voice: highly chromatic; few skips; rhythmically straightforward
Piano: 4–6-voice texture; highly chromatic; doubles vocal line
Diff: chromatic lines
Uses: a good setting; useful for a Shakespeare group
Rec: D#52

B. WHERE THE BEE SUCKS, Op. 3, No. 2. [66, vol.4]; 1st©1907. F♯maj; c♯'–f♯"; Tess-M; 2/4, Allegretto moderato; 30meas; Diff-V/m, P/md.

For: soprano; possibly tenor
Mood: light; playful; enchanted
Voice: mostly stepwise; light texture
Piano: fast and light; r.h. triplets and syncopation; l.h. some duplets and triplets; middle and high register
Diff: some rhythmic problems
Uses: useful to lighten a heavy voice on fast, soft passages
Rec: D#52

C. COME UNTO THESE YELLOW SANDS, Op. 3, No. 3. [66, vol.5]; 1st©1907. Emaj; c♯'–e"; Tess-M; 3/4, Andantino grazioso–Poco vivace; 35 meas; Diff-V/m, P/m.

For: medium voice
Mood: graceful; dance-like
Voice: movement by step or 3rds; some triplets
Piano: mostly 6-note chords; figure includes a triplet rhythm
Diff: singer must be able to divide beat into 2, 3, & 4 parts
Uses: useful in a Shakespeare group; interesting interplay between voice and piano

BABBITT, MILTON
(b. Philadelphia, PA, 1916)

61. **SOUNDS AND WORDS.** [49]; 1st©1964. Serial; c♯'–c'''; Tess-uses entire range more or less equally; regular and irregular changing meters, ♩ = 60; 7pp; Diff-V/dd, P/dd.
For: high soprano
Mood: text consists entirely of vowel and consonant sounds and short, unrelated words
Voice: fragmented; disjunct; extremely chromatic; large intervals; sudden dynamic changes
Piano: basically 2-voice texture; fragmented; extremely chromatic; pointillistic
Diff: perfect pitch desirable; frequent use of extreme high notes; complicated rhythms; pianist needs great skill
Uses: effective for performers competent in this idiom

62. **THREE THEATRICAL SONGS.** C. F. Peters, 1981. cmp ca.1946. Set of 3 songs from an unproduced musical play entitled *Fabulous Voyage*, an adaptation of Homer's *Odyssey*. Major keys predominate; b♭–f''; Tess-M; 2/2; 5min; Diff-V/m,P/m.
For: mezzo-soprano best
Mood: portrays 3 facets of "womankind"–Calypso, Penelope, and Circe (to be sung by the same singing actress); texts are in popular song language
Voice: skips up to an 8ve; many accidentals; syncopation; syllabic
Piano: "pop" style; doubles vocal line; many accidentals; syncopation
Diff: rhythms; pitch patterns and wide tessitura in (c.); characterization
Uses: for singer who is effective in this style, which resembles George Gershwin or Cole Porter

  a. *As Long as It Isn't Love* (Milton Babbitt). Mostly Cmaj; b♭–e''; 2/2; 3pp; portrays Calypso.
  b. *Penelope's Night Song* (Richard S. Childs). Fmaj; c'–f''; 2/2; 3pp.
  c. *Now You See It* (Richard Koch & Milton Babbitt). E♭maj; b♭–f''; 2/2; 5pp; portrays Circe.

63. **THE WIDOW'S LAMENT IN SPRINGTIME** (William Carlos Williams). Boelke-Bomart, 1959. Serial; f♯–f♯''; Tess-covers the range; 2/4 with changes, ♩ = 42; 2+min; Diff-V/dd, P/dd.
For: composer specifies soprano; perhaps better for mezzo-soprano
Mood: sad
Voice: angular, disjunct lines; various rhythmic divisions; many accidentals
Piano: typical serial style–rhythmic difficulties, disjunct,

covers the keyboard
Diff: perfect pitch desirable; absolute rhythmic security needed; control of dynamics
Uses: interesting and effective piece for mature performers secure in the idiom
Rec: D#58

BACH, P. D. Q. [See Schickele, Peter]
(1807–1742)

BACON, ERNST
(b. Chicago, IL, 1898; d. Orinda, CA, 1990)

[Songs in more than one collection are often in different versions and usually in different keys. Key given is that of the first collection # listed.]

[See Appendix for songs with German texts]

64. **ANCIENT CHRISTMAS CAROL.** [72, 74, 78]. cmp ca.1942. C♯min; b♯–e''; Tess-mL; 3/4, Lento ma non troppo; 2pp; Diff-V/m, P/m.
For: mezzo-soprano; baritone
Mood: lyrical; well-known Christmas text–"He came so still where His Mother was"
Voice: lyrical; much movement by 3rds; outlines triads
Piano: chordal, becoming somewhat contrapuntal; a little chromaticism
Uses: useful for recital or for church

65. **AS IF THE SEA SHOULD PART** (Emily Dickinson). [76]. cmp ca.1931. F; f'–a♭''; Tess-mH; 4/4, Andante maestoso; 1+pp; Diff-V/md, P/m.
For: soprano
Mood: spacious; majestic; the imagined vast reaches of eternity
Voice: sustained; chromatic; full
Piano: repeated chords and melody in r.h. over bass line 8ves
Diff: text with many similar vowels ("ee"); diction
Uses: majestic short song

66. **AT THE LAST** (Walt Whitman). [72]. cmp1926–1928. "To Roland Hayes." Dmaj; a–d♭''; Tess-mL; 4/4, 3/2, Sostenuto; 2pp; Diff-V/md, P/d.
For: alto; baritone; bass
Mood: dramatic poem dealing with death
Voice: line fragmented by rests; somewhat declamatory; short phrases; some chromaticism
Piano: chordal; sustained; chromatic
Diff: requires clear low tones; dramatic, yet soft
Uses: effective recital song

67. **THE BALLAD OF BILLY IN THE DARBIES** (Herman Melville, from *Billy Budd*). Classical Vocal Reprints, 2001. cmp1976 for William Parker. Minor tonalities with sliding harmonies; A–g♭' (♯); Tess-H-HH; 12/8, 10/8 (piano), 4/4 (voice), ♩. = ca.60 (voice ♩ = piano ♩.); 9+min; Diff-V/d, P/d.
For: baritone (high)
Mood: lyrical; dream-like; Billy Budd's soliloquy during his

last hour before hanging

Voice: extremely lyrical; mostly conjunct lines; some long phrases; speech rhythms make numerous divisions of the beat, 8th- & quarter-note triplets most frequent, often with syncopation; vocal line in 4/4 over piano in 12/8 or 10/8; syllabic except for two long, flowing melismas, one ascending on "dreaming" and the other descending from g♭' in the previous phrase to A on "sinking"(6 meas.); vocal line independent, though sometimes shadowed in inner voices of piano part; many accidentals; operatic in scope though intimate in nature; two spoken lines

Piano: linear 1–4 voice texture under voice, thicker chords in one dramatic interlude; constant 8th-note motion in 12/8 and 10/8 depicts the ceaseless motion of the sea as well as the wandering of Billy's thoughts; 28-meas. prelude, four interludes of 6–11 meas. each, 3-meas. postlude; many accidentals for the sliding, dream-like harmonies; some cross-hands; large reach helpful

Diff: some pitches and rhythms; high tessitura; ensemble

Uses: a wonderful song-scene for an advanced singer who has a smooth line from low A to high g♭ and exquisite expressive abilities

Rec: D#s 34, 45

68. **THE BANKS OF THE YELLOW SEA** (Emily Dickinson). For Alto or Baritone. [74, 78]. cmp1930s. "To John Charles Thomas." E♭min; b♭–d♭'; Tess-L; 6/8, With a slow and nostalgic swing; 2pp; Diff-V/md, P/m.

For: alto; baritone; bass

Mood: lyrical; descriptive

Voice: swinging rhythms; syncopation; several fairly long melismas; rather chromatic

Piano: syncopated afterbeat figures; fairly chromatic; independent of vocal line

Diff: requires clear low tones without heaviness

Rec: D#18

69. **THE BAT** (Emily Dickinson). [72, 78]. cmp ca.1970. "To Marni Nixon." B♭-centered; d♭'–g♭"; Tess-M; 3/8, Allegro; 3pp; Diff-V/d, P/dd.

For: soprano

Mood: humorous; descriptive; rather abstract

Voice: line fragmented by rests; melismas; somewhat disjunct

Piano: pointillistic; r.h. melody over chords; rapid ascending and descending scales in postlude suggest flight of bat

Diff: good sense of pitch and rhythm required

Uses: groups well with "The Spider" and "The Swamp," also by Bacon

70. **BEAT! BEAT! DRUMS!** (Walt Whitman). [77]. cmp ca.1920s. Chromatic on B; B–g'; Tess-mH-H; 6/4, 5/4, 4/4, Alla marcia (molto moderato) ♩ = 104; 7pp; Diff-V/d, P/d.

For: dramatic baritone

Mood: powerful; dramatic; driving; brutal; dominance of war

Voice: long sections of driving phrases, often in ascending patterns; many high phrases; mostly syllabic in speech rhythms; wide dynamic range; needs vocal weight

Piano: thick texture; drumbeat rhythmic motives; chords in r.h., 8ves in l.h.; some polyrhythms; dynamic variety

Diff: high tessitura; relentless forward motion demands endurance; ensemble

Uses: fine song in many settings (e.g., Whitman group or war songs group); good group ender

71. **BRADY** (Ernst Bacon). Boosey & Hawkes, 1949. B♭maj; A–f♭'; Tess-L; 2/4, Stepping along leisurely; 6pp; Diff-V/m, P/m.

For: bass; baritone

Mood: humorous narrative about a gambler

Voice: chiefly declamatory in style; some chromaticism

Piano: staccato; r.h. melody independent of voice; descriptive

Diff: requires command of declamatory, narrative style; rather low tessitura

Uses: good for a young bass

72. **A CLEAR MIDNIGHT** (Walt Whitman). For Bass or Alto. [74]. cmp1930s. C♯min; G♯–c♯'; Tess-mL; 4/2, Slow; 2pp; Diff-V/m, P/m.

For: bass perhaps better than alto

Mood: lyrical; philosophical; sad; poem about death

Voice: broad, flowing phrases; somewhat fragmented

Piano: chordal, basically 4-voice; occasionally contrapuntal; lengthy postlude

Diff: sustained phrases; singer's attention in long postlude

Uses: beautiful recital song

73. **THE COMMONPLACE** (Walt Whitman). Associated, 1946. [4]. Cmin (orig. Amin); d♭'–g"; Tess-M-mH; 6/8, With an easy but resolute swing; 3pp; Diff-V/m, P/m.

For: high baritone; tenor

Mood: declamatory

Voice: repeated tones and skips; three spoken phrases; sustained g", f", and e♭"; speech rhythms

Piano: chordal; swing rhythm; 10-meas. postlude

Diff: sustained high tones; good declamatory sense needed

Uses: patriotic song of democracy; usable in appropriate situations

74. **DAREST THOU NOW, O SOUL** (Walt Whitman). [75]. cmp1920s. Fmaj; g–f"; Tess-L-mH; 3/4, Andante sostenuto; 6pp; Diff-V/md, P/m.

For: bass; bass-baritone

Mood: broad; open; suspended; transcendent; dramatic; life's ultimate adventure

Voice: long, sustained lines; whole phrases on one pitch; alternate notes given in several phrases for medium-low and low voices

Piano: chordal; some unison three-8ve passages; some movement in broken 8ves; chromatic; sets and maintains mood with harmonic texture and movement in open intervals

Diff: text demands maturity and a spiritual view of life; sustaining full, rich sound at all dynamic levels

Uses: for a mature singer in many performance venues

75. **THE DIVINE SHIP** (Walt Whitman). [73, 78]. cmp ca.1927. Dmin; c'–e♭"; Tess-M; 4/4, Stately (♩ = 88–100); 1p; Diff-V/m, P/m.

For: medium or low voice; baritone best

Mood: a solemn and profound testament to our common

voyage and destination

Voice: long-phrased cantus firmus vocal line moving in half and whole notes

Piano: contrapuntal structure and open texture underlie the chorale-like setting

Diff: long vocal lines

Uses: good for teaching breath control; program with other songs on Whitman poems

Rec: D#67 [same song as "One Thought Ever at the Fore"]

76. **EDEN** (Emily Dickinson). [72, 73, 78, 167]. cmp1952. Two keys: Gmin & F♯min [73]; c♯'–a♭" & b♯–g♯"; Tess-M; 6/8, Languidly (two to the bar ♩. = 69–76); 3pp; Diff-V/d, P/d. [Note: This song exists in the two different collections noted above in two slightly different versions. The higher key version has a different ending from "And is lost in balms" to the end, ending with a 16-meas. section vocalized on "oo."]

For: tenor; soprano

Mood: lyrical love poem using nature imagery

Voice: lyrical and sustained but rather disjunct; fairly chromatic; closes with vocalise on "oo" vowel

Piano: chordal with much syncopation

Diff: singer needs good sense of pitch and rhythmic stability, as accomp. does not often help; duplets in 6/8; soft a♭"

Rec: D#s 18, 89

77. **ETERNITY** (Emily Dickinson). [72, 78]. cmp ca.1926–1928. "To Paul Horgan." X; f'–a♭"; Tess-mH; 4/4, 3/2, 6/4, Andante maestoso; 1p; Diff-V/m, P/md.

For: soprano; tenor

Mood: philosophical, using nature imagery

Voice: fragmented; chromatic; rising in pitch to climax in penultimate phrase

Piano: chordal; chromatic; dotted rhythms

Diff: pitches

Rec: D#89

78. **FAREWELL** (Emily Dickinson). [72]. cmp ca.1926–1928. F♯min; c♯'–f"; Tess-mL; 10/8 , 4/4, 5/8, Tranquillo; 3pp; Diff-V/m, P/d.

For: mezzo-soprano

Mood: lyrical; philosophical poem dealing with death

Voice: lyrical and sustained; generally soft

Piano: disjunct 8th-note patterns accomp. by chords; some independent melody

Diff: rhythms

Rec: D#3

79. **FIRST DAY** (Mary Prentice Lillie). [77]. cmp1920s. Bmin; c'–g♭"; Tess-M; 3/4, 4/4, Molto appassionato ma non troppo vivace ♩ = 92; 5pp; Diff-V/md, P/md.

For: mezzo-soprano; full lyric soprano

Mood: agitated; passionate, yet fearful, love song

Voice: rushing chromatic line in flexible word rhythms; large dynamic range

Piano: rapid repeated chord patterns divided between hands; some arpeggiation; polyrhythms; countermelodies

Diff: ensemble; difficult piano part

Uses: big romantic song for English group; excellent for mature singer

80. **FIVE POEMS BY EMILY DICKINSON.** G. Schirmer, 1944. [51]. Traditional keys with mild dissonance, sometimes modal; c'–g"(a"); Tess-M; regular meters; slow and moderate tempos; 10pp; Diff-V/m, P/m-md.

For: lyric soprano; high mezzo-soprano

Mood: lyrical; introspective; nature images; quiet

Voice: easy skips predominate, with some conjunct motion; many 2- & 3-note slurs; wide-ranged phrases; some syncopation and hemiola

Piano: chordal and linear; accidentals; quite pianistic

Uses: a nice set; some of Bacon's best material

    a. *It's All I Have to Bring.* (Same as *This and My Heart* in [78]). B♭maj; c'–f"; Tess-cs; 2/4 with changes, Andante; 2pp. [**Rec:** D#s 10, 59, 89]

    b. *So Bashful.* F♯maj; c♯'–g"(g♯"); Tess-M; 6/8, Allegretto grazioso; 2pp. [**Rec:** D#s 59, 89]

    c. *Poor Little Heart.* Amin; c'–f"; Tess-mH; 2/4, Rather slowly; 2pp. [**Rec:** D#18]

    d. *To Make a Prairie.* (Same as *If Bees Are Few* in [78]). X, C♯-centered; d♯'–g"(a"); Tess-M; 3/4, Quasi allegretto; 2pp. [**Rec:** D#s 59, 89]

    e. *And This of All My Hopes.* Fmin; e♭'–f"; Tess-M; 6/8, Rather slowly, lilting; 2pp. [**Rec:** D#s10, 59]

81. **FLOWERS AND MOONLIGHT** (Yang-ti, early Chinese). [72]. cmp1926–1928. A-centered; c♯'–e♭"; Tess-mL; 4/4, Placido; 2pp; Diff-V/me, P/d.

For: any medium voice

Mood: lyrical nature picture

Voice: sustained and static; phrases begin low and rise slowly; some chromaticism

Piano: open 5ths; afterbeats; disjunct 8th-note and triplet figures

82. **FOND AFFECTION** (anon.). [73]. D♭maj; c♯'–f"; Tess-M; 6/8, With quiet tenderness (but in 2); 2+min; Diff-V/m, P/m.

For: soprano; mezzo-soprano

Mood: folk-like; lyrical; somber

Voice: stepwise and small skips; some long-ranged phrases; syncopation; 17-meas. vocalized section

Piano: linear; 2-voice texture; arpeggios and countermelody; some 2 vs. 3; varied registers; no vocal line doubling

Diff: control of soft dynamics; several phrases end on sustained f"

Uses: effective song

83. **FROM BLANK TO BLANK** (Emily Dickinson). [76]. cmp ca.1931. A♭maj; d♭–f"; Tess-M; 4/4, Andante (♩ = 76); 1+pp; Diff-V/me, P/me.

For: soprano

Mood: fragile; sense of hopelessness

Voice: soft floating vocal lines that give impression of a blind, groping movement in its dotted rhythms; somewhat chromatic

Piano: thin texture; alternating 2-note groups

Diff: maintaining line in dotted rhythms

Uses: in Dickinson group

84. **GENTLE GREETING** (Emily Brontë). [73]. cmp

ca.1927. Dmaj; c♯'–g"; Tess-M; 4/4, Larghetto; 2min; Diff-V/m, P/md.

For: soprano

Mood: lyrical; simple; somber

Voice: many skips (up to 8ve); some long-ranged phrases; syncopation

Piano: countermelody and repeated chords; syncopation; spare texture

Diff: needs good register control

Uses: nice lyric song for recital use

85. **GRAND IS THE SEEN** (Walt Whitman). (Same as "The Unseen Soul" in [78]). [75]. cmp1920s. "To Povla Frijsch." Dmin; b–e"; Tess-M; 3/4, Sostenuto e con grand' espressione; 3pp; Diff-V/md, P/m.

For: baritone

Mood: spacious; philosophical; hymn-like; compares grandeur of the universe to the greater grandeur of the individual soul

Voice: sustained vocal lines often move up chromatically

Piano: repeated chords give way to increased space of soft, legato syncopated chords in r.h. over slowly moving bass line; two endings given

Diff: creation of appropriate mood with sustained vocal line and flexible dynamic range

Uses: fine song for mature singer; good recital material

86. **THE GRASS SO LITTLE HAS TO DO** (Emily Dickinson). [76, 78, 167]. cmp1931. Two keys: Bmin & Amin (final setting); d'–b" & c'–a"; Tess-M-mH; 4/4, Allegretto moderato (♩ = 108–116); 4pp; Diff-V/m, P/m.

For: soprano

Mood: playful; desultory

Voice: many 2-note slurs; repeated figures; soft dynamics; one descending melisma; some polyrhythms; syncopated rhythms

Piano: fairly thin texture; broken-chord patterns; melodic patterns; staccato passages; reflects imagery of poem

Diff: projection of meaning of the text in a childlike, transparent way

Uses: excellent recital material

Rec: D#89

87. **THE HEART** (Emily Dickinson). ("The Heart Asks Pleasure First") [73, 76]. cmp ca.1927. Two keys: E♭min [73] & Cmin [76]; d♭'–e♭" & b♭'–c"; Tess-mL-M; 6/8, Slowly; 1+min; Diff-V/m, P/me.

For: mezzo-soprano; some sopranos

Mood: quiet; motionless; the heart's longing for peace

Voice: skips on chord lines; accidentals; 2-note slurs

Piano: block chords; wide spacing; no doubling of vocal line

Uses: beautiful quiet song in a Bacon or Dickinson group, or a group of songs about the heart

Rec: D#18

88. **HOW STILL THE BELLS** (Emily Dickinson). [76]. cmp ca.1931. Chromatic; c'–e"; Tess-M; 4/4, Lento (♩ = 84); 2+pp; Diff-V/me, P/md.

For: mezzo-soprano

Mood: agitated

Voice: chromatic ascending vocal line

Piano: rhythms and harmonies evoke the sound of bells; chromatic; quartal; 21-meas. postlude

Diff: only two vocal phrases; singer must deal with a long postlude

Uses: in Dickinson, Bacon, or songs about bells group

89. **I'M NOBODY** (Emily Dickinson). [72, 76]. cmp1926–1928. Two keys: X; e'–g" [72] & c'–d♯" [76]; Tess-M; 4/4, 6/4, Allegretto; 3pp; Diff-V/d, P/d. [NOTE: This song exists in the collections noted above in two slightly different versions. The version in 72 has a whispered line for the singer not found in the other version, and some different piano figurations, in addition to being in a higher key.]

For: soprano

Mood: humorously philosophical

Voice: fragmented; parlando; whispered phrase; melisma on final word

Piano: 2-voice counterpoint; chromatic; disjunct

Diff: needs a good vocal actor

Uses: good for humor in a group

Rec: D#s 18, 89

90. **IS THERE SUCH A THING AS DAY?** (Emily Dickinson). [76]. cmp ca.1940. F♯maj; d♯'–f♯"; Tess-M; 4/4, Andantino; 1min; Diff-V/m, P/m.

For: soprano

Mood: naive, child-like expression; philosophical questions

Voice: skips along chord lines; mostly quarter-note movement; some slurred 8ths; long-ranged phrases

Piano: 2-voice texture; r.h. doubles vocal line; l.h. syncopated; no prelude

Diff: breathing needs careful planning

Uses: usable for a young singer or in a group of Dickinson songs; see also setting by Vincent Persichetti

Rec: D#s 3, 89

91. **IT'S COMING–THE POSTPONELESS CREATURE** (Emily Dickinson). [76, 78]. cmp ca.1931. Two keys: B♭min & 4♯s; c'–b♭' & c♯'–d♯"; Tess-L; 4/4; 4pp; Diff-V/m, P/m.

For: contralto; mezzo-soprano

Mood: quietly dramatic; dirge

Voice: sustained; several phrases on single pitches

Piano: death-march dotted rhythms; chordal; thick texture; soft dynamics

Diff: projecting dramatic material in a hushed manner

Uses: in Dickinson, Bacon, or death songs group

92. **JOY, SHIPMATE, JOY!** (Walt Whitman). [75]. cmp1920s. Cmin; e♭'–a♭"; Tess-mH; 3/4, ♩ in slow walking time; 2pp; Diff-V/m, P/md.

For: tenor

Mood: triumphant; dramatic; majestic approach to death

Voice: soaring, declamatory vocal line; *f–ff* dynamic level

Piano: chromatic; shifting harmonies; thick texture

Diff: voice must have sufficient size and sustaining power to ride over dense piano part

Uses: in set or separately; mature voice

93. **THE LAMB** (William Blake). [16, 73]. cmp ca.1927. X; c♯'–f♯"; Tess-M; 3/4, 4/4, Andante con moto;

2+min; Diff-V/md, P/m.

For: mezzo-soprano; soprano
Mood: child-like; innocent
Voice: many leaps of up to 7th; 2-note slurs; one melisma; triplets; hemiola
Piano: block- and broken-chord patterns; duplets and triplets; hemiola; many accidentals;13-meas. interlude; no doubling of vocal line
Diff: needs good register control; some difficult intervals; 2 vs. 3 & 3 vs. 2
Uses: nice song; see also Chanler, Nordoff, and Clifford Shaw settings of this text

94.   **THE LAST INVOCATION** (Walt Whitman). [75, 78]. cmp1920s. Two keys: Dmaj & E♭maj; g–d♭" & b♭–d"; Tess-L-M; 4/4, 3/2, 6/4, Lento; 2pp; Diff-V/m, P/m.

For: bass; bass-baritone
Mood: broad; deep; quiet; a moving appeal for a peaceful death
Voice: mostly conjunct vocal line; *pp-mf* dynamic range; syllabic with a few 2-note slurs; very legato
Piano: chordal structure; chromatic; some wide reaches
Diff: creating hushed quality needed without sacrificing flow of rich sound
Uses: good recital material for mature singer

95.   **LET DOWN THE BARS** (Emily Dickinson). [76]. cmp ca.1931. D; c'–d"; Tess-M; 3/4, Molto tranquillo ma non troppo lento; 3pp; Diff-V/m, P/e.

For: mezzo-soprano
Mood: somber, yet tender; suspended feeling
Voice: falling phrases hover between maj. and min. modes; sustained soft singing
Piano: chordal; soft and floating; 7-meas. postlude
Diff: sustaining intense expressiveness *ppp*
Uses: in Dickinson, Bacon, or death songs group

96.   **LINGERING LAST DROPS** (Walt Whitman). [72, 78]. cmp1926–1928. Two keys: Bmin & Amin; d♯'–g" & c'–f"; Tess-M; 4/4, Andante; 2pp; Diff-V/m, P/d.

For: lyric soprano; tenor
Mood: lyrical; philosophical, using nature imagery
Voice: lyrical and sustained; soft; opt. humming phrase at end
Piano: chordal; afterbeats; syncopation; 2-voice counterpoint at end

97.   **THE LITTLE STONE** (Emily Dickinson). [73]. cmp ca.1927. C♯maj; c♯'–g"; Tess-mL; 2/4, Allegretto; 1+min; Diff-V/m, P/m.

For: soprano
Mood: cheerful; sprightly; child-like
Voice: many small skips; accidentals; easy rhythms
Piano: linear, 2-voice texture; syncopation; l.h. staccato; r.h. mostly 16ths; does not double vocal line
Uses: nice recital song
Rec: D#s 3, 18

98.   **MIRANDA'S SONG** (suggested by Shakespeare's *Tempest*). [72, 78]. cmp1926–1928. "To Phyllis Curtin." E♭maj; c'–b♭"; Tess-mH; 6/8, 9/8, Larghetto; 3pp; Diff-V/d, P/m.

For: lyric or coloratura soprano
Mood: lyrical and lilting
Voice: vocalise; lyrical, sweeping phrases; much syncopation
Piano: l.h. short chords; r.h. melody often doubles vocal line; very light and delicate
Diff: ability to control vowel sounds over long phrases; flexibility and agility

99.   **MY RIVER RUNS TO THEE** (Emily Dickinson). [76]. cmp ca.1931. Fmaj; f'–f"; Tess-M; 3/4, Andantino; 2pp; Diff-V/e, P/me.

For: soprano; mezzo-soprano
Mood: searching; water imagery
Voice: simple melody alternates between maj. and min. modes in descending lines
Piano: mostly three voice texture; descending motives give water imagery
Uses: in Dickinson, Bacon, or water songs group

100.   **NO DEW UPON THE GRASS** (Emily Dickinson). [74]. cmp ca.1935. "To Radiana Pazmor." D♭min; a♭–d♭"; Tess-mL; 3/4, Grave; 3pp; Diff-V/d, P/md.

For: contralto; bass
Mood: sad; philosophical song about death
Voice: recit.-like; "Recite with freedom but do not disturb the regular flow of the accompaniment"
Piano: broadly sustained; contrapuntal; disjunct; chromatic
Diff: requires command of a recit.-like, declamatory style with imprecise rhythms, indicated by much syncopation, triplets, quadruplets, etc.
Uses: effective song for a fine musician

101.   **OF LOVE** (Robert Herrick). [73]. cmp ca.1927. "To Eva Gauthier." A-centered; d'–f"; Tess-M; 4/4, Andantino; 1min; Diff-V/m, P/m.

For: any voice except extreme ranges
Mood: cynical love song
Voice: mostly stepwise; easy rhythms; accidentals; 2-note slurs; one melisma
Piano: countermelody in 8ves; fluid rhythms; ties, triplets, and syncopation; no doubling of vocal line
Uses: in a group of love songs or in an American song group

102.   **O FRIEND** ("Alter? When the hills do") (Emily Dickinson). [76, 167]. cmp ca.1940. Two keys: Amaj & B♭maj; c♯'–g" & d'–a♭"; Tess-cs; 2/2, Sustained and with fervour (♩ = 45–50); 3pp; Diff-V/m, P/m.

For: soprano
Mood: calm; spacious; certain; questioning final chord
Voice: short question phrases; long, soaring answer phrases; wide range; long final note
Piano: slow r.h. broken-chord pattern over sustained l.h. 8ves; then arpeggiated l.h. under r.h. countermelody in 8ves
Diff: long phrases
Uses: excellent for any Dickinson or other American group
Rec: D#89

103.   **OMAHA** (Carl Sandburg). [74]. cmp1930s. Amin; c'–f "(a♭"); Tess-M; 2/2, Moderato (♩ = 88); 3pp; Diff-V/md, P/md.

For: baritone; tenor
Mood: rough and driving; depicts the ceaseless work "to get

Voice: declamatory in strict rhythm; *mf–ff* dynamic range; two melismas for tone painting; some polyrhythms; large, solid voice needed

Piano: syncopated and dotted rhythms set up working motion; accidentals; accents give rough quality

Diff: sufficient vocal weight to partner the piano

Uses: unusually strong song in Bacon catalog; group ender

104. ONE THOUGHT EVER AT THE FORE (Walt Whitman). [75]. Same song as "The Divine Ship" [**Rec**: D#67]

105. ON THE FRONTIERS (Walt Whitman). [72]. cmp1926–1928. "To Radiana Pazmor." E♭-centered; b♭–e♭"; Tess-mL; 3/2, 4/4, Lento; 3pp; Diff-V/d, P/dd.

For: mezzo-soprano

Mood: dramatic; nature imagery dealing with death

Voice: recit.-like; building in intensity; broad and lyrical in final section

Piano: staccato quarters in 8ves under chords; chromatic 8th-note figures

Diff: needs good vocal actor with command of parlando style

106. THE RED ROSE (Robert Burns). [78, 167]; 1st©1949. Two keys: Dmin & F♯min; (c')a–f" & (e')c♯'–a"; Tess-mL, mH; 4/4, Andantino; 1+min; Diff-V/md, P/e.

For: composer says medium voice; tenor seems best; baritone; soprano

Mood: folk-like; love song; simple; tender

Voice: many skips; one leap of 12th; long-ranged phrases; independent of piano part

Piano: countermelody supported by chords and broken chords; syncopation

Diff: long-ranged phrases; *pp* and *ppp* dynamics

Uses: effective song

107. SAILING HOMEWARD (Chang-Fang-Shen, A.D. 400; trans. A. Waley). [72]. cmp ca.1927. X; c'–f♯"; Tess-mL; 4/4, Lento; 2pp; Diff-V/m, P/d.

For: any medium or high voice

Mood: lyrical; philosophical, using nature imagery

Voice: phrases separated by rests; chromatic; melisma on last phrase

Piano: 2-voice; wide intervals; continuous 8th-note movement; delicate

Diff: control and clarity in *pp* and softer dynamics

108. SAVIOR (Emily Dickinson). [76]. cmp ca.1931. Fmin; b♭♭–a"; Tess-M; 3/4, Adagio; 3pp; Diff-V/m, P/m.

For: soprano; mezzo-soprano

Mood: prayer of giving up a heavy heart

Voice: no introduction; slow descending vocal lines; chromatic; sustained

Piano: falling broken-chord figures; some 8ve melody in r.h.; wide reach helpful; postlude

Diff: no prelude

Uses: in Dickinson group or group of prayers

109. SHE WENT (Emily Dickinson). [72]. cmp ca.1931. B♭min; e♭'–a♭"; Tess-M; 3/4, Un poco lento; 2pp;

Diff-V/m, P/md.

For: soprano

Mood: lament; floating; vanishing; philosophical poem about death

Voice: broad and sustained; several phrases begin high; generally soft dynamics

Piano: begins with bass pedal tone, adds voices; last section a disjunct 8th-note pattern

Diff: soft high tones; one phrase begins on a♭"

Uses: to study phrases beginning high and descending; good for elegy group

Rec: D#89

110. SHE WENT AS QUIET AS THE DEW (Emily Dickinson). [76]. cmp ca.1931. Gmin-maj; c'–f"; Tess-mL; 3/4, Semplice; 3pp; Diff-V/m, P/m. (Same song as "She Went" except for different key)

111. SLEEP (William Shakespeare). [72, 78]. cmp1926–1928. X; a(b)–d"; Tess-L; 4/4, Lento; 1p; Diff-V/m, P/me.

For: contralto

Mood: lyrical and sweet

Voice: lyrical, but disjunct; sustained; generally soft dynamics

Piano: 2-voice counterpoint with some 8ve doubling; chromatic

Diff: requires clear but not heavy low tones

112. SNOWFALL (Emily Dickinson). (Same as "Alabaster Wool" in [78]). [72]. cmp1926–1928. B♭-centered; c♯'–b♭"(g♭"); Tess-M-mH; 6/8, Allegretto; 4pp; Diff-V/md, P/d.

For: lyric soprano

Mood: lyrical description of nature

Voice: lyrical and flowing; long phrases; long and short melismas, several on low pitches

Piano: disjunct; afterbeat figure; chromatic and diatonic scale passages in 16ths; 2-voice texture

Diff: clear low tones; flexibility and agility

Uses: fine recital song

113. THE SOBBING OF THE BELLS (Walt Whitman). [75]. cmp1920s. X; a–f♭"; Tess-cs; 4/4, Andante; 5pp; Diff-V/md, P/md.

For: bass; bass-baritone

Mood: ponderous dirge; poem mourns assassination of President James Garfield, September 19, 1881

Voice: dramatic declamation; wide range; some recit.

Piano: repeated 8ves present bell imagery; thick texture in last half; chromatic

Diff: vocal weight needed to partner piano; dramatic singing at both extremes of range

Uses: in set or in a group of songs on the subject of assassination or mourning of national figures

114. SOLITUDE (Emily Dickinson). [72]. cmp1926–1928. "To Florence Kopleff." X; g♭–c♯"; Tess-LL; 2/2, Grave; 2pp; Diff-V/m, P/m.

For: contralto

Mood: somber; philosophical

Voice: very sustained; long note values; rather static

Piano: broad, sustained chords; chromatic

Diff: requires fine low tones, but not heavy chest voice
Uses: good for teaching low tones

115. **SONG OF SNOW-WHITE HEADS** (Cho Wen-chün; trans. A. Waley). [73, 78]. cmp ca.1927. Two keys: Dmin (modal flavor) & Emin; c'–f" & d'–g"; Tess-M; 4/4 (voice), 12/8 (piano), Quasi allegretto; 2min; Diff-V/m, P/m.
For: mezzo-soprano (woman's text)
Mood: sorrowful love song; introspective; quiet
Voice: skips along chord lines; accidentals; 2 vs. piano 3; duplets and triplets; syncopation
Piano: 2-voice linear texture; some 2 vs. 3; many accidentals; various registers; 7-meas. postlude
Diff: some phrases hard to hear against piano
Uses: nice song; translation does not always flow well

116. **SONNET** (Elizabeth Barrett Browning). [72]. cmp1926–1928. F♯-centered; c♯'–f♯"; Tess-M; 3/4, 4/4, Andante; 3pp; Diff-V/md, P/d.
For: soprano; mezzo-soprano
Mood: lyrical love poem: "How do I love thee?"
Voice: lyrical and flowing; somewhat chromatic
Piano: chordal with independent but related r.h. melody
Diff: requires clear low tones

117. **A SPIDER** (Emily Dickinson). [72]. cmp1926–1928. X; e'–a♭"; Tess-M; 3/4, Un poco vivace; 3pp; Diff-V/m, P/dd.
For: lyric soprano; tenor
Mood: humorously philosophical
Voice: sustained, beginning low and rising chromatically to climax
Piano: rapid chromatic scale passages in 8ves in contrary motion; lengthy interlude and postlude
Diff: mostly in the accomp.; high tessitura at climax
Uses: good for teaching chromatic scale; humorous; encore; makes nice group with "The Bat" and "The Swamp," also by Bacon
Rec: D#89

118. **STARS** (A. E. Housman). [16, 73]. cmp ca.1927. E♭-centered (min.); c'–f"; Tess-M; 2/4, 3/4, Placido; 2min; Diff-V/m, P/m.
For: mezzo-soprano; soprano; high baritone
Mood: lyrical; philosophical; space and eternity
Voice: many leaps, esp. 6th & 7th; some dotted notes; some long and long-ranged phrases
Piano: 3–4-voice texture, broken-chord pattern; many accidentals; does not double vocal line
Diff: irregular meter; long phrases; sustained long tones over several measures
Uses: good for a voice with ample sound and great warmth

119. **SUMMER'S LAPSE** (Emily Dickinson). [72, 78]. cmp1926–1928. "To Helen Boatwright." Dmaj; c♯'–g"; Tess-M; 6/8, 9/8, Larghetto; 3pp; Diff-V/md, P/md.
For: soprano
Mood: lyrical; nature imagery
Voice: lyrical and flowing; some long phrases; long melisma on final phrase; mostly stepwise
Piano: 2-voice counterpoint; intricate rhythms; disjunct with

large register changes
Diff: ensemble
Uses: good recital song
Rec: D#89

120. **SUNSET** (Emily Dickinson). [72, 78]. cmp1926–1928. "To Elisabeth Schwarzkopf." Two versions: X; c'–f" & c'–a♭"; Tess-M; 3/4, Sostenuto; 2pp; Diff-V/m, P/m.
For: soprano; mezzo-soprano [Same text as "The Sun Went Down" (see below), except in a higher key]

121. **THE SUN WENT DOWN** (Emily Dickinson). [76]. cmp ca.1931. Gmin; a–c"; Tess-L; 3/4, Grave; 2+pp; Diff-V/me, P/m.
For: contralto; mezzo-soprano
Mood: mysterious aloneness
Voice: very sustained, almost static; low in the voice; somewhat chromatic
Piano: chordal; movement on beats 1 & 3; 8th-note motive reflects image of flying bird
Diff: sustained phrases
Uses: in Dickinson, Bacon, or nature songs group
Rec: D#89

122. **THE SWAMP** (Emily Dickinson). [72]. cmp1926–1928. X; b–g"; Tess-M; 4/4, Allegretto, un poco rubato; 2pp; Diff-V/d, P/d.
For: soprano; mezzo-soprano
Mood: humorous, nature imagery–in particular, the snake
Voice: disjunct and chromatic; long, chromatic melisma on final word
Piano: 2-voice counterpoint; chromatic; triplets; tremolo
Diff: song begins on g"; also has phrase beginning on b
Uses: humorous; encore; makes a nice group with "The Bat" and "A Spider," by Bacon

123. **A THREADLESS WAY** (Emily Dickinson). [72]. cmp1926–1928. A♭maj; e♭'–f"; Tess-mH; 4/4, 6/4, Andante; 1p; Diff-V/m, P/m.
For: any high or medium lyric voice
Mood: philosophical, using blindness as a metaphor
Voice: lyrical with dotted rhythms; features descending phrases
Piano: chordal with dotted rhythms; fairly chromatic
Rec: D#89

124. **TO MUSIC: A FRAGMENT** (Percy Bysshe Shelley). [72]. cmp1926–1928. X; c'–g♯"; Tess-M; 4/4, Larghetto; 1p; Diff-V/d, P/d.
For: lyric soprano; tenor
Mood: lyrical; philosophical
Voice: lyrical and sustained; chromatic; long, cadenza-like melisma on final word
Piano: 2-voice counterpoint; chromatic; delicate
Diff: flexibility and control of soft dynamics

125. **TO MUSIQUE, TO BECALME HIS FEVER** (Robert Herrick). [73]. cmp ca.1927. X; c♯'–g♯"; Tess-M-mH; 4/4, Tranquillo; 4min; Diff-V/md, P/m.
For: tenor
Mood: philosophical; in praise of the power of music
Voice: stepwise and small skips; syncopation; some 2-note

slurs; one long melisma
Piano: block chords; syncopation; accidentals; some tremolo; incidental doubling of vocal line
Diff: cross-relations; fluid, speech-like rhythms; ensemble; register and dynamic control
Uses: lovely, effective song

126. **TWILIGHT** (Sara Teasdale). [73]. cmp ca.1927. C♯ (Mixolydian); c♯'–e"; Tess-M; 2/4, Grave; 1min; Diff-V/me, P/me.
For: mezzo-soprano; baritone; some sopranos
Mood: lyrical; descriptive; an impression
Voice: skips along chord lines; easy rhythms
Piano: block chords; countermelody; quiet; wide spacing; does not double vocal line
Diff: one entire 4-meas. phrase is on e"
Uses: effective short song

127. **TWILIGHT** (Walt Whitman). [75]. cmp1920s. Dmaj; c♯'–c"; Tess-mL; 3/4, Larghetto; 2pp; Diff-V/m, P/m.
For: any medium voice
Mood: twilight compared to life's end; delicate haze lingering after the light is gone
Voice: short syllabic phrases; small range; chromatic and quartal; soft
Piano: highly chromatic; thin texture
Diff: dissonances; very soft dynamic level
Uses: good contrast to bigger songs in Whitman group

128. **THE UNSEEN SOUL** (Walt Whitman). (Same as "Grand Is the Seen"). [72, 78]. cmp1926–1928. Dmin; b–e"; Tess-mL; 3/4, Maestoso; 3pp; Diff-V/m, P/md.
For: any medium or low voice
Mood: philosophical
Voice: broad and lyrical; 2-note slurs; somewhat declamatory; some chromaticism.
Piano: big chords; chromatic; syncopation

129. **VELVET PEOPLE** (Emily Dickinson). Carl Fischer, 1948. C♯min; c'–e"; Tess-M-mL; 3/4, Rather fast; 1+min; Diff-V/m, P/m.
For: medium voices; contralto
Mood: lyrical; descriptive
Voice: mostly conjunct; 2–4-note slurs; two longer melismas; syncopation; dotted rhythms
Piano: broken-chord patterns; accent pattern varies; accidentals; staccato; various registers; does not double vocal line
Diff: cross-accents in voice and piano; poem needs explanation
Uses: effective song for a young singer as well as the more mature singer; quiet ending

130. **WEEPING AND SIGHING** (Emily Dickinson). [72]. cmp1926–1928. Cmaj; d'–g"; Tess-mH; 5/8, Animato, ma non troppo vivace; 3pp; Diff-V/d, P/d.
For: lyric soprano
Mood: humorously philosophical
Voice: lyrical; "la-la" refrain has carefree bounce; humming at end is sustained
Piano: 2-voice; r.h. melody related to "la-la" refrain
Diff: lines with sung text are quite high in tessitura; rhythms

Uses: encore
Rec: D#s 3, 89

131. **WE NEVER KNOW** (Emily Dickinson). [72]. cmp1926–1928. X; b–g"; Tess-mL; 3/2, 3/4, Sostenuto; 1p; Diff-V/m, P/md.
For: mezzo-soprano
Mood: philosophical; fate and death
Voice: sustained; several large intervals; somewhat fragmented by rests
Piano: chordal with independent r.h. melody; syncopation
Diff: requires clear, soft low tones

132. **WHISPERS OF HEAVENLY DEATH** (Walt Whitman). [75]. cmp1920s. E♭maj; e♭'–e♭"; Tess-M; 3/2, 4/4, Adagio; 2pp; Diff-V/m, P/me.
For: tenor; baritone
Mood: transcendental
Voice: sustained vocal line in medium length phrases; *pp* throughout; last lines recited softly
Piano: slow r.h. chords over rising bass 8ves; hymn-like in second half of song
Diff: keeping intense presence in sustained soft singing; effective and convincing spoken phrase at end
Uses: in set for mature singer

133. **WILD NIGHTS** (Emily Dickinson). [76]. cmp ca.1931. Chromatic; d♭'–g♭"; Tess-M; 2/2, 3/3, Con fuoco (♩= 96); 4+pp; Diff-V/md, P/md.
For: soprano; mezzo-soprano
Mood: passionate; tempestuous
Voice: fast ascending chromatic phrases; last phrase a melisma arching down to d♭'
Piano: fast; chromatic; parallel 4ths; wide reach helpful
Diff: pitches against chromatic piano part; ensemble
Uses: big song; good group ender

134. **WORLD TAKE GOOD NOTICE** (Walt Whitman). For Baritone or Alto. [74, 78]. cmp ca.1942. E-centered; d♭'–e"; Tess-mL; 2/4, 3/4, In deliberate march time (piano in 6/8 & 9/8); 2pp; Diff-V/m, P/md.
For: baritone; mezzo-soprano
Mood: abstract; philosophical
Voice: short, clipped, fragmented phrases; some chromaticism
Piano: irregular and march-like with syncopated afterbeats; somewhat chromatic
Diff: rhythms; constant 2 vs. 3 between voice and piano

BAKER, DAVID N.
(b. Indianapolis, IN, 1931)

135. **EARLY IN THE MORNIN'** (Mari Evans). From the Cycle, *The Black Experience*. [6]; 1st©1977. X; d'–a♭"; Tess-M; 4/4, alternating short slow and fast sections; 6pp; Diff-V/md, P/d.
For: soprano; mezzo-soprano
Mood: both sad and humorous, philosophical and descriptive
Voice: many accidentals; blues style; features descending m3rd; a few words spoken; triplets; phrases fragmented by rests
Piano: generally chordal and chromatic with several rapid

16th-note passages; triplets
Diff: requires excellent vocal actor
Uses: effective in a variety of performance situations

136. **A GOOD ASSASSINATION SHOULD BE QUIET**
(Mari Evans). From the Cycle, *The Black Experience.*
[6]; 1st©1977. X; c'–a♭"; Tess-M; 4/4, 3/4, 2/4, 5/4,
Moderate tempo; 3pp; Diff-V/d, P/m.
For: soprano; mezzo-soprano
Mood: bitter; refers to death of Martin Luther King, Jr.
Voice: chromatic; disjunct with large leaps; moves mostly in
8th notes; phrases fragmented by rests
Piano: chordal texture; chromatic; disjunct; some triplets;
covers keyboard
Diff: many important low tones; perfect pitch helpful;
dramatic flair needed
Uses: effective song for singer with the above qualities

137. **STATUS SYMBOL** (Mari Evans). From the Cycle,
The Black Experience. [6]; 1st©1977. X; c'–f♯";
Tess-M; 4/4, 3/4, 7/8, 2/4, 5/8, Rhythm and blues feel;
4pp; Diff-V/md, P/m.
For: mezzo-soprano
Mood: sarcastic; topical
Voice: disjunct and chromatic; short, fragmented phrases;
spoken words; sliding pitches; strives for natural,
semi-spoken style
Piano: thin texture; chromatic; rapid 16th-note and triplet
passages; broken by frequent rests
Diff: singer must slip easily and naturally from singing to
speaking; strong, pointed text about racism from the
African-American point of view
Uses: could be an effective song for the right singer

BAKSA, ROBERT
(b. New York, NY, 1938)

138. **A CYNIC'S CYCLE.** Four Songs to Poetry from *The
Devil's Dictionary* by Ambrose Bierce for Voice and
Piano, Op. 41. Composers Library Editions, 1978
(Theodore Presser). cmp1968. Tonal; c'–a"; Tess-mH;
mostly regular meters;14pp; Diff-V/md, P/m.
For: tenor; some baritones
Mood: cynical, but humorous
Voice: stepwise and small skips; some syncopation and
speech-like rhythms; syllabic; changing meters in (b.)
Piano: each song has 5–11 meas. prelude and at least 4 meas.
of interlude or postlude; block and broken chords; some
linear writing; dotted rhythms; some 3 vs. 4
Diff: range (low notes for tenor, high notes for baritones);
rhythms and possibly ensemble in (b.) & (c.)
Uses: usable cycle for recital; has quick song at the end

    a. *Allah's Good Laws.* Cmaj; c'–e"; Tess-M; 2/2,
Slow, devotional; 2pp.
    b. *To Men.* D-centered; d'–g"; Tess-wide; 4/4 with
changes, Flexible; 3pp.
    c. *The Grave Robber.* Amin. predominates; e'–a";
Tess-wide; 4/4, Mysterious, then outraged; 4pp.
    d. *The Troutlet.* D-centered, then B♭; f'–g"; Tess-H;
3/4, With a lilt; 5pp.

139. **HOUSMAN SONGS** (A. E. Housman). Cycle for Low
Voice. Complete Edition. Composers Library Editions,
1967, 1982, 1999 (Presser). Tonal; b♭–f♯"; Tess-cs, M;
regular meters; varied tempos (♩ = 50–144); 38pp; Diff-
V/me-md, P/e-md.
For: baritone (lyric)
Mood: the young man's mind; fresh and young; undertones of
experiences to come
Voice: flexible lyric recit.; relatively short phrases; a few long
tones; syllabic setting; speech rhythms
Piano: supportive but does not double vocal line; accidentals;
some syncopation; mostly linear; some repeated-chord
patterns; grace notes in fast tempos
Diff: singer needs easy top; endurance for whole cycle (11
songs); piano part in fast songs
Uses: good recital material for senior or graduate level

    a. *When I Was One-and-Twenty.* G-Bmaj; c'–e";
Tess-M; 4/4, Moderate ♩ = 72; 3pp.
    b. *When the Lad for Longing Sighs.* Gmaj; d'–f♯";
Tess-cs; 4/4, Brightly, not too fast ♩ = 126; 3pp.
    c. *On Your Midnight Pallet Lying.* Lydian on C;
c'–f♯"; Tess-cs; 3/4, Moderately slow ♩ = 52; 3+pp.
    d. *Oh, Sick Am I to See You.* X; b♭–e♭"; Tess-M;
3/4, Agitated ♩ = 126; 3+pp.
    e. *White in the Moon.* Floating harmonies on G;
d'–d"; Tess-M; 4/4, Steady ♩ = 56; 3+pp.
    f. *Others, I Am Not the First.* B minorish; d'–f♯";
Tess-cs; 4/4, Agitated ♩ = 120; 4+pp.
    g. *Oh, Fair Enough Are Sky and Plain.* Dmaj; d'–e";
Tess-cs; 4/4, Fluid, not too slow ♩ = 86; 4+pp.
    h. *If It Chance Your Eye Offend You.* X; c'–e♭";
Tess-cs; 4/4, Moderate march ♩ = 108; 3pp.
    i. *Oh, When I Was in Love with You.* E♭maj; c'–e♭";
Tess-M; 6/8 (voice in 2/4), Freely, not too slow
♩ = 50; 2pp.
    j. *Think No More, Lad!* X; b–f"; Tess-cs; 4/4, Fast
♩ = 144; 4+pp.
    k. *Loveliest of Trees.* Gmaj; e'–f♯"; Tess-mH; 4/4,
Freely, gradually slowing ♩ = 120–In tempo ♩ = 86;
2+pp.

140. **MORE SONGS TO POEMS OF EMILY
DICKINSON,** Opus 40. Composers Library Editions,
1978 (Theodore Presser). [Now pub. in 1 vol.: *Emily
Dickinson Songs*, First Complete Edition–Newly
Revised. Composers Library Editions, 2000 (Theodore
Presser).] cmp1967. "For Carolyn Reyer." Traditional
keys; b♭–g"; Tess-M-mH; regular meters, varied
tempos; 24pp, 14min; Diff-V/m, P/m-md.
For: mezzo-soprano; soprano
Mood: theme of transience–passing of day, night, and autumn;
foreboding of death
Voice: stepwise and chord-member skips; some syncopation;
accidentals
Piano: little doubling of vocal line; mostly chordal texture;
broken-chord patterns; many accidentals; solo passages
Uses: nice recital group for student

    a. *Two Butterflies Went Out at Noon.* Cmaj; f'–f";
3/4, Lively; 4pp.
    b. *Heart! We Will Forget Him!* Tonal; c♯'–f♯"; 4/4,

    Moderately slow; 3pp.

  c. ***The Morns Are Meeker Than They Were.*** Fmaj; e'–a"; 4/4, Moderate; 2+pp.

  d. ***There's a Certain Slant of Light.*** E♭min; b♭–e♭"; 4/4, Slow; 2+pp.

  e. ***Poor Little Heart!*** B♭maj; d'–g"; 4/4, Moderate; 3pp.

  f. ***No Matter–Now–Sweet.*** Amaj; d♯'–f"; 3/4, Fast; 3pp.

  g. ***When Night Is Almost Done.*** Dmaj-Emaj; c'–f♯"; 4/4, Tranquil; 2pp.

  h. ***Who Robbed the Woods?*** Fmin-maj; f'–g"; 4/4, Quite fast; 4pp.

141. SEVEN SONGS TO POEMS OF EMILY DICKINSON, Opus 38. Composers Library Editions, 1977 (Theodore Presser). [Now pub. in 1 vol.: *Emily Dickinson Songs*, First Complete Edition–Newly Revised. Composers Library Editions, 2000 (Theodore Presser).] cmp1963–1966. Traditional keys; a♯–g"; Tess-M; regular meters, moderate tempos; 14min; Diff-V/d, P/md-d.

For: mezzo-soprano; lyric soprano
Mood: generally philosophical; introspective
Voice: mostly stepwise; some wide leaps; some pitches hard to find; many accidentals; some speech-like rhythms; quite singable
Piano: mostly linear, lying in the middle of the keyboard; independent of vocal line
Diff: singer needs security in pitch and rhythms; poems require special understanding and may not appeal to everyone; not for beginners
Uses: fine recital group; could also be shortened

  a. ***Much Madness Is Divinest Sense.*** Tonal; c♯'–f♯"; 3/4, 2/4, Moderate; 27meas.

  b. ***What Inn Is This.*** X; c♯'–e"; 4/4, Agitated; 3pp.

  c. ***I Took My Power in My Hand.*** B♭maj-min; f'–f"; 4/4, Moderate; 3pp.

  d. ***I Died for Beauty.*** Dmaj; a♯–f♯"; 2/4, Moderately slow; 3pp.

  e. ***A Shady Friend for Torrid Days.*** Gmin; f♯'–g"; 9/8, Bouncy (moderately fast); 4pp.

  f. ***The Soul Selects Her Own Society.*** Gmin-B♭maj; d'–g♭"; 4/4, Rubato (rather slow); 3pp.

  g. ***I'm Nobody.*** E♭maj-Gmin; d'–f"; 6/4, Moderate; 24meas.

142. THIS IS MY LETTER TO THE WORLD (Emily Dickinson). In *Emily Dickinson Songs*, First Complete Edition–Newly Revised. Composers Library Editions, 2000 (Theodore Presser). cmp1999. Gmaj; e'–g"; Tess-M; 4/4, Moderately ♩= 72–76; 2pp; Diff-V/me, P/m.

For: soprano; mezzo-soprano
Mood: tender; simple
Voice: straightforward lyrical melody; short phrases; triadic structure; syllabic
Piano: l.h. chords, r.h. melodic material; opening phrase recurs throughout song as a motif
Uses: pleasant song; good for beginning students

143. THREE PORTRAITS for Low Male Voice with Piano to Prose Poems of Fenton Johnson. Composers Library Editions, 1996 (Theodore Presser). Mostly major keys; A–e'; Tess-mH-H; 4/4, 2/4; tempos ♩= 72–138; 15pp; Diff-V/m, P/m.

For: baritone
Mood: character pieces: the banjo player (rollicking), the drunkard (inebriated), and the minister (reverent/angry)
Voice: mostly short phrases lying in the upper middle range; tuneful; expressive of text; some repeated-note, chant-like lines
Piano: piano parts constructed on motives that reflect the texts and give energy and shape to the music; third song parodies Handel's "Hallelujah Chorus" in a dissonant figure
Diff: mostly in the piano–tricky figures and fast passages
Uses: excellent set for an undergraduate baritone who is good with character portrayal; should be attractive to any American audience

  a. ***The Banjo Player.*** Dmaj; c♯–e'; Tess-mH-H; 4/4, Rollicking ♩= 132–138; 5+pp.

  b. ***The Drunkard.*** X; A–d'; Tess-mH-H; 2/2, Fairly slow, unsteady; 3pp.

  c. ***The Minister.*** E♭maj; B–e♭'; Tess-mH-H; 4/4, With reverence ♩= 72; 6+pp.

BALES, RICHARD
(b. Alexandria, VA, 1915; d. 1998)

144. OZYMANDIAS (Percy Bysshe Shelley). Peer International, 1953. [65]. Minor tonalities; d'–f"; Tess-M; 3/4 with changing meters, Slowly; Allegro con moto; 3pp; Diff-V/m, P/m.

For: baritone; possibly mezzo-soprano
Mood: dramatic; descriptive
Voice: declamatory; recit.-like; speech rhythms; accidentals; large dynamic contrasts
Piano: chordal; mostly doubles vocal line
Diff: dramatic climax on f"
Uses: effective song for the right singer; quiet ending

BALLANTINE, EDWARD
(b. Oberlin, OH, 1886; d. Martha's Vineyard, MA, 1971)

145. THE OAK-TREE (trans. from the Greek by Lilla Cabot Perry). Ditson, 1922. H & M keys: A♭maj & Fmaj; f'–a♭" & d'–f"; Tess-M; 3/2, 4/4, Largamente; Diff-V/m, P/m.

For: tenor, soprano; baritone, mezzo-soprano
Mood: lyrical
Voice: ascending lines; short phrases; climactic high tone; soft high tones
Piano: chordal; modulation; supports voice
Diff: controlling ascending phrases
Uses: good for use of head voice and dynamic contrasts

BALLOU, ESTHER W.
(b. Elmira, NY, 1915; d. Chichester, England, 1973)

146. **A SONG** (John Ciardi). For Alto or Mezzo-soprano
Voice. American Composers Alliance (Composers
Facsimile Edition), 1967. cmp1967. E-centered
(quartal, quintal, and tertian structures); b–f♯"; Tess-M;
4/4; 2+pp; Diff-V/md, P/md.

For: mezzo-soprano; contralto
Mood: love song; gentle, subdued, and relaxed
Voice: stepwise motion predominates, with many skips of 4ths
& 5ths; several long-ranged phrases (c'–f" and b–d");
speech-like rhythms, juxtaposing duplets and triplets;
some 2 vs. 3 & 3 vs. 4 against piano; phrases
interrupted by rests; syllabic; quiet (*pp–mp*)
Piano: linear; 1–3-voice textures; some countermelody in
8ves; juxtaposes rhythmic groupings of 2 vs. 3 and 4
vs. 3; quiet dynamics; some doubling of vocal line;
6-meas. prelude
Diff: rhythms; probably ensemble
Uses: would be effective in recital group of love songs, or in
a group by U.S. women composers

BARAB, SEYMOUR
(b. Chicago, IL, 1921)

147. **A CHILD'S GARDEN OF VERSES** (Robert Louis
Stevenson). Medium Voice & Piano. Boosey &
Hawkes, 1985. vol. 1 of 2. Conventional keys; d'–f";
Tess-M; regular meters; 15min; Diff-V/e-me, P/me-m.

For: mezzo-soprano; soprano; baritone, if interested
Mood: well-known poems from a child's point of view;
various moods
Voice: mostly stepwise and easy skips; uncomplicated
rhythms; some dotted rhythms; (g.) has most
complications–3 vs. 4 and many accidentals; mostly
syllabic, except end of (g.)
Piano: (a.) has 25-meas. prelude; broken-chord and
repeated-chord or afterbeat styles of accomp.
predominate; doubling of vocal line rare, except in (a.,
d., i., & l.); (g.) has polyrhythms and many accidentals,
in imitation of a "railway carriage"; (g.) is indebted to
Copland's "I Felt a Funeral in My Brain"
Diff: (f.), numerous modulations; (g.), potential ensemble
problems; a few intervals here and there may be
troublesome to inexperienced singers (e.g., (k.))
Uses: could be excerpted to make a light group to end a
recital; these songs seem to be intended for adults
(orchestral accomp. available); several could be done
by children and young adults
Rec: D#90

a. *Introduction and Marching Song.* B♭maj; f'–f";
4/4, 2/2, Alla marcia; 5pp.
b. *At the Sea-Side.* Modulatory; f'–d"; 4/4, Moderato;
2pp.
c. *The Moon.* A♭maj; e♭'–e♭"; 2/4, Grazioso; 3pp.
d. *The Swing.* Dmaj; d'–d"; 6/8, Andante con moto;
2pp.
e. *Windy Nights.* Gmaj; d'–d"; 6/8, Allegro assai; 3pp.
f. *Foreign Lands.* Cmaj; e'–e"; 6/8, Allegro non
troppo; 4pp.
g. *From a Railway Carriage.* B♭-centered; f'–f"; 6/8,
Allegro molto; 5pp.

h. *Where Go the Boats?* Dmaj; d'–d"; 6/8, Andante;
3pp.
i. *A Good Boy.* Gmaj/Dmaj; f'–e♭"; 2/4, Allegretto;
4pp.
j. *The Land of Nod.* Dmaj-D♭maj; f'–e"; 2/4, Lento;
3pp.
k. *The Cow.* Modulatory; d'–e"; 3/4, Andante
maestoso; 3pp.
l. *Time to Rise.* Cmaj-D♭maj; d'–f"; 6/8, Andantino;
1p.

148. **A CHILD'S GARDEN OF VERSES** (Robert Louis
Stevenson). Medium Voice & Piano. Boosey &
Hawkes, 1985. vol. 2 of 2. Conventional keys; c♯'–f";
Tess-M; regular meters; 15min; Diff-V/e-m, P/me-md.

For: mezzo-soprano; soprano; baritone
Mood: well-known poems; child's point of view
Voice: mostly stepwise and easy skips, but more skips than
vol. 1; uncomplicated rhythms; mostly syllabic; (m.),
portamentos and a spoken line; (p.) & (s.), many
accidentals
Piano: repeated chords and afterbeat accomp. styles
predominate; doubling of vocal line in (p.) & (w.); this
volume has many accidentals and is harder to read than
vol. 1; (p.), pentatonic touches and 35 meas. of piano
solo in prelude, interludes, and postlude; (s.) is a canon
for l.h. only with voice; (u.) opens with chromatic 6ths
in r.h. and is in 6♯'s with accidentals; (x.), wide
reaches
Diff: many accidentals and modulations
Uses: whole volume could be done as a set, as it is more
varied musically than vol. 1, or several songs could be
excerpted to make a group; songs are more difficult
than those in vol. 1, but a few could be done by
children (o., q., v.)

m. *Pirate Story.* Emaj; e'–e"; 2/2, Presto; 3pp.
n. *Autumn Fires.* Fmaj; f'–e"; 4/4, Andante
tranquillo; 2pp.
o. *The Sun's Travels.* Dmaj; e'–e"; 2/4, Allegretto;
4pp.
p. *Foreign Children.* Modulatory, sometimes
pentatonic; e'–e"; 6/8, Vivace; 5pp.
q. *Fairy Bread.* Emin-Gmaj; e'–d"; 3/4, Andantino;
2pp.
r. *Young Night Thought.* B♭maj; e♭'–f"; 12/8,
Tempo di marcia; 3pp.
s. *My Shadow.* F♯maj-Fmaj, modulatory; c♯'–f"; 2/4,
3/4, Moderately fast; 4pp.
t. *Singing.* A♭maj; g'–f"; 3/4, Allegretto; 2pp.
u. *The Wind.* F♯maj-C♯maj; e♯'–e♯"; 12/8, Allegro
non troppo; 4pp.
v. *Bed in Summer.* Amaj; e'–e"; 4/4, Moderato; 2pp.
w. *Picture-Books in Winter.* Amin; e'–e"; 9/8, Adagio;
3pp (with repeat).
x. *Farewell to the Farm.* Cmaj-A♭maj; g♭'–f"; 4/4,
Allegro vivace; 3pp.

149. **AN EXPLANATION** (Walter Learned). Boosey &
Hawkes, 1964. G-centered; d'–e♭"; Tess-M; 2/4, Con
moto; 36meas; Diff-V/m, P/me.

For: baritone; possibly tenor; man's text

Mood: humorous
Voice: some skips of 6th & 8ve; triplets; accidentals
Piano: chordal, 4-voice texture; smooth
Diff: syncopated entrances; independent of piano
Uses: for short-ranged singer; descending phrases; humorous; encore

150. **A FINE LINE** (Thomas Moore). [43]. D-centered; g'–g"; Tess-mH; 4/4, Andante con moto; 2pp; Diff-V/m, P/m.
For: soprano; tenor
Mood: sarcastically humorous text about love and hate
Voice: conjunct and disjunct motion, but no difficult intervals; numerous accidentals
Piano: chordal, with some figuration; numerous accidentals; supports vocal line at crucial points
Diff: some pitches for singer
Uses: good humorous song in the right situation

151. **FOUR SONGS.** Boosey & Hawkes, 1955. Separate entries below.

A. **GO, LOVELY ROSE** (Edmund Waller). Dmaj; d'–f#"; Tess-M; 4/4 (with changes almost every meas.), Andante; 3pp; Diff-V/m, P/m.
For: medium voices best–baritone; mezzo-soprano; some sopranos
Mood: lyrical
Voice: uncomplicated pitch patterns; frequent meter changes, but patterns not difficult; syllabic and 2-note slurs
Piano: arpeggiated patterning; some passages in 3rds in r.h.
Diff: possibly changing meters; ensemble
Uses: lovely lyrical song for intermediate or advanced student; use with other songs from this set or excerpt; see also settings by S. Adler, J. A. Carpenter, R. Cumming, A. Foote, Halsey Stevens, and others

B. **SHE'S SOMEWHERE IN THE SUNLIGHT STRONG** (Richard LeGallienne). A-centered–Eb-centered; e'–g"; Tess-mH; 5/4, Allegretto; 3pp; Diff-V/m, P/m.
For: tenor or soprano best; some mezzo-sopranos
Mood: elegiac; lyrical
Voice: many small skips; some dotted rhythms; melismas
Piano: afterbeat style predominates; many accidentals
Diff: meter, for some singers; flexible, accurate melismas
Uses: lyrical song for flexible voice

C. **MINSTREL'S SONG** (Thomas Chatterton). Amin; b–g"; Tess-M, wide; 12/8, Moderato; 6pp; Diff-V/md, P/m.
For: soprano; mezzo-soprano (woman's text)
Mood: lyrical; dirge-like
Voice: many small skips; some 8ve leaps; two 2-beat g"s; one 2-beat f#"; several low b's and c's, one sustained; accidentals; syllabic with 2-note slurs
Piano: entire song built on a–e" rocking figure in l.h.; r.h. countermelody, sometimes in 3rds; many accidentals
Diff: wide tessitura; refrain has different pattern each time it appears; irregular phrase lengths

D. **I CAN'T BE TALKIN' OF LOVE** (Esther Mathews).

Emaj; c#'–d#"; Tess-M; 6/8, Allegretto; 3pp; Diff-V/m, P/me.
For: medium voices
Mood: lighthearted love song
Voice: conjunct; some syncopation and dotted rhythms; some hemiola
Piano: broken-chord patterning with some countermelody; hemiola; short prelude and postlude
Diff: rhythms and ensemble
Uses: good recital song; could be paired with "Go, Lovely Rose" or "Minstrel's Song" (see above); see also setting by J. Duke

152. **A MAID ME LOVED** (Patrick Hannay). Boosey & Hawkes, 1964. X, ends on F; c'–e"; Tess-M; 2/2, 3/2, Allegro commodo; 6pp; Diff-V/m, P/m.
For: baritone; bass-baritone (must be flexible)
Mood: ironic love; disdain reversed; uneasy
Voice: many skips, esp. 5ths; duplets and triplets; somewhat fragmented; 2–6-note slurs; syncopation
Diff: secure sense of pitch needed; both low and high notes sustained
Uses: good song; sets mood of text very well

153. **MOMENTS MACABRES** (*Oxford Book of Light Verse*. Chosen by W. H. Auden). For Voice and Chamber Ensemble (piano-vocal score by the composer). Galaxy, 1981. Tonal; d'–b"; Tess-mH; regular meters; 22pp; Diff-V/m, P/m-md.
For: tenor; soprano
Mood: macabre humor
Voice: skips usually small; repetitions of pitch patterns and sequence much used in most songs; rhythms usually easy; (e.) more complicated; a number of long tones, some high; a number of accidentals, sometimes involving change of mode
Piano: various stock accomp. styles–repeated, broken, and rolled chords; ostinato in (f.); (e.), 19-meas. gypsy-like prelude; others have lesser amounts of solo material
Diff: getting the pitch, at times; long high notes (f" and a"); syncopation in (e.); ensemble in (a.) involves polyrhythms
Uses: as a macabre group; three or four could be excerpted

a. *Old Roger.* Amaj; e'–b"; 6/8, Robust, Not Too Fast; 3pp.
b. *Down by the Green Wood Shady.* Gmaj-min; g'–e"; 2/2, With sweet simplicity; 3pp.
c. *The Walk.* Emaj–Ab; f#'–a"; 4/4, Ceremonial marching tempo–Allegro possibile; 3pp.
d. *A Man of Words and Not of Deeds.* Gmaj; d'–g"; 6/4, Moderately fast, Legato, non rubato; 3pp.
e. *Gypsies in the Wood.* Fmaj; f'–g"; 6/8, Brilliantly fast; 4pp.
f. *Elegy for Frederick the Great.* Bbmaj; f'–g"; 4/4, Majestic; 3pp.
g. *Mama Had a Baby.* Ends Cmaj; g'–f"; 2/4, Breathlessly fast; 3pp.

154. **PARODIES.** As some traditional jump-rope rhymes might have been set to music by the Masters. For High Voice & Piano. Boosey & Hawkes, 1986. Traditional

keys; b–b"; Tess-M-H; regular meters; 27pp; Diff-V/m-md, P/m-d.

For: high voice specified; soprano; possibly tenor

Mood: humorous; clever

Voice: (a.), includes recit. section and fast aria-like section with runs in Handelian style; (b.), looks like a shortened aria by Donizetti, with ornaments, cadenzas, and key, meter, and tempo changes; (c.), mostly conjunct with accidentals, supposedly in the style of Hugo Wolf; (d.) in the style of Mussorgsky–mostly conjunct but with some long-ranged phrases and meter and tempo changes; (e.), easy skips, accidentals, and sustained lines in the style of Duparc; (f.), flamenco-style ornaments in the style of Falla and a long, sustained b" at end

Piano: (a.), mostly chordal, with some doubling of vocal line and quotes from Handel's "Hallelujah Chorus"; (b.), very much like piano reduction of a Donizetti aria; (c.), has 4-voice chordal sections and sections with repeated chords and syncopation; (d.) has 4- & 5-voice block chords, sections of melody or countermelody in 8ves, and some doubling of vocal line; (e.), looks like a shortened and simplified version of Duparc's "L'Invitation au voyage" and "Chanson triste"; (f.), looks like Falla's *Seven Spanish Folk Songs*, particularly the "Jota," and has a 20-meas. prelude and various broken-chord patterns in Spanish-style rhythms

Diff: (a.) & (b.) need flexibility and accuracy in runs; (f.) needs flexibility in ornaments and has a long, sustained b"; in order to be believable in the six different styles the ensemble will require significant preparation

Uses: humorous; can excerpt three or four songs

    a. *I'll Never Go to Macy's* (traditional, style of George Friedrich Handel). Dmaj; d'–a"; 4/4, 2/2, Recitativo and Allegro; 2+min.

    b. *Miss Lucy* (traditional, style of Gaetano Donizetti). Sectional: Fmaj-Dmaj-Gmin-Fmaj-B♭maj; b–b♭"; 4/4, 6/8, Andante–Allegretto–Molto vivace; 3+min.

    c. *I Was Standing on the Corner* (traditional, style of Hugo Wolf). Dmin; g'–g"; 6/8, Sehr mässig; 2+min.

    d. *Poor Old Lady* (traditional, style of Modest Mussorgsky). Fmin; d'–a♭"; 5/4, 4/4 & other changes, Maestoso non troppo lento; 4+min.

    e. *Charlie Chaplin* (traditional, style of Henri Duparc). Dmin-Cmaj; g'–g"; 4/4, Mouvement modéré; 2min.

    f. *Spanish Dancer* (traditional, style of Manuel de Falla). F♯maj-Amaj-Emaj; e'–b"; 3/8, Allegretto vivace; 1min.

155. **THE RIVALS** (James Stephens). Four Songs for High Voice. Cycle. Theodore Presser, 1971. Traditional harmonic structures with altered chords; d'–b♭"; Tess-M; regular meters; varied tempos; 14pp; Diff-V/m, P/md.

For: lyric tenor with light flexibility; soprano

Mood: generally light in mood and character; central theme of rivalry

Voice: normal pitch and rhythm patterns; some chromaticism; flexibility needed; good approach to b♭"

Piano: mostly 8th-note motion; chordal and linear; accidentals;

(a.), perpetual motion; (d.), staccato 8th-note 3rds with countermelody

Diff: a few high tones; vocalizing passages

Uses: teaching and performance material; program ender

    a. *The Daisies.* Fmaj-F♯maj; f'–f♯"; Tess-M; 6/8, Allegro moderato; 5pp.

    b. *The Rose in the Wind.* Gmin; d'–g"; Tess-M; 6/8, Slow; 2pp.

    c. *The Hawk.* Cmaj-D♭maj; e♭'–a♭"; Tess-M; 4/4, Allegretto–Andante–Lento–Adagio; 2pp.

    d. *The Rivals.* Fmaj-E♭maj; e'–b♭"; Tess-mH; 4/4, Allegro moderato; 5pp.

156. **SONGS OF PERFECT PROPRIETY** (Dorothy Parker). For Medium Voice and Piano. Cycle. Boosey & Hawkes, 1959. Vol. I. Few key sigs, but largely diatonic material; c'–f♯"; Tess-M; regular meters (one song in 5/4); varied tempos, begins and ends fast; 23min; Diff-V/e-m; P/e-md.

For: mezzo-soprano best; some sopranos with full middle and low voice

Mood: humorous; wry commentary on the many facets of womanhood; final phrase, the famous sarcastic ". . . and I am Marie of Rumania"

Voice: vocal line generally easy with no strenuous singing and few musical problems; singer must have voice of many colors, however, to express the various moods; some speaking; easy style

Piano: generally outlines chord structure and supports vocal line; frequent doubling of vocal line

Diff: avoidance of "pop" style; songs need straightforwardness of delivery for the punch lines

Uses: good for the right singer; a light touch on any program; could excerpt smaller sets

    a. *Song of Perfect Propriety.* c'–e"; 2/2, Allegro barbaro; 3pp.

    b. *Now at Liberty.* e'–f"; 3/4, Moderato; 3pp (3 stanzas).

    c. *Ultimatum.* c'–e"; 6/8, Andante maestoso; 3pp.

    d. *Renunciation.* e'–e"; 2/4, Moderato; 3pp.

    e. *Inventory.* c'–d"; 3/4, Lento; 3pp.

    f. *Social Note.* c'–f"; 4/4, Lento; 2pp.

    g. *A Very Short Song.* d'–f♯"; 5/4, Andante; 2pp.

    h. *One Perfect Rose.* d'–f"; 4/4, Andante con moto; 3pp.

    i. *Wisdom.* e'–f♯"; 4/4, Lento; 3pp.

    j. *Men.* b–f"; 4/4, Andante; 3pp.

    k. *Lullaby.* d'–e♭"; 4/4, Lento; 4pp.

    l. *Comment.* d♭'–f"; 3/4, Allegro giocoso; 2pp.

157. **SONGS OF PERFECT PROPRIETY** (Dorothy Parker). For Medium Voice and Piano. Boosey & Hawkes, 1984. Vol. II. Tonal; b♭–f♯"; Tess-M; regular meters; 20min; Diff-V/m, P/m-md.

For: mezzo-soprano

Mood: humorous; cynical; ironic; sometimes reveals pathos behind humor

Voice: skips not difficult; range in some phrases exceeds 8ve; rhythms uncomplicated; (u.), chant-like; many accidentals; mostly syllabic

Piano: doubling of vocal line rare; various accomp. styles, incl. afterbeat, 4-voice chordal texture, and broken chords; (v.), trill-like ornaments and rapid scales; (x.), features highly ornamented piano part

Diff: exact mood and characterization of each song

Uses: as a group; excerpt to make a shorter group or combine with songs from Vol. I of this title

    m. *Symptom Recital.* B-centered; b'–e♭"; 2/2, Allegro moderato; 3pp.

    n. *The False Friends.* Shifting tonalities, ends Fmaj; c'–f "; 3/4, Allegretto; 3pp.

    o. *Love Song.* F–Emaj; c'–e"; 4/4, Molto rubato, allegro; 4pp.

    p. *Indian Summer.* Cmaj; d'–e"; 2/4, Allegro vivace; 2pp.

    q. *Somebody's Song.* Shifting tonalities; b–e"; 4/4, Andante; 5pp.

    r. *Song of One of the Girls.* Shifting tonalities, ends E♭; b♭–e"; 6/8, Andante, molto rubato; 3pp.

    s. *Bric-a-Brac.* Shifting tonalities, ends F; b–d"; 3/4, Lento; 2pp.

    t. *They Part.* F–E♭; c'–f♯"; 4/4, Allegro non troppo; 3pp.

    u. *Chant for Dark Hours.* Shifting tonalities, ends F; c'–f "; 3/4, Lento; 3pp.

    v. *The Choice.* Shifting tonalities; c'–d♯"; 6/8, Andante, un poco lento; 3pp.

    w. *The Trusting Heart.* D-centered; d'–e"; 5/4, Allegretto, molto rubato; 3pp.

    x. *Coda.* Shifting tonalities, ends D; c'–f "; Allegretto mosso; 4pp.

BARBER, SAMUEL
(b. West Chester, PA, 1910; d. New York, NY, 1981)

[See Appendix for songs with French texts]

[See also D#s 41 & 50; no titles given]

158. **BEGGAR'S SONG** (William Henry Davies). [80]. cmp1936. E♭maj; d'–e♭"; Tess-mH; 2/4, Andante, with mock solemnity; Allegro moderato; 4pp; Diff-V/m, P/md.

For: baritone

Mood: humorous

Voice: conjunct; several melismas; long tones on d" and e♭"

Piano: 16th-note motion predominates; double note in r.h., often 3rds; one rapid passage of descending 3-voice chords; chromaticism; some doubling of vocal line

Diff: long notes, esp. sustained d"–e♭" for 6 meas. at end while piano harmonies change

Uses: group ender; possibly group with two other Davies poems in this volume

Rec: D#102

159. **BESSIE BOBTAIL,** Op. 2, No. 3 (James Stephens). [79]. Dmin; c'–f "; Tess-mL; 2/2, 3/2, 5/2, Andante, un poco mosso; 4pp; Diff-V/m, P/m.

For: all voices except extremely low

Mood: dramatic; descriptive and narrative

Voice: dramatic; short phrases fragmented by rests

Piano: chordal–mostly broken; scale fragments; features contrary motion

Diff: requires considerable dramatic and descriptive skill; two speakers: narrator and Bessie Bobtail

Uses: effective song for the right singer

Rec: D#s 10, 24, 31, 39, 92, 102, 103

160. **THE DAISIES,** Op. 2, No. 1 (James Stephens). [24, 35, 48, 79]. H & L Keys: Fmaj & Dmaj; c'–f " & a–d"; Tess-M; 3/4, 4/4, Allegretto con grazia; 2pp; Diff-V/m, P/m.

For: all voices

Mood: lyrical love song; nature imagery

Voice: lyrical and smooth

Piano: broken chords; contrapuntal figures; expressive of text

Uses: good for young lyric voice

Rec: D#s 31, 48, 92, 98, 102, 103

161. **DESPITE AND STILL.** Song Cycle for Voice and Piano, Op. 41. G. Schirmer, 1969. [79]. "To my friend Leontyne Price." Traditional harmonic structures with many altered chords; c'–b♭" (medium key available); Tess-M-mH; irregular and changing meters; tempos vary from slow to fast; 9min; Diff-V/d, P/d.

For: soprano best; tenor; other voices in medium key

Mood: generally melancholy; various facets of love's endurance

Voice: rarely conjunct; patterned with many skips and leaps; difficult pitches; speech rhythms; irregular, changing meters; dramatic in places

Piano: typical Barber piano score; pianistic, but solid technique in solo literature demanded; large reaches

Diff: pitch; rhythm; ensemble; interpretation; for advanced musician and mature singer

Uses: a work of substance and variety for graduate or concert programming; not for young or inexperienced singers

Rec: D#s 91, 102, 103

    a. *A Last Song* (Robert Graves). d'–g♯"; 3/4, 5/4, 3/2, Moderato; 1+min.

    b. *My Lizard* (Theodore Roethke). d'–b♭"; 3/4, Fast and light; 1min.

    c. *In the Wilderness* (Robert Graves). c'–g"; 6/8, 9/8, 5/8, 8/8, Flowing, in 2; 2min.

    d. *Solitary Hotel* (James Joyce). c'–f "; 2/2, Like a rather fast tango in 2; 2min. [**Rec:** D#s 92, 106]

    e. *Despite and Still* (Robert Graves). e'–a"; 4/8, 5/8, Fast and darkly impassioned; 1+min.

162. **HERMIT SONGS,** Op. 29, Nos. 1–10 (anon. Irish texts, 8th–13th centuries; various trans.). Cycle. G. Schirmer, 1954. [79]. cmp1952–1953. H & L eds. Mostly traditional keys with many altered-chord structures; c'–b♭" & g♯–f♯"; Tess-M; no meter sigs., ♪ constant throughout; variety of tempos; 17min; Diff-V/d, P/d.

For: soprano; medium voices

Mood: reflection of life in a monastery and the passage of time in a microcosmic world

Voice: great variety of styles and techniques; speech rhythms; some recit.; some awkward pitches to hear; many rhythmic intricacies; comfortable range

Piano: pianist needs full command of technique; many delicate bell figures; cross-hands; solo passages; accomp. interprets, illustrates, and provides background for text; great skill and sensitivity needed

Diff: mostly rhythmic; good ensemble will require two superior musicians and plenty of rehearsal time

Uses: enormously varied and attractive work; one of the most important American song cycles; not for amateurs or inexperienced intermediate singers

Rec: D#s 14, 93, 94, 95, 96, 97, 98, 102, 103

     a. *At Saint Patrick's Purgatory.* G♯min; c♯'–f♯"; Allegretto, in steady rhythm; 3pp.

     b. *Church Bell at Night.* [43]. X; d♯'–c♯"; Molto adagio; 1p.

     c. *St. Ita's Vision.* H & L keys: D-Cmin & C-B♭min; c'–a♭" & b♭'–g♭"; Recit.–Andante con moto; 4pp.

     d. *The Heavenly Banquet.* H & L keys: Fmaj & E♭maj; d'–a♭" & c'–g♭"; Lively, with good humor; 3pp.

     e. *The Crucifixion.* [24, 28]. Amin; d'–f"; Moderato; 2pp.

     f. *Sea-Snatch.* H & L keys: Cmin & G♯min; c'–b♭" & g♯'–f♯"; Allegro con fuoco, surging; 2pp. [**Rec:** D#24]

     g. *Promiscuity.* [43]. Amin; g♯'–c"; Sostenuto–Allegro moderato; 1p.

     h. *The Monk and His Cat.* [24]. Fmaj; d'–e"; Moderato, flowing; 4pp.

     i. *The Praises of God.* H & L keys: Cmaj & B♭maj; e'–g" & d'–f"; Un poco allegro; 2pp.

     j. *The Desire for Hermitage.* H & L keys: Cmin & B♭min; e'–g" & c'–f"; Calmo e sostenuto; 4pp.

163. **I HEAR AN ARMY,** Op. 10, No. 3 (James Joyce). [79]. H & L keys: Cmin (orig.) & Amin; d'–a♭" & b–f"; Tess-M; 4/4, 2/4, 5/8, 3/4, Allegro con fuoco (♩ = 116); 7pp; Diff-V/d, P/dd.

For: baritone; dramatic tenor

Mood: dramatic; descriptive; despairing love song using battle imagery

Voice: disjunct; many dotted rhythms; sustained at end; dramatic and powerful

Piano: contrapuntal figures; broken chords; features a "hoof-beat" rhythm; large reach helpful

Diff: requires great dramatic skill and a strong middle voice; powerful, ringing a♭"(f")

Uses: very effective for the mature dramatic voice; the three songs of Op. 10 make a good set

Rec: D#s 2, 10, 24, 31, 39, 48, 54, 92, 101, 102, 103, 104, 105, 106

164. **IN THE DARK PINEWOOD** (James Joyce). [80]. cmp1937. Cmaj; c'–f"; Tess-M; 9/8, 12/8, 6/8, Moderato; 2pp; Diff-V/m, P/md.

For: medium voices; baritone best

Mood: love song

Voice: conjunct; several phrases encompass range of 10th; scale passages ascend in one key, descend in another; legato; melismas; augmentation of opening scale near end of song; some cross rhythms

Piano: 3-voice block chords; 8th notes in r.h. usually double vocal line; l.h. rather static; many accidentals; 2 meas. cross-hands and cross rhythms

Diff: long-ranged phrases; achieving legato in both parts

Uses: to teach legato line and smooth registration

Rec: D#102

165. **LOVE AT THE DOOR** (from the Greek: *Meleager*, trans. John Addington Symonds). [80]. cmp1934. G♯min; d♯'–e"; Tess-M; 3/4, Allegro; with passion; 3pp; Diff-V/me, P/m.

For: all voices

Mood: disappointed love

Voice: stepwise and small skips; easy rhythms; needs legato and dynamic control

Piano: 16th-repeated-note pattern shared between hands; hemiola; 2-meas. prelude, 3-meas. postlude

Diff: cross-rhythms with piano; soft high notes near end

Uses: good student song; recital material

Rec: D#102

166. **LOVE'S CAUTION** (William Henry Davies). [80]. cmp1935. C♯min; b–e♯"; Tess-mL; 4/4, 5/4, 3/4, 6/4, 2/2, 3/2, [Moderato]; 4pp; Diff-V/m, P/m.

For: medium voices

Mood: secret love

Voice: speech-like rhythms; melody outlines chords or is stepwise; mostly syllabic

Piano: rolled and block chords, slow arpeggiation; many accidentals; no prelude, interludes, or postlude

Diff: somewhat irregular phrasing; singer's entrance to central section

Uses: to teach legato and smooth register changes

Rec: D#102

167. **MONKS AND RAISINS,** Op. 18, No. 2 (Jose García Villa). [79]. Dmin; d'–f"; Tess-M; 7/8 ,4/4, Allegro (♩. = 40); 4pp; Diff-V/d, P/d.

For: any medium or high voice

Mood: humorous; descriptive; nonsense song

Voice: frequently outlines 7th chords; flowing 8th-note motion

Piano: continuous contrapuntal 8th-note movement; difficult rhythms

Diff: rhythms; ensemble

Uses: effective humorous recital song; good song for teaching 7/8 meter

Rec: D#s 48, 102, 103

168. **NIGHT WANDERERS** (William Henry Davies). [80]. cmp1935. Cmin; c'–e♭"; Tess-M; 2/4, 3/8, [Moderato]; 4pp; Diff-V/md, P/md.

For: dramatic baritone

Mood: macabre

Voice: somewhat disjunct; mostly syllabic; two 32nd-note melismas; syncopation

Piano: syncopated basic pattern in 8th and quarter notes features 32nd-note flourishes; center section has 32nd-note motion; 6-meas. prelude; short postlude; many accidentals

Diff: communicating this text properly; ensemble in middle section

Uses: recital material for mature singer

Rec: D#102

169. **NOCTURNE,** Op. 13, No. 4 (Frederic Prokosch). [79]. H & L keys: D♯min & C♯min; d♯'–a♭" & c♯'–f♯"; Tess-M; 4/4, 3/2, 5/4, Andante, un poco mosso (♩ = 58); 6pp; Diff-V/d, P/dd.
For: all voices except very low
Mood: lyrical; passionate love song
Voice: broad and sustained; somewhat disjunct; some difficult intervals; long phrases
Piano: broken-chord figures using a sextuplet grouping; much 2 vs. 3; large reach helpful
Diff: frequent meter changes; irregular rhythms; pitches; requires easy a♭"(f♯"); poem needs insight
Uses: excellent song for a mature singer
Rec: D#s 10, 28, 48, 92, 98, 101, 102, 103, 104, 105, 106, 107

170. **A NUN TAKES THE VEIL** (Heaven-Haven), Op. 13, No. 1 (Gerard Manley Hopkins). [29, 79]. H & L keys: Dmin & B♭min (orig.); g'–g" & e♭'–e♭"; Tess-mH; 3/4, 4/4, 2/4, Broad and sustained, in exact rhythm; 2pp; Diff-Vm, P/me.
For: any female voice
Mood: lyrical; philosophical; nature imagery
Voice: mostly stepwise; sustained phrases; slow movement reflects calm resolution
Piano: chordal; many rolled chords; large reach helpful
Diff: sustained, hovering phrases
Uses: effective recital song
Rec: D#s 31, 102, 103, 104, 105, 106, 107

171. **NUVOLETTA,** Opus 25 (James Joyce). [79]. F♯maj; b♯–b♯"; Tess-mH-H; 3/8, 2/4, 3/4, 4/4, Allegretto (♩. = 72); 9pp; Diff-V/d, P/d.
For: lyric or coloratura soprano
Mood: humorous; descriptive; word play; fantasy
Voice: disjunct; chromatic; recit. section; cadenza covering two 8ves; pitches elusive; some vocalizing
Piano: chordal; waltz rhythm; arpeggiation; rapid scales (diatonic and chromatic); highly chromatic; independent and descriptive
Diff: pitches; rhythms; demands great flexibility; text needs acquaintance with Joyce
Uses: brilliant aria-like showpiece
Rec: D#s 59, 98, 100, 102, 103

172. **OF THAT SO SWEET IMPRISONMENT** (James Joyce). [80]. cmp1935. Dmin/maj; a♯–d"; Tess-M; 2/4, 3/8, 3/4, 4/4, Con moto; 3pp; Diff-V/m, P/m.
For: medium voices; baritone best
Mood: lyric love song
Voice: two strophes, second varied; mixed meter but rhythms not difficult
Piano: block chords, some rolled; some arpeggiation and new harmonies in second strophe; mostly doubles vocal line
Diff: mixed meter; both performers must be precise; some strange mis-accented words
Uses: in a group of James Joyce songs, or pair with "Strings in the Earth and Air"
Rec: D#102

173. **THE QUEEN'S FACE ON THE SUMMERY COIN,** Op. 18, No. 1 (Robert Horan). [79]. F♯maj; c'–e"; Tess-mL; 4/4, 3/2, 7/4, 6/4, 11/8, 7/8, 5/4, Andante con moto (♩ = 84); 4pp; Diff-V/dd, P/dd.
For: mezzo-soprano
Mood: lyrical; abstract love poem; nature imagery
Voice: most movement by 2nds & 3rds; very chromatic; fragmented
Piano: broken chords; chromatic motives; generally 8th-note movement
Diff: pitches; meter changes; text
Uses: effective recital song
Rec: D#s 102, 103

174. **RAIN HAS FALLEN,** Op. 10, No. 1(James Joyce). [79]. H & L keys: X; f'–g" & d'–e" (orig.); Tess-mH; 4/4, 3/2, Moderato (♩ = 50); 5pp; Diff-V/d, P/dd.
For: any lyric voice
Mood: lyrical love poem; nature imagery
Voice: very sustained; builds to dramatic climax, then subsides
Piano: broken chords and arpeggiations; quite chromatic; independent of voice; evokes picture of rain
Diff: high phrase ending, g"–f♯" (e"–d♯") with cresc.; pitches elusive; rhythm requires care
Uses: fine recital song for secure musician
Rec: D#s 39, 48, 54, 92, 102, 103, 106

175. **THE SECRETS OF THE OLD,** Op. 13, No. 2 (William Butler Yeats). [79]. H & L keys: Cmin & Amin (orig.); e♭'–g" & c'–e"; Tess-M; 5/8, 2/4, 3/8, 3/4, Allegro giocoso; 4pp; Diff-V/d, P/m.
For: mezzo-soprano; soprano
Mood: reminiscent; descriptive; gossipy
Voice: mostly conjunct with some skips; irregular phrasing; sustained middle section
Piano: continuous 8th-note afterbeat pattern; chordal; changing meters
Diff: constantly shifting meters; ensemble; character delineation
Uses: excellent song for a good musician and interpreter
Rec: D#s 31, 102, 103, 104, 105, 106, 107

176. **SERENADER** (George Dillon). [80]. cmp1934. B♭maj; c'–f"; Tess-M; 6/8, Andante con moto; 3pp; Diff-V/m, P/m.
For: baritone (high)
Mood: the gift of song
Voice: some rhythmic complexity; many skips involving unexpected intervals and tritones
Piano: 8ve patterning and other broken-chord patterns; visually awkward; middle section has some vocal line doubling
Diff: rhythms; some intervals
Uses: in a group about making music or writing poems
Rec: D#102

177. **SLEEP NOW,** Op. 10, No. 2 (James Joyce). [79]. H & L keys: X; e♭'–g" & c'–e" (orig.); Tess-M; 4/4, 3/4, 5/8, 5/4, Andante tranquillo (♩ = 40-46)–Più mosso e agitato (♩ = 72); 4pp; Diff-V/d, P/dd.
For: all voices except extremely low
Mood: lyrical; cry for peace of heart

Voice: many skips and leaps; fragmented phrases; large dynamic contrasts

Piano: chordal and contrapuntal; rather chromatic; 32nd-note figures in middle section

Diff: pitches; vocal expressiveness to handle contrasts of drama and lyricism; ensemble

Uses: haunting song for a singer with good dynamic control; group with other two songs from Op. 10

Rec: D#s 2, 39, 48, 70, 92, 98, 102, 104, 105, 106

178. **A SLUMBER SONG OF THE MADONNA** (Alfred Noyes). [80]. cmp1925. A♭maj; c♯'–e♭"; Tess-M; 3/8, Moderato; 3pp; Diff-V/me, P/m.

For: female voices

Mood: lullaby

Voice: mostly stepwise; small skips; one m7th; several accidentals; mostly 8th-note motion; syllabic

Piano: block repeated chords; brief arpeggiated l.h. passage; 4-meas. prelude

Diff: dynamics *pp–ff*; some intervals might challenge a young student

Uses: a simple but interesting song to teach dynamic control, legato, and expression

Rec: D#102

179. **STRINGS IN THE EARTH AND AIR** (James Joyce). [80]. cmp1935. Cmaj; d'–f"; Tess-mH; 3/4, 4/4, 5/4, [Moderato]; 2pp; Diff-V/me, P/me.

For: any voice

Mood: music in nature

Voice: stepwise and easy skips; easy rhythms; syllabic

Piano: doubles vocal line; 3rds in one hand, 8ves or single notes in the other; some syncopation

Uses: nice song for study or recital; simple but expressive

Rec: D#102

180. **SURE ON THIS SHINING NIGHT,** Op. 13, No. 3 (James Agee). [24, 59, 79]. H & L keys: B♭maj & Gmaj (orig.); d'–g" & b–e"; Tess-M; 3/4, 4/4, Andante (♩ = 50); 3pp; Diff-V/m, P/me.

For: all lyric voices

Mood: lyrical; philosophical; nature imagery

Voice: broad, sustained phrases; several phrases begin high

Piano: repeated chords throughout; melody in canon with the voice; bits of countermelody

Diff: high tessitura in middle section; dynamics; breathing

Uses: excellent teaching and recital song for a vibrant lyric voice

Rec: D#s 10, 16, 24, 28, 31, 39, 48, 65, 92, 101, 102, 103, 104, 105, 106, 107

181. **THERE'S NAE LARK** (Algernon Swinburne). [80]. cmp1927. E♭maj; b♭–e♭"; Tess-wide; 4/4, Moderato; 2pp; Diff-V/m, P/m.

For: medium and low voices

Mood: love song

Voice: mostly quarter-note motion; much stepwise motion; some large leaps of 9th, 8ve, 10th; legato

Piano: single-voice broken chords in r.h., some widely spaced; l.h. 2–3-voice chords

Diff: wide leaps in middle of phrases

Uses: good student song for register and dynamic control

Rec: D#102

182. **THREE SONGS, OPUS 45.** [79]. First performed by Gerard Souzay. H & L keys: traditional keys; d '–g" & b♭–e"; Tess-M-mH; 9min; Diff-V/m-md, P/m-d. Separate entries below.

A. **NOW HAVE I FED AND EATEN UP THE ROSE,** Op. 45, No. 1 (James Joyce, from the German of Gottfried Keller). H & L keys: Bmin & Amin; f♯'–f♯" & e'–e"; Tess-mH; 4/4, 2/4, 3/4, Moderato; 2+min; Diff-V/m-md, P/m.

For: tenor; baritone; man's text

Mood: lyrical

Voice: many skips; some chromaticism; syncopation

Piano: chordal-linear combination; many accidentals; various registers; some triplets; does not double vocal line

Diff: some pitch patterns; poem somewhat obscure

Uses: nice romantic song; quiet ending

Rec: D#s 92, 102, 104, 105, 108

B. **A GREEN LOWLAND OF PIANOS,** Op. 45, No. 2 (Czeslaw Milosz, from the Polish of Jerzy Harasymowicz). H & L keys: B♭maj & A♭maj; d'(f')–f♯" & c'(e♭')–e"; Tess-mH; 2min; Diff-V/md, P/md.

For: tenor; baritone; soprano; mezzo-soprano

Mood: humorous; nonsense

Voice: many leaps; 2-note slurs; dotted rhythms; syncopation; interrupted phrases

Piano: linear; unifying repetitive rhythmic pattern in l.h.; some rapid scales, trills, and staccato make sound effects; does not double vocal line

Diff: rhythms; some melodic intervals; ensemble

Uses: good humorous song

Rec: D#s 92, 102, 104, 105, 108

C. **O BOUNDLESS, BOUNDLESS EVENING,** Op.45, No. 3 (Christopher Middleton, from the German of George Heym). H & L keys: B♭maj & Gmaj; d♭'–g" & b♭–e"; Tess-M; 6/8, 9/8, Tranquillo, un poco mosso; 4min; Diff-V/md, P/md-d.

For: tenor; baritone; soprano; mezzo-soprano

Mood: lyrical; descriptive

Voice: stepwise and chord-member skips; some 2-note slurs; syncopation

Piano: broken-chord patterning; some countermelody; various registers; 16th-note motion; accidentals; rolled chords; does not double vocal line

Uses: nice lyric song; quiet ending

Rec: D#s 70, 92, 102, 104, 105, 108

183. **WITH RUE MY HEART IS LADEN,** Op. 2, No. 2 (A. E. Housman). [79]. H & L keys: Dmin & Bmin; e'–f" & c♯'–d"; Tess-M; 3/4, 4/4, 5/4, Andante cantabile; 2pp; Diff-V/m, P/m.

For: any lyric voice

Mood: lyrical; melancholy poem about death

Voice: lyrical and sustained; irregular rhythms; some elusive pitches

Piano: broken-chord figures throughout

Diff: rhythms and phrasing

Uses: fine recital song
Rec: D#s 48, 92, 102, 103, 106

BARNETT, ALICE
(b. Lewiston, IL, 1886; d. San Diego, CA, 1975)

184. **BEYOND** (Thomas S. Jones, Jr.). G. Schirmer, 1918. Emaj; e'–g♯"; Tess-M; 6/8, Poco animato; Diff-V/m, P/m-d.
For: lyric soprano
Mood: lyrical; philosophical spring song
Voice: graceful vocal line; some chromaticism; soft high climax
Piano: some large reaches; accidentals
Diff: demands good chromatic intonation; soft high tones
Uses: teaching soft head tones; attractive song

185. **CHANSON OF THE BELLS OF OSENÈY** (Cale Young Rice). G. Schirmer, 1924. Gmaj-Cmaj; c'–e"(a"); Tess-M; 5/4, Placidamente; Diff-V/md, P/md.
For: mezzo-soprano; baritone
Mood: declamatory; descriptive
Voice: declamatory style
Piano: much bell imagery
Diff: 5/4 meter
Uses: good for teaching declamation and irregular meter

186. **THE COOL OF THE NIGHT:** A Nocturne for Voice and Piano (Egmont H. Arens). G. Schirmer, 1919. Cmaj; c'–f♯"; Tess-M; 6/8, 9/8, 3/4, 4/8, Andante calmato; Diff-V/md, P/d.
For: mezzo-soprano
Mood: lyrical; summer nocturne
Voice: modulating phrases; rhythmically complicated
Piano: many 3rds; syncopation; large leaps; accidentals; highly descriptive
Diff: intonation; rhythms
Uses: good atmospheric song

187. **NIGHTINGALE LANE** (William Sharp). G. Schirmer, 1918. Amaj; b♯–g♯"; Tess-L-M; 12/8, Vivace; Diff-V/md, P/md.
For: soprano; tenor
Mood: lyrical night piece
Voice: fast movement; chromatic
Piano: much arpeggiation
Diff: fast articulation
Uses: teaching fast articulation and accurate intonation

188. **NIRVANA** (John Hall Wheelock). G. Schirmer, 1932. Dmaj; d'–f"; Tess-M; 4/4, Con moto tranquillo; Diff-V/md, P/md.
For: mezzo-soprano; baritone; possibly for soprano with mellow, full lower voice
Mood: lyrical; philosophical; quiet
Voice: flowing lines; some decoration
Piano: chordal; many harmonic excursions
Uses: good song; slightly popular flavor to harmonic structure

189. **PANELS FROM A CHINESE SCREEN.** Three Songs. Carl Fischer, 1924. Pub. separately. Traditional keys; c'–f"; Tess-M; 10pp; Diff-V/m, P/m.
For: mezzo-soprano
Mood: lyrical; descriptive; narrative
Voice: much conjunct motion; some skips; easy rhythms; melismatic passages; long-ranged phrases; duplets and triplets; long notes
Piano: chordal–block, rolled, broken; some cross-hands; wide reaches; parallel triads; little doubling of vocal line
Diff: melismatic passages; some long tones
Uses: nice set; rather impressionistic in style; good for teaching legato singing

    a. *The Singing Girl of Shan.* Cmaj; c'–e"; 2/4, Allegretto con moto.
    b. *On a Moonlit River.* Emaj; c♯'–e"; 3/4, Tranquillo.
    c. *In the Time of Saffron Moons.* Fmaj; c'–f"; 12/8, Andante grazioso.

190. **TWO SONGS FOR MEDIUM VOICE AND PIANO.** G. Schirmer, 1924. Pub. separately. Traditional keys; d'–g"; Tess-M; regular meters, moderate tempos; Diff-V/e-md, P/m-md.
For: mezzo-soprano
Mood: lyrical; narrative; descriptive; quasi-Middle-Eastern flavor
Voice: no problems; melodically repetitious
Piano: chordal; "Oriental" sounds
Uses: somewhat dated, but good teaching material for young singers

    a. *A Caravan from China Comes* (Richard LeGallienne). Gmaj; d'–g"; 2/4, Allegretto.
    b. *As I Came Down from Lebanon* (Clinton Scollard). Dmaj; d'–f♯"; 4/4, Tranquillamente mosso.

BARTLETT, HOMER N.
(b. Olive, NY, 1845; d. Hoboken, NJ, 1920)

191. **AN AUTUMN SONG,** Op. 121. Ditson, 1893. E♭maj; g–e♭"; Tess-M; 4/4, Andante; 6pp; Diff-V/m, P/m.
For: alto; bass
Mood: lyrical; thanksgiving for fruitful harvest
Voice: stepwise and chord-member skips; dotted notes; repetitive rhythms; 2–3-note slurs
Piano: repeated chords; some large reaches; many accidentals; some arpeggios; does not double vocal line
Uses: usable period piece

192. **DEAREST ROBIN,** Op. 134, No. 2; G. Schirmer, 1894. Gmin; d'–f♯"; Tess-M; 4/4, Allegretto con moto; 4pp; Diff-V/m, P/m.
For: soprano
Mood: lyrical; humorous; character song–maiden and robin
Voice: conjunct; repetitive; four stanzas; two speakers
Piano: linear; a bit archaic sounding
Uses: humorous song usable for young, expressive singer

193. **THE TWO LOVERS,** Op. 237 (Shaemas O'Sheel). G. Schirmer, 1911. Gmin; d'–a"; Tess-mH; 6/8, 4/4, Allegro moderato; 7pp; Diff-V/m, P/m.
For: soprano; tenor

Mood: lyrical; loneliness
Voice: sustained; long phrases; long tones at phrase ends; word and phrase repetition; "oo" and "ee" vowels frequent
Piano: arpeggiation; some repeated 8ves and chords; one chordal section
Diff: long phrases; sustained high phrases
Uses: a good "singing" song for a big, romantic voice; period piece

BARTON, GERARD
(b. 1861–?)

194. **IT WAS A LOVER AND HIS LASS** (William Shakespeare). [5]. Cmaj; g–c"; Tess-M; 4/4, Allegro commodo (♩ = 160); 2pp; Diff-V/e, P/me.
For: bass; bass-baritone
Mood: jolly song of love in spring; well-known text
Voice: mostly conjunct motion; leap of m7th
Piano: chordal; doubles vocal line throughout
Uses: good song for a young bass

BASSETT, LESLIE
(b. Hanford, CA, 1923)

195. **FIVE LOVE SONGS.** Merion, 1977. Commissioned by MTNA for its Centennial year and the American Bicentennial. Atonal; c♯'–a"; Tess-M-H, wide; mostly unmetered; varied tempos; 13min (18+pp); Diff-V/dd, P/dd.
For: soprano
Mood: various moods of love–lighthearted to passionate
Voice: unpatterned pitches; staccato; complicated rhythms; whispering and whistling required
Piano: special notation and pedal effects; tone clusters; trills; tremolo; fast scales; disjunct; articulations important
Diff: singer must be secure technician and musician; careful dynamic markings in both parts; special notation in both parts; several sustained high tones
Uses: can be very effective group if both performers are secure in this idiom; not for young singers

    a. *Love, like a Mountain Wind* (anon., Greece). X; d'–a♭"; Tess-H, wide; unmetered, ♩ = 60; 3pp.
    b. *The Tides of Love* (Walter Savage Landor). X; c♯'–g♯"; Tess-M; unmetered, 4/4, 5/4, ♩ = 69; 2pp.
    c. *To My Dear and Loving Husband* (Anne Bradstreet). X; f'–g♯"; Tess-mH, wide; unmetered and changing meters, Fast; 5pp.
    d. *Teach Me Your Mood, O Patient Stars* (Ralph Waldo Emerson). X; e♭'–g"; Tess-wide; unmetered and changing meters, changing tempos; 2+pp.
    e. *Madrigal* (Henry Harrington). X; g'–a"(b♭" whistled); Tess-H; 3/4, ♩. = c.68; 6pp.

196. **THE JADE GARDEN.** Merion, 1977. Atonal with some pentatonic flavor; c♯'–g♯"; Tess-M, wide; mostly unmetered; fluctuating tempos; 9min; Diff-V/d, P/d.
For: soprano
Mood: quiet; introspective; philosophical; Eastern
Voice: many wide leaps; many accidentals; speech-like

rhythms; independent of piano part
Piano: wide piano range; often concentrates on high part of keyboard; special notation instructions; rapid scales and broken chords; some wide reaches; often disjunct; some stopped strings inside piano
Diff: although difficult, not so difficult as some scores that have similar appearance; singer needs secure technique and musicianship; ensemble will need much rehearsal; close attention to dynamics
Uses: very effective short set; evokes Far-Eastern atmosphere well

    a. *Maple Leaves* (Tsurayuki). d♭'–f♯"; unmetered and changing meters, changing tempos.
    b. *Pine Tree* (Hakutsu). d♯'–e♭"; 4/4, 9/8, 10/8, etc., ♩ = 66.
    c. *Night* (Li Po). d♯'–g"; unmetered, irregular tempos.
    d. *Nightingale* (anon., Japan). c♯'–g♯"; unmetered, irregular tempos ♩ = 76.

197. **TO MUSIC.** Three Songs for High Voice and Piano. Cycle. Galaxy, 1966. Atonal; b–a"; Tess-M-mH; mostly regular but changing meters–various divisions of the beat; slow–moderate–fast; 8min (16pp); Diff-V/d, P/d.
For: tenor; soprano
Mood: subject of cycle is the divine power of music; atonal idiom gives sense of mysticism
Voice: sustained phrases; melismatic passages; difficult pitches in atonal idiom; words hard to project; ensemble problems
Piano: virtuoso solo techniques required; solo passages; many accidentals
Diff: difficulties abound for any but the most advanced students; perfect pitch helpful
Uses: interesting atonal group

    a. *Slow, Slow, Fresh Fount* (Ben Jonson). b–f♯"; Tess-M; 4/4 with changes, Slow; 3pp.
    b. *To Music* (Robert Herrick). f♯'–f"; Tess-M; 4/4, 5/4, 3/4, Moderately slow; 5pp.
    c. *Great Art Thou, O Music* (William Billings). c♯'–a"; Tess-mH; 4/4, 3/4, Rather fast and with strong pulse; 8pp.

BAUER, MARION
(b. Walla Walla, WA, 1887; d. South Hadley, MA, 1955)

198. **BY THE INDUS** (Cale Young Rice). A. P. Schmidt, 1917. H & L keys: Cmin & Amin; c'–a♭" & a–f"; Tess-M; 3/4, 4/4, Molto moderato; 6pp; Diff-V/md, P/m.
For: mezzo-soprano; dramatic soprano
Mood: dramatic; intense; disappointed love
Voice: many skips; duplets and triplets; fragmented phrases; groups of 5 & 4 in 3/4 meter
Piano: chordal; broken chords; some countermelody; 2 vs. 3; large dynamic contrasts; does not double vocal line
Diff: control of dynamics; secure registration; long phrases; mature sound needed
Uses: good for the right singer

199. ORIENTALE (Sir Edwin Arnold). A. P. Schmidt, 1917. Amin; e'–a"; Tess-M-mH; 2/4, Presto e appassionato; 4pp; Diff-V/m, P/m.
For: soprano
Mood: lyrical; ode to music and dancing
Voice: conjunct, with some leaps; some vocalizing; long trill; ends a"; flexible tempo; melodic-minor scale structure
Piano: broken-chord afterbeat figures; some intermittent melodic material
Diff: trill
Uses: easy coloratura; flashy ending

BAUER, ROSS
(b. 1951)

200. FOUR HONIG SONGS (Edwin Honig). C. F. Peters, 1991. cmp1989. Atonal; a♯–b♭"; Tess-wide; regular and irregular meters with many changes; slow-fast-fast-slow; 11min; Diff-V/dd, P/dd.
For: soprano
Mood: esoteric contemplation of the nature of being a tree
Voice: vocal line often disjunct; much 8ve displacement in phrases; many wide intervals; some speech rhythms, but mostly arbitrary patterns; occasional pitch help from the piano; melismas; many tempo and expressive markings; sustained high tones
Piano: atonal techniques in all areas; chordal; some ostinato patterns; some linear textures; facsimile score; many tempo, dynamic, and expressive markings
Diff: in all areas: poetry, pitch, rhythm, diction, meaning; perfect pitch helpful to the singer
Uses: an exercise in atonality for those who enjoy the challenge

  a. *Teetering.* X; b♭–g"; Tess-wide; 4/4, 3/4, 5/4, etc., Liberamente, molto espressivo, ♩ = 58; 4pp.
  b. *A Wind Dies.* X; b♭–a"; Tess-wide; 3/4, 4/4, 5/8, etc., Lightly, fantastically, ♩ = 126+; 5pp.
  c. *Another.* X; b–b♭"; Tess-wide; 4/4, 3/4, 5/8, etc., Animato, ♩ = 126–132; 6pp.
  d. *Teetering.* X; a♯–a"; Tess-wide; 7/8, 4/4, 3/4, etc., Liberamente, molto espressivo, ♩ = 58; 4pp.

BEACH, AMY MARCY CHENEY (MRS. H. H. A.)
(b. Henniker, NH, 1867; d. New York, NY, 1944)

[See Appendix for songs with French and German texts]

201. ARIETTE, Op. 1, No. 4 (To a lady singing to her accompaniment on the guitar) (Percy Bysshe Shelley). 1886. Reprint: Classical Vocal Reprints. [61, 82, vol. 1]. G♭maj; c♯'–f♯"; Tess-M; 3/8, Allegretto ma non troppo; 4pp; Diff-V/me, P/m.
For: soprano; mezzo-soprano; tenor
Mood: lyrical; nocturnal
Voice: stepwise and small skips; easy rhythms
Piano: imitates guitar; some accidentals; two key sig. changes
Uses: good student song; useful in a period group
Rec: D#s 52, 109

202. CANZONETTA (Armand Silvestre; Eng. text by Amy Beach). [11, Vol. 1]. A♭maj; f♭'–a♭"; Tess-M; 4/4, Tranquillo; 3pp; Diff-V/m, P/m.
For: soprano; tenor
Mood: comparison of eternal love to the vanishing beauties of nature
Voice: lyrical, conjunct lines; climax on a♭" approached from 7th below; sustained quiet ending
Piano: slow chords give way to broken-chord patterns; punctuating chords; syncopated climax
Uses: good song for teaching line and dynamics (*pp–ff*); French or English text usable

203. ECSTASY, Op. 19, No. 2 (Mrs. H. H. A. Beach). 1893. Reprint: Classical Vocal Reprints. [45, 82, vol. 2]. H & L keys: E♭maj. [82] & D♭maj; c'–g" & b♭–f"; Tess-M; 3/4, Andantino con molto espressione; 3pp; Diff-V/e, P/me.
For: any high or medium voice
Mood: lyrical; sentimental love song
Voice: short phrases; waltz-like rhythm
Piano: repeated chords; afterbeats; independent melody and countermelody; somewhat chromatic
Uses: usable recital song
Rec: D#109

204. ELLE ET MOI, Op. 21, No. 3 (Félix Bovet). [81]; 1st©1893. Reprint: Classical Vocal Reprints. H & L keys: Fmaj (Fr. & Eng.) & E♭maj (Eng. only); c'–c''' & b♭–g(b♭'); Tess-mH-H; 2/4, Allegro leggiero; 6pp; Diff-V/d, P/m.
For: soprano; mezzo-soprano
Mood: joyful; the approach of love
Voice: stepwise and skips along chord lines; coloratura passages (legato and staccato melismas); long trills; echo effects; some long high notes; final phrase 2-meas. trill on f" followed by a" and c''' and a staccato cadenza down; Fr. text only in [81], Eng. trans. given
Piano: graceful, non-legato broken-chord pattern with snatches of melody; shifting harmonies
Diff: coloratura techniques
Uses: a charming song; nice showpiece for coloratura with a good trill
Rec: D#109

205. FAIRY LULLABY, Op. 37, No. 3 (William Shakespeare). 1897. Reprint: Classical Vocal Reprints. Single and in *3 Shakespeare Songs*, Op. 37. [81, 82, vol.3]. Fmaj; e'–f"(a"); Tess-mH; 3/8, Allegro ma non troppo; 4pp; Diff-V/m, P/me.
For: soprano
Mood: delicate
Voice: stepwise motion with small skips; some syncopation; many 2-note slurs with some longer melismas; several long notes; final note is a"(f") sustained 4 meas.
Piano: guitar-like afterbeat pattern; some rolled chords; some countermelody; 4-meas. prelude, interlude, and postlude; does not double vocal line
Diff: syncopation, esp. in the refrain
Uses: lovely song for a young, flexible voice
Rec: D#110

206. **FAR AWA'!** Op. 43, No. 4 (Robert Burns). [82, vol.3]. D♭maj; f'–g♭"; Tess-mH; 3/4, Andantino; 2pp; Diff-V/me, P/me.

For: soprano

Mood: plaintive; song of separation; introspective

Voice: stepwise and small skips; easy rhythms; several 2–3-note slurs; quiet ending

Piano: block- and broken-chord accomp.; some doubling and outlining of vocal line; 4-meas. prelude; one interlude

Diff: some long notes; dynamic control; some Scottish dialect

Uses: excellent short, simple song; effective

Rec: D#110

207. **FORGET-ME-NOT,** Op. 35, No. 4 (H. H. A. Beach). [82, vol.4]. Fmaj; e♭'(f')–a"; Tess-mH; 6/8, Andante con grazia; 5pp; Diff-V/m, P/md.

For: tenor

Mood: lyrical love song

Voice: mostly stepwise and chordal skips; accidentals; some dotted rhythms; several long notes (e", f", g", and a"); ends on a" ff sustained 2 meas.; short melismas on "ah"

Piano: mostly arpeggiated with short repeated-chord section; accidentals, incl. double ♭s; two 4-meas. interludes; does not double vocal line

Diff: floating high notes (e.g., g" pp)

Uses: for recital or as student song for lyric tenor; somewhat overblown ending, but typical of the period

208. **FOR ME THE JASMINE BUDS UNFOLD** (Florence Earle Coates). [82, vol. 4]. E♭maj; c'(e♭')–g"(f"); Tess-M; 4/4, Allegro ma non troppo; 5pp; Diff-V/m, P/md.

For: mezzo-soprano; with alternative higher and/or lower pitches–baritone, soprano, or tenor

Mood: ecstatic love song

Voice: stepwise motion and chordal skips; many triplets and duplets; some 2 vs. 3 in piano; syllabic with some 2-note slurs; dynamics range pp–ff; big ending

Piano: afterbeat pattern and repeated chords in triplets; thick accomp.; some outlining of vocal line; short prelude; three short interludes

Diff: dynamics; needs a voice with good dynamic range and control

Uses: ecstatic song; possible group ender

209. **GO NOT TOO FAR,** Op. 56, No. 2 (Florence Earle Coates). A. P. Schmidt, 1904. Reprint: Classical Vocal Reprints. H & L keys: E♭maj. & B♭maj; d'–f" & a–c"; Tess-M; 4/4, Largo ma non troppo, sempre espressivo; 3pp; Diff-V/m, P/m.

For: any voice

Mood: lyrical; gentle; serious; love song

Voice: stepwise and small skips; some leaps of 7th; duplets vs. piano triplets

Piano: broken-chord pattern in triplets; 2 vs. 3; accidentals; does not double vocal line

Diff: 2 vs. 3 in piano; soft dynamics

Uses: nice song; simple expression; straightforward

210. **HYMN OF TRUST** (Oliver Wendell Holmes). Reprint: Classical Vocal Reprints (M). [82, vol. 2].

B♭maj; b♭–f"; Tess-M; 4/4, Andante; 4pp; Diff-V/m, P/m.

For: mezzo-soprano; baritone

Mood: reverent; trusting in divine love

Voice: stepwise motion and chordal skips; rhythms not complex; mostly syllabic with several 2-note slurs; quiet ending

Piano: repeated chords and afterbeat style; some countermelody; syncopation; does not double vocal line

Diff: possibly pp–ff dynamic control

Uses: for recital; possibly church use

211. **THE LOTOS ISLES** (Alfred Lord Tennyson). G. Schirmer, 1914. Reprint: T.I.S. (H). [51]. D♭maj; d♭'–g♭"; Tess-mL; 4/4, Lento, molto tranquillo; 4pp; Diff-V/m, P/md.

For: any medium voice

Mood: dreamy; nature imagery

Voice: mostly conjunct motion; a few skips; very sustained; generally soft dynamic level

Piano: chordal; moving 8ths in r.h., mostly parallel 3rds; some accidentals; supports vocal line well

Diff: maintaining optimal vocal sound at soft dynamic levels throughout

Uses: good teaching or recital song

212. **MEADOW-LARKS,** Op. 79, No. 1 (Ina Coobrith). [48]; 1st©1917. H & L keys: Fmaj & Cmaj; e♭'–c'" & b♭–g'"; Tess-mH; 4/4, 3/4, Allegro ma non troppo; 6pp; Diff-V/md, P/md.

For: lyric or coloratura soprano; lyric mezzo-soprano

Mood: joyful nature song

Voice: intervals outline chords; sustained high tones

Piano: broken and arpeggiated chords; bird-call melody in several places

Diff: easy agility; easy c'" (g") necessary for full effect, although lower option is provided

Uses: good training song for above voices, but may have limited audience appeal

213. **MY LUVE IS LIKE A RED, RED ROSE,** Op. 12, No. 3 (Robert Burns). Reprint: Masters Music Publications (In *Three Songs*, Op. 12). D♭maj; d♭'–a♭"; Tess-wide; 3/4, Allegretto espressivo; 6pp; Diff-V/md, P/md.

For: tenor

Mood: love song

Voice: many small skips; many 2-note slurs; a few melismas; rhythms include both duplet and triplet divisions of beat; legato style; many expressive markings; dramatic buildup at end

Piano: mostly arpeggiated triplet patterning; some block chords; harmonically supports and sometimes doubles vocal line; short prelude and interludes; 15-meas. postlude, winding down from climactic vocal ending

Diff: rhythms; ensemble; dialect; control of dynamics

Uses: program with two other Burns poems set by Beach ("Wilt Thou Be My Dearie" and "Ye Banks and Braes o' Bonnie Doon")

214. **NIGHT (Nachts),** Op. 35, No. 1 (Scherenberg). [82, vol 3]; 1st©1897. E♭maj; d'–g"; Tess-M; 4/4, Adagio e tranquillo; 3pp; Diff-V/m, P/me.

For: soprano; mezzo-soprano; tenor
Mood: lyrical; descriptive; tranquil; quiet
Voice: stepwise or chord-member skips; easy rhythms; smooth, sustained lines; 2- & 3-note slurs; English text nicely singable
Piano: broken-chord patterning; some countermelody; some accidentals; syncopated repeated tones; does not double vocal line
Diff: dynamic control; registration; smooth legato style
Uses: nice uncluttered lyric setting; recital use
Rec: D#110

215. **OH WERE MY LOVE YON LILAC FAIR!** Op. 43, No. 3 (Robert Burns). 1899. Reprint: Classical Vocal Reprints. [82, vol. 3]. H & M keys: Fmaj & E♭maj; c'–f" & b♭–e♭"; Tess-M; 4/4, Allegretto semplice; 2pp; Diff-V/m, P/m.

For: baritone; possibly some tenors
Mood: lyrical love song
Voice: stepwise motion and small skips; some dotted rhythms; a few triplets; some 2-note slurs; very soft ending (9-beat f" ppp)
Piano: block chords; some countermelody; accidentals; some doubling of vocal line
Diff: probably dynamics
Uses: useful song; setting suits text very well

216. **O MISTRESS MINE,** Op. 37, No. 1 (William Shakespeare). 1897. Reprint: Classical Vocal Reprints (H) in *Three Shakespeare Songs*. [55, 61, 81, 82, vol. 4]. H & L keys: Gmaj & E♭maj; f♯'–a"(g") & d'–f"(e♭"); Tess-M-H; 2/4, Allegretto grazioso; 5pp; Diff-V/m-md, P/m.

For: lyric tenor; man's text
Mood: graceful; sprightly
Voice: stepwise and chord-member skips; easy rhythms; syncopation; grace notes; several melismas include 16th notes
Piano: chordal, 4-voice; much staccato; articulations important; repetitive rhythms; interplay with voice; does not double vocal line
Diff: melismas on various syllables; soft and loud high tones
Uses: useful song; could end a group
Rec: D#s 52, 109

217. **PRAYER OF A TIRED CHILD,** Op. 75, No. 4 (Abbie Farwell Brown). [81]. E♭maj; c'–e♭"; Tess-mL; 4/4, Molto tranquillo; 3pp; Diff-V/e, P/e.

For: any medium or medium-low voice
Mood: lyrical; distracted prayer
Voice: conjunct; a few intervals of 4th; small range; syllabic; 2-note slurs
Piano: 2-voice broken-chord ostinato pattern in treble clef; 8th-note motion throughout
Uses: lovely song for a beginning student; also nice for a group of prayer songs

218. **THE SECRET (Le Secret)** (Le Comte Jules de Besseguier). [82, vol.1]. Fmin; e♭'–a"; Tess-mH; 3/8; 5pp; Diff-V/md, P/m.

For: soprano

Mood: plaintive
Voice: mostly stepwise with small skips outlining chords; rhythms not difficult; several 2-note slurs; two long melismas on "ah"; soft ending on a" sustained 4 meas.; dynamics ppp–f
Piano: combination of afterbeat and broken-chord patterning; accidentals; 4-meas. prelude, 8-meas. interlude, and 8-meas. postlude; does not double vocal line
Diff: dynamic control
Uses: English text usable but seems a bit better in French; for young soprano with flexibility and floating high tones, or to develop these qualities

219. **SPRING,** Op. 26, No. 3 (Cora Fabbri). Arthur P. Schmidt, 1894. Reprint: Classical Vocal Reprints. E♭maj; g'–a♭"; Tess-mH; 9/8, Allegro molto; 3pp; Diff-V/m, P/m.

For: soprano; tenor (?)
Mood: joyous spring song
Voice: lyrical, fast-moving line; stepwise and larger intervals up to an 8ve; an occasional duplet in compound meter; high ending, rit. on a♭" before cadence; syllabic; some irregular phrase lengths; some similar phrases begin on different beats of the measure
Piano: broken chords in triplet afterbeat pattern; some hemiola; some unexpected harmonies; delicate, pp–mf–ff at end
Diff: some entrances; changing phrase lengths in similar melodic material; possibly ensemble for less advanced musicians
Uses: spring song; could end group; good for teaching phrasing and dynamics

220. **SPRINGTIME** (Susan Merrick Heywood). [51]; 1st©1929. "To Arthur Kraft." H & L keys: A♭maj-min. & E♭maj-min; f'–a♭" & c'–e♭"; Tess-M; 6/8, Limpido; 1+min; Diff-V/m, P/md.

For: any voice except extremely low; text slightly better for a woman
Mood: lyrical; song about love
Voice: many skips; some 2-note slurs; dotted notes
Piano: broken-chord pattern; rapid; 4-voice measured tremolo figure; many accidentals; does not double vocal line
Diff: high tones sustained

221. **THE SUMMER WIND** (Walter Learned). [82, vol. 2]. A♭maj; e♭'–f"; Tess-M; 12/8, Allegro con delicatezza; 3pp; Diff-V/m, P/md.

For: soprano; mezzo-soprano; tenor
Mood: gentle and soothing
Voice: stepwise motion with skips not exceeding 8ve; easy rhythms; some 2-note slurs; quiet ending
Piano: repeated chords in 8ths; some accidentals; does not double vocal line
Diff: possibly dynamic control
Uses: good student and recital song; useful to develop dynamic control

222. **TAKE, O TAKE THOSE LIPS AWAY,** Op. 37, No. 2 (William Shakespeare). Arthur P. Schmidt, 1897. Reprint: *Three Shakespeare Songs, Op. 37.* Classical Vocal Reprints. [30, 56, 61, 81, 82, vol. 4]. H & M

keys: Emin [single, 81, 82, & CVR] & Cmin [56]. e'–a"(g") & c'–f"(e♭"); Tess-M-H; 6/8, Andantino con espressione; 3pp; Diff-V/m, P/m.

For: tenor; soprano
Mood: serious; disappointed love song
Voice: mostly chord-member skips; easy rhythms; interrupted phrases; one 3-meas. melisma
Piano: chordal; rolled chords; imitation of strummed instrument; does not double vocal line
Diff: dynamic control needed for textual repetition; both soft and loud high notes
Uses: fine setting of this text for Shakespeare group
Rec: D#s 52, 110

223. **THOUGH I TAKE THE WINGS OF MORNING,** Op. 152 (Robert Nelson Spencer, paraphrase of Psalm 139). Seesaw, 1941. Emin; d'–a"(f♯"); Tess-M; 4/4, Lento con molto espressione; 3+min; Diff-V/m, P/m.

For: soprano; tenor
Mood: lyrical; sacred; affirmation of faith
Voice: stepwise and skips along chord lines; dotted rhythms; some afterbeat entrances
Piano: linear-chordal combination; many accidentals; some doubling of vocal line
Diff: good dynamic control
Uses: useful for religious services or in a group of songs by Beach; quiet ending

224. **THREE BROWNING SONGS,** Opus 44, Nos. 1–3 (Robert Browning). Arthur, P. Schmidt, 1900. Reprints: Classical Vocal Reprints; Masters Music Publications (H & L); T.I.S. H & M keys. Traditional keys; d♭'(e♭')–b♭"(a") & b♭(c')–g"(f♯"); Tess-mH-H; regular meters, fast–slow–moderate tempos; 12pp; Diff-V/m-md, P/m-md.

For: dramatic voices
Mood: dramatic; ecstatic love songs
Voice: sustained lines; many leaps; dotted rhythms; triplets; 2 vs. piano 3; ascending lines; dynamic contrasts
Piano: mostly chordal–repeated, arpeggiated, etc.; triplet figures; some countermelody; incidental doubling of vocal line
Diff: sustained high tones; extreme dynamics; endurance
Uses: effective "singing" songs; good program material for a big, romantic voice
Rec: D#18

　　a. *The Year's at the Spring.* 1900? Reprint: Classical Vocal Reprints. [68, Bk.1; 81]. H, M, & L keys: D♭maj, B♭maj, & A♭maj; a♭'–a♭", f'–f", & e♭'–e♭"; Tess-H; 3/4, Allegro di molto; 3pp. [**Rec:** D#s 2, 11, 65, 69]
　　b. *Ah, Love, But a Day!* 1900. Reprint: Classical Vocal Reprints. H, M, & L keys: Fmin, Dmin, & Bmin; e♭'–a", c'–f♯", & a–d♯"; Tess-mH; 4/4, Lento con molto espressione; 4pp. [**Rec:** D#109]
　　c. *I Send My Heart Up to Thee!* 1900? Reprint: Classical Vocal Reprints, 1991. H & M keys: D♭maj & B♭maj; d♭'(e♭')–b♭"(a♭") & b♭(c')–g"(f"); Tess-mH-H (depending on opt. notes taken); 9/8, Andante con affetto; 5pp.

225. **THREE SONGS, Op. 2** (H. H. A. Beach). Reprint: Masters Music Publications. Traditional keys; b♭–g"; Tess-mL-H; regular meters, varied tempos; 10pp; Diff-V/m, P/m-md. Separate entries below.

A. **TWILIGHT,** Op. 2, No. 1. E♭min; b♭–e♭"; Tess-mL; 4/4, Adagio quasi andante; 4pp; Diff-V/m, P/m.

For: any medium or low voice
Mood: descriptive; tranquil; lyrical
Voice: mostly stepwise and small skips between chord members; 2–5 note slurs; some accidentals; easy rhythms; dynamics *pp–ff*; some long notes at extremes of song range
Piano: syncopated patterns in 8th- and quarter-note chords; some countermelody; some doubling of vocal line; short prelude and short interludes
Diff: many dynamic changes
Uses: recital material; a well structured song

B. **WHEN FAR FROM HER,** Op. 2, No. 2. Gmin; c'–g"; Tess-M; 6/8, Andantino; 3pp; Diff-V/m, P/m.

For: tenor; some high baritones
Mood: lyrical; exhorts moon to watch over the distant beloved
Voice: easy rhythms in compound meter; skips outline chords; several accidentals; many dynamic marks; several long notes; long g" has alternate d"; some 2–3 note slurs
Piano: some 16th-note descending scale passages, but mostly a syncopated afterbeat pattern; many accidentals; vocal line not doubled, but supported; short prelude, interlude and postlude
Diff: dynamic control
Uses: recital material; pair with Op. 2, No. 3, another song about the moon

C. **EMPRESS OF NIGHT,** Op. 2, No. 3. [82, vol.1]. Gmaj; f♯'–g"; Tess-H; 4/4, Allegretto ma non troppo; 3pp; Diff-V/m, P/md.

For: tenor; soprano
Mood: describes the moon
Voice: mostly stepwise motion with small skips; some dotted notes, 16th notes, and syncopation; some long notes; mostly syllabic with some 2–3-note slurs; dynamic range *pp–f*
Piano: broken chords and arpeggiation in constant 16ths; many accidentals; does not double vocal line
Diff: rhythms; a few modulations
Uses: useful for teaching and performance; could pair with Op. 2, No. 2
Rec: D#11

226. **THREE SONGS, Op. 11.** Reprint: Masters Music Publications. Traditional keys; e'–b"; Tess-mH-H; regular meters; moderate tempos; 13pp; Diff-V/m, P/m-md. Separate entries below.

A. **DARK IS THE NIGHT** (William Ernest Henley). [82, vol 1]. Emin; e'–b"; Tess-H; 6/8, Allegro con fuoco; 5pp; Diff-V/m, P/md.

For: tenor; soprano; not for a light voice
Mood: restless and stormy; dramatic
Voice: many skips, up to a 6th; rhythms not complex; b" approached by leap and sustained 2 meas.; mostly

syllabic; some 2-note slurs

Piano: "stormy" broken-chord pattern; some repeated chords; does not double vocal line

Diff: singer must count–there are many long notes

Uses: sizeable voice best; group with other songs by Mrs. Beach or in a mixed group from this period

Rec: D#109

B. THE WESTERN WIND (William Ernest Henley). [82, vol. 1]. Gmaj; f'–a"; Tess-H; 3/4, Allegretto ma non troppo; 4pp; Diff-V/m, P/m.

For: tenor

Mood: gentle song of longing for distant beloved

Voice: stepwise motion predominates; some leaps; rhythms not difficult; several long notes with dynamic markings; soft ending

Piano: afterbeat pattern; triplets and quadruplet groupings in interludes; does not double vocal line; 9-meas. prelude, one 6-meas. and several shorter interludes

Diff: long notes with dynamic changes

Uses: good recital song; teaches dynamic control

Rec: D#110

C. THE BLACKBIRD (William Ernest Henley). [82, vol. 2]. Dmaj; e'–g"; Tess-mH; 2/4, Allegretto quasi andante; 4pp; Diff-V/m, P/m.

For: soprano

Mood: happy

Voice: stepwise motion and skips among chord members; easy rhythms; syllabic

Piano: afterbeat style; some rolled chords and arpeggiation; staccato in manner of guitar or mandolin; does not double vocal line

Uses: suitable for teaching and performance

227. THE THRUSH (E. R. Sill). [82, vol. 1]. B♭maj; c'–f"; Tess-M; 6/8, Allegro con leggerezza; 6pp; Diff-V/m, P/m.

For: mezzo-soprano; soprano

Mood: observation of nature

Voice: mostly stepwise with small skips; accidentals; some duplets; some long notes; syllabic; some 2-note slurs

Piano: broken-chord pattern, somewhat like Mendelssohn; accidentals; does not double vocal line; two interludes; 7-meas. postlude

Diff: possibly ensemble; low notes if sung by soprano

Uses: good student song; possible recital use

228. THY BEAUTY, Op. 41, No. 2 (Harriett Prescott Spofford). Arthur P. Schmidt, 1898. Reprint: Classical Vocal Reprints. B♭maj; b♭–e♭"; Tess-mL-L; 4/4, Adagio espressivo; 4pp; Diff-V/m, P/m.

For: baritone; contralto

Mood: quiet waiting; night song

Voice: lyrical, flowing phrases; a few large intervals, up to 7th; soft dynamics until the last two phrases; syllabic

Piano: broken-chord patterns; some melodic material; some doubling of vocal line; frequent syncopation in l.h. or inner voices; repeated chords at end

Diff: dynamic control of *p–pp*

Uses: lovely song for a low voice; *ff* ending seems contrary to mood of song; consider ending softly; good teaching

song for legato and dynamic control

229. WHEN SOUL IS JOINED TO SOUL, Op. 62 (Elizabeth Barrett Browning). [81]. "to Madame Emma Eames." G♭maj; d♭'–b♭"; Tess-mH-H; 4/4, Andante con molto espressione; 6pp; Diff-V/md, P/m.

For: soprano

Mood: romantic love song

Voice: lyrical; sustained; numerous long tones, some high (a♯", g♭"); slow melismas on "ah" at end rise softly to b♭" f; last phrase sustained g♭" *f*

Piano: chordal; syncopated accomp. pattern; some arpeggiated broken chords; repeated chords at end; some modulatory passages have numerous accidentals

230. WILT THOU BE MY DEARIE?, Op. 12, No. 1 (Robert Burns). Reprint: Masters Music Publications. [82, vol.2]. Gmaj; e'–a"; Tess-mH; 4/4, Andante espressivo; 4pp; Diff-V/md, P/md.

For: tenor

Mood: love song

Voice: fairly conjunct; some leaps of up to 7th; speech-like rhythms; syncopation; through-composed; Scottish dialect; many dynamic markings

Piano: chordal accomp. in quarters & 8ths; often doubles vocal line; many accidentals; short prelude, interlude, and postlude

Diff: dialect; expressive dynamics; fragmented phrases

Uses: use with other Burns poems by Beach

231. WIND O' THE WESTLAND (Dana Burnet). G. Schirmer, 1916. Reprint: T.I.S. [51]. B♭maj; f♯'–a♭"; Tess-H; 4/4, Andantino espressive; 4pp; Diff-V/d, P/m.

For: soprano; lyric tenor

Mood: somewhat sentimental and nostalgic; nature imagery

Voice: somewhat disjunct; many small intervals; a few large ones, some difficult; many accidentals; 3 vs. 2 in piano; most phrases 2 meas. long

Piano: chordal; broken-chord figures in 8ths almost throughout; syncopation; much chromaticism; supports vocal line but does not double

Diff: pitches and rhythms for singer; sustaining the tessitura, esp. if sung by a tenor; accomp. may be more difficult to read than to play

Uses: an effective song for the right voice

232. WITHIN THY HEART, Op. 29, No. 1 (Mrs. H. H. A. Beach). [82, vol. 3]. Fmaj; c'(d')–a"(g"); Tess-M; 4/4, Lento con molto espressione; 3pp; Diff-V/m, P/m.

For: soprano; mezzo-soprano

Mood: sincere declaration of love

Voice: small skips predominate; a few dotted rhythms; several 2-note slurs; dynamics vary *pp–ff*

Piano: broken- and repeated-chord pattern in 8th notes; does not double vocal line; 4-meas. prelude and postlude, 3-meas. interlude

Diff: dynamics

Uses: for recital or study

233. YE BANKS AND BRAES O' BONNIE DOON (Robert Burns). Reprint: Masters Music Publications. [82, vol. 2]. Cmin; d'–a♭"; Tess-mH; 6/8, Andante quasi allegretto; 4pp; Diff-V/m, P/m.

For: soprano
Mood: plaintive song of lost love
Voice: stepwise motion and small skips; some 8ve leaps; some long notes; g" (3 beats *pp*) and a♭" (5 beats *ff*); many 2–3-note slurs; dynamics range *pp–ff*
Piano: mostly block chords; some arpeggiation; accidentals; does not double vocal line
Diff: dynamics; understanding some Scottish-dialect words
Uses: for recital or study; somewhat overblown when compared to other settings of this simple text, e.g., Roger Quilter
Rec: D#109

BEACH, BENNIE
(b. Mississippi, 1925)

234.   PEACE (Sara Teasdale). [17]. H & L keys: Tonal; e♭'–f" & d♭'–e♭"; Tess-M; 4/4, 3/4, ♩=ca.60; 3pp; Diff-V/m, P/m.
For: high or medium voices
Mood: lyrical; peaceful; philosophical; quiet
Voice: short phrases; frequent rests; somewhat chromatic
Piano: chordal; chromatic; some rolled chords; supports voice
Diff: some pitches.
Uses: nice song; recital material for undergraduates

BEACH, JOHN PARSONS
(b. Gloversville, NY, 1877; d. Pasadena, CA, 1953)

235.   AUTUMN SONG (Dante Gabriel Rossetti). [66, vol.2]; 1st©1904. Dmin; d♭'–e♭"; Tess-M; 6/8, Quieto; 41meas.; Diff-V/md, P/m.
For: mezzo-soprano; baritone
Mood: quiet
Voice: mostly stepwise; many accidentals; hard to hear; some duplets
Piano: 4-voice texture; repetitive rhythm; many accidentals; much doubling of vocal line
Diff: unexpected modulations
Uses: effective short-ranged song; use in interior of group (no introduction; final cadence on dominant)

236.   IS SHE NOT PURE GOLD (Robert Browning). [66, vol.4]; 1st©1907. G♭maj; c♯'–e♭"; Tess-M; 3/4, Andante; 40meas; Diff-V/m, P/m.
For: baritone
Mood: declamatory; masculine in expression
Voice: many skips, some large; interrupted phrases; some sustained phrases
Piano: 4–5-voice texture, block chords; some arpeggiation
Diff: metric freedom; needs a mature sound
Uses: good song to teach dynamic control and declamation; quite effective for the right singer

BEASER, ROBERT
(b. Boston, MA, 1954)

237.   THE OLD MEN ADMIRING THEMSELVES IN

THE WATER (William Butler Yeats). Helicon Music Corp., 1986. cmp1986. X (bitonal); c♯'–b♭"; Tess-wide; 5/4, 6/4, 4/4, 3/4, Stately; with dignity ♩=50+; 4pp; Diff-V/md, P/md.
For: tenor seems best; soprano (composer says for voice or flute)
Mood: philosophical; transience of life
Voice: 8th-note motion predominates; some dotted rhythms; several melismas; rubato, and other tempo variations for expressive reasons; many skips of 4th; many accidentals
Piano: partly block chords, partly linear; some doubling of vocal line, some imitation; many accidentals; many l.h. 8ves; quiet ending
Diff: some rhythms and entrances; perhaps wide tessitura; singer should have mature sound and technique
Uses: recital material
Rec: D#50(?)

238.   THE SEVEN DEADLY SINS (Anthony Hecht). For Tenor or Baritone and Piano. Helicon Music Corp., 1979. Cycle of 7 songs to be performed continuously (pauses between as short as possible). X; tenor: b♭–a", baritone: A–g'; Tess-wide; changing meters and unmetered; 29pp; Diff-V/d, P/dd.
For: tenor; baritone
Mood: dramatic
Voice: skips often wide; rhythms often complicated; *Sprechstimme*; jazz-like "rhythm and pitch-bending" required in (c.) & (d.); portamentos; special directions concerning rhythm in (b.)
Piano: no doubling of vocal line; (a., d., e., & f.) use fairly conventional style; special notation and directions given for (b.) & (g.); tone clusters played by arm or side of hand; pedal often blurs
Diff: ensemble; rhythms; wide leaps such as 10th; low notes for some tenors [b]; sustained dramatic singing
Uses: set for mature performers; although the tenor and baritone versions are written in separate clefs, the pitch is usually the same (at times the baritone option is one 8ve lower); some sections of the set have different pitches for the two options
Rec: D#s 49, 111

  a. *Pride.* X; ten.: b♭–d", bar.: B♭–d'; changing meters, Pomposo; 2pp.
  b. *Envy.* X; ten.: a♭'–g", bar.: B♭–g'; mostly unmetered, Flautando, 6pp.
  c. *Wrath.* X; ten.: d♯'–a", bar.: d♯–g'; changing meters, Con fuoco (Jazz); 4pp.
  d. *Sloth.* X; ten.: b–f♯", bar.: B–f♯'; changing meters, Tempo rubato; 3pp.
  e. *Avarice.* X; ten.: d♯'–g", bar.: A–g'; changing meters, Lightly and rhythmically; 6pp.
  f. *Gluttony.* X; ten.: b–g", bar.: A–f'; changing meters, Cantando; 4pp.
  g. *Lust.* X; ten.: d'–f♯", bar.: d–f♯'; unmetered, Molto presto; 4pp.

BECK, JOHN NESS
(b. Warren, OH, 1930; d. Columbus, OH, 1987)

239. **SONG OF DEVOTION** (text adapted from Philippians I:3–11). [20]; 1st©1968. Amaj; c♯'–f♯"; Tess-L; 4/4, Slow (♩ = 80); 3pp; Diff-V/m, P/m.
For: any medium voice
Mood: song of thanksgiving
Voice: broad and lyrical; somewhat static and recit.-like in middle section
Piano: chordal; chiefly quarter-note movement; independent of voice
Diff: rather low tessitura
Uses: suitable for church or recital
Rec: D#70

240. **SONG OF JOY** (adapted from Psalm 40). C. F. Peters, 1970. B♭maj; b♭–g"; Tess-M; 6/8, Joyfully (♩ = 92); 2min; Diff-V/m, P/m.
For: mezzo-soprano; some sopranos or tenors
Mood: joyous song of praise
Voice: brilliant; some long phrases; some difficult intervals
Piano: chordal; organ accomp. could work
Diff: requires brilliant sound; sustained, loud high tones; ascending phrase at end
Uses: recital or church

BECKER, JOHN
(b. Henderson, KY, 1886; d. Wilmette, IL, 1961)

241. **AT DIEPPE** (Arthur Symons). Song Cycle for Voice and Piano. C. F. Peters, 1992. cmp1959. Quasi-tonal; e♭'–g"; Tess-M-mH; mostly regular meters; slow-fast-moderate-slow; 8min; Diff-V/m-md, P/e-md.
For: soprano; tenor
Mood: descriptive; muted; questioning; reflections on the sea at sunset
Voice: somewhat chromatic line; some 8ve displacement in melody; syllabic; rhythmically straightforward; mostly lyrical
Piano: (a., c., d.) chordal; many accidentals; slow harmonic oscillation; dissonance combined with clear tonalities; (b.), linear–rapid triplet figures divided between hands with subtle changes imitate sound of raindrops
Diff: perhaps hearing vocal melody through a haze of light dissonance
Uses: an interesting short cycle to contrast with more romantic works

    a. *After Sunset.* F♯-centered; g♯'–g"; Tess-mH; 4/4, 5/4, Slowly and quietly; 2pp; Diff-V/m, P/e.
    b. *On the Beach.* X; e♭'–g"; Tess-mH; 4/4, Fast; 5pp; Diff-V/md, P/md.
    c. *Before the Squall.* X-B♭min; f'–f"; Tess-M; 4/4, 3/4, Moderately; 3pp; Diff-V/md, P/m.
    d. *Requies.* F♯; e'–f"; Tess-M; 4/4, Slowly; 3pp; Diff-V/m, P/me.

BEESON, JACK
(b. Muncie, IN, 1921)

242. **AGAINST IDLENESS AND MISCHIEF AND IN PRAISE OF LABOR** (A Practice Session for Voice and Piano) (Isaak Watts). Boosey & Hawkes, 1973. "For Madeleine Marshall." A-centered; d'–c"'; Tess-mH; 2/4, 3/4, 5/8, 3/8; 3min; Diff-V/d, P/d.
For: soprano–coloratura or flexible lyric
Mood: sprightly; exuberant
Voice: stepwise and chord-member skips; many melismas, often staccato; syncopation; dotted rhythms
Piano: 16th-note motion; scales in 3rds & 10ths; arpeggios; parallel 3rds & tritones in r.h.; articulations and accents important; ornaments; does not double vocal line
Diff: rapid scales, legato and staccato; sustained c"'s (opt. 8th-note c"')
Uses: very good song; fun to sing; excellent group ender

243. **BIG CRASH OUT WEST** for Baritone Voice and Piano (Peter Viereck). Galaxy Music Corporation, 1989. cmp1951. Ambiguous; c–e' (♭); Tess-mH; 3/4, 2/4, Vigorously (♩ = 58); 3pp; Diff-V/d, P/md.
For: baritone
Mood: descriptive, harsh; concerns traffic accident; dramatic
Voice: speech-like rhythms; syncopation; small melodic intervals; a few leaps of 6th; many accidentals
Piano: some 3-stave scoring; mostly quarter-note chords with large reach; dissonant; some 16th-note scale passages; quiet ending; no doubling of vocal line
Diff: singing vocal line without many pitch clues from piano
Uses: group with other Beeson songs; dissonant and somewhat unexpected musical events illustrate text well; nice illustration of accelerating motor

244. **CALVINISTIC EVENSONG** for Baritone and Piano (John Betjeman). Boosey & Hawkes, 1962, 1979. X; (A)c–f'(♭); Tess-mH; 4/4, 5/4, 2/2, 3/2, Heavily ♩ = 72; 3min; Diff-V/md, P/m.
For: baritone; some tenors
Mood: solemn; descriptive; uncertainty of time of death
Voice: speech-like rhythms with syncopation; often stepwise and small skips; a few leaps of 8ve or 7th; many accidentals
Piano: chordal; mostly half- and quarter-note motion; middle section more active with 8th-note accomp. to half-note chords; pedaling important; uses the melody of Psalm 50 at beginning and in middle section; many accidentals; simulates organ sound; many low sounds; no doubling of vocal line
Diff: rhythms; lack of repetition in melodic pattern; finding some pitches
Uses: in a Beeson group
Rec: D#59

245. **COWBOY SONG** for Baritone Voice and Piano (Charles Causley). Galaxy, 1989. G (liberal chromaticism, some bitonality, deceptive ending); A♯–f'(g'); Tess-wide, H; 2/2, 3/2, Rolling along (♩ = c.63); 9pp; Diff-V/d, P/md.
For: baritone
Mood: seemingly hearty, but fatalistic and surreal; dramatic
Voice: melody mostly built of upward (or downward) chains of successive m2nds and m or M 3rds; most phrases encompass 8ve or more; many accidentals; mostly syllabic; mostly straightforward rhythms; quarter-note triplets in center section create cross-rhythms with

piano duplets and other subdivisions

Piano: quarter-note/8th-note motion predominates; quarter-note triplets in center section result in some 2 vs. 3 & 3 vs. 4; rests and articulations important part of mood and text painting; many accidentals; 4 meas. r.h. in parallel tritones; minimal doubling of vocal line; some bitonal chords; 6-meas. prelude; two interludes; short postlude

Diff: tessitura; communicating mental state of persona; needs a mature technique and good musicianship; ensemble

Uses: best in a group of songs by Beeson; could stand alone

246. **DEATH BY OWL-EYES** (Richard Hughes). Boosey & Hawkes, 1973. X; d'–g"; Tess-mH; 2/4, Straightforwardly (♩ = c.60); 5pp; Diff-V/d, P/dd.

For: tenor

Mood: abstract; descriptive

Voice: disjunct; chromatic; melismatic phrases; fragmented

Piano: highly chromatic; many rapid passages; unmeasured at end

Diff: pitch; rhythms; trill on e♭"; text

Uses: good program material; teaches flexibility

Rec: D#18

247. **ELDORADO** (Edgar Allan Poe). [3]. cmp1951; rev.1967 & 1977. B-centered; c♯'–a"; Tess-mH; 3/4, 4/4, Swinging; 2min (4pp); Diff-V/md, P/md.

For: tenor; soprano

Mood: dramatic narrative; somewhat mysterious

Voice: stepwise and skips of 6th or smaller; many accidentals; phrasing masked when "at variance with metrical indications"; some irregular subdivisions of the beat

Piano: combination of chords and countermelody; little doubling of vocal line; many accidentals; l.h. changes clef often

Diff: ensemble; meter

Uses: good recital song

Rec: D#18

248. **FIVE SONGS** (Francis Quarles). Cycle. Peer International, 1954. Mostly modal–floating harmonies; c'–a♭"; Tess-M-mH; irregular changing meters; varied tempos; 7min; Diff-V/m-md, P/md.

For: lyric tenor with full lower voice

Mood: lyrical; unrest; hopeful

Voice: mostly conjunct; some skips; numerous accidentals; rhythmic intricacies based largely on word rhythms within a flowing metrical framework; comfortable range; several low pitches for tenor (e, d, c)

Piano: flowing; always moving–creating a dream-like effect; feverish; reflects the poetry well

Diff: changing meters; floating high tones; metaphysical poetry

Uses: good cycle for an advanced musician; lyrical, serious group for recital

  a. *On a Spiritual Fever.* Modal on F; c♯'–a♭"; Tess-M; 13/8 with many changes, Agitato; 2pp.
  b. *A Good Night.* Modal; c'–g"; Tess-mH; 3/4, 4/4, 5/4, Larghetto; 2pp.
  c. *On the World.* Modal; f♯'–g"; Tess-M; 6/8 in piano, 2/4 in voice, Vivace; 2pp.
  d. *Epigram.* X; e'–g♯"; Tess-M; 4/4, 3/4, 5/8, 2/4,

  Adagio molto; 1p.
  e. *On Death.* X-Cmaj; c'–g"; Tess-M; 4/4, 3/4, 5/4, Andantino sostenuto; 3pp.

249. **FROM A WATCHTOWER.** A Cycle of Five Songs for Soprano and Piano. Boosey & Hawkes, 1993. cmp1976. X in general; c'–b♭"; Tess-cs; regular meters with changes; slow to moderate tempos; 15min; Diff-V/m-dd, P/m-dd.

For: soprano

Mood: somewhat dark and lonely; theme of towers as places of siege, sorties, refuge, and the crumbling effects of time

Voice: largely disjunct vocal lines; many large leaps; many accidentals; melodic outlining of chord structures; syllabic setting; quite dissonant; some quarter-tones; singer will need good ear; many different rhythmic groupings for word stress

Piano: beginning motive of (a.) returns near end of last song, slightly altered; many accidentals; frequent 3-stave scoring; many different rhythmic groupings; chromatic passages contain unexpected patterns that change; dissonant harmonies

Diff: pitches; rhythmic structure of vocal line; many accidentals for pianist; ensemble; some unusual texts

Uses: challenging and interesting work for the graduate to professional level singer

  a. *Mutability* (William Wordsworth). X; c♯'–g♭"; Tess-cs; 4/4, Pensively ♩ = 42ca; 4pp.
  b. *Ballad: O What Is That Sound?* (W. H. Auden). X on G; c♯'–b♭"; Tess-cs; changing meters, Simply: Apprehensively: Terror-stricken ♩ = 54; 11pp.
  c. *Heaven-Haven* (Gerard Manley Hopkins). X on D; d♭'–g♭"; Tess-cs; 2/4, 3/4, With repressed sensuality ♩ = 36; 2pp.
  d. *Ballad: O Where Are You Going?* (W. H. Auden). X-chromatic; d'–g"; Tess-cs; 6/8, 9/8, Ironically ♩. = 82; 5pp.
  e. *The Listeners* (Walter de la Mare). X on E; c'–a"; Tess-cs; 4/4, 12/8, With inscape ♩ = 46 varying constantly; 8pp.

250. **INDIANA HOMECOMING** (Abraham Lincoln). Boosey & Hawkes, 1973. Amin; B–e'; Tess-M; 4/4, 5/4, 3/4, Slowly; 1+min; Diff-V/md, P/md.

For: baritone with full sound

Mood: soliloquy; remembrance of childhood; strong

Voice: somewhat angular lines; duplets and triplets; syncopation; dotted rhythms; long-ranged phrases

Piano: 5-voice block-chord texture; some broken chords and scales in 16ths; does not double vocal line

Diff: pitch; changing meters; cluster chords; ensemble

Uses: strong vehicle for the right singer

251. **SENEX** (John Betjeman). Boosey & Hawkes, 1979. Chromatic (somewhat G-centered); c–e'; Tess-H; 2/4, 3/4; Quick and repressed; 2+min (5pp); Diff-V/m, P/md.

For: baritone specified

Mood: masculine; somewhat humorous with serious undertone; descriptive

Voice: predominantly conjunct; chromatic; some syncopation;

much use of pitches c'–e'
Piano: 4–5-voice chordal texture; syncopation; l.h. scale
passages in 6ths
Diff: making unusual text understood; some high phrases
Uses: recital song

252. **TO A SINISTER POTATO** (Peter Viereck). Boosey
& Hawkes, 1973. X; B♭–f'; Tess-mH; 4/4,
Purposefully (♩ = c.48); 3+min; Diff-V/dd, P/dd.
For: baritone
Mood: abstract; philosophical; humorous description of the
potato
Voice: extremely disjunct; chromatic; difficult intervals; many
short note values
Piano: highly chromatic; tone clusters; virtuosic
Diff: pitch; tessitura; text; serious delivery
Uses: effective for the right singer

253. **THE YOU SHOULD OF DONE IT BLUES** (Peter
Viereck). Boosey & Hawkes, 1973. E♭-centered; b–g";
Tess-mH; 4/4, Slow and bluesy; 2+min; Diff-V/dd, P/d.
For: soprano; mezzo-soprano
Mood: not intense; somewhat amusing
Voice: syncopation; rhythmically complex; difficult intervals
Piano: linear, 3–4-voice texture; low and middle registers;
rhythmically complex; does not double vocal line
Diff: bluesy mood and style; ensemble; flexible tempo
Uses: good for right singer with knowledge of style
Rec: D#18

BELCHER, SUPPLY (See Special Section)

BENSHOOF, KENNETH
(b. Nebraska, 1933)

254. **THE COW** (Theodore Roethke). [3]. X; d♯'–g♯";
Tess-mH; unmetered, Grand; 1min (2pp); Diff-V/md,
P/d.
For: tenor; soprano
Mood: humorous
Voice: somewhat disjunct; syncopation; various subdivisions
of beat; one 21-note melisma; a 6-note melisma ending
in portamento down a 10th
Piano: afterbeat style; trills, rapid scales, and glissandos; many
accidentals
Diff: ensemble
Uses: humorous recital song; see another setting by Harris
Lindenfeld
Rec: D#6

255. **THE FOX** (English folk-song). [3]. G majorish; f♯'–g";
Tess-H; 4/4, Crisp; 2+min (7pp); Diff-V/m, P/d.
For: tenor seems best
Mood: tells story
Voice: nine strophes, one in B♭; small skips; some
syncopation; syllabic
Piano: much broken-8ve patterning; chromaticism; repetitive;
no doubling of vocal line
Diff: rapid delivery of clear diction
Uses: change-of-pace recital song; good practice for diction

and telling a story
Rec: D#6

BENSON, WARREN F.
(b. Detroit, MI, 1924)

256. **THREE SOLITARY SONGS.** For Medium Voice and
Piano. Carl Fischer Facsimile Edition, 1978. Tonal;
g–e♭"; Tess-mH; regular meters with changes; 6pp;
Diff-V/m, P/me.
For: baritone best; texts generally masculine, esp. (a.)
Mood: folk-like; music and text well matched
Voice: skips not difficult; syncopation; various subdivisions of
beat create polyrhythms; (c.) features many triplets;
syllabic; glissandos
Piano: mostly block chords; 4–5-voice texture; no doubling of
vocal line
Diff: facsimile MS, but easy to read; rhythms most difficult
factor
Uses: for rhythmically secure young baritone (or more mature
singer); definite "American" flavor

a. *From the Hazel Bough* (Earle Birney). Cmin;
g–e♭"; 4/4, Slow and easy; 2pp.
b. *American Primitive* (William Jay Smith).
Gmin-B♭maj; c'–e♭"; 4/4, 5/4, 3/4, Simply; 2pp.
c. *Lonesome Boy Blues* (Kenneth Patchen). Cmin;
c'–e♭"; changing meters, Very freely, very slowly;
2pp.

BERG, CHRISTOPHER
(b. Detroit, MI, 1949)

[See Appendix for songs with French texts]

257. **LAST LETTER** (Tim Dlugos). [3]. F-centered; c'–b♭';
Tess-wide; changing meters, often polymetric between
voice and piano; beginning very slowly, gradually
increase tempo; 6pp; Diff-V/d, P/md.
For: tenor; soprano
Mood: farewell to a lover
Voice: some pitches hard to find; speech-like rhythms;
irregular divisions of beat; syncopation; portamentos;
special instructions, e.g. "non vibrato" and "head
voice"
Piano: most of song written on one stave; arpeggiated triads &
7th chords in various rhythms and "in a wash of pedal";
ends with 2-stave writing of block chords and
simultaneous M2nds
Diff: rhythms and polymetric aspect of song; special vocal
effects
Uses: in group of contemporary American songs; perhaps a
good vehicle for singer who wants to learn
contemporary techniques; requires good musician with
flexible voice

258. **ODE ON A GRECIAN URN** (John Keats). Tender
Tender Music, 2000 (Classical Vocal Reprints).
cmp2000. Commissioned for Judith Bettina. G-
centered; b♭–g"; Tess-M; 7/8, 4/4, 3/2, 2/2, ♪ = 160

(♩ = 40); 12pp; Diff-V/md, P/m-md.

For: mezzo-soprano; soprano; tenor

Mood: romantic and impressionistic; the timelessness of the marble scene a reminder of the timelessness of Beauty and Truth to all generations

Voice: wide-ranging phrases in flowing melody; some large intervals; syllabic; rhythms reflect both word stress and movement of the text; many different rhythmic groupings, some syncopation and slow triplets; 7/8 section describes the scene; regular-metered sections comment on it

Piano: chordal, some countermelody; motion increases with triplet and quadruplet figures in middle voices; some polyrhythms; many expressive markings; much use of pedal; impressionistic harmonies

Diff: keeping track of 8th-note pulse in 7/8 section

Uses: lovely extended song for advanced singer; could stand alone or group with shorter romantic poems; music expresses text well

259. **SONGS ON POEMS OF FRANK O'HARA,** Opus 16, in three volumes (12 songs). Tender Tender Music, 1987; Classical Vocal Reprints, 1991. cmp1985–1987. "In memory of Chris DeBlasio (1959–1993)." Mostly major tonalities; a–a"(b" falsetto); Tess-mL-mH-H; regular meters with various 50s and 60s popular music rhythms; tempos vary from "Very slow" to "Very fast (eighths)"; 68pp; Diff-V/d, P/d.

For: baritone (high)

Mood: cycle traces a young poet's life from his lonely childhood through leaving home, going to New York, reveling in the city; being with others like himself, falling in love, and realizing that he is a good poet; many different moods expressed–all relate to the poet's intense feelings about his own life and experiences

Voice: flexible lyric recit.; conversational speech rhythms; some conjunct, smooth lines; some chromatic lines with large leaps; syncopated, jazzy lines; melodically and rhythmically expressive of the text; wide range; some spoken phrases; popular American styles require virtuoso technique

Piano: a variety of American popular forms and classic dance rhythms (Rumba, Samba, Blues, Soft Shoe, Fast Show Tune, Slow 2) filled with classical techniques and substance; dissonant; rhythmically complex; cross rhythms; improvisatory; piano highly expressive of text

Diff: large pitch, color, and dynamic range for singer; intricate rhythms; improvisatory piano style; ensemble

Uses: best for professional level performers to whom Frank O'Hara's poetic subject matter appeals

Rec: D#s 49, 112 [These recordings contain 6 songs on poems of Frank O'Hara–no titles given]

  a. *Autobiographia Literaria.* Major tonality; c#'–b"(falsetto); Tess-mL; 4/4, In a simple, declarative manner (♩ = 96); 2pp; Diff-V/md, P/md.

  b. *Song (1951).* Fmaj; c'–a"; Tess-mH-H; 2/2, Fast "show tune" (♩ = 132); 4pp; Diff-V/md, P/md.

  c. *Pearl Harbor.* Dmin; a–f"; Tess-M; 2/2, Tropically (slow, sexy 2) but menacing; 4pp; Diff-V/md, P/md.

  d. *A Warm Day for December.* Fmaj; c'–f"; Tess-M-

mH; 4/4, Exuberantly (a cool samba); 6pp; Diff-V/md, P/m.

  e. *Poem ("Lana Turner Has Collapsed!").* Emin; b–g"; Tess-mL-M; 4/4, Urgent, a la Western Union; 4pp; Diff-V/m, P/m.

  f. *Prelude and Song (July 29, 1960).* Major tonalities; bb–f#"; Tess-cs; changing meters, ♩ remains constant, Very freely; 4pp; Diff-V/m, P/m.

  g. *Song ("Is it Dirty").* C minorish; c'–f"; Tess-M; 2/2, Very slow 2; 3pp; Diff-V/md, P/e.

  h. *Steps.* Major keys (Eb-C); bb–f#"; Tess-M; 12/8, 3/4, Softshoe tempo–Ad lib, a la cocktail bar–Tempo of Satie's *Gymnopedies*–Tempo I, but more easygoing; 10pp; Diff-V/d, P/d.

  i. *Having a Coke with You.* Eb-Gmaj; c#–g"; Tess-cs; 2/2, Tempo di Rumba (♩ = 158); 8pp; Diff-V/d, P/d.

  j. *To You.* Gbmaj; db'–g"; Tess-mH-H; 3/2, Evenly, flowing; 5pp; Diff-V/md, P/m.

  k. *St. Paul and All That.* No clear key center; bb–f#"; Tess-mL-mH; 3/8, 3/4 with changes; fast introduction, then mostly ♩ = 58–63; 6pp; Diff-V/d, P/d.

  l. *A True Account of Talking to the Sun at Fire Island.* Major tonalities; a#–g"; Tess-L-M; 4/4, Tempo of Song No. 1 ("Autobiographia Literaria"); 12pp; Diff-V/d, P/d.

260. **TWO OSCAR WILDE SONNETS** (Oscar Wilde) for medium low voice and piano. Tender Tender Music, 1999 (Classical Vocal Reprints). cmp1999. X; a–e"; Tess-M; unmeasured, slow-faster; 8pp; Diff-V/md-d, P/md-d.

For: bass-baritone

Mood: angry; political protest against loss of Liberty

Voice: measured dramatic recit.; speech rhythms; angular vocal lines; syllabic; many accidentals; dissonant

Piano: chordal structure; thick texture with many accidentals; chord clusters; unmetered throughout; sets mood of anger and determination not to be moved

Diff: dissonant harmonies; many accidentals in vocal line; ensemble

Uses: an interesting pair of songs to contrast with more positive texts; could be quite powerful for the mature singer

  a. *Theoretikos.* Sliding harmonies; b–eb"; Tess-M; unmeasured, Lento ♩ = 56; 4pp; Diff-V/md, P/md.

  b. *Sonnet to Liberty.* X; a–e"; Tess-M; unmeasured, A little hurried, perhaps (but in 9); 4pp; Diff-V/d, P/d.

261. **TWO POEMS BY NELLIE HILL** (Nellie Hill) for Voice and Piano, Opus 9. Tender Tender Music, 1995 (Classical Vocal Reprints). cmp1978. H & L keys: Tonal; c'–a" & g#–f"; Tess-M, cs; changing meters, moderate and fast; 10pp; Diff-V/m-md, P/m-md.

For: soprano; mezzo-soprano; baritone

Mood: despairing: unhappy love affair; humorous: make-believe in real life

Voice: lyrical and narrative; melodic; meter changes frequent; some wide intervals; accidentals

Piano: a flavor of jazz style harmonically; patterned structure

seems somewhat improvisational at times; some
parallel 3rds; descriptive of text

Diff: some rhythms

Uses: interesting pair of songs for an intimate setting and an
audience open to the details of love affairs

    a. *Boyfriend.* F minorish & C♯ minorish; c'–a" &
g♯–e♭"; Tess-M; 6/4, 5/4, 4/4, 3/4, Andante
♩ = 100; 5pp; Diff-V/m, P/m.

    b. *Selling Techniques.* D minorish & C minorish;
c'–g" & b♭–f"; Tess-cs; 3/4, 2/4, 3/8, 6/8, Alla
spagnola ♩. = 58; 5pp; Diff-V/md, P/md.

BERGER, JEAN
(b. Hamm, Germany, 1909)

[See Appendix for songs with French texts]

262. **FIVE SHELLEY POEMS** (Percy Bysshe Shelley).
Sheppard, 1975. Traditional keys with added notes;
much parallel harmony and sequential harmonic
pattern; (e)g–e"; Tess-L; regular meters; varied tempos;
23pp; Diff-V/me, P/me.

For: bass; contralto

Mood: lyrical; straightforward; theme of passing time; last
song humorous

Voice: vocal line simplistic; repeated notes; mostly syllabic;
some 2-note slurs; chord outlining and stepwise
motion; much sequence

Piano: accomps. simplistic and highly patterned with much
sequence and parallel chord structure; afterbeat patterns
and broken-chord figurations with some scale patterns

Diff: repetitive character of music

Uses: for low voices; (e.), humorous song for a young bass

    a. *Where Art Thou?* Amin; a–d♯"; 6/4, Quite slowly
and with flexible rhythm; 3pp.

    b. *The Fountains Mingle with the River.* Gmin; g–e";
3/4, 4/4, Fast and boisterously; 6pp.

    c. *The Flower That Smiles Today.* E♭min; b♭–d";
6/4, 3/2, 7/4, At a gently flowing pace; 4pp.

    d. *Of Times Past.* B♭-Emin; (e)a–e"; 4/4, Not too
slowly; 4pp.

    e. *On a Cat.* Amin; a♭–d"; 6/4, Quite fast; 6pp.

263. **FOUR SONGS** (Langston Hughes). Broude Bros.,
1951. Traditional keys; b–f"; Tess-L-mL-M; regular
meters; varied tempos;12pp; Diff-V/me-m, P/me-m.

For: mezzo-soprano; baritone; contralto

Mood: lyrical; melancholy; descriptive; narrative

Voice: skips along chord lines; some irregular rhythms; some
interrupted phrasing; some dotted rhythms

Piano: mostly chordal; some chromaticism; melodic material

Diff: numerous low tones

Uses: good teaching material for young singer of limited
range; may be performed separately

    a. *In Time of Silver Rain.* Fmaj; c'–f"; Tess-M; 4/4,
Allegro commodo; 4pp.

    b. *Heart.* Amin; c'–e"; Tess-M; 3/4, 4/4, 2/4, Andante;
2pp.

    c. *Carolina Cabin.* Cmaj; b–e"; Tess-mL; 4/4, 5/4,
Poco allegro; 3pp.

    d. *Lonely People.* Emin; b–b'; Tess-L; 3/4, Lento;
3pp.

264. **FOUR SONNETS BY LUIS DE CAMOENS** (Set for
a Medium Voice and Piano or String Quartet with
Portuguese and English Words). Sheppard, 1942, 1970.
Traditional keys (with much parallelism common to the
guitar idiom); b♭–g"; Tess-mL-M; regular but changing
meters; 22pp; Diff-V/m-md, P/d.

For: baritone best; mezzo-soprano

Mood: love poetry, expressed in an extravagant "Latin"
manner

Voice: conjunct and flowing; rhythmic structure based on
Portuguese stress and inflection (longer tones and stress
toward ends of phrases); some recit.; very singable

Piano: guitar idiom and figurations; playable and effective
reduction from string quartet score

Uses: good set for right singer; Portuguese text flows better,
as some English words are oddly stressed

    a. *Although the Ancient Poets.* Dmin-maj; d'–f"; 3/4,
4/4, 2/4, Allegro, ma non troppo; 5pp.

    b. *Where Can Eyes Like Mine.* Emin; b–g"; 3/4, 4/4,
5/4, etc., Andante; 5pp.

    c. *All of My Life.* Bmin-maj; b–e"; 4/4, 2/4, Andante
con moto; 6pp.

    d. *O Lovely Eyes.* Amaj; b–g"; 6/4, 3/4, Poco allegro.

265. **OF LOVE.** Five Songs for High Voice and Piano.
Cycle. Sheppard, 1970. Traditional tertian harmonies
with color elements; c'–b♭"; Tess-mH-H; regular
meters with some changes; varied tempos; 15pp;
Diff-V/m-md (depending on singer's ease in high
tessitura), P/m.

For: high lyric tenor

Mood: various references to the beauty of womanhood

Voice: mostly diatonic movement; some accidentals; much
melodic repetition and sequence; much singing at top
of staff and above; much word repetition

Piano: patterned accomp. provides background for the voice;
little illustration of text; broken-chord figures; many
accidentals; parallel triads; large reach helpful

Diff: high tessitura

Uses: usable for a young, light, lyric tenor

    a. *He or She That Hopes to Gain* (anon., 17th
century). Ends C; e♭'–b♭"; 3/4, 4/4, 5/4, Fairly fast;
3pp.

    b. *Fair Julia* (Philipott, 16th century). Ends B; c♯'–a";
3/4, 5/4, At a gentle pace; 2+pp.

    c. *A Little Ground Well Tilled* (anon., ca. 1575). Ends
F; f'–a"; 5/8 with changes, Moderately fast; 3pp.

    d. *When I Admire the Rose* (Thomas Lodge,
1558–1625). Ends G; d'–f♯"; 4/4, Very slow; 2pp.

    e. *My Love in Her Attire* (anon., 17th century). Ends
G; d'–a"; 3/4, Quite animated; 4+pp.

BERGSMA, WILLIAM
(b. Oakland, CA, 1921; d. Seattle, WA, 1994)

266. BETHSABE BATHING (George Peele). Galaxy, 1962. cmp1961. C-centered; b–f‴; Tess-mL-mH; 3/2, with changes, ♩ = ca.60–66; 3min; Diff-V/d, P/d.

For: mezzo-soprano

Mood: sensuous; surreal; inner soliloquy; fire and heat imagery

Voice: disjunct with wide leaps; long-ranged phrases; syncopation; humming and vocalizing

Piano: percussive; uses piano harmonics; rapid repeated notes (like drum-rolls); careful articulation and dynamic markings

Diff: perfect pitch desirable; ensemble; security of registration and dynamics

Uses: colorful; effective; imaginative use of both vocal and piano sonorities; excellent for the right singer

267. CANTILENA FROM *IN SPACE*. For Soprano with Piano Accompaniment (piano reduction by composer). Galaxy, 1977, 1981. X and bitonal; b–c‴; Tess-H; changing meters, many tempo changes; 8+min; Diff-V/d, P/d.

For: lyric or coloratura soprano

Mood: lyric; other-worldly

Voice: vocalization on "ah" or "appropriate vowels or meaningless syllables" of singer's choice; many skips, incl. leaps of 7th, 9th, 10th; most melodic motives repeat at different pitch levels; some syncopation; some small divisions of beat (16ths); melodic fragmentation; many accidentals; phrasing important; opens with 16 meas. voice alone; closes with 12 meas. of g′ in whole notes, divided by rests, over piano chords

Piano: mostly linear; much imitation; some rolled chords; grace notes; many accidentals; wide pitch range; some staccato; tone clusters; some rhythmic complexities

Diff: some intervals; ensemble

Uses: nice recital piece for a floaty, flexible voice. NOTE: *In Space* is a multimedia work for soprano and orchestra. "In the first half, the soprano mimes various idiomatic motifs played by individual orchestral instruments that have been placed throughout the hall. In the second half, these seemingly random vocal pantomimes are merged and expanded with a full instrumental texture into a serious vocalise, the lyric Cantilena . . ."

268. LULLEE, LULLAY (Janet Lewis). [21]; 1st©1950. H & L keys: X; e′–g″ & c′–e♭″; Tess-M; 8/8, 6/8, 5/8, 3/4, 2/4, Andante; 2+min; Diff-V/md, P/md.

For: lyric soprano; mezzo-soprano

Mood: lullaby for the Christ-child

Voice: lyrical and flowing; syncopation; some rhythmic difficulties

Piano: chordal with independent melodic material; chromatic

Diff: meter changes; soft singing

Uses: good teaching song; recital use

Rec: D#59

269. SIX SONGS TO POEMS BY E. E. CUMMINGS for Voice and Piano. Carl Fischer, 1947. [No. 2 available separately]. Tonal centers; d♯′–b♭″; Tess-M-mH-H; regular and irregular changing meters; varied tempos; 22pp; Diff-V/d, P/d.

For: soprano; tenor

Mood: lyrical; descriptive; humorous; nonsensical; philosophical

Voice: variety of vocal techniques; disjunct movement; chromatic; fragmented phrasing; melismas; whispered and shouted phrases; some parlando; many triplet rhythms; some declamatory style

Piano: somewhat contrapuntal; chromatic; disjunct; ornaments; irregular note groupings; special pedal effects; independent of voice

Diff: pitches; rhythms; special vocal effects

Uses: use separately or as set; excellent group for advanced musician who is an imaginative and expressive singer with an affinity for the poetry of e. e. cummings

    a. *when god lets my body be.* X; e′–a″; Tess-M; 2/2 with changes, ♩ = 48; 4pp.

    b. *doll's boy's asleep.* X; f♯′–b♭″; Tess-mH; 2/2 with changes, ♩ = 42, but freely; 3pp.

    c. *hist whist.* Amin; d♯′–f″; Tess-M; 4/4 with changes, ♩ = 176–200; 4pp.

    d. *thy fingers make early flowers.* X; e′–a″; Tess-M; 5/8 with changes, ♪ = 112, but freely; 4pp.

    e. *it may not always be so.* X; e′–g♯″; Tess-M; 3/4 with changes, ♪ = 72; 4pp.

    f. *jimmie's got a goil.* D-centered; g′–a″; Tess-H; 5/8 with changes, Presto ♩ = 176; 3pp.

BERNSTEIN, LEONARD
(b. Lawrence, MA, 1918; d. New York, NY, 1990)

270. AFTERTHOUGHT (Leonard Bernstein). Study for the ballet *Facsimile*. Boosey & Hawkes, n.d. cmp1945. D-centered; a–g♯″; Tess-mH, wide; 4/4, 3/2, Lento; 4pp; Diff-V/md, P/m.

For: mezzo-soprano (dramatic voice best)

Mood: dramatic

Voice: most phrases begin with large leap (9th or 10th); demands control of wide tessitura and *pp–ff* dynamic range; some dotted rhythms and triplets; syllabic

Piano: block chords; some broken chords; some countermelody; many accidentals; does not double vocal line, but exchanges melodies with it

Diff: tessitura and dynamics–gradual and sudden changes

Uses: effective song for large voice with secure wide range

271. LA BONNE CUISINE (Four Recipes) (from *La Bonne Cuisine Française*, by Emile Dumont; English version by Leonard Bernstein). G. Schirmer, 1949. [83]. "For Jennie Tourel. The only begetter of these songs." Traditional key structures with altered chords; b–b″; Tess-L-M (sop), M-H (mez); mostly regular but changing meters; varied tempos; 13pp; Diff-V/d, P/d.

For: mezzo-soprano with good high voice; soprano with good low voice

Mood: humorous; reading of recipes

Voice: vocal line patterned in each song; many skips and leaps; many accidentals; sequential melodic treatment; long range; fast articulation; clear diction required; set ends on low b

Piano: patterned; illustrates text with humor; many accidentals; two songs very fast

Diff: some pitch patterns; long range; speed of articulation; making text clear will require great precision; only a long-ranged voice should attempt this set

Uses: good for freeing up a cumbersome voice, as the speed of articulation leaves no time for excessive effort; good for teaching clear, fast diction; a sure-fire audience pleaser; program ender; French or English

Rec: D#118

    a. *Plum Pudding.* [59]. Emin; e'–b"; 4/4, 2/4, 3/4, 3/2, Allegro molto, matematico ♩ = 192; 3pp.

    b. *Queues de Boeuf (Ox-Tails).* Fmaj; c'–a"; 6/8, 3/8, 9/8, Allegretto ♩. = 88; 3pp.

    c. *Tavouk Gueunksis.* E♭min-maj; d♭'–f♯"; 4/4, 5/8, 5/4, Adagio–Allegretto alla Turca ♩ = 63; 3pp.

    d. *Civet a Toute Vitesse (Rabbit at Top Speed).* [40]. Emin-maj; b–e"; 4/8, Presto ♪= 208; 4pp. [**Rec:** D#31]

272. **I HATE MUSIC!** A Cycle of 5 Kid Songs for Soprano (Leonard Bernstein?). Witmark, 1943. Traditional key structures with some stretching; c'–a"; Tess-M; changing meters and irregular rhythms; varied tempos; 5min; Diff-V/d, P/md.

For: lyric soprano

Mood: lyrical; childlike; humorous

Voice: many pitch and rhythmic challenges; some speaking; somewhat disjunct lines; changing meters

Piano: nimble fingers and accurate metric sense necessary

Diff: pitches; rhythms; ensemble

Uses: good teaching material for young sopranos to sharpen the ear, encourage attention to specific rhythmic details, and practice characterization

Rec: D#s 113, 114, 115, 116, 117, 118

    a. *My Mother Says That Babies Come in Bottles.* Emaj; e'–a"; Tess-mH; 2/2, 3/4, Moderato; 2pp.

    b. *Jupiter Has Seven Moons.* F-centered; c'–a"; Tess-M; 5/8, 4/8, Allegretto vivace; 4pp.

    c. *I Hate Music! But I Like to Sing.* X; c'–g"; Tess-M; 4/4, 2/4, Sostenuto–Allegro molto; 3pp.

    d. *A Big Indian and a Little Indian.* Cmaj; c'–a"; Tess-mH; 7/8, 8/8, 9/8, 5/8, 3/8, Con brio; 2+pp.

    e. *I Just Found Out Today.* Fmaj; c'–a"; Tess-mH; 4/4, 3/4, 1/4, Moderato, alla marcia; 3+pp.

273. **SILHOUETTE** (Galilee). [83]; 1st ©1951. "For Jennie Tourel . . ." F♯min-B♭min; b♭–g♯"; Tess-M; 5/8 with changes, Allegretto, molto ritmico; 7pp; Diff-V/md, P/md.

For: mezzo-soprano; soprano

Mood: descriptive

Voice: stepwise and skips along chord lines; melismas on "ee," "oo," and "ah"; some staccato and trills; Arabic phrases

Piano: chordal-linear combination; Middle Eastern flavor; large dynamic contrasts; articulations important; some doubling of vocal line

Diff: soft high tones; some spoken measures; Middle Eastern sounds and techniques

Uses: usable for one who can pronounce the text

Rec: D#118

274. **SO PRETTY** (Betty Comden & Adolph Green). Amberson, 1968. First performed by Barbra Streisand & Leonard Bernstein in Philharmonic Hall, New York. B♭maj-min; b♭–e♭"; Tess-M; 3/4, Very slowly; 3pp; Diff-V/me, P/me.

For: mezzo-soprano

Mood: lyrical protest against war in a child's words; earnest and naive

Voice: predominantly moves by step and 3rds; many accidentals; uncomplicated rhythms; syllabic, except for four 2-note slurs; dynamics important; some soft high tones

Piano: 4-voice structures; chordal-linear combination; doubles vocal line

Diff: possibly soft high tones

Uses: although "pop" influence is discernible, can be effectively used on a recital program for young singers

Rec: D#31

275. **TWO LOVE SONGS** (Rainer Maria Rilke; trans. Jessie Lemont). [20, 83]. cmp1949. "For Jennie [Tourel]." X; c'–g"; Tess-M-mH; regular and irregular changing meters; contrasting tempos; 7pp; Diff-V/md-d, P/d.

For: soprano; mezzo-soprano; tenor

Mood: lyrical love songs; philosophical

Voice: (a.), rather disjunct with large intervals, chromaticism, and some complex rhythms; (b.), stepwise with long phrases

Piano: mostly chordal; some contrapuntal figuration independent of voice; chromatic

Diff: pitch; rhythm; long phrases; large leaps; extremes of range

Uses: good recital material

Rec: D#118

    a. *Extinguish My Eyes . . .* X; c'–g"; Tess-mH; 6/8 with changes, Fast (♩. = 132); 4pp.

    b. *When My Soul Touches Yours . . .* X; c'–g♭"; Tess-M; 4/4 with changes, Moderately slow (♩ = 63); 3pp.

BEZANSON, PHILIP
(b. Athol, MA, 1916; d. Hadley, MA, 1975)

276. **THE WORD OF LOVE** (Paul Engle). Song Cycle. American Composers Alliance (Composers Facsimile Edition), 1962. X; c'–a" (b♭"); Tess-mH, wide; changing meters; varied tempos; 15min; Diff-V/d, P/md.

For: tenor specified

Mood: tense and intense

Voice: many small skips; many accidentals; dotted rhythms, syncopation, and triplets; rhythms not especially complicated, however; several sections have high tessitura; several low phrases lie between c' and f '; syllabic setting predominates

Piano: broken- and repeated-chord styles predominate; some linear style; some syncopation but uncomplicated rhythms; does not double vocal line but provides some pitch cues; although key center is obscured in most songs, all but one end on a maj or min chord

Diff: endurance in this tessitura; low phrases may be too low for some tenors

Uses: as a recital set when something in an unusual mood is wanted; cycle has melodic motives that recur throughout

    a. *Robber.* X; d'–g"; 4/4 with changes, Allegretto con moto; 3+pp.

    b. *Cornered.* X; c♯'–f♯"; changing meters, Allegro con fuoco; 3+pp.

    c. *Night Scene.* X; c'–f"; 4/4 with changes, Adagietto; 2+pp.

    d. *Grass.* X; c'–g♭"; voice in 4/4, piano in 12/8, both with changes, Allegretto con moto; 5+pp.

    e. *Fight.* X; d'–a"; 2/4 with changes, Con fuoco; 5pp.

    f. *City.* X; d♯'–a"; 5/4 with changes, Andante; 5pp.

    g. *Felon.* X; d'–a"(b♭"); 4/4 with changes, Giocoso; 4+pp.

BIALOSKY, MARSHALL
(b. Cleveland, OH, 1923)

277. **AN OLD PICTURE** (Howard Nemerov). [17]; 1st©1960. H & L keys: B♭ & G♭; f'–g" & d♭'–e♭"; Tess-M; 4/4, 3/2, Alla marcia (♩ = c.112–116); 3pp; Diff-V/m, P/m.

For: any medium or high voice.

Mood: descriptive

Voice: disjunct; much use of dotted rhythms

Piano: march-like; some chromaticism; staccato; not obviously related to the text

Diff: several high-lying phrases; one phrase begins on highest note of song

BIGGS, HAYS
(b. Huntsville, AL, 1957)

278. **SEPHESTIA'S SONG TO HER CHILD** (Robert Greene). Soprano and Piano. C. F. Peters, 1994. cmp1991. X; g♯'–a♭"; Tess-wide; 7/8, 5/8, 3/4, 4/4, ♩ = ca.100; ♩ = ca.66; 9pp; Diff-V/dd, P/dd.

For: soprano; mezzo-soprano (probably better)

Mood: troubled lullaby

Voice: many wide leaps; angular; difficult rhythms; meas. often divided differently from piano (4 vs. 6, 5 vs. 6, 6 vs. 4, etc.); syllabic; many dynamic markings

Piano: much 8th and dotted 8th-note motion followed by 16th-note section; refrain accompanied by chords; otherwise mostly linear; many accidentals; complex score; atonal patterning; some cluster chords

Diff: ensemble; refrain repetitions include 8ve displacement, key change, or other variations; wicked rhythms; few pitch clues from the piano

Uses: usable by two excellent musicians willing to put time into rehearsing this score

BILLINGS, WILLIAM (See Special Section)

BINKERD, GORDON
(b. Lynch, NE, 1916)

279. **ALLELUIA FOR ST. FRANCIS** (from the *Roman-Seraphic Missal*). Boosey & Hawkes, 1977. Fmaj; c'(b♭)–f"; Tess-M; 3/4, Moderato–lilting; 5pp; Diff-V/m, P/m.

For: mezzo-soprano; soprano; possibly baritone

Mood: reverent

Voice: flowing, chant-like line; stepwise with small skips; melismas; "alleluia" sections at beginning and end; 6 meas. unaccomp.

Piano: linear; flowing, chant-like lines; mostly 4-voice texture; does not double vocal line; many accidentals

Diff: seamless rhythmic fluidity, in the manner of chant, could be difficult for the student unacquainted with Gregorian chant

Uses: not for church; recital use in sacred group or group of Binkerd songs; quiet ending

280. **AND I AM OLD TO KNOW** (Pauline Hanson). Boosey & Hawkes, 1971. E-centered; c♯'–b♭"(a♭"); Tess-M; 2/2, ♩ = 40; 6min; Diff-V/d, P/md.

For: soprano with ample sound

Mood: transcendent love; song about death; intense

Voice: disjunct; long-ranged phrases; syncopation; many long tones; downward portamento

Piano: linear; wide spacing; many accidentals; some 2 vs. 3; 12-meas. postlude; very little doubling of vocal line

Diff: loud, sustained and soft, floating high tones; intensity in soft passages

Uses: limited use; needs a "Donna Anna" voice and seasoned performers; quiet ending

281. **THE FAIR MORNING** (Jones Very). [84]; 1st©1971. C-centered; b–f♭'''; Tess-mH; 3/4, 3/2, Allegro moderato (with many changes); 7min; Diff-V/d, P/d.

For: coloratura soprano

Mood: joyful; enthusiastic; describes beauties of morning

Voice: stepwise and skips on chord lines; fragmented phrases; much word repetition; many 2-note slurs and longer melismas; several unbarred cadenzas; repetitive

Piano: linear-chordal combination; sectional; covers keyboard; articulations important; disjunct; imitation; several solo passages

Diff: complex piece; singer must be secure in every way; ensemble; many high notes

Uses: can stand alone in a program; resembles short solo cantata in sectional construction; various expressive possibilities; useful for the right voice

282. **HEART SONGS.** Five Songs for Tenor and Piano (Robert Burns). Boosey & Hawkes, 1980. "To Clifton and Bettye Ware." Tonal; d'–a"; Tess-M-H; regular meters; 20min; Diff-V/m, P/m-md.

For: tenor specified

Mood: love songs

Voice: some phrases have wide range (e.g., e♭'–a♭"); skips not difficult; rhythms not difficult; Scotch snap used in (d.); mostly syllabic, but many 2- & 3-note slurs; a few long high notes (e.g., (b.) at end); tunes based on traditional Scottish airs

Piano: (a.) uses canonic devices; other songs use various chordal and linear types of accomp.; doubling of vocal line incidental; (d.), 20 meas. solo material; (e.), 40 meas. piano solo, 22 as postlude

Diff: range, for a young singer; long-ranged phrases; dramatic dynamics in (b.); breath management in (c.) (long phrases with melismas at ends); Scottish dialect

Uses: effective group for a mature singer

    a. *Bonie Bell.* A♭maj; e♭'–a♭"; 3/4; 2min.
    b. *Long, Long the Night.* Cmaj; e'–g"; 3/2, Very broad; 6min.
    c. *Wilt Thou Be My Dearie.* Fmin-A♭maj; d'–a"; 4/8; 4min.
    d. *Ae Fond Kiss.* [62]. H & M keys: Emaj & D♭maj; e'–g♯" & c♯–f"; 6/8, With a lilt; 4min.
    e. *Blythe Hae I Been.* A♭maj; e♭'–a"; 9/8; 4min.

283. **HER DEFINITION** (Thomas Hardy). Boosey & Hawkes, 1968. X–Gmaj; G–e♭'; Tess-mH; 4/4, 5/8, 7/8, 8/8, Moderato; 5pp; Diff-V/d, P/m.

For: bass-baritone

Mood: subdued restlessness; searching

Voice: very much like a cello line in its phrasing; many consecutive 3rds connected by m2nds; disjunct, yet flowing; changing meters; emphasis on m2nd

Piano: linear, 2–5-voice; chromatic; creates mood of unrest and wakefulness; arrives at restful final cadence

Diff: pitch; perfect legato line on ascending phrases

Uses: good song; a different kind of love song

284. **HER SILVER WILL** (Looking Back at Sposalizio) (Emily Dickinson). Boosey & Hawkes, 1976. cmp1974. H & M keys: G♭maj [84] & E♭maj (orig.); d♭'–a" & b♭–f♯"; Tess-M; 4/4, Andante sognante; 3pp; Diff-V/me, P/m.

For: mezzo-soprano; soprano

Mood: lyrical; contemplation of the moon

Voice: stepwise; repetitive; hypnotic; some chromaticism; 8th-note motion; some slurs

Piano: chordal background; some moving lines; a few triplets; incidental doubling of vocal line

Diff: piano and voice share melody in fragments on last page

Uses: nice song; easier than many Binkerd songs

285. **IF THOU WILT EASE THINE HEART** (Thomas L. Beddoes). Boosey & Hawkes, 1971. X; A–f'; Tess-M; 3/4 with many changes, ♩ = ca.52; 6pp; Diff-V/d, P/d.

For: baritone

Mood: lyrical; philosophical poem of love and death

Voice: stepwise; flowing phrases; somewhat chromatic; many meter changes

Piano: contemporary counterpoint; independent, but enhances text; wide register changes on keyboard

Diff: rhythm within frequent meter changes

Uses: fine recital song for lyric baritone

286. **IS IT YOU I DREAM ABOUT?** (Kate Flores). For Medium Voice and Piano. Boosey & Hawkes, 1980. Dmin/Fmaj; c♯'–f♯"; Tess-M; 2/4, Moderato; 4min; Diff-V/m, P/md.

For: mezzo-soprano; baritone; some sopranos

Mood: lost love

Voice: mostly small skips; some phrases have range of 10th; easy rhythms; mostly syllabic; many accidentals; one entire section repeats

Piano: many accidentals; opens with 7-meas. prelude; has 22-meas. interlude–to be played "in the manner of a cadenza"; various chordal patterns; occasional doubling of vocal line

Diff: some intervals difficult to read because of accidentals

Uses: good recital song; lyric with dramatic climax in accomp. during interlude

287. **LIGHTLY LIKE MUSIC RUNNING** (Jean Garrigue). [84]. cmp1973. X; g♯'–c♭'''; Tess-H; 3/4, ♩ = ca.46; 7pp; Diff-V/md, P/md.

For: high soprano

Mood: sensuous

Voice: mostly stepwise; several melismas; long high tones; one spoken line; syncopation; many accidentals

Piano: linear; many accidentals; 14-meas. interlude

Diff: singer must be comfortable in high tessitura (stays high); long, high, sustained tones, mostly soft

Uses: recital; possibly pair with "Her Silver Will" from same collection

288. **MERMAID REMEMBERED** (Babette Deutsch). [84]. X; d♯'–d'''; Tess-H; 9/8; 5+min (11pp); Diff-V/d, P/d.

For: high soprano

Mood: hypnotic; descriptive fantasy

Voice: some 2 vs. 3 in piano; syncopation; some difficult intervals; several melismas; one near 2-8ve phrase

Piano: musical imagery of guitar and water; many accidentals; several short interludes; wide piano range; no doubling of vocal line

Diff: sustained d'''; some long phrases; must have agile voice, be able to sing difficult intervals and long-ranged phrases rapidly; needs good dynamic control

Uses: could stand alone; recital use; effective program ender

289. **NURSERY ODE** (Ambrose Philips). Boosey & Hawkes, 1971. X; F–f♯'; Tess-M; 3/4, 9/8, ♩ = ca.50; 8pp; Diff-V/dd, P/dd.

For: baritone; bass-baritone

Mood: lyrical; philosophical description of young lady

Voice: disjunct; highly chromatic; large intervals; complex rhythms

Piano: virtuosic; complex rhythms; independent of voice, but enhances text

Diff: extremes of range; perfect pitch desirable; rhythms

Uses: good for teaching rhythmic accuracy; fine recital song for baritone with wide range

290. **O DARLING ROOM** (Alfred, Lord Tennyson). Boosey & Hawkes, 1977. G♭maj; d♭'–g♭"; Tess-M; 3/4, 2/4, 6/8, Moderato; 4pp; Diff-V/m, P/m.

For: medium voice specified; mezzo-soprano; soprano

Mood: lyrical; warm and contented

Voice: well-shaped vocal lines; mostly small skips; syllabic; syncopation; several *pp* phrases

Piano: chordal texture; some imitation of vocal line; extensive doubling of vocal line; syncopation

Diff: needs good dynamic control
Uses: nice song; recital use

291. ONE FOOT IN EDEN (Edwin Muir). Boosey & Hawkes, 1977. Cmin–maj; c'–eb"; Tess-M; 2/4, Broad; 9pp, 8+min; Diff-V/m, P/m.
For: baritone; mezzo-soprano; possibly contralto
Mood: retrospective–looking back on the nature of life
Voice: many small skips; some dotted rhythms; some syncopation; some recit.-like passages; contains melodic quotations from well-known hymns
Piano: block-chordal texture; some imitation of vocal line; sectional; many accidentals; several key sig. changes; rolled chords
Diff: needs mature vocal sound and wide range of dynamic control; several sustained eb"s
Uses: could stand alone

292. PEACE (Henry Vaughan). Boosey & Hawkes, 1968. H & L keys: C- & G-centered; cb'–ab" & gb–eb"; Tess-mH or M (depending on which option is taken in final 6 meas.); 3/4, Moderato–Emphatic and sonorous; 4pp; Diff-V/d, P/md.
For: soprano; mezzo-soprano; baritone (not for extremely light voices)
Mood: metaphysical poem concerns heaven
Voice: many skips; many accidentals; syncopation; dotted rhythms; many 2–4-note slurs
Piano: linear-chordal combination; covers the keyboard; large reaches; irregular phrase groupings; many accidentals; syncopation; dotted rhythms; grace notes; does not double vocal line
Diff: difficult intervals; sudden 8ve leaps; long-ranged phrases
Uses: effective for the right singer

293. SHUT OUT THAT MOON. A Song Cycle (Thomas Hardy). Boosey & Hawkes, 1968. cmp1965. Tonal centers; b–a"; Tess-mH; regular meters (except (b.)), varied tempos; 16min; Diff-V/d, P/md-d.
For: lyric soprano with easy high tessitura
Mood: lyrical; bittersweet quality of memory
Voice: skips and leaps predominate; many sustained phrases; (b.) in fast tempo with changing meters; numerous high phrases; melodic repetition and sequence; word repetition; accidentals
Piano: mostly linear; somewhat contrapuntal; thin, open, widely-spaced texture; articulation important; accidentals; rhythmic security and wide reach needed
Diff: various technical difficulties for both performers in addition to the demands of textual interpretation; for mature, advanced performers
Uses: a good cycle–effective, interesting, poignant

    a. *She, to Him.* E-centered; b–ab"; Tess-M-mH; 4/4, Slow; 5pp.
    b. *Shut Out That Moon.* A-centered; cb'–a"; Tess-M-mH; 2/2, Fast, light and rhythmic (many meter changes); 13pp.
    c. *A Bygone Occasion.* G-centered; c'–gb"; Tess-M; 2/2, ♩=ca.46; 4pp. (also pub. separately: E-centered; a–eb").

    d. *The Riddle.* E-centered; d'–g♯"; Tess-M; 4/4,Tempo rubato; 5pp.

294. SOMEWHERE I HAVE NEVER TRAVELLED (e. e. cummings). Boosey & Hawkes, 1969. A-centered; bb–ab"; Tess-mH; 6/8,9/8, 4/8, Andante con moto (in 6); 8+min; Diff-V/d, P/d.
For: tenor; man's text
Mood: love song
Voice: disjunct; syncopation; irregular rhythms; fragmented phrases; many accidentals
Piano: linear-chordal combination; large reaches; imitation; several important solo passages; many accidentals; wide spacing
Diff: rhythms; disjunct vocal line; wide dynamic variety; poem needs study; perhaps tenor could take low Bb up an 8ve, as composer uses 8ve displacement elsewhere in song
Uses: effective song for some voices

295. SONG OF PRAISE AND PRAYER (Children's Hymn) (William Cowper). Boosey & Hawkes, 1972. Cmin; eb'–f"; Tess-mH; 5/8, 6/8, Flowing; 4pp (with repeat); Diff-V/e, P/e.
For: any high or medium voice
Mood: sacred song
Voice: flowing; several high-lying phrases
Piano: somewhat contrapuntal; workable on organ
Uses: useful for young voices; church

296. WHAT SWEETER MUSICK (Robert Herrick). Boosey & Hawkes, 1968, 1971. (same music as "A Bygone Occasion" with a different text). H & L keys: Emin/Gmaj & C♯min/Emaj; c'–gb" & a–eb"; Tess-M; 2/2, ♩=ca.46; 2+min; Diff-V/md, P/m.
For: contralto; baritone; bass; higher voices in high key
Mood: lyrical and quiet
Voice: rather disjunct; large intervals; long phrases
Piano: canon-like imitation at beginning, otherwise chordal and chromatic
Diff: low tessitura; long, sustained phrases; 8ve leaps
Uses: useful quiet Christmas song

297. THE WISHING-CAPS (Rudyard Kipling). Boosey & Hawkes, 1971. "For Bruce Foote and Eric Dalheim." X; B–f'; Tess-mH; 3/4, 4/4, 9/8, 6/8, Allegro moderato (♩.=c.60)–Più allegro (♩.=84); 16pp; Diff-V/d, P/d.
For: baritone
Mood: dramatic; narrative; philosophical
Voice: disjunct; chromatic; triplets; staccato; fragmented phrases
Piano: chordal; fragmented; chromatic; triplets; syncopation; independent of vocal line
Diff: dramatic weight of voice, with fairly high tessitura; staccato; text may be difficult for some
Uses: a real *tour-de-force* for baritone

BIRCH, ROBERT FAIRFAX
(b. Chevy Chase, MD, 1917)

298. HAIKU. Japanese Poems Set to Music (various Haiku

poets). 8 vols. Patelson & Presser, 1963–1985. Traditional keys; g–b"(c'''); Tess-mL-H; regular meters; varied tempos; individual songs approx. 30sec. each; Diff-V/e-m, P/e-m.

For: all voices
Mood: lyrical; various moods of nature, animals, insects, as well as personal moods
Voice: highly varied; many different styles
Piano: highly varied; many different styles
Uses: short songs useful for teaching young singers to form mental pictures of the songs they sing; extreme brevity is both novel and attractive; small cycles could be created around various themes

A. **HAIKU,** Vol. 1. (58 songs).
B. **ALL SNOW,** Vol. 2. (57 songs).
C. **BUGS!** Vol. 3. (57 songs).
D. **ANOTHER FLOWER,** Vol. 4.
E. **AMONG THE BAMBOOS,** Vol. 5. (98 songs).
F. **RIPPLING SOUNDS,** Vol. 6.
G. **NOW FOR CHERRY BLOOM!** Vol 7. (124 songs).
H. **THE WAY OF HAIKU,** Vol. 8. (119 songs).
I. **FOOLISH YEARS OF SONG,** Vol. 9.

299. **HOW SLEEP THE BRAVE,** Op. 29, No. 3 (William Collins, 1721–1759). Patelson, 1952 (Theodore Presser). "To Walter Cassel." X; a–e"; Tess-M; 4/4, Sustained (Largo); 2pp; Diff-V/m, P/me.

For: baritone; bass
Mood: dirge for fallen heroes
Voice: stepwise and small skips; many accidentals; easy rhythms
Piano: block chords in half-notes; many accidentals; does not double vocal line
Uses: usable subdued song for interior of a group

300. **IF THERE WERE DREAMS,** Op. 27, No. 1 (Thomas L. Beddoes). Presser, 1956. B♭maj; f♯'–g♯"; Tess-H; 4/4, Andante (flowing smoothly); 2+min; Diff-V/md, P/md.

For: soprano; tenor
Mood: lyrical; quiet longing
Voice: some skips of 5th & 6th; syncopation; quick ornaments, written out
Piano: chordal; broken-chord patterns; some syncopation; dotted rhythms; many accidentals; some doubling of vocal line
Diff: long phrases; sustained singing
Uses: good song; big ending

301. **I LONG TO SEE A FLOWER,** Op. 43, No. 7 (Alfred Lord Tennyson). Theodore Presser, 1960. Dmaj; d'–a"; Tess-mH; 4/8, 6/8, Gently; 2min; Diff-V/m, P/me.

For: soprano; tenor
Mood: gentle poem about death
Voice: some skips; some dotted rhythms
Piano: 4–6-voice block chordal texture; syncopation; some repeated chords; does not double vocal line
Diff: climax is sustained a"; subtle dynamics
Uses: quiet song; use in interior of group

302. **THE PHILOSOPHIST,** Op. 32, No. 3 (Sir Walter Raleigh). Presser, 1956. "To Alexander Kipnis." Cmin; b–e♭"; Tess-M; 2/4, ♪ = 108 (with satire); 1+min; Diff-V/m, P/m.

For: baritone; bass
Mood: misanthropic; ironic
Voice: 2-note slurs predominate; some dotted rhythms
Piano: chordal–afterbeat and some rolled; some counter-melody; staccato, like strummed instrument; does not double vocal line
Diff: needs a rather "crusty" delivery
Uses: humorous song for a final group

303. **REPOSE** (Erasmus Darwin). Patelson, 1952 (Theodore Presser). D♭-G♭maj; d♭'–g♭"; Tess-M; 2/4, Slowly and quietly; 1+min; Diff-V/e-m, P/e-m.

For: soprano; tenor
Mood: lyrical; tranquil; subdued
Voice: easy skips; slurs; 2 slow, short trills, written out
Piano: broken-chord pattern; many accidentals; does not double vocal line
Diff: varieties of soft dynamics
Uses: useful to teach legato style and variations of soft dynamics; quiet ending

304. **THE RIVER** (Patrick MacDonogh). Theodore Presser, 1953. "To Gladys Swarthout." Amaj; a–f♯"; Tess-mH; 3/8, Flowing, moderato; 4pp; Diff-V/m, P/m.

For: mezzo-soprano; some sopranos
Mood: lyrical; serene; limpid
Voice: small skips, many 4ths; legato lines; some dotted rhythms
Piano: 2-voice 16th-note water figure; some rolled chords; incidental doubling of vocal line
Diff: meter changes; 7 f♯"s
Uses: interior of group; quiet ending

305. **SONNET** (Robert Nathan). Theodore Presser, 1956. "To Walter Carringer." E♭maj; e♭'–g"; Tess-mH; 3/4, Slow; 3+min; Diff-V/md, P/e.

For: tenor; soprano
Mood: lyrical; philosophical; the nature of beauty
Voice: smooth lines; long phrases; repetitive rhythms; accidentals; some recit.-like phrases
Piano: broken-chord pattern; some rolled chords; lute-like; does not double vocal line
Diff: long phrases; duplet vs. triplets in piano
Uses: nice song; beautiful singing lines

306. **THERE IS SWEET MUSIC,** Op. 31, No. 3 (Alfred, Lord Tennyson). Theodore Presser, 1956. E♭–G♭maj; d♭'–g♭"; Tess-M-mH; 4/4, 6/8, Andante; 3min; Diff-V/m, P/m.

For: tenor; soprano
Mood: lyrical; descriptive; quiet
Voice: stepwise and small skips; dotted rhythms; syncopation
Piano: block- and broken-chord patterns; duplets and triplets; syncopation; does not double vocal line
Uses: usable lyric song; fits the voice well

307. **WOO NOT THE WORLD,** Op. 40, No. 1 (Mu'tamid II, King of Seville, 1040–1095, trans. D. L. Smith). Theodore Presser, 1957. "To Lotte Lehmann." Emin;

e'–e" ; Tess-M; 2/4, Adagio sostenuto; 2min;
Diff-V/m-md, P/m.

For: mezzo-soprano; baritone; soprano; tenor
Mood: dramatic; philosophical; all things change
Voice: stepwise and chord-member skips; interrupted phrases; syncopation; triplets; 2–4-note slurs
Piano: chordal, broken and block; syncopation; 2 vs. 3; does not double vocal line
Uses: good dramatic song; fits the voice

BISCARDI, CHESTER
(b. Kenosha, WI, 1948)

308. **THE GIFT OF LIFE** (Emily Dickinson, Denise Levertov, Thornton Wilder). [continuous cycle; no individual titles]. C. F. Peters, 1996. cmp1990–1993. Tonal; b–a"; Tess-mL-mH; changing meters, (♩= ca. 48–72, varying throughout); 10min; Diff-V/m, P/md.

For: soprano
Mood: reflective and gentle; birth, life, memory, loss, death, and love
Voice: lyrical; some phrases cover the staff; some measured recit.; many skips and leaps; accidentals; several phrases low in the range; syllabic; specific expressive markings
Piano: mostly linear and melodic; some chordal sections with mildly dissonant tone clusters; many accidentals; wide reach helpful
Diff: some pitches; some wide intervals (9ths & 10ths) for singer; some polyrhythms
Uses: attractive and accessible cycle for both performers and audience; meaningful texts; good work for graduate level soprano with an even scale
Rec: D#119

BLAKE, DOROTHY GAYNOR
(b. St. Louis, MO, 1893; d. Webster Groves, MO, 19-?)

309. **AN EXPLANATION** (Walter Learned). Church, 1914. Emaj; e'–f♯" ; Tess-M; 4/4, no tempo indication (but fairly fast); 15meas; Diff-V/me, P/e.

For: tenor
Mood: humorous; light; conversational
Voice: many small skips; fragmented phrases; several fermatas
Piano: chordal; 4–5-voice texture; staccato; some doubling of vocal line
Uses: encore or short, light song for a group

BLANK, ALLAN
(b. New York, NY, 1925)

310. **THE CAT AND THE WIND.** For Soprano and Piano (Thom Gunn). American Composers Alliance (Composers Facsimile Edition), 1979. cmp1979. X; b♭–g"; Tess-wide; 2/2 with a few changes; Agile and very light; 2min; Diff-V/d, P/d.

For: soprano
Mood: descriptive
Voice: disjunct; descriptive of movement of things in the

wind; leaps of tritones & dim. 8ves; two quarter-tones; speech-like rhythms also describe movements; various complex subdivisions of beat and meas; polyrhythms with piano; syncopation; several 2- & 3-note slurs
Piano: mostly broken-chord patterns (non-tertian structures); many accidentals; very descriptive–quiet, delicate, much staccato; highly complex with irregular rhythms; does not double vocal line; some half-pedaling
Diff: pitches (perfect pitch seems necessary); rhythms
Uses: for two excellent imaginative musicians with an appreciation for cats and the wind

311. **IN JUST** (e. e. cummings). American Composers Alliance (Composers Facsimile Edition), 1965. cmp1956; rev.1964. X; c♯'–b"; Tess-wide; 3/8, 4/8 & other changes, ♪ = 112; 4min; Diff-V/d, P/d.

For: soprano
Mood: child-like description of spring; exuberant
Voice: disjunct; some long-ranged phrases (c♯'–b"); rhythmic complexities include syncopation and some triplets; words separated by rests; several high notes on "ee" and "oo"; many 2- & 3-note slurs; several longer melismas; slow downward glissando at end on "wee"
Piano: non-tertian harmonies; block, broken, and rolled chords; covers the entire keyboard; complex rhythms; much staccato; many other articulation marks; does not double vocal line
Diff: ensemble and rhythms; wide tessitura; perfect pitch would be helpful.
Uses: for two secure musicians; singer must have easy technique, flexibility, and command of this tessitura; see other settings of this text by J. Duke, Cage, and Argento

BLITZSTEIN, MARC
(b. Philadelphia, PA, 1905; d. Fort-de-France, Martinique, 1964)

312. **FROM MARION'S BOOK** (e. e. cummings). Cycle. Chappell, 1962. cmp1960. "To Alice Estey." Polytonal with many altered chords and cluster-like structures; no key sigs.; a♯–f"; Tess-M; regular but changing meters; varied tempos; 12min; Diff-V/d, P/md-d.

For: mezzo-soprano; some sopranos; lyric baritone
Mood: reflections of eternity, love, change, and rebirth; many images of nature
Voice: mostly conjunct; many accidentals; some skips; pitch patterns difficult to hear with piano; speech rhythms
Piano: no key sigs. and many accidentals make reading difficult; linear; transparency and delicacy required; facility and affinity for the modern score helpful
Diff: pitch perception; meaning of the poetry
Uses: for intellectually and poetically sophisticated performers; selections could be made

a. *o by the by.* a♯–e" ; 2/4 with changes, Allegro; 3pp. [**Rec:** D#120]
b. *when life is quite through with.* d♯'–b'; 9/8, Andantino; 2pp.
c. *what if a much of a which of a wind.* c'–e" ; 2/2, Vivace; 5pp.
d. *silent unday by silently not night.* b♭–e" ; 4/4 with

changes, Calmo; 4pp.

- **e.** ***until and I heard.*** b♭–f"; 6/8 with changes, Allegro (leggierissimo); 3pp. [**Rec:** D#120]
- **f.** ***yes is a pleasant country.*** b–e"; 2/2, Allegretto; 2pp.
- **g.** ***open your heart.*** c'–f"; 3/2 with changes, Molto moderato; 3pp. [**Rec:** D#120]

313. **JIMMIE'S GOT A GOIL** (e. e. cummings). [22]; 1st©1935. Bitonal; c'–f♯"; Tess-M; 2/2, Vivo; 3pp; Diff-V/d, P/d.
For: tenor; high baritone
Mood: humorous dialect song; "popular" song flavor
Voice: forceful and brilliant; chromatic
Piano: 3-voice texture; afterbeats; chromatic
Diff: dissonances make pitch perception elusive; rhythmic complexities; pronunciation
Uses: good humorous song; program ender
Rec: D#120

BOATWRIGHT, HOWARD
(b. Newport News, VA, 1918; d. Syracuse, NY, 1999)

314. **FIVE EARLY SONGS.** Walnut Grove Press, 2000 (Classical Vocal Reprints). cmp1946–1954. Tonal with modal and bitonal references; d'–a"; Tess-mH-H; changing meters; varied tempos; 21pp; Diff-V/m-d, P/me-md.
For: soprano; tenor
Mood: various (see songs)
Voice: pitches/intervals often not in piano part; many accidentals; melismas; some speech-like rhythms, chant-like sections; many meter changes, hemiola ties across bar lines; 2 vs. 3; some unaccomp. lines; melodic fragmentation; many long high notes
Piano: mostly linear, some 2-voice, hands 8ve or two 8ves apart; some block or broken tertian, quartal chords; imitation/interaction with vocal line; various subdivisions of beat; doubly dotted rhythms, hemiola; many accidentals; much solo piano, e.g., preludes 1–6 meas; interludes 1–18 meas; postludes 0–12 meas; last song ends quietly
Diff: rhythms, meter changes; some pitches; no stopping places in (c.); long high notes
Uses: use as a recital group, or excerpt from set; for an intelligent singer with good technique and musicianship

- **a.** ***Requiescat*** (Oscar Wilde). D minorish; f'–a♭"; Tess-M; 2/2, 3/2, Dirge-like (not too slow); 5pp; V/md, P/m; (lyrical).
- **b.** ***On Hearing the Birds*** (Irish–Anon.). F♯-centered; d'–g♯"; Tess-mH; 6/4, 4/4, 5/4, 3/4, 7/4, 2/4, Quiet, rather free; 2pp; V/m, P/me; (lyrical nature prayer).
- **c.** ***o by the by*** (e. e. cummings). D-centered, somewhat modal; d'–g"; Tess-H; 9/8, 6/8, 7/8, 5/8, 3/4, etc., Sprightly (but not too fast); 3pp; V/d, P/md; (enigmatic–a wish given up).
- **d.** ***At the Round Earth's Imagined Corners*** (John Donne). F♯-centered; d'–a"; Tess-H; 6/8, Vigorous–3/4, 6/8, 4/4, 2/4, 5/4, with gradually increasing agitation; 5+pp; V/md, P/m; (dramatic).

- **e.** ***Revelation*** (B. T. Coler). F♯-centered; e'–a"; Tess-H; 3/4, 2/4, 5/8, Slow (♩ = 40)–6/8, Light and gay (♩ = 96); 5pp; V/md, P/md; (close of winter, awakening of spring).

BOLCOM, WILLIAM
(b. Seattle, WA, 1938)

315. **BRIEFLY IT ENTERS,** a Cycle of Songs from the Poems of Jane Kenyon. Edward B. Marks & Bolcom Music, 1997 (Hal Leonard). cmp1994–1996 for Benita Valente. Mostly X, some clear keys; c'–b"; Tess-mH-H, cs; changing meters; varied tempos: ♩ = 56–132; 32pp; Diff-V/m-d, P/m-d.
For: soprano
Mood: a remembrance of the life and work of poet Jane Kenyon; background of grief at her early death and certainty of her eternal presence
Voice: lyrical but often angular lines; large leaps to *pp* high tones; direction and movement of vocal line paints text; syllabic setting; word rhythms; dissonant, but vocal entrances well prepared by piano; one song in 10/16
Piano: motivic musical construction; dissonant harmonies in some familiar forms (chaconne, waltz); linear and chordal; many accidentals
Diff: pitches, rhythms; ensemble; many soft high notes
Uses: excellent cycle for graduate or professional lyric soprano with good ear and floating high tones
Rec: D#337

- **a.** ***Who.*** X; d'–b"; Tess-cs; 3/4, 2/4, Moderately slow; 2pp.
- **b.** ***The Clearing.*** X; e♭'–b♭"; Tess-mH; 4/8, 6/8, 3/4, 3/8, Dancelike, spirited, a little bumptious ♪ = 144; 6pp.
- **c.** ***Otherwise.*** G♯min; c♯'–g♯"; Tess-M-mH; 3/2, 2/2, ♩ = 36 (♩ = 72) exactly; 3pp.
- **d.** ***February: Thinking of Flowers.*** X; e'–a"; Tess-mH; 10/16, 5/8, Calm, flowing, but not slow ♩. = ca.54; 3pp.
- **e.** ***Twilight: After Haying.*** X; c♯'–g♯"; Tess-M; 3/4, Stately ♩ = 80 (in 1); 4pp.
- **f.** ***Man Eating.*** X-C♯; c'–g"; Tess-M; 2/2, Tempo giusto (♩ = 66); 2pp.
- **g.** ***The Sick Wife.*** Amin; d'–a♭"; Tess-M; 4/4, ♩ = 56, mesto; 4pp.
- **h.** ***Peonies at Dusk.*** X; f'–b♭"; Tess-mH-H; 3/8, Like a leisurely waltz (♪ = 152); 4pp.
- **i.** ***Briefly It Enters, and Briefly Speaks.*** Fmaj; d'–b♭"; Tess-M-mH; 4/4, Stately (♩ = 66) but not dragging; ecstatic; 4pp.

316. **CABARET SONGS** (Arnold Weinstein). Vols.1 & 2. For Medium Voice and Piano. Marks, 1979 (Vol. 1) & 1985 (Vol. 2); Vol. 1 cmp1977–1978; Vol. 2 cmp1979–1983. "For Joan Morris." Tonal; Vol. 1: a♭–a", Vol. 2: a–f"; Tess-M; changing meters; various tempos; Vol. 1: 33pp, Vol. 2: 28pp; Diff-V/d, P/d-dd.
For: mezzo-soprano
Mood: unvarnished scenes and characters from life seen as though in a cracked mirror

Voice: stepwise motion and small skips predominate; some large skips, up to a 9th; some long-ranged phrases (b–d″, a♭–c″, a–a″); rhythms include syncopation, dotted notes, and triplets; some fragmented phrases; some portamentos; some spoken sections; some scat singing; some staccato; syllabic articulations predominate with some 3-note slurs; many accidentals; key sigs. often not used; each song seems to have its own style and also to reflect the style of a composer of semi-classical or popular music, such as Kurt Weill, Cole Porter, George Gershwin, Vincent Youmans, etc., distorted by contemporary tonality and harmony; composer's notes recommend that the focus of the singer be more on words than on tone

Piano: in cabaret and music-hall styles, but more elaborate and less repetitive; includes afterbeat-style accomps., broken and rolled chords, repeated patterning using dotted rhythms, and use of ostinato and countermelody; many accidentals; polytonal touches and much use of 9th, 11th, & 13th chords; some use of quartal harmony and octatonic scale; most songs in dance rhythms with ragtime and jazz-like references; most songs have prelude, interlude, and postlude material, e.g., (a.) has 7-meas. prelude, 14-meas. interlude, and end-tag marked "Play like the closing signature of a piano set before the union break"; many accomps. have an improvisatory sound; in his introductory notes Arnold Weinstein tells the pianist to "Play the words"

Diff: style; tessitura (although composer suggests transposing some songs if necessary); rhythms; delivering words clearly

Uses: use as one set, or two sets, or select your own group from the 12 songs (vol. 2 has narrower range); for singer who enjoys cabaret style and is experienced in these idioms; pianist must be likewise experienced; composer says that either the "trained" or "untrained" voice can be used (singer would need to be trained musician, however); composer says "they can be fairly efficacious training in theater-style performance for voice students"; introductory notes by Arnold Weinstein are helpful in defining style

Rec: D#s 37, 121

Vol. 1:

   a. *Over the Piano.* X; b–d″; 3/4, Swoopy, with rubato–Sentimental waltz-tempo; 4pp. [**Rec:** D#28]

   b. *Fur (Murray the Furrier).* X; a♭–e♭″; 2/4, 3/4, A lively one-step-Waltz-time; 7pp. [**Rec:** D#28]

   c. *He Tipped the Waiter.* X; a–f″; 3/8 with changes, Leggero (♩ = 72 or slower–Clear in texture–Slow polka [and other tempo changes]); 7pp.

   d. *Waitin'.* B♭maj; b♭–d″; 4/4, Simply (♩ = 60 or slower); 1p. [**Rec:** D#58]

   e. *Song of Black Max* (As Told by the De Kooning Boys). B-minorish; b♭–d″; 4/4 with changes, March tempo (♩ = 132), inflexible; 7pp. [**Rec:** D#28]

   f. *Amor.* Amaj; a–a″; 4/4, Light, rhythmic–Pachanga tempo; 7pp. [**Rec:** D#21]

Vol. 2:

   g. *Places to Live.* D majorish; a–e″; 2/2, Light, serene; 5pp.

   h. *Toothbrush Time.* E♭min-maj; a–e♭″; 4/4 with changes; Not too slow, slightly swing; 6pp.

   i. *Surprise!* X; b♭–e″; 3/8, Wild waltz; 2pp.

   j. *The Actor.* X; a–e″; 4/4, Slowly, freely; 2pp.

   k. *Oh Close the Curtain.* D-centered; a–f″; 3/4, Slow jazz waltz tempo (with some variations); 7pp.

   l. *George.* E♭majorish; b♭–e♭″; 4/4, Fox trot (with many fluctuations); 6pp.

317. **CABARET SONGS** (Arnold Weinstein). Vols. 3 & 4. For Medium Voice and Piano. Edward B. Marks Music Co. and Bolcom Music, 1997 (Hal Leonard). cmp1963–1997. Mostly tonal; Vol. 3: g–e♭″, Vol. 4: g–f♯″; Tess-mL & L (lower than Vols. 1 & 2); simple meters with some changes; varied tempos; Vol. 3: 29pp, Vol. 4: 20pp; Diff-V/m-d, P/m-d.

For: low and medium voices

Mood: scenes from life and nature in both serious and whimsical treatment; irony (see songs)

Voice: similar to Vols. 1 & 2 above; more *Sprechstimme*

Piano: see Vols. 1 & 2 above; fewer difficulties

Diff: see Vols. 1 & 2 above

Uses: use as two sets or one set; groups can be constructed from both vols.

Rec: D#337

Vol. 3

   a. *The Total Stranger in the Garden.* Cmin-Amin; g–d♭″; Tess-L; 4/4, 3/4, Allegretto comodo ♩ = c.80; 4pp; V/D, P/d. (Dialogue between husband and wife)

   b. *Love in the Thirties.* E-centered; a♯–c♯″; Tess-mL; 4/4, 2/4, With an Easy Swing ♩ = c.100; 8pp; V/d, P/d. (Dialogue between boy and his father)

   c. *Thius King of Orf.* X; *Sprechstimme*; 0, Free, not slow; 1p; V/m, P/md.

   d. *Miracle Song.* Dmin; a–e♭″; Tess-mL; 3/4, Mahlerian Jazz Waltz Tempo, ♩ = 116; 5pp; V/d, P/d; (Death is all around)

   e. *Satisfaction.* D-centered; c♯′–d″; Tess-L; 4/4, 3/4, 2/4, Fast ♩ = 120; 2pp; V/m, P/md. (Nature)

   f. *Radical Sally.* Cmin; g–e♭″; Tess-mL; 4/4, 2/4, 3/4, Bright ♩ = 112 or slower; 9pp; V/d, P/d. (Former demonstrator looking for a cause)

Vol. 4

   g. *Angels Are the Highest Form of Virtue.* X; a–c″; Tess-L; 4/4, Languorous (♩ = c.66); 2pp; V/d, P/md. (Nature)

   h. *Poet Pal of Mine.* X; g–f♯″; Tess-wide; 2/2, 4/4, 3/4, Lively (♩ = c.60); 4pp; V/d, P/d. (Permanence of poetry after author is gone)

   i. *Can't Sleep.* X; a–c″; Tess-L; 3/4, Like a lullaby (♩ = c.66); 2pp; V/m, P/m. (Love song)

   j. *At the Last Lousy Moments of Love.* X; a–d♭″; Tess-L; 4/4, 2/4, 3/4, Slow March ♩ = 76; 5pp; V/md, P/d. (Unfaithful lover)

   k. *Lady Luck.* F-centered; b–d″; Tess-mL; 4/4, 5/4, 3/4, Bright & light ♩ = 72; 2pp; V/md, P/m. (Luck)

   l. *Blue.* C-centered; g–d″; Tess-L; 2/2, 3/2, 4/4, Easily (♩ = 46); 4pp; V/d, P/md. (Quiet moment alone)

318. **I WILL BREATHE A MOUNTAIN:** A Song Cycle from American Women Poets. Edward B. Marks Music Co. and Bolcom Music, 1995 (Hal Leonard). cmp1989–1990. Commissioned for Marilyn Horne and premiered by her in 1996. Tonal and X; g–a"(b♭"); Tess-M, wide; changing meters; varied tempos; 42pp; Diff-V/me-dd, P/m-dd.

For: mezzo-soprano
Mood: variety: humorous, whimsical, commentaries on parting; mutability
Voice: some wide-ranged phrases; some disjunct melodies, others conjunct; many rhythmic complexities; some free rhythms; *Sprechstimme*; some speaking; portamentos; many accidentals; several options given for high notes; many words
Piano: many accidentals; variety of articulations; tone clusters; tremolo; rhythmic complexity; orchestral effects; piano score similar to score of *Cabaret Songs*, though less jazz-influenced; doubling of vocal line rare; 7-meas. postlude in (i.)
Diff: rhythms; pitches; entrances; mood; understanding poetry in some songs
Uses: an excellent set; some songs could be excerpted effectively; cycle would end a recital well
Rec: D#122

  a. *Pity Me Not Because the Light of Day* (Edna St. Vincent Millay). X; a–f"; Tess-M; 3/4, Moderato, flexible tempo; 3pp; V/d, P/d.
  b. *How to Swing Those Obbligatos Around* (Alice Fulton). E♭-centered/bitonal; g–f"; Tess-wide; 4/4, 5/8, 5+4/8, 3/4, 2/4, 7/8, Lively (straight eighths) (♪ = c.138); 6pp; V/d, P/d.
  c. *The Crazy Woman* (Gwendolyn Brooks). X; f♯–a"; Tess-wide; 0, 4/4, 3/4, 2/4, Not slow– slow– fast and wild–Grave; 3pp; V/dd, P/d.
  d. *Just Once* (Anne Sexton). X; a–g♯"(f♯"); Tess-wide; 2/2, 3/4, 5/4, 3/2, Agitato (♩ = 72–80); 4pp; V/d, P/d.
  e. *Never More Will the Wind* (H.D. [Hilda Doolittle]). E♭maj; c'–b♭"; Tess-M; 3/4, 5/8, 7/8, 4/4, 6/8, 3/8, 2/4, Slow and mournful–Adagio (♪ = c.72); 2pp; V/m, P/md. **[Rec: D#s 7, 65]**
  f. *The Sage* (Denise Levertov). F♯-centered; b–e♭"; Tess-M; 8/8 (3+3+2), Lazily, not too slow (♪ = c.104); 2pp; V/d, P/d.
  g. *O to Be a Dragon* (Marianne Moore). X; (g)c'–f♯"; Tess-wide; 0, 3/4, 2/4, Free, fast, with Oriental stateliness (♩ = c.58); 2pp; V/d, P/d.
  h. *The Bustle in a House* (Emily Dickinson). D♭maj; e♭'–e♭"; Tess-M; 5/8, 4/8, 6/8, 7/8, Largo, semplice; 2pp; V/me, P/m.
  i. *I Saw Eternity* (Louise Bogan). X; g–a♭"; Tess-wide; 4/4, 5/4, Fast, violent, in bursts– Slower, ironic–Faster, emphatic–Maestoso–Presto delirando; 4pp; V/dd, P/dd.
  j. *Night Practice* (May Swenson). D-centered; g–g"; Tess-wide; 8/4, 6/4, Stately, tranquil–with strength–Very steady; 4pp; V/d, P/d.
  k. *The Fish* (Elizabeth Bishop). D-centered; a–g♭"; Tess-M; 4/8, 3/4, 2/4, 3/8, Allegro vivo, scherzando (♪ = 138); 10pp; V/d, P/d.

[VASLAV'S SONG. See entry # 15 I]

BOND, CARRIE JACOBS
(b. Janesville, WI, 1861; d. Hollywood, CA, 1946)

319. **HALF MINUTE SONGS** (Carrie Jacobs Bond). [5]. 12 "songs," each but four measures in length. Traditional keys; c'–f"; Tess-M-mL; regular meters, varied tempos; 5pp; Diff-V/e, P/e.
For: any voice
Mood: short aphorisms, some in rhyme, some not, dealing with character and conduct in a semi-humorous fashion
Voice: mostly conjunct, with a few larger intervals; one song in recit. style
Piano: chordal; doubles vocal line entirely, except for one recit.
Diff: vocal line incorporated into great staff, except for recit., and is assumed to be the top line of the piano score
Uses: although the sayings are usually serious, the treatment of them results in a humorous small set useful in a variety of programs; should be performed in its entirety

  a. *Making the Best of It.*
  b. *First Ask Yourself.*
  c. *To Understand.*
  d. *Doan' Yo' Lis'n.*
  e. *How to Find Success.*
  f. *The Pleasure of Giving.*
  g. *Answer the First Rap.*
  h. *A Good Exercise.*
  i. *A Present from Yourself.*
  j. *Now and Then.*
  k. *When They Say Unkind Things.*
  l. *Keep Awake.*

BONDS, MARGARET
(b. Chicago, IL, 1913; d. Los Angeles, CA, 1972)

320. **THE NEGRO SPEAKS OF RIVERS** (Langston Hughes). [10]. cmp1942. Dmin; a–f"; Tess-M; 4/4, Moderato con moto; 7pp; Diff-V/m, P/m.
For: baritone; possibly any medium voice
Mood: relating the African-American to great rivers of the world with which he has been associated
Voice: legato, flowing, and somewhat dramatic
Piano: chordal with some melodic passages; supports the vocal line, incidental doubling; special pedal instructions
Diff: some pitches
Uses: very effective recital or concert song for many audiences

321. **THREE DREAM PORTRAITS** (Langston Hughes). [6, 10]; 1st©1959. Traditional keys; b–g♭"; Tess-mL, M; regular meters, moderate tempos; 9pp; Diff-V/me-m, P/me-m.
For: mezzo-soprano; baritone
Mood: joy and sadness mixed; pain, problems of being black
Voice: lyrical with flowing lines; some dancing rhythms; arching phrases ending in a long tone
Piano: both linear and chordal textures; some chromaticism;

Uses: effective recital song
Rec: D#12

    a. *Minstrel Man.*
    b. *Dream Variation.*
    c. *I, Too.*

BONE, GENE and
(b. Newman, CA, 1905; d. New York, NY, 1992)
FENTON, HOWARD
(b. New York, NY)

322. **THE APRIL HILL** (Janet Lewis). Carl Fischer, 1947.
D–Bmaj; c'–f♯"; Tess-M; 3/2, 4/2, 3/4, 2/4, 5/8,
Slow–con moto (and other changes); 4pp; Diff-V/md,
P/m.
For: mezzo-soprano; soprano
Mood: delicate lyricism; a beautiful and sensitive poem
dealing with death
Voice: lyrical line with skips and leaps that must float;
changing meters
Piano: sets mood; illustrates and interprets text with various
figures
Diff: floating legato line
Uses: interesting song to include in a group showing various
attitudes toward death

323. **CAPTAIN KIDD** (Stephen Vincent Benét). Carl
Fischer, 1948. Amin-maj; c♯'–f"; Tess-M; 2/4, 4/4,
Allegro ma non troppo; 5pp; Diff-V/m, P/md.
For: mezzo-soprano; baritone
Mood: humorous narrative
Voice: some awkward leaps, but effective; sectional
Piano: awkward chord leaps; countermelody in r.h. with
broken-chord support
Diff: characterization
Uses: good for teaching flexibility of tempo and narrative
style; humorous

324. **DEBORAH** (Alice Kilmer). [21]; 1st ©1947. H & L
keys: Gmin & Emin; c♯'–f♯"; & b♭–d♯"; Tess-M; 3/8,
2/4, lively, with a lilt; 1+min; Diff-V/me, P/md.
For: any female voice
Mood: lyrical; humorous; affectionate description of a
precocious little girl
Voice: somewhat disjunct; dance-like
Piano: afterbeat style; melody in 8ves; some doubling of vocal
line; arpeggiations
Diff: rhythms; some pitches; good vocal actor required
Uses: good song for a light moment in recital

325. **EVERYTHING THAT I CAN SPY** (James
Stephens). Morris, 1946. Dmin-Amin; d'–f♭"; Tess-M;
6/8, Allegro non troppo; 4pp; Diff-V/m,P/m.
For: baritone
Mood: lilting.
Voice: many skips of 4th & 5th; duplets and triplets; long
notes at phrase ends; chromatic
Piano: block and broken chords; countermelody; wide-ranged
and -spaced; passages in 3rds

Diff: sustained tones at phrase endings
Uses: good song; interior or end of group

326. **POETIC JUSTICE** (Gene Bone and Howard Fenton).
Carl Fischer, 1947. Emin; b–f"; Tess-M-mH; 4/4, 2/4,
Slow; 2pp; Diff-V/m, P/m.
For: baritone
Mood: dramatic; declamatory
Voice: skips and leaps; somewhat chromatic; two speakers
Piano: chordal; descriptive prelude, interlude, and postlude;
tremolo; glissando; specific articulations; tempo and
dynamic changes abrupt
Diff: some awkward pitches
Uses: odd text; short dramatic song, perhaps useful as a
surprise change of pace

327. **TRYST** (Countee Cullen). Carl Fischer, 1950.
Bmin-Dmaj; f♯'–g"; Tess-M; 6/8 with changes, Con
moto; 3pp; Diff-V/m, P/m.
For: soprano; tenor
Mood: lyrical; elegy in reverse
Voice: skips along chord lines; some modulating phrases; long
tones at ends of phrases
Piano: linear; arpeggiated figures in l.h.; some chordal
sections; delicate
Uses: lovely, sensitive song; good for lyric voices

BOOTT, FRANCIS
(b. Boston, MA, 1813; d. Boston, MA, 1904)

328. **BREAK, BREAK AT THE FOOT OF THY**
CRAGS, O SEA (Alfred, Lord Tennyson). [42, 85];
1st©1857. Fmin; c'–f"; Tess-M; 6/8, Andantino; 4+pp;
Diff-V/m, P/e.
For: baritone; mezzo-soprano
Mood: dramatic; sorrowful; declamatory; lyrical
Voice: many skips and leaps of up to 6th; strong climax on f"
followed by leap down to c'
Piano: chords in afterbeat patterns; doubling and some echoing
of vocal line
Diff: some leaps
Uses: good for developing legato line in declamatory style;
interesting comparison with setting by Sidney Homer

329. **JENNY KISSED ME** (Leigh Hunt). [85]; 1st©1887.
A♭maj; e♭'–e♭"; Tess-M; 2/4, Allegretto moderato;
2pp; Diff-V/e, P/e.
For: baritone; tenor
Mood: playful
Voice: stepwise with a few skips
Piano: afterbeat style; some imitation; some doubling of vocal
line
Uses: a clever, easy short song for an opening group

330. **KING MACBETH** (Owen Meredith). [85]; 1st©1870.
Cmin; c'–e♭"; Tess-M; 6/8, Andantino con moto; 3pp;
Diff-V/me, P/e.
For: baritone specified
Mood: dramatic; ballad; dark and bleak
Voice: conjunct, with easy skips; some dotted rhythms; one
long-ranged phrase

Piano: open 8ves and block chords; some doubling of vocal line; register differences for color

Uses: easy ballad; good to teach ballad style; effective

331. **THE SANDS OF DEE** (Alton Locke). [85]; 1st©1857. Dmin; a–d"; Tess-M; 4/4, Andante con moto; 3pp (4 stanzas); Diff-V/e, P/e.

For: alto specified; bass

Mood: ballad of maiden and the sea

Voice: stepwise and easy skips; repeated notes and words; dotted rhythms; declamatory ballad style

Piano: chordal; some 8ve tremolo in l.h.; some doubling of vocal line

Uses: good for developing the imagination for ballad style; program in a ballad group

BORROFF, EDITH
(b. New York, 1925)

332. **FROM *MODERN LOVE: SEVEN LYRICS BY KEATS AND SHELLEY.*** [11, Vol. 3]. cmp1979. Blurred tonalities and bitonality; d♭'–b"; Tess-M; regular meters; slow-fast; 2pp. each; Diff-V/m-md, P/me-m.

For: tenor; soprano

Mood: sad; angry

Voice: chromatic and triadic melodic lines; melismas; one descending glissando; fairly short phrases; one phrase in each song begins high

Piano: long, slow white-note glissandos; thin texture; folk-like afterbeat patterns

Diff: chromatic and bitonal (vs. piano) vocal lines; piano glissando

Uses: interesting pair of songs to initiate the young singer into non-traditional harmonies

    a. *A Dirge* (Percy Bysshe Shelley). Blurred harmonies; d'–a♭"; Tess-M; 3/4, Soft, blurred, dreamlike throughout; 2pp.

    b. *A Hate-Song: Improvised* (Percy Bysshe Shelley). Bitonal; d♭'–b"; Tess-M; 6/8, 9/8, Fast and with exaggerated expression; 2pp.

333. **SONG** (Robert Burns). [11, Vol. 3]. cmp1947. Amin; e'–e"; Tess-M; 3/4, 2/4, 5/8; 2pp; Diff-V/me, P/me.

For: any medium voice

Mood: sad; lost love

Voice: folk-like melody with atypical rhythmic structure; syncopation; added beats; conjunct

Piano: chordal; 4-part harmony; parallel chords

Diff: rhythmic flow

Uses: relatively easy song for young singer; teaches irregular rhythmic and metric flow

BOWLES, PAUL
(b. Jamaica, NY, 1910; d. Tangiers, Morocco, 1999)

[See Appendix for songs with Spanish texts]

[See also D#s 123 & 124; no titles given]

334. **BLUE MOUNTAIN BALLADS** (Tennessee Williams). G. Schirmer, 1946, 1979 (Hal Leonard). Modal flavors and blues alterations of keys; b–f♯"; Tess-mL-mH; meters regular but changing, varied tempos; 6+min; Diff-V/me-md, P/m-md.

For: mezzo-soprano; baritone

Mood: lyrical; folk-like; descriptive; blues

Voice: mostly stepwise with easy skips; easy rhythms; some chromaticism; mostly syllabic

Piano: predominantly chordal; folk and jazz elements in harmonies, rhythms, and spacing; large reaches

Diff: singer must feel at home in this folksy style and be secure rhythmically

Uses: useful group; could end a program

Rec: D#s 24, 56, 59

    a. *Heavenly Grass.* [20, 24]. H & L Keys: E-centered & D-centered; b–e" & a–d'; Tess-M; 3/4 with changes, With flowing simplicity; 2min. [**Rec:** D#10]

    b. *Lonesome Man.* [86]. E♭maj; d♭'–e♭"; Tess-M; 4/8, 7/16, Very rhythmically; 4pp.

    c. *Cabin.* [24, 64]. H & L keys: Cmaj/Amin & Amaj/F♯min; e'–e" & c♯'–c♯"; Tess-mL; 6/8, 9/8, Like a ballad; 1+min. [**Rec:** D#10]

    d. *Sugar in the Cane.* [86]. E-centered; d'–f♯"; Tess-M-mH; 4/4, In absolutely strict tempo; 2min. [**Rec:** D#7]

335. **DAVID** (Frances Frost). [86]; 1st©1945. Begins and ends D-centered, with chromaticism and bitonality; e'–d"; Tess-M; 4/4, Adagio, molto tranquillo; 2min; Diff-V/me, P/me.

For: medium or low voice

Mood: quiet; night-song; serene

Voice: almost always stepwise; chromatic; some syncopation; syllabic

Piano: block chords; pedal-tones; rare doubling of vocal line

Diff: syncopation; chromaticism

Uses: good song for well-prepared musician with a short vocal range

336. **FARTHER FROM THE HEART** (Jane Bowles). [86]. cmp1942. C♯min with chromaticism and bitonal touches; c♯'–e"; Tess-M; 4/4, Andante; 2min; Diff-V/me, P/m.

For: mezzo-soprano; baritone

Mood: folksy; melancholy; somewhat tense

Voice: stepwise and small skips; chromaticism; syncopation; some triplets; a-b-a form, repeating words of "a"

Piano: doubles vocal line; block and broken chords; 2 vs. 3

Uses: when easy folk-like song is needed

337. **THE FEATHERS OF THE WILLOW** (Canon Dixon). [86]. cmp1944. C-centered; e'–g"; Tess-mH; 4/4, ♩ = 66; 1+min; Diff-V/me, P/me.

For: high voices

Mood: autumn picture; descriptive; quiet

Voice: predominantly stepwise and small skips; leap of 9th & 8ve at climax; simple rhythms

Piano: some broken and block chords

Diff: leap up of 9th, then down 8ve (occurs twice)

Uses: young soprano; tenor

338. **THE HEART GROWS OLD** (Villiers David). [86].
A- & F-centered; d♭'–f"; Tess-mH; 4/4, ♩ = 88; 1min;
Diff-V/m, P/md.
For: any voice except very low
Mood: philosophical
Voice: stepwise and small skips; some irregular phrase lengths
Piano: constant motion in 16th notes; no doubling of vocal
line; some syncopation; some rapid, thick chords in r.h.
Diff: possibly ensemble

339. **IN THE WOODS** (Paul Bowles). [4, 86]. cmp1944. X;
g♯'–b"(f♯") (whistled b" is preferred); Tess-mH, or H
(if singer does not whistle); 4/4, Adagio, molto
semplice; 3pp; Diff-V/m, P/m.
For: high soprano
Mood: lonely; subdued
Voice: skips of 7th & 8ve; accidentals; two whistling sections,
which can be sung on "ah"
Piano: chordal; doubles vocal line; chromatic; soft dynamics
Diff: pitch; long phrases; whistling
Uses: good for a young singer; quiet ending

340. **LETTER TO FREDDY** (Gertrude Stein). [86]. cmp
early 1930's. D♭maj; e♭'–e♭"; Tess-M; 3/4,
Lento–Allegro; 1+min; Diff-V/m, P/me.
For: mezzo-soprano; contralto; possibly baritone
Mood: lyrical; conversational message; overbearing
Voice: stepwise and easy skips; some irregular rhythms
Piano: afterbeats in waltz meter; some ornaments; many
accidentals; does not double vocal line
Diff: series of sustained c"s at end
Uses: interesting change of pace
Rec: D#s 51, 56

341. **A LITTLE CLOSER, PLEASE** (The Pitchman's
Song) (William Saroyan). [86]; 1st©1941. C- & A-
centered; c'–e"; Tess-M; 4/4, 3/4, ♩ = 120–♩ = 80;
1+min; Diff-V/m, P/m.
For: baritone
Mood: somewhat tense; loneliness behind the pitchman's
facade
Voice: stepwise and small skips; some accidentals;
syncopation; dotted rhythms
Piano: first section in afterbeat style; second section in block
chords with vocal melody doubled; jazz influence
Diff: possibly rhythms
Uses: in an American group; a facet of American life
Rec: D#56

342. **ON A QUIET CONSCIENCE** (Charles the First).
[86]. cmp1945. X; a–e"; Tess-L-M; 4/8, 5/8, ♪ = 120;
1+min; Diff-V/me, P/m.
For: medium and low voices
Mood: serene; gentle; quiet
Voice: stepwise and skips up to a 7th; syllabic
Piano: some doubling of vocal line; block chords;
arpeggiation; middle to medium-high registers
Diff: 5/8 meter; MS reproduction may be hard to read
Uses: an attractive soft song

343. **ONCE A LADY WAS HERE** (Paul Bowles). [59, 86];
1st©1946. H & L keys: E♭maj-min & Cmaj-min;
e♭'–g♭" & c'–e♭"; Tess-M; 4/8-5/8 alternation, 2/8,
Slowly and easily; 4pp; Diff-V/md, P/m.
For: all voices
Mood: languid; reflective
Voice: rather chromatic; features descending lines with
difficult intervals
Piano: chromatic; afterbeat style; rhythmic difficulties
Diff: constant meter alternation; chromatic vocal line
Uses: good for ear and rhythm training for young singers
Rec: D#s 11, 16, 51

344. **THE PIPER** (Seumas O'Sullivan). [86]. cmp1944.
Amaj-min; e'–g"; Tess-mH; 3/8, ♩. = 100; 2min;
Diff-V/me, P/e.
For: soprano; tenor
Mood: active; happy
Voice: mostly small skips and easy rhythms; syllabic
Piano: afterbeat patterns; some syncopation
Diff: soft ending features sustained e"
Uses: possible recital material; see also settings by J. Duke
and Michael Head; voice and guitar version also incl. in
this volume

345. **SLEEPING SONG** (Paul Bowles). [86]. cmp1946.
B♭maj; f'–f"; Tess-H; 4/8, ♪ = 96; 1+min; Diff-V/e,
P/e.
For: tenor; soprano
Mood: folksy lullaby
Voice: stepwise and small skips; some skips of 6th & 7th;
dotted rhythms
Piano: 8-meas. prelude; 4-meas. interlude; broken-chord
patterns; block chords in places
Diff: high soft singing for some voices
Rec: D#56

346. **THREE** (Tennessee Williams). [86]; 1st©1947. X;
e'–d"; Tess-M; 3/4, ♩ = 54; 1+min; Diff-V/ee, P/me.
For: any voice; man better
Mood: introspective; subdued; folk-like
Voice: simple skips; simple rhythms; legato
Piano: chordal; doubles vocal line
Uses: good song; use anywhere
Rec: D#56

BRANDEIS, FREDERICK
(b. Vienna, Austria, 1832; d. New York, NY, 1899)

347. **LADY BIRD,** Op. 66, No. 1. Brentano's Literary
Emporium, 1881. Emin-maj; f♯'–g♯"(a"); Tess-mH;
2/4, Allegro scherzando; 4pp; Diff-V/m, P/m.
For: soprano–lyric or coloratura
Mood: sprightly; variations of the children's rhyme
Voice: stepwise and skips along chord lines; 2-note slurs; easy
rhythms
Piano: chordal; staccato; soft dynamics; grace notes
Diff: several phrases end on high note; rapid diction
Uses: good for a young high voice; useful to establish
flexibility and *leggiero* singing

348. **MY LOVE IS LIKE THE RED, RED, ROSE**
(Robert Burns). Pond, 1886. Emin; e'–g♯"; Tess-mH;
4/4, Appassionato; 4pp; Diff-V/m, P/m.

For: tenor specified
Mood: lyrical; love song
Voice: stepwise and skips along chord lines; 2-note slurs; final
minor phrase repeated in major
Piano: 5-voice chordal and broken-chord textures; doubles
vocal line
Uses: use in historical group, or perhaps in an opening group

BRANSCOMBE, GENA
(b. Picton, Ontario, Canada, 1881; d. New York, NY, 1977)

349. **BLUEBELLS DROWSILY RINGING.** A. P.
Schmidt, 1916. H & L keys: Dmaj & B♭maj; e'–g" &
c'–e♭"; Tess-M; 6/8, Andantino rhythmique; Diff-V/e,
P/m.

For: soprano; mezzo-soprano
Mood: lullaby
Voice: conjunct; rocking rhythms
Piano: patterned accomp. throughout
Diff: soft high tones
Uses: good teaching song for young girls

350. **HAIL YE TYME OF HOLIE-DAYES** (Kendall
Banning). A. P. Schmidt, 1912. "Dedicated to David
Bispham." H & L keys: E♭maj & Cmaj; e♭'–f" &
c'–d"; Tess-M; 4/4, Allegretto; Diff-V/e, P/e.

For: all voices
Mood: lyrical Christmas song
Voice: almost hymn-like
Piano: chordal
Uses: Christmas song with English flavor; good teaching
song

351. **LOVE IN A LIFE** (Elizabeth Barrett Browning). A
Song-Cycle for Medium Voice. Words from *Sonnets
from the Portuguese*. Reprint: Recital Publications,
1985. Traditional keys; c'–g"; Tess-M; traditional
meters; moderate tempos; 17pp; Diff-V/me-m, P/me.

For: mezzo-soprano
Mood: Victorian love poetry
Voice: vocal lines reminiscent of 1920s and 1930s stage music
(i.e., Sigmund Romberg); easy rhythms; some recit.;
syllabic
Piano: chordal; somewhat thick texture; numerous accidentals;
rather Victorian-sounding in general
Uses: illustrates Victorian-era songs by a female composer
and poet

    a. *I Thought Once How Theocritus Had Sung.* Cmaj;
c'–e"; 4/4, Moderato; 3pp.

    b. *But Only Three in All God's Universe.* E♭maj;
c♯'–g"; 4/4; 2pp.

    c. *How Do I Love Thee?* Fmaj; c'–f"; 4/4, Andante;
3pp.

    d. *The Widest Land.* Cmaj; d'–f"; 4/4, Moderato; 2pp.

    e. *The Face of All the World Is Changed.* Fmaj;
c'–e"; 3/4, Allegretto, ma non troppo; 3pp.

    f. *My Own Beloved.* Cmaj; c'–f"; 4/4, 3/4, Moderato.

352. **OLD WOMAN RAIN** (Louise Driscoll). [17]. H & L
keys: Amaj & Fmaj; f'–g♯" & d♭'–e"; Tess-mL; 4/4,
Andantino–Lento; 4pp; Diff-V/md, P/d.

For: high or medium female voice
Mood: humorously descriptive
Voice: stepwise; a few difficult intervals
Piano: broken chords and arpeggiations; descriptive of text
Diff: aug.4ths in middle section; high climax
Uses: good recital material

BRANTLEY, ROYAL
(b. Yorktown, TX, 1922)

353. **SIX SHORT SONGS.** For High Voice and Piano. In
Collected Songs, Recital Publications, 1998.
Traditional keys; c♯'–a"; Tess-M–mH; regular meters
with few changes; moderate tempos; 19pp; Diff-V/e-m,
P/me-md.

For: soprano; tenor
Mood: heavy; warm; humorous; pensive; exuberant
Voice: lyrical; declamatory; talkative (some spoken phrases);
some melismas; some speech rhythms; numerous
accidentals; some phrases soar above the staff
Piano: mostly chordal; numerous accidentals; r.h. 6ths & 3rds
in compound meter
Diff: some rhythmic groupings
Uses: excellent for young students; good teaching songs

    a. *To Stand Up Straight* (A. E. Housman). Gmaj;
d'–g"; Tess-M; 2/4, Heavy-Mechanical Approx.
♩ = 92; 3pp.

    b. *First Fig* (Edna St. Vincent Millay). Dmaj; e'–d";
Tess-mL; 3/4, 2/4, Steadily, lightly, warmly ♩ = 60;
2pp.

    c. *Quatrain* (Benjamin Franklin). E♭maj; e♭'–a♭";
Tess-mH; 2/4, Theatrically, ♩ = 92; 2+pp.

    d. *The Silver Swan* (Anonymous). Gmin-B♭maj;
e♭'–a♭"; Tess-mH; 3/4, Molto legato, Approx.
♩ = 50; 4pp.

    e. *Things I Treasure* (Harold Orr). C♯min-maj;
c♯'–f♯"; Tess-M; 4/4, 2/4, Very slowly–Freely;
1+pp.

    f. *The Year's at the Spring* (Robert Browning).
C♯/D♭maj; e♯'–a"; Tess-mH; 6/8, 9/8, Brightly
animated ♩. = 80; 5pp.

BRICETTI, THOMAS G.
(b. Mt. Kisco, NY, 1936; d. Perugia, Italy, 1999)

354. **THREE SONGS, OPUS 2** (Elizabeth Royce).
McGinnis & Marx, 1963. Traditional keys; e♭'–a";
Tess-M; regular and irregular meters; varied tempos;
8pp; Diff-V/m, P/m.

For: tenor; soprano
Mood: grim songs; dark thoughts and music; all concern death
Voice: many small skips; some pitches hard to find; many
accidentals; vocalizing on "ah" and "oo"; humming;
some staccato
Piano: many accidentals; linear and chordal textures;
arpeggiation and afterbeats

Diff: sustained a"; needs good dynamic control
Uses: usable short group for recital program in need of something different

    a. *Epitaph.* Amin; e'–a"; 2/2, 3/2, Lento ma non troppo; 2pp.
    b. *Verse.* E♭min; e♭'–f♯"; 5/4, 4/4, 3/4, Allegro d'un modo suspettoso; 2pp.
    c. *Portrait.* Cmin–maj; f♯'–a"; 2/4, Largo espressivo; 4pp.

BRINGS, ALLEN
(b. New York, NY, 1934)

355. **THREE SONGS.** Mira, 1976. cmp1954, 1956. These three songs could be done as a set by soprano or tenor, but all are slow in tempo and need very good dynamic control. Separate entries below.

A. **A CRADLE SONG** (William Blake). Traditional harmonies; d'–f♯"; Tess-M; Andante (♩ = 48); 2+pp; Diff-V/me, P/m.
For: any voice with this range
Mood: quiet, soothing lullaby
Voice: stepwise motion and small skips; easy rhythms; several short and longer (8 notes) melismas; soft dynamics
Piano: 2–6-voice chordal texture with constant motion in 8ths; countermelodies; several accidentals; doubling of vocal line incidental; large reach helpful
Diff: singer must be independent; a few abrupt modulations
Uses: nice neo-romantic song for recital or study

B. **NEVER SEEK TO TELL THY LOVE** (William Blake). Tertian and non-tertian structures; d♯'–f♯"; Tess-mH; 4/4 with changes, Andante (♩ = 48); 3pp; Diff-V/m, P/m.
For: tenor
Mood: song of disappointment in love; dramatic
Voice: many small skips; many accidentals; dotted rhythms and syncopation; dynamics range *ppp–ff*; soft ending; syllabic with a few 2-note slurs
Piano: 4–6-note block-chordal structures; many accidentals; some triplets and dotted rhythms; large dynamic contrasts; does not double vocal line
Diff: dynamic control
Uses: effective recital or student song for voice with wide dynamic range; perhaps pair with "Song"

C. **SONG** (John Donne). C♯maj; c'–g♯"; Tess-mH; 4/4 with changes, Largo (♪ = 60), with changes and fluctuations; 4+pp; Diff-V/md, P/md.
For: tenor; soprano
Mood: song of parting
Voice: many skips; many accidentals; dotted rhythms and syncopation; many tempo changes; some 2-note slurs; expressive dynamics, *p–ff*
Piano: block- and broken-chord structures; subdivisions of beat include duplets, triplets and quadruplets; doubling of vocal line incidental
Diff: some intervals; rhythms; making the text understood
Uses: perhaps pair with "Never Seek to Tell Thy Love"

BROOK, CLAIRE
(b. New York, 1925)

356. **FOUR SONGS from *SIX SIGNIFICANT LANDSCAPES*** (Wallace Stevens). [11, Vol. 8]. Tonal; a–f♯"; Tess-M; regular meters; varied tempos; 9pp; Diff-V/m-md, P/ me-m.
For: medium voices
Mood: atmospheric pictures
Voice: (a.), conjunct; others have skips up to an 8ve; (b.), dramatic and speech-like; some melismas, some 2-note slurs; rhythms fairly easy
Piano: (a., b., & c.), progressions built in 4ths & 5ths; (d.), tertian in an afterbeat style; (a., c., & d.), preludes; (a., b., & d.), postludes, lengthy in (a.)
Diff: while not dissonant, some pitches will be difficult; (b.), begins with voice alone; poetic imagery unusual
Uses: nice recital group

    a. *I (The Night Is of the Color . . .).* X; e'–e"; Tess-M; 3/4, Vif (♩. = 66); 3pp.
    b. *II (I Measure Myself . . .).* C-centered; a–e"; Tess-M; 4/4, Maestoso; 2pp.
    c. *III (When My Dream Was near the Moon . . .).* Dmaj; c'–f"; Tess-M; 4/4, Adagio (♩ = 63); 2pp.
    d. *IV (Not All the Knives of the Lamp Posts . . .).* Gmaj; f♯'–f♯"; Tess-mH; 4/8, 5/8, Presto (♩ = 168); 2pp.

BROUTMAN, EMANUEL
(fl. 20th century)

357. **NIGHT** (Arthur Symons). Composers Press, 1955. Received Honorable Mention in the 1954 Contest sponsored by the Composers Press. Bmin-centered; b♭–e"; Tess-M; 4/4, ♩ = 58; 2+min; Diff-V/m, P/m.
For: mezzo-soprano; baritone; contralto; bass
Mood: lyrical; changelessness; suspension of time
Voice: stepwise and small skips; fragmented phrases
Piano: chordal, mostly 5-voice; syncopation; large reaches; articulations important; some doubling of vocal line
Diff: fragmentation of phrases; ensemble
Uses: imaginative song; useful for teaching

BROWN, CHARLES
(b. Marianna, AR, 1940)

358. **THE BARRIER** (Claude McKay). [6]. Bmin; c'–e♭"; Tess-mL; 3/4, 2/4, Slowly and very rubato, Improvisatory; 3pp; Diff-V/m, P/md.
For: any medium or low voice
Mood: sadly philosophical and lyrical; dealing with racial barriers
Voice: moves generally in 8ths & 16ths; some chromaticism
Piano: chordal with triplet figures; more improvisatory in sound than vocal line, which it supports (no doubling)
Diff: text possibly difficult for young singer
Uses: effective piece for many occasions

359. **A SONG WITHOUT WORDS** (Based on the singing

of Blind Willie Johnson). [6]; 1st©1974. D♭maj; a♭–d♭"; Tess-mL; 3/4, 2/4, 4/4, Very slow and improvisatory, not strict; 2pp; Diff-V/md, P/m.

For: any low voice

Mood: blues style

Voice: vocalise on "ah" or humming; short phrases; grace notes and blue notes; dotted rhythms and triplets; largely diatonic

Piano: chordal texture; chromatic; free and improvisatory

Diff: requires understanding of and ability to perform blues style on part of both performers

Uses: could be effective for the right performers in a variety of situations

BROWN, ELIZABETH C. (See entry #15 N)

BROWNE, AUGUSTA
(b. Dublin, Ireland, 1820; d. Washington, DC, 1882)

360. THE SUN HAS SET (A Boat Song) (Roswell Park). Osbourn's Music Saloon, 183-?. Amaj; e'–f♯"; Tess-M; 2/4, Rowing time; 4pp; Diff-V/me, P/me.

For: soprano; tenor; mezzo-soprano

Mood: lyrical; tranquil

Voice: conjunct; 2-note slurs; some ornaments

Piano: chordal, some broken, some block; thin texture; wide spacing; some doubling of vocal line

Uses: attractive, usable period song

BRUSH, RUTH
(b. Fairfax, OK, 1910)

361. ENCHANTMENT (Gene Lindberg). Bartlesville Publishing Co., 1992. Gmin; b–d "; Tess-M; 6/8, Andante espressivo; 4pp; Diff-V/me, P/m.

For: medium voices

Mood: serene, lyrical night nature scene

Voice: many sequences and repeated patterns; easy skips and rhythms; mostly 8th-note motion

Piano: repeated patterns; 16th-note motion; double notes in r.h.; some l.h. arpeggiation; no doubling of vocal line, but does support; 1-meas. prelude

Uses: good student song; attractive text

362. SONG CYCLE, Part I (only part pub.). Bartlesville Publishing Co., 1982. Traditional harmony & keys; c'–g"; Tess-M; 6/8, slow, slow, fast; 15pp; Diff-V/me-m, P/m-md.

For: soprano; mezzo-soprano

Mood: nature pictures

Voice: stepwise and chord-member skips; many accidentals; uncomplicated rhythms, but some syncopations and a few duplet divisions of beat (in 6/8); syllabic; a few 2-note slurs; (c.) has several long high notes

Piano: broken-chord patterns and arpeggiation; accidentals; doubling of vocal line incidental

Diff: chromaticism and endurance in (c.) for some singers.

Uses: (a.) & (b.) work well for students with little experience; (c.) requires more experienced musician with more

vocal technique; use as a group or separately; "Velvet Shoes" is set quite differently from the settings by J. Duke, Mary Howe, and R. Thompson

   a. *Twilight* (Sara Teasdale). Amaj; f♯'–f♯"; 6/8, Andante espressivo; 3pp.

   b. *Velvet Shoes* (Elinor Wylie). Fmin; c'–e♭"; 6/8, Andante tranquillo; 4pp.

   c. *Give Me the Sea* (Berta Huish Christensen). D♭maj; c'–g"; 6/8, Allegro con brio–Andante; 8pp.

BUCK, DUDLEY
(Hartford, CT, 1869; d. West Orange, NJ, 1941)

363. THE CAPTURE OF BACCHUS, Op. 87, No. 3 (Charles Swain). [61]. Amaj; c♯'–g♯"(a"); Tess-M; 2/4, Allegretto giocoso; 8pp; Diff-V/m, P/m.

For: tenor

Mood: high-spirited; tells story; hearty

Voice: stepwise and small skips; opt. sustained a" at end; some dotted rhythms

Piano: afterbeat pattern; prelude; several short interludes; accidentals

Uses: to end a group of period songs

Rec: D#52

BULLARD, FREDERIC FIELD
(b. Boston, MA, 1864; d. Boston, MA, 1904)

364. BEAM FROM YONDER STAR. A Serenade (William Prescott Foster). [58]; 1st©1896. H & L keys: Amaj & Gmaj (orig.); d♯'–g♯" & c♯'–f♯"; Tess-M; 3/4, Poco Larghetto; 3pp; Diff-V/m, P/me.

For: tenor

Mood: lyrical; serenade

Voice: scalar lines with easy skips; soaring

Piano: chordal; some arpeggiation; some repeated chords; syncopation; does not double vocal line

Diff: rhythmic freedom; good dynamic control

Uses: good lyric song

365. HERE'S A HEALTH TO THEE, ROBERTS! (Richard Hovey). Boston Music Co., 1897. Fmaj; B♭–f'; Tess-mH; 2/4, Andante con moto; 5pp; Diff-V/md, P/m.

For: baritone (high, but not light)

Mood: hearty, masculine drinking song

Voice: 16th-note scales and chord-member skips of up to10th; many 8ve leaps; dotted rhythms; several long melismas

Piano: linear-chordal combination; many short 16th-note scales; moves around keyboard; some doubling of vocal line

Diff: flexibility; scales involve false sequence; repeated high e's and f's

Uses: harmonically interesting; fun to sing; group ender

366. THE INDIFFERENT MARINER (Arthur Macy). Ditson, 1898. E♭maj; G–e♭'; Tess-M; 4/4, Andante non troppo; 5pp; Diff-V/m-md, P/m.

For: bass; bass-baritone

Mood: sailor's song; crusty; "devil-may-care"
Voice: stepwise and easy skips; repetition and sequence;
dotted rhythms; triplets; one melisma ends refrain
Piano: linear-chordal combination; scale passages; 8ve
passages; accidentals; doubles vocal line
Diff: flexibility; characterization
Uses: vigorous masculine song; could close a group

BURGE, DAVID
(b. Evanston, IL, 1930)

367. **A SONG OF SIXPENCE.** Broude, 1969. cmp1967. X;
g–c♯'''; Tess-not applicable; unmetered; 10min; Diff-
V/dd, P/dd.
For: soprano
Mood: various moods
Voice: avant-garde techniques: wide range; extreme dynamics;
speaking; humming; vocalizing; laughing; movement
from one "station" to another; gestures; sarna bell and
gong played; finger snapping; strumming of piano
strings; many words and syllables possibly Japanese,
possibly meaningless; some English words
Piano: avant-garde techniques: cluster chords; rapid repeated
notes; glissando; pedal techniques; section of Pierre
Boulez' *Sonate III*; finger-snapping; hand-clapping;
laughing; some acting
Diff: vocal and pianistic techniques per se, plus the lack of
inhibition to follow the extra-musical directions; singer
needs easy access to wide vocal and expressive ranges
Uses: interesting piece; usable for those wishing to explore
the realm of the avant-garde

BURLEIGH, HENRY THACKER
(b. Erie, PA, 1866; d. Stamford, CT, 1949)

[See also D#s 67, 69, & 126 for songs not listed below]

368. **FIVE SONGS OF LAURENCE HOPE.** G. Ricordi,
1915. Reprint: Classical Vocal Reprints. Major and
minor keys; d'–b♭''; Tess-M-H; simple meters; mostly
slow tempos; 20pp; Diff-V/m-md, P/m-md.
For: tenor
Mood: nostalgic; past love remembered with emotion; love
and death
Voice: uncomplicated rhythms–some speech-like, many
dotted; irregular phrase lengths as in poems; melody
well grounded in harmonic plan; many color chords
and modulations; skips up to 8ve; many dynamic
markings; options for some high notes in (c.) & (e.)
Piano: interesting harmonies, 7th & 9th chords, some
augmented triads; fairly thick texture at times, with
chord/broken chord combinations; syncopation; often
doubles vocal line; 2–8 meas. preludes and 2–4 meas.
postludes in each song; four have interludes; some
large reaches
Diff: some pitch patterns; many high notes for some singers–
(e.) has two 3-count b♭"s and two a"s
Uses: an interesting recital group; unexpected harmonic
touches; romanticism; poem of (a.) uses "thee" and
"thou," otherwise not dated

Rec: D#127

   a. ***Worth While.*** Dmaj; d'–a"; Tess-mH; 3/4, Andante
cantabile; 3pp. [**Rec:** D#70]
   b. ***The Jungle Flower.*** Fmin; f'–f"; Tess-mH; 3/4,
Larghetto (♩ = 80); 4pp.
   c. ***Kashmiri Song.*** Bmin; e♭b'–a"(e"); Tess-M/mH
(opt. notes); 4/4, Mesto quasi Andantino; 4pp.
   d. ***Among the Fuchsias.*** Fmin; e'–g"; Tess-H; 3/4,
Andante teneramente; 4pp. [**Rec:** D#70]
   e. ***Till I Wake.*** Dmin; e'–b♭"; Tess-H; 3/4, 2/4,
Larghetto; 5pp. [**Rec:** D#70]

369. **THE GREY WOLF** (Arthur Symons). G. Ricordi,
1915. Reprint: Classical Vocal Reprints. Gmin-maj;
b♭–g"; Tess-M; 4/4, Moderato; 10pp; Diff-V/m, P/m.
For: high baritone; tenor (dramatic)
Mood: romantic desperation; symbolic of the ravenous
demands of addiction
Voice: dramatic lines; skips and leaps along chord lines; some
chromaticism; some long phrases; long sustained g" in
penultimate phrase; syllabic
Piano: patterned chordal texture; syncopated inner voice
chords with 8ve melody in r.h. that sometimes doubles,
sometimes counters vocal line; romantic harmonies
with color chords
Diff: perhaps conveying the symbolism
Uses: a big song; could group with other Symons poems
Rec: D#125

370. **JEAN** (Frank L. Stanton). William Maxwell Co., 1903.
Reprint: Classical Vocal Reprints. D♭maj; d♭'–f";
Tess-M; 3/4, Fervently, with good rhythm; 3pp; Diff-
V/me, P/me.
For: high baritone; tenor
Mood: lyrical love song; nostalgic
Voice: straightforward rhythms and melody; some dotted
notes; some accidentals; a b a' form
Piano: chords and some arpeggiation; often doubles vocal line;
accidentals; 4-meas. prelude
Diff: perhaps reading double flats and finding those intervals
for some students
Uses: very nice student song; quiet encore or in Burleigh art-
song group

371. **PASSIONALE** (James Weldon Johnson). Four Songs
for Tenor. G. Ricordi, 1915. Reprint: Classical Vocal
Reprints, 2000. Traditional keys; e'–b♭"; Tess-M-mH;
regular meters; moderate tempos; 16pp; Diff-V/m-md,
P/m.
For: tenor
Mood: romantic praise of the beloved's eyes, lips, face, voice,
and smile; the devastation of her betrayal
Voice: extremely lyrical, flowing, and expressive vocal lines;
repeated phrases in different harmonic colors; short to
medium phrases; some chromaticism; syllabic; some
soft high passages
Piano: chordal in various patterns, some countermelody; some
syncopated patterns with melody in top voice; abrupt
modulations, similar to Hugo Wolf; subtle harmonic
differences in chords of similar phrases
Diff: subtle harmonic differences and abrupt modulations

Uses: lovely set of early 20th-century romantic style with unusual and interesting harmonic coloration; good for a warm tenor voice capable of projecting passion with delicacy

    a. *Her Eyes Twin Pools.* "To Mr. John McCormack." Gmaj; g'–g"; Tess-mH; 4/4, Andante con moto; 3pp.

    b. *Your Lips Are Wine.* Gmin; f'–b♭"; Tess-M; 3/4, Maestoso; 4pp.

    c. *Your Eyes So Deep.* Gmin; f♯'–g"; Tess-M; 3/4, Andante sostenuto; 5pp.

    d. *The Glory of the Day Was in Her Face.* "To Mr. George Hamlin." E♭maj; e'–g"; Tess-M; 3/4, Andante cantabile; 4pp.

372. THE SAILOR'S WIFE (Mary Stewart Cutting). G. Ricordi, 1917. Reprint: Classical Vocal Reprints. A♭maj; e♭'–f"; Tess-M; 3/4, Andante sostenuto; 6pp; Diff-V/m, P/m.

For: soprano; mezzo-soprano
Mood: dramatic
Voice: melody somewhat chromatic; dotted rhythms; many rests; mostly syllabic; large dynamic range
Piano: block chords, many 7th & 9th chords; some arpeggiation; text painting with some rolled chords, tremolo, trills, short fast chromatic scales in l.h.; cross-hands; register changes; rarely doubles vocal line; 4-meas. prelude; two interludes
Diff: voice mainly independent of piano; some rhythms; ensemble
Uses: recital song in romantic style
Rec: D#125

373. SARACEN SONGS (Fred G. Bowles). G. Ricordi, 1914. Reprint: Classical Vocal Reprints. Traditional keys; d♭'–a"; Tess-M–mH; regular meters; moderate tempos; 19pp; Diff-V/m, P/me–m.

For: soprano; tenor
Mood: romantic Orientalism; love songs in a Middle Eastern setting
Voice: lyrical; vocal line follows chord members–many skips, a few larger leaps of 7ths & 8ves; some tritones; sequential construction in numerous phrases; syllabic; easy rhythms; four different characters, one woman and three men; wide dynamic range includes *ff* high notes and some *pp* endings
Piano: chordal construction–some afterbeat rhythmic patterning, a little arpeggiation; unusual harmonies for this period; melodic material sometimes doubles vocal line, sometimes countermelody; some grace notes; syncopation in patterns
Diff: dealing with dated poetic style
Uses: example of Orientalism prevalent during late 19th and early 20th centuries; a good vehicle for undergraduate singers to develop line, dynamic control, and character portrayal in lyrical material; could also be performed as a soprano-tenor cycle
Rec: D#127

    a. *Almona* (Song of Hassan). Amaj; e'–a"; Tess-cs; 3/4, Andante con moto; 3pp.

    b. *O, Night of Dream and Wonder* (Almona's Song).

B♭min–maj; d♭'–f"; Tess-M; 4/4, Molto tranquillo e ben sostenuto; 2pp.

    c. *His Helmet's Blaze* (Almona's Song of Yussouf to Hassan). Amin; g♭'–a"; Tess-mH; 6/8, Allegro agitato; 2pp.

    d. *I Hear His Footsteps, Music Sweet* (Almona's Song of Delight). Emin; d♯'–f"; Tess-M; 3/4, Allegretto ben ritmato; 3pp. [**Rec:** D#125]

    e. *Thou Art Weary* (Almona's Song to Yussouf). G♭maj; d♭'–e♭"; Tess-M; 4/4, Andante cantabile; 2pp.

    f. *This Is Nirvana* (Yussouf's Song to Almona). E♭maj; e♭'–g"; Tess-mH; 6/8, Allegretto; 3pp.

    g. *Ahmed's Song of Farewell.* Bmin-maj; e'–a"; Tess-mH; 3/4, 4/4, Andante doloroso; 4pp.

374. THREE SHADOWS (Dante Gabriel Rossetti). G. Ricordi, 1916. Reprint: Classical Vocal Reprints. A♭maj; c'–e♭"; Tess-mL; 3/4, Andante cantabile; 6pp; Diff-V/m, P/m.

For: baritone
Mood: love song, lyrical with dramatic climax
Voice: easy rhythms, some dotted and tied; mostly conjunct; some accidentals; big climax, quiet ending
Piano: block- and broken-chord patterning, some arpeggiation; some doubling of vocal line, some imitation; some thick chords; 4-meas. prelude; two interludes
Diff: dynamic range and control; making the quiet question at the end clear
Uses: in a group of Burleigh songs, or a group of songs by various composers on poems of D. G. Rossetti; text slightly dated

BUSCH, CARL
(b. Bjerre, Denmark, 1862; d. Kansas City, MO, 1943)

375. ORPHEUS WITH HIS LUTE (William Shakespeare). [26]; 1st©1903. Gmaj; c♯'–g"; Tess-M; 3/4, Allegretto; 3pp; Diff-V/m, P/me.

For: soprano; tenor
Mood: lyrical; tribute to music
Voice: stepwise and easy skips; some sustained tones
Piano: chordal, 4–5-voice texture; some doubling of vocal line
Uses: to teach mood changes; suitable for performance

376. UNDER THE GREENWOOD TREE (William Shakespeare). [26]; 1st©1900. "To George Hamlin." Gmaj; d'–g"; Tess-M; 4/4, Allegretto; 3pp; Diff-V/e, P/me.

For: tenor
Mood: hearty; cheerful
Voice: stepwise and easy skips; somewhat fragmented; lyrical and dancing
Piano: chordal; some countermelody; articulation important; does not double vocal line
Diff: some rhythms; sustained high tones
Uses: effective song; recital use

BYRON, CARL (See entry #15 L)

CADMAN, CHARLES WAKEFIELD
(b. Johnstown PA, 1881; d. Los Angeles, CA, 1946)

377. AS IN A ROSE JAR (Thomas S. Jones, Jr.). Reprint: T.I.S., 1998. Fmaj; d'–f"; Tess-mH; 4/4; 3pp; Diff-V/m, P/m.

For: tenor seems best
Mood: nostalgic
Voice: many small skips; some larger intervals, up to 8ve; mainly 8th- & quarter-note rhythms; syllabic
Piano: chords in 8th- & quarter-note motion–many span 8ve in r.h.; some accidentals; some doubling of vocal line
Diff: skips in melody will challenge some singers
Uses: somewhat dated, but a nice period song; first or second year material

378. AT DAWNING, Op. 29, No. 1 (Nelle Richmond Eberhart). [87]; 1st©1906. H & M keys: A♭maj & G♭maj; e♭'–g" & d♭'–f"; Tess-mH; 3/4; 2pp; Diff-V/me, P/m.

For: any high or medium voice
Mood: a well-known love song using nature imagery
Voice: lyrical with frequent intervals of 4th or larger; a few accidentals; two strophes
Piano: block, broken, and rolled chords with melodic material; doubles vocal line at climax of each strophe, otherwise supports it clearly
Uses: possible use in a variety of situations
Rec: D#s 47, 69

379. COULD ROSES SPEAK, Op. 26, No. 1 (George R. Rose). [87]; 1st ©1906. H & M keys: Gmaj & E♭maj; d'–f"& b♭–d"; Tess-mL; 4/4, Moderato e con gusto; 3pp; Diff-V/m, P/me.

For: any voice
Mood: sweetly sentimental and old-fashioned love song
Voice: lyrical but somewhat disjunct; characterized by 8ve leaps up and down; some 6ths & 7ths
Piano: chordal with some countermelodic material; some accidentals; supports vocal line clearly, no doubling
Diff: large intervals for the singer; warm (but not heavy) low tones needed
Uses: useful for learning to maintain legato in large intervals; possible performance use

380. FROM THE LAND OF THE SKY-BLUE WATER (from *Four American Indian Songs*, Op. 45) (Nelle Richmond Eberhart). White-Smith, 1909. Reprints: Classical Vocal Reprints (H & L); Masters Music Publications. [5]. A♭maj; e♭'–e♭"; Tess-M; 3/4, Moderately; 4pp; Diff-V/me; P/me.

For: any high or medium voice; mezzo-soprano best
Mood: descriptive; sad love song
Voice: characterized by a 16th/dotted-8th rhythm; one m7th
Piano: chordal; characterized by a 16th/dotted-8th rhythm; imitation of Native American flute at beginning and end; supports vocal line well
Uses: a good example of the pseudo-Native American style and subject matter popular in the early 20th century; useful from a historical standpoint
Rec: D#s 43, 46, 52

381. I HEAR A THRUSH AT EVE (Serenade) (Nelle Richmond Eberhart). White-Smith, 1913. Reprint: Classical Vocal Reprints. "Written for my friend John McCormack." H, M, & L keys: A♭maj, Fmaj, & E♭maj; e♭'–a♭", c'–f", & b♭–e♭"; Tess-M; 3/4, Grazioso anima; 45meas; Diff-V/m, P/m.

For: any male voice; best for tenor
Mood: waltz-like; slightly Viennese
Voice: leaps; some conjunct motion; fermatas
Piano: waltz rhythm; 3rds in r.h.; parallel chords; ornaments
Diff: good taste with style
Uses: effective if tastefully done; perhaps a good encore

382. IN A GARDEN (Douglas Hemingway). [87]; 1st ©1906. H & M keys: E♭maj & Cmaj; d'–g" & b–e"; Tess-M; 3/4, Tempo rubato; 2pp; Diff-V/me, P/me.

For: any high or medium male voice
Mood: old-fashioned love song using nature imagery
Voice: lyrical and legato, with some large intervals; flexible tempos and rhythms
Piano: chordal; doubles vocal line throughout much of song
Uses: possible performance use

383. LILACS (Nelle Richmond Eberhart). Presser, 1912. H & L keys: Fmaj & Dmaj; c'–f" & a–d"; Tess-M; 3/4, Moderato cantabile; 4pp; Diff-V/me, P/me.

For: medium or low voice
Mood: lyrical; history of the lilac
Voice: stepwise and small skips; repetitive rhythms, some dotted
Piano: chordal; afterbeat pattern; doubles vocal line
Uses: somewhat sentimental and dated; usable in a historical group

384. MEMORIES (Nelle Richmond Eberhart). [87]; 1st ©1906. H & M keys: A♭maj & Fmaj; d♭'–f" & b♭–d"; Tess-M; 4/4, Andante affettuoso; 3pp; Diff-V/me, P/me.

For: any male voice
Mood: tender song on the death of a beloved
Voice: lyrical and legato with a few large intervals
Piano: chordal; melodic and countermelodic material; incidental doubling of vocal line; some accidentals
Diff: downward leaps of m7th in vocal line
Uses: possible performance use

385. THE MOON BEHIND THE COTTONWOOD (from the Song Cycle, *The Morning of the Year*) (Nelle Richmond Eberhard). G. Schirmer, 1910. H & L keys: Cmaj & Gmaj ; e'–g" & b–d"; Tess-M; 4/4, Allegro moderato; Diff-V/m, P/m.

For: all voices
Mood: lyrical; increasingly ecstatic love song
Voice: soaring vocal line
Piano: repeated chords
Uses: usable for teaching student to soar and build long ascent to emotional climax

386. A MOONLIGHT SONG, Op. 42, No. 2 (John Proctor Mills). [14, 48]; 1st©1908. H, M, & L keys: G♭maj, E♭maj, & Cmaj [14]; f♭'–a♭", d'–f", & b–d"; Tess-mH; 2/2, Andante sostenuto; 2pp; Diff-V/m, P/m.

For: any male voice
Mood: lyrical; ecstatic love song
Voice: broadly flowing
Piano: chordal; somewhat chromatic; supports vocal line without doubling
Diff: *mezza-voce*; high tessitura of last phrase; soft dynamics
Uses: good for teaching soft, floating tone quality

387. MY LOVELY ROSE, Op. 26, No. 2 (Flora W. Thomas). [87]; 1st©1906. H & M keys: Fmaj & Dmaj; c'–f''("e") & a–d''; Tess-M; 4/4, Andante moderato; 4pp; Diff-V/me, P/e.
For: any voice
Mood: love song using rose imagery
Voice: lyrical; mostly conjunct motion with small intervals; a few large leaps that are not difficult; short phrases, several high in the range
Piano: chordal; vocal line doubled throughout much of song, often in an inner voice
Uses: nice example of early 20th-century style

CAGE, JOHN
(b. Los Angeles, CA, 1912; d. New York, NY, 1992)

[See also D#s 131 & 132; no titles given]

388. 5 SONGS FOR CONTRALTO (e. e. cummings). Henmar (facsimile), 1960. cmp1938. X; g♭–f♯''; Tess-L; changing meters; fast tempos; 12min; Diff-V/d, P/dd.
For: contralto; mezzo-soprano with easy, strong low voice
Mood: innocent, child-like expressions
Voice: fairly conjunct; lines stay around bottom of staff most of the time; (b.), several melismas; (c.), only three pitches, chant-like; (d.), ends with scales on "whee!"; (e.), shortest and most chromatic; score very difficult to read (printed texts included on separate page)
Piano: complex score, difficult to read; many accidentals; (a.), some passages in double 3rds; (b.), most difficult–linear, fragmentary, rhythmically complex; (d.), uses wide range of the keyboard; (e.), entirely in treble clef; highly independent of vocal line
Diff: pitches; rhythms; ensemble; extremely rapid tempos with constantly changing meters
Uses: for the advanced musician interested in the early avant-garde; perfect pitch desirable; good for true contralto; interesting settings of these texts
Rec: D#4

  a. *little four-paws.* X; b♭–c''; Tess-mL; changing meters, ♪ = 120; 2+pp. **[Rec: D#58]**
  b. *little christmas tree.* X; g♭–e''; Tess-L; changing meters, ♪ = 106; 9pp.
  c. *in just-spring.* X; a–c'; Tess-L; changing meters, ♩ = 152; 4pp.
  d. *hist whist.* X; g–f♯''; Tess-L; changing meters, ♩ = 200; 4+pp.
  e. *another comes.* X; g–c''; Tess-L; changing meters, ♩ = 60; 1p.

389. A FLOWER. Henmar, 1960. cmp1950. X (but built

around G); c'–c''; (can be transposed to any pitch level, should be "low and comfortable"); Tess-M; 5/4, ♩ = 84; 4min; Diff-V/d, P/md.
For: mezzo-soprano; soprano
Mood: vocalise using vowels and syllables
Voice: only c', g', a', b', and c'' are used; many special effects relating to dynamics and vibrato; instructions preceding song; generally soft dynamic level
Piano: played on closed piano; instructions given for two levels, fingers or knuckles
Diff: special vocal effects; control of soft dynamics
Uses: in modern group; for singer with good musicianship and interest in the unusual and avant-garde; large range or tonal beauty not required
Rec: D#s 128, 129, 130, 133

390. THE WONDERFUL WIDOW OF EIGHTEEN SPRINGS (James Joyce). C. F. Peters, 1961. X (but built around A); a'–e'' (can be transposed to any pitch level–should be "low and comfortable"); Tess-M (composer wants L); 4/4, ♩ = 58; 2min; Diff-V/d, P/md.
For: mezzo-soprano
Mood: intense, though quiet
Voice: pitches are all a', b', and e''; rhythmically complicated
Piano: played on closed piano; instructions given; for four levels, fingers or knuckles
Diff: rhythms; no pitch support for singer
Uses: useful in a modern group, or perhaps as an "awakener"
Rec: D#s 129, 130, 133

CALABRO, LOUIS
(b. Brooklyn, NY, 1926)

391. MACABRE REFLECTIONS (Howard Nemerov). A Cycle of Six Songs for Mezzo-soprano and Piano. Elkan-Vogel, 1969. X; g♭–g''; Tess-L, H; mostly regular but changing meters; varied tempos, begins and ends slow; 16min; Diff-V/d, P/md.
For: mezzo-soprano; contralto
Mood: macabre reflections on one's own death
Voice: many skips and leaps; conjunct passages often chromatic; low on the staff and below much of the time; many accidentals; much use of chest voice necessary; a few high tones; pitch perception sometimes difficult; speech rhythms; whispering
Piano: linear; fairly thin texture; much 8ve doubling; glissando; parallel chords; pictorial; frequent doubling of vocal line
Diff: pitch; nature of poetry–very personal; perhaps difficult to interpret with the proper distance
Uses: for a mature singer

  a. *The Ground Swayed.* b♭–f''; 4/4, 5/4, 6/4, Adagio; 3pp.
  b. *The Officer.* c'–f♯''; 4/4, Allegro; 3pp.
  c. *Each a Rose.* [16]. c'–g''; 5/4, Slow; 2pp.
  d. *No More Than Dust.* g♭–f♯''; 2/4, 3/8, 5/8, 6/8, Presto; 5pp.
  e. *It Is Forbidden.* [16]. c'–g''; 3/2, 3/4, 5/4, 7/4, Lento; 3pp.
  f. *The Sunlight Pierced.* a♭–e''; 4/4, Molto adagio.

CAMPBELL-TIPTON, LOUIS
(b. Chicago, IL, 1877; d. Paris, France, 1921)

392.   AT THE TOMB (Walt Whitman). Boston Music Co., 1918. Amaj; d'–a"; Tess-mH; 2/2, Molto appassionato, non strascinando; Diff-V/md, P/md.
For: tenor
Mood: dramatic; lament
Voice: declamatory
Piano: descriptive
Diff: high tones; declamatory style
Uses: for teaching and possible programming

393.   ELEGY (Walt Whitman). Boston Music Co., 1918. Reprint: Classical Vocal Reprints (H). H & L keys: F♯min & Emin; c♯'–f♯"(b") & b–e"(a"); Tess-mL; 3/4, Moderato; 5pp; Diff-V/md, P/m.
For: baritone; tenor; possibly contralto, mezzo-soprano, or dramatic soprano
Mood: dramatic; declamatory
Voice: many skips; duplets and triplets
Piano: chordal; duplets and triplets; chromatic lines; articulations important; grace notes; large dynamic contrasts; 2 vs. 3
Diff: pitches; rhythms; ensemble
Uses: for big voice with dramatic expressive abilities; quiet ending

394.   FOUR SEA LYRICS (Arthur Symons). Cycle. Wa-Wan Press, 1907. Reprint: Classical Vocal Reprints (H). [53, vol. 4]. "Written for and Dedicated to George Hamlin." Traditional key structures with late Romantic harmonies, French coloration; d'–a"; Tess-M-mH; compound meters; varied tempos; 21pp; Diff-V/d, P/md.
For: tenor (very full romantic sound needed)
Mood: lyrical; moods of the sea reflect poet's moods
Voice: typical Romantic vocal line: skips and leaps along modulating chord lines; many loud high climaxes; also much soft singing; many expressive markings
Piano: Romantic keyboard techniques; wide range of dynamics and color; many expressive markings
Diff: wide dynamic range; sustained phrases and high tones; for advanced singers only
Uses: a good work; for Romantic group on program; could be thrilling with the right voice

   a. *After Sunset.* [5]. Emaj; d♯'–a"; Tess-M; 6/8, Andante espressivo; 4pp.
   b. *Darkness.* Bmin; d'–a"; Tess-M; 6/8, 2/4, Allegro moderato–Andante misterioso; 6pp.
   c. *The Crying of Water.* [29, 48]. Bmaj; f♯'–g♯"; Tess-H; 12/8, Moderato ma con passione; 5pp.
   d. *Requies.* Emaj; e'–a"; Tess-mH; 12/8, Andante; 6pp.

395.   I WILL GIVE THANKS UNTO THE LORD, Op. 25, No. 2 (Psalm IX:1, 2, 10). G. Schirmer, 1936. H, M, & L keys: D♭, B♭, & A♭; d♭'–a♭", b♭–f", & a♭–e♭"; Tess-M-mH; 4/4, Moderato; 40meas.; Diff-V/md, P/m.
For: any voice that can sustain the high tones
Mood: reverent
Voice: most phrases cover an 8ve or more; many 2-note slurs; dramatic, sustained high tones
Piano: chordal, broken and repeated; syncopated; countermelody; some doubling of vocal line
Diff: intense high tones; dynamics
Uses: suitable for recital

396.   THE OPIUM-SMOKER: Tone Poem (Arthur Symons). G. Schirmer, 1907. Reprint: Classical Vocal Reprints. Modulatory, ends F♯maj; c'–f♯"; Tess-mH, cs; 12/8, Allegro molto (♩ = 70 maximum); 7pp; Diff-V/md, P/md.
For: tenor
Mood: impressionistic; romantic; dramatic picture of both the timeless high and the desperate low of the opium addict
Voice: both sustained phrases and speech-like phrases; extreme dynamics (*pp* followed by *ff*) and all in between express the opium dream state; syllabic; dramatic; chromatic
Piano: arpeggiation; chromatic l.h. scales; chordal; repeated chords; tremolo; many dynamic and expressive markings; modulatory; some melodic material in 2 vs. 3 with the accomp. pattern; big, romantic-impressionistic piano scoring
Diff: ensemble; dynamic range; some polyrhythms; some *ppp* high notes; needs many vocal colors and a good sense of drama
Uses: an interesting song of its style period; perhaps use in a group of French-influenced composers; needs mature singer

397.   RHAPSODIE, Op. 32, No. 1 (Walt Whitman). G. Schirmer, 1913. Reprint: Classical Vocal Reprints. E-Bmaj; d'–a"; Tess-cs; 6/8, Very fast, with joyous abandon (♩. = 80); 7pp; Diff-V/md, P/md.
For: tenor; soprano
Mood: joyful paean to the beauty of the earth
Voice: romantic, sweeping lines; chordal outlining; some 8ve leaps in each direction; syllabic; sustained g♯" cresc. *mf–ff*; key changes
Piano: downward arpeggiation; some short 8ve passages; some afterbeat figurations; changing keys and shifting harmonies; quiet ending
Diff: some odd word stresses; some large intervals
Uses: a big romantic song; different approach to Whitman; useful in a mixed-composer Whitman group

398.   A SPIRIT FLOWER (B. Martin Stanton; German text also). G. Schirmer. Reprint: Classical Vocal Reprints (H, M, & L). [29]. Emaj-Emin; b–g"; Tess-M; 4/4, Moderato; 4pp; Diff-V/m, P/md.
For: mezzo-soprano; soprano
Mood: dramatic poem about the death of a loved one
Voice: conjunct motion and small intervals with several larger leaps (incl. 8ves) within a phrase; powerful long tones on f♯" and g"; one low b has alternative, but not the other; a few accidentals
Piano: chordal with melodic material in prelude, interludes, and postlude; broken-chord figures and afterbeats; numerous accidentals; supports vocal line, doubling through much of song
Diff: young soprano will need both a well-developed high voice and a usable low b; avoidance of sentimentality

Uses: performance material for a tasteful singer

CARPENTER, JOHN ALDEN
(b. Park Ridge, IL, 1876; d. Chicago, IL, 1951)

399.   BID ME TO LIVE (Robert Herrick; French version by Maurice Maeterlinck). [88]; 1st©1912. D♭maj; b♭–d"; Tess-M; 4/4, Lento; 2min; Diff-V/m, P/m.
For: mezzo-soprano; contralto; baritone; bass
Mood: love-song; dedication
Voice: afterbeat entrances; repetitive rhythms; dotted notes; accidentals
Piano: chordal–block, repeated, arpeggiated; some cross-hands; accidentals; does not double vocal line
Uses: romantic style and mood; good singing song

400.   THE COCK SHALL CROW (DITTY) (Robert Louis Stevenson). Charles Scribner's Sons, 1896. Reprint: Classical Vocal Reprints. [88]. Amaj; b–e"; Tess-M; 2/2, Animato (♩ = 126); 3pp; Diff-V/e, P/me.
For: tenor; high baritone
Mood: somewhat jaunty in a folk-like way, but with sad undertones
Voice: straightforward syllabic setting; folk-like tempo fluctuations; stepwise and chordal skips; one 8ve leap down; sustained e"
Piano: running 8th notes in r.h. over 2-note chords or single notes in l.h.; some tempo fluctuations
Uses: easy song for young beginning student

401.   A CRADLE SONG (William Blake). [88]; 1st©1912. A♭maj; c'–e♭"; Tess-M; 4/4, Largo; 3min; Diff-V/e, P/e.
For: mezzo-soprano; contralto
Mood: tranquil; lullaby
Voice: stepwise and small skips; relatively motionless; many long notes; easy rhythms
Piano: chordal; some countermelody; center section has rocking bass; quiet
Diff: long, soft phrases
Uses: nice cradle song

402.   THE DAY IS NO MORE (Rabindranath Tagore). G. Schirmer, 1915. Reprints: Classical Vocal Reprints (L); Masters Music Publications. cmp1914. G♯min; g♯–d♯"; Tess-mL; 3/4, Larghetto (♩ = 80); 4pp; Diff-V/m, P/m.
For: contralto
Mood: lyrical; melancholy nature picture
Voice: broad, sustained phrases; many long notes; some phrases broken by rests
Piano: chordal, like plucked lute; independent melody in dotted rhythm; does not double vocal line
Diff: some odd declamation must be handled with care; 4-meas. sustained low g♯
Uses: good recital material for contralto with rich voice

403.   FOG WRAITHS (Mildred Howells). [89];1st©1913. Emin, shifting harmonies; b–d"; Tess-mL; 4/4, Lento Mistico; 4pp; Diff-V/m, P/m.
For: bass; contralto; baritone; mezzo-soprano

Mood: ghostly; those lost at sea return to homes and graves when sea fog rolls in
Voice: stepwise and small skips; one descending M7th and one ascending 8ve; ends low; slow, sustained phrases; syllabic; soft dynamics (p–mf)
Piano: chordal; ostinato ♩♩♩ pattern in first and last sections; middle section changes to quarter-note movement; modulatory; numerous accidentals; dynamics pp–mf
Diff: sustaining intensity at soft dynamic levels with an even flow of sound
Uses: fine song for bass or contralto; good recital material

404.   GITANJALI (Song-Offerings) (Rabindranath Tagore). Cycle. G. Schirmer, 1914. Reprints: Masters Music Publications; T.I.S. (a. & c., Med.). cmp1913. Traditional keys; b♭–g"; Tess-M-mH; regular meters; varied tempos; 35pp; Diff-V/md, P/d.
For: mezzo-soprano; some sopranos
Mood: rich images of life with philosophical overtones
Voice: opulent vocal line both melodically and harmonically; many long phrases in the middle range; some sustained high tones; rhythms flexible, but not difficult (French influence); ends on g" fff
Piano: Impressionistic keyboard techniques; parallel chords; tremolo and arpeggiation; running 16th-note figures, etc.; rich score; solid technique plus great sensitivity to tonal colors needed; many tempo changes, much rubato
Diff: vocal endurance for the whole cycle; proper capturing of moods and meaning of poetry; ensemble
Uses: fine work for an opulent mezzo-soprano voice; mature singer with strong, warm middle register best; cycle could end program; good teaching material for students of various levels
Rec: D#134

   a.   *When I Bring to You Colour'd Toys.* [5, 20]. F♯maj; c♯'–f♯"; 3/4, Animato; 5pp. [**Rec:** D#s 2, 10, 69, 137, 138]
   b.   *On the Day When Death Will Knock at Thy Door.* Dmin; c'–f "; 4/4, Grave maestoso; 3pp.
   c.   *The Sleep That Flits on Baby's Eyes.* [2, 25, 32, 41]. Dmaj; b–f♯"; 2/2, 3/2, 4/4, Lento–Poco più animato; 3pp. [**Rec:** D#s 5, 11]
   d.   *I Am like a Remnant of a Cloud of Autumn.* B♭min-D♭maj; b♭–f "; Grave; 5pp.
   e.   *On the Seashore of Endless Worlds.* A♭maj; c'–f♯"; 4/4, 6/8, Andantino, con moto grazioso; 11pp. [**Rec:** D#s 2, 11]
   f.   *Light, My Light.* Cmaj; e'–g"; 3/4, Presto giocoso; 8pp. [**Rec:** D#69]

405.   GO, LOVELY ROSE (Edmund Waller). G. Schirmer, 1912. Reprint: Classical Vocal Reprints (M). [88]. D♭maj; d♭'–e♭"; Tess-M; 2/4, 4/4, Larghetto grazioso; 2+min; Diff-V/m, P/m.
For: baritone best; some tenors
Mood: lyrical
Voice: some skips; duplets and triplets; some dotted rhythms; duplets vs. piano triplets
Piano: chordal, block- and broken-chord triplets; some doubling of vocal line
Diff: polyrhythms

Uses: nice song for American group

406. **THE GREEN RIVER** (Lord Alfred Douglas). G. Schirmer, 1912. Reprints: Classical Vocal Reprints (M); T.I.S. (M). [88]. Bmaj; b–e"; Tess-mL; 4/4, 3/4, Slowly (♩ = 60)–Più animato (♩ = 92); 4pp; Diff-V/m-md, P/m-md.

For: mezzo-soprano; baritone
Mood: lyrical; idyllic; philosophical; melancholy
Voice: sustained; soft singing; fairly chromatic; loud climax
Piano: chordal, rolled and arpeggiated; spare texture; chromatic; independent of voice
Diff: mood creation
Uses: good song for teaching and programming

407. **THE HEART'S COUNTRY** (Florence Wilkinson). Ditson, 1912. H & L keys: Amin & Fmin; e'–g" & c'–eb"; Tess-mH; 4/4, 3/4, Andante (♩ = 66); 2pp; Diff-V/m, P/m.

For: soprano; mezzo-soprano; tenor
Mood: lyrical; philosophical love song
Voice: short phrases; triplets; some chromaticism
Piano: chordal; repetitive; countermelody in inner voices
Diff: rhythms

408. **HER VOICE** (Oscar Wilde). [89]; 1st©1913. Ebmaj; b–g"; Tess-M; 3/4, Allegro giocoso (♩ = 152); 6pp; Diff-V/m, P/m.

For: mezzo-soprano
Mood: rueful but calm; the end of a love relationship between two lovers who need a bigger world
Voice: mostly conjunct; two or three leaps of 6th; syllabic; numerous repeated-note phrases; some low phrases; final note choice of g" or bb'
Piano: 5-meas. prelude presents a happy 16th/8th-note motive that accompanies the first section and returns at two points and in the 5-meas. postlude; second and third stanzas slower in repeated chords and then a syncopated figure suggesting the passage of time; some l.h. arpeggios; modulatory
Diff: syncopation in piano may confuse some inexperienced singers
Uses: an excellent song; interesting musical treatment of the poem; needs singer who can make the listeners feel they are the characters being presented

409. **IN SPRING** ("It was a lover and his lass") (William Shakespeare). Stevens, 1896. Amaj; b–f#"; Tess-M; 4/4, Animato; 3pp; Diff-V/m, P/m-md.

For: baritone; mezzo-soprano
Mood: lighthearted; cheerful
Voice: stepwise and easy skips; dotted rhythms; 2-note slurs
Piano: chordal; accidentals; several long pedal tones; some doubling of vocal line
Diff: fermata on f#"
Uses: lively song; very different in style from Carpenter's later, better-known songs

410. **LITTLE FLY** (William Blake). G. Schirmer, 1912. Reprint: Classical Vocal Reprints (M). [88]. Dbmaj; c'–db"; Tess-M; 3/4, 2/4, Allegretto grazioso; 1min; Diff-V/m, P/md.

For: baritone
Mood: analogy; philosophical
Voice: mostly stepwise; some dotted rhythms
Piano: broken-chord pattern in 16ths; no vocal line doubling
Uses: usable recital song

411. **LITTLE JOHN'S SONG** (Nora Hopper). Stevens, 1897. Gmaj; d'–f#"; Tess-mL; 6/8, Allegretto; 5pp; Diff-V/m, P/m.

For: baritone with ample sound
Mood: hearty; full of spirit
Voice: stepwise and chord-member skips; easy rhythms; 2-note slurs
Piano: chordal; some countermelody; staccato; many accidentals; does not double vocal line
Diff: dynamic control (pp–ff)
Uses: effective song; group ender; quite different in style from Carpenter's later songs

412. **LOOKING-GLASS RIVER** (Robert Louis Stevenson). G. Schirmer, 1912. Reprint: Classical Vocal Reprints (M). [5, 48, 88]. H & L keys: Fmaj & Dmaj; d'(c')–f"; & b(a)–d"; Tess-M; 4/4, Largo (♩ = 44); 3pp; Diff-V/m, P/md.

For: all voices
Mood: lyrical; peaceful; nature picture
Voice: broadly flowing; several large intervals
Piano: chordal; arpeggiation; some chromaticism; syncopation
Diff: large intervals taken softly
Uses: good for teaching soft, legato style; fine recital song
Rec: D#59

413. **MAY, THE MAIDEN** (Sidney Lanier). Oliver Ditson, 1912. Reprint: Classical Vocal Reprints (M). [53]. "To Miss Maggie Teyte." H & M keys: Fmaj & Dmaj (orig.); d'–g" & b–e"; Tess-mL; 3/4, Largo (♩ = 44); 3pp; Diff-V/me, P/m.

For: baritone; tenor
Mood: lyrical; simple, tender love song; nature imagery
Voice: lyrical and graceful; rocking rhythm
Piano: chordal; rocking rhythm; independent melodic material
Uses: lovely, quiet song for a lyric voice

414. **MORNING FAIR** (James Agee). [51]. cmp1935. D-Dbmaj; c#'–g#"; Tess-M; 3/4, Moderato, many tempo changes; 6pp; Diff-V/md, P/md.

For: soprano
Mood: dramatic; dawn song
Voice: many skips; various rhythmic subdivisions; accidentals
Piano: broken chords; tremolo; some countermelody; many contrasts; does not double vocal line
Diff: sectional construction; sustained high climaxes; dynamic contrasts

415. **THE PLAYER QUEEN** (William Butler Yeats). G. Schirmer, 1915. Reprints: Classical Vocal Reprints (M); T.I.S. (M). Ebmin; bb–f#"; Tess-M; 4/4, Lento; 5pp; Diff-V/m, P/md.

For: mezzo-soprano
Mood: ballad-like; haunting
Voice: conjunct; some melismas; sustained; three stanzas
Piano: patterned ostinato figure l.h.; background for

story-telling

Diff: text somewhat obscure, from an unfinished play; singer should read play for characterization

Uses: a superb song; interesting harmonic changes; very different style from other Carpenter songs

Rec: D#6

416. **REST** (Mable Simpson). [51]. cmp1934. A-centered; c'–g"; Tess-mL; 3/2, 4/4, Lento (♩ = 72); 3pp; Diff-V/m, P/m.

For: soprano; mezzo-soprano

Mood: lyrical; philosophical; nature imagery

Voice: sustained phrases; a few large intervals

Piano: chordal; repetition in inner voices; some independent melodic lines; fairly chromatic

Diff: very sustained phrases

Uses: good for teaching soft high tones and long phrasing

417. **LES SILHOUETTES** (Oscar Wilde). [5, 89]; 1st©1913. E♭maj(long-delayed); d'–g"; Tess-mH; 3/4, Largo mistico; Diff-V/m, P/md; English text.

For: soprano; tenor

Mood: lyrical; descriptive

Voice: long tones in every phrase; sustained

Piano: chordal; descriptive; quiet

Diff: breath control

Uses: beautiful song; good for teaching breath control, steady long tones, and an ear for color

418. **TO ONE UNKNOWN** (Helen Dudley). [89]; 1st©1913. Bmin; a–d#"; Tess-M; 3/2, Moderato; 3+min; Diff-V/m, P/m.

For: baritone; mezzo-soprano

Mood: narrative; mysterious; quiet

Voice: stepwise and easy skips; phrases begin after down-beat; fragmented

Piano: chordal, repeated and broken; various registers; some 8ve passages; does not double vocal line

Diff: ensemble; long tones at phrase endings

Uses: good song; useful for recital

419. **TREAT ME NICE** (Paul Laurence Dunbar). Frank K. Root & Co., 1905. Reprint: Classical Vocal Reprints. [8]. mH & L keys: Gmaj & Dmaj; d'–f#" & a–c#"; Tess-mL; 4/4, Slowly; 3pp; Diff-V/e, P/me.

For: baritone; bass-baritone; bass

Mood: a lover asks his beloved to treat him "nice"; humorously serious

Voice: folk-like with jazz influences; dotted rhythms; syllabic in dialect

Piano: chordal; mild jazz flavor; dotted rhythms; some melodic material in r.h.

Diff: dialect

Uses: easy song for a low voice if dialect is appropriate

420. **TWO NIGHT SONGS** (Siegfried Sassoon). G. Schirmer, 1921. Reprint: T.I.S. (H). cmp1920. [51]. H & L keys: Major keys; b–c"'(a") & a♭–a"(f#"); Tess-mH–H; regular meters, moderate tempos; 15pp; Diff-V/m-d, P/md-d.

For: baritone (orig. key low); tenor; soprano (a. only)

Mood: (a.) lyrical; (b.) dramatic

Voice: broad, flowing phrases; sustained; chromaticism; powerful, high climax

Piano: chordal–broken, afterbeat, thick texture; cross-hands; chromatic; modulating; rich harmonies

Diff: (a.), soft singing; long phrases; (b.), powerful c"'(a")

Uses: excellent songs; work well as a pair for performance purposes; for mature singers with secure technique and endurance

    a. *Slumber-Song.* H & L keys: Emaj & D♭maj (orig.); b–g#" & a♭–f"; Tess-H; 4/4, Slowly–Poco più animato–Poco più lento; 6pp; Diff-V/d, P/d.

    b. *Serenade.* [59]. H & L keys: Fmaj & Dmaj (orig.); c#'–c"'(a") & b♭–a"(f#"); Tess-mH–H; 6/8, 2/4, Moderato; 9pp; Diff-V/d, P/d. [**Rec:** D#s 11, 135]

421. **WATER COLORS.** Four Chinese Tone Poems (trans. from the Chinese by Herbert A. Giles). G. Schirmer, 1916. Reprints: Classical Vocal Reprints; Masters Music Publications. Traditional key structures–impressionistic harmonic colors; b♭–f"; Tess-M; regular meters; varied and flexible tempos; 20pp; Diff-V/m, P/m.

For: mezzo-soprano

Mood: impressionistic; descriptive; humorous

Voice: conjunct movement; long tones at ends of phrases; flexible rhythmic groupings; some ad lib

Piano: sets mood; paints background; delicate

Diff: creation of moods and projection of scenes

Uses: good work for young singer with lovely vocal quality and sensitivity to visual images; could end program humorously

    a. *On a Screen* (Li-Po). Fmin-maj; b♭–d♭"; Tess-mL; 2/2, 3/4, 4/4, Larghetto; 3pp. [**Rec:** D#136]

    b. *The Odalisque* (Yü-hsi). A♭ maj; e♭'–e♭"; Tess-M; 3/4, Grazioso; 5pp. [**Rec:** D#136]

    c. *Highwaymen* (Li-Shê). Dmin-Fmaj; c'–f"; Tess-M; 4/4, Largo; 3pp.

    d. *To a Young Gentleman* (coll. by Confucius). D♭maj; e♭'–e♭"; Tess-M; 4/4, Vivo, giocoso; 7pp.

422. **WHEN THE MISTY SHADOWS GLIDE** (En sourdine) (Paul Verlaine; trans. John Alden Carpenter). Ditson, 1912. H & L keys: A♭maj & Fmaj; c'–f" & a–d"; Tess-L; 3/2, 2/2, Slowly and in pensive mood (♩ = 42); 4pp; Diff-V/m, P/m.

For: mezzo-soprano; baritone; contralto; bass

Mood: lyrical; sad; philosophical; nature imagery

Voice: sweeping phrases; sustained; triplets; rather static; repeated tones

Piano: chordal; drone bass

Diff: very sustained, legato singing

Uses: good for teaching breath control; good low voice song, esp. for bass; English or French text

CARR, BENJAMIN (See Special Section)

CARTER, ELLIOTT
(b. New York, NY, 1908)

[See also D#50–no titles given]

423. **THREE POEMS OF ROBERT FROST.** Associated, 1947. cmp1942. Pub. together with collective title, but not really a set; separate entries below (a mezzo-soprano could do all 3).

A. **DUST OF SNOW.** [4]. X-Emaj; d♯'–e"; Tess-M; 4/4, Allegro; 35meas.; Diff-V/me, P/m.
For: baritone; mezzo-soprano; contralto; some high voices
Mood: cheerful; introspective
Voice: small skips; sustained long tones
Piano: chordal; syncopation; some countermelody; articulations important
Diff: long tones and their dynamic treatment
Uses: interior of group
Rec: D#s 4, 58, 139, 140, 141, 142

B. **THE LINE-GANG.** Emaj; b–f♯"; Tess-mH; 4/4, Vigorously (fast ♩'s); 71meas.; Diff-V/md-d, P/md.
For: mezzo-soprano; dramatic soprano; some tenors
Mood: dramatic; declamatory; descriptive
Voice: many skips; syncopation; declamation
Piano: almost constant 8ves; some imitation; articulations important; cross-rhythms and accents with vocal line but no doubling
Diff: ensemble; sustained soft singing
Uses: good group ender
Rec: D#s 4, 139, 141, 142

C. **THE ROSE FAMILY.** [4]. A♭maj; e♭'–f"; Tess-M; 5/8, Allegretto con moto; 38meas.; Diff-V/md, P/md.
For: tenor; mezzo-soprano; soprano possible
Mood: light; humorous
Voice: small skips; many accidentals; asymmetrical rhythms
Piano: linear with some chordal; many accidentals; articulations important
Diff: meter–divisions include 2+2+1, 3+2, & 2+1+2
Uses: effective song; quiet ending
Rec: D#s 4, 58, 139, 140, 141, 142

424. **VOYAGE** (Hart Crane). Associated, 1973. cmp1945. X, B-centered; c♯'–g"; Tess-M; 2/2, Andante espressivo; 3+min; Diff-V/d, P/md.
For: soprano; mezzo-soprano; possibly tenor
Mood: lyrical; love song
Voice: many skips, some difficult; rhythmic complexity; some long phrases
Piano: chordal; smooth; 4-voice texture, two moving voices
Diff: complex poem; rhythms; dissonance; dynamic control
Uses: effective song for mature singer who believes the poem
Rec: D#s 4, 53, 141, 142

425. **WARBLE FOR LILAC-TIME** (Walt Whitman). Peer International, 1956. cmp1943. E♭maj; b♭(e♭')–a"; Tess-M-mH; 12/8 predominates, with changes, Vivace–Slowly; 16pp; Diff-V/md, P/md.
For: tenor; soprano (not light)
Mood: lyrical; reminiscence; nostalgia for spring
Voice: many skips, often small; duplets against piano triplets or vice versa; syncopation; staccato; some melismas
Piano: chordal-linear combination; various registers; 8th-note

motion predominates; many accidentals; solo sections; does not double vocal line
Diff: rhythms; ensemble; dynamic control
Uses: cantata-like (sectional); should stand alone on program; has various moods; big ending in piano postlude
Rec: D#141

CARTER, JOHN
(b. St. Louis, MO, 1937)

426. **CANTATA.** For Voice and Piano (Traditional Black Spirituals). Cycle. (Peer)Southern, 1964. Vocal melodies in traditional key structure with somewhat dissonant accomp.; c'–b"; Tess-M, H; regular meters (one in 5/4); varied tempos, ends fast; 28pp; Diff-V/d, P/d-dd.
For: soprano; tenor (big voice capable of many colors)
Mood: succession of moods projected by traditional spirituals; yearning; mournful; prayerful; exultant
Voice: traditional melodies embellished; high tessitura in spots
Piano: virtuoso technique in modern idiom for first and last sections; much perpetual motion; broken-chord triplet figures with countermelody; last section mostly in 5/4; chord clusters; brilliant finish
Diff: rhythms; endurance for high tessitura; ensemble
Uses: very effective work for the right singer; must have both musical security and a deep feeling for the spirituals used; good rhythmic sense required; excellent program ender

   a. *Prelude.* (piano alone); no meter signature, Andante con moto e sostenuto; 1p.
   b. *Rondo "Peter Go Ring Dem Bells."* Emin-Amaj; e'–b"; Tess-M, H; 8/8, 9/8, 6/8, Allegro; 11+pp.
   c. *Recitative "Sometimes I Feel like a Motherless Child."* Gmin; c'–g"; Tess-M; 4/4, Lento; 2+pp.
   d. *Air "Let Us Break Bread Together on Our Knees."* A♭maj; e♭'–a♭"; Tess-mH; 4/4, 3/4, Andante con moto (sereno e semplice); 5pp.
   e. *Toccata "Ride on King Jesus."* Dmin-Fmaj; c'–a♭"; Tess-M, H; 5/4, 3/4, 4/4, Allegro feroce e forte; 8pp.

CHADWICK, GEORGE WHITEFIELD
(b. Lowell, MA, 1854; d. Boston, MA, 1931)

427. **ADVERSITY** (Arthur Macy). [5]; 1st©1902. Fmaj; d♭'–f"; Tess-M; 3/4, Tempo di Valse lento; 2pp; Diff-V/e, P/e.
For: baritone
Mood: gentle reverie
Voice: lyrical; soft dynamics; short phrases
Piano: slow waltz
Diff: high f" (can be taken in soft head voice or falsetto)
Uses: very interesting short song; interior of group

428. **ALLAH** (Henry Wadsworth Longfellow). [45, 90, 91]; 1st©1887. H & M keys: Emaj & D♭maj; c♯'–g♯" & b♭–f"; Tess-mL; 3/4, Serioso; 2pp; Diff-V/me, P/me.
For: any high or medium voice

Mood: lyrical and philosophical poem on death
Voice: conjunct motion and small intervals with one 8ve leap downward from highest note; triplets
Piano: chordal–block and broken; some irregular note groupings; supports vocal line, incidental doubling
Diff: a few dissonances with piano in vocal line
Uses: possible recital material

429. **BEDOUIN LOVE SONG** (Bayard Taylor). [90, 91]; 1st©1890. H & L keys: Dmin-maj & B♭min-maj; b–a" & g–f"; Tess-mH; 4/4, Animato assai; Diff-V/md, P/d.
For: tenor; baritone
Mood: wild; ecstatic; quasi-Middle-Eastern
Voice: vigorous first section; strong, lyrical second
Piano: horse-hoof figure in first section; harp-like arpeggios in second
Diff: big voice needed
Uses: good vigorous period piece; somewhat dated, but a fun song to sing

430. **BEFORE THE DAWN,** Op. 8, No. 3 (Arlo Bates). [90, 91]; 1st©1882. H & M keys: D♭maj & B♭maj; e♭'–a♭" & c'–f"; Tess-mH; 3/4, Andante con tenerezza; 6pp; Diff-V/m, P/m.
For: any high or medium voice
Mood: ecstatic love song using nature imagery
Voice: mostly conjunct motion and small intervals; long phrases, often building upwards
Piano: chordal, with afterbeats and some broken-chord figuration; supports vocal line clearly; considerable doubling in more difficult sections
Diff: sustaining the phrases
Uses: possible recital song

431. **A BONNY CURL** (Amelie Rives). [91]; 1st©1889. B♭maj; g(a)–d"; Tess-L; 4/4, Alla scozzese; 3pp; Diff-V/m, P/e.
For: alto
Mood: wishing for absent beloved; somewhat folksong-like with Scottish details in language and music
Voice: somewhat disjunct, with small intervals and leap of 7th downwards; dotted rhythms with Scotch snaps and grace-note ornaments
Piano: chordal; incidental doubling of vocal line
Diff: Scottish dialect; some rhythms for singer
Uses: could be effective in performance

432. **THE DANZA,** Op. 14, No. 1 (Arlo Bates). [5, 90, 91]; 1st©1885. H & L keys: Fmaj & D♭maj; f'–g"(b♭") & d♭'–e♭"(g♭"); Tess-mH; 3/8, Allegretto grazioso; 110meas.; Diff-V/md, P/md.
For: tenor; baritone; man's text
Mood: dance-like; Spanish; rhythmic; happy
Voice: many skips of 5th, 6th, & 7th; many slurs
Piano: broken chords in triplet pattern; some syncopation; some countermelody
Diff: good dynamic control
Uses: good rhythmical song for teaching and programming
Rec: D#s 2, 52

433. **EUTHANASIA** (Arthur Macy). [61]. A♭maj; c'–e♭"; Tess-M; 4/4, Lusinghiero; 2pp; Diff-V/me, P/m.

For: baritone
Mood: lighthearted love song
Voice: stepwise and skips up to 7th; some dotted rhythms
Piano: broken- and block-chord patterning; little doubling of vocal line
Uses: period group
Rec: D#52

434. **A FLOWER CYCLE** (Arlo Bates). Earlier American Music, vol. XVI, ed. by H. Wiley Hitchcock. Da Capo, 1980. 1st©1892. 12 songs for two or three singers. Traditional keys; c'–a"; Tess-varied; regular meters; 42pp; Diff-V/m, P/m-md.
For: soprano, mezzo-soprano, and tenor (each song specified)
Mood: nature poems with spring and summer background; likening natural and human events
Voice: predominantly stepwise and small skips; some dotted rhythms; occasional triplets; predominantly syllabic; one opt. trill (in "The Trilliums")
Piano: 6 songs have broken-chord accomps., each in a distinctive pattern; 6 have block chords in repeated-chord or afterbeat patterns; some doubling of vocal line in "The Cyclamen," "The Foxglove," "The Lupine," "The Meadow Rue," and "The Jasmine"
Diff: some extended high notes, as in "The Cyclamen"; some polyrhythms– 2 vs. 3, 4 vs. 3
Uses: as a shared cycle for three (or two–soprano and tenor) singers; groups for each of the voices can also be excerpted: Soprano: "The Trilliums," "The Cyclamen," "The Wild Briar," "The Cardinal Flower"; Mezzo-soprano: "The Crocus," "The Columbine," "The Foxglove," "The Meadow Rue"; Tenor: "The Waterlily," "The Lupine," "The Jasmine," "The Jacqueminot Rose" NOTE: If soprano and tenor share the cycle, add "The Columbine" and "The Foxglove" for the soprano and "The Crocus" and "The Meadow Rue" for the tenor

a. *The Crocus.* Emin; d'–e"; 3/4, Andante; 2pp.
b. *The Trilliums.* Fmaj; d'–a"; 6/8, Vivace; 5pp.
c. *The Waterlily.* A♭maj; e♭'–a♭"; 4/4, Affetuoso; 5pp.
d. *The Cyclamen.* Cmin-A♭maj; e♭'–a♭"; 4/4, Lento con moto; 3pp.
e. *The Wild Briar.* Cmaj; f'–g"; 6/8, Animato assai; 4pp.
f. *The Columbine.* Fmaj; c'–g"; 2/4, Allegretto; 3pp (3 stanzas).
g. *The Foxglove.* Fmaj; d'–g"; 3/4, Semplice, quasi menuetto; 3pp.
h. *The Cardinal Flower.* Dmin-Fmaj-Dmaj-F♯maj; f'–g♯"; 3/4, Andantino; 3pp.
i. *The Lupine.* B♭maj; e'–f"; 9/8, Allegro; 3pp.
j. *The Meadow Rue.* Amin; c'–g"; 4/4, Lento; 2pp.
k. *The Jasmine.* E♭maj; f'–a♭"; 9/8, Amabile; 4pp.
l. *The Jacqueminot Rose.* Cmin-maj; c'–a♭"; 3/4, Allegretto; 5pp.

435. **GREEN GROWS THE WILLOW** (Hamilton Aïdé). [5]. Amin; g–e"; Tess-M; 2/4, Andante; 5pp; Diff-V/me, P/me.

For: any low voice
Mood: lyrical nature imagery
Voice: mostly conjunct with intervals of a 4th upwards; a few larger leaps, incl. an 11th (if opt. notes are taken); several low-lying phrases (one extremely so)
Piano: chordal with broken-chord figuration and some counterpoint; doubles vocal line almost throughout
Diff: requires singer with a rich and strong low voice
Uses: good song for a low voice with a wide range

436. **IN BYGONE DAYS** (John Leslie Breck). [90, 91]; 1st©1885. H & M keys: E♭maj & Cmaj; f'–a♭"(b♭") & d'–f"(g"); Tess-mH; 4/4, Andantino; 2pp; Diff-V/m, P/me.
For: any male voice
Mood: lyrical poem about unrequited love
Voice: conjunct motion and small intervals with one 8ve leap upwards; a few accidentals
Piano: block chords with some melodic material; afterbeat figures in l.h.; some accidentals; supports vocal line well; some doubling
Diff: possibly some pitches in vocal line
Uses: possible recital song

437. **THE LAMENT** (Egyptian Song from *Ben Hur*) (Lew Wallace). [90, 91]; 1st©1887. H & M keys: Cmin-maj & Amin-maj; c'–g"(a") & a–e"(f♯"); Tess-M; 9/8, 12/8, Moderato con moto; 4pp; Diff-V/m, P/m.
For: any strong high or medium voice
Mood: nostalgic poem; imagery of ancient Egypt
Voice: conjunct motion with small intervals; begins low, becomes higher in tessitura as song progresses; large dynamic contrasts
Piano: chordal, block and broken, with repetitions; some accidentals; supports vocal line; incidental doubling
Diff: vocal stamina; wide dynamic range
Uses: could be effective for a strong voice

438. **THE LILY** (A. Salvini; trans. T. R. Sullivan). [90]; 1st©1887. Gmaj; d♯'–g"; Tess-mH; 3/4, Poco allegretto; 2pp; Diff-V/md, P/me.
For: soprano; tenor
Mood: lyrical, naive love song
Voice: conjunct motion with several leaps of 7th downward; a few accidentals; sustained g"
Piano: block chords with melodic material; some accidentals; supports vocal line; considerable doubling
Diff: intervals of 7th, not doubled by piano
Uses: a charming example of its kind

439. **LOVE'S IMAGE** (James Thomson). A. P. Schmidt, 1910. "To Mme. Schumann-Heink." H & L keys: F♯maj & E♭maj (orig); d♯'–g"(f♯") & c'–e"(e♭"); Tess-M; 4/4, Andantino; 3pp; Diff-V/m, P/m.
For: baritone; tenor; man's text
Mood: lyrical; love song
Voice: stepwise and small skips; duplets and triplets vs. opposite in piano
Piano: broken-chord pattern; 2 vs. 3; some large reaches
Diff: rhythms
Uses: nice lyric song for recital use

440. **LYRICS FROM *TOLD IN THE GATE*** (Arlo Bates). Earlier American Music, vol. XVI, ed. by H. Wiley Hitchcock. Da Capo, 1980. 1st ©1897. Many of these lyrics have Middle-Eastern flavor. Not meant to be performed together; separate entries below.

A. **SWEETHEART, THY LIPS ARE TOUCHED WITH FLAME.** B♭maj; c'–f"(g"); Tess-mH; 4/4, Molto appassionato; 5pp; Diff-V/md, P/md.
For: tenor; soprano (needs sizeable sound)
Mood: passionate love song; dramatic
Voice: chromaticism; leaps of 6th, 7th, & 8ve; dotted rhythms against triplets in accomp.; duplets; dynamics *pp–ff*
Piano: broken- and repeated-chord accomp.; triplets and 2 vs. 3; large dynamic contrasts; some doubling of vocal line
Diff: rhythms; dynamics for some singers
Uses: period piece; dated text

B. **SINGS THE NIGHTINGALE TO THE ROSE.** Cmaj; b–e"; Tess-M; 3/4, Andante con moto; 3pp (2 stanzas); Diff-V/me, P/me.
For: mezzo-soprano
Mood: sentimental love song
Voice: stepwise motion and skips within the chord; a few dotted rhythms
Piano: block- and broken-chords; often doubles vocal line
Uses: period piece

C. **THE ROSE LEANS OVER THE POOL.** Emaj; b–e"; Tess-M; 6/8, Scherzando; 3pp (2 stanzas); Diff-V/m, P/m.
For: mezzo-soprano
Mood: lyrical; coy; teasing
Voice: stepwise and easy skips; syncopation; fragmented phrases
Piano: block- and broken-chord figures; some dotted rhythms and triplets
Diff: rhythms; possibly ensemble
Uses: nice song; lighthearted

D. **LOVE'S LIKE A SUMMER ROSE.** Gmaj; b–e"; Tess-M; 2/4, Andantino; 4pp; Diff-V/m, P/m.
For: baritone; mezzo-soprano
Mood: lyric; fleeting quality of love
Voice: stepwise and small skips; repetitive rhythms; mostly syllabic
Piano: block- and broken-chords; often doubles vocal line
Uses: attractive in its simplicity; has folk-like quality; useful song; somewhat dated text

E. **AS IN WAVES WITHOUT NUMBER.** B♭maj; a–f"; Tess-M; 12/8, Molto moderato e sostenuto; 4pp; Diff-V/md, P/md.
For: baritone
Mood: love song; passionate
Voice: predominantly stepwise and small skips; several 8ve leaps; some duplets; features crescendos
Piano: arpeggiation; some repeated chords and tremolo; some doubling of vocal line
Diff: control of dynamics; rhythms

F. **DEAR LOVE, WHEN IN THINE ARMS I LIE.**

D♭maj; b♭–f"; Tess-M; 3/8, Larghetto, molto espressivo; 4pp; Diff-V/m, P/m.

For: mezzo-soprano; baritone
Mood: lyric love song
Voice: easy skips; some accidentals; some triplets and dotted rhythms
Piano: block chords; much doubling of vocal line
Uses: dated text; limited use

G. WAS I NOT THINE. E♭maj; b♭–e♭"; Tess-M; 4/4, Andante maestoso; 3pp; Diff-V/m, P/m.

For: mezzo-soprano; baritone
Mood: somewhat dramatic; theme of undying love; Middle-Eastern flavor in text
Voice: stepwise motion and easy skips; easy rhythms
Piano: block chords and arpeggiation; syncopation; key sig.changes
Uses: in a period group, possibly to show Middle-Eastern flavor common to the period

H. IN MEAD WHERE ROSES BLOOM. Amin; a–e"; Tess-M; 2/4, Moderato e mesto; 3pp; Diff-V/m, P/m.

For: mezzo-soprano
Mood: lyric; lost love
Voice: stepwise motion and easy skips; some dotted rhythms
Piano: Schumannesque; block chords, afterbeats, and syncopation; some doubling of vocal line
Diff: long range for some singers
Uses: useful student song

I. SISTER FAIREST, WHY ART THOU SIGHING. Amin; c'–f"; Tess-M; 4/4,Andante–Allegro agitato; 3pp; Diff-V/me, P/m.

For: mezzo-soprano; soprano
Mood: tragic; two speakers–questioner, woman who answers
Voice: stepwise motion and easy skips; easy rhythms; three short recit.-like sections
Piano: broken-chord pattern, afterbeat style; block chords
Uses: in a period group

J. OH, LET NIGHT SPEAK OF ME. D♭maj; c'–f"; Tess-M; 4/4, Molto moderato; 3pp; Diff-V/m, P/m.

For: baritone; mezzo-soprano
Mood: dramatic
Voice: accidentals; some 7ths & 8ves; some dotted rhythms
Piano: block chords in 8ths; some doubling of vocal line
Diff: some wide intervals
Uses: in a period group
Rec: D#10

K. I SAID TO THE WIND OF THE SOUTH. A♭maj-Emaj-D♭maj-Fmin-Cmaj; g–e"; Tess-M; 2/4, 4/4, Allegretto con moto, with changes; 5pp; Diff-V/m, P/m.

For: mezzo-soprano
Mood: lyrical love song; separation of lovers
Voice: mostly stepwise motion and easy skips; a few leaps of over an 8ve; uncomplicated rhythms
Piano: broken-chord patterning; several 4-meas. interludes
Diff: range (lowest notes have higher options); large leaps
Uses: in a period group; dated text

L. WERE I A PRINCE EGYPTIAN. Fmin-maj; b♭–f"; Tess-M; 3/4, Andante moderato; 3pp; Diff-V/m, P/m.

For: baritone
Mood: dramatic love song
Voice: stepwise motion and easy skips; duplets and triplets; some dotted rhythms; dynamics vary *pp–ff*
Piano: block chords; duplets and triplets
Diff: some rhythms; dynamics
Uses: Middle-Eastern flavor; dated period piece

441. THE MILLER'S DAUGHTER (Alfred , Lord Tennyson). [91]; 1st©1881. Cmaj; b–e♭"; Tess-mL; 3/4, Andante non troppo; 4pp; Diff-V/me, P/m.

For: any medium or medium-low male voice
Mood: the lover wishes to be the ornaments worn by his beloved; a charming, even provocative poem
Voice: mostly conjunct motion with small intervals; some accidentals; several dim.5ths
Piano: chordal, with melodic material in prelude and interludes; some accidentals; supports vocal line clearly; some doubling
Diff: a few intervals for the singer
Uses: charming period piece

442. O LOVE AND JOY (anon.). [91]; 1st©1892. Gmin; c'–f"; Tess-M; 2/4, Moderato assai (♪ = 69); 2pp; Diff-V/me, P/me.

For: any medium voice
Mood: a philosophical poem about the fleeting nature of love and its joys; labeled "folk-song"; in folk-song style; source not given
Voice: conjunct motion; a few skips; dotted rhythms; one 16th-note triplet
Piano: chordal with countermelodic material; doubles vocal line through much of song
Diff: lowered 7th may be difficult for some singers
Uses: possible recital song

443. REQUEST (poet not given). [90]; 1st©1883. Fmaj; c'–a"; Tess-M; 2/4, Allegretto semplice; 4pp; Diff-V/m, P/m.

For: soprano; some mezzo-sopranos
Mood: lyrical; plea for the beloved at sea
Voice: mostly conjunct motion; small intervals and several leaps of 7th upward and downward; sustained a"
Piano: chordal, afterbeat figures; generally supports or doubles vocal line
Diff: "eh" vowel on a"
Uses: possible recital use

444. SERENADE (Arlo Bates). [90]; 1st©1882. E♭maj; e♭'–g"; Tess-M; 3/4, Andante tranquillo; 4pp; Diff-V/m, P/m.

For: soprano; tenor
Mood: old-fashioned love song using nature imagery; three strophes with refrain
Voice: conjunct; small intervals; one 8ve leap upward within a phrase; two strophes superimposed, followed by the third (repeat not marked, but *da capo* at end of p. 2)
Piano: broken chords and afterbeat figures; some accidentals; supports vocal line but little actual doubling
Diff: frequent returns to highest notes of song

Uses: possible recital song

445. THE STRANGER-MAN (from *Six Songs*) (Arthur Macy). [5]. Gmin-maj; b–e"; Tess-M; 2/2, Alla burla (Allegretto, ♩ = 72); 4pp; Diff-V/m, P/m.
For: mezzo-soprano
Mood: humorous conversation between mother and daughter about kissing a stranger
Voice: conjunct and disjunct motion; a few large intervals; two characters alternate
Piano: chordal, with melodic material and figuration; sometimes doubles vocal line
Diff: differentiation of the characters
Uses: a useful humorous song

446. SWEET WIND THAT BLOWS (Oscar Leighton). [90, 91]; 1st©1885. H & M keys: B♭maj & G♭maj; d'–a" & b♭–f"; Tess-M; 3/4; 2pp; Diff-V/me, P/e.
For: any high or medium voice
Mood: lyrical song of an absent love using sea imagery; three strophes in somewhat folk-like style
Voice: conjunct motion; easy intervals; one dim.4th
Piano: block chords with repetition; a few accidentals; supports vocal line; incidental doubling; same music for all strophes
Diff: "ee" vowel on some higher pitches
Uses: useful teaching song; possible recital song

447. THOU ART SO LIKE A FLOWER (anon. translation of "Du bist wie eine Blume" by Heinrich Heine). [90, 91]; 1st©1883. H & M keys: Emaj & D♭maj; f♯'–g♯" & e♭'–f"; Tess-mH; 6/8, Dolce semplice; 2pp; Diff-V/me, P/m.
For: any male voice
Mood: lyrical love song; serviceable translation of the well-known Heine poem; original text provided; translation suits the music a little better
Voice: conjunct motion; small intervals; some obvious parallels with the Schumann setting
Piano: chordal–block, broken, and rolled; melodic material in prelude and postlude; some accidentals; supports vocal line, incidental doubling
Uses: interesting alternative to the Schumann setting; possible recital song
Rec: D#2

448. WHEN I AM DEAD (Christina Rossetti). A. P. Schmidt, 1910. H & L keys: G♭maj & E♭maj; (e♭')b♭–a♭" & (c')g–f"; Tess-mH, covers range; 4/4, Molto sostenuto e calmato; 4pp; Diff-V/m, P/m.
For: soprano; mezzo-soprano; tenor; baritone; best for women
Mood: lyrical; philosophical
Piano: block and broken chords; syncopation; many accidentals; r.h. 8ves; much doubling of vocal line
Diff: some leaps upward on slurred syllables; wide range
Uses: usable recital song

CHANLER, THEODORE
(b. Newport, RI, 1902; d. Boston, MA, 1961)

449. THE CHILDREN. Nine Songs for Medium Voice & Piano (Leonard Feeney). G. Schirmer, 1946. [92]. Traditional keys; c'–g"; Tess-M-mH; regular meters; varied tempos; 17+min (42pp); Diff-V/m-md, P/m-md.
For: mezzo-soprano; baritone; some sopranos
Mood: children's thoughts about the world and life expressed in a child-like way and/or adult thoughts about childhood
Voice: predominantly conjunct; (b.), some chant-like phrases; some accidentals, particularly in (c.) & (i.); many dotted rhythms, some syncopation, some mixing of duplet and triplet subdivisions of beat; mostly syllabic; some rapid articulations; (h.), opt. harmony part for a second singer
Piano: great variety in accomp. styles; based on broken-chord patterning, afterbeat style, and repeated chords; interesting to play; accidentals; many articulation markings; some doubling of vocal line, esp. in (e., g., & i.); (d.), 60 meas. solo piano, mostly in interludes
Diff: entrances in (a.) and others; irregular phrase lengths or piano overlaps; mood changes from child-like to adult commentary; fast tempo in (c.)
Uses: possibly as a set; probably more practical to excerpt four or five songs

   a. *The Children.* Cmaj; d'–f"; Tess-M; 3/8, Allegro; 3pp. [**Rec:** D#s 16, 65]
   b. *Once upon a Time.* Fmaj; c'–f"; Tess-M; 2/4, Moderato; 6pp. [**Rec:** D#16]
   c. *Wind.* B♭maj; c'–g"; Tess-mH; 2/4, Animato; 5pp.
   d. *Sleep.* D♭maj with modulations; c♯'–f"; Tess-M; 3/8, Andante; 8pp.
   e. *The Rose.* Emaj; c'–f♯"; Tess-mH; 4/4, Lento; 3pp. [**Rec:** D#16, 59]
   f. *Grandma.* [29]. Amin; c'–f"; Tess-M; 3/4, Allegro; 4pp.
   g. *Spick and Span..* Fmaj; d'–f"; Tess-M; 4/4, Lento moderato; 1p.
   h. *Moo Is a Cow.* D♭maj; d♭'–f"; Tess-mH; 2/4, Allegretto; 9pp. [**Rec:** D#16]
   i. *One of Us.* E♭maj, with modulations; c'–f"; Tess-M; 3/4, Molto lento; 3pp.

450. CRADLE SONG (William Blake). [92]. G♭maj; d♭'–g♭"; Tess-M; 6/4, Andante; 4pp; Diff-V/m, P/m.
For: soprano; mezzo-soprano
Mood: lyrical lullaby
Voice: sustained legato; many long tones; ends g♭" *pp*
Piano: chordal; almost continuous slow trill figure on d♭"–e♭"; some accidentals
Diff: soft high ending for singer
Uses: an effective song for a variety of occasions

451. EIGHT EPITAPHS (Walter de la Mare). Cycle. Boosey & Hawkes, 1939. Traditional keys with many altered chord structures; b–f"; Tess-L; regular and irregular changing meters; varied tempos, ends slow; 11min; Diff-V/d, P/m-d.
For: mezzo-soprano; some sopranos (comfortable in lower range)
Mood: small pictures of personalities of the deceased; poignant; humorous

Voice: short phrases; speech rhythms; some difficult pitches; rhythmic intricacies in fast songs; numerous low notes
Piano: generally moderate technical demands, but three central songs call for facility and rapid finger work, rhythmic changes, and precise articulation
Diff: pitch perception; rhythmic intricacies; ensemble; low tessitura; diction
Uses: excellent cycle for the advanced musician; appealing to audience; not a program ender
Rec: D#s 14, 143, 144

   a. *Alice Rodd.* D♯min; b–e"; 4/4, Non troppo lento; 2pp.
   b. *Susannah Fry.* G♯min; b–d♯"; 6/8, 4/8, Lento; 2pp.
   c. *Three Sisters.* Tonal-Cmaj; d'–e"; 3/4, Molto vivace; 6pp.
   d. *Thomas Logge.* F-centered; b–f"; 2/8 with many changes, Allegro assai, alla burla; 6pp. [**Rec:** D#16]
   e. *A Midget.* B♭min; c'–f"; 4/4, Molto moderato; 3pp.
   f. *No Voice to Scold.* D♭maj; f♭'–f"; 4/4, Tranquillo; 1p.
   g. *Ann Poverty.* Fmin; c'–d"; 4/4, Un poco più andante; 1p.
   h. *Be Very Quiet Now.* F♯maj; c♯'–d♯"; 3/2, Largo; 1p.

452. THE FLIGHT (Leonard Feeney). Associated, 1948. cmp1944. Fmaj; c'–g"; Tess-M; 5/16, 2/8, 8/16, 7/16, etc., Allegro moderato; 8pp; Diff-V/md, P/md.
For: soprano; mezzo-soprano; tenor; high baritone
Mood: New Testament story of angel warning Joseph to flee with his family
Voice: stepwise and skips on chord lines; asymmetrical meters and rhythms
Piano: linear; 16th-note motion; accidentals; does not double vocal line
Diff: changing meters; rhythms; ensemble; three speakers

453. FOUR RHYMES FROM PEACOCK PIE (Walter de la Mare). Associated, 1948. [92]. Traditional keys; b–f♯"; Tess-M; regular meters, varied tempos; 5min; Diff-V/m, P/m–md.
For: mezzo-soprano; soprano; high baritone
Mood: lighthearted
Voice: many easy skips; somewhat fragmented phrasing; syncopation; accidentals; some dotted rhythms
Piano: mostly chordal, some linear; some countermelody; syncopation; accidentals; does not double vocal line
Diff: various speakers; ensemble
Uses: effective songs; can be done separately or as set; good final group for recital
Rec: D#s 34, 44

   a. *The Ship of Rio.* F♯maj; b–f♯"; 2/4, Allegro vivace ♩ = 132; 1min.
   b. *Old Shellover.* A♭maj; e♭'–f♭"; 3/8, Andante con moto ♩. = 50; 1+min.
   c. *Cake and Sack.* B♭min; e♭'–f"; 2/4, Allegretto ♩ = 60; 1min.
   d. *Tillie.* Dmaj; d'–f♯"; 3/4, Waltz ♩. = 56; 1+min.

454. I RISE WHEN YOU ENTER (Leonard Feeney). [92]; 1st©1945. Gmaj; c♯'–g"; Tess-mH; 2/2, Allegro assai; 1+min; Diff-V/md, P/md.
For: tenor
Mood: bright; humorous; conversational; a city love song
Voice: many skips; ascending phrases; declamation; syncopation
Piano: fast off-beat afterbeat pattern; staccato; rhythm seems irregular, ungainly
Diff: ensemble
Uses: good final song in group; encore; good in a group concerning modern living
Rec: D#s 51, 59

455. THE LAMB (William Blake). [24, 31, 92]; 1st©1946. H & L keys: Gmin & Fmin; d'–e" & c'–d"; Tess-M; 4/4, Andante; 3pp; Diff-V/e, P/e.
For: medium or low voice
Mood: lyrical; child-like; innocent
Voice: stepwise and small skips; easy rhythms; short phrases
Piano: broken-chord and afterbeat patterning; does not double vocal line
Uses: very good short-ranged song for students; effective setting of this text with modal, somewhat archaic flavor

456. MEET DOCTOR LIVERMORE (Leonard Feeney). [4, 92]. Cmaj; c'–f"; Tess-mL; 4/4, Allegretto (♩ = 126); 5pp; Diff-V/md, P/d.
For: any medium voice
Mood: humorous description of a psychiatrist
Voice: somewhat disjunct; a few difficult intervals; short phrases separated by rests; almost speech-like; some staccato
Piano: chordal with some melodic figures; many accidentals; staccato and legato contrasted; support and/or doubling of vocal line incidental
Diff: pitches and rhythms for singer; rhythms for pianist; needs good vocal actor
Uses: useful humorous song (if care is taken not to offend mental health professionals and their clients)

457. MEMORY (William Blake). [92]; 1st©1946. F♯min; c'–f♯"; Tess-mL; 4/8, 3/8, Andantino; 3pp; Diff-V/md, P/md.
For: mezzo-soprano
Mood: introspective; daydreaming
Voice: stepwise and easy skips; 2–7-note slurs; duplet and triplet subdivisions; 2 vs. 3 in piano
Piano: constant 16ths in triplet figures; some 2 vs. 3; accidentals; does not double vocal line
Diff: 2 vs. 3; 4 vs. 3
Uses: pleasant song; mood piece
Rec: D#51

458. MY HANDS ARE EMPTY (Purchit Swami). [92]. B♭min; a–f"; Tess-mL; 4/8, 5/16, 3/4, 11/16, 4/4, 6/16, Lento (♪ = 84); 7pp; Diff-V/d, P/dd.
For: any medium or low voice
Mood: contemplative; a touch of Eastern philosophy
Voice: rather disjunct; some large intervals; many accidentals; frequent meter changes; short phrases separated by rests

Piano: chordal and contrapuntal; many accidentals; frequent meter changes; complex rhythms
Diff: pitches and rhythms
Uses: effective song for excellent musicians

459. **O MISTRESS MINE** (William Shakespeare). [92]. cmp1936. "To Eva Gauthier." D♭maj; c'–g♭"; Tess-mH; 3/4, Vivace; 1+min; Diff-V/m, P/md.
For: tenor
Mood: lyrical; "time is fleeting"
Voice: many small skips; syncopation; piano separates singer's phrases; many accidentals
Piano: perpetual motion in 16ths; broken chords; some countermelody; does not double vocal line
Diff: ensemble
Uses: effective song; good in Shakespeare group or elsewhere; soft ending
Rec: D#51

460. **THE POLICEMAN IN THE PARK** (Leonard Feeney). [92]; 1st©1948. D♭maj; a♭–d"; Tess-mL; 2/2, Andante; 3min; Diff-V/m, P/m.
For: bass; bass-baritone
Mood: declamatory; first-person narrative; humorous, with pathos in background
Voice: chromatic lines; some skips; syncopation; duplets and triplets; dotted rhythms; many accidentals
Piano: chordal; syncopated repeated and broken chords; some countermelody; various articulations; cross-hands; many accidentals; some doubling of vocal line
Diff: rhythms
Uses: colorful song for mature singer with dramatic sense; useful in final group or as change of pace; quiet ending

461. **THESE, MY OPHELIA** (Archibald MacLeish). [22, 92]; 1st©1935. E♭maj; e♭'–g♭"; Tess-mH; 9/8 with many changes, Andante; 3pp; Diff-V/d, P/d.
For: tenor
Mood: lyrical; philosophical
Voice: lyrical and flowing; closes with melisma on "ah"
Piano: chordal; steady, syncopated rhythm; chromatic
Diff: pitches; meter changes; rhythms; soft singing
Uses: good for teaching quiet, lyrical line; fine recital song
Rec: D#s 16, 51, 65

462. **THREE EPITAPHS** (Walter de la Mare). [92]. Not all for the same voice; separate entries below.

A. **MISTRESS HEW.** Emin; c'–g"; Tess-mL; 4/4, Andante cantabile; 3pp; Diff-V/m, P/me.
For: soprano; mezzo-soprano
Mood: tender description of the deceased with children
Voice: smooth, but characterized by 4ths & 5ths up and down
Piano: chordal; wide reach needed; syncopated
Diff: triplets in voice against duplets in piano
Uses: fine song for any singer

B. **A SHEPHERD.** Fmin; c'–f"; Tess-M; 6/8, Lento; 2pp; Diff-V/me, P/e.
For: mezzo-soprano; tenor; baritone
Mood: description of shepherd with his dog
Voice: mostly conjunct motion with a few modest intervals; folksong flavor
Piano: chordal; melodic and countermelodic passages; supports vocal line, sometimes doubling
Uses: good song for a young singer

C. **A ONE-EYED TAILOR.** Emaj; B-b; Tess-M; 12/8, Allegretto; 1p; Diff-V/me, P/me.
For: baritone; bass
Mood: extremely short description; could be interpreted in a humorous fashion
Voice: outlines E major triad, then stepwise descent
Piano: chordal with dotted-rhythm melodic line; supports vocal line except at beginning
Diff: despite simplicity of song, a few pitches may be difficult for some singers
Uses: good song for performance in a variety of situations

463. **THREE HUSBANDS.** Epitaph No. 9 (Walter de la Mare). Boosey & Hawkes, 1962. [92]. cmp1940. Cmaj; c'–g"; Tess-M; 5/4, Allegro vivace; 3pp; Diff-V/d, P/d.
For: soprano
Mood: lyrical; humorous
Voice: conjunct with some skips; fragmented phrasing; rhythmically intricate; various groupings of 5
Piano: linear; melody with staccato chords; rhythmically tricky; many accidentals and modulations
Diff: rhythmic groupings; ensemble
Uses: fine song; appealing group ender; encore
Rec: D#144

464. **THREE MONTHS AND A RABBIT** (Daniel Sargent). [92]. Could be performed as a set by one singer, although the varying tessituras and text of the last song might suggest otherwise. Traditional keys; c'–a♭"; Tess-mH-mL; regular meters; generally quick tempos; 20pp; Diff-V/m, P/md.
For: mezzo-soprano; tenor, if sung as a set; otherwise (b.) better for soprano; (d.), alto or baritone
Mood: tender; ecstatic; descriptive; modestly humorous
Voice: conjunct motion; moderate intervals; some high-lying phrases; numerous accidentals in (c.)
Piano: chordal with 16th-note passage work; rapid broken-chord figuration
Diff: tessituras, if sung by one person; some pitches and rhythms, esp. in (c.)
Uses: songs about months of the year and animals; probably best excerpted

　a. *April.* E♭maj-Cmin; c'–g"; Tess-M; 2/4, Allegretto (♩=96); 5pp.
　b. *May.* D♭maj; e♭'–a♭"; Tess-mH; 4/4, Molto vivace (♩=132); 9pp.
　c. *June.* "To Eva Gauthier." Fmin; c'–g"; Tess-M; 6/8, Andantino; 4pp.
　d. *Cottony Cottony.* F♯maj; c♯'–e"; Tess-mL; 6/8, Allegretto con moto; 2pp.

465. **VOYAGE IN PROVENCE** (Archibald MacLeish). [92]. Emin; e'–g"; Tess-mH; 6/8, Comodo; 2pp; Diff-V/m, P/me.
For: soprano; tenor
Mood: lyrical description of Provence

Voice: conjunct and intervals of 4th & 5th upward and downward; duplet rhythms
Piano: chordal with melodic fragments; supports vocal line fairly well
Diff: modal flavor may be hard for some singers to hear
Uses: an effective short song for recital

CHARLES, ERNEST
(b. Minneapolis, MN, 1895; d. Beverly Hills, CA, 1984)

466. **AND SO, GOODBYE** (Ernest Charles). [48, 93]; 1st©1938. H & L keys: D♭maj & A♭maj; e♭'–a♭" & b♭–e♭"; Tess-mH; 4/4, Restless–Calm, but not slow–Agitated; 4pp; Diff-V/m, P/md.
For: any voice of sufficient size; good for dramatic voices
Mood: emotional parting of lovers; sentimental
Voice: opens with upward leap of m7th, as do several other phrases; several high-lying phrases; climactic a♭" on "eh" vowel *ff*; final phrase *fff*; some accidentals
Piano: chordal with some melodic material; quarter-note triplets in second section; many accidentals; supports vocal line but does not double
Diff: some pitches for singer; vocal stamina needed
Uses: appealing to some singers and audiences

467. **BEAUTY** (Sunset) (William Bruno). [51]; 1st©1941. G♭maj; d♭'–g♭"; Tess-M; 4/4, Moderato (♩ = 96); 2pp; Diff-V/me, P/me.
For: any medium voice
Mood: descriptive; sentimental
Voice: legato phrases; overall pitch level gradually ascends to final g♭"; quarter-note triplets
Piano: chordal; some accidentals; supports vocal line, no doubling
Diff: accurate triplets for singer
Uses: possible performance use

468. **BON VOYAGE** (Velma Hitchcock). [93]; 1st©1939. H & L keys: Emaj-Dmaj-E♭maj & B♭maj-A♭maj-Amaj; f♯'–a" & c'–e♭"; Tess-M; 4/4, 3/4, Calm; 6pp; Diff-V/m, P/m.
For: any voice
Mood: parting and predicted return
Voice: mostly conjunct motion and small intervals; duple rhythms against triplets in piano; a few accidentals; numerous changes of tonal center
Piano: chordal–broken and block, with triplet figures almost throughout; 2 vs. 3; many accidentals; supports vocal line well, little doubling
Diff: pitches; rhythms
Uses: possible recital song

469. **CLOUDS** (anon). [32, 93]; 1st©1932. H, M, & L keys: D♭maj, B♭maj, & A♭maj; f'–a♭", d'–f", & c'–e♭"; Tess-mL; 4/4, 3/4, Tranquillo; 3pp; Diff-V/me, P/m.
For: any lyric voice, except very low
Mood: lyrical; nature picture
Voice: static; dreamy, with many repeated notes; somewhat more melodic in middle section
Piano: chordal–afterbeats, repeated, arpeggiated; some independent melodic motives

Uses: useful teaching song for young singers
Rec: D#145

470. **CRESCENT MOON** (Mona Modini Wood). [93]. H & L keys: Emaj & D♭maj; e'–f"♯ &; d♭'–e♭"; Tess-M; 4/4, Slowly and dreamily; 2pp; Diff-V/me, P/me.
For: any medium voice
Mood: dreamy nature imagery
Voice: mostly conjunct motion and small intervals; leap of m7th upward at end; triplets; long final note on "ee" vowel and e" or d♭"
Piano: chordal–broken-chord figuration in 8ths; some accidentals; supports vocal line without doubling
Diff: a few pitches; tone quality on final note
Uses: possible recital song

471. **L'ENVOI** (Sarojini Naidu). [93]; 1st©1939. H & L keys: Amaj & Fmaj ; e'–f♯"(a ") & c'–d"(f"); Tess-M; 4/4, Tranquillo (♩ = 72); 3pp; Diff-V/me, P/m.
For: any light voice
Mood: lyrical nature imagery
Voice: short, lyrical phrases; opt. g♯" and a"
Piano: chordal; some broken-chord figures in 32nd notes; triplets; numerous accidentals; often doubles vocal line
Diff: possibly rhythms for singer
Uses: could be effective in performance

472. **FRUSTRATION** (anon.). [51]; 1st©1941. E♭maj; e♭'–e♭"; Tess-M; 4/4, Vaguely (♩ = 76); 2pp; Diff-V/m, P/m.
For: soprano; mezzo-soprano
Mood: humorous; sarcastic image of dealing with small children
Voice: mostly conjunct motion; intervals of 5th, 6th, & 8ve; triplets; "almost spoken" at end; dissonances with piano
Piano: chordal; some triplets and a little broken-chord figuration; some accidentals; supports vocal line, but is sometimes dissonant to it
Diff: some pitches for singer
Uses: very short song; could be effective in some situations

473. **IF YOU ONLY KNEW** (George Johnson-Jervis). [93]; 1st©1935. H & L keys: Amaj & Fmaj; f♯'–f♯" & d'–d"; Tess-M; 4/4, Moderato; 3pp; Diff-V/me, P/me.
For: any high or medium voice
Mood: lyrical love song; nature imagery
Voice: many phrases begin high and descend in small intervals; mostly 2-meas. phrases
Piano: chordal; melody in prelude and interludes; some countermelody; syncopated afterbeats; a few accidentals; supports vocal line, does not double
Uses: an effective old-fashioned song for performance; useful teaching song

474. **LET MY SONG FILL YOUR HEART** (Viennese Waltz) (Ernest Charles). [28, 93]; 1st©1936. [Also available as a single] H & L keys: D♭maj & B♭maj; c'–a♭" & a–f"; Tess-M; 3/4, Alla Valzer; 5pp; Diff-V/md, P/d.
For: best for soprano
Mood: somewhat sentimental love song, in waltz-song style
Voice: conjunct and disjunct motion; many phrases descend by

6th or 7th, then ascend; frequent motion by half-step; some accidentals

Piano: chordal; some afterbeat figures; many accidentals; doubles vocal line throughout

Diff: articulation of words in waltz tempo; needs skillful pianist

Uses: could be a most effective recital song; group or program ender; encore

Rec: D#s 23, 33, 40

475. **LORD OF THE YEARS** (Velma Hitchcock). [93]; 1st©1938. H & L keys: G♭maj & D♭maj; e'–g♭" & b–d♭"; Tess-M; 4/4, Andante; 5pp; Diff-V/m, P/m.

For: any voice

Mood: a song of praise using nature imagery

Voice: mostly conjunct motion; a few small intervals; easy rhythms; highest pitch recurs on various vowels; some accidentals

Piano: chordal; supports vocal line, occasional doubling; many accidentals

Diff: pitches may not be as obvious for singer as they appear

Uses: in a variety of situations, incl. church

476. **MESSAGE** (Sara Teasdale). [51, 93]; 1st©1941. Gmin-Dmaj; e'–g"; Tess-mH; 6/8, Moderato; 3pp; Diff-V/m, P/m.

For: soprano

Mood: poem originally titled "To One Away"; romantic depiction of communication between distant lovers

Voice: high-lying phrases at beginning and end, each ending on a long note in upper-middle voice; some difficult intervals, incl. m7th

Piano: block and broken chords in 16ths; some accidentals; supports vocal line well, does not double

Diff: tessitura; long f♯" at end

Uses: possible recital song

477. **MY LADY WALKS IN LOVELINESS** (Mona Modini Wood). G. Schirmer, 1932. [34, 93]. "To John Charles Thomas." H & L keys: Fmaj & D♭maj; e'–g"(a") & c'–e♭"(f"); Tess-M; 4/4, Andante; 4pp; Diff-V/m, P/m.

For: baritone; tenor

Mood: lyrical; tribute to a lady

Voice: stepwise and easy skips; numerous 2-note slurs; lyrical and flowing

Piano: chordal; repetitive pattern in 3rds; countermelody; repeated chords; 8ve passages

Diff: fragmented phrasing

Uses: effective for an artistic singer

Rec: D#48

478. **NIGHT** (Sydney King Russell). [93]; 1st©1944. H & L keys: E♭min & Cmin; f'–a♭" & d'–f"; Tess-M; 4/4, Poco lento (♩ = 72); 4pp; Diff-V/m, P/m.

For: any high or medium voice

Mood: lyrical love song

Voice: sustained legato phrases with frequent 2- and 3-beat (or more) note values; final two phrases lie quite high with long note values; a few accidentals

Piano: chordal; broken chords in triplets throughout; some accidentals in middle section; supports vocal line; does

not double

Diff: 2 in vocal line vs. 3 in piano; tessitura at end of song

Uses: possible recital song

479. **O LOVELY WORLD** (Velma Hitchcock). [59]; 1st©1947. H & L keys: Emin-maj & Cmin-maj; f♯'–a" & d'–f"; Tess-M; 4/4, 3/4, Broad; 4pp; Diff-V/m, P/m.

For: all voices; some dramatic weight desirable

Mood: somewhat dramatic; reflection on the "world that we have lost"

Voice: long, sweeping phrases; sustained high tones; some chromaticism

Piano: chordal; some chromaticism

Diff: sustained high tone

Uses: useful teaching song for sustained high tones, phrasing, and breath control

480. **THE SUSSEX SAILOR** (Alfred Noyes). [59, 93]; 1st©1933. H & L keys: Gmaj & Dmaj; d'–g" & a–d"; Tess-mL; 4/4, 2/4; 9pp; Diff-V/m, P/d.

For: any male voice

Mood: descriptive; somewhat melancholy

Voice: long phrases; some triplets

Piano: partly chordal, partly rapid arpeggiation

Diff: contrasting moods require interpretive facility

Uses: good for young male singers

481. **WHEN I HAVE SUNG MY SONGS** (Ernest Charles). G. Schirmer, 1934. [24, 28, 93]. H & L keys: Fmaj & D♭maj; d'–g" & b♭–e♭"; Tess-M; 4/4, Calmly; 2+min; Diff-V/me, P/m.

For: any voice

Mood: lyrical; love song; sentimental

Voice: stepwise and small skips; afterbeat phrase beginnings

Piano: chordal; 5–6-voice block and broken patterns; some doubling of vocal line

Uses: text more suitable for mature than young singers; encore; in group of American songs

Rec: D#s 23, 47, 64, 65, 69, 146, 147, 148, 149

482. **THE WHITE SWAN** (Mona Bonelli). [51, 93]; 1st©1941. H & M keys: Bmin-Dmaj & Gmin-B♭maj; e'–a" & c'–f"; Tess-M; 4/4, Dreamily; 2min; Diff-V/m, P/md.

For: mezzo-soprano; soprano; baritone; tenor

Mood: descriptive; remembrance

Voice: stepwise; small skips; 2-note slurs; syncopation; dotted rhythms; dramatic climax

Piano: broken and block chords; cross-hands; does not double vocal line

Diff: some long phrases; sustained f" *ff*

Uses: effective song; lyric; big climax near end; quiet ending

483. **WHO KEEPS THE YEARS** (Clarence Olmstead). [93]; 1st©1940. H & L keys: A♭maj & E♭maj; e♭'–a♭" & b♭–e♭"; Tess-M; 4/4, Moderato; 4pp; Diff-V/m, P/m.

For: any voice

Mood: nostalgic; sentimental

Voice: mostly conjunct; small intervals; one 8ve leap; most phrases short, some ascending; low ending

Piano: broken-chord duplets & triplets; syncopation; melodies in prelude and interlude; doubles vocal line in first section, then incidental doubling; some accidentals

Diff: a few pitches for singer

Uses: possible recital song

484. YOUTH (Sarojini Naidu). [93]; 1st©1935. H & L keys: D♭maj-Bmaj & B♭maj-A♭maj; d♭'-a♭" & b♭-f"; Tess-M; 4/4, Appassionato (♩= ca.96); 4pp; Diff-V/md, P/d.

For: best for tenor or baritone

Mood: nostalgic commentary on the passing of youth

Voice: mostly conjunct motion; long phrase sweeps upward to first climax; triplets; some accidentals; high ending *ff*

Piano: chordal; broken-chord figures in 8ths &16ths; many accidentals; some doubling of vocal line

Diff: vocal stamina needed for climaxes of song

Uses: might be a good song for singers of a certain age

CHASALOW, ERIC
(b. Newark, NJ, 1955)

485. RAIN TOWARDS MORNING (Elizabeth Bishop). [9]. cmp1984. X; c'-a"; Tess-M; mostly regular changing meters; occasional irregular measure (5/8, 3/32); accel. to ♩= ca.66; 2min; Diff-V/d, P/d.

For: soprano

Mood: somewhat disoriented, as though being awakened suddenly; images of birds, rain at dawn, and a gentle companion

Voice: syllabic setting; speech rhythms; disjunct melodic line; many medium and large intervals; accidentals; dissonant

Piano: composer describes piano part as "filigree" beneath the long line of the vocal melody; much staccato; complex rhythms; dissonant figures; wide range on keyboard

Diff: perfect pitch helpful for singer

Uses: challenging song for graduate level performers

CHENOWETH, WILBUR
(b. Tecumseh, NE, 1899; d. Los Angeles, CA, 1980)

486. VOCALISE. [20]; 1st©1962. Gmaj; e'-b"; Tess-H; 6/8, Allegretto; 5pp; Diff-V/d, P/me.

For: coloratura soprano

Mood: lyrical

Voice: very florid; numerous triplet figures; grace notes

Piano: chordal; regular rhythm; supports voice

Diff: agility; high tones must be sung with ease

Uses: interesting showpiece

CHILDS, BARNEY
(b. Spokane, WA, 1926; d. Redlands, CA, 2000)

487. VIRTUE (George Herbert). [3]. Cmaj; c'-g"; Tess-M; unmetered, Evenly steady, no rubato, all durations precise (♩= 120); 2+min; Diff-V/d, P/m.

For: soprano; mezzo-soprano; possibly high baritone

Mood: all things must perish–only the soul survives

Voice: complex speech-like rhythms; final phrase uses entire

range of song; dynamics *p–ff*; special instructions for dynamics and timbre

Piano: spare; fragmentary staves appear only as needed

Diff: making durations precise as called for in score (for both performers); ensemble; possibly the unusual appearance of the score

Rec: D#150 contains 37 songs by Childs–no titles in source but may contain above song

CHING, J. MICHAEL
(b. Honolulu, HI, 1958)

488. RIDDLES WITHIN RIDDLES. Four Settings of Anglo-Saxon Riddles for Baritone and Piano. Columbia Univ. Press, 1984. X; (A)B♭–g♭'; Tess-M; changing meters; 7+min; Diff-V/d, P/d.

For: baritone

Mood: riddles (musical as well as verbal); answers for both given at end of set

Voice: many accidentals; many skips, some awkward; various subdivisions of the beat juxtaposed; mostly syllabic; some speaking; each song bears a resemblance, or contains a reference, to the answer to the musical riddle (e.g., (a.) opens with patterning similar to Schubert's "Ständchen")

Piano: many accidentals; complex rhythms in (a.); various subdivisions of beat juxtaposed in all four songs; trills in (b.) & (c.); large reach helpful; doubling of vocal line rare; piano often answers the riddle

Diff: complexities of rhythm and pitch; ensemble

Uses: interesting group to program for audience with some musical sophistication

    a. *I ("I Saw a Being . . .")*. X; B–g♭'; changing meters, Moderately; 3min; [The moon and the sun; Schubert: "Serenade," French overture style].

    b. *II ("It is a splendid thing when one knows not its ways")*. X; (A)B♭–e'; 2/2 with changes, Moderately slow; 1+min; [Shepherd's pipe; Debussy: "Syrinx"].

    c. *III ("I have a puffed breast and a swollen neck")*. X; E♭–e'; 6/8 with changes, Not too fast; 1+min; [Weathercock; Schubert: "Die Wetterfahne," from *Die Winterreise*].

    d. *IV ("A warrior is wondrously brought into the world . . .")*. X; B♭–e"; changing meters, Freely; 2min; [Fire; Scriabin: "Vers la flamme," op. 72].

CITKOWITZ, ISRAEL
(b. Skierniewice, Russia [now in Poland], 1909; d. London, England, 1974)

489. FIVE SONGS FROM *CHAMBER MUSIC* (James Joyce). Boosey & Hawkes, 1930. Polytonality; d'-a"; Tess-mH; irregular and changing meters throughout; moderate and fast tempos; 13pp; Diff-V/md, P/d.

For: tenor (light lyric)

Mood: delicate moods; love songs trace the development of a relationship

Voice: mostly conjunct; accidentals; some high tessitura;

pitches elusive; irregular word rhythms; 8th-note beat throughout

Piano: irregular rhythmic patterns within constant 8th-note motion; many accidentals; linear; constantly changing meters; delicate

Diff: pitches; rhythms; ensemble; declamation needs care

Uses: good set for singer attuned to the poetry of James Joyce

Rec: D#s 16, 17

    a. *Strings in the Earth and Air.* d'–f♯"; 8/8, 7/8, 5/8, Very lightly; 3pp.

    b. *When the Shy Star Goes Forth in Heaven.* d'–g♯"; 3/4, ♩ = 80; 3pp.

    c. *O It Was Out by Donneycarney.* f♯'–g♯"; 8/8, 10/8, 7/8, 11/8, Light and flowing eighths; 2pp.

    d. *Bid Adieu.* e'–a"; 4/4, 3/4, 6/8, Gayly; 3pp.

    e. *My Love Is in a Light Attire.* e'–a"; 10/8, 9/8, 8/8, 11/8, Flowing eighths; 2pp.

490. **GENTLE LADY** (James Joyce). [22]. cmp1925. G-centered; f'–d"; Tess-mL; 3/4 with many changes, Rubato (♪ = c.144); 3pp; Diff-V/md, P/md.

For: any medium voice

Mood: lyrical; quiet; song of dead lovers

Voice: lyrical; little movement; many repeated notes

Piano: single voice texture at beginning, later 2-voice; independent melody

Diff: pitches; frequent meter changes

Uses: good for fine musician of limited vocal range

CLARKE, HENRY LELAND
(b. Dover, NH, 1907; d. Greenfield, MA, 1992)

491. **TWO SONGS.** Conatus, 1977. cmp1941 & 1950. Modal structure (simultaneous quartal and tertian harmony); c'–g"; Tess-M–mH; regular meters; moderate tempos; 7pp; Diff-V/md, P/me.

For: dramatic baritone

Mood: declamatory; dramatic; call to freedom

Voice: mostly conjunct; some chord outlining and easy leaps; several f"s and g"s on easy vowels

Piano: chordal texture; slightly archaic sound; vigorously rhythmic

Uses: good material for dramatic baritone, or younger singer with a solid voice and authoritative presentation

    a. *Ah! Freedom Is a Noble Thing* (from *The Bruce* by John Barbour, d. ca.1385). c'–f"; 6/4, Risoluto; 3pp.

    b. *These Are the Times That Try Men's Souls* (Thomas Paine). d'–g"; 4/4, Moderato; 4pp.

CLOKEY, JOSEPH W.
(b. New Albany, IN, 1890; d. Covina, CA, 1960)

492. **THE STORKE.** A Christmas Carol, Op. 36. J. Fischer, 1926. Dmin; c'–d"; Tess-M; 4/4, Andante con moto; 56meas.; Diff-V/me, P/me.

For: mezzo-soprano; baritone; contralto

Mood: quiet; Christmas carol

Voice: stepwise and easy skips; 2-note slurs; old spellings of text but easy to pronounce

Piano: block chords; some 8th-note passages

Uses: nice seasonal song

CLOUGH-LEIGHTER, HENRY
(b. Washington, DC, 1874; d. Wollaston, MA, 1956)

493. **I DRINK THE FRAGRANCE OF THE ROSE,** Op. 19, No. 1 (Charles Hanson Towne). [58]; 1st©1902. Amaj; e♭'–f♯"; Tess-M; 4/4, Allegretto grazioso; 5pp; Diff-V/m, P/m.

For: tenor

Mood: lyrical; intimate

Voice: stepwise and skips, esp. 5th & 8ve; 2-note slurs; easy rhythms

Piano: repeated chords in 16th-note pattern; countermelody, l.h.; incidental doubling of vocal line

Uses: rather effective; interesting harmonies

494. **IT WAS A LOVER AND HIS LASS** (William Shakespeare). Oliver Ditson, 1906. Reprint: T.I.S. (H & M). [5, 26]. Gmaj; d'–a"; Tess-mH; 2/4, Poco allegro animoso; 4pp; Diff-V/m, P/m.

For: soprano; tenor

Mood: happy; joyful; sprightly; nature imagery

Voice: many skips; 2-note slurs; light, dancing melody

Piano: linear 4-voice texture; trills; articulations important; independent melodic motives; doubles vocal line

Diff: dynamic changes

Uses: interesting song; use anywhere

Rec: D#52

495. **REQUIESCAT** (Oscar Wilde). Boston Music Co., 1914. E♭min; e♭'–g♭"; Tess-M; 4/4, Lento, pensieroso e mesto; 3pp; Diff-V/m, P/m.

For: tenor

Mood: lyrical; elegy

Voice: conjunct; slow and sustained; floating lines; not much rhythmic word stress; soft, gentle singing

Piano: linear, 1–5-voice texture; recurring bell-like ornament; large reach helpful; light touch needed

Diff: sustaining proper mood

Uses: good song for teaching gentle approach and soft singing

496. **SEA GYPSY,** Op. 65, No. 1 (Richard Hovey). Boston Music Co., 1919. D♭maj; d–e♭'; Tess-mH; 6/8, Con moto, animato e vigoroso; 1+min; Diff-V/m, P/md.

For: baritone with ample sound

Mood: dramatic; sailor's song; powerful; compelling

Voice: many skips; portamento; repetitive rhythms; long tones

Piano: chordal-linear combination; some rolled chords; fast ornaments; dotted rhythms; many accidentals; does not double vocal line

Diff: ending demands stamina

Uses: big ending; could end group or program

COHEN, CECIL
(b. Chicago, IL, 1894; d. 1967)

497. **DEATH OF AN OLD SEAMAN** (Langston Hughes). [6]; 1st©1977. B♭min; c'–f"; Tess-M; 4/4, Larghetto, ♩ = 66; 2pp; Diff-V/m, P/me.
For: mezzo-soprano; baritone
Mood: dirge-like
Voice: generally diatonic; a few downward leaps of 6ths & 7ths; moves in quarters & 8ths; some chromaticism
Piano: chordal, like a funeral march; chromaticism; some melodic interest in prelude and interlude
Diff: two speakers in the poem require two different characterizations in the voice
Uses: possible recital material

CONE, EDWARD T.
(b. Greensboro, NC, 1917)

498. **SILENT NOON** (Dante Gabriel Rossetti). [49]. X; b–b"; Tess-M; 4/4 with perpetual meter changes, Molto tranquillo (♩ = 60); 6pp; Diff-V/dd, P/dd.
For: lyric soprano
Mood: lyrical; love song
Voice: flowing but disjunct; large intervals; extremely chromatic
Piano: contrapuntal; broken chords and arpeggios; extremely chromatic; some fragmentation
Diff: pitches; rhythms; meter changes; vocal flexibility; needs very accomplished pianist
Uses: effective for the advanced musician

CONTE, DAVID
(b. U. S. A., 1955)

499. **ALLELUIA.** Medium Voice and Piano. E. C. Schirmer, 1987. D-centered; b–f♯"; Tess-M; 4/4, 8/8, 5/4, With spirit ♩ = 132–Expressively ♪ = 112; 4pp; Diff-V/d, P/d.
For: mezzo-soprano; baritone; some sopranos
Mood: joyful
Voice: syncopation and various rhythmic groupings, such as 3+2+3; many small skips; many melismas; a b a form; ends on long f♯"
Piano: syncopation; asymmetrical rhythmic groups; irregular accents; 8th-note motion; repeated block chords in central section; large l.h. reaches; no doubling of vocal line; one interlude
Diff: rhythms; dynamic control; ensemble; final long f♯" could be a problem for a medium voice
Uses: group ender, perhaps for a group of religious songs; similarity to Rorem's "Alleluia" is immediately apparent

CONVERSE, FREDERIC SHEPHERD
(b. Newton, MA, 1871; d. Westwood, MA, 1940)

500. **BRIGHT STAR,** Op. 14, No. 3 (John Keats). Boston Music Co., 1903. A♭maj; B–f'; Tess-M; 4/4, Molto moderato e tranquillo; 4pp; Diff-V/m-md, P/md.
For: baritone specified
Mood: lyrical; contemplative

Voice: many leaps; duplets and triplets; 2 vs. 3 in piano; some dotted rhythms
Piano: block and arpeggiated chords; incidental doubling of vocal line
Diff: secure registration; dynamic control
Uses: good singing song; effective; quiet ending

501. **SILENT NOON,** Op. 20, No. 2 (Dante Gabriel Rossetti). Boston Music Co., 1906. Fmaj; c'–e♭"; Tess-M; 6/8, Molto moderato e tranquillo; 5pp; Diff-V/m, P/md.
For: mezzo-soprano; baritone
Mood: lyrical; serene
Voice: many skips; interrupted phrases; some long-ranged phrases; 2–3-note slurs
Piano: chordal; broken-chord patterning; rocking figures; measured trills; does not double vocal line; 8th- & 16th-note motion
Diff: some long phrases
Uses: impressionistic setting; see also settings by Edward T. Cone and Elinor Remick Warren

COOPER, ESTHER
(b. Boston, MA, 1897)

502. **ENOUGH** (Sara Teasdale). [21]; 1st©1950. H & L keys: Cmaj & A♭maj; d'–f"(g") & b♭–d♭"(e♭"); Tess-M; 4/4, Con sentimento; 1+min; Diff-V/m, P/d.
For: any female voice
Mood: lyrical; somewhat sentimental love song
Voice: sweeping phrases; becomes dramatic at end
Piano: chordal; broad melody in 8ves; 16th-note arpeggios; generally independent of voice
Diff: powerful g" at climax (e♭" low key)

COPLAND, AARON
(b. Brooklyn, NY, 1900; d. N. Tarrytown, NY, 1990)

[See also D#s 4, 21, 28, & 39; no titles given]

503. **DIRGE IN WOODS** (George Meredith). Boosey & Hawkes, 1957. cmp1954. E♭-centered; d'–b♭"; Tess-M; 4/4, 3/4, 12/8, 6/8, 5/4 for voice, 12/8, 9/8, 4/4, 3/4, 6/8, 15/8 for piano, Not too slow; 1+min; Diff-V/md, P/md.
For: tenor; soprano
Mood: somber; intense; somewhat dramatic
Voice: many skips; triplet and duplet subdivisions; syncopation
Piano: broken-chord patterns; some scale patterns; varied registers; incidental doubling of vocal line
Diff: ensemble; 2 vs. 3; sustained high tones
Uses: good recital song; groups well with other single Copland songs or other American songs
Rec: D#59

504. **FOUR EARLY SONGS.** [94]. cmp1918–1922. Tonal; c'–g"; Tess-mH-H; regular meters, slow tempos; 12pp; Diff-V/m-d, P/m-d. Separate entries below. [**Rec:** D#156]

A.   **NIGHT** (Aaron Schaffer). D♭maj (modal flavoring); c'–g"; Tess-mH; 4/4, Adagio molto; 5pp; Diff-V/d, P/d.
For: high or medium-high voices
Mood: peaceful nature description; impressionistic
Voice: chromaticism; some difficult intervals; some syncopation, dotted and double-dotted rhythms; ends long f "; many atmospheric dynamics
Piano: impressionistic score; mostly 8th-note motion; r.h. double-note pattern diminished to 32nd notes for 4 meas.; some arpeggios; some countermelody; no doubling of vocal line; some pitch clues; essentially quiet playing
Diff: chromaticism; rhythms; some entrances; ensemble
Uses: student or recital song; group with other three songs in this publisher's group, or the other two Schaffer poems

B.   **A SUMMER VACATION** (Aaron Schaffer). A♭maj; g'–g"; Tess-H; 4/4, 2/4, 12/8, Moderato; 3pp; Diff-V/m, P/d.
For: soprano; tenor
Mood: summer joys remembered
Voice: two strophes, strophic variation; mostly follows chord structure in accomp.; easy rhythms
Piano: arpeggiation in 8th-note duplets and triplets in l.h. with countermelody in quarters & 8ths; some 4 vs. 3; 16th-note arpeggiation in l.h. combined with broken chords in r.h. in 12/8 section; short prelude, interludes, postlude; does not double vocal line
Diff: perhaps ensemble transition to 12/8
Uses: group with (a.) & (c.) of this set; useful student song for young soprano or tenor with good musical skills

C.   **MY HEART IS IN THE EAST** (Aaron Schaffer). Gmaj/Emin–maj; d♯'–g"; Tess-H; 2/2, Mournfully; 2pp; Diff-V/m, P/m.
For: tenor; soprano
Mood: longing to be in Arabian lands; mournful
Voice: stepwise and easy skips; mostly quarter notes; straightforward rhythms
Piano: block chords with countermelody; some syncopation; does not double vocal line but includes most pitches in texture; short prelude and interludes
Diff: perhaps a few dotted rhythms
Uses: group with other songs in this set

D.   **ALONE** (Arabic text by John Duncan; trans. E. Powys Mathers). E-centered; d'–f♯'; Tess-mH; 2/2, Lento; 2pp; Diff-V/d, P/md.
For: tenor; soprano
Mood: longing; love song
Voice: quarter & 8th-note motion; some dotted rhythms; chromaticism; often dissonant with piano
Piano: broken-chord patterns in 8th notes; some countermelody; many accidentals; wide reach in l.h.; 4 meas. difficult syncopated chords; mostly quiet dynamics; somewhat impressionistic; does not double vocal line
Diff: finding pitches not in piano texture; ends on long f♯" with decresc.
Uses: very nice song for a love song group; pair with (a.) for an impressionistic pair

505.   **OLD POEM** (Chinese; trans. by A. Waley). Edition Salabert, 1923. cmp1920. Emin; e'–g"; Tess-mH; 3/4, 4/4, Very slowly; 3pp; Diff-V/md, P/md.
For: soprano
Mood: lyrical; lonely; introspective
Voice: stepwise and skips of up to 7th; some difficult intervals; duple and triple divisions of beat; some syncopation
Diff: intervals; fragmentary phrasing
Uses: good song; recital material; groups well with other single Copland songs listed here
Rec: D#156

506.   **PASTORALE** (trans. from the Kafiristan by E. P. Mathers). [95]. cmp1921. Quartal harmony; d'–a"; Tess-mH; 4/4 with changes, Not too slowly, serenely; 3min; Diff-V/m, P/m.
For: high voice
Mood: love song
Voice: mostly stepwise and small skips; a few leaps of 7th & 9th; quiet song
Piano: syncopated patterns; quiet; many tempo variations; wide pitch range
Diff: long legato line; subtle dynamic control on high notes
Uses: to practice floating high tones, or to display mastery of this technique; group with other single Copland songs or use in a mixed-composer group of love songs; could pair with Copland's "Vocalise"
Rec: D#35

507.   **SONG** (e. e. cummings). [22, 95]. cmp1927; also pub. separately as "Poet's Song" by Boosey & Hawkes. X; e'–a"; Tess-M; 3/2, 4/2, 2/2, Lento molto; 3pp; Diff-V/md, P/m.
For: soprano; tenor
Voice: long, flowing phrases occasionally broken by rests; some large intervals
Piano: smooth and sustained; chromatic; 4-voice texture; does not double vocal line
Diff: melodic intervals difficult; *messa di voce* on e" at end
Uses: good recital material and for teaching above techniques; groups well with the other single Copland songs listed here
Rec: D#s 4, 16

508.   **TWELVE POEMS OF EMILY DICKINSON.** Cycle. Boosey & Hawkes, 1951. Traditional keys with many altered chords and modulations; a–b♭"; Tess-M, mH, mL, wide; mostly regular meters with changes; varied tempos, begins and ends slow; 30min; Diff-V/d, P/d.
For: lyric mezzo-soprano; soprano (with strong low voice)
Mood: various moods and subjects: nature, life, death, eternity
Voice: often disjunct, but legato; wide range; large intervals; long phrases; some difficult pitch patterns; flexible tempos; rhythmic intricacies; many long tones
Piano: programmatic in nature; much linear texture; requires a variety of techniques; many tempo changes; much rubato; large reach helpful; rhythmic security required; many expressive and articulation markings; some fingerings; demands skillful pianist accustomed to modern score and sensitive both to the voice and to the poetry; "Sleep Is Supposed to Be" and "The Chariot"

share musical motives

Diff: range; pitch; rhythm; endurance; ensemble; for advanced singer, preferably with warm, beautiful sound, esp. in the chest voice

Uses: one of the best cycles by an American composer; can teach many techniques; an audience favorite; whole cycle fills half a program; very effective as a whole, but selections can be made [8 of the 12 songs orchestrated by the composer and recorded by several singers–D#s 14, 151, 152, 153, 154]

Rec: D#s 155, 156, 157, 158, 159 (12 songs)

   a. *Nature, the Gentlest Mother.* E♭maj; b♭–g"; 4/4, Quite slow; 4min. [**Rec:** D#s 14, 65, 151, 152, 153, 154]

   b. *There Came a Wind like a Bugle.* Amaj; b–g"; 2/4, 6/8, Quite fast; 1+min. [**Rec:** D#s 14, 58, 151, 152, 153, 154]

   c. *Why Do They Shut Me Out of Heaven?* [95]. C–A♭maj; b♭–a♭"; 4/4, 3/4, 2/4, Moderately; 2min.

   d. *The World Feels Dusty.* Modal on D; a♯–f♯"; 3/4, Very slowly; 1+min. [**Rec:** D#s 14, 151, 152, 153, 154]

   e. *Heart, We Will Forget Him.* E♭maj; b♭–g"; 4/4, Very slowly (dragging), 2min. [**Rec:** D#s 14, 151, 152, 153, 154]

   f. *Dear March, Come In!* F♯maj; a–f♯"; 6/8, 9/8, With exuberance; 2+min. [**Rec:** D#s 14, 151, 152, 153, 154]

   g. *Sleep Is Supposed to Be.* B♭-centered; b♭–b♭"; 4/4, Moderately slow, with dignity; 3min. [**Rec:** D#s 14, 151, 152, 153, 154]

   h. *When They Come Back.* Fmaj; c'–f♯"; 2/4, Moderately (beginning slowly); 1+min. [**Rec:** D#10]

   i. *I Felt a Funeral in My Brain.* Bitonal; c♯'–g"; 2/4, Rather fast–heavy, with foreboding; 2min.

   j. *I've Heard an Organ Talk Sometimes.* B♭-centered; b♭–f"; 3/4, Gently flowing; 2min.

   k. *Going to Heaven!* B♭maj; a–f"; 6/8, Fast; 2min. [**Rec:** D#s 14, 151, 152, 153, 154]

   l. *The Chariot.* Bmaj; b–f♯"; 4/4, With quiet grace; 3min. [**Rec:** D#s 10, 14, 151, 152, 153, 154]

509. **VOCALISE.** Boosey & Hawkes, 1929, 1956. [95]. E-centered; c'–b♭"(a"); Tess-mH; changing meters, Con moto, several tempo changes; 5pp; Diff-V/d, P/md.

For: soprano (voice must be flexible)

Mood: lyrical

Voice: motion in 8ths, quarters, and half notes; many accidentals; leaps up to 11th & 12th

Piano: linear; many accidentals; thin texture; does not double vocal line

Diff: singer needs excellent musicianship and vocal technique; dynamic control; tempo changes challenging

Uses: effective piece; fits well with other single Copland songs listed here: "Dirge in Woods," "Old Poem," and "Song"

Rec: D#160

CORIGLIANO, JOHN
(b. New York, NY, 1938)

510. **THE CLOISTERS** (William Hoffman). Cycle. G. Schirmer, 1967. Pub. separately. Tonal centers; a–g"; Tess-M-mH; unmetered, ♪& ♩ remaining steady; varied tempos, slow ending; 14pp; Diff-V/md-d, P/md.

For: mezzo-soprano

Mood: moods embrace disillusionment, irony, and sensuality

Voice: skips and leaps; flowing lines; dramatic climaxes; many accidentals; various phrase lengths; demanding of vocal size and endurance as well as flexibility

Piano: pianist must make sense from no key sig. and no meter sig.; not overly difficult, but a good rhythmic sense required

Diff: vocal endurance in the cycle as a whole; rhythmic irregularities; ensemble

Uses: good songs; work well as a group; program in interior of recital (quiet ending); can be sung separately, as two are published in [20]

Rec: D#20

   a. *Fort Tryon Park: September.* Fmin-maj; d♭'–g♭"; Tess-M, H; ♪unit of pulse; 4/8 & 3/8 alternate, Andante; 2pp. [**Rec:** D#7]

   b. *Song to the Witch of the Cloisters.* X; b–f"; Tess-M; ♩ unit, Allegro; 4pp. [**Rec:** D#65]

   c. *Christmas at the Cloisters.* [20]. G majorish; a–g"; Tess-mH; ♩ unit; 4pp.

   d. *The Unicorn.* [20]. Dmin/maj; a–g"; Tess-M; ♪unit, Andante; 4pp.

511. **DODECAPHONIA** (Mark Adamo). G. Schirmer, 1997. "To Joan Morris and Bill Bolcom." Tonal (Emin-succession of keys–ends inconclusively); f–f"; Tess-M; 4/4, 3/2, 6/8, 12/8, ♩= ca. 96–Presto ♩= 138–Broadly ♩. = 72–Adagio-Presto ♩= 152; 7min; Diff-V/md, P/m.

For: mezzo-soprano probably best; baritone; bass-baritone

Mood: text spoofs serial composition in mock-mysterious, private-eye style

Voice: speech-like patterns; many repeated pitches, as in recit.; some syncopation; sectional; mostly 8th-note motion; some quick repeated 16ths in Presto section at end; some gestures required in the score; two spoken lines

Piano: block chords, sustained or repeated, in 6/8 & 2/4; rolled chords; many sound effects in various registers; some tremolo; some counterpoint; many accidentals; some doubling of vocal line, always supportive; pianist has an acting bit; important dynamics for effect

Diff: needs good actress/actor who can bring this to life and a musically knowledgeable audience; understanding of cabaret style helpful for both performers

Uses: fine piece for performers and audience who enjoy spoofs of compositional styles

512. **PETIT FOURS** (A Song Cyclette). G. Schirmer, 1981. X; b♭–a"; Tess-M; regular meters with changes; 5pp; Diff-V/md, P/m-md.

For: tenor; high baritone

Mood: lyrical (a. & c.); humorous (b. & d.)

Voice: some difficult intervals; several portamentos; some syncopation; syllabic and 2–3-note slurs; many dynamic markings; some staccato

Piano: 4–5-voice textures; (a.), somewhat contrapuntal with some doubling of vocal line; (b.), afterbeat style, many accidentals, much staccato, little doubling of vocal line; (c.), chordal texture, legato, doubles vocal line; (d.), afterbeat style, polytonality, juxtaposition of unrelated keys, quotations from "The Drunken Sailor"

Diff: pitch patterns in (a.); relationship of vocal line and accomp. (polytonality) in (b.) and (d.); a few rhythms

Uses: attractive short group for closing a recital

  a. *Upon Julia's Clothes* (Robert Herrick). G-centered; c'–a"; 6/8, Gently; 1min.
  b. *The Turtle* (Ogden Nash). Polytonal; e♭'–e"; changing meters, With plodding facility; 30sec.
  c. *Une allée du Luxembourg* (Aloysius Bertrand). X; b♭–f"; 6/8, With simplicity; 30sec; text in French.
  d. *The Ancient Mariner* (Verse 1) (Samuel Taylor Coleridge). X; e'–g♭"; 4/4 with changes, With vigor; 45sec.

513.   POEM IN OCTOBER for Voice and Orchestra (piano reduction by composer) (Dylan Thomas). G. Schirmer, 1974. X; d'–a"; Tess-M; regular and irregular meters with frequent changes, varied tempos; 14+min; Diff-V/d, P/dd.

For: tenor; soprano; mezzo-soprano

Mood: lyrical; philosophical; uses nature imagery

Voice: both conjunct and disjunct motion; 8ve leaps common; chromatic; triplets; 3 & 6 in voice vs. 5 in piano; dynamics *pp–fff*; syllabic with occasional short melismas

Piano: chordal-linear combination; broken-chord patterns; chromatic; triplets and quintuplets; 3 vs. 5; tremolo; grace notes; many dynamic markings; large reach helpful; does not double vocal line

Diff: frequent changes of meter; complex rhythms; ensemble; control of dynamics

Uses: probably best in orchestral version; would stand alone on recital; excellent program material

CORTÉS, RAMIRO
(b. Dallas, TX, 1933; d. Salt Lake City, UT, 1984)

[See Appendix for songs with Spanish texts]

514.   THE FALCON (anon.). C. F. Peters, 1958. X; c♯'–b♭"; Tess-mH; 3/4, 4/4, 3/8, Lento, contemplativo; 5pp; Diff-V/d, P/d.

For: soprano specified

Mood: dramatic; somber; dirge; uses lullaby refrain

Voice: disjunct; complex rhythms; long-ranged phrases; 2-note slurs

Piano: linear; various structures in parallel motion; complex rhythms; large reaches; does not double vocal line; uses *Dies irae* theme throughout

Diff: text; every aspect will need extra work

Uses: effective song for the right singer; quiet ending

CORY, GEORGE
(b. Syracuse, NY, 1920)

515.   AND THIS SHALL BE FOR MUSIC. (Robert Louis Stevenson). General, 1955. D♭maj; b♭–d♭"; Tess-M; 6/8, 4/4, 6/4, Allegretto; 4pp; Diff-V/m, P/m.

For: baritone

Mood: lyrical; love song

Voice: conjunct; some large leaps; somewhat chromatic; straightforward rhythms

Piano: patterned; repeated rhythmic figure in arpeggiated l.h.; chords in r.h.

Uses: nice romantic song for intermediate student

516.   ANOTHER AMERICA (Douglass Cross). General, 1971. Cmaj; a–e♭"; Tess-mL; 2/2, Quietly, not fast; 8pp; Diff-V/me, P/me.

For: any low voice

Mood: sad; speaks of injustices toward native Americans

Voice: phrases broken down into 2-meas. motives ending in a relatively long note; declamatory style in middle section; some chromaticism

Piano: chordal texture; broken-chord or afterbeat figures in r.h. throughout much of song

Uses: somewhat popular in style; could fit in a group of songs about the dark side of Americana

517.   FOUR SONGS OF THE NIGHT. General, 1945, 1970. Pub. separately. No. 1–"For Maggie Teyte." Traditional key structures; b–f"; Tess-M; regular but changing meters, moderate tempos; 14pp; Diff-V/m,P/m.

For: set best for baritone; other possibilities below

Mood: quiet

Voice: mostly stepwise with small skips; accidentals; some repetitive rhythms; easy ranges

Piano: use of pedal-point, ostinato, block chords, and repeated motives; some wide reaches; some polyrhythms

Uses: nice set for senior recital; useful separately for various singers

  a. *Boat Song* (Douglass Cross). Emaj; c♯'–e"; 6/8, Lento e con leggierezza; 3pp; also for mezzo-soprano and some sopranos.
  b. *So We'll Go No More A-Roving* (Lord Byron). Cmaj; c'–c"; 2/4, 6/8, Allegretto; 3pp; also for mezzo-soprano or contralto.
  c. *Good-Night* (Percy Bysshe Shelley). X-E♭maj; b–d♭"; 3/4, Moderato ed intimo; 3pp; also for mezzo-soprano.
  d. *Equinox* (Robert Adams). Dmin; c'–f"; changing meters, Andante, & other changing tempos; 5pp; also possibly for tenor.

518.   MUSIC I HEARD WITH YOU (Conrad Aiken). General, 1945. "For Eileen Farrell." E♭maj; c'–g"; Tess-M; 12/8, Moderato con passione; 6pp; Diff-V/m, P/m-d.

For: soprano; tenor; text better for a man, but one low phrase could be uncomfortable for tenor

Mood: romantic; lush; lost love

Voice: stepwise with small skips; irregular phrase lengths;

some speech-like rhythms; soft high tones

Piano: chordal texture; rapid broken chords in one section; syncopation; many accidentals; sectional

Diff: needs good dynamic control

Uses: usable in a group; somewhat popular in style; see also setting by Richard Hageman

519. **REQUIESCAT** (Oscar Wilde). Associated, 1951. "For Marie Powers." E♭maj; b♭–e♭"; Tess-mL; 3/4, 2/4, 4/4, At a quiet, walking pace; 3min; Diff-V/m, P/m.

For: baritone; mezzo-soprano

Mood: dirge

Voice: many small skips; duplets and triplets; syncopation

Piano: chordal–block, rolled, cluster; syncopation; large reaches; does not double vocal line

Diff: fluid meter and rhythms

Uses: effective setting; recital material

COWELL, HENRY
(b. Menlo Park, CA, 1897; d. Shady, NY, 1965)

[See also D#s 59 & 161 for songs not listed below]

520. **DAYBREAK** (William Blake). Peer International, 1950. Gmin-B♭maj; d'–g"; Tess-mH; 4/4, Andante; 1+min; Diff-V/m, P/m.

For: tenor best; soprano possible

Mood: lyrical; daybreak as symbol of reawakening of soul

Voice: stepwise and small skips; 2–3-note slurs

Piano: chordal; 8th-note motion; some passages in 10ths; little doubling of vocal line

Diff: dynamic control

Uses: effective song; strong setting; quiet ending

Rec: D#161

521. **FIRELIGHT AND LAMP** (Gene Baro). C. F. Peters, 1964. "For Theodore Uppman." Cmin; c'–g"; Tess-mH; 4/4, Andante; 3pp; Diff-V/m, P/m.

For: soprano or tenor with solid low c

Mood: lyrical, with dramatic climax; mood piece

Voice: many skips; two downward portamentos of 10th; some dotted rhythms; duplets and triplets

Piano: chordal; 6–7-voice block chords; some broken chords

Diff: dynamic contrasts

Uses: quiet ending; interior of group

Rec: D#s 53, 161

522. **THE LITTLE BLACK BOY** (William Blake). C. F. Peters, 1964. "For Roland Hayes." Dmin; d'–a"(f"); Tess-M or mH (depending on opt. notes chosen); 4pp; Diff-V/md, P/md.

For: tenor

Mood: a parable

Voice: many skips; 2-note slurs; dotted rhythms; duplets and triplets

Piano: linear/block-chord combinations; covers keyboard; many accidentals; 12-meas. prelude; does not double vocal line

Diff: irregular meters; 2 vs. 3; two speakers; large dynamic changes

Uses: interpret in the light of Blake's *Songs of Innocence*; see

also settings by Clifford Shaw, Ernest Lubin, Virgil Thomson, and others

Rec: D#161

523. **THE PASTURE** (Robert Frost). [49]. Gmaj; e'–a"; Tess-mH; 4/4, Andante; 2pp; Diff-V/m, P/d.

For: lyric soprano

Mood: lyrical; description of nature

Voice: chiefly 2nds & 3rds; 8th-note movement; light and lyrical

Piano: r.h. melody in high register over l.h. chords

Uses: good song for a light, agile voice

Rec: D#161

524. **SPRING COMES SINGING** (Dora Hagemeyer). Associated, 1958. [4]. cmp1954. X; d'–a"; Tess-H; 6/8, Allegro; 7pp; Diff-V/md, P/md.

For: soprano; tenor

Mood: renewal; joy

Voice: small skips; many 2–3-note slurs; sustained high tones; dramatic climaxes

Piano: 3–6-voice chordal texture; some clusters; minimal doubling of vocal line

Diff: sustained high notes; final phrase ascends to f♯", g", a" over 6 meas.

Uses: group or program ender

525. **ST. AGNES MORNING** (Maxwell Anderson). Mercury, 1947. Fmaj; c'–g"; Tess-M; 4/4, Andante con moto; 4pp; Diff-V/m, P/me.

For: medium voices; baritone best

Mood: dramatic; uneasy; restless

Voice: stepwise and easy skips; repetitive rhythms

Piano: chordal; repetitive syncopated rhythmic pattern throughout

Diff: intensity of expression; dynamic control

Uses: nice song; quiet ending

Rec: D#s 53, 161

526. **THREE ANTI-MODERNIST SONGS** [for] Voice and Piano, ed. H. Wiley Hitchcock. (Poems from American newspapers, c. 1884–1924). C. F. Peters, 1996. cmp1938. Tonal, chromatic, quartal; c'–g"; Tess-cs; mostly regular meters; varied tempos; 7min; Diff-V/m-md, P/m-md.

For: soprano

Mood: humorous, sarcastic musical caricatures of Wagner, Strauss, and Stravinsky

Voice: disjunct vocal lines; frequent large ascending intervals followed by long descending line; chromaticism; repeated rhythmic patterns; some *Sprechstimme*

Piano: like simplified orchestral reductions of works of composers satirized

Diff: substantial voice needed with knowledge of the appropriate musical styles; ensemble

Uses: excellent for humorous group for musically knowledgeable audiences

   a. *A Sharp Where You'd Expect a Natural.* Wagnerian chromatic; c'–g"; Tess-cs; 4/4, Moderato pomposo; 6pp.

   b. *Hark! From the Pit a Fearsome Sound.* Straussian

chromatic; c'–g"; Tess-cs; 4/4, Presto misterioso; 7pp.

c. *Who Wrote This Fiendish Rite of Spring?* Quartal; d'–g"; Tess-cs; 2/4, 5/8, Allegro Moderato; 3pp.

CRAWFORD-SEEGER, RUTH (See SEEGER, RUTH CRAWFORD)

CRESTON, PAUL
(b. New York, NY, 1906; d. San Diego, CA, 1985)

[See Appendix for songs with French texts]

527. **THE BIRD OF THE WILDERNESS** (Rabindranath Tagore). [59]; 1st©1950. H & L keys: X; f♯'–a" & d'–f"; Tess-M; 3/4, 2/4, 4/4, Andante; 5pp; Diff-V/d, P/d.
For: all voices
Mood: lyrical; philosophical
Voice: disjunct; chromatic
Piano: much use of rapid chromatic passages
Diff: pitch; intonation; sustained high tone
Uses: teaching all phases of musicianship; good recital song; see also Horsman setting of this text
Rec: D#11

528. **PSALM XXIII,** Op. 27. [64]; 1st©1945. X; d'–f"; Tess-M; 6/8, With tranquillity; 8pp; Diff-V/dd, P/d.
For: mezzo-soprano; tenor with good low tones; baritone
Mood: lyrical; familiar text
Voice: flowing phrases, becoming more dramatic at end; duplets
Piano: chordal; broken, repeated, arpeggiated; somewhat chromatic; independent
Diff: rhythm; pitches; long phrases
Uses: good for church or recital
Rec: D#11

529. **A SONG OF JOYS** (Walt Whitman). Colombo, 1963. Dmaj; e♭'–g♭"; Tess-M; 6/8, Moderately fast; 6pp; Diff-V/m, P/md.
For: tenor; soprano
Mood: lyrical; ecstatic
Voice: conjunct with some leaps; modulations; some sustained high tones; some rhythmic irregularities
Piano: chordal–broken and arpeggiated; polyrhythms; wide reaches; accidentals; good finger technique needed
Diff: rhythmic groupings
Uses: sweeping song of joy; group or program ender

530. **THREE SONGS,** Op. 46. Leeds, 1952. Pub. separately. [**Rec:** D#11, all three songs listed below]

A. **SERENADE** (Edward C. Pinkney). A♭maj; f'–a♭"; Tess-M; 3/4, Rather fast; 5pp; Diff-V/m, P/md.
For: tenor
Mood: lyrical; serenade
Voice: mostly conjunct; accidentals; 4 & 2 in voice vs. 3 in piano; long tones; ends a♭" on "day"; comfortable tessitura

Piano: patterned, with characteristic rhythmic figures repeated; accidentals; nimble fingers needed
Diff: ensemble, for inexperienced performers
Uses: nice serenade for young tenor with secure a♭"

B. **LULLABY** (John G. Neihardt). Fmaj; f'–f"; Tess-M; 2/4, Slow; 3pp; Diff-V/m, P/m.
For: soprano; mezzo-soprano
Mood: lullaby using nature imagery
Voice: several phrases begin on highest notes of range and descend; some accidentals
Piano: arpeggiation in l.h.; independent melody in top voice; moving16ths in inner voice
Diff: well-controlled soft tone
Uses: good for phrases that begin high and descend; good recital song

C. **FOUNTAIN SONG** (John G. Neihardt). Emin-maj; e'–b"; Tess-mH; 6/4, With spirit; 8pp; Diff-V/d, P/dd.
For: lyric or coloratura soprano
Mood: joyous
Voice: flowing phrases; chromaticism; duplets
Piano: continuous arpeggiation and other 16th-note figurations; chromaticism
Diff: sustained b" at end; sustained tones at phrase ends
Uses: effective recital song of the showpiece type

CRIST, BAINBRIDGE
(b. Lawrenceburg, IN, 1883; d. Barnstable, MA, 1969)

531. **APRIL RAIN** (Conrad Aiken). Carl Fischer, 1915. Reprint: Classical Vocal Reprints (H). H & L keys: B♭maj & Gmaj; f'–g" & d'–e"; Tess-M; 4/8, Allegretto; 5pp; Diff-V/me, P/md.
For: lyric soprano
Mood: lyrical; ecstatic love song
Voice: many phrases begin high and descend stepwise; 8th-note movement throughout to final phrase
Piano: afterbeat pattern; arpeggiation at end
Diff: soft dynamics; some chromaticism
Uses: teaching; many descending phrases

532. **A BAG OF WHISTLES** (Edward J. O'Brien). Ditson, 1915. H & L keys: Cmaj & Amaj (orig); g'–f" & e'–d"; Tess-M; 3/8, Allegretto; 1min; Diff-V/e, P/me.
For: mezzo-soprano; soprano
Mood: sprightly; clever; "Irish"
Voice: stepwise; easy rhythms; lightly accented
Piano: chordal; spare texture; high register imitation of whistles; some doubling of vocal line

533. **BLUE BIRD** (Emily Selinger). [54]; 1st©1920. Amaj; a'–g♯"(opt. C♯'" & a"); Tess-mH; 6/8, Allegro vivace; 21meas.; Diff-V/e, P/me.
For: soprano
Mood: lighthearted; youthful
Voice: stepwise and skips of 3rd; not complicated
Piano: 3–5-voice texture
Uses: good for young, high, light voice

534. **CHINESE MOTHER GOOSE RHYMES** (from the

Chinese; trans. Prof. I. T. Headland, Peking University). Carl Fischer, 1917. Reprint: Classical Vocal Reprints (M). Traditional keys; c'–g"; Tess-M; regular meters, moderate to brisk tempos; 11pp; Diff-V/e, P/e.

For: mezzo-soprano; soprano
Mood: humorous rhymes
Voice: conjunct with some skips in pentatonic mode; some small ornaments; melodies based on Chinese themes
Piano: chordal; some ostinato; some ornaments; pentatonic
Uses: teaching pieces for young beginners; humorous and expressive songs

    a. *Lady-Bug.* Gmaj; d'–g"; 2/4, Allegretto grazioso; 1p.
    b. *Baby Is Sleeping.* Fmaj; c'–f "; 4/4, Moderately, without dragging; 2pp.
    c. *What the Old Cow Said.* Amin; d'–e"; 2/4, Allegretto; 2pp.
    d. *The Mouse.* Cmin; c'–e"; 2/4, Allegretto; 2pp.
    e. *Of What Use Is a Girl?* B♭min; f'–d♭"; 2/4, Moderately, without dragging; 1p.
    f. *Pat a Cake.* E♭maj; e♭'–e♭"; 2/4, Moderately, without dragging; 1p.
    g. *The Old Woman.* A♭maj; e♭'–e♭"; 2/4, Allegretto; 2pp.

535. **COLOURED STARS** (from the Chinese; trans. E. Powys Mathers). Carl Fischer, 1921. Reprint: Classical Vocal Reprints (H). G♭maj; d♭'–g♭"(b♭"); Tess-M; 3/4, 4/4, Allegretto; 6pp; Diff-V/m, P/md.

For: tenor
Mood: lyrical; ecstatic romantic song
Voice: conjunct; soaring line; triplets
Piano: arpeggiated; some 8ve and chordal countermelody; various rhythmic groupings; accidentals; 16th- & 32nd-note movement; secure technique needed
Diff: ensemble; chromaticism
Uses: good for a lyric tenor; could end a group nicely with the opt. b♭"

536. **THE DARK KING'S DAUGHTER** (Conrad Aiken). Church, 1920. Emaj; d'–b"; Tess-M, H; 4/4, 3/4, 5/4, 6/4, Allegretto; Diff-V/d, P/d.

For: tenor
Mood: magical
Voice: sustained lines; rhythmic intricacies
Piano: arpeggiated throughout (rather like Duparc)
Diff: big sound; good high tones
Uses: fine song for a substantial tenor voice

537. **DROLLERIES FROM AN ORIENTAL DOLL'S HOUSE** (Japanese and Chinese texts in English trans.). Carl Fischer, 1920. Reprint: Classical Vocal Reprints (M). Musical material based on Japanese and Chinese melodic themes (given for each song), mostly pentatonic; c'–g" (mostly only to e"); Tess-M; 2/4, 4/4; various tempo indications; 15pp; Diff-V/e-m, P/e-m.

For: medium voices; mezzo-soprano best
Mood: whimsical; some narrative; some dialogues
Voice: conjunct, easy skips; regular rhythms; some syncopation; occasional triplets; much repetition

Piano: 4ths & 5ths; some drum effects; mostly chordal with some decorative devices
Uses: good for teaching young students; light songs with humor and an Oriental flavor

    a. *The Moon-Child* (Japanese).
    b. *The Dancer* (Japanese).
    c. *Watching* (Japanese).
    d. *Unfortunate* (Chinese).
    e. *Little Small-Feet* (Chinese).
    f. *Bald Head Lee* (Chinese).

538. **EVENING** (Conrad Aiken). G. Schirmer, 1934. Fmaj; c'–a"(g"); Tess-M-mH; 3/4, Andante; 1+min; Diff-V/me, P/e.

For: soprano; tenor
Mood: lyrical; nostalgic
Voice: scale lines and easy skips; easy rhythms; legato
Piano: chordal–block and rolled; spare texture; many accidentals; quiet
Diff: preferred final note is a" *pp*, sustained over 2 meas.
Uses: conventional song; not one of Crist's best, but usable

539. **INTO A SHIP, DREAMING** (Walter de la Mare). Carl Fischer, 1918. Reprint: Classical Vocal Reprints (H & M). "Dedicated to Reinald Werrenrath." H, M, & L keys: A♭maj, G♭maj, & E♭maj; e♭'–g♯", d♭'–f♯", & b♭–d♯"; Tess-M; 4/4, Moderato, non troppo allegro; 4pp; Diff-V/m, P/m.

For: soprano; tenor; other voices in lower keys
Mood: lyrical; dream-like
Voice: conjunct with some skips; melody modulates; some difficult pitches; soft climax on g♯"
Piano: broken chords with countermelody; some syncopation; modulatory arpeggiated sections; 2 vs. 3; delicate
Uses: lovely song, perhaps Crist's best; very useful for young lyric sopranos; interior of group

540. **KNOCK ON THE DOOR** (Conrad Aiken). [48]; 1st©1934. H & L keys: Fmin & Dmin; e♭'–a♭" & c'–f"; Tess-M; 2/4, Presto; 3pp; Diff-V/md, P/m.

For: all voices with dramatic weight
Mood: dramatic; philosophical
Voice: disjunct; large intervals; declamatory
Piano: chordal; triplet figures; needs incisive, powerful tone
Diff: text; 8ve leaps downward
Uses: programming possibilities for the right voice

541. **LANGUOR** (Li-Tai-Pe; trans. E. Powys Mathers). Carl Fischer, 1923. Amaj; e♭'–f"; Tess-M; 4/4, 2/4, Lento, e molto tranquillo; 3pp; Diff-V/m, P/m.

For: mezzo-soprano; tenor; some baritones
Mood: lyrical; sensuous, descriptive song
Voice: conjunct; somewhat chromatic; speech rhythms; many triplets; repeated tones
Piano: chordal; wide-spread over keyboard; bass grace-note chords; slow quarter-note movement with some 8ths; large reach helpful; atmospheric
Diff: creation of mood; floating, legato line
Uses: sensuously lovely miniature; useful, esp. in an Oriental group

542. **LEILA** (Song of Nepal; trans. E. Powys Mathers). Carl Fischer, 1921, 1951. Gmin; d♭'–g♯"; Tess-M; 2/4, 5/4, Moderato; 8pp; Diff-V/m-md, P/m.
For: tenor
Mood: lyrico-dramatic; bitter love song
Voice: conjunct with leaps; ornaments; speech rhythms; various divisions of the beat; soaring line; strong final climax on g" sustained
Piano: chordal; syncopated pattern; tremolo with bass-line countermelody; big ending, 8ves and chords
Diff: dramatic emotional involvement with text; some passages low for a tenor
Uses: good romantic period piece for a full tenor voice

543. **O COME HITHER!** (George Darley). Carl Fischer, 1918. Reprint: Classical Vocal Reprints (H & M). Gmaj; d'–b"(d'''); Tess-H; 3/8, Allegro, con grazia; Diff-V/d, P/m.
For: coloratura soprano
Mood: coloratura showpiece, trinket size
Voice: much florid singing; chromaticism; trills; high tones; some staccato
Piano: patterned accomp.
Diff: typical feats of agility
Uses: useful for young coloratura; good ear training; agility

544. **QUEER YARNS** (Walter de la Mare). Carl Fischer, 1925. Traditional keys; c'–g"; Tess-M; 2/4, 6/8, moderate tempos; 10pp; Diff-V/m, P/md.
For: mezzo-soprano; tenor
Mood: humorous; odd; narrative
Voice: conjunct lines; some chromaticism; speech rhythms
Piano: chordal in various figurations; a little arpeggiation; accidentals; some tremolo
Diff: speech rhythms; chromatic melody
Uses: nice light group; enough variety of mood, tempo, etc., to be effective

    a. *Alas, Alack.* Dmin; 2/4, Allegro.
    b. *Tired Jim.* Emin; 2/4, Andante.
    c. *Five Eyes.* C♯min; 6/8, Allegretto.
    d. *Jim Jay.* Fmaj; 2/4, Allegretto.

545. **THE SHIP OF RIO** (Walter de la Mare). G. Schirmer, 1940. H & L keys: Gmaj & Emaj; d'–g" & b–e"; Tess-mH; 2/4, Allegro; 1min; Diff-V/m, P/md.
For: tenor
Mood: humorous nonsense; a sailor's tall tale
Voice: many small skips; a few triplets
Piano: broken-chord pattern; glissando and trill in bass; fast; does not double vocal line
Diff: fast articulation.
Uses: good for young students; humorous song for final group on program

CROCKETT, DONALD
(b. Pasadena, CA, 1951)

546. **THE PENSIVE TRAVELLER.** Six Songs on Poems by Henry David Thoreau for High Voice and Piano. Cycle. Serenissima, 1983. cmp1981. "For Jonathan Mack." X; c♯'–a"; Tess-mH; traditional meters, changing meters, and unmetered; tempos given in metronome markings; 14min; Diff-V/d, P/d.
For: tenor; soprano
Mood: philosophical nature poems; transcendental; oneness with nature; somewhat dramatic
Voice: mostly conjunct except for opening and closing songs; some chant-like writing in (b.); some rhythmic complexity; small divisions of the beat in (c.); special rhythmic notation in (d.); many accidentals; somewhat melismatic
Piano: some linear-style accomps.; some broken-chord and repeated-note accomps.; many trill or tremolo figures; non-tertian harmonies; some polyrhythms; various divisions of beat; some figures accelerate (d.); much staccato in (e.); sometimes imitates but does not double vocal line
Diff: ensemble; rhythmic complexity; (e.) hovers around register break; voice needs flexibility
Uses: effective group for a flexible lyric voice
Rec: D#162

    a. *I Was Born upon Thy Bank River.* X; d♭'–g"; 4/4 with changes, ♩ = 88, with fluctuations; 2pp; (attacca no.2).
    b. *For Though the Caves Were Rabitted.* X; a'–f"; 5/4, ♩ = 132–♩ = 80; 5pp.
    c. *On the Sun Coming Out in the Afternoon.* X; g'–g"; 3/4, Semplice (♩ = 52–56); 5pp.
    d. *What's the Railroad to Me?* X; c♯'–g♭"; unmetered, Not without humor ♩ = 88 (many changes and fluctuations); 6pp.
    e. *Sic Vita.* X; g'–g"; 4/4 with some changes, Deftly (♩ = 132); 10pp; (attaca (f.)).
    f. *I Was Born upon Thy Bank River* (II). X; e'–a"; unmetered, Freely, with gravity (♩ = 52) (with many tempo fluctuations); 2pp.

CRUMB, GEORGE
(b. Charleston, WV, 1929)

[See also D#s 58 & 71 for songs not listed below]

547. **THREE EARLY SONGS.** C. F. Peters, 1986. cmp1947. Tonal; b–f♯"; Tess-M; metered, with changes; varied tempos; 7min; Diff-V/m, P/m-md.
For: soprano; mezzo-soprano
Mood: descriptive; lyric; sadly nostalgic
Voice: stepwise and skips along chord lines; easy rhythms, duplet and triplet divisions of beat; some fragmented phrases; many *ppp–ff* dynamics; lyrical; (b.) & (c.) folk-like
Piano: arpeggiation; block and broken chords; other 16th-note figuration; many accidentals; little doubling of vocal line, but always supports; brief interludes; delicate coloristic harmonies and figurations often "glitter"
Diff: ensemble may take time
Uses: beautiful lyric group for a recital
Rec: D#s 163, 164

    a. *Night* (Robert Southey). F♯min; c♯'–e"; Tess-M;

12/8, 9/8, 4/4, Animato, misterioso (♩.= 86)–più lento (♩ = 52); 4pp.

b. *Let It Be Forgotten* (Sara Teasdale). Emaj (unsettled); b–f♯"; Tess-M; 4/4, 5/4, 3/4, 3/2, Lentamente, con delicatezza (♩ = 54)–pochiss. agitato (♩ = 70)–lento, esitante (♩ = 44); 3pp.

c. *Wind Elegy* (Sara Teasdale). E♭min; e♭'–d♭"; Tess-M; 12/8, 9/8, Tranquillamente mosso (♩. = 66); 4pp.

CUMBERWORTH, STARLING
(b. Remson Corners, OH, 1915)

548. **SLEEP, CHILD** (James Agee). Carl Fischer, 1956. cmp1954. C-centered; c♭'–g"; Tess-M; 4/4, ♩ = 76; 2+min; Diff-V/m, P/m.
For: mezzo-soprano; soprano
Mood: lyrical; sad; philosophical
Voice: conjunct with some skips; some chromaticism; interrupted phrasing; speech rhythms
Piano: chordal; broken chords in 8th-note motion; restless; some doubling of vocal line
Diff: some abrupt modulations; ensemble
Uses: beautiful song expressing the sorrow of reality; usable in many situations

549. **THREE CHINESE LOVE LYRICS** (from the Chinese; trans. Gertrude L. Joerissen and Ch'u Ta Kao). [18]. Mostly not in traditional key structure; e'–a"; Tess-M; regular meters; moderate tempos; 7pp; Diff-V/m-md, P/m-d.
For: soprano
Mood: lyrical; descriptive love songs
Voice: (a.), sustained and static; (b.), irregular phrase lengths, some chromaticism, recit. in middle section; (c.), rapid 8th-note movement, a few small melismas, chromaticism, several high-lying phrases
Piano: (a.), broken chords l.h., independent melodic line in 3rds r.h., somewhat chromatic; (b.), contrapuntal, melodic motive in parallel 9ths at beginning, some chromaticism; (c.), chordal, independent melodic material, rather chromatic
Diff: sustained singing; easy high tones; command of descriptive style
Uses: good recital material

a. *The Shadow of a Leaf* (Ting Tun-Ling, 8th-9th century). X; f'–g"; 2/2, Rocking rhythm; 2+pp.
b. *When the Sun Rose* (Li Chuang-Chia, 18th century). Emaj; e'–a"; 4/4, With movement; 2pp.
c. *Tiptoeing to Her Lover* (Prince Li Yu, 10th century). X; f'–a"; 4/4, 6/4, Lightly; 2+pp.

550. **TWO MACABRE WHIMS.** [19]. Minor keys; b♭–f"; Tess-M; regular meters, slow and faster; 4pp; Diff-V/m, P/m.
For: mezzo-soprano; baritone
Mood: humorous; mock-serious
Voice: conjunct with some skips; interrupted phrasing; speech rhythms; syncopation; one spoken phrase
Piano: (a.), borrowed from *Dies irae* in parallel 5ths, 4ths, &

triads low on keyboard; (b.), linear-chordal combination, many parallel 3rds, one double 8ve passage; does not double vocal line
Diff: ensemble; dynamic changes
Uses: in an American group; could end a recital

a. *A Reasonable Affliction* (Matthew Prior). Fmin; b♭–f"; Tess-M; 3/4, Slowly; 2pp.
b. *The Purist* (Ogden Nash). Amin; c'–e♭"; Tess-M; 4/4, ♩ = 96; 2pp.

CUMMING, RICHARD
(b. Shanghai, China, 1928, of American parents)

551. **FIVE TZU-YEH SONGS** (Tzu-yeh, trans. Arthur Waley). A Cycle of Chinese Love Poems for Woman's Voice and Piano. Mezzo-Soprano Voice. Classical Vocal Reprints, 1999. cmp1953; rev1981. Tonal; b–f♯"; Tess-mL-M; regular meters; slow–moderate tempos (♩ = 46–92); 11pp; Diff-V/e-me, P/e-m.
For: mezzo-soprano
Mood: longing for love; brief impressions
Voice: syllabic; a few short melismas; speech rhythms; narrow range; easy pitches
Piano: motives capture the mood of each song; easy patterns; pentatonic
Uses: attractive easy short cycle for young mezzo-soprano, high school or early college

a. *At the Time When Blossoms Fall . . . .* G; e'–e"; Tess-M; 3/4, 2/4, 4/4, Andante molto (♩ = circa 66); 3pp.
b. *All Night I Could Not Sleep . . . .* C♯min; c♯'–f♯"; Tess-M; 3/4, 4/4, Calmo (♩ = circa 56); 2pp.
c. *I Will Carry My Coat . . . .* Pentatonic; e'–f♯"; Tess-M; 2/4, Poco Animato (♩ = circa 92); 2pp.
d. *I Heard My Love Was Going . . . .* Pentatonic; e'–e"; Tess-M; 2/4, Moderato (♪ = circa 112); 2pp.
e. *I Have Brought My Pillow . . . .* Tonal; b–f♯"; Tess-mL, 2/4, 3/4, 5/4, Adagio (♩ = circa 46); 1+pp.

552. **GO, LOVELY ROSE!** (Edmund Waller). Boosey & Hawkes, 1956. cmp1949. Fmaj; c'–g"; Tess-M; 4/4, Allegro moderato; 3min; Diff-V/m, P/me.
For: baritone (high lyric)
Mood: lyrical; love song
Voice: conjunct; easy rhythms; some triplets; legato; many long tones; some 2–3-note slurs
Piano: chordal; parallel 3rds with countermelody; some arpeggiation; some doubling of vocal line
Diff: one high phrase (c"–g")
Uses: nice lyric song; setting has virtue of simplicity
Rec: D#10

553. **THE LITTLE BLACK BOY** (William Blake). For Medium Voice & Piano. Boosey & Hawkes, 1966. cmp1963. "To Helen Vanni." D-centered; c'–c'''(a"); Tess-M; 2/2, Ritmico e poco allegro (♩ = ca. 80); 4+min; Diff-V/md, P/md.
For: soprano
Mood: parable

Voice: many skips, up to 8ve; syncopation; various rhythmic groupings; cross-accents with piano
Piano: chordal texture and ostinato in 8ths; 8ths grouped irregularly within meas. (3+3+2, 5+3, 3+2+3); cross-accents; many accidentals; trills; no doubling of vocal line
Diff: complex rhythmic texture which adds much interest to song; needs extra ensemble work
Uses: good song; see also settings by Henry Cowell and Ernest Lubin
Rec: D#s 10, 165

554. MEMORY, HITHER COME (William Blake). Boosey & Hawkes, 1966. cmp1956. Emaj; b–e"; Tess-M; 4/4, 3/2, Allegro moderato; 3pp; Diff-V/e, P/e.
For: mezzo-soprano; baritone; some sopranos with mellow chest voice
Mood: lyrical; melancholy memory
Voice: conjunct and skips outlining triads; quarter-note movement in easy rhythms; ends on b
Piano: written out measured tremolo pattern with changing chords; constant 8th-note motion until final 10 meas.; delicate
Uses: lovely song for teaching and programming; quiet
Rec: D#10

555. OTHER LOVES. 3 Songs to Poems by Philip Minor. [3]. cmp1974. "For Helen Vanni." X; b♭–a♭"; Tess-M-mH; traditional meters; 9pp; Diff-V/md, P/d.
For: baritone; mezzo-soprano
Mood: languorous; forsaken love; anger
Voice: predominantly stepwise and small skips; some phrases have range of 9th; many accidentals (no key sigs.); syncopations; dotted rhythms in (c.)
Piano: (a.), broken-chord patterns; (b.), 5-voice block chords in quarter notes; (c.), repeated block chords in 16th notes with some countermelody and melodic material between vocal phrases; accidentals; incidental doubling of vocal line
Diff: rhythms (a.); chromaticism (b.); long f" (11 beats) ending in shout at end
Uses: as a set; language includes some cursing
Rec: D#165

   a. *Summer Song.* X; c'–f"; 5/4, Lento e languido; 3pp.
   b. *Night Song.* X, D♭-centered; b–f"; 4/4, Molto moderato; 3pp.
   c. *Love Song.* B♭-centered; b♭–a♭"; 2/4, Allegro comodo; 3pp.

556. TOMBSTONES IN THE STARLIGHT (Dorothy Parker). A Set of Six Songs. Medium Voice. Classical Vocal Reprints, 1998. cmp1997. Traditional keys; a–f♯"; Tess-M; regular meters; slow tempos; 13pp; Diff-V/me-m, P/me.
For: mezzo-soprano
Mood: satirical epitaphs
Voice: syllabic; short phrases; some wide intervals
Piano: repeated patterns that reflect the mood of the text; straightforward rhythms; chordal texture
Uses: amusing set when something easy and musically very

light is needed; good for young mezzo with a flair for humor and satire

   a. *The Minor Poet.* Gmaj; b–e"; Tess-M; 3/4, Minuet; molto andante; 2pp.
   b. *The Pretty Lady.* Cmaj; c'–e"; Tess-M; 3/4, Slow; lazy waltz; 2pp.
   c. *The Very Rich Man.* F; c'–d"; Tess-mL; 4/4, Dirge; slow; 2pp.
   d. *The Fisherwoman.* E♭maj; b–d"; Tess-M; 4/4, Allegretto; 2pp.
   e. *The Crusader.* D; a–f♯"; Tess-M; 4/4, Broad, grand; 3pp.
   f. *The Actress.* A; c♯'–e"; Tess-M; 4/4, Very slow; 2pp.

557. WE HAPPY FEW. Ten Songs for Voice and Piano. Cycle. Boosey & Hawkes, 1969. cmp1963. Commissioned and performed by Donald Gramm. Mostly traditional key structures; g–e" (gliss. down to d[D] and up to shouted f♯"); Tess-mL-M; mostly regular meters with some changes; varied tempos; 23min; Diff-V/d, P/d.
For: bass-baritone
Mood: lyric-dramatic-declamatory; varied moods of war, tending toward praise of honor and valor; final song triumphant
Voice: mostly conjunct movement; sequential treatment of melody frequent; straightforward rhythms, except for irregular patterns of last song; accidentals; one half-spoken passage; two glissandos
Piano: chordal and linear; some patterning; open 8ve movements; sequential and ostinato treatments; many accidentals; wide-spread over keyboard; one dissonant waltz-meter song; rhythmic security and wide reach necessary
Diff: largely in interpretation and endurance; some rhythmic problems
Uses: a moving, singable cycle for the mature bass-baritone; not so difficult vocally as either Ned Rorem's *War Scenes* or Hugo Weisgall's *Soldier Songs*, and has a different viewpoint from either; good program material for graduate student
Rec: D#s 165, 166

   a. *The Feast of Crispian* (William Shakespeare). Dmaj; g–e"; Tess-M; 6/4 with changes, Maestoso; 5pp.
   b. *To Whom Can I Speak Today?* (anon. Egyptian, ca.3000 B.C.). E♭min; a–c"; Tess-M; 2/2, Adagio; 3pp.
   c. *Fife Tune* (John Manifold). D-centered; a–e♭"; Tess-mL, M; 6/8, Andante amabile; 4pp.
   d. *Here Dead Lie We* (A. E. Housman). A♭ pedal tone throughout; c♭'–b'; Tess-M; 4/4, 6/4, Adagio; 1p.
   e. *A Ballad of the Good Lord Nelson* (Lawrence Durrell). Dmaj; a–d"; Tess-M; 2/4, Allegro moderato; 10pp.
   f. *Going to the Warres (to Lucasta)* (Richard Lovelace). Gmaj; a–d"; Tess-M; 3/4, Allegro comodo; 2pp.

g. *A Sight in Camp* (Walt Whitman). Fmin; ab–e";
Tess-mL; 2/2 with changes, Lento e misterioso;
5pp.

h. *The End of the World* (Archibald MacLeish). E-
centered; a–eb"(f#" shout); Tess-M; 3/4, Moderate
waltz-time; 5pp.

i. *Grave Hour* (Rainer Maria Rilke). G#min; b–e";
Tess-mL, M; 4/4, Adagio; 2pp.

j. *The Song of Moses* (from Exodus 15). Dorian &
Dmaj; g–e"; Tess-M; 5/8, 6/8, Rather fast–With
joyous exultation; 10pp.

CURRAN, PEARL G.
(b. Denver, CO, 1875; d. New Rochelle, NY, 1941)

558. **EVENING** (Pearl G. Curran). G. Schirmer, 1921. H &
L keys: Gmaj & Ebmaj; d'–f"(g") & bb–db"(eb");
Tess-M; 6/8, 4/4, Moderato–Allegretto–Moderato;
48meas.; Diff-V/e, P/me.
- **For:** baritone; mezzo-soprano; tenor; soprano
- **Mood:** introspective; retrospective
- **Voice:** stepwise and easy skips
- **Piano:** chordal–block and broken
- **Uses:** for a voice of limited range

559. **NOCTURNE** (Pearl G. Curran). Reprint: Tichenor
Publishing, (T.I.S.), 1998. Bmaj; b–d#" (f#"); Tess-
mL; 3/4, Andante tranquillo ♩ = 60; 6pp; Diff-V/me,
P/m.
- **For:** any voice in this range (alternate male/female word
choices)
- **Mood:** serene love song
- **Voice:** mostly conjunct; one leap of 7th; syllabic; a few triplets
to accommodate text
- **Piano:** broken-chord 8th-note patterning and 8th-note triplet
arpeggiation; some doubling of vocal line; 5-meas.
prelude
- **Uses:** nice romantic song for teaching or recital

560. **RAIN** (Pearl G. Curran). G. Schirmer, 1920. H & L
keys: Ebmaj & Cmaj; eb'–g" & c'–e"; Tess-mL; 4/4,
Allegretto; 5pp; Diff-V/e, P/e.
- **For:** any female voice except heavy, low voices
- **Mood:** child-like; cheerful; animated
- **Voice:** stepwise and easy skips; patter song
- **Piano:** 4-voice texture; arpeggiation; cross-hands; staccato;
repeated notes; covers the keyboard
- **Diff:** clear, rapid diction; one portamento
- **Uses:** good for teaching diction and portamento; usable for
young girls

DaCOSTA, NOEL
(b. Lagos, Nigeria, 1933)

561. **TWO SONGS FOR JULIE-JU** (George Houston
Bass). [6]. X; c'–b"; Tess-M; mostly regular but
changing meters; fast tempos; 7pp; Diff-V/md-d, P/md.
- **For:** tenor
- **Mood:** lyrical; light, happy, and jazzy
- **Voice:** somewhat disjunct but lyrical; short phrases; tricky

rhythms; chromatic
- **Piano:** generally chordal texture; chromatic; complex rhythms
- **Diff:** good sense of pitch and rhythm needed, as well as long
range; singer must understand jazz style, incl. the use of
jazz syllables
- **Uses:** good possibilities for a singer fluent in jazz singing;
should be performed together, as (b.) ends with a
musical quotation from (a.)

a. *I. ("Such a pretty black girl is my Julie-Ju").* X;
c'–bb"; Tess-M; 9/8, 3/4, 2/4, ♪ = 144; 3pp.

b. *II. ("It's time to sleep and dream the dreams").* G;
c'–b"; Tess-M; 9/8, 6/8, 3/8, 8/8, 11/8, ♪ = 112; 4pp.

DANA, C. HENSHAW
(b. West Newton, MA, 1846; d. Worcester, MA, 1883)

562. **IT WAS A KNIGHT OF ARAGON** (Thomas Bailey
Aldrich). A. P. Schmidt, 1878. Cmin-maj; G–e';
Tess-M; 4/4, Allegro brilliante–3/4, Allegretto; 4pp;
Diff-V/m-md, P/m.
- **For:** bass; bass-baritone
- **Mood:** narrative, concluding with humorous moral
- **Voice:** stepwise and chord-member skips; some accidentals;
many 2-note slurs; some dotted rhythms
- **Piano:** linear-chordal combination; some phrases in double
8ves & double 3rds
- **Diff:** characterization; mood contrasts
- **Uses:** usable recital song; could end a group

DANIELS, M. L.
(b. Cleburne, TX, 1931)

563. **DORIAN WINDSONG** (M. L. Daniels). [12]. D-
centered (Dorian mode); c'–d"; Tess-mL; 4/4, Gently
(♩ = c.76); 5pp; Diff-V/me, P/m.
- **For:** any medium or low voice
- **Mood:** lyrical love song
- **Voice:** mostly conjunct motion; a few intervals; frequent 2-
note slurs
- **Piano:** chordal; sections of continuously-moving 8ths alternate
with section more homophonic in style; sometimes
doubles vocal line
- **Diff:** most singers will need careful concentration to sing the
modal scale
- **Uses:** possible recital song

564. **LISTEN TO THE PIPER PLAY** (Carolyn M.
Daniels). [12]. Emin; b–d"; Tess-mL; 3/4, 4/4,
(♩ = c.76); 4pp; Diff-V/me, P/e.
- **For:** any medium or low voice
- **Mood:** lyrical love song in a folk-like style
- **Voice:** conjunct motion and small intervals, many outlining the
E-minor triad
- **Piano:** chordal; moving 8th notes
- **Diff:** most phrases end on "in' " on a sustained long tone
- **Uses:** good for a young singer

DAVIS, KATHERINE K.
(b. St. Joseph, MO, 1892; d. Littleton, MA, 1980)

565.   **I HAVE A FAWN** (Thomas Moore). Galaxy, 1966. X;
        c'–e''; Tess-M; 3/4, 4/4, Moving gently and flexibly;
        2+min; Diff-V/md, P/md.
For: mezzo-soprano; baritone
Mood: lyrical; love song; nature imagery
Voice: flowing phrases, often beginning low and ending high;
        somewhat chromatic; small melismas
Piano: broken-chord figures; repeated motives; chromatic;
        continuous 8th-note movement
Diff: pitches; flexibility
Uses: good recital song

566.   **NANCY HANKS** (Abraham Lincoln's Mother)
        (Rosemary Benét). Galaxy, 1941. Emin; d'–g''; Tess-M;
        3/4, Slowly; 3pp; Diff-V/me, P/me.
For: soprano
Mood: lyrical; questioning; poignant
Voice: folksong style
Piano: chordal; legato; somewhat independent of voice
Uses: effective song for contrast on program

DAVIS, SHARON
(b. North Hollywood, CA, 1937)

567.   **A BIRTHDAY** (Christina Rossetti). Avant, 1987.
        cmp1986. D- & A-centered; g'–g''; Tess-M; 3/4, 5/4,
        4/4, Andante grazioso (♩ = 69-72); 5pp; Diff-V/m, P/d.
For: tenor; soprano
Mood: joyous love song using nature imagery
Voice: stepwise and easy skips; some chromaticism; triplets; 3
        vs. 4 & 8 in piano; lyrical and flowing; syllabic
Piano: chordal–block and broken; a little chromaticism;
        broken-chord figures in 16th-note quintuplets, triplets,
        and sextuplets; 2 vs. 3 & 3 vs. 4; melody partially
        doubles vocal line in second section
Diff: ensemble; good sense of rhythm needed by both
        performers
Uses: excellent recital material

568.   **SIX SONGS ON POEMS OF WILLIAM PILLIN**
        for High Voice and Piano. Avant, 1983. "For Delcina
        Stevenson." 15min; separate entries below. [**Rec:**
        D#167, contains all 6 songs]

A.   **LOVE'S WILDEST TALENT.** X; c♯'–a''; Tess-M;
        4/4, 3/4, 5/4, 3/2, Andante con moto (♩ = 92); 2+min;
        Diff-V/md, P/m.
For: soprano; tenor
Mood: lyrical love song
Voice: chiefly conjunct but with leaps of M & m7th; rather
        chromatic; easy rhythms with a few triplets; lyrical and
        flowing; syllabic with slow melisma on "ah" at end
Piano: chordal–block and broken; 3–4-voice texture;
        countermelodies; passing tones in l.h.; rather
        chromatic; some doubling of vocal line
Diff: good sense of pitch needed; ends on sustained d'
Uses: excellent recital material

B.   **I DREAM.** X; e♭'–b'; Tess-mL; 2/2, 3/2, Andante
        (♩ = 96); 1+min; Diff-V/m, P/md.
For: all voices
Mood: philosophical; brooding
Voice: stepwise and small skips; some chromaticism; triplets;
        2 vs. 3 & 3 vs. 8 in piano; very sustained with many
        long tones; syllabic
Piano: chordal–block and broken; chromatic with
        arpeggiations in 16ths & 32nds; no vocal line doubling
Diff: low tessitura for high voices; ends on sustained e♭'
Uses: very limited range of aug.5th; could be used as a
        training piece for sustained tones in middle voice; good
        recital material; group with other songs from this set

C.   **THE TRUTH.** C♯min-Emaj; e'–b''; Tess-mH; 2/4, 3/4,
        In strict time (♪ = 108)–Più mosso (♪ = 126); 2+min;
        Diff-V/m, P/dd.
For: soprano
Mood: philosophical; dual nature of one's personality
Voice: stepwise and small skips with several 8ve leaps; a little
        chromaticism; dotted rhythms; lyrical and flowing;
        second section has melismatic passages with two final
        high coloratura phrases on "ah"
Piano: chordal and linear; block, broken, and afterbeat chords;
        somewhat chromatic; dotted rhythms; 16th-note triplets
        in l.h. in two sections; 2 vs. 3; syncopation; lengthy
        prelude and interlude; does not double vocal line
Diff: vocal agility needed; ensemble may be difficult
Uses: excellent recital material

D.   **BALLADE.** Modal, E-centered; d'–g''; Tess-M; 6/8,
        2/4, 3/4, 9/8, ♩ = 48 with changes; 3+min; Diff-V/md,
        P/m.
For: soprano; tenor; mezzo-soprano
Mood: mysterious; three characterizations
Voice: stepwise and small skips; a little chromaticism; duplets
        and triplets; three melodic styles–almost recit.-like,
        lyrical and flowing, light and dancing; syllabic
Piano: chordal–block, broken, and afterbeat; rather chromatic;
        duplets; special pedal instructions; does not double
        vocal line
Diff: good vocal actor needed; difficult to interpret
Uses: possible recital material

E.   **THE LEAF.** A-centered; e♭'–g♭''; Tess-M; 7/4,
        Tranquil, as if in a trance (♩ = 92); 2+min; Diff-V/m,
        P/m.
For: soprano; tenor; mezzo-soprano
Mood: philosophical love song; moody; sad
Voice: quite static; slow repeated-note passages on a' and other
        long tones; a little chromaticism; syllabic
Piano: chordal and linear; chromatic ostinato in treble in first
        and last sections; continuously moving quarters; cross-
        hands; large reach helpful; does not double vocal line
Diff: steady tone and excellent legato needed for long
        sustained tones; ends on 17-beat f♯'
Uses: could serve as training piece in middle voice; possible
        recital material

F.   **POEM.** F♯maj; c♯''–g♯''; Tess-M; 4/4, 2/4, Brillante
        (♩ = 66); 2min; Diff-V/m, P/dd.
For: soprano; tenor

Mood: philosophical; joyous
Voice: almost entirely stepwise motion, only a few small skips; a little chromaticism; rising phrases–one ending on 4-beat g♯", another on 3-beat f♯"; lyrical and flowing; syllabic with some 2-note slurs
Piano: broken chords in shimmering 32nds in first and last sections, and in triplet 16ths in middle section; quite chromatic; prelude, long interlude and postlude; melody in l.h. in interlude, r.h. 8ves in postlude; does not double vocal line
Diff: showpiece for pianist; singer will need good breath management for phrases that end high
Uses: excellent recital material

DeBLASIO, CHRIS. (See entry # 15 E)

DE BOHUN, LYLE [Clara Lyle Boone]
(b. Stanton, KY, 1927)

569. **BEYOND THE STARS** (Gwen Frostic). Arsis, 1975. X; c'–f♯"; Tess-M; 3/4, Solenne; 3pp; Diff-V/m, P/e.
For: any medium voice
Mood: lyrical and philosophical; nature imagery
Voice: stepwise and small skips; chromatic; considerable use of aug.2nd; easy rhythms; rising phrases; last 8 meas. vocal line climbs from lowest to highest note of song, ending ff
Piano: chordal-linear combination; chromatic; some doubling of vocal line
Diff: some pitches hard to hear; excellent breath control needed for phrases that climb slowly to high pitch
Uses: possible recital material

570. **FANTASIA** (Lyle de Bohun). Arsis, 1976. B♭min; a♭–f"; Tess-M; 4/4, Andante misterioso; 5pp; Diff-V/m, P/m.
For: contralto; mezzo-soprano; baritone
Mood: lyrical and philosophical love song; nature imagery
Voice: stepwise and chord-member skips; triplets and syncopation; 2 vs. 3 in piano; syllabic
Piano: broken-chord patterns in triplets almost throughout; 2-voice texture; little chromaticism; 2 vs. 3; incidental doubling of vocal line but good support
Diff: climax of song in final phrase begins with ascending 8ve to f"; 2 vs. 3; good low tones needed
Uses: recital possibilities

571. **LOVELY HEART** for High Soprano (Loren K. Davidson). Arsis, 1976. Amin–Dmin; c'–b♭"; Tess-mH, mL; 4/4, 3/4, Gracefully; 4pp; Diff-V/m, P/me.
For: soprano
Mood: lyrical and philosophical; nature imagery
Voice: stepwise and small skips; much movement in 8ths; 2 in voice vs. 3 in piano; lyrical and flowing; syllabic
Piano: contrapuntal; 2-voice texture; continuous movement in 8ths; middle section in triplets; both hands in treble clef throughout; incidental doubling of vocal line
Diff: overall tessitura may be a bit low for high soprano; good low tones needed; words difficult to project in high-tessitura phrases; 2 vs. 3

Uses: possible recital material for singer who has requisite vocal characteristics

572. **MIRRORED LOVE** (Lyle de Bohun). Arsis, 1975. X; d♭'–f"; Tess-M; 7/8, 5/8, Andante sostenuto; 2pp; Diff-V/md, P/m.
For: any high or medium voice
Mood: lyrical song about love; sad
Voice: stepwise and small skips; chromatic; flowing phrases without clearly-indicated breath points; syllabic with a few 2-note slurs
Piano: chordal and contrapuntal; 2–3-voice texture; prelude is 2-voice canon (vocal line then takes up this melody); chromatic; some doubling of vocal line
Diff: good sense of pitch needed, esp. where piano does not double vocal line; each half of song is one long phrase of text and music–singer will have to work out breath points
Uses: recital possibilities

573. **SONNET** (William Shakespeare). Arsis, 1974. A-centered; c'–g"; Tess-M; 4/4, Andante; 3pp; Diff-V/m, P/me.
For: tenor; soprano; mezzo-soprano
Mood: lyrical and philosophical love song
Voice: stepwise and small skips; intervals include aug.2nd & dim.3rd; some chromaticism; easy rhythms; syllabic
Piano: contrapuntal; 4-voice texture; somewhat chromatic; incidental doubling of vocal line but good support
Diff: some pitches hard to hear
Uses: good recital material

574. **WHEN ALL SONGS HAVE BEEN SUNG** (Loren K. Davidson). Arsis, 1976. Dmaj; c♯'–e"; Tess-mL; 4/4, 3/4, 5/4, Moderato; 2pp; Diff-V/me, P/e.
For: baritone; mezzo-soprano; contralto
Mood: lyrical and philosophical
Voice: stepwise and small skips; one 8ve leap downward; easy rhythms; syllabic
Piano: contrapuntal; 4-voice texture; continuous movement in 8ths; a little chromaticism; incidental doubling of vocal line but strong support
Uses: good for younger students; recital possibilities

DE GASTYNE, SERGE
(b. Paris, France, 1930)

575. **MAY MY HEART** (e. e. cummings). Elkan-Vogel, 1958. X, B-centered; b(e)–f♯"(g"); Tess-M; 7/4 with changes, Andante; 34meas.; Diff-V/md, P/m.
For: mezzo-soprano; soprano; baritone
Mood: lyrical; introspective
Voice: skips of 5th, 6th, & 7th; somewhat fragmentary; speech rhythms
Piano: 3–4-voice texture; moving lines; 8ves & 9ths; much use of M & m2nds
Diff: poem needs study; ensemble; changing meters; irregular rhythms
Uses: useful for programming and to teach modern idioms

576. **THREE YOUNG MAIDENS** (Tres Morillas), Op. 32,

No. 1 (from the *Cancioneros*, 15th century). Elkan-Vogel, 1961. "To Mildred Miller." Dmin; f'–a"; Tess-M-mH; 3/4, Vivace; 6pp; Diff-V/d, P/m.

For: tenor
Mood: flamenco expression of folk poem
Voice: sustained; conjunct, with flamenco ornamentation; florid passages in flamenco style; final phrase descends from a" to d", sustained
Piano: guitar figurations in patterned accomp., with rhythmic and harmonic structures common to flamenco style; specific pedal and articulation markings
Diff: flamenco style flexibility; high tessitura; not for a beginner
Uses: good song for tenor with flair for Spanish music; could end a program

577.   TWO ELEGIES (In Memoriam Magyarorszag) for Medium Voice and Piano. Elkan-Vogel, 1958. "To Mildred Miller." No key sigs., ambivalent harmonies turning on 2nds; b♭–f "; Tess-M-mH; regular meters; moderate tempos; 7pp; Diff-V/m, P/m-d.

For: mezzo-soprano; contralto
Mood: lyrical; elegiac; descriptive
Voice: many skips; accidentals; fragmentary; tempo changes
Piano: chordal; bell-like figurations; large reach helpful; ambivalent harmonies
Diff: fragmentary nature of vocal lines; dialogue; many tempo changes
Uses: effective pair of songs for a mature singer

   a. *The Last Words* (Maurice Maeterlinck; trans. F. Y. Powell). X; b♭–d"; Tess-M; 6/4, Andante; 3pp.
   b. *The Sleeper of the Valley* (Arthur Rimbaud; trans. Ludwig Lewisohn). X, D-centered; e'–f "; Tess-M-mH; 3/4, Andante con moto; 4pp.

DEIS, CARL
(b. New York, NY, 1883; d. New York, NY, 1960)

578.   THE FLIGHT OF THE MOON (La Fuite de la Lune) (Oscar Wilde). G. Schirmer, 1914. "To Mme. Julia Culp." E♭maj; a♭–g"; Tess-M; 3/4, Dreamily; 2+min; Diff-V/md, P/m.

For: mezzo-soprano
Mood: lyrical; atmospheric night song
Voice: sustained; subdued; mostly triple metric divisions
Piano: chordal–block, some rolled; cross-hands; some rapid arpeggiated soft ornaments; trill-like figures; does not double vocal line
Diff: range; sustained high and low tones
Uses: effective, if not overdone; quiet ending

579.   A LOVER'S LAMENT (William M. Johnson). [48]; 1st©1920. H & L keys: B♭maj & Fmaj; e♯'–a" & b♯–e"; Tess-M; 9/8, 3/4, Languido; 4pp; Diff-V/d, P/m.

For: tenor; baritone
Mood: lyrical; philosophical; love song
Voice: short phrases; stepwise movement; fragmented
Piano: rolled chords with some independent melodic interest
Diff: pitches; floating high tones

580.   MUSIC, WHEN SOFT VOICES DIE (Percy Bysshe Shelley). G. Schirmer, 1914. Gmaj; c♯'–a"; Tess-mH; 3/4, Moderato; 2+min; Diff-V/m, P/m.

For: tenor; soprano
Mood: ethereal; quiet love song
Voice: stepwise with some skips; many long tones; some syncopation; floating lines
Piano: arpeggiated texture with some countermelody; thin texture; does not double vocal line
Diff: soft high tones
Uses: approach conservatively

DE KOVEN, REGINALD
(b. Middletown, CT, 1859; d. Chicago, IL, 1920)

581.   ADOWN THE WOODLAND WAY (G. Hubi-Newcombe). G. Schirmer, 1911. Gmaj; d'–g"; Tess-M; 6/8, Allegro moderato; 8pp; Diff-V/m, P/m.

For: tenor
Mood: lyrical; an aubade
Voice: skips along chord lines; good vowels on high tones
Piano: arpeggiated throughout; numerous modulations, some abrupt; large reach helpful
Uses: nice example of the romantic aubade

582.   CRADLE SONG (Thomas Bailey Aldrich). [58]; 1st©1896. Gmaj; d'–g"; Tess-M; 6/8, Allegretto, marcato il movimento; 3pp; Diff-V/e, P/m.

For: soprano
Mood: quiet; serene
Voice: easy skips; easy rhythms
Piano: 16th-note chord figuration in r.h.; l.h. rocking figures; simple harmonies
Uses: useful for "ee" vowel on high, medium, and low pitches; good song

DELLO JOIO, NORMAN
(b. New York, NY, 1913)

583.   THE ASSASSINATION (Two Fates Discuss a Human Problem) (adapted by the composer from the poem by Robert Hillyer). Carl Fischer, 1949. cmp1947. Gmin; a♭–d"; Tess-L; 4/4, 6/4, 3/4, 5/4, Andante; 4min; Diff-V/md, P/m.

For: bass; contralto
Mood: dramatic; two speakers; fates discuss the killing of hope
Voice: short phrases; dialogue; recit.-like melodic patterns; speech rhythms
Piano: linear; punctuating chords; chordal mid-section; dissonant; accidentals
Diff: interpretation; text requires mature singer with philosophical mind
Uses: a powerful song for the right singer

584.   BALLAD OF THOMAS JEFFERSON (Louis Lerman). Weaver-Levant, 1943. Dmaj; a–d"; Tess-M; 4/4, With spirit; 2min; Diff-V/m, P/m.

For: bass-baritone; baritone
Mood: declamatory; narrative
Voice: many skips; dotted rhythms; syncopation; 3rd & 7th

Piano: afterbeat pattern; jazz-like bass line; does not double vocal line
Diff: story-telling
Uses: good for right voice and personality; must have folksy touch

585. **BRIGHT STAR** (Light of the World). Marks, 1968. E♭-centered; f'–g"; Tess-mH; 6/8, Andante semplice; 2+min; Diff-V/m, P/m.
For: soprano; tenor
Mood: Christmas song
Voice: siciliana figuration
Piano: chordal; many parallel altered chords
Uses: Christmas song for light, floating, lyric voice with easy f"s and g"s; good for teaching head voice

586. **A CHRISTMAS CAROL** (Gilbert Keith Chesterton). Marks, 1967. Modal; e♭'–g"; Tess-mH; 6/8, Adagio, con tenerezza; 4min; Diff-V/md, P/m.
For: soprano; tenor
Mood: Christmas song
Voice: siciliana figuration
Piano: chordal; some figuration; written-out ornaments
Diff: many phrases end high; voice must float
Uses: seasonal

587. **THE HOLY INFANT'S LULLABY.** Marks, 1967. Fmaj; f'–f"; Tess-mH; 12/8, Andantino; 3+min; Diff-V/m, P/m.
For: soprano
Mood: Christmas lullaby
Voice: 2 vs. 3; many phrases at top of staff; nonsense syllable refrain; ends on a hum
Piano: triplet "rustling" figures; countermelody in r.h.
Diff: many f"s
Uses: good song for floating lyric voice; seasonal

588. **LAMENT** (Chidiock Tichborne). Carl Fischer, 1959. E♭min; c'–f"; Tess-M; 4/4, 3/4, 6/4, Adagio; 4min; Diff-V/m-d, P/md.
For: medium voice; dramatic baritone
Mood: dramatic poem about death; "Written on the eve of the poet's execution"
Voice: subdued declamatory style; speech rhythms; some chromaticism; interrupted phrasing
Piano: chordal; some broken-chord figures; grace notes; several 8ve passages; large reach helpful
Diff: intensity of expression
Uses: good dramatic song for singer who can sustain mood of strength in hopelessness

589. **THE LISTENERS** (Walter de la Mare). Carl Fischer, 1960. X; c'–f"; Tess-mL; 4/4, 3/4, 3/2, 5/4, Allegro non troppo e misterioso; 6min; Diff-V/d, P/dd.
For: mezzo-soprano; baritone
Mood: dramatic; philosophical; abstract
Voice: declamatory; recit. style
Piano: chordal; difficult figurations; rapid repeated notes; virtuosic; long prelude
Diff: meter changes; declamatory style
Uses: for a mature singer

Rec: D#s 34, 44

590. **MILL DOORS** (Carl Sandburg). [21]; 1st©1948. H & L keys: X; e'–f♯" & d'–e"; Tess-M; 4/4, 5/4, 2/4, Very slow; 3min; Diff-V/m, P/m.
For: all voices
Mood: lyrical; philosophical
Voice: fragmented phrases; triplet figures
Piano: chordal; broken 8ves in bass
Diff: text; fragmented phrasing
Uses: effective song

591. **NEW BORN** (Lenore G. Marshall). Carl Fischer, 1948. cmp1946. Fmaj; c'–d"; Tess-M; 6/8, Andante con tenerezza; 2min; Diff-V/m, P/m.
For: medium and low voices
Mood: descriptive; quiet; serene; newborn child
Voice: stepwise and easy skips; 3/4 vs. 6/8 in piano; humming at end
Piano: rocking accomp. figures; countermelody
Uses: nice cradle song; quiet ending

592. **NOTE LEFT ON A DOOR-STEP** (Lily Peter). Marks, 1969. X; e♭'–f"; Tess-mH; 3/4, 4/4, Lento espressivo; 3pp; Diff-V/m, P/md.
For: mezzo-soprano
Mood: serene view of death
Voice: conjunct; speech rhythms
Piano: parallel chords; figured middle section; atmospheric
Diff: high phrases
Uses: sensitive song; teaches head voice and word stress

593. **SIX LOVE SONGS.** Cycle. Carl Fischer, 1954, 1955. Pub. separately. Traditional keys (but no key sigs.); d♭'–g"; Tess-M; mostly regular meters; varied tempos; 12–14min; Diff-V/m-md, P/m-md.
For: lyric tenor, if done as a cycle; single songs for soprano
Mood: lyrical; various aspects of love relationship
Voice: mostly conjunct lines with some skips along chord lines; much 16th-note subdivision of beat; characteristic syncopated figure recurs
Piano: patterned accomps. with characteristic rhythmic figures; many accidentals; various figurations; wide reach helpful; delicate dynamics and articulations
Diff: pitch perception; rhythmic intricacies
Uses: excellent songs, either singly or as a cycle; for an advanced undergraduate or graduate student; good recital material, esp. as a cycle

    a. *Eyebright* (J. Addington Symonds). Gmaj; e♭'–f"; 2/4, 3/4, Andante, con tenerezza; 2+min. [**Rec:** D#10]
    b. *Why So Pale and Wan, Fond Lover?* (John Suckling). [60]. H, M, & L keys: Bmin, Amin, & Fmin; e'–f♯", d'–e", & b♭–c"; 2/4, Andante movendo; 2min.
    c. *Meeting at Night* (Robert Browning). Gmin; f'–g"; 2/2, Allegro, molto deciso; 2min. [**Rec:** D#10]
    d. *The Dying Nightingale* (Stark Young). X; d♭'–g♭"; 5/4, 4/4, 6/4, Molto Adagio; 4+min.
    e. *All Things Leave Me* (Waltz Song) (Arthur Symons). D♭maj; f'–f"; 3/4, Allegro grazioso;

1+min.

f. *How Do I Love Thee?* (Elizabeth Barrett Browning). [60, 63]. H & L keys: Cmaj & Amaj; d'–g" & b–e"; 4/4, 6/4, 5/4, Andante, molto espressivo; 2+min.

594. **UN SONETTO DI PETRARCA** (A Sonnet by Petrarch) (English trans. Harold Heiberg). [49]. X; f♯'–b♭"; Tess-H; 4/4, 5/4, Andante appassionato; 4pp; Diff-V/d, P/dd.
For: lyric tenor; lyric soprano
Mood: lyrical; love poem
Voice: long phrases; many triplets; several melismas; some chromaticism
Piano: broken and rolled chords; 32nd notes; some counterpoint; 2 vs. 3; quintuplets
Diff: if sung by tenor, voice must have great flexibility and brilliant *ff* b♭" at end
Uses: beautiful recital song for the right singer

595. **SONGS OF REMEMBRANCE** (John Hall Wheelock). Cycle. Associated, 1979. C-centered (as a total work); c'–g"; Tess-H, mH; regular meters with a few changes; varied tempos; 33pp; Diff-V/d, P/dd.
For: seems to be intended for lyric baritone, but range and tessitura also suited to many tenors
Mood: remembering past love and childhood; nature imagery; philosophical
Voice: stepwise with skips rarely exceeding a 6th; fairly chromatic; triplets; 3 vs. 4 in piano; *senza misura* section in (c.); syllabic with occasional 2-note slurs
Piano: primarily chordal; 3–5-voice texture with doublings; some 3-stave notation; chromatic; triplets, tremolo, and rapid repeated notes and chords; many articulations; large reach necessary
Diff: tessitura lies high for baritone and would be tiring; (c.), extremely long and strenuous to perform; both loud and soft g' required; excellent musicianship needed by both singer and pianist; ensemble will require work
Uses: fine recital material for mature performers; (c.) could be performed alone

a. *The Revenant.* C- & G-centered; c–f'; Tess-H; 3/4, Andante moderato (♩ = 88); 5+pp.
b. *The Lion House.* E♭-centered; E♭–f♯'; Tess-mH; 3/4, 4/4, Lento (♩ = 52); 5+pp.
c. *Storm and Sea.* C-centered; c–g'; Tess-M, H; 4/4, Allegro, con intensità (♩ = 100) with changes; 18pp.
d. *Farewell to the House in Bonac.* C-centered; d–g'; Tess-H; 6/8, 9/8, Andantino semplice (♪= 84); 4pp.

596. **THERE IS A LADY SWEET AND KIND** (anon. Elizabethan). [21, 63]; 1st©1948. H & L keys: Gmaj & Fmaj; d'–g" & c'–f"; Tess-M; 2/2, 3/2, Amabile; 2min; Diff-V/m, P/m.
For: tenor; baritone
Mood: lyrical; descriptive
Voice: short phrases; several 8ve leaps; soft
Piano: chordal; long prelude and interludes; independent melody in 3rds
Diff: rhythms and pitches not always as simple as they seem
Uses: useful for a young singer

597. **THREE SONGS OF ADIEU.** Cycle. Marks, 1962. No key sigs., many accidentals; f'–b♭"; Tess-HH; regular meters with some changes; slow and moderate tempos; 6min; Diff-V/d, P/md.
For: high soprano
Mood: lyrico-dramatic; anguished farewell
Voice: vocal line lies extremely high, more than two-thirds of all phrases rising to top of staff and above; speech rhythms; dissonant pitch groups; diction difficult because of tessitura; somewhat dramatic
Piano: many accidentals; ostinato figure in (b.) requires good coordination; rhythmic precision necessary; wide-spread over keyboard
Diff: pitch perception; some rhythms; high tessitura; ensemble; mature singers
Uses: good short cycle for a high lyric voice; could end a program–high climax near end, but ends quietly

a. *After Love* (Arthur Symons). X; g'–b♭"; Tess-HH; 4/4, 3/4, 5/4, Lento, ma non troppo; 2pp.
b. *Fade, Vision Bright* (anon.). Cmin; g'–b♭"; Tess-HH; 4/4, Allegro moderato; 3pp.
c. *Farewell* (John Addington Symonds). Gmin; f'–b♭"; Tess-HH; 3/4, Adagio, molto espressivo; 2pp.

DEL TREDICI, DAVID
(b. Cloverdale, CA, 1937)

598. **CHANA'S STORY** (Chana Bloch). Boosey & Hawkes, 2000. cmp1996 & 1998. Commissioned for Miriam Abramowitsch. Tonal, fluctuating romantic harmonies; f–b♭"; Tess-wide, M, L; regular meters; varied tempos; 35min (79pp); Diff-V/m-d, P/md-d.
For: mezzo-soprano
Mood: cycle of love relationship from beginning to dissolution, from a woman's point of view: infatuation, the newborn child, beginnings of dissolution of relationship, family dysfunction, dying relationship, woman's rebirth
Voice: very wide-ranging vocal line; repeated-note sections; many large intervals; melodically repetitive and sequential; syllabic; many repeated words and phrases for emotional effect; wide dynamic range; extreme low and high notes; numerous rhythmic groupings reflecting word stress; many passages do not reflect word stress
Piano: a symphonic piano score–uses all of keyboard and needs many colors; much 3-stave scoring; widely-spaced chords; motivic structure; specific dynamic markings; many trills; some tremolo
Diff: length; wide leaps for singer; wide-ranging piano score
Uses: large work (half a recital program) for a mature singer with a large voice of many colors and expressive possibilities

a. *The Fever of Love* (*The Song of Songs* 5:14–16, 6–8, trans. by Chana Bloch and Ariel Bloch). D♭-centered with many fluctuations; f–a"; Tess-cs, wide; 3/4, 6/4, 3/2, Allegro maestoso (♩ = 138); 15pp.

b. *Eating Babies.* A♭maj; a♭–a♭"; Tess-wide, L; 2/2, 3/4, Allegretto amoroso, rubato (♩ = 76); 13pp.

c. *Tired Sex.* Chromatic–ends E♭min; e'–e♭"; Tess-M; 2/4, Allegretto, poco marcato (♩ = 112); 5pp.

d. *The Stutter.* B♭-centered; b♭–b♭"; Tess-wide; 2/2, Vivace (♩ = 108-112); 18pp.

e. *Clear and Cold.* Fluctuating harmonies, ends Amaj; g♯–b♭"; Tess-wide; 6/8, 3/4, Allegro agitato (♩. =116); 15pp.

f. *Alone on the Mountain.* A-centered; g♯–a♭"; Tess-M; 4/4, Andante (♩ = 92); 13pp.

599. FOUR SONGS ON POEMS OF JAMES JOYCE.
Boosey & Hawkes, 1974. cmp1958–1960. Atonal; a–a"; Tess-cs; regular and irregular changing meters; 26pp; Diff-V/dd, P/dd.

For: soprano with avant-garde technique
Mood: lyrical; delicate; somber
Voice: lyrical avant-garde techniques; extreme range; disjunct; rhythmically complicated
Piano: highly programmatic; many trills, tremolos, and other ornaments; changing meters; many accidentals
Diff: avant-garde; for advanced performers; perfect pitch desirable
Uses: probably effective for the right performers; use individually or as a set

a. *Dove Song.* a–f♯"; 4/4 with many changes, Andante frullante; 9pp.

b. *She Weeps Over Rahoon.* b♭–g♭"; 3/4, 4/4, 2/4, Lento languido; 5pp.

c. *A Flower Given to My Daughter.* a–a♭"; 2/4 with changes, Allegretto scherzando; 5pp.

d. *Monotone.* c'–a"; 6/8 with many changes, Adagio improvisando; 7pp.

600. TWO SONGS ON POEMS OF JAMES JOYCE.
Boosey & Hawkes, 1984. cmp1959. No key sigs.; a–a"; Tess-wide; changing meters; 10pp; Diff-V/dd, P/dd.

For: mezzo-soprano; soprano; high baritone
Mood: tense; nostalgic
Voice: many large skips; many accidentals; pitches often unrelated to piano and hard to find; complex rhythms; many dynamic markings; both loud and soft high notes
Piano: 2-voice disjunct counterpoint; tone color effects, incl. trills, tremolo, rolled chords; polyrhythms; tempo fluctuations; many accidentals; many dynamic markings; second song opens with canon; staccato
Diff: pitch patterns and finding pitches; rhythms; wide tessitura; both soft and loud high notes; ensemble
Uses: as a pair or separately; for advanced, mature singers who are skilled in this idiom

a. *Bahnhofstrasse.* [Eng. text] X; b–a"; 2/4 with changes, Largo; 2min.

b. *Alone.* X; a–g♭"; 4/4 with changes, Adagio–Molto più mosso; 3min.

DE PUE, WALLACE E.
(b. Columbus, OH, 1932)

601. ELDORADO (Edgar Allan Poe). [41]. X; c'–f"(a♭"); Tess-mL; 6/8, ♩. = ca. 116; 4pp; Diff-V/md, P/md.

For: baritone; tenor with low tones
Mood: dramatic; descriptive
Voice: disjunct; chromatic
Piano: chromatic; difficult chord figurations; independent of vocal line
Diff: dramatic expression; high ending
Uses: good for teaching ballad style to young singer; possible recital piece

602. LULLABY. [41]. Gmaj; d–e"; Tess-M; 6/8, ♩. = ca.60; 3pp; Diff-V/e, P/md.

For: high or medium female voice
Mood: simple; child-like
Voice: short phrases
Piano: 2-voice texture; arpeggiated chords
Uses: useful for very young student

DeVITO, ALBERT
(b. Hartford, CT, 1919; d. 1999)

603. SEA FEVER (John Masefield). Kenyon, 1961. H & L keys: Gmaj & E♭maj; d'–g" & b♭–e♭"; Tess-M; 6/8, Andante; 4pp; Diff-V/me, P/me.

For: baritone; tenor
Mood: masculine; hearty; simple
Voice: easy skips; melisma at end; easy rhythms with some syncopation
Piano: chordal texture–block and broken; "outlines" vocal line but does not double
Diff: calls for g" (e♭") five times
Uses: attractive, simple setting of this popular poem; useful for young baritone or tenor; good for high school contest or first recital piece and for gaining dynamic control

DeWITT, STAN
(b. Denver, CO, 1963)

604. THREE FITZGERALD SONGS (F. Scott Fitzgerald). For High Voice and Piano. Delamo Music, 1996 (Voice of the Rockies). Tonal; c♯'–g"; Tess-M-H; changing meters; fast–slow–fast tempos; 11pp; Diff-V/m, P/me-m.

For: tenor
Mood: two nostalgic love songs; one humorous song
Voice: stepwise motion and many small skips; duplet and triplet 8th notes; irregular meter sections in (a.); syllabic
Piano: block chords alone or in combination with countermelody; third song has dissonant afterbeat pattern; rare doubling of vocal line; 3–4 meas. preludes in each song; short interludes
Diff: rhythms, irregular note groupings (a.); word stress (b.)
Uses: as a group for a student; excerpt (a.) in a group of songs about love; (c.), humorous

a. *First Love.* Fmaj/G minorish; e♭'–f"; Tess-mH; 10/8, 8/8, Allegro ♩ = 144; 4pp.

b. *Thousand-and-First-Ship.* Unsettled; c♯'–g"; Tess-H; 2/2, Largo ♩ = 60; 5pp.

c. *Fragment.* Dmaj; e'–f♯"; Tess-H; 3/4, 2/4, Allegro ♩ = 152; 2pp.

DIAMOND, DAVID
(b. Rochester, NY, 1915)

605.   ANNIVERSARY IN A COUNTRY CEMETERY
(Katherine Anne Porter). Boosey & Hawkes, 1942.
cmp1940. Emin; c'–g"; Tess-M; 5/4. 3/4, 6/4, 3/2, Lento
e mesto; 2pp; Diff-V/m, P/me.

For:	soprano; tenor
Mood:	lyrical; dirge
Voice:	skips; some 8ve leaps; quarter-note movement
Piano:	chordal
Diff:	5/4 for inexperienced musicians
Uses:	good teaching song

606.   AS LIFE WHAT IS SO SWEET (anon., ca. 1624).
Arrow, 1941. cmp1940. Bmin; d♭'–g"; Tess-M;
changing meters, ♩ unit, Andante; 1+min; Diff-V/m,
P/me.

For:	soprano; tenor; mezzo-soprano
Mood:	lyrical; quiet
Voice:	stepwise and small skips; fluid, speech-like rhythms
Piano:	3–4-part texture, some chordal, some moving lines; does not double vocal line
Diff:	changing meters; poetic language
Uses:	setting well-suited to poem; interior of group

607.   BE MUSIC, NIGHT (Kenneth Patchen). Carl Fischer,
1948. cmp1944. Bmin; d'–a"; Tess-mL; 6/8, 9/8; 2min;
Diff-V/m, P/m.

For:	tenor
Mood:	lyrical
Voice:	some leaps; syncopation; duplets and triplets
Piano:	linear, mostly three voices; 14 meas. solo material; does not double vocal line
Diff:	2 vs. 3; ensemble
Uses:	less difficult than some Diamond songs; lovely setting of this beautiful text; quiet ending

608.   BILLY IN THE DARBIES (Herman Melville, from
Billy Budd). Elkan-Vogel, 1946. cmp1944. G-centered;
c'–g"; Tess-mL; 6/8, Allegretto; 3min; Diff-V/m, P/m.

For:	high baritone best; some tenors
Mood:	dramatic; first-person narrative of prisoner's last night before hanging
Voice:	mostly conjunct; some 8ve skips; some 2 vs. 3 in piano; dramatic dynamics
Piano:	chordal-linear combination; 8th-note motion; passages in 4ths & 5ths; does not double vocal line
Diff:	dramatic expression
Uses:	very good song for dramatic singer; less complex than some Diamond songs; see also setting by Bacon

609.   BRIGID'S SONG (James Joyce). Mercury, 1947. [16].
cmp1946. Amin; c'–g"; Tess-mH; 2/2, Andante; 1min;
Diff-V/me, P/e.

For:	soprano

Mood:	lyrical; dirge; surreal
Voice:	stepwise and small skips; two leaps of a 10th
Piano:	4-voice block chords; varied registers; bell-like sounds; does not double vocal line
Diff:	fragmented phrases at beginning
Uses:	effective simple song; useful for recital
Rec:	D#59

610.   CHATTERTON (John Keats). (Peer)Southern Music,
1950. cmp1946. Bmin-Amin-Dmaj; b–b"; Tess-M; 3/4,
2/4, 4/4, 5/4, Adagio non troppo (♩ = 69)–Poco più
mosso (♩ = 76)–Ancora più mosso (♩ = 80); 4pp; Diff-
V/m, P/me.

For:	dramatic soprano; mezzo-soprano; tenor
Mood:	lament on the death of Chatterton
Voice:	chiefly short phrases, some sweeping upward; regular rhythms with dotted patterns; quite dramatic
Piano:	entirely chordal; supports clearly but does not double vocal line
Diff:	needs strong voice with powerful b" and dramatic flair
Uses:	interesting recital song

611.   THE CHILDREN OF THE POOR (Victor Hugo;
trans. Algernon Charles Swinburne). Leeds, 1950.
cmp1950. X; b–a♯"(a"); Tess-M; changing meters
(♩ unit of beat), Adagio non troppo (♩ = 63); 3min;
Diff-V/d, P/md.

For:	dramatic soprano
Mood:	narrative; dramatic
Voice:	speech-like rhythms; fragmented; some difficult skips; many accidentals; polyrhythms with piano
Piano:	many accidentals; linear; independent of vocal line; parallel 4th & 5th passages; 2 vs. 3
Diff:	fluid rhythms; needs good control of registration; lowest note is final note of piece, a 16th which must be heard; ensemble will be difficult; highly complex and dissonant piece
Uses:	could open a group

612.   DAVID MOURNS FOR ABSALOM (II Samuel,
18:33). Mercury, 1947. cmp1946. Fmaj-Cmin;
c'–a"(g"); Tess-M; 2/2, Andantino; 3min; Diff-V/md,
P/m.

For:	tenor; soprano–dramatic voices
Mood:	dramatic lament
Voice:	stepwise and small skips; sustained
Piano:	5-voice chordal texture; moving bass line in 8ves throughout
Diff:	dynamic range (*p–fff*); loud high climaxes; very dramatic singing
Uses:	effective song for anyone who can do it
Rec:	D#59

613.   DO I LOVE YOU? (Theme and Variations) (Jack
Larson). (Peer)Southern, 1971. cmp1968. X, chromatic;
b–a"; Tess-mH-H; changing meters, Allegretto; 13pp;
Diff-V/dd, P/dd.

For:	soprano
Mood:	love song
Voice:	disjunct; 2-note slurs; duplets and triplets; many accidentals; 2 vs. piano 3
Piano:	linear-chordal combination; 2–5 voices; articulations

important; rapid scale and chordal patterns; does not double vocal line

Diff: pitch; rhythm; ensemble; for a virtuoso singer; perfect pitch desirable

Uses: approaches the limits of contemporary use of traditional materials, mediums, and techniques; use accordingly

614. **EPITAPH** (On the Grave of a Young Cavalry Officer Killed in the Valley of Virginia) (Herman Melville). Associated, 1946. [4]. cmp1945. Gmaj; c'–g"; Tess-M; 3/4, 4/4, 5/4, Poco adagio;1+min; Diff-V/m, P/me.

For: soprano; tenor

Mood: lyrical; subdued

Voice: small skips; easy rhythms; fragmented phrases

Piano: block chords; recurring 8th-note motive; does not double vocal line

Diff: ensemble; irregular phrase lengths; soft dynamics

Uses: nice song; usable for recital

615. **THE EPITAPH** (Logan P. Smith). Elkan-Vogel, 1947. cmp1946. Fmaj; b♭–f"; Tess-M; 3/4, 4/4, Allegretto; 1+min; Diff-V/m, P/me.

For: baritone

Mood: first-person narrative; poet imagines his own funeral

Voice: many small skips; speech-like rhythms

Piano: chordal-linear combination; imitation; staccato-legato differentiation; does not double vocal line

Uses: good song; useful

616. **EVEN THOUGH THE WORLD KEEPS CHANGING** (Rainer Maria Rilke; trans. M. D. Herter Norton). Carl Fischer, 1948. cmp1946. F♯min; c♯'–a"; Tess-M; 3/4 with changes, Andante; 2+min; Diff-V/md, P/m.

For: tenor; soprano

Mood: philosophical; in praise of song

Voice: many skips of 5th or less; fragmentary; speech rhythms

Piano: chordal-linear combination; awkward in spots

Diff: rhythms

Uses: in group about song

617. **A FLOWER GIVEN TO MY DAUGHTER** (James Joyce). Boosey & Hawkes, 1942. cmp1940. E♭; d'–f"; Tess-M; 4/4, Lento teneramente; 2pp; Diff-V/me, P/e.

For: tenor; soprano

Mood: lyrical; gentle

Voice: skips outlining triads; some conjunct lines; simple rhythms; some syncopation

Piano: chordal; some accidentals

Uses: good teaching song for student who likes poetry of James Joyce

618. **FOR AN OLD MAN** (T. S. Eliot). (Peer)Southern, 1951. [65]. cmp1943. X; d'–f"; Tess-M; changing meters, Allegro barbaro; 1min; Diff-V/m-d, P/m-d.

For: dramatic baritone

Mood: dramatic; intense; vigorous; rather vicious

Piano: 4–5-voice chordal texture; accidentals; syncopation; articulations important

Diff: dynamics up to *fff*

Uses: effective for the right voice

619. **FOUR LADIES** (Ezra Pound). (Peer)Southern, 1966. cmp1962. No key sigs.; a–d♯"; Tess-M; mostly regular meters, one in 7/8, varied tempos; 6pp; Diff-V/m, P/m.

For: baritone

Mood: lyrical; small portraits of women past their prime

Voice: mostly conjunct; some skips; short phrases

Piano: linear, 3–4-voice texture; some arpeggiated chords; some embellishment; accidentals; mildly dissonant; 2 vs. 3; staccato vs. legato

Diff: pitch; some rhythmic irregularities

Uses: good pieces for young baritone with some experience with women

  a. ***Agathas.*** B-centered; d'–d"; 3/4, 2/4, Molto moderato; 13meas.
  b. ***Young Lady.*** G-centered; a–d"; 3/4, 2/4, Lento; 13meas.
  c. ***Lesbia Illa.*** X; d'–d"; 7/8 with changes, Allegro moderato; 13meas.
  d. ***Passing.*** X; d'–e♭"; 5/4, 3/4, Lento; 10meas.

620. **HEBREW MELODIES** (Lord Byron). Cycle. (Peer)Southern, 1969. Basically atonal; a–b"; Tess-very wide (many phrases span 1½ 8ves); regular and irregular meters, constantly changing; slow and moderate tempos; 30pp; Diff-V/dd, P/dd.

For: dramatic baritone with secure a♭" (opt. lower notes provided for notes above a♭"); although the texts are definitely masculine, a mezzo-soprano or dramatic soprano could handle the vocal lines much more easily than a male voice

Mood: dramatic; anguished; poems seem to center on the personality of King Saul

Voice: typical vocal line of Diamond's dissonant style: large leaps and m2nds dominate; complex rhythmic structure; atonal idiom, though a flash of tonality here and there; many loud climaxes; bombastic

Piano: typical Diamond accomp.: constant movement; dissonant; a number of solo passages; many accidentals; complete modern score technique required

Diff: in every area; vocal endurance of any but very large voice questionable; for virtuoso singer with long-ranged, dramatic voice only

Uses: powerful texts; example of dissonant style

  a. ***My Soul Is Dark.*** a–f"; 3/2 with changes, Adagio, piuttosto moderato e drammatico; 7pp.
  b. ***If That High World.*** b–b"; 4/4 with changes, Andante; 6pp.
  c. ***Saul.*** c'–b♭"; 4/4 with changes, Maestoso, adagio; 10pp.
  d. ***All Is Vanity*** (Ciaconna). a♯–b"; 7/4 with changes, Andante; 7pp.

621. **HOMAGE TO PAUL KLEE** (Babette Deutsch). Elkan-Vogel, 1973. cmp1970. X; b♭–a♯"; Tess-M; changing meters, Allegretto; 2min; Diff-V/dd, P/dd.

For: dramatic soprano; lyric soprano

Mood: fragmentary; surrealistic; lighthearted

Voice: wide leaps, some difficult; fragmentary; much staccato

Piano: linear; covers keyboard; life of its own; articulations and dynamics very important; cross-hands

Diff: pitches; dynamic markings up to *fff*; staccato; smooth registration

Uses: interesting recital song for anyone who can handle it

622. **HOW IT WAS WITH THEM** (Walt Whitman); Leeds Music, 1950. cmp1950. X; b–f♯"; Tess-M; 2/4 with changes, Allegro pesante (♩ = 104), Meno mosso (♩ = 84, ♪ = 84); 3pp; Diff-V/d, P/d.

For: mezzo-soprano; baritone

Mood: thoughtful social statement

Voice: mostly conjunct motion; small intervals; a few larger leaps; some accidentals; speech-like rhythmic patterns; short phrases

Piano: chordal with melodic material; many accidentals; strong accents; rather independent of vocal line

Diff: singer will need secure sense of pitch and rhythm

Uses: unusual song; could be effective in the right setting

623. **I AM ROSE** (Gertrude Stein). Elkan-Vogel, 1973. cmp1971. E-centered; d'–e"; Tess-M; 3/4, Andante, molto semplice; 1+min; Diff-V/m-md, P/m.

For: mezzo-soprano; soprano

Mood: lyrical; whimsical; introspective setting

Voice: many skips, often awkward; easy rhythms

Piano: repetitive pattern mostly over pedal tone; strummed instrument effect; 7-meas. postlude; does not double vocal line

Diff: complex rhythms; tempo fluctuation

Uses: see Rorem for extroverted setting of this text

624. **I HAVE LONGED TO MOVE AWAY** (Dylan Thomas). (Peer)Southern, 1968. cmp1944. X; d'–g"; Tess-M; changing meters, Andante con moto; 1+min; Diff-V/md, P/m.

For: dramatic tenor; dramatic soprano

Mood: intense; dramatic

Voice: small skips; speech-like, irregular rhythms

Piano: 3–5-voice chordal texture; does not double vocal line

Diff: complex rhythms; tempo fluctuation

625. **I SHALL IMAGINE LIFE** (e. e. cummings). (Peer)Southern, 1968. cmp1962. X; b–f♯"; Tess-M; changing meters, Andante; 1min; Diff-V/md, P/m.

For: high baritone; mezzo-soprano; soprano

Mood: lyrical; philosophical; subdued

Voice: many skips; many accidentals; syncopation; speech rhythms

Piano: chordal; some clusters, some quartal; many accidentals; spare texture

Diff: rhythms; changing meters

Uses: usable subdued song; simpler Diamond song

626. **LET NOTHING DISTURB THEE** (St. Teresa of Avila, Henry Wadsworth Longfellow). Associated, 1946. cmp1945. Fmin; c'–f"; Tess-M-mH; 3/4, 4/4, 5/4, Adagio tranquillo; 1+min; Diff-V/m, P/m.

For: soprano; tenor; mezzo-soprano

Mood: prayer

Voice: stepwise and small skips; syncopation; fluid rhythms

Piano: 3–4-voice linear texture; some block chords; accidentals; does not double vocal line

Diff: fragmented phrases; ensemble

Uses: good song; usable in a recital group

627. **LIFE AND DEATH** (Chidiock Tichborne). (Peer) Southern, 1971. cmp1969. X; a–g"; Tess-M; 3/4, 5/4, 4/4, Andante; 6pp; Diff-V/d, P/d.

For: mezzo-soprano

Mood: lyrical; philosophical

Voice: disjunct; several leaps of over an 8ve; chromatic

Piano: chromatic; dissonant; 16th-note melodic motives; does not double vocal line

Diff: large range; clear low tones

628. **LIFT NOT THE PAINTED VEIL** (Percy Bysshe Shelley). (Peer)Southern, 1949. cmp1946. X; a–g"; Tess-mL; changing meters, Adagio; 2+min; Diff-V/md, P/md.

For: mezzo-soprano; dramatic soprano

Mood: dramatic; somber

Voice: stepwise and small skips; fragmentary; difficult rhythms

Piano: chordal, thick in parts; some moving lines; does not double vocal line

Diff: dramatic intensity

629. **LOVE AND TIME** (Katie Louchheim). Cycle. (Peer)Southern, 1971. cmp1967-68. "For Carolyn Reyer." Atonal; a–a"; Tess-cs; regular but changing meters; moderate to fast tempos; 13pp; Diff-V/d, P/d.

For: mezzo-soprano with long range

Mood: various views of love

Voice: mostly disjunct and spread over staff, most phrases encompass more than an 8ve; pitches difficult; word rhythms tend to be mechanical, perhaps due to absence of dotted rhythms; constant motion

Piano: many accidentals; polyrhythms; constant motion; little interpretation of text

Diff: in all areas; perfect pitch desirable; mature singer needed, although it is perhaps easier than most of Diamond's cycles

Uses: attractive poetry but the music does not seem to match it; shorter than the other cycles; an exercise in ear-training, rhythmic sharpness, and range for an advanced singer

    a. *The Incredible Hour.* a–a"; 3/2 with changes, Andante; 5pp.

    b. *Whither Thou Goest.* c♯'–f♯"; 4/4, 3/4, Allegretto; 1+pp.

    c. *Love's Worth.* c♯'–f♯"; 5/8 with changes, Allegretto; 3+pp.

    d. *Spring Talk.* d'–e"; 2/2, 3/2, 4/2, Scorrevole; 3pp.

630. **THE LOVER AS MIRROR** (Edward Stringham). Elkan-Vogel, 1946. cmp1944. "To Jennie Tourel." X; c'–g"; Tess-M; changing meters, Andante; 2min; Diff-V/md, P/m.

For: soprano; tenor; mezzo-soprano (not light)

Mood: lyrical; philosophical

Voice: small skips and stepwise; fluid rhythms; various subdivisions of quarter note; fragmentary

Piano: linear; fluid rhythms; changing meters; does not double vocal line

Diff: poetry; rhythms; g" sustained *ff*
Uses: effective change of pace in a group, esp. with other Diamond songs

631. LOVE IS MORE (e. e. cummings). (Peer)Southern, 1954. cmp1950. X; b–g"; Tess-M; 3/4 predominates, Andante con tenerezza; 2+min; Diff-V/d, P/d.
For: mezzo-soprano; soprano
Mood: lighthearted
Voice: complex rhythms; final phrase uses extremes of range
Piano: 4–5-voice chordal texture; some moving lines; complex rhythms; does not double vocal line
Diff: complex poem; rhythms
Uses: effective song

632. THE MIDNIGHT MEDITATION (Elder Olson). Cycle. (Peer)Southern, 1954. cmp1951. "For William Warfield." X, very dissonant; F–f'; Tess-cs, wide; regular and irregular changing meters; varied tempos; 18min; Diff-V/dd, P/dd.
For: dramatic bass-baritone
Mood: dramatic contemplation of the void and meaninglessness of life; highly pessimistic
Voice: disjunct; chromatic; speech inflection rhythms well set; melodic motives recur; frequent use of d', e♭', and e'; many articulations
Piano: 13-meas. prelude and other solo passages; multiple accidentals in every measure; many specific articulation markings; quite programmatic and illustrative of the text; complex rhythms; for a pianist with solid technique and an ear for dissonance
Diff: in every area; perfect pitch desirable; ensemble will be difficult
Uses: probably the most effective of Diamond's cycles; powerful poetry well-matched by the music; usable for an advanced graduate singer; reflects the intellectual pessimism of the time

  a. *Midnight: I Pluck the Curtains Back.* F–d'; 2/4, 3/4, 4/4, Lento; 5pp.
  b. *Immensity, Like the Darkness.* F♯–f'; 3/2 with many changes, Moderato; 7pp.
  c. *Let Children Ride the Year's Sweet Carrousel.* F♯–e'; 2/4 with changes, Allegretto; 6pp.
  d. *I Thought Once I Should Have at a Man's Age.* F–e"; 4/4 with changes, Gravemente; solenne; 4+pp.

633. THE MILLENNIUM (Isak Dinesen). (Peer)Southern, 1969. [65]. cmp1960. X; a–f♯"; Tess-M; changing meters, Adagio; 2+min; Diff-V/d, P/d.
For: baritone; mezzo-soprano; contralto
Mood: dramatic; narrative
Voice: difficult melodic intervals; wide-ranged; speech rhythms; declamatory
Piano: chordal, 3–5-voice texture; some open 8ves, 5ths & 4ths; chromatic; syncopation
Diff: ensemble; rhythmic groupings; metaphysical text
Uses: usable for singer attracted to this text

634. MONODY (Herman Melville). Elkan-Vogel, 1947. cmp1945. X; b♭–e♭"; Tess-M; 4/4, Adagio non troppo; 2min; Diff-V/m, P/md.

For: baritone; mezzo-soprano
Mood: lyrical; elegy
Voice: many skips; fluid, speech rhythms; fragmented
Piano: 4–5-voice chordal texture with moving 8th-note part; lush chords
Diff: ensemble

635. MUSIC, WHEN SOFT VOICES DIE (Percy Bysshe Shelley). Associated, 1944. [4]. X; c'–e"; Tess-M; 6/8, Moderato; 1min; Diff-V/m, P/m.
For: baritone best; mezzo-soprano; contralto
Mood: lyrical; lush setting
Voice: many leaps, esp. 5ths & 7ths; rhythmic groupings vary within measures
Piano: linear, 3–4 voices; legato; does not double vocal line
Diff: phrases end with ascending interval; rhythmic groupings
Uses: nice setting of this text; romantic

636. MY LITTLE MOTHER (Katherine Mansfield). Elkan-Vogel, 1946. cmp1943. X; c'–f "; Tess-M; 2/4, 3/4, 4/4, Andante tranquillo; 2pp; Diff-V/m, P/m.
For: any high or medium voice
Mood: lyrical; philosophical; somewhat abstract
Voice: smoother, more regular, and easier than most Diamond songs
Piano: contrapuntal; 2-voice; independent of voice
Uses: effective contemporary song for young voices

637. MY PAPA'S WALTZ (Theodore Roethke). (Peer)Southern, 1968. cmp1964. X; b–e"; Tess-M; 3/4, Tempo di valzer triste, un po' macabro; 1+min; Diff-V/m, P/m.
For: baritone
Mood: tense; animated; macabre
Voice: smoother, more regular, and easier than most Diamond songs
Piano: waltz-style; much staccato; thin texture
Diff: ensemble
Uses: effective; soft ending; rather different from Rorem's setting

638. MY SPIRIT WILL NOT HAUNT THE MOUND (Thomas Hardy). (Peer)Southern, 1952. cmp1946. X; c'–e"; Tess-M; 4/4, Adagio; 2min; Diff-V/md, P/md.
For: baritone; mezzo-soprano (better for a man)
Mood: lyrical; solemn
Voice: small skips; speech rhythms; lyrical style
Piano: chordal, 4–5 voices
Uses: nice song

639. ODE (Arthur W. E. O'Shaughnessy). (Peer)Southern, 1971. cmp1969. X; b–a♭"; Tess-covers the range; 6/8 with many changes, Tempo moderato; 2+min; Diff-V/d, P/d.
For: dramatic soprano; tenor
Mood: dramatic; philosophical; narrative (describes artist/poet/musician)
Voice: many wide skips and leaps; angular; chromatic; juxtaposing of duplet and triplet subdivisions
Piano: linear, 3–4-voice texture; articulations important; covers the keyboard; does not double vocal line

Diff: pitch; rhythms

640. ON DEATH (John Clare). Associated, 1944. [4]. cmp1943. X; c'–g"; Tess-M; 3/4, Adagio e mesto; 2+min; Diff-V/m, P/me.

For: high baritone; soprano; mezzo-soprano

Mood: somber; welcomes death

Voice: stepwise and easy skips; first 5 meas. unaccomp.; some long-ranged phrases

Piano: chordal and linear; irregular rhythmic groupings; syncopation; does not double vocal line

Uses: effective death song

641. A PORTRAIT (The Marchioness of Brinvilliers) (Herman Melville). Elkan-Vogel, 1947. cmp1946. B♭maj-Gmin; c'–g"; 6/8, 5/8, Allegretto grazioso; 1min; Diff-V/m, P/md.

For: mezzo-soprano; soprano; tenor

Mood: lyrical; describes painter's concept

Voice: many skips; fluid rhythms

Piano: linear; delicate; constant 16th notes; life of its own

Diff: changing meters; legato

Uses: program within a group

642. PRAYER (Theodore Roethke). (Peer)Southern, 1968. cmp1964. X; a–e"; Tess-M; 3/4 with changes, Adagio; 2+min; Diff-V/md, P/m.

For: baritone (full, mature sound necessary)

Mood: dramatic; declamatory; humorous

Voice: speech rhythms; phrase fragmentation; declamatory

Piano: chordal 3–4-voice texture; some linear texture; 8ves; independent of vocal line

Diff: ensemble; dynamic control; dramatic concept

Uses: effective song; quiet ending

643. THE SHEPHERD BOY SINGS IN THE VALLEY OF HUMILIATION (John Bunyan). (Peer)Southern, 1949. cmp1946. D♭maj; c♯'–b"(g♯"); Tess-M; 3/8 predominates, Allegretto grazioso; 1+min; Diff-V/m, P/m.

For: soprano; tenor

Mood: simple; humble; straightforward

Voice: stepwise and small skips; much simpler than most Diamond songs

Piano: linear-chordal combination, 2–4 voices independent of vocal line

Diff: some syncopation; good dynamic control

Uses: effective song; recital use

644. SOMEWHERE from *More Trivia* (Logan Pearsall Smith). Elkan-Vogel, 1947. cmp1946. Bmin-Gmaj; a–g"; Tess-M; 4/4, 3/4, Adagio non troppo (♩ = 69); 1+min; Diff-V/m, P/md.

For: mezzo-soprano; dramatic soprano; high baritone

Mood: philosophical and introspective; sea voyage metaphor; dramatic at climax

Voice: many skips; fluid speech-like rhythms; fragmented phrases; triplets; lyrical and flowing; a number of phrases begin low and rise, one to g" *ff*

Piano: chordal and linear; 4-voice texture; almost continuous 8th-note movement; some chromaticism; independent of vocal line

Diff: requires good breath management for high tones at ends of rising phrases; ensemble

Uses: good teaching and recital material

645. THIS WORLD IS NOT MY HOME (anon.). Elkan-Vogel, 1947. cmp1946. B♭maj; d'–f"; Tess-M; 3/4, 4/4, Andante sostenuto; 1min; Diff-V/me, P/me.

For: baritone; mezzo-soprano; some tenors

Mood: lyrical; somber; folk flavor

Voice: stepwise and small skips; syncopation

Piano: block chords with bass countermelody; does not double vocal line

Uses: effective song; simpler texture and concept than other Diamond songs

646. TO LUCASTA GOING TO THE WARS (Richard Lovelace). Associated, 1946. C–Gmaj; c'–g"; Tess-M; 4/4, Andante con moto; 2pp; Diff-V/m, P/m.

For: tenor; high baritone

Mood: lyrical; love song

Voice: conjunct; speech rhythms

Piano: linear; many 2nds; 16th-note l.h. passages; quiet ending; does not double vocal line

Uses: nice song; usable

647. THE TWISTED TRINITY (Carson McCullers). Elkan-Vogel, 1946. cmp1943. C-centered; c'–g"; Tess-M; 3/4 with changes, Lento; 2min; Diff-V/m, P/e-m.

For: dramatic soprano; tenor; mezzo-soprano

Mood: dramatic; surrealistic poem; introspective

Voice: easy skips; fluid rhythms; irregular rhythms

Piano: chordal-linear combination, 2-voice linear predominates; rhythmic complexity

Diff: poem needs study; dynamic control (*p–ff*); g" decresc.

Uses: quiet ending; interior of group

648. WE TWO. A Song Cycle (William Shakespeare). (Peer)Southern, 1967. "For Carolyn Reyer." No key sigs., dissonant; g–a"; Tess-wide; regular and irregular changing meters; varied tempos; 21min; Diff-V/dd, P/dd.

For: mezzo-soprano

Mood: lyrico-dramatic; love songs; various moods and attitudes of love relationship found in selected sonnets

Voice: largely disjunct; most phrases begin low and ascend 1 to 1½ 8ves, covering all registers of the voice; pitches difficult; rhythmic patterns sometimes complex; semi-speech rhythms, but somewhat mechanical; many accidentals

Piano: linear, contrapuntal score; many accidentals; variety of figures and articulations, some illustrative of text; pianist needs thorough grasp of the modern score

Diff: many; this work for mature singer with literary and intellectual leanings; vocal endurance a strong factor

Uses: usable for advanced singer; selections could also be made for Shakespeare program

    a. *Shall I Compare Thee to a Summer's Day?* a–g"; 4/4, 3/4, Andante; 3pp.

    b. *Let Me Confess That We Two Must Be Twain.* a–g"; 2/4, 3/4, Allegretto; 4pp.

c. *Those Pretty Wrongs That Liberty Commits.*
a♯–g"; 4/4, 3/4, 5/4, Allegretto; 4+pp.

d. *For Shame Deny That Thou Bear'st Love to Any.*
c'–a"; 6/8, 4/4, 3/4, Moderato; 5pp.

e. *O from What Power Hast Thou This Powerful
Might.* a–a"; 4/4, 3/4, 5/4, Adagio afflitto; 4pp.

f. *My Love Is as a Fever Longing Still.* b♭–g"; 2/2,
3/2, 4/2, Lento; 5pp.

g. *No Longer Mourn for Me When I Am Dead.*
a♭–a"; 5/8, 6/8, 7/8, 8/8, Allegretto; 4+pp.

h. *When in Disgrace with Fortune and Men's Eyes.*
g–a"; 3/2, 4/2, 2/2, 5/2, Adagio; 4pp.

i. *When to the Sessions of Sweet Silent Thought.*
b–g"; 4/4, 3/4, 3/2, 5/4, Andante; 4+pp.

DI CHIERA, DAVID
(b. McKeesport, PA, 1937)

649. **BLACK BEADS.** Three Songs for Mezzo-soprano and
Piano (Richard Kubinski). Cycle. Peer International,
1970. X, dissonant; a♭–b♭"; Tess-cs; regular and
changing meters; moderate tempos; 10pp; Diff-V/md,
P/e-m.
For: mezzo-soprano
Mood: dramatic; anguished
Voice: disjunct; wide range; not especially strenuous, except
for final b♭" on word "pity"
Piano: linear; contrapuntal; (a.), two voices, treble clef; (b.),
chordal ostinato pattern treated sequentially; (c.),
1–3-voice texture, drooping figure, chord clusters at
end support same falling half-step figure
Diff: pitch; solid high voice; simplicity required
Uses: short cycle to give contrast to more lively material on a
program; not a program ender

a. *Black Bead I.* a♭–f"; 2/4, 3/4, 4/4, Moderato; 4pp.

b. *Black Bead II.* c'–f♯"; 6/4, 4/4, ♩ = 96 (Rubato);
3pp.

c. *Black Bead III.* b♭–b♭"; 4/4, 6/4, With great
intensity; 3pp.

DICKINSON, CLARENCE
(b. Lafayette, TN, 1873; d. New York, NY, 1969)

650. **SIX EMILY DICKINSON SONGS.** For High Voice
(ed. Walter Foster). Reprint: Recital Publications.
Traditional keys; d♭'–g"; Tess-M; traditional meters;
varied tempos; 15pp; Diff-V/e-m, P/me-m.
For: soprano; mezzo-soprano
Mood: mostly nature-centered; expressed in a simple,
child-like way
Voice: stepwise motion and skips that outline chords
predominate; rhythms generally easy; some dotted
rhythms and syncopation (e.); some 16th-note
subdivisions (f.); mostly syllabic with some 2-note slurs
Piano: block-chord, arpeggiated, and broken-chord patterning;
(c.) features imitation; (f.), somewhat contrapuntal;
many accidentals; doubles or outlines vocal line;
3–8-meas. preludes & 3–5-meas. postludes
Diff: (e.), features several phrases with range of 9th; final

phrase has range of 11th; misprint in clef signs in (e.)
Uses: for singer of limited musical experience; simplest
settings seem best, particularly (b.)

a. *The Lovers.* Amaj; d♯'–e"; 4/4, Allegro moderato;
3pp.

b. *Poor Little Heart.* E♭maj; e♭'–f♯"; 6/8, Andante;
2pp.

c. *Summer Shower.* Gmaj; f'–g"; 2/4, Vivace; 3pp.

d. *A Train Went Through a Burial Gate.* Gmin;
d'–f"; 4/4, Andantino; 2pp.

e. *I Taste a Liquor Never Brewed.* Gmaj; d'–g"; 6/8,
Scherzando; 2pp.

f. *Have You Got a Brook in Your Little Heart?*
D♭maj; d♭'–f"; 2/4, Allegretto; 3pp.

DIEMER, EMMA LOU
(b. Kansas City, MO, 1927)

651. **THE FOUR SEASONS** (from *The Fairy Queen*, based
on *A Midsummer Night's Dream*, by William
Shakespeare). Seesaw, 1982. cmp1969. X; d'–b♭";
Tess-mH-H; changing meters and tempos, Moderately
slow–Lively–Very slow–Moderately slow; 20pp;
Diff-V/md, P/d.
For: tenor; soprano
Mood: descriptive
Voice: many small skips; many accidentals; both duplet and
triplet subdivisions of beat; syncopation; some staccato;
soft ending; syllabic
Piano: some 2-voice counterpoint; some broken-chord,
afterbeat, and block-chord patterning; some 2 vs. 3 & 4
vs. 6; "Winter" section has trills and grace notes; some
doubling or outlining of vocal line
Diff: ensemble; 5-beat high note (b♭")
Uses: good for recital; stands by itself

652. **TWO SONGS.** [11, Vol. 4]. Separate entries below.

A. **SHALL I COMPARE THEE TO A SUMMER'S
DAY?** (William Shakespeare). cmp1972. Dmin; d'–g";
Tess-M; 3/4, 2/4, 4/4, Not too slow ♩ = 96; 4pp; Diff-
V/m, P/m.
For: soprano; tenor
Mood: love song
Voice: mostly conjunct, one leap of 9th; mostly 8th-note
rhythms; several scale passages; 15-count a' at end
while piano changes harmonies
Piano: mostly 8th-note motion, broken chords; some doubling
of vocal line
Diff: possibly mixed meters; some long-ranged phrases
Uses: recital material, perhaps in a Shakespeare group

B. **OCTOBER WIND (IN NEW YORK)** (Dorothy
Diemer Hendry). cmp1948. X; d'–a"; Tess-mH; 3/4,
5/4, 4/4, Moderately slow ♩ = 76; 5pp; Diff-V/md, P/d.
For: soprano; tenor
Mood: imagined scenes of autumn; nostalgic
Voice: conjunct; skips up to 6th; easy rhythms; long a"; not
easy to find pitches
Piano: many accidentals; accomp. often high (both hands 𝄞);

widely spaced at times; interludes very chromatic; tone clusters

Diff: finding pitches at beginnings of some phrases
Uses: group with other songs of similar poetic subjects

DIERCKS, JOHN
(b. Montclair, NJ, 1927)

653. **ABOUT A LAMB.** Four Poems by Blake (William Blake). Theodore Presser, 1962. Traditional keys; b–f" (opt. lower tones); Tess-M; regular meters with some changes; varied tempos; 6+min; Diff-V/e, P/e.
For: mezzo-soprano
Mood: lyrical; pastoral; all concern the lamb symbol
Voice: mostly conjunct; some triadic skips; repetitive figures
Piano: chordal; rhythms same as voice; doubles vocal line
Uses: teaching material for young singer

  a. *Piping.* Emin; b–f"; 2/4, 3/4, Fast and light; 1min.
  b. *Little Lamb.* Bmaj; b–e"; 2/4, 2/2, Moving gently; 1+min.
  c. *Sweet Babe.* Gmaj; b–e"; 2/4, 3/4, Tenderly, with simplicity; 2+min.
  d. *Merrily* ("Sound the Flute"). Emaj; e'–e"; 3/8, Fast, light, joyful, 1+min.

DIERS, ANN MacDONALD
(b. Concord, MA, 20th Century)

654. **STOPPING BY WOODS ON A SNOWY EVENING** (Robert Frost). Galaxy, 1953. Emin; d'–f♯"; Tess-mL; 4/4, Thoughtfully, not too slowly; 2+min; Diff-V/e, P/e.
For: mezzo-soprano; baritone; some sopranos
Mood: lyrical; introspective
Voice: stepwise and easy skips; rhythms not complicated
Piano: chordal; afterbeats bell-like
Uses: very nice song for beginning older student; usable for young student also

DiGIOVANNI, ROCCO
[See Appendix for songs with Italian texts]

DITON, CARL
(b. Philadelphia, 1886; d. Philadelphia, PA, 1969)

655. **ENTREATY** (William Henley). [47]. Emin; e'–e"; Tess-M; 2/4, Andante con sentimento; 2min; Diff-V/e, P/me.
For: all voices that can sustain e"
Mood: lyrical; tender love song
Voice: easy skips; 2-note slurs; easy rhythms
Piano: 8-meas. prelude; some countermelody, mostly afterbeat chordal style; syncopation and repeated chords
Diff: e" is the basis of two phrases
Uses: suitable for beginning students of any age; tasteful, simple setting

DOBSON, TOM
(b. Portland, OR, 1890; d. New York, NY, 1918)

656. **AT THE EDGE OF THE SEA** (James Stephens). G. Schirmer, 1920. D♭maj; d♭'–f"; Tess-M-mH; 9/8, Scorrendo con tenerezza; 2+min; Diff-V/m, P/md.
For: lyric baritone; tenor with good lower middle tones
Mood: lyrical; philosophical
Voice: conjunct; modulating line; 6/8 rhythms
Piano: arpeggiated throughout; various rhythmic groupings
Uses: nice song for a man

657. **CARGOES** (John Masefield). G. Schirmer, 1920, 1948. H & L keys: Fmaj & E♭maj; d'–f" & c'–e♭"; Tess-M; 6/8, Allegretto grazioso; 4pp; Diff-V/m, P/m.
For: any voice; best for men
Mood: descriptive; colorful
Voice: stepwise and small skips; duplets and triplets; syncopation
Piano: chordal–broken and rolled; large reaches; some chord clusters; two arpeggios; does not double vocal line
Diff: rhythmic subdivisions; unusual place names and other 19th-century British colonial terminology
Uses: good song for near-beginner and for teaching 6/8 meter in various rhythmic groupings

658. **AN OLD SONG RE-SUNG** (John Masefield). G. Schirmer, 1916. Gmin; d'–g"; Tess-M-mH; 4/4, Moderato; 4pp; Diff-V/m, P/m.
For: lyric baritone best; tenor with full lower middle voice
Mood: lyrical
Voice: conjunct with some skips; dotted rhythms; three stanzas; highest tones not sustained
Piano: chordal and linear; countermelody; doubles vocal line
Uses: good teaching song; easy vowels on high tones; straightforward

DONAHUE, BERTHA TERRY
(b. New York, NY, 1917)

659. **THE CASTLE YONDER.** A Cycle of Songs for Soprano with Piano Accompaniment. Arsis, 1982. Traditional tonal centers and harmonies; a–a"; Tess-mL; chiefly regular meters with changes; varied tempos; 14pp; Diff-V/m, P/m.
For: soprano specified; range and tessitura would seem more suitable for mezzo-soprano
Mood: poems by children; "reflect a mother's comprehension of a child's world interwoven with her own"
Voice: stepwise and easy skips; somewhat chromatic; easy rhythms; flowing phrases; considerable word repetition to enhance child-like quality; syllabic with occasional 2–3-note slurs and several small melismas
Piano: primarily chordal, some contrapuntal movement; easy rhythms; chromatic; incidental doubling of vocal line
Diff: good sense of pitch required; good vocal actor needed
Uses: possible recital material for a change of pace

  a. *The Castle Yonder* (John Dudley). D-centered; a–f♯"; Tess-mL; 4/4, 2/4, 3/4, Freely–Con moto (♩ = 120); 4+pp.

b. *The Dew* (Amy Epstein). Cmin; c'–e♭"; Tess-mL;
2/4, 3/4, Lento e sostenuto (♪ = 100); 1+pp.

c. *Household Problems* (Larry Haft). G-centered;
d'–g"; Tess-M; 6/8, 3/8, 9/8, Allegretto leggiero ma
ben marcato (♩. = 80); 2pp.

d. *Rain* (Jocelyn Klein). Dmin; c'–d"; Tess-mL; 3/4,
4/4, Lento (♪ = 84); 1p.

e. *A Cat* (John Gittings). E-centered; c♯'–f ";
Tess-mL; 5/4, 3/4, 2/4, 4/4, Con moto, ma dolce;
2+pp.

f. *The Four Winds* (Shirley Gash). Amin; b–a";
Tess-M; 3/4, 4/4, 2/4, Molto allegro (♩ = 60); 2+pp.

DONATO, ANTHONY
(b. Prague, NE, 1909)

660. **TO MY NEIGHBOR AT THE CONCERT** (Jeanne
DeLamarter). [17]. H & L keys: X; d'–g" & b♭–e♭";
Tess-M; 4/4, Slowly–Quite fast; 4pp; Diff-V/d, P/d.

For: all voices
Mood: humorous; descriptive
Voice: somewhat disjunct; semi-declamatory
Piano: chordal; syncopated; afterbeats; rapid arpeggios
Diff: high tessitura at end; interpretation
Uses: good closing or encore song

DONOVAN, RICHARD
(b. New Haven, CT, 1891; d. New Haven, CT, 1970)

661. **FOUR SONGS.** Valley, 1951. Traditional keys;
d'–a♭"; Tess-M-mH; regular meters with some changes;
varied tempos; 10pp; Diff-V/m, P/m.

For: soprano; tenor
Mood: various moods range from philosophical to lively,
joyful, and slightly risqué
Voice: flowing, sustained, and dancing phrases; some irregular
phrase lengths; some 2 vs. 3; some chromaticism
Piano: mostly 2–3-voice counterpoint; some chordal textures;
some chromaticism
Diff: some meter changes; some long phrases; ensemble
Uses: good introductory songs for students new to
contemporary idiom

a. *Away, Delights!* (John Fletcher). Cmin; f'–g";
generally 4/4, Not too slowly; 3pp.

b. *Song for a Dance* (Francis Beaumont). A♭maj;
e♭'–a♭"; 3/4, 2/4, Con moto; 1p (repeated).

c. *O Love, How Thou Art Tired Out with Rhyme!*
Bmaj; d♯'–e"; 6/4, 9/4, Andante; 2pp.

d. *Here Comes a Lusty Wooer* (old rhyme). E♭maj;
d'–g"; 2/2, 3/4, Con brio; 4pp.

DOUGHERTY, CELIUS
(b. Glenwood, MN, 1902; d. Effort, PA, 1986)

[See also D#s 10, 50, 55 for songs not listed below]

662. **BEAUTY IS NOT CAUSED** (Emily Dickinson). [4];
1st©1948. "For Eva Gauthier." Cmaj; d♯'–g"; Tess-M;

4/4, Sustained and expressive; 1+min; Diff-V/m, P/m.

For: tenor; soprano
Mood: lyrical and whimsical nature poem
Voice: conjunct with small skips; syncopation; some triplets
Piano: repeated chords; some l.h. melody; does not double
vocal line
Diff: some off-beat entrances; strong dynamics at end
Uses: big chordal ending; could end a group; useful to
develop dynamic control *p–ff*

663. **THE BIRD AND THE BEAST** (*The Atlantic
Monthly*, from Sir Ernest Gowers "Plain Words"). G.
Schirmer, 1953. Fmaj; c'–e"; Tess-mL; 2/4, Allegretto;
71meas.; Diff-V/m, P/m.

For: mezzo-soprano; contralto; baritone; bass
Mood: humorous; child-like; narrative
Voice: easy skips; speech rhythms
Piano: broken-chord pattern; syncopation; some rapid scales;
some doubling of vocal line two 8ves lower
Diff: rhythms; text
Uses: in a final group or humorous encore for the right singer

664. **THE CHILDREN'S LETTER TO THE UNITED
NATIONS** (Public School No. 90, Queens, N. Y.,
Kindergarten Class, Oct. 1946). G. Schirmer, 1950.
Cmin-maj; c'–g"; Tess-M; 6/8, With fervent conviction;
6pp; Diff-V/e, P/m.

For: soprano
Mood: simply stated truths; child-like expression
Voice: stepwise and easy skips; sustained notes at ends of
phrases; syncopation
Piano: chordal; large reaches; bombastic ending; doubles
vocal line
Uses: simple, but suits text; useful for a young singer

665. **GREEN MEADOWS** (anon.). G. Schirmer, 1925. H &
L keys: Bmaj & Amaj; f♯'–g♯" & e'–f♯"; Tess-mH;
2/4, Andante; 4pp; Diff-V/me, P/m.

For: soprano; tenor
Mood: subdued; introspective; longing
Voice: stepwise and easy skips; repetitive; dotted rhythms;
some melismas
Piano: chordal; 16th-note motion in bass; broken chords in
rocking motion; large reaches; doubles vocal line
Uses: effective lyric song; quiet ending; simpler than many
Dougherty songs

666. **HEAVEN-HAVEN** (Gerard Manley Hopkins). [60];
1st©1956. H & L keys: E♭maj & Cmaj; e♭'–f " &
c'–d"; Tess-mL; 4/4, Very quietly and very sustained;
3pp; Diff-V/me, P/e.

For: all voices
Mood: lyrical; philosophical poem about death
Voice: broad and sustained; each phrase partially unaccomp.
Piano: chordal; sustained; "In the manner of a medieval
organ"
Diff: long phrases

667. **HUSH'D BE THE CAMPS TODAY** (Walt
Whitman). G. Schirmer, 1948. E♭maj; b♭–g"; Tess-M;
4/4, With simple fervor; 5min; Diff-V/m, P/m.

For: high baritone

Mood: somber; sustained; dirge
Voice: stepwise and chant-like with small skips; some dotted rhythms; long phrases; many notes
Piano: chordal; syncopated; repeated chords; cross-hands; large reaches
Diff: sustained tones
Uses: effective song for the right singer

668. **THE K'E** (from the Chinese, 718 B.C.). [28, 64]; 1st©1954. Amin; d'–f"; Tess-M; 2/4, Slowly; 5pp; Diff-V/m, P/me.
For: soprano
Mood: melancholy; lost love; nature imagery
Voice: some long phrases; sustained, floating lines
Piano: broken chords; grace notes; some chromaticism
Diff: phrasing; breath control
Uses: effective song for teaching and recital; good contest piece for young singers

669. **LISTEN! THE WIND** (Humbert Wolfe). Boosey & Hawkes, 1958. Cmin-maj; b–g"; Tess-M; 4/4, ♩ = 126; 5pp; Diff-V/m-md, P/md.
For: lyric baritone with good g"
Mood: dramatic; impression of autumn season of life
Voice: mostly conjunct; some 8ve leaps; breathless feeling of motion; climax sustained g" ff
Piano: broken-chord figurations; some repeated chords; some arpeggiation; measured tremolo; chromatic; fast tempo; good rhythmic sense and coordination needed; somewhat programmatic
Diff: ensemble
Uses: exciting song; could close a group

670. **LOVE IN THE DICTIONARY** (*Funk and Wagnalls Students' Standard Dictionary*). [59]; 1st©1949. "For Blanche Thebom." H & L keys: E♭maj & Cmaj; c'–g" & a–e"; Tess-mH; 3/4, Leisurely at first . . . In spirited waltz rhythm; 6pp; Diff-V/m-d, P/m-d.
For: lyric soprano; mezzo-soprano
Mood: lyrical; light; humorous
Voice: large intervals; interrupted phrases; somewhat chromatic
Piano: chordal; afterbeat waltz style
Diff: good pitch and rhythmic sense needed
Uses: good light number for closing a group; encore
Rec: D#s 70, 168

671. **LOVELIEST OF TREES** (A. E. Housman). Boosey & Hawkes, 1948. Dmin-Fmaj; d'–f"(a"); Tess-M; 4/4, With rapture, but quietly; 3min; Diff-V/m, P/m.
For: any medium or high voice
Mood: lyrical; quiet; in awe of the scene
Voice: skips; dotted notes; repetitive rhythms
Piano: chordal; some countermelody; repetitive rhythm; polyrhythms–4 vs. 6; does not double vocal line
Uses: effective song; interior of group

672. **MADONNA OF THE EVENING FLOWERS** (Amy Lowell). Boosey & Hawkes, 1949. Cmaj; c'–g"; Tess-M; 4/4, Broadly; 65meas.; Diff-V/md, P/md.
For: tenor; high baritone
Mood: dramatic; descriptive; love song

Voice: declamatory; speech rhythms; divisions of beat into 2, 3, & 4
Piano: chordal; thick scoring; covers the keyboard; repeated, syncopated, and broken-chord patterns
Diff: constant crescendo over final 38 meas., beginning *pp*

673. **A MINOR BIRD** (Robert Frost). [64]; 1st©1958. Fmin; f'–e♭"; Tess-mL; 4/4, Melancholy (♩ = 76); 3pp; Diff-V/me, P/me.
For: mezzo-soprano
Mood: melancholy; philosophical
Voice: short phrases separated by rests; broad lines in second section
Piano: open 5ths sustained by pedal; "bird-call" motive; repeated chords
Diff: interpretive insight
Uses: effective song; good for teaching

674. **MUSIC** (Amy Lowell). R. D. Row, 1953. Dmin; c'–f"; Tess-mL; 4/4, Quietly, not dragging; 6pp; Diff-V/md, P/md.
For: mezzo-soprano; some sopranos; contralto
Mood: declamatory; narrative; child's imaginary world
Voice: many skips of 5th, 6th, & 7th; speech rhythms; some chant-like and fragmented sections
Piano: chordal; imitates sound of flute over block chords; does not double vocal line
Diff: ensemble
Uses: good setting; quiet ending

675. **NEW ENGLAND PASTORAL** (Emily Dickinson). Boosey & Hawkes, 1949. "For Eva Gauthier." Fmaj; c'–f"; Tess-M; 12/8, 4/4, Delicately chiming; 3min; Diff-V/m, P/m.
For: mezzo-soprano; soprano
Mood: simple, naive view of heaven; quiet
Voice: duplets in voice vs. triplets in piano; some 2-note slurs
Piano: juxtaposition of duplets and triplets; chordal; some chorale-like phrases
Diff: long phrases; 2 vs. 3
Uses: useful song, if not Dougherty's best; soft ending

676. **ONCET IN A MUSEUM** (Two Ways) (John V. A. Weaver). R. D. Row, 1953. Gmaj; d'–g"; Tess-M; 4/4, 6pp; Diff-V/md, P/md.
For: soprano; tenor
Mood: philosophical; nature of love; colloquial expressions
Voice: many skips; duplets and triplets; many accidentals; syncopation
Piano: chordal; thick texture; some imitation of vocal line, some doubling; large reaches; marked "like a blues"; climax of song in a piano interlude
Diff: jazz-like rhythmic effects; long phrases
Uses: quiet ending; useful for some singers

677. **PIANISSIMO** (Eli Ives Collins). G. Schirmer, 1948. "For Eva Gauthier." Emaj; c'–g"; Tess-M; 2/2, With steady pulsing rhythm; 3min; Diff-V/md-d, P/md.
For: mezzo-soprano; dramatic or lyric soprano
Mood: descriptive; jazz-like rhythm
Voice: many skips; complex rhythms; syncopation; interrupted phrases

Piano: chordal with some counterpoint; syncopated; some triplets; complex texture and rhythms; dramatic dynamic contrasts; does not double vocal line
Diff: rhythms; style; ensemble

678. PORTRAIT (Robert Browning). G. Schirmer, 1948. H & L keys: Fmaj & E♭maj; c'–a" & b♭–g"; Tess-mH; 4/4, Improvisatory, with increasing intensity; 4pp; Diff-V/md, P/m-d.
For: tenor; high baritone
Mood: dramatic; love song
Voice: angular; many leaps of 5th & 6th; syncopation; duplets vs. piano triplets; some chromaticism
Piano: broken- and repeated-chord patterns in triplets; some countermelody; thick texture; some doubling of vocal line, more imitation
Diff: ensemble; 2 vs. 3; phrases end on high tones
Uses: effective song for mature voice

679. PORTRAIT OF A LADY (Amy Lowell). R. D. Row, 1953. H & L keys: E♭maj & Cmaj; d'–g" & b–e"; Tess-M; 4/4, Andantino (quasi un arioso); 5pp; Diff-V/m, P/md.
For: tenor; baritone
Mood: lyrical; descriptive of an old painting
Voice: stepwise and small skips; fragmented; is an obbligato to the accomp.; some dotted notes; syncopation
Piano: somewhat like a Bellini aria; broken-chord figure; countermelody in 3rds; 8ves and trills; other ornaments; some repeated chords; does not double vocal line
Diff: ensemble; dramatic climax
Uses: effective setting of this text; recital use

680. PRIMAVERA (Amy Lowell). [59]; 1st©1948. H & L keys: A♭maj & Fmaj; c'–b♭" & a–g"; Tess-M; 4/4, With joyous enthusiasm; 9pp; Diff-V/d, P/d.
For: lyric soprano
Mood: joyful spring song
Voice: chromatic; large intervals; rapid notes in fast tempo
Piano: chordal; rapid chromatic passages
Diff: increasingly high tessitura to climactic b♭" and long a♭" at end (high key)
Uses: good showpiece for voice and piano

681. SONATINA (Rose Fyleman). G. Schirmer, 1948. Amaj; e'–f♯"; Tess-M; 4/4, Allegro moderato; 2min; Diff-V/m, P/m.
For: soprano; mezzo-soprano
Mood: humorous; child's negative statements
Voice: is an obbligato to the piano accomp.; mostly stepwise with small skips; easy rhythms
Piano: piano piece which the speaker is "practicing"; in classical style; no vocal line doubling
Diff: ensemble
Uses: clever song for a humorous group; encore

682. SONG FOR AUTUMN (Mary Webb). G. Schirmer, 1962. Gmaj; e'–g"(a"); Tess-M; 4/4, 6/4, With exuberance; 1min; Diff-V/m, P/md.
For: soprano; tenor; dramatic voice needed
Mood: dramatic
Voice: many skips; 2-note slurs; duplets and triplets

Piano: rocking repeated-chord figures in triplets; arpeggiated figures; trills; some doubling of vocal line
Diff: long sustained tones
Uses: big ending; could close a group

683. THE SONG OF THE JASMINE (from *The Book of the Thousand and One Nights*). Boosey & Hawkes, 1957. "For Povla Frijsh." G♭maj; d♭'–a♭"; Tess-M-mH; 6/4, Dolcissimo; 2+min; Diff-V/md, P/md.
For: soprano
Mood: lyrical; descriptive; floating
Voice: many leaps and sustained tones; long phrases; subdued
Piano: chordal; repetitive pattern in triplets; varied registers; no doubling of vocal line
Diff: long tones; breath control
Uses: effective song for the right voice

684. SONGS BY E. E. CUMMINGS. G. Schirmer, 1966. 4 songs pub. separately; separate entries below. NOTE: These 4 songs group nicely as follows (and can be done well as a group by a soprano): 1. thy fingers make early flowers. 2. o by the by. 3. little fourpaws. 4. until and i heard.

A. THY FINGERS MAKE EARLY FLOWERS. [64]. E♭maj; e♭'–g"; Tess-mL; 6/8, Andantino; 5pp; Diff-V/d, P/md.
For: tenor; soprano
Mood: lyrical; descriptive; philosophical; love song
Voice: flowing phrases; somewhat fragmented; syncopation
Piano: contrapuntal; somewhat chromatic
Diff: rhythm; pitches; text
Uses: separately or with others in this set

B. UNTIL AND I HEARD. Fmaj; f'–b♭"; Tess-mH-H; 9/8, 6/8, 12/8, Allegretto; 1+min; Diff-V/md-d, P/d.
For: soprano
Mood: exuberant; vital; concerns bird's song
Voice: stepwise and skips on chord lines; syncopation; irregular phrase lengths; 2–5-note slurs
Piano: chordal with rapid countermelody; some ornaments; imitates birdsong; middle and high registers
Diff: ensemble; climaxes on sustained b♭" leading to a" *ff*
Uses: effective song for American group, group about song or singing, or with other songs of this set

C. O BY THE BY. Fmaj; c'–g"; Tess-M; 4/4, Leggero; 1min; Diff-V/md, P/md.
For: soprano; mezzo-soprano
Mood: light; exuberant; a wish given up
Voice: leaps; fragmented; dotted notes; syncopation
Piano: linear-chordal combination; middle and high registers; staccato important; does not double vocal line
Diff: ensemble; poem requires study; dynamics
Uses: good song; use separately or with others in this set

D. LITTLE FOURPAWS. Fmin; d♭'–e♭"; Tess-M; 3/4, Moderato; 21meas.; Diff-V/m, P/m.
For: baritone; mezzo-soprano; any voice comfortable in the range and tessitura
Mood: quiet; delicate; song about a kitten's death
Voice: small skips; fragmentary phrases

Piano: 2–4-voice texture; constant 16ths; medium and high registers; soft dynamics
Uses: good soft song (*p–pp*); interior of group

685. SOUND THE FLUTE! (William Blake). [20]; 1st©1957. Fmaj; f'–d"; Tess-M; 3/8, 4/8, Quickly and lightly (♪ = 184); 3pp; Diff-V/e, P/m.
For: any light lyric voice
Mood: light; joyful New Year's song
Voice: light and dancing; punctuated by rests; many dotted rhythms
Piano: light and staccato; chordal
Uses: good for singer of limited range

686. THE TAXI (Amy Lowell). [60]; 1st©1961. H & L keys: Emin & C#min; d#'–e" & b#–c#"; Tess-mL; 4/4, Monotonously (♩ = 120-126); 2min; Diff-V/m, P/d.
For: all voices
Mood: abstract description of the poet leaving a lover (presumably in a taxi)
Voice: rather static; more dramatic at end
Piano: chordal with continuous trill figures
Diff: interpretation of text
Uses: for students with short ranges who understand this text

687. UPSTREAM (Carl Sandburg). G. Schirmer, 1960. "For Louis Nicholas." Gmaj with many modulations; d'–f"; Tess-M; 4/4, With drive (♩ = 128); 3pp; Diff-V/me, P/m.
For: tenor; high baritone
Mood: dramatic; powerful; philosophical; patriotic
Voice: vigorous; several powerful long tones; fragmented
Piano: chordal; fairly chromatic; supportive of voice, little doubling
Diff: loud dynamics
Uses: good song; recital use

DUKE, JOHN
(b. Cumberland, MD, 1899; d. Northampton, MA, 1984)

[See also D#s 50, 171, 173; titles not given]

688. ACQUAINTED WITH THE NIGHT (Robert Frost). (Peer)Southern, 1964. [65]. G-centered; b–f"; Tess-M; 4/4, At the rate of a slow, casual walk; 3min; Diff-V/md, P/md.
For: baritone; mezzo-soprano
Mood: dramatic; declamatory; intense
Voice: many leaps; syncopation; afterbeat entrances; speech rhythms
Piano: chordal with repetitive countermelody; short tremolos, written out; does not double vocal line
Diff: duplets in voice vs. triplets in piano; some long phrases
Uses: effective song; quiet ending
Rec: D#172

689. APRIL ELEGY (Alfred Young Fisher). G. Schirmer, 1965. [100]. H & L keys: Emin (orig.) & C#min; c'–g" & a–e"; Tess-M; 9/8, 6/8, With very quiet and steady motion; 2+min; Diff-V/m, P/m-md.
For: tenor; possibly soprano

Mood: lyrical; elegiac
Voice: many skips, esp. 6ths; several long-ranged phrases; some syncopation
Piano: r.h. 2-voice vertical structures and 16th-note trills, written out; l.h. syncopated arpeggios and repeated notes; many accidentals; does not double vocal line
Diff: soft dynamics; register control
Uses: lovely subdued song

690. AT THE AQUARIUM (Max Eastman). [98]. cmp1947. F#-centered; c#'–f#"; Tess-M; 4/4, With wan and wary motion; 4pp; Diff-V/d, P/d.
For: mezzo-soprano; baritone; soprano
Mood: descriptive; quiet
Voice: many skips; some long-ranged phrases; syncopation; speech-like rhythms
Piano: broken-chord patterning; features 2 vs. 3; duplets and triplets switch hands several times in a difficult pattern; some long reaches; many accidentals; does not double vocal line
Diff: intervals; rhythms; ensemble
Uses: interesting recital song for two competent musicians

691. THE BABE (Edward Carpenter). [100]; 1st©1925. H & L keys: Emaj & Dmaj; d#'–f" & c#'–eb"; Tess-M; 12/8, 4/4, Broadly (♩. = 72); 3pp; Diff-V/me, P/m.
For: all voices
Mood: wonder at the birth of a child
Voice: somewhat disjunct, but legato
Piano: numerous accidentals; broken chord figuration; supports vocal line well
Diff: legato 8ves and other large intervals in voice; several long phrases
Uses: effective recital song

692. BELLS IN THE RAIN (Elinor Wylie). [21]; 1st©1948. H & L keys: X; d'–g" & c'–eb"; Tess-mH; 4/4, Quietly, with bell-like evenness (♩ = 69); 2+min; Diff-V/m, P/d.
For: soprano; mezzo-soprano
Mood: lyrical; philosophical; nature imagery
Voice: some large intervals; phrases often begin high
Piano: arpeggiations and broken-chord figurations throughout in r.h.
Diff: ensemble; dynamics
Rec: D#11

693. BE STILL AS YOU ARE BEAUTIFUL (Patrick MacDonogh). [60]; 1st©1968. H & L keys: Dmaj & Cmaj; c'–f" & bb–eb"; Tess-mH; 4/4, Quiet and flowing (♩ = 84); 3pp; Diff-V/m, P/m.
For: any high or medium voice
Mood: lyrical; love poem
Voice: short phrases; somewhat chromatic
Piano: arpeggiated and broken chords; somewhat chromatic
Diff: some pitches; soft singing
Uses: good recital song
Rec: D#s 11, 171

694. THE BETTER PART (George Santayana). [97]. cmp1977. Abmaj; db'–ab"; Tess-mH; 4/4, Con passione, ma non troppo allegro (slower center section); 6pp; Diff-V/m, P/m.

For: dramatic tenor; soprano
Mood: philosophical
Voice: more melodic than many Duke songs; syncopation; some 2 vs. 3 in piano; many accidentals; ends with 11-beat sustained a♭" *ff*; dramatic ending
Piano: arpeggiation in duplets, triplets, and quadruplets; dramatic, modernized plagal cadence at end
Diff: possibly ensemble when polyrhythms are involved
Uses: text seems to require a mature singer

695. THE BIRD (Elinor Wylie). [100]; 1st©1947. Bmin/Dmaj (high); f'–a" [not in L vol.]; Tess-H; 4/4, Simply and very quietly (♩ = about 80); 3pp; Diff-V/m, P/m.

For: high soprano
Mood: lyrical and ecstatic
Voice: somewhat disjunct, but legato
Piano: chordal, with some accidentals
Diff: some large leaps; both loud and soft high tones needed
Uses: development of light high register and for recital
Rec: D#s 21, 30, 169

696. THE BLACK PANTHER (John Hall Wheelock). [98]. cmp1971. Emin; a–f"; Tess-M; 3/4, Tempo giusto–Più mosso; 6pp; Diff-V/m, P/m.

For: baritone best
Mood: dramatic
Voice: many skips; some syncopation; climax is 3-beat f" *ff*; quiet ending
Piano: detached block chords and legato broken-chord patterns; accidentals, no key sig.
Diff: possibly some rhythms
Uses: for a mature singer

697. BREAD AND MUSIC (Conrad Aiken). [98]. cmp1956. Fmin-Fmaj; d'–g♭"; Tess-M; 12/8, Moderate tempo, quiet, flowing rhythm; 4pp; Diff-V/m, P/m.

For: baritone; mezzo-soprano; soprano
Mood: nostalgic for lost love
Voice: many skips but not difficult; duple and triple subdivisions of beat; syncopation; 2 vs. 3 in piano
Diff: rhythms
Uses: good recital song; for other settings of poem see "Music I Heard With You" by Richard Hageman and Paul Nordoff

698. BREDON HILL (A. E. Housman). [99]. cmp1981. B-centered; b♭–e"; Tess-mL; 2/2, Moderato (♩ = 44); 5pp; Diff-V/md, P/m.

For: any medium voice
Mood: dark poem; the dead lover narrates
Voice: somewhat disjunct, but needs to be very legato and sustained at a slow tempo; several long phrases; some large intervals; many accidentals
Piano: chordal; many accidentals; does not always clearly support vocal line
Diff: pitches; long sustained phrases; maintaining mood at slow tempo
Uses: fine recital song
Rec: D#173

699. BROWN PENNY (William Butler Yeats). Carl Fischer, 1976. D♯maj[!]; a♯–e"; Tess-M; 12/8, Moderato; 6pp; Diff-V/md, P/md.

For: medium voice specified; man's text
Mood: philosophical; concerns love
Voice: many small skips; some chromaticism; some duplet subdivisions; lines of poetry separated; off-beat entrances
Piano: broken-chord patterns; many accidentals; independent of vocal line; wide piano range; rather difficult to read
Diff: some entrances difficult rhythmically; d♭" sustained *pp*
Uses: for rhythmically secure young student; possibly pair with "The Song of Wandering Aengus" by Duke

700. CALVARY (Edward Arlington Robinson). Carl Fischer, 1948. Dmin; g–f"; Tess-L, M, H; 4/4, With heavy and measured tread; 6pp; Diff-V/d, P/d.

For: bass-baritone
Mood: dramatic
Voice: sustained phrases; some large leaps; chromatic in spots; climax on f" for 10 beats + 2 to end word "writhing," *ff*; low ending
Piano: recurrent ornamental figure; rolled chords in spots; large reach helpful; broken-chord figurations increase in speed to measured tremolo; somewhat bombastic
Diff: long phrases; high climax followed by low, quiet ending
Uses: rather melodramatic; useful for certain situations, given the right voice; not for young singers

701. CAPRI (Sara Teasdale). Boosey & Hawkes, 1949. [96]. cmp1947. D♭-centered; c'–a♭"; Tess-M-mH; 2/4, Slowly and with intense feeling; 2pp; Diff-V/md, P/m.

For: soprano
Mood: lyrical; contemplative; longing
Voice: rather disjunct; many leaps of 5th or 8ve; many accidentals; syncopation; dotted rhythms
Piano: many accidentals; broken chords; syncopation; does not double vocal line
Diff: dynamic control; secure registration
Uses: effective setting of this text; quiet ending; one of Duke's best songs

702. CENTRAL PARK AT DUSK (Sara Teasdale). Boosey & Hawkes, 1949. [96]. cmp1947. X; e'–g"; Tess-M; 4/4, Hushed and tense; 1+min; Diff-V/m-md, P/m.

For: composer says medium voice; soprano best
Mood: lyrical; descriptive; quiet
Voice: many skips; dotted rhythms; syncopation; soft, sustained high tones
Piano: block chords; large reaches; soft dynamics; does not double vocal line
Diff: soft dynamics; some pitches hard to hear
Uses: effective song for recital group

703. COUNTING THE BEATS (Robert Graves). [98]. cmp1974. C-centered; c'–f♯"; Tess-M; 4/4, Tempo giusto; 4pp; Diff-V/m, P/m.

For: mezzo-soprano; baritone
Mood: somber; premonitions of death
Voice: many skips; both duplet and triplet subdivisions of

beat; syncopation; many accidentals (no key signature); climax is 4-beat f♯" *ff*

Piano: mostly block chords; steady and march-like; does not double vocal line

Diff: possibly dynamics (*pp–ff*), rhythms, and some intervals

Uses: good recital song; mature subject

704. **THE DARK HILLS** (Edward Arlington Robinson). [98]. cmp1966. C♯maj; b♯–e"; Tess-M; 5/4 with changes, Lento e tranquillo; 3pp; Diff-V/m, P/m.

For: mezzo-soprano; baritone; contralto; bass

Mood: peaceful sunset

Voice: fairly conjunct; many accidentals; irregular phrase lengths; dynamics *pp–f*

Piano: 4–5-voice block chords; does not double vocal line

Diff: rhythms

Uses: a well-made song

705. **DIRGE** (Adelaide Crapsey). [98]. cmp1935. Amin; c♯'–g"; Tess-M; 3/4, Slow and sustained; 2pp; Diff-V/m, P/me.

For: mezzo-soprano; soprano

Mood: lyrical and sad

Voice: many skips; syncopation; long notes on f♯" and g" *ff*; dynamics range *pp–ff*; quiet ending

Piano: sparse linear accomp.; many accidentals

Diff: range and dynamics

Uses: effective song; well-written; see also other settings by Harrison Kerr and Hugo Weisgall

706. **THE DOOR** (Orrick Johns). [96]. cmp1956. Dmaj; a♯–f"; Tess-mL; 4/4, Quiet and steady; 4pp; Diff-V/m, P/me.

For: mezzo-soprano; baritone

Mood: lyrical description of love

Voice: conjunct and disjunct motion; intervals often outline triads; dramatic ending

Piano: both block and broken chords; many accidentals

Diff: requires singer with effective low tones

Uses: general use; excellent recital material

707. **EIGHT SONGS ON TRANSLATIONS FROM THE GREEK AND LATIN LYRIC POETS.** For Baritone and Piano. Recital Publications, 1984. Separate entries below.

A. **THREE GREEK EPITAPHS.** Traditional keys and harmonies; A–e'; Tess-M-mH; 4/4, 3/4, slow tempos; 8pp; Diff-V/m-md, P/me-m.

For: baritone specified

Mood: epitaphs for a sailor, a problem drinker, a happy man

Voice: disjunct; many accidentals (no key sigs.); syncopation and dotted rhythms; syllabic

Piano: (a.), block chords; (b.), contrapuntal with some rolled chords; (c.), repeated 8th-note chords; accidentals; syncopation; does not double vocal line; some prelude and interlude material

Diff: irregularities in rhythms; some intervals; ensemble

Uses: composer states these are intended as a group, but that "any one of them could easily be combined with some of the other songs to make a varied group for recital purposes"

a. *An Inscription by the Sea* (Edward Arlington Robinson, from Greek of Glaucus). B♭min-maj; A–e♭'; Tess-M; 4/4, Lento e mesto; 2pp.

b. *Undying Thirst* (Robert Bland, from Greek of Antipater). Gmin; B–e'; Tess-mH; 3/4, Andante sostentuo; 3pp.

c. *A Happy Man* (Edward Arlington Robinson, from Greek of Carphyllides). B♭maj; A–e♭'; Tess-M; 4/4, Molto tranquillo; 3pp.

B. **HESPERUS** (Lord Byron, from Sappho). Bmin-Dmaj; c♯'–e♭"; Tess-M; 4/4, Quiet, but not too slow; 2pp; Diff-V/md, P/m.

For: baritone specified; mezzo-soprano possible

Mood: tribute to the evening star

Voice: somewhat disjunct; many accidentals; speech-like rhythms; syllabic; dynamic range *pp–ff*

Piano: broken-chord patterning; some countermelody; accidentals; does not double vocal line

Diff: dynamics; possibly rhythms and ensemble

Uses: in a group from this volume

C. **LESBIA RAILING** (Jonathan Swift, from Latin of Catullus). Cmaj; c'–f"; Tess-M; unmetered but barred (6/4, 4/4), Agitato; 3pp; Diff-V/m, P/m.

For: baritone specified

Mood: irony and contradictions of love; energetic

Voice: stepwise motion with small skips; some accidentals; rhythms not complex but some syncopation; 5-beat f" *ff*; syllabic

Piano: broken chords in constant 8th notes with countermelody; accidentals; does not double vocal line; 6-meas. prelude; 5-meas. interlude

Diff: possibly high note on "love"

Uses: could end group about women, or group from this volume; would pair well with "To Cloe" (see below)

D. **EROTION** (Kirby Flower Smith, from Latin of Martial). Fmaj; a–e♭"; Tess-M; 4/4, Con moto; 3pp; Diff-V/md, P/md.

For: baritone specified

Mood: epitaph on girl-child of six; plaintive

Voice: somewhat disjunct; many accidentals; rhythms often speech-like; dynamics *pp–f*; quiet ending; syllabic

Piano: afterbeat and broken-chord patterning; some countermelody; texture fairly thick; syncopation; 9-meas. section requiring cross-hands; does not double vocal line; two interludes

Diff: fragmentary nature of some phrases; ensemble

Uses: group with other songs from this volume

E. **TO CLOE** (Thomas Moore, from Latin of Martial). Emin; b–e"; Tess-mH; unmetered but irregularly barred, ♪unit of beat, Giocoso; 3pp; Diff-V/d, P/md.

For: baritone specified

Mood: ironic; describes Cloe's attractions, which poet realizes he can live without

Voice: stepwise with skips, often of 8ve; irregular rhythms, often speech-like; syncopation; syllabic

Piano: some afterbeat style; uses repeated short scale/block-chord motive; mostly staccato; does not double vocal line; 6-meas. prelude

Diff: rhythms and ensemble
Uses: in group from this volume; would pair well with "Lesbia Railing" (see above)

F. **THE LONELY ISLE** (Howard Mumford Jones, from Latin of Claudius Claudianus). Bmin-maj; a♯–e″; Tess-M; 4/4, Molto tranquillo; 3pp; Diff-V/me, P/m.
For: baritone specified; also mezzo-soprano or contralto
Mood: serene description of nature
Voice: stepwise motion and skips outlining chords; accidentals; many long notes; some syncopation; several cresc. and decresc.; syllabic
Piano: broken-chord patterning; many accidentals (no key sig.); does not double vocal line
Uses: to develop dynamic control; for recital use, group with others from this volume

708. **ELAINE** (Edna St. Vincent Millay). [100]; 1st©1989. H & L keys: Bmin & Amin; d′–e″ & c′–d″; Tess-mL; unmetered, Andante espressivo (♪ = 138), 5pp; Diff-V/m, P/m.
For: mezzo-soprano; contralto
Mood: lyrical love song; reference to well-known poems by Tennyson
Voice: mostly conjunct with a few leaps
Piano: contrapuntal with broken chords
Diff: irregular meter: 5, 6, or 7 eighth-notes per measure
Uses: excellent recital material

709. **THE END OF THE WORLD** (Archibald MacLeish). Valley, 1953. Fmin; c′–f″; Tess-M; 4/4, Allegro giusto; 3min; Diff-V/md, P/md.
For: soprano; mezzo-soprano
Mood: surrealistic; somewhat humorous
Voice: declamatory, patter-like section followed by smooth, sustained section
Piano: linear; staccato passage in 8ves; afterbeat section; polyrhythms; some sustained chords
Diff: diction; poem needs explanation
Uses: perhaps to open a group or as a change of pace
Rec: D#171

710. **EVENING** (Frederic Prokosch). [60]; 1st©1954. H & L keys: shifting tonalities; a–g″ & f♯–e″; Tess-mL; 4/4, With a quiet steady swing–Faster and very agitated–Broad; 2+min; Diff-V/md, P/d.
For: dramatic soprano; mezzo-soprano
Mood: lyrical description of a scene grows into dramatic and emotional outburst
Voice: flowing; dramatic and disjunct
Piano: chordal; arpeggiated; more rapid arpeggiation and scales toward end
Diff: dramatic expression
Uses: illustration of sharply contrasting dynamics and style in a single song

711. **FEBRUARY TWILIGHT** (Sara Teasdale) [51, 100]; 1st©1926. H & L keys: F♯maj & Emaj; f♯′–f♯″ & e′–e″; Tess-M; 6/8, 4/4, Very sustained (♩. = 52); 3pp; Diff-V/m, P/me.
For: any medium voice
Mood: lyrical landscape

Voice: slow and sustained; many repeated notes, a few leaps; short middle section *quasi recitativo*
Piano: chordal, with syncopation; some accidentals; supports vocal line completely
Diff: accurate rhythm for singer against piano syncopation
Uses: good recital song

712. **FIVE LEWIS CARROLL POEMS.** For Medium Voice and Piano. Recital Publications, 1986. Traditional keys; a♭–f″; Tess-M; regular meters; varied tempos; 30pp (MS); Diff-V/m, P/m.
For: medium voice specified
Mood: humorous
Voice: many small skips; several 8ve leaps; (a.) & (b.) include dotted rhythms and syncopation; many accidentals; (b.), recit. section; (a.) & (d.), refrains; syllabic
Piano: afterbeat style (a.) and block- and broken-chord patterns and combinations; many accidentals (only (d.) uses key sig.); some trill-like and tremolo-like sections (b.); does not double vocal line; all have prelude, interlude, and postlude material (e., 10-meas. prelude, 9-meas. interlude, & 3-meas. postlude)
Diff: pronunciation of (b.); delivery with the right touches of humor
Uses: can be used as a set for a humorous, light recital group; any songs could be excerpted; good encore material, particularly (a., b., & d.); (b.) marvelous musical parody of sectional ballad style, matching the poetic parody of the style

a. *The Lobster Quadrille.* B♭maj; a♭–f″; 4/4, Moderato, ma con anima; 7pp.
b. *Jabberwocky.* Emin; a–f″; 4/4, Dolce e misterioso–Moderato ma risoluto–Allegro marcato–Allegro con brio, with changes and fluctuations; 9pp.
c. *The Little Crocodile.* Fmaj; c′–e♭″; 4/4, Andante placido; 4pp.
d. *The Mock Turtle's Song.* A♭maj; c′–f″(e♭″); 3/4, Andante doloroso; 6pp.
e. *The Duchess' Lullaby.* Dmin; c♯′–f″; 3/4, Molto energico; 4pp.

713. **FOUR POEMS BY EMILY DICKINSON.** [97]. cmp1975. Traditional keys; c♯′–a″; Tess-M; traditional meters; 18pp; Diff-V/m, P/m-md.
For: soprano; tenor
Mood: themes of nature, young love, and life
Voice: intervals not difficult; some syncopation; some speech rhythms; irregular phrase lengths; syllabic
Piano: (a.), block chords and bird calls; (b.), afterbeat style and 2 vs. 3; (c.), broken-chord "brook" patterns; (d.), broken-chord patterns and countermelody; does not double vocal line
Diff: irregular phrase lengths; ensemble in (b.)
Uses: as a group, or any of the four could be sung alone; see another setting of (a.) by Ronald C. Perera (in *Five Summer Songs*)
Rec: D#170

a. *New Feet within My Garden Go.* E-centered; d′–g″; 3/4, Tranquillo; 3pp.

b. ***The Rose Did Caper on Her Cheek.*** Dmaj; c♯'–a"; 4/4, Scherzoso; 4pp. [**Rec:** D#3]

c. ***Have You Got a Brook in Your Little Heart?*** Fmaj-Fmin; e♭'–g♯"; 4/4, Allegretto; 5pp.

d. ***I Taste a Liquor Never Brewed.*** Cmaj; e'–a♭"; 6/8, Giocoso; 6pp.

714. **FRAGMENT** (Adelaide Crapsey). [100]; 1st©1989. H & L keys: F♯min & Emin; c♯'–e" & b–d"; Tess-mL; 6/8, With a quiet swing; 2pp; V/md, P/e.
For: any medium or low voice
Mood: lyrical; night scene
Voice: legato; some leaps
Piano: two voices; r.h. melody with l.h. broken chords
Diff: duplets and leap of m9th between phrases in voice
Uses: a very short song

715. **FROM THE SEA.** Five Songs for Soprano (Sara Teasdale). Cycle. [97]. cmp1962. Traditional keys; b–a"; Tess-M; traditional meters; 18pp; Diff-V/md, P/m-md.
For: soprano
Mood: a love that could not be uttered; sublimation
Voice: many skips; word rhythms cause many different types of beat subdivision; irregular rhythms and polyrhythms with piano; much syncopation; many accidentals
Piano: mostly broken-chord patterning; some block chords; many accidentals (no key sigs.); various subdivisions of beat; (d.), features 2 vs. 3; little doubling of vocal line
Diff: pitch patterns (a. & c.); rhythms; ensemble (b. & d.)
Uses: best to use as a group; those most attractive to excerpt might be (a.) & (b.); (e.), deals with lost love as inspiration for poetry; cf. Rorem's setting of Whitman's "Sometimes With One I Love"
Rec: D#170

a. ***All Beauty Calls You to Me.*** A♭maj; c♭'–g"; 4/4, Molto tranquillo; 3pp.

b. ***Listen, I Love You.*** Cmaj; b–g♯"; 6/8, Allegretto con moto; 4pp.

c. ***I Am So Weak a Thing.*** Amaj; c♯'–g"; 4/4, Moderato ma con molto espressione; 4pp.

d. ***All Things in All the World Can Rest, but I.*** E♭maj; d'–a"; 3/4, Agitato; 4pp.

e. ***Oh, My Love.*** A♭maj; c'–a♭"; 4/4, Andante; 3pp.

716. **GIVE ME YOUR HAND** (John Hall Wheelock). [98]. cmp1971. Gmin; a–e♭"; Tess-M; 6/4, Lento, ma con molto (♩=44); 3pp; Diff-V/me, P/me.
For: contralto; mezzo-soprano; baritone; bass
Mood: somber and quiet
Voice: stepwise motion and small skips; many dynamic markings
Piano: block chords; 4–5-voice texture; accidentals instead of key sig.; does not double vocal line
Diff: possibly sustaining slow tempo
Uses: mature text; good recital song for low voice

717. **GOOD MORNING** (6 Songs for Soprano) (Mark Van Doren). [99]. cmp1974. Traditional tonal centers, frequent changes; e'–a"; Tess-mH; regular meters and varied tempos; 28pp; Diff-V/d, P/dd.

For: soprano; possibly tenor
Mood: somewhat child-like views of the joys of nature
Voice: many short phrases; some large intervals; all songs have sustained tones in high or middle voice at end; numerous accidentals; some high-lying phrases
Piano: mostly chordal; broken-chord figurations, very rapid in (d.) & (e.); afterbeats in (f.); (b.) in two parts, melody with broken-chords in l.h.; many accidentals; usually supports vocal line quite well
Diff: some pitches; needs singer with easy high voice and smooth passaggio
Uses: could be an effective recital group

a. ***Good Morning.*** G-centered; f♯'–g"; Tess-mH; 3/4, Moderato–ma con anima (♩=84); 4pp.

b. ***Walking in the Rain.*** Dmin; e'–a"; Tess-mH; 12/8, Andante commodo (♩.=84); 5pp.

c. ***Those Great Clouds There.*** Emin; f'–a"; 6/8, Lento e molto quieto (♩.=44); 4pp.

d. ***Water That Falls and Runs Away.*** C-centered; e'–g"; Tess-M; 2/2, Allegro moderato (♩=92); 5pp.

e. ***Listen to Us, the Leaves Say.*** Amin; e'–g♯"; Tess-mH; 4/4, Allegretto (♩=72); 4pp.

f. ***Merry-Go-Round.*** A♭-centered; d'–a♭"; 6/8, Giocoso (♩.=76); 6pp.

718. **THE GRUNCHIN' WITCH** (Jessica Jackson). [100]; 1st©1926. Cmin; b–g" (H & L vols.); Tess-M; 2/4, With a great rush (♩=160, 126); 4pp; Diff-V/md, P/d.
For: any but very light voices
Mood: humorously descriptive
Voice: rather disjunct; intensively rolled [r] with glissando; ends low
Piano: chordal, some broken; dotted rhythms; many accidentals
Diff: requires excellent vocal actor capable of varied vocal sounds
Uses: fine humorous song

719. **HERE IN THIS SPOT WITH YOU** (Robert Nathan). G. Schirmer, 1949. [100, H & L]. X-Fmaj; b–f"; Tess-M; 4/4, Quietly and tenderly; 2min; Diff-V/md, P/md.
For: baritone
Mood: strong; love song
Voice: angular; many skips; dotted rhythms; long-ranged phrases; many accidentals
Piano: chordal; broken and afterbeat patterns; modulation; accidentals; thick texture at climax; does not double vocal line
Diff: long phrases; some pitches; ensemble; dynamic control; not for a beginner
Uses: useful in recital; quiet ending

720. **HIST . . . WHIST** (e. e. cummings). (Peer)Southern, 1957. [65]. Amin; (a)b–g"; Tess-M; 2/2, Very lively; 1min; Diff-V/md, P/md.
For: mezzo-soprano; soprano; possibly high baritone
Mood: lighthearted; describes doings of goblins and witches
Voice: fragmented phrases; duplets and triplets; many skips; spoken and whispered tones; a "squeal" at the end
Piano: afterbeat pattern; large dynamic contrasts; moves

around keyboard; always staccato

Diff: ensemble; special effects

Uses: very effective song; useful to help overcome singer's inhibitions and develop imagination; could end a group

Rec: D#170

721. I CAN'T BE TALKIN' OF LOVE (Esther Mathews). G. Schirmer, 1950. [100]. H & L keys: F♯maj & E♭maj; c♯'–g" & b♭–e"; Tess-M; 4/4, With a quiet and steady swing; 1+min; Diff-V/m, P/m.

For: soprano; can be transposed effectively for lower voice; women's voices best

Mood: whimsical; love song

Voice: many skips; accidentals; duplets and triplets; syncopation

Piano: broken-chord pattern with some countermelody; constant dotted rhythm; accidentals; does not double vocal line

Diff: 3 in voice vs. 4 in piano

Uses: effective song; light touch; could end a group quietly

722. I CARRY YOUR HEART (e. e. cummings). [100]; 1st©1962. H & L keys: E-centered & D-centered; c'–g♯" & b♭–f♯"; Tess-M-mH; 6/8, Andantino; 2min; Diff-V/md, P/m.

For: soprano

Mood: lyrical; love song

Voice: skips; duplet and triplet subdivisions of beat; many accidentals

Diff: some intervals; 2 vs. 3 in piano

Uses: nice lyric song; useful for Duke or e. e. cummings group; easier poem than cummings' usual style

Rec: D#s 10, 30, 170

723. I LOST MY HEART (A. E. Housman). [99]. cmp1976. B♭-centered; a–f"; Tess-mL; 4/4, Poco lento e giusto (♩ = 63); 3pp; Diff-V/m, P/md.

For: mezzo-soprano; contralto

Mood: dark text; speaker falls in love with enemy soldier

Voice: short phrases; rather disjunct with some difficult intervals; some accidentals; mostly independent of piano accomp.

Piano: chordal; melodic material in prelude and interludes; numerous accidentals; support of vocal line incidental

Diff: pitches

Uses: possible recital material

724. I LOVE THE LORD (Psalm 116). [96]. cmp1961. Amaj-Gmin-Dmaj; b♭–e"; Tess-mL; 4/4, 2/2, Allegro maestoso (♩ = 144); 6pp; Diff-V/m, P/m.

For: mezzo-soprano; baritone

Mood: thankfulness for deliverance from sorrow and trouble (well-known Psalm text)

Voice: conjunct and disjunct motion; a few large leaps and difficult intervals

Piano: block chords and broken-chord figuration; numerous accidentals

Diff: wide dynamic range with frequent changes; ability to convey a dramatic religious text

Uses: possible recital and church use

725. IN THE FIELDS (Charlotte Mew). Carl Fischer, 1960. Gmaj; a–e"; Tess-mL; 5/4 with changes, Slow and quiet; 2+min; Diff-V/m, P/me.

For: low voices; good for contralto or bass-baritone with warm, beautiful sound

Mood: lyrical; prayerful; spring song

Voice: many skips; speech rhythms; sustained

Piano: block-chord texture with some countermelody; some large reaches; dynamic control important; does not double vocal line

Diff: ensemble; good dynamic control; sustained phrases

Uses: excellent lyric song; good for recital

Rec: D#s 39, 172

726. I RIDE THE GREAT BLACK HORSES (Robert Nathan). G. Schirmer, 1949. [100]. H & L keys: F♯-centered & E-centered; c♯'–g♯" & d♯'–f♯"; Tess-M; 4/4, With a firm tempo and great rhythmic drive; 2min; Diff-V/md, P/md.

For: baritone

Mood: dramatic; powerful; intense

Voice: many skips; dramatic high tones; dotted rhythms; duplets vs. piano triplets

Piano: chordal; repeated-chord pattern in triplets; some rolled chords; great dynamic contrasts

Diff: sustained high tones; dynamic control

Uses: dramatic, exciting song; good program ender

Rec: D#171

727. I WATCHED THE LADY CAROLINE (Walter de la Mare). [64, 100, H & L]; 1st©1961. X; b♭–e♭"; Tess-M; unmetered, with flowing rhythm and flexible tempo (♪ = c.184); 4pp; Diff-V/md, P/d.

For: baritone; contralto

Mood: lyrical; rather abstract; descriptive

Voice: flowing phrases; much up and down movement; some chromaticism

Piano: 2-voice texture; chromatic

Diff: rhythm and meter; text

Uses: good teaching song

728. JUST-SPRING (e. e. cummings). [60, 63], 1st©1954. H & L keys: major tonalities; d'–b♭" & a–f"; Tess-M; 2/4, Joyous(♩ = 116); 1+min; Diff-V/d, P/d.

For: soprano

Mood: lighthearted and imaginative

Voice: disjunct; many large leaps; soft high tones; large dynamic contrasts

Piano: broken chords and rapid passage-work; some complicated rhythms

Diff: *messa di voce* on b♭"

Uses: good song to end a group

Rec: D#s 10, 11, 170

729. THE LAST WORD OF A BLUEBIRD (as told to a child) (Robert Frost). G. Schirmer, 1959. [100]. "For Louis Nicholas." H & L keys: Cmin-maj & B♭min-maj; a–f" & g–e♭"; Tess-M; 2/2, Strict tempo; 1min; Diff-V/d, P/d.

For: mezzo-soprano; baritone; some sopranos and tenors

Mood: child-like; lighthearted; lightly humorous; narrative

Voice: many skips; duplets and triplets; conversational

Piano: broken-chord patterns; many arpeggios; cross-rhythms and accents; articulations important; does not double vocal line

Diff: rhythms

Uses: useful for student who has trouble being expressive, as this song is easy to make come alive; good for a final light group; encore

730. **LITTLE ELEGY** (Elinor Wylie). [28, 51, 100]; 1st©1949. H & L keys: Dmin & Bmin; f'–a" & d'–f♯"; Tess-mH; 2/4, Plaintively; 2pp; Diff-V/m, P/me.

For: soprano; tenor; mezzo-soprano; baritone

Mood: elegiac; sad; plaintive

Voice: small skips; m6th leap to *p* a"; *pp–mf* dynamic range; syllabic

Piano: chordal and broken-chord figures; modulatory; snatches of melody; soft dynamics

Diff: floating soft dynamics in high phrases; modulations may throw singers who have only a fair ear

Uses: very lovely song; teaches soft singing, modulatory passages, floating phrases; many performance uses

Rec: D#30

731. **LOVELIEST OF TREES** (A. E. Housman). [24, 31, 59, 100]; 1st©1934. "To Lawrence Tibbett." H & L keys: A♭maj & Fmaj; d♯'–f " & c'–d"; Tess-mL; 2/4, Allegretto grazioso; 6pp; Diff-V/me, P/m.

For: all lyric voices

Mood: lyrical; philosophical

Voice: many skips along chord lines; legato

Piano: broken-chord figuration throughout

Diff: good legato line

Uses: good for teaching legato line; excellent recital song for a quiet mood

Rec: D#s 10, 171

732. **LOVELY** (Mary Lillian Fortson). [99]. cmp1970. Gmaj-min; c♯'–a"; Tess-M; 6/8, Andantino (♩.= 60); 5pp; Diff-V/m, P/me.

For: soprano

Mood: lyrical love song

Voice: somewhat disjunct, but legato; broken into short phrases; some accidentals

Piano: chordal; broken 8ves and afterbeats; supports vocal line, no doubling

Diff: maintaining legato through frequent small leaps, and musical connection through many short phrases separated by rests

Uses: useful song for recital

733. **LOVE'S SECRET** (William Blake). Boosey & Hawkes, 1955. [62, 96]. cmp1953. Dmin; a–f "; Tess-M; 6/8, In gently rocking rhythm; 1+min; Diff-V/m, P/m.

For: baritone; mezzo-soprano

Mood: lyrical; somber; nostalgic

Voice: many leaps; some long-ranged phrases

Piano: broken and block chords; some tremolo; trills; thin texture.

Diff: irregular phrase lengths; ensemble; soft dynamics

Uses: good song; quiet ending

734. **LUKE HAVERGAL** (Edward Arlington Robinson).

[21]; 1st©1948. H & L keys: Gmaj & E♭maj; e♭'–a" & b–f "; Tess-mH; 2/4, Sadly, tenderly; 4min; Diff-V/d, P/d.

For: tenor; soprano; baritone; mezzo-soprano

Mood: lyrico-dramatic; philosophical; poem about death

Voice: mostly stepwise movement; triplet figures; sweeping phrases; dynamic contrasts

Piano: chordal with melodic material; arpeggiations and broken chords; increasingly complex texture

Diff: easy high tones; dramatic weight; color and dynamic contrasts; sustained phrases

Uses: excellent song; recital material

Rec: D#s 16, 17, 47, 48

735. **MINIVER CHEEVY** (A Satire in the form of Variations) (Edward Arlington Robinson). Carl Fischer, 1948. Gmin; g–f "; Tess-M; 4/4, 12/8, ♩ = 80 with a different tempo for each variation; 6pp; Diff-V/md, P/d.

For: baritone

Mood: humorously descriptive

Voice: ten sections; generally short phrases with fragmentation; triplets

Piano: chordal–afterbeats, broken chords; dotted rhythms; staccato; parallel 10ths

Diff: excellent vocal actor required; 9th variation portrays Miniver Cheevy inebriated

Uses: very effective recital song

Rec: D#s 16, 17

736. **MORNING IN PARIS** (Robert Hillyer). Carl Fischer, 1956. Fmaj; e♭'–a"; Tess-mH; 6/8, Quiet and graceful; 1+min; Diff-V/m, P/m.

For: lyric tenor

Mood: lyrical; descriptive

Voice: many leaps; irregular phrase lengths; fluid rhythms

Piano: chordal-linear combination; 3–4-voice texture; many accidentals; does not double vocal line

Diff: ensemble; floating high tones

Uses: effective song; quiet ending; more energetic than Rorem's setting ("Early in the Morning")

737. **THE MOUNTAINS ARE DANCING** (e. e. cummings). Carl Fischer, 1956. Gmaj; d'–a"; Tess-mH; 3/8, Very lively and joyous; 7pp; Diff-V/d, P/d.

For: soprano

Mood: lyrical; joyful spring song

Voice: constant skipping along modulating chord lines; pitches somewhat difficult; some rhythmic intricacies at fast tempo; poem develops like a musical theme–phrases begin with same words, then change; difficult to remember

Piano: linear; patterned with broken-chord figures; various rhythmic groupings; irregular phrases among regular ones; ends with flourish; nimble fingers needed

Diff: pitch patterns; word sequence; speed of articulation; ensemble; for advanced musician facile with words

Uses: wonderful song for high lyric soprano; program ender

Rec: D#s 10, 170

738. **MY SOUL IS AN ENCHANTED BOAT** (Percy Bysshe Shelley). Valley, 1953. D-centered; d♭'–g"; Tess-mL; 4/4, ♩ = 72; 1+min; Diff-V/md, P/me.

For: soprano; lyric mezzo-soprano
Mood: lyrical; serene; introspective
Voice: stepwise and small skips; irregular phrase lengths; many accidentals
Piano: single stave; blurred pedaling; 8ve pattern in constant repetitive rhythm; various registers; very thin texture; does not double vocal line
Diff: exposed vocal line; soft; pitches
Uses: effective quiet song for recital group

739. NIGHT COMING OUT OF A GARDEN (Lord Alfred Douglas). [98]. cmp1954. G-centered; b♭–g"; Tess-mH; 12/8, Very quiet and sustained but not too slow–Faster, with increasing excitement until the end; 7pp; Diff-V/md, P/md.
For: mezzo-soprano; soprano (with sizeable sound)
Mood: anticipation of dawn
Voice: many small skips–vocal opening resembles fanfare; duplets and triplets; dynamic control crucial–many cresc.; sustained f♯" and g"; 10-beat final g"
Piano: broken-chord patterning; second section has staccato repeated chords; some 2 vs. 3; quiet 4-meas. prelude; big ending; does not double vocal line
Diff: rhythms; dynamics
Uses: effective song for singer with sizeable sound and good dynamic control; could end a group or program

740. O, IT WAS OUT BY DONNYCARNEY (James Joyce). [98]. cmp1953. E♭maj; c'–f"; Tess-M; 4/4, With simplicity and tenderness; 2pp; Diff-V/m, P/m.
For: baritone; mezzo-soprano; tenor; soprano
Mood: lyric nostalgia; delicate
Voice: mostly small skips; rather melodic; syncopation featured; many accidentals; begins with a 7-beat *messa di voce* on b♭'
Piano: broken-chord patterning; 4-meas. interlude; does not double vocal line
Diff: possibly rhythms
Uses: very nice lyrical song; tasteful setting; see also setting by Israel Citkowitz

741. OLD BEN GOLLIDAY (Mark Van Doren). [99]. cmp1971. Fmaj; c'–e"; Tess-mL; 4/4,12/8, Moderato (♩ = 104-92-72); 5pp; Diff-V/m, P/m.
For: any medium voice
Mood: strange song about a man oblivious to the loss of his wife
Voice: somewhat folk-like; mostly conjunct and diatonic
Piano: chordal; countermelodies and figuration in dotted rhythms; broken-chord figuration; syncopation; some accidentals; supports vocal line well
Diff: will require a skillful interpreter
Uses: possible recital material

742. ON A MARCH DAY (Sara Teasdale). Boosey & Hawkes, 1949. [96]. cmp1947. "To Eva Gauthier." Emaj-min; b–g♭"; Tess-M; 2/2, With great sweep and energy; 7pp; Diff-V/d, P/d.
For: mezzo-soprano
Mood: exuberant nature song; philosophical tone
Voice: long, sweeping phrases; sustained tones; somewhat chromatic; occasional triplet quarters

Piano: sweeping arpeggios and other figuration in 8ves, 16ths, & 32nds; a few rhythmic complexities
Diff: sustained legato singing; *ff* low tones
Uses: effective recital song

743. ONE RED ROSE (Mark Van Doren). Carl Fischer, 1970. Cmaj; b♭–f"; Tess-M; 2/2, Affettuoso (♩ = 80); 6pp; Diff-V/me, P/m.
For: baritone
Mood: lyrical; love song; nature imagery
Voice: sustained; long phrases
Piano: broken-chord patterns throughout
Diff: easy, powerful f" required

744. ONLY FOR ME (Mark Van Doren). Boosey & Hawkes, 1955. [96]. cmp1954. B-centered; c'–g"; Tess-mH; 6/8, Moderato; 2+min; Diff-V/md, P/m.
For: tenor
Mood: narrative; somber; a small drama
Voice: many skips; accidentals; syncopation
Piano: chordal; 16th-note patterns; many accidentals; does not double vocal line
Diff: long phrases at end; sustained f♯"
Uses: somewhat sentimental but usable; slow-paced song

745. O WORLD (Mark Van Doren). Carl Fischer, 1970. E-centered; d'–f"; Tess-mH; 4/4, Allegro maestoso; 2min; Diff-V/md, P/md.
For: high baritone; tenor; soprano; mezzo-soprano
Mood: dramatic; strong
Voice: many leaps, esp. 6ths; long tones
Piano: chordal; various subdivisions of the beat; syncopation; does not double vocal line
Diff: long tones at phrase endings; dynamic control
Uses: effective song for voices with ample sound

746. PEGGY MITCHELL (James Stephens). [20, 100]; 1st©1965. "To John Hanks." H & L keys: X; c♯'–f' & b–e♭"; Tess-M; 5/4, 6/4, Tenderly, with flexible and flowing rhythm; 4pp; Diff-V/md, P/md.
For: tenor; lyric baritone
Mood: lyrical; philosophical; descriptive
Voice: flowing, but disjunct; large intervals; quite chromatic
Piano: contrapuntal; expressive of the text; does not double vocal line
Diff: intervals; soft, delicate singing required
Uses: good for musicianship training; excellent recital song

747. PENGUIN GEOMETRY (Donald Wheelock). [99]. cmp1980. B♭maj, with changes; b♭–f"; Tess-M; 4/4, Allegro moderato (♩ = 116); 7pp; Diff-V/m, P/me.
For: any medium voice
Mood: humorous; traveler seeks directions at the South Pole
Voice: somewhat disjunct; broken into short phrases; some accidentals; dialogue between penguins and the traveler
Piano: chordal; afterbeats and broken 8ves; numerous accidentals; supports vocal line without doubling
Diff: some pitches; needs a good vocal actor
Uses: humorous song

748. A PIPER (Seumas O'Sullivan). [59, 100]; 1st©1949. H & L keys: Dmaj & B♭maj; c♯'–b" & a–g"; Tess-HH;

6/8, In brisk march tempo; 5pp; Diff-V/d, P/m.
For: coloratura soprano; lyric mezzo-soprano
Mood: descriptive; joyous
Voice: somewhat disjunct; a little chromaticism; much use of 2 vs. 3; first note is b" (g" in low key)
Piano: chordal; some arpeggiation; somewhat chromatic
Diff: high tessitura; opening b" (in high key)
Uses: composer suggests if not singable in its original form, the highest parts of the vocal line may be omitted by the singer and added to the accomp.

749. POLITICS (William Butler Yeats). [99]. cmp1974. Amin-Cmaj; c'-e"; Tess-mL; 6/8, In waltz style (♩. = 72); 3pp; Diff-V/m, P/m.
For: any medium male voice
Mood: man is distracted from serious matters by thoughts about a beautiful girl
Voice: alternating long sustained phrases with short, almost recit.-like phrases
Piano: chordal–afterbeats and broken chords; countermelodies; numerous accidentals; mostly supports vocal line well, does not double
Diff: some pitches; making the meaning entirely clear
Uses: unusual song; could be effective in recital

750. THE PURITAN'S BALLAD (Elinor Wylie). [97]. cmp1946. Gmin predominates; c'-a"; Tess-mH; 4/4 with changes, With a firm and vigorous tread; 10pp; Diff-V/md, P/d.
For: dramatic soprano; lyric soprano with sizeable sound
Mood: dramatic; powerful; suspenseful
Voice: many accidentals; few repetitions in fairly disjunct melody; syncopation; some triplets; dotted rhythms; pp–ff dynamics important; three a"s of 3–5 beats
Piano: through-composed; sectional; various broken-chord, chordal, and linear accomp. styles used; many accidentals; various rhythmic groupings, some complex; some 3 vs. 4; some 2 vs. 3 combined with syncopation; 8-meas. prelude; several interludes; many clef changes for l.h.; vocal line ends quietly; piano has short bombastic postlude
Diff: ensemble; lack of patterning in melody; dynamics; getting proper mood
Uses: effective for singer who can control dynamics and use drama in text and music to advantage; resembles "Luke Havergal" in its drama, but seems harder to bring off

751. RAPUNZEL (Adelaide Crapsey). Mercury, 1947. cmp1935. Amin; e'-a"; Tess-mH; 6/8, Lento–quasi recitativo; 2+min; Diff-V/me, P/me.
For: soprano
Mood: dramatic; mysterious; intense; sensuous
Voice: easy skips; fragmented phrases; sustained soft phrases; high sustained climax at end
Piano: countermelody in 8ves throughout; pianist changes tempo; dynamics important
Diff: ensemble; pitches; poem needs explanation

752. REALITY (Dorothy Duke). [99]. cmp1922, rev1972. Amaj-min; c♯'-f♯"; Tess-mL; 4/4, Lento espressive (♩ = 60); 3pp; Diff-V/m, P/me.
For: mezzo-soprano; tenor; baritone

Mood: romantic song to an absent beloved
Voice: somewhat disjunct but legato; several leaps of 6th upwards; variable phrase lengths; numerous accidentals
Piano: chordal, in repeated 8ths almost throughout; many accidentals; mostly supports vocal line well
Diff: some pitches
Uses: mildly modern-sounding song, with text reminiscent of the early 20th century

753. RENOUNCEMENT (Alice Meynell). [97]. cmp1964. C♯min-maj; c♯'-a"; Tess-mH; 4/4, Andante moderato (♩ = 56); 5pp; Diff-V/md, P/md.
For: soprano; tenor (needs sizeable sound for effective dynamics)
Mood: dramatic love song
Voice: many skips; many accidentals (no key sig.); speech-like rhythms; big ending on a" (4 beats) ff; long c♯" (9 beats) ff; dynamics p–ff
Piano: mostly repeated chords with recurrent countermelody; rather thick texture at times; big, dramatic ending; does not double vocal line
Diff: no repetition or sequence; rhythms; ensemble
Uses: possibly effective for large lyric or dramatic voice

754. THE RETURN FROM TOWN (Edna St. Vincent Millay). [99]. cmp1980. B♭maj; d'-g"; Tess-mL; 4/4, Moderato (♩ = 96); 4pp; Diff-V/me, P/me.
For: soprano; mezzo-soprano
Mood: humorous, folk-like poem; young woman passes up opportunities to be unfaithful to husband
Voice: somewhat like a folksong; generally short phrases, with last word of phrase sometimes detached by an 8th rest
Piano: countermelody with broken chords in l.h.; some accidentals; supports vocal line, incidental doubling
Uses: versatile humorous song

755. REVEILLE (A. E. Housman). [98]. cmp1947. Dmin-maj; a-f♯"; Tess-mH; 4/4, Urgent, restless, but not too free in tempo; 8pp; Diff-V/md, P/md.
For: baritone; mezzo-soprano
Mood: hearty; joy of nature and life
Voice: many skips, mostly with chordal outlines; much syncopation; irregular phrase lengths; many expressive dynamic markings, pp–ff
Piano: broken-chord patterning alternating with staccato chords; many accidentals (no key sig.); 7-meas. prelude; 2 interludes; does not double vocal line
Diff: ensemble; rhythms
Uses: good recital material

756. RICHARD CORY (Edward Arlington Robinson). Carl Fischer, 1948. B♭maj; a-e"; Tess-M; 6/8 (piano), 2/4 (voice), Quietly and decorously with an elegant swing; 2min; Diff-V/md, P/m.
For: baritone; mezzo-soprano; contralto
Mood: narrative; descriptive
Voice: straightforward but elegant syllabic vocal line; 2 vs. 3 in the piano throughout; rhythmic pointing of important words; intense pp singing at end
Piano: 3–5-voice texture; long introduction sets scene; elegant 6/8 metrical structure with some syncopation portrays a strolling motion; key changes

Diff: ensemble; dynamic control; rhythms
Uses: clever setting–piano characterizes Richard Cory while vocal line (narrator) tells the story; groups well with "Luke Havergal" and "Miniver Cheevy"
Rec: D#s 16, 17

757.   THE SHEAVES (Edward Arlington Robinson). [99]. cmp1978. Db-centered; c'–fb"; Tess-mL; 2/2, Molto tranquillo (♩ = ca.60); 5pp; Diff-V/m, P/m.
For: any medium or low voice
Mood: lyrical and philosophical; nature imagery
Voice: conjunct and sustained; occasional intervals of 4th or 5th; much of song at a soft dynamic level
Piano: chordal; some sustained, some broken-chord figuration; syncopation; many accidentals (more difficult to read than play); supports vocal line; does not double
Diff: some pitches; maintaining vocal quality at soft dynamic level
Uses: excellent recital material

758.   SHELLING PEAS (Jessica Jackson). [100]. cmp1926. H & L keys: Cmin & Amin; c'–ab" & a–f"; Tess-mH; 3/4, 4/4, 5/4, Allegro (♩ = 84); 6pp; Diff-V/m, P/md.
For: all but very light voices
Mood: humorously descriptive
Voice: many leaps of 4th & 5th; ends low
Piano: chordal–afterbeats and broken chords
Diff: meter changes; some high-lying phrases; good vocal actor needed
Uses: good humorous song

759.   SHE'S SOMEWHERE IN THE SUNLIGHT STRONG (Richard LeGallienne). [99]. cmp1984 (the last song written by Duke before his death). Ab maj; f'–ab"; Tess-mH; 6/8, Lento e teneramente (♪ = 108); 2pp; Diff-V/m, P/me.
For: tenor
Mood: lyrical love song; nature imagery
Voice: lyrical and legato; a few upward leaps, incl. m9th; accidentals; dissonances with piano; pp ending on ab"
Piano: chordal; 8ths throughout; accidentals; more difficult to read than play; supports vocal line without doubling
Diff: some pitches
Uses: fine recital song

760.   SILVER (Walter de la Mare). [64, 100 (L)]; 1st©1961. Amin; a–d"; Tess-mL; 3/4, Slowly, with hushed intensity (♩ = 42); 4pp; Diff-V/m, P/m.
For: contralto; bass
Mood: lyrical; poetic nature description
Voice: sustained; fragmented in middle section; generally soft dynamics
Piano: sustained chords; afterbeats; broken chords; 32nd-note motives
Diff: beautiful control of soft tone
Uses: effective song for low voice

761.   SIX POEMS BY EMILY DICKINSON for Soprano Voice and Piano. (Peer)Southern, 1978. Traditional keys; b♯–a"; Tess-M; regular meters; 25pp; Diff-V/m-md, P/m-md.
For: soprano

Mood: themes of nature, lost love, and death
Voice: small skips; many accidentals; considerable syncopation; dotted rhythms; syllabic; some fragmented phrases
Piano: (a.), repeated-chord pattern, after-beat style, some countermelody; (b., d., e., & f.), various broken-chord patterns; (c.), block chords; many accidentals; little doubling of vocal line
Diff: (a.), rhythms, ensemble, low notes for some singers; (c.), soft dynamics (pp–mp); (d.), most difficult–rhythms, fast tempo, alternation of 5/8, 4/8; capturing moods of these rather diverse songs
Uses: effective set; good senior recital material; any could be excerpted for use in an all-Duke or American group
Rec: D#170 [contains all six listed below]

a.   Good Morning, Midnight. Cmin; c'–gb"; 4/4, Allegretto; 4pp. [**Rec:** D#3]
b.   Heart! We Will Forget Him! Emin; eb'–a"; 4/4, Passionato; 3pp. [**Rec:** D#s 3, 39]
c.   Let Down the Bars, Oh Death. C♯min-maj; b♯–f♯"; 5/4, Grave e molto tranquillo; 3pp.
d.   An Awful Tempest Mashed the Air. Amin-maj; eb'–a"; 5/8, 4/8, 4/4, Tempo giusto ma molto agitato–Lento e molto tranquillo; 7pp.
e.   Nobody Knows This Little Rose. Gmaj; c♯'–g♯"; 4/4, Andantino; 4pp. [**Rec:** D#3]
f.   Bee! I'm Expecting You! Fmaj predominates; db'–f"; 2/2, Molto vivace; 4pp. [**Rec:** D#s 3, 7]

762.   SIX SONGS ON POEMS BY EMILY BRONTË. (Peer)Southern, 1977 (b. pub. singly, 1966). Traditional keys; ab–g♯"; Tess-M, wide; regular meters; varied tempos; 19min (43pp); Diff-V/m-md, P/m-d.
For: best for mezzo-soprano
Mood: philosophical; generally dark
Voice: many skips; several wide-ranged phrases; many accidentals; not doubled by piano
Piano: block- and broken-chord patterns; many accidentals
Diff: endurance; range; dynamics
Uses: as set, or excerpt; final song dramatic

a.   Love and Friendship. Eb maj; c'–eb"; 3/4, Moderato; 6pp.
b.   Remembrance. Eb min-maj; ab–g"; 4/4, Grave più mosso; 2+min.
c.   On the Moors. Gmin-Dmin; bb–g"; 3/4, Allegro giusto ma molto animato; 2+min.
d.   Worlds of Light. Eb maj; db'–gb"; 4/4, Molto quieto–Più mosso e molto appassionato–Molto più mosso; 3min.
e.   The Old Stoic. Cmin-maj; c'–f"; 4/4, Grave; 2min.
f.   The Messenger. F♯maj; b–g♯"; 3/4, 4/4, 3/4, Quasi recitativo–Allegro–Largo–Allegro; 6min.

763.   THE SONG OF WANDERING AENGUS (William Butler Yeats). Carl Fischer, 1976. Amin; c'–f"; Tess-M; 3/4, 4/4, Moderato; 6pp; Diff-V/md, P/md.
For: baritone best; man's text
Mood: nostalgic remembrance; fantasy
Voice: stepwise and small skips; a few difficult intervals; some syncopation; some dotted rhythms

Piano: broken-chord patterns; independent of vocal line; many accidentals; short prelude; interludes

Diff: enharmonic notation for inexperienced singers; many accidentals; symbolism in the poem; needs good dynamic control *pp–ff*

Uses: dramatic group ender; possibly pair with "Brown Penny" by Duke

764. **SONGS OUT OF SORROW** (Sara Teasdale). Cycle. [98]. cmp1967. Tonal with traditional harmonies; a–f♯"; Tess-M; traditional meters; 22pp; Diff-V/m-md, P/m-md.

For: mezzo-soprano; contralto

Mood: despondency; sorrow; sublimation

Voice: many skips, up to 8ve; speech rhythms in (b.); duplet and triplet subdivisions in (e.); some syncopation; long notes on e", f ", and f♯"

Piano: (a.), mostly block chords, some broken; (b.), broken-chord patterning; (c.), predominantly linear; (d.), block chords; (e.), arpeggiation and "bird-call" sound effects; (f.), broken-chord patterning; little doubling of vocal line; set has quiet ending

Diff: rhythms; meter in (c.); subject matter

Uses: set for a mature singer

    a. *Spirit's House.* G-centered; a–e"; 3/4, Lento; 4pp.
    b. *Mastery.* E♭maj; b♭–f "; 4/4, Moderato ma molto animato; 4pp.
    c. *Lessons.* C-centered; b–e"; 7/8, Moderato; 3pp.
    d. *In a Burying Ground.* G♯min; c'–e♭"; 4/4, Lento e giusto; 4pp.
    e. *Wood Song.* Dmaj; e'–f♯"; 6/8, Gioioso; 3pp.
    f. *Refuge.* G-centered–E♭; c♯'–f "; 4/4, Largo e mesto; 4pp.

765. **SPRAY** (Sara Teasdale). Boosey & Hawkes, 1949. [96]. cmp1947. A-centered; c♯'–a"; Tess-mL; 2/4, Light and lively (♩ = c.80); 5pp; Diff-V/m, P/d.

For: soprano; mezzo-soprano; tenor

Mood: joyous love song; nature imagery

Voice: some large leaps; a few chromatic tones

Piano: chordal; broken chords and other figuration in 32nds throughout; some chromaticism

Diff: easy a" at climax

Uses: effective recital song

766. **SPRING THUNDER** (Mark Van Doren). [60]; 1st©1968. H & L keys: X; e♭'–g" & c'–e"; Tess-M; 4/4, Moderato; 2pp; Diff-V/md, P/d.

For: all voices

Mood: dramatic; descriptive

Voice: disjunct; fragmented by rests

Piano: chordal–rolled and broken; descriptive of text; does not double vocal line

Diff: dynamic contrast

Uses: good for a singer with dramatic skill

767. **STILLNESS** (Karen Duke). [99]. cmp1949. A-centered; d '–g"; Tess-M; 4/4, Very quiet and sustained; 3pp; Diff-V/m, P/m.

For: soprano; tenor

Mood: delicate nature scene

Voice: conjunct motion; some intervals of 5th & 6th; one 8ve leap; some accidentals, but few dissonances with accomp.; even 8ths against 3 vs. 4 in piano

Piano: chordal; broken-chord figuration; some melodic material; triplet 8ths vs.16ths in middle section; numerous accidentals; supports vocal line well

Diff: pitches; rhythms for singer and pianist

Uses: recital material

768. **STOPPING BY WOODS ON A SNOWY EVENING** (Robert Frost). [97]. cmp1967. G♯min; d♯'–a"; Tess-mH; 4/4, Tempo giusto e molto dolce; 6pp; Diff-V/md, P/dd.

For: soprano; tenor

Mood: lyrical; introspective

Voice: not a patterned melody; resembles Hugo Wolf's melodic concepts and text rhythms; many accidentals; long a" with *messa di voce*; soft ending

Piano: almost constant 4 vs. 3 between hands; many accidentals; soft dynamics; needs excellent pianist

Diff: ensemble; soft dynamics for both performers

Uses: good treatment of this well-known poem; quite different in concept from settings by Ann MacDonald Diers, John LaMontaine, and Paul Sargent

Rec: D#170

769. **THERE WILL BE STARS** (Sara Teasdale). Boosey & Hawkes, 1953. [96]. cmp1951. Emin-maj; b–g♯"; Tess-mH; 4/4, ♩ = ca.92; 2min; Diff-V/md, P/m.

For: soprano; some tenors

Mood: intense; somewhat declamatory; night and death

Voice: many leaps; speech rhythms; long-ranged phrases

Piano: chordal–block and broken; some countermelody; accidentals; no prelude or postlude; does not double vocal line

Diff: dynamic control

Uses: effective song; quiet ending; mature sound needed; one of Duke's best songs

Rec: D#10

770. **THREE CHINESE LOVE LYRICS.** For Tenor (poets from Ch'ing dynasty; trans. Henry H. Hart & James Whitall). [97]. cmp1964. Tonal; d♯'–a"; Tess-mH; regular meters; 10pp; Diff-V/md, P/m-md.

For: tenor specified

Mood: lyrical

Voice: many skips, usually neither large nor difficult; many accidentals (no key sigs.); speech-like rhythms in (a.); some polyrhythms; syncopation; long high notes (g", a♭", a")

Piano: repeated- and broken-chord patterning; many accidentals; (b.) imitates lute; (c.), rather thick and has dramatic ending; does not double vocal line

Diff: rhythms; dynamics in (b.) & (c.)

Uses: as a set

    a. *Noonday* (Fan Tseng-Hsiang; trans. Henry H. Hart). B-centered; e♭'–g"; 4/4, Moderato; 4pp.
    b. *Through Your Window* (Tzu Yeh; trans. Henry H. Hart). Emaj; d♯'–a"; 4/4, Tempo giusto; 2pp.
    c. *The Shoreless Sea* (Li Hung-Chang; trans. James Whitall). Gmin-maj; d♯'–a"; 9/8, Allegro

appassionato; 4pp.

771. **THREE GOTHIC BALLADS** (John Heath-Stubbs). Cycle. Peer-Southern, 1959. Minor keys; a–f"; Tess-M, mL, mH; regular meters, slow tempos; 10min; Diff-V/md, P/md-d.

For: baritone

Mood: lyrical declamation; despair; remoteness

Voice: conjunct; skips and leaps; speech rhythms; interrupted phrasing; climactic f"s

Piano: linear; ornamentation; rapid, short arpeggiated figures; various rhythmic groupings; good facility and rhythmic precision necessary

Diff: ensemble; rhythmic groupings; proper moods; easy high f" required; for advanced singers only

Uses: excellent recital material for an imaginative, mature singer with full-bodied, somewhat dark voice

    a. *The Old King.* Dmin; b♭–f"; Tess-mL-M; 6/8, 2/4, Very quietly, like a lullaby; 5pp.

    b. *The Mad Knight's Song.* Fmin; a–f"; Tess-M, H; 4/4, Weird-grotesque, but with steady, relentless rhythm; 8pp.

    c. *The Coward's Lament.* Emin; b♭–f"; Tess-M; 4/4, Slow and mournful; 4pp.

772. **THREE POEMS BY MARK VAN DOREN.** For Medium Voice and Piano. New Valley, 1982. Traditional keys; a–f"; Tess-mH; traditional meters; rather slow tempos; 11pp; Diff-V/m, P/m-d.

For: baritone; mezzo-soprano

Mood: philosophical; theme of wisdom connects the songs

Voice: small skips and stepwise motion; syncopation; accidentals; 5-beat f"; syllabic

Piano: (a.), broken-chord patterning; (b.), begins with 2-voice linear accomp. and ends with arpeggiation and countermelody; (c.), arpeggiation and tremolo-like patterning; accidentals (no key sig.); does not double vocal line

Diff: rhythms in (a.) & (c.); some intervals (e.g., tritone) and dynamics in (c.)

Uses: as a group

    a. *Slowly, Slowly Wisdom Gathers.* Gmin-maj; a–f"; 4/4, Andante moderato; 4pp.

    b. *So Simple.* Amin-maj; c'–e"; 4/4, Moderato; 2pp.

    c. *Dunce's Song.* Dmin; c'–f"; 4/4, Lento e misterioso; 5pp.

773. **THREE SONGS** (Richard Nickson). Southern Music Co. (San Antonio), 1989. Tonal (shifting key centers); d'–a"; Tess-M; regular meters; varied tempos; 12pp; Diff-V/m, P/m.

For: tenor; soprano (high voice specified)

Mood: three aspects of love

Voice: (a.) & (b.), simple rhythms; (c.), features 12/8 piano part with 4/4 vocal line; chromaticism; skips along chord lines; (a.), most complex

Piano: arpeggiation and broken-chord patterns; many accidentals; supports vocal line; does not double; 2–4 meas. preludes and interludes

Diff: a few isolated speech-like rhythms; chromaticism in

(a.); 2 vs. 3 in (c.)

Uses: nice undergraduate recital group for lyrical voice with good legato line

    a. *Fantasy.* F♯, modulating; e♯'–g"; Tess-M; 4/4, moderato (♩ = c.60); 4pp.

    b. *All Music, All Delight.* Emin; d'–g"; Tess-M; 6/8, Lento e molto tranquillo (♪ = c.100); 5pp.

    c. *Aubade.* Dmaj; d'–a"; Tess-M; 12/8 (piano), 4/4 (voice), Giocoso-ma non troppo presto (♩. = c.104); 3pp. [**Rec:** D#30]

774. **TIGER! TIGER!** (William Blake). [99]. cmp1984. X; c♭'–g♭"; Tess-M; 4/4, Allegro energico (♩ = 120); 4pp; Diff-V/d, P/d.

For: any medium voice

Mood: descriptive and philosophical, with reference to the Creator

Voice: somewhat disjunct; frequent leaps up and down, some difficult; many accidentals

Piano: chordal; broken-chord figuration; syncopation; many accidentals; supports vocal line fairly well, no doubling

Diff: pitches; rhythms

Uses: good setting of this text for recital

775. **TO KAREN, SINGING** (John Duke). Elkan-Vogel, 1946. Dmaj; c♯'–g"(a"); Tess-M; 4/4, Quiet and sustained; 2min; Diff-V/m-md, P/m.

For: soprano; tenor

Mood: lyrical; gentle child's song

Voice: many small skips; some dotted rhythms

Piano: broken-chord patterning; irregular slurring and grouping makes meter seem irregular; accidentals; countermelody; does not double vocal line

Diff: rhythmic security needed; soft dynamics

Uses: effective song for recital group; reflective; quiet ending

776. **TO THE THAWING WIND** (Robert Frost). (Peer)Southern, 1964. Amin; c'–g"; Tess-M; 4/4, With great excitement but in steady tempo; 5pp; Diff-V/m, P/md.

For: dramatic tenor; high baritone

Mood: dramatic; intense; animated

Voice: many leaps; dotted rhythms; syncopation; many long-ranged phrases; declamatory

Piano: broken-chord patterning in 16ths; various groupings; varied registers; some countermelody; does not double vocal line

Diff: registration; dynamic control

Uses: big ending–good program ender; effective song

Rec: D#172

777. **TWO LYRICS BY ELINOR WYLIE.** R. D. Row, 1950. Separate entries below.

A. **VELVET SHOES.** Amaj; d'–a"; Tess-mH; 4/4, 3/4 (usually alternating), At a tranquil pace; and with a muted effect throughout; 4pp; Diff-V/m, P/m.

For: soprano

Mood: tranquil; subdued; white "silent" imagery

Voice: stepwise and easy skips; duplets and triplets; floating tones; accidentals

Piano: broken-chord texture; large reaches; some triplets; subdued and muted; does not double vocal line

Diff: mixed meters; soft high tones

Uses: pairs well with "Viennese Waltz"; see also settings by Mary Howe and Randall Thompson; this setting contains a stanza not set by Thompson

B. VIENNESE WALTZ. G♭maj; c'–a♭"; Tess-M; 3/4, Dreamily, in moderate waltz tempo; 8pp; Diff-V/d, P/d.

For: soprano

Mood: sadly philosophical

Voice: disjunct; chromatic; regular waltz rhythm with occasional duplet quarters; irregular phrase lengths

Piano: waltz-like afterbeats; arpeggios; highly chromatic; does not double vocal line

Diff: requires soft g" and powerful a♭"

Uses: pair with "Velvet Shoes"

Rec: D#10

778. **TWO SONGS.** Valley, 1948. cmp1935. X; c'–e"; Tess-M; no meter sigs., irregularly barred; 6pp; Diff-V/m-md, P/me-m.

For: (a.), any voice; (b.), baritone

Mood: (a.), relentless–pace of modern life; (b.), relentless, wandering, lonely

Voice: stepwise and many small skips; accidentals; triplet divisions vs. duplets in piano

Piano: linear textures; many accidentals; restless 8th-note motion; does not double vocal line

Diff: irregular meter; ensemble; some pitches

Uses: usable recital material; see also Martin Kalmanoff setting of "XXth Century"

    a. *XXth Century* (Robert Hillyer). X, E-centered; c'–e"; Tess-M; ♩ = 116; 2pp. [**Rec:** D#s 39, 171]

    b. *White in the Moon the Long Road Lies* (A. E. Housman). X; c'–e♭"; Tess-M; ♩ = 116; 4pp. [**Rec:** D#10]

779. **TWO SONGS** (Richard Nickson). Southern Music Co. (San Antonio), 1989. Traditional keys; a♯–f"; Tess-M; 4/4; slow; 7pp; Diff-V/m, P/me-md.

For: baritone specified

Mood: love songs

Voice: some chromaticism; some large chordal skips; some long-ranged phrases, up to 10th; rhythms not difficult; some syncopation

Piano: (a.), polyrhythms, 2 vs. 3; arpeggio passage in 32nds; no doubling of vocal line; mostly arpeggiation; 5-meas. prelude; (b.), chordal; some countermelody; 4-meas. prelude and interlude; many accidentals

Diff: piano does not double vocal line; long-ranged phrases

Uses: could be used as a pair, although both are slow; can be used separately

    a. *Farewell.* Bmin; a♯–f"; Tess-M; 4/4, Andante mesto ♩ = c.69; 4pp.

    b. *Love's Mirror.* Gmaj; b–e"; Tess-M; 4/4, Molto quieto e teneramente ♩ = c. 66; 3pp.

780. **VOICES** (Witter Bynner). Boosey & Hawkes, 1949. [96]. cmp1946. Ends Amaj; f♯'–a"; Tess-mH; 3/4,

Gracefully, in waltz rhythm; 4pp; Diff-V/m-d, P/m.

For: tenor; soprano

Mood: lyrical; reminiscent

Voice: sustained; many long tones; many skips; triplets and duplets; accidentals

Piano: broken-chord pattern with double-stemmed melody over block chords; wide range; no vocal line doubling

Diff: long phrases; breath control; climax on a"; sustained g♭" decresc.; pitches sometimes elusive

Uses: good song; suitable setting for the text; quiet ending; see also Hageman setting

781. **WHEN, IN DISGRACE WITH FORTUNE** (William Shakespeare). [99]. cmp1976. Cmin-X; b–f"; Tess-M; 4/4, Moderato e molto doloroso (♩ = 56), Molto animato e gioioso (♩ = 80); 4pp; Diff-V/md, P/md.

For: baritone

Mood: rather dramatic love song, beginning darkly and becoming ecstatic at the end

Voice: dramatic; chromatic; some large intervals; somewhat independent of piano; final phrase covers entire range of song *ff*, ending low

Piano: chordal; section of broken-chord figuration in 16ths; many accidentals; usually supports vocal line; does not always provide cues for pitches

Diff: pitches; strong low voice and ability to project a variety of moods needed

Uses: fine recital song

782. **WHEN I SET OUT FOR LYONNESSE** (Thomas Hardy). R. D. Row, 1953. H & L keys: Cmaj & Amaj; c'–a♭" & a–f"; Tess-L; 3/4, With steady, well-measured rhythm; 6pp; Diff-V/m, P/d.

For: any except high, light voices; best for baritone

Mood: jaunty; ecstatic song of traveling

Voice: disjunct; large leaps; short phrases

Piano: chordal with some difficult figurations; 2 vs. 3; triplets; does not double vocal line

Diff: requires solid low tones

Uses: good song for opening or closing a group

783. **WHEN I WAS ONE AND TWENTY** (A. E. Housman). G. Schirmer, 1972. [100, H & L]. X; c'–f"; Tess-M; unmetered (variable number of beats per measure), Andantino; 2min; Diff-V/md, P/md.

For: any voice except extremely low

Mood: regretful; conversational; uneasy

Voice: many skips, esp. 4ths & 5ths; cross-accents with piano

Piano: linear; cross-accents; does not double vocal line

Diff: reading difficult because of barring; irregular meter; ensemble

Uses: attractive song; rhythms give somewhat surreal effect in comparison to more straightforward settings of this text

784. **WHEN SLIM SOPHIA MOUNTS HER HORSE** (Walter de la Mare). Mercury, 1965. [16]. cmp1959. Gmaj; c'–e♭"; Tess-M; 4/4, At a steady pace; 2min; Diff-V/md, P/m.

For: baritone; mezzo-soprano; contralto

Mood: lyrical; descriptive

Voice: many skips, esp. 6ths; fragmented phrasing; speech rhythms

Piano: clever horse figure; linear texture; does not double vocal line; harmonically very tame

Diff: ensemble; some rhythms

Uses: nice song for Duke or other American group

785. **WHEN THE ROSE IS BRIGHTEST** (Nathaniel Parker Willis). [97]. cmp1970. "To Giulia Grisi." D♭maj; d♯'–a"; Tess-mH; 4/4, Affettuoso; 3pp; Diff-V/m, P/m.

For: soprano; tenor

Mood: lyrical

Voice: many skips, up to 8ve; easy rhythms; syllabic; several high notes of 4 or more beats (g♭", g", a♭", and a")–some *f*, some *p*; soft ending

Piano: syncopated chordal pattern; repeated chords; many accidentals (no key sig.); does not double vocal line

Diff: possibly sustaining the high notes

Uses: nice lyric song for voice with beautiful high tones

786. **THE WHITE DRESS** (Humbert Wolfe). G. Schirmer, 1967. [100, H & L]. Bmin; a♯–e"; Tess-M; unmetered but barred (3/4, 4/4, 5/4 groupings), Very quietly, but not too slowly; 2+min; Diff-V/m, P/m.

For: baritone

Mood: lyrical; tranquil; love song

Voice: stepwise and small skips; many accidentals

Piano: chordal texture; broken-chord pattern with countermelody; does not double vocal line

Diff: meterless aspect; ensemble; sustained low tones

Uses: effective song

Rec: D#171

787. **WILD SWANS** (Edna St. Vincent Millay). Mercury, 1947. cmp1935. A-centered; d♭'–a"; Tess-M; meter barred irregularly, With great abandon; 4pp; Diff-V/md, P/m.

For: soprano best; some tenors

Mood: descriptive; restless; questing

Voice: stepwise and easy skips; 6ths & 7ths; irregular rhythms and meters; some accidentals

Piano: linear, mostly 2-voice texture; 8th-note motion; some countermelody; dotted rhythms; triplet subdivisions; many accidentals; 24 meas. solo material; does not double vocal line

Diff: irregular rhythmic flow; ensemble; a" sustained *ff*

Uses: effective song

788. **THE WIND HAS CHANGED** (South Wind) (Mark Van Doren). [99]. cmp1966. Fmin-X; c'–e"; Tess-M; 12/8, Vivace (♩ = 104); 5pp; Diff-V/md, P/d.

For: any medium voice

Mood: lyrical and descriptive

Voice: lyrical, flowing phrases; occasional difficult intervals; some accidentals

Piano: 16th-note figuration throughout, sometimes in broken chords; melody or countermelody in top voice needs to be emphasized; numerous accidentals; usually supports vocal line well, no doubling

Diff: some pitches; pianist needs excellent, secure technique

Uses: good recital material

789. **A WINTER NIGHT** (Sara Teasdale). [99]. cmp1967. Bmin; d '–a"; Tess-M; 4/4, Andante sostenuto (♩ = 63); 5pp; Diff-V/d, P/d.

For: soprano

Mood: descriptive scene, contrasting poet in her comfortable home with plight of the poor and homeless

Voice: much conjunct motion; few intervals larger than a 5th; builds to *f* or *ff* climax several times, each time reaching a higher pitch; long a" at final climax; some accidentals; rather independent of piano

Piano: chordal, with grace notes; streams of parallel intervals; 2-voice counterpoint in last section; numerous accidentals; clear pitches for singer not always given

Diff: pitches

Uses: useful in a variety of situations

790. **YELLOW HAIR** (William Butler Yeats). R. D. Row, 1953. B♭maj; c'–g♭"; Tess-M; 4/4 (voice), 12/8 (piano), Allegro; 2+min; Diff-V/md, P/m.

For: tenor; high baritone

Mood: whimsical; dialogue between poet and girl

Voice: many skips, esp. 5ths & 6ths; duplets vs. piano triplets

Piano: afterbeat pattern; arpeggios; accidentals; does not double vocal line

Diff: 2 in voice vs. 3 in piano; sustained high tones

Uses: clever poem; usable recital material

Rec: D#10

DUKE, VERNON [Vladimir Dukelsky]
(b. Parfianovka, Russia, 1903; d. Santa Monica, CA, 1969)

[See also D#s 50 & 173; no titles given]

791. **FOUR SONGS** (William Blake). Broude Bros., 1955. Mostly traditional keys; c'–g♯"; Tess-M-mH; regular and changing meters; moderate tempos; 7pp; Diff-V/m-d, P/m-d.

For: soprano; mezzo-soprano

Mood: lyrical; philosophical; humorous; texts generally for children

Voice: some stepwise motion; some disjunct; somewhat chromatic; some fragmentation

Piano: mostly chordal; some contrapuntal textures; chromaticism; does not double vocal line

Diff: pitches; some rhythms; agility

Uses: effective recital group

    a. *Nurse's Song.* X; c'–f♯"; Tess-M; 4/4, Semplice; 1p.
    b. *The Fly.* X; e♭'–g"; Tess-M; 3/4, Con moto; 2pp.
    c. *The Blossom.* F♯min; e'–g♯"; Tess-M; 4/4, 3/2, Allegretto; 1p.
    d. *How Sweet I Roam'd.* Fmaj; c♯'–g"; Tess-M-mH; 4/4 with changes, Commodo–Poco meno mosso; 3pp.

792. **AN ITALIAN VOYAGE** (orig. Russian texts by M. Kuzmin; English lyrics by Merrill Sparks). General, 1976. cmp1932. Tonally unsettled; c'–g♯"; Tess-M; mostly regular meters; moderate tempos; 13pp; Diff-V/md, P/md.

For: soprano
Mood: lyrical; descriptive of visual scenes and ephemeral emotions
Voice: mostly skips; some stepwise motion; syllabic; some rhythmic complexity
Piano: mostly linear; broken-chord and afterbeat figurations; uncertain harmonic structures; many accidentals; light texture; some 3rds
Diff: mostly in pitch patterns and distinct enunciation; giving melodic and harmonic shape to the songs may require extra skill; not for beginners
Uses: usable set

   a. *Invitation.* e'–g♯"; 4/4 with changes, Amoroso; 3pp.
   b. *Morning in Florence.* c'–g♭"; 2/4, 3/8, Allegro; 3pp.
   c. *A Trip to Assisi.* b–f"; 4/4, Commodo; 4pp.
   d. *The Venice Moon.* c'–g"; 6/8, Tempo moderato (Barcarolla); 3pp.

793. SIX SONGS FROM "A SHROPSHIRE LAD" (A. E. Housman). Cycle. Broude Bros., 1955. cmp1945. Traditional keys with many altered chords; b♭–g♯"; Tess-M-mH; regular meters with changes; 8min; Diff-V/m, P/e-m.
For: lyric baritone best (highest tones generally not sustained)
Mood: lyrical; moods reflect lost youth and love, and approaching death
Voice: conjunct with skips and a few leaps; accidentals; uncomplicated rhythms
Piano: generally patterned with various figures; accidentals; some semi-cluster chords; large reach helpful for l.h. of last song
Uses: nice work–attractive and usable for secure intermediate student; could close a program

   a. *Into My Heart.* B♭min; c'–g♯"; 4/4, Andantino; 2pp.
   b. *With Rue My Heart Is Laden.* A-centered; c♯'–f"; 3/4, Con moto; 2pp.
   c. *When I Watch the Living.* F-centered/C; b♭–e♭"; 4/4, 3/2; Commodo; 2pp.
   d. *Loveliest of Trees.* A♭-centered; d'–e"; 6/8, 9/8, Amabile; 2pp.
   e. *Oh, When I Was in Love.* B♭-centered; c'–f"; 4/4, Calmato; 2pp.
   f. *Now Hollow Fires.* Emin/C; d'–g"; 3/4, 4/4, Pesante; 2pp.

EATON, JOHN
(b. Bryn Mawr, PA, 1935)

794. HOLY SONNETS OF JOHN DONNE. A Song Cycle for Dramatic Soprano and Piano or Symphony Orchestra. Shawnee, 1960. No key sigs., very dissonant; c'–b"; Tess-M-mH; irregular and changing meters; varied tempos; 12min; Diff-V/d, P/d.
For: dramatic soprano
Mood: dramatic; anguished pleading for God's grace and pardon

Voice: rather serpentine vocal line; highly chromatic; complex rhythmic patterns; polymeters between voice and piano; words difficult to project; melismatic phrases
Piano: rather thick keyboard texture, alternately contrapuntal and chordal; rhythmic precision needed; infested with multiple accidentals in every measure; pianist needs secure grasp of modern score
Diff: in every area; perfect pitch desirable; strong rhythmic sense vital for singer; large voice necessary
Uses: powerful poetry and dissonant setting requires a mature and passionate personality to project this cycle

   a. *(XIV) Batter My Heart, Three Person'd God.* c'–a"; 3/4 with many changes, Pesante; 5pp.
   b. *(XI) Spit in My Face You Jewes.* d♯'–b♭"; 4/4, Agitato; 3pp.
   c. *(IV) Oh, My Black Soule!* f'–a"; 4/4 with many changes, Freely declaimed; 3pp.
   d. *(XIII) What If This Present Were the World's Last Night?* c'–f"; some spoken phrases; 3/8, 2/4, Tranquillo; 5pp.
   e. *(VII) At the Round Earth's Imagined Corners.* d'–b"; 4/4 with changes, Moderato maestoso; 3pp.

EDMUNDS, JOHN
(b. San Francisco, CA, 1913; d. Berkeley, CA, 1986)

[See also D#s 59 & 174 for songs not listed below]

795. CANTICLE (John Norris). [101]. cmp1946. Fmaj; d'–f"; Tess-mL; 3/2, 2/4, Allegretto leggiero; 3pp; Diff-V/me, P/me.
For: mezzo-soprano
Mood: lyrical; love song; nature imagery
Voice: flowing phrases
Piano: chordal, 3-voice texture; supports voice
Diff: frequent meter changes
Uses: good for young singers

796. CLOSE NOW THINE EYES (Francis Quarles). [101]. cmp1951. Cmaj; c'–f♯"; Tess-M; 3/2, Largo; 3pp; Diff-V/m, P/m.
For: baritone
Mood: lyrical; peaceful love song
Voice: long phrases; very sustained
Piano: chordal–organ-like; somewhat chromatic
Diff: long phrases; sustained tones

797. COME AWAY, DEATH (William Shakespeare). [101]. cmp1936. Gmaj; e♭'–g♭"; Tess-M; 4/4, 3/2, 2/4, 5/4, Allegretto sospirando; 4pp; Diff-V/m, P/d.
For: soprano; tenor
Mood: lyrical; poem about death
Voice: flowing phrases; some large intervals
Piano: continuous broken-chord pattern in 16ths in r.h.; chordal in l.h.

798. GLORY BE TO THE GRACES (Robert Herrick). [101]. cmp1959. B♭maj; b♭–f"; Tess-mL; 5/8, 7/8, 2/4, 3/8, Brisk and strong (♪ = 120); 3pp; Diff-V/m, P/md.

For: mezzo-soprano; contralto; baritone
Mood: lyrical; lively song in praise of the Graces
Voice: ascending and descending scale passages; 8ve leaps downward
Piano: chordal; dotted rhythms; 16th-note patterns
Diff: frequent meter changes; text
Uses: possible encore song

799. **HALLELUJAH** (Old Testament). [101]. cmp1949. Gmaj; c♯'–a"; Tess-M; 3/4, 2/4, 4/4, Fast (♩. = 60); 5pp; Diff-V/d, P/d.
For: soprano
Mood: jubilant
Voice: brilliant; disjunct; sustained tones; melismas
Piano: chordal; some independent melodic material
Diff: flexibility; sustained high tones, ascending
Uses: showpiece in contemporary idiom

800. **HAVE THESE FOR YOURS** (A. E. Housman). (Peer)Southern, 1957. X; f'–g♭"; Tess-mH; 4/4, 2/4, Quietly; 3pp; Diff-V/md, P/d.
For: soprano; tenor
Mood: lyrical; philosophical poem about death
Voice: flowing phrases; somewhat chromatic
Piano: rapid arpeggiations; somewhat chromatic
Uses: good for soprano; tenor of limited range; requires good musicianship

801. **HEAR THE VOICE OF THE BARD** (William Blake). [101]. cmp1938. Fmin; e♭'–a♭"; Tess-mH; 3/4, 5/4, Moderato; 3pp; Diff-V/d, P/md.
For: soprano; tenor
Mood: somewhat dramatic; philosophical
Voice: fairly chromatic; features descending scalewise passages
Piano: chordal; supports voice; melodic only in short prelude and under final phrase
Diff: large upward leaps; rhythms; sustained high phrase at end
Uses: good for vocalization beginning high and descending; recital possibilities

802. **HELEN** (Edgar Allan Poe). [101]. cmp1935. D♭maj; d♭'–e♭"; Tess-mL; 2/2, 3/2, Andante con moto; 4pp; Diff-V/m, P/d.
For: baritone
Mood: lyrical; descriptive
Voice: flowing phrases; sustained; some chromaticism
Piano: chordal with independent contrapuntal movement; syncopation; rather chromatic
Diff: frequent meter changes
Uses: useful song for those unable to sustain long phrases

803. **HERE SHE LIES IN A BED OF SPICE** (Robert Herrick). [101]. cmp1934. Gmaj; d'–f♯"; Tess-M; 3/4, 2/4, Allegretto; 2pp; Diff-V/m, P/d.
For: tenor
Mood: lyrical; poem in praise of a dead lover
Voice: short vocal melismas
Piano: rapid 16th-note figures; somewhat chromatic
Diff: frequent meter changes; delicacy

804. **THE ISLE OF PORTLAND** (The Star-Filled Seas) (A. E. Housman). Boosey & Hawkes, 1950. cmp1935. Cmaj with changing modes; c'–e"; Tess-M; 4/4, Very slow; 2pp; Diff-V/me, P/me.
For: baritone; mezzo-soprano
Mood: lyrical; elegy
Voice: conjunct; easy rhythms; change of mode in mid-stanza; 2- & 4-note slurs
Piano: chordal; change of mode; smooth; soft
Uses: lovely song for teaching and programming
Rec: D#174

805. **THE LONELY** (Æ–George William Russell). [21]; 1st©1948. "To Janet Fairbank." H & L keys: X; e♭'–f" & c♭'–d"; Tess-M; 6/8, 9/8, Gently (♩. = 50); 1+min; Diff-V/m, P/m.
For: any lyric voice
Mood: lyrical; sad
Voice: flowing phrases; syncopation; some chromaticism
Piano: broken-chord figurations throughout; somewhat chromatic
Diff: meter alternations; rhythmic patterns
Uses: effective recital song

806. **MILKMAIDS** (anon.). Mercury, 1957. cmp1946. G♭maj; d♭'–f"; Tess-M; meter not indicated, Briskly (♩ = 116); 3pp; Diff-V/m, P/d.
For: tenor; baritone
Mood: humorous; descriptive; twist at end
Voice: flowing phrases; much ascending and descending movement
Piano: 2-voice texture in 8th-notes; sometimes contrapuntal
Diff: rhythm
Uses: group ender; encore
Rec: D#174

807. **O DEATH, ROCK ME ASLEEP** (Anne Boleyn?). (Peer)Southern, 1955. Cmaj; d♯'–e"; Tess-M; no meter sig., Slow; 2pp; Diff-V/me, P/md.
For: any medium voice
Mood: philosophical; poem about death
Voice: sustained; somewhat chromatic
Piano: chordal; chromatic; supports voice
Diff: pitch
Uses: good for student of limited range; useful for recitals
Rec: D#174

808. **PRAISE YE THE LORD** (Psalm 113, King James Vesion). [101]. cmp1960. Cmaj-Fmaj; c'–a"; Tess-M; 2/2, 2/4, 5/4, Moderato; 4pp; Diff-V/md, P/d.
For: dramatic soprano; mezzo-soprano
Mood: joyful; praise
Voice: dramatic; brilliant; somewhat disjunct; a few melismatic passages
Piano: chordal with independent melody; organ-like
Diff: voice needs dramatic weight; solid low tones
Uses: recital or church

809. **SEAL UP HER EYES, O SLEEP** (William Cartwright). [101]. cmp1952. "For Eva Gauthier." Cmin; c'–e"; Tess-L; 4/4, Very slow (♩ = 52); 3pp; Diff-V/dd, P/dd.

For: mezzo-soprano; baritone
Mood: lyrical; poem about love
Voice: very florid, with short melismas and descending scales in 32nds
Piano: extremely florid and ornamented
Diff: florid passages low in pitch; for mature singer
Uses: unique song for any recital

810. **STAY, O SWEET** (John Donne). [101]. cmp1935. E♭maj; d♭'–g"; Tess-mL; 3/2 with changes, Largo (♩ = 94); 2pp; Diff-V/m, P/m.
For: tenor; high baritone
Mood: lyrical; poem about love
Voice: flowing phrases; several 8ve leaps; frequent meter changes
Piano: chordal; chromatic; supports voice without doubling
Diff: meter changes; 8ve leaps

811. **TAKE, O TAKE THOSE LIPS AWAY** (William Shakespeare). [101]. cmp1934. X; e♭'–g"; Tess-mH; 6/8, 9/8, Allegro con brio; 3pp; Diff-V/m, P/m.
For: soprano; tenor
Mood: lyrical
Voice: long flowing phrases begin high
Piano: repeated chords; fairly chromatic; 2 vs. 3
Diff: pitches; rhythms; sustained last tone
Uses: good recital song

812. **TO ELECTRA** (Robert Herrick). [101]. cmp1934. X; b–a♭"; Tess-H, L; 4/4, 5/4, 3/2, Allegro moderato; 3pp; Diff-V/d, P/d.
For: tenor
Mood: lyrical; poetic; love song
Voice: somewhat disjunct; chromatic; a few small melismas
Piano: chordal; broken-chord patterns; chromatic; doubles vocal line throughout
Diff: frequent meter changes; range; flexibility
Uses: recital song for mature voice

813. **TO MUSIC** (Robert Herrick). [101]. cmp1935. Dmaj; d'–g♭"; Tess-M; 2/4, 5/8, 3/4, Andantino; 2pp; Diff-V/m, P/md.
For: soprano; mezzo-soprano; tenor
Mood: lyrical; in praise of music
Voice: flowing phrases; rather chromatic
Piano: chordal; broken chords in l.h.; chromatic; partially doubles vocal line
Diff: frequent meter changes

814. **UPON JULIA'S HAIR** (Robert Herrick). [101]. cmp1935. D♭maj; c–a♭"; Tess-M; 3/4, 4/4, 2/4, 5/4, 3/2, Allegro animato ma non troppo; 3pp; Diff-V/d, P/dd.
For: tenor
Mood: lyrical; poem about love
Voice: flowing phrases; chromatic; somewhat disjunct; long, sustained final phrase
Piano: arpeggiated figures in 16ths; descriptive of text
Diff: rhythms; intervals; frequent meter changes
Uses: good song for an excellent musician

815. **WEEP YOU NO MORE, SAD FOUNTAINS**
(anon.). [101]. cmp1938. E♭maj; e♭'–g"; Tess-mH; 6/8, Evenly, with motion (♪ = 88); 3pp; Diff-V/m, P/md.
For: soprano; tenor
Mood: lyrical; love song
Voice: short phrases; chromatic
Piano: chordal; chromatic; 8th-note motion
Uses: good recital song

816. **WHENAS IN SILKS MY JULIA GOES** (Robert Herrick). [101]. cmp1937. Gmaj; e♭'–e♭"; Tess-M; 6/8, 9/8, Allegro moderato; 2pp; Diff-V/me, P/d.
For: baritone
Mood: lyrical; love song
Voice: flowing phrases; little chromaticism
Piano: arpeggiations in 16ths; independent but supports voice
Uses: the Herrick poems can be made into a fine recital group

817. **WHEN DAISIES PIED** (William Shakespeare). [101]. cmp1936. X; e♭'–a♭"; Tess-mH; 6/8, 9/8, Lively (♩ = 92); 4pp; Diff-V/md, P/md.
For: tenor
Mood: pastoral; lyrical
Voice: chromatic; some difficult intervals
Piano: 2-voice texture; independent melodies
Diff: highest tones light and short

EDWARDS, CLARA
(b. Mankato, MN, 1887; d. New York, NY, 1974)

818. **THE FISHER'S WIDOW** (Arthur Symons). G. Schirmer, 1929. Cmin; (b)f♯'–g "(a♭"); Tess-mH; 2/4, Allegro moderato; 45meas.; Diff-V/m, P/m.
For: soprano
Mood: dramatic; somber; animated
Voice: small skips; chromatic; some triplets
Piano: chordal, some broken; some rapid afterbeat figures; some doubling of vocal line
Diff: several note options eliminate possible high- or low-note problems
Uses: usable fast song for recital group

819. **GIPSY LIFE** (Clara Edwards). G. Schirmer, 1932. H & L keys: Emin & Bmin; e'–b" (g") & b–f♯"(d"); Tess-M; 3/4, Allegro con brio; 2min; Diff-V/m, P/m.
For: soprano; mezzo-soprano
Mood: sprightly; Spanish-gypsy flavor
Voice: stepwise and small skips; duplets and triplets; three vocalized sections
Piano: habanera rhythms; guitar-like accomp. figures; does not double vocal line
Uses: effective group ender; fun to sing

820. **INTO THE NIGHT** (Clara Edwards). [25, 59]; 1st©1939. H, M (also pub. separately by G. Schirmer), & L keys: Gmaj, Fmaj, & E♭maj; e'–f"(g"), d'–e♭"(f") & c'–d♭"(e♭"); Tess-M; 4/4, Tranquillo; 4pp; Diff-V/me, P/me.
For: all voices
Mood: lyrical; sentimental love song
Voice: lyrical; sustained; duplet and triplet division of beat
Piano: chordal; supportive

Diff: triplets in vocal line
Uses: good for young singers

821. THE LITTLE SHEPHERD'S SONG (William Percy). Mills, 1922. H, M & L keys: E♭maj, D♭maj, & B♭maj; e♭'–a♭", d♭'–g♭", & b♭–e♭"; Tess-M; 6/8, 3/8, Con moto e grazioso; 4pp; Diff-V/me, P/md.
For: lyric soprano
Mood: joyous song about nature
Voice: lyrical; a few chromatic tones
Piano: chordal; first-inversion triads descending chromatically in solo passages; broken-chord figures under voice; occasional doubling of vocal line
Diff: requires agility
Uses: good for young soprano

EDWARDS, LEO
(b. Cincinnati, OH, 1937)

822. LULLABY (from *Harriet Taubman*) (Anthony Martone). For High Voice with Piano. Willis, 1983. E-centered; b–b"; Tess-wide; 6/4 predominates, Adagio; 5pp; Diff-V/m, P/m.
For: soprano
Mood: lullaby, with tension in background
Voice: opens with recit.-like passage; mostly stepwise with skips up to an 8ve; 8-meas. humming section; several 2–5-note slurs; portamento; ends on sustained b"
Piano: broken-chord patterning; l.h. has rocking figures; syncopation; doubling of vocal line incidental
Diff: needs soft, floating high tones; soft dynamics throughout
Uses: recital; good song to practice soft singing

ELMORE, ROBERT
(b. Ramapatnam, India, 1913; d. Philadelphia, PA, 1985)

823. ARISE, MY LOVE (Song of Solomon). Composers Press, 1951. cmp ca.1949. "This song won First Place in the 1949 Contest sponsored by the Composers Press, Inc." Cmaj (with changes); d'–a"; Tess-mH; 4/4, 3/4, Largo–Più mosso–Allegretto molto; 6pp; Diff-V/md, P/m.
For: tenor; soprano
Mood: ecstatic, sensuous love song
Voice: stepwise; small skips; a few larger leaps; modest number of accidentals, but key sig. changes frequently; triplets; some polyrhythms against piano; lyrical and flowing; sustained a"ƒƒ; syllabic; a few 2-note slurs
Piano: chordal–block and broken; several countermelodic figures in 8ves; somewhat chromatic; key sig. changes frequently; triplets and sextuplets; incidental doubling of vocal line
Diff: pitches; rhythms; a"ƒƒ on "fair"
Uses: good recital song

ELWELL, HERBERT
(b. Minneapolis, MN, 1898; d. Cleveland, OH, 1974)

824. AGAMEDE'S SONG (Arthur Upson). Valley, 1948. Cmaj; f'–f"; Tess-M; 2/2, Moderato, tranquillo e semplice; 2pp; Diff-V/me, P/e.
For: soprano
Mood: lyrical; elegiac
Voice: simple line; some long tones
Piano: open 8ves until near end; some chords; rather bare

825. IN THE MOUNTAINS (Chang Yu). Broadcast Music, 1946. G♭maj; d♭'–f"; Tess-M; 3/4, Moderato; Diff-V/m, P/d.
For: soprano; tenor
Mood: lyrical; quiet; solitary
Voice: conjunct; sustained
Piano: arpeggiated throughout with changing patterns
Uses: beautiful song for teaching and programming

826. RENOUNCEMENT (Alice Meynell). G. Schirmer, 1942. Gmaj; g(b)–g"; Tess-M; 4/4, Comodo; 3min; Diff-V/md, P/m-md.
For: mezzo-soprano
Mood: dramatic; putting past love out of mind
Voice: recit.-like vocal line; many skips; some long-ranged phrases; some chromatic lines
Piano: chordal–block and broken; syncopation; 8ve passages; accidentals; some thick texture
Diff: ƒƒ climax on g"; dynamics
Uses: good song for singer with ample voice and dramatic flair; big ending

827. THE ROAD NOT TAKEN (Robert Frost). G. Schirmer, 1942. Amaj-F♯min; b–f♯"; Tess-M; 4/4, Allegretto; 6pp; Diff-V/m, P/md.
For: mezzo-soprano; high baritone; some sopranos
Mood: somewhat declamatory; introspective
Voice: recit.-like; speech rhythms; some long-ranged phrases
Piano: chordal-linear combination; scale passages; many accidentals; does not double vocal line
Diff: rhythm; ensemble; unequal phrase lengths
Uses: effective use of voice and piano sonorities; useful song

828. THE SUFFOLK OWL (Thomas Vautor). Valley, 1948. Emin; d'–g"; Tess-M; 4/4, Lento; 2pp; Diff-V/d, P/d.
For: soprano
Mood: philosophical; descriptive; night and death
Voice: disjunct; dotted rhythms; triplets; small melismas; some chromaticism
Diff: rhythms; irregular phrase lengths; ensemble
Uses: effective song; good sonorous effects

829. THREE POEMS OF ROBERT LIDDELL LOWE. Cycle. Fema, 1969. Traditional keys; d'–a"; Tess-M; regular meters, varied tempos; 9min; Diff-V/m, P/m.
For: tenor; soprano; tenor perhaps better for text
Mood: lyrical; death and regeneration images in nature
Voice: diatonic vocal line, mostly conjunct; some melismatic passages; some long tones; ends on sustained a"ƒƒ
Piano: much linear and some chordal texture
Uses: attractive cycle; not difficult; could close a program

    a. *All Foxes.* Gmaj; d'–g♯"; 2/2, 3/2, Allegro; 5pp.

b. *This Glittering Grief.* Phrygian on A; d'–g"; 3/4; 5pp. [**Rec:** D#175]

c. *Phoenix Afire.* Amaj; d'–a"; 3/4, Moderato; 5pp.

ENDERS, HARVEY
(b. St. Louis, MO, 1892; d. New York, NY, 1947)

830. **DIRGE** (Adelaide Crapsey). G. Schirmer, 1927. Dmin; d'–f"; Tess-mL-M; 4/4, Lento; 2pp; Diff-V/m, P/m.

For: mezzo-soprano; baritone; some sopranos
Mood: somber; intense, though a quiet song
Voice: skips along chord lines; chromatic; syncopation; duplets and triplets; 2-note slurs
Piano: chordal–block and arpeggiated; 2 vs. 3; some doubling of vocal line; dramatic climax of song in solo section
Diff: sustained f" with cresc.

831. **THE LITTLE TURTLE** (A Tale) (Vachel Lindsay). G. Schirmer, 1926. A♭ maj; d♭'–a♭"(f"); Tess-mH; 4/4, Slowly and darkly–Faster and brighter; 2pp; Diff-V/m, P/m.

For: soprano
Mood: humorous; colorful; child's verse
Voice: stepwise and skips along chord lines; some long-ranged phrases; beat subdivided into 2, 3, & 4
Piano: chordal; 2-note repeated pattern; some doubling of vocal line
Diff: several mood changes; staccato and legato
Uses: colorful setting; for final group; encore

832. **RUSSIAN PICNIC** (Harvey Enders). [35]; 1st©1946. Cmaj-A♭ maj; c'–g"; Tess-M; 4/4, At a gay and fast gait (♩ = 160); 6pp; Diff-V/d, P/md.

For: tenor
Mood: joyous love song in the style of a Russian dance; describes Russian scene
Voice: numerous leaps upward; strong accents and dynamic contrasts; Russian names and pseudo-Russian words; shouting; chromatic scale covering a 10th; final long g"
Piano: chordal and contrapuntal; broken and afterbeat chords; often doubles vocal line, incl. the chromatic scale
Diff: capturing the necessary sense of abandonment in the style for both singer and pianist; singer needs solid technique and vocal and interpretive freedom
Uses: an interesting addition to a program

ENDICOTT, SAMUEL (S. C. Colburn)
(b. Boston, MA, 19th Century)

833. **HER SONGS** (B. Preston Clark, Jr.). Boston Music Co., 1916. Bmaj; d♯'–g♯"; Tess-M; 4/8, Lento; 3pp; Diff-V/m, P/m.

For: tenor; soprano
Mood: lyrical lullaby
Voice: conjunct with some skips along chord lines; speech rhythms
Piano: recurring bass in a rocking figure; countermelody; incidental doubling of vocal line
Uses: nice romantic song; usable

834. **NOCTURNE** (B. Preston Clark, Jr.). Boston Music Co., 1916. Cmaj; d'–f♯"; Tess-M; 4/4, 3/4, 5/4, Lento; 6pp; Diff-V/m, P/md.

For: lyric baritone; tenor
Mood: lyrical nocturne
Voice: conjunct; soft dynamics; sustained e" on "ee" vowel; very quiet ending
Piano: arpeggiated or measured tremolo in l.h. throughout; five 16th notes per beat; r.h. chords
Diff: accomp. a bit awkward in rhythm; lulling
Uses: nice song; quiet

ENGEL, CARL
(b. Paris, France, 1883; d. New York, NY, 1944)

835. **"MY HEART," I SAID** (Cora Fabbri). G. Schirmer, 1908. Fmaj; d'–g"; Tess-M; 4/4, Poco agitato–Poco lento; 2pp; Diff-V/m, P/m.

For: soprano; tenor
Mood: lyrical; nostalgic
Voice: stepwise and skips along chord lines; some phrase fragmentation
Piano: chordal; countermelody in 3rds; many accidentals
Uses: use within a group; very quiet ending (*pppp*)

836. **A SPRIG OF ROSEMARY** (Amy Lowell). G. Schirmer, 1922. E♭maj; e♭'–f"; Tess-M; 4/4, Andante flessibile; 3pp; Diff-V/m, P/m.

For: tenor
Mood: lyrical; descriptive; somewhat declamatory
Voice: many small skips; duplets and triplets; 3 vs. piano 2
Piano: unusual broken-chord pattern (a bit awkward); some syncopation; does not double vocal line

837. **TWO LYRICS** (Amy Lowell). G. Schirmer, 1911. Pub. separately; separate entries below.

A. **SEA-SHELL.** [25, 41]. G♭ maj; e♭'–e♭"; Tess-M; 6/8, Con moto ondeggiante e ben sentito; 3pp; Diff-V/me, P/md.

For: mezzo-soprano; soprano
Mood: descriptive; song of the sea
Voice: rocking rhythm; some chromaticism
Piano: arpeggiated 16th-note figures; syncopation; cross-hands
Diff: tricky modulation for singer meas. 17–20
Uses: good for students of limited range; could be paired with "The Trout"

B. **THE TROUT.** Gmaj; g'–g"; Tess-mH; 4/8, Allegretto e furbescamente; 3pp; Diff-V/md, P/md.

For: soprano
Mood: humorous; questioning; child-like
Voice: stepwise and small skips; chromatic; 8th- & 16th-note motion; some ornaments; many accidentals
Piano: chordal; chromatic 16th-note figure repeated in countermelody; large reaches; articulations important; does not double vocal line
Diff: flexibility; rapid articulation and diction
Uses: encore or pair with "Sea-Shell"

ENGLE, DAVID
(b. Detroit, MI, 1938)

838. NIGHT SONG (SILENT, SILENT NIGHT)
(William Blake). The Willis Music Co., 1987. Aeolian on E; e'–g"; Tess-mH; 6/8, 4/8, 5/8, 7/8, etc., Andante, con moto tranquillo (♪ = 132); 4pp; Diff-V/d, P/d.

For: soprano; tenor
Mood: lyrical; ironic
Voice: stepwise and small skips; syllabic; changing meters with 8th-note pulse
Piano: "crystalline" outer sections feature block and broken chords in mostly 8th- & 16th-note motion; some irregular groupings; active central section begins contrapuntally, then has subdivisions that create cross-rhythms between the hands (e.g. 4 vs. 6); two quartal arpeggios; some doubling of vocal line
Diff: changing meters make rhythms challenging; ensemble; communicating the text
Uses: perhaps combine with other composers' settings of Blake poems, other than *Songs of Innocence*

ENGLISH, GRANVILLE
(b. Louisville, KY, 1895; d. New York, NY, 1968)

839. WINGS OF A DOVE (Henry Van Dyke). Composers Press, 1947. First Prize, 1946 Composers Press Song Competition. Emaj; d♯'–g"; Tess-M; 3/4, Andante con moto e poco rubato; 3min; Diff-V/m, P/m-d.

For: tenor; soprano
Mood: lyrical; philosophical
Voice: some skips; some triplets
Piano: chordal, 5-voice texture; some broken chords; cross-hands; rolled chords
Diff: meter changes; triplets in voice vs. duplets in piano
Uses: mood piece; quiet ending

EVERSOLE, JAMES
(b. Lexington, KY, 1929)

840. ANNE RUTLEDGE (Edgar Lee Masters). [57]. C-centered; g'–g"; Tess-mH; 2/2, 3/2, ♩ = 68-72; 2pp; Diff-V/m, P/m.

For: soprano
Mood: introspective; young girl speaks of what might have been
Voice: chant-like; small skips; speech-like rhythms; accidentals
Piano: block and broken chords; many accidentals; does not double vocal line
Diff: possibly rhythms
Uses: nice song about a legendary American

FAIRCHILD, BLAIR
(b. Belmont, MA, 1877; d. Paris, France, 1933)

841. LAMENT OF MAHOMET AKRAM (Lawrence Hope). C. W. Thompson, 1909. Gmin; d'–f"; Tess-M; 4/4, Andante; 5pp; Diff-V/m, P/m.

For: baritone; some tenors
Mood: regretful memory; lost love
Voice: stepwise and small skips; dotted rhythms, duplets vs. piano triplets
Piano: chordal–broken-block mixture in asymmetrical triplet patterns; "Eastern" ornamentation; some accidentals; does not double vocal line
Diff: some long phrases
Uses: usable period piece

842. A MEMORY, Op. 22, No. 3 (William Allingham). C. W. Thompson, 1909. E♭maj; d'–e♭"; Tess-M; 3/4, Moderato; 2pp; Diff-V/e, P/e.

For: mezzo-soprano; soprano
Mood: lyrical; nostalgic; a scene remembered
Voice: stepwise and small skips; dotted rhythms
Piano: broken-chord figure; some block chords; thin texture; incidental doubling of vocal line
Uses: usable in a group of American songs

843. SONGS FROM THE CHINESE (English Version by M. Waley). For Medium Voice. Durand et Cie., 1922. Reprint: Recital Publications, 1998. cmp ca.1920–22. Tonal, mostly whole-tone; c♯'–g"; Tess-M-mH; regular meters; slow to moderate tempos; 22pp; Diff-V/me-m, P/me-m.

For: soprano; tenor
Mood: impressionistic; transitory nature of life; nature images; the passing of time and inevitable loss
Voice: lyrical; mostly conjunct lines; whole-tone structures; syllabic; polyrhythms
Piano: chordal and broken-chord repeated patterns; whole-tone harmonies; chromaticism
Diff: vocal pitches against a hazy harmonic background
Uses: example of impressionistic influence on American composers and the fascination with Oriental texts and imagery

    a. *Sailing Homeward* (Chan-fang-scheng, 4th century). F; e'–g"; Tess-M-mH; 6/4, Andante con moto; 3pp.
    b. *The Red Cockatoo* (Po-chu-I, 772-846). Whole-tone; d'–f♯"; Tess-cs; 2/2, 3/2, Poco moderato (scherzando); 2pp.
    c. *Night* (Meï-scheng, 1st century). E; d'–g"; Tess-M; 2/4, Andante ma non troppo; 4pp.
    d. *Old Poem* (Anon., 1st century). F; f♯'–g"; Tess-M; 2/2, Commodo; 3pp.
    e. *Plucking Rushes* (Anon., 4th century). Whole-tone on G; d'–g"; Tess-M; 4/4, 3/3, Andantino; 2pp.
    f. *Cock-Crow Song* (Anon., 1st century). Whole-tone on F♯; d'–g"; Tess-mH; 3/4, 4/4, Soave; 3pp.
    g. *New Corn* (T'ao Ch'ien, 365-427). Dmin; d'–f♯"; Tess-M; 4/4, Molto Andante; 2pp.
    h. *A Bad Bargain* (T'ao Ch'ien). Whole-tone; c♯'–f♯"; Tess-M; 4/4, 2/4, Giocoso; 3pp.

844. WHEN I WAS ONE AND TWENTY (A. E. Housman). C. W. Thompson, 1905. Dmaj; d'–d"; Tess-M; 4/4, Con moto; 3pp; Diff-V/m, P/me.

For: baritone; mezzo-soprano
Mood: lyrical

Voice: 8th-note motion; many dotted rhythms; syncopation; accidentals; 2-note slurs
Piano: chordal; many accidentals; incidental doubling of vocal line
Uses: useful recital material, perhaps in a Housman group

FAITH, RICHARD
(b. Evansville, IN, 1926)

845. DOVER BEACH (Matthew Arnold). [103]. E♭-chromatic; d'–a♯"; Tess-cs; 3/4, Moderato ♩ = c.100; 13pp; Diff-V/d, P/d.
For: tenor
Mood: dramatic; foreboding, turbulent, and majestic qualities of the sea
Voice: long phrases; sustained chromatic lines; many phrases hang in passaggio; dramatic climax on a♯"
Piano: initial slowly moving chords in long prelude; chromatic broken-chord patterns; many accidentals; long interlude; returns to chords at final climax; piano takes the role of the sea
Diff: long philosophical poem; singer needs ease at various dynamic levels in passaggio
Uses: good dramatic-philosophical song for mature singer with substantial sound

846. IF I WERE (Traditional). [103]. Gmaj; f'–f"; Tess-mH; 2/4, 3/8, 3/4, Allegretto ♩ = c.108; 4pp; Diff-V/md, P/m.
For: soprano; tenor
Mood: lighthearted love song
Voice: vocal line soars to long tones at phrase ends; syllabic
Piano: chordal; broken-chord patterns; some countermelodies
Diff: sustained tones in passaggio
Uses: good for young bright soprano or tenor voice

847. IT IS A BEAUTEOUS EVENING (William Wordsworth). [103]. A♭–Dmaj; d'–a♭"; Tess-M; 6/8, 9/8, Andantino ♩ = c. 42; 5pp; Diff-V/m, P/md.
For: tenor
Mood: majestic; solemn; sunset at the ocean
Voice: sustained; syllabic; conjunct, with a few large intervals
Piano: almost constant 16th-note motion in wave-like figuration; many accidentals
Diff: balance of voice and piano
Uses: good for a group of sea songs; mature singer

848. IT WAS A LOVER AND HIS LASS (William Shakespeare). [102]. Gmaj; f♯'–a"(b"); Tess-H; 2/4, 3/4, 3/8, Allegro, ma non troppo ♩ = c.126; 5pp; Diff-V/m, P/m.
For: soprano
Mood: jocular; bouncy
Voice: rhythmic; high tessitura; "hey" on b" with a glissando down to c"; ends on sustained g"
Piano: motivic construction; much staccato; fairly thin texture
Diff: high passages; 3/8 measures
Uses: interesting contrast with other settings of poem; good for high soprano

849. MOTHER GOOSE LYRICS. [103]. Traditional keys; d♭'–b♭"; Tess-M, mH; regular meters; medium to fast tempos; 10pp; Diff-V/me-m, P/me-m.
For: soprano; tenor
Mood: humorous; character songs
Voice: syllabic; tuneful; some large leaps; some 2 vs. 3; speech rhythms
Piano: mixed accomp. patterns; some doubling of vocal line
Diff: character delineation; some rhythmic patterns
Uses: good songs for college freshmen or advanced high school singers

    a. *Where Are You Going To, My Pretty Maid?* B♭maj; d'–b♭"; Tess-mH; 2/4, Allegro; 2pp.
    b. *Jenny Wren.* G♭maj; d♭'–a♭"; Tess-cs; 4/4, Allegretto; 3pp.
    c. *The Queen of Hearts.* Cmaj; g'–a"; Tess-cs; 6/8, Allegro, ma non troppo ♩ = c.132; 3pp.
    d. *I Saw a Ship A-Sailing.* Emin; d'–g"; Tess-M; 2/4, Moving; 2pp.

850. MUSIC, WHEN SOFT VOICES DIE (Percy Bysshe Shelley). [102]. Amin; e'–g"; Tess-M; 2/2, 3/2, Moderato, espress.; 3pp; Diff-V/m, P/m.
For: soprano; tenor
Mood: dark and somber
Voice: conjunct; chromatic; lyrical; some polyrhythms
Piano: broken-chord patterns; prelude and postlude same material; some countermelodies
Diff: tuning of chromatic approach to last note of vocal line; polyrhythms
Uses: interesting contrast to settings by Porter, Gold, Quilter, and others

851. THE OWL AND THE PUSSYCAT (Edward Lear). [102]. Phrygian on G; (b♭)c'–g"; Tess-M; 6/8, Allegretto; 5pp; Diff-V/m, P/m.
For: soprano; tenor
Mood: humorous
Voice: many 4ths & 5ths in vocal line; chromatic movement; final phrase hangs on g" and f"
Piano: broken-chord patterns; some 8ve r.h. melody; chordal sections; 16th-note r.h. finish
Diff: Phrygian mode in vocal line may be new to some students; ending phrase high and sustained
Uses: good humorous song

852. RETURN OF SPRING (ssü-K'ung T'u). [103]. Pentatonic on E & G; d'–g♯"; Tess-mH; 4/4, Quasi allegretto ♩ = c.104; 4pp; Diff-V/m, P/m.
For: tenor; soprano
Mood: hypnotic spring song
Voice: flowing vocal line; mostly conjunct; a few large intervals; ends on soft sustained g" approached chromatically from d"
Piano: perpetual motion 16th-note pattern in r.h.; some l.h. countermelody; heavily pedaled for hypnotic effect
Diff: sustained vocal lines
Uses: good spring song for light, floating, high voice

853. SONNET LIV (William Shakespeare). [102]. Fmin; e'–a"; Tess-mH; 4/4, 2/4, 3/4, Andantino, espress.; 4pp; Diff-V/m, P/m.

For: tenor; soprano
Mood: restrained passion
Voice: sustained, flowing line; some short melismas; several high phrases; many dynamic nuances; one-chord introduction
Piano: block and broken-chord accomp.; two interludes and postlude; accidentals
Diff: *p–mf* dynamics throughout; decresc. on sustained high tones
Uses: good song for lyric voice with easy top

854. SPRING, THE SWEET SPRING (Thomas Nashe). [102]. Gmaj; d'–g"; Tess-mH; 6/8, 9/8, Allegretto ♩.= ca.68; 5pp; Diff-V/m, P/m.
For: soprano; tenor
Mood: heralding of spring
Voice: straightforward vocal line; three large ascending intervals in refrain; modified strophic form
Piano: 16th-note arpeggiated figuration with repeated notes
Diff: ensemble
Uses: good spring song for undergraduate singers; cf. Argento's "Spring"

855. THE SUN HAS SET (Emily Brontë). [103]. Dmin.-chromatic; c♯'–f♯"; Tess-L, mH; 3/8, Andantino ♩.= c.46; 4pp; Diff-V/m, P/m.
For: soprano
Mood: mournful; dark; empty
Voice: very sustained; ascending chromatic lines; soft dynamics
Piano: arpeggiated figurations with repeated notes in pattern; chromatic; constant 16th-note motion
Diff: long rising chromatic vocal phrase
Uses: good song for a soprano with dark colors in the voice

856. TO CLORIS (Sir Charles Sedley). [103]. Fmaj; c'–g"; Tess-mH; 3/4, 4/4, 3/2, Allegretto ♩= c.88; 4pp; Diff-V/m, P/me.
For: tenor
Mood: witty; half lighthearted, half serious
Voice: syllabic; some irregular phrasing
Piano: downward rolled chords; broken-chord and afterbeat patterns
Uses: good song for a light, nimble tenor voice

857. WILLIAM BUTLER YEATS LYRICS. [103]. Separate entries below.

A. THE LAKE ISLE OF INNISFREE. Pentatonic; d♯'–f"; Tess-M; 3/4, 2/4, 4/4, Andantino ♩= c.84; 5pp; Diff-V/m, P/md.
For: tenor; soprano
Mood: reverie; remembrance of most beautiful place
Voice: mostly conjunct, small skips; relatively small range; quiet (*pp–mf*); syllabic setting; accidentals
Piano: broken chord patterns with various spacings; 2 vs. 3; 16th-note figurations; accidentals; some doubling of vocal line
Diff: many accidentals; some enharmonic notation; soft dynamics
Uses: use in group of Yeats songs or separately

B. THE SONG OF WANDERING AENGUS. A♭maj; d♭'–g♭"; Tess-cs; 3/4, 4/4, 3/2, 5/4, Allegretto, quasi Allegro; 4pp; Diff-V/m, P/m.
For: tenor
Mood: an old man's fantasy
Voice: no prelude; vocal line outlines parallel triads; somewhat folk-like; modified strophic form; unusual harmonic shifts; syllabic; melody governs word stress
Piano: mostly 2-voice texture; r.h. doubles vocal line in first strophe; afterbeat structure in second; rolled chords in third; postlude
Diff: tuning of parallel triad outlines in vocal line
Uses: in Yeats group or separately; good for ear training

C. THE WIND BLOWS OUT OF THE GATES OF DAY. E♭min–B♭maj; d♯'–f♯"; Tess-M; 4/4, 3/4, 6/8, 3/2, Moving, espress. ♩= c.104; 4pp; Diff-V/m, P/m.
For: soprano; tenor
Mood: fantasy; loneliness; fairies dancing
Voice: mostly conjunct; some 8ve leaps; syllabic; long final note
Piano: long prelude; 16th-note patterns; rolled short chords; some broken chord patterns; wide spacing
Diff: creating mood
Uses: in Yeats group, group of fantasy songs, or separately

D. I HEAR THE SHADOWY HORSES. G♯min; d♯'–a♭"; Tess-M; 4/4, 3/4, 3/2, 5/4, Allegro con brio ♩= c.138; 5pp; Diff-V/md, P/md.
For: tenor
Mood: tumultuous; passionate
Voice: sustained; many ascending phrases; dramatic
Piano: r.h. chords over widely-spaced l.h. 8ths; arpeggiated patterns; fast repeated notes; alternating 8ves; dramatic postlude
Diff: ensemble
Uses: fine dramatic song for Yeats group; cf. "Michael Robartes Bids His Beloved Be at Peace" by Sidney Homer (same text)

E. THE WILD SWANS AT COOLE. Pentatonic and chromatic; c'–g"; Tess-M; 4/4, 3/4, 5/4, Andantino ♩= ca.72; 8pp; Diff-V/md, P/md.
For: soprano; tenor
Mood: observation of wild swans' annual visit gives wonder and beauty
Voice: syllabic; speech rhythms shape rhythmic line; some tone painting; accidentals; some long phrases; quiet, sustained ending
Piano: paints imagery of the poem; mostly linear; arpeggiated figuration in triplets; pentatonic
Diff: frequent 2 vs. 3 between voice and piano
Uses: excellent recital material for graduate level soprano or tenor; cf. setting by Suskind

858. WINTER JOURNEY (William Lavonis). [103]. G-B♭min; e♭'–a"; Tess-mH-H; 9/8, 6/8, Andante ♩= c.58-60; 6pp; Diff-V/md, P/m.
For: tenor; soprano
Mood: grief; loss
Voice: sustained; 2 vs. 3; repeated notes; floating rising phrases; syllabic

Piano: broken-chord patterns in various metrical divisions; delicate textures; dissonant; many accidentals
Diff: sustained phrase endings; ensemble
Uses: lament

FARWELL, ARTHUR
(b. St. Paul, MN, 1872; d. New York, NY, 1952)

[See also D#s 43 & 46 for songs not listed below]

859. DRAKE'S DRUM (Henry Newbolt). [66, vol.4]; 1st©1907. Dmin; b♭–f"; Tess-M; 4/4, With spirit, not too fast; 66meas.; Diff-V/md, P/md.
For: baritone specified
Mood: dramatic; hearty; masculine; sailor's song
Voice: many skips; dotted rhythms; syncopation; declamatory
Piano: dotted rhythms; drum imitation; interlude in fast 8ves
Diff: dynamic range; sailor-talk dialect; rhythmic freedom at cadences
Uses: in a final group

860. LOVE'S SECRET (William Blake). [66, vol.2]; 1st©1903. Fmaj; c'–f"; Tess-M; 4/4, Moderato; 25meas.; Diff-V/m, P/m.
For: baritone; possibly tenor
Mood: lyrical
Voice: mostly stepwise; some leaps of 6th & 7th; sustained
Piano: chordal; chromatic; fairly thick texture
Diff: baritone needs good f"s
Uses: usable song for mature singer

861. ON A FADED VIOLET, Op. 43, No. 2 (Percy Bysshe Shelley). [48]; 1st©1927. H & L keys: A♭maj & Fmaj; c♯'–f" & b♭–d"; Tess-mL; 4/4, Quietly, simply; 3pp; Diff-V/m, P/md.
For: all voices
Mood: lyrical
Voice: short phrases; some chromaticism
Piano: chordal; lines imitate or answer vocal melodies; chromatic
Uses: good for student with limited ability to sustain phrases

862. REQUIESCAT (Katherine R. Heyman). [66, vol.2]; 1st©1904. A♭maj; c'–e♭"; Tess-mH; 4/4, Adagio; 12meas.; Diff-V/e, P/m.
For: soprano; mezzo-soprano
Mood: lyrical; lullaby
Voice: stepwise and skips of 3rd; some 8ve leaps
Piano: chordal, 4–5-voices; countermelody; quiet; no prelude or postlude
Diff: must be very slow to be effective
Uses: useful in interior of group

863. RESURGAM (Emily Dickinson). G. Schirmer, 1926. D♭maj; b♭–a♭"; Tess-mH; 6/8 (piano), 2/4 (voice), Rapidly; 2pp; Diff-V/md, P/d.
For: dramatic soprano; dramatic mezzo-soprano
Mood: exultant
Voice: short, dramatic phrases; one long cresc. from beginning to end; ends a♭" on "day"
Piano: chordal; harmonic progression unusual and somewhat

illogical; driving dotted-8th/16th triplet pattern repeated throughout; big sound
Diff: pitches; ensemble
Uses: excellent song for big voice; program ender; good final song for a Dickinson group

864. THIRTY-FOUR SONGS ON POEMS OF EMILY DICKINSON. Vol. I (cmp1930s & 1940s) & Vol. II (cmp1941–1949). Boosey & Hawkes, 1983. Separate entries by opus and/or title below.

VOL. I

A. OPUS 101 (Vol. I). Traditional keys; c'–a"; Tess-M-mH; 4/4, mostly slow tempos; 9pp; Diff-V/m-md, P/me-d.
For: medium voice; (c.) also for high voice (bigger voice); (d.) also for med. high voice
Mood: religious (a. & b.); dramatic (b. & c.); doleful (d.)
Voice: skips and some large leaps; (a.), triplets, dotted rhythms, syncopation; (b.) & (d.), many short phrases; chromaticism, esp. in (d.); sustained high notes in (c.) & (d.)
Piano: chordal; highly chromatic; (a.), triplets in inner voices; (c.), triplets combined with dotted-note figures and some rapid 9- & 10-note scale passages; (c.), is the most difficult; wide piano range; short postlude
Diff: chromaticism and reading accidentals; (c.), somewhat ungrateful vocal line
Uses: probably not enough variety to perform as a group; songs from this opus can combine with others in the two vols.; (a.) sounds like Victorian church style; Wagnerian harmonic influence overblows the poem; (c.), group ender, if the Victorian style is desirable

    a. *A Savior!* (Op. 101, No. 1). Fmaj; c'–f"; Tess-M; 4/4, Slowly; 2pp; Diff-V/m, P/me.
    b. *Unto Me* (Op. 101, No. 2). Cmaj; c'–f"; Tess-M; 4/4, Slowly; 2pp; Diff-V/m, P/m.
    c. *As If the Sea* (Op. 101, No.3). Fmaj; f'–a"; Tess-mH; 4/4, With dash and sweep; 3pp; Diff-V/md, P/d.
    d. *Good Morning, Midnight!* (Op. 101, No. 4). E♭min; d♭'–g♭"; Tess-M; 4/4, Slowly; 2pp; Diff-V/m, P/m.

B. OPUS 105 (Vol. I). Mostly major keys; b–g"; Tess-L-mH; traditional meters; various tempos; 30pp; Diff-V/e-md, P/e-md.
For: medium voice (a., b., c., d., f., h.); medium-low voice (e. & l.); low voice (g.); medium-high voice (j. & k.)
Mood: various moods (see titles)
Voice: many skips that outline chords combined with stepwise movement; chromatic progressions; (c.), large skips; (e.) & (j.) (first stanza), narrow-ranged melody; many dotted rhythms and repetitive rhythm patterns; syncopation; some polyrhythms against piano (2 vs. 3 & 4 vs. 3); (l.), speech-like rhythms; generally syllabic; (i.), some long high tones near end; (j.) needs easy g" and f♯" (not sustained)
Piano: block- and broken-chord figures, often with repeated rhythmic motif; (f.), constant 8th-note motion; (j.) &

(k.), constant 16th-note motion; highly chromatic; text-painting includes bird motif (c.), sea waves (e.), buzzing bee (j.); (i., j., & k.) feature 2 vs. 3; generally outlines or doubles vocal line (except (g.) and parts of a., b., & i.); noticeable absence of "lude" material; (i.) has 4-meas. prelude and 2 short interludes; (j.) has 6-meas. postlude

Diff: many accidentals for both performers; interpretation of some of the poems (d. & h.)

Uses: not meant to be a performance group; choose songs from this and the other opuses to make various groups; best and most appealing songs in the opus seem to be (b., c., d., g., i., j., k., & l.); (b.), an effective descriptive song–good in a group of songs about death or in other Dickinson groups; (d.), also a beautiful song about death; (e., g. & l.), effective short songs; poem of (e.) also set by Isadore Freed (see "Chartless"); (f.), good group or program ender; (k.), good song for young singer who can project sweetness and innocence; good teaching songs

a. ***I'll Tell You How the Sun Rose*** (Op. 105, No. 1). E♭maj; e♭'–e♭"; Tess-M; 4/4, Buoyant and elastic; 2pp; Diff-V/me, P/me; playful.

b. ***Safe in Their Alabaster Chambers*** (Op. 105, No. 2). E♭min; e♭'–e"; Tess-M; 6/8, Slowly; 3pp; Diff-V/m, P/m; timeless and haunting. [**Rec:** D#51]

c. ***The Sabbath*** (Op. 105, No.3). E♭maj; b–e♭"; Tess-M; 4/4, Moderately; 3pp; Diff-V/me, P/m; conversational; whimsical. [**Rec:** D#3]

d. ***These Saw Vision*** (Op. 105, No. 4). Cmaj; c'–e"; Tess-mL; 2/2, Slowly; 2pp; Diff-V/me, P/e; loving, quiet grief.

e. ***I Never Saw a Moor*** (Op. 105, No.5). Cmaj; b–d♭"; Tess-mL; 4/4, Very slowly; 1p; Diff-V/e, P/m; affirmation.

f. ***The Little Tippler*** (Op. 105, No.6). D♭maj; d♯'–f"; Tess-M; 12/8, With motion; 3pp; Diff-V/m, P/md; exuberance.

g. ***Aristocracy*** (Op. 105, No. 7). Cmaj; b–c"; Tess-L; 4/4, Slowly; 1p; Diff-V/e, P/e; sweetly matter-of-fact. [**Rec:** D#3]

h. ***The Test*** (Op. 105, No. 8). Modulating (Amin–D♭maj); e♭'–e"; Tess-M; 4/4, Slowly; 2pp; Diff-V/m, P/m; intense.

i. ***Summer's Armies*** (Op. 105, No. 9). D♭maj; c♯'–g♭"; Tess-M; 6/8, Slowly and smoothly; 6pp; Diff-V/md, P/md; descriptive; intense with dramatic ending. [**Rec:** D#51]

j. ***The Level Bee*** (Op. 105, No. 10). Cmaj; c'–g"; Tess-M; 6/8, With motion; 4pp; Diff-V/m, P/md; descriptive and philosophical. [**Rec:** D#51]

k. ***With a Flower*** (Op. 105, No. 11). Fmaj; f'–f"; Tess-mH; 6/8, Simply, with motion; 2pp; Diff-V/m, P/m; delicate.

l. ***Presentiment*** (Op. 105, No. 12). X; b–d"; Tess-mL; 4/4, Very slowly; 1p; Diff-V/me, P/me; foreboding. [**Rec:** D#51]

VOL. II

C.   I HAD NO TIME TO HATE (Vol. II). Cmin-maj; b–d"; Tess-mL; 4/4, Very slowly; 1p; Diff-V/me, P/me.

For: any medium or low voice

Mood: subdued and introspective

Voice: stepwise motion and small skips; dotted rhythms; syllabic

Piano: block chords; many accidentals; outlines vocal melody

Diff: none for a mature singer

Uses: mature subject; a striking song in its simplicity; group with other songs from these 2 vols.

D.   OPUS 107 (Vol. II). Traditional keys; c'–b♭♭"; Tess-M-mH; traditional meters; varied tempos with fluctuations; 12pp; Diff-V/m, P/m-md.

For: soprano; mezzo-soprano seems best

Mood: songs of life, death, nature; dramatic mood predominates

Voice: stepwise motion and skips along chordal lines; (d.), quite chromatic; dotted rhythms and syncopation; syllabic; b♭♭" sustained 2 meas.

Piano: block- and broken-chord patterning; many accidentals; some polyrhythms; some chromatic scales in (b.) & (c.); (a.) does not double vocal line; other songs either double or outline vocal line

Diff: some rhythms and dynamics; wide tessitura in (c.)

Uses: can be used as a group, or excerpt some of this opus to combine with other songs from the 2 vols.; (d.) could be program ender

a. ***On This Long Storm*** (Op. 107, No. 1). Gmin; d'–f"; 4/4, Slowly; 2pp.

b. ***Tie the Strings to My Life*** (Op. 107, No. 2). Gmaj; d'–g"; 12/8, With agitation; 4pp. [**Rec:** D#51]

c. ***On This Wondrous Sea*** (Op. 107, No.3). D♭maj; c'–b♭♭"; 6/8, Slowly; 3pp.

d. ***Blazing in Gold*** (Op. 107, No. 4). D♭maj; d♭'–a♭"; 6/8, 12/8, Rather fast (with several fluctuations); 3pp.

E.   OPUS 108 (Vol. II). Traditional keys; b♯–g♯"; Tess-M; traditional meters; slow to moderate tempos; 19pp; Diff-V/m, P/m-md.

For: medium voice (mezzo-soprano seems best); soprano

Mood: often child-like views of nature, death, and eternity; humorous touches in (i.) & (j.); some nostalgia

Voice: stepwise motion and skips along chord lines; (d.) & (i.), more disjunct; many accidentals; dotted rhythms and syncopation; some speech-like rhythms; duplet and triplet subdivisions of beat in (j.); phrases somewhat fragmented in (c.) & (h.); syllabic; some long high notes (g" 4 beats and g♯" 2+ beats)

Piano: block- and broken-chord patterning predominate; many accidentals; (e.), chromatic scale patterning; sea and brook sound effects in 8th- & 16th-note duplets and triplets; (h.), some "frog" imagery; (i.), "mouse-like'" musical imagery; (j.), opens with 2-meas. prelude of chromatic scales in 32nds; generally either outlines or doubles vocal line; little prelude, interlude, or postlude material

Diff: rhythms; reading accidentals; melodic intervals in (d.) & (j.); ensemble, (e., h., i., & j.)

Uses: does not cohere as a single group; excerpt songs from this opus to combine with other songs in the two vols.

a. *Heart, We Will Forget Him!* (Op. 108, No. 1).
E♭min; e♭'–e♭"; 4/4, Slowly (with fluctuations);
1p.

b. *The Butterfly* (Op. 108, No. 2). Dmaj; d'–e♭"; 2/4,
Rather slowly (with fluctuations); 2pp.

c. *I Never Felt at Home Below* (Op. 108, No.3).
Cmin; c'–g"; 4/4, Moderately (with fluctuations);
3pp.

d. *And I'm a Rose!* (Op. 108, No. 4). Emaj; d♯'–g♯";
2/4, Moderately; 1p.

e. *The Sea Said "Come" to the Brook* (Op. 108,
No.5). Amaj; b♯–g"; 3/4, Slowly; 2pp.

f. *We Should Not Mind So Small a Flower* (Op. 108,
No.6). Cmaj; e'–e"; 2/4, Slowly, simply; 2pp.

g. *Ample Make This Bed* (Op. 108, No. 7). E♭min;
e'–f"; 12/8, Very slowly; 1p. [**Rec:** D#51]

h. *I'm Nobody! Who Are You?* (Op. 108, No. 8).
B♭maj-min; d'–e♭"; 6/8, Very moderately; 2pp.

i. *Papa Above!* (Op. 108, No. 9). F♯min; b–f♯"; 2/4,
Slowly; 3pp.

j. *Dropped into the Ether Acre* (Op. 108, No. 10).
E♭min; c'–g♭"; 4/4, 6/4, Very slowly; 2pp.

F. **OPUS 112** (Vol. II). Traditional keys; c♭'–g";
Tess-mH; traditional meters; 8pp; Diff-V/m-md, P/md.
For: soprano–dramatic or lyric with sizeable sound
Mood: dramatic (a. & c.) and lyric (b.)
Voice: (a.) & (b.), predominantly conjunct with many
accidentals; (c.), many skips; many dotted rhythms;
syncopation; each song ends on a high note (g", e♭",
and f♯"); syllabic
Piano: broken-chord patterning; both duplet and triplet
subdivisions of beat; (c.) includes chromatic scales,
some in 8ve 16th notes; passages for r.h. in fast parallel
4ths; some doubling of vocal line; little prelude,
interlude, or postlude material
Diff: ensemble; polyrhythms in all songs–2 vs. 3, 4 vs. 3, &
4 vs. 6
Uses: could be an effective group for a sizeable voice with
control of soft as well as louder dynamics; can also
excerpt with other songs from these two vols; cf. (b.)
with setting by Vincent Persichetti

a. *Wild Nights! Wild Nights!* (Op. 112, No. 1).
E♭min-maj; c♭'–g"; 2/4, Fast; 2pp. [**Rec:** D#70]

b. *The Grass So Little Has to Do* (Op. 112, No. 2).
E♭maj; d'–g"; 4/4, Moderately fast; 3pp. [**Rec:**
D#51]

c. *An Awful Tempest Mashed the Air* (Op. 112,
No.3). Dmin-maj; c♯'–f♯"; 4/4, Stormy; 3pp.

865. **THE WILD FLOWER'S SONG** (William Blake).
Church, 1920. B♭maj; f'–e"; Tess-M; 3/4, Simply; 4pp;
Diff-V/m, P/m.
For: any voice
Mood: lyrical; despair
Voice: stepwise and leaps on chord lines; 2–3-note slurs;
dotted rhythms
Piano: chordal–block and broken; thin texture; many
accidentals; incidental doubling of vocal line
Uses: usable in an American group

FAX, MARK
(b. Baltimore, MD, 1911; d. Washington, DC, 1974)

866. **LOVE** (from *Five Black Songs*) (Jo Ann Harris). [6].
X, G-centered; d'–f"; Tess-M; 2/2, 5/4, 3/2, 4/2,
Leisurely, freely (♩ = 50); 3pp; Diff-V/me, P/me.
For: any voice except extremely low
Mood: lyrical love song
Voice: phrases somewhat fragmented by rests; emphasizes
m3rds e'–g' and a'–c"; rather static; almost recit.-like
Piano: chordal texture; fragmented by rests; a few grace notes
Uses: recital possibilities

FENNIMORE, JOSEPH
(b. New York, NY, 1940)

[See Appendix for *Berlitz: Introduction to French*]

867. **INFANT JOY** (William Blake). Fennimore-Hibberd
Publishing, 1977 (Classical Vocal Reprints). cmp1977.
C♯/D♭; d'–g♭"; Tess-M; 4/4, 2/4, Gentle, Childlike;
3pp(MS); Diff-V/md, P/d.
For: mezzo-soprano; soprano
Mood: delicate, joyful; dialogue
Voice: "infant" lines marked "no vibrato"; narrator lines
marked "naturale"; stepwise movement predominates; a
few skips; many accidentals; fragmented phrases;
speech-like rhythms
Piano: mostly in middle register and above; somewhat linear;
some broken-chord patterns; many accidentals; many
articulations; quarter-note motion progresses through
8ths to 16th-note patterns; shared patterns between
hands difficult to read; flutter pedal effects; does not
double vocal line but many pitches are in texture
Diff: ensemble; some rhythms; piano part; differentiating the
two voices
Uses: quiet recital song for a Fennimore group or for a
mixed-composer group of Blake poems
Rec: D#176

868. **INSCAPE.** For Medium High Voice and Piano.
Selected Poems of Gerard Manley Hopkins.
Fennimore-Hibberd Publishing Co., 1990 (Classical
Vocal Reprints). cmp1963–1977. Tonal, some
bitonality and modal touches; b♭–a"; Tess-mH, wide;
regular meters with some changes; varied tempos; 35pp
(MS); Diff-V/m-dd, P/m-dd.
For: mezzo-soprano; soprano; mature, sizeable voice
Mood: philosophic; nostalgic, despairing, death, nature (see
composer's tempo indications)
Voice: difficult intervals in most songs; various rhythmic
divisions of measures create polyrhythms with piano;
speech-like passages; syncopation; chromaticism; large
dynamic range; several long high notes
Piano: much broken-chord/arpeggiated patterning, often in
rapid 32nds; repeated chords (some grouped in five
16ths); some counterpoint; staccato, trills, tremolo and
tremolo-like effects; many register changes, some quick
large reaches in both hands; many accidentals; little
doubling of vocal line; preludes and postludes; 1–6
meas. interludes in some songs; many notes

Diff: requires excellent singer and pianist with fleet fingers; difficulties include pitches, rhythms, ensemble, and understanding the poetry

Uses: recital group, or excerpt songs; (a.) a possible student song; cf. Rorem "Spring and Fall"

Rec: D#176

   a. *Spring and Fall: To a Young Child.* Cmaj/Amin/modal; d'–f"; Tess-mH; 3/4, Calm, contemplative (♩ = c.104); 3pp.

   b. *The Times Are Nightfall.* b–f"; Tess-wide; 3/4, 4/4, 2/4, Hushed, with an inner despair (♩ = c.88); 2+pp.

   c. *Spring and Death.* Unsettled; b♭–f"; Tess-wide; 6/8, 3/4, 4/4, 9/8, 2/4, Mysterious (♪ = c.126); 9+pp.

   d. *Dry Were Her Sad Eyes.* E♭-centered; d'–g"; Tess-mH; 3/4, 2/4, Quietly, calmly, sadly (♩ = c.76); 3pp.

   e. *The Windhover: To Christ Our Lord.* Unsettled; e'–a"; Tess-H; 3/4, 3/8, 2/4, 4/4, Ecstatic (♩ = c.72); 7pp.

   f. *A Windy Day in Summer.* E-centered; e'–g"; Tess-mH; 3/8, Breezy, easy, light (♪ = c.152); 3+pp.

   g. *No Worst, There Is None.* Unsettled; b♭–g♯"; Tess-wide; 3/4, Despairing, bitter (♩ = c.63); 7pp.

869. **MARY WEEPS FOR HER CHILD** (Anon., early 16th century) for Medium-High Voice and Piano. Fennimore-Hibberd Publishing Co., 1990 (Classical Vocal Reprints). cmp1976. C♯min; c♯'–g♯"; Tess-wide; 3/4 with changes, ♩ = c.58; somewhat sad, but with fervor–♩ = 92; 4+pp(MS); Diff-V/md, P/m.

For: soprano; tenor

Mood: somewhat sad; four speakers: narrator, Mary, Joseph, Child Jesus

Voice: fairly conjunct; some leaps of 6th & 7th; many accidentals; some speech-like rhythms, triple rhythms, triplets, syncopation; many unaccomp. meas.

Piano: block chords; 16th-note counterpoint; many accidentals; both hands in bass clef for most of song; does not double vocal line

Diff: meter changes; 16th-century English words (trans. given for some in score; check pronunciations); unaccomp. sections for some singers; tessitura (singer should be comfortable with "ee" vowels on g♯")

Uses: text well set; good recital song

Rec: D#176

870. **MY HEART** (Sappho). Fennimore-Hibberd Publishing Co., 1990 (Classical Vocal Reprints). cmp1984. X; b–a"; Tess-mH; 3/4, 4/4, 2/4, Quasi parlando (♩ = c.58); 5pp (MS); Diff-V/d, P/d.

For: tenor; soprano; some mezzo-sopranos

Mood: love song

Voice: speech-like rhythms; many accidentals; difficult intervals; several melismas; opt. spoken line

Piano: textural variety; some repeated patterning in 16th notes; trills, rolled chords, register changes, staccato for color effects; r.h. crosses over left for 5 meas.; does not double vocal line

Diff: rhythms; intervals; ensemble; facsimile not hard to read

Uses: recital piece for advanced performers

Rec: D#176

871. **SCARLATTI** (Herbert Martin). Fennimore-Hibberd Publishing, n.d. (Classical Vocal Reprints) cmp1977. A-centered, unsettled; f♯'–f"; Tess-M; 6/8, 3/8, ♩. = 112; 4pp(MS); Diff-V/md, P/md.

For: mezzo-soprano; soprano; baritone; tenor (sonority seems best for woman's voice)

Mood: lost love as inspiration for art; constant motion and energy

Voice: stepwise and small skips; various subdivisions of measures; includes hemiola; mostly syllabic

Piano: independent of vocal line; mostly 2–3-voice texture; patterned; much staccato; cross-accents; one 6-meas. legato section; both hands in treble clef mostly; requires good facility in perpetual motion; 8-meas. prelude, 6-meas. postlude

Diff: changing rhythms in vocal line create possible ensemble difficulty; pianist controls this song

Uses: in any group of American songs; encore; group ender

872. **THE SNOW GREW OUT OF THE SKY LAST NIGHT** (Herbert Woodward Martin). Fennimore-Hibberd Publishing, 1990 (Classical Vocal Reprints). cmp1976. Begins and ends on F–transitory; d'–a♭"; Tess-mH; 3/4, 2/4, 4/4, 5/8, 7/8, 3/8, ♩ = 72, with wonder and awe; 5pp(MS); Diff-V/dd, P/dd.

For: soprano; tenor

Mood: lyrical nature description

Voice: speech-like rhythms; syncopation; many accidentals; some difficult intervals in context; mostly syllabic

Piano: some patterned and unpatterned sections; many passages in 16ths & 32nds, some grouped in 7's; staccato "raindrop" pattern in triplet 16ths; many accidentals; register changes; does not double vocal line; 4-meas. prelude, 5-meas. interlude

Diff: rhythms; melodic intervals; ensemble; pitch at some entrances

Uses: for experienced performers with excellent musicianship and technique

Rec: D#176

873. **WINTER LOVE** (Herbert Woodward Martin). Fennimore Hibberd Publishing, 1990. cmp1976. Begins Amin–transitory; d♯'–e"; Tess-M; 3/4, 2/4, ♩ = c.138, light, bright, and cheerful; 2+pp(MS); Diff-V/m, P/m.

For: medium voices; baritone seems best

Mood: lighthearted farewell to winter and winter love

Voice: repetitive melody with meter changes; many accidentals; syllabic; repetitious words

Piano: mostly 2–3-voice texture, 8th-note motion; considerable doubling of vocal line

Diff: possibly changing meters

Uses: nice student song; lacks complication, but introduces some aspects of 20th-century writing; recital material

Rec: D#176

FERKO, FRANK
(b. Barberton, OH, 1950)

[See Appendix for songs with French texts]

874. FOR MY BROTHER: REPORTED MISSING IN ACTION, 1943 (Thomas Merton). For Baritone and Piano. E. C. Schirmer, 2000. cmp1981. X; c–a' (ten. clef); Tess-M; 4/4, 3/4, Moderately slow; 7min; Diff-V/m, P/m.

For: lyric baritone; dramatic tenor
Mood: grief; faith
Voice: lyrical, chant-like line; mostly flowing 8th-note motion; many repeated notes; conjunct; a few skips of 3rd & 4th; leaps of 7th, 2 to a' ("gently")
Piano: open texture; dirge-like bass line in 8ves low on the keyboard; r.h. melody sometimes doubles vocal line; some dissonant and cluster chords; some 3-stave scoring; mostly soft dynamics; accidentals
Diff: some pitches; finding the appropriate chant-like approach
Uses: a powerful song; use in group of elegies or songs about war experiences; needs mature singer

FINE, IRVING
(b. Boston, MA, 1914; d. Boston, MA, 1962)

875. CHILDHOOD FABLES FOR GROWNUPS, Set 1 (Gertrude Norman). Boosey & Hawkes, 1955, 1958. Traditional keys; a–f"; Tess-M; regular meters with some changes; varied tempos; 17pp; Diff-V/md, P/md.

For: contralto; mezzo-soprano; large voice best
Mood: humorous declamation; animal character sketches
Voice: quite disjunct in two songs, conjunct in one, mixed in one; word rhythms; fragmented phrases; occasional difficult pitches; fast articulation
Piano: patterned; 8ves, broken-chord patterns, repeated chords; fast tempos in 3 of 4; (c.) lyrical and melodic; good rhythmic sense required; many wide register changes on keyboard
Diff: difficulties mainly in the learning stage; singer should have good chest voice and strong tones at top of staff, as well as full middle voice; large leaps in vocal line can be difficult
Uses: excellent group for the right singer; flair for comedy needed; good program ender
Rec: D#s 34, 177

    a. *Polaroli.* Dmaj; a–d"; 4/4 with changes, Moderato; 4pp. [**Rec:** D#59]
    b. *Tigeroo.* Dmin; b♭'–f"; 2/4 with changes, Allegro moderato; 4pp. [**Rec:** D#44]
    c. *Lenny the Leopard.* C–Emin; c'–e♭"; 4/4 with changes, Andante; 4pp. [**Rec:** D#44]
    d. *The Frog and the Snake.* Dmaj; d'–e♭"; 2/4, 3/4, Allegro vivace; 5pp. [**Rec:** D#59]

876. CHILDHOOD FABLES FOR GROWNUPS, Set 2 (Two Arias for Medium Voice and Piano) (Gertrude Norman). Boosey & Hawkes, 1959. Tonal; b♭–f"; Tess-M-mH; traditional meters with changes; 18pp; Diff-V/md, P/md.

For: mezzo-soprano; possibly baritone or contralto
Mood: humorous animal character sketches
Voice: (a.), many skips and rhythmic complications (syncopation and various subdivisions of beat); (b.),

many chant-like passages and sections featuring movement by half-step, long f" dimin.–cresc.; ends on 4-meas. d♯"; predominantly syllabic, a few melismas
Piano: (a.), humorous "wiggly" effects (trills, tremolo, rapid triplets); (b.), special pedal effects, much staccato, many scale passages; broken- and repeated-chord patterning; numerous accidentals; each song has ca.24 meas. solo material for piano (prelude, interludes).
Diff: possibly register changes, esp. in (b.); getting the subtleties and complexities of this score exactly right for the best comic and musical effects
Uses: can stand alone or be combined with one or two songs from Set 1 for a longer group; program ender; talent for comedy needed; although composer calls these "arias," they fall within the definition of "art songs"
Rec: D#177

    a. *Two Worms.* A♭maj; d'–f"; 6/8 with changes, Andante–Allegretto; 8pp. [**Rec:** D#44]
    b. *The Duck and the Yak.* A-minorish; b♭–f"; 4/4 with changes, Allegro–Allegro vivace; 10pp. [**Rec:** D#44]

877. MUTABILITY. Six Songs based on Poems by Irene Orgel for Mezzo-Soprano and Piano. Mills Music, 1959. (Written with Eunice Alberts, contralto, in mind.) Romantic harmonies with a rather dissonant halo; g–g♭"; Tess-cs; regular and irregular changing meters; varied tempos; 12min; Diff-V/d, P/d.

For: contralto; mezzo-soprano
Mood: dramatic; searching; philosophical; mutability of life
Voice: difficult intervals; many large leaps; accidentals; one long melisma; intricate speech rhythms; many low passages
Piano: linear; many accidentals; some speech rhythms in accomp.; rhythmic complexity; pianist should be accustomed to reading modern score
Diff: many, but probably mostly in the learning stage; ensemble will require work
Uses: effective work for philosophically inclined mature singer
Rec: D#178

    a. *I Have Heard the Hoofbeats of Happiness.* a–f♯"; 2/4, Allegro; 2pp.
    b. *My Father.* b♭–e♭"; 3/4, Andante; 2pp. [**Rec:** D#58]
    c. *The Weed.* b♭–g♭"; 4/4 with changes, Adagio; 4pp.
    d. *Peregrine.* g–e"; 6/8 with changes, Allegro; 4pp.
    e. *Jubilation.* b♭–f"; 4/8 with changes, Andante; 4pp.
    f. *Now God Be Thanked for Mutability.* a–e♭"; 4/4 with changes, Adagio; 3pp.

878. TWO SONGS FROM DOÑA ROSITA (Federico García Lorca, trans. James Graham-Lujan and Richard L. O'Connell–English settings). Ed. Leo Smit. Joclem Music Publishing, 1998 (Boosey & Hawkes). cmp1943. Tonal/Modal; e'–e"; Tess-M; regular meters; moderate tempos; 5+min; Diff-V/e-me, P/m.

For: medium voices; some high voices
Mood: melancholy
Voice: dotted rhythms; some long phrases

Piano: dance-like rhythms; accidentals; staccato and legato; doubles vocal line in (b.)
Diff: a few long phrases
Uses: a nice pair of songs; Spanish text not given

    a. *Because I Caught a Glimpse of You.* Dmin; e'–e"; Tess-M; 3/4, Moderately (♩= c.96-100); 2+min.
    b. *Song of the Flowers.* Phrygian on A; e'–e"; Tess-M; 2/4, 4/4, Allegretto (♩= c.92); 3+min.

FINK, MICHAEL
(b. Long Beach, CA, 1939)

879. RAIN COMES DOWN (Edna St. Vincent Millay). E. C. Schirmer, 1969. cmp1963. X; d♯'–f"; Tess-M; 2/2, 3/2, ♩= 48; 3min; Diff-V/md, P/m.
For: soprano specified
Mood: somber; intense; quiet
Voice: many skips; portions of phrases separated; some triplets
Piano: chordal; wide-spread sonority; grace notes; various registers; many accidentals; delicate; does not double vocal line
Diff: ensemble; pitches
Uses: effective mood piece

880. WHAT LIPS MY LIPS HAVE KISSED (Edna St. Vincent Millay). E. C. Schirmer, 1963. Cmp1959. F-centered; e♭'–b♭"(g"); Tess-mH; 4/4, 2/4, Poco adagio; 2+min; Diff-V/md, P/m.
For: soprano specified, but not a light voice
Mood: introspective; nostalgic; somber
Voice: many skips; several long-ranged phrases; many accidentals; somewhat declamatory
Piano: linear-chordal combination; many accidentals; repetitive rhythmic unit; phrase endings do not coincide with voice phrasing; does not double vocal line
Diff: ensemble; dynamic control

FINNEY, ROSS LEE
(b. Wells, MN, 1906; d. Carmel, CA, 1997)

881. CHAMBER MUSIC (James Joyce). High Voice and Piano. Cycle. C. F. Peters, 1985. cmp1952. Tonal with traditional key sigs. (keys and modes often obscured with delicate dissonance); a(c')–a"; Tess-mH-M; traditional meters with changes; wide variety of tempos; 1hr; Diff-V/md-d, P/me-d.
For: high voice; texts better for lyric tenor; music fits soprano voice well also
Mood: cycle of love: (a.–c.) set the scene; (d. & e.) crystallize a man-woman relationship; (f.–m.) are courting songs of spring and virginity; (n.–p.) are passionate songs of physical love (end of first part); second part deals with disillusionment and the bitterness of death of love, ending in loneliness and despair
Voice: conjunct melodic lines with some accidentals; rhythmically challenging in traditional terms; mostly syllabic settings; vocally grateful; expressive of texts
Piano: good balance of linear and chordal; generally thin textures; a few dramatic songs with more dense

textures; tonal harmonies; most dissonances created by use of M & m2nds; expressive of texts
Diff: some 2 vs. 3; some very low notes in vocal line (although upper 8ve alternatives given); a few awkward spots for pianist; endurance for both singer and pianist; interpretation needs maturity and long preparation
Uses: excellent long work (a complete recital program) for mature singer whose voice reflects every emotional nuance of texts and who has a special affinity for James Joyce; pianist also must have sensitivity to texts and command of many colors
Rec: D#179

    a. *I. Strings in the earth and air.* Emaj; e'–f♯"; 3/4, 4/4, Gently; 2pp.
    b. *II. The twilight turns from amethyst.* G♯min-Amin; a(d')–f♯"; 4/4, 5/4, Tranquilly; 3pp.
    c. *III. As that hour when all things have repose.* Emaj; b(d')–g"; 2/4, Mysteriously; 4pp.
    d. *IV. When the shy star goes forth in heaven.* Cmaj; d'–g"; 4/4, With madrigalesque restraint; 3pp.
    e. *V. Lean out of the window, Goldenhair.* Quartal; e'–g"; 3/8, Joyously; 3pp.
    f. *VI. I would in that sweet bosom be.* Bmin; d'–g"; 6/8, 9/8, Reflectively; 3pp.
    g. *VII. My love is in a light attire.* F♯-centered; f♯'–f♯"; 6/8, Very lightly; 3pp.
    h. *VIII. Who goes amid the green wood.* A-centered; c♯'(d')–f♯"; 6/8, 9/8, With simplicity; 3pp.
    i. *IX. Winds of May, that dance on the sea.* Bmin; d'–a♭"; 3/4, Lightly and capriciously; 3pp.
    j. *X. Bright cap and streamers.* Emaj; e'–e"; 3/4, A little stiffly; 3pp.
    k. *XI. Bid adieu, adieu, adieu.* F♯min; f♯'–f♯"; 6/8, 9/8, Persuasively; 3pp.
    l. *XII. What counsel has the hooded moon.* Dorian; c'–f"; 4/4, 6/8, 9/8, Languidly argumentative; 3pp.
    m. *XIII. Go seek her out all courteously.* Cmaj; e'–g"; 6/8, Buoyantly; 3pp.
    n. *XIV. My dove, my beautiful one.* Cmin-D♭min; b♭(c')–f"; 4/4, Sensuously; 2pp.
    o. *XV. From dewy dreams, my soul, arise.* X-Emaj; b(c')–f"; 4/4, 3/4, From deep exhaustion; 2pp.
    p. *XVI. O cool is the valley now.* Emin; c'–e"; 3/4, 2/4, 4/4, Relaxed; 2pp.
    q. *XVII. Because your voice was at my side.* Gmaj; d'–g"; 2/4, With tension; 1p.
    r. *XVIII. O sweetheart, hear you your lover's tale.* Gmaj-Emin; d'–f"; 6/8, 9/8, With shallow sentiment; 2pp.
    s. *XIX. Be not sad because all men . . .* Emin-Gmaj; b(d')–g"; 4/4, Confused; 1p.
    t. *XX. In the dark pinewood I would we lay.* X, chromatic; b♭(c')–f"; 4/4, With nostalgic desire; 2pp.
    u. *XXI. He who hath glory lost.* E-centered; d'–f"; 3/8, With struggle; 2pp.
    v. *XXII. Of that so sweet imprisonment.* Gmaj; d'–g"; 4/4, 3/2, Calmly; 2pp.
    w. *XXIII. This heart that flutters near my heart.* F♯min; f♯'–f♯"; 4/4, With tender sadness; 2pp.
    x. *XXIV. Silently she's combing.* C♯maj; d♯'–f♯";

y. *XXV. Lightly come or lightly go.* Emaj; e'–g"; 3/8, Very lightly; 3pp.

z. *XXVI. Thou leavest to the shell of night.* Bmaj; d'–g"; 5/4, 3/4, 7/8, 4/4, Lyric becoming dramatic; 2pp.

aa. *XXVII. Though I thy Mithridates were.* Emin; e'–g"; 3/8, Verbosely; 3pp.

bb. *XXVIII. Gentle lady, do not sing sad songs . . .* Amin; d'–g"; 3/4, Wearily; 2pp.

cc. *XXIX. Dear heart, why will you use me so?* Gmaj-min; d'–a"; 3/4, 4/4, Complainingly; 3pp.

dd. *XXX. Love came to us in time gone by.* Emaj; b(e')–f"; 4/4, With nostalgia; 2pp.

ee. *XXXI. O, it was out by Donnycarney.* Modal; d'–g"; 6/8, 9/8, Reminiscently; 2pp.

ff. *XXXII. Rain has fallen . . .* Amin; d'–g"; 4/4, Lonely; 2pp.

gg. *XXXIII. Now, o now, in this brown land.* Amin; c♯'–f"; 4/4, Desolately; 4pp.

hh. *XXXIV. Sleep now . . .* A-centered; c♯'–g"; 4/4, Tormented; 4pp.

ii. *XXXV. All day I hear the noise of waters.* Modal; a(d')–a♭"; 2/2, 3/2, Dolorously; 2pp.

jj. *XXXVI. I hear an army . . .* Based on tritone; d'–g♯"; 9/8, 12/8, 6/8, Tempestuously; 6pp.

882. **A CYCLE OF SONGS TO POEMS BY ARCHIBALD MacLEISH.** American Music Edition, 1955. cmp1934. Traditional keys; d'–g"; Tess-M; regular and changing meters; slow tempos predominate; 13min; Diff-V/m-md, P/m.
For: lyric tenor
Mood: lyrical; theme of regeneration
Voice: mostly conjunct with some repeated tones; speech rhythms; occasional chromaticism
Piano: linear; 2–4 voices; 8th-note motion predominates; large reach helpful
Diff: rhythmic groupings; poetry
Uses: beautiful cycle for lyric tenor with mature and sensitive poetic and musical instincts; extreme lyricism predominates; not a program ender

a. *They Seemed to Be Waiting.* Emin; e'–f♯"; 4/4, 3/2, Adagio; 3pp.

b. *Go Secretly.* Emin; e'–g"; 4/4, Largo; 2pp.

c. *The Flowers of the Sea.* Amin; d'–f"; 3/4, 4/4, 2/4, Lento e doloroso; 2pp.

d. *Salute.* Cmaj; e'–g"; 6/8, 3/4, Presto; 4pp.

e. *These, My Ophelia.* Emin; e'–a"; 4/4, 3/4, 5/4, Adagio molto espressivo; 2pp.

883. **POOR RICHARD.** Seven Songs to Words by Benjamin Franklin. G. Schirmer, 1950 (H), L ed. pub. by Independent Music Pub. cmp1946. H & L keys: Traditional keys; e'–a" & c'–f"; Tess-M; regular meters; moderate tempos; 21pp; Diff-V/me, P/m.
For: baritone; tenor
Mood: lyrical; wry; humorous; typical Franklinisms
Voice: conjunct; few skips; easy rhythms; some long tones; a few melismas
Piano: linear; 2–4 voices; contrapuntal; generally 8th-note

motion
Diff: a few rhythmic irregularities between voice and piano
Uses: good cycle for students; not difficult; attractive subject; undergraduate recital material, or a "breather" group for advanced student singing a strenuous program

a. *Epitaph.* Cmin; c'–f"; 6/8, Moderato; 3pp.

b. *Here Skugg Lies.* Gmin; g'–e♭"; 2/4, Moderato; 1p.

c. *Epitaph on a Talkative Old Maid.* Dmin; d'–e♭"; 2/4, Moderato; 3+ pp.

d. *When Mars and Venus.* Emin; e'–d"; 6/8, Andante; 1p.

e. *Drinking Song.* Fmaj; c'–d"; 4/4, Allegro; 5pp. [**Rec:** D#10]

f. *Wedlock, as Old Men Note.* C-Amaj; c♯'–d"; 6/8, Moderato; 3pp. [**Rec:** D#10]

g. *In Praise of Wives.* Fmaj; c'–f"; 6/8, Moderato; 4pp.

884. **THREE LOVE SONGS TO WORDS BY JOHN DONNE.** Valley, 1957. Traditional keys; d'–a"; Tess-M; regular meters, some changing; slow tempos; 7min; Diff-V/m, P/m.
For: lyric tenor
Mood: lyrical; love songs; metaphysical
Voice: supremely lyrical; some leaps; text contains some archaic words and pronunciations
Piano: linear; 2–5-voice texture; generally moving 8th-note patterns; some accidentals
Diff: flawless legato line; clear diction; understanding the poetry
Uses: very lovely cycle; needs exquisite handling and clear, flowing sound; intermediate to advanced singers should find this group useful; quiet group on a program

a. *A Valediction: Of Weeping.* Emin; e'–g"; 2/4, 3/4, ♪ = 80; 2pp.

b. *A Valediction: Forbidding Mourning.* Bmin; e'–f♯"; 4/4, 3/4, ♩ = ca.42 but with freedom; 3pp.

c. *Love's Growth.* Gmaj; d'–a"; 4/4, 5/4, 3/2, ♩ = 54; 3pp.

885. **THREE 17TH CENTURY LYRICS.** Valley, 1948. cmp1936–1938. Traditional keys; b–f♯"; Tess-M; mostly regular meters with some changes; moderate tempos; 6pp; Diff-V/me-m, P/md.
For: tenor best; soprano; mezzo-soprano
Mood: lyrical; philosophical; joyous
Voice: short phrases; many 16ths; some dotted rhythms; some syncopation; duplets in compound meter; some fragmentation of phrases
Piano: linear-chordal combination; syncopation; somewhat disjunct; chromatic
Diff: ensemble; some pitches and rhythms
Uses: good cycle; recital material for competent musician

a. *On the Life of Man* (Henry Vaughan). Bmin; b–f♯"; 4/8, 5/8, 3/8, 2/8, Andante (with a spherical motion; ♪ = c.126); 2pp.

b. *Look How the Floor of Heaven* (William Shakespeare). Emin-Bmin; c♯'–f♯"; 6/8, Andante (with a gentle rolling motion; ♪ = c.152); 2pp.

c. *On May Morning* (John Milton). Emaj; e'–f♯"; 4/4, Larghetto (with movement; ♩ = 76); 2pp.

FISHER, WILLIAMS ARMS
(b. San Francisco, CA, 1861; d. Boston, MA, 1948)

886. **BLOW, BLOW, THOU WINTER WIND** (William Shakespeare). [5, 26]; 1st©1897. H & L keys: E♭maj & Cmaj (orig.); e♭'–g" & c'–e"; Tess-mH; 4/4, Andante–Allegro; 2pp; Diff-V/m, P/me.
For: tenor; baritone
Mood: dramatic; strong; cynical; false
Voice: many skips; 2–6-note slurs; dotted rhythms
Piano: chordal, 4-voice block and some afterbeat; doubles vocal line
Diff: tempo changes; short 16th-note runs
Uses: good for Shakespeare group; group ender

887. **I HEARD A CRY,** Op. 18, No. 1 (Sara Teasdale). [13 (2nd yr.), 53]. cmp1915. H & L keys: Cmaj (orig.) & A♭ maj; e'–a"(g") & c'–f "(e♭"); Tess-mH; 6/4, Moderato ma non troppo; 2pp; Diff-V/m, P/md.
For: all voices except very low
Mood: dramatic; love song
Voice: disjunct; 8ve & 7th leaps; sharp accents
Piano: chordal; chromatic; much independent material; some doubling of vocal line
Diff: 8ve leaps; clear, ringing a"(f ")

888. **SIGH NO MORE, LADIES** (William Shakespeare). [5, 26, 55]. cmp1896. H, M, & L keys: Amin, Gmin, & F♯min (orig.); e'–f", d'–e♭", & c♯'–d"; Tess-mH; 2/4, Con brio; 3pp (with repeat); Diff-V/me, P/me.
For: tenor; baritone; bass
Mood: humorously philosophical
Voice: stepwise and easy skips; much repetition and sequence; 2-note slurs; fast diction
Piano: afterbeat figure with 8ve melody; staccato; much doubling of vocal line
Uses: to encourage lightness and flexibility; in Shakespeare group

889. **UNDER THE ROSE** (Richard H. Stoddard). [13 (1st yr.)]; 1st©1925. H & L keys: Fmaj & Dmaj; c'(e')–g" & a(c♯')–e"; Tess-M; 6/4, Moderato; 2pp; Diff-V/e, P/me.
For: tenor; baritone
Mood: lyrical; love song; rather sentimental
Voice: features phrases ascending in 3rds
Piano: chordal; sustained; some chromaticism; many 7th chords; frequent doubling of vocal line

890. **A WIDOW BIRD SATE MOURNING,** Op. 3, No.1 (Percy Bysshe Shelley). G. Schirmer, 1895. B♭min; b♭–d♭"; Tess-mL-M; 4/4, Moderato; 2pp; Diff-V/m, P/m.
For: contralto; mezzo-soprano
Mood: descriptive; somber; quiet
Voice: skips; some dotted rhythms; 2-note slurs
Piano: chordal; many accidentals; some doubling of vocal line
Diff: good register control
Uses: usable recital song

FISKE, DWIGHT
(b. Providence, RI, 1892(?); d. New York, NY, 1959)

891. **THE BIRD,** Op. 2 (D. L. F.). Ditson, 1917. "To Geraldine Farrar." Dmin; d'–g♭"; Tess-M; 3/4, 6/8, Moderato con moto; 2pp; Diff-V/m, P/m.
For: soprano
Mood: lyrical; descriptive; atmospheric
Voice: floating phrases; speech rhythms; climax on g♭" on "bird"
Piano: chordal; some ornamentation; sectional
Uses: usable for young singer; needs floating, lyric sound

FLAGELLO, NICOLAS
(b. New York, NY, 1928; d. New Rochelle, NY, 1994)

892. **SONGS FROM WILLIAM BLAKE'S *AN ISLAND IN THE MOON.*** General, 1965. Pub. separately (6). cmp1964. Mostly traditional keys with altered structures; b–b♭"; Tess-mL, M, mH: regular and irregular changing meters; varied tempos; 30 pp; Diff-V/m-md, P/m-d.
For: tenor
Mood: lyrical; sad; humorous; ghostly; love song
Voice: skips and leaps; chromaticism; some speech rhythms
Piano: mostly chordal; various figurations; large leaps; chromaticism; considerable solo work; some difficult rhythms
Diff: some pitches; some rhythms
Uses: good songs; interesting group for recital; more suitable for advanced students
Rec: D#180

a. *As I Walked Forth.* Amaj-min; f♯'–f♯"; Tess-mL; 6/8, 9/8, Andantino–Lento; 3pp. [**Rec:** D#32]
b. *This Frog He Would A-Wooing Ride.* Gmin; d'–g"; Tess-M; 4/4, 5/4, 7/4, Allegretto; 5pp.
c. *O Father, O Father.* F♯min; c♯'–a"; Tess-M-mH; 4/4, 6/4, Allegro giusto; 5pp.
d. *Good English Hospitality.* Amaj; d'–a"; Tess-M; 4/4, 5/4, 6/4, Allegro giocoso; 7pp. [**Rec:** D#32]
e. *Leave, O Leave Me to My Sorrows.* X; b–g"; Tess-mL; 3/4, 4/4, 2/4, 5/4, Andante–Lento; 3pp. [**Rec:** D#32]
f. *Dr. Clash and Signor Falalasole.* Gmin-Cmaj; d'–b♭"; Tess-M; 3/4 with changes, Allegro energico; 7pp.

FLANAGAN, WILLIAM
(b. Detroit, MI, 1926; d. New York, NY, 1969)

[See also D#50; no titles given]

893. **THE DUGOUT** (Siegfried Sassoon). Peer International, 1953. cmp1946. D♭-centered; e♭'–g"; Tess-M; 5/8, 6/8, 3/8, 7/8, Andante con moto; 1+min; Diff-V/m, P/m.
For: tenor; soprano
Mood: subdued; foreshadowing of death
Voice: stepwise and chord-member skips; 2–3-note slurs;

many accidentals

Piano: broken-chord patterning; many accidentals; various registers

Diff: irregular meter

Uses: effective within appropriate group; quiet

894. **GO AND CATCH A FALLING STAR** (John Donne). Peer International, 1954. cmp1949. D♭maj; e'–b♭"; Tess-H; 4/4, 3/4, 5/4, Moderato; 1min; Diff-V/d, P/md.

For: tenor

Mood: cynical

Voice: many leaps; 2–3-note slurs; duplets, triplets, and quadruplets

Piano: chordal-linear combination; some large reaches; some cluster chords; little doubling of vocal line

Diff: register and dynamic control

Uses: interesting song

895. **HEAVEN-HAVEN** (Gerard Manley Hopkins). Peer International, 1952. cmp1947. X; f'–f♯"; Tess-M; 5/4, 3/4, 4/4, Andante con moto; 1+min; Diff-V/m, P/m.

For: soprano; tenor

Mood: quiet; solitude

Voice: speech rhythms; syncopations; some dotted notes

Piano: chordal-linear combination; 8th-note motion; staccato; thin texture; does not double vocal line

Diff: irregular meter and rhythms

Uses: effective recital song; see also settings by Barber, Dougherty, and Ward (in *Sacred Songs for Pantheists*)

896. **HORROR MOVIE** (Howard Moss). C. F. Peters, 1965. cmp1962. X; c'–g"; Tess-mH; 4/4, 6/4, 6/8, 9/8, 10/8, Largo misterioso; 4+min; Diff-V/d, P/md.

For: best for dramatic soprano; possibly tenor

Mood: narrative; humorous juxtaposition of stock characters; draws moral

Voice: disjunct; declamatory; various subdivisions of beat; long-ranged phrases

Piano: orchestral use of instrument–covers keyboard, large dynamic differences, large reaches; articulations important; various styles; does not double vocal line

Diff: changing meters; singer must be vocally and musically secure and have enthusiasm for text

Uses: change of pace song; group or program ender; excellent for the right singer

Rec: D#s 53, 181

897. **IF YOU CAN** (Howard Moss). C. F. Peters, 1963. Pub. with "Plants Cannot Travel." cmp1961. F♯-centered; d♭'–a"; Tess-M-mH; 4/4, 3/4, 5/8, 2/4, Largo andante; 2+min; Diff-V/md, P/md.

For: tenor; soprano

Mood: dramatic; questions love

Voice: disjunct; skips not exceeding 9th; complex rhythms; 2–3-note slurs; refrain

Piano: linear-chordal combination; wide spacing; various registers; wide reaches; triplets; no vocal line doubling

Diff: ensemble; must be secure musician

Uses: pairs well with "Plants Cannot Travel"

Rec: D#181

898. **PLANTS CANNOT TRAVEL** (Howard Moss). C. F. Peters, 1963. Pub. with "If You Can." cmp1959. C-centered; e'–a"; Tess-mH; 3/8, 4/8, 5/8, Allegretto; 1p; Diff-V/m, P/m.

For: soprano; tenor

Mood: quiet; subdued; love can do the impossible

Voice: stepwise and easy skips; phrases descend; 8th-note motion

Piano: chordal–afterbeat style; some chromaticism; wide spacing; does not double vocal line

Diff: irregular meters and rhythms; breathing

Uses: pairs well with "If You Can"

Rec: D#181

899. **SEE HOW THEY LOVE ME** (Howard Moss). C. F. Peters, 1965. cmp1961. F-centered; d'–a"; Tess-mH; 4/4, ♩ = 54; 2min; Diff-V/d, P/md.

For: tenor; soprano

Mood: transcendental view of man and nature

Voice: disjunct; skips up to 10th; long-ranged phrases; duplets and triplets; 2-note slurs

Piano: linear-chordal combination; imitation; wide spacing; various registers; large reaches; repetitive triplet figures; does not double vocal line

Diff: intervals; *subito* extreme dynamics

Uses: quiet ending; usable song; see also setting by Rorem

Rec: D#181

900. **SEND HOME MY LONG STRAYED EYES** (John Donne). Peer International, 1955. cmp1949. X; e'–g"; Tess-M-H; 3/4, 2/4, 4/4, Andante; 2min; Diff-V/d, P/md.

For: tenor

Mood: lyrical; intellectual

Voice: disjunct; many accidentals; 2–3-note slurs; complex rhythms

Diff: rhythmic complexities; changing meters

Uses: intellectual song for singer attuned to Donne's poetry

Rec: D#59

901. **SONG FOR A WINTER CHILD** (Edward Albee). Peer International, 1964. cmp1950. E-F-F♯maj. progression; d'–a"; Tess-M; 3/4 with changes, Very slow; 1+min; Diff-V/md, P/m.

For: tenor; soprano

Mood: lyrical; gentle; quiet

Voice: many skips; rather disjunct; some triplets; quietly declamatory; 2-note slurs

Piano: block chords; 8th-note motion; 8ve passages; large reaches; does not double vocal line

Diff: changing meters; speech rhythms

Uses: effective quiet song; quiet ending

902. **THE UPSIDE-DOWN MAN** (Howard Moss). Peer International, 1964. [65]. cmp1962. X; c'–a"; Tess-M; 4/4, 3/4, 6/4, 5/4, ♩ = 92; 3+min; Diff-V/d, P/d.

For: tenor best; soprano (dramatic or substantial lyric voice)

Mood: dramatic; somber; upside-down

Voice: disjunct; long-ranged phrases; mostly 8th-note motion; some triplets; awkward intervals

Piano: linear; some counterpoint in double 8ves; large reaches; bitonality; 2 vs. 3; some doubling of vocal line with 8ve

displacement
Diff: dramatic and complex; for secure singer and musician
Uses: clever setting of poem; good for appropriate singer
Rec: D#181

903. VALENTINE TO SHERWOOD ANDERSON
(Gertrude Stein). Peer International, 1951. cmp1947.
"For Florence Kopleff." Dmaj; b–e"; Tess-M; 5/8, 7/8,
3/4, 4/4, Moderato; 1+min; Diff-V/m, P/m.
For: contralto; mezzo-soprano; baritone
Mood: lyrical
Voice: many skips; speech rhythms
Piano: chordal; 4-voice texture with countermelody; incidental
doubling of vocal line
Diff: irregular metric patterns
Uses: fine song; interior of group
Rec: D#s 53, 59

FLOYD, CARLISLE
(b. Latta, SC, 1926)

904. THE MYSTERY. Five Songs of Motherhood
(Gabriela Mistral). Cycle. Boosey & Hawkes, 1966.
cmp1960. "For Phyllis Curtin." Ambiguous tonalities,
usually ending with open 5ths; e'–b"; Tess-H; 17min;
Diff-V/d, P/dd.
For: high lyric soprano
Mood: lyrico-dramatic; cycle of motherhood–conception to
lullaby
Voice: many skips and some leaps predominate; accidentals;
many f#"s and g"s; chromatic; various divisions of the
beat; some short vocalizing passages; long phrases
Piano: orchestral reduction playable by pianist with very large
hands; 3-stave notation frequent; mostly thick chordal
texture; double trills; tremolo; many accidentals; some
arpeggiation
Diff: piano score; high tessitura; for mature performers only
Uses: very personal work; emotionally not for every high
soprano
Rec: D#182

  a. *He Has Kissed Me.* f#'–a"; Tess-mH; 3/4 with
  changes, Andante; 3pp.
  b. *Gentleness.* f'–ab"; Tess-mH; 6/8, Andante
  moderato; 4pp.
  c. *To My Husband.* e'–b"; Tess-mH-H; 12/8, 6/8, 9/8,
  5/4, Lento; 6pp.
  d. *At Dawn.* f#'–b"; Tess-HH; 4/4, Allegro deciso;
  5pp.
  e. *Rocking.* f#'–g"; Tess-H; 6/8, 5/8, 5/4, 6/4, Adagio
  ma con moto; 3pp.

905. PILGRIMAGE. Solo Cantata on Biblical Texts for
Low Voice and Piano. Cycle. Boosey & Hawkes, 1959.
cmp1955. "To Mack Harrell." Traditional keys with
many parallel harmonies; G#–f#'(a'); Tess-mH-HH;
regular meters; varied tempos; 20min; Diff-V/d, P/d.
For: bass-baritone with easy, brilliant high voice
Mood: lyrico-dramatic; man's dependence on God
Voice: skips along chord lines; speech rhythms; long passages
at top of staff and above; (d.), the highest, only 2 meas.

rest, no breathing rests; (d.) ends f#', (e.) begins on A
Piano: large reach necessary; many large, thick chords; some
3-stave passages; countermelodies; composer says "not
orchestral reduction," but it has problems of a
reduction; repeated notes; arpeggiated figures;
wide-spaced chords; parallel harmonies
Diff: tessitura and endurance for singer; calls for easy and
brilliant high tones; hand size for pianist
Uses: good for recital and church programs; could end a
recital in spite of slow, soft closing; orchestral material
available on rental
Rec: D#183

  a. *Man That Is Born of a Woman* (Job 14). Dmin;
  A–f'; Tess-M-mH; 3/4, Adagio molto sostenuto;
  4pp.
  b. *Save Me, O Lord, for the Waters Are Come In
  unto My Soul* (Psalm 69). C#min-maj; G#–f';
  Tess-H; 4/4, 2/4, 3/4, Andante e molto largamente;
  6pp.
  c. *O Lord, Thou Hast Searched Me and Known Me*
  (Psalm 139). Eb-Bbmaj; c–gb'; Tess-mH-H; 4/4,
  Andante; 6pp.
  d. *Praise the Lord, O My Soul* (Psalms 148–149).
  F#maj; d–f#'; Tess-HH; 4/4, Allegro; 5pp.
  e. *For I Am Persuaded* (Romans 8). Dmaj; A–a'(e');
  Tess-L, M, H (ends low A); 4/4, Largo, molto
  tranquillo; 4pp.

FOERSTER, ADOLPH M.
(b. Pittsburgh, PA, 1854; d. Pittsburgh, PA, 1927)

906. TRISTRAM AND ISEULT, Op. 60 (Matthew
Arnold). [58]; 1st©1904. Cmaj (with many
modulations); db'–a"(g"); Tess-mH; 3/4; 8pp;
Diff-V/md, P/md.
For: dramatic soprano; tenor
Mood: dramatic; narrative; ballad
Voice: many leaps; sequential passages; dotted rhythms;
sustained high tones; long phrases
Piano: chordal; sectional; varied patterning; opens with
Wagnerian-style passage; little doubling of vocal line
Diff: dynamic control; high tones; mature sound needed
Uses: colorful; Wagnerian harmonies, modulations, and
melodic turns

FONTRIER, GABRIEL
(b. Bucharest, Rumania, 1918, American father)

907. SLEEP NOW, DREAM NOW (Lullaby). General,
1964. Gmaj; e'–f#"; Tess-M; 6/4, 4/4, 5/4, 7/4,
Moderato; 2pp (2 stanzas); Diff-V/e, P/e.
For: soprano
Mood: lyrical; lullaby
Voice: skips; easy rhythms; meter changes; quiet
Piano: chordal; rocking l.h. pattern; large reach helpful; abrupt
modulations
Uses: attractive, simple lullaby; good for young singer

FOOTE, ARTHUR
(b. Salem, MA, 1853; d. Boston, MA, 1937)

908. **CONSTANCY,** Op. 55, No. 1 (Anonymous). Arthur P.
 Schmidt, 1904. Reprint: Classical Vocal Reprints.
 [104]. Cmaj/min; c'–f"; Tess-M; 4/4, Rather fast, with
 free diction (♩ = 120); 4pp; Diff-V/m, P/m.
For: baritone; mezzo-soprano
Mood: pledge of constant love; comparisons to natural
 phenomena
Voice: syllabic; melody outlines chords; each stanza really one
 extended phrase; middle section in Cmin; 2-meas.
 interlude between stanzas 1& 2, otherwise no rests in
 the vocal line
Piano: broken- and repeated-chord patterns support and
 frequently double the vocal line
Diff: phrasing; breathing places
Uses: interesting and pleasant song for young singers;
 somewhat folk-like in the English style

909. **A DITTY** ("My true love hath my heart") (Sir Philip
 Sidney). [104, 105]; 1st©1892. H & L keys: Amaj &
 Fmaj; c♯'–f♯" & a–d"; Tess-M; 2/4, Allegretto
 grazioso; 2pp; Diff-V/me, P/e.
For: soprano; mezzo-soprano; contralto
Mood: lyrical; quiet love song
Voice: many skips; easy rhythms
Piano: block-chord texture; some doubling of vocal line
Uses: good easy song; nice for young girl

910. **THE EDEN-ROSE,** Op. 26, No. 4 ("The Poem is
 quoted by Rudyard Kipling in 'Mrs. Hauksbee sits
 out'."). [105]; 1st©1892. Fmin; c'–g"; Tess-M; 9/8, 6/8,
 Comodo–Più lento; 5pp; Diff-V/m, P/md.
For: mezzo-soprano
Mood: lyrical; narrative; sentimental love song
Voice: flowing phrases; some chromaticism
Piano: rolled and arpeggiated chords; rather chromatic and
 expressive

911. **GO, LOVELY ROSE** (Edmund Waller). [104];
 1st©1884. H & L keys: E♭maj & Cmaj; d♭'–g" &
 b♭–e"; Tess-M; 4/4, Moderately fast; 6pp; Diff-V/m,
 P/m.
For: tenor; baritone
Mood: lyrical; love song; intense expression
Voice: stepwise and skips along chord lines; dotted and
 repetitive rhythms; 2 vs. piano 3
Piano: repeated, arpeggiated, and block chords; sectional;
 doubles half of vocal line
Diff: dynamic control
Uses: nice lyric song; good for teaching–has descending
 phrases; quiet ending

912. **I ARISE FROM DREAMS OF THEE,** Op. 26, No.
 11 (Percy Bysshe Shelley). [105]; 1st©1892. Fmin;
 c'–f"; Tess-M; 4/4, Non troppo allegro, comodo; 4pp;
 Diff-V/me, P/m.
For: tenor; baritone
Mood: lyrical; sentimental love song
Voice: vigorous, marked rhythm in first and last sections;
 sweeping phrases in middle

Piano: chordal first and last sections; arpeggiated in middle

913. **I'M WEARING AWA' TO THE LAND O' THE
 LEAL,** Op. 13, No. 2 (Lady Nairn). 1887. Reprint:
 Classical Vocal Reprints (M). [1, 68, 4 bks., 104]. H &
 L keys: D♭maj & B♭maj; d♭'–f" & b♭–d"; Tess-mL;
 9/8, Not too slowly; 2pp; Diff-V/me, P/me.
For: all voices
Mood: lyrical; Scottish dialect
Voice: flowing phrases; some quadruplets in compound meter
Piano: chordal; a little chromaticism; quadruplet groupings;
 occasional doubling of vocal line
Diff: quadruplets in compound meter; dialect
Uses: period piece

914. **IN A BOWER** (Louise C. Moulton). [105]; 1st©1892.
 Emin; c♯'–f"; Tess-M; 6/8, Con moto, grazioso; 5pp;
 Diff-V/m, P/m.
For: mezzo-soprano; baritone
Mood: mysterious; foreboding; narrative
Voice: chord-member skips; easy rhythms
Piano: broken- and block-chord patterns; continuous 16th
 notes; does not double vocal line
Diff: sustained tones; breath control
Uses: short ballad-like song; period piece

915. **IN PICARDIE** (Graham R. Tomson). A. P. Schmidt,
 1896. [104]. Amaj; d♯'–d"; Tess-M; 4/4, Non troppo
 allegro, ma con moto; Diff-V/e, P/e.
For: baritone; mezzo-soprano
Mood: lyrical; descriptive
Voice: downward skips at phrase beginnings
Piano: syncopated chordal figure; supports voice
Diff: some phrases bound over with a moving 4th beat
Uses: excellent teaching song for a young baritone or
 mezzo-soprano; descending phrases

916. **IT WAS A LOVER AND HIS LASS,** Op. 10, No. 1
 (William Shakespeare). Arthur P. Schmidt, 1885.
 Reprints: Classical Vocal Reprints (mH); Masters
 Music Publications. [5]. Fmin; e'–g♭"; Tess-mH; 4/4,
 Grazioso (♩ = 112); 2pp; Diff-V/m, P/me.
For: soprano; tenor
Mood: cheerful song of love in springtime
Voice: conjunct motion with modest intervals, but with
 ascending 8ve leap at a rapid tempo; 2-note slurs; some
 high-lying phrases
Piano: chordal; some broken-chords; occasional doubling of
 vocal line
Diff: song will require care to achieve musical accuracy
Uses: an interesting setting of this text
Rec: D#52

917. **THE LAKE ISLE OF INNISFREE** (William Butler
 Yeats). A. P. Schmidt, 1921. Amin-Cmaj; e♭'–a";
 Tess-mH; 3/4, In meditative, steady movement;
 Diff-V/m, P/m.
For: tenor; soprano
Mood: lyrical; meditative
Voice: flowing line; rather high
Piano: flowing; supportive; some nice modulations
Diff: requires easy production of g" and a"

Uses: good light lyric tenor song

918. LILAC TIME (Alfred Noyes). A. P. Schmidt, 1917. Reprint: Classical Vocal Reprints. H & L keys: Fmaj & Cmaj; e'–a" & b–e"; Tess-mL; 4/4, Moderately fast; gracefully; Diff-V/e, P/e.
For: all voices; baritone or tenor best
Mood: descriptive
Voice: simple syllabic setting
Piano: some melodic material; mostly supports vocal line
Uses: could teach visualization of a scene

919. ON THE WAY TO KEW (William E. Henley). A. P. Schmidt, 1894. Reprint: Classical Vocal Reprints (H). [104]. Cmaj; c'–e"; Tess-M; 4/4, Moderato con moto; Diff-V/m, P/e.
For: baritone; mezzo-soprano
Mood: reminiscent; hopeful
Voice: lyrical
Piano: syncopated "walking" pattern; modulations
Uses: very pleasant song; good for young voices

920. O SWALLOW, SWALLOW, FLYING SOUTH (Alfred, Lord Tennyson). Arthur P. Schmidt, 1896. Reprint: Classical Vocal Reprints (H). [5]. Dbmaj-Fmaj; c'–ab"; Tess-M; 4/4, Allegretto grazioso; 5pp; Diff-V/m, P/md.
For: tenor
Mood: love song using nature imagery; "life is brief, but love is long"
Voice: flowing, legato phrases, building to a dramatic climax
Piano: broken-chord figuration in outer sections; homophonic chords, with l.h. melody in middle section; supports vocal line; little actual doubling; some accidentals
Diff: a few pitches; good interpretive skills needed
Uses: effective song for performance
Rec: D#52

921. THE ROSE AND THE GARDENER, Op. 51, No. 1 (Austin Dobson). A. P. Schmidt, 1902. Cmaj; b–e"; Tess-L; 2/4, Gracefully; not fast; Diff-V/e, P/e.
For: mezzo-soprano
Mood: lyrical; narrative; flower song (somewhat resembling Mozart's "Das Veilchen")
Voice: conjunct; many // before quotations in phrases
Piano: chordal; arpeggios in minor section; supports voice
Diff: registration, for some singers
Uses: small, graceful song with a moral concerning beauty and time

922. A SONG OF FOUR SEASONS (Austin Dobson). A. P. Schmidt, 1898. [104]. H & L keys: Dmaj & Bbmaj; d'–g" & bb–eb"; Tess-mH; 4/4, Allegro; 6pp; Diff-V/m, P/e.
For: all voices
Mood: lyrical and descriptive; the seasons of love
Voice: lyrical and sprightly
Piano: syncopated figure; section of repeated 8th notes
Uses: usable for students; easy to understand

923. SONG OF THE FORGE (Gilbert Parker). Arthur P. Schmidt, 1895. Reprint: Classical Vocal Reprints (M).

[5]. Bbmin-maj; db'–eb"; Tess-M; 6/8, Allegro assai (♩= 104); 6pp; Diff-V/m, P/md.
For: baritone, possibly mezzo-soprano
Mood: dramatic and descriptive; longing to travel far from home
Voice: conjunct and disjunct motion; a few intervals larger than 5th; many dynamic changes; powerful ending in middle voice
Piano: chordal; dotted rhythms almost throughout; broken 8ves and other figuration; supports vocal line well, occasionally doubling it
Diff: requires singer with well-developed middle range and ability to achieve vocal contrasts
Uses: could be an impressive song for recital

924. TRANQUILLITY (Mary Van Orden). A. P. Schmidt, 1915. H & L keys: Dbmaj & Bbmaj; db'–g" & bb–e"; Tess-mH; 3/4, Grazioso, molto moderato; 3min; Diff-V/m,P/m.
For: any voice except extremely low
Mood: lyrical; descriptive; sea scene
Voice: many skips; dotted rhythms
Piano: broken-chord and rocking figures; duplets and triplets; middle and high registers; does not double vocal line
Diff: long phrases; climax ff on g"
Uses: usable lyric song; quiet ending

925. A TWILIGHT FEAR (C. G. Blanden). A. P. Schmidt, 1918. H & L keys: Gmaj & Ebmaj; f#'–g#" & d'–e"; Tess-M; 6/4, Simply and expressively; 2pp; Diff-V/me, P/e.
For: all voices; text perhaps best for a man
Mood: lyrical; gentle fear of loss
Voice: skips along chord lines; some accidentals; sustained; quiet
Piano: chordal; pulsing rhythm; some accidentals
Diff: simplicity of expression; needs smooth and beautiful voice; text delicately colored and metaphorical
Uses: unusual song; useful quiet song in the right group

FORNUTO, DONATO D.
(b. New York, NY, 1931)

926. CHRISTINA'S SONGS (Christina Rossetti). For Coloratura Soprano and Piano. Filpat Publishing, 1982. Tonal; d'–eb'''; Tess-M–H; mostly regular meters with some changes; fast and slow tempos; 22pp; Diff-V/m-d, P/me-d.
For: coloratura soprano (also published for soprano with a few altered phrases)
Mood: brilliant; lyrical; agitated; somber; elegiac
Voice: high tessitura; many different melodic motives; many phrases above the staff; much wordless coloratura; singer leaves stage slowly while singing "oo" and "ah" in last song; final phrases sung offstage; ends on d'''
Piano: almost constant motion, usually in 8ths; many accidentals; broken-chord patterns; rolled chords; arpeggiation; fast tempos
Diff: ensemble; text on very high phrases for voice; wandering harmonic structure
Uses: challenge for advanced coloratura soprano

a. *Birthday Song.* Tonal; d'–c'''; Tess-M, H; 4/4, 6/4, 5/4, 9/4, 8/4, Brightly ♩ = 120; 5pp.

b. *Seasons.* Tonal; d'–b"; Tess-mH-H; 3/4, 4/4, 5/8, Flowing ♩ = 120; 5pp.

c. *Who Has Seen the Wind?* Tonal; d'–a"; Tess-mH; 3/4, 5/8, 4/4, 6/8, 5/4, Agitato ♩ = 132-138; 5pp.

d. *May.* Tonal; eb'–bb"; Tess-mH; 5/4, 5/8, 3/4, Freely ♩ = 60 ca.; 2pp.

e. *Sing No Sad Songs for Me.* Tonal; d'–eb'''; Tess-M,H; 4/4, 7/4, Slowly and Freely ♩ = 63-69; 5pp.

927. SONGS OF INNOCENCE AND EXPERIENCE
(William Blake). Cycle. Harold Branch, 1973. Traditional keys; a–a"; Tess-M-mH; regular and irregular meters with some changes; varied tempos; 24pp; Diff-V/md-d, P/m-md.

For: lyric mezzo-soprano
Mood: lyrical; one song declamatory; well-known Blake poems
Voice: largely conjunct with a few large leaps; modulating harmonies; speech rhythms and motor rhythms; wide range; syllabic
Piano: chordal texture; much quartal harmony; changing meters; numerous accidentals
Diff: one song in 7/8, very fast
Uses: excellent songs for a lyric mezzo-soprano with an easy top; attractive settings of varied group of poems; intermediate and advanced singers

a. *Piping Down the Valleys Wild.* Amaj; bb–a"; 6/8, Allegro moderato; 5pp.

b. *The Lamb.* [57]. Abmaj; c'–eb"; 5/4, 6/4, 3/4, 2/4, 4/4, Andante; 4pp.

c. *A Cradle Song.* a–e"; 4/4, Moderato; 4pp.

d. *The Sick Rose.* Fmin; a–a"; 3/4, Lento; 2pp.

e. *Little Fly.* Ebmin; d'–g"; 2/4, 9/8, Allegretto rubato; 3pp.

f. *The Tiger.* Dmin; b–g"; 7/8. 3/4, 5/4, 6/4, Vivace; 6pp.

FOSS, LUKAS
(b. Berlin, Germany, 1922)

928. WHERE THE BEE SUCKS (William Shakespeare). G. Schirmer, 1951. cmp1940. G-centered; d'–g"; Tess-M; 4/4, Allegretto; 3pp (1st 2pp. can be repeated ad lib); Diff-V/m, P/m.

For: soprano; mezzo-soprano
Mood: lighthearted; energetic; sprightly
Voice: small skips; dotted rhythms; syncopation; 2-note slurs
Piano: broken-chord and 8ve patterns; double 3rds; imitation of vocal line; duplets and triplets
Diff: irregular phrase lengths; ensemble
Uses: good song for Shakespeare group or elsewhere in recital

FOSTER, FAY
(b. Leavenworth, KS, 1886; d. Bayport, NY, 1960)

929. DUSK IN JUNE (Sara Teasdale). Bryant, 1917. H & L

keys: Gmaj & Dmaj; d'–g" & a–d"; Tess-L; 3/2, 4/4, With great feeling, but not too slowly; 2pp; Diff-V/me, P/m.

For: lyric soprano; contralto
Mood: lyrical; nature picture
Voice: stepwise ascending phrases; some phrases broken by rests
Piano: broken-chord figures; independent melody; somewhat chromatic; expresses text
Uses: could be effectively and tastefully performed

FOSTER, STEPHEN COLLINS
(b. Pittsburgh, PA, 1826; d. New York, NY, 1864)

NOTE: In [106, 107, 108] (as well as elsewhere) one can find a large number of additional songs of Stephen Collins Foster, generally similar in style of vocal line (lyrical, simple, and strophic), piano accompaniment (chordal, mostly with broken and afterbeat figures, and with related melodic material in solo passages), and mood (lyrical, melancholy, and sentimental). They are suitable for most medium and high lyric voices, with the texts varying in suitability for men or women.

[See also D#50; no titles given]

930. AH! MAY THE RED ROSE LIVE ALWAY
(Stephen Collins Foster). Reprint: Classical Vocal Reprints. [106, 107, 108]. cmp1850. Gmaj; c♯'–f♯"; Tess-M; 6/8, Not too fast; 2+pp (3 strophes); Diff-V/me, P/m.

For: any medium lyric voice
Mood: lyrical; sad; nature imagery
Voice: flowing; some phrases begin high; opt. turn ornament
Piano: repeated chords with related melody in solo passages
Uses: useful for students or any suitable occasion
Rec: D#s 5, 47, 184, 185, 186, 188

931. BEAUTIFUL DREAMER (Stephen Collins Foster). [54, 106, 107, 108]. cmp1864. Ebmaj; d'–f"; Tess-M; 9/8, Moderato; 4pp; Diff-V/me, P/e.

For: any medium or high lyric voice
Mood: lyrical; dreaming
Voice: flowing phrases; many begin high
Piano: arpeggiation and afterbeat chords; vocal melody in solo passages
Uses: useful for teaching or any suitable occasion
Rec: D#s 5, 184, 185, 186, 187, 188

932. COME WHERE MY LOVE LIES DREAMING
(poet not given). [63, 108]. H & L keys: F-Cmaj & Eb-Bbmaj; f'–f" & eb'–eb"; Tess-mH; 4/4, Moderato; 5pp; Diff-V/me, P/e.

For: tenor; baritone
Mood: lyrical, dreamy love song
Voice: mostly conjunct motion; several large intervals, incl. 8ve leaps upwards in mid-phrase; a b a structure in text and music
Piano: chordal–block, rolled, and broken–with bits of melodic and countermelodic material; few accidentals; supports vocal line very clearly; incidental doubling
Diff: maintaining vocal line in upward and downward leaps

Uses: good example of its style; useful in a variety of situations, and for teaching
Rec: D#s 185, 189

933. **GENTLE ANNIE** (Stephen Collins Foster). [106, 107, 108]. cmp1856. E♭maj; d'–f"; Tess-M; 2pp (3 strophes); Diff-V/m, P/e.
For: lyric baritone; tenor
Mood: lyrical; sad; sentimental
Voice: leap of 6th upward at phrase ends
Piano: broken- and block-chord patterns
Diff: upward leap of 6th
Uses: for students or any suitable occasion
Rec: D#s 24, 187, 188

934. **IF YOU'VE ONLY GOT A MOUSTACHE** (Comic Song) (George Cooper). [43, 106, 107, 108]. cmp1864. Dmaj; d'–f♯"; Tess-M; 6/8, Con esprit; 2pp (4 strophes); Diff-V/me, P/m.
For: all voices; male voices perhaps best
Mood: humorous; descriptive
Voice: light and dancing; somewhat parlando
Piano: repeated afterbeat chords; independent melody in solo passages
Uses: good for student with comic flair
Rec: D#s 5, 21, 24, 184, 188

935. **JEANIE WITH THE LIGHT BROWN HAIR** (Stephen Collins Foster). [63, 106, 107, 108]. cmp1854. H & M keys: Gmaj & Fmaj; d'–g" & c'–f"; Tess-M; 4/4, Moderato; 5pp; Diff-V/me, P/me.
For: baritone; tenor
Mood: lyrical; dreaming; descriptive; nature imagery
Voice: title phrase broken by rest; long ascending portamento; mostly conjunct with skips of 6th in both directions
Piano: broken- and block-chord figures; related melody in solo passages
Diff: portamento
Uses: useful in many situations; good for students
Rec: D#s 184, 185, 186, 187, 188

936. **MY WIFE IS A MOST KNOWING WOMAN** (George Cooper). [43, 106, 107]. cmp1863. E♭maj; e♭'–f"; Tess-M; 6/8, Vivace; 2+pp (5 strophes); Diff-V/e, P/m.
For: tenor; high baritone
Mood: humorously descriptive
Voice: short phrases separated by rests; light and bouncing
Piano: broken chords and repeated afterbeat figure; related melody in solo passages
Uses: good for singer with comic flair

937. **NOTHING BUT A PLAIN OLD SOLDIER** (Patriotic Ballad) (Stephen Collins Foster). [106, 107]. cmp1863. Fmaj; c'–f"; Tess-M; 4/4, Moderato; 3pp (3 strophes); Diff-V/me, P/me.
For: baritone
Mood: humorously descriptive; patriotic in tone
Voice: march-like and vigorous; odd declamation of "George Washington" adds to humor
Piano: broken- and repeated-chord patterns; related melody in solo passages

Uses: good for singer with comic flair
Rec: D#s 186, 188

938. **OPEN THY LATTICE LOVE** (George P. Morris). [27, 106, 107, 108]. cmp1844. Cmaj; c'–e"; Tess-M; 6/8, Allegretto; 2pp (2 strophes); Diff-V/e, P/e.
For: all voices
Mood: simple serenade; nature imagery
Voice: conjunct with a few large intervals
Piano: chordal; 4-voice texture with some afterbeats; some doubling of melody
Rec: D#187

939. **SOME FOLKS** (Stephen Collins Foster). [106, 108]. cmp1855. Fmaj; f'–f"; Tess-M; 2/4, Moderato; 2pp (5 strophes); Diff-V/e, P/e.
For: any high or medium voice
Mood: happy; humorous
Voice: light and bouncing; short phrases
Piano: broken-chord and afterbeat patterns; related melody in solo passages
Uses: good light song for Foster group
Rec: D#s 6, 184, 188

940. **THE SONG OF ALL SONGS** (Stephen Collins Foster). [106, 107]; 1st ed. 1863. Fmaj; c'–f"; Tess-M, Moderato; 2pp (5 strophes); Diff-V/e, P/me.
For: any medium voice
Mood: light; humorous; describes popular songs of the day
Voice: light and bouncing
Piano: repeated and broken chords; afterbeat pattern; related melody in solo passages

941. **SWEETLY SHE SLEEPS, MY ALICE FAIR** (Charles G. Eastman). [106, 108]; 1st ed. 1851. B♭maj; d'–d"; Tess-M; 6/8, Andantino; 3pp; Diff-V/e, P/e.
For: lyric baritone; tenor
Mood: lyrical; sentimental love song
Voice: characteristic phrase begins on d" and descends through the 8ve
Piano: broken- and repeated-chord patterns; related melody in solo passages; some doubling of vocal line
Uses: good teaching song; descending phrases
Rec: D#188

942. **THAT'S WHAT'S THE MATTER** (Stephen Collins Foster). [106, 107, 108]; 1st ed. 1862. Dmaj; c'–e"; Tess-M; 2/4, Moderato; 2pp (5 strophes); Diff-V/e, P/me.
For: baritone; tenor
Mood: vigorous; patriotic tone (Civil War)
Voice: short phrases; sturdy rhythm
Piano: afterbeat pattern; related melody in solo passages
Uses: period piece
Rec: D#188

943. **THERE ARE PLENTY OF FISH IN THE SEA** (George Cooper). [106, 107]; 1st ed. 1862?. Cmaj; c'–e"; Tess-mL; 6/8, Vivace; 2+pp (3 strophes); Diff-V/e, P/e.
For: mezzo-soprano; tenor; high baritone
Mood: humorously descriptive–of the girl who did not want to

be caught

Voice: light and dancing
Piano: broken and block chords; afterbeat pattern; related melody in solo passages
Uses: good for singer with comic flair
Rec: D#189

944.   THERE'S A GOOD TIME COMING (from the London *Daily News*). [106, 107]; 1st ed.1846. B♭maj; d'–f"; Tess-M; 4/4, Moderato; 1p (8 strophes); Diff-V/me, P/m.
For: any high or medium voice
Mood: joyful; optimistic
Voice: short phrases separated by rests; vigorous and strongly accented, making extensive use of Scotch snap rhythmic figure
Piano: afterbeat chords; scale passages in 8ves; related melody in solo passages
Uses: good song for students or any suitable occasion
Rec: D#188

945.   WHY NO ONE TO LOVE? (Stephen C. Foster). Reprint: Classical Vocal Reprints. [106, 108]. cmp1862. Cmaj; c'–e"; Tess-M; 3/4, Moderato; 3pp; Diff-V/e, P/ee.
For: any voice (easily transposed)
Mood: lyric; regretful; sentimental
Voice: quarter-note motion, easy rhythms; easy intervals, one skip of a M6th; three strophes
Piano: waltz style afterbeat accomp.; does not double vocal line; 8-meas. prelude, interlude, postlude
Uses: period parlor song; graceful, attractive to beginning students; nice to teach legato for a light voice
Rec: D#s 6, 35

FOSTER, WALTER CHARLES
(b. Olmsted Falls, OH, 1934)

946.   INNERMOST NAME (Walter Foster). [109]. Dmaj-min; d'–c'''; Tess-wide; 4/4, ♩ = 48; 1+pp; Diff-V/md, P/m.
For: lyric tenor; soprano
Mood: lyrical love song; the stranger never met
Voice: many skips and leaps; rather chromatic; triplets; sustained c'''; flexible vocal line; syllabic with a few 2-note slurs
Piano: chordal–block and rolled; some arpeggiation and scales; grace notes; somewhat chromatic; triplets; some doubling of vocal line
Diff: tenor needs easy high voice or falsetto

947.   IN THE TIME OF YOUR SORROW (Martha Weber). [109]. E♭min; e♭'–b"; Tess-H; 4/4, Andante; 2pp; Diff-V/d, P/md.
For: high soprano
Mood: mourning
Voice: some stepwise motion; many skips; syllabic
Piano: chords with arpeggiated l.h.; accidentals; awkward key; r.h. doubles vocal line throughout; MS occasionally hard to read
Diff: high tessitura; accidentals

Uses: in a recital group

948.   LINES TO A FRIEND LONG ABSENT (Martha Weber). [109]. A-centered (mostly dissonant); d♭'–g♯"; Tess-M; 4/4, Lento; 1p; Diff-V/md, P/me.
For: soprano
Mood: loss of a friend
Voice: dissonant line; many accidentals; only pitch reference in the piano part is A; rhythms oddly notated; syllabic
Piano: repeated A's in three 8ves in an oddly-syncopated pattern
Diff: pitches of vocal line; ensemble, if song is meant to be rhythmically strict
Uses: in a recital group for expressive singer with good ear

949.   MOMENTS (Paula Roxburgh). [109]. Various keys; f'–d'''; Tess-H; 3/4 with changes; various tempos; 9pp; Diff-V/d, P/d.
For: coloratura soprano
Mood: sensuous; very intimate
Voice: skips and leaps; written-out ornaments; coloratura passages; very high passages; sustained d'''; many accidentals; polyrhythms; alternate version given in lower key
Piano: arpeggiation and rolled chords; tremolo; many accidentals; polyrhythms; demands sweeping style
Diff: many accidentals; hard to read; long
Uses: big song; needs an uninhibited singer

950.   POEMS OF A COUNTRY GIRL (7 Songs) (Holly Wynn Walker). Recital Publications, 2000. cmp1999–2000. Mostly tonal; b–b♭"; Tess-M-H, cs, wide; mostly regular meters; varied tempos; 50pp; Diff-V/m-md, P/me-md.
For: high soprano (coloratura or lyric-coloratura)
Mood: love songs; sensual; self-absorbed
Voice: conjunct and chord outlining; some large leaps; sustained lines; many melismas; ornaments; sustained high phrases; (e.) atonal
Piano: romantic piano techniques; much patterned arpeggiation, repeated chords, 8ve melody, tremolo; melodic material in lengthy preludes, interludes and postludes; considerable doubling of vocal line in texture or directly
Diff: many notes; text clarity in high-lying and melismatic phrases; possibly balance in arpegg. piano sections; personal nature of poetry may not suit everyone
Uses: technical showpiece set for high soprano with coloratura flexibility and pianist with fleet fingers

    a. *In the Barn.* Succession of M & m keys; c♯'–a"; Tess-mH-H; 3/4, ♩ = 66; 6+pp.
    b. *Fingertips.* Emaj-Cmin; d'–a"; Tess-cs; 4/4, 3/4, ♩ = 56; 2pp.
    c. *Bedtime.* Changing keys–E♭; e'–b♭"; Tess-mH; 3/4, ♪ = 76; 4+pp.
    d. *Disease.* F minorish–G; b–b♭"; Tess-mH-H; 6/4, 4/4, ♩ = c.112; 8pp.
    e. *The Branch.* X; d♭'–a♭"; Tess-M; 4/4, 5/4, 6/4, ♩ = 50 Very free; 3pp.
    f. *Hidden* (orig. and transp. keys). Ends D♭ & E♭; c♯'–g♯" & d♯'–a♯"; Tess-wide; 4/4, 7/4, ♩ = 96

With warmth; 2pp.
g. *Sweet Youth.* D minorish, shifting harmonies;
d'–b♭"; Tess-wide; 4/4, ♩ = 44 Freely; 10+pp.

951. RAIN SONG (Martha Weber). [109]. X-Amin; e♭'–c'''; Tess-H; 4/4, Lento; 3pp; Diff-V/md, P/m.
For: high soprano
Mood: memory of love
Voice: skips; arpeggio; melisma; accidentals
Piano: arpeggiated patterns; slow, trilling rain pattern
Diff: pitches; words on high tones; high tones must float
Uses: nice quiet song

952. THE SOLITARY PATHWAY (Walter Foster). [109]. E-E♭maj; d♯'–b♭"; Tess-M; 3/4, 4/4, ♩ = 40; 2+pp; Diff-V/m, P/m.
For: lyric tenor; soprano
Mood: lyrical love song
Voice: stepwise, skips, and leaps of 7th & 9th; written-out ornaments; diatonic; triplets; b♭" is held; syllabic with small melismas created by the ornaments
Piano: chordal–chiefly arpeggiated, a few broken; almost entirely diatonic; triplets; some rapid scalar passages; incidental doubling of vocal line
Diff: some large intervals
Uses: group with other songs by this composer

953. TO THE UNBORN (Martha Weber). [109]. Ends Emaj; c'–d'''(b"); Tess-H; 3/4, 4/4, 5/4, 6/4, Allegro; 8pp; Diff-V/d, P/d.
For: high soprano with coloratura
Mood: from agitation to calmness
Voice: mostly skips and leaps; some rapid scales and ornaments; words on very high notes
Piano: broken-chord patterns; arpeggios; melody in 8ves with arpeggios; scales; many accidentals; difficult to read; 63 meas. of solo material
Diff: high tessitura; melismatic passage; piano accomp.
Uses: big song for a recital group

954. THE WELCOME (Martha Weber). [109]. B♭min-Gmin-E♭maj; d'–b"; Tess-H; 4/4, ♩ = 76; 4pp; Diff-V/md, P/d.
For: high soprano
Mood: ecstatic love song
Voice: skips and leaps; easy rhythms; sustained b♭" at end; syllabic
Piano: wide arpeggiation; rhythmic chord patterns
Diff: high tessitura for voice; words on extreme notes
Uses: as a group ender

FRACKENPOHL, ARTHUR
(b. Irvington, NJ, 1924)

955. RISE UP, MY LOVE, MY FAIR ONE (Thomas John Carlisle); Shawnee Press, 1981. Cmaj; b♭-e"; Tess-mL; 4/4, 3/4, 2/4, Warmly (♩ = ca.69); 3+min; Diff-V/m, P/m.
For: baritone; bass-baritone; any medium voice
Mood: tender love song; an adaptation of Boaz's song to Ruth
Voice: mostly stepwise in motion–some 3rds, two 5ths; some

accidentals
Piano: broken-chord patterns almost throughout; occasional melodic material; numerous accidentals; incidental doubling of vocal line, but clear support throughout
Diff: possibly some pitches
Uses: probably intended as a wedding song; recital use also

FREED, ARNOLD
(b. New York, NY, 1926)

956. ACQUAINTED WITH THE NIGHT (Robert Frost). Boosey & Hawkes, 1965. Fmin; c'–a♭"; Tess-M; 2/4, Adagio; 6pp; Diff-V/d, P/d.
For: dramatic soprano; mezzo-soprano; some tenors; some high baritones
Mood: dramatic; somber; intense
Voice: disjunct; leaps not exceeding 8ve; dotted notes; syncopation; large dynamic changes
Piano: linear; colorful use of registers and articulations; sustained tones; ornaments; complex rhythms; large reaches; does not double vocal line
Diff: sustained low and high tones; dynamic control; opening unaccomp.
Uses: effective song for mature voice; quiet ending; see also setting by J. Duke

FREED, ISADORE
(b. Brest-Litovsk, Russia, 1900; d. Rockville Center, NY, 1960)

957. CHARTLESS (Emily Dickinson). [21]; 1st©1946. H & L keys: Dmaj &B♭maj; c'–f♯" & a♭–d"; Tess-M; 9/8, 6/8, Andante sostenuto; 2min; Diff-V/me, P/m.
For: all voices except very high
Mood: philosophical; poem of faith and insight
Voice: flowing phrases in first section; *quasi parlando* in last
Piano: chordal; somewhat chromatic; melody and contrapuntal figures related to vocal melody
Diff: duplets in compound meter
Uses: good teaching song

958. CROSSING THE PLAINS (Joaquin Miller). Carl Fischer, 1947. Amin; d'–f♯"; Tess-M-mH; 2/2, Maestoso; 6pp; Diff-V/m, P/m.
For: dramatic baritone
Mood: dramatic; descriptive; ponderous
Voice: skips and leaps along chord lines; repetitive both melodically and textually; strongly accented tones at top of staff
Piano: chordal; somewhat ponderous; accidentals
Diff: endurance in strongly-accented high phrases; for mature voices
Uses: perhaps an effective song for a group about various American phenomena, scenes, moods, etc.; creates strong sense of the westward migration

959. NOVEMBER (Thomas Hood). (Peer)Southern, 1953. Amin; e♭'–g"; Tess-M; 4/4, Allegretto; 1+min; Diff-V/m, P/m.
For: tenor; soprano
Mood: descriptive

Voice: afterbeat phrase beginnings; stepwise and small skips; easy rhythms; 8th-note motion
Piano: chordal, afterbeat style; some accidentals; does not double vocal line
Uses: effective song for seasonal or American group; big ending

960. **PSALM VIII.** (Peer)Southern, 1954. Fmin; c'–f"; Tess-M; 4/4, 3/2, Andante; 4pp; Diff-V/m, P/m.
For: mezzo-soprano; baritone; some sopranos
Mood: declamatory; praise of God
Voice: easy skips; many repeated tones; speech rhythms; recit. style; duplets and triplets
Piano: block chords; some repeated tones; countermelody; incidental doubling of vocal line
Diff: speech rhythms
Uses: good sacred song; useful for recital or church

961. **WHEN I WAS ONE-AND-TWENTY** (A. E. Housman). (Peer)Southern, 1960. cmp1953. Gmaj; d'–g"; Tess-mH; 4/4, Allegretto; 1+min; Diff-V/md, P/m-md.
For: tenor; soprano
Mood: lyrical
Voice: stepwise and small skips; 2–4-note slurs; interrupted phrasing
Piano: chordal-linear combination; parallel structures in parallel motion; accidentals; some vocal line doubling
Diff: ensemble
Uses: good setting

FREER, ELEANOR EVEREST
(b. Philadelphia, PA, 1864; d. Chicago, IL, 1942)

962. **FIVE SONGS TO SPRING,** Op. 6. For Medium Voice. William A. Kaun Music Co., 1905. Reprint: Recital Publications, 1985. Traditional keys; c'–f♯"(e"); Tess-M; traditional meters with changes; varied tempos; 16pp; Diff-V/m-md, P/m-md.
For: medium voices
Mood: concerns nature and thoughts about spring
Voice: mostly stepwise motion with small skips; both duplet and triplet subdivisions of beat; (c.), quite chromatic; (d.), recit. sections; (e.), dialogue between shepherd and shepherdess; mostly syllabic.
Piano: block chords; arpeggios and broken-chord patterns; some rolled chords; tremolo; (e.) imitates shepherd's pipe; many accidentals; does not double vocal line
Diff: chromaticism in (c.); vocabulary of the poems; many textural changes and sectional structure of the songs cause problems with continuity
Uses: as a set; possibly excerpt (a.)

   a. *The Eternal Spring* (John Milton). Amaj; e'–e"; 3/4, Largo (with fluctuations); 2pp.
   b. *Song in March* (William Gilmore Simms). Cmaj; c'–e"; 3/4, Andante quasi allegretto; 5pp.
   c. *Song* (William Watson). X; e♭'–e♭"; 3/4, Allegro; 2pp.
   d. *Incipit Vita Nova* (William Morton Payne). Gmaj; d'–e"; 4/4 with changes, Andante con moto–

Moderato–Allegro–Moderato molto; 3pp.
   e. *An April Pastoral* (Austin Dobson). F♯maj; d♯'–f♯"(e"); 9/4 with changes, Capriccioso; 4pp.

FREIBERGER, KATHERINE
(b. U. S. A., 1927)

963. **THE COFFEE POT FACE** (Aileen Fisher). A Cycle of Seven songs for Medium High Voice and Piano. The Willis Music Company, 1994. Major tonalities with delicate dissonances; b–g"; Tess-M; regular meters; steady tempos with a few changes; 14pp; Diff-V/m-d, P/md.
For: soprano (very light, with a young sound)
Mood: whimsical; fleeting; thoughts from a child's perspective (or adult memories of childhood)
Voice: lyrical; some easy vocal lines; some folk-like tunes; a few songs require good ear
Piano: delicate; interesting; some cross-hand playing; some playing inside the piano; articulations
Diff: intervals; lack of piano support; length of phrases with final high tones; songs require delicate, childlike touch
Uses: very interesting short cycle for a young, light soprano

   a. *The Coffee Pot Face.* C; c'–e♭"; Tess-M; 2/2, Lightly (♩ = 88); 1p.
   b. *Otherwise.* Amin; d'–f"; Tess-M; 3/4, Very sustained, moderately slow (♩ = 66); 2pp.
   c. *I Never Had a Pony.* A minorish; e'–f"; Tess-M; 6/8, With rollicking good humor (♩ = 96); 4pp.
   d. *Stars.* X; b–g"; Tess-cs; 4/4, Tempo ad lib; 1p.
   e. *Moon.* X; e♭'–f"; Tess-M; 4/4, Mechanically. Strictly marked tempo (♩ = 66); 2pp.
   f. *Dreams.* A minorish; e'–g"; Tess-cs; 2/2, Adagio sostenuto (♩ = 50); 1p.
   g. *Rainy Day.* C; c'–e"; Tess-M; 2/4, Moderately fast (♩ = 88); 3pp.

FRIEDELL, HAROLD
(b. New York, NY, 1905; d. Hastings-on-Hudson, NY, 1958)

964. **THE SHEPHERDESS** (Alice Meynell). H. W. Gray, 1959. Fmaj; e♭'–a"(g"); Tess-mH; 3/4, Flowing; 3min; Diff-V/m, P/m.
For: tenor
Mood: lyrical; descriptive; love song
Voice: easy skips; one long melisma; 2–4-note slurs; duplets and triplets
Piano: broken and block chords; large reaches
Diff: smooth legato style; a"(opt. f") sustained *pp*
Uses: good singing song with consonant harmony; usable for young singer as well as more mature voice

FROMM, HERBERT
(b. Kitzingen, Germany, 1905; d. Brookline, MA, 1995)

965. **THE CRIMSON SAP.** Song Cycle for Medium Voice and Piano (Jean Harper). Carl Fischer, 1956. Traditional keys ("hollow" tonalities; most songs end on 8ves or open 5ths); g–a"; Tess-M-mH; changing meters, varied tempos; 21min; Diff-V/m-md, P/m.

For: lyric baritone; possible for mezzo-soprano; texts seem better for man

Mood: lyrical; dream-like; complete cycle of love relationship from inception to emptiness

Voice: modal in character; prominence of m2nd in melodic phrases; generally not difficult

Piano: creates dream-like moods, delicate touch needed

Diff: creating the introspective quality of the cycle

Uses: interesting cycle with references to music; good for imaginative, smooth lyric baritone; not a program ender

    a. *I Shall Not Sing of Hearts.* Amin; b♭–f"; Tess-M; 2/2, ♩= 66; 2+min.

    b. *Cut Me a Twig.* Gmin-maj; c'–f"; Tess-M-mH; 3/4, 2/4, 4/4, ♩= 176; 2min.

    c. *A Golden Band.* Lydian mode; f'–d"; Tess-M; 2/4, 3/4, ♩= 84–78; 2min.

    d. *Love for the Ankle Bone.* Emaj; b–e♯"; Tess-mH; 3/4, ♩= 164; 45sec.

    e. *Come Away with Me.* G-centered; g–g♭"; Tess-M; 6/4, 3/4, 4/4, 5/4, ♩= 184; 2+min.

    f. *The Devil Has a Forked Tongue.* Gmin; g–f"; Tess-M (ends low G); 4/4, ♪= 168; 2min.

    g. *A Veil Is over the Moon.* G- & E♭-centered; d♭'–f"; Tess-M; 6/8, 3/8, 2/4, ♪= 100; 2min .

    h. *I Was Sick.* B♭min; b♭–e♭"; Tess-M; unmetered, ♩= 88; 3+min.

    i. *I Am the Fever.* Amin; a–a"(e"); Tess-M-mH; 3/4, 2/4, 3/8, ♩= 144; 1+min.

    j. *Some Are Now Secret.* Cmaj; e'–d♭"; Tess-M; 3/4, ♩= 76; 3min.

FROST, ANNE KLANDERMAN
(b. U. S. A., 20th Century)

966. **SONGS FOR WALLACE** (Wallace Stevens). Three Art Songs for Soprano & Piano. Voice of the Rockies (BMI), 1993. Tonal references, but non-tertian harmony; a♯–g"; Tess-M; regular meters; varied tempos; 10pp; Diff-V/m, P/me-m.

For: soprano specified; mezzo-soprano seems better

Mood: philosophical

Voice: mostly conjunct; some skips of 7th & 8ve; fragmentary; some rhythmic complexity; syllabic; a few melismas; many accidentals

Piano: non-tertian structures; some wide reaches; broken-chord, repeated-chord, and afterbeat patterning; doubling of vocal line mostly incidental; many accidentals; longer than usual prelude, interlude, and postlude material; long interlude in (b.)

Diff: entrances, because of fragmentary writing; some rhythms; understanding the texts

Uses: as a group, or excerpt (b.) in a humorous group

    a. *Nevertheless.* F-centered; a♯–f"; Tess-M; 4/4, moderato (♩= 63); 3pp.

    b. *Rationalists.* A♭-centered; c'–g♭"; Tess-M; 4/4, 6/8, Moderato (♩= 120–♪= 176); 4pp.

    c. *Reasons for Moving.* X; d'–g"; Tess-M; 4/4, 3/4,

Adagio (♩= 58); 3pp.

GABURO, KENNETH
(b. Somerville, NJ, 1927; d. Iowa City, IA, 1993)

967. **THE NIGHT IS STILL** (Rabindranath Tagore). Carl Fischer, 1956. cmp1952. X; d'–a♭"; Tess-M; 3/4 with changes, Slow (♩= 76); 3+min;Diff-V/m-md, P/m-md.

For: soprano; tenor

Mood: lyrical; nocturne

Voice: leaps; long tones; dissonant intervals; two high climaxes; chromatic

Piano: linear with ornamental scale and turn figures; some 4-stave notation; numerous accidentals; rhythmic intricacies; quiet ending

Diff: pitch perception; some meter changes

Uses: usable song for student with good pitch and rhythmic sense and a ringing a♭"

GANZ, RUDOLF
(b. Zurich, Switzerland, 1877; d. Chicago, IL, 1972)

968. **IF ROSES NEVER BLOOMED AGAIN** (Franz Evers; English version by Francesca Falk Miller). H. W. Gray, 1959. Modal, Lydian on G with modulations; f♯'–g"; Tess-mH; 2/2, 3/2, Andante; 3pp; Diff-V/m, P/me.

For: soprano; tenor

Mood: lyrical; love song

Voice: conjunct with triadic skips; quiet

Piano: arpeggiated chords with short chordal section; delicate; mostly treble clef; specific pedalings and fingerings

Diff: some pitches

Uses: lovely song; usable for any high lyric voice; good teaching piece

969. **A MEMORY** (Minnie K. Breid). [25]; 1st©1919. Gmaj; f♯'–g"; Tess-M; 6/8, Quietly; 2pp; Diff-V/me, P/me.

For: soprano; tenor

Mood: lyrical; love song

Voice: rather static, featuring repeated b'; one phrase builds to g"; melisma

Piano: chordal; syncopation; some chromaticism; arpeggiations at end; some doubling of vocal line

Uses: good short song for young lyric soprano

970. **A SEASON CYCLE OF SONGS**, Op. 7, for High Voice (anon.; includes German trans.). Clayton F. Summy, 1904. Reprint: Recital Publications, 1986. last 3 songs cmp1902. Traditional keys; c'–a"; Tess-M-mH; regular meters, varied tempos; 21pp; Diff-V/m, P/me-md.

For: soprano; tenor

Mood: lyrical and philosophical; nature imagery

Voice: stepwise and small skips; leaps of m7th & 8ve; a little chromaticism; duplets and triplets lyrical and flowing; (c.) features voice in 2/4, piano in 6/8; (d.) features short phrases separated by rests; a few 2- & 3-note slurs

Piano: chordal and linear; block, broken, rolled and repeated chords; countermelodies; patterned; some chromaticism; triplets and groupings of 6 & 7; cross-hands; strong support and some doubling of vocal line

Uses: an example of its period; could be used in recital

    a. *Spring* (Frühling). Gmaj; d'–a"; 4/4, 3/4, 2/4, Allegro non troppo (♩ = 92); 5pp.

    b. *Summer* (Sommer). Bmaj–Gmaj; g'–b" (g♯"); 4/4, 6/4, Con slancio (♩ = 152); 7pp.

    c. *Autumn* (Herbst). Emin; c♯'–a♭"; 6/8, 2/4, Andantino (♩. = 69); 5pp.

    d. *Winter*. Gmin; c'–g"; 4/4, 6/4, Lento assai (♩ = 56); 3pp.

GARWOOD, MARGARET
(b. Haddonfield, NJ, 1927)

971. **THE CLIFF'S EDGE** (Songs of a Psychotic) (Eithne Tabor). Songflower Press, 1988 (Hildegard Publishing Company). X; b♭–b"; Tess-M-mH, cs; changing meters; varied tempos; 19pp; Diff-V/m-d, P/m-md.

For: soprano

Mood: despair; record of young woman's descent into madness

Voice: angular lines; syllabic setting; large intervals ascend to sustained high tones; dissonant; polyrhythms

Piano: motivically structured; mostly linear; some chordal passages; many accidentals; broken-chord patterns; 8ve countermelodies

Diff: dissonance; intensity of poetic subject matter

Uses: cycle gives heartbreaking view of the poet's descent into madness; probably very effective to program with happier groups before and after; graduate level

    a. *O Thou Twin-Blossoming Rose (Schizophrenia).* X; e'–a"; Tess-M; 3/4, 4/4, 2/4, Mysterioso; 3+pp.

    b. *The Child in the Sunlight (Hebephrenia).* X; e♭'–a"; Tess-mH; 3/4, 2/4, Allegretto ♩. = 80; 5pp.

    c. *And Is There Anyone at All? (Loneliness).* X; c♯'–a"; Tess-cs; 4/4, 3/4, 7/8, 5/8, 4/8, Lento; 3pp.

    d. *This Is How It Starts (Breakdown).* X; e'–b"; Tess-wide; 4/4, 3/4, Quasi Recitative–In tempo ♩ = 88; 5pp.

    e. *And with What Silence (Asylum).* X; b♭–f♯"; Tess-wide; 3/8, 4/4, 7/8, 3/4, Lento (dreamlike) ♪ = 72; 2pp.

972. **SPRINGSONGS.** Five Songs to Poems of E. E. Cummings for Soprano and Piano. Songflower Press, 1994 (Hildegard Publishing Company). Partly tonal, partly X; d♭'–b"; Tess-M-H; changing meters, ♩ = 48–♩. = 72; 24pp; Diff-V/md, P/m-d.

For: soprano (light lyric or lyric-coloratura)

Mood: romantic; ecstatic; songs of love and rebirth

Voice: lyrical and melodic; many phrases above the staff; sustained high tones; some large intervals; syllabic

Piano: mostly linear; patterned structures; some motor rhythms under 8ve melodies; afterbeat patterns in changing meters; numerous accidentals; counter-melodies

Diff: grasping and projecting meaning of poems with their

fragmented lines; mild dissonances; some rhythms

Uses: fine set for graduate or advanced undergraduate light soprano with flawless diction and a floating top

    a. *o sweet spontaneous.* Lydian on A; e'–a"; Tess-mH; 5/4, 3/4, 2/4, 7/8, Con brio ♩ = 132; 5pp.

    b. *trees were in (give, give).* G majorish; d♭'–a"; Tess-mH; 4/4, 2/4, Andantino ♩ = 60; 3pp.

    c. *until and I heard.* X; f♯'–b♭"; Tess-H; 3/4, 2/4, Scherzando ♩. = 72; 7pp.

    d. *thy fingers make early flowers.* X; e'–b"; Tess-H; 2/4, 3/4, 7/8, 6/8, Larghetto ♩ = 56; 5pp.

    e. *before the fragile gradual throne.* X; d'–a"; Tess-M; 4/4, 2/4, 3/4, Calmo ♩ = 48; 4pp.

973. **WHAT A PROUD DREAMHORSE** (e. e. cummings). Songflower Press, 1994 (Hildegard). Tonal but unsettled; c♯'–b♭"; Tess-wide, H; 4/4, 3/4, Allegro deciso ♩ = 152; 12pp; Diff-V/d, P/d.

For: soprano specified

Mood: surreal; dream-like

Voice: syncopation and mixed meter; some very long high tones; many phrases move by step and small skips; some large leaps; fragmented; somewhat like an aria

Piano: syncopation; varied afterbeat pattern suggests movements of horse; many accidentals; incidental doubling of vocal line

Diff: long high notes; ensemble; rhythms

Uses: group with other songs on poems by e. e. cummings or can stand alone

GETTY, GORDON
(b. Los Angeles, CA, 1933)

974. **THE WHITE ELECTION.** A Song Cycle for Soprano and Piano on 32 Poems of Emily Dickinson. Rork, 1985, 1986. Traditional keys with many modulations; b–a"; Tess-mH-M; traditional meters; varied tempos characterized by many changes and fluctuations; 81pp; 60min; Diff-V/m, P/me.

For: soprano; high mezzo-soprano (composer's specification)

Mood: tells Emily's story in her own words; "the white election meant a renunciation of the world . . . [and] probably also meant a shadow marriage to be perfected at death"; theme is union in death

Voice: mostly a type of recit. style in 8th notes with many repetitions of a single pitch, stepwise motion, and small skips; easy rhythms; in strophic songs some rhythmic variants for second stanza printed in smaller notes; occasional phrases have range of up to10th; most songs have several tempo changes or fluctuations; some of the many modulations (usually done with changes of key signature) are to distant keys; a few songs have many dynamic marks; vocal line intended to represent Emily's "chipper, chatty, conversational idiom"

Piano: thin score, sometimes to suggest Emily's piano (which was one 8ve shorter on both ends than the modern instrument), at other times to hear the piano play one note at a time "as we hear a violin or human voice"; sometimes spare block and broken chords; sometimes thinly-supported countermelody; occasional linear sections; some chords tied for 4 or 5 meas. (pianist instructed not to re-strike); some 3- or 4-stave writing; occasional solo material (c. has 20-meas. postlude); some doubling of vocal line

Diff: sustaining the attention of an audience for sixty minutes will require an excellent actress; vocal endurance; music here simply serves to carry text; Emily's words stand with spare and simple support

Uses: complete cycle constitutes entire recital for an unusually talented singer-actress; individual parts of the cycle could stand alone as smaller groups (it is divided into four parts, each with a subtitle); in the wrong hands performance of the entire cycle could be tedious; composer has supplied 10 pp. of notes on the poetry and music, which should be invaluable to performers; appears to be a unique work in its concept of presenting the poet's words in spare, simple musical forms, tonality, melody, harmony, and rhythms to match the aesthetic quality of the poetry, as well as the simplicity and purity of the poet's lifestyle and person

Rec: D#190

[Most of the songs have several tempo changes or fluctuations not noted below.]

PART ONE: THE PENSIVE SPRING

a. *I Sing to Use the Waiting* (major setting). Amaj; c♯'–e"; 4/4, Largo–Allegretto; 1+pp.

b. *There Is a Morn by Men Unseen.* Dmin-maj; c'–f"; 3/4, Andantino, grazioso; 3+pp (2 strophes).

c. *I Had a Guinea Golden.* Fmaj-Dmaj; d'–g"; 4/4, Allegretto grazioso libero; 3pp (2 strophes).

d. *If She Had Been the Mistletoe.* Amin-maj; c'–f♯"; 4/4, Allegro; 1p.

e. *New Feet within My Garden Go.* Cmaj; d'–f"; 4/4, Moderato libero; 1+pp.

f. *She Bore It.* E♭maj; d–g"; 4/4, Comodo; 2pp (2 strophes).

g. *I Taste a Liquor Never Brewed.* Dmaj; d'–f♯"; 4/4, Moderato; 1p (2 strophes).

h. *I Should Not Dare to Leave My Friend.* Fmin; e'–d♭"; 4/4, Recit.: Presto agitato; 2pp.

PART TWO: SO WE MUST MEET APART

i. *There Came a Day at Summer's Full.* Cmaj; c'–g"; 4/4, Recit.: Allegro; 4pp.

j. *The First Day's Night Had Come.* Amaj; e'–e"; 2/4, 3/8, Largo–Recit.: Allegretto; 4pp.

k. *The Soul Selects Her Own Society.* Dmin-maj; d'–e"; 4/4, Moderate libero; 2pp.

l. *It Was Not Death, for I Stood Up.* D♭maj; b–g♭"; 4/4, Recit.: Presto agitato; 3pp.

m. *When I Was Small, a Woman Died.* Cmaj; c♯'–g"; 2/4, Tempo di marcia–Recit: Allegretto; 5pp.

n. *I Cried at Pity, Not at Pain.* Fmin; c'–g"; 4/4, Recit.: Presto agitato; 3pp.

o. *The Night Was Wide.* Amin; d'–e"; 4/4, Presto con forza–Andante libero; 3pp.

p. *I Cannot Live with You.* Fmin; c'–a"; 4/4, Recit.: Allegro agitato–Andante, tempo giusto; 5pp.

PART THREE: ALMOST PEACE

q. *My First Well Day, Since Many Ill.* A♭maj; e♭'–g"; 4/4, Andantino–Moderato; 5pp.

r. *It Ceased to Hurt Me.* Amin; c'–f"; 4/4, Recit.: Moderato; 2pp.

s. *I Like to See It Lap the Miles.* Fmaj; e'–f"; 2/4, Allegro non troppo; 5pp.

t. *Split the Lark and You'll Find Music.* D♭maj; c'–f♯"; 4/4, Allegro con forza–Adagio grazioso; 1+pp.

u. *The Crickets Sang.* Emaj; e'–f♯"; 4/4, Moderato; 2pp.

v. *After a Hundred Years.* F♯min; d'–e"; 4/4, Adagio libero; 2pp.

w. *The Clouds Their Backs Together Laid.* Cmin; g'–g"; 4/4, Presto–Adagio; 1+pp.

x. *I Shall Not Murmur.* Gmaj; d'–f♯"; 4/4, Moderato; 1+pp.

PART FOUR: MY FEET SLIP NEARER

y. *The Grave My Little Cottage Is.* Cmaj-min; d'–g"; 4/4, Andante, tempo giusto; 1p.

z. *I Did Not Reach Thee.* Amaj; b–g"; 4/4, Largo–Recit.: Allegretto; 4pp.

aa. *My Wars Are Laid Away in Books.* Amaj; c♯'–f♯"; 4/4, Allegretto maestoso; 2pp.

bb. *There Came a Wind like a Bugle.* Gmin; d'–a"; 3/4, 4/4, Moderato–Presto; 4pp.

cc. *The Going from a World We Know.* Cmaj; c'–e♭"; 4+2+4/4, Tempo di marcia; 2pp.

dd. *Upon His Saddle Sprung a Bird.* Fmaj; f'–e♭"; 5/4 with changes, Allegro; 1p.

ee. *Beauty Crowds Me.* Fmaj; e'–f"; 4/4, Andante; 1p.

ff. *I Sing to Use the Waiting* (minor setting). Cmin; c'–a♭"; 4/4, Allegretto; 2pp.

GIANNINI, VITTORIO
(b. Philadelphia, PA, 1903; d. New York, NY, 1966)

975. **FAR ABOVE THE PURPLE HILLS** (Karl Flaster). [110]; 1st©1939. F♯min; c♯'–a"; Tess-mL; 4/4, Moderato; 3pp; Diff-V/m, P/m.

For: soprano

Mood: despairing; song of lost love

Voice: stepwise and chord-line skips; several descending scale passages; beat divided into 2, 3, & 4; 2–4-note slurs

Piano: chordal–broken, repeated block, rolled; some countermelody; does not double vocal line

Diff: some triplets vs. 2 or 4 in piano; dynamics

Uses: recital use

Rec: D#191

976. **HEART CRY** (Karl Flaster). [110]; 1st©1929. E♭min; e♭'–b♭"; Tess-M; 4/4, 3/4, Adagio-recitativo–Più mosso; 4pp; Diff-V/md, P/m.

For: tenor; soprano

Mood: declamatory; despairing; intense bereaved love

Voice: scalar and chord-line melody; speech rhythms

Piano: chordal; often low register; syncopation; chromatic

pattern in 8ves; duplets vs. vocal triplets; does not double vocal line
Diff: sustained high tones; intensely personal expression
Uses: very romantic; usable in a group; quiet ending
Rec: D#191

977. **I DID NOT KNOW** (Karl Flaster). [110]; 1st©1950. G♭maj; d♭'–a♭"; Tess-mH; 4/4, Adagio con molto espressione; 2pp; Diff-V/m, P/m.
For: soprano; some mezzo-sopranos
Mood: love song; quiet but intense
Voice: many skips; syncopation; dotted notes; 2-note slurs; low ending
Piano: chordal; broken-chord pattern; some countermelody; accidentals; no prelude or postlude; does not double vocal line
Diff: low ending
Uses: effective song; quiet ending
Rec: D#191

978. **I ONLY KNOW** (Karl Flaster). [110]. H & M keys: C♯min-Emaj; & Amin-Cmaj; f♯'–a" & d'–f"; Tess-mH/M; 4/4, Cantabile; 3pp; Diff-V/m, P/md.
For: tenor; baritone
Mood: recovery from unhappy love affair; affirmative but somewhat bitter
Voice: nicely balanced phrases, often encompassing a 7th or 8ve; syllabic; many accidentals; a b a' form; center section somewhat dramatic
Piano: block chords and arpeggiation; 8ve 8th-note triplets; many accidentals; short prelude and dramatic interlude; no doubling of vocal line; reaches of 9th & 10th
Diff: ensemble; a few duplets against piano triplets
Uses: possible recital song
Rec: D#191

979. **I SHALL THINK OF YOU** (Karl Flaster). [110]; 1st©1935. Cmaj; d'–g"; Tess-mL; 4/4, 5/4, Adagio–recitativo; 2pp; Diff-V/m, P/me.
For: tenor; high baritone
Mood: lyrical; nostalgic; love song
Voice: many skips; most phrases long ranged; speech rhythms; duplets and triplets
Piano: chordal; some large reaches; does not double vocal line
Uses: usable in a recital group; recit.-like style
Rec: D#191

980. **IT IS A SPRING NIGHT** (Karl Flaster). [110]; 1st©1942. D♭maj; e♭'–a"; Tess-M-mH; 4/4, Andante sostenuto; 5min; Diff-V/d, P/d.
For: tenor; soprano
Mood: lyrical; nocturne; ecstatic love song
Voice: richly romantic; chromatic; modulating; builds to high climax; aria-like intensity; soaring lines; quiet ending
Piano: highly romantic, much like Rachmaninoff; chordal; syncopation; arpeggiation; countermelodies; modulations; romantic piano technique required
Diff: similar to those of an operatic aria, with added requirement of lyricism of song; for advanced singers
Uses: wonderful song for the romantic singer; demands big lyric voice with plenty of endurance
Rec: D#191

981. **LONGING** (Karl Flaster). [110]; 1st©1950. X; b–g♭"; Tess-M; 3/4, Adagio (dolce e nostalgico); 4pp; Diff-V/md, P/md.
For: soprano; mezzo-soprano
Mood: lyrical; reminiscent
Voice: stepwise with some skips up to 7th; repetitive rhythms; many accidentals
Piano: broken-chord pattern moves in 16ths, mostly descending; some countermelody; many accidentals; does not double vocal line
Diff: ends on lowest note of range
Uses: rather delicate song; effective; not so complex as some of Giannini's songs; good singing lines
Rec: D#191

982. **SING TO MY HEART A SONG** (Karl Flaster). [110]; 1st©1944. H & M keys: Gmaj & Emaj; d'–b" & b–g♯"; Tess-M; 4/4, Allegro moderato; 3pp; Diff-V/md, P/md.
For: soprano; tenor; dramatic or ample lyric sound
Mood: ecstatic love song
Voice: many leaps; many long tones; long-ranged phrases; duplets and triplets; accidentals
Piano: repeated triplet block chords; thick texture; some countermelody; 8ve passages; large reaches; arpeggios in groups of 5; some 2 vs. 3; many accidentals; does not double vocal line
Diff: some duplets vs. piano triplets; needs mature sound
Uses: big song; program ender; exciting with the right singer
Rec: D#s 40, 191

983. **TELL ME, OH BLUE, BLUE SKY!** (Karl Flaster). [110]; 1st©1927. "To Madam Marcella Sembrich." F♯min-B♭maj; c♯'(f♯')–g♯"; Tess-mH; 4/4, 3/4, 5/4, 6/4, Adagio; 4pp; Diff-V/m, P/m.
For: soprano
Mood: lyrical; introspective; lost love
Voice: many small skips; some tritones; fragmented phrases; some syncopation
Piano: broken-chord patterns; rolled chords; some countermelody; syncopated repeated chords; 4-meas. interlude contains the climax of the song; incidental doubling of vocal line
Diff: phrases need to be "spun out"
Uses: effective song if tastefully done; somewhat sentimental
Rec: D#s 47, 191, 192

984. **THERE WERE TWO SWANS** (Karl Flaster). [110]; 1st©1944. H & M keys: Tonal; c'–g♯" & a♭–e"; Tess-mH; 4/4, Moderato; 3pp; Diff-V/m, P/m.
For: soprano (not light)
Mood: descriptive; somber
Voice: leaps include 7th & 8ve; much stepwise motion also; some recit.-like phrases; triplets vs. piano duplets or quadruplets
Piano: chordal–block, broken, rolled; syncopated repeated tone; varied texture and register; some doubling of vocal line
Diff: sustained high tones; dramatic climax on g"*ff*
Uses: effective if tastefully done; somewhat sentimental; quiet ending
Rec: D#191

985. THREE POEMS OF THE SEA (Karl Flaster). [110]; 1st©1935. Traditional key structures with late Romantic modulations; c♯'–b"; Tess-M-H; regular changing meters; tempos increase in speed throughout set; 9+min; Diff-V/m-d, P/m-d.
For: big lyric tenor voice with ringing b"
Mood: lyrical; background and elements of the sea in two love poems and one metaphorical poem
Voice: stepwise, skips, and leaps; short and long phrases; ascending phrases; sustained tones at ends of phrases; loud and soft high tones
Piano: Romantic piano technique required; much broken-chord and arpeggiated patterning; large reaches; changing meters; accidentals; motion suggests movement of the sea; cross-hands; much modulation
Diff: tessitura; endurance; ensemble; meter changes
Uses: showpiece set for the right tenor; singer can display full control of a beautiful lyric voice; both soft high singing and ringing a"s and one b"; good final group
Rec: D#191

  a. *Sea Dream.* D♭maj; e'–a♭"; Tess-M; 4/4, Andante sonnolento; 2pp.
  b. *Waiting.* Emaj; c♯'–g♯"; Tess-M-mH; 5/4, 3/4, 4/4, 3/2, 2/4, Andante; 3pp.
  c. *Song of the Albatross.* Amin-Emaj; e♯'–b"; Tess-mH; 2/2, 3/2, 6/4, Allegro; 6pp.

GIASSON, PAUL E. [Guy Paulson]
(b. New Bedford, MA, 1921)

986. VOCALISE. Galleon, 1962. Emaj-centered; g♯'–b♭"; Tess-M-H; 6/8, 2/4, Moderato; 3+min; Diff-V/m-md, P/m.
For: soprano; tenor
Mood: somewhat dramatic
Voice: some awkward intervals; center section dramatic and doubled by piano one 8ve lower
Piano: chordal texture; many accidentals; some wide l.h. reaches; syncopation; many parallel 3rds & 10ths
Diff: to be done on "ah" would require many vowel modifications; calls for dynamics pp–ff (both called for on a♭"); some sudden dynamic changes
Uses: good vocalise for tenor who can float soft ending on g♯", or soprano who can do same and also handle a♭" ff; quiet ending

GIDEON, MIRIAM
(b. Greeley, CO, 1906 d. New York, NY, 1996)

987. BELLS (William Jones). American Composers Alliance (Composers Facsimile Edition), 1966. X; a–b'; Tess-L; 3/4, 4/4, Moderato; 2pp; Diff-V/md, P/m.
For: bass; bass-baritone; contralto
Mood: somber; concerns Abraham Lincoln
Voice: stepwise motion and small skips; many accidentals; speech-like rhythms; syllabic with a few 2–4-note slurs; subdued dynamics except for one f phrase
Piano: broken-chord figures; non-traditional harmony; many accidentals; both duplet and triplet subdivisions of beat; some 2 vs. 3; does not double vocal line but helps singer find pitches
Diff: perhaps ensemble
Uses: as part of recital group about Lincoln and/or other famous persons; for musical student with short range

988. EPITAPHS FROM ROBERT BURNS. For High Voice. American Composers Alliance (Composers Facsimile Edition). cmp1952. X; c'–a" (also available in med.-low & low eds.); Tess-wide; traditional meters with changes; varied tempos; 7pp; Diff-V/d, P/md.
For: soprano; tenor (also med. or low voices)
Mood: wry; humorous
Voice: mostly disjunct; some long-ranged phrases (e.g., d'–g♭", f'–a♭"); (d.) has several phrases sung on a single pitch; rhythms uncomplicated; Scotch snap used; (a.) & (b.) contain several 2-note slurs; (c.) & (d.), syllabic; several sudden dynamic changes; several soft high notes; has big ending
Piano: linear and linear-chordal combinations; often bitonal; many accidentals; doubling of vocal line incidental
Diff: pitches; ensemble; pronunciation of words and place names in Scottish dialect
Uses: a set for a singer comfortable in wide tessitura
Rec: D#193

  a. *Epitaph for a Wag in Mauchline.* D-centered; d'–a♭"; 4/4, Boldly; 2pp.
  b. *Epitaph on Wee Johnie.* A-centered; c'–a"; 5/8, 6/8, 4/8, Tenderly, not too slowly; 1p.
  c. *Epitaph on the Author.* X; d'–f♯" (also available in med. voice ed.); 4/4, 3/4, 5/4, Gravely; 1p.
  d. *Monody on a Lady Famed for Her Caprice.* X; c♯'–a♭"; 3/4, Gaily, somewhat boisterously; 3pp.

989. THE SEASONS OF TIME. Songs on Tanka Poems of Ancient Japan. Cycle. General, 1971. X (much dissonance, many 2nds); e'–a"; Tess-M-mH; regular and frequently-changing meters, some irregular meters; varied tempos; 12pp; Diff-V/dd, P/dd.
For: soprano; tenor
Mood: moods of the seasons, almost all bittersweet; nature pictures; philosophical
Voice: highly chromatic vocal line, difficult to hear; speech rhythms; 16th/dotted-8th recurring rhythmic figure; high soft singing
Piano: much delicate tremolo; mostly in treble clef; linear; delicate textures; dissonant; many accidentals; light touch needed
Diff: perfect pitch desirable; much soft singing; singer needs appreciation for Japanese poetry and imagery
Uses: interesting cycle for advanced musician and superior singer with feeling for these texts
Rec: D#s 194, 195

  a. *Now It Is Spring.* 2/4, 3/4, Radiante ♩ = 72; 1p.
  b. *The Wild Geese Returning.* 2/4, 3/4, Pensierosamente ♩ = 63; 1p.
  c. *Can It Be That There Is No Moon.* 3/4 with changes, Tristamente ♩ = 50; 1p.
  d. *Gossip Grows like Weeds in a Summer Meadow.* 2/4, 3/4, Gaimente ♩ = 120; 1p.

e. *Each Season More Lovely.* 4/4 with changes, Estatico ♩ = 84; 5pp.

f. *In the Leafy Treetops of the Summer Mountain.* 4/4, 5/4, Da lontano ♩ = 72; 1/2p.

g. *I Have Always Known That at Last I Would Take This Road.* 5/8 with changes, Affectivo ♩ = 60; 1p.

h. *To What Shall I Compare This World?* 4/4 with changes, Transparamente ♩ = 72; 1p.

i. *Yonder in the Plum Tree.* 2/4 with changes, Leggiero ♩ = 66; 1p.

990. SONGS OF VOYAGE. High Voice and Piano. American Composers Alliance (Composers Facsimile Edition), 1964. cmp1961. X; d'(e♭')–a" (also available in low-voice ed.); Tess-mH-H; changing meters, contrasting tempos; 13+pp; Diff-V/d, P/d.

For: soprano; tenor (in this range)
Mood: see individual annotations
Voice: highly chromatic, many small skips; speech-like rhythms; duplet and triplet subdivisions of beat, complicated by meter changes; 2 vs. 3 in piano; syllabic; one 6-note melisma with leaps of 7th in (a.)
Piano: (a.), linear style, mostly 2–3-voice texture, many accidentals, and occasional doubling of vocal line; (b.), mostly non-tertian vertical structures in broken-chord patterns; triplet and duplet subdivisions of beat; asymmetrical rhythmic groups
Diff: ensemble; many pitches hard to find; perfect pitch helpful; rhythms; irregular phrase lengths in (a.)
Uses: could be programmed separately or as a pair

a. *Farewell Tablet to Agathocles* (Florence Wilkinson). X; e'–g♯"; Tess-H; 6/8, 2/4 and many changes, Andantino (with several changes); 5pp; (death and mourning).

b. *The Nightingale Unheard.* (Josephine Preston Peabody). X; d'(e♭')–a"; Tess-mH; changing meters, Con movimento (with fluctuations); 8+pp; (entreats the nightingale to sing for the world's downtrodden rather than the world's kings).

991. SONNETS FROM *FATAL INTERVIEW* (Edna St. Vincent Millay). American Composers Alliance (Composers Facsimile Edition), 1961. cmp1952. X; d'–a♭"; Tess-M-mH; changing meters, varied tempos; 10pp; Diff-V/d, P/d.

For: mezzo-soprano
Mood: loneliness; lost love
Voice: highly chromatic; many accidentals; rhythmic complications from changing meters and mixture of duplet and triplet subdivisions of beat; predominantly syllabic; some melismas; dramatic ending
Piano: predominantly linear; some afterbeat style; some countermelody; many accidentals; r.h. of (b.) has many 3rds; occasional doubling of vocal line; some interlude material
Diff: ensemble; rhythms
Uses: as a recital set; dramatic ending

a. *I. (Gone in good sooth you are).* [3]. X; d♯'–a♭"; Tess-M; changing meters, Distant (♪ = 92); 3pp.

b. *II. (Night is my sister).* X; d'–g♭"; Tess-mH;

changing meters, Tumultuous (♩ = 66); 4pp.

c. *III. (Moon that against the lintel of the west . . .).* X; e'–a♭"; Tess-mH; changing meters, Impassioned (♩ = 88); 3pp.

992. TO MUSIC. High Voice and Piano (Robert Herrick). American Composers Edition (Composers Facsimile Edition), 1964. cmp1957. X; c♯'(d♯')–a♭" (also available in L & M eds.); Tess-mH; 2/4 with many changes, Dolce ma un poco agitato (followed by many changes), 7pp; Diff-V/d, P/d.

For: high voice (in this range)
Mood: lyrical tribute to the power of music
Voice: chromatic; many accidentals; syncopation and dotted rhythms; irregular meters; complicated rhythms; several melismas, often for text-painting; ends on sustained g♯"
Piano: mixture of linear and chordal texture; many accidentals; many vertical structures based on 2nds, 5ths, & 7ths; some 3-stave writing; does not double vocal line; 7-meas. prelude and 7-meas. interlude
Diff: ensemble; hearing the intervals; rhythms
Uses: recital use in a group concerning music
Rec: D#193

GILBERT, HENRY F.
(b. Somerville, MA, 1868; d. Cambridge, MA, 1928)

993. THE OWL (Alfred, Lord Tennyson). [5, 66, vol. 5]; 1st©1910. Emin; d'–e"; Tess-M; 4/4, Andante ma con moto e con uomore; 37meas.; Diff-V/me, P/me.

For: any voice
Mood: descriptive; dignified
Voice: scalar and small skips; some 2-note slurs
Piano: chordal; 4–6-voice texture
Uses: good range for inexperienced singers; useful in American group

994. PIRATE SONG (Robert Louis Stevenson). [61, 66, vol. 1]; 1st©1902. Cmin; c'–g"(f"); Tess-M; 2/4, Allegro energico e con brio; 71meas.; Diff-V/m, P/md.

For: tenor; high baritone
Mood: masculine; drinking song
Voice: skips; some scales; some 2-note slurs; some odd intervals
Piano: r.h. often has fast melody in 8ves; many accidentals
Uses: good encore song; group ender

995. TELL ME WHERE IS FANCY BRED (William Shakespeare). [61]. Emin-Gmaj (many modulations); d'–g"; Tess-mH; 3/4, Moderato; 6pp; Diff-V/md, P/md.

For: tenor; soprano
Mood: rather dramatic
Voice: skips of up to 8ve; many accidentals; dotted rhythms; some triplets
Piano: block and broken chords; 9-meas. prelude, 21 meas. of interludes; many accidentals
Diff: some intervals; a few rhythms
Uses: in a Shakespeare group; period piece

GLANVILLE-HICKS, PEGGY
(b. Melbourne, Australia, 1912; d. Sydney, Australia, 1990; naturalized American citizen, 1948)

996.   FIVE SONGS (A. E. Housman). Weintraub, 1952. cmp1944. Traditional keys with altered chords; b–a"; Tess-M-mH; regular meters with changes; moderate tempos; 11pp; Diff-V/m-md, P/m.
For: tenor; soprano; texts slightly better for men
Mood: lyrical; somewhat melancholy
Voice: numerous sustained high tones; some leaps; accidentals
Piano: broken-chord figurations; many accidentals; some glissando passages
Uses: attractive program ender

    a. *Mimic Heaven.* Dmaj-min; d'–a"; Tess-M; 4/8, 3/8, ♪ = 138; 2pp.
    b. *He Would Not Stay.* b–g"; Tess-M; 3/4, 2/4, 4/4, 1/4, ♩ = 60; 2pp.
    c. *Stars.* B♭maj; d'–g"; Tess-M; 4/8, ♩ = 72; 2pp.
    d. *Unlucky Love.* e'–e"; Tess-M; 6/8, ♩ = 72; 2pp.
    e. *Homespun Collars.* Amaj; f♯'–a"; Tess-mH; 4/8, 6/8, ♩ = 116; 3pp.

997.   PROFILES FROM CHINA (Eunice Tietjens). Weintraub, 1951. Tonal and bitonal; e'–a"; Tess-M-mH; regular meters; moderate tempos; 5+min; Diff-V/md, P/m.
For: soprano; tenor
Mood: Oriental; fragile images and descriptions of China
Voice: some difficult intervals; pitches hard to find; syncopation; dotted rhythms; mostly syllabic; requires dynamic range *pp–ff*
Piano: pianistic–mostly broken-chord figures; many accidentals; many 4ths & 5ths in harmonic structures; does not double vocal line
Diff: score somewhat difficult to read; singer should have good dynamic control
Uses: nice set for senior or graduate recital

    a. *Poetics.* B-centered; f♯'–a"; Tess-mH; 3/8; 1min.
    b. *A Lament of Scarlet Cloud.* D♯-centered; e'–g"; Tess-M; 4/4; 1min.
    c. *The Dream.* Bitonal; e'–f"; Tess-M; 4/4, Lento recitativo–Maestoso; 1min.
    d. *Crepuscule.* F-centered; f'–e"; Tess-M; 2/4, Andantino; 45sec.
    e. *The Son of Heaven.* B-centered; a'–g♯"; Tess-mH; 6/8, 3/4; 1min.

998.   13 WAYS OF LOOKING AT A BLACKBIRD (Wallace Stevens). Weintraub, 1951. Traditional keys with some dissonance; a–g♯"; Tess-M; regular meters with a few changes; varied tempos and moods; 10min; Diff-V/me, P/m.
For: all except very low voices
Mood: lyrical; 13 portraits of a blackbird; very brief scenes and images
Voice: sustained tones; a few large leaps; mostly conjunct; some melismatic phrases; one spoken text
Piano: mostly linear; various figures and patterns–octaves, scale passages, repeated tones, trills, arpeggiation

Diff: quick succession of different moods
Uses: very interesting work; excellent for teaching students to study, absorb, and reflect the text of a song; usable for both younger and older students; recital material

GLEASON, FREDERICK GRANT
(b. Middletown, CT, 1848; d. Chicago, IL, 1903)

999.   EVENING SONG (Bianca di Medici). [67, vol. 3]; 1st©1890. A♭maj; c'–a♭"; Tess-M; 4/4; 4pp; Diff-V/m, P/m.
For: lyric soprano
Mood: quiet
Voice: chord-member skips; duplets and triplets; recit.-like central section
Piano: chordal–broken and repeated; vocal melody used in prelude, interlude, and postlude
Diff: sustained a♭" occurs twice
Uses: usable quiet song

GLICKMAN, SYLVIA
(b. New York , NY, 1932)

1000.   BLACK CAKE, A RECIPE BY EMILY DICKINSON. Hildegard Publishing Co., 1994. cmp1978. X; d'–a♯"; Tess-mH; 3/4, 4/4, 5/4, 2/4, 7/8, etc., Moderato ♩ = 100 with changes; 6pp; Diff-V/md, P/md.
For: soprano; high mezzo-soprano
Mood: humorous and/or matter of fact (your choice)
Voice: sequential construction unifies; some leaps of m7th & M10th; patter passages in staccato; short cadenza-like staccato passage; many crescendos; some spoken lines
Piano: some doubling and imitation of vocal line; variety of articulations; many accidentals; 4+3+2/8 section seems to imitate mixing bowl action; 4-meas. prelude and 10-meas. postlude; several interludes
Diff: singer needs good ear and flair for comedy; ensemble–both performers have to handle many tempo and dynamic changes
Uses: good recital song

1001.   EMILY DICKINSON SONGS. Hildegard Publishing Co., 1991. cmp1979-1983. Tonal; a♯–b"; Tess-wide; regular meters; slow to moderate tempos; 17pp; Diff-V/md-d, P/md-d.
For: soprano; mezzo-soprano (c.)
Mood: nature; philosophical
Voice: mixture of conjunct and disjunct intervals; syllabic; rhythms somewhat speech-like; many accidentals; (a.) & (c.), varied ternary form; (b.), through-composed
Piano: awkward l.h. arpeggiation (wide intervals); r.h. arpeggiation in aug. triads and quartal and quintal chords; some block chords; chromaticism; colorful; 16th- & 8th-note motion; rare vocal doubling
Diff: ensemble; difficult to find pitch on some entries; speech-like rhythms create fragmentation in (a.) & (c.); range of (c.) for some sopranos
Uses: a set for the long-ranged soprano; (c.) could be excerpted by mezzos (or baritones) into a group of

Dickinson poems set by other composers

a. *From Cocoon Forth.* Emaj-C♯min; e'–b"; Tess-H; 6/8, 4/8, Slowly lilting, hesitant; 8pp.

b. *After Great Pain.* F♯ centered; c'–a"; Tess-wide; 4/4, 3/4, Molto moderato; 4pp.

c. *It Will Be Summer.* Chromatic-ends Emaj; a♯–e"; Tess-M; 3/4, In lazy waltz time; 5pp.

GOETSCHIUS, PERCY
(b. Paterson, NJ, 1853; d. Manchester, NH, 1943)

1002. **O! MY LOVE'S LIKE A RED, RED ROSE** (Robert Burns). [1]; 1st©1898. Amaj; e'–f♯"; Tess-M; 4/4, Allegro con brio; 3pp; Diff-V/m, P/m.
For: tenor specified
Mood: exuberant love song; folk-like flavor
Voice: repetitive melody and rhythms; dotted rhythms; some grace notes; some 2-note slurs
Piano: rolled- and broken-chord patterning; does not double vocal line
Uses: usable simple setting

GOLD, ERNEST
(b. Vienna, Austria, 1921; d. Santa Monica, CA 1999)

1003. **SONGS OF LOVE AND PARTING.** For High Voice and Piano. Cycle. G. Schirmer, 1963. Pub. separately. Traditional keys; a–b"; Tess-M, mH, L; generally regular meters with some changes; varied tempos; 16min; Diff-V/md-d, P/m-md.
For: tenor and soprano if done as a cycle (seems best as a double cycle, based on the texts and their sequence–tenor: 1–3; soprano: 4–7)
Mood: lyrical and dramatic; various moods of a broken love relationship
Voice: wide range of both pitch and dynamics; highly expressive of the texts; many wide leaps
Piano: much melodic material; sets moods
Diff: range; some high tones; ensemble
Uses: very beautiful and well-written cycle; should add interest to any program as a double cycle; can also be sung separately
Rec: D#s 41, 196, 197

a. *Gifts* (James Thomson). Emaj; d'–a"; Tess-M; 6/8, 9/8, Allegretto; 2min .

b. *Shall I Compare Thee* (William Shakespeare). C♯min-maj; c♯'–b"; Tess-M; 4/4, 3/4, 6/4, Leisurely; 3+min.

c. *A Red, Red Rose* (Robert Burns). Bmin; b–a"; Tess-L,M,H; 4/4, Allegretto con grazia; 3+min.

d. *Peace* (Emily Dickinson). Gmin; f♯'–a♭"; Tess-mH; 3/4, 4/4, 5/4, Allegro agitato; 1min.

e. *Parting* (Emily Dickinson). [64]. B♭min; a–a♭"; Tess-mL with H phrases; unmetered, Tempo rubato; 1+min.

f. *Time Does Not Bring Relief* (Edna St. Vincent Millay). G-centered; a–g"; Tess-M,H; 6/4, 4/4, Appassionato; 3+min.

g. *Music, When Soft Voices Die* (Percy Bysshe Shelley). [64]. E♭min-B♭maj; e♭'–g♭"; Tess-M-mH; 4/4, Tempo rubato; 1min.

GOLDE, WALTER
(b. Brooklyn, NY, 1887; d. Chapel Hill, NC, 1963)

1004. **O BEAUTY, PASSING BEAUTY** (Alfred Lord Tennyson). Brodt, 1958. Bmin; b–f♯"; Tess-M; 3/4, Andante sostenuto e rubato; 2+min; Diff-V/m, P/m.
For: high baritone
Mood: lyrical; love song
Voice: many skips, esp. 5ths & 7ths; dotted rhythms; some triplets
Piano: repeated chords; various registers; many accidentals; some countermelody; 2 vs. 3; some doubling of vocal line
Diff: f♯" sustained with crescendo
Uses: usable lyric song

GOLDMAN, RICHARD FRANKO
(b. New York, NY, 1910; d. Baltimore, MD, 1980)

1005. **MY KINGDOM** (Robert Louis Stevenson). Mercury, 1952. Amin; e'–g"; Tess-M; 4/2, 2/2, 3/2, ♩ = 63 Simply and unaffectedly; 3pp; Diff-V/m, P/e.
For: tenor
Mood: lyrical; childish fancy
Voice: many skips; easy rhythms; quiet dynamics
Piano: linear; 2–4 voices; easy rhythms
Uses: pleasant song; useful for young tenor; child's text

1006. **TWO POEMS OF WILLIAM BLAKE.** Mercury, 1952. cmp1929. Amin/Gmaj; d'–g"; Tess-M; regular meters; 4pp; Diff-V/me, P/e.
For: lyric soprano; tenor
Mood: lyrical; pastoral
Voice: skips along chord lines; some melismas
Piano: linear; patterned, or chorale-like
Uses: two nice songs for young singer; good teaching pieces

a. *To a Lovely Myrtle Bound.* Amin; f'–f"; 6/8, Slow ♩ = 54; 2pp.

b. *The Shepherd.* Gmaj; d'–g"; 4/4, ♩ = 66; 2pp.

1007. **THE WEARY YEARE** (Edmund Spenser). Mercury, 1956. cmp1955. Amaj; d'–a"; Tess-M; 4/4, 2/4, 3/4, Allegro moderato; 3pp; Diff-V/m, P/m.
For: tenor; soprano
Mood: lyrical; New Year's song
Voice: many skips along chord lines; easy rhythms
Piano: chordal-linear combination; somewhat march-like

GORDON, RICKY IAN
(b. Long Island, NY, 1956)

[See also D#53 for songs not listed below]

1008. **GENIUS CHILD** (Langston Hughes). A Cycle of 10

Songs for High Voice. Williamson Music, 1995 (Hal Leonard). Composed for Harolyn Blackwell. Major keys; c'–b♭"; Tess-M-mH-H; mostly regular meters; varied tempos ♩ = 44–138; 50pp; Diff-V/md-d, P/md.

For: soprano

Mood: poignant; impressions of city life in Harlem; many scenes, characters, and moods

Voice: lyrical; low- and high-lying phrases; many different types of vocal expression; jazz syncopation; glissandos and embellishments that suggest blues improvisation

Piano: popular music forms; piano is background for voice and has its own role in solo sections; continuous throughout each song; usually syncopated

Diff: singer needs good sense of blues style

Uses: good cycle for a high soprano acquainted with Langston Hughes's poetry; example of distinctly American style with popular music roots

    a. ***Winter Moon.*** X; c'–a"; Tess-mH; 3/4, 4/4, 2/4, Strangely Atmospheric; 2pp.

    b. ***Genius Child.*** Cmaj; c'–g"; Tess-M; 4/4, 3/2, 6/8, Rhythmic ♩ = 120; 4pp.

    c. ***Kid in the Park.*** A minorish; d'–f"; Tess-M; 4/4, Slow, Desolate ♩ = 58; 3pp.

    d. ***To Be Somebody.*** Cmaj; c'–a"; Tess-mH; 6/8, Sprightly ♩. = 66; 6pp.

    e. ***Troubled Woman.*** Emin; e'–g"; Tess-M; 3/4, Andante ♩ = 80; 3pp.

    f. ***Strange Hurt.*** Dmin; d'–g♭"(a♭"); Tess-M-mH; 4/4, Tango ♩ = 120; 2+pp.

    g. ***Prayer.*** E♭maj; d'–g"; Tess-M; 4/4, Solemn ♩ = 66; 6pp.

    h. ***Border Line.*** A♭maj-Amin; c'–b♭"; Tess-H, L; 4/4, Rhythmic, Brisk ♩ = 138; 8pp.

    i. ***My People.*** A♭maj; d♭'–a♭"; Tess-cs; 3/4, Slow Dreamy ♩ = 58; 4pp.

    j. ***Joy.*** B♭-G♭maj; f'–b♭"; Tess-mH-H; 4/4, 6/8, Exhuberant and Accented ♩ = 132; 8pp.

[I NEVER KNEW. See entry #15 O]

1009.   **THE LAKE ISLE OF INNISFREE** (William Butler Yeats). [111]. cmp1987. Tonal; d'–g♭"; Tess-M; 4/4, 2/4, Dreamlike ♩ = 48; 6pp; Diff-V/md, P/md.

For: soprano; tenor

Mood: dreamy; longing for the natural world

Voice: lyric recitative; mostly conjunct; a few intervals larger than 5th; syllabic; speech rhythms

Piano: built on duplet pattern that creates a dreamlike haze of harmony; many accidentals; some double 3rds & 4ths; 5-meas. interlude; descriptive; impressionistic

Uses: interesting late 20th-century setting of this poem; good for a warm soprano or tenor voice

1010.   **POEM (LANA TURNER HAS COLLAPSED)** (Frank O'Hara). [111]. cmp1985. C-A♭major; d'–b"; Tess-mH-H; 4/4, 2/4, Abrupt ♩ = 132; 5pp; Diff-V/md, P/md.

For: soprano; tenor

Mood: raucous; abrupt; jazzy

Voice: disjunct; chord outlines interspersed with chromatic conjunct phrases; wide range in single phrases (d'–b♭");

---

syllabic; energetic

Piano: syncopation; punctuating chords and other motives; accidentals; jazzy rhythmic structure

Diff: vocal range (ends on b"); some rhythms

Uses: effective setting of this poem; advanced undergraduate or graduate level singer; see also Christopher Berg setting

1011.   **THE SPRING AND THE FALL** (Edna St. Vincent Millay). [111]. cmp1984. Tonal; b–a"; Tess-M; 4/4, Slow and Languid ♩ = 69; 5pp; Diff-V/md, P/md.

For: soprano

Mood: gentle sadness at love's slow demise

Voice: a rather simple melody, quasi-ballad style; some large descending intervals; numerous accidentals

Piano: chromatic; constant 8th-note motion in duplet figures; many accidentals; some doubling of vocal line

Diff: constant motion of piano with many accidentals

Uses: interesting contemporary ballad setting of this poem; cf. Lekberg setting

1012.   **WILL THERE REALLY BE A MORNING** (Emily Dickinson). [111]. cmp1983. B♭maj; a–f"; Tess-cs; 4/4, Lento ♪ = 96-free eighth notes–pedal throughout; 5pp; Diff-V/m, P/m.

For: mezzo-soprano

Mood: slow ballad; questioning of life

Voice: disjunct lines; wide-ranged melody in most phrases; syllabic; words conform to melody; simple expression; entire text and music repeated

Piano: slow ballad style; broken-chord figuration; some melodic material

Diff: making the direct repeat effective

Uses: undergraduate level; contrast with other settings of this poem (Persichetti: "Out of the Morning"; Bacon: "Is There Such a Thing as Day?")

GOTTLIEB, JACK
(b. New Rochelle, NY, 1930)

1013.   **HAIKU SOUVENIRS.** For Voice and Piano (Leonard Bernstein). Amberson, 1978 (copyright assigned to Theophilous). cmp1967. X; g♯–g"; Tess-wide; traditional meters with some changes and unmetered; varied tempos; 6+min; Diff-V/d, P/md-d.

For: baritone seems best; mezzo-soprano

Mood: (a.–c.): descriptive; (d.): humorous; (e.): philosophical; some fragility but more of a full-bodied, Western approach than might be expected

Voice: some large leaps (M & m7ths & 9ths); melismas common; (a.), trill which accelerates and retards twice; (c.), two portamentos; (d.), grace notes; (e.), portamentos ending with "back in the throat"; (c.–e.), short repeated sections; other ornaments; several *senza misura* sections; one section sung into piano strings

Piano: mostly spare; (b.), three staves; (c.), thickest texture; (e.), imitates Japanese *sho*; mixture of linear and block-chord styles; some staccato; some special instructions, incl. use of harmonics; does not double vocal line

Diff: detailed above; some dynamic changes are sudden and *fp* required twice; wide tessitura

Uses: as a set; an attractive group for singer who can handle the tessitura (g", 1 beat *ff*, g♯ is 16th note occurring three times)

    a. *Haiku I.* Nearly Amin; d'–d"; 4/8, 3/8, Semplice e gentile; 1p.

    b. *Haiku II.* A♭-centered; e'–f♯"; 3/4, 2/4, 4/4, Piacevole e legato; 2½pp.

    c. *Haiku III.* X; g♯–g"; 2/4, Con slancio; 1+pp.

    d. *Haiku IV.* X; e♭'–f♯"; 7/8 with many changes, Scherzando; 2pp.

    e. *Haiku V.* X; f♯'–f"; unmetered, Freely, without measure; 2pp.

GOTTSCHALK, LOUIS FERDINAND
(b. St. Louis, MO, 1868; d. Rio de Janeiro, 1934)

1014. **AT THE SIGN OF THE THREE BLACK CROWS.** Bass Song (William H. Gardner). White-Smith, 1901. Dmaj; A–d'; Tess-M–mH; 6/8, Con anima; 2 stanzas with refrain; Diff-V/m, P/e.

For: bass

Mood: drinking song

Voice: conjunct with some skips; constant dotted rhythms with long tones at phrase ends; typical drinking-song style

Piano: open-8ve doubling of vocal line, with small flourish at cadences; some punctuating chords

Uses: rousing song for bass; could end light group

GRAHAM, ROBERT
(b. Eldorado, KS, 1912)

1015. **AFTER A RAIN AT MOKANSHAN** (Witter Bynner). Associated, 1958. [4]. cmp1956. B♭-centered; d'–f"; Tess-mH; 4/4, Slow; 2min; Diff-V/m, P/m.

For: all except lowest voices

Mood: tranquil; delicate; Oriental flavor

Voice: stepwise and small skips; regular rhythms; many accidentals

Piano: 2–4-voice texture; delicate; many accidentals; independent of vocal line

Diff: begins f"; dynamic control

Uses: usable for student or more advanced singer

GREEN, RAY
(b. Cavendish, MO, 1908; d. 1997)

1016. **I LOVED MY FRIEND** (Langston Hughes). [3]. cmp1935; rev.1970. X–F; f'–a"; Tess-H; 2/4, ♩ = 100 with many changes; 3pp; Diff-V/m, P/m.

For: soprano; tenor

Mood: lyric

Voice: easy skips; syncopations; repetitive

Piano: mostly block chords; many accidentals; 14-meas. prelude; 22 meas. interludes

Diff: rhythms

Uses: student song for high soprano

GRIFFES, CHARLES TOMLINSON
(b. Elmira, NY, 1884; d. New York, NY, 1920)

[See Appendix for songs with German texts]

1017. **LES BALLONS** (Oscar Wilde). [112]. cmp1912?; rev.1915; ("reconstructed" by Donna K. Anderson from composer's sketches). A♭maj; e♭'–a♭"; Tess-mH; 6/4, Gently throughout; 6pp; Diff-V/m, P/md.

For: soprano; tenor

Mood: descriptive; gentle; delicate, floating quality

Voice: stepwise and skips along chord lines; some accidentals and minor colorations; easy rhythms; 2–3-note slurs

Piano: most of song has both hands in treble clef; arpeggiated in triplets with some duplets; some 2 vs. 3; 6-meas. interlude

Diff: voice needs to float; ending has long g" and a♭" (with opt. lower notes)

Uses: lovely lyrical song for recital; as with many Oscar Wilde poems, title is French but text is English

Rec: D#203

[BY A LONELY FOREST PATHWAY. See Appendix, #A40 B]

1018. **CLEOPATRA TO THE ASP** (John B. Tabb). [112]. cmp ca.1912; ("reconstructed" by Donna K. Anderson from composer's sketches). E♭min; d♭'–g"; Tess-mH; 4/4, Languido; 4pp; Diff-V/md, P/d.

For: soprano; mezzo-soprano

Mood: despairing; quietly suicidal

Voice: mostly stepwise with small skips; some accidentals; some dotted rhythms and syncopation; mostly syllabic

Piano: several different repeated- and broken-chord patterns; one 5-note pattern like a turn ornament; features groupings of 2, 3, 4, & 5 eighth notes; 2 vs. 3, 3 vs. 5, & 4 vs. 5; accidentals; rare doubling of vocal line

Diff: most problems in accomp.–may cause ensemble problems; polyrhythms in combining voice and piano

Uses: possible recital song for mature singer; mature subject

1019. **ELVES** (Elfe) (Joseph von Eichendorff; English version by L. Untermeyer). G. Schirmer, 1941. [168]. cmp pre-1911. A♭maj; g♯'–a♭"; Tess-mH; 6/8, Allegro vivace; 45sec; Diff-V/m, P/md.

For: high soprano–lyric or coloratura; possibly tenor

Mood: animated; sprightly; mysterious

Voice: stepwise and skips on chord lines; repetitive rhythms; some sustained high tones

Piano: broken-chord patterns; staccato; articulations important; cross-hands; many accidentals; some doubling of vocal line

Diff: sustained high tones; ensemble; dynamics

Uses: excellent animated, lighthearted song for young singer

Rec: D#s 66, 203

1020. **EVENING SONG** (Sidney Lanier). G. Schirmer, 1941. [114]. cmp1912. C♯maj; d♯'–g♯"; Tess-M; 12/8, Quietly but not too slowly; 6pp; Diff-V/md, P/d.

For: soprano; tenor

Mood: lyrical; ecstatic love song; nature imagery

Voice: flowing phrases; highly chromatic

Piano: repeated- and broken-chord figures throughout; highly chromatic; somewhat long solo sections
Diff: pitches; brilliant g♯"
Uses: good recital song
Rec: D#s 11, 24, 64, 201, 203

1021. THE FIRST SNOWFALL (John B. Tabb). G. Schirmer, 1941. [115]. cmp ca.1912. Dmin; d'–f "; Tess-M-mH; 4/4, Slowly and softly; 2pp; Diff-V/m, P/m.
For: mezzo-soprano; soprano
Mood: lyrical; philosophical; subdued; somber
Voice: many skips of 5th & 7th; 2-note slurs; dotted rhythms; floating line
Piano: unusual broken-chord pattern; syncopation; many accidentals; large reaches; does not double vocal line
Diff: entire song *pp*; soft high tones
Uses: nice impressionistic song; interesting harmonies
Rec: D#s 45, 46, 203

1022. FIVE POEMS OF THE ANCIENT FAR EAST. [variously titled *5 Poems of Ancient China and Japan* and *5 Chinese Songs*] For Medium Voice and Piano. G. Schirmer, 1917. Reprints: Masters Music Publications; T.I.S. (c., d., & e.). [115]. cmp1916-17. Pentatonic harmony; a♯–e"; Tess-mL-M; regular meters, varied tempos; 14pp; Diff-V/me-m, P/m-d.
For: mezzo-soprano; baritone
Mood: lyrical; descriptive; love song; spring song
Voice: sustained; long phrases; flowing
Piano: broken-chord figures; independent melodic material; some Chinese themes used; some parallel movement
Diff: some rhythms
Uses: good teaching and recital material
Rec: D#203

  a. *So-fei Gathering Flowers* (Wang Chang-Ling, ca.750 A.D.). c'–d"; 2/4, Con moto e gaiezza (♩ = 132); 4pp.
  b. *Landscape* (Sada-ihe, Japanese, 13th century). c'–e"; 4/4, 3/4, Dolente (♩ = c.80); 2pp.
  c. *The Old Temple among the Mountains* (Chang Wen-Chung, T'ang Dynasty, 905-618 B.C.). b♭–e♭"; 4/4, Misterioso, ma non troppo lento (♩ = 52); 4pp.
  d. *Tears* (Wang Seng-Ju, 6th century). a♯–d♯"; 6/4, 4/4, Lento (♩ = c.66); 2pp.
  e. *A Feast of Lanterns* (Yuan Mei, 18th century). c♯'–d♯"; 4/4, Molto vivace (♩ = 138-144); 4pp.

1023. FOUR IMPRESSIONS (Oscar Wilde). C. F. Peters, 1970. cmp1912–1915; ed. Donna K. Anderson. Impressionistic harmonies; d'–b♭"; Tess-M-mH; regular meters with some changes; slow, fast, and moderate tempos; 17pp; Diff-V/d, P/d; titles French, texts English.
For: lyric soprano; tenor
Mood: lyrical; visual impressions: autumn, morning, winter at sea, dawn
Voice: much conjunct motion; numerous skips and repeated tones; chromatic; long, modulating phrases; sustained high tones (2 b♭"s)

Piano: chordal-linear combination with impressionistic harmonies and techniques
Diff: sustained singing with high tones
Uses: excellent group for mature singer with a warm, lyric voice with easy high notes
Rec: D#s 202, 203

  a. *Le Jardin* (The Garden). E♭min; d'–b♭"; Tess-M; 3/4, 5/4, 4/4, Mesto ♩ = 63-66; 4pp.
  b. *Impression du Matin* (Early Morning in London). Ambiguous tonality; d'–f♯"; Tess-M; 4/4, 5/4, 3/4, Tranquillo ♩ = 60; 4pp.
  c. *La Mer* (The Sea). B♭min; e♭'–g"; Tess-M; 6/8, Molto tempestoso ♩. = 112-116; 4pp.
  d. *Le Réveillon* (Dawn). Gmin-Cmaj; e♭'–b♭"; Tess-mH; 2/2, ♩ = 58-60; 5pp.

1024. THE HALF-RING MOON (John B. Tabb). [115]; 1st© 1941. Emin; d♯'–e"; Tess-M; 4/4, With a very quick movement; 2pp; Diff-V/m, P/m.
For: soprano; mezzo-soprano
Mood: lyrical; sung by girl whose love has gone to sea and does not return
Voice: two strophes, the second sung more slowly and sadly; a number of leaps, incl. two dim. 5ths; some accidentals; duplets against triplets in piano
Piano: chordal, with repeated chords in triplets throughout; melodic lines in r.h.; 2 vs. 3; supports vocal line well, does not double
Diff: a few pitches; rhythm for singer and pianist
Uses: limited range useful for young singers who are good musicians
Rec: D#203

1025. IN THE HAREM (Chu Ch'ing-yu; trans. Herbert A. Giles). [113]. cmp ca.1917. Pentatonic; b♭–e♭"; Tess-M; 4/4, Moderato; 3pp; Diff-V/me, P/m.
For: mezzo-soprano; baritone
Mood: descriptive; rather delicate
Voice: stepwise and small skips in pentatonic scale; easy rhythms; requires smooth singing; 5-beat e♭"
Piano: most of song has both hands in treble clef; pentatonic patterning in 8ths & 16ths; does not double vocal line
Diff: possibly getting the pitch in the pentatonic schema
Uses: nice student song
Rec: D#203

1026. PHANTOMS (John B. Tabb). [different text from "Phantoms" of *Three Poems for Voice and Piano*, Op. 9 below]. [112]. cmp ca.1912. A♭- & F-centered (with many alterations); e♭'–f"(a♭"); Tess-mH; 4/4, Rather slowly and with tender sadness; 5pp; Diff-V/m, P/d.
For: soprano; tenor (lyric)
Mood: the "phantoms" are snowflakes; delicate, quiet, and introspective
Voice: stepwise and small skips; accidentals; easy rhythms
Piano: arpeggios in quick notes (16ths or 32nds, often in groups of 6 or 7); delicate figurations; mostly both hands in treble clef; does not double vocal line
Diff: ensemble; polyrhythms
Uses: to develop smooth lyrical approach to singing
Rec: D#203

1027. **PIERROT** (Sara Teasdale). [112]. cmp1912. Bmin-maj; d'–g♯"; Tess-mH; 3/8, Allegretto scherzando; 3pp; Diff-V/me, P/m.
For: soprano
Mood: narrative; lyrical
Voice: mostly conjunct; several phrases end in sustained syllable (4 meas.); some accidentals; easy rhythms
Piano: broken-chord patterning; some rolled chords; staccato; delicate; does not double vocal line
Uses: good student song
Rec: D#203

1028. **SONG OF THE DAGGER** (Roumanian folk poem; trans. Carmen Sylva and Alma Strettell). Henmar, 1983. cmp1912–1916. Gmin; A♭–f'; Tess-M; 4/4, 5/4; ♩ = ca.168–Presto–Lento; 4min; Diff-V/md, P/md.
For: dramatic baritone; bass-baritone
Mood: "a bitter and savage outburst of rejection, hate, jealousy and revenge" [Donna K. Anderson, ed.]
Voice: melody mostly diatonic with some chromaticism; uncomplicated rhythms predominate with a few triplets; some 2 vs. 3 in piano; dynamics important (*pp–ff*); many cresc.; 3-beat f', 7-beat e♭'
Piano: repeated block chords; broken-chord patterning with and without countermelody; tremolo; 4-meas. prelude, three short interludes, 7-meas. postlude; duplet and triplet subdivisions of beat
Diff: controlling the excitement in song, esp. in dynamics and tempos
Uses: mature, or advanced college-age singer
Rec: D#s 24, 202, 203

1029. **THREE POEMS BY FIONA MacLEOD,** Opus 11. G. Schirmer, 1918. Reprints: Classical Vocal Reprints (A., low); Masters Music Publications; T.I.S. (H). [114]. Separate entries below.

A. **THE LAMENT OF IAN THE PROUD.** [48, 59]. H & L keys: F♯min (orig.) & Dmin; f♯'–a♯" & d'–f♯"; Tess-mH; 4/4, Lento (Poco più mosso e agitato); 6pp; Diff-V/d, P/md.
For: tenor; baritone; some dramatic weight required
Mood: dramatic; poem about death
Voice: long sustained phrases; somewhat declamatory; two long, dramatic high tones
Piano: arpeggiations; afterbeat chords; triplet figures; considerable interpretive skill needed
Diff: long phrases; climactic high tones– second must be felt as climax of song
Uses: superb recital song; good for teaching dramatic interpretation
Rec: D#s 6, 10, 24, 48, 199, 200, 202, 203

B. **THY DARK EYES TO MINE.** A♭maj; e♭'–a♭"; Tess-H; 4/4, Andantino; Diff-V/d, P/d.
For: tenor
Mood: ecstatic but quiet love song
Voice: sustained; leaps; sustained soft high tones
Piano: triplet figures in r.h.; melodic fragments in l.h.; thick texture
Diff: soft head tones
Uses: lovely song; useful recital material

Rec: D#s 200, 201, 202, 203

C. **THE ROSE OF THE NIGHT.** X; c♯'–a"; Tess-mH; 3/4, 4/4, Moderato; Diff-V/dd, P/d.
For: tenor
Mood: dramatic; ecstatic; mystical
Voice: sustained; ever ascending; big high climaxes; meter changes; duplets juxtaposed with triplets
Piano: chromatic triplet figurations; passage work; thick texture; dramatic postlude; irregular rhythmic groupings; 2 vs. 3; some doubling of voice
Diff: endurance; aria-like; many difficulties
Uses: fine recital song for advanced performers
Rec: D#s 200, 202, 203

1030. **THREE POEMS FOR VOICE AND PIANO, OPUS 9.** G. Schirmer, 1918. Reprints: Masters Music Publications; T.I.S. (A., high). cmp1916 & 1912. Pub. separately; separate entries below.

A. **IN A MYRTLE SHADE** (William Blake). [51, 114]. Emaj; f♯'–a"; Tess-H; 4/4, Tranquillo; Diff-V/md, P/m.
For: tenor; soprano
Mood: tranquil reflection
Voice: high, floating, sustained phrases; some long tones
Piano: triplet pattern throughout; rippling effect
Diff: easy head tones
Uses: wonderful song; excellent recital material
Rec: D#s 11, 70, 201, 203

B. **WAIKIKI** (Rupert Brooke). [51, 114]. X; d♯'–g♯"; Tess-mH; 3/4, Andante con moto; 6pp; Diff-V/md, P/md.
For: tenor
Mood: lyrical; descriptive; evocative of island scene and story lost to memory
Voice: skips, small and large; speech rhythms; big dynamic climax
Piano: chordal; fast ornaments; 3 vs. 4 & 3 vs. 2; wide reaches; many accidentals; rather thick; incidental doubling of vocal line
Diff: complex song; needs mature sound, understanding, and technique
Uses: effective for the right singer
Rec: D#s 59, 201, 203

C. **PHANTOMS** (Arturo Giovanitti). [115]. Dmin; b♭–f"; Tess-M; 4/4, 3/2, Moderato; 5pp; Diff-V/md, P/md.
For: baritone
Mood: dramatic; anguished night song; memory of lost love
Voice: declamatory; speech rhythms; many skips; chromatic lines; 2-note slurs
Piano: chordal; repeated chords both hands; thick texture; 2 vs. 3; syncopation; arpeggios and rocking bass; large dynamic contrasts; does not double vocal line
Diff: dynamics; register control; dramatic sense; rhythmic security needed
Uses: good song for singer with ample sound; quiet ending
Rec: D#203

1031. **TONE IMAGES, OPUS 3.** G. Schirmer, 1915.

Reprints: Masters Music Publications; T.I.S. (B., H & M). cmp ca.1912. Pub. separately; separate entries below (probably not a performance set, although the first two seem to pair well).

A. **LA FUITE DE LA LUNE** (Oscar Wilde). [115]. D♭maj; d♭'–f"; Tess-M; 3/4, Tranquillo; 4pp; Diff-V/m, P/md.
For: soprano; tenor
Mood: lyrical; lonely; impression of silence
Voice: English text; stepwise; some leaps; 2–3-note slurs
Piano: chordal; broken and block patterns; syncopation; 2 vs. 3; large reaches; many accidentals; hazy pedaling; some countermelody; does not double vocal line
Diff: dynamic control
Uses: good impressionistic song; harmonic tints interesting and subdued
Rec: D#203

B. **SYMPHONY IN YELLOW** (Oscar Wilde). [51, 64, 114]. Bmaj; d♯'–g♭"; Tess-mL; 4/4, 3/4, Languidamente; 3pp; Diff-V/m, P/d.
For: soprano; tenor
Mood: lyrical; descriptive; British scene
Voice: sustained; somewhat static; large intervals; generally soft dynamics
Piano: sustained chords; thick texture; hazy impressionistic sound; broken chords in middle section
Diff: long phrases; soft singing; pitches
Uses: effective song; good for recital
Rec: D#s 10, 203

C. **WE'LL TO THE WOODS AND GATHER MAY** (William E. Henley). [52, vol. 6, 115]. H & L keys: Emaj & Dmaj (M ed. in E♭maj pub. by G. Schirmer); e'–f♯" & d'–e"; Tess-M; 9/8, 3/4, Molto vivace; 4pp; Diff-V/me, P/m.
For: all voices except very low
Mood: merry; descriptive of nature
Voice: flowing phrases; some chromaticism
Piano: broken- and repeated-chord figures
Uses: good teaching song
Rec: D#s 11, 203

1032. TWO BIRDS FLEW INTO THE SUNSET GLOW. (Roumanian folk text). [112]. cmp1914. Gmin; c'–f"; Tess-M; 2/4, ♩=ca.80; 4pp; Diff-V/me, P/m.
For: any voice with this range
Mood: spare and simple; despairing thoughts; quiet and plaintive
Voice: many small skips along chord lines; easy rhythms; soft-medium dynamics
Piano: block chords; some broken-chord patterning; 2 vs. 3
Uses: good student song for young mezzo-soprano or soprano with this range
Rec: D#203

1033. TWO KINGS SAT TOGETHER IN ORKADAL (Zwei Könige sassen auf Orkadal) (Emanuel Geibel; English version by Henry G. Chapman). G. Schirmer, 1910. Reprint: Masters Music Publications (Ger. and Eng.) in *Songs to German Poems*. [168]. Emin; b♭–e"; Tess-L; 2/4, Moderato; 5pp; Diff-V/m, P/m.
For: baritone; bass-baritone
Mood: dramatic; gloomy; ballad–narrative with three speakers
Voice: stepwise and chordal skips; easy rhythms; 2-note slurs
Piano: chordal; some open 8ves; syncopated open 8ves; various articulations; doubles vocal line
Diff: character differentiation; sustained e♭" ff
Uses: good for a dramatic singer
Rec: D#s 45, 46, 66

1034. TWO POEMS BY JOHN MASEFIELD. G. Schirmer, 1920. Reprints: Masters Music Publications; T.I.S. (A., M & L). [115]. cmp1918. Pub. separately; separate entries below.

A. **AN OLD SONG RESUNG.** H & L keys: Fmaj & A♭maj; e♭'–f" & c'–d"; Tess-M; 4/4, Giocoso, ma non troppo presto; Diff-V/e, P/m.
For: tenor; baritone
Mood: narrative; sturdy sea song
Voice: energetic
Piano: chordal
Uses: good song for young men and for teaching diction
Rec: D#s 2, 10, 24, 45, 46, 47, 65, 203

B. **SORROW OF MYDATH.** Bmin; b–f♯"; Tess-M; 4/4, Molto appassionato, ma non troppo allegro; 3min; Diff-V/d, P/d.
For: high baritone
Mood: dramatic; death-wish; sea imagery; intense
Voice: declamatory; complex rhythms; chromatic; portamento
Piano: thick texture; low and murky; arpeggiated; rocking bass line; chromatic 16th-note pattern; large reaches; sectional texture and dynamic contrasts; some melodic doubling
Diff: ensemble; dynamic climax on long f♯"; quiet ending
Uses: effective for singer with dramatic flair
Rec: D#203

1035. TWO RONDELS for a Soprano Voice with Piano Accompaniment, Op. 4. G. Schirmer, 1915. Reprints: Classical Vocal Reprints; Masters Music Publications; T.I.S. (b.). [114]. Traditional keys; c♯'–f♯"; Tess-M; regular meters; contrasting tempos; 7pp; Diff-V/m, P/m.
For: soprano
Mood: lyrical
Voice: stepwise and easy skips; easy rhythms; 2-note slurs
Piano: chordal; some linear sections; duplets and triplets; some imitation; little doubling of vocal line
Diff: long phrases; dynamic control; sustained f♯" climax
Uses: nice pair of songs for a young singer
Rec: D#203

a. *This Book of Hours* (Walter Crane). F♯min; c♯'–f♯"; 2/4, Molto moderato e semplicemente; 3pp.
b. *Come, Love, across the Sunlit Land* (Clinton Scollard). Amaj; e'–f♯"; 4/4, Allegro con spirito; 4pp.

1036. UPON THEIR GRAVE (Auf ihrem Grab) (Heinrich

Heine; trans. Louis Untermeyer). G. Schirmer, 1941. [61, 168]. cmp pre-1911. D♭maj; c'–g"; Tess-M; 12/8, Moderato (without dragging); 4pp; Diff-V/md, P/md.
- **For:** soprano
- **Mood:** lyrical; descriptive; somber
- **Voice:** stepwise and skips along chord lines; easy rhythms; many accidentals
- **Piano:** broken- and repeated-chord patterns; some large reaches; many accidentals; 11-meas. postlude; quiet ending; does not double vocal line
- **Diff:** some long phrases; dynamics; registration
- **Uses:** usable song in a group
- **Rec:** D#s 66, 203

1037. **THE WATER-LILY** (John B. Tabb). [112]. cmp1911. Mostly Cmin; d♯'–g♯"; Tess-mH; 6/4, With a quiet movement; 4pp; Diff-V/m, P/m.
- **For:** soprano; tenor
- **Mood:** descriptive; lyrical and graceful
- **Voice:** skips along chord lines; accidentals; easy rhythms; syllabic with a few 2–3-note slurs; language has archaic touches ("art thou," "methinks")
- **Piano:** block chords; some broken chords in quarter notes; syncopation; accidentals; incidental vocal line doubling
- **Diff:** irregular phrase lengths
- **Uses:** lyrical student song
- **Rec:** D#203

GRIFFIS, ELLIOT
(b. Boston, MA, 1893; d. Los Angeles, CA, 1967)

1038. **ELDORADO** (Edgar Allan Poe). Composers Press, 1937. Bmin; b–f♯"; Tess-M; 12/8 , 4/4, Poco lento (♩. = 80)–Allegro furioso (♩. = 116)–Allegro (♩. =100)–Recitative (♪ = 84); 6pp; Diff-V/m, P/d.
- **For:** baritone
- **Mood:** dramatic narrative; philosophical
- **Voice:** stepwise and small skips; a little chromaticism; swinging rhythmic feeling typical of compound meters; dramatic with a central recit.; syllabic; "demonic laughter *ad libitum*" indicated during postlude
- **Piano:** broken-chord figures in first and last sections; block and rolled chords in recit. section; patterned; some chromaticism; two septuplets; 13-meas. prelude with opt. cut, two short interludes, 4-meas. postlude; supports vocal line well with incidental doubling
- **Diff:** avoiding a "sing-song" effect because of the meter; achieving drama without becoming overblown
- **Uses:** dramatic song; cf. setting by Edgar Stillman Kelley

1039. **TO HELEN** (Edgar Allan Poe). Composers Press, 1946. Fmaj; d'–e"(g"); Tess-mL; 4/4, 2/4, Slow (♩ = 60) (with fluctuations); 3min; Diff-V/m, P/m.
- **For:** tenor; lyric baritone
- **Mood:** lyrical; likening the beauties of Helen to the glories of the ancient world
- **Voice:** stepwise and small skips; several phrases lie low and are static, almost recit.-like; a little chromaticism; triplets; rhythms otherwise not difficult; syllabic
- **Piano:** chordal–block, broken, and rolled; melodic material in prelude and interludes; rather chromatic in middle

section; triplets; incidental doubling of vocal line
- **Diff:** tenor would need a very solid middle and low range
- **Uses:** possible recital material

GRIMM, JOHANN (See Special Section)

GROSSMAN, DEENA
(b. Fairfield, CA, 1955)

1040. **TWO SONGS FROM *LEOPARD FLOWERS*** (Ono no Komachi, 844-880; trans. from Japanese by Arthur Waley). [11, Vol. 6]. cmp1983. X; c♯'–f♯"; Tess-cs; 2/4, slow (♩ = 60, 48); 4pp; Diff-V/m, P/e–m.
- **For:** soprano; mezzo-soprano
- **Mood:** emptiness of heart; loneliness of soul
- **Voice:** lyrical; chromatic; onomatopoetic vocal lines; numerous rhythmic divisions in melismas
- **Piano:** linear; thin texture; dissonant; grace notes
- **Diff:** chromaticism
- **Uses:** interesting brief songs on Oriental texts

   a. *Something Which Fades.* X; c♯'–f♯"; Tess-M; 2/4, ♩ = 60; 2pp.
   b. *Floating Weed.* X; c♯'–f "; Tess-cs; 2/4, ♩ = 48; 2pp.

GROSSMAN, RAPHAEL
(American, 20th Century)

1041. **A WOMAN OF VALOR** (Biblical Proverb text). [57]. E♭maj; e♭'–e♭"; Tess-M; 4/4, Moderato, flowing; 2pp; Diff-V/m, P/me.
- **For:** all voices except very low; baritone or tenor best
- **Mood:** proverb; respectful
- **Voice:** chant-like (melody partially based on a Hebrew chant); stepwise and small skips; duplets and triplets; 2–4-note slurs
- **Piano:** block chords with some l.h. animation
- **Uses:** good student song

GRUENBERG, LOUIS
(b. near Brest-Litovsk, Poland, 1884; d. Los Angeles, CA, 1964)

1042. **ANIMALS AND INSECTS,** Op. 22. Seven Songs for a Medium Voice and Piano Accompaniment (Vachel Lindsay). Universal-Edition, 1925. cmp1924. Key sigs. (most end in definite key, but the many accidentals obscure key feeling); a–a"; Tess-L, H; regular meters (but with many small and complex subdivisions of beat); various degrees of Allegro and Allegretto; 21pp; Diff-V/dd, P/dd.
- **For:** soprano
- **Mood:** whimsical; sad; humorous; philosophical; portraits of animals and insects
- **Voice:** much chromatic movement; many large leaps and other skips; repeated tones, esp. at top of staff; many sustained high tones on closed vowels; speech rhythms; many small note values; some long slurs with many

notes; vocal noises; stuttering

Piano: complex score; linear; many accidentals; rhythmic difficulties; much passage-work; piano illustrates text; fine pianist needed

Diff: see above; also clear enunciation will be difficult, as many phrases lie high; ensemble

Uses: excellent work (set or excerpts) for an advanced singer with flawless diction; very good for light group on a recital; should be interesting to the audience

Rec: D#49

    a. *The Lion.* 2/4, Allegretto giocoso; 3pp.
    b. *An Explanation of the Grasshopper.* 4/4, Moderato giocoso; 1p.
    c. *The Spider and the Ghost of the Fly.* 4/4, Allegro moderato e misterioso; 3pp.
    d. *A Dirge for a Righteous Kitten.* 4/4, Allegretto funebre; 3pp.
    e. *The Mysterious Cat.* 2/4, Allegro delicato; 3pp.
    f. *The Mouse That Gnawed the Oak-Tree Down.* 2/4, Allegro marcato; 4pp.
    g. *Two Old Crows.* 4/4, Allegro moderato; 5pp.

GUION, DAVID W.
(b. Ballinger, TX, 1892; d. Dallas, TX, 1981)

1043. ALL DAY ON THE PRAIRIE (Texas cowboy song). [8, 34]; 1st©1930. H & L keys: B♭maj & A♭maj; f'–e♭" & e♭'–d♭"; Tess-M; 6/8, Leisurely, with typical Western drawl (♩.= 63); 6pp; Diff-V/me, P/me.

For: tenor; baritone
Mood: semi-humorous description of the life of a cowboy
Voice: conjunct motion; small intervals; four strophes are essentially repetition; whistling at end
Piano: chordal; afterbeats; melodic interludes between strophes; supports vocal line quite clearly
Diff: uninhibited singer who can whistle needed
Uses: could be effective in performance; very limited range; useful for young men

1044. AT THE CRY OF THE FIRST BIRD (Ancient Irish Poetry). [64]; 1st©1924. Bmin; d'–g"; Tess-M; 4/4, Slowly, with great dignity and feeling; 6pp; Diff-V/m, P/m.

For: any high or medium voice
Mood: lyrical; somber
Voice: long sustained phrases; features b'; quiet and somewhat static; one dramatic climax
Piano: chordal; dramatic prelude; r.h. in 6ths, partially doubling vocal line, over sustained B in a and a' sections; syncopated repeated chords in b sections
Diff: long phrases; ƒ8ve leap g'–g"–g'
Uses: recital and church; good for teaching breath control; cf. Barber "The Crucifixion"

HADLEY, HENRY K.
(b. Somerville, MA, 1871; d. New York, NY, 1937)

1045. EVENING SONG (Sidney Lanier). G. Schirmer. 1915. Reprint: Classical Vocal Reprints (H & M). Fmaj;

c'–f"; Tess-mH; 6/4, Very slowly and peacefully; Diff-V/m, P/e.

For: mezzo-soprano
Mood: lyrical; calm
Voice: sustained; many f"s
Piano: arpeggiated pattern
Diff: perfect legato line
Uses: beautiful song; recital use

1046. FILL A GLASS WITH GOLDEN WINE (William E. Henley). G. Schirmer, 1910. H & L keys: G♭maj & E♭maj; g♭'–b♭" & e♭'–g"; Tess-M; 4/4, Moderato; Diff-V/m, P/e.

For: all voices
Mood: lyrical; philosophical; quiet love song
Voice: very lyrical line
Piano: chordal with melodic motives
Uses: a somewhat sentimental song, rather like some of R. Strauss's song texts

1047. HOW DO I LOVE THEE? Op. 20, No. 3 (Elizabeth Barrett Browning). [58]; 1st©1900. B♭maj; d'–a"(b♭"); Tess-M-mH; 3/4, Allegro appassionato; 6pp; Diff-V/d, P/d.

For: soprano; tenor
Mood: dramatic; passionate love song
Voice: long, smooth phrases; sustained high tones; intervals and rhythms not difficult
Piano: somewhat awkward arpeggiation; constant 16ths; little doubling of vocal line
Diff: dynamic control; sustained high tones
Uses: usable song for a big voice

1048. IF YOU WOULD HAVE IT SO, Op. 84, No.3 (Rabindranath Tagore). Carl Fischer, 1921. H & M keys: Cmin & Amin; f'–a♭" & d'–f"; Tess-H; 6/8, 3/8, Allegretto scherzando; Diff-V/m, P/m.

For: tenor; soprano
Mood: lyrical; descriptive
Voice: short phrases; some rhythmic intricacies
Piano: descriptive of text
Diff: high tessitura; light tone
Uses: excellent song; usable for recital and teaching

1049. I HEARD A MAID WITH HER GUITAR, Op. 44, No. 3 (Clinton Scollard). Church, 1909. Reprint: Classical Vocal Reprints (H). Gmaj; d'–g"; Tess-M; 3/4, 4/4, Allegretto; Diff-V/m, P/md.

For: tenor
Mood: lyrical
Voice: many skips; phrases end on long tones
Piano: guitar effects; 3rds; staccato
Uses: excellent song; good guitar effects on piano

1050. IN THE TIME OF ROSEBUD'S BLOOMING, Op. 53, No. 2 (Die junge Rose blühte) (Heinrich Heine; English version by Harriet Betty Boas). G. Schirmer, 1911. A♭maj; d'–a♭"; Tess-M; 3/4, Ruhig bewegt; Diff-V/md, P/m.

For: soprano; tenor
Mood: lyrical; longing
Voice: lyrico-dramatic; descending phrases; leaps to sustained

climax

Piano: syncopated figure; fairly thick; doubles vocal line

Uses: good song; shows heavy German stylistic influence

1051. THE LUTE PLAYER OF CASA BLANCA, Op. 84, No. 1 (Laurence Hope). Carl Fischer, 1921. H & L keys: Gmin & Emin; f'–a" & d'–f♯"; Tess-mH; 3/4, Allegretto con gentilezza; 4pp; Diff-V/m, P/m.

For: soprano; mezzo-soprano

Mood: lyrical; sprightly; love song

Voice: scalar melody with easy skips; sustained high tones; some dotted rhythms

Piano: lute figure has staccato and rolled chords; some block chords

Diff: diction somewhat awkward; sustained a"; needs good register and dynamic control

Uses: effective piece for light, flexible voice

1052. MY SHADOW (Robert Louis Stevenson). [45, vol. 1]; 1st© 1912. Gmaj; d'–e"; Tess-M; 4/4, Allegro giocoso; 4pp; Diff-V/m, P/e.

For: all voices

Mood: humorous patter song

Voice: rapid 8th notes; conjunct with skips and leaps

Piano: chordal–sustaining and punctuating

Diff: speed of enunciation

Uses: wonderful teaching song for rapid diction; good encore

1053. MY TRUE LOVE, Op. 94, No. 1 (Sir Philip Sidney). Carl Fischer, 1924. H & L keys: D♭maj & B♭maj; c'–a♭" & a–f"; Tess-H; 4/4, Allegro giocoso; Diff-V/m, P/m.

For: soprano

Mood: joyful

Voice: soaring, leaping, running line

Piano: triplet figuration

Diff: easy f", g", and a"; some staccato singing

Uses: good song for a young soprano

1054. PROSPICE, Op. 105, No. 1 (Robert Browning). Carl Fischer, 1926. Cmaj; c'–g"; Tess-M; 4/4, Grave; Diff-V/d, P/d.

For: dramatic baritone

Mood: dramatic; majestic; poem about death

Voice: dramatic declamatory style

Piano: chordal; a bit bombastic; weak postlude

Diff: endurance; large dramatic voice with full command of technique needed

Uses: excellent dramatic song if tastefully done; consider cutting weak postlude

1055. THE ROSE-LEAVES ARE FALLING LIKE RAIN, Op. 49, No. 2 (Il pleut des petales de fleurs) (Alfred Samain; English version by Henry G. Chapman). G. Schirmer, 1909. Reprint: Classical Vocal Reprints. [48]. H & L keys: Emin & Cmin; e'–g" & c'–e♭"; Tess-mH; 6/8, Lente, avec langueur; 4pp; Diff-V/m, P/md.

For: tenor; baritone

Mood: lyrical, sentimental song of dying roses and lost love

Voice: flowing phrases; extremely legato

Piano: chordal; broken-chord figurations with changing mode;

arpeggiations

Diff: English version not as good as French

Uses: beautiful song; recital material

1056. SENTIMENTAL COLLOQUY, Op. 82, No. 2 (Colloque sentimental) (Paul Verlaine; English version by Alice Mattullath). Carl Fischer, 1923. H & L keys: F♯min & Emin; c'–g♯" & b♭–f♯"; Tess-mH; 3/4, Broadly with dignity; 6pp; Diff-V/md, P/md.

For: any voice except extremely low or light

Mood: dramatic; dialogue; remembrance of past love

Voice: many small skips; duplets and triplets; some triplets vs. piano duplets and vice versa

Piano: chordal–block and broken; many accidentals; 7-meas. prelude; 2 vs. 3; some doubling of vocal line

Diff: phrases beginning after downbeat

Uses: useful song; probably better sung in French; strong French influence in texture, word rhythms, stress, piano patterning, and color

1057. A SPRING NIGHT (Charles H. Towne). Carl Fischer, 1918. H & L keys: Fmaj & Dmaj; d'–g" & b–e"; Tess-mH; 9/8, Allegro appassionato; Diff-V/m, P/m.

For: tenor; soprano

Mood: lyrical

Voice: lilting lines; some sustained phrases; ending features f"

Piano: arpeggiated figuration; some repeated triplets

Diff: features f" and g"

Uses: good song; useful

1058. THE TIME OF PARTING, Op. 84, No. 2 (Rabindranath Tagore). Carl Fischer, 1921. H, mH, & M keys: F♯maj, Fmaj, & E♭maj; e♯'–g♯", e'–g", & d'–f"; Tess-M; 3/4, Andante teneramente; Diff-V/md, P/m.

For: tenor; soprano

Mood: lyrical; tender; quiet song about death

Voice: soft; much 2 vs. 3 & 3 vs. 4

Piano: patterned, moving 16ths; illustrates passage of time

Diff: 2 vs. 3 and 3 vs. 4

Uses: exquisite song in many ways

1059. UNDER THE APRIL MOON, Op. 112, No. 3 (Bliss Carman). Carl Fischer, 1929. "For Margaret Matzenauer." Fmaj; e♭'–g"; Tess-M; 9/8, Con moto; 35meas.; Diff-V/m, P/md.

For: soprano; tenor; presumably contralto in a lower key

Mood: lyrical; tranquil; floating

Voice: easy skips; many long sustained tones; quiet

Piano: chordal with 16th-note perpetual-motion pattern; does not double vocal line

Diff: long phrases; sustained style; soft singing

Uses: nice lyric song; quiet ending; useful at beginning or interior of group

1060. THE YEAR'S AT THE SPRING (Robert Browning). Church, 1909. B♭maj; c'(b♭)–f"; Tess-M; 4/4, Very slowly and tenderly; 26meas.; Diff-V/m, P/m.

For: soprano; mezzo-soprano; tenor; baritone

Mood: lyrical; optimistic

Voice: many skips; 7th & 8ves; fragmentary phrases; much sequence

Piano: linear-chordal combination; does not double vocal line

Uses: interesting slow, lyrical setting of this poem, often set as a quick, dramatic song; see settings by Beach, Rorem ("Pippa's Song"), and others

HAGEMAN, RICHARD
(b. Netherlands, 1882; d. Beverly Hills, CA, 1966)

1061. ALL PATHS LEAD TO YOU (Blanche S. Wagstaff). Galaxy, 1953. Ebmaj; f'–bb"(g"); Tess-mH-H (depending on options taken); 4/4, Slowly; 2min; Diff-V/m, P/m.

For: tenor; possibly soprano

Mood: lyrical; love song

Voice: many skips on chord lines; easy rhythms

Piano: chordal; constant 16th-note broken-chord motion; does not double vocal line

Uses: effective song for recital group

1062. ANIMAL CRACKERS (Christopher Morley). G. Schirmer, 1922. [29]. H & L keys: Ebmaj & Cmaj; eb'–f" & c'–d"; Tess-M; 6/8, Allegro; 5pp; Diff-V/me, P/m.

For: soprano; mezzo-soprano; men who feel comfortable with text

Mood: narrative; simple description; speaker is a child

Voice: scalar with easy skips

Piano: afterbeat chordal style; 16th-note scale patterns; some doubling of vocal line

Uses: useful for a young singer; encore

1063. AT THE WELL (Rabindranath Tagore). G. Schirmer, 1919. Reprints: Classical Vocal Reprints (H & M); T.I.S. (H). [25]. "To Amparito Farrar." H & L keys: Gbmaj & Dbmaj; eb'–c'"(ab") & bb–gb"(eb"); Tess–mH; 5/8, 6/8, Allegro; 7pp; Diff-V/d, P/dd.

For: lyric or coloratura soprano

Mood: lyrical; descriptive; narrative

Voice: sweeping phrases; rapid diction; some chromaticism

Piano: broken-chord figuration; rapid 16th- & 32nd-note motion; chromatic; does not double vocal line

Diff: agility; easy bb" and c'" in high key; 5/8 rhythms

Uses: good showpiece for high soprano; program ender

Rec: D#11

1064. BEGGAR'S LOVE (Bettler Liebe). (Theodor Storm; English version by Robert Nathan). G. Schirmer, 1958. Abmaj; eb'–ab"; Tess-mH; 4/4, Adagio; 3pp; Diff-V/m, P/md.

For: tenor

Mood: lyrical; love poem

Voice: flowing phrases, mostly short; probably set to the English version

Piano: arpeggiated chords in triplets

Uses: lyrical love song; highest phrases not dramatic; good for teaching

1065. DO NOT GO, MY LOVE (Rabindranath Tagore). G. Schirmer, 1917. Reprints: Classical Vocal Reprints (H & L); T.I.S. (H). [24, 51, 59]. "To George Hamlin." H & L keys: F#min & Dmin; d#'–g" & b–eb"; Tess-M; 3/4, Adagio; 4pp; Diff-V/m, P/m.

For: all voices

Mood: lyrico-dramatic; love song

Voice: lyrical and sustained; declamatory middle section; soft high tones on "ee" vowel; some fragmented phrases

Piano: chordal; syncopation; arpeggiation

Diff: soft high tones; ascending phrases; some difficult irregular entrances over piano syncopation

Uses: good song for sustained singing; recital material

Rec: D#s 10, 47, 48, 64, 65, 69, 204, 205

1066. HUSH (Robert Nathan). Galaxy, 1951. Fmaj; c'–g"; Tess-M; 4/4, Molto tranquillo; 2min; Diff-V/m, P/m.

For: soprano

Mood: lyrical; quiet love song

Voice: many skips; fragmented phrasing; syncopation

Piano: linear-chordal combination; syncopated repeated chords; some cross-hands; some 3rds

Diff: ensemble

Uses: effective quiet song

1067. LOVE IN THE WINDS (Richard Hovey). Galaxy, 1941. Ebmaj-Emaj-Dbmaj; eb'–bb"; Tess-H; 4/4, Allegro con fuoco; 2min; Diff-V/md, P/d.

For: dramatic tenor (man's text)

Mood: exultant love song; dramatic and forceful

Voice: many leaps, esp. of 5th; many accidentals; some 2 vs. 3 in piano; sustained high tones; big ending

Piano: various chord figurations; repeated chords; rapid scale passages; rapid repeated notes; various rhythmic subdivisions of beat; 4 vs. 3; wind and water color effects; large reaches; some doubling of vocal line

Diff: sectional; many tempo changes; many sustained high notes; needs robust, mature sound; balance

Uses: for robust tenor; good encore or program ender

1068. ME COMPANY ALONG (James Stephens). Carl Fischer, 1925. H & L keys: Bbmaj & Fmaj; f'–bb" & c'–f"; Tess-M; 6/8, Allegro non troppo; 92 meas.; Diff-V/d, P/dd.

For: any voice except extremely low

Mood: happy; exuberant

Voice: many skips; needs legato; lilting, dances along

Piano: fast; many notes; covers the keyboard; arpeggios; broken-chord patterning

Diff: high sustained ending; irregular rhythmic groupings; tempo fluctuations

Uses: good group ender

1069. MIRANDA (Hillaire Belloc). Galaxy, 1940. H & L keys: Amaj & Fmaj; e'–a" & c'–f"; Tess-M; 3/8, Con spirito (♩.= 76); 2+min; Diff-V/m, P/d.

For: soprano; mezzo-soprano

Mood: vigorous; descriptive

Voice: dance-like; melismas; grace notes

Piano: 32nd- & 64th-note figures; rapid scale passages; some chromaticism; enhances the text

Diff: agility; easy a"(f")

Uses: group or program ender

Rec: D#s 11, 33

1070. MUSIC I HEARD WITH YOU (Conrad Aiken).

Galaxy, 1938. H & L keys: Gmin & Ebmin; e'–a" & c'–f"; Tess-M-mH; 4/4, Andante; 5pp; Diff-V/m, P/md.

For: tenor; baritone
Mood: nostalgic; somber
Voice: stepwise and some skips; syncopation; interrupted phrasing
Piano: chordal–broken and block; duplets and triplets; repetitive; sectional; little doubling of vocal line
Diff: continuity; sustained a"
Uses: haunting song; quiet ending, but could end group
Rec: D#206

1071. NATURE'S HOLIDAY (T[homas] Nash). [51]; 1st©1921. Emaj-Cmaj-Amaj; g'–c♯'''; Tess-HH; 4/4, Allegro giocoso (♩= 112); 10pp; Diff-V/dd, P/dd.

For: for high soprano
Mood: a joyous song of nature; imitates various bird-calls
Voice: rather disjunct vocal line; many short phrases; many high-lying phrases; 3 sustained b"s; trills and other figures imitative of bird-calls
Piano: chordal; rapid broken-chord and scalar passages; dance-like dotted rhythms; triplets, grace notes, and other ornamental figures; a *tour de force* for the pianist, somewhat in the style of Liszt
Diff: requires soprano with easy high voice up to b" (c♯''' touched lightly); pitches and rhythms; articulation of many words in high tessitura; ability to trill highly desirable; voice will need enough heft so as not to be swamped by the showy piano accomp.
Uses: brilliant showpiece for the right singer

1072. THE NIGHT HAS A THOUSAND EYES (Francis William Bourdillon). Boosey & Hawkes, 1935. H & L keys: Ebmaj & Dbmaj; f'–ab" & eb'–gb"; Tess-H; 4/4, Very quietly; 3pp; Diff-V/m, P/md.

For: soprano; tenor; mezzo-soprano; high baritone
Mood: lyrical; philosophical poem about love
Voice: stepwise and small skips; uncomplicated rhythms
Piano: arpeggios and double arpeggios; no vocal line doubling
Diff: sustained high tones
Uses: a rouser, but has quiet ending

1073. O WHY DO YOU WALK? (To a Fat Lady Seen from the Train) (Frances Comford). Galaxy, 1950. Amaj; e'–f♯"; Tess-M; 4/4, Molto tranquillo; 2min; Diff-V/m, P/md.

For: any high or medium voice
Mood: philosophical; satirical
Voice: mostly stepwise; short phrases; triplets
Piano: chromatic; triplets; largely doubles vocal line
Diff: text
Uses: humorous song; text may not be suitable for all occasions

1074. PRAISE (Seumas O'Sullivan). [51]; 1st©1956. Ebmaj-Bmaj; f'–bb"; Tess-mH; 4/4, Tenderly–Più lento; 3pp; Diff-V/md, P/m.

For: tenor
Mood: lyrical love song
Voice: short phrases, some containing large intervals; some accidentals and unexpected turns of phrase; several triplets; one quarter-note triplet

Piano: chordal; broken-chord figures; countermelodic material; 3 vs. 2 ; many accidentals; supports vocal line, does not double
Diff: some pitches
Uses: good recital possibilities

1075. THE RICH MAN (Franklin P. Adams). Galaxy, 1937. Cmaj; b–d"; Tess-M; 4/4, Moderato; 3pp; Diff-V/m, P/m.

For: bass; baritone
Mood: humorous; colorful
Voice: patter treatment of text; 5-note slur on "fate"; leaps of 6th & 7th; sustained tones
Piano: afterbeat style; parallel motion of parallel structures; glissandos; large reaches; many accidentals; does not double vocal line
Diff: entrances in irregular phrase lengths
Uses: change-of-pace song in a group; encore

1076. THE TOWN (Theodor Storm; English version by Robert Nathan). G. Schirmer, 1958. Amin–Bmaj; e'–g♯"; Tess-M-mH; 3/4, Quasi adagio; 4pp; Diff-V/m, P/md.

For: tenor; soprano
Mood: lyrical; somber; descriptive; quiet
Voice: English version good; legato; long lines; 8ve leaps
Piano: repeated-chord pattern; 3rds in 16th notes; some arpeggiation
Diff: ensemble

1077. UNDER THE WILLOWS (Shoshone love song; trans. Mary Austin). G. Schirmer, 1957. [51]. Amin (with changes); d♯'–a"; Tess-M; 2/4, 6/8, 3/4, Andantino; 5pp; Diff-V/m, P/md.

For: tenor
Mood: lyrical love song; nature imagery
Voice: stepwise and small skips; triplets; 3 vs. 2 in piano; undulating phrases; syllabic
Piano: chordal–block and rolled; somewhat chromatic; dotted rhythms, triplets, 32nd-note figures; supports vocal line, incidental doubling
Diff: rhythms
Uses: could be effectively programmed

1078. VOICES (Witter Bynner). Galaxy, 1943. Abmaj; eb'–f"; Tess-M; 3/4, Tempo di valse animato; 1+min; Diff-V/m, P/m.

For: mezzo-soprano; soprano; tenor; baritone
Mood: lyrical; descriptive; a memory
Voice: vocal line fits into the piano texture; chordal outlines; accidentals; easy rhythms
Piano: half the song is piano solo–a piece of its own in waltz style; does not double vocal line
Diff: ensemble; vocal line often interrupted
Uses: effective change of pace; chance to show off a tasteful accompanist; soft ending

1079. WHEN THE WIND IS LOW (Cale Young Rice). Galaxy, 1957. Fmaj; c'–a"; Tess-M; 4/4, Dreamily; 3pp; Diff-V/md, P/d.

For: soprano; tenor
Mood: lyrical; philosophical; love song; nature imagery

Voice: sweeping phrases; triplets; several large intervals; somewhat chromatic

Piano: contrapuntal; triplet figures; syncopation; broken chords; does not double vocal line

Diff: some notes and rhythms; *pp* a"; several long phrases

Uses: good for teaching soft high tones and legato approach to disjunct intervals

HAGEN, DARON
(b. Milwaukee, WI, 1961)

1080. ECHO'S SONGS. Voice & Piano. Cycle. E. C. Schirmer, 1992. cmp1979–1983. Tonal; b♭–a"; Tess-M-mH, cs; regular meters, some changes; varied tempos (♩ = 30–144); 17pp; Diff-V/e-md, P/e-m.

For: soprano; tenor

Mood: loss of love, of another, of self, of life

Voice: lyrical; wide-ranged melodic lines; many different rhythmic divisions; mostly syllabic; some melismas; some unaccomp. lines (one complete song); mild dissonance with piano; mostly slow tempos; much freedom in vocal lines

Piano: establishes mood of song; some chordal, some linear textures; some parts only punctuations of vocal line; mild dissonance

Diff: some pitches and rhythmic patterns; smooth transitions between songs that flow into each other

Uses: interesting cycle for advanced undergraduate or graduate level singer; attractive poetry, though somber throughout; d., e., j., & k. also set by Rorem

Rec: D#207

   a. *Never Pain to Tell Thy Love* (William Blake). Cmin; c'–g"; Tess-cs; 4/4, Warmly ♩ = a free 54; 2pp.

   b. *I Am Not Yours* (Sara Teasdale). X; c'–a"; Tess-cs; 3/4, 2/4, Bright and Flexible ♩ = 144; 2pp.

   c. *A Dream within a Dream* (Edgar Allan Poe). A; b♭–f♯"; Tess-M; 4/4, 3/4, 5/4, 2/4, Conversational, freely effusive ♩ = c.69; 4pp.

   d. *Echo's Song* (Ben Jonson). E♭min; b♭–a♭"; Tess-mH; 3/4, 2/4, Ardent and Blue ♩ = 72; 2pp.

   e. *I Am Rose* (Gertrude Stein). Gmaj; g'–g"; Tess-mH; 4/4, Quick ♩ = 126; 1p.

   f. *Lost* (Carl Sandburg). Amin; c'–a"; Tess-cs; 4/4, Adagio ♩ = 64 or less; 1p.

   g. *why did you go?* (e. e. cummings). Dmin; d'–g"; Tess-M; 2/4, 5/4, 4/4, Straightforward, simple ♩ = c. 60; ½p (unaccomp.).

   h. *Since You Went Away* (Shu Ch'i-siang, trans. Kenneth Rexroth). Emin; e'–f"; Tess-M; 4/4, 5/4, Even more restrained ♩ = c.60; ½p (single line accomp.).

   i. *Thou Wouldst Be Loved* (Edgar Allan Poe). G; c♯'–f♯"; Tess-M; 3/4, 3/2, 4/4, Andante; 2pp.

   j. *Look Down, Fair Moon* (Walt Whitman). X; e'–f♯"; Tess-M; 12/4, Numb, sluggish, always harsh ♩ = c. 64; 1p.

   k. *The Mild Mother* (Anonymous 16th century). Tonal; b–f"; Tess-cs; 4/4, 8/4, 3/4, Very, very slow, tender, and intimate ♩ = c.30; 1p.

1081. LOVE IN A LIFE. Eight Songs for Voice and Piano. Carl Fischer, 1999. cmp1981–1998. X and tonal; a–f♯"(g"); Tess-M, wide, cs; mostly regular but changing meters; moderate tempos; 28pp; Diff-V/me-md, P/e-m.

For: baritone

Mood: expressions of the elusiveness of love and truth in life, yet the eternal omnipresence of Love

Voice: patterned melodies with subtle changes; some stepwise motion; many skips; frequent leaps of 8ve; some wide-ranged phrases; many different divisions of beat; some polyrhythms; syllabic; some speech rhythms, many melodic rhythms; mixture of dissonant and quasi-popular styles

Piano: mostly chordal construction; some linear 2–4-voice scoring; accidentals; open texture; does not double vocal line

Diff: pitches in some songs; rhythms in changing meters; divisions within the meas.

Uses: interesting cycle with considerable variety; four poems are the same as set by Rorem; good cycle for advanced undergraduate or graduate recital

Rec: D#208

   a. *Love in a Life* (Robert Browning). X; b–f♯"; Tess-M; 9/8, 6/8, Restless, Elastic, Smooth; 4pp.

   b. *Youth, Day, Old Age, and Night* (Walt Whitman). X; a–e"; Tess-M; 3/4, 4/4, Moderately Fast, Mercurial (in 1); 2pp.

   c. *Congedo* (Nuar Alsadir). Fmaj; c'–g"; Tess-cs; 3/4, 4/4, Freely; 3pp.

   d. *Ample Make This Bed* (Emily Dickinson). A♭maj; c'–g♭"; Tess-wide; 2/2, Simple, Direct ♩ = 63; 2pp.

   e. *The Green for Pamela* (Roland Flint). Tonal; c'–g"; Tess-M; 4/4, Freely; 5pp.

   f. *The Waking* (Theodore Roethke). X; b–g"; Tess-M, cs; 4/4, Slowly; 4pp.

   g. *Just Once* (Anne Sexton). D minorish with repeated g'" in piano sounding throughout; a–e♭"; Tess-cs; 10/2, 6/2, 4/2, 2/2, 3/2, Adagio, quasi andante ♩ = 52; 4pp.

   h. *Love* (Thomas Lodge). X; b♭–e"(f", g"); Tess-cs; 9/8, 3/4, 6/8, Passionate, yet rueful ♩ = 116 (♪ = ♪); 4pp.

1082. LOVE SONGS. A Cycle of Eight Songs for High Voice & Piano. E. C. Schirmer, 1992. cmp1984–1987. "for Ned Rorem, on his 63rd birthday." Mostly tonal, but no clear key centers; c'–c♭'"; Tess-M-H; regular changing meters, varied tempos (♩ = 42–152); 23pp; Diff-V/me-d, P/me-md.

For: soprano

Mood: romantic; many aspects of love: being loved, troubled love, depressed love, lost love, loving care of another, remembered love, decaying love, creative pain of love

Voice: predominantly lyrical; conjunct and disjunct vocal lines; large intervals frequent; chromatic and whole-tone passages; many accidentals; syllabic; a few melismas; speech rhythms; melodic repetition in different rhythms frequent; many expressive markings

Piano: melodic and rhythmic repeated-motive structure; linear and chordal textures; many accidentals; variety of figuration; wide reach helpful for some rolled chords

Diff: some pitch patterns; dissonances between voice and piano; some sustained ascending high phrases

Uses: good cycle for graduate level soprano

Rec: D#207

 a. *I Am Loved* (Gwen Hagen). Tonal on F; c'–c♭'''; Tess-cs, H; 5/4, 6/4, Allegro frescamente (♩ = 116); 3pp.
 b. *Little Uneasy Song* (Reine Hauser). E; d'–a''; Tess-M; 2/2, 6/4, 12/8, Drowsy (♪ = 84); 3pp.
 c. *Ah! Sun-Flower* (William Blake). G; d'–f''; Tess-M; 2/2, 3/2, Allegretto (♩ = 88–108); 2pp.
 d. *Lost Love* (Ze'ev Dunei). Blurred harmonies; e♭'–g♯''; Tess-M; 8/8, 12/8, Simple (♪ = 88); 2pp.
 e. *Washing Her Hair* (Sarah Gorham). X; d'–a''; Tess-M; 3/4, Allegretto, ma non troppo (♩ = 120); 4pp.
 f. *Requiem* (Ze'ev Dunei). Bitonal; f♯'–f♯''; Tess-M; 3/4, Andante (♩ = 58); 2pp.
 g. *The Satyr* (Gwen Hagen). X; e♭'–b''; Tess-mH; 4/4, 6/4, 3/4, Quick and Sharp (♩ = 152); 3pp.
 h. *Sonnet* (Gardner McFall). X; d'–a''; Tess-mH; 2/2, 3/2, Flowing Calmly (♩ = ca.63); 4pp.

1083. **MERRILL SONGS** (James Merrill). For High Voice and Piano. E. C. Schirmer, 1997. cmp1995. Commissioned by William Weaver for countertenor Charles Maxwell. Tonal; a–a♭''; Tess-L, M, H; mostly regular meters with changes; varied tempos (♩ = 54–♩. = 138); 33pp; Diff-V/m-md, P/e-m.

For: countertenor; soprano (recorded by a soprano)

Mood: philosophical reflections on old age, divorce, the deterioration of the body, death and renewal; some mysticism

Voice: singable, straightforward melodies; long phrases; little word inflection; numerous large intervals; short melismas; some angular lines; two songs with unaccomp. vocal lines (these texts set in speech rhythms); wide range

Piano: mostly linear, spare textures; jazz flavor in two songs; syncopated figures; numerous accidentals

Diff: difficult poetry to grasp, interpret, and communicate; unusual imagery will require superior diction

Uses: excellent late 20th-century work for graduate level singer

Rec: D#207

 a. *A Downward Look.* Bmin; d♯'–g''; Tess-cs; 4/4, 3/2, 2/2, Weightless, floating ♩ = 54; 3+pp.
 b. *Body.* B; b–f♯''; Tess-M; 4/4, 3/2, 2/4, 3/4, Allegretto ♩ = 108; 2pp.
 c. *The Instilling.* Emin; d'–g''; Tess-cs; 4/4, 3/2, ♩ = 56; 3pp.
 d. *On the Block: Mantel Clock, Imitation Sèvres.* A♭maj; e♭'–a♭''; Tess-cs; 4/4, 3/2, Allegretto ♩ = 108; 4pp.
 e. *Vol. XLIV, No. 3.* X; a–g''; Tess-mH, L; 3/4, Freely effusive, but not slow ♩ = 69; 2+pp.
 f. *On the Block: Lamp, Terracotta Base, US, Ca. 1925.* X; a–e''; Tess-L–mH; 9/8, 12/8, Allegro ♩. = 138; 5+pp.
 g. *Pledge.* Bmin; b–f♯''; Tess-cs; 4/4, 3/4, 2/2, ♩ = 54;

6+pp.
 h. *An Upward Look.* Gmaj; d'–a♭''; Tess-M; 2/2, Nobile, con dignità ♩ = 54; 4pp.

1084. **MULDOON SONGS** (Paul Muldoon). Carl Fischer, 2000. cmp1989. Tonal, mostly traditional keys with added notes; (a)b–a♭''; Tess-M, wide, cs; regular meters with some changes; varied tempos (♩ = 56–156); 12min; Diff-V/me-md, P/e-m.

For: tenor

Mood: somewhat philosophical; seeing and experiencing incidents in a slightly skewed way; the scene behind the scene

Voice: some stepwise movement; many skips; numerous 8ve leaps; melodies patterned and frequently repetitive; numerous rhythmic divisions for word stress; many expressive and dynamic markings; mostly syllabic; a few slow melismas

Piano: mostly chordal with melodic material; some afterbeat patterning; numerous harmonic shifts using same musical material; numerous accidentals; wide reaches

Diff: understanding of poetic images; rhythmic patterns and changing meters in (a.); wide-ranged phrases with many 8ve leaps, some with specific dynamic markings

Uses: attractive set; good recital material for senior or graduate tenor with solid command of his range to a♭'' and understanding of the poetry

Rec: D#208

 a. *The Waking Father.* Dmaj; c♯'–g''; Tess-wide; 4/4, 3/4, Big, exuberant (♩ = 156); 4pp.
 b. *Thrush.* Emin; b–f''; Tess-M; 4/4, 3/2, Hypnotic, languorous (♩ = 56); 2pp.
 c. *Blemish.* Tonal; e♭'–e''; Tess-M; 12/8, Smooth and quick (♩. = 88); 1p.
 d. *Mink.* C minorish; e♭'–d''; Tess-M; 4/4, Quick, but turgid (♩ = 144); 1p.
 e. *Bran.* Tonal; a(a')–g''; Tess-wide; 3/4, 4/4, Moderately (♩ = 72); 2pp.
 f. *Holy Thursday.* Fmaj; c'–a♭''; Tess-M, cs; 2/2, Simply expressive (♩ = 40); 3+pp.

HAILSTORK, ADOLPHUS C.
(b. Rochester, NY, 1941)

1085. **A CHARM AT PARTING** (from the cycle *A Charm at Parting*) (Mary Phelps). [6]. X; c♯'–g''; Tess-M; 4/4, 5/4, 6/4, ♩ = 52; 3pp; Diff-V/md, P/md.

For: soprano; mezzo-soprano

Mood: lyrical; dreamy

Voice: very lyrical, legato, and flowing; some chromaticism; a few difficult intervals

Piano: chordal texture with moving 8th-note counterpoint, becoming more complex

Diff: legato line requires good control

Uses: good recital song

1086. **' LOVED YOU** (from the cycle *A Charm at Parting*) (Alexander Pushkin; trans. Zola Essman). [6]. X; b–f''; Tess-M; 3/4, 2/4, 4/4, ♩ = 60; 3pp; Diff-V/md, P/d.

For: mezzo-soprano; baritone

Mood: lyrical love song; sadness of lost love
Voice: phrases static at first, becoming more disjunct and dramatic, then returning to quietness; rather chromatic; some large leaps; fragmented phrasing
Piano: linear texture, 4-voice contrapuntal writing; chromatic; triplets and quintuplets in 16ths
Diff: good sense of pitch and rhythm needed
Uses: excellent recital material

HAMM, CHARLES
(b. Charlottesville, VA, 1925)

1087. **ANYONE LIVED IN A PRETTY HOW TOWN** (e. e. cummings). Valley, 1956. X; f'–g"; Tess-mH; 6/8, Easily; 3pp; Diff-V/m, P/m.
For: soprano; tenor
Mood: ironic commentary on personal relationships
Voice: small skips; easy rhythms
Piano: repeated-chord pattern; rolled chords; varied registers; does not double vocal line
Diff: text
Uses: interesting song; useful in an e. e. cummings group

HAMMOND, WILLIAM G.
(b. Melville, NY, 1874; d. New York, NY, 1945)

1088. **THE PIPES OF GORDON'S MEN** (J. Scott Glasgow). G. Schirmer, 1911. H & L keys: Fmin & Dmin; f'–ab" & d'–f"; Tess-M; 6/8, 2/4, Con spirito; 5pp; Diff-V/me, P/e.
For: tenor; baritone; dramatic voices best; can be easily transposed for bass
Mood: dramatic ballad; narrator and three characters
Voice: easy skips; repetitive rhythms; Scotch snap
Piano: drone bass with high melody, like bagpipes; measured and unmeasured tremolo; block chords; large reaches
Diff: characterization; large dynamic differences; sustained high tones at end
Uses: effective for singer with large voice and dramatic flair

HANCOCK, EUGENE W.
(b. St. Louis, MO, 1929; d. 1994)

1089. **ABSALOM** (Second Book of Samuel). [6]. X; F#–eb'; Tess-M; 3/4, 4/4, 7/4, 9/4, 11/4, 5/4, Slowly, with much expression; 3pp; Diff-V/d, P/me.
For: bass
Mood: sad; familiar text
Voice: steady motion; longer tones at ends of phrases; large leaps; difficult intervals; sustained; ends on lowest pitch
Piano: chordal texture; quarter-note motion; organ-like
Diff: intervals, low tones, sustained vocal line
Uses: recital material for bass

HANSON, HOWARD
(b. Wahoo, NE, 1896; d. Rochester, NY, 1981)

1090. **FOUR PSALMS** for Baritone Solo with Accompaniment for Piano or Organ, Op. 50. Cycle (continuous). Carl Fischer, 1965. No key sigs. (modal, with much quartal and parallel harmony); A–f'; Tess-M, mH, H; regular meters, some unmeasured sections; varied tempos; 21min; Diff-V/d, P/d.
For: baritone with strong top (many e's and f's)
Mood: declamatory; some lyrical sections
Voice: mostly conjunct; some 8ve leaps; tessitura concentrates in upper third of range much of the time; rhapsodic in nature; speech rhythms; a few melismatic passages; chant-like
Piano: much solo material; sections connected with rhapsodic piano line; largely chordal texture with various figurations; wide reach helpful
Diff: high tessitura sections; length
Uses: probably very effective work as a whole or four separate Psalms; sections connected by solo piano material, but each could stand alone; needs mature baritone voice for best effect; too many f's for young singers

  a. *Psalm XLVI: God Is Our Refuge and Strength.*
  b. *Psalm VI: O Lord, Rebuke Me Not in Thine Anger.*
  c. *Psalm XLVII: O Clap Your Hands.*
  d. *Psalm VIII: O Lord Our Lord, How Excellent Is Thy Name.*

HARBISON, JOHN
(b. Orange, NJ, 1938)

[THE FLUTE OF INTERIOR TIME. See entry #15 K]

1091. **MIRABAI SONGS** (Mirabai, 16th-century India; Eng. versions by Robert Bly). For Soprano (or Mezzo-Soprano) and Piano. Associated, 1983 (Hal Leonard). cmp1982. X; b–ab"; Tess-M, cs; changing meters, ($\downarrow$ = 66–144+); 17min; Diff-V/d, P/d.
For: soprano; mezzo-soprano
Mood: mystical union with the "Dark One"–Lord Krishna
Voice: many disjunct phrases; repeated-note phrases; some sustained high phrases; polyrhythms; dissonant harmonic texture throughout; mostly syllabic; some tone-painting
Piano: motivic structure in repeated patterns; dissonant; many accidentals; piano creates haze of sound; motor rhythms
Diff: dissonance; pitches; some rhythms; ensemble; projecting poetry through haze of dissonance; perfect pitch perhaps helpful
Uses: a challenging cycle for the singer attracted to Indian mysticism
Rec: D#s 209, 210

  a. *It's True, I Went to the Market.* X; b–g#"; Tess-cs; 4/4, Allegro ($\downarrow$ = 108); 5pp.
  b. *All I Was Doing Was Breathing.* X; d'–g"; Tess-M; 3/4, 4/4, 5/4, 3/8, 5/8, Tranquillo ($\downarrow$ = 108); 5pp.
  c. *Why Mira Can't Go Back to Her Old House.* X; d'–ab"; Tess-cs, H; 4/4, 9/8, 12/8, 10/8, 5/8, 7/8,

Con brio (♩ = 144+); 5pp.
  d. *Where Did You Go?* X; c'–g"; Tess-M; 4/4, Recitando, rubato (♩ = 66); 2pp.
  e. *The Clouds.* X; c'–g"; Tess-M; 5/8, 3/8, 4/8, Andante velato (♩ = 88); 5pp.
  f. *Don't Go, Don't Go.* X; c♯'–g"; Tess-M; 4/4, 5/8, Lento (♩ = 66); 3pp.

1092. SIMPLE DAYLIGHT (Michael Fried); Associated Music Publishers, 1990 (Hal Leonard). First performed in 1990 by Dawn Upshaw, to whom the work is dedicated. X, dissonant; b–b"; Tess-cs; mostly regular meters with changes; varied tempos; 16min; Diff-V/dd, P/dd.
For: soprano specified
Mood: ranges from lyrical expression of love and beauty to rather angry and bitter alienation, incorporating a vulgar phrase
Voice: much disjunct motion; some intervals of 6th, 7th, 8ve & 9th; many accidentals; phrases very short to very long; frequent sustained singing; words sometimes interrupted by rests; lengthy but not fast melismas in several songs; specific dynamic and tempo markings
Piano: chordal and contrapuntal; highly dissonant; many accidentals; triplets and irregular groupings; many specific articulation, dynamic and tempo markings
Diff: perfect pitch desirable for singer, secure musicianship necessary; strength needed throughout vocal range; highly-skilled pianist with thorough grasp of the modern score required
Uses: could be impressive for the right voice in the appropriate setting
Rec: D#s 211, 212

  a. *Japan.* b–b♭"; 4/4, Mesto, andante (♩ = 69); 6pp.
  b. *Simple Daylight.* b♭–f♯"; 3/2, 4/2, Semplice, intenso (♩ = 52); 3pp.
  c. *Somewhere a Seed.* d♭'–b"; 2/2, Bollente (♩ = 80); 4pp.
  d. *Your Name.* c♯'–a"; 5/2, Posato (♩ = 69); 3pp.
  e. *The Wild Irises.* c♯'–a♭"; 9/4, Con fervore, rubato (♩. = 63); 3pp.
  f. *Odor.* d♯'–a" 2/2, Allegro (♩ = 92); 6pp.

HARLING, W. FRANKE
(b. London, England, 1887; d. Sierra Madre, CA, 1958)

1093. THE DIVAN OF HAFIZ, Op. 15. Four Persian Love Lyrics (Richard LeGallienne). Cycle. Boston Music Co., 1912. Traditional keys; f'–a"; Tess-M; regular meters; varied tempos; 16pp; Diff-V/m, P/m.
For: lyric tenor
Mood: lyrical; spring love poems
Voice: grateful for the voice; conjunct; a few skips; three 8ve leaps to a"; very lyrical
Piano: chordal with countermelody; 2pp fast, light arpeggiation; tremolo; some turn-of-the-century idioms and clichés, but not overdone
Diff: no technical difficulties, but texts quite dated
Uses: highly romantic cycle; text and music of (a.) & (b.) better than those of (c.) & (d.); first two would be

excellent teaching pieces for head tones, lyricism, and beautiful sound; cycle is really a period piece of the Middle-Eastern-poetry genre, but perfect for singing

  a. *Heart! Have You Heard the News!* Gmaj; g'–g"; 9/8, 6/8, Allegro movimento giocoso; 3pp.
  b. *O Love, the Beauty of the Moon Is Thine.* Dmin-Fmaj; f'–a"; 2/2, Andante languido; 3pp.
  c. *Winds of the East.* Fmaj-Dmaj; f'–a"; 6/8, Vivo; 6pp.
  d. *Love, If for Nothing Else.* A♭maj; f'–g"; 3/4, Andante affettuoso; 4pp.

HARRIS, DONALD
(b. St. Paul, MN, 1931)

[See Appendix for songs with French texts]

1094. OF HARTFORD IN A PURPLE LIGHT (Wallace Stevens). Presser, 1979. cmp1979. "...First performed and broadcast on the poet's 100th birthday by Susan Davenny Wyner, soprano, and Yehudi Wyner, piano." X; a–c♯'''; Tess-wide; 3/4, Adagietto; 5+min; Diff-V/dd, P/dd.
For: soprano with wide range and flexibility
Mood: descriptive and dramatic
Voice: disjunct; leaps, often 7ths or 9ths; highly complex in most ways–pitches, rhythms, ensemble, tessitura, and diction; perfect pitch almost essential; many gradual tempo fluctuations; many dynamic markings
Piano: linear and disjunct; harmonic structure usually includes 2nds, 7ths, 9ths, or tritones; complex in most ways; bristles with accidentals; many rolled vertical structures; grace notes; some 3- & 4-stave writing
Diff: ensemble extremely difficult; both performers must be excellent musicians and experienced in reading contemporary scores; singer must have flexible, easy technique
Uses: only for the mature performers described above
Rec: D#213

HARRIS, EDWARD C.
(b. Elizabeth, NJ, 1899; deceased)

1095. SEA CHARM (Langston Hughes). Boosey & Hawkes, 1950. G♯min-Bmaj; d♯'–d♯"; Tess-M; 3/4, Moderately slowly, with unchanging motion; 3pp; Diff-V/me, P/me.
For: baritone; mezzo-soprano
Mood: declamatory
Voice: conjunct; short phrases
Piano: ostinato bass under parallel triads

HARRIS, ROY
(b. Lincoln County, OK, 1898; d. Santa Monica, CA, 1979)

1096. EVENING SONG (Alfred Lord Tennyson). [116]; 1st©1942. Fmaj; c'–g♭"; Tess-M; 6/8 with changes, Lento; 4min; Diff-V/m-d, P/m-d.

For: mezzo-soprano; soprano
Mood: lullaby
Voice: small skips; chromaticism; 2–3-note slurs
Piano: chordal-linear combination; many accidentals; large reaches; sostenuto pedal; dotted rhythms; duplets and triplets; does not double vocal line
Diff: changing meters; ensemble
Uses: rather dissonant setting of this text; quiet ending

1097. **FOG** (Carl Sandburg). [21]; 1st©1948. H & L keys: Bitonal; d'–f" & c'–eb"; Tess- mL; 5/4, 4/4, ♩ = 52; 2+min; Diff-V/md, P/d.
For: any voice except very high
Mood: poetic description of nature
Voice: somewhat disjunct; chromatic; fragmented
Piano: chordal; chromatic; 3-stave notation
Uses: good recital song for singer with good ear

1098. **FREEDOM'S LAND.** For Solo Voice or Unison Chorus (Archibald MacLeish). [116]. cmp1941. Fmaj (with alterations); c'–d"; Tess-M; 4/4, ♩ = 120; 3pp; Diff-V/me, P/m.
For: baritone
Mood: patriotic song; march
Voice: stepwise and small skips; some accidentals; syncopation
Piano: block chords; 5–6-voice texture; accidentals; moves predominantly in quarters; doubles vocal line
Uses: patriotic song

1099. **WAITIN'** (Roy Harris). [116]. cmp1941. "For Igor Gorin, Russian bass." F-centered; c'–f"; Tess-mH; 2/2, ♩ = ca.60; 3pp; Diff-V/md, P/m.
For: baritone seems best; mezzo-soprano
Mood: "latter-day spiritual"; bleak
Voice: many skips along chord lines; many accidentals; syncopation; many 2-note slurs; informal diction
Piano: block chords; many accidentals; moves predominantly in quarter notes; polytonal touches; 5-voice texture predominates; incidental doubling of vocal line
Diff: rhythms; phrasing (many fragments)
Uses: needs sizeable sound; very "American" in expression

HARRIS, VICTOR
(b. New York, NY, 1869; d. New York, NY, 1943)

1100. **NOD** (Walter de la Mare). J. Fischer, 1921. Ebmaj (also pub. in Db & Bb); f'–g"; Tess-mH; 4/4, In a gentle rhythm; 5pp; Diff-V/m, P/m.
For: any voice that can sing softly
Mood: quiet; serene; night song
Voice: stepwise and easy skips; 2-note slurs; accidentals
Piano: chordal–broken and block; some doubling of vocal line
Diff: features f"
Uses: effective atmospheric song; quiet ending

1101. **SILVER** (Walter de la Mare). J. Fischer, 1921. Fmaj (also pub. in Eb); f'–g"(ab"); Tess-mH; 3/4, Slow and tender; 6pp; Diff-V/m, P/m.
For: soprano; tenor; mezzo-soprano; baritone
Mood: lyrical; descriptive; quiet night song

Voice: many skips along chord lines; dotted rhythms; accidentals; subdued
Piano: chordal–block and rolled; moving 8th notes; dotted-rhythm motive; some parallel structures move chromatically; does not double vocal line
Diff: dynamic range ppp–f
Uses: effective song; very quiet ending (ppp)

HARTLEY, WALTER S.
(b. Washington, DC, 1927)

1102. **TWO SONGS AFTER WILLIAM BLAKE.** Fema, 1958. cmp1954. Traditional keys; c'–g"; Tess-mL-M; regular meters with some changes; 5min; Diff-V/me-m, P/m.
For: soprano specified; also lyric mezzo-soprano
Mood: innocent, child-like, joyful; somber, regretful, love in retrospect
Voice: mostly stepwise with small skips; some 2-note slurs and melismas; some unaccomp. passages; some dramatic sections; independent of the piano; some syncopation
Piano: (a.), mostly 16ths in scales and arpeggios; short sustained chordal section; (b.), chordal texture–block and arpeggiated; afterbeat styles; atmospheric; in first section, misalignment of meter of piano and voice gives uneasy effect
Diff: possibly getting pitches in unaccomp. sections
Uses: nice settings, together or separately; good student songs

    a. *The Lamb.* Emaj; c#'–f#"; 2/4, Allegro giojoso; 1+min.
    b. *Love's Secret.* Cmin; c'–g"; 3/4, 4/4, 3/2, 5/4; 3+min.

HAUBIEL, CHARLES
(b. Delta, OH, 1892; d. Los Angeles, CA, 1978)

1103. **FOG** (Grace Hoffman White). Composers Press, 1935. Gmin; c'–eb"; Tess-M; 3/4, Andantino con dolore; 4pp; Diff-V/md, P/d.
For: mezzo-soprano
Mood: lyrical; nature picture with note of sadness
Voice: long, sustained phrases; several large intervals
Piano: 16th-note arpeggios throughout, almost all in descending patterns; somewhat chromatic
Diff: long phrases; long tones at phrase endings
Uses: possibly recital material

1104. **SEA GULLS** (Grace Hoffman White). Southern (San Antonio), 1935, 1962, 1967. H & L keys: Ebmaj & Bbmaj; d'–g" & a–d"; Tess-mH; 3/4 with changes, A piacere; 6pp; Diff-V/md, P/md.
For: any voice
Mood: lyrical; descriptive; atmospheric
Voice: many skips; accidentals; duplet and triplet subdivisions of beat juxtaposed
Piano: chordal–broken and rolled; countermelody; covers keyboard; does not double vocal line
Diff: complicated rhythms; ensemble; irregular phrase lengths

Uses: usable song for recital

HAUSSERMANN, JOHN
(b. Manila, Philippines, 1909; d. Denver, CO, 1986)

1105. THREE MOODS FOR MEDIUM VOICE AND PIANO, Op. 18 (poets not identified). Composers Press, 1940. cmp1938–1939. X; b♭–f♯"; Tess-mL, M; regular meters with changes; varied tempos; 6+min; Diff-V/md, P/d.

For: baritone
Mood: love songs: narrative, sorrowful, joyous
Voice: sectional; somewhat declamatory; chromatic; fragmented; triplets; some large intervals
Piano: chordal–broken, arpeggiated, and rolled figures; triplets; chromaticism
Diff: pitches; rhythms; recit. style
Uses: should be performed together

  a. *The Wind and the Song.* X; b♭–e"; Tess-mL; 4/4, 6/4, Quickly–Moderately fast–Swiftly–Slower; 3min.
  b. *Return.* X; b♭–e♭"; Tess-M; 6/8, 4/4, Slowly–Freely–Faster and a little agitated–More movement– Faster, with abandon; 2min.
  c. *At Eastertide.* X; b♯–f♯"; Tess-M; 3/4, 6/8, 4/4, Moderate tempo– Faster–Joyously–Quickly; 1+min.

HAWLEY, CHARLES BEACH
(b. Brookfield, MA, 1858; d. Red Bank, NJ, 1915)

1106. NOON AND NIGHT (Herbert Trench). [15]; 1st©1905. Amaj; a–c"; Tess-LL; 4/4, 2/4, 3/4, Moderato; 2pp; Diff-V/e, P/me.

For: bass
Mood: lyrical; love song; nature imagery
Voice: simple and lyrical; several meter changes
Piano: chordal; supports voice with some doubling
Diff: meter changes could pose some problems to singers for whom the song is best suited
Uses: good for young students or other beginners

HAYS, DORIS
(b. Memphis, TN, 1941)

1107. 7 BLUES FRAGMENTS from *Southern Voices.* Soprano and Piano. Henmar, 1982. cmp1981. X; c♯'–a♭"; Tess-M; regular and irregular meters with changes; slow to moderate tempos; 8+min; Diff-V/d, P/d.

For: soprano
Mood: "*Southern Voices* for orchestra is based on the melodies and rhythms of southern speech and utterance. Blues references are both to the musical heritage and to an impression of certain southern dialects. The soprano solos in *Southern Voices* are not synchronous with the orchestra and provide a sometimes ironic commentary on the sentimental view of many natives about their region. . . . The performance style of "Blues

Fragments" is free, almost spoken and semi-improvisational." [Doris Hays]
Voice: chromatic; mostly conjunct with small skips; "blue-notes" and other special instructions; many phrases begin high and descend; syllabic with short melismas
Piano: chiefly chordal texture; rhythmically complex; 2 vs. 3 & 2 vs. 5; special instructions for pedaling; independent of vocal line
Diff: blues style and "blue-notes" may not come naturally; other pitches and rhythms; needs good vocal actor
Uses: excellent recital material for performers who can handle the style
Rec: D#214

HEGGIE, JAKE
(b. Florida, 1961)

1108. ENCOUNTERTENOR (John Hall). [169 , Bk. 3]. "for Brian Asawa." Tonal; f–f♯"; Tess-M, wide; changing meters; two fast, one slow; 21pp; Diff-V/md-d, P/md-d.

For: countertenor
Mood: facets of being a countertenor; various moods
Voice: constructed mostly with steps and small skips, a few large skips; several long-ranged phrases; many melismas, some cadenza-like; rhythms generally not difficult; some polyrhythms vs. piano; some unaccomp. phrases
Piano: block and broken chords; rapid scale passages; some accomp. material common to (a.) & (c.); linear writing in parts of (b.); tremolo, staccato; some parallel 3-voice (no 5th) 7th chords; does not double vocal line; 4–6 meas. preludes in (a.) & (c.)
Diff: requires excellent vocal technique; phrase lengths; range; tessitura; rhythms in parts of (b.); length
Uses: a fine group for two excellent performers; while (a.) & (b.) must be sung by a countertenor, the subject of (c.) (how will it be when I can sing no more?) is of interest to all singers; any medium voice

  a. *Countertenor's Conundrum.* Emin, many shifts; f–f"; Tess-M; 4/4, 6/8, 4/8, Quasi una fantasia–Allegretto grazioso–Allegro; 9pp. [**Rec:** D#215]
  b. *The Trouble with Trebles in Trousers.* Unsettled/B♭; g–f♯"; Tess-wide; 4/4, 2/4, 3/4, Allegretto (not too fast); 8pp. [**Rec:** D#215]
  c. *A Gift to Share.* F-centered; b–e♭"; Tess-M; 3/4, slow–6/8, Allegretto grazioso; 4pp.

1109. EVE-SONG (Philip Littell). Cycle. [169, Bk.1]. "for Kristin Clayton." Tonal; c'–b♭"; Tess-M-H; regular meters with changes; mostly moderate tempos with fluctuations within songs; 33pp; Diff-V/m-d, P/m-d.

For: soprano specified
Mood: various; viewpoints of Eve in Paradise and after; dramatic, lyrical, nostalgic
Voice: fairly conjunct lines (b. & d.); angular lines (a. & g.); syncopation; some jazzy rhythms (e. & f.); hemiola; various rhythmic divisions of the beat; speech-like (a. & h.); humming on "oo" or "ah"; other melismas in 4

songs; scat singing in (f.); many tempo changes;
unaccomp. meas. in 4 songs

Piano: longer songs (a., f., & g.) have thicker texture than
other Heggie songs for soprano; many accidentals;
block chords, some repeated; broken chords; jazz
elements; waltz and other dance-like sections; various
arpeggiations; vocal line not doubled; 7-meas. prelude
to (b.); shorter preludes to (c., d., e., g., & h.); short
postludes in two songs; (d.) & (e.) join

Diff: rhythms; some pitch patterns; ensemble

Uses: some cyclic procedure ties songs (a.) & (f.); brief
musical quotations from (a.) & (b.) in (h.); use as a
cycle, or excerpt (*The Faces of Love* recording excerpts
b., d., & e. in a nice group; others could be added)

  a. *My Name.* Unsettled; c♯'–a"; Tess-H; 3/4 with
  many changes, Moderately (with fluctuations); 7pp;
  Diff-V/d, P/d; dramatic, questioning.

  b. *Even.* Unsettled; d'–a♭"; Tess-mH; 8/8,
  Moderately–not too slow; A little faster; 5pp; Diff-
  V/md, P/md; peaceful evening description. [**Rec:**
  D#215]

  c. *Good.* B♭-centered; d'–g♯"; Tess-mH; 4/4,
  Moderately–with a lilt; Slower, Faster, Very fast,
  Slower; 3pp; Diff-V/d, P/md; questioning.

  d. *Listen.* Bitonal; c'–g♯"; Tess-M; 4/4, Like a
  recitative; A bit faster; Seductively; 3pp; Diff-V/m,
  P/m; dialogue of Eve and the serpent. (segue to next
  song). [**Rec:** D#215]

  e. *Snake.* Fmin–Bmin; (b)c'–a"; Tess-wide; 4/4, Cool
  and Jazzy; 5pp; Diff-V/d, P/md; Eve is tempted.
  [**Rec:** D#215]

  f. *Woe to Man.* Unsettled; e'–b♭"; Tess-H; 4/4,
  Slowly; A cocky stride; 3/2, Very fast; 3/4, A broad
  waltz; Slower stride; Fast; Stride tempo; 5pp; Diff-
  V/d, P/d; dramatic.

  g. *The Wound.* Unsettled; e'–g♯"; Tess-mH; 6/8,
  Moderately–like a lullaby; 3pp; Diff-V/d, P/d;
  anxious; Eve carrying a child.

  h. *The Farm.* Dmaj/Bmin; d'–f♯"; Tess-M; 4/4, 6/4,
  3/4, Moderately–not slow; 2pp; Diff-V/m, P/m;
  memory of paradise.

1110. **THE FACES OF LOVE** (Emily Dickinson). [169, Bk.
1]. Tonal; c'–a"(b"); Tess-H, wide; 15pp; Diff-V/md-d,
P/md-d. Separate entries below.

A. **I SHALL NOT LIVE IN VAIN.** "for Renée Fleming."
4♯s, unsettled; d'–a"; Tess-H, wide; 4/4, Moderately
(♩=ca.69); 3pp; Diff-V/d, P/md.
For: soprano specified
Mood: love of mankind and nature
Voice: angular melody; many skips; syncopation; long notes
on g♯" and a"; mostly syllabic; tempo fluctuations;
short poetic text repeated with variant of original
melody
Piano: block chords; some countermelody; duplet and triplet
8ths; some rolled chords; large reaches; accidentals;
does not double vocal line
Diff: melodic intervals; rhythms; high notes on "pain" and
"vain"
Uses: with other songs in the group or separately, perhaps in a

multi-composer Dickinson group
Rec: D#215

B. **AS WELL AS JESUS?** "for Kristin Clayton." E-
centered, but shifting; e'–g"; Tess-mH; 4/4, Moderately
slow–with deep intensity (♩=ca.48); 2pp; Diff-V/md,
P/md.
For: soprano specified
Mood: questioning; earthly love compared to love of Jesus for
mankind
Voice: rather angular and somewhat chromatic melody;
speech-like rhythms; syllabic
Piano: repeated 8th-note vertical intervals, mostly in l.h.;
countermelodies; quiet song except at climax (thicker
texture); does not double vocal line; 5-meas. prelude
and postlude; some resemblance to Chopin's *Prelude in
E minor* for piano
Diff: beginning pitches of phrases may be hard to find
Uses: in the set or separately in a Dickinson group
Rec: D#215

C. **IF YOU WERE COMING IN THE FALL.** [9].
Quartal on A; c♯'–a"; Tess-M-mH; 6/8, 9/8, 2/4, Quick
and bright; 3min; Diff-V/md, P/md.
For: soprano
Mood: passion and uncertainty; the desire to be united with a
beloved other
Voice: largely conjunct, very melodic vocal line; syllabic
setting in rhythms that reflect meaning and images of
the text
Piano: evolves from opening vocal melodic phrase, an
exuberant and rhythmic "motto"; reminiscent of
Copland's "Going to Heaven"
Diff: none for secure performers
Uses: excellent song for undergraduate singer; recital material
Rec: D#215

D. **IT MAKES NO DIFFERENCE ABROAD.** "for
Carol Vaness." 2♭s, unsettled; c'–g"; Tess-wide; 3/2,
2/2, Directly; ♩=ca.112; 2pp; Diff-V/md, P/md.
For: soprano specified
Mood: nature goes on despite personal loss; lyrical
Voice: many skips among chord members, incl. 7ths; wide-
ranged phrases; some syncopation; syllabic
Piano: 4–5-voice texture moving mostly in quarters; linear;
some widely-spaced chords built in 4ths or 5ths;
doubles only a few individual notes of vocal line
Diff: range; intervals
Uses: in the set or separately in a Dickinson group
Rec: D#215

E. **AT LAST TO BE IDENTIFIED!** "for Nicolle
Foland." Bitonal; e'–a♭"(b"); Tess-H; 3/4, 4/4,
Ecstatically (with many broadenings, etc.)–Slow, with
accel. to end; 3pp; Diff-V/md, P/d.
For: soprano specified
Mood: dramatic; eternity theme
Voice: many skips, incl. 6ths & 7ths; speech-like free
measures; 3-meas. melisma on "ah"; accidentals; 2 vs.
3; long note on "ee" on a♭"; opt. ending on long f♯" or
b" on "day"
Piano: triplet arpeggiation of chords often lacking 3rds, hands

6th or 10th apart; also triplets at other intervals in contrary motion; a few block chords, widely spaced; accidentals; does not double vocal line; 7-meas. interlude; short prelude and postlude

Diff: melodic intervals; finding beginning pitch of some phrases; long high notes

Uses: group ender for this set; in a group of Dickinson poems

1111. MY TRUE LOVE HATH MY HEART (Sir Philip Sidney). [169, Bk. 3]. Emaj; e'–f#"(g#"); Tess-mH; 3/2, 4/2, Moderately, not slow; 4pp; Diff-V/m, P/m.

For: soprano

Mood: lyrical love song

Voice: many skips within chord structures; easy rhythms; two strophes, second varied slightly; use of Lydian 4th

Piano: block chords in 4–5 voices; some broken chords, some countermelody; accidentals; opt. cello part included

Diff: legato technique; good breath and dynamic control

Uses: pretty song; use where a happy love song is needed (also included is a duet version with cello obbligato)

Rec: D#215 (duet version)

1112. NATURAL SELECTION (Gini Savage). Cycle. [169, Bk.1]. "for Nicolle Foland." Tonal; c#'–a"; Tess-mH-H; regular meters, some changes; varied tempos; 24pp; Diff-V/md-d, P/m-d.

For: soprano specified

Mood: energetic, often dramatic

Voice: speech-like rhythms incl. syncopation, dotted rhythms, various divisions and subdivisions of beat, fragmentation of phrases; angular melodies, except in final song; melismas, some on "ah" and "oo"; some portamentos; many dynamic markings and tempo changes; (c.) refers to opera characters

Piano: repeated block chord and other piano figures connect first and last song; some countermelody; arpeggiation; (b.), tango with some big chords and tone clusters; (c.), thinner texture with broken and block chords; (d.), features a "boogie" bass and/or beat in either or both hands, sometimes accomp. by quartal chords in r.h.; other jazzy elements; rare incidental doubling of vocal line; some solo material in each song, 1–4 meas.

Diff: ensemble; speech-like rhythms; communication of a variety of moods

Uses: probably meant to be done as a cycle, but songs are effectively excerpted on the recording; "Joy Alone" is a beautiful lyric song; "Alas! Alack!" is humorous in an ironic sense

   a. *Creation.* Unsettled; d'–a"; Tess-H; 3/2 with changes; ♩=ca.48; 3pp; Diff-V/md, P/m; (coming of age).

   b. *Animal Passion.* Amin; d'–g#"; Tess-mH; 4/4 predominates, With fantasy–tango rhythm; 6pp; Diff-V/d, P/d; (longing for a lover; dramatic, energetic). [**Rec:** D#215]

   c. *Alas! Alack!* Unsettled; c#'–g#"; Tess-mH; 4/4, Quick (♩=ca.126); 6pp; Diff-V/d, P/md; (wanting the wrong man; ironic). [**Rec:** D#215]

   d. *Indian Summer–Blue.* Unsettled; d'–g"; Tess-mH; 4/4, Lazy; Quick–with a swing (♩=ca.132–168–ca.132); Slow (♩=66); Quick (♩=168); ♩=♩; 5pp;

(curiosity about husband's previous marriages [Blue refers to Bluebeard]; somewhat resentful).

   e. *Joy Alone (Connection).* Dmaj; d'–a"; Tess-H; 4/2, 7/4, 5/4, 4/4, Moderately (♩=ca.108); 3/4, Gentle waltz (♩=ca.144); Tempo I (2/2, 3/2, 4/2); 4pp; Diff-V/md, P/md; (solitude in nature; lyrical). [**Rec:** D#215]

1113. OF GODS AND CATS (Gavin Geoffrey Dillard). [169, Bk.2]. Tonal; a–g#"; Tess-wide; 4/4 with changing meters; moderate and fast tempos; 10pp; Diff-V/md-d, P/md-d.

For: mezzo-soprano specified

Mood: both humorous; (b.), gently irreverent interpretation of God as a child

Voice: jazzy rhythms (syncopation, dotted rhythms, 3 vs. 2, ties over bar lines); conjunct; some skips to a 7th; some melismas; portamentos; scat singing; (a.), voice often alone or accomp. by a single slinky line

Piano: thin textures; chromatic scales in triplets; M2nd & m2nd in harmony; various divisions of beat; (b.), mostly 2-voice linear in 8ths, staccato/legato juxtaposition; Emaj scale in 10ths; some 8ves and block chords; many accidentals; does not double vocal line; 6-meas. preludes; short interludes and postludes

Diff: rhythms; ensemble; changing meter in (b.); long phrases ("alleluia" ends on g", 7-meas. phrase)

Uses: good pair for recital, or use separately

Rec: D#215

   a. *In the Beginning . . . .* Amin; a–f#"; Tess-wide; 4/4, Stealthily; 4pp; (creation of the cat).

   b. *Once upon a Universe.* E♭maj; b♭–g#"; Tess-wide; 5/8, 6/8, 4/8, 4/4, etc., With humor (♩=ca.160); 6pp; (God, the naughty child, admonished by his mother).

1114. PAPER WINGS (Frederica von Stade). [169, Bk.2]. Tonal; c'–g"; Tess-M-mH; 4/4, 6/8 predominate; varied tempos; 14pp; Diff-V/m-md, P/m-md.

For: mezzo-soprano specified

Mood: about children and childhood

Voice: stepwise; small skips; accidentals; some syncopation; dotted rhythms; some 3 vs. 2 & 2 vs. 3; (d.), most jazzy and complex; mostly syllabic; some melismas on "ah" or humming; one spoken line; stage directions; (a.) briefly quotes Canteloube's "Brezairola" at beginning; some recit.-like phrases

Piano: broken chords in tertian, quartal, and quintal harmony; mostly 8th-note motion, some 16ths; block chords; countermelodies, some in 8ves; some staccato; chromatic scales in triplets; texture relatively spare; ethnic flavor in (b.); jazzy (d.); "Für Elise" quotation in (d.); does not double voice but pitches not hard to find; one 8-meas. interlude; other shorter solo material

Diff: some intervals; some rhythms; ensemble in (d.)

Uses: as a set or excerpt

Rec: D#215

   a. *Bedtime Story.* E♭maj/B♭maj; d#'–f#"; Tess-mH; 6/8 (♪=ca.100), 4/4 (♩=112); 4pp; (story told to a child about herself).

    b. *Paper Wings.* Cmin; c'–g"; Tess-mH; 6/8, Allegretto–with spirit (♩. = 72)–More gently; 3pp; (remembrance of childhood).

    c. *Mitten Smitten.* Gmaj; d'–d"; Tess-M; 4/4, Moderately (♩ = ca.100); 2pp; (memory of childhood). [segues to next song]

    d. *A Route to the Sky.* Cmin; c'–g"; Tess-M; 4/4, ♩ = ca.100–Presto (♩ = 152)–Tempo I; 5pp; (rescuing a child from the roof).

1115. **SONGS TO THE MOON** (Vachel Lindsay). [169, Bk.2]. "for Flicka" [von Stade]. Tonal; g–a"(a♭"); Tess-M-H, wide; simple meters; varied tempos; 25pp; Diff-V/m–md, P/me–md.

For: mezzo-soprano specified

Mood: whimsical; some humorous; views of the moon by various animals and persons

Voice: generally stepwise and easy skips; some leaps up to 9th; syncopation; jazzy rhythms in 3 songs; poly-rhythms; hemiola; irregular phrasing; portamentos; melismas on "ah"; many sustained long notes, some high; some spoken lines; scat singing; one song a "sing-song" jump-rope chant on indefinite pitches

Piano: generally thin textures, some 2–3 voices; syncopation; jazzy piano and rhythmic elements; chromatic scales in triplets and other chromaticism; some arpeggios, tremolo, and trill-like passages; colorful variety of piano registers; in (e.), pianist must clap and "heel stomp"; 12-meas. prelude in (a.); other preludes, interludes, postludes are short; (a.–d.) joined

Diff: some rhythms; scat singing and interpretation for some singers; characterization needed; range (some alternatives to long high notes)

Uses: a good set; songs can be excerpted; recording incl. (a., b., c., & g.)

    a. *Prologue: Once More–to Gloriana.* Gmaj; d'–g"; Tess-mH; 3/4, Gently–with quiet reverence; 3pp; (ethereal). [**Rec:** D#215]

    b. *Fairy-Tales for the Children: Euclid.* Gmin; c'–f"; Tess-M; 4/4, Quick and rhythmic (♩ = 88)–Half tempo (♩ = 88); 3pp; (whimsical). [**Rec:** D#215]

    c. *The Haughty Snail-King (What Uncle William Told the Children).* Cmin; g–f♯"; Tess-M; 4/4, Pompously; 4pp; (humorous, "with a jazzy, bluesy feel"). [**Rec:** D#215]

    d. *What the Rattlesnake Said.* Fmin; c'–f♭"; Tess-M; 4/4, Mysteriously ♩ = ca.138; 3pp; (humorous).

    e. *The Moon's the North Wind's Cooky (What the Little Girl Said).* F-centered; c'–f"; Tess-M; 4/4, Spirited ♩ = 92–♩ = 92–freely with an easy, jazzy feel–Tempo I, Lazier, Slower, Softer; 2pp; ("hopscotch or jump rope song").

    f. *What the Scarecrow Said.* G minorish; d'–a"(g♯"); Tess-H; 3/4, Mysteriously ♩ = ca.116; 3pp; (whimsical).

    g. *What the Gray-Winged Fairy Said.* F minorish; e♭'–f"(g"); Tess-M; 4/4, unmetered, freely–chant-like; 2pp; (imaginative; colorful). [**Rec:** D#215]

    h. *Yet Gentle Will the Griffin Be (What Grandpa Told the Children).* Fmin; c'–a♭"; Tess-wide; 3/4, Rather creepy–Very fast and rather wild

(spooky)–much slower–mysterious–Fast; 5pp; (mysterious, excited).

1116. **SOPHIE'S SONG** (Frederica von Stade). [169, Bk.2]. "for Jennifer Larmore." B♭maj; b–e"; Tess-M; 4/4, 5/4, Easy going ♩ = ca.60–moving a little ♩ = ca.72–Tempo I; 3pp; Diff-V/md, P/m.

For: mezzo-soprano

Mood: describes an opera star

Voice: angular; many skips of 3rd, 4th, 5th, 6th; syncopation; duplet and triplet 8ths; pairs of 16ths; some phrases range to a 10th; syllabic; somewhat speech-like

Piano: a b a' form; ostinato-like l.h. in a-section with syncopated melody above; b-section has afterbeat pattern in l.h., r.h. imitates composers mentioned (Mozart, Strauss)

Diff: rhythms; angularity of vocal line

Uses: attractive personality song for group about singers, singing, or with other character pieces

Rec: D#215

1117. **WHITE IN THE MOON** (A. E. Housman). [169, Bk.2]. Bmin; a–d♯"; Tess-mL; 6/8, Moderately (♪ = 120); 3pp; Diff-V/m, P/m.

For: baritone; mezzo-soprano

Mood: stark; lonely wandering

Voice: stepwise and skips among chord members; some dotted rhythms; 2 vs. 3; syncopation; syllabic

Piano: 3–6-voice mostly linear texture in 8ths; some block chords in dotted-quarters; first inversion chords in parallel motion; rare doubling of vocal line; 2-meas. prelude; 3 interludes of 1–5+meas.

Diff: rhythms when duplet dotted-8ths are 4 vs. 6 against piano; syncopation

Uses: teaching or recital; cf. J. Duke and A. Somervell settings

Rec: D#39

HEILNER, IRWIN
(b. New York, NY, 1908; d. Clifton, NJ, 1991)

1118. **THE TIDE RISES** (Henry Wadsworth Longfellow). [22]; 1st©1935. X; d♭'–g"; Tess-L; 4/4, 6/4, Grave–Più mosso; 3pp; Diff-V/m, P/md.

For: soprano; mezzo-soprano; tenor

Mood: strange and sorrowful song about death

Voice: more intoned than sung; many repeated tones; quiet, with one outburst

Piano: chordal; some figuration; chromatic

Diff: several loud high phrases; otherwise low and recit.-like

Uses: good for teaching this style

HEINRICH, ANTHONY PHILIP [Anton Philipp Heinrich]
(b. Schönbüchel, Bohemia, 1781; d. New York, NY, 1861)

1119. **THE MUSICAL BACHELOR** (The Poetry by a Gentleman of Kentucky). [50]. cmp ca.1820; harmonization and accompaniment by John Tasker Howard. Gmaj; g'–g"; Tess-M-mH; 2/4, Con moto; 2pp (2 strophes); Diff-V/m, P/e.

For: tenor
Mood: humorous; a gentleman's standards for a wife
Voice: conjunct; two 16th-note passages on important words; several g"s; scale passages
Piano: simple support of melody; doubles vocal line
Uses: good period piece; fun to sing; recital material

HELLER, ALFRED
(b. New York, NY, 1931)

1120.   **TWO HEINE SONGS.** Mercury, 1967. cmp1953. (Heinrich Heine; trans. Aaron Kramer; songs appear to be set to English translations). Separate entries below.

A.   **EIN FICHTENBAUM STEHT EINSAM.** X; c♯'–e"; Tess-mL; 4/4, 6/4, Slow; 2pp; Diff-V/m, P/m.
For: mezzo-soprano; baritone
Mood: lyrical; descriptive of pine tree and palm tree
Voice: mostly stepwise; somewhat fragmented; some chromaticism
Piano: chordal; independent melodic movement
Diff: pitches

B.   **DER TOD, DAS IST DIE KÜHLE NACHT.** X; e♭'–g"; Tess-mL; 4/4, Slow; 2pp; Diff-V/m, P/m.
For: soprano; mezzo-soprano; tenor
Mood: lyrical; philosophical; poem about death
Voice: mostly stepwise; somewhat fragmented; some chromaticism
Piano: chordal; independent of voice
Diff: recit. style
Uses: although these two songs appear to call for slightly different voice types, a mezzo-soprano, low tenor, or high baritone could sing both

HELLER, JAMES G.
(b. New Orleans, LA, 1891; d. Cincinnati, OH, 1971)

1121.   **THREE SONGS FOR BARITONE** (Robert Nathan). Affiliated Musicians, 1953. Traditional keys; c♯–f'; Tess-M-mH; regular meters; moderate tempos; 10min; Diff-V/m, P/m-md.
For: baritone
Mood: quiet; somber; central song a love song
Voice: many skips; some slurs; mostly easy rhythms; accidentals; dramatic climax
Piano: broken-chord texture; many accidentals; some countermelody; does not double vocal line
Diff: accidentals sometimes seem awkward
Uses: could be an effective set for undergraduate recital or more advanced singer

   a.   *When in the Evening.* C♯min; c♯–f'; 3/4, Quieto e poco malinconico; 3min.
   b.   *The Secret.* Amaj; d–e'; 4/4, Andante contemplativo; 4min.
   c.   *Where I Am Going.* Cmin; d–d'; 6/4, Lento; 3min.

1122.   **THREE SONGS FOR SOPRANO** (Robert Nathan). Affiliated Musicians, 1953. Traditional keys; f'–f";

Tess-M; regular and irregular meters; moderate tempos; 5min; Diff-V/e-me, P/e-me.
For: soprano
Mood: serene; tranquil; introspective; somber
Voice: stepwise and small skips; some speech rhythms; accidentals
Piano: chordal; some broken chords; syncopation; duplet and triplet divisions; accidentals; does not double vocal line
Uses: useful for a beginner, young or older; set could also be done by a mezzo-soprano or tenor

   a.   *Epitaph for a Poet.* Dmin; f'–f"; 4/4, Andante elegiaco; 2min.
   b.   *Bells in the Country.* Fmin; f'–e♭"; 5/4, Molto moderato; 1+min.
   c.   *The Waves of Quiet.* B♭min; f'–e♭"; 4/8, Andante molto tranquillo; 2min.

HELM, EVERETT
(b. Minneapolis, MN, 1913; d. Berlin, Germany, 1999)

1123.   **PRAIRIE WATERS BY NIGHT** (Carl Sandburg). [21]; 1st©1950. Gmin; d'–e♭"; Tess-M; 4/4, 3/2, 3/4, Not too fast (♩ = 144)–Slower (♩ = 112); 2+min; Diff-V/m, P/m.
For: any medium voice
Mood: lyrical; descriptive of nature
Voice: sustained and declamatory; recit. section; two melismatic phrases
Piano: chordal; chromatic; independent of voice
Diff: legato singing
Uses: could be used effectively in recital

1124.   **TWO LOVE SONGS** (e. e. cummings). Theodore Presser, 1947. cmp1946. Traditional keys; e'–f♯"; Tess-M; regular meters with some changes; 6pp; Diff-V/m, P/m.
For: tenor; high lyric baritone
Mood: lyrical; philosophical; love songs
Voice: conjunct with skips and repeated tones; accidentals; some speech rhythms
Piano: chordal-linear combination; broken-chord figures; large reach needed
Diff: some pitch and rhythm problems for insecure musician; last phrase of (b.), ascending Fmaj scale to f" *pp*
Uses: romantic songs usable for intermediate students; fairly simple e. e. cummings settings

   a.   *it is so long.* X-Gmaj; e'–f♯"; 4/4, 3/4, 5/8, 2/4, Lento; 3pp.
   b.   *for my lady.* Fmaj; f'–f"; 4/4, 2/4, 3/4, 7/8, 6/4, Broadly; 3pp.

HELPS, ROBERT
(b. Passaic, NJ, 1928)

1125.   **THE RUNNING SUN.** Soprano and Piano (James Purdy). Cycle. C. F. Peters, 1976. cmp1972. Each song dedicated to different person–(c.) "to Helen Boatwright," (d.) "to Bethany Beardslee." X; g–b";

Tess-wide; unmetered, traditional, & changing meters; varied tempos; 7+min; Diff-V/m-d, P/d.

For: soprano; mezzo-soprano (difficult range to handle; must have flexibility and an easy technique)

Mood: the permanence of nature and its cycles, and the impermanence of human life

Voice: contemporary score, but not so complex as many others; has the expected wide leaps but also some conjunct sections; (b.), sung entirely on one pitch (b♭'); rhythmic complexities incl. irregular subdivisions of beat and "regular" rhythms in (e.), after opening with recit. passage; several long-ranged phrases; many accidentals; extreme tempos in (d.)

Piano: some linear sections (as in (a.)); some block and broken vertical structures; harmonies of 4th, 5th, 7th, 9th, etc. common; many accidentals; various subdivisions of beat cause polyrhythms with voice; tremolo; (a.) & (e.), totally in treble clef; some 5 vs. 2 & 3 vs. 4; difficult, but not so difficult as many other scores

Diff: rhythms, pitches, and ensemble; needs good sense of relative pitch or perfect pitch

Uses: for two performers who have experience in performing modern scores; singer must have ease in all parts of wide range; student who can handle this is unusual

Rec: D#16

a. *I (We who are under the ground . . .).* X; g♯–b"; unmetered, Slow (a piacere); 2pp.

b. *II (When the chief shepherd counts his sheep . . .).* B♭-centered; b♭' only pitch; 2/4, Slow; 1p.

c. *III (I miss you in the evening hours . . .).* X; a–g♯"; 3/4, 2/4, Espressivo; 3pp.

d. *IV (All along the meadow . . .).* X; g–a♭"; changing meters, Fast (♩ = 54) (with changes); 4pp.

e. *V (And there is so much more than could be said . . .).* G-centered; g'–b♭"; 3/4, Slow; 3pp.

HERBST, JOHANNES (See Special Section)

HERSCH, FRED (See entry #15 B)

HERVIG, RICHARD
(b. Story City, IA, 1917)

1126. **FIVE ROMANTIC SONGS** (British Romantic poets). Associated, 1985. NATS Vocal Composition Award, 1984. No key sigs.; d'–a♭"; Tess-M; changing meters; medium to slow tempos; 8+min; Diff-V/d, P/d.

For: soprano; tenor; some mezzo-sopranos

Mood: songs of love and lost love

Voice: wide range in many phrases; melodies based on non-tertian harmonies; melismatic in places; many accidentals; irregular rhythms and phrasing; syncopation

Piano: predominantly linear; some widely-spaced writing; some tone clusters; some use of harmonics; essential to use marked pedaling; requires reach of 9th; complex

Diff: ensemble; pitch patterns; free, flowing rhythms; some long phrases; quickly changing dynamics; opening of

(b.) includes trill of perfect 4th (c♯"–g♯') and is the most difficult and dramatic of the songs

Uses: rewarding set of songs for mature performers and sophisticated audiences; interesting for both performers

a. *So, We'll Go No More Aroving . . .* (Lord Byron). d'–f♯"; meter changes, ♩ = ca.56; 3pp.

b. *O, That 'Twere Possible . . .* (Alfred Lord Tennyson). e♭'–a♭"; meter changes, ♩ = ca.66; 3pp.

c. *Lament* (Percy Bysshe Shelley). e♭'–g♭"; 2/4, 3/4, ♩ = ca.52-54; 3pp;

d. *From "Lucy."* (William Wordsworth). f'–f"; predominantly 4/4 with changes, ♩ = ca.56; 3pp.

e. *Music When Soft Voices Die . . .* (Percy Bysshe Shelley). e♭'–f♯"; meter changes, ♩ = ca.80-84; 3pp.

HESS, BENTON
(b. Parkersburg, WV, 1947)

1127. **METAMORPHOSIS** (Christopher Hewitt). High Voice and Piano. daringdiva press, 1989; Classical Vocal Reprints, 1990. cmp1989. Commissioned and premiered by Carol Webber, soprano. Mostly X; g♯–b♭"; Tess-M, cs, wide; regular meters with changes; slow to moderate tempos; 21pp; Diff-V/m-d, P/m-d.

For: soprano

Mood: nebulous; wishing to be something else, somewhere else; desire to change one's surroundings

Voice: mostly angular and somewhat chromatic lines; not recognizably melodic; nebulous, floating dissonance reflects the mood of the texts; wide range; syllabic

Piano: built of repeated patterns that set mood of text; chromatic; some awkward hand crossing; mostly linear

Diff: pitches; defining individual songs against sameness of harmonic background; ensemble

Uses: suitable for graduate level soprano for contrasting material to more romantic or classical groups

a. *This Spring.* X; c♯'–a♭"; Tess-cs; 4/4, Quite slowly; 2pp.

b. *Ophelia.* Quartal on B♭; d'–g♯"; Tess-M;3/4, 2/4, 4/4, Andante mosso; 3pp.

c. *Metamorphosis: Fish.* X; d♭'–a"; Tess-M, cs; 4/4, Lento (♩ = c.50); 5pp.

d. *The Lake.* X; b–g"; Tess-wide; 12/8, 4/4, Moderato; 3pp.

e. *When I Am Old.* B♭-centered; g♯–b♭"; Tess-wide; 3/4, 4/4, 6/8, 12/8, Quite slowly; 6pp.

HEWITT, JAMES (See Special Section)

HEWITT, JOHN HILL
(b. New York, NY, 1801; d. Baltimore, MD, 1890)

1128. **THE KNIGHT OF THE RAVEN BLACK PLUME.** [50]. cmp pre-1835; harmonization and accompaniment by John Tasker Howard. Gmaj; d'–e"; Tess-M; 6/8, Moderato; 3pp (3 strophes); Diff-V/e, P/me.

For: baritone
Mood: ballad with refrain; three characters
Voice: conjunct with a few skips along chord lines; folk-like melody
Piano: broken-chord pattern (lute-like); arpeggiation; bass line prominent; weak postlude
Diff: characterization
Uses: good period piece; to teach ballad style; usable as encore to program of American song

1129. **THE MINSTREL.** [50]. cmp1825; harmonization and accompaniment by John Tasker Howard. Cmaj; e'–g"; Tess-M; 2/2, Maestoso; 3pp (3 strophes); Diff-V/m, P/e.

For: tenor; soprano possible
Mood: ballad-like narrative song; three speakers
Voice: conjunct; some skips; one ascending 1-4-6-8 phrase to g"; moving 8ths; some 2-note slurs
Piano: simple broken-chord accomp. with short introduction
Diff: characterization
Uses: good for teaching storytelling in song; period piece

HOAG, CHARLES K.
(b. Chicago, IL, 1931)

1130. **DIRGE** ("Fear no more the heat o' the sun") (William Shakespeare). Boosey & Hawkes, 1964. Mostly Emin (much bitonality); c'–g"; Tess-mH; 4/4, 3/4, Freely; 3min; Diff-V/md, P/md.

For: tenor; mezzo-soprano; some sopranos
Mood: dramatic; somewhat uneasy
Voice: many skips, esp. 5ths; fragmented; two unaccomp. phrases; accidentals; beat subdivided into 2, 3, & 4
Piano: bitonal 4-voice chordal texture; 19 meas. solo material; many accidentals; wide skips; 2 vs. 3; does not double vocal line
Diff: rhythms; some awkward intervals; highest passage *ff*
Uses: soft ending; useful for Shakespeare group

1131. **THREE SONGS–TO WORDS BY THOMAS WYATT.** New Valley, 1962. X; b–a♭"; Tess-M, H; regular and irregular meters with changes; varied tempos; 9pp; Diff-V/d-dd, P/d.

For: soprano; mezzo-soprano; tenor
Mood: philosophical; one humorous; one dealing with love
Voice: somewhat disjunct; chromatic; short phrases; triplets; some sextuplets
Piano: (a.), imitative counterpoint, short chords, short melodic motives; (b.), rolled chords, afterbeat patterns, irregular note groupings, long interlude; (c.), dissonant chords, little melodic material
Diff: pitches; rhythms; melismas in voice
Uses: good recital material; can be performed separately or as a set

    a. *Words.* b–f"; Tess-M; 5/8, ♪ = 152; 3pp.
    b. *What Menys Thys?* c'–g"; Tess-M; 4/4, 5/4, 3/4, 2/4, Moderately–Faster; 3pp.
    c. *Love's Snare.* f♯'–a♭"; Tess-H; 2/2, 1/2, Slowly; 3pp.

HOEKMAN, TIMOTHY
(b. Racine, WI, 1954)

1132. **AMERICAN LYRICS.** Five Songs for High Voice and Piano. Recital Publications, 1992. cmp1989–1990. Traditional keys; c'–c'''; Tess-M-H; mostly regular meters (one song in 11/8); varied tempos (♩ = 40–120); 32pp; Diff-V/m-d, P/e-d.

For: lyric-coloratura soprano; coloratura soprano
Mood: romantic; exuberant; philosophical; dramatic; tender; breathless and joyous
Voice: long, flowing lines; setting both syllabic and with expressive melismas; much coloratura in last song, legato and staccato; wide intervals; sustained high notes; wide expressive range; polyrhythms; last song ends sustained c'''
Piano: both chordal and linear; much melodic material; many interludes; polyrhythms; accidentals; broken-chord patterns in double notes, both hands
Diff: many nuances in a virtuoso context for the singer
Uses: fine set for graduate level coloratura soprano

    a. *When June Is Here* (James Whitcomb Riley). E♭maj; e♭'–a♭"; Tess-mH; 4/4, Exuberantly, with rubato (♩ = approx.120); 7+pp.
    b. *The Philosopher* (Edna St. Vincent Millay). Gmin-maj; d'–b♭"; Tess-mH-H; 3/4, Moderately (♩ = 92); 6+pp.
    c. *Mend the World* (Louis Untermeyer). Dmin; d'–b"; Tess-cs; 4/4, 3/4, Slowly (♩ = approx. 44); 6pp.
    d. *Come Slowly, Eden* (Emily Dickinson). Bmaj; f♯'–f♯"; Tess-M; 4/4, Very slowly and tenderly (♩ = 40); 2pp.
    e. *i am so glad and very* (e. e. cummings). Cmaj; c'–c'''; Tess-cs, H; 11/8, Allegro (♩. = 108-120); 7+pp.

1133. **THE NASH MENAGERIE.** Seven Poems of Ogden Nash for Countertenor (or Mezzo-Soprano) and Piano (Ogden Nash). Recital Publications, 1999. cmp1995–1996. Tonal; f♯'–g"; Tess-M, cs; regular meters with changes; varied tempos (♩ = 48–126); 32pp; Diff-V/m-d, P/m-d.

For: countertenor; mezzo-soprano
Mood: humorous musical portraits
Voice: both conjunct and disjunct extremes; chromatic; melismatic; wide intervals; abundant tone painting; free melismatic passages; many different rhythmic divisions; baroque-style ornamentation; accidentals
Piano: musical motives express character of animal portrayed; rhythmic structure reflects the motion of the animal portrayed; some free passage work; many accidentals
Diff: extreme vocal flexibility demanded
Uses: a wonderfully humorous set of songs for an advanced singer with an affinity for animals and Ogden Nash; should be easily accessible to any audience

    a. *The Wombat.* Bitonal (G & A♭); d'–e♭"; Tess-M; 4/4, Alla marcia ♩ = 112; 3pp.
    b. *The Turkey.* Amin; c♯'–f"; Tess-m; 4/4, Pompously ♩ = 88; 4pp.
    c. *The Hippopotamus.* Chromatic; a♭–e"; Tess-cs;

    4/4, 6/4, Slowly ♩ = 48; 3pp.

  d. *The Kangaroo.* E♭min; b♭–f♭"; Tess-cs; 4/4, 6/4, Bouncy ♩ = 126; 2pp.

  e. *The Fly.* E; g♯–g♭"; Tess-cs; unmeasured, slowly and very freely; 6pp.

  f. *The Caterpillar.* B♭maj; c'–f "; Tess-cs; 3/4, 4/4, Gracefully ♩ = 66; 4+pp.

  g. *The Germ.* Amaj; f♯–g"; Tess-cs; 4/4, 7/4, Moderately fast ♩ = 88; 8+pp.

1134. **SEVEN HOUSMAN SONGS** (A. E. Housman). Poetry from *A Shropshire Lad.* For High Voice/ For Medium Voice (2 separate vols.). Recital Publications, 1988. cmp1980–1982. H & M keys: Traditional keys; c♯'–b♭" & b♭–g" (5 songs m3rd down; 2, whole-step down); Tess-M-H; regular and irregular meters; varied tempos; 34pp; Diff-V/m-md, P/e-d.

For: tenor; baritone
Mood: melancholy; meditations on life's inevitable losses
Voice: lyrical; mostly conjunct lines; many 2- & 3-note slurs and short melismas; wide range; numerous high phrases; very melodic and grateful for the voice
Piano: patterns that express the mood of the poem consistent within each song; linear and chordal textures; last song arpeggiated throughout in fairly rapidly changing harmonies; lies well under the hand
Diff: some high phrases
Uses: a lovely set of songs for an advanced undergraduate or graduate level tenor or baritone; should be attractive to any audience; can excerpt single songs

  a. *Loveliest of Trees.* Amaj; d'–g♯"; Tess-M; 2/2, 3/2, 5/4, Andante; 3pp.

  b. *When I Was One-and-Twenty.* Gmaj-min; d'–g"; Tess-M-mH; 4/2, Allegretto; 3pp.

  c. *There Pass the Careless People.* Amin; d'–g"; Tess-M-mH; 4/4, 3/2, 3/4, Adagio; 6pp.

  d. *Oh, When I Was in Love with You.* C♯maj; c♯'–a♯"; Tess-cs; 3/4, Allegro; 2pp.

  e. *The Lent Lily.* D♭maj; f'–a♭"; Tess-mH; 6/8, Allegretto; 3+pp.

  f. *Look Not into My Eyes.* Fmin; e'–b♭"; Tess-mH-H; 3/4, 4/4, 5/4, 3/2, 7/4, Largo; 4pp.

  g. *From Far, from Eve and Morning.* Gmin; a♭'–a"; Tess-H; 4/4, Allegro; 12pp.

HOFFMAN, STANLEY M.
(b. Baltimore, MD, 1929)

1135. **A PSALM BEYOND THE SILENCES** (A Piece for Jewish Holocaust Remembrance) (Joseph H. Albeck). E. C. Schirmer, Ione Press, 1999. Minor/Modal; c'–b"(g"); Tess-M-mH; 3/4, 4/4, 6/4, Lento ♩ = 72; 7pp; Diff-V/md, P/md.

For: tenor; soprano; some mezzo-sopranos
Mood: somber; somewhat dramatic
Voice: mostly conjunct; some melismas; subdivisions of beat into duplets, triplets, and 16ths; one Hebrew word
Piano: r.h. chords mostly double the melody; many octave 4-voice chords in r.h.; l.h. has chords and arpeggiation;

some 2 vs. 3; accidentals and key changes; short prelude and interludes
Diff: many dynamic changes; balance (big chords in piano could cover a smaller voice)
Uses: possible recital song, perhaps to end a group of Psalms, or stand alone

HOGAN, DAVID
(b. Petersburg, VA, 1949; d. TWA Flight 800, 1996)

1136. **THREE LOVE SONGS** for Medium Voice and Piano. E. C. Schirmer, 1994. Winning Vocal Category Composition, 1993 Delius Composer's Competition. Tonal; c♯'–f♯"; Tess-M; regular and irregular changing meters; tempos range from "Slow and Expressive" to ♪ = 152-168; 10min; Diff-V/md, P/md.

For: mezzo-soprano
Mood: mysterious; direct; joyful; distillations of the great themes of Divine Love, truth to oneself, and faithful union with another
Voice: chant-like melody; sharply defined short phrases; irregular rhythms; some syncopation; some large leaps
Piano: thin textures; delicate harmonies; subdued dynamics; constantly changing meters and rhythmic stresses
Diff: mostly rhythmic
Uses: excellent short set of songs for advanced undergraduate or graduate singer

  a. *Love on My Heart from Heaven Fell* (Robert Bridges). G & G♯-centered; c♯'–e"; Tess-M; 5+5/8, 5/8, 6/8, 2/4, 7/8, etc., Without dragging ♪ = 152; 5pp.

  b. *Perjury* (Emily Dickinson). B-centered; e'–e"; Tess-M; 4/4, 6/4, 5/4, 2/4, 3/4, Slow and expressive; 2pp.

  c. *My True Love Has My Heart* (Sir Philip Sidney). B♭maj; f'–f♯"; Tess-cs; 6/8, 5/8, 9/8, 3/4, etc., Bright, jauntily ♪ = 168; 7pp.

HOIBY, LEE
(b. Madison, WI, 1926)

[See Appendix for songs with French and German texts]

1137. **ALWAYS IT'S SPRING** (e. e. cummings). [120]. cmp1985. X-Cmaj; d♯'–b♭"; Tess-mH; 2/2, 5/4, 3/4, 3/2, Allegro molto (♩ = 76); 1+min; Diff-V/d, P/dd.
For: soprano
Mood: lyrical and descriptive
Voice: lyrical and flowing; leaps of 7th & 10th; some chromaticism; triplets; portamentos; numerous sustained high tones, climaxing on b♭" (7 beats); chiefly syllabic
Piano: rippling 16th-note figures in groupings of 4, 9, 10, 13, & 14 in outer sections; middle sections have r.h. melodic material in 3rds & 6ths with rolled afterbeat chords l.h.; triplets; both hands often in treble clef; does not double vocal line
Diff: requires easy, light high voice; good sense of pitch needed; ensemble may present problems
Uses: excellent recital material

Rec: D#s 3, 70

1138.   **AUTUMN** (Rainer Maria Rilke). [119]. cmp1979. G♯min–A♭maj; d♯'–g"; Tess-H; 4/4, Andante sostenuto–Un poco agitato–Molto lento–Doppio più mosso; 4min; Diff-V/md, P/md.

For: soprano; tenor
Mood: philosophical
Voice: predominantly stepwise but some large leaps (7th, 9th, 10th); accidentals; various divisions of beat; irregular phrase lengths; syllabic
Piano: broken-chord patterns in 8th & 16th notes; 16th-note triplets; accidentals; wide-ranging on keyboard; does not double vocal line
Diff: high-tessitura phrases; ensemble
Uses: recital song
Rec: D#216

1139.   **BERMUDAS: A SONG OF PRAISE** (Andrew Marvell). [118, vol.3]. Piano quartet accomp. and version for duet (H & M voices) also available. Traditional chordal structures with various tonal centers; b♭–a♭"; Tess-M–mH; 9/8 with changes, Moderato, in 3 (♩= 46)–Allegretto (♩= 100)–Moderato, come prima (♩= 72); 16pp; Diff-V/d, P/d.

For: mezzo-soprano; tenor
Mood: lyrical and philosophical; in praise of God
Voice: stepwise and small skips; leaps of 7th & 8ve; some chromaticism; duplets and 2 vs. 3 in piano; syncopation; lyrical and flowing; leaps from low voice to upper middle voice and vice versa; chiefly syllabic with 2–4-note slurs; several small melismas
Piano: chordal and linear; block, broken, and rolled chords; scalar passages; melodic material; contrapuntal sections; chromatic; triplets; irregular groupings; 2 vs. 3 & 3 vs. 7; grace notes; some doubling of vocal line
Diff: good sense of pitch and rhythm needed; length of song demands vocal stamina
Uses: interesting recital material; could stand alone

1140.   **A CHRISTMAS SONG** (Jacques Mitchell). [65]. cmp1970. Dmin; c'–a"; Tess-M; 3/4, Not too fast (♩. = 52); 3pp; Diff-V/m, P/m.

For: soprano
Mood: humorous; sibling relationship before Christmas
Voice: stepwise and easy skips; some chromaticism; syncopation; phrases generally rise higher as song progresses; text intentionally ungrammatical
Piano: chordal-linear combination; broken, rolled, and afterbeat chords; countermelody alternates between l.h. & r.h.; somewhat chromatic; triplets; incidental doubling of vocal line
Diff: good vocal actor needed
Uses: encore; good for occasional entertainment purposes

1141.   **DAPHNE** (Harry Duncan). [118, vol. 2]. cmp1955. G-centered; d'–g"; Tess-M, mH; 5/8, 6/8, 8/8, 7/8, Andante (♪= 76); 5pp; Diff-V/md, P/d.

For: soprano
Mood: lyrical; nature imagery; ancient Greek "Daphne" myth
Voice: stepwise and small skips; somewhat chromatic; movement in 8ths & 16ths; several ascending scalar

phrases in unison or 3rds with piano; 2 vs. 3 in piano; lyrical and flowing; primarily syllabic
Piano: contrapuntal; 2–4-voice texture; chromatic; movement in 8ths, 16ths, & 32nds; syncopation; triplets; 2 vs. 3; grace notes; some doubling of vocal line
Diff: good sense of rhythm and pitch needed (despite doubling in piano)
Uses: possible recital material

1142.   **THE DOE** (John Fandel). [119]. cmp1950; rev.1983. E♭-centered; d'–g"; Tess-mH; 2/2, Allegro moderato (♩= 69); 1min; Diff-V/m, P/md.

For: soprano
Mood: descriptive; graceful
Voice: many skips along chord lines; requires smooth singing; portamento; *messa di voce*; easy rhythms; dynamics generally quiet; many accidentals
Piano: arpeggiated patterning in 8ths, 16ths, & 8th-note triplets; some l.h. staccato; many color modulations; many accidentals; does not double vocal line
Diff: dynamic control; long final phrase (4 meas. on "go," 3 meas. e♭")
Uses: recital material for voice with good a♭", f♯", and g"; to open or within a group
Rec: D#s 3, 216

1143.   **THE DUST OF SNOW** (Robert Frost). [118, vol. 2]. C♯-centered; e'–g"; Tess-M; 4/4, 3/4, 2/4, Allegretto; 2pp; Diff-V/m, P/m.

For: soprano; tenor
Mood: lyrical; nature imagery
Voice: stepwise and easy skips; little chromaticism; legato and sustained, chiefly in half and quarter notes; syllabic
Piano: chordal-linear combination; double-dotted 8th/32nd rhythmic pattern in r.h. throughout, with wide register changes; l.h. sustained single tones and 3-voice rolled chords; some chromaticism; both hands in treble clef or cross-hands throughout much of song; incidental doubling of vocal line
Diff: good sense of pitch needed; phrase lengths–entire song is a single statement with only one rest in vocal line
Uses: good recital material

1144.   **EVENING** (Wallace Stevens). [119]. cmp1963. Bmin; f'–a"; Tess-H; 6/4 with changes, Still–Agitato–Meno mosso; 4+min; Diff-V/md, P/d.

For: soprano; tenor
Mood: dramatic
Voice: predominantly conjunct; syncopation; various divisions of beat; mostly syllabic; 2–4-note slurs; many sustained high notes
Piano: block-chord, arpeggiated, and broken-chord patterning; divisions of beat vary from 2 to 13; many accidentals; polyrhythms; 1-meas. prelude and two short interludes; doubling of vocal line incidental
Diff: fragmented nature of several phrases; long high notes; ensemble
Uses: effective recital song

1145.   **FOUR DICKINSON SONGS** (Emily Dickinson). (Peer)Southern, 1988. cmp1986–1987. Pub. under one cover; separate entries below.

A. **A LETTER.** cmp1987. Gmaj; b–f♯"; Tess-M; 4/4, 3/4, Moderato (♩ = 108); 5pp; Diff-V/md, P/m.
For: mezzo-soprano; tenor
Mood: descriptive of family situation; philosophical
Voice: stepwise and small skips; chromatic in middle section; triplets; 3 vs. 4 in piano; syllabic, one small melisma
Piano: broken-chord figures; some block chords; chromatic middle section; triplets; does not double vocal line
Uses: good recital material
Rec: D#39

B. **HOW THE WATERS CLOSED.** X; d'–g"; Tess-M; 3/4, 2/4, 4/4, Mesto (♩ = 54); 2pp; Diff-V/md, P/m.
For: soprano; tenor
Mood: somber; describes scene of a drowning
Voice: mostly stepwise; many accidentals; 2-note slurs; some dotted rhythms and syncopation
Piano: quarter-note chords with 8th-note countermelody; many accidentals; wide-ranged; some doubling of vocal line
Diff: intensity of situation; dynamic range (pp–ff)
Uses: separately or in group; recital material

C. **WILD NIGHTS.** cmp1986. X; c'–g"; Tess-M; 2/4, 3/4, Allegro (♩ = 72); 5pp; Diff-V/d, P/dd.
For: soprano; tenor
Mood: ecstatic love song
Voice: primarily conjunct with occasional leaps of 7th & 8ve; little chromaticism; triplets; soaring lyrical phrases; syllabic; 8-beat sustained e" & 10-beat b'
Piano: broken-chord figures in 32nds in first half and in 16th-note triplets in second half; 2 vs. 3; chromatic; does not double vocal line
Diff: good legato line and breath management needed
Uses: recital material

D. **THERE CAME A WIND LIKE A BUGLE.** cmp1987. Cmaj; e'–a"; Tess-mH; 4/4, 3/4, 2/4, Molto allegro (♩ = 108); 4pp; Diff-V/md, P/dd.
For: soprano; tenor
Mood: lyrical and philosophical; song about death
Voice: lyrical and flowing; several leaps of M7th & 8ve; some chromaticism; 3 vs. 4 & 5 in piano; syllabic with melisma on "fly"
Piano: broken-chord, broken-8ve, scalar, and trill figures; block and rolled chords; chromatic; groupings of 3, 5, 6, & 10; does not double vocal line
Diff: excellent sense of pitch and rhythm needed; ensemble will be tricky
Uses: excellent recital material

1146. **GO, AND CATCH A FALLING STAR** (John Donne). Boosey & Hawkes, 1965. D♭maj; d♭'–a♭"; Tess-M; 2/4, 3/4, Vivace; 6pp; Diff-V/d, P/d.
For: tenor
Mood: lyrical; philosophical; pertaining to love
Voice: very disjunct; numerous 8ve leaps; short phrases; chromatic
Piano: disjunct; chromatic; contrapuntal; 16th-note figures almost throughout; does not double vocal line
Diff: vocal agility; light and easy a♭"
Uses: good for teaching agility; excellent recital song

1147. **AN IMMORALITY** (Ezra Pound). [20, 117, 120]. cmp1952. H & L keys: A♭maj & Gmaj; e♭'–g" & d–f♯"; Tess-M; 2/2, 3/2, 7/4, 5/4, Poco allegro; 3pp; Diff-V/m, P/md.
For: tenor; soprano
Mood: abstract; perhaps humorous; moral about love
Voice: short phrases; some large intervals
Piano: chordal figurations; quite chromatic
Diff: meter changes; some difficult pitches
Uses: short humorous song to add contrast to a group
Rec: D#218

1148. **IN THE WAND OF THE WIND** (John Fandel). [119]. cmp1952. F-centered; e♭'–a♭"; Tess-mH; 3/2 with changes, Allegro molto; 1min; Diff-V/md, P/md.
For: soprano; tenor
Mood: dramatic and descriptive
Voice: stepwise and skips along chord lines; accidentals; uncomplicated rhythms; some triplets
Piano: scalar and block- and broken-chord patterns; some tremolo; accidentals; does not double vocal line
Diff: ensemble
Uses: nice short song; useful in seasonal group
Rec: D#216

[INVESTITURE AT CECCONI'S. See entry #15 M]

1149. **I WAS THERE** (Walt Whitman). Five Poems of Walt Whitman. Baritone and Piano. G. Schirmer, 1993 (Hal Leonard). Traditional keys; B♭–g'; Tess-M-H; changing meters, varied tempos (♩ = 46–♩ = 160); 5min; Diff-V/m-d, P/me-d.
For: baritone
Mood: vintage Whitman: the joy of writing poems; oneness of all in suffering; contemplation of the soul; Lincoln's death; the joy of venturing into the unknown
Voice: lyrical and dramatic; conjunct and disjunct lines; long sustained high tones; some high tessitura; syllabic; romantic treatment called for
Piano: highly repetitive piano parts; each song built on a simple motive; sets mood and provides motion of the text; romantic piano techniques
Diff: high tessitura; endurance
Uses: an accessible set for a fairly mature Verdi baritone; program as a group or separately
Rec: D#s 217, 218

  a. *Beginning My Studies.* [117]. E♭maj; B♭–f'; Tess-mH; 9/8, 6/8, 3/4, 4/4, Allegretto; 4pp.
  b. *I Was There.* Bmin; B–e'; Tess-mH; 2/2, 3/2, 5/2, Steady ♩ = 76; 6pp.
  c. *A Clear Midnight.* [117]. D♭min; B–c♭'; Tess-M; 5/2, 3/2, 4/2, 7/4, Lento ♩ = 46; 2pp.
  d. *O Captain! My Captain!* Cmin; B♭–f♯'; Tess-mH-H; 2/4, 4/4, 3/4, Lento ♩ = 54; 8pp.
  e. *Joy, Shipmate, Joy!* Cmaj; d–g'; Tess-H; 3/4, Allegro molto ♩ = 160; 4pp.

1150. **JABBERWOCKY** (Lewis Carroll). [117, 120]. cmp1986. H & M keys: X; c'–a" & b♭–g"; Tess-M, mH; 2/2, 3/2, Molto moderato (♩ = 92); 4+min; Diff-V/d, P/d.

For: soprano
Mood: nonsensical
Voice: generally conjunct at beginning and end; middle section features 8ve leaps and other large intervals; somewhat chromatic; portamento; easy rhythms; short phrases separated by rests; syllabic
Piano: chordal and linear; block and broken chords; chromatic; much 2-voice texture; tremolo; scale passages; glissandos; triplets; does not double vocal line
Diff: good sense of pitch, strong low and high tones, and vocal stamina needed; pronunciation of text; nonsense text calls for good vocal actor
Rec: D#s 22, 56

1151. LADY OF THE HARBOR (Emma Lazarus). [117, 120]. cmp1985. H & M keys: Cmaj & Amaj; e'–a" & c♯'–f♯"; Tess-M; 9/8, Moderato, rocking (♩ = c.60); 3pp; Diff-V/m, P/m.
For: soprano; mezzo-soprano
Mood: dramatic and inspiring; familiar poem ("Give me your tired, your poor . . .")
Voice: most phrases include a long sustained tone, often at the end; one leap of m9th
Piano: chordal; a rocking compound meter; several 16th-note flourishes
Diff: duplets in compound meter; several high-lying phrases
Uses: useful in its relationship to the cultural diversity of the United States
Rec: D#217

1152. LOVE LOVE TODAY (Charlotte Mew). [118, vol. 2]. cmp1970. Fmin; c'–g"; Tess-M; 4/4, Moderato (♩ = ca.92); 2pp; Diff-V/m, P/me.
For: soprano; tenor
Mood: lyrical love song
Voice: lyrical and flowing; stepwise and easy skips, several 7ths; a little chromaticism; portamento; syllabic
Piano: broken-chord figures in 8ths in much of song; some chromaticism; supports vocal line, incidental doubling
Uses: good recital material

1153. THE MESSAGE (John Donne). [120]. cmp1977. X; d♭'–g♯"; Tess-M; 3/2, 2/2, Con moto espressivo; 6pp; Diff-V/md, P/m.
For: soprano; tenor
Mood: lyrical and philosophical; unrequited love
Voice: lyrical and flowing; several 8ve leaps; chromatic; many sustained tones; triplets; syllabic; a few 2-note slurs
Piano: chordal-linear combination; countermelodies in r.h.; block and broken chords; chromatic; triplets; supports vocal line; incidental doubling
Diff: good sense of pitch needed; good legato and breath management needed
Uses: excellent recital material

1154. NIGHT SONGS (Adelaide Crapsey). Cycle. Rock Valley Music Company, 1996 (Classical Vocal Reprints). cmp1984. X with various tonal centers; c♯'–a♭"; Tess-M; regular and irregular meters; varied tempos; 10min; Diff-V/d, P/d.
For: mezzo-soprano; tenor
Mood: lyrical and philosophical; somber; deal with death

Voice: stepwise and small skips; leaps of 7th & 8ve; chromatic; triplets; syncopation; 3 vs. 2 & 4 in piano; lyrical and flowing; syllabic with small melismas in (d.); 9-beat c♯', 10-beat e', sustained g♯"
Piano: chordal and linear; r.h. semi-ostinato bass line in first and last sections of (d.); block, broken, and rolled chords; r.h. countermelodies; chromatic; triplets; dotted rhythms; grace notes; cross-hands; occasional incidental doubling of vocal line
Diff: excellent sense of pitch and rhythm needed; sustained low tones
Uses: good recital material; very somber mood
Rec: D#18

   a. *Night.* E-centered; e'–e"; 3/4, 2/4, Andante (♩ = 54); 2pp. [**Rec:** D#218]
   b. *Pierrot.* C♯-centered; c♯'–e"; 3/4, Moderato (♩ = 100); 3pp.
   c. *Angélique.* X; d'–a♭"; 3/8 with changes, Moderato con moto (♪ = 108); 4pp.
   d. *The Shroud.* A-centered; c♯'–g"; 3/4, 2/4, 4/4, Moderato (♩ = 72); 3pp.

1155. O FLORIDA. Five Songs to Poems of Wallace Stevens for Middle Voice. Cycle. Rock Valley Music Company, 1996 (Classical Vocal Reprints). cmp1983 (also available for voice and string quartet). X with some tonal centers; a–g♭"; Tess-M, mL; 22min; Diff-V/d, P/d.
For: mezzo-soprano; baritone; contralto
Mood: strangely philosophical; enigmatic; heavy, dark, humid, and sensuous tropical imagery
Voice: both conjunct and disjunct; chromatic; triplets; 2 vs. 3 & 3 vs. 2 in piano; syncopation; portamentos; grace notes; numerous large leaps from low to upper middle voice and vice versa; sustained high tones; syllabic; a few 2- & 3-note slurs; one small melisma
Piano: chordal and linear; block, broken, and rolled chords; scalar passages; melodic fragments; chromatic; triplets; irregular groupings; 2 vs. 3 & 3 vs. 4; grace notes; trill; some incidental doubling of vocal line
Diff: excellent sense of pitch and rhythm required; secure technique needed for abrupt register changes; mature and imaginative interpreter needed for difficult texts; taxing accomp.
Uses: possible recital material for performers attracted to these texts
Rec: D#218

   a. *Floral Decorations for Bananas.* X, F♯-centered; b♭–f"; Tess-M; 4/4, 3/2, Languid (♩ = ca.88); 5+pp.
   b. *Gubbinal.* X-D minorish; c'–f"; Tess-mL; 2/2, 5/4, 3/2, Con moto marcato (♩ = 76); 3pp.
   c. *Continual Conversation with a Silent Man.* X, F-centered; c'–f"; Tess-mL; 3/4 with changes, Con moto espressivo (♩ = 96); 5pp.
   d. *Contrary Theses.* X, E♭-centered; d♭'–g♭"; Tess-M; 4/4 with changes, Con moto sostenuto (♩ = 84); 5pp.
   e. *O Florida, Venereal Soil.* X; a–f♭"; Tess-mL; 6/4 with changes, Moderato (♩. = 44); 14pp.

1156. **O STAR** (John Fandel). [118, vol. 2]. cmp1951; rev.1979. C-centered; c'–g"; Tess-M; 2/2, 3/2, 3/4, Lento (♩ = 44); 2pp; Diff-V/md, P/m.
For: soprano; mezzo-soprano; tenor
Mood: lyrical and philosophical
Voice: lyrical and flowing; stepwise and small skips; some chromaticism; triplets; syllabic
Piano: chordal with melodic passages; chromatic; easy rhythms; some 3-stave writing; incidental doubling of vocal line
Diff: good sense of pitch needed
Uses: good recital material

1157. **PAS DANS MON COEUR** (Marcia Nardi). [118, vol. 2]. cmp1961. X; c'–f✗"; Tess-mL; 4/4, 5/4, 2/4, Adagio (♩ = 80); 4pp; Diff-V/md, P/md.
For: mezzo-soprano
Mood: gloomy and moody; rain imagery; absence of lover; French flavor
Voice: somewhat disjunct with tritones, aug.5th, 7th, etc.; chromatic; triplets; short phrases separated by rests; syllabic with a few 2–3-note slurs; text English with a few French phrases
Piano: contrapuntal; 2-voice texture; chromatic; triplets; afterbeat pattern of three 16ths; grace notes; some doubling of vocal line
Diff: good sense of pitch needed (despite doubling by piano)
Uses: possible recital material

1158. **THE RIVER-MERCHANT'S WIFE: A LETTER** (Rihaku; trans. Ezra Pound). [65]. cmp1956; rev.1981. X; d'–a"; Tess-M; changing meters, Andante (♩ = 44), Allegretto (♪ = 160); 8pp; Diff-V/d, P/dd.
For: soprano
Mood: philosophical, in the manner of Japanese poetry; letter to an absent husband
Voice: conjunct and disjunct motion; chromatic; some recit.-like phrases
Piano: contrapuntal motion; many accidentals
Diff: pitches and rhythms; both high- and low-lying phrases
Uses: effective song

1159. **THE SERPENT** (Theodore Roethke). [119]. cmp1979. "For Leontyne Price." B♭maj; c'–b♭"; Tess-H; 7/8 with many changes; Allegro giocoso; 4min; Diff-V/d, P/d.
For: soprano
Mood: humorous–a serpent "takes up" singing
Voice: movement predominantly by step and half-step; many skips, esp. 8ves; staccato; portamento; both sudden and gradual dynamic changes; ends on sustained b♭" (on "week"–5 meas.); several melismas; pitch patterning in both parts has "serpentine" motions
Piano: linear and some broken-chord and scale patterning (some scales in 10ths); articulations carefully marked; sudden and gradual dynamic changes; many accidentals; tremolo; trills, and other sound effects; 4-meas. prelude
Diff: changing meters and asymmetrical rhythmic subdivisions (e.g., 4/4 as 3+3+2 8ths) make rhythmic complications; long, sustained high notes (in addition to b♭" at end, 5-meas. f " and 2- & 3-meas. a♭"s)
Uses: excellent song in every way; well-crafted for both

performers; musically and expressively interesting to audience and performers; see also settings by Gail Kubik and Ned Rorem
Rec: D#s 3, 216

1160. **SHE TELLS HER LOVE WHILE HALF-ASLEEP** (Robert Graves). [117, 120]. cmp1952. H & M keys: C♯- & B-centered; d'–e" & c'–d"; Tess-M; 3/4, 2/4, Moderato (♩ = 100); 3pp; Diff-V/m, P/m.
For: any medium voice
Mood: lyrical; nature imagery
Voice: lyrical and flowing; easy skips with one M7th; some chromaticism; syllabic; several 2-note slurs
Piano: chordal-linear combination; 2–4-voice texture; chromatic; r.h. countermelody against l.h. broken chords; triplets; does not double vocal line
Diff: good sense of pitch needed
Uses: good recital material
Rec: D#3

1161. **SUMMER SONG** (John Fandel). [120]. cmp1952; rev. 1967. A-centered; e'–g"; Tess-mH; 3/4 with changes, Serene (♩ = ca.46); 2pp; Diff-V/m, P/md.
For: soprano; tenor
Mood: lyrical; nature imagery
Voice: stepwise and small skips; some chromaticism; lyrical and flowing; short phrases; syllabic
Piano: chordal-linear combination; block, broken, and rolled chords; r.h. melody in 8ves; chromatic; 32nd/double-dotted-8th rhythm; grace notes; incidental doubling of vocal line
Diff: good sense of pitch needed
Uses: good recital material

1162. **THREE AGES OF WOMAN** (Elizabeth Bishop). (Peer)Southern, 1994. cmp1990. Commissioned for Phyllis Bryn-Julson. Tonal; c–a"(g"); Tess-M-mH; changing meters; varied tempos; 16pp; Diff-V/md, P/md.
For: soprano; some mezzo-sopranos
Mood: three scenes from a woman's life (two from childhood)
Voice: much stepwise and easy skip movement; leaps up to an 8ve; syncopation and other rhythms from jazz; many accidentals in (b.) & (c.); mostly syllabic; some portamentos
Piano: imitates a ride in a horse-drawn wagon in (a.) in a 2-voice 16th/8th-note pattern; syncopation; staccato; linear writing, block chords, many articulations in (b.); (c.), blues with a dotted-quarter/8th pattern; many accidentals and dynamic marks throughout; large reach needed; some doubling of vocal line in each song
Diff: rhythms; fragmented phrases; reality-based texts; low tessitura in parts of (c.); ensemble
Uses: nice recital group; unusual

    a. *Manners.* Cmaj; c'–g"; Tess-mH; 5/4, 2/4, 4/4, Moderato (♩ = 80); 6pp.
    b. *Filling Station.* Emin/Amin; c♯'–a"; Tess-mH; 3/2, 4/4, 5/4, 3/4, 9/4, 6/4, 2/2, Moderato (♩ = 108); 6pp.
    c. *Insomnia.* Cmin; c'–f "; Tess-mL-M; 4/4, 3/4, 2/4, 3/2, Slow blues; 4pp.

1163. **TO AN ISLE IN THE WATER** (William Butler Yeats). [117, 120]. cmp1950. H & M keys: Fmaj & E♭maj; c'–g" & b♭–f"; Tess-M; 2/4, 3/4, Moderato (♩ = 72); 4pp; Diff-V/m, P/m.
For: tenor; lyric baritone; ideal for tenor-baritone
Mood: lyrical love song
Voice: stepwise and easy skips; leaps of 8ve & 10th; a little chromaticism; easy rhythms; lyrical and flowing; syllabic with 2- & 3-note slurs
Piano: chordal-linear combination; l.h. countermelody; r.h. flowing 16th-note pattern; some chromaticism; easy rhythms; both hands in treble clef in several sections; supports vocal line strongly; incidental doubling
Diff: lies awkwardly for some tenors, with low phrases and phrases in passaggio
Uses: excellent recital material for the right voice

1164. **TWENTY-EIGHT YOUNG MEN** (Walt Whitman). [120]. cmp1983. E♭maj-X; e♭'–b♭"; Tess-mH; 2/2, 7/4, 3/4, 3/2, Moderato (♩ = 66), Languid (♩ = 60); 6pp; Diff-V/md, P/md.
For: soprano
Mood: descriptive in a voyeuristic way
Voice: short phrases, gradually becoming higher and building to a climax, then subsiding and building again to an even higher climax; both high and low long tones
Piano: primarily chordal; some figuration; supports vocal line fairly well; some doubling
Diff: some pitches and high-lying phrases; subject matter
Uses: could be quite effective in the right situation

1165. **TWO POEMS OF WILLIAM BLAKE.** [117, 120]. cmp1987. Traditional tonal centers; d♭'–g♭"; Tess-M-mL; regular meters, moderate tempos; 6pp; Diff-V/m, P/m.
For: any medium voice
Mood: innocent; child-like; peaceful
Voice: stepwise and easy skips; some chromaticism; dotted rhythms and syncopation; (a.), many duplets, lyrical, flowing, sustained tones in middle voice; 2 vs. 3 in piano; syllabic
Piano: chordal–block and broken; l.h. syncopation; r.h. melody often doubles vocal line; some chromaticism
Diff: duplets in compound meter
Uses: good for students and for recital

    a. *The Shepherd.* H & M keys; D-centered & C-centered ; f'–g" & e♭'–f" ; Tess-mL; 9/8, 6/8, Peaceful (♩. = 60); 3pp. [**Rec:** D#217]
    b. *The Lamb.* H & M keys: E♭maj & D♭maj; e♭'–a♭" & d♭'–g♭"; Tess-M; 4/8, 3/4, Serene (♪ = 84); 3pp. [**Rec:** D#s 28, 218]

1166. **WHAT IF . . .** (Samuel Taylor Coleridge). [117, 120]. cmp1986. H & M keys: C♯min-X & B♭min-X; d♯'–g♯" & c'–f"; Tess-M; 6/4, 9/4, Con moto espressivo (♩ = c.116); 4pp; Diff-V/md, P/md.
For: any high or medium voice
Mood: the implications of a dream
Voice: gradually building to high point; long tones
Piano: various broken-chord patterns; many accidentals; supports vocal line fairly well

Diff: pitches and sustained tones at top of staff
Uses: good recital material
Rec: D#s 3, 56, 218

1167. **WHERE THE MUSIC COMES FROM** (Lee Hoiby). [117, 120]. cmp1973. H & M keys: G-D-Bmaj & E-B♭-Gmaj; f'–a" & d'–f" [the key relationships between high and middle keys do not appear to match]; Tess-M; 3/4, Moderato (♩ = 84); 6pp; Diff-V/m, P/md.
For: soprano; mezzo-soprano
Mood: joyous; ecstatic
Voice: mostly short phrases, building to high climax near the end; several long tones in middle range
Piano: chordal, with embellishments; dotted rhythms; dance-like; supports vocal line well
Uses: good to open or close a program
Rec: D#s 70, 218

1168. **WHY DON'T YOU?** (Robert Beers). [118, vols. 2 & 3]. cmp1984. X; c'–f"; Tess-M-mL; 4/4 with changes, Bouncy (♩ = 152)–Poco più mosso (♩ = 168); 3min; Diff-V/d, P/d.
For: any high or medium voice
Mood: nonsensical; humorous; sarcastic; "off-the-wall[!]"
Voice: conjunct and disjunct; "bouncy"; somewhat chromatic; duplets, triplets, syncopation; portamentos; varied phrase lengths; syllabic
Piano: chordal-linear combination; chromatic; broken-chord figures progressing in rising 5ths; continuously moving 8th notes; pedal tones; very little doubling of vocal line
Diff: good sense of pitch and rhythm needed; requires good vocal actor, perhaps with a rather odd sense of humor
Uses: possible program material; could end a group; encore
Rec: D#218

1169. **WINTER SONG** (Wilfred Owen). [119]. cmp1950; rev.1983. Dmin; d'–a♭"; Tess-mH; 2/2, Andante–Più mosso; 3min; Diff-V/m, P/m.
For: soprano; tenor
Mood: descriptive; love song; lyric
Voice: stepwise and skips along chord lines; accidental; syllabic; some 2–3-note slurs; uncomplicated rhythms; some syncopation; two 2-beat a♭"s
Piano: broken-chord patterning in 8ths with a few scales; some accidentals; does not double vocal line
Uses: singer needs floating high notes
Rec: D#s 39, 216

HOLMBERG, PATRICIA T.
(b. Denton, MT, 1934)

1170. **OUTWITTED** (Edwin Markham). For Soprano and Piano. Voice of the Rockies (BMI), 1995. Emin-D♭maj; d'–a♭"; Tess-wide; 4/4, 3/4, Andante–Allegro; 5pp; Diff-V/m, P/md.
For: soprano; sizeable sound needed
Mood: dramatic; energetic
Voice: some dotted notes; syncopation; mostly conjunct; several 8ve or dim.8ve leaps; 6-meas. a♭" ends song; other long notes
Piano: 16th- & 8th-note motion predominates; 8 meas. 32nds

& 16ths in r.h. near the end, followed by a tricky 3-meas. broken chord passage; mostly 2-voice texture

Diff: long high notes; finding pitches in first half of song

Uses: composer suggests pairing it with the Val-Schmidt setting of the same text

HOMER, SIDNEY
(b. Boston, MA, 1864; d. Winter Park, FL, 1953)

1171. BREAK, BREAK, BREAK, Op. 6, No. 1 (Alfred Lord Tennyson). G. Schirmer, 1901. H & L keys: B♭min & Gmin (orig.); e♭'–g♭" & c'–e♭"; Tess-mH; 4/4, Adagio non molto; 2pp; Diff-V/d, P/m.

For: contralto; bass; mezzo-soprano; baritone

Mood: dramatic; anguished

Voice: dramatic declamation and lyrical phrases of great tenderness; descending skips; conjunct in middle section

Piano: chordal; thick texture; melodic interest; some doubling of vocal line

Diff: dramatic style; best for advanced singer

Uses: quite a good song; recital use

1172. THE COUNTRY OF THE CAMISARDS, Op. 15, No.5 (Robert Louis Stevenson). G. Schirmer, 1904. Reprint: Classical Vocal Reprints (H & L). D♭maj; b♭–b♭'; Tess-L; 2/4, Moderato; Diff-V/e, P/e.

For: bass; contralto

Mood: reflective

Voice: simple line; sustained

Piano: chordal

Uses: good teaching song for low voice; easy range

Rec: D#2

1173. DOWN BYE STREET (John Masefield). [48]; 1st©1928. H & L keys: Fmin & Dmin; e♭'–a♭" & c'–f"; Tess-mL; 2/4, 4/4, Allegro, eagerly–Andante; 9pp; Diff-V/m, P/md.

For: all voices

Mood: narrative; ballad-like song of a poor widow and her son

Voice: sectional–alternating narrative section with chromatic section of ascending phrases

Piano: broken-chord figurations in one section, chromatic chords in the other.

Diff: high-lying phrase with powerful g" and a♭"(e" and f") at climax

Uses: one of several songs showing Homer's sociological interests–a protest song of its era

1174. THE HOUSE THAT JACK BUILT, Op. 36 (from *Mother Goose*). Church, 1920. H & L keys: G♭maj & E♭maj; c'–a♭" & a–f"; Tess-mL; 12/8, Allegro–Gaily, with increasing animation throughout; 39meas.; Diff-V/m, P/m.

For: any voice that has the range

Mood: narrative; cumulative story

Voice: continuous singing; largest skip is 7th, otherwise stepwise and small skips

Piano: 2–6-voice chordal texture; doubles vocal line

Diff: breathing; sustained singing on g♭"

Uses: good group ender; encore

Rec: D#219

1175. MICHAEL ROBARTES BIDS HIS BELOVED BE AT PEACE, Op. 17, No.3 (William Butler Yeats). G. Schirmer, 1906. Reprint: Classical Vocal Reprints. H & L keys: Amin & Gmin (orig.); e'–e" & d'–d"; Tess-M; 9/8, 6/8, 12/8, 4/4, 3/4, Allegro molto–With passion; Diff-V/md, P/m.

For: baritone

Mood: dramatic; passionate love song

Voice: syllabic; conjunct and disjunct phrases; expressive and dramatic; many tempo and meter changes; some 2 vs. 3 in piano; chromatic; numerous dynamic and expressive markings

Piano: chordal r.h over repeated motivic phrase in l.h.; some block chords in chromatic progressions

Diff: combination of passionate intensity and tenderness

Uses: imaginative song for an expressive singer; quiet ending; cf. "I Hear the Shadowy Horses" by Richard Faith

Rec: D#2

1176. PIRATE STORY (*A Child's Garden of Verses*), Op. 16, No. 1 (Robert Louis Stevenson). G. Schirmer, 1906. Reprint: Classical Vocal Reprints. Cmaj; c'–d"; Tess-M; 3/4, 2/4, Allegro (with grace and merriment); 4pp; Diff-V/me, P/m.

For: baritone; bass-baritone

Mood: merry; children's make-believe game

Voice: syllabic; fast diction; repetitive rhythms except in meter changes; children as characters

Piano: chordal; block and afterbeat patterns; some alternating 8ves in l.h.

Diff: rhythmic variations within patterns for some young singers; becoming the child character

Uses: a charming song from a child's viewpoint; good for young singers

1177. REQUIEM (*Underwoods*), Op. 15, No. 2 (Robert Louis Stevenson). G. Schirmer, 1904. Reprints: Classical Vocal Reprints (H & L); T.I.S. (H). [8, 68, bks. 3 & 4]. cmp1904. H & M keys: Amaj & G♭maj; f♯'–e" & e♭'–d♭"; Tess-M; 4/4, Adagio; 2pp; Diff-V/e, P/e.

For: any male voice

Mood: philosophical; nature imagery

Voice: stately; many dotted rhythms; some chromaticism

Piano: chordal; doubles vocal line almost throughout

Uses: good short song for young men

Rec: D#219

1178. SEVENTEEN LYRICS FROM *SING-SONG* (Christina Rossetti). G. Schirmer, 1908. Reprint: Classical Vocal Reprints. Traditional keys; a–f"(f♯") (low ed.); Tess-M; Regular meters (predominantly 4/4); varied tempos; 31pp (I & II); Diff-V/me-m, P/me-m.

For: medium voice; probably better suited to a woman

Mood: 17 very short songs, one only 4 meas., longest, 44 mas.; child-like poems; tender, naive, droll, humorous

Voice: conjunct motion and small intervals; a few leaps of 6th; some songs have ranges of less than 8ve; several high-lying and low-lying phrases; few accidentals, except for last song of Part II, more difficult than the others

Piano: chordal–mostly block- and broken-chord figures; melodic material in short postludes; no preludes; considerable doubling of vocal line; few accidentals, except for last song of Part II

Diff: not for a very young voice, despite text material; if one person sings all, or a significant portion of this set, both high and low voice will need to be well developed

Uses: effective as a set or excerpted to form small groups

PART I:

a. *Eight o'Clock; the Postman's Knock!* Fmaj; a–c"; Tess-L; 4/4, Allegro (♩ = 104); 1p.

b. *Baby Cry–Oh Fie!* Fmaj; f'–c"; Tess-M; 4/4, Allegro (♩ = 116); 1p.

c. *Dead in the Cold, a Song-Singing Thrush.* Cmaj; c'–a'; Tess-L; 4/4, Lento (♩ = 84); 1p.

d. *Love Me,–I Love You.* Dmaj; d'–c♯"; Tess-mL; 4/4, Lento (♩=98); 1p.

e. *Kookoorookoo! Kookoorookoo!* Cmaj; c'–f"; Tess-M; 12/8, Vivace (♩.=1 38); 2pp.

f. *Boats Sail on the Rivers.* Fmaj; c'–d"; Tess-mL; 4/4, Lento (♩ = 58); 2pp.

g. *In the Meadow–What in the Meadow?* Gmaj; d'–e"; Tess-M; 4/4, Vivace (♩=104); 2pp. [**Rec:** D#2]

h. *The Dog Lies in His Kennel.* Gmaj; b–d"; Tess-L; 4/4, Allegro (♩ = 144); 2pp.

i. *Lie Abed, Sleepy Head.* Gmaj; d'–d"; Tess-M; 4/4, Lento (♩ = 60); 1p.

j. *Mix a Pancake, Stir a Pancake.* Fmaj; c'–f"; Tess-M; 2/4, Vivace (♩ = 144).

PART II:

k. *Who Has Seen the Wind?* A♭maj; d♭'–d♭"; Tess-mL; 2/2, Andante con moto (♩ = 58); 2pp.

l. *Dancing on the Hilltops.* Gmaj; a–e"; Tess-L or M (depending on options taken); 3/4, Animato (♩. = 56); 2pp.

m. *A Pocket Handkerchief to Hem.* B♭maj; f'–f"; Tess-M; 4/4, Allegro molto, con amore (♩ = 138); 2pp.

n. *A Motherless Soft Lambkin.* E♭maj; b♭–d♭"; Tess-M; 4/4, Molto lento (♩ = 60); 2pp.

o. *Lullaby, Oh Lullaby!* Amin; c'–c"; Tess-mL; 4/4, Molto lento (♩ = 52); 2pp.

p. *Hurt No Living Thing.* Fmaj; a♯–d"; Tess-L; Allegretto (♩ = 106); 1p.

q. *Minnie and Mattie and Fat Little May.* Dmaj; e♯'–d"(f♯"); Tess-M; 6/8, Allegro (♩. = 76); 4pp.

1179. THE SICK ROSE, Op. 26, No. 1 (William Blake). G. Schirmer, 1913. Reprint: Classical Vocal Reprints (H & L). [121]. C♯min; c♯'–g"; Tess-M; 4/4, Molto lento; 2pp; Diff-V/m, P/md.

For: soprano; tenor
Mood: dramatic
Voice: chromatic; leaps of 7th & 8ve
Piano: chordal; thick texture; many accidentals; large reach helpful; doubles vocal line
Diff: dynamic control; register control
Uses: good short dramatic song; needs mature, substantial sound

Rec: D#48

1180. SING ME A SONG OF A LAD THAT IS GONE, Op. 15, No. 1 (Robert Louis Stevenson). Classical Vocal Reprints. E♭maj; c'–e♭"; Tess-cs; 6/8, 9/8, Allegro. Spirited; 5pp; Diff-V/m, P/m.

For: baritone
Mood: bittersweet; loss of youth
Voice: stepwise and chord outlining; some chromatic phrases; repetitive rhythms reflect poetic rhythm; syllabic
Piano: block chords in 8th-quarter rhythmic pattern give effect of rowing in waves; repeated chords in middle section; last stanza takes on more movement
Diff: many phrases begin on e♭"
Uses: an old-fashioned masculine song; could fit into various groups for undergraduate baritone

1181. THREE SONGS. [122]. Separate entries below.

A. THE FIDDLER OF DOONEY, Op. 20 (William Butler Yeats). [121, 122]. Gmin (orig.); d'–g"; Tess-M; 4/4, Allegro molto; 4pp; Diff-V/m-md, P/m.

For: tenor
Mood: narrative; exuberant; humorous
Voice: many skips of 3rd, 4th, 5th–like a fiddling tune
Piano: afterbeat chordal pattern; fiddle figuration; continuous motion in 8ths; big ending; doubles vocal line
Diff: dynamics; most long notes crescendo; ends on g" *ff*
Uses: a rouser; group or program ender

B. SING TO ME, SING, Op. 28 (William E. Henley). [122]. "For Louise Homer." E♭maj; e♭'–a♭"(b♭); Tess-M; 3/4, Allegro molto; 4pp; Diff-V/m, P/md.

For: soprano; mezzo-soprano; tenor (ample voice required)
Mood: exuberant; ecstatic love song; dramatic
Voice: many skips (up to 8ve) within chords; rhythms not difficult; include dotted 8th &16th notes, 16ths in pairs; other dotted rhythms; dynamics *p–fff* (thick chordal accomp.)
Piano: block and arpeggiated chords; some 16th-note patterns combine scale and arpeggio; some 8-voice chords; mostly doubles the vocal line
Diff: requires ample vocal sound, capable of *p–fff*
Uses: group or recital ender; encore for dramatic voice
Rec: D#s 23, 33, 219

C. SHEEP AND LAMBS (Katherine R. Hinkson). G. Schirmer, 1911. Reprint: Classical Vocal Reprints. [122]. H & L keys: A♭maj & G♭maj (orig.); c'–f♯" & b♭–e"; Tess-mH; 4/4, Andante (not dragging), tenderly; 25meas.; Diff-V/md, P/md.

For: any voice
Mood: innocent; devout; descriptive
Voice: many skips, esp. 6ths; dotted rhythms
Piano: continuous 16ths, both hands, in broken-chord pattern; sustained bass notes; no prelude; no vocal line doubling
Diff: dynamic range; fairly big climax
Uses: recital or church use; good song; quiet ending

1182. THE UNFORGOTTEN (*Underwoods*), Op. 15, No. 3 (Robert Louis Stevenson). G. Schirmer, 1904. Reprint: Classical Vocal Reprints. [121]. H & L keys: Gmaj &

Emaj (orig.); d'–d" & b–b'; Tess-M; 4/4, Andante, simply; 3pp; Diff-V/e, P/e.
For: bass; baritone; some tenors
Mood: nostalgic; quiet; plaintive
Voice: stepwise and easy skips; easy rhythms
Piano: bass and treble lines duet with syncopated repeated note in inner voice; thin texture; doubles vocal line
Uses: usable lyric song

1183. **WHEN DEATH TO EITHER SHALL COME,** Op. 34, No. 2 (Robert Bridges). G. Schirmer, 1917. H & L keys: Emaj & D♭maj; e'–e" & d♭'–d♭"; Tess-M; 2/4, Lento (calm, sustained); Diff-V/e, P/e.
For: tenor
Mood: lyrical; simple
Voice: descending lines
Piano: simple patterned accomp.
Uses: simple song; good for teaching

HOPKINS, HARRY P.
(b. Baltimore, MD, 1873; d. Baltimore, MD, 1954)

1184. **THE VIOLET** (trans. from Goethe). [1]; 1st©1898. E♭maj; d'–f"; Tess-mH; 4/4, Moderato; 4pp; Diff-V/me, P/me.
For: soprano
Mood: lyrical
Voice: stepwise and easy skips; 2–4-note slurs
Piano: chordal; thin texture; some doubling of vocal line
Diff: soft dynamics; voice must be flexible
Uses: interesting comparison with other settings of "Das Veilchen" (e.g., Mozart)

HOPKINSON, FRANCIS (See Special Section)

HORN, CHARLES EDWARD
(b. London, England, 1786; d. Boston, MA, 1849)

1185. **LEAVE ME DEAR ONE** (Flaccus). Davis & Horn, 1839. E♭maj; d'–f"; Tess-M; 2/4, Suave lamentevuole; 4pp (2 strophes); Diff-V/e, P/me.
For: any voice
Mood: lyrical love song
Voice: stepwise; a few chordal skips; much repetition and sequence; easy rhythms
Piano: chordal; broken-chord texture with octaves in l.h.; doubles vocal line; melody elaborated.
Uses: period piece

1186. **A SOUTHERN REFRAIN** ("Long Time Ago") (George P. Morris). [50]; arr. from pre-existing melody ca.1853. B♭maj; f'–f"; Tess-M; 2/4, Andante; 3pp (3 strophes); Diff-V/m, P/e.
For: tenor, if all strophes sung; soprano, with word changes
Mood: fond reminiscence; sad
Voice: sustained vocal line; conjunct; leaps of 6th at phrase ends [octave leap and triplet figure of the Copland arr. is original notation, according to John Tasker Howard]
Piano: very simple broken-chord accomp. by J. T. Howard

Diff: orig. key tends to lie "in the cracks" vocally; transposing up or down half-step helps
Uses: one of the loveliest of the early songs; needs a steady voice of sweet, clear quality; useful in many situations

1187. **WHAT CAN A POOR MAIDEN DO?** (harmonization & accomp. by John Tasker Howard). [50]. cmp ca.1850. Amaj; e'–f♯"; Tess-M; 6/8, Con spirito; 2 strophes; Diff-V/e, P/e.
For: soprano; mezzo-soprano
Mood: humorous; coy; young woman's song
Voice: conjunct; some skips; patter song
Piano: simple chordal accomp.; incidental doubling of vocal line
Uses: good for teaching direct expression to an audience; humorous

HORSMAN, EDWARD
(b. New York, NY, 1873; d. Summit, NJ, 1918)

1188. **THE BIRD OF THE WILDERNESS** (Rabindranath Tagore). G. Schirmer, 1914. Reprint: Classical Vocal Reprints (H, M, & L). [48]. "To Miss Alma Gluck." H, M, & L keys: D♭maj, B♭maj, & A♭maj; d♭'–b♭"(a♭"), b♭–g"(f"), & a♭–f"(e♭"); Tess-M; 12/8, Moderato, quasi allegretto; 4pp; Diff-V/m, P/d.
For: all voices
Mood: joyous love song
Voice: flowing phrases; ascending patterns to b♭"(g", f")
Piano: arpeggiated chords; rather chromatic
Diff: singer needs ringing sound on highest tones; lower options provided
Rec: D#63

1189. **IN THE YELLOW DUSK** (from the Chinese of Li Po, ca. A.D. 700). G. Schirmer, 1916. H & L keys: Emaj & Dmaj; f♯'–a♭" & e'–g♭"; Tess-M; 3/4, 4/4, 2/4, Tranquillamente–Meno mosso; 2+min; Diff-V/md, P/d.
For: soprano; mezzo-soprano; tenor
Mood: lyrical; descriptive scene
Voice: recitative-like phrases; fragmented; chromatic; triplets
Piano: chordal; syncopated afterbeats; triplets; chromaticism; impressionistic
Diff: pitches; rhythms; good dynamic control

1190. **THE SHEPHERDESS** (Alice Meynell). G. Schirmer, 1916. H & L keys: G♭maj & Emaj; d♭'–a♭" & b–e"; Tess-M; 4/4, Larghetto semplice; 4pp; Diff-V/m, P/m.
For: tenor; baritone; man's text
Mood: lyrical; serene; quiet
Voice: stepwise and skips on chord lines; 2–3-note slurs
Piano: chordal; accidentals; large reaches; 8th-note motion; some doubling of vocal line
Uses: usable lyric song; quiet ending

HORVIT, MICHAEL
(b. Brooklyn, NY, 1932)

1191. **THREE FACES OF LOVE** for Soprano and Piano. Southern (San Antonio), 1990. Tonal; d♭'–b♭"; Tess-

M-H; regular meters; slow to moderate tempos; 22pp;
Diff-V/m-md, P/me-m.

For: lyric soprano
Mood: romantic; broad and lush, with some dissonant tension
Voice: long, sweeping lines; folk-like melody in very high
 tessitura in (b.); some large leaps; sustained high tones;
 syllabic; some short melismas; melody dominates text
Piano: outlines harmonies in mostly arpeggio and broken-
 chord patterns; some bitonality; repeated patterns in
 slowly moving harmony
Diff: some long phrases; sustained b♭"s and a"s
Uses: beautiful and not too difficult set for full lyric soprano
 with even scale and great warmth; good contrast to
 more dissonant groups
Rec: D#220

 a. *She Walks in Beauty* (Lord Byron). D♭-centered;
 e♭'–a♭"; Tess-M; 4/4, 3/4, 2/4, Moderately
 (♩ = circa 84); 8pp.
 b. *We'll Go No More A-Roving* (Lord Byron). Amaj;
 g'–b♭"; Tess-H; 2/4, 3/4, With spirit, but not too
 fast (♩ = circa 116); 4pp.
 c. *The Indian Serenade* (Percy Bysshe Shelley).
 Fmaj; d♭'–b♭"; Tess-cs; 4/4, 3/4, 2/4, Somewhat
 slow (♩ = circa 72)–very freely; 10pp.

1192. THREE SONGS OF ELEGY for Soprano Solo and
 Piano (Emily Dickinson). Cycle. E. C. Schirmer, 1970.
 cmp1964. Traditional keys with dissonant altered
 chords; d♭'–g♭"; Tess-M; regular meters; slow tempos;
 9pp; Diff-V/m, P/m.

For: soprano (not light)
Mood: dramatic; anguish at another's death; somewhat
 deranged; numb
Voice: disjunct; dissonant intervals; forceful high tones; heavy
 weight; for a "Donna Anna" voice
Piano: supports voice and creates moods; mostly chordal with
 some broken-chord passages; many accidentals
Diff: pitch patterns; some rhythmic irregularity; proper mood
Uses: good cycle for many situations; not a program ender

 a. *I Felt a Cleavage in My Mind.* E♭-centered;
 e♭'–f♯"; 4/4 with changes, Moderately (♩ = ca.120);
 3pp.
 b. *Ample Make This Bed.* Amin; f'–e"; 2/4, With ease
 (♩ = ca.104); 2pp.
 c. *I Felt a Funeral in My Brain.* Cmin-Cmaj;
 d♭'–g♭"; 2/2, Slowly (♩ = ca.66); 4pp.

HOUTZ, STEVEN (See entry #15 R)

HOVHANESS, ALAN
(b. Somerville, MA, 1911; d. Seattle, WA, 2000)

1193. BLACK POOL OF CAT, Op. 84, No. 1 (Jean
 Harper). C. F. Peters, 1960. Built around A; g'–f♭";
 Tess-mH; 7/4, constantly changing; 7pp; Diff-V/m,
 P/dd.
For: any voice
Mood: tranquil and calm, but pulsating

Voice: conjunct melody; repetitive; some very long phrases
Piano: fast repeated notes and other patterns; high and middle
 register; 2-page solo prelude
Diff: long phrases; very long melismas; Middle-Eastern
 flavor
Rec: D#221

1194. I HEARD THEE SINGING (Consuelo Cloos). C. F.
 Peters, 1960. X; c♯'–g♯"; Tess-M; 4/4, 3/4, Allegretto;
 95meas.; Diff-V/d, P/d.
For: soprano
Mood: Middle-Eastern; unreal world
Voice: long phrases; long melismas; much use of aug.2nd
Piano: one stave; repeated notes; many ornaments; 2-page solo
 prelude
Diff: Middle-Eastern scale intervals; long phrases; awkward
 melismas
Uses: usable for a "different" song; perhaps in a group about
 song or singing

1195. INNISFALLEN, Op. 95, No. 4 (Jean Harper). C. F.
 Peters, 1960. X; d'–e"; Tess-M; 2/2, ♩ = 72–76; 2+min;
 Diff-V/dd, P/e.
For: medium voice
Mood: lyrical; nature
Voice: many skips; microtones (approached by skip)
Piano: thin texture; pedal tones in bass; thin high part; many
 sustained tones.
Diff: microtones (even harder when approached by skip);
 some long phrases; Middle-Eastern flavor
Uses: usable for student with unusually good ear

1196. LOVE'S PHILOSOPHY (WEDDING SONG), Op.
 370 (Percy Bysshe Shelley). C. F. Peters, 1994.
 cmp1984. Amin; e'–a"; Tess-mH; 2/4, Andante
 ♩ = ca.76; 4pp; Diff-V/m, P/me.
For: soprano; tenor
Mood: love song; enthusiastic
Voice: stepwise and small skips; many 2-note slurs; easy
 rhythms; repetitious melody
Piano: 8th-quarter-note motion; r.h. block chords double vocal
 melody; l.h. single melodic line; 12-meas. prelude, 9-
 meas. postlude
Uses: pleasant setting of this well-known text; neither as
 ecstatic nor as "busy" as the Quilter setting; recital,
 student, or wedding use

1197. LULLABY OF THE LAKE (Consuelo Cloos). C. F.
 Peters, 1960. A-centered; g'–e"; Tess-mH; 4/4, Allegro;
 49meas.; Diff-V/me, P/m.
For: all voices; somewhat better for men
Mood: lyrical; hypnotic; love song
Voice: stepwise or small skips; long phrases; repetitive
Piano: high register; single stave, one hand; dance-like quick
 16th/8th-note repetitive pattern
Diff: long phrases; long melismas; Middle-Eastern flavor
Uses: useful in some groups
Rec: D#221

1198. THE MOON HAS A FACE, Op. 156 (Robert Louis
 Stevenson). C. F. Peters, 1968. X; e'–e♯"; Tess-M; 4/4,
 6/8, Lento–Misterioso; 2min; Diff-V/me-m, P/m.

For: mezzo-soprano; soprano; baritone
Mood: lyrical; descriptive; childlike
Voice: stepwise and easy skips; accidentals
Piano: chordal-linear combination; 1–4-voice texture; delicate; series of parallel 5ths & tritones
Uses: nice song; approach to new idiom for young student

1199. O GODDESS OF THE SEA, Op. 151 (Alan Hovhaness). C. F. Peters, 1968. Bitonal, voice in D♭, piano X; a♭–f"; Tess-L; meterless, Very free with a strange and fierce expression; 4min; Diff-V/m, P/m.
For: bass; contralto
Mood: invocation to "Goddess of the Sea"
Voice: long phrases; some staccato
Piano: 3–4-voice texture; rather static; many dynamic markings
Diff: long phrases
Uses: usable for the right voice

1200. OUT OF THE DEPTHS, Op. 142, No. 3 (from *Psalm CXXX*). C. F. Peters, 1958. Amin; e'–a"; Tess-M; 4/4, Andante; 2+min; Diff-V/m, P/m.
For: soprano; tenor
Mood: devotional; supplication
Voice: long-lined melody; phrases often exceed 8ve
Piano: chordal; 4–6-voice texture; final page features block chords in both hands
Diff: long phrases; dynamic range wide
Uses: in a recital group or church; needs a big voice

1201. O WORLD, Op. 32, No. 2 (Percy Bysshe Shelley). C. F. Peters, 1969. X; F♯–e'; Tess-mL; unmetered; chant-like flow; 5pp; Diff-V/dd, P/md.
For: bass specified
Mood: despair; introspective
Voice: long melismas with little support from the piano; chant-like groupings
Piano: 4-voice repeated chords; quick group followed by long, sustained chord
Diff: very long phrases; pitches; *ff* climax on sustained e' near end
Uses: effective for the right singer; aria-like; perhaps could stand alone or be in a short group

1202. PAGAN SAINT (Consuelo Cloos). C. F. Peters, 1960. G is central pitch of scale: G A B♭ C♯ D E F; g'–g"; Tess-mH; Piano prelude (2pp): changing meters, Presto; Song: 7/8, Allegro; 4pp; Diff-V/d, P/md.
For: soprano
Mood: excited; wild; ecstatic
Voice: uses scale illustrated above; perpetual motion; long melismas
Piano: 2-page piano prelude; doubles vocal line; imitates Middle-Eastern instruments
Diff: breathing; long phrases and melismas; difficult scale for Western ears
Uses: perhaps an effective final song in a group
Rec: D#221

1203. RAVEN RIVER (Consuelo Cloos). C. F. Peters, 1960. Amin; e–a'; Tess-LL; Piano: 4/4, 7/8, 3/4, 2/4, 3/8, Allegro, Voice: unmetered, Andante; 4pp; Diff-V/m,

P/md.
For: bass; contralto
Mood: lyrical; song about death
Voice: melismatic; quarter note unit of measure; repetitious and chant-like; begins on low e; almost entirely chest voice for contralto; singer must strike gong at places marked
Piano: separate piano piece; 2pp. solo introduction; fast 16ths; 16th-note patterns in 8ves in treble above singer
Diff: initial experience of singer and piano performing two separate compositions at the same time may be confusing
Uses: interesting song for very low, dark, rich voice

1204. THREE SONGS (Jean Harper). C. F. Peters, 1960. E-centered; b–e"; Tess-mL, M, mH; regular meters; moderate tempos; 4+min; Diff-V/m-d, P/m-md.
For: medium voice
Mood: descriptive
Voice: stepwise and small skips; long phrases; melismas; microtones
Piano: largely perpetual motion; much ostinato
Diff: microtones; long phrases; melismas; texts
Uses: effective as a group for the singer with an unusually good ear

   a. *Describe Me!* E-centered; d'–e"; Tess-mH; 2/2, Allegro; 2min.
   b. *Green Stones.* D-centered; d'–c"; Tess-mL; 2/2, Allegro; 1min.
   c. *Fans of Blue.* E-centered; b–e"; Tess-M; 2/2, Andante; 2min.

HOWE, MARY
(b. Richmond, VA, 1882; d. Washington, DC, 1964)

[See Appendix for song in German]

1205. AVALON (Nancy Byrd Turner). [126]. Cmaj; d'–g"; Tess-M; 3/4, Andante comodo; 4pp; Diff-V/m, P/m.
For: soprano; tenor
Mood: philosophical; nature imagery
Voice: largely conjunct; sustained phrases
Piano: broken-chord patterns in l.h. with chordal or single-line countermelodic material in r.h.
Diff: climactic g" on somewhat unimportant word and problematic vowel
Uses: recital possibilities

1206. THE BAILEY AND THE BELL (anon., 15th century). [124]. X; d'–a"; Tess-M; 2/2, 6/8, Gravely–Allegretto; 6pp; Diff-V/m, P/md.
For: tenor
Mood: mystical
Voice: broad opening and closing with dancing middle section; somewhat chromatic
Piano: organ-like chords at beginning and end; dancing middle section; quite chromatic
Diff: some rhythmic problems
Uses: recital possibilities; poem also set by Peter Warlock

1207. THE BIRDS. [124]. Dmaj; e'–g"; Tess-M; 4/4, Slowly; 3pp; Diff-V/me, P/e.

For: soprano; tenor
Mood: lyrical; happy
Voice: short phrases; recit.-like; largely diatonic
Piano: sustained chords with countermelodic motives
Uses: good for younger students

1208. FAIR ANNET'S SONG (Elinor Wylie). [124]. X; c'–g"; Tess-M; 4/4, 3/2; 5pp; Diff-V/m, P/md.

For: mezzo-soprano
Mood: merry but wistful; nature imagery
Voice: somewhat marcato and disjunct at first, then more sustained and conjunct
Piano: chordal texture; somewhat chromatic; supports vocal line without doubling
Diff: long descresc. from _f_ to _pp_ on final g"
Uses: recital possibilities

1209. FRAGMENT (Cecilia Lee). [124]. X; c'–f♯"; Tess-M; 4/4, Moderato; 6pp; Diff-V/m, P/m.

For: mezzo-soprano
Mood: lyrical; joyous; full of nature imagery
Voice: long, flowing phrases; some chromaticism; long, powerful e♭" at climax
Piano: broken-chord figures in triplets throughout; rather chromatic
Diff: a few rhythmic problems
Uses: good legato study; recital material

1210. HORSES (Rose Fyleman; trans. from an old Danish rhyme). [124]. A♭maj; e♭'–f"; Tess-M; 6/8, Allegretto; 2pp; Diff-V/e, P/me.

For: any high or medium voice
Mood: simple and child-like
Voice: lyrical; dancing
Piano: chordal
Uses: good for younger students

1211. HYMNE (John Donne). [125]. X-B♭min; e♭'–a"; Tess-mH; 4/4, 3/4, Grave; 4+min; Diff-V/md, P/d.

For: tenor
Mood: dramatic; intense
Voice: many skips; speech rhythms; duplets and triplets; triplets vs. piano duplets
Piano: chordal; clusters; large reaches; many accidentals; does not double vocal line
Diff: sustained a"; rhythms; long phrases; dynamics
Uses: powerful song for the right voice and personality

1212. IN TAURIS (Euripides, from _Iphigenia in Tauris_; trans. Gilbert Murray). [125]. X; d♭'–g"; Tess-M; 2/2, 3/2, Larghetto serioso–Poco andantino–Maestoso; 10pp; Diff-V/d, P/md.

For: mezzo-soprano; dramatic soprano
Mood: sorrowful; grieving for lost love
Voice: chromatic; flowing phrases of varying lengths; rather static; quarter-note triplets; recit.-like sections
Piano: chordal and organ-like; chromatic; triplets; lengthy interlude
Diff: pitches and rhythms; requires excellent breath control; needs advanced interpretive skills

Uses: dramatic recital piece for a skilled singer

1213. IRISH LULLABY (In a Low Rocking Chair) (Helen Coale Crew). Carl Fischer, 1948. E♭maj; e♭'–f"; Tess-M; 4/4, Commodo; 5pp; Diff-V/m, P/m.

For: soprano; mezzo-soprano
Mood: tranquil; subdued; imagines Mary rocking the Christ child
Voice: scalar and skips along chord lines; duplets and triplets; syncopation
Piano: chordal with countermelody; large reaches; moves around keyboard; does not double vocal line
Diff: gradations of soft dynamics
Uses: usable quiet song

1214. LET US WALK IN THE WHITE SNOW (Velvet Shoes) (Elinor Wylie). [21]; 1st©1948. H & L keys: Cmaj & A♭maj; d'–g" & b♭–e♭"; Tess-M; 5/8, 4/8, 2/8, 8/8, Andantino, molto tranquillo; 4min; Diff-V/md, P/md.

For: any female voice
Mood: lyrical; descriptive
Voice: short phrases; several 8ve leaps downward
Piano: chordal; independent contrapuntal figures; features parallel 7ths
Diff: frequent meter changes; much soft singing
Uses: interesting comparison with other settings of the poem (R. Thompson, J. Duke, and others)

1215. LITTLE ELEGY (Elinor Wylie). [11, vol. 7]. Amin; e'–e"; Tess-M; 4/4, Andantino; 3pp. Diff-V/me, P/m.

For: all voices
Mood: lyrical poem of loss
Voice: stepwise and easy skips; easy rhythms; long note on e"
Piano: some doubling of vocal line; some l.h. arpeggiation; short prelude and interludes
Uses: for study or recital; study in cresc. and decresc.

1216. MEN (Dorothy Reid). [125]. B♭maj; f'–f"; Tess-M; 4/4, Casually–not too fast; 2pp; Diff-V/me, P/me.

For: soprano; mezzo-soprano
Mood: cute; descriptive
Voice: short phrases separated by rests; several large leaps; a few staccato notes
Piano: chordal; moving 8th-note motives in inner voices
Uses: humorous song for students with limited range
Rec: D#13

1217. MY LADY COMES (Chard Powers Smith). [125]. Fmaj; d'–g"; Tess-M–mH; 3/4, Tranquillo; 3pp; Diff-V/m, P/me.

For: tenor
Mood: quiet love song; introspective
Voice: stepwise motion; some syncopation; sustained tones
Piano: chordal; spare texture; climax has chromatic movement
Diff: climax on sustained g"; variations of soft dynamics
Uses: good tenor song

1218. OLD ENGLISH LULLABY (15th century). [126]. Amaj; c♯'–f♯"; Tess-M; 4/4, Andante semplice; 2pp; Diff-V/e, P/me.

For: any medium voice

Mood: lullaby
Voice: folksong-like; regular, repeated rhythmic patterns
Piano: 4-voice; broken-chord figures in inner voices
Diff: some Old English spellings and pronunciations
Uses: useful for younger students

1219. **O MISTRESS MINE** (William Shakespeare). [126]. Dmaj; d'-e"(f♯"); Tess-M; 2/4, 2pp; Diff-V/e, P/me.
For: any high or medium voice
Mood: light; joyful; a touch of humor
Voice: lyrical; 8th-note motion; numerous small leaps; reminiscent of the Quilter setting
Piano: chordal; mostly 4-voice texture; much doubling of vocal line
Uses: teaching and recital possibilities

1220. **O PROSERPINA** (William Shakespeare). [124]. X; g'-a"; Tess-mL; 4/4, 3/4, Slowly; 4pp; Diff-V/me, P/me.
For: tenor; soprano
Mood: lyrical love song; nature imagery
Voice: lyrical; rather short phrases; several triplets
Piano: chordal texture; 2-voice moving 8ths in r.h. in much of song; somewhat chromatic
Uses: good recital possibilities

1221. **THE PRINKIN' LEDDIE** (Elinor Wylie). [126]. Cmin-maj; d'-g"; Tess-mH; 6/8, 2/4, 3/8, Vivo; 9pp; Diff-V/d, P/d.
For: tenor
Mood: excited; text is like a Scottish folksong
Voice: energetic rhythms with moderate use of Scotch snap figure; becomes more irregular toward end; contrasts of staccato and legato passages
Piano: chordal; melodic material in prelude and interludes; independent of vocal line; bagpipe-like drones, horn 5ths, etc.; some chromaticism
Diff: some notes and rhythms; many Scottish word forms
Uses: excellent song for tenor to whom Scottish dialect appeals; also brilliant song for tenor who lacks higher tones of the usual range

1222. **RED FIELDS OF FRANCE** (Charles Going). [126]. Dmin; d'-f"; Tess-mL; 2/4, 3/4, Andante comodo; 2pp; Diff-V/e, P/e.
For: any high or medium voice
Mood: sad
Voice: short, lyrical phrases separated by rests; final phrase highest and most powerful
Piano: chordal and simple; supports voice
Uses: good for younger students

1223. **THERE HAS FALLEN A SPLENDID TEAR** (Alfred Lord Tennyson). [124]. B♭maj; d'-f"(b♭"); Tess-mL; 9/8, Allegro ma non troppo; 4pp; Diff-V/m, P/md.
For: lyric tenor
Mood: excited love song; nature imagery
Voice: lyrical, but with many small breaks suggesting breathless excitement; duplets
Piano: repeated- and broken-chord figures; supports but does not double vocal line

Uses: good recital song

1224. **THREE HOKKU** (from the Japanese, Amy Lowell). [125]. "To Adele Addison." X; g'-g"; Tess-M-mH; regular meters; moderate tempos; 3pp; Diff-V/me, P/me.
For: best for soprano; possibly lyric tenor
Mood: delicate impressions; flower images
Voice: stepwise motion and small skips; many sustained tones
Piano: chordal—block and broken; thin textures; wide-spread sonorities; many accidentals
Diff: delicate dynamic gradations; light-textured sound
Uses: nice short set (no individual titles)

1225. **VIENNESE WALTZ** (Elinor Wylie). [125]. Dmin; d'-g♯"; Tess-M; 4/4, 3/4, Andantino penseroso–Tempo di valse triste; 6pp; Diff-V/d, P/d.
For: soprano; mezzo-soprano; tenor
Mood: sad; descriptive; unhappy lovers
Voice: recit.-like at beginning, changing to waltz melody; chromatic; phrases often separated by rests
Piano: chordal texture; chromatic; some waltz-like afterbeats; independent of vocal line; important interlude
Diff: pitches; requires good interpreter of words; text somewhat obscure
Uses: recital possibilities
Rec: D#13

1226. **WERE I TO DIE TO-NIGHT** ("Utterance") (Marie Valeur). [126]. G-centered; d'-g"; Tess-M; 2/2, Moderato; 4pp; Diff-V/m, P/me.
For: soprano; tenor
Mood: serene; loving
Voice: sustained phrases; many long note values
Piano: chordal texture; sustained; broken-chord figures in triplets in l.h.; somewhat chromatic
Diff: requires very sustained legato singing
Uses: effective piece for recital

1227. **WHEN I DIED IN BERNERS STREET (A STRANGE STORY)** (Elinor Wylie). [11, vol. 7]. Fmin/maj; c'-g"; Tess-mH; 4/4; 6pp; Diff-V/m, P/m.
For: soprano; tenor
Mood: death scenes; fantasy of persona's six previous deaths
Voice: mostly conjunct; accidentals; fairly easy rhythms; a few triplet divisions of the measure; some staccato; other expressive articulation markings
Piano: sets scene and changes scene for each of six verses; accomp. style and texture changes for each verse; some block chords, some afterbeat style; some doubling and support of vocal line
Diff: characterization; changes in mood and dynamics
Uses: effective for singer who understands this text

1228. **YOU** (Alice Dows). [125]. Amin; e'-g"; Tess-M; 4/4, 3/4, Deeply-slowly; 3pp; Diff-V/m, P/m.
For: soprano; mezzo-soprano; tenor
Mood: song of love and death; intense and somber
Voice: many skips; some syncopation; many dynamic markings; long-ranged phrases
Piano: chordal—block and broken; 2 vs. 3; bare-sounding except at climax; syncopation; large reaches; incidental

doubling of vocal line
Diff: climax is sustained g" with cresc.
Uses: recital material
Rec: D#13

HUGHES, RUPERT
(b. Lancaster, MO, 1872; d. Los Angeles, CA, 1956)

1229. **A RILEY ALBUM.** Ten Songs by James Whitcomb Riley. For Medium Voice. E. Schuberth, 1902. Reprint: Recital Publications, 1986. Traditional keys; b♭–f"(a"); Tess-M; regular meters; varied tempos; 29pp; Diff-V/me, P/e-m.
For: any medium voice
Mood: child-like and naive; mostly humorous
Voice: stepwise and easy skips; a little chromaticism; duplets and triplets; (d.) recit.-like; syllabic with some 2-note slurs; sustained d", e♭", e", and f".
Piano: chordal and linear; block, broken, rolled, and afterbeat chords; melodies and countermelodies; scalar passages, some rapid; triplets; grace notes; glissando; cross-hands; a little chromaticism; some doubling of vocal line; strong support elsewhere
Diff: a great deal of "Hoosier" dialect, some of which does not immediately make sense
Uses: as period pieces, could add a touch of humor to a program; whole set perhaps too similar in nature; shorter sets could be selected; might appeal to a singer with Indiana connections

  a. *A Scrawl* (from *Afterwhiles*). E♭maj; b♭–e♭"; 4/4, Molto rubato; 3pp.
  b. *Griggsby's Station* (from *Afterwhiles*). Cmaj; c'–e"; 4/4, Rather fast but with much expression; 5pp (with repeats).
  c. *Coffee like Mother Used to Make: A Hoosier Ditty* (from *Afterwhiles*). Fmaj; c'–d"; 2/4, 3/4; 3pp.
  d. *Our Own: A Chant* (from *Armazindy*). G♭maj; d♭'–f"(e♭"); 2/4, Lento; 2pp.
  e. *The Dead Lover: A Recitation* (from *Afterwhiles*). Fmin-Amaj-Fmaj; c'–f"(d♭"); 6/8, 2/4, Andante; 3pp.
  f. *The Little Tiny Kickshaw* (from *Rhymes of Childhood*). G♭maj; c'–e♭"; 4/4, 4pp.
  g. *Uncle Sidney* (from *Rhymes of Childhood*). A♭maj; g♭'–e♭"; 2/4, 2pp.
  h. *An Impetuous Resolve* (from *Rhymes of Childhood*). Amaj; e'–d"(e"); 4/4, Allegro; 2pp (with repeat).
  i. *Billie Goodin* (from *Rhymes of Childhood*). Amaj; c♯'–e"; 6/8, Allegro; 3pp (with repeat).
  j. *Granny's Come to Our House* (from *Rhymes of Childhood*). Amaj; e'–e"(a"); 4/4, Very fast; 2pp (with repeat).

HUHN, BRUNO
(b. London, England, 1871; d. New York, NY, 1950)

1230. **CATO'S ADVICE** (18th-century drinking-song) (Henry Cary). G. Schirmer, 1905. H & L keys: Gmaj & Cmaj; d'–g"(a") & G–c'; Tess-M; 3/4, Brightly and with strongly marked rhythm; 2min; Diff-V/m, P/e.
For: tenor; baritone; bass
Mood: rousing
Voice: diatonic melody outlines chords
Piano: rather 18th-century in style
Uses: undistinguished song, but perhaps useful as a simple, straightforward song for a young singer; helpful to loosen up a tight approach

HUNDLEY, RICHARD
(b. Cincinnati, OH, 1931)

1231. **THE ASTRONOMERS** (An Epitaph) (Based on an inscription found in Allegheny, Pa.). [127]. cmp1959; rev.1970. F♯min; c♯'–f♯"; Tess-M; 3/2, 2/2, ♩= 52; 1+min; Diff-V/me, P/m.
For: soprano; tenor
Mood: epitaph; tranquil; subdued
Voice: first part intoned on one pitch; one long-ranged phrase; duplets and triplets; syncopation
Piano: short free-rhythm introduction; sonority wide-spread; 4-voice block chords; some broken chords
Diff: final tone is f♯" sustained with cresc.–decresc.
Uses: beautiful text; nice song
Rec: D#s 39, 51, 222

1232. **BALLAD ON QUEEN ANNE'S DEATH** (anon.). General, 1964. cmp1962. Dmin; b♭–d"; Tess-M; changing meters, Allegretto; 2pp; Diff-V/m, P/m.
For: baritone; mezzo-soprano; contralto
Mood: lyrical; lament
Voice: stepwise and small skips; fluid, speech-like rhythms
Piano: broken-chord and afterbeat figures; guitar-like; 3-voice texture
Diff: fluid rhythms; changing meters
Uses: very nice song
Rec: D#s 51, 223

1233. **BARTHOLOMEW GREEN** (James Purdy). [127]. cmp1978. Dmin; d'–f"; Tess-mH; 5/4 with changes, Lively and spirited; 3pp; Diff-V/m, P/me.
For: soprano; tenor; high baritone
Mood: lighthearted; poem rhymes several person's names with an attribute, in the manner once popular on tombstones
Voice: many small skips; easy rhythms
Piano: block chords in afterbeat pattern; some countermelody; cross-accents; some staccato; doubling of vocal line incidental
Diff: changing meters create some rhythm and ensemble complexities
Uses: attractive song; a "light" touch for a group of epitaphs
Rec: D#51

1234. **BIRDS, U. S. A.** (James Purdy). [127]. cmp1972. Fmaj; f'–f"; Tess-mH; 2/2, Grandly–Lively; 2pp; Diff-V/m, P/m.
For: soprano; tenor
Mood: wry statement about birds; light
Voice: small skips and stepwise motion; syncopation; Scotch snap; triplets; 2½-meas. final f"; somewhat fragmented

Piano: block chords; some broken chords; some
countermelody; accidentals; some doubling of vocal
line; accents; some staccato; 4-meas. prelude
Diff: mostly rhythmic
Uses: in a Hundley group

1235. COME READY AND SEE ME (James Purdy). [127,
128]. cmp1971. H & L keys: G♭maj & E♭maj;
d♭'–g♭" & b♭–e♭"; Tess-mH; 2/2, (♩ = ca.56); 4pp;
Diff-V/m, P/m.
For: all voices in range; woman's text
Mood: longing for an unfound love; lyrical
Voice: stepwise and skips along chord lines; syncopation;
some triplet divisions of beat; legato; dynamics *mp–f*
Piano: arpeggiated patterns with occasional countermelody;
some accidentals; doubling of vocal line incidental
Diff: rhythm
Uses: nice lyric song for a student; has a folk-like flavor
Rec: D#s 7, 51, 70

1236. EPITAPH ON A WIFE (Anon.). [128]. cmp1957.
Cmaj; c–e♭' (𝄢); Tess-mH; 3/4, 4/4, 5/4, 7/4, 2/4,
Spirited, rhythmic, without rushing (steady) ♩ = 108;
2pp; Diff-V/e, P/e.
For: male voice; baritone best
Mood: humorous
Voice: quarter-note motion; skips outline chords; quotes first
phrase of *Doxology*
Piano: staccato counterpoint to vocal line in 8th & 16th notes;
block chords under *Doxology* phrase; glissandos at the
end; 5-meas. introduction sets tone
Diff: three leaps of a 7th; a few dissonant intervals
Uses: humorous song; other group of epitaphs; Hundley's
other epitaphs are higher, but some medium voices
could do them as a group; see "The Astronomers,"
"Bartholomew Green," and "Isaac Greentree"
Rec: D#51

1237. EVENING HOURS (James Purdy). [128]. cmp1975.
Commissioned by tenor Kenneth Riegel. F-F♯maj;
c'–f♯"; Tess-M; 2/2, 3/2, Nostalgic ♩ = ca. 54; 5pp;
Diff-V/m, P/m.
For: tenor; soprano; mezzo-soprano
Mood: longing for the past; yearning
Voice: mostly stepwise or small skips and quarter-note motion
Piano: broken chords; some block chords; somewhat
impressionistic; supports vocal line, rarely doubles;
accidentals
Diff: some tempo changes may challenge ensemble
Uses: group of love songs, time-of-day songs, or songs on
texts by Purdy ("Come Ready and See Me"; "I Do")

1238. FOR YOUR DELIGHT (A Romance) (Robert Louis
Stevenson). General, 1962. E♭maj; c'–f"; Tess-M; 3/4,
4/4, Gracefully; 5pp; Diff-V/m, P/m.
For: lyric baritone
Mood: lyrical; love song
Voice: conjunct with some skips; some sustained tones at ends
of phrases; ends on 15-beat e♭" sustained softly
Piano: linear-chordal combination; open texture; melodic
interest; 10-meas. postlude
Diff: some unexpected pitches

Uses: nice song; useful for teaching young singers
Rec: D#32

1239. I DO (James Purdy). [127]. cmp1974. "To Paul
Sperry." D♭maj; (f')g♭'–a♭"; Tess-H; 2/2, Allegro
grazioso; 2pp; Diff-V/m, P/m.
For: tenor
Mood: lighthearted, jazzy marriage proposal
Voice: stepwise and skips along chord lines; syncopation;
some triplets; some polyrhythms
Piano: block chords and broken-chord patterns; some staccato;
some accidentals; doubling of vocal line incidental;
5-meas. prelude
Diff: rhythms
Uses: "off-beat" love song
Rec: D#51

1240. ISAAC GREENTREE (Based upon an epitaph found
in Samuel Palmer's collection, *Epitaphs and Epigrams:
Curious, Quaint, Amusing*). [127]. cmp1960. "To Paul
Sperry." A♭maj; c'–g♭"; Tess-mH; 4/4 with changes,
♩ = ca.108; 2pp; Diff-V/m, P/m.
For: soprano; tenor
Mood: epitaph; lyric and gentle
Voice: many accidentals; many small skips; triplets
Piano: block chords; accidentals; spare accomp.; some rolled
chords; does not double vocal line
Diff: chromaticism in melody
Uses: lovely song; group with "The Astronomers" and
"Bartholomew Green" for a short group of epitaphs, or
with other Hundley songs
Rec: D#51

1241. MAIDEN SNOW (Kenneth Patchen). General, 1961.
cmp1960. "To Anna Moffo." Gmin; d'–g"; Tess-mH;
changing meters, Andante sostenuto; 2pp; Diff-V/m,
P/e.
For: soprano; tenor
Mood: lyrical; tranquil; introspective
Voice: mostly stepwise; some wide skips; speech rhythms
Piano: 3–5-voice texture; chordal; some arpeggios; melody in
interludes
Diff: fluid rhythms
Uses: nice song for a recital group

1242. MY MASTER HATH A GARDEN (anon.
Elizabethan verses). [127]. cmp1963. Fmaj; d'–g";
Tess-mH; 2/2 with changes, Brightly ♩ = 96–Sostenuto
cantabile; 4pp; Diff-V/m, P/m.
For: soprano
Mood: prayerful
Voice: many small skips; easy rhythms; changing meters
create a few rhythmic and accent complications;
syllabic; 2–5-note slurs
Piano: block chords; 3–5-voice texture; some staccato;
5-meas. prelude; 4-meas. interlude; some doubling of
vocal line; high notes somewhat sustained
Diff: some rhythms
Uses: for young lyric soprano with easy floating high notes;
see other settings by R. Thompson and V. Thomson (in
Praises and Prayers)

1243. **OCTAVES AND SWEET SOUNDS.** [129, H & M eds.]. cmp1989–1990. NOTE: Composer calls this a collection of songs, but says they may be sung as a whole or separately; composed for Glenda Maurice, mezzo-soprano, and premiered as a group in 1990; listed here both as a group and as a collection.

A. **STRINGS IN THE EARTH AND AIR** (James Joyce). H & M keys: D♭maj & Bmaj; d'–f" & c'–e♭"; Tess-M; 3/4, Sustained, but not too slowly ♩ = 80–84; 4pp; Diff-V/m, P/m.
For: medium voices; high voices
Mood: love and nature vibrating as music
Voice: some syncopation; melismas; lyrical lines; accidentals; several phrases an inverted arch
Piano: impressionistic pedaling; quarter-note motion predominates; many accidentals; some doubling of vocal line, some imitation; strong downbeats; 4-meas. prelude, 2 interludes, lyrical postlude
Diff: few; interwoven parts on final page
Uses: as part of set or singly; teaching legato line
Rec: D#70

B. **SEASHORE GIRLS** ["maggie and milly and molly and may"] (e. e. cummings). H & M keys: Cmaj & B♭maj; e♭'–f♯" & d♭'–e"; Tess-M; 6/8, 5/8, 7/8, 9/8, 4/4, etc., ♩. = 80–♩. = 112–Fast & lively–♩. = 72–76–♩. = 63–66–Scherzando ♩. = 84; 5pp; Diff-V/md, P/md.
For: medium voices; high voices
Mood: spirited and philosophical
Voice: mostly syllabic; small skips and stepwise motion; some rhythmic complications
Piano: various and many articulations; somewhat linear; some doubling of vocal line; prelude; 3 interludes; 12-meas. postlude requires bold pianism
Diff: rhythms; ensemble; entrances; many meter changes; demands clear, quick diction
Uses: separately; with other songs from this set; in set of songs on e. e. cummings texts

C. **MOONLIGHT'S WATERMELON** (Jose García Villa). H & M keys: Dmaj & Cmaj; d'–f♯" & c'–e"; Tess-M; 3/4, 2/4, Elegantly, with good rhythm ♩ = 138; 5pp; Diff-V/m, P/m.
For: medium voices; high voices
Mood: nonsense text; lyrical approach
Voice: mostly syllabic; stepwise and skips on chord lines; rests interrupt many lines; some syncopation
Piano: waltz; afterbeat style; accidentals abound; 4-meas. prelude; 6 interludes of 2–8 meas. 9-meas. postlude; many expressive and articulation markings
Diff: memorizing this text; some rhythms
Uses: in a Hundley group
Rec: D#53

D. **STRAIGHTWAY BEAUTY ON ME WAITS** (James Purdy). H & M keys: Indefinite, ends A♭maj(G♭maj); d'–g" & c'–f"; Tess-wide; 4/4, 3/4, 7/8, 5/4, ♩ = 60 with changes; 4pp; Diff-V/d, P/d.
For: medium voices; high voices
Mood: rhapsodic love song; dramatic
Voice: somewhat disjunct; many expression marks; melismas; long-ranged phrases
Piano: many changes in texture, register, articulation, and rhythmic subdivisions; many accidentals and enharmonic juxtapositions
Diff: intervals; ensemble
Uses: in a Hundley group, to create dramatic mood
Rec: D#53

E. **WELL WELCOME** (Gertrude Stein). H & M keys: Cmaj with color chords, suggesting bitonality; c'–a♭"; Tess-wide; 3/2, 4/2, 5/4, 3/4, ♩ = 92 ("calm" center section); 6pp; Diff-V/d, P/md.
For: medium voices; high voices
Mood: dramatic; personal choice theme
Voice: dramatic recitative; speech rhythms; aria-like section; disjunct; many accidentals; mostly syllabic; a few melismas; one phrase encompasses range of song
Piano: sustained chords on one level, fanfare figures above (at beginning and end) in 8ths & 16ths; center section simpler, doubling much of vocal line; fanfare figures make up the postlude
Diff: comprehending and communicating text; rhythms; ensemble; pianist must cover keyboard quickly
Uses: group ender

1244. **POSTCARD FROM SPAIN** (Richard Hundley). General, 1964. cmp1963. Cmaj; f'–a"; Tess-H; mostly 3/4, ♩ = 66–freely; 1min; Diff-V/m, P/e.
For: tenor
Mood: lyrical; humorous; waltz song
Voice: many skips; some syncopation; fragmentary
Piano: waltz style; some tremolo; some 5/4 meas.; independent of vocal line
Diff: rhythms; sustained g" at end
Uses: nice encore; final song in a group; anywhere something light is needed
Rec: D#32

1245. **SOFTLY THE SUMMER.** (R. Hundley) General, 1963. cmp1957. D♭maj; f'–b♭"; Tess-H; 3/4, Tempo a piacere (gently flowing); 3pp; Diff-V/m-md, P/m.
For: high soprano
Mood: lyrical; descriptive; lazy
Voice: several leaps of 6th & 7th; dotted notes; repetitive rhythmic and melodic patterns
Piano: broken-chord patterning; thin texture; incidental doubling of vocal line
Diff: high tessitura; needs floating high tones
Uses: nice lyric song for high soprano

1246. **SPRING** ("When daisies pied . . .") (William Shakespeare). General, 1963. cmp1962. Fmaj; f'–a"; Tess-mH; 3/4, Light, airy and with sparkle; 1min; Diff-V/m, P/m.
For: tenor; soprano
Mood: humorous; cheerful; lively
Voice: some skips of a 6th
Piano: 2-voice texture; waltz rhythm; r.h. countermelody
Diff: poem
Uses: lively song for a recital group
Rec: D#s 51, 223

1247. SWEET SUFFOLK OWL (anon. verses, 1619).
[127]. cmp1979. "To Paul Sperry." Fmin-Emin; c'-f";
Tess-M; 2/4, Deliberately (♪= 92–96); 2pp; Diff-V/md,
P/m.

For: soprano; tenor
Mood: philosophical
Voice: stepwise and small skips; dotted rhythms; syncopation; triplets; 2–5-note slurs; mostly syllabic
Piano: afterbeat-style chords; does not double vocal line
Diff: rhythms quite complex
Uses: excellent song; see also setting of this text by Herbert Elwell ("The Suffolk Owl")
Rec: D#s 7, 51, 56

1248. WHEN ORPHEUS PLAYED (William Shakespeare).
[128]. cmp1979. "To Paul Sperry." C♯min; c♯'-f♯";
Tess-M; 3/4, 2/4, 4/4, Rapturous ♩= 88; 4pp; Diff-V/m,
P/m.

For: high and medium voices
Mood: power of music
Voice: stepwise and chordal skips; some melismas; some accidentals; long c♯" at end
Piano: waltz-like; somewhat impressionistic; some vocal line doubling; short prelude, interlude, and postlude
Diff: tempo fluctuations for ensemble
Uses: cf. setting of text "Orpheus With His Lute" by other composers (Wm. Schuman, Vaughan Williams, A. Sullivan, etc.)

1249. WILD PLUM (Orrick Johns). General, 1961. Fmaj;
d'-f "; Tess-M; changing meters, Allegretto; 1min;
Diff-V/m, P/m.

For: all voices except extremely low or heavy
Mood: lyrical; delicate
Voice: many skips; some 7ths; speech rhythms
Piano: 2–4-voice texture; linear; staccato; articulations important; some doubling of the vocal line
Diff: speech-like, fluid rhythms; syncopation; two meas. unaccomp. voice
Uses: useful in a recital group
Rec: D#223

HYSON, WINIFRED
(b. Schenectady, NY, 1925)

1250. SONGS OF JOB'S DAUGHTER. For Soprano with Piano Accompaniment (Jean Starr Untermeyer). Cycle. Arsis, 1983. Generally traditional tonal centers and harmonies; c♯'-a"; Tess-M; regular and irregular meters with changes; varied tempos; 17pp; Diff-V/d, P/d.

For: soprano
Mood: philosophical; nature imagery
Voice: conjunct and disjunct motion; some chromaticism; triplets; 3 vs. 2 & 6 in piano; rising phrases; syllabic; one portamento slur 8ve downward in (d.)
Piano: chordal-linear combination; block, broken, rolled, and afterbeat chords; countermelodies; chromatic; triplets and groupings of 6 & 10; 2 vs. 3; tremolo; grace notes; special instructions for tone clusters in (f.)
Diff: excellent sense of pitch and rhythm needed; both singer

and pianist must be secure musicians; interpretive skills and insight esp. needed for this poetry
Uses: excellent recital material

   a. **Injunction.** B♭min; g'-a♭"; 3/4, 4/4, Sustained (♩= 63); 2pp.
   b. **High Tide.** F♯min; c♯'-g"; 4/4, 5/4, 3/4, 2/4, ♩= 104 (with changes); 3pp.
   c. **Lullaby for a Man-Child.** E-centered; d'-a"; 6/8, 5/8, 8/8, Tenderly (♪= 104); 2+pp.
   d. **Two and a Child.** Emin; d'-a"; 2/4, Lightly and rhythmically as in a dance (♩= 88) (with changes); 3+pp.
   e. **Birthday.** X; d♭'-a"; 4/4, 5/4, 3/4, 6/4, With great feeling, and with motion, as in a waltz (♩= 144) (with changes); 4pp.
   f. **My Phoenix.** B♭min; e♭'-a♭"; 4/4, 3/4, 5/4, Maestoso (♩= 80); 1+pp.

IDE, CHESTER EDWARD
(b. Springfield, IL, 1878; d. 1944)

1251. LOVERS OF THE WILD (Robert Louis Stevenson).
[66, vol. 4]; 1st©1907. Amaj; e'-f♯"; Tess-mH; 3/4,
Allegro ma graziosa; 2min; Diff-V/m, P/m.

For: tenor
Mood: lyrical; mildly ecstatic
Voice: mixed skips and stepwise motion
Piano: basic 4-voice chordal texture; some rolled chords and other patterns
Uses: usable in American group of the period

1252. NAMES (Samuel Taylor Coleridge). [5, 66, vol. 4];
1st©1907. A♭maj; e♭'-a♭"; Tess-mH; 3/4, Allegro; 72
meas.; Diff-V/md, P/m.

For: soprano specified
Mood: lighthearted; graceful waltz
Voice: many skips; syncopation
Piano: waltz style; almost a piece by itself
Diff: ensemble; some intervals; unusual modulations
Uses: lively song; group ender or encore; possible for tenor; a "he"/ "she" character song

ILGENFRITZ, McNAIR
(b. 1887?; d. New York, NY, 1953)

1253. BLOW, BLOW, THOU WINTER WIND (William Shakespeare). Schuberth, 1922. Dmin-Fmaj; f'-a"(f "); Tess-mH; 4/4, Presto assai; 4pp (repeated); Diff-V/m, P/m.

For: tenor.
Mood: vigorous; cynical; falsely jaunty
Voice: some leaps; 2–3-note slurs; easy rhythms
Piano: rapid afterbeat pattern; compound meter; covers the keyboard; some doubling of vocal line
Diff: sustained high climaxes
Uses: good group ender

IMBRIE, ANDREW
(b. New York, NY, 1921)

1254. ROETHKE SONGS (Theodore Roethke). C. F. Peters, 1990. X (atonal); a♯–b"; Tess-wide; regular meters with complex divisions of beat for text setting; varied tempos; 15min; Diff-V/dd, P/dd.

For: soprano
Mood: progression of young love, lost love, aftermath
Voice: angular; many leaps; complex rhythms; fragmented phrases; many accidentals; melismas for text or mood painting in each song but the last
Piano: complex piano score in every way; linear approach; block chords and broken chords; bitonality and atonality; many accidentals; many articulations; many dynamics; unusual pedal effects and careful attention to pedaling details; some incidental doubling of vocal pitches; rhythms most complex aspect
Diff: singer should have perfect pitch; both performers must be excellent musicians; score requires considerable preparation from both performers
Uses: recital group for advanced performers who enjoy this idiom
Rec: D#224

a. *The Young Girl.* X; c♯'–a"; Tess-wide; 3/4, Allegro non troppo ♩ = 104; 4pp.
b. *Her Words.* X; c♯'–b"; Tess-wide; 6/8, Allegro ♩. = 112; 6pp.
c. *The Apparition.* X; b–g"; Tess-wide; 4/4, Andantino ♩ = 100; 3pp.
d. *Her Longing.* X; b–b"; Tess-wide; 4/4, Allegro ♩ = 120; 7pp.
e. *Her Time.* X; a♯–a"; Tess-wide; 5/4, Quasi adagio ♩ = 96; 5pp.

INGALLS, JEREMIAH (See Special Section)

IVES, CHARLES
(b. Danbury, CT, 1874; d. New York, NY, 1954)

[Only the songs on English texts are annotated; however, many of Ives's German songs have been recorded on D#s 66, 227, & 238; other foreign language songs appear on D#s 19, 27, 42, 46, 230, 231, 232, 235, & 245]

1255. AFTERGLOW (James Fenimore Cooper, Jr.). [134, 136]. cmp1919. X; e♭'–d"; Tess-mL; meter not indicated, Slowly and very quietly;1p; Diff-V/d, P/dd.

For: any lyric voice
Mood: lyrical; philosophical
Voice: flowing; chromatic; generally soft
Piano: tone clusters; highly chromatic; rolled chords
Diff: sustained phrasing; soft singing; pitches; rhythm
Uses: effective recital song; good for student who is fine musician but has limited range
Rec: D#s 225, 227, 229, 236, 241, 245, 248

1256. ALLEGRO (Ives?). [134]. cmp1900. Fmaj; c'–g"; Tess-M; 2/4, Allegro–Largo; 3pp (with repeat); Diff-V/m, P/d.

For: soprano; mezzo-soprano
Mood: happy; optimistic; nature imagery
Voice: light and dancing; phrases separated by short rests; 2-note slurs; final phrase of each strophe is "Largo"
Piano: rapid 32nd-note figures on afterbeats in r.h.; single line of moving 8ths in l.h.
Diff: delicacy; vocal flexibility
Rec: D#227

1257. ANN STREET (Maurice Morris). [134, 136]. cmp1921. X; e'–e"; Tess-mL; meter not indicated, Fast and noisily; 2pp; Diff-V/md, P/d.

For: all voices
Mood: humorously descriptive
Voice: fragmented short phrases; chromatic; a few ornaments; syncopated rhythms
Piano: tone clusters; highly chromatic; grace notes; cross-hands; tremolo
Diff: pitch; rhythm; ensemble
Uses: unusual short song
Rec: D#s 3, 227, 229, 232, 233, 234, 235, 237, 238, 239, 240, 241, 247

1258. AT SEA (Robert Underwood Johnson). [134, 136]. cmp1921. X; c'–d"; Tess-M; 4/4, 3/4, tempo not indicated; 1p; Diff-V/m, P/md.

For: mezzo-soprano; baritone
Mood: lyrical; love poem
Voice: broad phrases; some chromaticism
Piano: chordal; many rolled chords; cross-hands; independent melodic fragments
Rec: D#s 227, 232, 248

1259. AT THE RIVER: from *4th Violin Sonata* (text and tune from "Shall We Gather at the River?" by Robert Lowry). [134, 136]. cmp1916. G-centered; e♭'–e♭"; Tess-mL; 12/8, Allegretto; 2pp; Diff-V/m, P/d.

For: all voices
Mood: well-known gospel hymn in lyrical setting
Voice: follows the contour of the hymn-tune with "wrong" notes and rhythms
Piano: chordal; rolled chords, widely spaced
Diff: needs careful attention to notes and rhythms, esp. for singer to whom the original tune is familiar
Uses: good song to introduce students to Ives
Rec: D#s 44, 46, 225, 227, 229, 232, 234, 237, 238, 240, 242, 244, 245

1260. AUGUST (Folgore da San Geminiano, from Rossetti's *Early Italian Poets*). [134, 136, 138]. cmp1920. X; c'–e"; Tess-M; meter not indicated, Con grazia–Andante vivo–Meno mosso; 3pp; Diff-V/d, P/dd.

For: mezzo-soprano; baritone
Mood: descriptive; nature imagery
Voice: disjunct; highly chromatic; large leaps; somewhat declamatory
Piano: dissonant; chromatic; primarily chordal
Diff: pitches; rhythms
Uses: effective recital song
Rec: D#s 227, 230, 248

1261. AUTUMN (Ives?). [134]. cmp1908. D♭maj; b♭–f";
Tess-mL; 4/4, Adagio; 2pp; Diff-V/m, P/m.
For: mezzo-soprano; baritone
Mood: lyrical; descriptive of nature
Voice: short phrases, often separated by rests; leap downward from highest to lowest note of song (between phrases)
Piano: syncopated chords in l.h.; independent melody in r.h.; very expressive
Diff: requires easy, brilliant f" with immediate shift to low register
Uses: effective recital song; possibly in a seasons group
Rec: D#s 225, 227, 231, 234, 238, 248

1262. THE CAGE (Charles Ives). [132, 134]. cmp1906. X; d'–e"; Tess-M; meter not indicated, evenly and mechanically, no ritard, decresc., accel., etc.; 1p; Diff-V/m, P/m.
For: any high or medium voice
Mood: philosophical
Voice: continuous 8th-note movement; only one rest in vocal line; undulating
Piano: chordal; tone clusters
Diff: pitches
Uses: unusual recital song
Rec: D#s 227, 229, 231, 235, 237, 239, 240, 241, 245, 246, 248

1263. THE CAMP-MEETING (from a movement of *Symphony No. 3*) (Charlotte Elliott, in part). [134]. cmp1912. partially B♭maj; a♭–e"; Tess-mL; 6/8, 9/8, 7/8, 10/8, Largo cantabile; 4pp; Diff-V/md, P/dd.
For: mezzo-soprano; contralto; baritone
Mood: descriptive; philosophical; religious tone
Voice: somewhat disjunct and chromatic at beginning; hymn-tune quotation at end
Piano: lengthy prelude; chromatic; dissonant; complicated rhythms
Diff: pitches; rhythms; understanding "gospel hymn" style
Uses: could be effectively programmed
Rec: D#s 44, 46, 227, 229, 230, 232, 239, 245

1264. CANON (Thomas Moore). [133, 134]. cmp1894. Emaj; d♯'–f♯"(b"); Tess-mL; 3/4, Allegro; 2pp; Diff-V/m, P/m.
For: soprano; mezzo-soprano; tenor
Mood: lyrical; philosophical; recalling past youth and love
Voice: rather emphatic, considering the nature of the text; generally loud dynamics; staccato; small melismas; dotted rhythms
Piano: l.h. forms canon at the 8ve at distance of one measure with vocal line; r.h. chordal, often syncopated
Diff: ensemble
Rec: D#s 10, 226, 227, 241, 248

1265. CHARLIE RUTLAGE (Cowboy Ballad). [134, 135]. cmp1914–1915(?). X (with suggestions of Dmin); d'–d"; Tess-mL; 4/4, In moderate time; 4pp; Diff-V/md, P/d.
For: all voices; better for men
Mood: narrative; descriptive; ballad style
Voice: folksong-like, becoming declamatory and dramatic; partially spoken

Piano: chordal; afterbeat pattern, becoming highly chromatic and dissonant; tone clusters; tremolos; chords struck with fists
Diff: requires excellent vocal actor; pianist acquainted with Ives's style
Uses: adds variety to a program; good for a singer with excellent histrionic ability
Rec: D#s 2, 10, 225, 227, 229, 231, 233, 239, 240, 241, 242, 245, 248

1266. THE CHILDREN'S HOUR (Henry Wadsworth Longfellow). [134, 136]. cmp1901. E-centered; d'–d"; Tess-L; 4/4, 3/4, 6/8, 9/8, Adagio sostenuto; 3pp; Diff-V/m, P/md.
For: all voices
Mood: lyrical; descriptive
Voice: broad phrases; almost recit.-like; repeated notes; triplets
Piano: undulating 16th-note pattern, r.h.; syncopated accomp., l.h.; chordal middle section
Uses: effective recital song
Rec: D#s 225, 227, 232, 234, 238, 241, 242, 245, 247

1267. THE CIRCUS BAND (Harmony Twichell [Ives]). [5, 134]. cmp1894. Amaj–Fmaj; c♯'–f♯"; Tess-M; 2/2, 6/8, In quickstep time; 3pp (with repeats); Diff-V/m, P/d.
For: soprano; mezzo-soprano; tenor; high baritone
Mood: humorously descriptive
Voice: imitative of circus-band tune; staccatos; syncopation
Piano: chordal–afterbeat style; parallel chromatic chords; imitations of circus band; flourishes; like a piano reduction of a band score
Diff: needs good vocal actor
Uses: good recital song for humorous contrast
Rec: D#s 5, 225, 227, 229, 232, 237, 242, 245, 247

1268. DECEMBER (Folgore da San Geminiano, from Rossetti's *Early Italian Poets*). [134, 136]. cmp1912–1913; arr. for voice and piano, 1920 (orig. for chorus and instruments). X; c♯'–d"; Tess-mL; meter not indicated, Allegro con spirito; 2pp; Diff-V/d, P/dd.
For: any medium voice
Mood: descriptive; philosophical
Voice: "roughly and in a half spoken way"; declamatory throughout; many short repeated notes; a vocal tone cluster is indicated, probably intending an inexact pitch
Piano: rapid parallel triads in r.h.; tone clusters; afterbeat figures; generally very short note values
Diff: pitches; rhythms; ensemble
Uses: effective recital song for advanced performers
Rec: D#s 227, 230, 239, 248

1269. DOWN EAST (Ives?). [134]. cmp1919. Partially Fmaj; c'–d"; Tess-mL; 6/8, 3/4, 7/4, 8/4, Very slowly–A little faster, but with a slow even rhythm; 2pp; Diff-V/m, P/md.
For: all voices
Mood: lyrical; nostalgic
Voice: chromatic at beginning; soft dynamics; quotation from "Nearer My God to Thee"
Piano: somewhat chromatic; contrapuntal; some rolled chords; cross-hands; generally soft
Diff: soft singing

Uses: effective nostalgic song
Rec: D#s 226, 227, 230, 231, 236, 244, 245

1270. **AN ELECTION** [also entitled: "It Strikes Me That . . . (November 2, 1920), for Medium Voice and Piano"] (Charles Ives). [133, 134]. cmp1920 (orig. for voice & orch.); arr. for piano, 1921. X; c'–f♯"; Tess-M; meter not indicated at beginning (many changes throughout), Slowly (many tempo changes); 6pp; Diff-V/dd, P/dd.
For: baritone; mezzo-soprano
Mood: narrative; philosophical; political commentary
Voice: disjunct; fragmented; declamatory; semi-spoken in places; highly chromatic; several descending chromatic scale passages; complex rhythms; dramatic ending
Piano: chordal; dense; dissonant; wide-spread over keyboard; highly chromatic; some 16th-note figurations; tremolo; rolled chords
Diff: pitches; rhythms; endurance, esp. in final phrases lying at top of staff; requires very accomplished pianist with large hands
Uses: striking song; graduate to professional level; Ives's opinionated political views
Rec: D#s 227, 235, 239, 241, 248

1271. **EVENING** (John Milton). [4, 7, 134, 135]. cmp1921. X; c♯'–d"; Tess-M; 3/4, 4/4, 3/2, Largo; 2pp; Diff-V/m, P/md.
For: soprano; mezzo-soprano
Mood: lyrical; philosophical; descriptive of nature
Voice: irregular phrase lengths; somewhat chromatic; generally soft
Piano: chordal; chromatic; some "bird-call" motives
Diff: soft singing
Uses: fine recital song; good contrast with other Ives songs
Rec: D#s 227, 229, 231, 233, 234, 240

1272. **EVIDENCE** (Ives?). [134]. cmp1910. B♭maj; b♭–e♭"; Tess-M; 4/4, Andante tenuto; 2pp; Diff-V/m, P/md.
For: mezzo-soprano; contralto
Mood: lyrical; philosophical; nature imagery
Voice: flowing phrases; a little chromaticism
Piano: broken-chord figures in sextuplets, l.h.; r.h. melody related to vocal line; 2 vs. 3 throughout
Diff: needs sensitive accompanist
Rec: D#s 227, 232

1273. **A FAREWELL TO LAND** (Lord Byron). [133]. cmp1925. X; g♯'–g"; Tess-M; 4/4, 3/4, Adagio–Allegro–Adagio; 1p; Diff-V/d, P/md.
For: mezzo-soprano
Mood: philosophical with patriotic tone; nature imagery
Voice: generally begins at top of range and descends to end of song; chromatic melismas in "Allegro" section; complex rhythms
Piano: follows contour of vocal line, beginning in extremely high register and ending very low; chromatic; complex rhythms; contrapuntal
Diff: pitches; rhythms; agility; begins on g♭"
Rec: D#s 227, 229, 232, 235, 237, 238, 240, 241

1274. **FROM "AMPHION"** (Alfred Lord Tennyson). [134]. cmp1896. E♭maj; d'–g"; Tess-M; 3/4, Allegretto con spirito; 2pp; Diff-V/md, P/m.
For: soprano; mezzo-soprano
Mood: poetic nature picture
Voice: a few large leaps; little chromaticism
Piano: chordal; arpeggios; occasional doubling of vocal line
Rec: D# 227

1275. **FROM "LINCOLN, THE GREAT COMMONER"** (Edwin Markham). [134]. cmp1921. X; c'–e"; Tess-M; meter not indicated, Firmly, but actively and with vigor; 4pp; Diff-V/d, P/dd.
For: mezzo-soprano; baritone
Mood: descriptive; patriotic tone
Voice: somewhat disjunct; chromatic; grace notes; short chromatic scale passages
Piano: highly chromatic and dissonant; tone clusters; dotted, march-like rhythms; rolled chords; trills; clusters struck with fists
Diff: pitches; rhythms; requires good vocal actor
Uses: effective recital song for the right singer
Rec: D#s 227, 241, 248

1276. **FROM "NIGHT OF FROST IN MAY"** (George Meredith). [134]. cmp1899. Gmin; b♭–e♭"; Tess-mL; 2/4, Andante con moto; 2pp; Diff-V/me, P/me.
For: mezzo-soprano; contralto; baritone
Mood: lyrical; philosophical; nature imagery
Voice: flowing phrases; irregular phrase lengths; stays close to the key
Piano: broken chords, l.h.; syncopated chords with melodic fragments, r.h.
Uses: could be effectively programmed
Rec: D#s 227, 232

1277. **FROM "PARACELSUS"** (taken from the latter part of Scene V) (Robert Browning). [133, 134]. cmp1912–1921. X; c♭'–f♯"; Tess-L, H; meter not indicated, Allegro–Andante molto; 3pp; Diff-V/d, P/dd.
For: mezzo-soprano; baritone
Mood: philosophical; religious tone
Voice: disjunct; large leaps; chromatic; dramatic at beginning, becoming lyrical at end
Piano: chordal; dissonant; highly chromatic; some counterpoint; rolled chords; tremolo
Diff: pitches; rhythms; requires dramatic weight in voice; excellent pianist necessary
Rec: D#s 10, 227, 229, 232, 237, 239, 241, 245, 247

1278. **FROM THE "INCANTATION"** (Lord Byron). [134, 136]; arr. for voice & piano, 1921 (orig. a song with instrumental accomp.). E♭-centered; e♭'–d"; Tess-mL; 13/16 with changes, Allegretto moderato; 3pp; Diff-V/md, P/d.
For: all voices
Mood: lyrical; philosophical; nature imagery
Voice: flowing phrases; rocking up-and-down motion in irregular rhythms
Piano: arpeggiated chromatic chords
Diff: rhythm
Uses: good Ives song for singers of limited range
Rec: D#s 226, 227, 229, 248

1279. **FROM "THE SWIMMERS"** (Louis Untermeyer). [134, 136]. cmp1915–1921. X; c♯'–e"; Tess-M; meter not indicated, slowly (as a barcarolle); 6pp; Diff-V/d, P/dd.

For: any high or medium voice
Mood: philosophical; descriptive; nature imagery
Voice: long, flowing phrases; chromatic; 2-note slurs and short melismas; triplets
Piano: 32nd-note figures in l.h. under barcarolle melody in r.h.; rapid scale passages; undulating arpeggios; rapid repeated tone clusters; r.h. and l.h. not always intended to be exactly coordinated; 2 pianists suggested for some parts of song; numerous explicit instructions
Diff: pitches; rhythms; ensemble; ends in a spoken line of text; demands superb accompanist
Uses: impressive recital material for the right performers
Rec: D#s 227, 234, 238, 239, 240, 241, 245, 247

1280. **GENERAL WILLIAM BOOTH ENTERS INTO HEAVEN** (Vachel Lindsay). [133]. cmp1914. X; b–e"; Tess-M; 4/4, 3/4, 2/4, 1/8, 3¼/4, Allegro moderato (many tempo changes); 6pp; Diff-V/d, P/dd.

For: baritone; other dramatic voices possible
Mood: dramatic; narrative; descriptive; religious fervor
Voice: marcato and march-like; contrasting slower, more lyrical sections; hymn-tune quotations; chromatic; irregular rhythms; dotted rhythms; syncopation; shouted lines
Piano: highly chromatic; tone clusters; imitation of drum beats; dotted rhythms; grace notes; rapid figurations; thick texture
Diff: for mature, advanced performers with dramatic flair
Uses: excellent recital material for advanced singer with mature dramatic voice
Rec: D#s 28, 59, 69, 227, 228, 234, 235, 239, 240, 241, 247

1281. **GOD BLESS AND KEEP THEE** (anon.) [130]. cmp1897? D♭maj; b♭(a♭)–b♭'; Tess-L; 4/4, 3/4, Andante sostenuto; 2pp; Diff-V/m, P/m.

For: any low voice
Mood: a rather charming, warm, and old-fashioned love song
Voice: conjunct motion and modest intervals, some outlining triads and 7th chords; middle section of each strophe shifts in tonality
Piano: chordal, mostly block, with bits of melody and countermelody; many accidentals; more difficult to read than play; supports vocal line, sometimes doubles
Diff: some pitches
Uses: useful for low voice of limited range
Rec: D#227

1282. **GRANTCHESTER** (with a quotation from Debussy) (Rupert Brooke). [134]. cmp1920. X; c'–c"; Tess-mL; meter not indicated, Adagio non tanto; 3pp; Diff-V/d, P/dd.

For: mezzo-soprano; contralto; baritone
Mood: descriptive; philosophical; nature imagery
Voice: lyrical; rather chromatic; spoken phrase; last section intoned
Piano: chordal; chromatic; impressionistic, with quotation from *L'Après midi d'un faune*; complex rhythms; cross-hands

Diff: pitches; rhythms
Uses: fine recital material
Rec: D#s 227, 239, 241, 246, 248

1283. **THE GREATEST MAN** (Anne Collins). [134, 136, 137]. cmp1921. E- & B-centered; e'–g"; Tess-M; 4/4, Allegro moderato; 4pp; Diff-V/md, P/md.

For: soprano; mezzo-soprano; tenor; high baritone
Mood: humorously descriptive of child's father
Voice: generally stepwise; chromatic; dotted rhythms; triplets
Piano: chordal; chromatic; dotted rhythms; generally doubles voice (partially opt.)
Diff: requires good vocal actor
Uses: recital song; audience-pleasing
Rec: D#s 225, 227, 231, 233, 234, 240, 248

1284. **HE IS THERE!** (also known as "They Are There") (Charles Ives?, with quotations from others). [134]. cmp1917. B♭maj; d'–g"; Tess-M; 4/4, In march time; 5pp (with repeat); Diff-V/m, P/d.

For: all voices except very low
Mood: patriotic
Voice: march-like; quotations from several patriotic songs; strong accents; highest pitch is to be yelled
Piano: chordal; somewhat chromatic; arpeggiation; afterbeats; syncopation; strong accents; opt. violin, flute, or fife obbligato
Diff: requires good vocal actor
Uses: effective to close an Ives group
Rec: D#s 225, 226, 227, 232, 234, 242, 245, 247

1285. **HIS EXALTATION** (adapted from *2nd Violin Sonata*) (Robert Robinson). [134]. cmp1913. X (vocal line in Amaj); a–e"; Tess-M; 3/2, Slowly (maestoso); 2pp; Diff-V/dm P/d.

For: mezzo-soprano; contralto; baritone
Mood: lyrical; philosophical; nature imagery; religious tone
Voice: broad, sweeping phrases; firmly in the key; triplets
Piano: lengthy prelude; chromatic; dissonant; triplets; strong accents
Diff: strong, clear low tones; powerful middle voice
Uses: good for transition from middle to low voice; effective recital song
Rec: D#s 44, 46, 227, 229, 230, 232, 239

1286. **THE HOUSATONIC AT STOCKBRIDGE** (Robert Underwood Johnson). [134, 138]. cmp1921. X; d♭'–f"; Tess-mL; 4/4, 5/4, Slowly and quietly; 5pp; Diff-V/d, P/dd.

For: mezzo-soprano; baritone
Mood: lyrical; descriptive
Voice: sustained; rather chromatic; phrases often separated by rests
Piano: chordal; chromatic; sustained; soft and delicate until near end
Diff: pitches; rhythms; piano score
Uses: colorful song for a nature group
Rec: D#s 225, 227, 230, 231, 237, 239, 243, 247

1287. **HYMN** (hymn text). [134, 136]. cmp1904; arr. for voice and piano, 1921 (orig. for cello with string quartet & bass). X; c♯'–e"; Tess-M; 4/4, 3/4, 7/8, 5/4,

Largo; 2pp; Diff-V/m, P/md.

For: any high or medium voice
Mood: lyrical; philosophical
Voice: somewhat disjunct; long lyrical phrases; chromatic
Piano: contrapuntal; chromatic; fragments of vocal melody; occasionally doubles vocal line
Diff: pitches; long phrases
Uses: effective recital song; probably not appropriate for church use
Rec: D#s 226, 227, 230, 245

1288. THE INDIANS (Charles Sprague). [134, 135]. arr.1921. X; d♭'–d"; Tess-M; 3/8, 4/8, 5/8, Very slowly; 2pp; Diff-V/md, P/d.

For: any medium voice
Mood: descriptive; philosophical; sad commentary on the plight of the Indians
Voice: generally moving in 8ths & 16ths; 2–3-note slurs; some syncopation
Piano: chordal; chromatic; dissonant; rolled chords
Diff: pitch; rhythm; soft singing
Uses: effective song
Rec: D#s 227, 229, 237, 241, 247

1289. IN FLANDERS FIELDS (John McCrae). [132, 134]. cmp1919. X, G- & D-centered; d'–e"; Tess-M; 4/4, Maestoso (but with energy and not too slowly); 3pp; Diff-V/m, P/d.

For: baritone (may also be sung by male chorus)
Mood: patriotic
Voice: lyrical; flowing; dramatic in middle section; regular rhythms
Piano: chords and tone clusters–some rolled, some sharp and march-like; chromatic; tremolo
Diff: voice needs dramatic weight
Uses: can be effectively performed; World War I subject
Rec: D#s 225, 227, 234, 238, 245, 247

1290. THE INNATE (Ives?). [133, 134]. cmp1908; arr. for voice & piano (or organ), 1916 (orig. for string quartet & piano). X; d'–e"; Tess-M; meter not indicated, Slowly; 1+pp; Diff-V/d, P/d.

For: any high or medium voice
Mood: philosophical; religious tone
Voice: short phrases; chromatic; quotation of hymn-tune "Nettleton" at end
Piano: somewhat contrapuntal; highly chromatic; generally 4-voice texture
Diff: pitches; rhythms
Rec: D#s 227, 230, 237, 245

1291. I TRAVELLED AMONG UNKNOWN MEN (William Wordsworth). [134]. cmp1901. Cmaj; c'–f"; Tess-M; 2/4, Andante con moto; 2pp; Diff-V/m, P/md.

For: baritone
Mood: lyrical; poetic song of love for England and a beloved who is dead
Voice: many 8ve leaps; movement in 8ths & 16ths; 2-note slurs; dotted rhythms; strong accents; some chromaticism; features c'
Piano: chordal; delicate texture; upper register; afterbeats; fairly chromatic

Diff: singer needs easy f"; portamento downward to g'
Uses: good program material
Rec: D#227

1292. KÄREN (anon.). [134, 138]. cmp1894. G♭maj; d♭'–g♭"; Tess-M; 3/4, 3/8, Allegro moderato; 2pp; Diff-V/me, P/me.

For: tenor; lyric baritone
Mood: lyrical; love song
Voice: generally stays in the key; regular rhythms
Piano: l.h. broken chords; r.h. independent melody in 3rds
Uses: one of the easier Ives songs for students
Rec: D#s 227, 245

1293. THE LAST READER (Oliver Wendell Holmes). [134, 136]. cmp1911; arr. for voice & piano, 1921 (orig. for instruments). Dmin-maj; d'–d"; Tess-M; 6/4, 4/4, 3/4, Andante con moto; 2pp; Diff-V/m, P/md.

For: any lyric voice
Mood: lyrical; peaceful; philosophical; happy
Voice: flowing phrases; quotations from Ludwig Spohr and Joseph Haydn; triplets; somewhat chromatic
Piano: chordal; fairly chromatic; triplets; irregular groupings
Diff: pitches; rhythms; sustained phrasing
Rec: D#s 225, 227, 230, 239

1294. THE LIGHT THAT IS FELT (John Greenleaf Whittier). For Medium Voice and Piano. [16, 134]. cmp1904. Bmaj; b–c♯"; Tess-L; 2/4, Slowly; 2pp; Diff-V/md, P/d.

For: contralto
Mood: lyrical; philosophical; religious sentiment
Voice: flowing phrases; many dotted rhythms; little chromaticism
Piano: arpeggiated 16ths, mostly descending; rolled chords; cross-hands; syncopation; little chromaticism
Diff: light, clear low tones
Uses: lovely memory of childhood for teaching and performance
Rec: D#s 225, 227, 230

1295. LIKE A SICK EAGLE (John Keats). [134, 136]. cmp1920. X; c'–d♭"; Tess-L; meter not indicated, Slowly; 1p; Diff-V/md, P/d.

For: any low or medium voice
Mood: oddly philosophical
Voice: chromatic; one leap of m9th; short, twisting phrases; singer may use sliding, indefinite pitches
Piano: contrapuntal; basically 4-voice texture; chromatic; dissonant
Diff: pitches; rhythms; sliding, indefinite pitches
Rec: D#s 227, 229, 231, 237, 241, 245

1296. LUCK AND WORK (Robert Underwood Johnson). [131, 134, 136]. cmp1916; arr. for voice & piano, 1920 (orig. for instruments). X; d'–e"; Tess-M; meter not indicated, Fast and hard; 1p; Diff-V/md, P/d.

For: all voices
Mood: humorously philosophical
Voice: chromatic; many short note values; a few ornaments
Piano: contrapuntal; highly chromatic; cross-hands
Diff: pitches; rhythms

Uses: effective recital song, perhaps to close an Ives group
Rec: D#s 226, 227, 239, 248

1297. **MAJORITY** (Ives?). [133, 134]. cmp1915; arr. for voice & piano, 1921 (orig. for chorus & orch). X; c#'–f "; Tess-M; meter not indicated at beginning (4/2, with changes), Slowly (with many tempo changes); 5pp; Diff-V/d, P/dd.
For: any medium voice
Mood: dramatic; philosophical
Voice: somewhat disjunct; fragmented; chromatic; sustained; dramatic at beginning, more lyrical in middle section
Piano: chordal; rolled and arpeggiated; tone clusters; highly chromatic; dissonant; lengthy introduction; instructions for playing massive chord clusters given at end of collection
Diff: pitches; rhythms; dramatic weight in low parts of voice; expert pianist required
Rec: D#s 227, 237, 239, 241

1298. **MAPLE LEAVES** (Thomas Bailey Aldrich). [134, 135]. cmp1920. X; c'–c"; Tess-mL; meter not indicated, Andante; 1p; Diff-V/md, P/d.
For: any lyric medium voice
Mood: lyrical; philosophical description of autumn
Voice: some phrase fragmentation; some chromaticism
Piano: broken and rolled chords; cross-hands; small melodic fragments
Diff: pitches; rhythms
Uses: attractive lyric song for recital
Rec: D#s 225, 227, 229, 231, 234, 241, 248

1299. **MEMORIES. A,–VERY PLEASANT B,–RATHER SAD** (Ives?). [134]. cmp1897. Cmaj–Ebmaj; b–e"; Tess-mL; 6/8, 4/4, Presto–Adagio; 4pp; Diff-V/m, P/me.
For: mezzo-soprano
Mood: A,- humorously descriptive; B,- sad and melancholy
Voice: A,- lively and bouncing; includes whistling; B,- lyrical and sustained; ends with a hum
Piano: A,- chordal with afterbeats; B,- flowing arpeggios
Diff: good vocal actor needed; ability to whistle
Uses: excellent double song; presents contrast in a group
Rec: D#s 3, 5, 39, 227, 229, 231, 237, 245, 247

1300. **MIRAGE** (Dante Gabriel Rossetti). [134]. cmp1902. Ebmaj; c'–f "; Tess-M; 4/4, 3/4, 2/4, Moderato; 1p; Diff-V/m, P/m.
For: mezzo-soprano
Mood: sadly philosophical
Voice: flowing phrases; features triplets; stays close to the key
Piano: broken-chord triplet pattern in l.h.; chords and melodic fragments in r.h.; some chromaticism
Diff: rhythm
Rec: D#s 227, 232, 248

1301. **MISTS** (Ives?). [134, 136]. cmp1910. Gmaj; e'–g"; Tess-M; 4/4, 3/4, Largo sostenuto; 2pp; Diff-V/m, P/d.
For: soprano; tenor
Mood: lyrical; philosophical
Voice: sustained phrases; some chromaticism; syncopation
Piano: chordal; parallel chords over pedal tones; chromatic

Diff: pitches; rhythms
Rec: D#s 226, 227, 241

1302. **MY NATIVE LAND** (traditional). [134, 138]. cmp1897. Ebmaj; (bb) eb'–c"; Tess-mL; 4/4, 3/4, Adagio; 1p; Diff-V/m, P/m.
For: any medium voice
Mood: patriotic
Voice: lyrical; short phrases separated by short rests; triplets; one quintuplet
Piano: chordal; independent melodic fragments in contrary motion to voice; rolled chords
Diff: rhythms
Uses: could be useful for student with limited range
Rec: D#s 39, 227

1303. **NATURE'S WAY** (Ives). [132, 134]. cmp1908. Fmaj; d'–f "; Tess-M; 3/4, Adagio moderato; 1p; Diff-V/md, P/md.
For: any high or medium voice
Mood: philosophical; nature imagery
Voice: lyrical; one leap of m10th; some dotted rhythms; some syncopation
Piano: broken chords in l.h. under 8ve F's in r.h.
Rec: D#227

1304. **THE NEW RIVER** (Ives?). [134, 136]. cmp1912; arr. for voice & piano, 1921 (orig. for instruments). X; db'–d#"(a#"); Tess-mL; 3/4, 5/4, 4/4, Fast and rough; 2pp; Diff-V/d, P/dd.
For: any high or medium voice, except light
Mood: dramatic; philosophical; deals with modern life
Voice: disjunct; chromatic; syncopated rhythms; triplets; opt. pitches a 5th higher in first part of song
Piano: highly chromatic; rapid 16th-note figures in 9ths; afterbeat pattern
Diff: pitches; rhythms; needs dramatic weight
Uses: effective recital song
Rec: D#s 226, 227, 229, 230, 239, 247

1305. **A NIGHT THOUGHT** (Thomas Moore). [134, 136]. cmp1895. Bmaj; b–d#"; Tess-mL; 3/8, 2/8, Adagio; 1p; Diff-V/m, P/md.
For: any medium voice
Mood: lyrical; philosophical
Voice: some long phrases; dotted rhythms; short note values; soft dynamics
Piano: contrapuntal; somewhat chromatic
Rec: D#227

1306. **NO MORE** (William Winter). [130]. cmp1897. Dmaj; c#'–d "; Tess-mL; 4/4, 3/8, Thoughtful; 4pp; Diff-V/m, P/m.
For: any medium voice
Mood: sad, lyrical poem of two lovers; one goes to sea and does not return
Voice: mostly conjunct motion; a few modest intervals; short phrases; few accidentals; ends f on a'
Piano: chordal; countermelody to the vocal line; broken-chord figures indicated as "wave-like;" some accidentals; supports vocal line clearly; no doubling
Diff: a few pitches

Uses: useful for a singer with limited range; emphasizes middle voice
Rec: D#s 226, 227

1307. **OLD HOME DAY** ('Ducite ab urbe domum, mea carmina, ducite Daphnin') (Charles Ives?). [134]. cmp1920. X-Gmaj; d'–e"; Tess-M; 4/4, Slowly–Moderately, and with even rhythm; 4pp (with repeats); Diff-V/m, P/d.
For: any high or medium voice
Mood: nostalgic; descriptive
Voice: broad, lyrical first section; following sections in style of vaudeville tunes, town band tunes, etc.
Piano: highly chromatic with sweeping arpeggiations at beginning; following sections in style of vaudeville, town band, church bell, etc.; opt. fife, violin, or flute obbligato
Diff: needs good vocal actor with feeling for the various styles
Uses: colorful program material
Rec: D#s 226, 227, 230, 245

1308. **"1, 2, 3."** (Ives?). [131, 134]. cmp1921. X; f'–d"; Tess-M; 3/8, 3/4, Fairly fast; 1p; Diff-V/m, P/d.
For: all voices
Mood: humorously philosophical
Voice: light and crisp; syncopation; staccato
Piano: pseudo-waltz; chromatic; dissonant; running 16ths; cross-hands; syncopation
Diff: ensemble
Uses: humorous recital song; group ender
Rec: D#s 227, 229, 231, 234, 239, 241, 245

1309. **THE ONE WAY** (The True Philosophy of all Nice Conservatories of Music and Nice "MUS. DOC'S" "IMBCDGODAMLILY"). [4, 130]. cmp1923(?). Fmaj-B♭maj; f'–g"; Tess-M; 2/4, 4/4, Andante–Allegro, tempo di marcia; 6pp; Diff-V/m, P/md.
For: any high voice
Mood: satire on conservatory musical training
Voice: simple and tuneful; melismas and chromaticism to suit text; somewhat disjunct
Piano: chordal; simple chords for verse; march-like with triplet afterbeats for refrain; some chromaticism
Uses: humorous addition to any program
Rec: D#s 226, 227, 229

1310. **ON THE ANTIPODES** (Ives?). [133]. cmp1915-23. X; a–a"; Tess-M; 4/4 with many changes, Adagio maestoso (with many changes); 4pp; Diff-V/dd, P/dd.
For: dramatic soprano; mezzo-soprano
Mood: philosophical discussion of "Nature"
Voice: disjunct; fragmented; large leaps; chromatic; intricate rhythms; divides into two parts (to be sung by chorus)
Piano: written for piano duet (two pianos); extremely chromatic and dissonant; tone clusters; complicated rhythmic patterns
Diff: pitches; rhythms; several words on final sustained a"; ensemble
Uses: could be very effectively programmed
Rec: D#s 227, 239, 241, 243

1311. **PEAKS** (Henry Bellamann). [4, 130]. cmp1923(?). X; d'–e"; Tess-M; 4/4, 5/4, 3/4, Andante con moto; 2pp; Diff-V/md, P/d.
For: any lyric medium voice
Mood: lyrical; philosophical; nature imagery
Voice: smooth and sustained; melismas in syncopated dotted rhythms; some chromaticism
Piano: chordal; chromatic; dissonant; syncopated dotted rhythms; triplets; other irregular groupings
Diff: pitches; rhythms
Rec: D#s 226, 227

1312. **PICTURES** (Monica Peveril Turnbull). [4, 130]. cmp1906? E♭maj, with changes; d♭'–e"; Tess-M; 9/8, Con moto; 4pp; Diff-V/md, P/d.
For: any medium voice
Mood: four contrasting nature scenes: "The Cornfield," "The Sea," "The Moor," and "Night"; outer pictures peaceful and serene, inner pictures somewhat dramatic
Voice: conjunct and disjunct motion, emphasizing intervals of 4th & 5th; numerous accidentals; duplets against compound meter in piano
Piano: chordal; variety of broken-chord figures; many accidentals (although key signature remains unchanged, the inner pictures are in G♭maj and Cmaj, respectively); supports vocal line well; does not double
Diff: pitches and rhythms; quick contrasts in interpretation
Uses: interesting to study and perform
Rec: D#s 226, 227, 247

1313. **PREMONITIONS** (Robert Underwood Johnson). [134, 136]. cmp1917; arr. for voice & piano, 1921 (orig. for instruments). X; c♯'–f"; Tess-mL; meter not indicated, Slowly; 2pp; Diff-V/d, P/d.
For: any medium voice
Mood: lyrical; philosophical; poem about death
Voice: flowing phrases; chromatic; declamatory and dramatic towards end
Piano: chordal; tone clusters; highly chromatic
Diff: rhythm; requires dramatic weight in voice at end
Rec: D#s 227, 229, 230, 248

1314. **THE RAINBOW** (William Wordsworth). [134, 136]. cmp1914; accomp. arr. for piano, 1921 (orig. for instruments). X; c'–f"; Tess-M; 5/4, 4/4, 3/4, 6/4, 8/4, Moderately fast; 2pp; Diff-V/md, P/dd.
For: any medium voice
Mood: philosophical
Voice: lyrical; flowing phrases; somewhat disjunct; chromatic; triplets
Piano: chordal; chromatic; tone clusters; rolled chords; cross-hands
Diff: pitches; frequent meter changes
Rec: D#227

1315. **REQUIEM** (Robert Louis Stevenson). [133]. cmp1911. X; d♭'–f"; Tess-M; 6/8, 9/8, 5/4, 2/4, Allegro moderato–Adagio; 2pp; Diff-V/md, P/d.
For: any medium or high voice
Mood: reflective; philosophical
Voice: disjunct; chromatic; syncopation; duplets; other irregular groupings; horn-call imitations at end

Piano: chordal; 16th- & 32nd-note figurations; duplets; other irregular groupings; extra pianist or instrument may be used for soft horn calls at end
Diff: pitches; rhythms
Uses: interesting contrast to well-known S. Homer setting
Rec: D#s 226, 227, 239, 241

1316. **ROUGH WIND** (Percy Bysshe Shelley). [134, 136]. cmp1898; arr. for voice & piano, 1922 (orig. from a symphony). D-centered; e♭'–a"; Tess-M; 3/4, Allegro; 3pp; Diff-V/md, P/dd.
For: soprano; tenor (not light)
Mood: philosophical; nature imagery
Voice: forceful and somewhat dramatic; little chromaticism; dotted rhythms
Piano: sextuplets; 16ths in l.h. under 2-voice contrapuntal r.h.; syncopation; chromaticism
Rec: D#s 227, 230

1308. **A SCOTCH LULLABY** (Charles Edmund Merrill, Jr.). [130]. cmp1896. Gmaj; c♯'–f♯"; Tess-M; 12/8, Andante sostenuto; 2pp; Diff-V/m, P/m.
For: any high or medium voice
Mood: lullaby, using a very broad form of Scottish dialect
Voice: mostly conjunct motion and small intervals; one 8ve leap upwards; few accidentals
Piano: chordal; with some countermelodic motives; supports vocal line; some doubling; some accidentals
Diff: a few pitches for singer; getting the language right
Uses: good for study emphasizing middle voice; possible recital song
Rec: D#227

1309. **A SEA DIRGE** (William Shakespeare). [4, 130]. cmp1925. E♭-centered; c'–e"; Tess-M; 9/8, 12/8, 6/8, In a slow swaying way; 2pp; Diff-V/md, P/d.
For: any lyric medium voice
Voice: disjunct; several melismas; flowing phrases; chromatic
Piano: chordal; dissonant; chromatic; independent melodic fragments
Diff: pitch; rhythm
Uses: could be effectively programmed
Rec: D#s 226, 227, 229, 239

1310. **THE SEE'R** (Charles Ives). [4, 134, 135, 136]. cmp1913–1920(?). X; c'–d"; Tess-M; meter not indicated at beginning, 5/8, 2/4, 1/4, Moderately fast; 2pp; Diff-V/d, P/d.
For: all voices
Mood: humorously descriptive
Voice: rapidly moving with syncopation and strong accents at beginning; short chromatic melismas; ends on syncopated repetitions of c"
Piano: chordal; chromatic; dissonant; syncopated independent melody in 16ths in latter part of song
Diff: pitches; rhythms
Uses: humorous addition to a program
Rec: D#s 227, 231, 234, 236, 239, 247

1311. **SEPTEMBER** (Folgore da San Geminiano, from Rossetti's *Early Italian Poets*). [134, 136]. cmp1920. X; d'–g♯"; Tess-M; meter not indicated, Presto; 2pp;

Diff-V/dd, P/dd.
For: soprano; tenor
Mood: philosophical; nature imagery
Voice: chromatic; very short note values; set to English translation
Piano: chromatic arpeggiations and broken chords throughout
Diff: pitches; rhythms
Rec: D#s 226, 227, 239, 241, 245, 248

1312. **SERENITY** (John Greenleaf Whittier). [134, 135]; adapted 1919. B-centered; f'–e"; Tess-M; 6/8, Very slowly, quietly and sustained, with little or no change in tempo or volume throughout; 1p; Diff-V/md, P/me.
For: any high or medium voice
Mood: religious text
Voice: very static; chant-like; only one interval larger than 2nd; many duplets in compound meter and across bar lines
Piano: high, bell-like chords; a little chromaticism
Diff: soft singing–preferably head voice in low range; rhythmic groupings
Uses: beautiful song; useful in many situations
Rec: D#s 225, 227, 229, 231, 234, 237, 241, 244, 245

1313. **THE SIDE SHOW** (Ives). [134, 138]. cmp1921. A♭maj; d'(d♭')–f"; Tess-M; 3/4, 2/4, 5/4, In a moderate waltz time; 1p; Diff-V/md, P/m.
For: any high or medium voice
Mood: humorously descriptive
Voice: off-balance waltz rhythm; little chromaticism; semi-popular swing to the tune
Piano: waltz style
Diff: rhythms
Uses: good recital song; encore
Rec: D#s 65, 225, 226, 227, 231, 236, 240, 241, 245, 246, 247

1314. **SLOW MARCH** (Inscribed to the Children's Faithful Friend) (Charles Ives). [134]. cmp1888. Fmaj; c'–c"; Tess-mL; 4/4, Largo; 1p; Diff-V/e, P/e.
For: any low or medium voice
Mood: sad; describes burial of family pet
Voice: rather static; many repeated tones; hymn-like
Piano: chordal–chiefly half notes; quotation from G. F. Handel in prelude and postlude
Diff: interpretive approach must be straightforward
Uses: unusual subject matter
Rec: D#s 226, 227, 229, 231, 242

1315. **SLUGGING A VAMPIRE** (same music as "Tarrant Moss," different text) (Charles Ives?). [133, 134]. cmp1902. Cmaj; b–f"; Tess-M; 4/4, 2/4, Allegro con fuoco; 1p; Diff-V/m, P/m.
For: baritone
Mood: humorously descriptive
Voice: short note values; patter style; stays close to the key
Piano: chordal; some doubling of vocal line
Diff: rapid diction; good vocal actor needed
Uses: effective humorous song; good Ives group ender
Rec: D#s 28, 227, 229, 231, 239 ("Tarrant Moss": D#s 227, 234, 248)

1316. SOLILOQUY: OR A STUDY IN 7ths AND OTHER THINGS (Ives). [136]. cmp1907. X; dᵇ'–b''; Tess-H, L; 4/16, 5/16, 1/16, 7/16, 8/16, 6/16, Adagio–Allegro; 1p; Diff-V/dd, P/dd.

For: soprano; tenor
Mood: humorously descriptive and philosophical; reflects on nature
Voice: chanted or half-spoken at beginning; faster and extremely disjunct; large leaps; complicated rhythms
Piano: highly chromatic; tone clusters; rapid broken chords; two pianists may be used
Diff: pitches; rhythms; large leaps to short high tones
Uses: impressive recital song; Ives group ender
Rec: D#s 227, 229, 239, 240, 243

1317. SONGS MY MOTHER TAUGHT ME (Adolf Heyduk; trans. adapted). [132, 134]. cmp1895. Eᵇmaj; bᵇ–c''; Tess-mL; 3/4, 2/4, Largo; 2pp; Diff-V/m, P/m.

For: contralto
Mood: lyrical; sentimental
Voice: skips among chord members; little chromaticism
Piano: chordal; afterbeat patterns
Rec: D#s 5, 227, 231, 236, 245

1318. SPRING SONG (Harmony T. Ives). [5, 134, 138]. cmp1904. Fmaj; c'–g''; Tess-M; 3/4, Allegretto; 2pp; Diff-V/me, P/me.

For: soprano; mezzo-soprano; tenor
Mood: lyrical; nature song
Voice: flowing phrases; a little chromaticism
Piano: chordal; repeated chords; some chromaticism
Rec: D#s 227, 231, 248

1319. THERE IS A CERTAIN GARDEN (anon.). [130]. cmp1893. Cmaj; a–e''; Tess-mL; 4/4, Allegretto con moto; 2pp; Diff-V/m, P/m.

For: mezzo-soprano; contralto
Mood: lyrical; descriptive; sentimental
Voice: flowing phrases; 2-note slurs; small melismas
Piano: chordal; some repetition; some chromaticism; occasional independent melodic lines
Rec: D#s 226, 227, 247

1320. THERE IS A LANE (Ives?). [134]. cmp1902. Bᵇmaj; c'–f''; Tess-M; 3/4, Adagio sostenuto; 1p; Diff-V/me, P/m.

For: mezzo-soprano
Mood: nostalgic; descriptive
Voice: lyrical, flowing phrases; one leap of m7th; vocal line stays close to the key
Piano: syncopated 3-voice chords in contrary motion, both hands; some chromaticism
Uses: effective to program; easier than most Ives songs
Rec: D#s 225, 226, 227

1321. THE THINGS OUR FATHERS LOVED (and the greatest of these was Liberty) (Charles Ives). [132, 134]. cmp1917. X; c'–d#''; Tess-M; meter not indicated, Slowly and sustained; 2pp; Diff-V/m, P/d.

For: mezzo-soprano; baritone
Mood: descriptive
Voice: disjunct; chromatic; suggestions of hymn tunes and village-band tunes
Piano: chordal and contrapuntal at beginning; rapid 16ths in final section
Diff: pitches; rhythms; ensemble
Uses: musically colorful study and performance piece
Rec: D#s 39, 225, 226, 227, 231, 237, 239, 247

1322. THOREAU (adapted from themes in *Second Pianoforte Sonata*) (Ives?). [134, 136]. cmp1915. X; c#'–d''; Tess-M; meter/tempo not given at beginning, Very slowly (given later); 1p; Diff-V/m, P/d.

For: all voices
Mood: philosophical description of the poet
Voice: sustained; static; recit.-like; many repeated notes; triplets
Piano: soft dissonant chords at beginning; contrapuntal texture accompanies voice
Uses: effective recital song
Rec: D#s 225, 227, 229, 230, 237, 244, 248

1323. THOSE EVENING BELLS (Thomas Moore). [132, 134]. cmp1907. Eᵇmaj-Cmin; c'–eᵇ''; Tess-M; 3/4, 6/8, Moderato con moto; 2pp; Diff-V/me, P/md.

For: any medium voice
Mood: lyrical; philosophical
Voice: flowing phrases; 8ve leaps downward, with anticipations; syncopation
Piano: rolled chords in r.h. over staccato 8ths in 4ths, 5ths, & 6ths in l.h.; some chromaticism
Diff: voice and piano form 2 vs. 3 rhythm almost throughout
Uses: one of the easier Ives songs
Rec: D#s 226, 227, 230

1324. TOM SAILS AWAY (Ives?). [133, 134]. cmp1917. X; c'–d''; Tess-mL; meter not indicated, Slowly (with many tempo changes); 3pp; Diff-V/d, P/dd.

For: all voices
Mood: narrative; descriptive; war theme
Voice: rambling; irregular phrases for narrative style; highly chromatic; quotation from "Over There" at end
Piano: highly chromatic; complex rhythmic patterns; somewhat contrapuntal; broken chords; arpeggiations
Diff: pitches; rhythms; ability to handle narrative style
Uses: can be effectively programmed; World War I song
Rec: D#s 225, 227, 229, 231, 234, 236, 238, 239, 241, 245, 246, 247

1325. TWO LITTLE FLOWERS (and dedicated to them) (Charles Ives). [133, 134, 137]. cmp1921. Dmaj; (bᵇ)d'–e''; Tess-M; 4/4, Allegretto; 2pp; Diff-V/m, P/m.

For: soprano; mezzo-soprano
Mood: lyrical; descriptive
Voice: flowing phrases; very graceful and melodic; some syncopation; a few chromatic tones
Piano: arpeggiated chords throughout; cross-hands; little chromaticism; pedaling specified
Diff: rhythms; ensemble
Uses: quiet impressionistic song
Rec: D#s 3, 28, 225, 227, 231, 233, 234, 236, 238, 241, 245, 247

1326. VOTE FOR NAMES! (Charles Ives). [65]. cmp1912.

X; b–a"; Tess-M; 9/16, Freely; 2pp; Diff-V/d, P/m.
For: soprano; mezzo-soprano; tenor
Mood: political satire
Voice: extremely disjunct; very large leaps; spoken phrases; glissandos.
Piano: mostly repeated chords; highly chromatic; large reaches
Diff: leaps of up to 15th in vocal line; "free singing words without bar lines, without reference to piano"; glissandos and "tremble"; speaking; accomp. more difficult to read than play
Uses: good for singer with excellent ear and ability to produce the vocal effects called for
Rec: D#227

1327. **WALKING** (Charles Ives). [134, 135]. cmp1900–1902(?). X; d'–f♯"; Tess-M; 4/4, 9/8, Allegro con spirito; 4pp; Diff-V/m, P/md.
For: baritone
Mood: narrative; descriptive; philosophical
Voice: marked; strong accents; several melismas
Piano: chordal; fairly chromatic; parallel 4ths & 5ths; arpeggiation; long, descriptive interlude
Uses: effective recital song
Rec: D#s 2, 225, 227, 234, 239, 241, 246, 248

1328. **WALT WHITMAN** (from 20th Stanza) (Walt Whitman). [134, 136]. cmp1921. X; c'–f"; Tess-H, L; meter not indicated, Fast and in a challenging way; 2pp; Diff-V/md, P/d.
For: baritone
Mood: abstract; philosophical; dramatic
Voice: disjunct; large leaps; chromatic; dramatic and declamatory
Piano: chromatic; tone clusters; generally loud and dramatic
Diff: text; dramatic weight needed
Rec: D#s 6, 67, 225, 227, 229, 239, 241, 248

1329. **WATCHMAN!** (from *First Sonata for Violin and Piano*) (John Bowring). [132, 134]. cmp1913. Dmaj-Bmin; d'–f♯"; Tess-mL; 4/4, 6/8, 3/4, Andante con moto; 2pp; Diff-V/m, P/md.
For: any high or medium voice
Mood: familiar hymn text–"Watchman, tell us of the night" by Lowell Mason
Voice: begins quoting hymn tune, then adds "wrong" notes and rhythms
Piano: chordal; contrapuntal; chromatic
Diff: careful attention to notes and rhythms for singer who knows the tune
Rec: D#s 44, 46, 227, 230, 232

1330. **WEST LONDON** (A Sonnet) (Matthew Arnold). [134, 136]. cmp1912; arr. for voice & piano, 1921 (orig. an uncompleted overture). X; (b) c'–f"; Tess-M; 4/4, Moderato; 3pp; Diff-V/md, P/md.
For: any high or medium voice
Mood: descriptive; philosophical; deals with poverty
Voice: somewhat disjunct; long, flowing phrases; dramatic accents; little chromaticism
Piano: broken chords; l.h. 16th-note figures; staccato; some chromaticism
Diff: requires good vocal actor, must be sung with dignity

Rec: D#s 226, 227, 229, 236, 238, 240, 241, 245, 247

1331. **WHERE THE EAGLE** (Monica Peveril Turnbull). [22, 134, 137]. cmp1900. E♭maj; d'–e"; Tess-M; 2/4, Adagio molto; 1p; Diff-V/m, P/d.
For: any high or medium voice
Mood: philosophical; religious tone
Voice: lyrical; flowing; 8th- & 16th-note movement; 2-note slurs
Piano: chordal; high register of piano; 16ths moving chromatically in contrary motion
Diff: delicate touch required of both performers
Rec: D#s 227, 234, 238, 247

1332. **THE WHITE GULLS** (from the Russian) (Maurice Morris). [134, 136]. cmp1921. X; b–e"; Tess-M; 4/2 with many changes, Largo; 2pp; Diff-V/md, P/md.
For: mezzo-soprano; baritone
Mood: lyrical; descriptive; philosophical; nature imagery
Voice: stepwise descending phrases; chromaticism; broad and flowing
Piano: chordal; chromatic; tone clusters; long note values with some filling in of inner voices
Diff: pitch
Uses: good for teaching sustained singing; many phrases begin high and descend
Rec: D#s 6, 227, 229, 234, 236, 238, 241, 247

1333. **THE WORLD'S WANDERERS** (Percy Bysshe Shelley). [134]. cmp1895. E♭maj; e♭'–e♭"; Tess-M; 2/4, Adagio sostenuto; 1p (with repeat); Diff-V/me, P/m.
For: any lyric high or medium voice
Mood: philosophical; questioning; nature imagery
Voice: flowing phrases; ascending scale-wise patterns
Piano: independent melody accomp. by syncopated chords
Uses: short and easy student song
Rec: D#227

1334. **YELLOW LEAVES** (Henry Bellamann). [130]. cmp1923(?). X; a♯–e"; Tess-mL; 3/4, 4/4, 5/8, tempo not indicated but fairly slow tempo implied; 2pp; Diff-V/md, P/d.
For: mezzo-soprano; contralto
Mood: lyrical; description of nature
Voice: flowing phrases; somewhat disjunct
Piano: impressionistic in style; broken and rolled chords; grace notes; wide spacing
Diff: pitch; rhythm; clear, light low tones
Uses: could be an effective recital song
Rec: D#s 226, 227, 247

IVEY, JEAN EICHELBERGER
(b. Washington, DC, 1923)

1335. **FROM WOMAN'S LOVE** (Sara Teasdale). [3]. cmp1962. Separate entries below.

A. **I WOULD LIVE IN YOUR LOVE.** Cmaj; c'–f"; Tess-M; 4/4, Molto tranquillo; 2pp; Diff-V/me, P/me.
For: any voice (mezzo-soprano might be best)

Mood: pledges love
Voice: mostly stepwise movement; many 2–9-note slurs; easy rhythms in 8th notes
Piano: mostly 4-voice texture, some 2-voice; moves in 8th-note scale-like passages
Diff: inexperienced singer may have trouble with entrances due to continual flow of piano 8ths
Uses: pair with "To One Away"; a contemporary-sounding pair that requires little experience

B. **TO ONE AWAY.** Unsettled; e'–e"; Tess-M; 4/4, Allegro giusto; 2pp; Diff-V/m, P/m.
For: any voice (mezzo-soprano or soprano seems best)
Mood: love song
Voice: chant-like patterning; syncopation; accidentals; short phrases
Piano: built over 1-meas. l.h. ostinato in 8ths; in r.h. all chords are major except one; often outlines singer's melody
Diff: rhythms most difficult aspect
Uses: pair with "I Would Live in Your Love"

JACOBI, FREDERICK
(b. San Francisco, CA, 1891; d. New York, NY, 1952)

1336. **THE LOOK** (Sara Teasdale). G. Schirmer, 1915. Emaj; c♯'–g♯"; Tess-M; 4/4, Gaily; 2pp; Diff-V/m, P/me.
For: soprano
Mood: lyrical; whimsical
Voice: skips along chord lines; leaps; some chromaticism; one small ornament; quiet ending
Piano: broken chords; rhythmically patterned; some melodic material; large reach helpful; flexible tempo
Diff: pitch–due to modulations
Uses: good song for teaching and programming; encore

1337. **THREE SONGS** (Philip Freneau). Valley, 1955. Traditional keys; d'–b♭"; Tess-M-mH; regular meters; contrasting tempos; 11pp; Diff-V/m-md, P/e-m.
For: soprano; tenor
Mood: lyrical; two gentle, one patriotic
Voice: vocal line varies: simple folksong style; rather archaic style; march-like patriotic tune; some ornamentation and coloratura; many rising phrases; soft high tones; some awkward pitches
Piano: one pure English folksong accomp.; other two mostly chordal; some accidentals
Diff: ascending phrases ending on b♭" and coloratura passages of third song
Uses: interesting settings of 18th-century poetry; tenor with beautiful, soft head tones could use them to good effect in second song; songs show great contrast; intermediate to advanced singers

    a. *On the Sleep of Plants* (1790). Gmaj; f'–g"; Tess-M; 4/4, Andante semplice, con tenerezza; 4pp.
    b. *Elegy* (1786). B♭min; d'–b♭"; Tess-M-mH; 4/4, Very slowly; 3pp.
    c. *Ode to Freedom* (1795). B♭maj; f'–b♭"; Tess-M-mH; 4/4, Briskly; 4pp.

1338. **TWO POEMS BY GEOFFREY CHAUCER.** G. Schirmer, 1923. Traditional keys; c♯'–a"; Tess-M; regular meters; contrasting tempos; 13pp; Diff-V/me-md, P/e-md.
For: tenor
Mood: lyrical; love song
Voice: skips and leaps within chords; chromaticism; archaic sound; phrases have characteristic rhythmic structure
Piano: (a.), linear, ostinato pattern in r.h. heard intermittently throughout, some wide-spread chords in l.h., large reach helpful; (b.), perpetual motion in 8th- & 16th-note patterns, cross-hands, tremolo, trills
Diff: some pitches; modal structure; texts in Middle English–pronunciation and meaning require study
Uses: interesting pair of songs; good recital material for the right lyric tenor (see Diff:)

    a. *Roundel.* Phrygian on D; d'–e♭"; 4/4, Not quickly; 3pp.
    b. *Ballade.* Dmaj; c♯'–a"; 2/2, Very quickly and with humor; 10pp.

JACOBS-BOND, CARRIE
(see Bond, Carrie Jacobs)

JAMES, PHILIP
(b. Jersey City, NJ, 1890; d. Southhampton, NY, 1975)

1339. **THE STRANGER** (Brychan B. Powell). Belwin-Mills, 1951. Emin; e'–g"; Tess-mH; 4/4, Andante pastorale; 4pp; Diff-V/m, P/m.
For: tenor; soprano
Mood: lyrical; restoring power of song
Voice: straightforward both melodically and rhythmically; numerous accidentals; 2-note slurs
Piano: linear; melodic material in r.h.; some broken-chord figures; many accidentals; some 8ves; wide reaches
Diff: sustained g" climax *ff* on "sing"
Uses: useful song for teaching and recital

JENNI, DONALD
(b. Milwaukee, WI, 1937)

1340. **ADAM LAY YBOUNDIN** (anon., 14th cent.). American Composers Alliance (Composers Facsimile Ed.), 1958. cmp1957. Lydian mode, c'–d"; Tess-M; 4/4 with changes, Lightly detached; 2pp; Diff-V/me, P/me.
For: medium and low voices
Mood: religious
Voice: mostly stepwise motion and small skips; one leap of 9th; easy rhythms; some syncopation; syllabic; a few 2–4-note slurs
Piano: 3-voice texture; moves in quarter notes; parallel motion in 4ths & 5ths suggests the period of the text; prelude and two interludes total 19 meas. of the 50-meas. song
Diff: text 14th-century English; composer includes trans. and pronunciations of several words
Uses: for someone interested in texts from this era

JOHNS, CLAYTON
(b. New Castle, DE, 1857; d. Boston, MA, 1932)

1341. **IF LOVE WERE NOT** (Florence Earle Coates). [5].
D♭maj; e♭'–g♭"; Tess-M; 4/4, Lento; 3pp; Diff-V/me,
P/e.
For: any high voice; many mezzo-sopranos
Mood: somewhat sentimental description of the absence of
love; nature imagery
Voice: mostly conjunct motion; a few large intervals
Piano: chordal; much parallel motion in an impressionistic
style; some accidentals; mostly doubles vocal line
Uses: could be good for young singers

1342. **NINE SONGS, OP. 20.** For High Voice. Boston Music
Co., 1896. Reprint: Recital Publications, 1986. Separate
entries below.

NOTE: Although this entire opus could be sung by a lyric
tenor, this would not seem the intent or best use of the set (some
songs are also suitable for other voices); songs vary
considerably in quality of text and music; the last two, in
particular, seem out of place with the others.

A. **PRINCESS PRETTY EYES** (Thomas D. Lister).
Gmaj; b(d')–g"; Tess-mH; 4/4, Un poco vivace; 4pp;
Diff-V/m, P/me.
For: tenor
Mood: lyrical love song
Voice: stepwise and easy skips; easy rhythms; undulating
phrases, some ascending to g", some descending; lyrical
and flowing; 2-note slurs; several scalar melismas
Piano: chordal-linear combination; little chromaticism;
melodic passages; considerable doubling of vocal line
Uses: charming period piece

B. **A BRIDAL MEASURE** (Thomas Bailey Aldrich).
A♭maj; e♭'–a♭"; Tess-M; 4/4, Poco vivace; 3pp;
Diff-V/me, P/e.
For: tenor; soprano
Mood: lyrical; in praise of Flora; nature imagery
Voice: stepwise and skips along chord lines; easy rhythms;
lyrical and flowing; a few 2-note slurs
Piano: chordal; melody in interlude and postlude; generally
doubles vocal line
Uses: charming period piece

C. **WHEN TO HER LUTE CORINNA SINGS** (words
from Campion and Rossiter's *Book of Airs*, 1601).
Gmaj; d'–g"; Tess-M; 6/8, Moderato con moto; 2pp;
Diff-V/e, P/me.
For: tenor
Mood: lyrical love song
Voice: stepwise with only a few easy skips; some
chromaticism; lyrical and flowing; a few 2-note slurs
Piano: chordal-linear combination; a little chromaticism;
4-voice texture; reminiscent of a lute-song; doubles
vocal line
Uses: useful for recital, perhaps in group of "modern" settings
of Campion's airs

D. **MY TRUE LOVE** (Florence Earle Coates). Dmaj;
a(d')–f♯"; Tess-M; 6/8, Vivace; 3pp; Diff-V/e, P/e.
For: tenor
Mood: lyrical love song
Voice: stepwise and easy skips; easy rhythms; lyrical and
flowing; a few 2-note slurs
Piano: chordal and linear; melody in prelude and interlude;
supports vocal line strongly; some doubling
Uses: possible recital material

E. **IN AUTUMN** (Frank Walcott Hutt). Amaj; c♯'–a";
Tess-M; 6/8, Vivace molto; 3pp; Diff-V/me, P/me.
For: tenor; soprano
Mood: lyrical song about nature
Voice: stepwise and skips along chord lines; dotted rhythms;
2-note slurs
Piano: chordal-linear combination; little chromaticism;
melody in prelude, interlude, and postlude; generally
doubles vocal line
Uses: charming period piece

F. **AN OLD RHYME** (Robert Herrick). E♭maj; d'–e♭";
Tess-mL; 3/4, Lento molto; 2pp; Diff-V/me, P/e.
For: any high or medium voice
Mood: lyrical love song
Voice: stepwise and small skips; leaps of dim.5th and m7th; a
few chromatic notes; lyrical, flowing, delicate; 2-note
slurs; 3 vs. 2 in piano
Piano: syncopated r.h. chords over sustained l.h. 8ves; little
chromaticism; considerable doubling of vocal line
Uses: charming period piece

G. **MORNING** (Emily Dickinson). D♭maj; c'–f ";
Tess-M; 4/4, 3/4, Moderato con moto; 2pp; Diff-V/m,
P/me.
For: tenor; soprano
Mood: lyrical and philosophical
Voice: stepwise and small skips; several tritones; some
chromaticism; lyrical and flowing; syllabic
Piano: l.h. bass line and countermelody with r.h. afterbeat
chords; somewhat chromatic; supports vocal line well
Uses: possible recital material

H. **THE SUNFLOWER** (anon.). Dmaj; d'–f♯"; Tess-M;
6/8, Poco vivace; 3pp; Diff-V/me, P/me.
For: tenor; soprano
Mood: sentimental nature scene
Voice: stepwise and easy skips; one m7th leap; a few
chromatic notes; dotted rhythms; a few 2-note slurs
Piano: chordal-linear combination; countermelody; some
chromaticism; dotted rhythms; supports vocal line
strongly; incidental doubling
Uses: period piece

I. **THE ROSEBUD** (anon.). E♭maj; c'–f "; Tess-M; 3/4,
Lento; 3pp; Diff-V/me, P/e.
For: tenor
Mood: sentimental love song
Voice: stepwise and easy skips; a few chromatic notes; lyrical
and flowing; syllabic
Piano: chordal–block, repeated, and one rolled; melody in
prelude, interlude, and postlude; doubles or supports
vocal line

Uses: period piece

JOHNSON, D. WAYNE
(b. Minneapolis, MN, 1926)

1343. **THREE ASPECTS OF JOY.** Leyerle Publications, 1982. Tonal; a–g"; Tess-M; traditional meters; various tempos; 14pp; Diff-V/md, P/md.
For: mezzo-soprano
Mood: joy of life, including joy of love
Voice: predominantly stepwise motion with small skips; some large leaps (e.g., M9th & 10th); many accidentals; some rhythmic complications in (a.) & (c.); syncopation; a few triplet subdivisions of beat; speech-like rhythms in (c.); predominantly syllabic
Piano: block and broken-chord patterning; some countermelody; many accidentals (no key sigs.); syncopation; (b.), asymmetrical division of 4/4 meter (3+3+2); (c.), needs large reach in r.h.; each song has prelude and interlude(s), (b.), postlude; little doubling of vocal line
Diff: (b.), polyrhythms created by asymmetrical groupings in piano; (c.), rhythms and dramatic dynamics
Uses: as a group

    a. *Poem* (Robert Bly). D-centered; a–g"; 4/4, 4/8, 6/8, ♩= 66; 4pp.
    b. *The Rain* (Robert Creeley). C-centered; d♭'–f"; 4/4, ♩= 138; 5pp.
    c. *An Aspect of Love* (Gwendolyn Brooks). X; d'–g"; 4/4 with some changes, ♩= ca.50; 5pp.

JOHNSTON, JACK
(b. Milwaukee, WI, 1935)

[See Appendix for songs with French texts]

1344. **DIVERSE VOICES OF HERRICK** for Medium Voice and Piano (Robert Herrick). Leyerle, 1986. cmp1986. Varied tonal centers; f–g"; Tess-mL-mH; mostly regular meters, some irregular with changes; varied tempos; 17+min; Diff-V/d, P/dd.
For: mezzo-soprano; baritone
Mood: philosophical; various voices of prayer and of love
Voice: much conjunct motion; many 8ve leaps; some tritones; other skips generally small and/or easy to hear; chromatic; considerable use of repeated-note passages or static phrases moving in a very limited range; almost entirely syllabic; a few 2-note slurs and one small melisma in (i.); rhythms generally easy; both loud and soft high tones; numerous recit.-like passages
Piano: chiefly chordal–block, broken, and afterbeat; patterned; linear material often rapid scalar passages, single line or 3rds; dissonant "bell-tone" chords in (b.); countermelodies in (d.); rapid broken 8ves in (c.) & (h.); grace notes in (i.); triplets and sextuplets; large reach helpful; independent of vocal line
Diff: entire cycle requires vocal endurance because of length and variable tessitura; requires easy production and control of low voice; needs excellent interpreter to

Uses: capture the various "voices"; ensemble requires care excellent recital material for advanced students or professionals; various "mini-cycles" could be selected from complete set to solve tessitura problems; entire cycle might be more effective shared by two singers, male and female

    a. *His Prayer For Absolution* (The Poet's Voice: Upper-class Oxonian). A-centered; c'–f"; Tess-M; 2/4, 4/4, 6/4, Fervently (♩= ca.56); 1+min.
    b. *The Bell-Man* (The Bell-man's Voice: North British). B♭-centered; b♭–f"; Tess-mL; 4/4, Slow and mysterious; 2+min.
    c. *The Frozen Heart* (The Voice of Callow Youth: Standard British). E♭-centered; e♭'–f"; Tess-M; 2/4, Fast and excited; 1min.
    d. *To Anthea* (The Voice of Experience: Standard British). E♭-centered; d'–g♭"; Tess-mH; 3/4, A piacere–Waltz-romance (in 3); 2min.
    e. *To His Mistresses* (The Voice of Decrepitude: London Cockney). X; f–f♯"; Tess-M; 3/4, 4/4, 6/4, A piacere ma sotto voce (decrepitly)–Slow and tremulous; 2min.
    f. *Grace for a Child* (A Pious Voice: Scots). D-centered; d'–e"; Tess-mL; 2/4, 3½/4, Simply (not loudly); 1min.
    g. *To Keep a True Lent* (The Voice of Rebuke: Irish Priest). F-centered; c'–f"; Tess-M; 2/4, 3/4, 4/4, 5/4, Fast and furious; 1min.
    h. *His Creed* (A Postulant's Voice: Youthful, educated). X; c'–f"; Tess-M; 4/4, 5/4, Fast as a penance; 1+min.
    i. *A Thanksgiving to God, for His House* (The Voice of Contentment: North British). B♭-centered; c'–g"; Tess-M; 4/4, 9/8, 12/8, 6/8, Leisurely; 4+min.
    j. *To God* (The Poet's Voice Again). A-centered; a–f"; Tess-M; 2/4, 4/4, Come prima; 2+min.

JONES, MARJORIE
(b. Portland, OR; d. 1998)

1345. **FOUR SHORT SOLOS** (Adelaide Crapsey). Gentry, 1971 (Theodore Presser). Tertian, quartal, and quintal harmonies; c♯'–e"; Tess-M; traditional meters; 4pp; Diff-V/e, P/e.
For: any medium voice
Mood: life and death
Voice: stepwise and small skips; uncomplicated rhythms
Piano: predominantly 4-voice block chords; doubling of vocal line incidental
Uses: for beginning singer with some maturity (not young singer); songs vocally and musically easy; poems need mature understanding

    a. *On Seeing Weather-Beaten Trees.* B♭-Fmaj; e♭'–d"; 4/4, Gently; 1p.
    b. *November Night.* Emaj; c♯'–c♯"; 4/4, Clear and clean; 10meas.
    c. *Triad.* G-centered; d'–d"; 4/4, Moderato; 10meas.
    d. *Little Sister Rose-Marie.* Emaj; e'–e"; 4/4, Brightly; 2pp.

JORDAN, ALICE
(b. Davenport, IA, 1916; d. 1999?)

1346. TAKE JOY HOME (Jean Ingelow). Heritage Music Press, Roger Dean Publishing, 1983. "For Sherrill Milnes." Fmaj; c'–f"; Tess-mH; 4/4, 3/4, Freely, with warmth and breadth of style; 4pp; Diff-V/me, P/md.
For: mezzo-soprano; soprano; baritone; some tenors
Mood: optimistic; joyful; somewhat religious
Voice: many small skips; several 8ve leaps; easy rhythms; a few triplets; mostly syllabic with a few 2-note slurs; ends on sustained f" (10 beats)
Piano: repeated chords in triplets; some duplet broken-chord patterning; some 8ve passages in l.h., one in r.h.; accidentals; does not double vocal line; has big, dramatic ending; 4-meas. prelude
Diff: tessitura for young baritone and some young mezzo-sopranos
Uses: group or recital ender; probably best in a religiously-focused group; could be used in church; will show off good high notes (eb" and f")

JORDAN, JULES
(b. Willimantic, CT, 1850; d. Providence, RI, 1927)

1347. DAFFODILS. G. Schirmer, 1887. Cmaj; a–e"; Tess-M-H; 9/8, 3/4, 4/4, Andantino; 5pp; Diff-V/me, P/me.
For: baritone; mezzo-soprano
Mood: sprightly; tribute to spring
Voice: stepwise and small skips; some dotted rhythms; several accidentals; 2-note slurs
Piano: chordal; some syncopation; rhythmic figure of trumpet call; some doubling of vocal line
Uses: period piece; in a group of earlier American songs

KAGEN, SERGIUS
(b. St. Petersburg, Russia, 1909; d. New York, NY, 1964)

1348. ALL DAY I HEAR (James Joyce). Weintraub, 1950. Ab-centered; f'–f#"; Tess-M; 4/4, Agitato; 1+min; Diff-V/m, P/m-d.
For: soprano; tenor
Mood: intense; dark; somber
Voice: stepwise and small skips; some syncopation
Piano: animated broken chords, l.h.; r.h. chords and simplified version of vocal melody
Uses: effective song; see also setting by Persichetti

1349. BECAUSE I COULD NOT STOP FOR DEATH (Emily Dickinson). Leeds, 1951. X; c'–f"; Tess-M-L; 4/4 with changes, Andante; 2+min; Diff-V/md, P/m.
For: soprano; mezzo-soprano; tenor; high baritone
Mood: somber; intense; unrelenting
Voice: many skips; accidentals; dotted rhythms; syncopation; phrases spaced apart
Piano: two sections: first, broken 8ves and many accidentals; second, sustained chords and staccato broken chords
Diff: rhythms; angular vocal line
Uses: within a group; quiet ending; see also Copland setting

1350. DRUM (Langston Hughes). Mercury, 1954. X on G; bb–eb"; Tess-mL; 2/2, Allegro; 3pp; Diff-V/m, P/me.
For: any medium or low voice
Mood: philosophical
Voice: rather disjunct; large and difficult leaps; some chromaticism; march-like
Piano: chordal texture; staccato bass, imitating drum
Diff: pitches
Uses: recital possibilities; useful for good musician with limited upper notes

1351. I'M NOBODY (Emily Dickinson). Weintraub, 1950. "To Mme. Povla Frijsh" B-centered (bitonal); d'–g"; Tess-mH; 3/4 with changes, With humor; 1min; Diff-V/m, P/m.
For: soprano
Mood: humorous; straightforward
Voice: many skips; fragmentary phrases; speech rhythms; tritones
Piano: linear; thin texture; staccato; medium and high registers; incidental doubling of vocal line
Diff: final phrase descends g"–d'; ensemble
Uses: good short song

1352. I THINK I COULD TURN (Walt Whitman). Mercury, 1952. X; A–d'; Tess-M; 4/4, 3/4, 2/4, 5/8, Slowly and heavily; 4pp; Diff-V/d, P/d.
For: bass
Mood: philosophical
Voice: generally parlando; many repeated notes; 16th-note movement; triplets; fragmented; some large intervals
Piano: 2-voice texture; moving 8ths in bass; dotted rhythms and syncopation in treble
Diff: pitch; rhythm; text
Uses: good bass song; recital material

1353. A JUNE DAY (Sara Teasdale). Weintraub, 1950. X (bitonal); f#'–bb"(a"); Tess-M-H; 3/8, Gently, not too slowly; 2pp; Diff-V/md, P/md.
For: soprano (lyric or coloratura)
Mood: descriptive; nostalgic
Voice: many skips; high soft sustained tones; some rhythmic complexities
Piano: chordal; block chords with countermelody; rapid notes resemble bird song; high and middle registers of piano
Diff: some awkward pitches; dynamic control
Uses: useful song for a high light voice

1354. LET IT BE FORGOTTEN (Sara Teasdale). Weintraub, 1950. B-centered; f'–f"; Tess-M; 2/2, 3/2, Andante; 1+min; Diff-V/me, P/e.
For: tenor; soprano; mezzo-soprano
Mood: quiet; subdued; time obliterates
Voice: conjunct; easy, repetitive rhythms; interrupted phrases; some triplets
Piano: chordal; many accidentals; outlines melody
Diff: irregular meter and phrase lengths
Uses: effective quiet song

1355. LONDON (William Blake). Mercury, 1954. "To Mack Harrell." X; b–f"; Tess-M; 3/2 with changes, Andante; 3pp; Diff-V/m, P/me.

For: mezzo-soprano; baritone
Mood: philosophical; pessimistic
Voice: fairly disjunct; some large leaps; generally quarter-note motion; chromatic
Piano: quarter-note movement in parallel 8ves in bass at beginning and end, otherwise 4-voice chordal texture; chromatic
Diff: pitches
Uses: possible recital piece

1356. **MAG** (Carl Sandburg). Weintraub, 1950. Bitonal; B♭–e'; Tess-mH; 4/4 with changes, Slowly and heavily; 2+min; Diff-V/d, P/m.
For: baritone (dramatic)
Mood: dramatic; bitter; intense
Voice: declamatory; complicated speech-like rhythms; many small skips
Piano: chordal; quarter-note 8ves & 7ths in l.h.; chords in r.h.
Diff: rhythms; e' a featured note
Uses: powerful song for a big, dramatic voice

1357. **MAYBE** (Carl Sandburg). Weintraub, 1950. Cmaj; d'–g"; Tess-M; 4/4 with changes, With great simplicity; 1+min; Diff-V/m, P/e.
For: soprano
Mood: uncertainty; lyrical; subdued
Voice: stepwise and small skips; speech rhythms; triplets and duplets; syncopation
Piano: 2–4-voice block-chordal texture; incidental doubling of vocal line; spare texture
Diff: rhythm
Uses: soft ending; interior of group

1358. **MEMORY, HITHER COME** (William Blake). Mercury, 1952. X; d'–f♯"; Tess-M; 4/4 with changes, Leisurely; 2pp; Diff-V/m, P/m-e.
For: soprano; tenor
Mood: lyrical; serene; somewhat wispy
Voice: stepwise and easy skips; irregular phrase lengths; speech rhythms; duplets and triplets
Piano: linear; very thin texture; repetitive; many accidentals; does not double vocal line
Diff: changing meters; irregular phrase lengths; ensemble

1359. **MISS T** (Walter de la Mare). Weintraub, 1950. E-centered; e'–e"; Tess-M; 2/4, Allegretto; 2pp; Diff-V/me, P/me.
For: all voices except very low
Mood: humorous
Voice: skips; repetitive; simple tune over mildly dissonant accomp.; speech rhythms
Piano: chordal; syncopated afterbeat pattern
Uses: attractive humorous song; good for a young singer

1360. **3 SATIRES.** Mercury, 1956. X (predominance of m2nds); a–e"; Tess-cs; regular and changing meters; varied tempos; 8pp; Diff-V/md, P/m.
For: baritone; mezzo-soprano
Mood: satirical
Voice: often disjunct vocal line emphasizes dissonance of 2nds & 7ths; speech rhythms
Piano: emphasis on m2nds; some rhythmic irregularities;

fairly thin texture
Diff: pitch
Uses: good for ear-training; humorous texts

a. *Persons of Intelligence and Culture* (Louis MacNeice). a–e"; 2/4, 3/4, Leisurely–In a manner of a music hall artist; 3pp.
b. *Yonder See the Morning Blink* (A. E. Housman). d'–e"; 4/4, 2/4, 3/4, 5/4, Slowly; 2pp.
c. *How Pleasant It Is to Have Money* (Arthur Hugh Clough). c'–e"; 2/4, 3/4, Andantino–Tempo di valzer; 3pp.

1361. **UPSTREAM** (Carl Sandburg). Weintraub, 1950. X; c♯'–f"; Tess-M; changing meters, Maestoso; 2pp; Diff-V/md, P/m.
For: high baritone; robust tenor
Mood: dramatic; robust; strong
Voice: many skips; accidentals; declamatory; speech rhythms
Piano: 4–6-voice chordal texture; outlines voice part; double 8ves throughout
Diff: changing meters; dynamic control
Uses: good song in dramatic style; group opener or closer; encore; see also setting by Dougherty

KALMANOFF, MARTIN
(b. Brooklyn, NY, 1920)

1362. **GEORGE WASHINGTON COMES TO DINNER** (adapted from George Washington). Carl Fischer, 1950. Cmaj; b–f"(g"); Tess-M-H; 4/4, Allegro (quaintly, but with veneration); 10pp; Diff-V/md, P/md.
For: baritone; mezzo-soprano; some sopranos
Mood: humorous (from *Rules of Civility and Decent Behaviour in Company and Conversation*)
Voice: many skips and melismas; humming; trill; much sequence
Piano: chordal-linear combination; Alberti bass; sectional mood changes; some doubling of vocal line; reminiscent of Handel, Haydn, and Mozart
Diff: long phrases; breathing; dynamics; agility
Uses: good program ender; could stand alone

1363. **TWENTIETH CENTURY** (Robert Hillyer). [17]. H & L keys: Cmaj & A♭maj; e'–g" & c'–e♭"; Tess-M; 2/2, Allegro furioso e strepitoso–Moderato; 3pp; Diff-V/m, P/md.
For: all voices except very low
Mood: agitated; philosophical; commentary on modern life
Voice: phrases broken by rests, giving a hurried, staccato effect
Piano: afterbeats; chromatic arpeggiations in middle section
Diff: rapid delivery
Uses: good fast song to close a group; encore; could open a group about modern life

KEELE, ROGER S.
(b. Minneapolis, MN, 1954)

1364. **THREE BRITISH POEMS** for Baritone and Piano.

Classical Vocal Reprints, 2000. cmp1993. Tonal; A–f';
Tess-M-mH; regular meters; slow tempos; 13+min;
Diff-V/m-md, P/m-d.

For: baritone
Mood: somber; death poems
Voice: combination of chant-like phrases on single notes and
more melodic phrases of larger range and intervals;
some speaking; some *Sprechstimme*; glissandos; mostly
uncomplicated rhythms; triplets and double-dotted
figures; trills in (a.); *ff* phrases on d♯' and e♯' in (c.)
Piano: (a.) linear; quasi-Baroque style giving way to more
modern jazz-like harmonic style; trills; scalar
flourishes; polyrhythms; (b.) block chords in quiet
repeated pattern; harmonically reminiscent of Poulenc;
some whole-tone coloration at end; (c.) a classic Bolero
in slow 3; repeated pitches "d" or "a" throughout until
key shift of final section; some thick chords; forearm
and palm cluster-chord glissandos; forceful ending;
some doubling of vocal line within chordal texture
Diff: vocal trills; various vocal techniques; length and
intensity of (c.); l.h. Bolero pattern could be taxing;
balance in (c.)
Uses: excellent set for mature performers; variety of mood
and musical treatment of the poems attractive

    a. *Do Not Go Gentle into That Good Night* (Dylan
       Thomas). E-centered; B–f'; Tess-M-mH; 4/4, 3/4,
       2/4, 5/4, Andante; 4min (7pp).
    b. *Fragment* (Wilfred Owen). Tonal, some whole-
       tone harmonies; d♭–e'; Tess-mH; 4/2, 3/2, 6/2, 4/4,
       Seductively slow, with a certain detachment of
       emotion ♩ = 63; 3min (2pp).
    c. *Titanic!* (The Convergence of the Twain-Lines on
       the Loss of the Titanic) (Thomas Hardy). Gmin-
       G♯; A–e♯'; Tess-M-mH; 3/4, Tempo di Bolero
       (slow 3); 7min (15pp).

KELLEY, EDGAR STILLMAN
(b. Sparta, WI, 1857; d. New York, NY, 1944)

1365. **ELDORADO,** Op. 8, No.1 (Edgar Allan Poe). [48, 66,
vol. 1]. cmp1891. H & L keys: Gmaj-Emin-Bmin &
Emaj-C♯min-G♯min; e'–g" & c♯'–e"; Tess-M; 4/4,
Allegro con spirito; 3+min; Diff-V/m, P/d.
For: baritone; tenor
Mood: dramatic; narrative; exciting
Voice: scalar and chordal intervals; easy rhythms
Piano: fast, repeated 8ves and chords, afterbeat style; some
countermelody; cross-hands; exciting and colorful
Diff: voice in simple meter while piano has a triplet-pattern
background; wide dynamic range needed; ballad style
Uses: effective song when well done; good for teaching
ballad style and characterization
Rec: D#48

1366. **ISRAFEL,** Op. 8, No.2 (Edgar Allan Poe). [66, vol. 1].
cmp1891. A♭maj (but unstable and modulating);
d♯'–g"; Tess-M; 6/4, 4/4, Lento (with 2 faster sections);
99meas.; Diff-V/m, P/d.
For: tenor; soprano
Mood: dramatic; lyrical sections

Voice: scalar or chordal intervals
Piano: chordal–arpeggiated, broken, and double-broken;
tremolo
Diff: sectional construction; dynamics; intense soft singing
Uses: effective teaching song for above characteristics

KENDRICK, VIRGINIA
(b. Minneapolis, MN, 1910)

1367. **APRIL WHIMSY** (Virginia Kendrick). Privately pub.,
1979; available from Schmitt Music Centers. Gmaj;
d'–e"(f♯"); Tess-M; 4/4; 3pp; Diff-V/m, P/m.
For: light soprano
Mood: joyous; welcomes springtime
Voice: stepwise and small skips; needs some flexibility for
16th notes; some 2-note slurs; easy rhythms
Piano: block- and broken-chord patterning; accidentals;
doubling of vocal line incidental
Uses: for a young singer

1368. **FROM MY WINDOW** (Virginia Kendrick). Fox,
1960. Emin; d'–f"(g"); Tess-M or mL (depending on
pitch options taken); 4/4, Moderato; 4pp; Diff-V/m,
P/m.
For: soprano; tenor; text better for woman
Mood: wakeful spring night poem
Voice: stepwise and easy skips; some syncopation; repetitive
rhythms
Piano: chordal–syncopated, repeated, and broken; counter-
melody; many accidentals; some doubling of vocal line
Uses: good song

1369. **HUSH LITTLE DAVID** (Lullaby for a Teething
Baby) (Virginia Kendrick). Privately pub., 1979;
available from Schmitt Music Centers. E♭maj; c'–d♭";
Tess-mL; 4/4, 2/4; 3pp; Diff-V/me, P/me.
For: any voice in this range
Mood: lullaby; quiet and soothing
Voice: fairly conjunct; a few accidentals; uncomplicated
rhythms; a few dotted notes; several fermatas; 2 meas.
of humming; mostly syllabic
Piano: block chords; bass line sometimes doubles or outlines
the melody; accidentals; three key changes
Diff: soft dynamics throughout
Uses: a "different" lullaby; nice for a change of pace

1370. **JADE SUMMER** (Virginia Kendrick). Schmitt, 1972.
X; highly chromatic, some bitonality; e'–d♯"; Tess-M;
6/8 with changes; 2min; Diff-V/m, P/md.
For: medium voice specified
Mood: descriptive of nature scene; lyrical
Voice: smooth conjunct line; many accidentals; supported
harmonically by piano but not doubled
Piano: chordal texture; many accidentals; uses dove-call as
repeated motive
Diff: reading and relating many accidentals
Uses: good for short-ranged singers; use in a group of
summer songs, nature songs, or seasonal songs; also
has opt. harp accomp.

1371. **WHITE SKY** (Virginia Kendrick). J. Fischer, 1972.

X-Dmaj-X; e'–g♯"; Tess-mH; 3/4, 2/4, 4/4, Almost free time; 2pp; Diff-V/md, P/m.

For: soprano; mezzo-soprano
Mood: lyrical; wintery spring night scene
Voice: skips and leaps; soft singing; much head voice
Piano: "frosty" chord clusters in treble clef; very free; quiet; accidentals
Diff: some pitches hard to hear; soft singing
Uses: very good song; a different view of spring; light lyric voice best; interior of group

KENNEDY, JOHN BRODBIN
(b. New York, NY, 1934)

1381. APRIL AND MAY (2 songs) (Samuel Menashe). Boosey & Hawkes, 1972. Major keys; c'–a"(g"); Tess-mH; regular meters; contrasting tempos; 3min; Diff-V/m, P/e-m.

For: soprano; tenor
Mood: lyrical; exuberant; spring song
Voice: scalar and chordal intervals; some leaps; syncopation; 2–7-note slurs; duplets and triplets
Piano: chordal; many 2nds & 7ths; scale passages; imitation of vocal line; thin texture; does not double vocal line
Diff: good register control for large leaps
Uses: use as a pair

    a. *April.* B♭maj; g'–a"(g"); 2/2, Gently lyric; 1+min.
    b. *May.* B♭maj; c'–a"(g"); 2/2, Gay and perky; 1+min.

1382. BROKEN DIALOG (Jean Garrigue). Boosey & Hawkes, 1966. "To Beverly Wolff." X-Cmin; e♭'–b♭"; Tess-mH-H; 6/2 with changes, Moderato; 2+min; Diff-V/d, P/d.

For: soprano; tenor
Mood: lyrical; somber; farewell
Voice: stepwise and small skips; many leaps of 7th; slurs; long, sustained phrases
Piano: linear; imitative; covers the keyboard; perpetual motion; does not double vocal line
Diff: long phrases; ensemble; triplets vs. piano duplets
Uses: effective for capable performers

KERR, HARRISON
(b. Cleveland, OH, 1897; d. Norman, OK, 1978)

1383. CAROL ON A FIFTEENTH-CENTURY TEXT ("He came all so still . .."). Conatus, 1975. cmp1940. Dissonant; f'–e"; Tess-M; 6/8 with changes, Tranquillamente ma con affetto; 3pp; Diff-V/me, P/e.

For: all voices
Mood: lyrical
Voice: conjunct; limited range
Piano: thin linear texture; rocking rhythmic figure; 2 vs. 3
Diff: rhythmic figures
Uses: another setting of a familiar text

1384. THE RUBÁIYAT OF OMAR KHAYYÁM (FitzGerald trans.). Cycle. Conatus, 1975. cmp1919. Traditional keys (with some occasional slight

dissonance); B–f♯'; Tess-M-mH; regular meters; moderate tempos; 6pp; Diff-V/m, P/m.

For: baritone with easy e' and f'
Mood: lyrical; melancholy; fleeting nature of life
Voice: spacious character, like a romantic solo cello line; sustained; some leaps
Piano: chordal texture; parallelism; simple movement; wide reach helpful
Diff: climactic and sustained high tone
Uses: good short work for lyric baritone with beautiful sound and easy top voice

    a. *Ah, Love!* Dmin; c♯–f'; 2/2; 2pp.
    b. *Yon Rising Moon.* Gmin–Dmaj; B–f♯'; 4/4, Scorrendo; 2pp.
    c. *When You and I.* Fmin; c–f'; 4/4, Andante; 2pp.

1385. SIX SONGS FOR VOICE AND PIANO TO POEMS BY ADELAIDE CRAPSEY. Cycle. Marks, 1952. Traditional keys (with many altered chords and dissonances); c♯'–a"; Tess-M-mH; mostly regular but changing meters; moderate to slow tempos; 6pp; Diff-V/md, P/md.

For: light lyric soprano
Mood: lyrical; grieving; anticipation of death (see titles)
Voice: conjunct; some skips and leaps; delicate; numerous soft high tones
Piano: chordal; arpeggiated figurations; melodic material; dissonant; delicate; atmospheric
Diff: pitch perception; interpretation of fragile moods of poetry
Uses: excellent short cycle for light soprano with good ear and poetic understanding; quiet

    a. *Triolet.* B♭min; f'–f"; Tess-M; 4/4, Con lenezza e sempre *p*; 1p; (melancholy).
    b. *Old Love.* Emin; d♯'–a"; Tess-M; 4/4, 3/4, 2/4, Moderato; 1p; (ghostly).
    c. *Dirge.* Amin; e'–a"; Tess-M; 4/4, 3/4, 5/4, 3/2, Andante mesto; 1p; (sadness of loss).
    d. *Fate.* F♯min; c♯'–f♯"; Tess-M; 3/4, Andante; 1p; (resignation).
    e. *The Old, Old Winds.* Ends Bmin; g'–a♭"; Tess-mH; 3/4, 5/8, 2/4, 4/4, Moderato; 2pp; (anguish).
    f. *A White Moth Flew.* Amin; a'–f♯"; Tess-mH; 6/8, 3/4, 3/8, 4/4, Andante; 1p; (premonition of death).

1386. THREE SONGS (Edna St. Vincent Millay). Conatus, 1975. cmp1927. Minor tonalities (pervaded with delicate dissonance throughout); c'–g"; Tess-M; regular meters, some irregular and changing; varied tempos; 10pp; Diff-V/md, P/d.

For: soprano
Mood: lyrical; passionate; melancholy; autumnal
Voice: rhythmically fluid; often outlines delicately dissonant chords; wide dynamic range; accidentals
Piano: linear texture; many accidentals; rhythmically intricate; needs light touch; large reach helpful; long trills
Diff: pitch patterns perhaps elusive to novice singer; ensemble will take work; rhythmic intricacies
Uses: good songs; music effectively complements poems with harmonic idiom capturing the poetic moods exquisitely;

excellent group for advanced student

a. *The Death of Autumn.* B♭min; c'–g♭"; 3/4 with changes, Adagio scioltamente; 4pp.
b. *Ebb.* X; f'–g"; 3/4 with changes, Lento; 2pp.
c. *Wild Swans.* Ends Gmin; c♯'–g"; 6/8 with changes, Allegretto; 4pp.

KERR, THOMAS
(b. Baltimore, MD, 1915; d. 1989)

1387. RIDING TO TOWN (Paul Laurence Dunbar). [6]. Dmaj; c'–f♯"; Tess-mL; 6/8, At a convenient, rollicking tempo; 7pp; Diff-V/m, P/d.
For: mezzo-soprano; baritone
Mood: joyous; descriptive; humorous
Voice: swinging dotted rhythms; "tra-la-la" refrain; final phrase lies high, although remainder of song lies in lower part of range; some chromaticism
Piano: quite chromatic; independent of voice; dotted rhythms; staccato
Diff: needs excellent accompanist and good vocal actor
Uses: good student song

KETTERING, EUNICE LEA
(b. Savannah, OH, 1906; d. Albuquerque, NM, 2000)

1388. COMPENSATION (Sara Teasdale). [17]. H & L keys: F♯min & Dmin; d♯'–f♯" & b–d"; Tess-mL; 4/2, ♩=c.60; 2pp; Diff-V/d, P/d.
For: all voices
Mood: lyrical; melancholy; nature imagery
Voice: short phrases, but broad and flowing; fairly chromatic
Piano: chordal; triplet figures; chromatic; some doubling of vocal line
Diff: some pitches; controlling dynamics
Uses: useful for students (short phrases)

KIM, EARL
(b. Dinuba, CA, 1920; d. Cambridge, MA, 1998)

1389. LETTERS FOUND NEAR A SUICIDE (Frank Horne). [49]. X; b♭–g"; Tess-mL; 3/4 with changes, Lento (♩=c.48); 8pp; Diff-V/dd, P/dd.
For: mezzo-soprano; tenor; high baritone
Mood: dramatic; philosophical; morbid
Voice: disjunct; highly chromatic; fragmented; melismas in complex rhythms
Piano: chromatic; fragmented; complex rhythms; trills; grace notes; pedal effects
Diff: frequent meter changes; pitches; rhythms
Uses: can be dramatic and effective for mature performers

KIMBELL, MICHAEL A.
(b. Glen Cove, NY, 1946)

1390. THREE SONNETS FROM THE PORTUGUESE (Elizabeth Barrett Browning). Michael and Edith Kimbell, Music Publishers (ASCAP), 2000. Tonal; c'–a"; Tess-M-mH; changing meters; varied tempos (♩=84–108); 14pp; Diff-V/m-md, P/m.
For: soprano
Mood: gentle and luminous; the love of another that awakens one to life
Voice: lyric recitative and sustained melody; speech rhythms; motion and direction of vocal line reflect inner emotions and meaning of text; some wide-ranged phrases; two songs unmetered
Piano: mostly chordal; some linear; various figurations; delicate dissonance; harmonic substance and motion expressive of inner emotions of text; many accidentals; some chord clusters
Diff: some pitches; dissonance; some rhythms
Uses: effective set for advanced undergraduate or graduate soprano seeking 20th-century songs

a. *When Our Two Souls.* E♭; c'–a"; Tess-M-mH; 3/4, 5/4, 2/4, Moderato ♩=108; 5pp.
b. *I Lived with Visions.* D-centered; d♭'–g"; Tess-M-mH; unmetered; 4pp.
c. *Beloved, Thou Hast Brought Me Many Flowers.* Tonal; e♭'–g♯"; Tess-M-mH; unmetered, Andante con moto ♩=84; 5pp.

KING, BETTY JACKSON
(b. Chicago, IL, 1928; d. 1994)

1391. IN THE SPRINGTIME (William Shakespeare). [10]. cmp1976. E♭maj-Emaj; e♭'–e"; Tess-M; 3/4, Tenderly; 4pp; Diff-V/me, P/me.
For: any high or medium voice
Mood: joyous song of love in springtime; well-known text
Voice: characterized by 8ve leaps upward; some 4ths & 5ths
Piano: chordal; broken 8ves and chords; contrapuntal figuration; melodic material; doubles vocal line, except for final two phrases
Diff: 8ve leaps
Uses: useful setting of this text for young singers; could be used for teaching 8ve intervals

KINGSFORD, CHARLES [Charles Cohen]
(b. Brooklyn, NY, 1907; d. 1996)

1392. DOWN HARLEY STREET (Benjamin Musser). [20, 38]; 1st©1942. Cmaj; c'–d"; Tess-mL; 6/8, Allegretto (♩.=c.60); 2pp; Diff-V/e, P/me.
For: any medium voice
Mood: light; humorous; descriptive
Voice: light and dancing; folk-like; swinging 6/8 rhythms
Piano: chordal, punctuated by rests; dance-like
Diff: opt. whistling in final two measures
Uses: "fun" song for students; recital possibilities

1393. WALL-PAPER (for a little girl's room). (Raymond Dresensky). [48]; 1st©1937. H & L keys: Fmaj & E♭maj; c'–g" & b♭–f"; Tess-M; 2/2, With lilt; 3pp; Diff-V/e, P/me.
For: any female voice

Mood: descriptive; cute
Voice: simple and bouncing, like a children's song; several "quasi recit." sections
Piano: chordal; supports voice
Uses: useful for a young girl

KIRCHNER, LEON
(b. Brooklyn, NY, 1919)

1385. THE TWILIGHT STOOD (Emily Dickinson). Song Cycle for Soprano and Piano. Associated Music Publishers, 1987. X (built on scale of alternating half and whole steps); f♯–d'''; Tess-cs, H, HH; constantly changing meters, ♪ = 60–♩ = 108; 18pp; Diff-V/dd, P/dd.
For: soprano (with extremely wide range and perfect pitch)
Mood: dark; violent; Dickinson's more pessimistic poems
Voice: disjunct; non-melodic; instrumentally conceived; extremely wide range; unusually high tessitura in many phrases; rhythmic groupings difficult with words; some wordless melismas
Piano: totally dissonant; see Kirchner's *Piano Sonata* for his general style
Diff: difficult in every way; voice merely a line with words in the overall texture; difficult poems; perfect pitch highly desirable; unrelieved dissonance; four songs connected to next song
Uses: musical and vocal challenge for virtuoso performers

    a. *The Auctioneer.* X; d'–d'''; Tess-cs, H; changing meters, ♩ = 100; 3pp.
    b. *He Scanned It.* X; f♯–c'''; Tess-cs, H; changing meters, ♩ = 60; 3pp.
    c. *The Crickets Sang.* X; a–d'''; Tess-L, H; changing meters, ♪ = 126; 5pp.
    d. *Partake As Doth the Bee.* X; c'–b''; Tess-cs; 3/4, ♪ = 60; 1p.
    e. *Much Madness.* X; b–b♭''; Tess-cs; changing meters, ♩ = 52; 2pp.
    f. *There Came a Wind (Coda).* X; e♭'–d'''; Tess-H-HH; changing meters, changing tempos (♩ = 108–69–96); 4pp.

KIRK, THERON
(b. Alamo, TX, 1919; d. San Antonio, TX, 1999)

1386. I CAN'T BE TALKIN' OF LOVE (Esther Mathews). [12]. Gmin; c'–d''; Tess-mL; 4/4, Andante (♩ = 100); 3pp; Diff-V/me, P/me.
For: any medium or low voice
Mood: whimsical love song
Voice: conjunct; modest intervals; triplets
Piano: continuous triplet figures; a few chords
Diff: lowered 7th scale step; words fit melody somewhat awkwardly in places
Uses: for a young singer; see also setting by J. Duke

1387. AN OLD PERSON OF DOVER (Edward Lear). [12]. Emin; e'–d''; Tess-M; 4/4, 3/4, Largo (♩ = 48); 2pp; Diff-V/me, P/e.

For: any medium voice
Mood: humorously descriptive; a "politically-correct" limerick
Voice: conjunct motion; a few intervals; many triplets
Piano: broken chord figures in triplets throughout
Diff: some pitches; switching between triplet and syncopated duplet rhythms in vocal line
Uses: good humorous song for a program

1388. PRAYERS FROM THE ARK (Carmen Bernos de Gastold; trans. Rumer Godden). Song Cycle for Soprano, Tenor, and Bass-baritone with Piano or Orchestra. Hinshaw Music, 1976. Pub. in 3 vols. for soprano, tenor, and bass-baritone, with piano accomp. Tonal and modal (with many altered chords), some parallel harmonies; ranges: sop.: c♯'–b''; ten.: f'–c'''; b-bar.: D–e♭'; Tess-sop.-M; ten.-mH-H; b-bar.-mH; regular meters; varied tempos; 52pp (complete), 45min; Diff-V/m-d, P/m-md.
For: soprano, tenor, and bass-baritone (bass with good top perhaps better in general; no option given for low D)
Mood: lyrical; some dramatic sections; prayers of the various animals in the ark
Voice: syllabic setting; speech-like rhythmic patterns; shape of line follows rise and fall of speech and suits the character of each animal; one trill for the tenor; some spoken passages for the bass-baritone
Piano: great variety of figurations, patterns, and textures; highly descriptive and programmatic–fits the characteristics of each animal very well; needs an accomplished pianist and sensitive musician with an ear for color and responsiveness to the text; good reduction from orchestral score
Diff: few for the soprano; high tessitura, three high c's, and a trill for the tenor; bass-baritone needs a low D and an easy upper range
Uses: different from anything else; a very effective work, whether done as a whole with three singers or as three separate sets or cycles by the individual voices; can be done by advanced students (graduate level); would be excellent vehicle for faculty performance; piano accomp. very effective; only the bass-baritone songs might not work as well alone, as all are slow

I. SONGS FOR SOPRANO, Vol. 1.

    a. *The Prayer of the Little Bird.* Amaj; d'–a''; Tess-M-mH; 4/4, Allegretto; 4pp.
    b. *The Prayer of the Goldfish.* Fmin; c♯'–d♭''; Tess-M-mH; 12/8, Adagio; 4pp.
    c. *The Prayer of the Cat.* Cmaj; d'–f''; Tess-cs; 4/4, Largo; 3pp.
    d. *The Prayer of the Lark.* Amaj; e'–f♯''; Tess-M-mH; 4/4, Allegro molto; 2pp.
    e. *The Prayer of the Butterfly.* Dmaj; f♯'–a''; Tess-mH; 3/4, Tempo di valse con moto rubato; 4pp.
    f. *The Prayer of the Dove.* Dmaj; d'–b''; Tess-mL-M; 4/4, Andante; 4pp.

II. SONGS FOR TENOR, Vol. 2.

    g. *The Prayer of the Monkey.* G♭-centered; f'–g''; Tess-M; 4/4, Allegro giocoso; 3pp.

h. *The Prayer of the Goat.* Fmaj; g'–c'''; Tess-H; 12/8, Allegro impetuoso; 5pp.

i. *The Prayer of the Dog.* X–F; f'–b♭''; Tess-H; 4/4, Moderato; 4pp.

j. *The Prayer of the Lark.* Cmaj; g'–a''; Tess-H; 4/4, Allegro molto; 2pp. [same as sop. title; higher key]

k. *The Prayer of the Cock.* C-centered; g'–c'''(g''); Tess-H; 6/8, Moderato; 3pp.

l. *The Prayer of the Dove.* Fmaj; f'–c'''; Tess- M, H; 4/4, Andante; 4pp. [same as sop. title; higher key]

III.   SONGS FOR BASS-BARITONE, Vol. 3.

m. *Noah's Prayer.* B♭min-centered; F–e♭'; Tess-L, M, H; 4/4, Allegro (with many tempo changes); 5pp.

n. *The Prayer of the Elephant.* X; A–d♭'; Tess-M; 4/4, Largo pesante; 3pp.

o. *The Prayer of the Donkey.* X–D; D–d'; Tess-M; 4/4, Largo sostenuto; 4pp.

p. *The Prayer of the Giraffe.* G-centered; e–d♯'; Tess-mH; 4/4, Allegro deciso; 4pp.

KIRKMAN (JONES), MERLE
(b. Kokomo, IN, 20th Century)

1389.   DEEP WET MOSS (Lew Sarett). Carl Fischer, 1948. cmp1947; Won W. W. Kimball Prize of the Chicago Singing Teachers Guild Competition, 1947. F♯maj; c♯'–e''; Tess-mL; 4/4, Andante; 4pp; Diff-V/m, P/m.

For: baritone; mezzo-soprano
Mood: lyrical; song about death
Voice: conjunct with some skips; modulating; sustained; romantic
Piano: linear; arpeggiated; syncopated chords in middle section; romantic harmonies
Uses: good subdued song

KLEIN, JOHN
(b. Rahns, PA, 1915; d. Rahns, PA, 1981)

1390.   ILLUSION (Jeanne Hislop). Associated, 1945. Fmaj-min; e'–f''; Tess-M; 4/8, 3/8, Allegretto commodo; 1+min; Diff-V/me, P/me.

For: soprano; tenor
Mood: lyrical; philosophical
Voice: stepwise and easy skips; both major and minor scales; easy rhythms; 2-note slurs
Piano: chordal; thin texture; doubles vocal line
Diff: irregular meter
Uses: good song; quiet ending

1391.   TO EVENING (Jeanne Hislop). Associated, 1947. G-centered; c'–g''; Tess-mH; 7/8, 8/8, 6/8, 5/8, Andante con moto; 4min; Diff-V/md, P/m.

For: soprano; mezzo-soprano; tenor
Mood: lyrical; poem about death
Voice: easy skips; arching phrases; free-flowing, chant-like meter and rhythms; 2-note slurs
Piano: chordal–quartal, quintal, tertian block structures; some countermelody; some arpeggiation; many accidentals;

Diff: large reaches; incidental doubling of vocal line rhythms; ensemble; dramatic climaxes *ff* on f' and g"
Uses: very effective song; music well-mated to text; resembles plainchant

KLEMM, GUSTAV
(b. Baltimore, MD, 1897; d. Baltimore, MD, 1947)

1392.   A CURIOUS THING (Mary Carolyn Davies). Galaxy, 1941. Gmaj; d'–e''; Tess-M; 4/4, Moderately; 2pp; Diff-V/me, P/e.

For: any high or medium voice
Mood: lyrical; sad; a touch of humor at end
Voice: lyrical; flowing phrases, frequently beginning with 8ve leap upward
Piano: repeated chords, with alternating D and E in upper voice of each hand
Diff: requires careful control of 8ve leaps
Uses: good for younger students

1393.   A HUNDRED LITTLE LOVES ("Dierdre" [permission of Mr. F. W. Woodruff & *The Chicago Tribune*]). Carl Fischer, 1944. Won W. W. Kimball Prize of the Chicago Singing Teachers Guild Competition, 1943–1944; Fmaj; c'–f''; Tess-mH; 3/4, With a gay lilt (Like a serenade); 72meas.; Diff-V/m, P/md.

For: high baritone; some tenors (need comfortable low c); man's song
Mood: narrative; dramatic ending, otherwise lighthearted
Voice: serenade-like at first; free recit. section; dramatic ending; many skips
Piano: guitar-like accomp. figure; some thick chords (both hands); some r.h. passages in rapid 8ves; tremolo; articulations important; some doubling of vocal line
Diff: recit.-like section changes mood and pace of song; ends on *ff* sustained f"
Uses: needs to be tastefully done; possible encore

1394.   SOUNDS (H. J. Pearl). Ditson, 1931. [53]. H & L keys: Cmaj (orig.) & A♭maj; g'–a" & e♭'–f"; Tess-H; 4/4, 3/4, Moderato–Più mosso; 2pp; Diff-V/me, P/m.

For: lyric or dramatic soprano
Mood: nature picture; melancholy to joy
Voice: lyrical, becoming more dramatic; triplets
Piano: chordal; triplet figures; somewhat chromatic; some doubling of vocal line
Diff: high tessitura in latter part of song; sustained g"s (e")

KOCH, FREDERICK
(b. Cleveland, OH, 1923)

1395.   5 SONGS FOR PREPARED PIANO & MEDIUM VOICE (Barbara Angell). Seesaw, 1973. cmp1970. X; b♭–a"; Tess-mL, M; 14pp; Diff-V/d-dd, P/d-dd.

For: mezzo-soprano
Mood: lyrical; love poems; some philosophical and abstract
Voice: disjunct; large leaps; fragmented; melismas; *Sprechstimme*; speaking; whispering; glissando
Piano: extensive instructions at beginning for the preparation

of the piano; also a group of "frames" in various meters, from which the pianist is to improvise the introduction and interlude to the first song; repeated notes; broken- and arpeggiated-chord figures; parallelism; thin textures

Diff: avant-garde techniques; perfect pitch desirable

Uses: effective recital material for performers experienced in the idiom

   a. *Re-Encounter.* bb–f"; 4/4, 5/4, 3/4, 2/4 ♩ = 60; 3pp.
   b. *Fox's Song.* b–g"; unmetered at beginning 5/4, 4/4, 2/4, 3/4, Freely (♩ = c.76–92); 4pp.
   c. *On the Rim of Sleep.* bb–a"; 2/4, 3/4, 4/4, ♩ = 92; 2pp.
   d. *Rooms.* b–a"; 4/4, 5/4, 3/4, ♩ = 88; 2+pp.
   e. *Passage.* d'–a"; 4/4, 3/4, 5/4, 2/4, ♩ = 112; 3pp.

1405. PRAYERS OF STEEL (Carl Sandburg). [19]. X; e'–f"; Tess-M; changing meters, 4/4 predominates, Andante con moto–Più mosso; 2min; Diff-V/d, P/md.

For: high baritone; tenor

Mood: declamatory; powerful

Voice: disjunct; declamatory; portamentos; melisma; syncopation; 5 meas. *Sprechstimme*

Piano: quarter-note hammer strokes; strident; l.h. 9ths (cannot be rolled); some chord clusters; 16th-note section; does not double vocal line

Diff: changing meters; irregular rhythms; pitch; portamentos; *Sprechstimme*

Uses: imaginative song for the right singer; useful in an American group

1406. THREE SONGS FROM *THE CHILDREN'S SET*, Op. 18 (Dorothy Aldis). [18]. Traditional keys; c'–g"; Tess-mL-M; regular and irregular changing meters; varied tempos; 6pp; Diff-V/m, P/md-d.

For: mezzo-soprano; soprano

Mood: humorous; descriptive

Voice: some leaps; 8th- & 16th- note movement; a little chromaticism; dotted rhythms; long tones at ends of phrases

Piano: contrapuntal and chordal; triplets; glissando; somewhat chromatic

Diff: meter changes; rapid diction; good vocal actor required

Uses: useful for beginning students

   a. *Whistles.* Fmaj; db'–g"; 2/4 with changes, Moderately fast–Slower; 1+pp.
   b. *The Sad Shoes.* Cmaj; c'–e"; 4/4, 5/7, 3/2, Rather slowly; 2pp.
   c. *Rolling Down a Hill.* Cmaj; d'–e"; 2/4 with changes, Fast–A little slower; 2pp.

KOCH, JOHN
(b. Haverhill, NH, 1928?)

1407. CALICO PIE (Edward Lear). General, 1965. [4]. X; c'–f♯"; Tess-M; 3/4, Moderately fast; 1min; Diff-V/me, P/m.

For: soprano; mezzo-soprano

Mood: light; nonsense

Voice: stepwise and easy skips; some syncopation

Piano: broken chords; waltz style; thin texture

Uses: useful for a young singer

1408. DITTY (Robert Louis Stevenson). General, 1965. Gmin; d'–f♯"; Tess-M; 4/4, Fast and vigorous; 1min; Diff-V/m, P/d.

For: tenor; high baritone

Mood: ironic

Voice: many skips, esp. 4ths & 5ths; 2–5-note slurs

Piano: some broken chords; 3rds, sometimes in both hands; imitation; many accidentals

Diff: irregular phrase lengths

Uses: good tenor song; useful for a young singer

1409. AN EPITAPH (Walter de la Mare). General, 1965. Abmin; f'–gb"; Tess-mH; 3/4, 4/4, Very sustained; 3pp; Diff-V/md, P/m.

For: tenor

Mood: lyrical; memorial to passing beauty

Voice: conjunct; 6/8 rhythms; quiet

Piano: linear; melodic material over 8th-note bass and tenor lines; spare texture; many 2nds

Diff: somewhat difficult to read

Uses: interesting, gentle song; good for young tenor

1410. AN IMMORALITY (Ezra Pound). General, 1965. [4]. F♯min; e'–d"; Tess-M; 2/2, Molto moderato; 2pp; Diff-V/e, P/e.

For: all voices; text slightly better for men

Mood: lyrical; praise of love

Voice: conjunct; easy rhythms; some abrupt modulations

Piano: broken-chord pattern in l.h.; 2-note chords or single melody in r.h.; accidentals

Uses: good teaching song for young students

Rec: D#32

1411. NEW SONGS OF OLD MOTHER GOOSE. General, 1968. Traditional keys, some bitonality; d'–g"; Tess-M; regular meters; varied tempos; 18pp; Diff-V/m, P/md.

For: soprano; mezzo-soprano; tenor

Mood: humorous and lighthearted, with other varied nursery-rhyme moods

Voice: mostly stepwise and small skips; syllabic; easy rhythms; some complications in (d.)

Piano: mostly chordal figurations; some linear writing with countermelodies; rather thin texture; snatches of familiar nursery-rhyme tunes; many accidentals

Uses: nice for light group in recital

   a. *The Old Woman.* Bitonal; d'–e"; 2/4, 3/4, Vivace, 3pp.
   b. *Poor Robin.* E-centered; gb'–f"; 4/4, Andantino; 2pp.
   c. *Good King Arthur.* Cmaj; eb'–g"; 4/4, Presto; 3pp.
   d. *Old Clothes to Sell.* Cmaj-Amin; a'–f"; 4/4, Andante; 3pp.
   e. *Lullaby.* Fmaj-Cmaj; d'–d"; 2/2, Adagio; 2pp.
   f. *As I Was Going to Derby.* Amin-Emaj; f♯'–f♯"; 4/4, Vivace; 5pp.

1412. **O MY LUVE IS LIKE A RED, RED ROSE** (Robert Burns). Orchesis, 1960. D♭maj; d♭'–f"; Tess-mH; 2/4, Molto andante e sostenuto; 36meas.; Diff-V/m, P/e.
For: tenor; soprano; mezzo-soprano; composer changes "lass" to "lad" as an option
Mood: folk-like; tender love song
Voice: small skips; many accidentals; syncopation
Piano: 4–6-voice block chords; many accidentals; some doubling of vocal line
Diff: most phrases cover 7th or 8ve
Uses: useful for a young student; see also settings by Ernst Bacon and Ernest Gold

1413. **SILVER** (Walter de la Mare). General, 1965. Dmin; e'–f"; Tess-M; 3/4, 4/4, 3/8, 3/2, Freely and smoothly ♩=c.72; 2+min; Diff-V/m, P/m.
For: soprano; tenor
Mood: lyrical; atmospheric
Voice: floating line; some leaps upward; repeated tones; speech rhythms; quiet
Piano: impressionistic harmonies; thin texture; mostly in treble clef; some ornaments; many 8ves, 3rds & 6ths; cross-hands; specific pedalings
Diff: legato line; some meter changes
Uses: interesting setting; see also J. Duke and Victor Harris
Rec: D#32

1414. **TAME CAT** (Ezra Pound). General, 1965. [4]. F-centered; e♭'–e♭"; Tess-M; 4/8, 3/8, 2/8, alternating tempos of ♪=112 & 144; 1min; Diff-V/me-m, P/m.
For: baritone; tenor
Mood: whimsical
Voice: stepwise and easy skips; some triplets; syncopation; triplets vs. piano duplets
Piano: broken quartal and quintal harmonies; much use of M & m2nds & dim.8ves; does not double vocal line
Uses: useful whimsical song; quiet ending
Rec: D#32

1415. **THE TEA SHOP** (Ezra Pound). General, 1965. D♭maj; e'–f"; Tess-M; 3/4, Moderato; 1+min; Diff-V/m, P/m.
For: tenor
Mood: lyrical; somewhat sad; transience of youth and beauty
Voice: stepwise and chord-member skips; dotted rhythms; syncopation
Piano: constant 8ths in triplets and duplets; many accidentals; repetitive patterning; does not double vocal line
Diff: some rhythmic complexities; long tones
Rec: D#32

KOEMMENICH, LOUIS
(b. Elberfeld, Germany, 1866; d. New York, NY, 1922)

1416. **O COOL IS THE VALLEY NOW** (James Joyce). J. Fischer, 1919. H & L keys: D♭maj (orig.) & B♭maj; g'–a♭" & e'–f"; Tess-M; 12/8, Calm with tenderness; 3pp; Diff-V/m, P/m.
For: tenor
Mood: lyrical; tender
Voice: conjunct diatonic line; sustained; some long tones;

climax on a♭"
Piano: broken-chord triplet figure; some repeated chords
Uses: lovely song; quiet; good for any lyric tenor

KOEPKE, PAUL
(b. Cleveland, OH, 1918)

1417. **THE IVORY TOWER** (Virginia Fager). Carl Fischer, 1943. Won W. W. Kimball Prize of the Chicago Singing Teachers Guild Competition, 1942–1943. E♭maj; e♭'–g"; Tess-M-mH; 4/4, Slowly, with expression; 4pp; Diff-V/m, P/m.
For: tenor; soprano
Mood: intense; night song of separation
Voice: stepwise and small skips; some triplets; dotted rhythms; dramatic ending
Piano: chordal–block and broken; duplets and triplets; dotted notes; big ending; some doubling of vocal line
Diff: needs to build intensity of expression gradually
Uses: in a group of night songs; group ender

KOHN, STEVEN MARK
(b. Cleveland, OH, 1957)

1418. **HAIKU** (Japanese Haiku Poets–17th and 18th centuries, trans. by Peter Beilenson) for Medium-high Voice and Piano [27 songs]. Classical Vocal Reprints, 1998. Tonal; c'–g"; Tess-M; regular meters with some changes; varied tempos; 28pp; Diff-V/e-m, P/e-m.
For: any medium voice
Mood: fleeting impressions of nature and human relationships
Voice: short phrases of syllabic lyric recitative; narrow ranges
Piano: mostly chordal; some linear; sets the mood of the poem and does some tone painting
Uses: attractive songs in any performance setting; may be sung as a cycle or selected and grouped as the singer wishes; good contrast to heavier works

a. *That Winter* (Jakushi). Dmin; Slowly; 1p.
b. *Defeated in the Fray* (Shiki). Gmin; With military airs; 1p.
c. *Enviable Leaves* (Shiki). Amin; Smooth and dreamy; 1p.
d. *Over the Ruins* (Basho). E; Slow and solemn; 1p.
e. *Behind the Moon* (Kikau). F♯min; Delicately; 1p.
f. *While I Turned My Head* (Shiki). D; Simply; 1p.
g. *Hill of Flowers* (Basho). Emin; With gentle lyricism; 1p.
h. *I'm Very Sorry* (Raizan). F♯min; Slow and very free; 1p.
i. *On the Temple's Great Bronze Bell* (Buson). Amin; Slowly and freely; 1p.
j. *Where Does He Wander?* (Chiyo). Amin; With childlike simplicity; 1p.
k. *Even in Castles* (Kyoriku). Emin; Stately and solemn, feel in slow "one"; 1p.
l. *Oh, the Tiny Cry* (Ransetsu). Very Fast; 1p.
m. *An Old Silent Pond* (Basho). Amin; Slow and very loose; 1p.
n. *Having Spoken Ill* (Basho). X; Freely; 1p.

o. *In My Small Village* (Issa). Dmin; Simply, 1p.

p. *From Watching the Moon* (Shiki). Gmaj; Very gently and freely; 1p.

q. *Thinking Comfortable Thoughts* (Hyakuchi). Cmaj; Simply, with sentiment; 1p.

r. *After Bells* (Basho). Fast; 1p.

s. *It Is Not Easy* (Kyorai). Simply, with humor; 1phrase.

t. *Mr. Toad* (Chora). Fast; 1p.

u. *Poppy Petals Fall* (Etsujin). Emin; Delicately flowing; 1p.

v. *Into a Cool Night* (Otsuji). Fmin; Slowly and freely; 1p.

w. *A Thousand Captains* (Basho). With fury; 2pp.

x. *The Exquisite Pure White Fan* (Buson). Plaintively; 1p.

y. *I Have Known Lovers* (Anon.). Amaj; With grace and repose; 1p.

z. *Live in Simple Faith* (Issa). E♭maj; With simple serenity; 1p.

aa. *Snow Whispering Down* (Joso). E♭min; Very smooth and dreamy; 1p.

KORTE, KARL
(b. Ossining, NY, 1928)

1419. SONGS OF WEN I-TO (20th-century Chinese poet; trans. by Kai-yu Hsu). E. C. Schirmer, 1973. cmp1968. No key sigs, (mildly dissonant, some modality); b–b"; Tess-M-mH; regular and irregular changing meters; moderate and slow tempos; 21pp; Diff-V/d, P/md.

For: tenor

Mood: dramatic; bitter; anguished

Voice: many disjunct intervals; accidentals; both modal and dissonant; high ending

Piano: mostly linear; fairly open texture; dissonant; many accidentals

Diff: pitch; mood of poetry; high ending

Uses: useful if a protest group seems appropriate; the songs are quite bitter and reflect ethnic problems as well as the personal life of the poet

a. *I Wanted to Come Home.* Modal on E♭; c'–a"; Tess-mH; 4/4 with changes, Flowing (♩ = 96-104); 6pp.

b. *The Laundry Song.* E-centered; b–b♭"; Tess-M; 2/2 with changes, Monotonously (♩ = 54); 9pp.

c. *Forget Her.* X; c'–b"; Tess-cs; 3/4 with changes, Somewhat free (♩ = 60-66); 6pp.

KRAKAUER, DAVID (See entry #15 F)

KRAMER, A. WALTER
(b. New York, NY, 1890; d. New York, NY, 1969)

1420. DARK AND WONDROUS NIGHT, Op. 44, No. 2 (Dunkle, schöne Nacht) (Otto Julius Bierbaum; trans. Frederick H. Martens). Ditson, 1917. cmp1916. "For Christine Miller." M & L keys: Dmin & Cmin (orig.);

c'–e" & b♭–d"; Tess-M; 4/4, Slowly–With devotion–Very calmly; 2pp; Diff-V/e-m, P/m.

For: any voice

Mood: tranquil; serene; Christmas text

Voice: stepwise and easy skips; easy rhythms

Piano: syncopated repeated-chord pattern; large reaches; incidental doubling of vocal line

Diff: soft singing; long phrases; starts high

Uses: displays a beautiful sound

1421. FOR A DREAM'S SAKE, Op. 38, No.1 (Christina Rossetti). J. Fischer, 1914. H & L keys: Gmin & E♭min; d'–g"; & b♭–e♭"; Tess-M; 6/4, 4/4, Slowly, with intense feeling; 3pp; Diff-V/me, P/md.

For: any voice

Mood: dramatic; somber

Voice: stepwise and easy skips; recit. style; dotted notes

Piano: block chords; duplets and triplets; large reaches; some doubling of vocal line

Uses: usable sentimental song

1422. I HAVE SEEN DAWN, Op. 48, No.1 (John Masefield) [48]. cmp1922. H & L keys: Constantly shifting; d♯'–f" & b♯–d"; Tess-M; 4/4, with changes, Freely declaimed, ardently; 4pp; Diff-V/m, P/m.

For: any medium or low voice

Mood: old-fashioned, romantic love song; nature imagery

Voice: somewhat recit.-like; numerous small intervals and larger leaps, some difficult; shifting tonal centers and rhythms

Piano: chordal–block, broken, and rolled; bits of melody and countermelody; numerous accidentals; supports vocal line clearly

Diff: pitches; rhythms

Uses: useful example of its era; modest range and lower tessitura song

1423. A NOCTURNE, Op. 34, No. 4 (Frederick H. Martens). Church, 1913. "To Miss Christine Miller." E♭maj; b♭–e♭"; Tess-mL; 9/8, Somewhat slowly, with passion; 36meas.; Diff-V/m, P/md.

For: mezzo-soprano; contralto; baritone; bass

Mood: tranquil; atmospheric; love song

Voice: stepwise; some skips of 6th; phrases often separated by interludes

Piano: broken-chord patterns; arpeggios; repeated chords; a "Wolfian" melody in 8ves; 10-meas. prelude; orchestral texture

Uses: for the subdued facet of a mature, rich voice

1424. A PHANTASY, Op. 29, No. 3a (from the Japanese). [44]. Cmaj; c'–e"; Tess-M; 3/4, 4/4, Slowly and simply; 15meas.; Diff-V/e, P/e.

For: baritone; mezzo-soprano

Mood: subdued love song

Voice: stepwise and easy skips; meter changes; quiet ending

Piano: 4–6-voice chordal texture, fairly thin; not the usual Kramer piano score; supports vocal line

Uses: Haiku-like mood; useful when something brief is needed

1425. PLEADING, Op. 48, No.2 (Hermann Hesse; English

version by J. E.). J. Fischer, 1923. cmp1922. H & L keys: G♭maj & E♭maj; e♭b'–g♭" & c♭'–e♭"; Tess-mH; 4/4, Moderately–Tenderly; 36meas.; Diff-V/md, P/m.

For: any voice; text better suited to a man
Mood: tender; lyrical; love song
Voice: many skips, some awkward; legato
Piano: repeated chords; 6-voice texture; many accidentals
Diff: good dynamic control; legato line
Uses: interior of group

1426. **THERE IS A GARDEN IN HER FACE,** Op. 34, No. 7 (anon.). J. Fischer, 1914. "To Mme. Alma Gluck." H, M, & L keys: Emaj, Dmaj, & Cmaj; e'–g♯", d'–f♯", & c'–e"; Tess-mH; 2/4, Moderately–Gracefully; 57meas.; Diff-V/me-m, P/m.

For: any male voice
Mood: lighthearted but tender love song
Voice: skips of 3rds & 6ths
Piano: 3–4-voice texture; chordal; arpeggiated near end
Diff: good diction on 16th notes; sustained g♯" at end
Uses: phrases begin high and descend; nice song for teaching; group opener

1427. **WE TWO** (Ernst Staus; singable English version provided). Carl Fischer, 1915. H & L keys: Cmaj & A♭maj; g'–a"; & e♭'–f"; Tess-M; 4/4, Free in time, with much warmth and color; 3pp; Diff-V/m, P/m.

For: tenor; soprano; mezzo-soprano; baritone
Mood: dramatic; love song
Voice: many small skips; recit. sections; dotted notes; syncopation
Piano: chordal–block, syncopated, repeated, and arpeggiated; no vocal line doubling; opt. dynamics and length of postlude
Diff: 9-beat sustained g" at end
Uses: dramatic song

KRAUSZ, SUSAN
(b. Stuttgart, Germany, 1914)

1428. **BERCEUSE** (H. L. Rittener; trans. by the composer). [18]. X (some aspects of D♭maj); b♭–a♭"; Tess-M; 6/8, 3/8, Moderato; 5pp; Diff-V/m, P/md.

For: mezzo-soprano
Mood: lyrical lullaby
Voice: flowing; long sustained tones; chromatic
Piano: chromatic; rocking rhythm with afterbeats; lengthy contrapuntal introduction
Diff: pitches; sustained singing
Uses: recital use

KRENEK, ERNST
(b. Vienna, Austria, 1900; d. Palm Springs, CA, 1991)

1429. **THE FLEA** (John Donne). [49]. cmp1960. Serial; b–c'''; Tess-mH, L; 1/2, ♩ = 48; 6pp; Diff-V/dd, P/dd.

For: high soprano; tenor
Mood: descriptive; philosophical; marked: "In expression ranging from the cynical to the phrenetic"

Voice: highly fragmented and disjunct; very large leaps; highly complex rhythms
Piano: fragmented; highly chromatic; numerous special effects
Diff: pitches; rhythms; text

KREUTZ, ROBERT
(b. LaCrosse, WI, 1922; d. 1996)

1430. **DECEMBER LARK** (Oliver Herford). [17]. H & L keys: B♭min & Gmin; e♭'–g♭" & c'–e♭"; Tess-M; 3/4, 5/4, Slowly; 2pp; Diff-V/m, P/m.

For: all voices except very low
Mood: lyrical; philosophical; nature imagery
Voice: stepwise with several large leaps
Piano: chordal; some arpeggiation; does not double vocal line
Diff: soft legato singing
Uses: good song for teaching; programming possibilities

1431. **FALL** (Ralph Wright). Willis Music, 1987. A-centered; b–g"; Tess-M; 4/4 with changes, Adagio e tranquillo (♩ = 66–69); 4pp; Diff-V/m, P/me.

For: mezzo-soprano; tenor (although specified for high voice, some phrases lie rather low for soprano)
Mood: lyrical; nature imagery
Voice: very smooth and conjunct; some 5ths & one 8ve; both high-lying and low-lying phrases; some accidentals; simple rhythms
Piano: homophonic and chordal, with some accidentals; organ or piano indicated–probably best for organ; supports vocal line clearly, some doubling
Uses: an effective, simple song

KUBIK, GAIL
(b. South Coffeyville, OK, 1914; d. Claremont, CA, 1984)

1432. **FABLES IN SONG** (Theodore Roethke). MCA, 1975. cmp1950 & 1969; pub. separately. X; g–g"; Tess-M, H; regular and changing meters; mostly fast tempos; 27pp; Diff-V/d, P/m-d.

For: mezzo-soprano; dramatic soprano with good chest voice
Mood: humorous; lively songs; some broad comedy
Voice: both conjunct-chromatic and disjunct; many repeated notes, esp. low; much staccato; interrupted phrases; many accidentals; features c" and c♯"; changing meters; some speaking; articulations important; much humorous narrative
Piano: detached figures; thin textures; much staccato with other articulations; specific pedaling, esp. sostenuto; accidentals; one spoken passage ("boom-boom"); wide reach helpful
Diff: pitches; some rhythms; ensemble
Uses: excellent set of humorous songs; good for teaching strict observance of composer's indications and getting a too-serious singer to "let go"; excellent program material for singer with comic flair

    a. *The Kitty-Cat Bird.* a–g"; Tess-M; 2/2, 3/2, 3/4, Fast, with lots of bounce; 8pp.
    b. *The Sloth.* g–d"; Tess-L; 3/4, 2/4, Slowly; 6pp.

c. *The Lamb.* b–g"; Tess-M; 2/4, 3/4, 3/8, 5/8, Fast, brightly; 3pp.

d. *The Serpent.* b♭–g♭"(a"); Tess-M, H; 4/4, 3/2, 2/4, 3/4, 2/2, With spirit and impudence; 10pp (see also settings by Hoiby and Rorem).

1433. SONGS ABOUT WOMEN. (Peer)Southern, 1951, 1950. cmp1938 & 1939. Tonal with altered chord structures; c♯'–g"; Tess-M; regular changing meters; contrasting tempos; 12pp; Diff-V/m, P/m.

For: mezzo-soprano; soprano; tenor(?); poems make it a hazy decision; third poem definitely spoken by a woman; first poem could be spoken by either sex

Mood: lyrical; small character sketches

Voice: conjunct; speech rhythms; some recit.

Piano: linear; patterned; sostenuto pedal

Diff: choice of singer to do entire set

Uses: rather good songs; useful for intermediate and advanced students

a. *Like a Clear, Deep Pool* (W. Somerset Maugham). D-centered; c♯'–g"; 2/4 with changes, Moderately fast, unhurried; 4pp.

b. *She Who Was All Piety* (Audrey Wurdemann). F♯min; e'–f♯"; 3/4 with changes, Moderately slow; 4pp.

c. *A Woman's Armor* (Mary Bickel). Amin-maj; c♯'–f"; 3/4, 4/4, Fast, with energy; 4pp.

KULP, JONATHAN (see Appendix for song with Spanish text)

KUPFERMAN, MEYER
(b. New York, NY, 1926)

1434. ISLAND IN A ROOM (1963) (Robert Winner). General, 1963. Atonal, serial techniques; b–a"; Tess-wide; changing meters, Lento ed intenso molto (with changes); 9min; Diff-V/dd, P/dd.

For: dramatic soprano

Mood: dramatic; sinister; distorted and disoriented; macabre

Voice: wide leaps and awkward intervals; complex rhythms; one section of free rhythms; many dynamic markings; independent of piano; dramatic ending

Piano: complex; thick texture; many accidentals; complex rhythms; many notes; somewhat hard to read; one free ostinato section; highly dramatic

Diff: very difficult to put together; singer needs perfect pitch, and absolute vocal and musical confidence, esp. with rhythms; pianist and singer will need much rehearsal

Uses: can stand alone; effective for big, dramatic voice

KURTZ, EUGENE
(b. Atlanta, GA, 1923)

1435. THREE SONGS FROM *MEDEA* (Robinson Jeffers). Editions Jobert, 1965. cmp1949–1951. X; a–a♯"; Tess-mL; regular and irregular meters with frequent changes; varied tempos; 9+min; Diff-V/d, P/dd.

For: dramatic

Mood: "from Robinson Jeffers' adaptation of the *Medea* of Euripides"; philosophical; brooding

Voice: mostly conjunct with a few large skips; leaps of 9th & 11th; triplets; chromatic; quasi-cadenza at end of (b.); syllabic with occasional 2–3-note slurs; many dynamic markings

Piano: both chordal and linear; much 3-stave notation; highly chromatic; complex rhythms; 2 vs. 3; triplets and sextuplets; cross-hands; grace notes; rolled chords; large reach necessary; large register changes; many dynamic markings; does not double vocal line

Diff: frequent changes of meter; complex rhythms; cresc. on final low a; requires excellent musicianship of singer, and a virtuoso pianist

Uses: excellent recital material for very advanced musicians; apparently intended as a set but could be performed separately, as each takes a different character in the drama and is somewhat different in its vocal demands

a. *I Wish the Long Ship Argo* (The Nurse, Act I). X; d'–a♯"; Tess-mL; 6/8, 9/8, 4/8, 1/8, Con moto (♩.= 50); 6pp.

b. *Unhappy One, Never Pray for Death* (Second woman, Act I). X; c♯'–a"; Tess-M; 2/4 with changes, Molto vivo (♩= 120) (with changes); 6pp.

c. *Children: It Is Evening* (Medea, Act II). X; a–a"; Tess-mL; 4/4 with changes, Lento (♩= 60) (with changes); 7pp.

LADERMAN, EZRA
(b. New York, NY, 1924)

1436. FROM THE PSALMS (Psalms 7, 9, 22, 39, 57, 61, 69, 103, 104, 119, Revised Standard Version). Cycle. Oxford, 1970. No key sigs., dissonant; b–a"; Tess-M-mH; regular and irregular changing meters; moderate tempos, ends fast; 11min; Diff-V/dd, P/d-dd.

For: soprano; tenor; texts perhaps best for tenor

Mood: dramatic; troubled; alienation

Voice: high tessitura phrases; many wide leaps; long, sustained tones; florid passages; grace notes; complicated rhythmic patterns; very forceful passages

Piano: many widely-spaced cluster chords demand a large reach; linear textures, generally 1–2 voices; running 16ths; many accidentals; very dissonant; many specific articulations

Diff: on all levels; perfect pitch desirable; diction probably easier for tenor than soprano; ensemble

Uses: for a virtuoso singer

Rec: D#249

a. *What I Did Not Steal.* c♯'–g"; Tess-M; 7/4 with many changes, Free (♩= ca.76); 4pp.

b. *Behold the Wicked Man.* f'–g♯"; Tess-mH; 4/4 with changes, ♩= 96; 4pp.

c. *From the End of the Earth.* b–g♭"; Tess-M-mH; 3/4, 2/4, ♩= 44; 4pp.

d. *Look Away from Me.* d♭'–a"; Tess-M-mH; 3/4, 2/4, 5/4, Forcefully, ♩= 84; 3pp.

e. *Thou Didst Set the Earth.* d♭'–a"; Tess-mH-H; 2/4,

3/4, ♩ = 100; 7pp.

1437. SONGS FOR EVE (Archibald MacLeish). Cycle. Oxford Univ. Press, 1968. "Affectionately dedicated to Judith Raskin." X (dissonant; one song in Emaj, cycle ends A♭maj); b♭–c'''; Tess-M-HH; regular and irregular changing meters; varied tempos; 20min; Diff-V/dd, P/d.

For: soprano
Mood: lyrical; Eve's reflections on identity of woman, of space and time
Voice: all kinds of intervalic structures; dissonant and large leaps frequent, as well as chromatic lines; many florid passages; speech rhythms; many phrases end high; complex
Piano: mostly linear; wide-spread over keyboard; infested with accidentals; a characteristic chord occurs throughout at crucial points
Diff: in every area; perfect pitch desirable; symbolic and philosophical insight into the poetry
Uses: extremely effective work for the virtuoso singer
Rec: D#249

  a. *What Eve Sang.* c'–a♭"; Tess-M; 6/4 with changes, Andante ♩ = 60; 3pp.
  b. *Eve's Exile.* b–g♯"; Tess-M; 4/4 with changes, Andante sostenuto ♩ = 58–60; 3pp.
  c. *Eve's Now-I-Lay-Me.* d'–b"; Tess- M-mH; 4/4 with changes, Floatingly ♩ = 80–Allegro con spirito ♩ = 132–138; 4pp.
  d. *Eve in the Dawn.* e♭'–a♭"; Tess-M; 4/4 with changes, Moderato e agitato ♩ = 80–84; 4pp.
  e. *The Riddles.* Emaj; b♭–a"; Tess-mH; 3/4 with changes, Allegretto ♩ = 144; 6pp. (pub. separately by Oxford; good for any soprano).
  f. *Eve's Rebuke to Her Child.* b–b"; Tess-mH; 4/4 with changes, Moderato, ma agitato ♩ = 80; 5pp.
  g. *Eve Quiets Her Children.* d♯'–a"; Tess-M-HH; 3/4 with changes, Deliberately ♩ = 69–72; 6pp.
  h. *Eve Explains to the Thrush Who Repeats Everything.* e♭'–c'''; Tess-HH (almost all high tones, a", b", c''', are on "ee" vowel); 4/4, 6/4, Plaintively ♩ = 88; 8pp.

1438. SONGS FROM MICHELANGELO (trans. Joseph Tusiani). Cycle. Oxford Univ. Press, 1975; First performed, 1973. Tonal, some songs in traditional keys with alterations; F–e'; Tess-M, LL, mH-H; regular and irregular changing meters; varied tempos; 23min; Diff-V/dd, P/d-dd.

For: bass preferred; composer says "for baritone," and 1st performance was by Sherrill Milnes, but this cycle needs a bass voice and lies perfectly for a basso cantante; too low to be effective for any but the "bassiest" of baritone voices; many upper tones are given as opt. to the lower, more effective ones
Mood: lyrical and dramatic; (a.–f.) about being in love; (g.), anguished; approaching death
Voice: many different techniques; large leaps, grace notes, melismas; descending arpeggios; wide ranges; speech rhythms; many accidentals; ends e' *pppp*; difficult but singable

Piano: mostly linear texture; motivic construction; often wide-spread over keyboard; many accidentals; wide reach helpful
Diff: range; handling of long-ranged phrases; vocal line very much like a cello line in places; some pitches
Uses: excellent for virtuoso singer with a rich, colorful voice

  a. *Who Is the One That Draws Me to You?* Amin; A–d'; Tess-M; 3/4, 2/4, Andantino ♩ = 66; 5pp.
  b. *Oh Sweeter a Sudden Death Would Be.* A–d♭'; Tess-M; 4/4 with changes, Presto ♩ = 144; 4pp.
  c. *Your Face Is Sweeter Than Mustard.* Gmaj; G♯–e'; Tess-mH; 4/4, 2/4, Gaily ♩ = 116; 8pp.
  d. *The More You See the Torment on My Face.* A♭; A♭–d♭'; Tess-M; 3/4, 2/4, 4/4, Moderato ♩ = 69; 4pp.
  e. *If in a Woman a Part Is Beautiful.* A♭; A♭–e'; Tess-mH; 6/8, ♩ = 69; 6pp.
  f. *For All This Anguish.* Bmin; F♯–d'; Tess-L, mH; 2/4 (voice), 6/8, 2/4 (piano); Grave ♩ = 50; 4pp.
  g. *Alas, Alas, for I Am Now Betrayed by All My Fleeting Days.* F–e♭'; Tess-LL, cs; 3/4, 2/4, 4/4, 5/4, Appassionato, ♩ = 60; 12pp (musical summary of previous songs).

LA FORGE, FRANK
(b. Rockford, IL, 1879; d. New York, NY, 1953)

1439. COME UNTO THESE YELLOW SANDS (William Shakespeare). G. Schirmer, 1907, 1936. Reprint: T.I.S. (H). Gmaj; f♯'–b"(d'''); Tess-H; 4/4, Allegretto; 5pp; Diff-V/md, P/md.

For: high soprano (coloratura or light lyric)
Mood: animated; light
Voice: stepwise and skips along chord lines; coloratura passages–staccato and legato melismas; long phrases
Piano: rapid scale passages; staccato chords; register varies; some doubling of vocal line
Diff: coloratura techniques; ensemble
Uses: good coloratura song

1440. RETREAT (Schlupfwinkel) (Princess Gabriele Wrede; English trans.). [48]; 1st©1906. H, M, & L keys: B♭maj, A♭maj, & Fmaj; e'–g", d'–f", & b–d"; Tess-M; 6/8, Langsam, düster; 2pp; Diff-V/me, P/m.

For: any voice
Mood: despairing; somber; introspective
Voice: stepwise; lyrical, with powerful climax
Piano: afterbeat chords; bass melody mostly doubles vocal line
Diff: good dynamic control

1441. SONG OF THE OPEN (Jessica H. Lowell). Ditson, 1919. Reprint: T.I.S. (M). [53]. "To Mme. Frances Alda." H & M keys: Fmin (orig.) & Dmin; e♭'–a♭"(c''') & c'–f "(a"); Tess-M; 4/4, Vivace e appassionato; 32meas.; Diff-V/md, P/d.

For: soprano; mezzo-soprano
Mood: ecstatic love song
Voice: many leaps; duplets and triplets; some staccato
Piano: rapid arpeggios in triplet 16ths; many accidentals
Diff: dynamic control; sustained c''' *ff* at end

Uses: effective song; crowd-pleaser; group ender; encore

1442. TO A MESSENGER (An einer Boten) (Princess Gabriele Wrede; English version). G. Schirmer, 1909. Emaj; e'–b"; Tess-mH; 4/4, Schnell mit Humor–Allegro giocoso; 4pp; Diff-V/m, P/m.
For: tenor
Mood: humorous
Voice: conjunct with chordal skips and leaps; 2-note slurs; sustained tones and climax on b" on "say"
Piano: reflects text well; thin texture; some arpeggiated passages
Diff: high tones; proper word inflection
Uses: good humorous song; program ender; encore; good for tenor to show off b"

LAITMAN, LORI
(b. Long Beach, NY, 1955)

1443. THE HOUR (Sara Teasdale). [170]. cmp1992? "For Lauren Wagner." Tonal, fluctuating harmonies; c'–g"; Tess-cs; 3/4, 7/8, 2/4, 4/4, ♩=63; 3+pp; Diff-V/m, P/m.
For: soprano
Mood: questioning; is the one to be loved pre-ordained?
Voice: skips along chord lines, some stepwise phrases; syllabic; text "based upon the poem . . ." and set to music in a rather "popular" style
Piano: single-voice, chord-outlining bass line under r.h. chords; some accidentals; harmonic background
Uses: an "easy listening" style perhaps useful for singers who have no classical style background
Rec: D#338

1444. THE METROPOLITAN TOWER (Sara Teasdale). [170]. cmp1991? "for Lauren Wagner." A♭-Amaj; d'–f"; Tess-M; 3/4 with changes; ♩=72 Lyrical, Legato; 4pp; Diff-V/me, P/m.
For: soprano
Mood: lyrical; first awareness of love
Voice: small skips outlining chords, some stepwise motion; syllabic; a b a form; lyrical phrases in melodic rhythm (some alterations for word stress)
Piano: chordal; patterned single 8th-note outlining of chords in l.h.; some countermelody in r.h.; much doubling of vocal line at the upper 8ve; some accidentals
Diff: shifting harmonies for some inexperienced musicians
Uses: relatively easy song for undergraduate students; attractive to program
Rec: D#338

1445. OLD TUNES (Sara Teasdale). [170]. "for Lauren Wagner." A- & E-centered; c♯'–g♯"; Tess-M; 3/4 with changes; ♩=100; 6+pp; Diff-V/m, P/m
For: soprano
Mood: nostalgic; bittersweet
Voice: stepwise and chord-outlining skips, one 8ve; syllabic; some fragmented phrases for word stress in waltz meter
Piano: mostly 2-voice texture; some 2-voice chords in irregular afterbeat pattern; slightly dissonant harmonic structure, sometimes bitonal; gives impression of elusive remembrance of melodies

Diff: some pitches; some rhythmic patterns for pianist
Uses: interesting setting for singer with good ear

1446. THE STRONG HOUSE (Sara Teasdale). [170]. cmp1992? "for Lauren Wagner." Tonal; d'–g"; Tess-M; 7/8, 4/8, 4/4, 3/4, 5/8, ♩=66; 3pp; Diff-V/m, P/m.
For: soprano
Mood: unstable; love has a shadow
Voice: mostly stepwise with a few descending large intervals (6th or 8ve); syllabic
Piano: single-voice, chord-outlining pattern in l.h. under some chords in r.h.; some 2-voice linear passages; functions mostly as harmonic background
Diff: perhaps some pitches in shifting harmonies for insecure musicians
Uses: pleasant setting of this text
Rec: D#338

1447. TO A LOOSE WOMAN (Sara Teasdale). [170]. cmp1992? "for Lauren Wagner." G-Dmaj; d'–a"; Tess-cs; 4/4, 3/4, 2/4, ♩=84; 3+pp; Diff-V/m, P/md.
For: soprano
Mood: sly; humorous; jazzy
Voice: skips and leaps, up to 8ve; mostly syllabic; 2 portamentos (probably "slides"); some syncopation; one phrase begins on a"
Piano: built on a jazzy, syncopated, chromatic chordal pattern; 2 vs. 3; one glissando
Diff: some pitches against piano chromaticism
Uses: clever setting for a jazzy group
Rec: D#338

1448. A WINTER NIGHT (Sara Teasdale). [170]. "for Lauren Wagner." X (Phrygian); d'–g"; Tess-M; 4/4, 3/4, 5/4, 2/4, Lyrical ♩=69; 4pp; Diff-V/m, P/m.
For: soprano
Mood: image of winter outside and in the heart
Voice: stepwise with a few skips–two 8ve leaps upward; modal melodic structure; syllabic
Piano: chordal and linear; some block chords, some outlining; motivically constructed bass line reflects bleakness of winter; some doubling of vocal line in inner voices
Diff: modal scale for singer against lightly dissonant chords
Uses: excellent song for teaching and performance; useful in a "winter" group

LA MONTAINE, JOHN
(b. Oak Park, IL, 1920)

1449. INVOCATION, Opus 4 (John La Montaine). Fredonia, 1950. cmp late 1940s. D♯-centered; b–e"; Tess-M; 2/2, 4/4, 3/2, , Allegro alla breve ma maestoso (with several changes); 6pp; Diff-V/m, P/m.
For: baritone
Mood: protest song against nuclear weapons and war; invokes ancient gods
Voice: mostly stepwise and easy skips; many long, sustained notes; many accidentals; some slow melismas
Piano: chordal texture; many accidentals; wide piano range; much use of parallel motion; great variety of dynamics
Diff: calls for powerful, mature sound; singer must have

good breath control and be able to sustain d♯" (6 meas.), c" (6 meas.), and d" (5 meas.)

Uses: useful if "protest" song is wanted

1450. SHALL I COMPARE THEE TO A SUMMER'S DAY? (William Shakespeare). Fredonia, 1962. Emaj; b–g♯"; Tess-M-H; 6/8, Gently flowing, soaringly lyrical; 4pp; Diff-V/m-md, P/m.

For: tenor; soprano
Mood: praises beauty; love song; lyrical
Voice: many small skips; some wide leaps; syncopation (meter obscured); many accidentals; often disregards poetic meter in manner of Renaissance composers
Piano: mostly linear; rather thin texture; wide piano range; many pedal points; some hemiola; countermelodies; some imitation of voice
Diff: rhythms and resulting ensemble problems; tenor may have trouble with low b (three syllables on this pitch)
Uses: beautiful setting of this sonnet; in a Shakespeare group

1451. SONGS OF THE ROSE OF SHARON. For High Voice with Piano Accompaniment, Op. 6 (Song of Solomon, Chapter 2 [King James Version]). Cycle. Broude Bros., 1962. cmp pre-1956. First performed by Leontyne Price. Traditional keys, centering on F♯ with many altered chords; b–bb"; Tess-M-mH-H; regular meters with some changes; varied tempos; 15min; Diff-V/d, P/dd.

For: high lyric soprano
Mood: lyrical; sensuous love songs
Voice: many skips; some leaps; repeated tones; long phrases; many sustained tones above the staff; many long tones
Piano: orchestral reduction–playable and probably effective, but difficult; chordal-linear combination; some difficult turns in inner voices; large reach necessary; many accidentals; some arpeggiation; repeated chords could be tiring
Diff: high tessitura; orchestral reduction for pianist; needs mature performers with adequate endurance
Uses: although best with orchestra, this cycle can work with piano; lovely work for big lyric voice of great warmth and beauty
Rec: D#250

  a. *I Am the Rose of Sharon and the Lily of the Valleys.* Amaj; d♯'–a"; Tess- mH; 4/4, Slowly but flowingly ♩ = 66; 3pp.
  b. *I Sat Down under His Shadow.* F♯min; f♯'–g"; Tess-mH; 6/8, 3/8, 9/8, In the manner of a slow dance ♩ = 116; 4pp.
  c. *His Left Hand Is under My Head, and His Right Hand Doth Embrace Me.* f♯'–d"; Tess-M; 4/4, Very slowly ♩ = 44-48; 1p.
  d. *O My Dove, That Art in the Clefts of the Rock.* D♯maj; e♯'–g♯"; Tess-M; 5/4, 3/4, 3/2, Moderately ♩ = 88; 3pp.
  e. *My Beloved Is Mine, and I Am His.* Amaj; b–ab"; Tess-M; 4/4, Serenely and flowingly ♩ = 104; 3pp.
  f. *The Voice of My Beloved! Behold, He Cometh.* c♯'–bb"; Tess-mH; 3/4, Very slowly ♩ = 46; 4pp.
  g. *Rise Up, My Love, My Fair One, and Come Away.* F♯min; d♯'–a"; 3/4, 2/4, Moderately fast and with

great fervor ♩ = 126; 4pp.

1452. STOPPING BY WOODS ON A SNOWY EVENING (Robert Frost). Galaxy, 1963. Gmaj; c'–eb"; Tess-M; 6/8, 9/8, Simply and rhythmically; 2min; Diff-V/m-md; P/m.

For: baritone; mezzo-soprano
Mood: subdued; tranquil
Voice: skips along chord lines; syncopation; quiet; legato lines
Piano: pedal tones; afterbeat chord pattern imitates sleigh bells; various registers; does not double vocal line
Diff: poem needs some thought; irregular rhythms and phrase lengths; ensemble
Uses: effective song; useful for young and more mature singers
Rec: D#59

1453. THREE POEMS OF HOLLY BEYE, Opus 15. Fredonia, 1954. Tonal; b–f♯"; Tess-M; mostly regular meters; varied tempos; 8pp; Diff-V/m, P/m.

For: medium voice specified; mezzo-soprano best (women's texts)
Mood: love songs
Voice: stepwise; easy skips; syllabic; syncopation; some triplet subdivisions; dotted rhythms
Piano: mostly linear; rather thin textures; wide piano range; many accidentals
Diff: range could be a problem for young mezzo-soprano due to sustained f" and f♯"
Uses: good short set; undergraduate material

  a. *Definition of the Highest.* Dmaj; c'–eb"; 3/4, 2/4, ♩ = 112; 2pp.
  b. *Happiness.* E-centered; b–f"; 4/4, 2/4, 3/4, 3/2, ♩ = 126; 3pp.
  c. *Song from the Bamboo Cycle.* F♯-centered; c♯'–f♯"; 4/4, ♩ = 66; 3pp.

LANE, RICHARD B.
(Paterson, NJ, 1933)

1454. FOUR SONGS (Mark Van Doren). Carl Fischer, 1957. "To Patricia Berlin." Traditional keys; a–a"; Tess-M; regular meters with some irregular groupings; 22pp; Diff-V/m-md, P/m-md.

For: soprano
Mood: lyrical; songs of loneliness
Voice: mostly conjunct; some 2- & 3-note slurs; soft high tones; some portamentos
Piano: orchestral reduction; wide-spread on keyboard; large reach helpful; linear texture; many open 8ves, 4ths & 5ths; some glissandos and tremolo; sustained trills in last song; rather romantic; extended piano interludes
Diff: continuity
Uses: attractive songs; usable with piano; mature lyric voice needed
Rec: D#251

  a. *Mountain House: December.* Bmin; a–g"; Tess-M; 4/4, Lento molto; 4pp.
  b. *Dunce's Song.* E-centered; d'–g"; Tess-M; 3/4,

Allegro molto; 7pp.

 c. *Down Dip the Branches.* G- & E-centered;
d♯'–g♯"; Tess-M; 4/4, Andante; 4pp.

 d. *Will He Come Back?* Ends Cmaj; c'–a"; Tess-M;
4/4 with changes, Allegro molto; 7pp.

LANG, MARGARET RUTHVEN
(b. Boston, 1867; d. Jamaica Plain, MA, 1972)

1455. **BETRAYED**, Op. 9, No. 4 (Lizette Woodworth
Reese). [139]. Amin; e'–a"; Tess-M; 6/8, 4/4, Allegro
appassionato; 4pp; Diff-V/m, P/m.
For: tenor
Mood: unhappy song of lost love; dramatic
Voice: stepwise and easy skips; leaps of 8ve; syllabic; little
chromaticism; duplets; short phrases separated by rests
Piano: chordal–block and broken; some chromaticism;
syncopation; incidental doubling of vocal line but
strong support
Diff: needs ringing tone on g" and a" on "death"
Uses: possible recital material; good period piece

1456. **FIVE SONGS, OP. 15.** Arthur P. Schmidt, 1898.
Reprint: Recital Publications, 1983. Separate entries.

A. **KING OLAF'S LILIES** (Lizette Woodworth Reese).
Emaj; b–f♯"(g♯"); Tess-M; 4/4, Andante con moto
(♩ = 76); 5pp; Diff-V/m, P/m.
For: mezzo-soprano
Mood: narrative and descriptive; ballad
Voice: stepwise and easy skips; 8ve leaps; a little
chromaticism; dotted rhythms; syllabic
Piano: chordal–block and broken; melodic material in prelude
and interlude; somewhat chromatic; tremolo; strong
support of vocal line; some doubling
Diff: narrator, female, male characters represented in text
Uses: usable ballad

B. **THE DEAD SHIP** (Lizette Woodworth Reese). Cmaj;
b(d')–e"; Tess-M; 6/8, Con moto (♩ = 58); 7pp;
Diff-V/m, P/m.
For: baritone
Mood: lyrical but gloomy; "ghost" ship; ends in death
Voice: stepwise and small skips; little chromaticism; swinging
rhythms; lyrical and flowing; syllabic; 2-note slurs;
small melismas
Piano: chordal–block and broken; melodic fragments; some
chromaticism; triplet 16ths; does not double vocal line
Uses: usable period piece

C. **APRIL WEATHER** (Lizette Woodworth Reese).
Gmaj; c♯'–g"; Tess-M; 4/4, Allegretto (♩ = 100); 4pp;
Diff-V/me, P/me.
For: tenor; mezzo-soprano
Mood: lyrical love song; nature imagery
Voice: stepwise and easy skips; some chromaticism; easy
rhythms; lyrical and flowing; grace notes; numerous
2-note slurs
Piano: chordal; somewhat chromatic; strong support of vocal
line, incidental doubling
Uses: possible recital material

D. **THE GARDEN OF ROSES** (F. Marion Crawford).
Emin; d'–e"; Tess-M; 12/8, 4/4, Moderato ma con moto
(♩ = 76); 6pp; Diff-V/me, P/me.
For: any medium voice
Mood: lyrical love song; nature imagery
Voice: stepwise and small skips; little chromaticism; triplets
and syncopation; syllabic; 2-note slurs; two small
melismas
Piano: chordal–block and broken; melodic material in prelude
and interludes; triplets; some chromaticism; tremolo;
strong support of vocal line; little doubling
Uses: possible use as period piece

E. **SPINNING SONG** (H. P. Kimball). Fmaj; c'–f";
Tess-M; 12/8, 4/4, Con moto (♩ = 84); 4pp; Diff-V/me,
P/me.
For: mezzo-soprano
Mood: lyrical; philosophical
Voice: stepwise and small skips; some chromaticism; dotted
rhythms; duplets; short phrases; syllabic; two important
melismas on "ah"
Piano: repeated broken-chord pattern characterizes spinning
wheel; duplets; some chromaticism; strong support of
vocal line, some doubling
Uses: possible recital material

1457. **I KNEW THE FLOWERS HAD DREAMED OF
YOU** (John B. Tabb). [44]. cmp pre-1930. A♭maj;
e♭'–g♭"; Tess-mH; 3/4, Andantino; 3pp; Diff-V/m,
P/m-md.
For: mezzo-soprano; soprano
Mood: lyrical
Voice: stepwise and easy skips; easy rhythms
Piano: block chords; arpeggios; some irregular rhythmic
groupings; much doubling of vocal line
Diff: voice duplets vs. groups of 6 & 7 in piano; subtle
dynamic control
Uses: good for a young voice

1458. **IN THE TWILIGHT** (H. Bowman). [139]. Emaj;
g'–e"; Tess-M; 4/4, Andantino con moto; 2pp; Diff-V/e,
P/e.
For: any high or medium voice
Mood: lyrical and philosophical
Voice: very static with many repeated notes; a few chromatic
tones; 3 vs. 4 in piano; ends on sustained e" *ppp*
Piano: repeated chords; some chromaticism; syncopation;
doubles or supports vocal line strongly
Diff: control of *ppp* sustained e"
Uses: useful for student with very limited range

1459. **NIGHT** (Louise Chandler Moulton). [139] . Bmaj;
d♯'–g"; Tess-M; 9/8, Con moto (♩ = 92); 5pp;
Diff-V/me, P/m.
For: soprano; tenor
Mood: lyrical; embracing the night
Voice: stepwise and easy skips; some chromaticism; lyrical
and flowing; syllabic; 2-note slurs
Piano: chordal–block, broken, and rolled; some chromaticism;
duplets; doubles or strongly supports vocal line
Uses: possible recital material

1460. **NONSENSE RHYMES AND PICTURES BY EDWARD LEAR,** Op. 42. Arthur P. Schmidt, 1905. Reprint: Recital Publications, 1985. Traditional keys; g–c'''; Tess-M-mL; regular meters; varied tempos; 32pp; Diff-V/m, P/md.

For: all voices except low, depending upon what options are taken (see below under Uses)

Mood: humorous miniatures in limerick style

Voice: stepwise and easy skips; some leaps; some chromaticism; easy rhythms; a few triplets; short phrases; speaking; vocalization on [z]; largely syllabic with 2-note slurs; several songs feature melismatic passages requiring vocal agility

Piano: chordal-linear combination; a little counterpoint; block, broken, rolled, and afterbeat chords; r.h. melodic passages; scalar passages; some chromaticism; triplets, quintuplets, and septuplets; trill figures; tremolo; grace notes; strongly supports and frequently doubles vocal line; lengthy prelude to final song

Diff: needs vocal agility for some songs, incl. ability to sing rapid passages on [z], and good vocal actor

Uses: could be an amusing addition to a program; entire set seems too similar in nature; shorter sets could be selected, allowing for adaptation to various voice types; final song makes the most effective ending, and could also end a program or serve as an encore; in context it limits the use of the set to soprano or possibly tenor

    a. *The Person of Filey.* Cmaj; c'–g"; Tess-M; 2/4, Slowly, and in exact time; 2pp.
    b. *The Old Man of Cape Horn.* Dmin; d'–e"; Tess-mL; 6/8, Slowly; 2pp.
    c. *The Person of Skye.* Emin; e'–e"; Tess-M; 3/4, In slow waltz time; 4pp.
    d. *The Old Man in the Kettle.* Dmaj; d'–d"; Tess-M; 6/8; 2pp.
    e. *The Old Man Who Said, "Well!"* B♭maj-Cmin; c'–g"; Tess-M; 2/4, Very fast; 2pp.
    f. *The Old Man Who Said, "Hush!"* Amin; a–e"; Tess-M; 6/8, Slowly and dramatically; 2pp.
    g. *The Old Man with a Gong.* Emaj; e'–f♯"; Tess-M; 4/4, With accent and deliberation; 4pp.
    h. *The Young Lady of Lucca.* Fmaj; c'–f"; Tess-M; 6/8, Very slowly, but gracefully; 2pp.
    i. *The Old Lady of France.* Dmaj; d'–f♯"(e"); M; 3/4, Tempo di minuetto; 2pp.
    j. *The Old Man in a Tree.* Emaj; c♯'–f"; Tess-mL; 3/4, Slow waltz-tempo; 4pp.
    k. *The Old Person of Cassel.* Amaj; e'–e"(a"); Tess-M; 2/4, Lightly & rhythmically (♩ = 92); 3pp.
    l. *The Lady of Riga* (anon.). A♭maj; g–c'''; Tess-mL; 6/8, Allegro moderato (♩. = 96); 3pp.

1461. **ON AN APRIL APPLE BOUGH** (Sylvia; ed. Arthur Gray). [44]. cmp pre-1930. E♭maj; e♭'–g"; Tess-M; 9/8, Allegretto grazioso; 3pp; Diff-V/m, P/m.

For: soprano

Mood: lyrical; cheerful; theme of renewal

Voice: stepwise and small skips; 2–7-note melismas; easy rhythms; repetitive patterns

Piano: chordal; rocking figure; repeated chords; incidental doubling of vocal line

Diff: long tones on words such as "sing" and "swing"

Uses: interesting song; useful for a young singer, recital material for mature singer

1462. **A POET GAZES ON THE MOON** (after Tang-Jo-Su; trans. Stuart Merrill). [139]. Cmin-A♭min; c'–e♭"; Tess-M; 3/4, 9/8, Andante con moto; 4pp; Diff-V/me, P/me.

For: baritone

Mood: lyrical love song

Voice: stepwise and small skips; little chromaticism; triplets; lyrical and flowing; 2–3-note slurs; small melismas

Piano: chordal; melodic material in interludes, often in 3rds; little chromaticism; triplets; strongly supports but does not double vocal line

Uses: possible recital material

LARSEN, LIBBY
(b. Wilmington, DE, 1950)

1463. **COWBOY SONGS** for Soprano Solo and Piano. E. C. Schirmer, 1994. Tonal pentatonic; c♯'–b♭"(d♭'''); Tess-M; regular meters; ♩ = 52–88; 6min; Diff-V/md, P/m.

For: soprano

Mood: cowboy life and loves; ironic, descriptive, dreamy, narrative

Voice: vocal line easily singable; some folk-like melodies; much legato; fast narrative in patterned tune in (c.); rhythmic patterns reflect word rhythms; some wide intervals

Piano: motivic structure reflects imagery of poetry; chordal; some wide spacing; accidentals

Diff: mostly rhythmic; singer will need rhythmic security

Uses: excellent short set for the vocally and musically secure singer; should appeal to all audiences

    a. *Bucking Bronco* (Belle Starr). D♭; d♭'–a"; Tess-M; 6/4, 3/4, 4/4, 4 meas. free, then ♩ = 88 strict tempo; 2+min.
    b. *Lift Me into Heaven Slowly* (Robert Creeley). D♭; d'–f"; Tess-M-mL; 6/4, ♩ = 52, slowly; 2 min.
    c. *Billy the Kid* (Anon.). Begins and ends Fmaj; c♯'–b♭"(d♭'''); Tess-M-mL; 4/4, ♩ = 84; 1min.

1464. **MARGARET SONGS.** Three Songs from *Willa Cather* for Soprano Solo and Piano (Willa Cather and Libby Larsen [(b.)]). Oxford University Press, 1998. Tonal; e♭'–a♭"; Tess-mH; regular meters with some changes; varied tempos; 18pp; Diff-V-m-md, P/m-md.

For: soprano

Mood: narrative; excited; reflective; remembrance of love

Voice: conjunct; some sustained phrases; short tone-painting melismas; speech rhythms; some wide intervals; 2 vs. 3; definite character telling her story

Piano: some motor rhythms evoking motion and sound of the train; numerous double thirds; trills; brief passage work; some cross-hand playing; accidentals; 16th-note motion in (c.); wide spacing in l.h.

Diff: ensemble in places; some rhythms

Uses: excellent set for advanced undergraduate or graduate soprano good at characterization; should be attractive to any audience

a. *Bright Rails* (Willa Cather). E♭ min; g♭'–a♭"; Tess-mH; 9/8, ♩ = 120, rhythmically, like a train; 6pp.

b. *So Little There* (Larsen adaptation). Tonal; e♭'–a♭"; Tess-mH; 3/4, 4/4, 5/4, recitative ♩ = 80; 7pp.

c. *Beneath the Hawthorne Tree* (Willa Cather). D majorish; f'–a"; Tess-mH; 6/8, ♩ = 50, rapturously; 5pp.

1465. ME (BRENDA UELAND). A Song Cycle for Soprano and Piano (from Brenda Ueland's 1938 autobiography). Oxford University Press, 1998. cmp1986–1987; first performance by Benita Valente. Tonal and X; b♭–c'''; Tess-M, mH, cs; regular meters; varied tempos (♩ = 46–132); 37min; Diff-V/md-dd, P/m-dd.

For: soprano

Mood: languid; bright; adolescent emotions; youthful arrogance; quiet; passionate; scenes from a woman's life in her own prose

Voice: lyric and dramatic recitative; long melodic lines; speech rhythms; mostly syllabic; some short and more sustained melismas; many large intervals; many high passages; very specific tempo and expressive markings; many accidentals; long texts; quite operatic in concept and scope; calls for all vocal techniques

Piano: patterned; motor rhythms and patterns; double 6ths & 3rds; arpeggiation; fast passage work; many accidentals; polyrhythms; very specific tempo, pedal, and expressive markings; motivically structured; romantic in nature

Diff: range; some pitches; rhythms; endurance; ensemble; pianist needs full command of concert technique

Uses: excellent cycle for advanced graduate or professional level soprano with warm, flexible sound, c'–c''', and flawless diction; would constitute half a recital program

a. *Why I Write This Book.* X; c'–g"; Tess-M; 6/8, Languidly, relaxed meter, ♪ = c.92; 4pp.

b. *Childhood.* X; d'–a"; Tess-cs; 4/4, 2/4, ♩ = 60, brightly; 13pp.

c. *Adolescence.* Tonal; d'–c'''; Tess-cs; 3/4, 4/4, As an awkward, halting waltz-interrupted from time to time with observations; 8pp.

d. *Greenwich Village.* Tonal; d♯'–g♯"; Tess-cs, M; 4/4, ♩ = 126-132, jaunty, with youthful arrogance; 10pp.

e. *Marriage . . . Divorce.* Tonal; c'–b"; Tess-cs; 6/8, ♪ = 96, quietly, flexibly, as if suspended; 5pp.

f. *Work.* X; c'–a"; Tess-cs; 4/4, ♩ = 126, with relentless passion; 9pp.

g. *Art (Life Is Love . . .).* Tonal; b♭–b♭"; Tess-cs; 4/4, 6/8, ♩ = 108, brilliantly, with vibrance; 18pp.

h. *The Present.* X; f♭'–a♭"; Tess-M-mH; 6/8, ♩ = 92, very freely; 6pp.

[PERINEO. See entry #15 Q]

1466. SONGS FROM LETTERS (Martha Jane Canary Hickock). Calamity Jane to her daughter Janey, 1880–1902, for Soprano and Piano. Oxford University Press, 1989. X; c'–c'''; Tess-M-mH, cs; regular meters; slow-moderate-very fast tempos; 13min; Diff-V/m-d, P/me-d.

For: soprano

Mood: narrative; five letters from Calamity Jane to her daughter telling about her own life; undercurrent of grief and sadness

Voice: lyric and dramatic melodic recitative; speech rhythms; lines often angular; expressive of the emotional content of the text; somewhat dissonant; some portamento; some wide leaps to high notes; numerous unaccomp. passages of free recitative; one high melisma on "ah";

Piano: motivically constructed with patterns expressive of different aspects of the text; many accidentals; some double 3rds; some wide spacing; mostly chordal texture; dissonant

Diff: some pitches; a few high phrases

Uses: an excellent cycle for a graduate level soprano; challenging musically and emotionally; should be attractive to audiences interested in Americana

a. *So Like Your Father's (1880).* X; e'–f"; Tess-M; 4/4, Freely, recitative–Quietly (♩ = 56); 1+pp.

b. *He Never Misses (1880).* X; f'–f"; Tess-M; 4/4, With abandon (♩ = 192-200); 4+pp.

c. *A Man Can Love Two Women (1880).* X; c♯'–b♭"; Tess-cs; 3/4, 2/4, Calmly (♩ = 56); 3+pp.

d. *A Working Woman (1882-1893).* X; d♭'–c'''; Tess-M-mH; 4/4, 3/4, Slowly, freely, recitative–Jaunty, as a tack piano (♩ = 100); 7+pp.

e. *All I Have (1902).* X; c'–b"; Tess-mH; 4/4, 3/4, 2/2, With flexibility throughout (♩ = 56); 4+pp.

1467. SONNETS FROM THE PORTUGUESE (Elizabeth Barrett Browning). Cycle. Oxford University Press, 1998. cmp1988–1989 for Arleen Augér. X, some centering on F and G; d'–b"; Tess-M, mH, cs; regular and irregular changing meters; varied tempos (♩ =54–144); 38pp; Diff-V/m-d, P/m-d.

For: soprano (lyric)

Mood: calm, peaceful; breathless, joyful; questioning; certain; love poems from Elizabeth Barrett to Robert Browning

Voice: lyrical; speech rhythms; melodic patterns recur; some long high phrases; syllabic; a few expressive melismas; many words, some repetition; very singable lines

Piano: patterned; polyrhythms; accidentals; somewhat dissonant with a romantic sweep of phrases and figures; double 3rds & 5ths in both hands; some wide spacing; chordal and linear

Diff: some pitches; ensemble; some tricky piano figurations; endurance

Uses: fine cycle for graduate or professional level soprano

Rec: D#8

a. *I Thought Once How Theocritus Had Sung.* X on F; f'–g♯"; Tess-M; 4/4, ♩ = 54-60, calmly, peacefully; 5pp.

b. *My Letters!* X on G; e♭'–a"; Tess-cs; 4/4, 3/4, 5/4, ♩ = 100 very lightly, as a soft tremor; 7pp.

c. *With the Same Heart, I Said, I'll Answer Thee.* X on G; d'–a"; Tess-M; 6/8, 3/8, 5/4, Slowly, freely–♩. = 54; 6pp.

d. *If I Leave All for Thee.* X (F minorish); d'–a";
Tess-M; 6/4, 8/4, 7/4, 9/4, ♩ = 80, Very legato,
mysteriously; 7pp.

e. *Oh, Yes!* X; e'–g"; Tess-mH; 4/4, 5/4, 7/4, 6/4,
♩ = 144; 5pp.

f. *How Do I Love Thee?* X; d'–b"; Tess-mH; 6/8, 2/4,
♪ = 92 very freely throughout; 4pp.

LARSON, ANNA
(b. Knoxville, TN, 1940)

1468. **THE LISTENERS** (Walter de la Mare). Arsis, 1984.
X; A–f'; Tess-M; 4/4 with changes, ♩ = 60–Con moto
(♩ = 80); 7min; Diff-V/d, P/d.

For: dramatic baritone
Mood: philosophical; dramatic
Voice: rather disjunct; frequent leaps of 7th & other large
intervals; frequent repeated-note passages; chromatic;
triplets; short phrases separated by rests; sections
separated by interludes; syllabic
Piano: chordal and linear; broken-chord figures; 8ve
doublings; chromatic; triplets; no vocal line doubling
Diff: secure musicianship required; interpretation will need
careful study
Uses: excellent material for mature singer; could stand alone

LATHAM, WILLIAM P.
(b. Shreveport, LA, 1917)

1469. **THE NEW LOVE AND THE OLD** (Arthur
O'Shaughnessy). [17]. H & L keys: Amin & Fmin;
d'–g" & bb–eb"; Tess-M; 6/8, Andante; 4pp; Diff-V/m,
P/m.

For: tenor; baritone
Mood: lyrical; sad
Voice: flowing phrases fragmented by rests; recit.-like section
with repeated notes; 8ve leaps upward
Piano: chordal; fragmented; some independent melodic lines
Diff: leaps; *sotto voce* on highest tones; ensemble
Uses: good teaching song; useful for recital

LATROBE, CHRISTIAN I. (See Special Section)

LAURIDSEN, MORTEN
(b. Colfax, WA, 1943)

1470. **A WINTER COME.** Six Songs on Poems by Howard
Moss for High Voice and Piano. peermusic classical,
1985. cmp1967. Tonal and X; bb–g#"; Tess-cs, M;
changing meters; varied tempos (♩ = 52–160); 15pp;
Diff-V/m-md, P/m-md.

For: tenor; soprano
Mood: crisp; sparkling; cold; images of winter
Voice: syllabic; melody governs word stress; some conjunct
lines; many large intervals
Piano: fairly thin textures; mostly linear; numerous
accidentals; various rhythmic groupings
Diff: some pitches; vocal lines somewhat instrumental in

nature
Uses: interesting cycle for graduate level singer; good group
for a "seasons" program
Rec: D#50 (no titles given)

a. *When Frost Moves Fast.* [65]. Ebmaj; bb–eb";
Tess-cs; 4/4, 6/8, 3/4, 7/4, Fast and delightful
(♩ = ca.160); 4pp.

b. *As Birds Come Nearer.* [65]. Bb-centered;
cb'–gb"; Tess-cs; 4/4, 3/4, 2/4, 6/4, ♩ = 76; 2pp.

c. *The Racing Waterfall.* A-centered; d'–f#"; Tess-M;
2/4, 3/4, Allegretto giocoso (♩ = 104); 2pp.

d. *A Child Lay Down.* X; f#'–f"; Tess-M; 7/4, 6/4,
5/4, Mysteriously (♩ = 52); 2pp.

e. *Who Reads by Starlight.* Fmin-maj; eb'–e"; Tess-
M; 3/2, 2/2, ♩ = ca.120 excitedly, as if revealing a
secret; 2pp.

f. *And What of Love.* X; c'–g#"; Tess-cs; 4/4, 3/4,
5/4, Warmly expressive (♩ = 60); 3pp.

LEES, BENJAMIN [Lysniatsky]
(b. Harbin, Manchuria, China, 1924)

1471. **CYPRIAN SONGS** (Richard Nickson). Boosey &
Hawkes, 1960. Cycle. Ambiguous tonalities; A–f#';
Tess-M-mH; regular and irregular changing meters;
slow tempos; 11min; Diff-V/md, P/md.

For: lyric baritone
Mood: lyrical; reflects the memory of love relationship
Voice: mostly conjunct and chromatic; sustained phrases;
many long tones; 3 & 4 in voice vs. 2, 3, & 4 in piano;
some pitches elusive; many phrases lie around g-a-bb;
three high phrases
Piano: linear-chordal combination; numerous ostinato figures;
subdued; emphasis on m2nds; 24-meas. trill
Diff: pitch; breath control; some rhythmic irregularities
Uses: subdued, dream-like cycle; good for learning breath
control; useful quiet group for recital; intermediate to
advanced students

a. *From What Green Island.* Bb–d'; Tess-M; 4/4 with
many changes, Andante; 4pp.

b. *Wake! For the Night of Shadows.* A–d'; Tess-mH;
3/4 with changes, Adagio; 4pp.

c. *Still Is It As It Was.* c–d#'; Tess-mH; 2/2, 3/2,
Moderato intimo; 5pp.

d. *Over Me like Soft Clouds.* Bb–f#'; Tess-M-mH;
5/4 with many changes, Adagio dolcemente; 5pp.

1472. **SONGS OF THE NIGHT** (Richard Nickson). Cycle.
Boosey & Hawkes, 1958. Minor keys (except for last
song); eb'–bb"; Tess-mH-HH; regular meters; varied
tempos; 12min; Diff-V/d, P/md.

For: soprano (high lyric with ample sound); tenor with same
qualities
Mood: lyrical; somber moods of night and death; last song is
approach of day
Voice: conjunct; some skips; a few upward leaps; long
phrases; many passages lie at top of staff and above;
last two songs climax on bb"; last song ends bb" on
"day"; speech rhythms; some pitches difficult

Piano: patterned in various ways, much repetition; (d.), perpetual motion piece–piano represents rain; some chordal passages; effective writing; large reach helpful

Diff: extremely high tessitura phrases, highest tones approached conjunctly rather than by leap; singer will need absolute ease and freedom eb"–bb" and ample sound on the staff

Uses: good cycle for advanced student; program ender

    a. *O Shade of Evening.* Ebmin; g'–bb"; Tess-HH; 6/8, Andante ♩. = circa 46; 2pp.

    b. *A Star Fell in Flames.* Gmin; ab'–a"; Tess-mH-H; 3/4, Moderato ♩ = circa 63; 2pp.

    c. *The Enemies.* Cmin; f'–g"; Tess-M; 2/2, Moderato ♩ = 76; 2pp.

    d. *A Whisper of Rain.* Fmin; f'–g♯"; Tess-M-H; 2/4, Con moto ♪ = circa 168; 8pp.

    e. *Fall to the Night Wind.* Bbmin; f'–bb"; Tess-mH-H; 6/8, Andante ♪ = 120; 2pp.

    f. *On Eastern Hills.* Ebmaj; eb'–bb"; Tess-M (ends high); 4/4, Commodo ♩ = 66; 2pp.

1473. **THREE SONGS FOR CONTRALTO AND PIANO.** Cycle. Boosey & Hawkes, 1968. First performed by Maureen Forrester. No key sigs., tonal F-, D- (A), Bb-centered; harmonic figures reminiscent of *Songs of the Night* (see above); f–f"; Tess-L, mL, M, mH; irregular and changing meters; moderate tempos; 17pp; Diff-V/md, P/md.

For: contralto

Mood: lyrical; dream-like; floating quality of youth

Voice: sustained phrases; many long tones; much chest voice; small conjunct intervals contrasted with leaps; slow speech rhythms; some slow melismatic passages; some difficult intervals

Piano: patterned with various figures; ornamental arpeggiation; repeated tones; detached and staccato 8ves; sustained chords and tones; broken-chord figures; articulations important; emphasis on m2nds

Diff: sustained phrases; good breath control necessary; solid low f necessary; interpretation of poetry requires insight into symbolism; some difficult intervals

Uses: good cycle; very effective for the right singer; quiet ending

    a. *The Moonlit Tree* (Richard Nickson). g♯–c"; Tess-mL-L; 3/4 with changes, Adagio ♩ = 58; 5pp.

    b. *Close All the Doors* (Richard Nickson). g–e"; Tess-M-mH; 5/4 with changes, Moderato ♩ = 112; 5pp.

    c. *The Angel* (William Blake). f–f"; Tess-M; 4/4 with many changes, Andante con moto ♩ = 96; 7pp.

LEICHTLING, ALAN
(b. Brooklyn, NY, 1947)

1474. **SONGS IN WINTER,** Op. 58. Cycle. Seesaw, 1972. cmp1971–1972. X; bb–a"; Tess-M; regular and irregular changing meters; varied tempos; 49pp; Diff-V/dd, P/dd.

For: mezzo-soprano

Mood: lyrical; philosophical; love songs; nature imagery

Voice: disjunct; chromatic; large intervals; much unaccompanied singing; rhythmic intricacies

Piano: dissonant; chromatic; chordal; tone clusters; some contrapuntal sections; some broken-chord figuration

Diff: perfect pitch desirable; rhythms; ensemble; length

Uses: rather long cycle; effective for advanced performers

    a. *Sonnet (To the Autumnal Moon)* (Samuel Taylor Coleridge). c'–g♯"; 3/4 with many changes, Molto moderato e scorrevole; 9pp.

    b. *Sonnet (When in Disgrace with Fortune and Men's Eyes)* (William Shakespeare). bb–a"; 1/4, 4/4, 3/4, 5/8, 3/8, etc., Adagio e solenelle; 7pp.

    c. *The Passionate Shepherd to His Love* (Christopher Marlowe). db'–g"; 4/4 with changes, Allegro ma non troppo; 9pp.

    d. *The Definition of Love* (Andrew Marvell). bb–ab"; 6/8 with changes, Rubato ma non troppo; 3+pp.

    e. *The Nymph's Reply to the Shepherd* (Sir Walter Raleigh). c'–ab"; 2/4 with changes, Andante con moto; 9pp.

    f. *Solitude* (Alexander Pope). c♯'–f"; 3/4, 2/4, Lento e piacevole; 5pp.

    g. *Song ("Go and Catch a Falling Star")* (John Donne). d'–f♯"; 9/8, 12/8, 6/8, Allegretto e leggero; 9pp.

LEKBERG, SVEN
(b. Chicago, IL, 1899; d. Indianola, IA, 1984)

1475. **BIRDS SINGING AT DUSK** (from the Chinese of Li Po). [17]. H & L keys: X; d♯'–f♯" & b–d"; Tess-M; 4/4, Lento assai; 3pp; Diff-V/m, P/m.

For: all voices

Mood: lyrical; descriptive; nature imagery

Voice: flowing phrases; parlando section

Piano: chordal; chromatic; some independent melodic lines; single-voice texture in middle

Diff: pitches; needs great delicacy of style

Uses: excellent for recital and for teaching *parlando* style

1476. **FOUR POEMS OF EDNA ST. VINCENT MILLAY.** [51]. Separate entries below. Could be sung as a group by a lyric or dramatic soprano.

A. **THE ROAD TO AVRILLÉ.** G. Schirmer, 1971. Gbmaj; db'–b"; Tess-H; 3/4, 4/4, In waltz time–Poco rubato; 2+min; Diff-V/m-md, P/m-md.

For: lyric soprano; tenor

Mood: descriptive; remembrance; parted lovers

Voice: stepwise and easy skips; many accidentals; repetitive rhythms; dotted notes; 2-note slurs

Piano: waltz style; countermelody in 3rds & 6ths; many accidentals; some doubling of vocal line

Diff: b" sustained

Uses: lovely song for recital group; quiet ending

B. **SWEET SOUNDS, OH, BEAUTIFUL MUSIC.** Dbmaj-Bmaj-Bbmaj; d♯'–bb"; Tess-M; 3/4, 4/4,

Joyously; 4pp; Diff-V/md, P/d.

For: soprano; tenor

Mood: joyous; in praise of music

Voice: sweeping phrases, many ascending; pitches usually clear, despite frequent changes of tonal center; some dissonances with piano; climactic b♭" on "live"

Piano: repeated and broken chords; broken 8ves; triplets; many accidentals; supports vocal line well

Diff: some pitches; several important upper-register tones on "ih" vowel

Uses: an effective recital song

C. I DRANK AT EVERY VINE. G♭maj-Cmaj-Emaj; e♭'-f♯"; Tess-M; 3/4, 4/4, Slowly and gently; 3pp; Diff-V/m, P/me.

For: any medium or high voice

Mood: lyrical; philosophical statement about hunger and thirst

Voice: mostly conjunct motion; some 4ths, one m7th; short phrases separated by rests

Piano: chordal; numerous accidentals; supports vocal line well

Diff: some pitches

Uses: could be an effective recital song

D. THE SPRING AND THE FALL. G. Schirmer, 1971. Fmin; e♭'-b♭"; Tess-H; 9/8, 6/8, With easy motion; 2+min; Diff-V/m, P/m-md.

For: dramatic or lyric soprano

Mood: lament for lost love

Voice: stepwise and small skips; easy rhythms; some long-ranged phrases; several sustained high tones

Piano: block chords–repeated and broken; many accidentals; large dynamic contrasts; big ending

Diff: sustained high tones (b♭" *fff*, final f", 11 beats); dynamic control (*p–fff*)

Uses: good song for high-lying voice; group or program ender

1477. O LORD, THOU HAST SEARCHED ME (Psalm 139:1, 4, 8). G. Schirmer, 1972. Cmin; b♭-g"; Tess-mH; 6/8, 4/4, Moderato; 3pp; Diff-V/m, P/m.

For: soprano; tenor

Mood: religious; devout

Voice: stepwise and small skips; some long-ranged phrases; some syncopation

Piano: 4–5-voice chordal texture over scale lines and other moving parts

Diff: some long phrases

Uses: recital material; good religious song

LESSARD, JOHN A.
(b. San Francisco, 1920)

1478. MORNING SONG (Claire Nicolas). General, 1964. B♭maj; e'-f"; Tess-M; 6/8; 2pp; Diff-V/me, P/me.

For: soprano; mezzo-soprano

Mood: lyrical; whimsical; ambivalent

Voice: conjunct; speech rhythms in usual 6/8 patterns; fairly rapid tempo; some vocalizing

Piano: 8ves in various combinations; linear; accidentals

Uses: short song; useful as teaching song for young students

1479. MOTHER GOOSE (Mother Goose Rhymes). Peer International, 1953. Traditional keys; a–e"; Tess-M, L; regular meters; varied tempos; 7pp; Diff-V/e, P/e.

For: mezzo-soprano

Mood: humorous

Voice: tuneful vocal lines; conjunct; short phrases

Piano: patterned; broken 8ves; simple texture; large reaches

Uses: easy set for young mezzo-soprano; program ender

    a. *There Was an Old Woman.* Emin; e'–c"; 6/8, ♩.= 66; 17meas.

    b. *Doctor Fell.* Amaj; e'–e"; 2/2, ♩= 100; 10meas.

    c. *Going to St. Ives.* Amaj; a–e"; 2/2, ♩= 88; 20meas.

    d. *The Man in the Moon.* Gmin; g'–e"; 2/2, ♩= 76; 22meas.

    e. *T'Other Little Tune.* G♭-B♭maj; e♭'–d♭"; 4/4, ♩= 144; 15meas.

    f. *Three Wise Men of Gotham.* Emin; e'–d"; 4/4, ♩= 152; 11meas.

1480. ORPHEUS (William Shakespeare). Mercury, 1952. Cmaj; c'–e"; Tess-mH; 4/4, 5/4, 2/4, Allegretto; 4pp; Diff-V/m, P/md.

For: mezzo-soprano; lyric baritone

Mood: lyrical; philosophical; nature imagery

Voice: long phrases; a few triplets; syncopation

Piano: some counterpoint; broken-chord figures; afterbeats; independent of voice

Uses: fine recital song

1481. RECUERDO (Edna St. Vincent Millay). General, 1964. G-centered; d'–g"; Tess-M; 4/4, 5/4, Con moto; 4pp; Diff-V/md, P/md.

For: soprano; tenor; mezzo-soprano

Mood: tired; discordant; disjunct; surrounded by bustling activity

Voice: stepwise and skips up to 6th; speech-like rhythms; some repetition; many accidentals

Piano: discordant and disjunct; describes environment, noises of ferry; block and broken chords; many accidentals; independent of vocal line

Diff: irregular rhythms; some pitches difficult against accomp.; both performers need to understand poem and setting; pianist must differentiate and balance harmonic support and sound effects and articulate carefully

Uses: in an American group or one describing modern city living; see also settings by Castelnuovo-Tedesco and Musto

1482. ROSE-CHEEK'D LAURA (Thomas Campion). General, 1969. X; b–g"; Tess-H, L; 4/4 with many changes, Allegretto; 3pp; Diff-V/d, P/d.

For: light lyric baritone best; mezzo-soprano

Mood: lyrical; transparent; praise of beauty

Voice: both conjunct and disjunct; many accidentals; changing meters, 8th note constant; many leaps

Piano: widely-spaced linear score; distinct articulations; many accidentals; thin texture

Diff: pitch; rhythm; ensemble; both performers must be rhythmically sophisticated, accurate, and stable

Uses: interesting song; not for a beginner

1483. **SONGS FROM SHAKESPEARE.** General, 1969.
Traditional keys with dissonance; b♭–f"; Tess-M-mL;
regular, changing meters; slow tempos; 5pp; Diff-V/m,
P/m.

For: baritone; mezzo-soprano
Mood: lyrical; transparent
Voice: many skips; speech rhythms; short phrases
Piano: linear; transparent 8ve textures; some trills;
articulations important; large reach helpful
Diff: pitches; rhythm
Uses: interesting songs; quite different in approach from other
settings of these texts

    a. *Ariel's Song.* E♭maj; b♭–e♭"; 3/4, 4/4, 5/4, 2/4,
Lento; 2pp.
    b. *Full Fathom Five.* G-centered; e'–f"; 3/4, 2/4,
Lento; 3pp.

1484. **WHENAS IN SILKS MY JULIA GOES** (Robert
Herrick). General, 1964. Emaj; e'–e"; Tess-M; 4/4, 3/4,
Lento; 2pp; Diff-V/m, P/md.

For: lyric baritone; tenor
Mood: descriptive; sensuous
Voice: somewhat fragmented but lyrical; rhythm somewhat
complex; easy intervals
Piano: rapid afterbeat pattern; some chromaticism
Diff: rhythms
Uses: good for singer with limited range but good
musicianship; teaching soft singing

LEYERLE, WILLIAM
(b. Cape Girardeau, MO, 1931)

1485. **BLACK IS THE COLOR OF MY TRUE LOVE'S
HAIR** (Traditional). [55]; 1st©1977. Cmin; c'–e♭";
Tess-mL; 4/4 (♩ = 72); 3pp; Diff-V/me, P/me.

For: baritone; bass-baritone
Mood: lyrical love song; familiar text in a new setting
Voice: somewhat disjunct, but legato; several 8ve leaps;
syncopation
Piano: melody doubles vocal line in r.h.; broken chords and
figuration in 8th notes in l.h.
Diff: rhythm and 8ve leaps for singer
Uses: teaching syncopation, modest rhythmic complexities,
and 8ve leaps; good recital song for young singer

1486. **THE TREASURE CHEST** (William Leyerle). (No.1
from *Hypochondria*, a Cycle of 6 Songs, apparently
unpublished). [56]. cmp1983. Amin; d♯'–g"; Tess-mH;
4/4, Adagio e sofferentemente–2/4, Largo; 3min;
Diff-V/m, P/me.

For: tenor; soprano
Mood: humorous; describes contents of medicine cabinet;
includes Latin and pseudo-Latin phrases
Voice: begins with melisma on "Oh!"; chant-like section lists
diseases and their remedies; small skips; uncomplicated
rhythms
Piano: spare accomp.–just 8ves under chant-like sections;
"Largo" section has l.h. countermelody and r.h.
afterbeat chords
Diff: requires *ff* on e♭", e", and f" several times

Uses: humorous song

LIEBERMANN, LOWELL
(b. New York, NY, 1961)

1487. **SIX SONGS ON POEMS OF HENRY W.
LONGFELLOW,** Op. 57, for Voice and Piano.
Theodore Presser, 2000. cmp1997. "For Robert White."
Mostly tonal, shifting harmonies; c'–a♭"; Tess-M, mH,
cs; regular and irregular changing meters; varied
tempos; 20min; Diff-V/m-md, P/m-md.

For: tenor; soprano
Mood: melancholy: the comfort of Night; the unfulfilled life;
snow as metaphor for despair; the troubled mind;
remembrance of a dead child; the renewal of hope
Voice: mostly very conjunct lines, a few skips, up to a 6th;
rhythmically fluid in changing meters; syllabic with a
few 2–3-note slurs; three 16th-note melismas
Piano: patterned; much arpeggiation in shifting harmonies;
filigree passages, as well as repeated notes and parallel
2-note chords in r.h.; some very soft passages in high
register; rhythmic groupings of 5, 6, 7, 9, 10, & 13;
many accidentals; some chromatic block chords in (f.)
Diff: some pitches; *pp* singing at top of staff; changing
meters; irregular note groupings; accidentals in rapid
arpeggiation
Uses: beautiful cycle in neo-romantic style for graduate level
lyric tenor (or soprano)

    a. *Hymn to the Night.* E♭-centered; d'–a♭"; Tess-M-
mH; 3/8, 2/8, 5/4, Allegro (♪ = c.108); 8pp.
    b. *Mezzo Cammin.* X; e'–g"; Tess-mH; 4/4, Lento
(♩ = c.40); 3pp.
    c. *Snow-Flakes.* X on G; f'–f♯"; Tess-M; 6/8, 9/8,
8/8, Lento (♪ = c.80); 3pp.
    d. *The Haunted Chamber.* X on F; c'–g♭"; Tess-cs;
5/4, 4/4, 3/4, 6/4, 7/8, 7/4, Moderato (♩ = c.80); 6pp.
    e. *Delia.* E♭maj; c♯'–g♭"; Tess-cs; 4/4, Largo
(♩ = c.50); 1p.
    f. *The Arrow and the Song.* C♯-centered, shifting;
e♭'–f♯"; Tess-M; 6/4, 9/4, Allegro (♩. = c.72); 5pp.

1488. **THREE DREAM SONGS** (Langston Hughes) for
Voice and Piano, Op. 53. Theodore Presser, 1999.
cmp1996. Tonal; b–g"; Tess-mL, cs; regular meters;
slow to medium tempos; 6min; Diff-V/m, P/e-m.

For: baritone; mezzo-soprano
Mood: present: dream as a metaphor; past: sleeping dream;
future: waking dream for the future
Voice: syllabic; short phrases; chromatic; one melisma; wide
range in (c.); ascending dramatic phrases
Piano: mostly chordal; chromatic; some countermelody
Diff: chromatic vocal line; dramatic structure of third song
Uses: good short set for a rich low voice

    a. *Ardella.* Tonal on B; b–e♭"; Tess-mL; 4/4, Adagio;
1p.
    b. *Dream.* Tonal; c'–c♯"; Tess-mL; 4/4, Andante; 1p.
    c. *I Dream a World.* Gmaj; b–g"; Tess-cs; 4/4, 3/2,
Nobile; 1p.

LINDENFELD, HARRIS
(b. Benton Harbor, MI, 1945)

1489. **THE COW** (from *Three Songs on Poems by Theodore Roethke*). [3]. cmp1973. X; d'–d♭'''; Tess-H; unmetered, 2/4, 4/4; 3pp; Diff-V/d, P/d.
For: soprano
Mood: humorous
Voice: requires acting; uses speaking, *Sprechstimme*, and singing; portamentos; difficult melisma; rhythms in sung section rather free
Piano: requires pianist to use head and arm movements in "exaggerated bravura"; highly chromatic; mostly 2-voice texture; some tone clusters; trills; grace notes; no doubling of vocal line
Diff: vocal techniques and pitch patterns; ensemble
Uses: change of pace; group ender

1490. **DOLOR** (from *Three Songs on Poems by Theodore Roethke*). [3]. cmp1972. X; b–f♯"; Tess-mH; 2/4, 3/4, 4/4, ♩ = ca.66 (with several changes); 5pp; Diff-V/md, P/md.
For: baritone; mezzo-soprano
Mood: wry commentary on life in the modern office
Voice: chant-like; conjunct–moves mostly by half and whole steps; various subdivisions of beat and meas.; many accidentals
Piano: block structures–7th, 2nds, 4ths, 8ves, clusters, etc; chromaticism; many clef changes; rhythmic complexities
Diff: rhythms; communication–getting the right mood
Uses: possible recital song for modern life theme group

LINDERMAN, ED
(b. Chicago, IL, 1947)

1491. **I SHALL PASS THROUGH THIS LIFE BUT ONCE** (Etien de Grelliet). Voice of the Rockies, 1995. cmp1982. Dmaj with Lydian 4th; g♯–f♯"; Tess-wide; 4/4, Andante; 2pp; Diff-V/m, P/e.
For: mezzo-soprano; some sopranos with low extension
Mood: lyrical but resolute
Voice: somewhat angular melody; skips of m9, M7, dim.5; quarter & 8th note motion; some triplets; ends on sustained e"; no option given for low g♯
Piano: l.h. broken chord patterns; r.h. 2–4 voice chords and countermelody; some octaves; incidental doubling of vocal line; 9-meas. prelude, 2-meas. postlude
Diff: tessitura; range
Uses: somewhat "popular" flavor; change of pace in a group; quiet encore

LIPPÉ, EDOUARD [Solomon Hirsch Lipschutz]
(fl. 20th Century)

1492. **HOW DO I LOVE THEE?** (Elizabeth Barrett Browning). Boston Music Co., 1941. H & L keys: E♭maj & D♭maj; e♭'–g♭"(a♭) & d♭'–e"(g♭); Tess-M; 4/4, Andante con moto; 5+pp; Diff-V/md, P/d.
For: any voice except extremely low or extremely light

Mood: narrative; ecstatic; intense; dramatic
Voice: chromatic lines; many skips; rhythms not difficult
Piano: big; large reaches; 6–8-voice chords; broken chords; arpeggios; afterbeat pattern; some countermelody; big ending; some doubling of vocal line
Diff: substantial sound needed; wide dynamic range; opt. a♭" sustained with fermata
Uses: versatile song; group ender; possible encore; possible wedding song
Rec: D#35

LIPSKY, ALEXANDER
(b. Poland, 1901)

1493. **LILAC-TIME** (Thomas S. Jones, Jr.). [22]. X; c'–e"; Tess-mL; 4/4, 3/4, Lento; 3pp; Diff-V/md, P/md.
For: mezzo-soprano; baritone
Mood: lyrical; somber spring song
Voice: fragmented; chromatic; generally short phrases
Piano: chordal, with some melodic interest; chromatic
Diff: soft tone control
Uses: good for singer with limited high tones

LIPTAK, DAVID
(b. Pittsburgh, PA, 1949)

1494. **SEVEN SONGS** (James Wright). For Medium Voice and Piano. MMB Music, Inc., 1984. cmp1984 "for William Sharp." X (atonal); g–e"; Tess-mL-mH; changing meters; alternating slow/fast tempos; 28pp; Diff-V/dd, P/dd.
For: baritone
Mood: surreal, dream-like texts and settings
Voice: complex pitch sequences and rhythm patterns; fragmented phrases; difficult to find pitches; many dynamic changes; many tempo changes in (d.); very difficult score depicts disparate poetic images
Piano: difficult rhythms; pitch sequences with many accidentals; many texture, articulation, and dynamic changes; pedaling carefully marked; wide reaches; 3-stave scoring in (d.); mostly linear, although last two songs have more block chords; covers keyboard
Diff: ensemble requires two excellent musicians; singer should have perfect pitch; difficult poetry; singer needs acting skills for (d.); difficult in every way
Uses: recital material for mature performers with outstanding musicianship
Rec: D#252

    a. *The Jewel.* X; g♯–e"; Tess-M; 4/4, 3/4, 5/8, ♪ = c.66 Slow, Mysterious; 1+pp.
    b. *Twilights.* X; g♯–d"; Tess-M; 3/4, 2/4, 4/4, 5/4, ♩ = c.92 With Energy; 3pp.
    c. *Beginning.* X; g–e"; Tess-M; 5/4, 6/4, 4/4, etc., ♪ = c.50 Slowly & peacefully; 3+pp.
    d. *Two Hangovers: Number One.* X; a–e"; Tess-wide; 6/4, 5/4, 5/8, 4/4, 3/4, etc., ♩ = c.66 (many changes range from ♪ = c.54 to ♩ = c.120); 7pp. Segues into ***Number Two: I Try to Waken And Greet the World Once Again.*** X; a–e"; Tess-mH; 7/8, 5/8,

3/8, 4/4, etc., ♩ = c.126 Fast, rhythmic, sprightly; 2pp.

e. *Milkweed.* X; a–e"; Tess-M; 3/4, 4/4, 2/4, ♪ = c.58 Slow, gentle; 4pp.

f. *Spring Images.* X; b♭–e"; Tess-M; 2/4, 5/8, 3/4, 7/8, 4/4, etc., ♩ = c.88 Mercurial, bright; 3pp.

g. *A Dream of Burial.* X; g♯–b'; Tess-mL; 3/4, 2/4, 4/4, 3/3, ♪ = c.44 Very slow: nearly motionless, recitative; 3pp.

LITTLE, ARTHUR REGINALD
(American, b. 19th Century)

1495. THE CITY OF SLEEP (Rudyard Kipling). [66, vol. 3]; 1st©1905. Fmin; d'–f"; Tess-M; 6/8, Solemnly, but not slowly; 71meas.; Diff-V/m, P/m.
For: tenor
Mood: rather dramatic; somber; intense
Voice: stepwise and small leaps; some odd accidentals; major-minor fluctuation
Piano: block chords; some countermelody
Diff: poem needs explaining; ensemble; dynamic control; major-minor fluctuation.
Uses: nice song; interesting rhythmic structure and harmonic color; useful for recital

1496. HELEN (Edgar Allan Poe). [66, vol. 1]; 1st©1902. Cmaj; e♭'–g"; Tess-mH; 4/4, Reposefully, with breadth; 20meas.; Diff-V/m, P/m.
For: tenor
Mood: lyrical
Voice: stepwise with small skips
Piano: block chords; interesting harmonic progressions; thick texture; large reach needed
Diff: dynamic control; sustained g" at end
Uses: American group

LLOYD, CHARLES, JR.
(b. Toledo, OH, 1948)

1497. COMPENSATION (Paul Laurence Dunbar). [6]. X; b♭–c♭"; Tess-mL; 3/4, Slowly with expression; 1p; Diff-V/m, P/me.
For: any medium or low voice; best for bass or contralto
Mood: lyrical; philosophical
Voice: very sustained phrases in half/quarter-note rhythmic pattern; features ascending m3rds & P5ths; chromatic
Piano: chordal; broken chords and afterbeats in l.h.; chromatic
Uses: good short song; meaningful text

LOCKWOOD, ANNEA (See entry #15 G)

LOCKWOOD, NORMAND
(b. New York, NY, 1906)

1498. THE GOLDEN LADY (Dorothy Lockwood). Broude Bros., 1954. cmp1953. Dmaj with altered chords; b♭–g♭"; Tess-M; 6/8, Moderately slow, in 6; 3pp;

Diff-V/m, P/m.
For: soprano; tenor
Mood: lyrical: "Lines to go with a Picture"
Voice: conjunct with some skips; one phrase encompasses g" and b♭; triplet and duplet groupings; some syncopation
Piano: chordal; some countermelody; accidentals; 8th-note movement; large reach helpful
Diff: rhythmic groupings may be difficult for weak musician
Uses: nice song; useful for teaching polyrhythms and visual imagery in a text

1499. JOSEPH, DEAREST JOSEPH (German carol; trans. by Percy Dearmek). [4];1st©1956. A♭maj; d♭'–g"; Tess-mH; 3/4, 6/4, 4/4, Andante; 3+min; Diff-V/m, P/me.
For: soprano; mezzo-soprano; tenor
Mood: reverent; two speakers–Mary and narrator
Voice: stepwise and small skips; two leaps of 9th; some syncopation
Piano: block chords; 4–6-voice texture; rarely doubles vocal line
Diff: legato long phrases in two sections; leap of 9th; descending scale on "frees"
Uses: church solo or Christmas recital

1500. OH, LADY, LET THE SAD TEARS FALL (Adelaide Crapsey). Seesaw, 1947. cmp1938. D♯min; f♯'–d♯"; Tess-mH; 4/4, Lamentevole; 34meas.; Diff-V/me, P/m.
For: mezzo-soprano; any voice with amplitude in the range shown
Mood: intense; sad; sustained; lament
Voice: stepwise and small skips; very legato; cresc. in ascending lines
Piano: 6-voice texture; constantly moving voices in 3rds; rich harmonies
Diff: many cresc.; *ff* on d♯"
Uses: beautiful song; good for student with big voice but short range; recital material

1501. RIVER MAGIC (Eva Byron). Seesaw, 1947. cmp1945. "For Janet Fairbank." X-Fmin-X; d'–f"; Tess-mH; 4/4, Slow–Moderato–Slow; 3min; Diff-V/d, P/md.
For: any voice except light and high
Mood: mood piece combined with narrative
Voice: syncopated; jazzy; many accidentals; dialect
Piano: syncopated; dotted rhythms; accidentals
Diff: some intervals; style

LOEFFLER, CHARLES MARTIN
(b. Mulhouse, Alsace, France, 1861; d. Medfield, MA, 1935)

[See Appendix for songs with French texts]

[See also D#s 253 & 254 for songs not listed below]

1502. FOUR SONGS, Opus 15. Reprints: Classical Vocal Reprints (b.); Masters Music Publications; Recital Publications, 1983. Traditional keys with whole-tone harmonies and many modulations; c'–f"; Tess-M;

regular meters with changes; slow to moderate tempos; 21pp; Diff-V/d, P/d.

For: baritone
Mood: dream-like love poetry, full of distant memory
Voice: fairly long lines; modulating melodies; chromatic; polyrhythms; mostly syllabic
Piano: score looks like a French piano score from the full-blown impressionistic style; thick texture alternates with more linear configurations; much arpeggiation; highly chromatic; many polyrhythms; pianist needs good ear for tonal color and weight
Diff: chromaticism; polyrhythms
Uses: wonderful set for lyric baritone with rich sound and good grasp of French style

    a. *Sudden Light* (Dante Gabriel Rossetti). D♭maj with much modulation; d♭'–e"; 3/2, Adagio –Vivo e molto leggiero; 5pp.

    b. *A Dream within a Dream* (Edgar Allan Poe). D♭maj with much modulation; c'–e♭"; 12/8, 9/8, 8/8, 6/8, Andante moderato; 6pp. [**Rec:** D#10]

    c. *To Helen* (Edgar Allan Poe). Fmaj with many modulations; d♭'–f "; 4/4, Andante, un poco allegretto; 4pp. [**Rec:** D#253]

    d. *Sonnet* (G. C. Lodge). Modulatory, ends Cmin; d♭'–f "; 3/4, 4/4, Andante; 6pp.

LOGAN, WENDELL
(b. Thomson, GA, 1940)

1503. **MARROW OF MY BONE . . . IF THERE BE SORROW** (Mari Evans). (from Cycle, *Ice and Fire* [It is not clear whether this is 1 song from the cycle or 2–both are extremely short and obviously for different voices.]) [6]. 2-part song for 2 different voices. X; 1:g♯'–b♭", 2: F–e♭'; Tess-1: H, 2: mL; 1: 3/4, 2/4, ♩ = ca.96, 2: unmetered–5/4, 4/4, 3/4, free–♩ = ca.60; 3pp; Diff-V/dd, P/dd.

For: 1: soprano; 2: baritone (or bass)
Mood: 1: passionate, dramatic; 2: lyrical; philosophical
Voice: 1 ("Marrow of My Bone"): strong accents, long tones on e", g", and b♭" (*sfz–p* with cresc., and several leaps of 7th; 2 ("If There Be Sorrow"): "Improvised quality" (with special performance notes for improvised opening passage), chromatic; large leaps
Piano: 1: moving 16ths almost throughout with sustained chords; chromatic; 2: chordal, improvisatory; white-key glissando
Diff: 1: high tessitura; good sense of pitch needed; 2: ability to deal with moderate avant-garde idiom; low tones and good sense of pitch needed
Uses: good recital possibilities

LOMBARDO, ROBERT
(b. Hartford, CT, 1932)

1504. **A SONG FOR MORPHEUS** (Kathleen Lombardo). Boosey & Hawkes, 1966. X; f♯–g♯"; Tess-M; 2/4 with many changes, ♩ = 56; 5pp; Diff-V/dd, P/dd.
For: mezzo-soprano; soprano with good low tones

Mood: philosophical
Voice: extremely disjunct and chromatic; difficult intervals; intricate rhythms; spoken section
Piano: fragmented; chromatic; pointillistic; rapid repeated notes; large leaps
Diff: long range; perfect pitch desirable
Uses: advanced singers experienced in avant-garde idiom

LONDON, EDWIN
(b. Philadelphia, PA, 1929)

1505. **THE BEAR'S SONG** (trans. from Haida, Queen Charlotte's Island, British Columbia). New Valley, 1968. cmp1960. Atonal (avant-garde dissonance); c♯'–b"; Tess-covers the range; 3/8, 2/8, 4/8, ♩ = ca.76; 6pp; Diff-V/dd, P/d.
For: tenor
Mood: dramatic
Voice: some large leaps; many skips; pitches difficult; intricate rhythms; several high tones; some humming
Piano: percussive chords; short figurations; extremely dissonant; score difficult to read
Diff: avant-garde techniques; perfect pitch desirable
Uses: strange song; composer says: "Whoever can sing this song is admitted forever to the friendship of the bears"; use accordingly

LOOMIS, CLARENCE
(b. Sioux Falls, SD, 1889; d. Aptos, CA, 1965)

1506. **EVOLUTION** (Clayton Quast). Carl Fischer, 1937. Gmaj; c♯'–e"; Tess-M; 2/4, Not too quickly; 4pp; Diff-V/m, P/m.
For: any voice
Mood: humorous; fish evolves to bull-frog
Voice: easy skips; talky; syncopation
Piano: chordal; block and afterbeat style; staccato-legato contrast important; some grace notes and arpeggios
Uses: good encore song; needs singer with flair for humor

LOOMIS, HARVEY WORTHINGTON
(b. Brooklyn, NY, 1865; d. Boston, MA, 1930)

1507. **AND LET ME THE CANAKIN CLINK** (Iago's Song), Op. 10, No.18 (William Shakespeare). [26]. Emaj; c♯'–e"; Tess-M; 6/8, Molto vivace; 2pp; Diff-V/e, P/me.
For: baritone; tenor
Mood: drinking song; lighthearted
Voice: robust; repetitive; easy rhythms
Piano: chordal; cross-hands; trills; does not double vocal line
Diff: features e"
Uses: useful to end a Shakespeare group; encore

1508. **HARK! HARK! THE LARK** (William Shakespeare). [61, 66, vol.1], 1st©1902. Fmaj; c'–f "; Tess-mL; 4/4, 3/4, Allegretto pastorale, alternating with Moderato con moto; 34 meas.; Diff-V/m, P/m.
For: medium voice

Mood: lyrical; pastoral; somewhat archaic
Voice: pentatonic melody
Piano: imitates harp and two flutes; imaginative use of colors
Diff: 8ve leaps; sustained f" at end
Uses: would be interesting in a Shakespeare group

1509. IN THE FOGGY DEW (poet not given). [58]; 1st©1902. Amin-maj; d'–a"; Tess-M; 4/4, Andante poco con moto e rubato; 5pp; Diff-V/m, P/m.
For: all voices except extremely light
Mood: nostalgic; longing for Irish homeland
Voice: folk flavor; scales and small skips; dotted rhythms; Scotch snap; vocalized ending
Piano: dotted rhythms; interplay with vocal line; one stanza has triplets; some doubling of vocal line
Diff: expressive freedom in tempo; vocalized high ending
Uses: effective song

1510. MORNING SONG ("The Year's at the Spring") (Robert Browning). [66, vol. 4]; 1st©1907. Emaj-Gmaj-Emaj; d♯'–f♯"; Tess-mH; 9/8, 3/4, Allegro con spirito; 31meas.; Diff-V/m, P/m.
For: soprano; tenor
Mood: ecstatic; vital; strong
Voice: mostly skips; sustained high tones; quite dramatic
Piano: 4-voice texture; contrapuntal motive in imitation; repeated 8ves
Diff: big crescendos
Uses: interesting setting; group or recital ender; see setting by Amy Marcy Beach

1511. O'ER THE SEA (Ludwig Tieck; English version). [66, vol. 1]; 1st©1902. Gmaj; d'–b"; Tess-L, H; 6/8, Allegro; 59meas.; Diff-V/md, P/md.
For: soprano; tenor
Mood: light; exciting
Voice: lyrical; high climax at end; mostly stepwise
Piano: broken chords; afterbeats; trills; moves around keyboard
Diff: both low and high sections; sustained b"; final note is sustained g" with cresc
Uses: group ender

LUBIN, ERNEST
(b. New York, NY, 1916; d. New York, NY, 1977)

1512. THREE SONGS OF INNOCENCE (William Blake). G. Schirmer, 1945; pub. separately. Traditional keys; b♭–a"; Tess-mL, M, mH; regular meters; varied tempos; 14pp; Diff-V/m, P/e-md.
For: soprano
Mood: lyrical; child-like; lullaby; narrative
Voice: stepwise and easy skips; melismas; easy rhythms; 2-note slurs; repetitious
Piano: chordal; parallelism; broken-chord patterns; (b.), subtle and expressive harmonies; countermelody
Diff: dynamic control
Uses: nice set for young voices

    a. *The Piper.* Fmaj; c'–a"; Tess-mH; 2/4, Allegro moderato; 4pp.

    b. *A Cradle Song.* Amin; d'–g"; Tess- mL; 3/4, Andante con moto; 4pp.
    c. *The Little Black Boy.* E♭maj; b♭–g♯"; Tess-M; 3/4, 4/4, Semplice (at a natural tempo); 6pp.

LUCKSTONE, ISIDORE
(b. Baltimore, MD, 1862; d. New York, NY, 1941)

1513. THE CLOWN'S SERENADE (Edward W. Bryant). Church, 1898. Fmaj; e'–g"; Tess-M-mL; 6/8, Allegretto; 71meas.; Diff-V/m-me, P/m.
For: tenor
Mood: serenade; love song; cheerful
Voice: small skips; simple rhythms; chromatic colorations in vocal line differ in each stanza
Piano: guitar-like; arpeggiated chords; some l.h. melody; no doubling of vocal line
Diff: sustained high tones at ends; variant modulations in each stanza
Uses: unusual serenade

LUENING, OTTO
(b. Milwaukee, WI, 1900; d. New York, NY, 1996)

1514. A FARM PICTURE (Walt Whitman). [4]; 1st©1944. Ends A♭maj; f'–f"; Tess-M; 4/4, 2/4, Allegro moderato; 2pp; Diff-V/me, P/me.
For: all medium and high voices
Mood: descriptive
Voice: straightforward melody; some chromaticism
Piano: chordal with many 2nds; syncopation; accidentals; l.h. mostly doubles r.h.
Diff: irregular phrase lengths; some pitches
Uses: short song (1 min.); could teach student to visualize scene in interpretation

1515. HEAR THE VOICE OF THE BARD (from *Songs of Experience*, William Blake) for Baritone and Piano. Highgate Press Facsimile Edition, 1986 (Galaxy). cmp1928. Tonal but transitory; c–c'; Tess-M; 6/4, 5/4, 3/4, 3/2, 9/4, Allegro moderato–Allegro vivace; 4+pp; Diff-V/md, P/md.
For: baritone specified; bass
Mood: dramatic
Voice: mostly conjunct; short melismas; easy rhythms; irregular phrase lengths; many accidentals
Piano: not patterned; some block chords, some counterpoint; some open 8ves; chromaticism; several register changes; mostly quarter- & 8th-note motion; considerable doubling of vocal line in various 8ves
Diff: chromaticism; irregular phrase lengths
Uses: in group of Blake poems or other British poems

1516. HERE THE FRAILEST LEAVES OF ME (Walt Whitman). Associated, 1944. X (floating harmonies, ends on F♯ center); f'–f"; Tess-M; 3/4, Andante; 2pp; Diff-V/m, P/m.
For: tenor; soprano
Mood: lyrical; subtle; subdued
Voice: duplets and triplets; 2 vs. 3 in piano

Piano: triplet broken chords, both hands; a few block chords; incidental doubling of vocal line
Diff: 2 vs. 3
Uses: good song; useful in a group about songs or poetry

1517. LOVE'S SECRET (William Blake). Marks, 1951. E♭maj; b♭–f"; Tess-M; 2/2, Slow, like a folksong; 3pp; Diff-V/e-m, P/e.
For: lyric baritone
Mood: lyrical; introspective; lost love
Voice: scale lines and small skips; easy rhythms; portamento
Piano: chordal; some countermelody; supports voice
Diff: portamento e♭"–g'
Uses: subtle harmonic coloring; folk flavor; very nice song; good teaching piece for young singers

1518. THREE SONGS FOR HIGH VOICE AND PIANO. G. Schirmer, 1944. Traditional keys; f'–b♭"; Tess-mH; regular meters with changes, moderate tempos; 5pp; Diff-V/m-md, P/e-me.
For: tenor; soprano
Mood: lyrical; philosophical
Voice: many skips; rhythms somewhat static
Piano: mostly chordal; some broken-chord patterns; modulating harmonies
Diff: range of first song; some pitches
Uses: nice short group

    a. *Gliding O'er All* (Walt Whitman). B♭maj; a♭'–b♭"; 4/4, 2/4, Broad, but not too slow; 2pp.
    b. *Young Love* (William Blake). Amaj-min; g'–f"; 3/4, 6/4, 4/4, Moderate; 2pp.
    c. *Auguries of Innocence* (William Blake). Cmaj-Gmaj; f'–f"; 4/4, Moderate; 1p.

LYBBERT, DONALD
(b. Cresco, IA, 1923; d. New York, NY, 1981)

1519. FROM HARMONIUM. A Song Cycle for High Voice and Piano (Wallace Stevens). Theodore Presser, 1970. Tonal centers (but emphasis on dissonance); a♭–b"; Tess-L, M, H; regular meters with some changes; varied tempos; 9min; Diff-V/d, P/m-md.
For: soprano (lyric with wide range)
Mood: lyrico-dramatic; moods of death
Voice: conjunct and chromatic; also disjunct and dissonant; many large leaps; wide pitch and dynamic range; sustained phrases
Piano: patterned in various figures; all create floating, unreal sensations; pianist needs facility
Diff: pitch; range; perfect pitch desirable; understanding of poetry; not for young singer
Uses: good cycle in the modern idiom; will show off both high and low range, as well as good ear and poetic sophistication

    a. *Another Weeping Woman.* C♯min; a–a"; Tess-mH, L; 4/4, 3/4, 2/4, ♩ = 72; 3pp.
    b. *The Death of a Soldier.* Amin; c'–f"; Tess-wide; 4/4, 3/4, ♩ = 48; 3pp.
    c. *To the Roaring Wind.* X; a♭–b"; Tess-mH-H; 4/4,

3/8, ♩ = 152; 4pp.
    d. *Valley Candle.* X; b–a"; Tess-wide; 3/4, ♩ = 58; 3pp.

LYON, JAMES (See Special Section)

MacDOWELL, EDWARD
(b. New York, NY, 1861; d. New York, NY, 1908)

[See Appendix for songs with German texts]

[See also D#s 41 (no titles given) & 27, 66 for German songs]

1520. CRADLE HYMN, Op. 33, No. 2 (Samuel Taylor Coleridge; trans. from the Latin). Breitkopf & Härtel, 1894. Reprint: Classical Vocal Reprints (M). Dmaj; e'–d"(f♯"); Tess-M; 6/8, Simply, with tenderness; 2pp; Diff-V/me, P/me.
For: any voice
Mood: subdued; gentle; in Latin, lullaby for the Christ-child; in English, just a lullaby
Voice: stepwise and chord-member skips; repetitive; dotted rhythms; some 2-note slurs
Piano: block chords with repeated tone; various registers; delicate; does not double vocal line
Diff: soft dynamics; legato line
Uses: lovely song for a young singer
Rec: D#258

1521. EIGHT SONGS, OPUS 47. [142]; 1st pub. under one cover, Breitkopf & Härtel, 1893. Reprints: Classical Vocal Reprints (M & L); T.I.S. (D. only). Separate entries below.

A. THE ROBIN SINGS IN THE APPLE-TREE, No. 1 (Edward MacDowell). [44]. Fmaj; e'–f"; Tess-mH; 6/8, Moderately, with feeling; 29meas.; Diff-V/e, P/me.
For: tenor; soprano (change "she" to "he" in text)
Mood: nostalgic; somber
Voice: stepwise and small skips; minor key coloration
Piano: 4-voice chordal texture; some countermelody; some doubling of vocal line
Uses: nice vocal line for a young voice; use in MacDowell or other group
Rec: D#s 258, 261

B. MIDSUMMER LULLABY, No. 2 (after Goethe). Amaj; e'–c♯"; Tess-M; 6/8, Dreamily; 35meas.; Diff-V/e, P/e.
For: any voice
Mood: serene; tranquil
Voice: easy skips; simple rhythms
Piano: 3–6-voice repeated-chord texture; doubles vocal line
Uses: for a young singer
Rec: D#s 257, 258, 261

C. FOLKSONG, No. 3 (William Dean Howells). Cmin; b–c"; Tess-M; 4/4, Slowly and simply, with pathos; 29meas.; Diff-V/e-m, P/e.
For: any voice
Mood: descriptive; sad

Voice: several phrases cover range of 8ve; some syncopation
Piano: 4–6-voice chordal texture; outlines vocal melody
Uses: useful for young singer or adult beginner
Rec: D#s 257, 258, 261

D.   CONFIDENCE, No. 4 (Edward MacDowell). Gmaj;
e'–e"; Tess-M; 3/4, Not too slow, gracefully; 37meas.;
Diff-V/m, P/m.
For: any voice
Mood: optimistic love song
Voice: many small skips; 2-note slurs
Piano: drone bass under much of song; 4–6-voice chordal
texture; some syncopation
Rec: D#s 257, 258, 261

**E.   THE WEST-WIND CROONS IN THE CEDAR-
TREES,** No. 5 (Edward MacDowell). Emaj; c#'–e";
Tess-M; 6/8, Not fast, with much character; 27meas.;
Diff-V/e-m, P/e.
For: baritone; tenor
Mood: despairing; somber; progress of love
Voice: small skips; grace notes; repetitive rhythms; ends on
sustained e"
Piano: 4–5-voice chordal texture; staccato-legato contrasts;
some doubling of vocal line
Diff: many dynamic markings; many phrases use *messa di
voce*; varieties of soft dynamics
Uses: good for teaching
Rec: D#s 258, 261

F.   IN THE WOODS, No. 6 (after Goethe). Amaj;
c#'–e"(a"); Tess-M; 3/4, Moderately, lightly; 69meas.;
Diff-V/m, P/e-m.
For: any light female voice
Mood: narrative
Voice: small skips; "la-la" refrain; grace notes; triplets
Piano: 4–5-voice chordal texture; staccato 8th-note
countermelody; outlines vocal melody
Diff: opt. high tone at end (a")
Uses: nice song for a young soprano and for more mature
singers
Rec: D#s 258, 261

G.   THE SEA, No. 7 (William Dean Howells). [27, 37].
Dmaj; d'–d"; Tess-mL; 6/8, Broadly, with rhythmic
swing; 35meas.; Diff-V/m, P/m.
For: baritone; mezzo-soprano; contralto
Mood: dramatic; somber; narrative
Voice: stepwise and easy skips; 8ve skips at climax; repetitive
rhythm
Piano: 4–6-voice chordal texture; grace notes; some
countermelody
Diff: dramatic song; good command of dynamics (*ppp–ff*)
and registration needed
Uses: good for teaching dramatic expression; music matches
text well; good recital material
Rec: D#s 10, 59, 256, 258, 261

H.   THROUGH THE MEADOW, No. 8 (William Dean
Howells). Dbmaj; eb'–eb"; Tess-M; 2/2, Not too slow,
piquantly; 35meas.; Diff-V/e, P/e.
For: baritone; tenor

Mood: descriptive; regretful
Voice: easy skips; easy rhythms; some 2–3-note slurs
Piano: 4–5-voice chordal texture; some staccato; some
doubling of vocal line
Rec: D#s 258, 261

1522.   FOUR SONGS, OPUS 56 (Edward MacDowell?).
Arthur P. Schmidt, 1898. Reprints: Classical Vocal
Reprints (H & L); Masters Music Publications. [142].
Separate entries below; no titles, 1st line given.

A.   No. I. Long ago sweetheart mine... [36, 61]. H & L
keys: Dmin & Bbmin; d'–g" & bb–eb"; Tess-M; 4/4,
Simply, with pathos; 1+min; Diff-V/m, P/e.
For: baritone; mezzo-soprano
Mood: nostalgic; sentimental; atmospheric
Voice: smooth lines; phrases have range of over an 8ve
Piano: 4–5-voice chordal texture; chords outline vocal melody
Diff: long-ranged phrases; soft dynamics
Uses: effective if done "simply," as composer suggests; quiet
ending
Rec: D#s 10, 69, 256, 258, 261

B.   No. II. The swan bent low to the lily... [141, L].
Bbmaj; c'–eb"; Tess-M; 6/8, With much feeling;
19meas.; Diff-V/e, P/e.
For: any voice
Mood: dramatic at climax; love song
Voice: easy skips; easy rhythms
Piano: 6-voice chordal texture; some rolled chords; large
reaches
Diff: dynamic control; register control
Rec: D#s 256, 257, 258, 261

C.   No. III. A maid sings light... [61, 141, H]. H & L
keys: Fmaj (pub. separately by A. P. Schmidt) & Dmaj;
d'–g" & b–e"; Tess-M; 2/4, Brightly, archly; 1min;
Diff-V/m, P/e-m.
For: any voice except extremely heavy
Mood: lighthearted; coy; advisory
Voice: stepwise and small skips; many 8ve leaps; staccato-
legato contrasts
Piano: 4–5-voice chordal texture; staccato; thin
Diff: many expressive fluctuations in tempo; rapid diction;
soft singing; lightness
Uses: best suits young soprano in high key
Rec: D#s 69, 256, 258, 261

D.   No. IV. As the gloaming shadows creep... Ebmaj;
c'–eb"; Tess-M; 4/4, Tenderly; 1+min; Diff-V/m,
P/m-me.
For: baritone; mezzo-soprano
Mood: descriptive; smooth style
Voice: legato style; some phrases cover range of 8ve; easy
rhythms; 2-note slurs
Piano: 5–7-voice chordal texture; register changes; large
reaches; mostly subdued
Diff: ends on sustained eb" *pp*
Rec: D#s 258, 261

1523.   FROM AN OLD GARDEN, Op. 26 (Margaret
Deland). G. Schirmer, 1887. Reprint: Classical Vocal

Reprints. Traditional keys; c'–f"; Tess-mL-M; regular meters, varied tempos; 14pp; Diff-V/e-me, P/e-md.

For: soprano perhaps best for entire set; other high or medium voices for separate songs

Mood: sentimental; nature imagery; some mild humor; some melancholy

Voice: lyrical; short phrases; some dotted rhythms; one waltz song; some dance-like figures; some duplets in compound meter

Piano: chordal textures; some rolled and broken chords; one waltz song; grace notes; some arpeggiation; some independent melodic material

Diff: good taste and simplicity in performance

Uses: useful for young singers of limited range; period piece

Rec: D#s 258, 261

    a. *The Pansy,* No. 1. B♭maj; f'–f"; 6/8, Daintily, tenderly (♩. = 66); 2pp.

    b. *The Myrtle,* No. 2. [56, vol. 6]. Fmin; c'–f"; 6/4, Sadly, wearily (♩. = 54); 2pp.

    c. *The Clover,* No. 3. Dmaj; f♯'–e"; 2/4, Sturdily, with feeling (♩ = 80); 2pp.

    d. *The Yellow Daisy,* No. 4. E♭maj; g'–f"; 3/4, Archly, yet with tenderness (♩ = 132); 2pp.

    e. *The Blue-Bell,* No. 5. [32 (Gmaj.), 52, vol. 6] Amaj; e'–e"; 6/8, Jocosely (♩. = 116); 2pp. [**Rec:** D#255]

    f. *The Mignonette,* No. 6. Emaj; c♯'–e"; 3/4, Quaintly: a la menuet (♩ = 126); 4pp.

1524. **IDYLL,** Op. 33, No. 3 (Johann Wolfgang von Goethe; trans. Edward MacDowell). Breitkopf & Härtel, 1894. Gmaj; d'–e"(g"); Tess-M; 2/4, 3/4, Lightly, daintily. Not too slow; 3pp; Diff-V/m, P/m.

For: young light soprano; mezzo-soprano

Mood: descriptive; naive; sprightly

Voice: many chord-member skips; dotted rhythms; repetitive patterns; 2-note slurs

Piano: staccato 8th-note chords; arpeggios; much med-high register; does not double vocal line

Diff: several long-ranged phrases; opt. g" ending, sustained *ppp*

Uses: useful for a young voice

Rec: D#258

1525. **MENIE,** Op. 34, No. 1 (Robert Burns). [7, 141, H];1st©1889. Dmin; d'–f"; Tess-M; 6/8, Sadly, despondently; 3pp; Diff-V/me, P/m.

For: tenor; baritone

Mood: sad; love's difficulties; nature imagery

Voice: lyrical; like a folksong; short phrases

Piano: broken and rolled chords; independent melody and countermelody

Diff: Scottish dialect pronunciation and meanings

Rec: D#258

1526. **MY JEAN,** Op. 34, No. 2 (Robert Burns). A. P. Schmidt, 1889. [141, L]. Amaj; e'–e"(g♯"); Tess-M; 3/4, Unaffectedly, tenderly; 3pp; Diff-V/m, P/m.

For: tenor; baritone

Mood: lyrical; love song

Voice: many chord-member skips; dotted and double-dotted

rhythms; 2–3-note slurs

Piano: chordal; various registers; some countermelody; double-dotted rhythms; some doubling of vocal line

Diff: dialect meanings

Uses: effective lyric song for American group

Rec: D#258

1527. **SIX LOVE SONGS, Op. 40** (W. H. Gardner). Cycle. Arthur P. Schmidt, 1890. Reprint: Classical Vocal Reprints. [142]. Traditional keys; c'–g"; Tess-M-mH; regular meters; varied tempos; 13pp; Diff-V/e-m, P/e-m; no titles; 1st lines given.

For: tenor

Mood: lyrical; various moods of love; sentimental

Voice: easy skips; easy and repetitive rhythms

Piano: 3-6-voice chordal texture; fairly thin; some syncopation; some doubling of vocal line

Uses: attractive for a light lyric tenor if done very simply and with exquisite taste

Rec: D#258

    a. *Sweet blue-eyed maid. . .* Cmaj; f'–f"; 2/4, Daintily, not too sentimentally; 69meas.

    b. *Sweetheart tell me. . .* A♭maj; f'–f"(g"); 2/4, Softly, tenderly; 50meas.

    c. *Thy beaming eyes. . .* [68, bks. 1, 2, 3]. H & M keys: Fmaj & E♭maj; c'–f" & b♭–e♭"; 4/4, With sentiment, passionately; 28meas. [**Rec:** D#s 10, 259, 260]

    d. *For sweet love's sake. . .* B♭maj; e'–g"; 6/8, Simply, with feeling; 21meas.

    e. *O lovely rose. . .* [45]. Gmaj; e'–e"; 2/2, Slowly, with great simplicity; 18meas.

    f. *I ask but this. . .* Cmaj; e♭'–f"; 2/4, Moderately fast, almost banteringly; 51meas.

1528. **THREE SONGS, OPUS 58** (Edward MacDowell?). Arthur P. Schmidt, 1899. Reprints: Classical Vocal Reprints (mH); T.I.S. (B. & C.). [5, 142]. Probably not meant to be sung together; separate entries below.

A. **CONSTANCY,** No. 1. Fmaj; d'–f"(a"); Tess-mH; 4/4, Simply, but with deep feeling; 2min; Diff-V/m, P/e.

For: tenor; soprano

Mood: nostalgic; sentimental

Voice: small skips, esp. 4ths; repetitive rhythms; maj-min colorations

Piano: 4-6-voice chordal texture; many accidentals; outlines vocal melody

Diff: opt. a" sustained at end *ppp*; very soft dynamics

Uses: soft ending; interior of group

Rec: D#s 258, 261

B. **SUNRISE,** No. 2. Amaj; e'–f♯"; Tess-mH; 4/4, With power and authority; 1+min; Diff-V/m, P/m.

For: tenor; soprano (not light)

Mood: descriptive; dramatic

Voice: stepwise and small skips; repetitive rhythms

Piano: 5-7-voice block-chord texture; large reaches; needs big sound; some doubling of vocal line

Diff: ends sustained e" crescendo to *ff* over two meas.; begins and ends *ff*

Rec: D#s 258, 261

C.   MERRY MAIDEN SPRING, No. 3. Fmaj; e♭'–g";
Tess-mH; 2/4, Lightly, gracefully; 1min; Diff-V/m,
P/m.
For: soprano
Mood: happy; bright
Voice: many small skips; 2–3-note slurs
Piano: 3–5-voice texture; some staccato countermelody; some
       chords; does not double vocal line
Diff: rapid diction; sustained f" and g" at end
Uses: good song for a young singer; group ender
Rec: D#s 258, 261

1529. THREE SONGS, Op. 60 (Edward MacDowell).
       Arthur P. Schmidt, 1902. Reprints: Classical Vocal
       Reprints (mH); T.I.S. [5, 142]. Traditional keys;
       c#'–a♭"; Tess-M-mH; regular meters; moderate
       tempos; 4min; Diff-V/m-md, P/m.
For: tenor; soprano
Mood: lyrical; center song dramatic; descriptive; nostalgic
Voice: many small skips; some syncopation; some 16th notes;
       2-note slurs
Piano: 3–6-voice chordal textures; some large reaches; some
       doubling of vocal line
Diff: dynamic control
Uses: not MacDowell's best songs, but useful period pieces
Rec: D#s 258, 261

       a. Tyrant Love. Fmaj; d'–g"; 3/4, Lightly, yet with
           tenderness; 1min.
       b. Fair Springtide. [141, H]. Dmin; c#'–f#"; 2/4, Very
           slow, with pathos; 1+min.
       c. To the Golden Rod. [141, L]. A♭maj; e♭'–f"(a♭");
           6/8, With tender grace; 1+min.

1530. TO A WILD ROSE, Op. 51, No. 1 (Herman
       Hagedorn). [29, 141, 142, H & L]; 1st©1896. H & L
       keys: G♭maj & Emaj; d♭'–g♭" & b–e"; Tess-mH; 2/4,
       With simple tenderness; 3pp; Diff-V/me, P/me.
For: any voice except extremely low
Mood: lullaby; tranquil; subdued
Voice: small skips; one opt. leap of 11th; easy rhythms
Piano: block chords; 8-meas. prelude; doubles vocal line
Diff: leap of 11th on 2-note slur; dynamic control
Uses: lovely lyrical melody; sweetly sentimental text; quiet
       ending
Rec: D#257

1531. TWO OLD SONGS, Op. 9. A. P. Schmidt, 1894.
       Reprints: Classical Vocal Reprints (M); T.I.S. (b., M).
       E♭maj; e♭'–e♭"; Tess-M; regular meters, slow tempos;
       5pp; Diff-V/e, P/e.
For: any voice
Mood: lyrical
Voice: simple folk-like vocal lines
Piano: simple 4-part accomp.; doubles voice
Diff: Scottish dialect
Uses: period pieces; useful as simple songs for young voices;
       interesting winter lullaby
Rec: D#258

       a. Deserted ("Ye Banks and Braes") (Robert Burns).
           [141, H & L]. 4/4, Slow, with pathos, yet simply;
           3pp.
       b. Slumber Song. 6/8, Tenderly, softly; 2pp; a winter
           lullaby.

MAHY, KENNETH
(b. Weihsien, China, 1937, of American parents)

1532. FOUR LOVE SONGS, Op. 4. Leyerle Publications,
       1990. Traditional keys; c'–f"; Tess-M; regular meters;
       slow–moderate tempos; 16pp; Diff-V/me-md, P/m-md.
For: baritone; mezzo-soprano; some sopranos
Mood: philosophical in several moods; admonition of a lover;
       in love with love; declaration of love
Voice: much stepwise motion; easy skips using chord
       members; some dotted rhythms; some syncopation;
       straightforward text settings, mostly syllabic
Piano: much arpeggiation/broken chord patterning in 8ths &
       16ths; some triplets; (a.), 4–5-voice linear texture;
       many accidentals; (b.), 18th-century flavor; (c.), rapid
       scalar ornaments; (d.), 14-meas. interlude; all have
       preludes; vocal line usually doubled in the texture
Diff: possibly a few rhythms in (a.) & (b.); ensemble in (b.)
Uses: as a set, or songs may be excerpted; charming and
       attractive, esp. (a.–c.); composer notes that (d.) has
       been used for weddings
Rec: D#262

       a. I Saw My Lady Weep (John Dowland). Emin;
           c'–f"; Tess-M; 44, Andante espressivo ♩= 76; 4pp.
       b. Go, Lovely Rose (Edmund Waller). Emin; d'–e";
           Tess-M; 4/4, 5/4, 2/4, Andante cantabile ♩= 66;
           4pp.
       c. Brown Penny (William Butler Yeats). Emin-Gmaj;
           d'–d"; Tess-M; 6/8, Andante affettuoso; 4pp.
       d. Thought of My Thoughts (Hans Christian
           Andersen, English version by the composer). Bmin;
           d'–d"; Tess-M; 4/4, 3/4, 3/2, Andante espressivo
           ♩= 72; 4pp.

MALOTTE, ALBERT HAY
(b. Philadelphia, PA, 1895; d. Los Angeles, CA, 1964)

1533. BLOW ME EYES (Wallace Irwin). G. Schirmer,
       1941. Fmaj; c'–g"; Tess-mL-M; 4/4, Fast and with a
       lusty vigor; 100meas.; Diff-V/md, P/md.
For: baritone
Mood: humorous sailor's song; narrative
Voice: declamatory; some speaking; syncopation; duplets and
       triplets
Piano: syncopated afterbeat style; hornpipe passages;
       glissando
Diff: freedom of tempo; sustained g" and f" ff
Uses: good song for teaching diction, humorous style, timing,
       mood changes, and narrative style; group ender; encore

1534. CONTRARY MARY (Nancy Byrd Turner). G.
       Schirmer, 1936. C#min-Emaj; d#'–g#"; Tess-M; 6/8,
       Allegro scherzando; 6pp; Diff-V/m, P/m-d.

For: soprano
Mood: humorous; sprightly; play on words of familiar nursery rhyme
Voice: some skips; easy rhythms; two recit.-like sections
Piano: 12-meas. prelude; 3-voice texture with 3rds in r.h.; block- and broken-chord sections; arpeggios; articulations important
Diff: expressive freedom; final 4-meas. on g♯"
Uses: encore; good for a young singer; "cute"

1535. SING A SONG OF SIXPENCE (traditional). G. Schirmer, 1938. Fmaj; d'–f"; Tess-M; 3/4, 6/8, 2/4, 4/4, many tempo changes; 6pp; Diff-V/md, P/md.
For: baritone; mezzo-soprano; soprano
Mood: humorous; nursery rhyme
Voice: exaggerated style; articulations important; some speaking; duplets and triplets
Piano: broken chords; afterbeat style; quick ornaments; glissando; block chords in duplets and triplets; sectional
Diff: final note f" sustained *ff*; some speaking
Uses: good song to develop comic talent; many mood and tempo changes develop comic timing; big ending; encore

1536. UPSTREAM (Carl Sandburg). [59]; 1st©1937. H & L keys: Dmin & B♭min; e'–a" & c'–f"; Tess-mH; 3/4, 4/4, 2/4, Moderato assai (with changes); 6pp; Diff-V/d, P/d.
For: dramatic tenor; baritone
Mood: dramatic; philosophical; patriotic tone
Voice: declamatory, with semi-spoken section; numerous long, loud high tones
Piano: chordal; rhythmically intricate; independent of voice
Diff: three sustained high tones; somewhat complex rhythms; voice needs much dramatic weight
Uses: teaches parlando style; good for dramatic voices; see also setting by Dougherty

MANA-ZUCCA [Augusta Zuckermann]
(b. New York, NY, 1887; d. Miami, FL, 1981)

1537. THE FIRST CONCERT (Sylvia Golden) [38]; 1st©1934. Cmaj; c'–c"; Tess-mL; 4/4, Moderately fast-Faster; 6pp; Diff-V/m, P/me.
For: any medium or low voice
Mood: humorous description of a child with a cold being taken to a concert
Voice: short phrases with pauses for other actions, as a child telling a story; somewhat recit.-like, with many repeated notes; speaking, coughing, and other actions
Piano: chordal; some broken-chord figures; doubles vocal line almost throughout
Diff: needs a good vocal actor; singer must manage "cough and choke and sputter" without losing vocal control; useful for singer-actor with a short-ranged voice
Uses: humorous song

1538. I LOVE LIFE (Irwin M. Cassel). Church, 1923. Reprint: T.I.S. (L). H & L keys: Fmaj & Dmaj; f'–a" & d'–f♯"; Tess-M; 12/8, Allegro; 5pp; Diff-V/me, P/md.
For: any high or medium voice; excellent for young baritone

Mood: sentimentally philosophical
Voice: vigorous movement; strong accents; good vowels on high tones; descending phrases
Piano: chordal; repeated and arpeggiated chords; somewhat chromatic; some doubling of vocal line
Uses: good for teaching vowel modification on high tones
Rec: D#s 33, 40, 263

MANDELBAUM, JOEL
(b. New York, NY, 1932)

1539. RAINBOWS OF DARKNESS (Laura Eliasoph). [57]. E-centered; (a)b–g"; Tess-M; 4/4, Lento; 3pp; Diff-V/m, P/m.
For: mezzo-soprano
Mood: introspective
Voice: stepwise and easy skips; some accidentals; a few triplets; dynamics *pp–ff*; mostly syllabic
Piano: block chords with countermelody; some 2 vs. 3; little doubling of vocal line
Diff: climactic phrase is *ff* with long g" (4½ beats)
Uses: lovely text with suitable musical setting; useful song

MANNEY, CHARLES FONTEYN
(b. Brooklyn, NY, 1872; d. New York, NY, 1951)

1540. ORPHEUS WITH HIS LUTE (William Shakespeare). [26, 58]; 1st©1897. H & L keys: E♭maj & D♭maj (orig.); e♭'–g" & d♭'–f"; Tess-mH; 3/4, Andante semplice; 3pp; Diff-V/me, P/e.
For: soprano; mezzo-soprano; tenor
Mood: lyrical; philosophical
Voice: flowing phrases; several 8ve leaps; several phrases begin high (f" or g") and descend
Piano: 4-voice chordal texture; some independent melodic material; some doubling of vocal line
Uses: useful for a Shakespeare group

MANNING, KATHLEEN LOCKHART
(b. near Hollywood, CA, 1890; d. Los Angeles, CA, 1951)

1541. SHOES (Kathleen Lockhart Manning). [48]. H & L keys: Fmaj & Cmaj; f'–g" & c'–d"; Tess-mH; 2/4, Allegro (♩ = 84); 3pp; Diff-V/me, P/me.
For: any female voice
Mood: child-like; quaint
Voice: simple phrases; many repeated notes; mostly conjunct motion; few intervals; 4-beat f" or c" at end
Piano: chordal; afterbeats; supports vocal line clearly, doubles in last part of song
Uses: good possibility for a very young student
Rec: D#41

1542. SKETCHES OF PARIS (Kathleen Lockhart Manning). A Cycle of Songs. G. Schirmer, 1925. Traditional keys with parallel harmonies; b–e♭"(g")(pub. in H & L keys); Tess-M–mL; regular meters; varied tempos; 22pp; Diff-V/e, P/m.
For: all voices; perhaps better for men

Mood: lyrical; small scenes of Paris
Voice: simple melodic lines; lyrical
Piano: generally chordal, broken-chord figures; accidentals; modulating harmonies; supportive of voice
Uses: numerous clichés, but a few of the songs are useful for young students; small scenes give opportunity to exercise imagination

    a. *River-Boats.* Fmaj; c'–d"; 4/4, Moderato ♩ = 104; 2pp.
    b. *Lamplighter.* Fmaj; c'–d"; 4/4, Slowly and mystically ♩ = 60; 2pp.
    c. *The Street Fair.* Gmaj; d'–g"(d"); 2/2, Vivace ♩ = 132; 7pp.
    d. *In the Luxembourg Gardens.* E♭maj; b♭–d"; 4/4, Moderato ♩ = 84; 3pp. [Rec: D#264]
    e. *Absinthe.* B♭maj; c'–c"; 4/4, Vague and wandering ♩ = 72; 4pp.
    f. *Paris: An Ode.* E♭maj; b♭–e♭"; 4/4, Molto appassionato ♩ = 69; 4pp.

1543. **A WINTER AFTERNOON** (Kathleen Lockhart Manning). G. Schirmer, 1933. cmp1932. H, M, & L keys: Gmaj, E♭maj, & Cmaj; d'–g", b♭–e♭", & (a)g–c"; Tess-M; 2/4, Allegretto; 1+min; Diff-V/e, P/me.
For: any voice
Mood: melancholy; subdued; rain song
Voice: stepwise and small skips; some syncopation; repetitive melodic patterns
Piano: repetitive;16th-note motion; parallel 6ths, 3rds, & 4ths with vocal line; syncopation
Uses: useful for young singers or adult beginners

MARKS, JAMES
(b. Denver, CO, 1924)

1544. **THREE SONGS** (e. e. cummings). Recital Publications, 1992. cmp1966. Tonal and X; c♯'–a"; Tess-M, mH, cs; regular and irregular changing meters; moderate tempos; 14pp; Diff-V/m-d, P/m-d.
For: tenor; soprano
Mood: tranquil; fierce; gentle
Voice: (a.) & (c.), lyrical and mostly conjunct; (b.), dramatic and angular; syllabic; some speech rhythms, some words governed by melodic rhythm; both soft and loud high phrases
Piano: patterned; arpeggiated l.h. with afterbeat chords in (a.); (b.), chordal with some arpeggiated sections; (c.), chordal; built on repeated rhythmic figure; dissonance
Diff: some pitches; dramatic ascending lines in (b.); difficult poems; diction
Uses: good set for graduate level singer

    a. *come nothing to my comparable soul.* E♭-centered; e♭'–a"; Tess-M; 6/4, 12/8, 3/8, 4/8, Tranquilly ♩ = 96; 4pp.
    b. *what if a much of a which of a wind.* X; c♯'–g♯"; Tess-cs; 6/8, 9/8, 4/4, 3/4, 5/8, Forcefully ♩ = 112; 5pp.
    c. *somewhere I have never travelled.* Tonal; d'–a"; Tess-mH; 3/2, Slowly ♩ = 84–90; 5pp.

MARTINO, DONALD
(b. Plainfield, NJ, 1931)

1545. **FROM *THE BAD CHILD'S BOOK OF BEASTS*** (Hilaire Belloc). For High Voice and Piano. Dantalian, 1978. Unconventional tonality; c'–a"; Tess-H, M; changing meters; 7pp; Diff-V/md, P/md.
For: soprano
Mood: humorous
Voice: each song has wide range; many skips; uncomplicated rhythms; (a.), syllabic and "talky"; (b.), folk-like; (c.), syllabic; expressive tempo changes
Piano: (a.), block chords, tremolo, many accidentals; 20 meas. piano solo; sinister; (b.), block- and broken-chord patterning; 9-meas. interlude; (c.), broken and afterbeat chords; features chromatic passage in double 3rds (1 meas.)
Diff: range and tessitura of (a.) & (b.) for many singers; diction in high tessitura
Uses: clever group; recital ender; see also "The Microbe" by Persichetti

    a. *The Lion; The Tiger.* F minorish; c'–a"; Tess-H; 12/8 with many changes, Vigorously; 1+min.
    b. *The Frog.* Modal flavor; d'–a"; Tess-H; 3/4, Freely, in ballad-style; 1+min.
    c. *The Microbe.* F-centered; e♭'–g"; Tess-M; 2/4, Gradually finding the tempo (followed by many changes); 1min.

1546. **SEPARATE SONGS.** For High Voice and Piano. Dantalian, 1978. cmp1951. Separate entries below.

A. **ALL DAY I HEAR THE NOISE OF WATERS** (James Joyce). F-centered; e'–g"; Tess-M; 3/4 with changes; Adagio, tranquillo; 2pp; Diff-V/md, P/md.
For: soprano; tenor
Mood: melancholy
Voice: stepwise and small skips; wide-ranged phrases; syncopation; some triplets; text-painting
Piano: broken-chord patterning; some rolled chords; both tertian and quartal harmony; does not double vocal line
Diff: range of several phrases; probably getting starting pitch
Uses: attractive song for a Joyce or American-composer group; see setting of same text by Persichetti

B. **THE HALF-MOON WESTERS LOW, MY LOVE** (A. E. Housman). D-centered; d'–c'''(a"); Tess-H; 3/8 with changes, Moderato; 3pp; Diff-V/m, P/md.
For: soprano
Mood: love song of separation
Voice: stepwise and small skips; some syncopation; two sections on "ah"; c''' is opt. in one of these sections; long a" at end; soft dynamics
Piano: broken-chord patterning; does not double vocal line
Diff: possibly rhythms; control of soft dynamics
Uses: nice song for a high voice

1547. **THREE SONGS** (James Joyce). E. C. Schirmer, 1970. Atonal (avant-garde techniques); H & L(orig.) keys: b♭–b♭" & F♯–f♯'; Tess-covers range; mostly regular meters; slow tempos; 9pp; Diff-V/dd, P/dd.

For: bass; tenor (composer says suitable for soprano)
Mood: nocturnal remembrance; macabre reflection
Voice: avant-garde techniques: highly complex rhythms; dissonant and large intervals; no support from accomp.; perfect pitch desirable; some whispering
Piano: avant-garde rhythmic and harmonic techniques; complex in every way; special instructions for pianist
Diff: for performers experienced in the atonal and avant-garde style
Uses: avant-garde recital; extreme contrast to other groups on a regular program

  a. *Alone.* bb–g" & G–eb'; 4/4 with changes, ♩ = 44–46; 3pp.
  b. *Tutto È Sciolto.* bb–g" & F♯–eb'; 2/4 with changes (voice), 6/8 with changes (piano), ♪ = 56–60; 3pp.
  c. *A Memory of the Players in a Mirror at Midnight.* b–bb" & G–f♯'; 2/4, ♩ = 56; 3pp.

1548. TWO RILKE SONGS. For Mezzo-Soprano and Piano (Rainer Maria Rilke; English text by Jean Lunn). E. C. Schirmer, 1970. Atonal (avant-garde); f–a"; Tess-wide; no meter; 6pp; Diff-V/dd, P/dd.
For: mezzo-soprano
Mood: poems: (a.), sensuous; (b.), dream-like remembrance
Voice: vocal line atonal and avant-garde; large dissonant leaps; various articulations; extreme range; many expressive markings; complex rhythms; English version singable
Piano: avant-garde harmonic and rhythmic techniques; many expressive markings; many accidentals; complex construction
Diff: for performers experienced in avant-garde techniques

  a. *Die Laute* (The Lute). f–a"; 2/4 with many changes, Lento (♩ = 30±–molto liberamente; 4pp.
  b. *Aus einer Sturmnacht VIII* (On a Stormy Night VIII). g–ab"; 2/4 with changes, Comodo ♩ = 72±; 2pp.

MASON, DANIEL GREGORY
(b. Brookline, MA, 1873; d. Greenwich, CT, 1953)

1549. THE CONSTANT CANNIBAL MAIDEN, Op. 38, No. 3 (Wallace Irwin). G. Schirmer, 1943. Ends Emaj; c–f♯"; Tess-M; 3/2, 3/4, 2/4, Sostenuto–Allegretto scherzando, etc.; 92meas.; Diff-V/md, P/m.
For: baritone
Mood: humorous sailor's song
Voice: many skips; many accidentals; some legato; some declamation
Piano: three basic patterns: one sustained rocking, others contain references to "Habañera," "The Ruins of Athens," and "Yankee Doodle"
Diff: several different styles; high phrases wordy
Uses: good for developing humorous style; clever, funny song; good group ender; encore

1550. THE QUEST, Op. 15, No. 1 (Mary Lord Mason). G. Schirmer, 1918. Bbmaj; c♯'–gb'; Tess-M; 3/4, Con moto, grazioso; 6pp; Diff-V/m, P/m-md.
For: tenor; soprano

Mood: lyrical; searching
Voice: triadic skips and conjunct lines; many accidentals; modulating line
Piano: linear; modulatory; constant 8th- & 16th-motion; some syncopation; large reach helpful
Uses: useful student song

McARTHUR, EDWIN
(b. Denver, CO, 1907; d. New York, NY, 1987)

1551. NIGHT (Charles H. Towne). [59]; 1st©1949. H & L keys: Dbmaj & Amaj; f'–ab" & c♯'–e"; Tess-mH; 4/4, 2/2, With moderate motion; 8pp; Diff-V/md, P/d.
For: all voices
Mood: philosophical poem about night
Voice: legato; sustained; long phrases; many long tones
Piano: chordal; arpeggiated section at end; somewhat independent of vocal line
Diff: careful pacing needed for long phrases and sustained high tones at end
Uses: useful to gain breath control

1552. SPRING DAY (Johan Egilsrud). [60, 63]; 1st©1969. H & L keys: Amaj & Fmaj; a'–a" & f'–f"; Tess-H; 4/4, Lento (majestic); 2pp; Diff-V/e, P/e.
For: soprano; tenor
Mood: joyous; descriptive
Voice: stepwise; sustained; builds continuously in pitch and drama
Piano: chordal; afterbeats
Diff: brilliant a" required
Uses: program possibilities for a young singer

McCALL, MAURICE
(b. Norfolk, VA, 1943)

1553. CHANSON TRISTE (Maurice McCall). [6]; 1st©1973. X; c'–c'''; Tess-wide; 3/4, ♩ = 54; 2pp; Diff-V/d, P/m.
For: lyric soprano
Mood: lyrical; a vocalise on various vowels
Voice: numerous large leaps; some difficult triplet patterns; generally high; also emphasizes some rather low tones; chromatic
Piano: chordal texture initially, somewhat contrapuntal later; chromatic; a few difficult rhythmic patterns
Diff: coloratura techniques; may have too many stressed low tones for some singers; good sense of pitch and rhythm needed
Uses: nice short piece for contrast on recital

1554. SWEET SORROW (Maurice McCall). [6]; 1st©1973. X; e'–bb"; Tess-wide; 4/4, 2/4, 3/4, 5/4, Vigorously ♩ = 72–60; 2pp; Diff-V/md, P/m.
For: lyric or coloratura soprano
Mood: lyrical; philosophical
Voice: declamatory phrases; strong rhythms alternating with lyrical, flowing phrases; fairly chromatic
Piano: strong chordal phrases, complex rhythmic patterns, alternate with flowing, contrapuntal phrases

Diff: pitches; rhythms
Uses: good recital song

McCOY, WILLIAM J.
(b. Crestline, OH, 1848; d. Oakland, CA, 1926)

1555. THE ONLY VOICE, Op. 51, No.1 (Oscar Weil). [66, vol. 3]; 1st©1905. Fmaj; f'–f"; Tess-mH; 6/4, Slowly, sadly; 30meas.; Diff-V/me, P/m.
For: soprano; tenor; mezzo-soprano
Mood: somber; introspective; sad
Voice: stepwise and easy skips; sustained; legato
Piano: 4-voice block chords; slow broken chords
Uses: easy short song; nicely-colored harmonies

1556. WHEN LOVE PASSED BY (J. W. Walsh). [15]; 1st©1902. D♭maj; b♭–d♭"; Tess-M; 3/4, no tempo indication; 3pp; Diff-V/e, P/me.
For: any medium or low voice
Mood: melancholy; lost love
Voice: simple and lyrical
Piano: chordal; some independent melodic material; some doubling of vocal line
Uses: good for young singers in early stages of development

McGILL, JOSEPHINE
(b. Louisville, KY, 1877; d. Louisville, KY, 1919)

1557. DUNA (Marjorie Pickthall). Boosey & Co., 1914. Reprint: Classical Vocal Reprints. H, mH, M, & L keys: E♭, D♭, C, & B♭; e♭'–g", d♭'–f", c'–e", & b♭–d"; Tess-M; 2/4, Con moto; 1+min; Diff-V/me, P/e.
For: any voice (word changes for women)
Mood: first person narrative; folk-like flavor
Voice: easy skips; one slurred 10th; some dotted rhythms; slightly archaic language
Piano: block chords–some rolled; needs 8ve span
Uses: famous period song; encore

1558. O SLEEP (Grace Fallow Norton). G. Schirmer, 1927. Dmaj; a–c♯"; Tess-mL; 3/4, Very quietly and slowly; 4pp; Diff-V/m, P/m.
For: contralto; bass
Mood: lyrical; entreaty to sleep
Voice: conjunct with some skips, one leap; polymetric feeling with accomp.; quiet; sustained; one small ornament
Piano: moving 8ths; polymetric feeling due to grouping in r.h. in 3s and l.h. in 2s; cross-hands; somnolent mood; some accidentals
Diff: creation of floating rhythms on two planes
Uses: lovely song; excellent quiet song for low voices

McKAY, NEIL
(b. Ashcroft, B.C., 1924 [naturalized American])

1559. THE DEAF MEN AND THE DIVA (Wm. D. Leyerle) for Soprano and Piano (Reduction from Chamber Ensemble). Leyerle Publications, 1996. Variety of maj and min keys framed at beginning and end by dissonance; d'–c'''(d'''); Tess-mH-H; regular meters, various tempos (♩ = 60–♩ = 92); 9min; Diff-V/d, P/md.
For: soprano (lyric-coloratura probably best)
Mood: humorous; what makes a "well-sung song" from the viewpoints of six academic voice teachers, each with tunnel vision and a disinclination to listen to what anyone else says
Voice: contains every style in the soprano repertoire; many musical parodies
Piano: various operatic and song accomp. styles
Diff: singer needs flexible instrument with good top, and a keen ear for pitch
Uses: the ultimate inside joke–a witty caricature of the voice teaching profession turned loose on unsuspecting singers; a natural for the faculty "mock recital"

1560. THERE ONCE WAS _____ : INTRODUCTION AND FIVE LIMERICKS for Medium Voice and Piano. Leyerle Publications, 1989. Mostly tonal; a–g"; Tess-mL-M, cs; mostly regular changing meters, ♩ = 100–♩. = 60; 8min; Diff-V/m, P/m.
For: baritone; mezzo-soprano
Mood: humorous; typical limericks
Voice: syllabic; speech rhythms and phrase rhythms expressive of the text; repeated-note recit; large leaps; one hummed passage; one downward glissando
Piano: some tricky rhythms; adds musical humor to textual humor; string plucking; knocking on wood
Diff: mostly rhythmic
Uses: excellent short cycle to add humor to any program for singer with wit and style

    a. *Introduction.* Cmaj; a–d"; Tess-M; 3/8, 2/8, 4/8, 7/8, Energico ♩ = 72; 2pp.
    b. _____ *A Woman Called Hannah.* Fmaj; c'–f"; Tess-cs; 6/8, 9/8, ♪ = c.100; 2pp.
    c. _____ *A Lady of Kent.* B♭maj; b♭–e♭"; Tess-M; 4/4, 5/4, 2/4, ♩ = 70 with steady tempo and stately manner; 2pp.
    d. _____ *A Spinster Named Tweed.* E♭maj; b♭–e♭"; Tess-M; 5/8, 6/8, 3/8, Whimsically ♩. = 84; 2pp.
    e. _____ *A Maid from Madras.* X; d♭'–f♭"; Tess-mL; 3/4, Slowly-A tempo ♩ = 120; 2pp.
    f. _____ *A Deb in St. Paul.* Cmaj; b–g"; Tess-cs; 3/4, Viennese Waltz ♩. = 60; 2pp.

MECHEM, KIRKE
(b. Wichita, KS, 1925)

1561. FOUR SONGS FOR BARITONE AND PIANO, Op. 10 (Kirke F. Mechem). E. C. Schirmer, 1972. "To Theodor Uppman." Tonal with definite key centers; B♭–f'; Tess-mH; regular and irregular changing meters; varied tempos; 17pp; Diff-V/m-md, P/m.
For: baritone
Mood: lyrico-dramatic; mostly somber moods
Voice: skips and leaps; 8ves frequent; long tones; speech rhythms; not very complicated
Piano: mostly linear; some cross-hands; some solo passages

Diff: some extended *mezza-voce* passages
Uses: interesting set; poetry fairly good; useful, but probably not to end a program

    a. *The Green-Blooded Fish.* Gmaj; B♭–e♭'; 5/8, 6/8, Allegretto (♩. = 60); 3pp.
    b. *July Rain.* Gmin; B–e'; 4/4 with changes, Lento (♩ = 40); 4pp.
    c. *Inferiority Complex.* B♭min; B♭–f'; 2/2, Agitato (♩ = 66); 5pp.
    d. *A Farewell.* B–e'; 2/2, Allegretto (♩ = 80); 5pp.

1562. **GOODBYE, FAREWELL AND ADIEU.** Three Songs of Parting, Op. 33. For Medium Voice and Piano. Carl Fischer, 1979. Tonal; b♭–g♭"; Tess-M; 4/4 with changes; varied tempos; 13pp; Diff-V/md, P/md.
For: mezzo-soprano; soprano
Mood: dramatic; lyric, nostalgic ending
Voice: (a.) & (b.), rather disjunct; (c.), predominantly conjunct; rhythms of (a.) & (c.), fairly regular; (b.) has recit. sections with speech-like rhythms; many accidentals and tempo changes; mostly syllabic; some 2–5-note slurs; many dynamic markings
Piano: linear-chordal combination; many accidentals; (a.), 11-meas. interlude, 2-meas. postlude; some doubling and imitation of vocal line; (c.), 2-meas. interlude; doubles or outlines vocal line
Diff: pitch patterns in (a.); style and drama in (b.); gradation of "soft" dynamics in (c.)
Uses: as a group; attractive to audience

    a. *Since There's No Help* (Michael Drayton). "To Jeanne Garson." Dmaj; b♭–f♯"; 4/4, Allegretto (with fluctuations); 5pp.
    b. *Parting, without a Sequel* (John Crowe Ransom). "To Shirley Verrett." E-centered; b–f"; 4/4 with changes, Recitativo (with many changes); 6pp.
    c. *Let It Be Forgotten* (Sara Teasdale). "To Margery Tede." Phrygian on F; c♭'–g♭"; 4/4, Molto lento; 2pp.

MEINEKE, CHRISTOPHER (See Special Section)

MENOTTI, GIAN CARLO
(b. Cadegliano, Italy, 1911)

[See Appendix for songs with Italian texts]

1563. **FIVE SONGS FOR VOICE AND PIANO** (Gian Carlo Menotti). [143]; 1st©1983. Traditional keys; d♭'–a"; Tess-M, mH, cs; mostly regular meters; varied tempos; 21pp; Diff-V/m-md, P/m-md.
For: tenor; soprano
Mood: romantically dark; all poems deal with life's approaching end
Voice: lyrical; fairly wide ranges; Italian vocal style (i.e., melody rules); needs warm, full sound
Piano: romantic figurations–repeated chords with melody in l.h., broken chords, afterbeat patterns, arpeggiated chord patterns; much modulation; lush harmonies

Diff: some pitches in (d.); some very personal poetry
Uses: recital material; program as a group or separately; good for teaching a smooth line
Rec: D#267

    a. *The Eternal Prisoner.* Emin; d♭'–a"; Tess-cs; 12/8, 9/8, Andante molto mosso e agitato; 3pp.
    b. *The Idle Gift.* C-C♯maj; d'–g♯"; Tess-M; 4/4, Allegretto mosso e scorrevole; 3pp.
    c. *The Longest Wait.* A♭-E♭maj; d'–a♭"; Tess-mH; 4/4, 2/4, Adagio, ma non troppo; 5pp.
    d. *My Ghost.* Cmaj-Amin; d'–g"; Tess-mH; 6/8, 9/8, Andante, molto moderato (with humor); 5pp.
    e. *The Swing.* D♭-Emaj; d'–a♭"; Tess-mH; 5/4, 4/4, 5/8, 3/4, Andante calmo; 5pp.

1564. **THE HERO** (Robert Horan). [64]; 1st©1952. "For Marie Powers." Gmin-B♭maj; c'–f"; Tess-M; 3/4 with changes, Lento; 4pp; Diff-V/md, P/md.
For: mezzo-soprano; contralto
Mood: cynical; ironic description
Voice: stepwise and small skips; several melismas; a dramatic study in dynamics
Piano: chordal; 4–8-voice texture; motion in 8th notes predominates; considerable doubling of vocal line; dramatic ending for pianist as well as singer
Diff: control of dynamics
Uses: dramatic song for the right voice; excellent audition, competition, or recital song

MERZ, KARL
(b. Bensheim, Germany, 1836; d. Wooster, OH, 1890)

1565. **OH TONIGHT MY SOUL IS LONGING** (Mr. Gustavus Hagewau). S. Brainard & Sons, 1866. Gmin-maj; d'–b"; Tess-H; 2/4, 3/4, Andante (Allegretto); 4pp; Diff-V/m-md, P/e-me.
For: light soprano
Mood: lyrical; longing
Voice: sectional; first part: simple dotted rhythms, skips, leaps; second part: more lyrical with ornamental melodic line; rather Mozartean; triplets and quadruplet figures on up-beats; trill and turn at final cadence; word repetition
Piano: chordal; some broken-chord figuration; many 3rds & 6ths; quiet ending
Diff: approach to b" by leap of 6th; ends on g"
Uses: period piece; could help develop flexibility in a young soprano

1566. **THE STARRY MIDNIGHT HOUR.** A Serenade. A. C. Peters & Bro., 1863. Amaj; e'–e"; Tess-M; 2/4, Tender; 4pp (2–4 strophes); Diff-V/e, P/e.
For: tenor; light baritone
Mood: lyrical; gentle serenade
Voice: conjunct with a few easy skips; good vowels on high tones; 18th-century flavor
Piano: 8-meas. introduction with melody in r.h. and afterbeat figure in bass; broken-chord figurations; simple chords; 18th-century style
Uses: nice song for young tenor or baritone with easy head voice; in a group of serenades; period piece

MEYEROWITZ, JAN
(b. Breslau, Germany [now Wroclaw, Poland], 1913
[naturalized American]; d. Colmar, France, 1998)

1567. **BRIGHT STAR** (John Keats). [49]. Atonal; b–b♭";
Tess-mH; 3/4, 4/4, 5/4, Adagio, senza emozione; 5pp;
Diff-V/dd, P/dd.
For: soprano
Mood: lyrical; philosophical
Voice: disjunct; chromatic; very large intervals; large dynamic
contrasts
Piano: extremely chromatic; chordal; difficult 16th-note
patterns
Diff: pitch; rhythm; ensemble
Uses: effective song for advanced performers

1568. **ON THE LAND AND ON THE SEA** (Christina
Rossetti). Broude Bros., 1952. Fmaj; c'–e"(f "); Tess-M;
4/4, Andante; 2pp; Diff-V/me, P/me.
For: mezzo-soprano; baritone
Mood: tranquil; simple; prayer
Voice: chromaticism; easy rhythms; many accidentals;
repetitious
Piano: chordal–block, a few rolled; some chromatic
harmonies; parallelism
Uses: nice song; quiet

MICHAEL, DAVID MORITZ (See Special Section)

MILLARD, HARRISON
(b. Boston, MA, 1829; d. Boston, MA, 1895)

1569. **NORAH ACUSHLA!** (George Cooper). [144];
1st©1876. Gmaj; d'–e"; Tess-M; 6/8, Moderato con
espress.; 2pp (3 strophes); Diff-V/e, P/e.
For: any voice
Mood: lyrical; love song; Irish lilt
Voice: stepwise and small skips; easy rhythms; grace notes
Piano: afterbeat and broken-chord styles; short prelude; does
not double vocal line
Uses: a once-popular parlor song; pleasant; easy; good
illustration of historical type

1570. **SLEEP, O DARLING** (Duerme o bella) (José Batres).
[144]. A♭maj; e♭'–f "; Tess-M-mH; 3/4, Tempo di
valse; 4pp; Diff-V/m, P/e.
For: tenor
Mood: lyrical; serenade
Voice: stepwise and skips along chord lines; some
chromaticism; easy rhythms
Piano: guitar-like waltz pattern; does not double vocal line
Uses: nice lyrical singing line; useful period piece

1571. **SLEEPING** (H. Ashland Kern). [144]; 1st©1873.
E♭maj; d'–f "(b♭"); Tess-M; 6/8, Larghetto con
espressione; 4pp; Diff-V/e, P/e.
For: tenor; high baritone
Mood: subdued; song about death
Voice: graceful melody; skips along chord lines; easy rhythms;
two small ornaments

Piano: 4–5-voice block chords; a few broken chords; doubles
vocal line
Uses: historical group

MITCHELL, FRANK
(b. Hollywood, CA, 1941)

1572. **THE EARTH, THE WIND, AND THE SKY.** 15
Poems by Emily Brontë. J. F. Mitchell, 1977. cmp1977.
Traditional tonal centers and harmonies (often with
modal flavor); d♭'–a" (also available in M & L eds.);
Tess-M, mL; regular meters; varied tempos; 36min;
Diff-V/m, P/me-d.
For: soprano; tenor; some mezzo-sopranos
Mood: lyrical and philosophical; nature imagery predominates
Voice: stepwise and small skips; little chromaticism; mostly
easy rhythms with occasional syncopation, duplets, or 3
vs. 4 in piano; (e.), irregular rhythmic pattern; lyrical
and flowing; syllabic with a few 2-note slurs
Piano: chordal and linear; block, broken, rolled, and afterbeat
chords; broken 8ves; scalar passages; melodic material
in interludes; some chromaticism; syncopation; dotted
rhythms; triplets and a few groupings of 5 or 7; 2 vs. 3;
trills and trill-like figures, grace notes and other
ornaments; incidental doubling of vocal line
Diff: musical difficulties primarily for pianist
Uses: set is rather long to be done as a cycle; small groups
could be selected

   a. *For the Moors.* D-centered, B, & A; d♭'–a";
     Tess-M; 3/4 with changes, Medium–Rather slowly–
     Faster; 4+min.
   b. *Winter Reflection.* Modal, E♭-centered; e♭'–f ";
     Tess-mL; 2/2, Slowly; 2min.
   c. *Tell Me, Smiling Child.* Modal, centers in G;
     e♭'–f♯"; Tess-M; 6/8, 2/4, 5/8, Medium, not too
     fast–Somewhat slowly; 2+min.
   d. *The Darkened Woods.* Fmin; f '–d♭"; Tess-mL; 4/4,
     Medium slow; 1+min.
   e. *Celebration.* A-centered; d'–f♯"; Tess-M;
     unmetered (equivalent to 14/8 [3+3+2+2+2+2]),
     2/4, 4/4, Fast; 3min.
   f. *Evening Landscape.* Modal, D-centered; d'–g";
     Tess-M; 3/4, Slow medium; 1+min.
   g. *I'm Happiest When Most Away.* G-centered-
     Bmaj-A-centered; f '–a"; Tess-M; 3/4, Medium fast;
     1min.
   h. *In Summer Moonlight.* G-centered; d'–g"; Tess-M;
     2/2, Flowing medium; 2min.
   i. *The Old Hall.* D-centered; d'–e"; Tess-mL; 4/4,
     Slowly; 2+min.
   j. *The Harp.* Centers on A & E; d♯'–e"; Tess-M;
     unmetered & 4/4, 3/4, Medium–Fast medium;
     2+min.
   k. *The Traveler.* G-centered; e♭'–f "; Tess-M; 6/8,
     Fast; 1+min.
   l. *A Spell.* Cmin; d'–f "; Tess-M; 4/2, Medium slow;
     3min.
   m. *The Caged Bird.* G-centered; d'–f "; Tess-M; 3/4,
     4/4, 2/4, Slow medium; 3min.
   n. *The Pessimist.* Amin; d'–g"; Tess-M; 4/4, 3/4, 2/4,

Medium slow; 2+min.

o. *No Coward Soul Is Mine.* E- & A-centered; e'–f"; Tess-M; 2/2, Fast medium; 4min.

1573. **FIVE LYRICS BY EDNA ST. VINCENT MILLAY.** J. F. Mitchell, 1983. cmp1983. Also available in M & L eds. Separate entries below.

A. **SUMMER, THE LOVELY.** B♭maj; f'–e♭"; Tess-M; 6/4, 4/4, 3/4, Medium; 2+pp; Diff-V/me, P/md.
For: any high or medium voice
Mood: lyrical; nature imagery
Voice: stepwise and easy skips; short phrases; syllabic with occasional 2-note slurs
Piano: chordal–block, broken, and rolled; rapid scale passages, incl. quintuplets and a sextuplet; syncopation; trills and trill figures; supports vocal line strongly, no doubling
Diff: introduction is challenging for pianist
Uses: short phrases and limited range useful for many students; recital possibilities

B. **THE WILD SWANS.** Dmin; d'–g"; Tess-M; 4/4, Medium; 1+pp; Diff-V/me, P/d.
For: soprano; mezzo-soprano; tenor
Mood: lyrical; nature imagery
Voice: stepwise and easy skips; short phrases; syllabic with occasional 2-note slurs
Piano: chordal–block and broken; rapid descending 2-voice scale passages in r.h.–upper voice in 32nds, lower voice in sextuplet 16ths (3 vs. 4); a little countermelody; does not double vocal line
Diff: difficult accomp.
Uses: recital possibilities

C. **TRAVEL.** B♭min; d♭'–e♭"; Tess-M; 4/4, 2/4, Fast medium; 2+pp; Diff-V/me, P/m.
For: any medium voice
Mood: philosophical; longing to go away
Voice: stepwise and skips within chords; a little chromaticism; short phrases move within limited range; syllabic
Piano: chordal–block and rolled; repeated-note or scale-wise triplets almost throughout; 3-note countermelodic figure recurs frequently; supports vocal line strongly, does not double
Diff: a few pitches may be hard to hear
Uses: short phrases and limited range useful for many students; recital possibilities

D. **THE DREAM.** Fmaj; d'–f"; Tess-mL; 4/4, Medium; 3+pp; Diff-V/me, P/me.
For: any medium voice
Mood: lyrical love song
Voice: stepwise and easy skips; short phrases; syllabic
Piano: broken-chord figure throughout; l.h. countermelody in middle section; supports vocal line, does not double
Uses: recital possibilities

E. **THE RETURN FROM TOWN.** A♭maj; e♭'–f"; Tess-M; 4/4, 2/4, Medium; 2pp (with repeat); Diff-V/e, P/m.
For: soprano; mezzo-soprano
Mood: like a folksong; humorous; "girl meets boy"

Voice: stepwise and easy skips; syllabic
Piano: chordal with descending melodic pattern in triplets in r.h.; staccato chords; incidental doubling of vocal line
Uses: good for younger students; recital possibilities; see also setting by J. Duke

1574. **FIVE SONNETS OF EDNA ST. VINCENT MILLAY.** J. F. Mitchell, 1983. cmp1983. Traditional tonal centers and harmonies, often with a modal flavor; d'–c'''; Tess-M, mH; mostly regular meters with a few changes; moderate tempos; 11+min; Diff-V/m-d, P/m-d.
For: soprano
Mood: lyrical and philosophical; life and love
Voice: mostly stepwise and small skips; little chromaticism; syncopation; duplets and triplets; 3 vs. 2 & 4 in piano; (b.), 4-note melismas with a longer one in 16ths; (c.), rising phrases; (d.), rapid melismas and trills; one spoken phrase; syllabic; occasional 2–3-note slurs
Piano: chordal and linear; block, broken, and afterbeat chords; scale passages; countermelodies; broken 8ves; some chromaticism; triplets and groupings of 7 & 9; 2 vs. 3 & 3 vs. 4; trills; grace notes; cross-hands; incidental doubling of vocal line
Diff: rhythms; some pitches; requires vocal agility
Uses: good recital material

a. *Night Is My Sister.* Amin; d'–b"; Tess-mH; 12/8, 6/8, Medium slow; 2+min.
b. *Columbine.* Emaj; e'–g♯"; Tess-M; 6/8, Fast medium; 2min.
c. *Time Does Not Bring Relief.* Gmin; e♭'–a♭"; Tess-M; 4/4, Slow medium; 3min.
d. *You'll Be Sorry.* Cmaj; e'–c'''; Tess-M; 2/4, 4/4, Fast medium–Fast–Medium; 2+min.
e. *Beauty.* E♭maj-Gmaj; d'–a"; Tess-mH; 4/4, 5/4, 3/4, 2/4, Medium; 2+min.

1575. **THE POOL OF SPIRIT.** Seven Poems by Cynthia Stuart. Cycle. J. F. Mitchell, 1980. cmp1980. Traditional keys and harmonies, often with a modal flavor; d'–a" (also pub. in M & L eds.); Tess-M-mL; regular meters with changes; moderate tempos; 18+pp; Diff-V/m, P/m.
For: tenor; soprano; mezzo-soprano
Mood: lyrical and philosophical
Voice: stepwise and easy skips; some chromaticism; lyrical and flowing; phrases generally quite short; (d.), recit.-like; syllabic
Piano: chordal and linear; block, broken, rolled, and repeated chords; some chromaticism; often a single-line melody as counterpoint to vocal line against chords; supports but does not double vocal line
Diff: frequent changes of meter in (c.)
Uses: good student material; limited range and short phrases of most of the songs useful in many situations; recital possibilities

a. *The Path.* D♭maj; e♭'–f"; Tess-mL; 4/4, 6/4, Medium slow (♩ = 72); 1+pp.
b. *Sleep.* Dmaj; e'–g♯"; Tess-M; 2/2, 4/4, Fast medium (♩ = 72); 3+pp.

c. *Eclipse.* E♭min; e♭'–f"; Tess-M; 4/4, 3/4, 2/4, Medium slow; 3+pp.

d. *Be Still.* Emin; d'–d"; Tess-mL; unmetered, Freely, rather slow; 1p.

e. *The Pool.* Emin; e'–f♯"; Tess-mL; 4/4, 3/4, Slow medium (♩ = 76); 2+pp.

f. *Morning.* Amaj; e'–a"; Tess-M; 2/2, Fast (♩ = 92); 3+pp.

g. *Earth.* Modal, E-centered; d'–e"; Tess-M; 4/4, Slow medium (♩ = 72); 2+pp.

1576. **SEVEN SONGS FROM WILLIAM BLAKE** (from *Poetical Sketches*, 1783). J. F. Mitchell, 1977. cmp1964 & 1977. Traditional keys and harmonies with modal flavor; c'–a♭" (also available in M & L eds.); Tess-M, mL; regular meters with changes; moderate to fast tempos; 26+pp; Diff-V/m, P/d.
For: mezzo-soprano; tenor
Mood: lyrical and philosophical; nature imagery
Voice: stepwise and easy skips; somewhat chromatic; triplets; syncopation; lyrical, flowing phrases, generally rather short; melisma at end of (c.); syllabic; occasional 2-note slurs.
Piano: chordal and linear; much broken-chord figuration; block and afterbeat chords; (c.) & (f.), quite chromatic; countermelodies; scalar passages; triplets; supports but does not double vocal line
Diff: frequent meter changes in (e.); some pitches hard to hear
Uses: good recital material

a. *To Morning.* X; e♭'–a♭"; Tess-M, mL; 2/2, Flowing medium (♩ = 66); 3+pp.

b. *Love and Harmony Combine.* Modal, F-centered; e♭'–f"; Tess-M; 2/4, 3/4, Fast medium (with delicacy) (♩ = 108); 4pp.

c. *My Silks and Fine Array.* Modal, G-centered; d'–a♭"; Tess-M; 4/4, Slow medium (♩ = 72); 4pp.

d. *Memory, Hither Come.* Fmin-F♯min; c♯'–f♯"; Tess-M, mL; 4/4, 6/4, Medium fast and sprightly (♩ = 168); 3+pp.

e. *How Sweet I Roamed.* Bmin; d'–f♯"; Tess-M; 3/4, 2/4, 6/8, Medium (♪ = ca.152–160); 3pp.

f. *The Wild Winds Weep.* Gmin-modal, E-centered; c'–g♯"; Tess-M; 4/4, 2/4, 3/4, Fast (♩ = 116); 5pp.

g. *I Love the Merry Dance.* Emaj; e'–g♯"; Tess-M, mL; 6/8, 4/4, Fast medium (♩. = ca.92–96); 3+pp.

1577. **THREE SONGS FROM *THE MYSTIC TRUMPETER*** for Baritone and Piano. (Walt Whitman). Cycle. J. F. Mitchell, 1984. cmp1984. Traditional tonal centers and harmonies, often with a modal flavor; B–g'; Tess-M; mostly regular meters; varied tempos; 20pp; Diff-V-m-md, P/md-d.
For: baritone specified
Mood: philosophical and dramatic
Voice: stepwise and small skips; little chromaticism; triplets and 3 vs. 4 in piano; (a.), quite dramatic with numerous recurrences of the dim.5th a'–e♭"; (b.), lyrical with melismas on "all"; (c.), again more dramatic; high tessitura at end and sustained 5-beat f' and 7-beat g'; syllabic with occasional 2-note slurs

Piano: chordal and linear; block, broken, and rolled chords; melodic fragments in short preludes and interludes; rapid scale passages; some chromaticism; syncopation; triplets and groupings of 7; (a.), fanfare-like opening; (b.), countermelody; (c.), both hands often in bass clef with repeated-note l.h. figure in 16ths and trills; incidental doubling of vocal line
Diff: good sense of pitch and interpretive insight needed
Uses: good recital cycle

a. *I Hear Thee Trumpeter.* A-centered; c–f'; 3/2, Medium–Medium fast; 8+pp.

b. *The All-Enclosing Theme.* Dmaj; B–e'; 4/4, 5/4, Medium slow; 3pp.

c. *A Culminating Song.* A- & C-centered; c–g'; 2/2, 6/4, 4/4, Medium–Fast; 6+pp.

1578. **THREE SONNETS OF KEATS** (John Keats). J. F. Mitchell, 1986. cmp1986. A- & E-centered; d'–a" (also available in M & L eds.); Tess-M, mH; regular meters; moderate tempos; 8pp; Diff-V/m, P/m.
For: soprano; tenor
Mood: lyrical and philosophical; nature imagery
Voice: stepwise and small skips; some chromaticism; triplets; syllabic with a few 2-note slurs
Piano: primarily chordal–block, broken, and rolled; a little countermelody; somewhat chromatic; incidental doubling of vocal line
Diff: good sense of pitch needed
Uses: useful recital group

a. *O Solitude.* Amaj; f♯'–g"; Tess-mH; 4/4, 3/4, Slow medium; 2+pp.

b. *In City Pent.* Amaj; e'–g"; Tess-M; 4/4, 2/4, 3/4, Firmly; 2pp.

c. *My Golden Pen.* E-centered; d'–a"; Tess-M; 4/2, 4/4, 3/4, 2/4, Medium; 3pp.

1579. **VISIONS FROM THE EARTH.** Ten Poems by Emily Brontë for High Voice and Piano. Cycle. J. F. Mitchell, 1976. cmp1976. Traditional tonal centers and harmonies, often with a modal flavor; c'–a" (also available in M & L eds.); Tess-M, mL; regular and irregular meters with changes; varied tempos; 47pp; Diff-V/m-md, P/me-dd.
For: soprano; tenor
Mood: lyrical and philosophical
Voice: stepwise and small skips; leaps of 7th, 8ve, & 10th; little chromaticism; generally easy rhythms with occasional syncopation or triplets; 2 vs. 3 & 3 vs. 4 in piano; (a.), static, recit.-like phrases at beginning; later phrases begin high or medium-high and descend scale-wise; (d.) & (h.), irregular meters with frequent changes; (f.), two quintuplet groupings; (h.), 3-meas. f♯" at end; syllabic with occasional 2–3-note slurs
Piano: chordal and linear; block, broken, rolled, and repeated chords; countermelodies; some chromaticism; scalar passages; syncopation, triplets, and 2 vs. 3; (h.), rapid trill figures and scale patterns in triplet 16ths in 8ves, suggesting the wind; (j.), 9-meas. postlude with opt. cut; incidental doubling of vocal line
Diff: good sense of pitch and rhythm needed; a rather long

cycle in which to sustain a somber mood

Uses: good recital material for performers who can handle the whole work; individual songs could be excerpted or a shorter set created

   a. *A Vision.* Dmin-Emaj; c♯'–a♭"; Tess- mL, M; 3/4, 4/4, Slow medium–Fast; 5+pp.

   b. *Cold in the Earth.* Emin-Fmaj-Amin; c'–a"; Tess-M; 4/4, 3/4, 6/4, Medium slow; 5pp.

   c. *To Imagination.* Gmaj; d'–g"; Tess-M; 2/2, Medium, not too fast; 3+pp.

   d. *Come, Walk with Me.* Fmaj-Amin-F♯min; e♭'–g"; Tess-M; 6/4 with changes, Medium; 4pp (with repeat).

   e. *Shall Earth No More Inspire Thee.* E-centered; f♯'–e"; M; 4/4, 2/4, Medium–Fast medium; 3+pp.

   f. *Child of Delight.* A♭maj; e♭'–f"; Tess-M; 3/4, 4/4, 2/4, 5/4, Medium; 5+pp.

   g. *Stars.* C-centered; d'–a"; Tess-M; 3/4, 2/4, 4/4, Medium slow–Fast (♩ = 92); 5pp.

   h. *The Night Wind.* Bmin; e'–f♯"; Tess- M; 4/4 with frequent changes, Fast (♩ = 108–112); 4pp.

   i. *How Clear She Shines.* Amaj; e'–g"; Tess-M; 4/4, 6/4, Slow medium; 2+pp.

   j. *The Messenger.* Dmaj; d♯'–a"; Tess-mL; 4/4, 6/4, 3/4, 5/4, Medium; 5+pp.

1580. **VISIONS FROM THE FLAME.** Ten Poems by William Blake. Cycle. J. F. Mitchell, 1977. cmp1977. Traditional keys, tonal centers, and harmonies, often with a modal flavor; d'–b♭" (also available in M & L eds.); Tess-M; mostly regular meters with changes; varied tempos; 39pp; Diff-V/md-md, P/me-d.

For: tenor best for complete cycle; possibly soprano; (b., c., g., & h.) could be sung by baritone or mezzo-soprano

Mood: lyrical and philosophical; sometimes moralizing in tone; nature imagery; (e.) mildly risqué in tone, somewhat in the manner of "Promiscuity" from Barber's *Hermit Songs*

Voice: stepwise and small skips; little chromaticism; generally easy rhythms with occasional triplets or syncopation; (b.), simple vocal line as befits text; (d.), 9-beat f♯"; (e.), two sextuplet melismas and one in broken 3rds; fragmented phrases; (f.), 6- & 7-beat a"s; (h.) & (i.), duplets and 2 vs. 3 in piano; (i.), descending scalar melismas; syllabic with occasional 2–3-note slurs.

Piano: chordal and linear; block, broken, and rolled chords; countermelodies in (a.) & (d.); some chromaticism; triplets and groupings of 5, 6, 7, 9, and 10; syncopation; (b.), melody in interludes; (d.), scales and trills in 3rds & 16th-note broken-chord patterns; (e.), afterbeat pattern with grace notes; (h.), 2-voice counterpoint; (i.), dotted rhythms afterbeat pattern rapid scales with irregular groupings; much staccato; incidental doubling of vocal line

Diff: good sense of pitch needed; some ensemble problems

Uses: possible recital group for a tenor; does not require extensive or expansive high voice

   a. *The Voice of the Bard.* Cmin; e♭'–b♭"; 4/4, 2/4, 3/4, Slow medium; 3+pp.

   b. *The Lamb.* Fmaj; f'–f"; 4/4, 3/4, 2/4, 6/8, Medium

(not too fast); 4+pp.

   c. *The Divine Image.* A-centered; e'–f♯"; 2/2, 2/4, 3/4, 4/4, Slow medium; 3+pp.

   d. *Ah! Sunflower.* G♯min-D♭maj; d♯'–g♯"; 3/4, 6/8, Slow medium; 2+pp.

   e. *I Asked a Thief.* A♭maj; e♭'–e♭"; 4/4, 3/4, 2/4, Medium–Fast; 3pp.

   f. *The Garden of Love.* Amin; d'–a"; 2/2, 6/4, 4/4, Fast medium; 5pp.

   g. *The Smile.* Emaj-Fmin; f'–f"; 4/4, Medium slow; 3pp.

   h. *Mock On, Mock On.* Cmaj; e♭'–e♭"; 6/8, 9/8, 12/8, Medium fast; 4pp.

   i. *The Tyger.* C♯-centered-Gmin; d'–g"; 12/8, 6/8, 9/8, Fast; 6pp.

   j. *Eternity.* A♭-& G-centered; e♭'–a♭"; 4/4, 12/16, Slowly; 1+pp.

MOEVS, ROBERT
(b. La Crosse, WI, 1920)

1581. **TIME** (William Shakespeare, from Sonnet LXIV). Marks, 1975. cmp1969. X; g–a"; Tess-H, M, L; changing meters; changing tempos; 3+min; Diff-V/dd, P/dd.

For: dramatic soprano

Mood: somber poem; fragmented mood

Voice: long sustained phrases; quarter tones; glissando; some speaking; each note marked dynamically

Piano: modern techniques, inside and outside piano; interlude pointillistic; covers keyboard

Diff: avant-garde techniques; quarter tones; vocalized consonants; dynamic control of each individual note; perfect pitch almost necessary

MOORE, DOUGLAS
(b. Cutchogue, NY, 1893; d. Long Island, NY, 1969)

1582. **ADAM WAS MY GRANDFATHER** (Stephen Vincent Benét). Galaxy, 1938. Fmin; c'–f♯"; Tess-M; 2/4, Allegro moderato; 5pp; Diff-V/m, P/m-md.

For: baritone

Mood: declamatory; rakish; humorous

Voice: conjunct with some skips; various rhythmic patterns repeated; sustained e♭"s and climax on f♯"

Piano: patterned rhythmically and somewhat harmonically; chordal; broken-chord figure in middle section; mostly staccato in outer sections

Diff: few difficulties; not for a young singer

Uses: vigorous song for baritone with flair for the style

1583. **DEAR DARK HEAD** (trans. from Irish of Sir Samuel Ferguson). Galaxy, 1963. Amaj (modal flavor); f♯'–a"; Tess-M-mH; 3/4, Andante con moto; 3pp; Diff-V/m, P/m.

For: tenor

Mood: lyrical; love song

Voice: many small skips; legato style; some slurs

Piano: chordal–broken chords; outlines vocal melody

Uses: interior of a group; quiet ending; mildly dissonant

1584. **OLD SONG** (Theodore Roethke). [21]; 1st©1950. H &
L keys: Fmaj & D♭maj; c'–f ″ & a♭–d♭″; 4/4, Andante
(♩ = 72); 2+min; Diff-V/m, P/m.
For: contralto; any medium or low voice
Mood: lyrical; love song; nature imagery
Voice: short phrases; somewhat disjunct
Piano: chords accompany independent melody, forming
counterpoint with the voice
Diff: long decresc. on last note (c″ or a♭')
Uses: effective song; recital material

1585. **SIGH NO MORE, LADIES** (William Shakespeare).
Boosey & Hawkes, 1944. Modal; d'–e″; Tess-M; 4/4,
Andante con moto; 2pp; Diff-V/e, P/e.
For: any voice
Mood: humorously philosophical
Voice: stepwise and small skips; easy rhythms; 2-note slurs
Piano: animated chordal background; some countermelody;
4-voice texture; does not double vocal line
Uses: nice song for a young singer

1586. **THREE SONNETS OF JOHN DONNE.** G.
Schirmer, 1944. [51]. Traditional keys; d'–a″; Tess-mH;
regular meters; contrasting tempos; 15pp; Diff-
V/m-md, P/e-md.
For: tenor (not light)
Mood: dramatic; strong; confident
Voice: many skips; angular; wide-ranged phrases; sustained
high tones; speech rhythms
Piano: mostly chordal; some linear; repeated and arpeggiated
chords; many accidentals; 3 vs. 4; duplets and triplets
juxtaposed
Diff: ensemble; rhythms; irregular phrase lengths
Uses: perform together; not as difficult as other settings of
Donne's sonnets (Britten, John Eaton, etc.).

  a. *Thou Hast Made Me.* Bmin; d'–g♯″; Tess-mH; 3/4,
  Adagio; 4pp.
  b. *Batter My Heart.* Gmaj; f'–g″; Tess-mH; 4/4,
  Allegro; 6pp.
  c. *Death, Be Not Proud.* Dmin; d'–a″; Tess-mH; 4/4,
  Andante; 5pp. [Rec: D#59]

1587. **UNDER THE GREENWOOD TREE** (William
Shakespeare). [21]; 1st©1950. H & L keys: Fmaj &
D♭maj; f'–a″ & d♭'–f″; Tess-mH; 3/4, Andantino
(♩ = 90); 2min; Diff-V/m, P/m.
For: tenor; baritone; lyric soprano
Mood: lyrical; nature imagery
Voice: generally lyrical; several dramatic phrases; small
melismas
Piano: broken-chord figuration
Uses: interesting setting; useful

MOORE, UNDINE S.
(b. Jarratt, VA, 1905; d. Petersburg, VA, 1989)

1588. **I AM IN DOUBT** (Florence Hynes Willeté). [10].
cmp1975. X; e'–a″; Tess-mH; 4/4, 2/4, 3/4, 6/4
(♩ = ca.58); 2pp; Diff-V/m, P/m.
For: soprano; tenor

Mood: rather intense love song
Voice: conjunct, disjunct, and recit.-like phrases; one melisma,
but not fast; some accidentals
Piano: chordal; triplet countermelody; many accidentals; large
reach needed; doubles vocal line at critical points
Diff: some pitches and rhythms
Uses: good song for recital

1589. **LOVE LET THE WIND CRY . . . HOW I ADORE
THEE** (Sappho; rendered by Bliss Carman; based on
prose trans. of H. Wharton). [6]; 1st©1977. D♭maj-
Emaj; d♭'–a″; Tess-M; 3/4 with changes, With
passion–Pressing forward ♩ = ca.88–92; 6pp;
Diff-V/md, P/d.
For: dramatic soprano
Mood: passionate; dramatic; descriptions from nature
Voice: expansive, soaring phrases; low-lying section; strong
accents; duplets and triplets; some phrases begin high
Piano: big chords at beginning and end; long passages of trill
and broken-chord figures; strongly supports and
doubles vocal line
Diff: needs dramatic voice and expressive ability; must soar
over heavy accomp.
Uses: fine song for dramatic soprano

MOPPER, IRVING
(b. Savannah, GA, 1914)

1590. **THE LEMON-COLORED DODO** (anon.) Boston
Music Co., 1947. B♭min; f'–g♭″; Tess-mH; 2/4,
Moderately fast, poutingly; 4pp; Diff-V/me, P/m.
For: light soprano
Mood: humorous; nonsense; narrative
Voice: stepwise and easy skips; interrupted phrases; some
dotted rhythms; 3-note slurs; repetitive
Piano: afterbeat chordal pattern; many 2nds; accidentals; does
not double vocal line
Diff: needs a simple, innocent delivery
Uses: best for a young soprano; encore

MORGENSTERN, SAM
(b. Louisville, KY, 1910; d. New York, NY, 1989)

1591. **EVENING STAR.** No. I of *Fragments from the Greek*
(Sappho; trans. Stackpoole) (unpub. cycle). [57]. X;
c'–e″; Tess-M; 3/4 with changes, Andante moderato;
1p; Diff-V/md, P/md.
For: all voices except very low or very high
Mood: "All things come to rest at eventide"
Voice: duplets and triplets juxtaposed; many small skips;
syllabic
Piano: linear; chiefly 2-voice texture; imitation; accidentals;
no doubling of vocal line
Diff: ensemble; rhythms
Uses: good song to introduce student to complexities of
contemporary art songs

1592. **MY APPLE TREE** (Federico García Lorca; trans.
Edwin Honig). [60]; 1st©1952. H & L keys: A-
centered & F-centered; f'–a″ & d♭'–f″; Tess-mH; 3/4,

2/4, Free; 2min; Diff-V/d, P/dd.
For: soprano; tenor
Mood: lyrical; nature description
Voice: florid with numerous short melismas; fairly chromatic
Piano: 2-voice texture; independent; short melismas; complex rhythms
Diff: pitch; flexibility
Uses: interesting coloratura song in modern idiom

MOSS, LAWRENCE
[See Appendix for songs with German texts]

MUNN, ZAE
(b. Moscow, ID, 1953)

1593. LAUBER LIEDER (Peg Carlson Lauber). Four songs for soprano and piano. Arsis Press, 1996. cmp1994. X; d'–ab"; Tess-M; regular changing meters, tempos ♪ = 80–♩. = 50; 12min; Diff-V/md, P/md.
For: lyric soprano
Mood: dark; depressed; dealing with the challenges of life
Voice: syllabic; chromatic and dissonant; large leaps; many tritones
Piano: accidentals; predictable patterns within hand positions; vocal line sometimes doubled
Diff: atonality; will need much imagination
Uses: interesting for a singer who finds the poems meaningful

    a. *The Slowly Opening Rose.* X; d'–f"; Tess-cs; 4/4, 2/4, 3/4, ♩ = 48; 3+min.
    b. *I Have Washed and Buttoned Up.* X; eb'–g"; Tess-M; 6/8, 8/8, 4/4, 9/8, 5/8, ♪ = 80; 2+min.
    c. *Geese along the Flowage.* X; eb'–g"; Tess-M; 4/4, 2/4, 3/4, 6/8, ♩ = 108; 3+min.
    d. *The Sermon.* X; d♯'–ab"; Tess-M; 3/4, 4/4, ♩ = 60; 3min.

MURRAY, BAIN
(b. Evanston, IL, 1926; d. 1993)

1594. FLAME AND SHADOW (Sara Teasdale). Teasdale Song Cycle for Soprano and Piano. Ludwig, 1974. cmp1956. No key sigs., many accidentals, delicate dissonances; b–bb"; Tess-M; regular and irregular changing meters; varied tempos; 23pp; Diff-V/d, P/md.
For: lyric soprano
Mood: lyrical; bright and dark aspects of love
Voice: conjunct; skips and small leaps; speech rhythms; some long phrases; some low phrases; constant meter changes; accidentals
Piano: predominantly linear texture; some repeated-note ostinato figures; cross-hands; many accidentals and meter changes; irregular meters; often contrapuntal; expressive of text
Diff: changing meters; pitch patterns; ensemble
Uses: interesting cycle; should be effective for a more advanced student with solid musicianship

    a. *The Look.* c'–ab"; Tess-M; 6/8 with some changes,

Andantino grazioso; 3pp.
    b. *The Long Hill.* c'–a♯"; Tess-M; 4/4, 8/8, 7/8, 5/8, etc., Andante espressivo; 3pp.
    c. *Joy.* d♯'–a"; Tess-M; 12/8, 10/8, 15/8 with changing accents, Allegro con fuoco; 3pp.
    d. *Alone.* b–g"; Tess-M; 4/4, 5/4, 3/4, Largo, with poignancy and restraint; 3+pp.
    e. *Youth and the Pilgrim.* b♯–g♯"; Tess-L, M; 4/4 with changes, Alla marcia andante; 3+pp.
    f. *Peace.* c'–bb"; Tess-wide; 6/8, with changes, Adagio tranquillo con espressione; 2+pp.
    g. *I Would Live in Your Love.* c'–bb"; Tess-M; 9/8, 6/8, Maestoso, appassionato e risoluto; 4+pp.

1595. NOW CLOSE THE WINDOWS (Robert Frost). [19]. D-Centered; a–e"; Tess-M; 4/4, Adagio tranquillo; 2min; Diff-V/m, P/m.
For: mezzo-soprano; contralto; baritone
Mood: quiet against uneasy background; shutting out the storm
Voice: many small skips; some long-ranged phrases; some syncopation
Piano: repetitive l.h. patterns; long pedal tones; syncopated r.h. counterpoint; thin texture; no vocal line doubling
Uses: effective somber song; quiet ending; in an American or other group

1596. THE PASTURE (Robert Frost). [17]. H & L keys: F & D; bb–g" & g–e"; Tess-M; 5/8, 7/8, 6/8, 9/8, Allegro; 4pp; Diff-V/d, P/d.
For: light lyric voices
Mood: naive; descriptive of nature
Voice: light, lyrical, dancing; some chromaticism
Piano: arpeggiations; chromatic
Diff: changing meters; 5/8 groupings; wide range
Uses: good song for lyric voices; best suited to women

MUSTO, JOHN
(b. Brooklyn, NY, 1954)

[See also D#s 28 & 50; no titles given]

1597. CANZONETTAS: THREE SONGS ON ANONYMOUS POEMS. Peer-Southern, 1987. Tonal; c'–a"; Tess-wide; mixed meters; slow to moderate tempos; 7pp; Diff-V/m-md, P/ md-m.
For: tenor best for set; soprano; (c.), high or medium voices
Mood: lyrical; (a.) & (b.) love songs
Voice: (a.), rather disjunct; wide skips; (b.) & (c.), more conjunct; some wide skips (up to 7th); rhythmic complexity; accidentals
Piano: (a.), 14-meas. prelude; others have shorter preludes and interludes; linear and chordal writing; (a.) & (c.), legato; (b.) features staccato afterbeat style; many accidentals
Diff: wide tessitura and long-ranged phrases in (a.); rhythms; lack of support from piano
Uses: as a group or separately; (a.) & (b.), a nice short pair; (c.), setting of familiar poem for medium voice

    a. *Western Wind.* A minorish; e'–a"; Tess-wide; 3/4 with changes, Slow, wistful (♩ = 50); 3pp.

b. *All Night by the Rose.* G♯maj; d♯'–g♯"; Tess-mH; 5/4 with changes, Allegretto (♩ = 80); 1p.

c. *The Silver Swan.* Tonal (sequential); c♯'–f♯"; Tess-M; 5/4 with changes, Slowly, sadly (♩ = 56); 3pp.

1598. **DOVE STA AMORE** for High Voice and Piano [English texts] (also published for Medium Voice and Piano). peermusic (Songs of Peer, Ltd.), 1998 (Presser). X; a–d♭'" & g–c♭'"; Tess-cs, L, H; mostly regular meters with changes; varied tempos; 28pp; Diff-V/m-d, P/me-d.

For: soprano; mezzo-soprano

Mood: dark and somewhat surreal; various circumstances in which love exists in tension with a disturbing setting

Voice: largely disjunct; rhythmically complex; very wide range; many wide intervals; tone-row construction in last song; long phrases; extreme low and high notes; mostly atonal; arpeggios; many accidentals; long coloratura passage on "ah" in last song; speech rhythms

Piano: wide range of techniques and figurations; many accidentals; some 3-stave notation; repeated patterns in fast harmonic motion; wide dynamic range; some popular style with atonal content

Diff: range; rhythms; atonality; wide intervals; ensemble; diction

Uses: for a graduate to professional level singer; best for a musically sophisticated audience

a. *Maybe* (Carl Sandburg). X; c'–a" & a'–f♯"; Tess-cs; 12/16, 6/16, Moderately (♪. = 82); 3pp.

b. *Sea Chest* (Carl Sandburg). Gmin; c'–a" & a'–f♯"; Tess-cs; 3/8, Gently rocking (♩= 40); 3pp.

c. *The Hangman at Home* (Carl Sandburg). X; b♭–b♭"& g–g"; Tess-cs; 2/4, 3/4, 3/8, 4/8, 5/8, Moderately (♪ = 90); 5pp.

d. *How Many Little Children Sleep* (James Agee). G majorish; a–a" & g–g"; Tess:cs; 6/8, 9/8, Simply, quietly (♪ = 115); 4pp.

e. *Dove Sta Amore . . .* (Lawrence Ferlinghetti). X (tone row); a–d♭'" & g–c♭'"; Tess-cs, L, H; 4/4, 3/4, 7/8, 6/4, Tempo rubato (♩ = ca. 92) and Tempo giusto (♩ = 140); 13pp.

1599. **ENOUGH ROPE** (Dorothy Parker). [145]. cmp1987. Tonal; a–b"; Tess-wide; mixed meters with changes; varied tempos; 7pp; Diff-V/m-d, P/m-d.

For: soprano

Mood: humorous; philosophical

Voice: many skips; frequent leaps of 7th or more; long-ranged phrases; easy rhythms in (a.); (b.), complex rhythms with syncopation and short phrases interrupted by rests; (c.) features syncopation in a legato context

Piano: (a.), busy 16ths, often alternating intervals of a 2nd; (b.), block chords, some rolled; large reach helpful; complex rhythm; (c.), broken chord pattern; cross-hand ornaments; 3-stave scoring

Diff: voice has little support from piano; complex rhythms; difficult intervals; pitches hard to find

Uses: a nice short set of songs, each one completely different; (c.), an unusually serious text for Dorothy Parker

a. *Social Note.* E-centered; e'–a"; Tess-mH; 2/4, 3/4,

Fast and restless (♩ = 144); 3pp. [**Rec:** D#7]

b. *Résumé.* X; a–a"; Tess-wide; 4/4, 7/8, 3/4, Slowly, with a blues feel (♩ = 40); 1p.

c. *The Sea.* F♯-centered; f♯'–b"; Tess-H; 3/2, 2/2, 5/4, Gently rocking (♩ = 30); 1p.

[**HEARTBEATS.** See entry #15 C]

1600. **LAMENT** (Edna St. Vincent Millay). [145]. cmp1988. E♭min, much chromaticism; e'–b"; Tess-wide; 2/4, 6/8, 7/8, Moderately (♩ = 76); 5pp; Diff-V/d, P/dd.

For: soprano (dramatic or lyric-spinto best)

Mood: life going on after bereavement

Voice: rather disjunct; dramatic; many accidentals; changing moods; slides of M3rd & m6th

Piano: sounds like a cabaret song; swing bass; bristles with accidentals; mood, key, and register changes; trill and tremolo in dramatic moments; 8-meas. prelude; 9-meas. interlude; two other short interludes

Diff: dramatic scene; mood changes; ensemble; fragmented phrases; phrase ranges over an 8ve; reading piano score

Uses: dramatic song with pathos for mature singer-actress

1601. **QUIET SONGS.** Peer-Southern, 1991. cmp1990. "To Amy [Burton]." Tonal with varied and transitory key structures; a–c♯'"; Tess-wide; mixed meters with many changes; varied tempos; 25pp; Diff-V/md-dd, P/me-dd.

For: soprano (if sung as a group)

Mood: various moods: spirited; love song; peace; cynical view of Christmas; ennui; death

Voice: wide-ranged phrases, except (b.); various divisions of the beat; syncopation; polyrhythms; little support from the piano; many leaps; a few unaccomp. meas.; some humming; dramatic

Piano: covers the keyboard; complex polyrhythms; many accidentals; (d.) scored on 3 staves; trills featured in (e.); solo material in (b.) & (c.) (4 complex meas.), (d.), & (f.) (7-meas. prelude); third hand would be helpful in (d.), as well as a wide reach

Diff: rhythms; intervals; tessitura; ensemble

Uses: songs for an advanced singer and pianist; mature viewpoints; not necessarily quiet songs; commissioned as a group, but could be sung separately; (b.) & (c.) pair nicely

a. *maggie and milly and molly and may* (e. e. cummings). E; d♭'–b"; Tess-H; 9/8 mixed, Breezily (♩. = 66); 4pp.

b. *Intermezzo* (Amy Elizabeth Burton). B♭; c'–g"; Tess-wide; 7/4 mixed, Slowly (♩ = 84); 1p.

c. *Quiet Song* (Eugene O'Neill). D; a–c♯'"; Tess-wide; 5/4 mixed, Moderately (♩ = 92); 6pp.

d. *Christmas Carol (To Jesus on His Birthday)* (Edna St. Vincent Millay). D; b–a"; Tess-wide; 5/4 mixed, Slowly (♩ = 54); 5pp.

e. *Palm Sunday: Naples* (Arthur Symons). B♭; c'–a"; Tess-wide; 6/8 mixed, Andante grazioso (♪ = 132); 5pp.

f. *Lullaby* (Léonie Adams). X; c'–a"; Tess-wide; 5/4 mixed, Slowly (♩ = 69); 4pp.

1602. **RECUERDO** (Three Songs on Poems By Christina

Rossetti, Edna St. Vincent Millay and Louise Bogan), for Medium Voice. [145]; 1st©1988. "For William Sharp and Steven Blier." Tonal; b–b♭"; Tess-mH, cs; regular and irregular changing meters; varied tempos; 20pp; Diff-V/d, P/d.

For: soprano; lyric mezzo-soprano
Mood: memories of a dead lover, an all-night date, a dead friend; longing, melancholy, fondness, loving remembrance
Voice: mostly disjunct and wide ranging; much syncopation; syllabic settings; some intricate rhythms; rhythms reflect both word stress and imagery
Piano: built on clear motives; ragtime style in second song rhythmically sophisticated; demands solid command of keyboard and familiarity with popular styles
Diff: rhythms; range; style; complexity of piano style
Uses: excellent set for advanced performers
Rec: D#s 7, 56

   a. *Echo* (Christina Rossetti). Major tonalities; d♭'–b♭"; Tess-M-mH, cs; changing regular and irregular simple and compound meters, Slow, mysterious, obsessive (♩ = 52); 8pp.
   b. *Recuerdo* (Edna St. Vincent Millay). Amaj in a crazy mirror; b–g♯"; Tess-M-mH, cs; changing regular and irregular meters, Moderately fast (♪ = 104); 9pp.
   c. *Last Song* (Louise Bogan). Tonal; d'–g"; Tess-mH, cs; changing regular and irregular meters, Slowly, simply (♩ = 50); 3pp.

1603. SHADOW OF THE BLUES (Langston Hughes). [145]. cmp1987. "For Christopher Trakas and Steven Blier." Kaleidoscope of harmonic materials with traditional triads and 7th chords often moving in parallel 3rds, 6ths, or 10ths; vocal line more tonally anchored than piano part; c♯'–g♯"; Tess-M-mH; mixed meters and 12/16; varied tempos; 13pp; Diff-V/md-dd, P/d-dd.

For: male voices best; tenor in the high key
Mood: lament and admonition; love for the down-trodden; sorrow; listlessness
Voice: various rhythmic subdivisions of the beat; much syncopation and other jazz rhythms; many wide-ranged phrases; leaps of 7th or more; many accidentals
Piano: block- and broken-chord patterns; syncopation; ostinato; polyrhythms; many parallel 6ths & 3rds; last song is jazz with fractured harmonies; (b.), solemn chorale-like prelude and postlude; prelude of (c.) sets up ostinato; jazzy prelude and interludes in last song
Diff: ensemble; singer must be independent of piano and have excellent sense of pitch and rhythm; final song more difficult than the others; requires excellent pianist; familiarity with jazz/blues styles helpful
Uses: an excellent recital group for mature musicians

   a. *Silhouette.* X; d'–g"; Tess-M; 4/4 6/4, 3/4, 5/4, Breezily (♩ = 112); 2pp.
   b. *Litany.* X; d♭'–f♯"; Tess-M; 3/4, 4/4, 5/4, 6/4, Slowly (♩ = 66); 3pp.
   c. *Island.* E♭-centered; e♭'–e♭"; Tess-mH; 5/8, 4/8, 11/16, 13/16, 15/16, etc., Fast and fleeting

(♪ = 208); 4pp.
   d. *Could Be.* X; c♯'–g♯"; Tess-wide; 12/16, 9/16, Smoothly, moderately (♪ = 92); 4pp.

1604. TRIOLET (Eugene O'Neill). [145]. cmp1987. "To Amy Burton." D♭; c♯'–g♯"; Tess-wide; 3/4, Slow ragtime waltz; 1p; Diff-V/m, P/me.
For: tenor; soprano
Mood: love song; lyric
Voice: stepwise and skips up to 8ve; short phrases; easy rhythms
Piano: repetitive accomp. pattern; many 6ths; 4-meas. prelude; no doubling of vocal line
Diff: lack of piano support; dissonances
Uses: nice short lyric song for recital or study
Rec: D#65

1605. TWO BY FROST (Robert Frost). [145]. cmp1982. "To Amy Burton." Tonal; c♯'–g♯"; Tess-M, mH; regular meters with changes; moderate tempos; 3pp; Diff-V/md, P/md.
For: high voices
Mood: nature
Voice: stepwise and skips of 4ths to 7ths; many accidentals; many short phrases; straightforward rhythms; tempo fluctuations
Piano: (a.), block and broken chords; many accidentals; no doubling of vocal line; (b.), somewhat linear; some staccato; many tempo fluctuations
Diff: singer should be independent of accomp., comfortable with leaps of 7ths, and singing unusual scales
Uses: as a short pair; possibly lyrical encore

   a. *Nothing Gold Can Stay.* X; c♯'–g"; Tess-mH; 2/4, 3/4, Moderately; 1p.
   b. *The Rose Family.* G♭; d♭'–g♯"; Tess-M; 4/4, 6/4, 3/4, Allegretto; 1p.

MYERS, GORDON
(b. Shell Rock, IA, 1919)

1606. CROWS AND OTHER PEOPLE (news fillers). A Micro-Song Cycle Based on the Wisdom that Comes from News Fillers. Eastlane, 1969. Traditional keys; a–e"; Tess-M; regular meters; varied tempos; 4pp; Diff-V/e, P/e.
For: all voices
Mood: humorous
Voice: diatonic, simple melodies with humorous phrasing; some syncopation
Piano: simple, patterned accomp.
Uses: short, humorous cycle; good for young students or for anyone who needs a light touch

   a. *Crows.* Gmaj; f'–d"; 4/4, Briskly, ♩ = 96; 2pp.
   b. *A Hippopotamus.* X; a–e"; 4/4, ♩ = 50.
   c. *A Thousand Species.* A♭maj; c'–e♭"; 3/4, ♩ = 84, In the style of a Viennese waltz.

1607. IN PURSUIT OF HAPPINESS. Ten Songs for Fun-from *The Art of Belly Canto* (various sources). Leyerle

Publications, 1990. cmp1954–1989. Tonal; (D)G/a♭–f"; Tess-M; mostly regular meters with changes; varied tempos; 27pp; Diff-V/e-md, P/e-m.

For: baritone; mezzo-soprano
Mood: humorous
Voice: syllabic; comic timing of phrases; mostly narrow ranges; last song wide ranged; tuneful
Piano: simple accomps. set mood, interact with and comment on text; some humorous quotations of familiar tunes
Diff: large range of last song (really a bass drinking song)
Uses: marvelous humorous set for general audiences; singer must have good comic skills

a. *Things Could Be Worse* (Myers). Emin-maj; e'–d"; Tess-M; 11/4, 9/4, 10/4, 15/4, ♩ = 72; 1p.

b. *Wanted: Good Woman* (L. Fisher Mann). D-Emaj; d'–e"; Tess-M; 4/4, ♩ = 76; 1p.

c. *Wedding Song* (Myers). Dmaj; d'–e"; Tess-M; 3/8, 4/4, ♩. = 88; 5pp.

d. *Mills, Thunder, Hammers* (Peter Valton, 1760s). A♭maj; A♭–f"; Tess-wide; 4/4, ♩ = 96; 2pp.

e. *Husband for Sale* (News Item: *Trenton Times*, Oct. 18, 1985). Gmin-maj; b–d"; Tess-M; 4/4, ♩ = 112; 3pp.

f. *Emma, Come On Home* (from Bill Dwyer's column in *The Trentonian*). Dmin-maj; f♯'–d"; Tess-M; 4/4, ♩ = 96; 1p.

g. *Ode from a Secretary.* Amin; f'–f"; Tess-M; 4/8, 5/8, 2/8, 6/8, ♩ = 108; 3pp.

h. *The Centipede* (Margaret Myers Kasai). F-Bmaj; c'–d"; Tess-cs; 4/4, ♩ = 120; 1p.

i. *They Tasted Prickley* (news-filler). Amin; b–f"; Tess-M; 4/4, 3/4, ♩ = 90; 3pp.

j. *We Have the Best Noses* (from *Wit and Mirth*, Vol. VI, ed. Thomas D'Urfey, 1719–1720). F-Gmaj; (D)G–e'; Tess-cs; 6/4, ♩ = 58; 7pp.

1608.   POOR RICHARD SAYS . . . Twenty Proverbs by Benjamin Franklin for Medium Voice and Glass Harmonica or Harpsichord or Piano or Whatever is Available. Leyerle Publications, 1997. cmp1985, 1991. Traditional keys, a few X; c'–f"; Tess-M; regular meters; varied tempos; 1p. each; Diff-V/e, P/e.

For: any voice
Mood: humorous proverbs
Voice: short phrases; small range
Piano: chordal–block and broken
Uses: humorous short group or as encores

If Your Head Is Wax; *God Heals*; *There Are More Old Drunkards*; *He That Scatters Thorns*; *A Country Man between Two Lawyers*; *Half Wits Talk Much*; *'Tis Hard for an Empty Sack*; *Learn from the Skillful*; *Tart Words Make No Friends*; *The Honey Is Sweet*; *Now I Have a Sheep and a Cow*; *An Egg Today*; *He That by the Plow Would Thrive*; *A Ploughman on His Legs*; *'Tis as Truly a Folly*; *For Want of a Nail*; *In Marriage without Love*; *Epitaph on a Scolding Wife*; *A Traveller*; *Early to Bed and Early to Rise*

1609.   THEY SAID . . . A Modern Song Sickle Cutting

through the Quotes of Time. For Medium Voice and Piano (20 one-page songs from various sources). Leyerle Publications, 1989. cmp1978–1989. (Also, **THEY SAID . . .** Volumes II and III. Leyerle Publications) Traditional keys; b♭–e"; Tess-M; regular meters, humorous expressive tempo indications; "ca.8 minutes, depending on laughter time" (1p. each); Diff-V/e, P/e.

For: baritone; mezzo-soprano
Mood: humorous quotations from famous people
Voice: recitative; quaint melodies; tone painting
Piano: easy technically but quite expressive of the moods of the texts
Uses: good short set for singer who has a fine sense of wit and humor and enjoys making an audience laugh; encores

[Titles and humorous tempo markings listed below; Vols. II & III in same style]

W. C. Fields (Seriosso); *Fred Allen* (Nasamoto); *Robert Benchley* (Puzzlemento); *Charlotte Rarich* (Dramatissimo); *Satchel Page* (In Quiet Desperation); *Phyllis Diller*; *Abe Lemons* (Jog E. Mosso); *Alicia M. Short* (Resoluto. Slow, Very Slow Waltz); *Gordon Myers[1]* (Baldemucho); *Sign in a New Orleans Bar* (No Bunko); *Sign in a Restaurant Window* (Mom's Inn); *Benjamin Franklin* (Proverbissimo); *Gloria Steinem* (Need-a-roso); *Dr. Lloyd M. Crustacean* (Snailargo); *Anonymous[1]* (With Wonder); *General Ulysses S. Grant* (Authentoso); *Anonymous[2]* (Roundelay); *George Bernard Shaw* (The Count Is 3 and 2); *Confucius* (With Assurance); *Gordon Myers[2]* (With Difficulty).

1610.   A WEDDING SONG (not to be sung in church) (Gordon Myers). Eastlane, 1969. Dmaj; d'–e"; Tess-M; 3/8, 4/4, ♩. = 88; 5pp.

For: any high or medium voice
Mood: humorous; children grow up, marry, and have children
Voice: chiefly stepwise; some small, easy skips; diatonic; easy rhythms; syllabic with a few 2-note slurs
Piano: dissonant broken-chord pattern in 8ths almost throughout; scale passage in interlude; duplet and quadruplets; does not double vocal line
Diff: some pitches hard to hear against accomp.; good vocal actor needed
Uses: occasional entertainment purposes

NAGINSKI, CHARLES
(b. Cairo, Egypt, 1909; d. Lennox, MA, 1940)

1611.   LOOK DOWN, FAIR MOON (Walt Whitman). G. Schirmer, 1942. cmp1940. Amin; d'–e"; Tess-mH; 4/4, Lento; 2+min; Diff-V/m,P/m.

For: baritone
Mood: intense but quiet
Voice: stepwise and easy skips; one high phrase; lyrical and smooth; dramatic and intense
Piano: repeated chords; solo material bitonal
Diff: controlled intensity, *mf* and below
Rec: D#67

1612. **THE PASTURE** (Robert Frost). [59]; 1st©1940. "To Mme. Povla Frijsh." H & L keys: Gmaj & E♭maj; d'–g" & b♭–e♭"; Tess-M; 4/4, Comodo ♩= 112; 3pp; Diff-V/me, P/me.
For: women's voices
Mood: simple; descriptive; nature imagery
Voice: light and delicate
Piano: afterbeat chords; thin texture; supports voice
Diff: interpretive skill required
Uses: good for young voices
Rec: D#s 23, 268

1613. **RICHARD CORY** (Edward Arlington Robinson). G. Schirmer, 1940. "To Mme. Povla Frijsh." Amaj; a–e"(g"); Tess-mL; 4/4, Allegretto, very slick; 1+min; Diff-V/d, P/d.
For: baritone; bass; mezzo-soprano; contralto
Mood: dramatic; narrative
Voice: rather detached; declamatory; some spoken phrases; many repeated tones
Piano: afterbeats; 16th-note runs; arpeggios; many accidentals
Diff: bitonality; mature sound needed
Uses: good song in declamatory style; useful in a final group
Rec: D#39

NELHYBEL, VACLAV
(b. Polandanad Odrau, Czechoslovakia, 1919; d. Scranton, PA, 1996)

1614. **BE NOT FAR FROM ME** (adapted from the Psalms). [146]. Dmin; d'–f"; Tess-M; 4/4, ♪= 146; 4pp; Diff-V/m, P/md.
For: mezzo-soprano; baritone; soprano
Mood: reverent
Voice: many small skips; syncopation; melismas in 8ths & 16ths; many accidentals; soft ending; neo-Baroque in style
Piano: 3-voice counterpoint in neo-Baroque style; some doubling of vocal line
Diff: singer must count; voice needs flexibility for melismas
Uses: recital sacred group; church

1615. **HEAR ME WHEN I CALL** (adapted from the Psalms). [146]. Cmaj-Amin; d'–f"; Tess-M; 9/8, 12/8, ♪= 144; 4pp; Diff-V/m, P/m.
For: mezzo-soprano; baritone; soprano
Mood: prayerful
Voice: stepwise; small skips; some syncopation; several melismas; neo-Baroque approach
Piano: 2–4-voice counterpoint in neo-Baroque style; most of vocal line doubled; 9-meas. prelude; 6-meas. interlude
Diff: possibly rhythms
Uses: church or recital

1616. **HEAR MY VOICE** (adapted from the Psalms). [146]. Cmin-maj; d'–e"; Tess-M; 3/4, ♪= 96; 4pp; Diff-V/m, P/m.
For: mezzo-soprano; baritone
Mood: prayerful
Voice: predominantly conjunct; some dotted rhythms; several melismas; dynamics *pp–f*

Piano: 3-voice counterpoint; many accidentals; most of vocal line doubled; 4-voice chordal ending
Diff: dynamic control; some rhythms
Uses: church or recital

1617. **THE HISTORY OF THE HOUSE THAT JACK BUILT, A DIVERTING STORY** (traditional nursery rhyme). For Baritone Voice and Piano. General, 1973. B♭maj; B♭–c'(d'); Tess-M; 2/4, Allegretto; 20pp; Diff-V/md, P/d.
For: baritone; possibly bass
Mood: humorous; familiar nursery rhyme
Voice: imitates bel canto style; extended melismatic passages; staccato; trill
Piano: chordal; many passages in 8ves; some ornamentation; extended "overture"
Diff: trill (c'–d'); rapid "patter" of words; needs good vocal actor
Uses: interesting addition to a program

1618. **THE LORD IS MY ROCK** (adapted from the Psalms). [146]. Gmin; d'–e♭"; Tess-M; 4/4, ♩= 90; 7pp; Diff-V/m, P/md.
For: baritone; mezzo-soprano
Mood: affirmation of faith; somewhat dramatic
Voice: many small skips; rhythms not complex; phrases often unconnected; several 2–4-note slurs
Piano: 2- & 3-voice counterpoint in neo-Baroque style; many accidentals; some doubling of vocal line; 7-meas. prelude; four short interludes; 4-meas. postlude
Diff: singer must count
Uses: seems best for a sizeable voice; recital or church

NEVIN, ETHELBERT
(b. Edgeworth, PA, 1862; d. New Haven, CT, 1901)

1619. **OH! THAT WE TWO WERE MAYING,** Op. 2, No. 8 (Kingsley). [61]. A♭maj; a♭'–f"; Tess-M-H; 6/8, Moderato e molto tranquillo; 4pp; Diff-V/me, P/md.
For: tenor; soprano
Mood: lyric and sentimental
Voice: stepwise with small skips; easy rhythms
Piano: broken-chord patterns; some repeated chords; countermelody duets with vocal line; little vocal line doubling
Uses: in a group of pre-1900 songs
Rec: D#s 52, 269

1620. **ONE SPRING MORNING,** Op. 3, No. 2 (Wolfgang von Goethe). G. Schirmer. Reprint: T.I.S. (H). [61]. Emin; d'–f#"; Tess-M; 2/4, Allegretto scherzando; 5pp; Diff-V/m, P/md.
For: soprano; mezzo-soprano
Mood: pastoral; lighthearted shepherdess
Voice: stepwise, small skips; easy rhythms; "tra-la-la" refrain
Piano: afterbeat style; some countermelodies; several interludes
Diff: articulating the "tra-la-la" sections; two refrain sections end on sustained f#"
Uses: nice recital song; English version of "Die Spröde" (set by Hugo Wolf); German text provided

1621. **ORSOLA'S SONG,** Op. 20, No. 9 (Jean Richepin). [61]. cmp1892. F♯maj-min; f♯'–f♯"; Tess-M; 6/8, Lento, con espressione; 5pp; Diff-V/me, P/m.

For: soprano; tenor
Mood: song of night
Voice: mostly stepwise; some chromatic passages; some dotted rhythms
Piano: some broken-chord patterning; some doubling of vocal line; several interludes
Uses: has singable English text; original French text provided

1622. **A SONG OF LOVE** (from *A Book of Songs*, Op. 20) (Edmond Lock Tomlin). [5]. Gmaj; d'–g"; Tess-M; 3/4, Comodo; 3pp; Diff-V/me, P/me.

For: tenor
Mood: lyrical, slightly sentimental love song; nature imagery
Voice: somewhat disjunct for a song of this type; 8ve leaps between phrases
Piano: chordal; some accidentals
Diff: "ee" on f♯" for two beats
Uses: good teaching song; possible performance use

1623. **STARS OF THE SUMMER NIGHT** (Henry Wadsworth Longfellow). [147]; 1st©1887. Emaj; g♯'–f♯"; Tess-mH; 4/4, Moderato; 3pp; Diff-V/me, P/me.

For: tenor
Mood: quiet love song
Voice: stepwise and some skips; 2-note slurs; dotted rhythms
Piano: chordal; afterbeat pattern; some countermelody
Uses: pleasant song; simple setting; useful

NILES, JOHN JACOB
(b. Louisville, KY, 1892; d. Lexington, KY, 1980)

1624. **THE BLUE MADONNA** (John Jacob Niles). G. Schirmer, 1948. [51]. "For Gladys Swarthout." Gmin; g'–b♭"; Tess-mH; 3/4, In the stately manner of the pavane; In the tempo of a Spanish waltz; 5pp; Diff-V/me, P/e.

For: soprano; tenor (easily transposed to suit other voices)
Mood: Spanish version of nativity scene
Voice: stepwise; repetitious; Spanish flavor in "tra-la" refrain; chant-like effect of word declamation; portamentos at end of refrain
Piano: block-chord and afterbeat style; stanzas, although barred in 3/4, are alternating 2/4, 4/4 meas.; does not double vocal line
Uses: effective song

1625. **CALM IS THE NIGHT** (John Jacob Niles). G. Schirmer, 1954. [51]. G♯min-Bmaj; b–e"; Tess-M; 4/4, Tranquillo; 3pp; Diff-V/me, P/m.

For: mezzo-soprano
Mood: lyrical; sad; nature picture
Voice: flowing phrases; 8th-note movement
Piano: broken-chord figuration; some independent melody in prelude
Uses: good recital song

1626. **CARELESS LOVE** (John Jacob Niles). [51];

1st©1955. Dmaj; d'–a"; Tess-M; 6/8, 2/4 (♩. = 52); 7pp; Diff-V/m, P/m.

For: soprano; tenor
Mood: narrative and descriptive of the title
Voice: somewhat folksong-like in style; characterized by a motive descending in half-steps; several leaps of 6th & 8ve; several high-lying phrases; ends on a"
Piano: chordal; broken-chord and syncopated figuration; most accidentals in the block-chord sections; sometimes doubles the vocal line, esp. in chromatically descending phrases
Diff: making words clear in high phrases
Uses: for teaching or recital

1627. **THE CAROL OF THE BIRDS** (John Jacob Niles). [32, 148]; 1st©1941. H & L keys: Fmaj & Dmaj; c'–f' & a–d"; Tess-M; 6/8, In graceful, pastoral style; 5pp; Diff-V/me, P/e.

For: mezzo-soprano; alto
Mood: tender; the birds visit the Christ-child
Voice: folksong-like style; conjunct; small intervals; larger leaps between phrases; frequently uses lowest and highest notes of song; imitation of birdcall as a refrain
Piano: chordal; often doubling vocal line
Uses: effective song for young singer; possible church use

1628. **COME GENTLE DARK** (John Jacob Niles). Hinshaw, 1975. B♭maj; d'–g"; Tess-mH; 4/4, ♩ = ca.88; 3pp; Diff-V/me, P/me.

For: soprano; mezzo-soprano; tenor
Mood: rather disjunct; irregular phrase lengths; small melismas
Piano: repeated chords; independent melodic motives
Diff: breath control for sustained phrases
Uses: good teaching material

1629. **EVENING** (Thomas Merton). [148]. Modal; d'–a"; Tess-M; 4/4, ♩ = 63; 4pp; Diff-V/me, P/e.

For: soprano
Mood: lyrical; descriptive; nature imagery
Voice: flowing; short melismas
Piano: chordal; reiterated 8th-note pattern
Diff: clear, floating tones above staff
Uses: good song for a young soprano
Rec: D#s 34, 45

1630. **FEE SIMPLE** (Cale Young Rice). Carl Fischer, 1955. "To Mack Harrell." H & L keys: D♭maj & B♭maj; d♭'–a♭" & b♭–f"; Tess-M; 4/4, 3/4, Lugubre; 3pp; Diff-V/m, P/me.

For: any high or medium voice
Mood: lyrical; naive; philosophical song about death
Voice: almost like a folksong; some chromaticism; generally soft dynamics
Piano: chordal; sustained; a few afterbeats; slow march rhythm in solo sections
Diff: ends on soft a♭"(f ")
Rec: D#39

1631. **GAMBLING SONGS.** G. Schirmer, 1940s. Pub. separately in different years. Indicated to be for different voices, but may be sung as a set by a lyric

baritone; also useful separately. Separate entries below.
[148]. [Four of the five recorded by Mack Harrell;
D#270]

A.   THE ROVIN' GAMBLER (folk-song). [37];
1st©1941. H & L keys: G♭maj & E♭maj; d♭'–g♭" &
b♭–e♭"; Tess-M; 2/4, Boldly (♩ = 108); 6pp; Diff-V/m,
P/m.
For: tenor; baritone
Mood: humorous; narrative; folksong
Voice: many skips; 2-note slurs; dynamic contrasts; three
          speakers; strophic
Piano: chordal; patterns vary from strophe to strophe; does not
          double vocal line
Diff: breathing; characterization
Uses: good teaching and performance material for young
          tenors and mature baritones

B.   THE GAMBLER'S LAMENT (John Jacob Niles).
1946. Gmin; d'–g"; Tess-M; 4/4, 3/4, Like a dirge
(♩ = 50)–A little lighter in mood (♩ = 120); 4pp;
Diff-V/m, P/e.
For: baritone; tenor
Mood: sad; philosophical song about death
Voice: folksong style; sharp contrast in tempo and mood in
          middle section
Piano: chordal; waltz-style middle section
Diff: proper mood changes
Uses: good teaching and recital material

C.   THE GAMBLER'S WIFE (By-Low) (John Jacob
Niles). 1942. "For Gladys Swarthout." G♭maj;
d♭'–g♭"; Tess-mH; 2/4, 3/4, 4/4, Fairly slow, tenderly
(♩ = 80); 3pp; Diff-V/me, P/m.
For: all voices
Mood: quiet; philosophical; lullaby
Voice: skips; highest tone soft on "ee" vowel; contrasting
          sections
Piano: chordal; broken chords descending
Diff: interpretive and dynamic flexibility; soft high tones
Uses: good recital song; effective sung by a man as part of the
          set or separately by a woman

D.   GAMBLER, DON'T YOU LOSE YOUR PLACE
(John Jacob Niles). 1941. Fmaj; c'–f"; Tess-M; 4/4, 2/4,
At a quiet pace (♩ = 92)–With emphasis (♩ = 132); 5pp;
Diff-V/m, P/m.
For: baritone; tenor
Mood: dramatic; fate of the gambler
Voice: conjunct; long phrases; fermatas; contrasting sections
Piano: stately; rather thick chordal texture; afterbeat style in
          contrasting section
Diff: dramatic, ff f" phrase occurs three times; baritones need
          good head-voice f"
Uses: good for teaching and recital

E.   GAMBLER'S SONG OF THE BIG SANDY RIVER
(John Jacob Niles). 1942. F♯min; c♯'–f♯"; Tess-M;
2/4, Rapidly (♩ = 144); 4pp; Diff-V/m, P/d.
For: tenor; high baritone
Mood: joyous; rollicking song of the better side of the
          gambler's life

Voice: like a folksong; some large leaps; f♯" in each strophe
Piano: chordal; afterbeat style; large register changes
Diff: rapid enunciation; solid f♯" at end, becoming a shout
Uses: group or program ender

1632.   I NEVER HAD BUT ONE LOVE (John Jacob Niles).
Carl Fischer, 1955. "To Gladys Swarthout."
Cmaj-Amin; c'–f"; Tess-mH; 4/4, Lamenting but not
too slow (♩ = 80); 4pp; Diff-V/e, P/me.
For: mezzo-soprano; baritone
Mood: sad; philosophical; song of lost love
Voice: like a folksong; lyrical and flowing; irregular phrase
          lengths
Piano: chordal; doubles voice throughout
Uses: good for students

1633.   THE LOTUS BLOOM (anon. adaptation from the
Chinese). [148]; 1st©1952. Dmin; f'–b♭"; Tess-H; 4/4,
5/4, 3/4, Slowly, with resignation; 3pp; Diff-V/m, P/m.
For: high soprano
Mood: philosophical poem of past love
Voice: phrases generally begin high and descend; flowing;
          lyrical
Piano: chordal; generally thin texture; florid melodies in 8ves
          in prelude and interludes
Diff: powerful g" and b♭" required
Uses: good recital song for the right voice

1634.   MY LOVER IS A FARMER LAD (John Jacob
Niles). [148]. Fmin; c'–a♭"; Tess-M; 2/4, 6/8, 4/4,
Flowing, In a storytelling manner (♩ = 76); 6pp; Diff-
V/m, P/m.
For: soprano
Mood: narrative, in a folksong-like style; the girl compares the
          farmer boy to her other suitors
Voice: moves in 8ths in 6/8 sections, dotted rhythms in 2/4
          sections, triplets in 4/4 section; conjunct motion; small
          intervals
Piano: chordal–block and broken; some vocal line doubling
Diff: a somewhat long song; few rests make it potentially
          tiring for young singers; some rhythms
Uses: charming song for a variety of occasions

1635.   REWARD (John Jacob Niles). G. Schirmer, 1968.
[51]. "As sung by Richard Tucker." Cmin-E♭maj;
e♭'–g"; Tess-mL; 4/4, 6/8, 2/4, Tenderly and with
feeling; 4pp; Diff-V/e, P/me.
For: soprano; mezzo-soprano; tenor
Mood: lyrical; tender love song
Voice: diatonic; arching phrases
Piano: chordal; broken and arpeggiated patterns; diatonic;
          occasionally independent of vocal line
Diff: legato; phrasing; sustained g" at end
Uses: good for less advanced students; moment of simplicity
          on a program

1636.   UNUSED I AM TO LOVERS (John Jacob Niles).
[148]. Gmin; f'–f"; Tess-M; 4/4, Tenderly, with great
yearning; 4pp; Diff-V/m, P/e.
For: soprano; mezzo-soprano
Mood: lyrical; song of first love
Voice: conjunct motion; frequent interval g'–d"; written-out

ornament that includes quintuplet 16ths and triplet 8ths

Piano: simple block chords throughout

Diff: rhythm for singers; modal flavor with e♮ and f♮ may be difficult for some singers

Uses: a good recital song

1637. **THE WILD RIDER** (John Jacob Niles). [148]. Cmin; c'–e♭"; Tess-mH; 3/4, Spirited, with a steady swing, a feeling of one beat to the measure; 6pp; Diff-V/me, P/me.

For: any medium female voice

Mood: a spirited song; describes the lover on horseback; somewhat humorous

Voice: conjunct motion; small intervals; an occasional 6th; moves mostly in quarter notes; much repetition of d" and e♭"

Piano: chordal, with afterbeat figures; supports vocal line clearly, does not double

Diff: tessitura for some lower voices

Uses: effective in group with western-U.S. theme

NORDOFF, PAUL
(b. Philadelphia, PA, 1909; d. Herdecke, Germany, 1977)

1638. **CAN LIFE BE A BLESSING** (John Dryden). Schott, 1938. Gmaj; d'–g"; Tess-M-mH; 4/4, 12/8, Moderato ♩ = 104; 4pp; Diff-V/m-md, P/m.

For: tenor; soprano

Mood: lyrical; humorous love behavior

Voice: duplets vs. piano triplets; triplets; many g"s and f♯"s; rapid diction; much word repetition

Piano: running triplet 8ths; large reach helpful

Diff: some modulations; rapid diction; high tessitura passages

Uses: rather a fun song; good for facile diction and technique

1639. **ELEGY** (Elinor Wylie). Schott, 1938. Fmaj; c'–f"; Tess-M; 4/4, Slowly; 1min; Diff-V/m, P/m.

For: mezzo-soprano; soprano

Mood: lyrical; subdued

Voice: leaps of 7th, 8ve, 9th; long-ranged phrases; easy rhythms

Piano: chordal-linear combination; large reaches; does not double vocal line

Diff: dynamic and register control; final note sustained c' pp

Uses: effective song; see also settings by Rorem and J. Duke

1640. **EMBROIDERY FOR A FAITHLESS FRIEND** (Walter Prude). [4]; 1st©1945. Emin; c'–a"; Tess-mH; 3/4, Allegro; 3pp; Diff-V/md, P/m.

For: soprano

Mood: uneasy; intense; descriptive

Voice: many leaps, often up or down an 8ve; dim. triads outlined; syncopation; asymmetrical phrasing; sustained long g♯" at end

Piano: basic waltz rhythms; articulation contrasts important

Diff: rhythms; leaps; dynamic changes, both gradual and sudden; long ff g♯" at end

Uses: effective recital song; group ender

Rec: D#70

1641. **FAIR ANNETTE'S SONG** (Elinor Wylie). Schott, 1933. Fmaj; c'–f"; Tess-mH; 4/4, Quickly; 30sec; Diff-V/m, P/m.

For: soprano

Mood: lyrical; quiet; ever-changing seasons

Voice: stepwise; skips on chord lines; easy rhythms; 2-note slurs; many accidentals

Piano: broken chords; thin texture; many high notes; short trills; accidentals; does not double vocal line

Uses: useful for a young singer; quiet ending

1642. **LACRIMA CHRISTI** (Marya Mannes). Mercury, 1947. cmp1932. Cmin-maj; c'–f"; Tess-M; 4/4, Very slowly; 3pp; Diff-V/m, P/m.

For: dramatic soprano; mezzo-soprano

Mood: anguished; sufferings of Christ; austere; archaic quality

Voice: stepwise; chord-member skips; syncopation; afterbeat phrase beginnings; 2-note slurs

Piano: chordal texture weaves around ostinato; large reaches; many accidentals; does not double vocal line

Diff: dynamic and register control; mature sound needed

Uses: effective song; music well-mated to text

1643. **MUSIC I HEARD WITH YOU** (Conrad Aiken). Schott, 1938. Bmin; d♯'–f♯"; Tess-M; 4/4, Slowly; 2min; Diff-V/m, P/m-d.

For: tenor

Mood: nostalgic

Voice: many skips; sudden harmonic-melodic coloration changes; speech rhythms

Piano: juxtaposed duplet and triplet divisions; many accidentals; block chords; does not double vocal line

Diff: some duplets vs. piano triplets; subtle dynamic control

Uses: soft ending; cf. Hagemann and Cory settings and J. Duke's "Bread and Music" (same text)

1644. **SERENADE** (Kathleen Millay). Schott, 1938. F♯maj-Bmaj; c♯'–f♯"; Tess-covers the range; 3/4 (like a waltz with some 4/4 meas.); 3pp; Diff-V/m, P/m.

For: soprano

Mood: introspective; somewhat sad

Voice: many skips and 8ve leaps; 2-note slurs; many accidentals

Piano: waltz style; block chords; many accidentals; high and middle registers; hard to read

Diff: some pitches hard to hear; sustained f♯'s

Uses: good soprano song

1645. **SONG** ("The bailey beareth the bell away") (anon.). Associated, 1938. Dmin; d♭'–a"; Tess-mH; 4/4, Andante; 3min; Diff-V/md, P/m.

For: tenor; soprano

Mood: lyrical; dramatic climax; somber

Voice: many skips; accidentals; irregular rhythms

Piano: 4–6-voice chordal texture; does not double vocal line

Diff: dynamic control (pp–ff); meaning of text

1646. **SONG OF INNOCENCE** (William Blake). [60]; 1st©1952. H & L keys: Amaj & Fmaj; d'–f♯" & b–d♯"; Tess-M; 2/2 3/2, Allegro–Meno mosso; 2+min; Diff-V/md, P/m.

For: all voices

Mood: lyrical; well-known poem
Voice: lyrical but somewhat disjunct; numerous long tones
Piano: chordal; legato; somewhat chromatic
Diff: ensemble; irregular phrase lengths; soft dynamics
Uses: good for young singers

1647. **TELL ME, THYRSIS** (John Dryden). Associated, 1938. Gmaj; e'–g"; Tess-M; 4/4, 12/8, Allegro ♩ = 132; 4pp; Diff-V/m, P/m.
For: tenor; soprano
Mood: lyrical
Voice: some skips; modulates abruptly to Emaj, back to Gmaj; two strophes; ends g" *ff* on "joy" (opt. d")
Piano: triplet figure with 2-note chords; large reach helpful; syncopated figure in Emaj section
Uses: nice song; good for young singer with easy g"

1648. **THERE SHALL BE MORE JOY** (Ford Madox Ford). Schott, 1938. F♯maj; c♯'–f♯"; Tess-M; 4/4 (voice), 12/8 (piano), Allegro; 1+min; Diff-V/m, P/d.
For: tenor; high baritone
Mood: descriptive; serene; picture of heaven
Voice: stepwise and easy skips; 2–3-note slurs; 2 vs. piano 3
Piano: chord figuration in 8th-note triplets; quiet; cross-hands
Diff: ensemble; 2 vs. 3; breathing
Uses: imaginative and interesting setting; quiet ending
Rec: D#23

1649. **THIS IS THE SHAPE OF THE LEAF** (Conrad Aiken). Schott, 1937. Emin; b–e"; Tess-L; 4/4, 12/8, 6/4, 3/4, Slowly; 5pp; Diff-V/d, P/d.
For: mezzo-soprano; contralto
Mood: lyrical; philosophical; nature imagery
Voice: triplets almost throughout; rather static; parlando style
Piano: repeated triplet pattern; chromatic chords; syncopation; somewhat static; compound meter throughout
Diff: pitches; rhythms
Uses: useful teaching song; performance possibilities

1650. **TIME, I DARE THEE TO DISCOVER** (John Dryden). Associated, 1938. Emin; d♯'–g"; Tess-M; 3/4, 2/4, 4/4, Adagio (♩ = 56); 3pp; Diff-V/m, P/me.
For: soprano; mezzo-soprano
Mood: lyrical love song
Voice: stepwise and easy skips; somewhat chromatic; flowing phrases; syllabic; several phrases begin *pp* on f♯"
Piano: primarily linear and flowing; countermelody in 3rds; somewhat chromatic; independent of vocal line
Diff: *pp* phrases beginning on f♯"
Uses: recital material

1651. **WHITE NOCTURNE** (Conrad Aiken). Ditson, 1942. Emaj-centered; c'–e"; Tess-M; 4/4, 5/4, 3/4, Andante; 3+min; Diff-V/m, P/m.
For: tenor or baritone best; possible for women
Mood: nostalgic remembrance; lyrical; quiet
Voice: skips of 6th & 7th; many accidentals; some triplets;
Piano: 6-voice chords with some moving lines; many accidentals; aug. triads; does not double vocal line
Diff: features e"; dynamic control (*ppp–f*)
Uses: good recital song; quiet ending
Rec: D#10

NUNLIST, JULI
(b. Montclair, NJ, 1916)

1652. **OH, WHEN I WAS IN LOVE WITH YOU** (A. E. Housman). [19]; 1st©1972. Fmaj-min; c'–d"; Tess-M; 3/4, Liltingly; 2pp; Diff-V/m, P/m.
For: baritone; bass
Mood: narrative; lively; passing of love
Voice: many skips and 8ve leaps; dotted rhythms; second strophe in minor
Piano: patterned block-chord texture; dotted rhythms; staccato; moves around keyboard; does not double vocal line
Uses: useful recital material; group ender

O'HARA, GEOFFREY
(b. Chatham, Ontario, Canada, 1882; d. St. Petersburg, FL, 1967)

1653. **THE BALLAD OF LITTLE BILLEE** (William Makepeace Thackeray). Harms, 1932. H, M, & L keys: E♭maj, Cmaj, & B♭maj; e♭'–g", c'–e", & b♭–d"; Tess-mL; 2/2, With vigor; 6pp; Diff-V/m, P/md.
For: tenor; baritone; bass
Mood: humorous narrative; sailor's song
Voice: vigorous, like a sea chantey; declamatory section
Piano: sectional; rolled chords; afterbeats; some melodic material in prelude; some chromaticism
Uses: good for young students; teaching narrative style

OLIVEROS, PAULINE
(b. Houston, TX, 1932)

1654. **THREE SONGS.** For Soprano and Piano. Smith Publications, 1976. cmp1957–1958. X; d♭'–a"; Tess-M-mH; changing meters; moderate to slow tempos; 5+pp; Diff-V/d, P/d.
For: soprano specified
Mood: philosophical
Voice: mostly small skips; some leaps up to 7th; many accidentals; rhythms somewhat complex with various divisions and subdivisions of beat; syllabic
Piano: linear; disjunct; not patterned; imitation; tremolo; rhythms somewhat complex; many dynamic markings; does not double vocal line
Diff: ensemble; rhythms; perfect pitch helpful
Uses: interesting recital group; possible use as introduction to modern compositional style

   a. *An Interlude of Rare Beauty* (Robert Duncan). X; d♭'–e"; 3/4 with changes, ♩ = ca.42; 2pp.
   b. *Spider Song* (Robert Duncan). X; d'–a"; 2/4 with changes; ♩ = 72; 3pp.
   c. *Song Number Six* (Charles Olson). X; f♯'–f "; 3/4, ♩ = ca.44–46; 4meas.

ORLAND, HENRY
(b. Saarbrücken, Germany, 1918; d. St. Louis, MO, 1999)

[See Appendix for songs with French and German texts]

1655. SIX OCCASIONAL SONGS, Op. 18. Seesaw, 197-. Although pub. together, these songs do not appear to be a set, nor are they for the same voice type; could perhaps be done together by several different singers. Separate entries below (No. 4 of the six omitted).

A.   DITTY ON A LITTLE SCOTCH VERSE, No. 1. X; c♯'–a"; Tess-mH; 4/4, Adagio; 1p; Diff-V/md, P/d.
For: soprano; tenor
Mood: folk-like text; dialect
Voice: undulating vocal line; somewhat chromatic; 8th- & 16th-note movement
Piano: somewhat chromatic and contrapuntal; ornamented by several mordents; suggests "water music"
Diff: needs light, easy high tones
Uses: recital material

B.   THE FIRST NOWELL, No. 2. Bmin; a♯–g"; Tess-mL; 3/4, Moderato assai; 1p; Diff-V/m, P/md.
For: mezzo-soprano; baritone
Mood: Christmas song
Voice: chiefly imitation of the familiar tune, in a minor key and with "wrong" notes
Piano: contrapuntal and chromatic; "recorders and viols ad libitum" indicated
Diff: pitches
Uses: fun; occasional use

C.   FROM PSALM 49, No. 3. E♭min; G♭–f'; Tess-mH; 4/4, Andante maestoso; 3pp; Diff-V/md, P/d.
For: baritone
Mood: an exhortation to the people
Voice: majestic; dotted rhythms; triplets; several 8ve leaps; short phrases
Piano: dotted marching rhythms in 8ves; much use of triplets; quite chromatic
Diff: some dramatic weight in voice needed
Uses: useful recital song

D.   THANKSGIVING, No. 5. X; F–f♯'; Tess-mH; 4/4, Grave ma non troppo lento–Larghetto; 2pp; Diff-V/md, P/md.
For: baritone; bass-baritone
Mood: song of thanksgiving; majestic
Voice: somewhat disjunct; fairly chromatic; dotted rhythms
Piano: chordal-contrapuntal combination; chromatic; dotted-rhythm melody accompanied by triplets
Diff: sustained, powerful f♯' at end
Uses: could be useful recital material

E.   AIR, No. 6. X; c♯'–g"; Tess-M; 3/8, Scherzando; 1+pp; Diff-V/md, P/d.
For: tenor; high baritone
Mood: lyrical; happy; love song
Voice: disjunct; somewhat chromatic; mordent on word "shake"; short phrases
Piano: chromatic; dissonant; repeated notes and chords; grace notes; both hands in treble clef; light, dancing quality
Diff: tenor needs clear low tones
Uses: good student song

OWEN, RICHARD
(b. New York, NY, 1922)

1656. THE IMPULSE (Robert Frost). General, 1966. D♭-centered; e♭'–f"; Tess-M; 4/4, 6/4, 2/4, 3/4, Andante con moto; 3pp; Diff-V/md, P/m.
For: any voice with the range, except very low
Mood: quietly declamatory; narrative; bleak
Voice: mostly conjunct; declamatory; speech rhythms; delicate, quiet; some difficult pitches
Piano: linear; spare texture; grace notes; soft dynamics
Diff: some pitch and rhythmic difficulty for the insecure musician; not for a young singer
Uses: interesting character song; good to teach clear, easy declamation; recital material

1657. I SAW A MAN PURSUING THE HORIZON (Stephen Crane). General, 1966. Dmin; g'–g"; Tess-M-mH; 6/8, Allegro; 2pp; Diff-V/m, P/e.
For: tenor; soprano
Mood: lyrical; short commentary on man's ambition
Voice: short phrases; somewhat declamatory; two speakers; short climax on g" ff
Piano: linear; 1–2 voices in 8th-note movement; accidentals
Uses: very short song; good for a young tenor
Rec: D#32

1658. PATTERNS (Amy Lowell). General, 1973. X; b♭–a"; Tess-mL-M; 4/4, 2/4, 3/4, 5/4, Andante (with several changes); 6+min; Diff-V/d, P/d.
For: mezzo-soprano; dramatic soprano
Mood: bitter; bereaved; dramatic; intense
Voice: some recit.-like passages; skips and leaps of up to an 8ve; duplet and triplet rhythms juxtaposed; polyrhythms with piano; many accidentals; some difficult intervals; voice ends alone
Piano: ostinato resembles B-A-C-H motive (one different interval); chordal-linear combination; sectional; triplets and duplets juxtaposed; grace notes; tremolo; many accidentals
Diff: singer needs dramatic flair and intensity; several sustained high tones; voice needs mature sound and weight; some ensemble problems likely
Uses: can stand alone; effective recital piece; dramatic program ender

1659. THERE WERE MANY WHO WENT IN HUDDLED PROCESSION (Stephen Crane). General, 1966. Cmin; c♭'–f♯"; Tess-cs; 2/2, 3/2, 3/4, 4/4, Andante; 2pp; Diff-V/md, P/m.
For: baritone; mezzo-soprano
Mood: declamatory; philosophical; quiet
Voice: numerous skips, esp. 4ths; soft 8ve leap to f♯" on "alone"; speech rhythms
Piano: chordal; parallel 5ths by half-step movement; dirge-like; some small ornamental and melodic passages
Diff: speech rhythms; some pitches; poem
Uses: very good song for mature singer
Rec: D#32

1660. TILL WE WATCH THE LAST LOW STAR (Witter Bynner). General, 1962. E♭maj; c'–g♭"; Tess-M; 4/4,

5/4, Andante; 2pp; Diff-V/m, P/m.

For: tenor; soprano
Mood: lyrical; song of parting
Voice: conjunct with one 8ve leap; modulations
Piano: linear; mild dissonance; accidentals; doubles voice most of the time
Uses: lovely short lyrical song for any singer

OWENS, ROBERT
(b. Denison, TX, 1925)

1661. FAITHFUL ONE (Langston Hughes). [6]; 1st©1969. Cmaj; d'-d"; Tess-M; 4/4, Melanconico moderato; 2pp; Diff-V/m, P/m.

For: baritone
Mood: humorously philosophical
Voice: syncopated, "drunken" rhythms and sharp accents; generally diatonic; one glissando
Piano: chordal in syncopated rhythms; rather independent of vocal line
Diff: rhythms and stresses; requires good vocal actor
Uses: could be used separately; probably best in context

1662. GENIUS CHILD (Langston Hughes). [6]; 1st©1969. E♭min; d♭'-f"; Tess-M; 4/4, 3/4, Vivace–Andante con moto–Vivace; 4pp; Diff-V/md, P/me.

For: mezzo-soprano; baritone; possibly dramatic soprano; tenor
Mood: angry; dramatic
Voice: many dotted rhythms and sharp accents in first and third sections; middle section more flowing; rapid ascending minor scale passage, with m2nd at end; long, loud final e♭"
Piano: initial rapid repeated chords in triplets; sustained chords in middle section
Diff: some low-lying phrases; rapid scale passages
Uses: dramatic song; see also setting by Ricky Ian Gordon

PAINE, JOHN KNOWLES
(b. Portland, ME, 1839; d. Cambridge, MA, 1906)

1663. A BIRD UPON A ROSY BOUGH, Op. 40, No.1 (Celia Thaxter). A. P. Schmidt, 1884. B♭maj; d'-g"; Tess-M-mH; 4/4, Allegretto; 4pp; Diff-V/m, P/m.

For: soprano; tenor
Mood: descriptive; somber
Voice: stepwise and chord-member skips; some dotted rhythms; 2–4-note slurs
Piano: broken-chord patterning; many accidentals; some doubling of vocal line
Diff: good dynamic control
Uses: usable period piece

1664. EARLY SPRING-TIME, Op. 29, No. 3 (Rev. Thomas Hill). Ditson, 1879. [5]. C♯min-G♯maj; e'-g♯"; Tess-mH; 2/4, 3/4, Moderato; 3pp; Diff-V/m, P/me.

For: tenor; soprano
Mood: longing; spring after winter; metaphoric
Voice: rather complicated rhythmically; syncopation; 2–3-note slurs

Piano: chordal–block and broken patterns; duplets and triplets; articulations important; doubles vocal line
Diff: rhythmic irregularity; polyrhythms
Uses: useful period piece for recital

1665. MATIN SONG, Op. 29, No.1 (Bayard Taylor). [58]. cmp1879. A♭maj; e♭'-f"; Tess-M; 3/4, Larghetto; 3pp; Diff-V/m, P/e.

For: lyric tenor; lyric soprano
Mood: lyrical; subdued love song
Voice: leaps of 5th & 6th; several arching phrases; triplets and duplets; dotted rhythms
Piano: afterbeat and repeated-chord patterns; does not double vocal line
Uses: one of the better songs of this period

1666. MOONLIGHT (Mondnacht), Op. 29, No. 4 (Joseph von Eichendorff; English trans.). Ditson, 1879. Emaj; e'-g♯"; Tess-mH; 3/4, Andante con moto; 4pp; Diff-V/m, P/m.

For: tenor; soprano
Mood: lyrical; delicate poem about night
Voice: flowing; conjunct; some leaps of 6th; phrases ascending to top of staff
Piano: delicate broken-chord figurations; rustling effect; two beats of introduction, 4-meas. postlude; quiet ending; gentle touch needed
Diff: control of upper middle voice tones in legato ascending phrases–somewhat like the Schumann setting, although not as sustained
Uses: nice song; useful; translation poor

PANETTI, JOAN
(b. New Haven, CT, 20th Century)

1667. THREE SONGS TO WORDS BY LYDIA FAKUNDINY. New Valley, 1964. Atonal; f♯–a"; Tess-cs; unmetered; varied tempos; 11pp; Diff-V/dd, P/d.

For: soprano
Mood: loneliness
Voice: avant-garde techniques; large leaps; fragmented phrases; staccato; glissandos; many instructions
Piano: partially played with a nail on the strings; dissonant; staccato; rather bare texture; some loud chords
Diff: avant-garde difficulties; score difficult to read
Uses: useful for someone interested in the idiom

　　a. *I Think.* Slow and easy, ♩ = 50.
　　b. *I Assure You.* Relaxed, ♩ = 112.
　　c. *What Are Words?* Fast, ♩ = 112 (with changes).

PARCHMAN, GEN LOUIS
(b. Cincinnati, OH, 1929)

1668. CYCLE OF NOVELTIES (Six Short Songs). Seesaw, 1971. cmp1964. X; c'-b♭"; Tess-M; mostly regular and changing meters; varied tempos; 6min; Diff-V/md, P/md.

For: soprano; tenor

Mood: humorous; tender and naive; nostalgic
Voice: some lyrical, some declamatory; chromatic
Piano: chromatic; afterbeats; repeated chords; many repeated meas.; trill-like figures; little doubling of vocal line
Diff: long range; good low tones; some pitches and rhythms
Uses: interesting group for a recital; should be sung together

    a. *It Couldn't Be Done* (poet not given). 3/4, Allegro molto (♩ = 80); 25sec.
    b. *The Flea* (Roland Young). 3/8, Allegretto (♪ = 126); 28sec.
    c. *Resumé* (Dorothy Parker). 2/4, Adagio (♩ = 60); 48sec.
    d. *Little Lamb* (William Blake). 3/4, Moderato (♩ = 144); 1min.
    e. *Just and the Unjust* (Lord Bomen). 2/4, 4/4, 5/4, 6/4, Adagio (♩ = 54); 38sec.
    f. *I Remember* (Thomas Hood). 4/4, Moderato (♩ = 96); 1min-45sec.

PARKER, HORATIO
(b. Auburndale, MA, 1863; d. Cedarhurst, NY, 1919)

1669. THE BLACKBIRD, Op. 59, No. 3 (William E. Henley). G. Schirmer, 1904. [5]. Amaj; d♯'–g"(g♯"); Tess-mH; 3/4, 2/4, Moderato–Allegretto; 3pp; Diff-V/md, P/md.
For: soprano
Mood: joyful; light
Voice: many skips; many accidentals; 2-note slurs; triplets; several long-ranged phrases
Piano: delicate quick arpeggios; other broken chords; staccato; bird-like sounds; some doubling of vocal line
Diff: rapid diction; flexibility; ends on sustained a"
Uses: nice for a high, flexible voice; probably best for a young singer

1670. GOOD-BYE, Op. 59, No. 4 (Christina Rossetti). G. Schirmer, 1904. Bmin-maj; b–d♯"; Tess-M; 2/4, Allegretto, poco agitato; 3pp; Diff-V/m, P/m.
For: baritone; mezzo-soprano
Mood: somber; dramatic; final parting
Voice: many skips; dotted rhythms; accidentals; 2-note slurs
Piano: syncopated afterbeat pattern; some arpeggios, some block chords; various registers; doubles vocal line
Diff: long sustained phrases; mature sound needed
Uses: useful dramatic song; use in a Parker or other American song group; good mood contrast for the period

1671. LOVE IN MAY, Op. 51, No.1 (Ella Higginson). Church, 1901. D♭maj; d♭'–g♭'(a♭'); Tess-mH; 3/4, Moderato; 3pp; Diff-V/m, P/md.
For: tenor; soprano
Mood: exuberant love song
Voice: many small skips; dotted rhythms
Piano: chordal–broken and repeated-chord patterns; tremolo; trills; fast melismas; 2 vs. 3; some accidentals; some doubling of vocal line
Diff: duplets vs. piano triplets; r.h. triplets over l.h. doubling of vocal line
Uses: effective for the right singer; tapered soft ending

Rec: D#69

1672. LUTE-SONG (from *Two Songs from Tennyson's "Queen Mary"*) (Alfred, Lord Tennyson). [5]. Cmin; b–c"; Tess-L; 4/4, Rather slow; 3pp; Diff-V/me, P/e.
For: any low voice
Mood: rather melancholy statement about love
Voice: mostly conjunct motion; two leaps of m7th downward
Piano: arpeggiated chords, imitating the lute; brief melodic interlude; supports the vocal line
Diff: needs a full and rich-sounding c'
Uses: possible recital song

1673. NIGHT-FALL (Martin Schütze). Boston Music Co., 1914. Emin; b–f"(g"); Tess-M; 4/4 (voice), 10/8 (piano), Moderato tranquillo molto; 3pp; Diff-V/md, P/md.
For: mezzo-soprano; soprano; baritone
Mood: quiet; dreaming; descriptive
Voice: many repeated notes in melody; half-steps and easy skips; sustained; easy rhythms
Piano: broken-chord style; one phrase of r.h. 3rds; subdued; does not double vocal line
Diff: 4/4 vs. 10/8
Uses: good song; two distinct levels of meaning

1674. OLD ENGLISH SONGS, OP. 47. John Church Co., 1899. Reprint: Recital Publications, 1983. All of these songs are good student material. A, B, & C make a group for mezzo-soprano; A, B, C, & F make a group for tenor; A, B, D, & E make a group for baritone. Separate entries below.

A. **LOVE IS A SICKNESS FULL OF WOES,** Op. 47, No. 1 (Samuel Daniel). H & L keys: Dmin & Cmin; d'–f" & c'–e♭"; Tess-M; 3/4, Moderately, in minuet time; 4pp; Diff-V/me, P/m.
For: mezzo-soprano; baritone; soprano; tenor
Mood: ironic
Voice: many small skips; easy rhythms; several 2–4-note slurs; a few accidentals; several dynamic markings
Piano: block chords; bass countermelody in quarter & 8th notes; doubles vocal line; 8-meas. prelude
Diff: possibly dynamics

B. **COME, O COME, MY LIFE'S DELIGHT,** Op. 47, No. 2 (Thomas Campion's *Third Book of Airs*). H & L keys: Dmaj & Cmaj; d'–e" & c'–d"; Tess-mH; 4/4, With animation; 3pp; Diff-V/m, P/m.
For: mezzo-soprano; baritone; soprano; tenor
Mood: ecstatic love song
Voice: stepwise motion and small skips; easy rhythms; long notes (6–8 beats) at some phrase endings; accidentals
Piano: block- and broken-chord patterning; staccato; doubles vocal line; 6-meas. prelude; 7-meas. interlude

C. **HE THAT LOVES A ROSY CHEEK,** Op. 47, No. 3 (Thomas Carew). H & L keys: Gmaj & E♭maj; d'–f♯"(e") & b♭–d"(c"); Tess-mH; 3/4, Contemplatively; 3pp; Diff-V/m, P/m.
For: mezzo-soprano; baritone; soprano; tenor
Mood: philosophical

Voice: many small skips; easy rhythms; a few dotted rhythms; a few accidentals; a few 2-note slurs; two strophes

Piano: block- and broken-chord patterning; some accidentals; doubles vocal line

D.   ONCE I LOVED A MAIDEN FAIR, Op. 47, No. 4 (old ballad, time of James I; condensed by Oxenford). H & L keys: Emaj & Dmaj; e'–e" & d'–d"; Tess-M; 3/4, Allegretto, Humorously; 4pp; Diff-V/me, P/m.

For: baritone; tenor

Mood: somewhat arrogant; a bit humorous

Voice: stepwise and many small skips; some accidentals; repetitive; easy rhythms; mostly syllabic with a few melismas

Piano: block chords; motion in 8th notes; staccato; 4-meas. prelude; 2-meas. interludes

E.   THE COMPLACENT LOVER, Op. 47, No. 5 (Sir Charles Selby). H & L keys: Fmaj & Dmaj; c'–f" & a–d"; Tess-M; 4/4, Cheerfully and rather fast; 3pp; Diff-V/m, P/m.

For: baritone; some tenors

Mood: hearty; realistic love song

Voice: many skips along chord lines; some dotted rhythms; several 2-note slurs

Piano: 2–4-voice texture; block chords in 8th notes; sections in 8ves; staccato; doubles vocal line; 3-meas. prelude; 3-meas. interlude; 2-meas. postlude

Diff: semi-disjunct pitch patterns

F.   THE LARK NOW LEAVES HIS WAT'RY NEST, Op. 47, No. 6 (Sir William Davenant). Also pub. separately by Church, 1899. H & L keys: E♭maj & Cmaj; c'–b♭"(g") & a–g"(e"); Tess-mH; 2/2, Allegro; 5pp; Diff-V/md, P/m.

For: coloratura or lyric soprano; tenor

Mood: cheerful; descriptive

Voice: many skips; several 8th-note runs; easy rhythms; trill on final cadence

Piano: linear; 2–3-voice texture; much doubling of vocal line

Diff: wide range; 3-meas. sustained b♭" *ff* (opt. lower note)

Uses: works well for young soprano; good contest material

Rec: D#69

1675.   SERENADE, Op. 59, No. 2 (Nathan H. Dole). G. Schirmer, 1904. Emin; d#'–g"; Tess-M; 6/8, Allegretto; 4pp; Diff-V/m, P/m.

For: tenor

Mood: love song

Voice: many leaps, esp. 5ths; some dotted rhythms; some slurs

Piano: block and afterbeat chords; 16th-note melody in solo material; some chromaticism

Uses: useful in historical or serenade group

1676.   SONG, Op. 59, No. 1 ["Bright Is the Ring of Words"] (Robert Louis Stevenson). G. Schirmer, 1904. Emaj; c#'–f#"; Tess-M; 3/4, 9/8, Con brio; 4pp; Diff-V/md, P/m.

For: baritone; some tenors

Mood: nostalgic; immortality of poetry and its power

Voice: many skips; 2-note slurs; duplets vs. piano triplets

Diff: long, sustained tones; voice 2 vs. piano 3; one 3-note

slur includes 8ve leap

Uses: good setting; see also setting by Vaughan Williams

PARKER, JAMES CUTLER DUNN
(b. Boston, MA, 1828; d. Brookline, MA, 1916)

1677.   SERENADE ("Come into the garden, Maud") (Alfred, Lord Tennyson). Ditson, 1855. Dmin-Fmaj; c'–f"; Tess-M; 6/8, Allegretto; 6pp; Diff-V/e, P/e.

For: baritone

Mood: descriptive; love song

Voice: stepwise and small skips; easy rhythms; some sustained tones

Piano: guitar-like broken-chord patterning; some staccato; some chromaticism; some block chords

Uses: useful in historical or serenade group

PASATIERI, THOMAS
(b. New York, NY, 1945)

[See Appendix for songs with German texts]

1678.   AGNES (Paul Enow, age 9). [150]. cmp1973. "Dedicated to all future American poets." Cmaj; c'–f"; Tess-M; 2/2, 5/4, 4/4, 3/4, Allegro molto; 3pp; Diff-V/m, P/m.

For: any voice

Mood: humorous; cute

Voice: diatonic and simple, in keeping with the child's text; some triplets; cadenza-like melisma

Piano: chordal; doubles vocal line

Diff: needs good vocal actor

Uses: could be fun in a variety of situations

1679.   AS IN A THEATRE (William Shakespeare; *Richard II*, V, ii). [151]. cmp1977. Polytonal; d♭'–g"; Tess-mH; 4/4, Andante; 3pp; Diff-V/md, P/md.

For: tenor; high baritone

Mood: dramatic; tense; descriptive

Voice: many small skips; some larger leaps; many accidentals; duple and triple subdivisions of beat; some syncopation; some dotted rhythms; syllabic

Piano: polyphonic texture predominates; some imitation; chordal sections, some 8-member chords; uses wide range of keyboard; doubles vocal line at unison or 8ve

Diff: pitch patterns; dramatic delivery of text for some singers

Uses: possible recital song; not one of the "songs" from Shakespeare's plays

1680.   BEAUTIFUL THE DAYS (Kirstin Van Cleave). [151]. cmp1978. Fmin; c'–b♭"; Tess-mH, wide; 4/4, Cantabile; 2pp; Diff-V/md, P/m.

For: soprano

Mood: nostalgic

Voice: many large and small skips; repeated dotted rhythmic patterns; syllabic; some high phrases, one soft

Piano: broken-chord and scale patterning in three voices; regular rhythms in 8th-note motion; triplet figure at some phrase endings; doubles vocal line

Diff: tessitura for some singers; dynamics *pp–f*
Uses: has a "popular song" flavor; good for a floaty voice with easy high tones

1681. **DAY OF LOVE.** A Song Cycle for Voice and Piano (Kirsten Van Cleave). G. Schirmer, 1983. Commissioned by and dedicated to Frederica von Stade. First performed by Frederica von Stade and Martin Katz, 1979. Tonal; a–b♭"; Tess-mH; traditional meters with changes; Moderato (with changes)–Allegro moderato–Andante triste; 26pp; Diff-V/md-d, P/d.
For: mezzo-soprano; soprano
Mood: loneliness; aftermath of broken relationship
Voice: stepwise; skips along chord lines; chromaticism; accidentals; uncomplicated rhythms predominate; some syncopation; 2 vs. 3 in piano; many melismas, some highly chromatic, some rapid; some soft phrases with long ranges (b–f"); other soft high notes (g♯"); soft ending (f")
Piano: linear and chordal sections; wide range on keyboard; many accidentals (incl. ♭♭ & ×), sometimes 5 or 6 accidentals per chord; often doubles or outlines vocal line; 34-meas. prelude; lengthy interlude-transitions divide the six vocal sections of this continuous work; two cadenza-like passages; dramatic piano part
Diff: some pitch patterns in melismas, as in "Jealousy" section and others; dynamics; final section has several *subito pp* high notes; requires flexibility and a sure ear and technique
Uses: must be used as a whole; an attractive recital group. NOTE: This is a continuous work; although called a "song cycle" by the composer, sections are not individually titled or separated except by piano interludes. It is cyclic in that both the opening piano and vocal themes appear again at the conclusion.

1682. **DIRGE FOR TWO VETERANS** (Walt Whitman). [150]. cmp1973. X; c♯'–g♭"; Tess-M; 4/4, 3/4, 2/4, 3/8, 5/8, Adagio, quasi recitativo–Un poco più mosso–Molto meno mosso–Maestoso; 7pp; Diff-V/dd, P/dd.
For: mezzo-soprano; baritone
Mood: narrative and descriptive; the two dead soldiers are father and son, mourned by wife and mother
Voice: lyrical at first, becoming more dramatic; many melismas in short note values
Piano: largely chordal; chromatic; often doubles voice; complex rhythms; sweeping passages in 32nds
Diff: pitches and rhythms; requires superb pianist; dramatic flair needed
Uses: excellent recital material for mature singer

1683. **DISCOVERY** (Anne Howard Bailey). [150]. cmp1973. Gmin; d'–b♭"; Tess-mH; 5/4, 4/4, 3/2, 2/4, 3/4, Adagio, 4pp; Diff-V/md, P/md.
For: soprano; tenor
Mood: lyrical love song
Voice: lyrical and flowing; some chromaticism; dotted rhythms; triplets
Piano: chordal; some 2-voice texture in running 16ths; usually doubles vocal line
Diff: pitches and rhythms
Uses: good for recital

1684. **THE HARP THAT ONCE THROUGH TARA'S HALLS** (Thomas Moore). [150]. cmp1975. "To Beverly Sills." A♭maj; e♭'–b♭"(d"'); Tess-mH; 6/8, Andantino; 3pp; Diff-V/m, P/m.
For: soprano
Mood: lyrical; sentimental
Voice: lyrical and flowing; some chromaticism; repetitious rhythmic pattern
Piano: chordal texture; doubles vocal line; countermelodies; some chromaticism
Diff: requires fine legato; difficult slur pattern throughout
Uses: interesting recital material

1685. **INSTEAD OF WORDS** (Gerald Walker). [150]. cmp1976. "To Joanna Simon." Gmin; d'–f"; Tess-M; 4/4, 2/4, 5/4, Andante con moto; 2pp; Diff-V/m, P/m.
For: any medium or high voice
Mood: lyrical love song
Voice: flowing phrases, each building higher to climax in middle of song, then subsiding to starting level
Piano: chordal; generally doubles voice; some chromaticism
Uses: good for students; recital possibilities

1686. **THE KISS** (Martin Dulman). [150]. cmp1976. "To Catherine Malfitano." Fmin; e'–a♭"; Tess-M; 3/8, Adagio fluido e cantabile; 3pp; Diff-V/md, P/m.
For: soprano
Mood: love song; analogies from nature
Voice: flowing phrases; fairly long melismas; coloratura-like song, but in middle range; not for coloratura soprano
Piano: like a slow dance; some doubling of vocal line; several countermelodies; some chromaticism
Diff: vocal flexibility; moderate agility
Uses: good for recital; agility study for soprano who lacks high notes

1687. **LULLABY FOR A LOST CHILD** (Josephine Schillig). [150]. cmp1969. Amin; e'–e"; Tess-M; 4/4, Andante triste; 3pp; Diff-V/me, P/m.
For: any voice
Mood: sad; somewhat sentimental
Voice: largely diatonic; regular and repetitious rhythms
Piano: continuous 8th-note movement in l.h., generally in broken-chord patterns; r.h. doubles vocal line
Uses: possibilities for students of limited vocal means

1688. **OPHELIA'S LAMENT** (Adapted from *Hamlet*) (William Shakespeare). [150]. cmp1975. "Commissioned by and dedicated to Joan Patenaude." Emaj-min; d'–b"; Tess-M; 9/8 with changes, Allegro violente, Andante misterioso (and many more changes); 10pp; Diff-V/dd, P/dd.
For: soprano
Mood: sad; dramatic; narrative
Voice: sweeping phrases; complex rhythms with triplets, quadruplets, etc.; chromatic; several melismas
Piano: great variety of textures and techniques; generally supports or doubles vocal line; complex rhythms
Diff: pitches and rhythms; requires sense of the dramatic and fine pianist
Uses: very effective for the mature singer

1689. OVERWEIGHT, OVERWROUGHT OVER YOU
(Sheila Nadler). [151]. cmp1977. Dmaj/Bmin; b♭–g";
Tess-M; 2/4, 3/4, Allegro; 4pp; Diff-V/md, P/m.
For: mezzo-soprano
Mood: humorous; somewhat grotesque
Voice: many skips; many accidentals; uncomplicated rhythms, a few triplets; syllabic except for cadenza (*Quasi recitativo a piacere*) at end
Piano: repeated-chord and linear sections; some tone clusters; trills; many accidentals; generally doubles vocal line
Diff: chromaticism
Uses: for the singer who dares

1690. PARTING (William Shakespeare). [149]. Gmaj; e'–f";
Tess-M; 3/4, Andante mosso; 2pp; Diff-V/rnd, P/e.
For: soprano; tenor; mezzo-soprano; high baritone
Mood: well-known lines from *Romeo and Juliet*
Voice: stepwise; some skips up to 7th; some syncopation; 2-note slurs
Piano: chordal, some rolled; indecisive final cadence; doubles vocal line
Uses: useful for near-beginner of any age

1691. REFLECTION (Emily Dickinson). [150]. cmp1975.
"To Gerard Souzay." X; e'–e'''; Tess-M; 4/4, Sostenuto; 2pp; Diff-V/m, P/me.
For: any voice except very low
Mood: rather melancholy
Voice: many phrases begin with leap upward of m7th, M6th, or dim 4th; otherwise diatonic; some chromaticism
Piano: chordal texture; generally supports, sometimes doubles vocal line
Diff: control of large leaps at soft dynamic level
Uses: recital possibilities; good for students of limited vocal means but good musicianship

1692. RITES DE PASSAGE (Louis Phillips) (For Voice and Chamber Orchestra, String Quartet, or Piano; piano ed. by the composer). Belwin-Mills, 1974. "To Elaine Bonazzi." Tonal; a♭–a♯"; Tess-wide; changing meters and tempos; 19pp; Diff-V/dd, P/dd; English text.
For: mezzo-soprano
Mood: realistic; maturity looking back at dreams of youth–returning to deserted home of youth
Voice: disjunct; detached phrases; fast scale passages; rapid chromatic passages; speech-like rhythms; trills
Piano: playable reduction, but complex; prelude, several interludes; large-reach chords; fast passages; tremolo
Diff: requires mature sound, solid musicianship, secure pitch, and rhythmic independence; entire range needs ease at all dynamic levels; voice must be flexible
Uses: effective; haunting and interesting work; dramatic; varied; should stand alone; however, Pasatieri published piano version

1693. THAT TIME OF YEAR (William Shakespeare, Sonnet 13). [149]. cmp1965. "To Jennie Tourel." C♯-centered; c♯'–a♭"; Tess-M; 4/4, 5/4, 3/4, Molto lento; 3pp; Diff-V/d, P/md.
For: mezzo-soprano; soprano; tenor
Mood: dramatic; concerns age and love
Voice: small note values, mostly 16ths; many accidentals; some long-ranged phrases; skips on chord lines
Piano: linear-chordal combination; syncopation; many accidentals; various registers; some large reaches; powerful dynamic climaxes; no vocal line doubling
Diff: many notes; some difficult pitch patterns
Uses: effective song for mature singer; quiet ending

1694. THERE CAME A DAY (Emily Dickinson). [151].
cmp1977. E majorish; b–e♭"; Tess-M; 4/4, Andante cantabile–Lento; 4pp; Diff-V/md, P/md.
For: mezzo-soprano with sizeable sound
Mood: theme: love to be perfected after death; dramatic
Voice: many small and large skips; many accidentals; some syncopation, triplets; dotted rhythms; syllabic; some 2–3-note slurs
Piano: broken-chord patterning supports doubling of vocal line; many accidentals; many dynamic contrasts; 2-meas. prelude
Diff: a few pitch patterns; dynamics
Uses: recital material for a singer who has good dynamic control; soft ending; possibly use in a mixed-composer group of Dickinson poems

1695. THESE ARE THE DAYS (Emily Dickinson). [150].
cmp1973. B♭maj; d♭'–g♭"; Tess-M; 4/4, 3/4, 5/4, 6/4, Andante moderato; 4pp; Diff-V/md, P/m.
For: all voices except alto or bass
Mood: lyrical nature pictures of spring
Voice: lyrical; flowing phrases of varying lengths; several melismas and trill-like figures
Piano: chordal with 8th-note broken-chord figures in l.h.; some chromaticism
Diff: vocal melismas in 32nds
Uses: excellent recital song

1696. THREE AMERICAN SONGS (Louis Phillips). [149].
cmp1969. Traditional keys; c'–a"; Tess-M; changing meters, varied tempos; 7pp; Diff-V/m, P/m.
For: soprano
Mood: esoteric; somber and lyrical; humorous
Voice: stepwise and small skips; many afterbeat entrances; mostly syllabic
Piano: thin textures; many 2nds & 7ths; subtle color effects
Diff: (b.) needs subtlety and delicacy; poetry needs thought
Uses: useful as a set or separately; (b.) seems particularly effective

    a. *Boundaries.* Fmaj; d'–e"; changing meters, Andantino; 2pp.
    b. *Haiku.* Fmin; d♭'–a"; 3/4, 2/4, Adagio; 3pp.
    c. *Critic's Privilege.* B♭maj; c'–f"; 6/8, Allegretto buffo; 2pp.

1697. THREE COLORATURA SONGS. [149].
cmp1966–1969. Tonal; d'–d'''; Tess-mH, H; regular meters with changes, varied tempos; 20pp; Diff-V/d, P/md.
For: coloratura soprano
Mood: (a.), cynical; (b.), bitter; (c.), lusty
Voice: coloratura techniques; staccato and legato articulations; soft and loud high tones; long-ranged phrases; divisions of beat into 2, 3, & 4; syncopation

Piano: rather thin textures; registers and spacing used for color effects; trills; tremolo; staccato; rolled chords; syncopation; many accidentals

Diff: singer needs good technique and solid musicianship; poem of (b.) difficult

Uses: for the coloratura soprano who is tired of singing sweet and light things and wants to do something mean and bitter– (a.) & (b.) fit this description; (c.), rather different–a song using sensuous nature symbols to signify ripeness for love

    a. *Miranda-Miranda* (Louis Phillips). Dmin-centered; e♭'–d'''; Tess-H; 3/4, 2/4, 4/4, Allegro molto; 9pp.

    b. *Lear and His Daughters* (Louis Phillips). X; e'–d'''; Tess-H; 3/4, 2/4, Lento; 6pp.

    c. *Love's Emblems* (John Fletcher). Dmaj; d'–b"; Tess-mH; 4/4, Allegro; 5pp; separately, would be a good program ender for lyric soprano with flexibility and easy b".

1698. **THREE POEMS BY KIRSTIN VAN CLEAVE.** [151]. cmp1978. "To Sheila Nadler." Tonal with many changes; b♭–a"; Tess-wide; changing meters, slow–fast–slow; 11pp; Diff-V/md, P/md.

For: mezzo-soprano

Mood: love songs; the agony and the ecstasy of love

Voice: somewhat disjunct, esp. (a.); many accidentals; uncomplicated rhythms; some dotted rhythms and triplets; syncopation; syllabic; several 2–6-note slurs

Piano: block and broken-chord figures; many accidentals; doubles or outlines vocal line; some tone clusters; some 8ves; uses wide keyboard range

Diff: some long-ranged phrases (c♯'–g", e'–e"); some intervals

Uses: as a set; recital material; somewhat popular flavor

    a. *A Night of Love.* Fmin; c♯'–g♯"; 2/4 with changes, Andante; 4pp.

    b. *You Know.* Bmin with changes; b–a♭"; 2/4, 3/4, Allegro moderato–Andantino; 4pp.

    c. *Give Me Then Your Hand.* Cmaj-Emaj; b♭–a"; 4/4, 3/4, Andante espressivo; 3pp.

1699. **THREE POEMS OF JAMES AGEE.** Cycle. Belwin-Mills, 1974. cmp1973. "To Shirley Verrett." Traditional keys (with altered chord structures and quite romantic harmonies); d♭'–a"; Tess-M, mH, H; regular but changing meters; moderate tempos; 11pp; Diff-V/d, P/md.

For: mezzo-soprano

Mood: lyrico-dramatic; somber

Voice: many skips; some chromatic alterations; a rather romantic sweep to many phrases; speech rhythms; some recit.; some melismatic phrases

Piano: chordal; modulations; some ornamental figures; big sound; piano used very romantically

Diff: perhaps some initial difficulties in learning pitches

Uses: good cycle for mature voice; singer needs great warmth of sound; could end a program (ends a"), but would be a depressing mood

Rec: D#s 15, 271

    a. *How Many Little Children Sleep.* A♭maj-E♭min; d♭'–g♭"; Tess-M; 4/4, ♩ = 72; 3pp.

    b. *A Lullaby.* Emin-Dmin; c♯'–f"; Tess-M; 4/4, 3/4, 2/4, 3/2, ♩ = 56; 4pp.

    c. *Sonnet.* Amin; e♭'–a"; Tess-mH-H; 4/4, 3/2, 5/4, 6/4, ♩ = 72; 4pp.

1700. **THREE POEMS OF THEODORE RAMSAY.** [171]. X; b–b"; Tess-wide; mostly regular meters with some changes; moderate and slow tempos; 14pp; Diff-V/d, P/d.

For: soprano

Mood: regret for a love relationship asked to bear too much

Voice: long flowing vocal lines; many large intervals; many phrases use same rhythmic pattern; melody dominates words; dramatic climaxes on high notes; three isolated high b♭s

Piano: constant 8th-note motion; many accidentals; bitonalities; romantic piano techniques; unclear harmonic direction creates a pall of sound; piano doubles vocal line throughout

Diff: finding natural word stress in melodic lines

Uses: possible recital material for full lyric soprano

    a. *Love.* X; c♯'–b"; Tess-wide; 4/4, 2/4, 3/4, 5/4, 3/2, Andante fluido; 5pp.

    b. *Remembering.* X on A♭; d♯'–a"; Tess-wide' 4/4, 3/2, 2/4, Moderato; 4pp.

    c. *On Parting.* X on E; b–b♭"; Tess-wide; 4/4, 3/4, 2/4, Adagio; 5pp.

1701. **THREE SONNETS FROM THE PORTUGUESE** (Elizabeth Barrett Browning). G. Schirmer, 1984. Tonal but unstable; b♭–g♯"; Tess-M; traditional meters with changes; medium, slow, and fast tempos; 15pp; Diff-V/md, P/md.

For: mezzo-soprano

Mood: love songs; lyric and dramatic moods

Voice: rather disjunct; many accidentals; some syncopation; a few irregular groupings; some 32nd notes; *pp–ff* dynamic range; mostly syllabic; some 2–5-note slurs

Piano: both linear and broken-chord sections; uses wide range on keyboard; many accidentals, often 4–5 per chord; frequent 8ves in one or both hands; vocal line almost always doubled; (a.), 18 meas., (b.), 9 meas., (c.), 6 meas. of prelude, interlude, and postlude

Diff: leaps of tritone, m9th, M7th, etc.; dynamics; some misprints in text

Uses: good short recital set; program ender

    a. *I (Go from me).* X; b♭–g♭"; 3/4 with changes, Moderato fluido; 5pp.

    b. *II (I see thine image through my tears tonight).* Begins B-centered; b–f♯"; 2/4 with changes, Lento; 4+pp.

    c. *III (I thank all who have loved me in their hearts).* Amaj-F♯min; c♯'–g♯"; 2/4, Allegro moderato; 5pp.

1702. **TO MUSIC BENT IS MY RETIRED MIND** (Thomas Campion). [151]. cmp1977. Amaj-F♯min; g♯–d"; Tess-M-mL; 4/4 with changes, Andante fluido; 3pp; Diff-V/md, P/md.

For: mezzo-soprano; baritone; contralto; bass
Mood: philosophical; thoughts about heaven
Voice: predominantly stepwise; small skips; beat subdivided into 2, 3, & 4 parts; syncopation; dotted rhythms; 16th-note melismas; many accidentals; humming
Piano: predominantly linear; some tone clusters; many accidentals; imitation; some triplets and 2 vs. 3; some doubling of vocal line; 4-meas. prelude; large reaches
Diff: melismatic lines
Uses: mature thoughts; possibly use in a group centered around "music"

1703. THE VERANDAHS (Kenward Elmslie). [151]. cmp1978. Emin; b–f♯"; Tess-wide; 3/4, Moderato ritmico; 3pp; Diff-V/md, P/d.
For: mezzo-soprano
Mood: grotesque; descriptive
Voice: many skips, some large; some long-ranged phrases (b–f♯", etc.); some dotted rhythms and triplets; syncopation; syllabic with some 2–4-note slurs; trills; many accidentals; very soft ending on high pitches
Piano: linear writing predominates; imitation; dotted rhythms; trills; tone clusters; many accidentals; wide keyboard range; some doubling of vocal line
Diff: wide-ranged soft sections
Uses: possible recital song for a nature group

1704. VOCAL MODESTY (Gerald Walker). [150]. cmp1976. "To Joanna Simon." Cmaj; c'–f♯"; Tess-mL; 3/4, Allegro; 2pp; Diff-V/m, P/m.
For: any female voice; possibly baritone
Mood: humorous; the singer in love with his/her voice; a "twist" at end
Voice: short phrases; somewhat disjunct; like a waltz; all phrases but one begin on beat two
Piano: chordal; fairly chromatic; doubles voice
Diff: needs good vocal actor
Uses: for singer who can act the part

1705. WINTER'S CHILD (Martin Dulman). [150]. cmp1976. X, A♭-centered; e♭'–g♭"; Tess-M; 3/4, A piacere, come improvvisando; 3pp; Diff-V/md, P/d.
For: any high or medium voice
Mood: rather abstract and mysterious
Voice: short phrases separated by rests; later phrases longer; flowing and legato; chromatic
Piano: chords formed by striking one note at a time in rapid succession and sustaining; otherwise generally block chords; very chromatic
Diff: pitches
Uses: good recital song

PASMORE, HENRY
(b. Jackson, WI, 1857; d. San Francisco, CA, 1944)

1706. A NORTHERN ROMANCE (Andrew Lang). [58]; 1st©1890. H & L keys: F♯min & E♭min (orig.); c♯'–g" & b♭–e"; Tess-M; 6/8, 4/4, Moderato; 5pp; Diff-V/m, P/me.
For: soprano; mezzo-soprano; contralto
Mood: reminiscence; narrative; bleak

Voice: scalar melody; some skips; much repetition and sequence; easy rhythms
Piano: block chords; both hands in 3rds; some open 8ves
Diff: several phrases end on sustained low tones
Uses: useful period piece

PATTISON, LEE
(b. Grand Rapids, WI, 1890; d. Claremont, CA, 1966)

1707. SLEEP NOW (James Joyce). G. Schirmer, 1926. Emin-Emaj; e'–g"; Tess-M-mH; 2/2, Larghetto; 2pp; Diff-V/m, P/m.
For: tenor; soprano
Mood: lyrical; passionate
Voice: skips and leaps; some conjunct; numerous triplets; opening sustained e" on "sleep"
Piano: "pulsing" accomp. rhythm; chordal with 8th-note motion throughout; rather thick texture
Diff: some pitches
Uses: interesting setting; for contrasting setting, see Barber

PAULUS, STEPHEN
(b. Summit, NJ, 1949)

1708. ALL MY PRETTY ONES. A Cycle of Eight Songs for Soprano and Piano (Michael Dennis Browne). European American (MS), 1984. Mostly tonal with blurred harmonies; c♯'–b"; Tess-M, mH, cs; mostly regular changing meters; varied tempos (♩ = 52–152); 25min; Diff-V/md-d, P/md-dd.
For: soprano (high lyric or coloratura)
Mood: an appreciation of birds; facets of the poet's love of and relationship to birds; symbolism of the singing of birds
Voice: lyric recitative; speech rhythms; melismas; some glissandos; many wide intervals; numerous sustained high tones; coloratura techniques
Piano: various birdsong figures, melodies, and patterns–trills, staccato motives, repeated notes, many accidentals; some 3-stave scoring; some overlapping 16th-note figures divided between hands; arpeggiated figurations
Diff: some words in high tessitura; some pitches and rhythms; ensemble
Uses: interesting and attractive cycle for an advanced graduate soprano; could be programmed with other songs about birds in various style periods and languages
Rec: D#272

a. *In a Tree at Dawn, to Listen to Birds.* X; c♯'–a"; Tess-cs; 4/4, 2/4, ♩ = ca. 52; 4pp.
b. *And the Birds Arrive.* Tonal; e'–b"; Tess-mH-H; 4/4, 5/4, 3/4, ♩ = 88; 8+pp.
c. *Purple Finch.* Tonal; c♭'–b♭"; Tess-M-mH; 3/4, 2/4, 4/4, ♩ = ca.60; 5+pp.
d. *Feeder.* Tonal; e'–a"; Tess-mH; 4/4, 2/4, 3/4, ♩ = 108; 4+pp.
e. *Little Life.* Tonal; d'–a"; Tess-mL, mH; 2/4, 3/4, 4/4, ♩ = 58; 4pp.
f. *The Bird Inside.* Tonal; c♯'–b♭"; Tess-cs; 3/4, 4/4, 5/4, ♩ = 56; 4pp.

g. *Night Bird.* Tonal; e♭'–a♭"; Tess-cs; 4/4, 2/4, ♩ = 152; 6+pp.

h. *All My Pretty Ones.* F♯maj; e'–b"; Tess-cs; 2/4, 4/4, 2/2, ♩ = 120; 9pp.

1709. ARTSONGS. For Tenor and Piano. Cycle. European-American (MS), 1983. cmp1983. "To Paul Sperry" (commissioned by Paul Sperry & the Schubert Club of St. Paul, MN, in honor of the Schubert Club's 100th Anniversary Year). X; c♯–a' (♭ tenor clef); Tess-M-mH; traditional meters with changes; varied tempos; 27min; Diff-V/dd, P/dd.

For: tenor specified
Mood: poems about the visual arts; each one comments "in some way" on a well-known work of art; various moods–dramatic, witty, philosophical, lyric
Voice: stepwise and small skips predominate; some large leaps; many accidentals; some portamentos, glissandos, staccato; 3 meas. humming; rhythms often complex and speech-like; various subdivisions of the beat and meas.; several melismas
Piano: block and broken vertical structures, often built in 4ths or 5ths; sometimes linear; countermelody supported by block structures; some trill-like patterning; some ostinato; many accidentals; both hands often in same clef; "Moor Swan" has lovely water imagery in the accomp.; complex rhythms create polyrhythms with voice; some grace notes, tremolo, rapid scale, arpeggio passages (one in 3 vs. 4 in piano); subdued ending; does not double vocal line; except for (e.), each song has a prelude and at least one interlude
Diff: vocal and mental endurance; cycle requires a great deal of singing; rhythms; finding pitches at beginning of many phrases; ensemble; reproduced MS
Uses: for two excellent musicians; an interesting concept which should interest both audience and performers; see *Nantucket Songs* by Rorem for another setting of (b.), "The Dance"
Rec: D#272

a. *Archaic Torso of Apollo* (Rainer Maria Rilke; trans. Stephen Mitchell). X; d–g'; 4/4 with changes, Majestic, stern; 6+pp. [Rec: D#9]
b. *The Dance* (William Carlos Williams). X; f–g'; 4/4 with changes, Energetic, charged; 6+pp. [Rec: D#9]
c. *Museum Piece* (Richard Wilbur). A♭-centered; e♭–g'; 12/8 with changes, ♩. = 63–♩ = ca.138 (with 2 more changes); 7pp.
d. *Seurat* (Ira Sadoff). X; c♯–a'; 3/4 with changes, ♩ = 56 (with changes); 13pp.
e. *On Seeing Larry Rivers' "Washington Crossing The Delaware" at The Museum of Modern Art* (Frank O'Hara). Polytonal touches; e♭–g♯'; 4/4 with changes, ♩ = 132; 8+pp.
f. *Moor Swan* (John Logan). D-centered; e–a'; 3/4 with changes, ♩ = 52; 5pp. [Rec: D#9]
g. *Warrior with Shield* (Michael Dennis Browne). X; c♯–g♯'; 4/4 with changes, ♩ = 80/72; 9pp.

1710. BITTERSUITE. Four Poems of Ogden Nash for Baritone and Piano. European American (MS), 1987. cmp1987 for Håkan Hagegård. X and quasi-tonal; A–g';

Tess-mH,H; regular meters with changes; varied tempos (♩ = 48–144); 35pp; Diff-V/m-d, P/m-dd.
For: high baritone
Mood: bittersweet; the passage of time; our inevitable death
Voice: syllabic; speech rhythms and straight melodic rhythms; line melodic but with unexpected turns and direction; high tessitura; mostly dissonant
Piano: patterned; mostly linear; some chordal texture; fast dissonant arpeggiation; fast 8ve changes; measured tremolos with 2nds & 3rds
Diff: dissonance; high tessitura; ensemble
Uses: interesting set for mature high lyric baritone
Rec: D#272

a. *For a Good Dog.* X; c♯–f♯'; Tess-mH-H; 4/4, 2/4, ♩ = ca.144; 8+pp.
b. *The Middle.* Quasi-tonal-Bmaj; c –e'; Tess-mH; 2/4, 4/4, 3/4, ♩ = ca.80; 5+pp.
c. *Time Marches On.* X; A–g'; Tess-mH-H; 4/4, ♩ = 144/138; 15+pp.
d. *Old Men.* Tonal; d–g'; Tess-mH; 4/4, 2/4, 3/8, 6/8, 5/8, ♩ = 48; 3+pp.

1711. SONGS OF LOVE AND LONGING for Soprano and Piano (various Japanese Tanka poets). European American (MS), 1992. X; b–a"; Tess-M, mH, H; mostly regular changing meters; varied tempos (♩ = 66–136); 10min; Diff-V/m-d, P/m-d.
For: soprano
Mood: images of longing, unrequited love, and lonely nights
Voice: mostly lyrical but disjunct lines; wide intervals; a few melismas; numerous sustained tones; glissandos; 5-meas. sustained a" with decres. to *mf* and cresc. to *ff*
Piano: repeated patterns; trills; tremolos; passages all in bass clef or all in treble clef; hands awkwardly entwined in some places; accidentals; groups of 5
Diff: pitches; some high phrases; some piano figurations
Uses: interesting cycle of Oriental poems; good short 20th-century group for graduate level soprano who likes Tanka poetry

a. *Endless Autumn Nights* (Anonymous). X; c♯'–g"; Tess-cs; 4/4, 2/4, 3/4, ♩ = 66; 3pp.
b. *The One Who Greets Me* (Otomo no Yakamachi). X; d♭'–e"; Tess-M; 2/4, 3/8, 4/4, ♩ = 120 freely, liquid; 2pp.
c. *Dark Seed* (Sosei). X; d'–a"; Tess-cs; 6/8, 3/4, ♩. = 84; 3pp.
d. *Echoes* (Mibu no Tadamine). X; d♭'–g♭"; Tess-M; 4/4, 3/4, ♩ = 112; 4pp.
e. *Moonless Nights* (Ono no Komachi). X; d'–a"; Tess-H; 4/4, 3/8, 2/4, 9/8, ♩ = 136 Driving; 4pp.
f. *The Bashful Moon* (Anonymous). X; b–f♯"; Tess-M; 4/4, 2/4, ♩ = ca.108; 2+pp.
g. *From This World* (Anonymous). G-centered; c'–g"; Tess-mH; 3/4, ♩ = 120; 3+pp.

PEASE, ALFRED H.
(b. Cleveland, OH, 1838; d. St. Louis, MO, 1882)

1712. BREAK, BREAK, BREAK (Alfred Lord Tennyson).

Pond (also Ditson), 1869, 1897. Emin; b–g";
Tess-M-mH; 6/8, Moderato; 4pp; Diff-V/m, P/e.
For: tenor; soprano
Mood: lyrical treatment of text
Voice: skips and leaps; repeated tones
Piano: 4-meas. intro. with "wave" figure in bass; repeated chords; afterbeat pattern; arpeggiation; cross-hands
Diff: features e" and f♯"
Uses: useful song for another setting of this text, although the musical setting does not seem really despairing enough; period piece

PEASLEE, RICHARD C.
(b. New York, NY, 1930)

1713. SONGS FROM THE CHINESE (various poets; trans. Arthur Waley). Magellan, 1972. Harmonically varied: pentatonic, vertical structures of 5th, 4th, 2nd, 7th; c'–a"; Tess-M-mH; changing meters; varied tempos; 15pp; Diff-V/m-md, P/m-md.
For: tenor; soprano
Mood: Oriental; poetry often wry or ironic; sometimes dramatic
Voice: speech-like rhythms; syncopation; some intervals hard to sing against piano; mostly small skips
Piano: both chordal and linear; many accidentals; long solo section in last song; syncopation; colorful
Diff: although poetry seems best for a tenor, vocal line may be uncomfortably low in spots; some abrupt dynamic changes
Uses: effective recital set

   a. *On the Birth of His Son* (Su Tung- p'o). eb'–a"; 4/4 with changes, Moderately fast; 2+pp.
   b. *Flowers and Moonlight on the Spring River* (Yang-ti). eb'–g"; 4/4 with changes, Slowly; 1+pp.
   c. *After Lunch* (Po Chu-i). d'–f"; 4/4 with changes, Moderately; 3pp.
   d. *Li Fu-Jen* (Wu-ti). f'–a"; 5/4 with changes, Slowly; 2pp.
   e. *The Red Cockatoo* (Po Chu-i). d'–g"; 4/4 with changes, Lively; 3pp.
   f. *The Little Lady of Ch'ing-hsi* (children's song). c'–f"; 6/8 with changes, Quietly flowing; 3pp.

PELISSIER, VICTOR (See Special Section)

PENDLETON, EDMUND
(b. U. S. A., 1899; d. Paris, France, 1987)

1714. DARK HILLS (Edward Arlington Robinson). G. Schirmer, 1931. Abmaj; d'–e"; Tess-M; 4/4, Moderato sostenuto; 6pp; Diff-V/me, P/m.
For: baritone; mezzo-soprano
Mood: descriptive; philosophical; concerns death
Voice: stepwise and easy skips; easy rhythms
Piano: broken chords in triplet pattern; 16th-note quadruplets; does not double vocal line
Diff: sustained phrases; long tones at ends of phrases

Uses: effective subdued song

PENHORWOOD, EDWIN
(b. Toledo, OH, 1939)

1715. AMERICA I LOVE YOU (Spike Milligan). [152]. cmp1983. Tonal; f'–a"; Tess-mH; 3/2, 4/2, ♩= 72; 2pp; Diff-V/m, P/m.
For: soprano
Mood: humorous with a twist; satire
Voice: syllabic; mostly conjunct in quarter-note motion; a few leaps of 6th or more; quarter-note triplets over running 8ths in piano; one spoken line; two characters (woman and man)
Piano: mostly 2-voice texture; some chords at end; built on melodic motives from "America the Beautiful" and "The Star-Spangled Banner" cleverly worked into the piano lines
Diff: some rhythms; ensemble
Uses: fine humorous song; good for teaching characterization

1716. COME WALK IN THE GARDEN WITH ME (Callum MacColl). [152]. cmp1978. A; d'–c♯'''; Tess-cs; 7/8, 4/4, 9/8, 3/4, 5/4, ♩= 126 (legato, but with energy and excitement); 10+pp; Diff-V/d, P/d.
For: soprano (coloratura or high lyric)
Mood: ecstatic love song; invitation to walk in the beauty of spring and love
Voice: syllabic throughout; rhythms reflect both speech and melodic contour; some wide-ranged phrase groups; mostly conjunct; some skips; a few leaps of 6th; accidentals; changing meters; many different rhythmic groupings; polyrhythms with piano (2 vs. 3, 3 vs. 4)
Piano: much widely spaced broken-chord figuration; parallel 4ths, 5ths, & 6ths frequent; linear motion and texture; meter changes from irregular to regular; some widely spaced contrary motion; covers the keyboard in a fairly fast tempo; doubling of vocal line incidental
Diff: rhythms; meter changes; fast diction in high tessitura; ensemble
Uses: an exciting song; good recital material for musically secure high soprano

1717. COUNTING THE BEATS (Robert Graves). [152]. cmp1965. X; c'–bb"; Tess-mH; 3/4, 5/4, 4/4, 5/8, 6/8, ♩= 138; 8pp; Diff-V/d, P/md.
For: soprano; tenor
Mood: wakeful; apprehensive of the passing of time; thoughts of two lovers about where they will be after death
Voice: mostly stepwise; some large leaps; syllabic; various rhythmic divisions, regular and irregular meters; syncopation over the barline; chromatic; some doubling of vocal line; ends on sustained bb" *fff*
Piano: 18-meas. prelude sets mood and motion of song; l.h. afterbeat style with wide spacing under r.h. melody in wide intervals; interlude dissolves into heartbeat motion in l.h.; chordal texture in center section; combination of motives at end; final meas. same as opening meas.
Diff: rhythms–an exercise in the title itself; some sustained phrases; loud ending on bb"

Uses: very active song for an advanced singer; group ender

1718. **EVEN** (Anne Morrow Lindbergh). [152]. cmp1964.
Emin, modulatory; e'–b"; Tess-mH-H; 3/4, 4/4, 3/2, 2/4,
♩ = 108–112; 6+pp; Diff-V/md, P/md.
For: soprano (lyric)
Mood: lyrical love song; authentic love gives freedom to the
beloved
Voice: sustained, slow-moving vocal line; conjunct
throughout; first 26 meas. voice alone with a single
note piano line; whole song builds from *p* beginning to
ff climax and returns to *p* opening melody; syllabic;
specific dynamic and expressive markings
Piano: begins with single line, then chordal in reverse afterbeat
pattern; some 2 vs. 3; next stanza, chromatic chordal
motion becoming repeated 8th-note figures that cover
three 8ves at climactic phrases; subsides to opening
single line
Diff: solo legato opening; sustained long phrases; power and
warmth for climactic meas. soaring to b" at midpoint of
6-meas. sustained e"–b" phrase
Uses: effective song, well constructed; powerful sentiment;
needs mature voice secure in *a cappella* singing

1719. **HAIKU.** A Song Cycle (various Japanese poets). T.I.S.
Publications, 2000. cmp1995–1996. Mostly X, quasi-
tonal; f♯–g"; Tess-L, M, cs; regular meters; varied
tempos; 12-14min; Diff-V/e-md, P/e-md.
For: mezzo-soprano; baritone
Mood: brief impressions; mostly nature images; fleeting
awarenesses
Voice: lyrical; short phrases; mostly disjunct; chromatic; some
wide intervals; syllabic
Piano: many different types of patterns and figurations, each
reflecting the mood of the poem; accidentals; some
bitonality; some fast arpeggiated figurations
Diff: pitches; some piano figurations
Uses: interesting cycle for singer with good ear who likes
Haiku poetry

a. *Summer Evening* (Shiki). X; b–e"; Tess-M; 3/4,
4/4, 7/4, ♩ = 54; 3pp.
b. *The Way of Zen* (Basho). Bitonal; c'–g"; Tess-cs;
4/4, 3/4, With excitement and brilliance ♩ =92; 1p.
c. *Clouds* (Basho). X; c'–d"; Tess-M; 4/4, 6/4, 8/4,
♩ = 66; 2pp.
d. *Coolness* (Basho). G minorish; c♯'–d♭"; Tess-M;
4/4, ♩ = 69; 1p.
e. *Onitsura's First Poem (Age 8)* (Onitsura). X; b–g";
Tess-cs; unmetered, Allegro; 1p.
f. *Loneliness* (Hashin). Fmin; f♯–e"; Tess-mL; 3/4,
Adagio, man non troppo ♩ = c.54 or 60; 2pp.
g. *Where the Cuckoo Flies* (Basho). B♭min; b♭–e";
Tess-cs; 4/4, 3/4, 7/8, Andante ♩ = 104; 3pp.
h. *Spring* (Ryota). G majorish; g'–e"; Tess-M; 2/4, 4/4,
Allegro; 3pp.
i. *The Sudden Chillness* (Buson). X; a–f"; Tess-cs;
3/4, 4/4, Allegro ♩ = c.144; 1p.
j. *Maple Leaves* (Shiko). X-B♭min; f'–f♯"; Tess-M;
3/4, 4/4, ♩ = 44; 2pp.
k. *Bell Tones* (Basho). X; a–g'; Tess-L; 2/2, ♩ = c.69;
1p.

l. *The Mushroom* (Issa). X; a♭–d"; Tess-M;
unmetered, freely; ½p.
m. *The Cuckoo* (Basho). X; c'–f "; Tess-M; unmetered,
2/4, 3/4, Allegro; 4+pp.

1720. **I HEARD A FLY BUZZ WHEN I DIED** (Emily
Dickinson). [152]. cmp1965. Emin; e'–f♯"; Tess-M;
4/4, ♩ = 72 quasi recitativo; 3pp; Diff-V/m, P/me.
For: soprano; mezzo-soprano
Mood: stillness; approaching the moment of death
Voice: stepwise and small skips; mostly 8th-note motion; some
dotted quarter/8th phrases; syllabic; a few accidentals;
several expressive markings
Piano: block chords; some wide spacing; contrary motion in
both opening and closing directions expresses points of
text; short melodic motif at beginning and end of song
Diff: singer needs good legato line and dynamic control;
piano does not provide motion
Uses: lovely song; expressive of the text in a direct way; good
for undergraduate singer

1721. **THE LADIES** (Low Voice). T.I.S. Publications, 2000.
cmp1998 (one in1963). Tonal; G♯–e'(g' falsetto) [(c.) -
⸦ d♭'–f "]; Tess-M, mH, cs; regular meters; varied
tempos; 27pp; Diff-V/m-md, P/md-md.
For: baritone
Mood: praise of Phyllis; infatuation with Julia; romantic love
of Helen; true love of Sally
Voice: lyrical; syllabic; melodic setting of words; grateful to
the voice
Piano: mostly chordal; one song arpeggiated throughout; some
bitonality; romantic textures in general
Diff: some ascending phrase endings
Uses: good set for senior or graduate baritone; attractive
recital material

a. *My Phyllis* (Thomas Lodge). F-F♯min; G♯–e';
Tess-cs; 4/2, 3/2, ♩ = 44; 4pp.
b. *Upon Julia's Clothes* (Robert Herrick). Bitonal;
c–e♯'; Tess-mH; 2/2, 2/4, 4/4, ♩ = 84; 4pp.
c. *To Helen* (Edgar Allan Poe). [152].D♭maj; d♭'–f ";
Tess-M; 4/4, 2/4, Gently and caressingly; 6pp.
d. *Sally in Our Alley* (Henry Carey). E♭maj; B♭–e' (g'
falsetto); Tess-cs; 4/4, ♩ = 100; 13pp.

1722. **A LUTE WILL LIE** (Callum MacColl). [152].
cmp1978. G♭maj; d♭'–b♭"; Tess-mH; 2/2, 3/2, ♩ = 52;
4+pp; Diff-V/m, P/m.
For: soprano; tenor
Mood: quiet love song; renewal of love through music;
comparison to lute
Voice: sustained, floating lines; syllabic; much conjunct
motion; some skips; leap of M6th to b♭" at end *mf*;
dynamics *p–f*, mostly *p*
Piano: chordal with melody; arpeggiated chords at beginning
and in two interludes (two 5-meas. interludes, one 10-
meas. interlude); 11-meas. postlude
Diff: floating last high phrases
Uses: nice song for a group about love, music, or the
relationship between love and music; for a warm lyric
voice with the ability to sustain floating phrases

1723. **THE NIGHT** (Francis William Bourdillon). [152].
cmp1992. Cmin; f#'–a"; Tess-mH; 6/4, 9/4, ♩ = 84; 4pp;
Diff-V/md, P/md.
For: soprano; tenor
Mood: luminous; upward floating comparison of the stars to
the mind and the sun to love
Voice: sustained; upward floating phrases; some slow
syncopation; two 8ve leaps to a" *mp*
Piano: chordal; some countermelody in r.h.; various divisions
of 6/4; wide spacing of chords, generally ascending
patterns; many modulations
Diff: floating sustained phrases and soft 8ve leap a"
Uses: beautiful song; needs an ample, luminous voice;
probably best for a mature singer

1724. **SHE TELLS HER LOVE WHILE HALF ASLEEP**
(Robert Graves). [152]. cmp1965. F-centered; f'–bb";
Tess-mH; 2/2, 3/2, ♩ = 52 in a flowing manner; 2pp;
Diff-V/m, P/me.
For: tenor (light lyric); soprano
Mood: love song; quiet description of nocturnal whispers
Voice: sustained; syllabic; climactic phrase rises to bb" *f*;
dynamic range: *ppp–f*
Piano: chordal; wide spacing; some 1-voice lines; soft
dynamics; little motion
Diff: maintaining mood demands full control of soft singing
as well as ease with high phrase; relatively motionless
Uses: effective dream-like love song; could fit into many
different kinds of groups

1725. **STRANGE LOVERS MAY CARESS YOU** (Spike
Milligan). [152]. cmp1983. Tonal; f'–gb"; Tess-M; 3/4,
♩ = 76; 4pp; Diff-V/m, P/me.
For: tenor; soprano
Mood: pleading; attempt to regain lost love
Voice: lyric recitative; stepwise motion; syllabic; word
repetition for expressive effect; *p–f*
Piano: chordal in slow syncopation (♩-♪) pattern; some r.h.
melody; shifting harmonies illuminate emotional state;
6-meas. prelude, 11-meas. postlude
Diff: long postlude demands singer's emotional attention
Uses: luminous love song; good for teaching legato line and
soft singing in passaggio

1726. **WHEN HEAVEN CRIES** (Callum MacColl). [152].
cmp1962. Cmaj/G#min; d#'–e"; Tess-M; 3/4, ♩ = 120;
3+pp; Diff-V/m, P/m.
For: tenor; soprano
Mood: somewhat self-pitying; comparison of rain (Heaven's
tears) to loss-of-love tears
Voice: syllabic; sustained and slow moving vocal line; some
triadic outlining, some stepwise motion; accidentals;
pp–mf dynamics
Piano: block chords in ostinato rhythmic pattern of ♩-♩ in each
measure; consonant-to-dissonant harmonic pattern
projects grief; wide spacing; dynamics, *pp–mf*
Diff: sustaining quiet intensity
Uses: expressive song; good for teaching slow legato line and
quiet intensity

1727. **WHO KNOWS IF THE MOON IS A BALLOON**
(e. e. cummings). [152]. cmp1966. X; db'–g"; Tess-

mH; 3/4, 4/4, 5/8, 2/4, 5/4, slowly and erratically
♪ = 132; 4pp; Diff-V/md, P/md.
For: soprano; tenor
Mood: whimsical; fantasy of finding another world where it's
always spring
Voice: mostly conjunct, some triadic outlining; rhythmic
patterns reflect both speech rhythms and motion of
words; many different divisions of beat; some
polyrhythms; mostly syllabic; one melisma
Piano: 8-meas. prelude with cross-hand playing; some
afterbeat style in l.h.; quartal and quintal chords in r.h.;
some melodic material in r.h. frequently doubles vocal
line; long trills; tremolo; grace notes; contrary-motion
flourishes; 2nd half of song all in treble clef
Diff: rhythms; some pitches
Uses: good e. e. cummings setting for fairly advanced singer

1728. **WILD NIGHTS!** (Emily Dickinson). [152]. cmp1993.
Cmin-maj; a'–c'''; Tess-H; 4/4, Allegro con fuoco
♩ = 120–132; 7pp; Diff-V/d, P/d.
For: high soprano
Mood: rapturous love song
Voice: high tessitura; fairly short phrases; 3 a"s, 2 bb"s, 1 c''',
half of them on "ee" vowel, half on "uh"; beginning
and 3 high phrases *ff*
Piano: fast arpeggiated patterns in both hands throughout in
16ths, 8th-note triplets, and some 32nd-note
figurations; occasional doubling of vocal line; many
accidentals; very romantic style
Diff: relentless tempo; dynamic variation will demand
control and thinking ahead; ensemble
Uses: exciting song for a mature singer and a pianist with
good concert level technique; group or program ender

PERERA, RONALD C.
(b. Boston, MA, 1941)

1729. **APOLLO CIRCLING.** Four Lyric Songs for High
Voice and Piano on a Poem by James Dicky. Cycle.
E.C. Schirmer, 1977. cmp1971–1972. Atonal; c'–c''';
Tess-L, M, H; regular and irregular meters with
changes; overall slow to moderate tempos with many
changes, 1 fast section; 28pp; Diff-V/dd, P/d-dd; MS
facsimile.
For: best for lyric tenor
Mood: predominantly lyrical with some dramatic passages;
poem ("For the First Manned Moon Orbit") is
descriptive of feelings of outer space and the moon
Voice: avant-garde idiom; disjunct with large leaps; short
phrases; syllabic with one melisma; many dynamic
markings with sudden extremes; some sustained tones;
speech rhythms
Piano: wide spacing; often pointillistic; rhythmically intricate;
some patterning; clusters; many dynamic markings;
some 3-stave scoring; large reach helpful; previous
acquaintance with avant-garde score very helpful
Diff: pitch patterns; range; large leaps; high tessitura
passages; great dynamic flexibility needed; text
projection; rhythmic patterns
Uses: for two advanced performers familiar with avant-garde
style; could be a stunning work; musical idiom fits

subject of poetry beautifully

Rec: D#273

    a. *So Long.* c'–f♯"; 2/2, 3/2, 12/16, 5/8, 4/4, 5/4,
Cold–Agitated, etc.; 7pp.

    b. *The Moon Comes.* c♯'–a"; 4/4 Hushed, fantastic;
4pp.

    c. *You Lean Back.* c♯'–b♭"; 8/8, 4/8, 3/8, 5/8, 6/8,
11/8, etc., With tenderness, but not sentimental–
Holding back the last a little; 7pp.

    d. *You Hang Mysteriously.* d'–c'''; 12/16, 4/8, 5/4, 4/4,
With controlled excitement–Passionately–
Broad–Still slower; 10pp.

1730. **FIVE SUMMER SONGS** on Poems of Emily
Dickinson. Cycle. E. C. Schirmer, 1976. cmp1969,
1972. Tonal (some whole-tone passages, parallel
harmonies, delicate dissonances); b–f♯"; Tess-M for
sop., mH-H for mezzo-sop.; regular meters with some
changes (1 song in 5/8); moderate tempos; 20pp;
Diff-V/md-d, P/md.

For: soprano; lyric mezzo-soprano with easy top

Mood: very lyrical; poems center on aspects of summer in the
poet's mind

Voice: irregular phrasing; some large intervals (8ve leaps);
some long sustained tones; much soft singing; some
rhythmic intricacies

Piano: fluid and linear; countermelodies with vocal line; many
arpeggiated figures; whole-tone scale figurations; trills;
cross-hands; much solo material; descriptive and
delicately romantic; wide reaches

Diff: some large leaps; soft passages; 5/8 song; ensemble;
text projection on long tones

Uses: lovely cycle; quite different from *Apollo Circling*;
excellent material for intermediate to advanced singers;
good musicianship needed

    a. *New Feet within My Garden Go.* B♭maj; c♯'–e♭";
3/4, 4/4, Sustained (♩ = 58–63); 3pp.

    b. *South Winds Jostle Them.* C (whole-tone); f'–f♯";
3/4, 2/2, Rippling (♩. = 52); 5pp.

    c. *I Know a Place.* b–f♯"; 4/4, 3/4, Gently rocking
(♩ = 72); 5pp.

    d. *To Make a Prairie.* Gmin-maj; d'–f"; 5/8, Bright (♩
+ ♪ = 48); 4pp.

    e. *The One That Could Repeat the Summer Day.*
c'–f"; 6/4, Floating, serene (♩ = ca.56, but free);
3pp.

1731. **SLEEP NOW** (James Joyce) for High Voice and
Piano. Boosey & Hawkes, 1993. cmp1985. NATS
Vocal Composition Award, 1990. "For Karen Smith
Emerson." Mostly tonal and modal; d'–b♭"; Tess-mH-
H; regular and irregular meters with changes; varied
tempos; 26pp; Diff-V/d, P/m-d.

For: high soprano

Mood: the "unquiet heart": anguished and dramatic; reflective;
lyrical; nostalgic; passionate

Voice: combination of very conjunct lines and large intervals,
esp. 8ves; repeated notes; chromatic; melismas in
various rhythmic patterns, mostly slow and floating;
descending portamentos; much tone painting; grace

notes; some long and long-ranged phrases; long notes
in high, low, and med. range; many different rhythmic
patterns; much syncopation in long lines; polyrhythms
with piano; many meter changes, accidentals, and high
phrases

Piano: chordal and linear; measured tremolo block chords,
arpeggiation, 8ve passages, tremolo with melody in l.h.,
repeated chords with melody in l.h.; 8th- and 16th-note
motion throughout except for (b.) in quarters; ostinato-
like 16th-note patterns in both hands in subtly changing
harmonies; many accidentals; specific pedaling
markings, incl. Sostenuto; much syncopation; many
short solo passages; piano sets mood, mostly dream-
like and floating; gives clues and cues to vocal line;
occasional doubling

Diff: pitches; high tessitura; flowing rhythmic line with
many different patterns; irregular and changing meters;
pianist's hands often close together and crossed;
ensemble

Uses: luminous, dream-like cycle for advanced singer and
pianist; "I Hear an Army" and "Sleep Now" very
different conceptions from Barber's settings

    a. *I Hear an Army.* X on A; d'–b♭"; Tess-wide, H;
4/4, 2/4, 6/4, 3/2, 2/2, With demonic energy
(♩ = c.116); 10pp.

    b. *Ecce Puer.* Whole tone & diatonic; e'–a"; Tess-cs;
7/4, 5/4, 9/4, 6/4, 3/4, 7/2, 2/2, 5/2, 4/2, Simply and
tenderly (♩ = 92); 3pp.

    c. *She Weeps Over Rahoon.* Pentatonic minor
(lowered 5th); d'–a♭"; Tess-M, mH; 4/4, 2/4, 8/8,
7/8, 3/8, 4+5/8, Smooth and plaintive (♩ = 132);
5pp.

    d. *The Twilight Turns from Amethyst.* C minorish–
ends on dominant; d'–b♭"; Tess-H; 3/4,
Reflectively (♩ = 63); 3pp.

    e. *Sleep Now.* Lydian on G; g'–a"; Tess-mH-H; 4/8,
6/8, 9/8, Flowing freely (♩. = 66); 5pp.

PERKINSON, COLERIDGE-TAYLOR
(b. New York, NY, 1932)

1732. **A CHILD'S GRACE** (Robert Herrick). [6]. Gmaj;
g'–f"; Tess-mH; 2/4, 3/4; 1p; Diff-V/e, P/m.

For: any voice except very low

Mood: simple; child's prayer

Voice: diatonic; general 8th-note movement

Piano: movement generally in 16ths high on keyboard; a little
more chromatic than the vocal line

Uses: good teaching piece for young singers

1733. **MELANCHOLY** (John Fletcher). [6]. Gmin; b♭–f";
Tess-M; 4/4 with changes; 6pp; Diff-V/m, P/m.

For: mezzo-soprano; lyric baritone

Mood: melancholy

Voice: lyrical; flowing; diatonic with conjunct motion;
generally 8th-note movement

Piano: chordal-contrapuntal combination; 4-voice texture

Diff: one high-lying phrase

Uses: good recital song

PERLE, GEORGE
(b. Bayonne, NJ, 1915)

1734. **THIRTEEN DICKINSON SONGS,** Vols. 1, 2, & 3
for Soprano and Piano (Emily Dickinson). Cycle.
Gunmar, 1981, 1983, & 1984. cmp1977–1978.
Commissioned for Bethany Beardslee by the National
Endowment for the Arts. X; f♯–c♯'''; Tess-wide (but M
predominates); traditional meters with changes and
unmetered; tempos given in metronome markings;
36min; Diff-V/dd, P/dd.
For: soprano specified; possibly mezzo-soprano
Mood: ranging from innocent and naive thoughts on life and
nature to deeply philosophical thoughts about death and
dying
Voice: overall disjunct; wide leaps; wide-ranged phrases (e.g.,
c♯'–c♯''', g♯–a''); several songs have sections chanted
on one pitch or within a range of a whole-step (e., g., &
k.); some speech-like rhythms; fragmentation; many
accidentals; irregular phrase lengths; perfect pitch
desirable; songs in vol.2 seem slightly less difficult
than the others; predominantly syllabic; some 2-note
slurs; several melismas; some soft high notes (a♭'',
c♯'''); some staccato
Piano: linear writing predominates; some imitation; some
sections in block chords; vertical structures often
feature 2nds, 4ths, or 7ths; many accidentals; many
pedal and dynamic markings; polyrhythms and other
rhythmic complexities; large reach needed; does not
double vocal line; most songs have some solo material
for piano, e.g., (e.), 14-meas. prelude; (i.), 16-meas.
prelude; (d.), trills; (i.), staccato; (j.), specific
instructions for sostenuto pedal
Diff: tessitura; pitches; ensemble; reading the rhythms, at
times (successions of dotted-8th or dotted-16th notes);
performers must note errata published with each vol.
Uses: use in entirety or make a selection of songs from the
cycle; performers must be excellent musicians; singer
must be secure in every way, with an easy technique
Rec: D#68

Vol. 1: FROM A CHILDHOOD

   a. *Perhaps You'd Like to Buy a Flower.* X; f♯–c♯''';
2/4 with changes, ♩= 60; 1+min.
   b. *I Like to See It Lap the Miles.* X; g–a''; 2/4 with
changes, ♩= 63 (with changes); 2+min.
   c. *I Know Some Lonely Houses Off the Road.* X;
g–c'''; unmetered and unbarred, ♩= 63 (with
changes); 4+min
   d. *There Came a Wind like a Bugle.* X; a♯–a'';
unmetered and unbarred, ♩= 112.5 (with changes);
2min.

Vol. 2: AUTUMN DAY

   e. *Beauty–Be Not Caused–It Is–.* X; b–f''; 5/8, 5/4,
♪= 110; 2+min.
   f. *The Wind–Tapped like a Tired Man–.* X; a–a'';
unmetered and unbarred, tempos constantly change;
3min.
   g. *These Are the Days When Birds Come Back–.* X;

b♭–b''; unmetered and unbarred, ♩= 69; 3min.
   h. *The Heart Asks Pleasure–First–.* X; b♭–g♭''; 9/8,
♩.= 54; 2+min.

Vol. 3: GRAVE HOUR

   i. *What If I Say I Shall Not Wait!* X; a–b'';
unmetered, ♩= 120; 2min.
   j. *If I'm Lost–Now–.* X; g–a♭''; changing meters,
♩= 80; 3min.
   k. *The Loneliness One Dare Not Sound–.* X; g–c♯''';
unmetered, ♩= 42 (with changes); 3min.
   l. *Under the Light, Yet Under.* X; g–a♭''; unmetered
and unbarred, ♩= 64–♩= 64; 2+min.
   m. *She Bore It Till the Simple Veins* (Closing Piece).
X; a♭–g♯''; changing meters, ♩= 51; 3min.

PERRY, JULIA
(b. Akron, OH, 1927; d. Akron, OH, 1979)

1735. **BY THE SEA** (Julia Perry). Galaxy, 1950. Emaj; e'–a'';
Tess-mH; 4/4; 2min; Diff-V/md, P/m.
For: soprano; tenor
Mood: lonely; plaintive; dreaming
Voice: many skips; one leap of 9th; duplets and triplets
juxtaposed; syncopation
Piano: 4–6-voice block chords; some arpeggiated and
broken-chord patterns; vocal line doubling incidental
Diff: wide range of several phrases; sustained a''
Uses: effective song

PERSICHETTI, VINCENT
(b. Philadelphia, PA, 1915; d. Philadelphia, PA, 1987)

1736. **EMILY DICKINSON SONGS,** Opus 77.
Elkan-Vogel, 1958. Pub. separately. Tonal; d♭'–f'';
Tess-M; regular meters, varied tempos; 6min;
Diff-V/me-m, P/me-m.
For: mezzo-soprano
Mood: lyrical; philosophical; humorous
Voice: stepwise and small skips; some syncopation; mostly
easy rhythms; some fragmentation
Piano: chordal and linear; syncopation; accidentals; some
sequence and repetition; little doubling of vocal line
Diff: ensemble; poems need thought
Uses: excellent set for a student with imagination

   a. *Out of the Morning.* [16]. A-centered; d'–e''; 4/4,
Andante; 2pp.
   b. *I'm Nobody.* Amaj; d'–e''; 2/4, Allegretto; 3pp.
   c. *When the Hills Do.* X; d'–d''; 4/4, Slowly; 2pp.
   d. *The Grass.* C-centered; d♭'–f''; 4/4, 3/4, Andante
affettuoso; 4pp. [**Rec:** D#10]

1737. **HARMONIUM.** Cycle for Soprano and Piano, Op. 50
(Wallace Stevens). Elkan-Vogel, 1959. cmp1951. No
key sigs. (dissonant harmonies emphasize 2nds &
tritones); c'–c'''; Tess-many tessituras; generally regular
meters (some changes), a few irregular; many different
tempos; 1hr; Diff-V/dd, P/dd.

For: soprano (with ample sound and endurance)

Mood: many different moods; most center on the loneliness of the individual against the backdrop of life

Voice: wide range; difficult pitch and rhythmic patterns; perfect pitch helpful; difficult poetry

Piano: various techniques; much linear, contrapuntal material; large reach helpful; pianist should have excellent technique and be accustomed to the 20th-century idiom

Diff: in all areas, incl. the poetry

Uses: entire recital program for the advanced, virtuoso singer; selections can be made to form effective smaller groups; in spite of dissonance, basically a lyrical work

a. *Valley Candle.* c'–g"; 2/4, ♩ = 40; 2pp.

b. *The Place of the Solitaires.* c♯'–g"; 4/4, ♩ = 132; 4pp.

c. *Theory.* e'–g"; 2/2, ♩ = 60; 2pp.

d. *Lunar Paraphrase.* c♯'–g"; 3/4, ♩ = 44; 3pp.

e. *The Death of a Soldier.* c'–g"; 4/4, ♩ = 76; 3pp. [Rec: D#10]

f. *The Wind Shifts.* c♯'–a"; 2/4, 6/8, ♩ = 54; 5pp.

g. *The Weeping Burgher.* e♭'–a"; 4/4, ♩ = 112; 5pp.

h. *Six Significant Landscapes.* c♯'–a"; 4/4, 3/4, 5/4, 6/4, ♩ = 54; 11pp; 6 sections.

i. *In the Clear Season of Grapes.* c'–g"; 4/4, ♩ = 92; 4pp.

j. *Tea.* d'–g"; 4/8, 2/8, 3/8, ♩ = 84; 3pp.

k. *The Snow Man.* c♯'–a"; 2/2, ♩ = 84; 4pp. [Rec: D#10]

l. *Tattoo.* e♭'–g♯"; 4/4, ♩ = 58; 2pp.

m. *Sonatina to Hans Christian.* d'–g"; 2/4, ♩ = 120; 4pp. [Rec: D#59]

n. *Infanta Marina.* d'–f"; 3/8, ♪ = 48; 3pp.

o. *Metaphors of a Magnifico.* d♯'–g"; 2/4, ♩ = 120; 7pp.

p. *Gubbinal.* e♭'–e"; 3/4, ♩ = 40; 2pp.

q. *Domination of Black.* c'–c"'; 3/4, 4/4, 2/4, 5/4, ♩ = 50 (various changes); 10pp; very dramatic.

r. *Earthy Anecdote.* c'–a"; 3/4, 4/8, 2/4, 3/8, ♩ = 144; 5pp.

s. *Of the Surface of Things.* d'–g"; 6/4, ♩ = 44; 3pp. [Rec: D#10]

t. *Thirteen Ways of Looking at a Blackbird.* c'–a"; 4/4, with many changes, 13 sections, each with a different tempo; 20pp; ends quietly; much piano solo material in connecting passages between sections.

1738. **HILAIRE BELLOC SONGS,** Opus 75. Elkan-Vogel, 1965. Very different in mood and subject; separate entries below.

A. **THOU CHILD SO WISE,** No. 1. [16]. Emin; c'–e♭"; Tess-M; 2/2, Slowly; 2pp; Diff-V/e, P/e.

For: mezzo-soprano; baritone

Mood: lyrical; mystical; concerns the child Jesus

Voice: simple phrases; somewhat dissonant with accomp.; sustained; one phrase unaccomp.

Piano: patterned; single line of arpeggiated chords; four chords punctuate ending

Uses: haunting song; simple, effective, quiet

Rec: D#10

B. **THE MICROBE,** No. 2. C-centered; c'–e"; Tess-mH; 2/2, Innocente; 1+min; Diff-V/md, P/m.

For: soprano; mezzo-soprano

Mood: humorous; child-like

Voice: stepwise and easy skips; complex and irregular rhythms

Piano: 3–4-voice chordal texture; articulations and phrasing important; quarter-note motion; no vocal line doubling

Diff: diction; irregular rhythms; ensemble

Uses: good humorous song; encore

1739. **JAMES JOYCE SONGS,** Opus 74. Elkan-Vogel, 1959. Tonal (but highly chromatic); c'–f♯"; Tess-M; regular and irregular meters; moderately slow tempos; 6+min; Diff-V/m-md, P/m-md.

For: mezzo-soprano for set; other voices can do single songs

Mood: lyrical; somber; restless

Voice: stepwise and easy skips; some chromaticism; some syncopation; speech rhythms; irregular rhythms; accidentals

Piano: chordal textures; somewhat irregular rhythmically; many accidentals; chromatic; some vocal line doubling

Diff: irregular rhythms; some pitches

Uses: good set for a mezzo-soprano; not for beginners

a. *Unquiet Heart,* No.1. [16]. B-centered; d♯'–f♯"; Tess-mH; 4/4, 5/4, Doloroso; 3min.

b. *Brigid's Song,* No.2. B♭-centered; c'–d"; Tess-mL; 5/4, Sostenuto; 1+min.

c. *Noise of Waters,* No.3. B-centered; c♯'–e"; Tess-M; 4/4, Andante; 2min. [Rec: D#54]

1740. **A NET OF FIREFLIES.** Song Cycle for Voice and Piano, Op. 115 (various Japanese Haiku poets; trans. H. Steward). Elkan-Vogel, 1972. Commissioned by Carolyn Reyer. No key sigs. (mildly dissonant and impressionistic); c'–g"; Tess-M; regular meters; varied tempos; 19min; Diff-V/m, P/m.

For: mezzo-soprano; soprano

Mood: lyrical; short, fleeting images and impressions of Haiku poetry; a succession of images in the course of a day

Voice: short phrases; conjunct and disjunct; delicate; mostly syllabic

Piano: spare texture; piano illustrates text; much pedaling gives haze of sound; somewhat pointillistic in places

Diff: pitch perception (not unduly difficult, but perfect pitch would simplify matters); creating proper moods somewhat difficult

Uses: nice songs; good for teaching soft singing and clear diction

a. *Waking at an Inn* (Sôseki). c'–e"; 4/8, Piacevole; 1p.

b. *The Pavilion on the Lake* (Rimpû). e♭'–e♭"; 3/4, Tranquillo; 1p.

c. *With Sharpened Senses* (Bashô). d'–e"; 4/4, Sonoro; 1p.

d. *Four Magpies* (Hô-ô). d'–g"; 4/4, Decisivo; 1p.

e. *A Whiteness* (Shikô). e'–e"; 2/4, Amabile; 1p.

f. *Noon* (Buson). c'–d"; 2/4, Semplice mesto; 1p.

g. *The Carp* (Raizan). c'–b♭"; 4/4, A bene placido; 1p.

h. *The Faun* (Issa). e'–e"; 9/8, Grazioso; 1+p.

i. *Hypothesis* (Zen Paradox). c♯'–e♭"; 4/4, Affabile;

13meas.

j. *Summer Grasses* (Bashô). d'–f"; 4/4, Declamando; 1p.

k. *Paper Wings* (Hô-ô). c'–e♭"; 4/4, Affettuoso; 1p.

l. *Its Netted Trail* (Hô-ô). d♯'–e♯"; 3/4, Sereno; 1p.

m. *Beneath the Net* (Buson-Sôgyo). d♯'–e"; 2/4, Con agilità; 2pp.

n. *Firefly* (Bashô). e'–e"; 2/4, Gioviale; 1p.

o. *After the Death of Her Small Son* (Chiyo). c♯'–d"; 3/4, Tristamente; 1+pp.

p. *Dewdrop* (Issa). e'–e"; 4/4, Dolce espressivo; 8meas.

q. *The Black Cat's Face* (Hô-ô). c♯'–c"; 3/4, Senza rigore di tempo; 1p.

1741. TWO CHINESE SONGS, Op. 29 (trans. Arthur Waley). Elkan-Vogel, 1979. Modal; a♭–d"; Tess-L; traditional meters; slow-fast; 2pp; Diff-V/e, P/e.

For: bass; bass-baritone
Mood: descriptive; wry; miniatures
Voice: conjunct; accidentals; speech-like rhythms; three short melismas; uncomplicated
Piano: single-voice piano part, in bass clef in (a.) and treble in (b.); (a.), a reiterated pedal tone that resolves at the end; (b.), some rhythmic complexities with 16th notes, syncopation, and dotted rhythms; staccato
Diff: these miniatures are easy but singer must be secure and independent; piano provides little help
Uses: as a change of pace and texture

a. *All Alone* (traditional). Dorian mode; a♭–b♭'; 5/4, 4/4, Slowly, but freely; 45sec.

b. *These Days* (Wang Chi). Dorian mode; c'–d"; 2/4, Spirited; 35sec.

PETER, JOHANN FRIEDRICH (See Special Section)

PFAUTSCH, LLOYD
(b. Washington, MO, 1921)

1742. BIRTH WISHES FOR THE CHRIST CHILD (Byron Herbert Reece). [12]. Emin-Gmaj; b–d"; Tess-L; Changing meters (regular and irregular), Calmly, with worshipful tenderness (♩ = 108); 4pp.; Diff-V/me, P/e.

For: any medium or low voice
Mood: worshipful; sheltering the Christ-child
Voice: mostly conjunct; intervals outlining triads; modal; *a cappella* phrases
Piano: chordal and simple
Diff: possibly changing meters; lowered 7th step of scale; pitch in *a cappella* phrases
Uses: for a beginning student; possible church use

1743. I-THOU SONGS (Emily Dickinson). [153]; 1st©1991. Two short songs, without individual titles; fluctuating tonal centers; b–e"; Tess-mL; 6pp; Diff-V/m, P/me.
For: mezzo-soprano; alto
Mood: philosophical reflections on death
Voice: mostly conjunct and flowing; ascending and descending

4ths; one M7th; (b.) characterized by 8ve leaps upward
Piano: broken chords in l.h. with melody (mostly in P5ths) in r.h. in (a.); sustained tone clusters, with simple chordal middle section, in (b.); numerous accidentals in both
Diff: some pitches; 8ve leaps
Uses: (b.) could be a useful exercise in 8ve leaps and associated vocal registration problems

a. A-centered; c–e♭"; 4/4, Smoothly flowing (♩ = c.50); 3pp.

b. B-centered; b–e"; Quasi recitative; 3pp.

1744. LUTE BOOK LULLABY (William Ballet). [17]. H & L keys: Emin & Dmin; d'–e" & c'–d"; Tess-mL; 4/4, With quiet simplicity; 2pp; Diff-V/me, P/me.
For: all voices
Mood: lyrical; simple; Virgin's cradle song
Voice: diatonic; small intervals
Piano: chordal; organ-like; 3-voice texture
Uses: good student song for Christmas

1745. THREE CHILD SONGS (Rabindranath Tagore). [153]; 1st©1991. Fluctuating tonal centers; d♭'–a♭"; Tess-mH; regular meters with a few changes; 9pp; Diff-V/m, P/m.
For: soprano
Mood: lyrical and tender in (a.) & (b.); humorous in (c.)
Voice: mostly conjunct; only a few intervals in (a.) & (b.); legato phrases; somewhat disjunct in (c.); short phrases separated by rests
Piano: flowing counterpoint in almost continuous 8ths in (a.), essentially in two voices and entirely in the treble clef; chordal in (b.); chordal with afterbeats in (c.)
Diff: modal scales, shifting tonal centers may be hard to hear; rhythms in (c.)
Uses: could be good for certain students

a. *The Gift.* E♭-centered; d♭'–a♭"; 4/4, 3/2, Adagio sereno e ben sentito (♩ = c.60–66); 3pp.

b. *My Song.* A-centered; e'–g♯"; 4/4, 2/4, Lento riposato (♩ = 66); 2pp.

c. *Superior.* C- & A♭-centered; d'–g"; 3/4, Allegro portato (♩ = c.116); 4pp.

1746. THE VIRGIN'S SLUMBER SONG (Francis Carlin). [153]; 1st©1991. Dmin; c'–c"; Tess-L; 4/4, 3/4, Very slow and tranquil (♩ = 66); 2pp; Diff-V/me, P/e.
For: alto; baritone; bass
Mood: lullaby
Voice: smooth legato phrases; almost entirely conjunct
Piano: chordal; occasional bits of melodic line
Diff: lowered 7th may be hard to hear against chords
Uses: good song for young singers; work on "oo" vowel

PIERCE, ALEXANDRA
(b. Philadelphia, PA, 1934)

1747. FOUR SONGS ON POEMS OF JAMES JOYCE. Center of Balance, 1981–1983. cmp1981–1983. Separate entries below.

A. **ALL DAY I HEAR THE NOISE OF WATERS.** C♯-centered; (G♯)A–e'(d" falsetto); Tess-M; 6/8, Tempo rubato (♩=ca.48); 3+min; Diff-V/d, P/m.
For: bass-baritone; baritone
Mood: lyrical and philosophical; nature imagery
Voice: stepwise; leaps up to 8ve; chromatic; duplet and triplet patterns; calls for high-lying falsetto singing; lyrical, flowing; syllabic; 2-note slurs; short melismas on "ah"
Piano: chordal–block and broken; chromatic; numerous pedal markings; incidental doubling of vocal line
Diff: good sense of pitch needed; easy and high falsetto needed to perform song as composer intends
Uses: excellent recital material

B. **ECCE PUER.** X; B♭–f♯'; Tess-mH; 4/4, 5/4, Con moto (♩=ca.80); 8min; Diff-V/d, P/m.
For: baritone
Mood: lyrical and philosophical
Voice: stepwise; leaps up to 8ve; chromatic; triplets; short phrases separated by rests; syllabic; some 2-note slurs; dramatic
Piano: chordal–block, broken, and rolled; lengthy prelude with melodic material; long postlude; numerous pedal markings and articulations; incidental doubling of vocal line
Diff: good sense of pitch needed; high-tessitura phrases
Uses: excellent recital material

C. **BAHNHOFSTRASSE.** X; A–g'; 3/4, Moderato; 3+min; Diff-V/d, P/md.
For: baritone
Mood: lyrical and philosophical
Voice: stepwise; skips up to 7th; chromatic; syllabic; a few 2-note slurs; phrases usually end in a long, sustained tone; lyrical and flowing; English text
Piano: chordal–block and broken; chromatic; triplets, quintuplets, and sextuplets; brief melodic passages in 8ves, r.h., l.h., or both; numerous pedal markings; prelude, three interludes (one quite long), and postlude; incidental doubling of vocal line
Diff: good sense of pitch needed; high tessitura
Uses: excellent recital material

D. **FLOOD.** B♭-centered; B♭–e♭'; Tess-M; 4/4, 5/4, ♩=ca.88; 3+min; Diff-V/d, P/m.
For: baritone
Mood: lyrical and philosophical; nature imagery
Voice: stepwise; skips up to 7ths; chromatic; syllabic; a few 2-note slurs; lyrical and flowing
Piano: primarily chordal–block and rolled; melodic passages, often in 8ves; chromatic; numerous pedal markings; does not double vocal line
Diff: good sense of pitch needed
Uses: excellent recital material

1748. **GREEN GROW THE RASHES** (Robert Burns). Center of Balance, 1986. cmp1986. M & L keys: A-centered & G-centered; a♯–g♭" & g♯–f"; Tess-M; 4/4, ♩=126; 6+min; Diff-V/d, P/d.
For: baritone; bass-baritone
Mood: lyrical; in praise of the "lasses"; like a folksong
Voice: stepwise; skips up to 8ve; chromatic; strophic with

modification; triplets; prominent use of tritone; lyrical and flowing; chiefly syllabic; occasional 2-note slurs
Piano: much use of open-5th bagpipe drone and Scotch snap; r.h. countermelody to vocal line; chromatic; incidental doubling of vocal line
Diff: accuracy of pitch needed; good vocal actor needed to carry strophic setting with text repetitions
Uses: possible recital material

1749. **SPRING AND FALL** (Gerard Manley Hopkins). Center of Balance, 1985. cmp1985. D-centered; a–e"; Tess-M; 5/4 with changes, ♩=ca.84; 5+min; Diff-V/d, P/m.
For: contralto; mezzo-soprano; baritone
Mood: lyrical and philosophical; seasons compared to life
Voice: chiefly stepwise; small skips; leaps of 7th, 8ve, & 9th; chromatic; syncopation; triplets; lyrical flowing phrases separated by rests; syllabic; occasional 2–3-note slurs
Piano: chordal and linear; 4–5-voice texture; melodic material in prelude and interludes; numerous pedal markings; does not double vocal line
Diff: good sense of pitch needed; frequent meter changes, often to irregular meters
Uses: excellent recital material

PINKHAM, DANIEL
(b. Lynn, MA, 1923)

1750. **ELEGY** (Robert Hillyer). E. C. Schirmer, 1964. "To Nell Tangeman." Emaj-min; b–e"; Tess-M; 4/4, Andante; 2pp; Diff-V/me, P/e.
For: baritone; mezzo-soprano; contralto; bass
Mood: lyrical; subdued
Voice: stepwise and easy skips; easy rhythms; M & m3rd scale degree
Piano: thin chordal texture; easy rhythms; some counter-melody; does not double vocal line
Uses: effective elegy; gentle; interior of a group

1751. **THE FAUCON** (anon.). R. D. Row, 1949. Modal, E♭-centered; e♭'–a♭"; Tess-mH; 6/8, Andante con moto, ma flessible; 3pp (with repeat); Diff-V/md, P/md.
For: soprano; tenor
Mood: archaic religious text (also known as the "Corpus Christi Carol")
Voice: rather free and florid; 16th-note movement; 2-note slurs; small melismas
Piano: chordal; some counterpoint; flowing, melismatic, independent melody in solo passages
Diff: vocal flexibility and agility; understanding of pronunciations and meanings of words
Uses: effective recital material; probably not for church use

1752. **THE HOUR GLASS** (Ben Jonson). E. C. Schirmer, 1964. Fmin; c'–g"; Tess-M; 3/4, 2/4, 4/4, 5/4, Andante, mesto; 2pp; Diff-V/m, P/e.
For: soprano; tenor
Mood: lyrical; philosophical
Voice: disjunct line interspersed with conjunct passages; changing meters
Piano: linear; 2–4 voices; some chordal passages; accidentals

Diff: legato wide intervals; some pitches difficult
Uses: good lyric song with introspective, philosophical flavor
Rec: D#274

1753. LETTERS FROM SAINT PAUL. E. C. Schirmer, 1971. Tonal; cb'–a"; Tess-M-mH; mostly changing meters; varied tempos; 12pp; Diff-V/d, P/m.
For: tenor best; soprano possible
Mood: theme: exhortation to Christians to follow the way of Christ
Voice: disjunct; complex speech-like rhythms; accomp. helps with pitches
Piano: for organ or piano; organ perhaps better because of widely-spaced sustained chords; many accidentals and subdivisions of the beat
Diff: for mature singer and musician with expressive skills
Uses: good for church recital or as service music in sophisticated musical situations

   a. *(Hebrews 12:1–2).* f♯'–ab"; changing meters, Con moto, ma flessibile; 1+min.
   b. *(Romans 8:35, 37, 38, 39).* c♯'–ab"; 4/4 with changes, Sostenuto; 2min.
   c. *(Colossians 3:16).* c'–g"; 3/4, 4/4, Andante sereno; 45sec.
   d. *(I Thessalonians 5:1–6).* db'–a"; changing meters, Quasi recitativo ma con moto; 2min.
   e. *(Philippians 4:4–7).* c'–g"; changing meters, Animato; 1min.
   f. *(Romans 12:11–12).* cb'–a"; changing meters, Andante flessibile; 1+min.

1754. MUSIC, THOU SOUL OF HEAVEN (anon., 17th century). E. C. Schirmer, 1978. cmp1953; rev.1977. "To Ned Rorem." Gmin; c'–g"; Tess-M-mH; 4/4, 3/4, 2/4, Andante; 2pp; Diff-V/m, P/me.
For: soprano; mezzo-soprano; possibly tenor
Mood: invocation to music
Voice: somewhat declamatory; skips mostly small with some unexpected intervals; irregular phrase lengths
Piano: chordal texture; many accidentals; many dynamic markings; supportive of voice
Diff: some long phrases; needs good dynamic control; tenor might wish to transpose up, as the c' is *ff*
Uses: nice song to open recital or group of songs about music
Rec: D#274

1755. MUSIC IN THE MANGER for Medium Voice and Piano (or Harpsichord) (Norma Farber). Ione Press, 1987 (E. C. Schirmer). cmp1981. X; a–e"; Tess-M, cs; regular meters; moderate tempos; 10min; Diff-V/m-md, P/m.
For: baritone; mezzo-soprano
Mood: invocation of music; questioning of Mary; praises of birds at the manger
Voice: syllabic; partly word stress, partly melodic rhythms; some phrases angular
Piano: built on repeated patterns; somewhat dissonant; chordal; broken-chord and arpeggiated figures
Diff: some pitches; texts have unusual imagery; clear diction necessary
Uses: an interesting cycle of songs for many situations; especially useful at Christmas

   a. *What's That Music in the Manger?* X; a–e"; Tess-M; 4/4, 12/8, Allegro ♩ = 120–132; 4+pp.
   b. *Mary, Did You Falter?* X; bb–e"; Tess-M; 2/2, 3/4, 3/2, ♩ = 46; 4+pp.
   c. *A Summoning Hosanna!* X; a–e"; Tess-cs; 4/4, 2/4, 3/8, 3/4, ♩ = 124; 10pp.

1756. NOW THE TRUMPET SUMMONS US AGAIN (from the *Inaugural Address* of John F. Kennedy). C. F. Peters, 1965. X, C-centered; d'–a"; Tess-covers range; 4/4, Lento flessibile; 2+min; Diff-V/d, P/md.
For: dramatic tenor; dramatic soprano
Mood: dramatic declamation
Voice: wide leaps; syncopation; duplets and triplets; speech rhythms
Piano: 1-minute prelude; many accidentals; wide reaches; linear-chordal combination; various rhythmic subdivisions; many dynamic markings; little doubling of vocal line
Diff: wide leaps; dramatic high tones; tempo fluctuations
Uses: effective dramatic song

1757. A PARTRIDGE IN A PEAR TREE (Old English). R. D. Row, 1948. X; d'–bb"; Tess-mH; 4/4, 6/8, 5/8, Allegro leggiero e scherzando; 1min; Diff-V/m, P/m.
For: soprano (lyric or coloratura)
Mood: sprightly; exuberant
Voice: stepwise; chord-member skips; syncopation; 2-note slurs; two longer melismas; two portamentos
Piano: chordal; articulation contrasts important; many 7ths, 9ths, & 2nds; moves around keyboard; does not double vocal line
Diff: voice begins alone (one meas.); bb" has fermata followed by downward portamento; sustained g" approached by upward glissando
Uses: useful song; group ender
Rec: D#274

1758. SING AGREEABLY OF LOVE (W. H. Auden). R. D. Row, 1949. Amin; e'–e"; Tess-M; 6/8, In the manner of a folk-song; 2min; Diff-V/m, P/me.
For: baritone; tenor
Mood: lighthearted love song
Voice: many accidentals; dotted rhythms; modal cadences
Piano: thin texture; afterbeat pattern; rolled chords; imitates strummed instruments; some cross-hands; interesting harmonic turns in refrain
Uses: good recital song in a group about love

1759. SLOW, SLOW, FRESH FOUNT (Ben Jonson). C. F. Peters, 1961. Bb-centered; f♯'–gb"; Tess-mH; changing meters (4/4 predominates), Andantino; 1+min; Diff-V/m, P/m.
For: tenor; soprano
Mood: lyrical; woeful; "pathetic fallacy"
Voice: short, falling phrases; duplets and triplets; syncopation; many accidentals; 2 unaccomp. meas.
Piano: block chordal texture; many accidentals; some doubling of vocal line
Diff: ensemble; rhythmic complexities

Uses: nice slow lyric song
Rec: D#s 59, 274

1760. STARS, I HAVE SEEN THEM FALL (A. E. Housman). Ione, 1983. cmp1946; rev.1973. F-centered; d'–f"; Tess-M; 3/4, 2/4, 4/4, Flexible (♩ = 48); 2pp; Diff-V/m, P/e.
For: any medium voice
Mood: philosophical; nature imagery
Voice: stepwise; skips outlining chords; short phrases; somewhat chromatic
Piano: chordal; 4–5-voice texture; chromatic
Uses: fine song for recital

1761. THREE ALLELUIAS for High Voice and Piano. Ione Press Reprint, 1988 (ECS Publishing). X; b–b"; Tess-cs, mH, H; changing meters; varied tempos (♩ = 58–112); 7pp; Diff-V/m-d, P/me-md.
For: soprano
Mood: exuberant; serene; jubilant
Voice: syllabic and melismatic; disjunct and repeated-note phrases; unusually wide leaps; (c.) in 7/4
Piano: chordal; irregular rhythmic patterns; many accidentals
Diff: some pitches; wide intervals; some rhythms
Uses: interesting set or use separately; advanced undergraduate or graduate
Rec: D#274

  a. *An Exuberant Alleluia.* X; c♯'–a"; Tess-cs; 4/4, 2/4, 3/8, ♩ = 112; 2pp.
  b. *A Serene Alleluia.* X-Dmaj; d'–g"; Tess-cs; 4/4, ♩ = 58; 1p.
  c. *A Jubilant Alleluia.* X; b–b"; Tess-mH-H; 7/8, 4/4, ♩ = 104; 4pp.

1762. THREE SONGS FROM ECCLESIASTES. For High Voice with Piano Accompaniment. E. C. Schirmer, 1963. "Commissioned by Phyllis Curtin." No key sigs. (somewhat dissonant but tonal); b♭–a"; Tess-M; changing meters; varied tempos; 11pp; Diff-V/m, P/m.
For: soprano; tenor
Mood: lyrical; philosophical
Voice: many leaps in (a.); skips in (b.); conjunct in (c.); some irregular rhythms; mostly syllabic
Piano: largely chordal with some punctuating linear figures; accidentals
Diff: some pitches hard to hear at first
Uses: mildly dissonant; recital use

  a. *Vanity of Vanities.* b♭–a"; 4/4 with many changes, Maestoso–Allegro ritmico, e brillante; 4pp.
  b. *Go Thy Way, Eat Thy Bread with Joy.* e'–g"; 4/4, 6/4, 3/4, Lento; 1p.
  c. *To Every Thing There Is a Season.* Ends Dmaj; d'–g"; 3/4 with changes, Allegro; 6pp.

1763. TRANSITIONS. For Medium Voice and Piano (Howard Holtzman). Cycle. E. C. Schirmer Facsimile Series, 1980; version for med. voice & piano completed 1979 (1st version for med. voice & bassoon). Tonal; a–f♯"; Tess-M; traditional meters with changes; flowing rhythms; varied tempos; 23pp; Diff-V/d, P/md-d.
For: mezzo-soprano seems best because of sonority; baritone possible
Mood: philosophical; transitions from dark to light, night to day, the passage of time
Voice: more conjunct than disjunct; contains leaps of 6th, 7th, dim.8ve, 9th, etc.; much chromaticism; rhythms seem less problematic than pitches; meter changes; many dynamic markings; a few melismas; several songs have melodic repetitions
Piano: countermelodies in bass (former bassoon part); 2–3-voice texture; linear; much doubling of vocal line by r.h.; many accidentals
Diff: dramatic dynamics in places; pitches
Uses: as a set—each song leads musically into the next

  a. *Grey.* E♭ & E-centered; c'–f♯"; 3/4, ♩ = 126; 3pp.
  b. *I Like the Light Diffused.* C-centered; a–f♯"; changing meters, ♩. = 60–72; 3pp.
  c. *Lullaby for a Shrouded Figure.* C- & F-centered; b–e"; 4/4 with changes, ♩ = 60; 3+pp.
  d. *Home Movies.* X; b–f"; 4/4 with changes, ♩ = 96; 3+pp.
  e. *Aubade.* B-centered; b–e"; changing meters, no tempo indication; 4pp.
  f. *Near This Stone.* B-centered; c♯'–d"; changing meters, ♩ = 69; 1p.
  g. *So, One by One.* E-centered; b–f"; changing meters, ♩. = 56; 4pp.

PLESKOW, RAOUL

[See Appendix for songs with Latin texts]

PORTER, QUINCY
(b. New Haven, CT, 1897; d. Bethany, CT, 1966)

1764. MUSIC, WHEN SOFT VOICES DIE (Percy Bysshe Shelley). Mercury, 1947. Unsettled; d'–c"; Tess-M; 4/4, ♩ = ca.60; 1+min; Diff-V/m, P/m.
For: bass; baritone; contralto; mezzo-soprano
Mood: lyrical; subdued
Voice: conjunct; easy rhythms
Piano: chordal; wide reaches; impressionistic; sophisticated pedaling; no doubling of vocal line
Diff: pitches
Uses: good subdued song for recital

1765. THREE ELIZABETHAN SONGS. Yale Univ. Press, 1961. cmp1959. "For the Elizabethan Club of Yale University." Composed for a masque; probably not all for one voice; separate entries below.

A. THE GOD OF LOVE (popular ballad of Shakespeare's time). Amin; d'–g"; Tess-M; 6/8, Moderato; 6min; Diff-V/m, P/md.
For: tenor; soprano
Mood: ballad style
Voice: stepwise; easy skips; repetitious; long phrases
Piano: different figure for each of 5 strophes; much doubling

of vocal line; some 16th-note scales

Diff: making all five strophes interesting

B. **WHEN I WAS FAIR AND YOUNG** (probably by Queen Elizabeth I). Emaj; d♯'–f♯"; Tess-mH; 2/4, Allegro; 2+min; Diff-V/md, P/md.

For: soprano
Mood: sprightly; repents of disdainfulness
Voice: small skips; much sequence; fragmented; staccato; legato; syncopation
Piano: 2–4-voice linear texture; articulations very important; some doubling of vocal line
Diff: fragmentary vocal line; ensemble; refrain of each strophe is high
Uses: good song

C. **SPRING** ("When daisies pied.") (William Shakespeare). Fmaj-Dmin; d'–f"; Tess-M; 2/4, Allegro; 2+min; Diff-V/m, P/md.

For: tenor; soprano; mezzo-soprano
Mood: humorous; bright; cheerful
Voice: stepwise; small skips; some syncopation
Piano: 2–4-voice linear texture; some chords; articulations important; does not double vocal line
Diff: ensemble; piano has irregular rhythms
Uses: effective setting

POWELL, JOHN
(b. Richmond, VA, 1882; d. Charlottesville, VA, 1963)

1766. **HEARTSEASE**, Op. 8, No. 2 (Lelia C. Stiles). [48]; 1st©1919. H & L keys: D♭maj & B♭maj; d♭'–g" & b♭–e"; Tess-mL; 3/4, Andante; 5pp; Diff-V/m, P/d.

For: all voices
Mood: philosophical; nature imagery
Voice: broad, flowing, lyrical phrases
Piano: broken- and arpeggiated-chord figurations; independent melody in prelude, interlude, and postlude
Uses: period piece

POWELL, MEL
(b. New York, NY, 1923; d. Sherman Oaks, CA, 1998)

1767. **HAIKU SETTINGS** (Japanese poems from 17th to 19th centuries; trans. Harold G. Henderson). G. Schirmer, 1961. X; b♭–e" (g♯" in falsetto); Tess-M-mH; changing meters; 17pp; Diff-V/dd, P/dd.

For: baritone probably best; mezzo-soprano
Mood: fleeting impressions typical of Haiku poetry
Voice: highly complex in every way; fragmented; angular
Piano: highly complex; 3-stave notation; many accidentals; several dynamic markings in each meas.; many articulations; covers keyboard; demands great facility; does not double vocal line
Diff: composer specifies light vocal quality (*voce di testa*)–"pure" sound quality, not dramatic; falsetto in spots; some speaking on pitch at four different levels; some whispering; has its own system of note value specifications; ensemble is very difficult (much is approximate); many directions given by composer;

singer must be secure vocalist and musician, experienced in this idiom

Uses: effective for performers who can handle it; set has four movements: *I. three haiku. II. two haiku. III. four haiku. IV. two haiku*
Rec: D#275

PRESSER, WILLIAM
(b. Saginaw, MI, 1916)

1768. **EAGER WEAPER** (anon.). [154]. cmp1945. Cmaj; (D)F♯–e'(g'); Tess-M; 4/4, ♩ = 116; 1+min; Diff-V/d, P/md.

For: bass; bass-baritone
Mood: humorous; based on version of a familiar nursery rhyme
Voice: stepwise; skips along chord lines; very rapid 16th-note passages, both syllabic and melismatic; humorous quasi-cadenza with sustained e' at end; final note shouted
Piano: chordal; rapid 16th-note scale passages in prelude, interlude, and postlude; afterbeats; does not double vocal line
Diff: coloratura passages for voice; extremes of range if low and high options are taken
Uses: good humorous song; group or program ender; encore

1769. **MADRIGAL** (anon.). [154]. cmp1969. Dmaj; G–e♭'; Tess-M; 3/4, ♩ = 92; 2min; Diff-V/m, P/m.

For: bass; bass-baritone
Mood: descriptive of one's beloved with humorous twist at end
Voice: stepwise; skips along chord lines; syllabic except for 1-meas.–16th-note melisma
Piano: chordal-linear combination; suggests Renaissance 2-voice polyphony at beginning; somewhat chromatic; does not double vocal line
Diff: sustained e♭' and d' on "ih" *f*
Uses: good for recital; unexpected humor; could be paired with "The Shoe Tying" (see below)

1770. **REQUIEM** (Robert Louis Stevenson). [154]. cmp1944. "For Louis Nicholas." Modal, C-centered; B♭–e♭'; Tess-mH; 4/4, 5/4, ♩ = 60; 2min; Diff-V/m, P/me.

For: bass specified; bass-baritone; baritone
Mood: sadly philosophical
Voice: stepwise; skips along chord lines; syllabic; 3-note slurs; arching phrases; 14-beat final note
Piano: 2–3-voice counterpoint; continuously moving 8ths; does not double vocal line
Diff: some series of pitches may be hard to hear because of modality; sustained final note (c)
Uses: very nice alternative to the familiar setting by S. Homer

1771. **THE SHOE TYING** (Robert Herrick). [154]. cmp1969. Modal, D-centered; F–d'; Tess-M; 3/4, ♩ = 60; 1+min; Diff-V/m, P/me.

For: bass; bass-baritone
Mood: humorously descriptive
Voice: stepwise; 8ve leaps at phrase beginnings; mostly short phrases; 6-meas. sustained final note (a)

Piano: chordal; partially r.h. melody with l.h. accomp.; syncopation
Diff: long tone at end
Uses: good for student needing short phrases; could be paired with "Madrigal" (see above)

1772. THREE EPITAPHS (Robert Herrick). Tenuto, 1964. cmp1947. Traditional keys; d'–g"; Tess-M; 4/4, med. and slow tempos; 4pp; Diff-V/me, P/me.
For: tenor; soprano
Mood: lyric; quiet; subdued
Voice: mostly stepwise; small skips, up to 6th; uncomplicated rhythms; some dotted rhythms and paired 8ths; mostly syllabic; some 2–3- note slurs
Piano: block- and broken-chord and scalar patterning; a few accidentals; movement mostly in 8ths in (a.) & (b.); (c.), mostly block chords in quarter notes; some imitation; some doubling of vocal line
Diff: controlling dynamics (mostly soft)
Uses: nice set when quiet songs are wanted

   a. *Upon a Maid.* E♭maj; e♭'–g"; 4/4, Allegretto (♩ = 72); 1+pp.
   b. *Upon a Child That Died.* Emin; d'–e"; 4/4, Allegretto (♩ = 63); 1+pp.
   c. *An Epitaph upon a Virgin.* Emin; e'–e"; 4/4, Adagio (♩ = 48); 1p.

1773. TO CELIA (Ben Jonson). [154]. cmp1971. Cmaj; c–c'; Tess-M; 6/4, ♩ = 80; 3min; Diff-V/e, P/e.
For: bass; bass-baritone; baritone
Mood: philosophical love song; setting of the words and melody of "Drink to me only with thine eyes"
Voice: stepwise; easy skips; syllabic; 2-note slurs
Piano: chordal; single line of l.h. like a basso continuo; supports but does not double vocal line
Uses: good for young student

1774. TO DAISIES (Robert Herrick). [154]. cmp1969. Cmaj; G–c'; Tess-mL; 4/4, ♩ = 52; 2+min; Diff-V/m, P/e.
For: bass
Mood: philosophical; hoping the beloved will not die too soon
Voice: stepwise; easy skips; a few large leaps; syllabic; sustained G (decresc.) at end
Piano: chordal; somewhat chromatic; supports but does not double vocal line
Diff: final sustained G
Uses: recital possibilities

1775. TO ELECTRA (Robert Herrick). [154]. cmp1969. Modal, C-centered; G–e♭'; Tess-M; 2/2, ♩ = 152; 2min; Diff-V/m, P/me.
For: bass; bass-baritone
Mood: philosophical love song
Voice: stepwise; easy skips; syllabic; one long melisma
Piano: 2–3-voice counterpoint; suggests the Renaissance style; much of song requires soft playing; does not double vocal line
Diff: control of soft dynamics
Uses: recital possibilities

PREVIN, ANDRE [Andreas Ludwig Priwin]
(b. Berlin, Germany, 1929)

1776. FIVE SONGS. For Mezzo-Soprano and Piano (Philip Larkin). Hansen, 1978. "To Dame Janet Baker." X; c'–g♯"; Tess-M; traditional meters with changes; varied tempos; 16pp; Diff-V/md-d, P/d.
For: mezzo-soprano; some sopranos
Mood: loneliness; isolation; new beginnings
Voice: stepwise motion and small skips predominate; some long-ranged phrases (e'–f♯", d'–g♯", f♯'–g"); many accidentals; some triplets; syncopation; (b.) & (d.), speech-like rhythms; 2-note slurs, 4–5-note melismas
Piano: bitonal effects; block- and broken- chord patterns; some afterbeat style (c., a waltz with "rinky-tink" accomp. adding atmosphere to text); many accidentals; some tone clusters; some passages in parallel structures (3rds, 6ths, 6/4 chords, and broken 8ves); large reach helpful; incidental doubling of vocal line
Diff: some pitches and rhythms (e.g., end of d.); passages which outline 9th chord (e.)
Uses: nice recital group

   a. *Morning Has Spread Again.* X; d'–f♯"; 3/4 with changes, (♩ = ca.112); 2+min.
   b. *Home Is So Sad.* X; d'–f"; 3/4 with changes, Slowly (♩ = ca.48); 2+min.
   c. *Friday Night in the Royal Station Hotel.* C-centered; c'–e"; 3/4 with changes, ♩ = 60; 4+min.
   d. *Talking in Bed.* X; d'–g♯"; 3/4 with changes, ♩ = ca.72; 2+min.
   e. *The Trees.* X; d'–g"; 3/4 with changes, ♩ = 92; 1+min.

PRICE, FLORENCE B.
(b. Little Rock, AR, 1888; d. Chicago, IL, 1953)

1777. MY DREAM (Langston Hughes.) [10]. cmp1935. Dmaj; a'–g"; Tess-M; 6/8, 2/4, Allegretto (♩. = 63, ♩ = 108); 5pp; Diff-V/d, P/dd.
For: mezzo-soprano; baritone (mature voices)
Mood: dramatic statement about being African-American
Voice: dramatic and wide-ranging; strong high and low tones needed; several large leaps; some accidentals
Piano: chordal; much broken-chord and 16th-note figuration; numerous accidentals; vocal line doubling incidental
Diff: pitches; range
Uses: very effective song for the right singer

1778. NIGHT (Louise C. Wallace). [6, 10, 47]; 1st©1946. Cmaj; c'–f"; Tess-M; 4/4, Andante; 2pp; Diff-V/m, P/m.
For: soprano; mezzo-soprano; tenor
Mood: lyrical; descriptive; atmospheric
Voice: many skips; some dotted rhythms; accidentals
Piano: broken-chord pattern, both hands; numerous accidentals; does not double vocal line
Diff: long phrases
Uses: useful short mood song; romantic
Rec: D#276

1779. OUT OF THE SOUTH BLEW A WIND (Fannie Carter Woods). [47]. E♭maj; c'–g"; Tess-M; 6/8, Allegretto; 3pp; Diff-V/me, P/me.

For: tenor; soprano
Mood: lyrical; descriptive
Voice: spun-out, long phrases; easy skips; good singing lines
Piano: broken chords and afterbeat pattern; some rapid soft runs imitating wind; some doubling of vocal line
Diff: sustained tones at end (f" and e♭")
Uses: good for teaching floating tones

1780. SONG TO THE DARK VIRGIN (Langston Hughes). [6, 10]; 1st©1977. Fmin-A♭maj; b♭–e♭"; Tess-mL; 4/4, Andante con moto; 4pp; Diff-V/me, P/md.

For: mezzo-soprano; contralto
Mood: lyrical; sensuous; not particularly prayer-like
Voice: largely diatonic; some triplets; climactic phrase low in pitch; lyrical and flowing
Piano: chordal texture–broken, arpeggiated, and rolled, moving in16ths
Diff: needs good low tones
Uses: recital possibilities
Rec: D#s 11, 276

1781. TWO SONGS. [11, Vol. 2]. Traditional keys; b–g♯"; Tess-M; regular meters; moderate tempos; 5pp; Diff-V/e-me, P/e-me.

For: any medium to medium-high voice
Mood: spiritual
Voice: traditional melodic form of the Black Spiritual; folk-like; dialect
Piano: chordal
Uses: in a group of spirituals

    a. *Feet O' Jesus* (Langston Hughes). Emaj; b–g♯"; Tess-M; 4/4, Tempo moderato; 3pp.
    b. *Trouble Done Come My Way* (Florence B. Price). "Dedicated to Marian Anderson." E♭maj; e♭'–e♭"; Tess-M; 2/2, Andantino; 2pp.

PRIMOSCH, JAMES
(b. Cleveland, OH, 1956)

1782. BEDTIME (Denise Levertov). [9]. Major tonalities; a♭–e"; Tess-mL; changing compound meters; ♪ = ca.88–92; 2+min; Diff-V/m, P/md.

For: mezzo-soprano
Mood: warm, drowsy, rich; lovers who are "singular and often lonely" by day become one at night
Voice: slow, sinuous, somewhat bluesy syncopated vocal line
Piano: entire part grows out of 7-note figure in introductory measures; creates aura of stillness and warmth
Diff: rhythms and length of phrases for singer; some 3-stave scoring for piano
Uses: slow, free song for a rich, smooth mezzo-soprano voice

PROTHEROE, DANIEL
(b. Ystradgynlais, South Wales, 1866; d. Chicago, IL, 1934)

1783. THREE LYRICS BY ROBERT BROWNING.

Gamble Hinged, 1910. Reprint: Classical Vocal Reprints. Traditional keys; f'–a"; Tess-mH-H; 3/4, 4/4; varied tempos; 10pp; Diff-V/m-md, P/m-md.

For: tenor; soprano
Mood: dramatic
Voice: stepwise; skips outlining chords; dotted rhythms, triplets; much repetition, sequence; many sustained high notes
Piano: block repeated chords; broken chords; rapid arpeggios; some doubling of vocal line; 4-meas. prelude to each song; chordal endings
Diff: sustained high notes; control of the many dynamics
Uses: as a period group, or excerpt any of the songs; (b.) & (c.) are good performance songs for young high voices without developed low notes; compare with Op. 44 of Amy Beach–same texts, different order

    a. *Ah, Love, But a Day.* G♯min-A♭maj; f'–a♭"; Tess-mH; 3/4, Andante con moto–4/4, Molto affectuoso; 4pp.
    b. *I Send My Heart Up to Thee.* Gmaj; f♯'–a♭"; Tess-H; 4/4, Moderato con moto; 3pp.
    c. *The Year's at the Spring.* Cmaj; g'–a"; Tess-H; 3/4, Allegro vivace; 3pp.

RAHN, FLICKA
(b. Corpus Christi, TX, 1944)

1784. TWO SONGS (Amy Lowell). [11, Vol. 10]. X; b♭–f"; Tess-M-mH; mixed meters; slow to moderate tempos; 5pp; Diff-V/m, P/m.

For: medium or high voice
Mood: love song; beach scene; atmospheric
Voice: many skips; many accidentals; mostly quarter and 8th notes; some long phrases; some melismas
Piano: atmosphere matches Oriental flavor of poems; some arpeggiation; some 3–4 part vertical chords; spare texture; countermelody; does not double vocal line
Diff: some intervals; skips up to m7th; some long-ranged phrases, up to a 10th; several melodic intervals of aug.2nd
Uses: nice songs for an imaginative student to sample mild modern compositional technique

    a. *Vicarious.* X; b♭–f"; Tess-M; 4/4, 2/4, 3/4, 6/4, ♩ = 69 Almost in Two; 3pp.
    b. *Shore Grass.* X; e'–f♭"; Tess-mH; 4/4, 5/4, 3/4, With repressed emotion (♩ = 96 approx.); 2pp.

RAKOWSKI, DAVID
(b. St. Albans, VT, 1958)

1785. SILENTLY, A WIND GOES OVER. Five "Wind" Songs for Soprano and Piano. C. F. Peters, 1997. cmp1994; rev1996. "For Susan Narucki." X; c'–b"; Tess-cs; regular and irregular changing meters; varied tempos; 13min; Diff-V/d-dd, P/d-dd.

For: soprano
Mood: various moods of, and thoughts evoked by, the wind
Voice: chromatic; long phrases; atonal; wide intervals;

numerous slow melismas; piano assists with some pitches; syncopation

Piano: dissonant throughout; little harmonic or metrical frame of reference; many different figurations; wide reach helpful; constant accidentals

Diff: pitch; rhythm; text; ensemble; perfect pitch desirable

Uses: representative of the atonal idiom

a. *Sudden Storm* (Joseph Duemer). X; e'–g♯"; Tess-mH; 4/4, 5/4, 7/4, Quasi recitativo: poco liberamente ♩ = 84–92; 4+pp.

b. *The Wind Shifts* (Wallace Stevens). X; c'–g♯"; Tess-cs; 4/4, 6/4, 3/4, 5/4, Allegro e capriccioso ♩ = 108–116; 10pp.

c. *Psalm of the Wind-Dweller* (April Bernard). X; d♭'–b"; Tess-cs; 6/8, 3/8, 9/8, Gently flowing, flessibile, ♩ = 56–66; 12pp.

d. *Windy Nights* (Robert Louis Stevenson). X; c'–a♭"; Tess-cs; 3/4, 4/4, 2/4, 6/4, Scherzando ♩ = 112–120; 7pp.

e. *For Wittgenstein* (Joseph Duemer). X; d♭'–a"; Tess-cs; 4/4, 5/4, 7/8, 6/4, etc., Liberamente, flessibile ♩ = 52–63; 7+pp.

RAPHLING, SAM
(b. Fort Worth, TX, 1910; d. New York, NY, 1988)

1786. AUTOGRAPH ALBUM. General, 1968. Amaj (with numerous changes); b♭–a♭"(f"); Tess-M; 3/4 with changes, Moderately slow (with many changes); 8pp.; Diff-V/md, P/d.

For: soprano; mezzo-soprano

Mood: humorous; made up of short quotations from a child's autograph book

Voice: short sections; somewhat disjunct; frequent key changes; short phrases

Piano: sectional; independent melodies; afterbeat pattern; broken chords; counterpoint

Diff: requires good vocal actor who can deal with this kind of text

Uses: clever informal addition to a program

1787. BEAT! BEAT! DRUMS! (Walt Whitman). General, 1968. X; c'–f"; Tess-M; 4/4, Lively ♩s; 5pp; Diff-V/dd, P/d.

For: dramatic baritone

Mood: dramatic; declamatory; call to war

Voice: many skips and leaps; accidentals; no tonal center; 2-note slurs; motor rhythms and speech rhythms; some poor mating of words and music

Piano: many rapid repeated chords in patterns; l.h. 8ves; motor rhythms; dissonant; many accidentals; awkward figurations

Diff: every area; vocal line is awkward and not idiomatic for the voice, esp. at the tempo indicated

Uses: possibly powerful song for advanced singer if taken at slower tempo than indicated

1788. CARL SANDBURG POEMS. Edition Musicus, 1952. pub. separately. Tonal (with some dissonance); b♭–g"; Tess-M-mL; regular and irregular changing meters; slow to moderate tempos; 16pp; Diff-V/e-m, P/e-m.

For: baritone best for set; other voices possible for separate songs

Mood: mostly lyrical; some declamatory; some narrative

Voice: predominantly skips; melody often outlines chords; speech rhythms; some awkward pitches, sustained phrases, and long tones; some declamatory singing

Piano: mostly chordal; some linear; some motivic construction; some patterning; generally does not double vocal line

Diff: some pitches; long phrases; declamatory style; relating the songs to each other as a set

Uses: interpretive challenge; voice needs many colors; not for beginners

a. *Gone.* Cmaj; c'–e"; Tess-M-mL; 4/4, 6/4, 5/4, Slowly; 3pp.

b. *Cool Tombs.* Emin; b–g"; Tess-M; 4/4, 3/4, 5/4, Slowly; 4pp.

c. *Fog.* c'–c"; Tess-mL; 3/4, Slowly, mysterious; 2pp.

d. *Mag.* b♭–d"; Tess-M-mL; 5/4, 6/4, 4/4, Moderately; 3pp.

e. *Washington Monument by Night.* Emin; c'–e"; Tess-M; 4/4, 6/4, 3/4, Moderately; 4pp.

1789. FUGUE ON "MONEY" (Richard Armour). [17]. H & L keys: X; e♭'–g" & c'–e"; Tess-M; 3/4, 5/4, 4/4, 2/4, Moderately lively–Bit slower doloroso–Faster; 3pp; Diff-V/d, P/d.

For: all voices except extremely low

Mood: humorously philosophical

Voice: fragmented; very short phrases; chromatic

Piano: contrapuntal; chromatic

Diff: pitches; meter changes

Uses: group or program ender; encore

1790. NEW SONGS ON 4 ROMANTIC POEMS. General, 1968. Harmonically chromatic; a–f♯"; Tess-M; mostly regular meters with changes; moderate tempos; 11pp; Diff-V/dd, P/dd.

For: mezzo-soprano; high lyric baritone if voice is flexible

Mood: love song; song of unchanging nature; in praise of gold; philosophically optimistic

Voice: disjunct; many awkward intervals; large leaps; speech-like rhythms; syncopation; much chromaticism

Piano: thick texture; rhythmically complex; mostly chordal; some linear writing; imitates sounds of nature

Diff: fast negotiation of unusual intervals; singer must be secure musician

Uses: as a group or separately

a. *Lover's Logic* (Percy Bysshe Shelley). b–f"; Tess-mH; 5/4 with changes, Moderately lively; 3pp.

b. *My Heart Leaps Up* (William Wordsworth). c♯'–f♯"; Tess-wide; 4/4, Lively, joyfully; 2pp.

c. *Gold* (George Lord Byron). a–f"; Tess-M; 4/4, Moderately slow; 2pp.

d. *Splendour in the Grass* (William Wordsworth). c'–d♯"; Tess-M; 3/4, Moderately lively–Joyfully; 4pp.

1791. SHADOWS IN THE SUN (Langston Hughes). Cycle.

General, 1971. Gently dissonant throughout; cb'–g♯"; Tess-M; regular meters; predominantly slow tempos; 22pp; Diff-V/m-md, P/m-md.

For: seems best for tenor
Mood: lyrical; sad; shadowy impressions of individual human beings, mostly women
Voice: largely conjunct; some skips; speech rhythms
Piano: each song patterned; clusters, broken-chord patterns; chromatic; linear; some cross-hands; accomp. sets mood; light touch necessary
Diff: few for good musician; singer needs deep understanding of the poetry of Langston Hughes
Uses: poignant songs; good cycle; singer must be able to sustain overall mood of sadness

    a. *Beggar Boy.* d♯'–f♯"; 2/4, Very moderately lively; 4pp.
    b. *Troubled Woman.* db'–g♯"; 3/4, Slowly; 2pp.
    c. *Suicide's Note.* c'–ab'; 4/4, 3/4, Slowly; 1p.
    d. *Sick Room.* eb'–f♯"; 2/4, Slowly; 1p.
    e. *Soledad* (A Cuban Portrait). eb'–f"; 4/4, Moderately slow–With movement and passionately; 2pp.
    f. *To the Dark Mercedes of "El Palacio de Amor."* d'–d♯"; 3/4, Moderately; 3pp.
    g. *Mexican Market Woman.* e'–gb"; 4/4, Moderately slow ♩s; 2pp.
    h. *After Many Springs.* c♯'–g♯"; 3/4, Lively and lightly; 2pp.
    i. *Young Bride.* cb'–db"; 4/4, Moderately moving–Tenderly–Sadly but sweetly; 2pp.
    j. *The Dream Keeper.* c♯'–d"; 4/4, Moderately slow; 1+pp.
    k. *Poem.* c'–eb"; 4/4, Slowly–With dignity; 1+pp.

1792. SHINE! GREAT SUN! (Walt Whitman). Mercury, 1963. Bbmaj; db–f'; Tess-mH; 2/2, Lively–Agitated–Brilliantly; 3pp; Diff-V/md, P/m-md.

For: baritone specified; some tenors
Mood: energetic; love song
Voice: many skips; dotted rhythms; many long tones; syncopation
Piano: block- and broken-chord patterns; constant 8ths; dotted notes; syncopation; does not double vocal line
Diff: long sustained tones; features f'
Uses: big ending; group or program ender

1793. SPOON RIVER ANTHOLOGY (Edgar Lee Masters). Edition Musicus, 1952. Pub. separately (6 titles listed on the music; only 3 available); separate entries below.

A. ANNE RUTLEDGE. Fmin; b–f"; Tess-M; 3/4, Very slow; 4pp; Diff-V/m, P/e.
For: mezzo-soprano
Mood: lyrical; declamatory
Voice: skips; speech rhythms; sustained phrases
Piano: chordal; sustained
Uses: interesting song

B. LUCINDA MATLOCK. Db-Dmaj; bb–a"; Tess-M; 4/4, 3/4, 6/4, Very moderately lively; 5pp; Diff-V/md,

P/d.
For: mezzo-soprano
Mood: spirited; happy; narrative
Voice: rather disjunct; intricate rhythms
Piano: independent; some difficult rhythms; rapid passages
Diff: rhythms; flexibility over a wide range
Uses: good recital possibilities

C. PENNIWIT, THE ARTIST. Emin; d'–a'(e"); Tess-L; 2/2, 3/4, 1/2, 5/4, Moderately lively (with humor); 2pp; Diff-V/m, P/m.
For: baritone
Mood: humorous; descriptive
Voice: rather static in pitch; very short range; declamatory
Piano: partly independent and melodic, partly supportive of the vocal line
Diff: meter changes; declamatory style; much syncopation
Uses: humorous song; useful for singer with limited range but good musicianship

1794. TERRA FIRMA (6 Poems of Evelyn Ames). Edition Musicus, 1985. X; d'–ab"; Tess-M-mH; regular meters; varied tempos; 22pp; Diff-V/md-d, P/md-d.
For: soprano probably best; tenor possible
Mood: love song; description; philosophical; nature; humor; descriptive
Voice: angular; many leaps of 8ve or more; chromatic; syncopation; speech-like rhythms
Piano: much chromaticism; polyrhythms; many different articulations; some broken-chord patterns; repeated chords; 16th-note motion predominates; each song has short prelude; (a.) & (c.) have short postludes; some doubling of vocal line can be found in texture
Diff: chromaticism; intervals; rhythms; ensemble
Uses: as a set of "energetic" songs; can be easily excerpted

    a. *Creation.* X; d♯'–g♯"; Tess-mH; 4/4, Moderately; 3pp.
    b. *Jet Pilot.* X; g♯'–g♯"; Tess-mH; 3/4, Fast; 2pp.
    c. *Terra Firma.* X; d'–ab"; Tess-wide; 2/2, Moderately lively; 4pp.
    d. *Hope.* X; f'–gb"; Tess-M; 4/4, Moderately slow; 2pp.
    e. *Dialogue (With a Cat).* X; d'–gb"; Tess-M; 4/4, 3/4, moderately lively; 6pp.
    f. *Give Her April.* X; d'–f♯"; Tess-mH; 4/4, Lively; 5pp.

RAUM, ELIZABETH
(b. U.S., 1944; became Canadian citizen)

1795. TWO SONGS from *Men I Have Known* (Elizabeth Raum). [11, Vol. 5]. Tonal; b–a"; Tess-M-mH; regular meters; moderate tempos; 10pp; Diff-V/m-d, P/m-d.
For: soprano
Mood: curiosity
Voice: various subdivisions of the beat; some 2 vs. 3 in accomp.; hemiola; some melismas; stepwise; small skips; accidentals, esp. in (b.), which also has short cadenza and speech-like rhythms
Piano: argeggiated; does not double vocal line; (b.), a tango;

Diff: many accidentals; preludes, interludes, and a postlude rhythms in both songs; ensemble in (b.)

Uses: amusing pair of songs

    a. *J.D.* D-centered; d'–a"; Tess-mH; 4/4, 3/4, 6/8, Andante; 6pp.

    b. *T.S.* B-centered; b–a"; Tess-M; 4/4, Tempo di tango; 4pp.

READ, GARDNER
(b. Evanston, IL, 1913)

1796. **ALL DAY I HEAR,** Op. 48, No. 2 (James Joyce). Boosey & Hawkes, 1950. X-Bmin; b–e"; Tess-mL; 4/4, Flowingly, with liquid motion; 2min; Diff-V/d, P/d.

For: baritone; mezzo-soprano; contralto; bass

Mood: somber; bleak; desolate; sad

Voice: many skips; sustained; triplets and duplets; two portamentos down

Piano: broken-chord patterns; arpeggios in groups of seven 16ths per beat; does not double vocal line

Diff: duplet and triplets vs. piano groupings of 7; ensemble; long phrases

Uses: good song; see setting of same text, "The Noise of Waters" by Persichetti

For: D#278

1797. **AT BEDTIME,** Op. 84, No. 1 (Irene Beyers). (Peer)Southern, 1951. D-centered; c♯'–d"; Tess-M; 6/8, Quietly, with gentle motion; 3+min; Diff-V/me, P/m.

For: mezzo-soprano

Mood: lyrical; lullaby; subdued

Voice: stepwise and small skips; easy rhythms; 2-note slurs

Piano: chordal texture; block, clusters, quartal and quintal structures; some rocking figures; some doubling of vocal line

Uses: quiet song; quiet ending

1798. **FROM A LUTE OF JADE,** Op. 36. Composers Press, 1943. Tonal (with many color chords, impressionistic and pentatonic); c'–f♯"; Tess-M; regular meters; contrasting tempos; 6min; Diff-V/m, P/m.

For: all voices–baritone or mezzo-soprano with easy f♯"; tenor or soprano with warm lower voice

Mood: lyrical; reminiscent; dream-like

Voice: skips along altered chord lines; some intervals hard to hear; some conjunct motion; mostly quiet singing; delicate poetry; big ending

Piano: mostly linear; patterned; countermelody; parallelism; arpeggiation; *glissando* to last note; big ending in Cmaj somewhat incongruous with foregoing delicacy

Diff: some pitch patterns

Uses: attractive songs; effective; rather romantic; useful in interior of program

Rec: D#s 277, 278

    a. *Tears* (Wang Seng-Ju, 6th century A.D.). c'–f♯"; 4/4, Andante, con mesto (♩ = 56); 2pp.

    b. *The River and the Leaf* (Po-Chu-I, 7th century A.D.). d'–f♯"; 6/4, 4/4, 3/4, Allegro moderato (♩ = 120); 3pp.

    c. *Ode* (Confucius, 5th century B.C.). c♯'–f"; 4/4, 3/4, Allegro leggiero (♩ = 88); 3pp.

1799. **IT IS PRETTY IN THE CITY,** Op. 84, No. 4 (Elizabeth Coatsworth). (Peer)Southern, 1953. Dmaj; b–g"; Tess-M; 3/4, Flowing, somewhat rubato; 2min; Diff-V/m, P/e.

For: mezzo-soprano; soprano

Mood: descriptive; narrative; naive and simple

Voice: many skips; short phrases; syncopation; triplets; repetitive rhythms

Piano: thin texture; broken-chord patterning; some countermelody; many accidentals; does not double vocal line

Diff: high phrase has sustained f♯"

Uses: good for a young singer; useful recital material

1800. **LULLABY FOR A MAN-CHILD,** Op. 76, No.1 (Jean Starr Untermeyer). Galaxy, 1957. Fmin; b♭–f"; Tess-M; 6/8, Slowly, with quiet feeling; 4+min; Diff-V/m, P/m.

For: mezzo-soprano; some sopranos with full lower voice

Mood: lyrical; sad lullaby; universal sentiment

Voice: many skips, esp. 4ths; sustained phrases; two 8ve leaps to f" softly; quiet ending on c'

Piano: rocking motion of parallel 5ths in l.h. with a characteristic rhythm; some linear passages with countermelody; quiet; one *ff* climax

Diff: consecutive 4ths perhaps hard to hear at first

Uses: lovely song; needs warm, womanly sound; interesting contrast with other lullabies

Rec: D#276

1801. **THE MOON,** Op. 23, No. 4 (William H. Davies). Associated, 1946. [51]. A♭maj; b♭–a♭"; Tess-mH; 4/4, Moderato con moto (some meter changes); 2+min; Diff-V/md, P/d.

For: soprano; some tenors

Mood: lyrical; descriptive; moonlight

Voice: many skips; long phrases; duplets and triplets; 2 vs. piano 3

Piano: chordal–broken in 16th-note triplet pattern; irregularly-grouped arpeggios; some syncopation; does not double vocal line

Diff: ensemble (polyrhythms and polymeters); very long last phrase

Rec: D#s 277, 278

1802. **NOCTURNAL VISIONS.** Three Songs for Baritone and Piano on Lyrics by Jesse Stuart, Rabindranath Tagore, and James Joyce. Boosey & Hawkes, 1988. cmp1985. NATS Vocal Composition Award, 1986. X (with various central pitches); B–a'(g'); Tess-mH-H; regular and irregular meters with changes; varied tempos; 23pp; Diff-V/dd, P/d-dd.

For: baritone specified; range and tessitura well-suited to dramatic tenor; possibly mezzo-soprano

Mood: (a.) & (b.), lyrical and philosophical, using nature imagery; (a.), ecstatic; (b.), reminiscences of childhood; (c.), dramatic, descriptive, and despairing love song using battle imagery

Voice: lyrical, flowing phrases in (a.) & (b.); (c.), dramatic and somewhat disjunct, becoming more lyrical towards end; many high-lying phrases; chromaticism increases through cycle; skips and leaps include aug.2nd, dim.5th, m7th, & 8ve; rhythmic complexity increases through cycle; triplets, some with internal dotted rhythm; 3 vs. 2, 4, 5, 7, & 8 and 4 vs. 6 in piano; voice in 4/4 or 3/4 with piano in 12/8 or 9/8 in (c.); recit.-like sections; syllabic; a few 2-note slurs

Piano: chordal and linear; block, broken, and rolled chords; (a.), somewhat chromatic; (b.), several key changes but little chromaticism; (c.), chromatic; patterned with melodic figures in 8th, 16th, or 32nd notes almost throughout; groupings of 3, 4 (in 3/4 meter), 5, 6, 7, 8, 10, & 14; duplets and triplets, 2 vs. 3 and other combinations; tremolo and trill figures; cross-hands in (a.); both hands frequently in treble clef in (b.); (c.), quite dramatic; articulations important; only incidental doubling of vocal line
Diff: mature and accomplished musicians with excellent sense of pitch and rhythm required; considerable vocal stamina required of baritone voice to handle the high tessitura and many sustained tones in passaggio; (c.) requires much more dramatic weight than the first two
Uses: excellent recital material for advanced musicians
Rec: D#277

   a. *Night of All Nights* (Jesse Stuart). D-centered; d–a'(g'); Tess-H; 6/4, Tempestuously (♩.= ca.52); 7pp.
   b. *The First Jasmine* (Rabindranath Tagore). X; c–f♯'; Tess-mH; 2/2, Moderately, somewhat freely–Rather simply, flowingly (♩=ca.50); 8+pp.
   c. *I Hear an Army* (James Joyce); X; B–g♭'; Tess-mH; 3/4 with changes, Driving and stormily (♩= ca.80) (with changes); 7+pp.

1803. NOCTURNE, Op. 48, No. 1 (Frances Frost). Associated, 1946. [4, 51]. X-Bmin; e♭'–f"; Tess-mH; 11/8, Slowly, with nostalgia; 2+min; Diff-V/md, P/md.
For: soprano; tenor
Mood: lyrical; quiet; nostalgic; regretful
Voice: stepwise and small skips; irregular meter; legato; short recit.-like section
Piano: chordal–block triad pattern, broken-chord pattern, sustained chords; does not double vocal line
Diff: irregular meter biggest challenge to both performers; ensemble
Uses: effective quiet song; good contrast in a group
Rec: D#278

1804. PIPING DOWN THE VALLEYS WILD, Op. 76, No. 3 (William Blake). Galaxy, 1950. Emin (modal flavor); d'–e"; Tess-mL; 6/8, Lightly, with simplicity; 2min; Diff-V/e, P/e.
For: mezzo-soprano
Mood: child-like; joyous
Voice: stepwise; chord outlines
Piano: 4-voice block 5ths & 4ths; several interludes; imitates vocal melody
Diff: ensemble; ends on sustained *f* e"
Uses: excellent song for a young voice
Rec: D#278

1805. THE UNKNOWN GOD, Op. 23, No. 2 (George W. Russell). Associated, 1946. [51]. Dmin; d'–e"; Tess-M; 3/4 predominates, Misterioso e poco lento; 1+min; Diff-V/m, P/d.
For: any voice; mezzo-soprano best
Mood: descriptive; animated
Voice: stepwise; small skips; some triplets
Piano: broken chords; duplets and triplets; long introduction; some doubling of vocal line
Diff: many tempo changes
Uses: quiet ending; could open a group
Rec: D#s 277, 278

1806. A WHITE BLOSSOM, Op. 23, No. 3 (Vail Read). [17]. cmp1946. H & L keys: X; d'–f♭" & b–d♭"; Tess-mL; 2/2, 3/2, Tranquilly; 4pp; Diff-V/md, P/d.
For: all voices
Mood: lyrical; descriptive
Voice: long and short phrases; flowing; chromatic
Piano: chordal; sweeping arpeggiations; highly chromatic
Diff: some pitches
Rec: D#s 277, 278

REED, H. OWEN
(b. Odessa, MO, 1910)

1807. MOUNTAIN MEDITATION (Marion M. Cuthbertson). Mills, 1960. C-centered; b♭–f"; Tess-M; 4/4, Meditatively and sustained (changing meters); 2min; Diff-V/md, P/md.
For: dramatic baritone
Mood: declamatory; descriptive; virile
Voice: many skips, esp. 4ths, 5ths, & 8ves; speech rhythms; long-ranged phrases
Piano: tertian, quartal, and quintal structures–block and broken; irregular rhythms and stresses; moves around on keyboard; does not double vocal line
Diff: several portamentos up an 8ve; sustained f"; ensemble
Uses: recital song for outdoor or nature group

1808. THE PASSING OF JOHN BLACKFEATHER (Merrick F. McCarthy). Mills, 1959. X; g–e"; Tess-mL; 7/4 with changes, Dolefully and sustained; 2+min; Diff-V/m, P/m.
For: bass; bass-baritone; contralto
Mood: declamatory; narrative; somber
Voice: many skips, often of more than a 5th; many sustained low tones; various rhythmic subdivisions
Piano: quartal and quintal structures–block and broken; syncopation; does not double vocal line
Diff: two speakers; final phrase spoken; dynamic control
Uses: recital; centerpiece of group or ender

REED, PHYLLIS LUIDENS
(b. Mineola, NY, 1931)

1809. I HAVE A DREAM (Martin Luther King, Jr.). Galaxy, 1970. D♭maj-C♯min-G♭maj; g♯(c♯')–g♭"(e"); Tess-M; 4/4, 3/2, ♩= 66; 4pp; Diff-V/m, P/me.
For: mezzo-soprano; baritone

Mood: philosophical; idealistic
Voice: rather static at first, becoming more melodic; speech rhythms
Piano: chordal texture; generally doubles vocal line
Uses: useful for many occasions

REIF, PAUL
(b. Prague, Czechoslovakia, 1910; d. New York, NY, 1978)

1810. AND BE MY LOVE [2 sections: 1. The Passionate Shepherd To His Love (Christopher Marlowe) & 2. Love Under the Republicans (Or Democrats) (Ogden Nash)]. General, 1962. X; d'–a♯"; Tess-H; 2/4, 4/4, 3/4, slow to fast with many changes; 13pp; Diff-V/d, P/d.
For: lyric soprano; tenor
Mood: 1, lyrical and pastoral; 2, humorous and satirical
Voice: disjunct; some difficult intervals; some staccato; fragmented
Piano: chordal; some figuration; dissonant; long prelude and interlude; does not double vocal line
Diff: many tempo and meter changes; high tessitura; interpretive skill required, esp. in second section
Uses: for a mature singer; group ender

1811. THE CIRCUS. A Cycle of 9 Songs (Kenneth Koch). Seesaw, 1970. X; d'–d'''; Tess-H; regular meters with changes; varied tempos; 28pp (individual songs quite short); Diff-V/dd, P/dd.
For: lyric or coloratura soprano
Mood: humorously descriptive
Voice: disjunct; highly chromatic; includes speaking and passages of indefinite pitch; declamatory style; complicated rhythms
Piano: extremely chromatic and dissonant; variety of styles; special effects inside piano; complex rhythms
Diff: wide range; high tessitura; excellent vocal actor required; perfect pitch a definite asset
Uses: unusual and effective group for soprano of singular talents; most effective performed in its entirety; songs not individually titled, first lines given below

  a. *The Circus. With what pomp and ceremony the circus arrived.*
  b. *The snoring circus master wakes up.*
  c. *Suddenly a great scream breaks out in the circus tent.*
  d. *Orville the midget tramped up and down.*
  e. *Minnie the rabbit fingered her machine gun.*
  f. *The circus girls form a cortege.*
  g. *Minnie the rabbit felt the blood leaving her little body as she lay in the snow.*
  h. *Soon through the forest came the impassioned bumble bee.*
  i. *Bang! went the fly-swatter.*

1812. LA FIGLIA CHE PIANGE (T. S. Eliot). General, 1957. C-centered; B♭–e'; Tess-M; 4/4, 2/4, 3/4, Tranquillo (with changes); 5+min(8pp); Diff-V/md, P/m; (English text).
For: baritone
Mood: somber; retrospective

Voice: many accidentals; some difficult intervals; mostly syllabic; straightforward rhythms; independent of the piano accomp.
Piano: chordal texture; 11-meas. prelude; interludes between sections; many accidentals; several 8ve passages
Diff: poem is somewhat difficult to interpret (English text); best with mature sound; begins with *ff* sustained e♭'
Uses: stands alone; would make quiet contrast to more forceful and/or faster material on recital

1813. THE FISHES AND THE POET'S HANDS. Cycle of 3 Songs (Frank Yerby). Seesaw, 1970. X; c'–a♯"; Tess-mH (with some emphasis on extreme low tones also); regular meters with changes; varied tempos; 12+pp; Diff-V/dd, P/dd.
For: soprano; tenor
Mood: macabre; concerns the death of a poet
Voice: highly chromatic and disjunct; *Sprechstimme*; speaking; many pitches inexact; special instructions at beginning of cycle
Piano: highly chromatic and dissonant; special effects with mallets, etc.; inexact pitches; glissandos; vibrato effect
Diff: avant-garde techniques necessary; perfect pitch advantageous; strange text
Uses: effective and unusual recital group for the right performer; songs not individually titled, first lines given below

  a. *They say that when they burned young Shelley's corpse.*
  b. *Now all the hungry broken men.*
  c. *You see this is ironical and light because I am so sick, so hurt inside.*

1814. FIVE FINGER EXERCISES. (A Song Cycle) (T. S. Eliot). General, 1957. Traditional keys; b♭–g"; Tess-M; regular meters with some changes; fast and moderate tempos; 15pp; Diff-V/m-md, P/m.
For: soprano; tenor
Mood: mostly lyrical; (a.–c.), melancholy; (d.) & (e.), sarcastic
Voice: many skips; some leaps, conjunct motion; repeated tones; accidentals; speech rhythms within simple meters; some elusive pitches
Piano: mostly chordal; various broken-chord figurations; some linear texture in (c.); (e.), waltz with dissonant harmonies; accidentals; lightly scored
Diff: some pitches; some ensemble
Uses: interesting and effective cycle for teaching and recital
Rec: D#32

  a. *Lines to a Persian Cat.* Cmin; c♯'–g"; 4/4, Lively; 2pp.
  b. *Lines to a Yorkshire Terrier.* B♭maj; b♭–g♭"; 3/4, 4/4, Moderato, ma non troppo; 3pp.
  c. *Lines to a Duck in the Park.* Bmin; b–g"; 4/4, Moderato; 3pp.
  d. *Lines to Ralph Hodgson, Esqre.* Fmaj; c'–g"(c''' falsetto); 2/4, 6/8, Allegretto; 4pp.
  e. *Lines to Mr. Eliot* ("Lines for Cuscuscaraway and Mirza Murad Ali Beg"). E♭maj; e♭'–g"; 3/4, Allegro giocoso; 3pp.

1815. GERMAN FOR AMERICANS. (Cycle of 7 Short
Songs or Scenes). Seesaw, 1971. X; c'–b"; Tess-M;
mostly regular meters with many changes; varied
tempos with many changes; 21pp; Diff-V/dd, P/dd.
For: soprano; tenor
Mood: humorous; hilarious mixture of German and English,
with actions, describing a visit to Germany
Voice: chromatic and disjunct; speaking; *Sprechstimme*;
fragmented; many meter and tempo changes
Piano: chromatic and dissonant; many styles of accomp.;
primarily chordal; afterbeats, broken chords, arpeggios
Diff: requires flexible voice, good sense of pitch, and ability
to alternate singing and speaking naturally and easily;
singer is instructed to "act out most of the scenes,
especially where there is an imaginary dialogue"
Uses: very effective cycle for the right singer; could end a
recital (possibly in pandemonium!); songs not
individually titled; first lines given below

    a. *Here we go–fasten your seat belt– no
smoking–Germany, here I come.*
    b. *Sprechen sie English, ja?*
    c. *Ist das nicht ein schöner room?*
    d. *Just the city tour, please.*
    e. *Herr waiter–more wine, please– Danke schön.*
    f. *Excuse me, who is the conductor? Oh, so das ist
Karajan!*
    g. *A call from overseas?*

1816. O YOU WHOM I OFTEN AND SILENTLY COME
(Walt Whitman). Seesaw, 1971. X; db'–bb"; Tess-M;
4/4, 2/4, 5/4, Very slow; 3+pp; Diff-V/dd, P/dd.
For: lyric tenor
Mood: lyrical; poem about love
Voice: highly chromatic and very disjunct; falsetto;
semi-spoken line; fragmented; grace notes
Piano: highly chromatic and dissonant; chordal; grace notes;
broken-chord figures; repeated chords
Diff: flexibility for large leaps; soft and loud high tones;
strong low tones
Uses: effective recital song for mature performers

1817. RICHARD CORY (Edward Arlington Robinson).
Seesaw, 1971. X; b–a"; Tess-mH; 2/4, 3/4, Fast (with
many changes); 5+pp; Diff-V/dd, P/dd.
For: mezzo-soprano; some sopranos
Mood: lyrical; descriptive; a twist at the end
Voice: chromatic and disjunct; fragmented by rests; many
tempo changes
Piano: highly chromatic and dissonant; primarily chordal with
broken-chord patterns; some complex rhythmic patterns
Diff: pitches; ensemble; requires highly-skilled pianist
Uses: could be an effective recital song; see also settings by J.
Duke and Naginski

REINAGLE, ALEXANDER (See Special Section)

RHODES, PHILLIP
(b. Forest City, NC, 1940)

1818. MOUNTAIN SONGS (A Ballad Cycle) (Texts from
traditional folk sources). C. F. Peters, 1979. cmp1974.
Commissioned by the National Association of Teachers
of Singing in celebration of the National Bicentennial.
Modal; ab–bb"; Tess-M; changing meters; 20min;
Diff-V/md, P/md.
For: soprano specified
Mood: southern Appalachian folk poetry
Voice: wide-ranging melody; some large leaps; rhythmically
active; some polyrhythms; much syncopation; (c.),
unmetered; (b.) requires whistling; mostly syllabic
Piano: no key sigs.; many accidentals; some awkward
patterns; nimble fingers and whistling required
Diff: accidental-strewn score difficult to read; some wide
intervals; rhythmically irregular
Uses: interesting cycle for advanced, versatile, expressive
singer; other voices might be used, as the five songs
seem unrelated as an actual cycle, e.g., (a.) &
(b.)–tenor; (c.)–baritone; (d.)–very lyric tenor
Rec: D#279

    a. *The Unquiet Grave.* Tritone relationships
throughout; d'–ab"; 3/4, 2/4, 3/8, Slow and eerie;
7pp.
    b. *The Old Man and the Devil.* Phrygian; d'–bb"; 6/8
with changes, Moderately fast (with many
changes); 9pp.
    c. *Guide Me, Oh Thou Great Jehovah.* Mixolydian;
c'–f#"; unmetered, notated to resemble folk
inflections of singer (not the familiar hymn-tune),
Slowly and freely (with majesty); 4pp.
    d. *The True Lover's Farewell.* Aeolian; ab–ab"; 3/4
with changes, Slow; 6pp.
    e. *Birdie Went A-Courting.* Mixolydian; d'–bb"; 2/4,
3/4, Fast and exuberant; 7pp.

RICH, GLADYS
(b. Philadelphia, PA, 1892; d. Salt Lake City, UT, 1972)

1819. AMERICAN LULLABY (Gladys Rich). [24, 31 (L),
59]; 1st©1932. H & L keys: Fmaj & Dmaj; c–f" &
a–d"; Tess-mL, mH; 4/4, Grazioso; 4pp; Diff-V/me,
P/m.
For: any female voice
Mood: humorous lullaby with the flavor of contemporary life
Voice: swinging rhythm with syncopation; several large leaps;
mostly conjunct
Piano: chordal; broken-chord afterbeats; chromatic scale
motives; swinging rhythm
Diff: accurate rhythms
Uses: good for young students; in a group about
contemporary life; encore
Rec: D#19

RIEGGER, WALLINGFORD
(b. Albany, GA, 1885; d. New York, NY, 1961)

1820. THE DYING OF THE LIGHT, Op. 59 (Dylan
Thomas). [4]; 1st©1956. Serial technique; b–a";
Tess-M-H; 4/4 with a few changes, Slowly and with

expression; 5pp; Diff-V/d, P/d.
For: dramatic tenor; dramatic soprano
Mood: stormy; song of rage against death
Voice: some awkward intervals (serial technique); non-repetitive speech rhythms; dramatic, sustained high notes; some spoken lines; tempo changes
Piano: disjunct; combines linear and chordal writing; some tone clusters; some canon with voice
Diff: intervals and pitch patterns; 8ve displacement of tone-row; ensemble; independence of voice and piano
Uses: effective expression of this well-known text for secure, mature musicians

1821. **THE SOMBER PINE** (Egmont Arens). Associated, 1961. cmp1902. Cmaj; e'–a"; Tess-mH; 9/8, 3/4, 2/4, ♩.= ca.72; 1min; Diff-V/m, P/m.
For: soprano (lyric or coloratura)
Mood: contrast of spring (cheerful) and winter (somber)
Voice: many skips, esp. 5ths & 6ths; triplets and duplets; long-ranged phrases
Piano: 5–6-voice chordal texture–block, broken, and repeated
Diff: sustained high tones; register control
Uses: good recital piece for high soprano

1822. **YE BANKS AND BRAES O' BONNIE DOON** (Robert Burns) [65]. cmp1910. F♯min-maj; b–f♯"; Tess-mL; 3/4, 2/4, Moderato; 6pp; Diff-V/me, P/m.
For: any medium voice
Mood: descriptive of nature; unhappy ending; poem in folksong style
Voice: folksong-like melody; modal; Scotch snap; triplet figures; a few large intervals; recit.-like phrases; low-lying phrases
Piano: chordal; triplet figures; largely doubles vocal line in first half of song
Diff: rhythms for singer; Scottish dialect
Uses: effective song; excellent example of contemporary setting in folk style

RIETI, VITTORIO
(b. Alexandria, Egypt, 1898; d. New York, NY, 1994)

1823. **FIVE ELIZABETHAN SONGS FOR MEDIUM-HIGH VOICE.** General, 1968. cmp1967. Tonal; a♯(c')–a♯"(g"); Tess-M; regular meters; varied tempos; 10pp; Diff-V/md, P/md.
For: high baritone; some tenors; mezzo-soprano
Mood: mostly lighthearted love songs; one dramatic song concerning jealousy
Voice: small skips; stepwise; chromaticism; some syncopation; some awkward intervals
Piano: homophonic with some linear writing; staccato; many accidentals; chromaticism; many modulations; some "wrong-note" technique; independent of vocal line
Diff: c' low for tenor; repeated f♯"s in (c.) high for baritone
Uses: nice set for high baritone or low tenor with the right tessitura

    a. *Madrigal* (anon., 16th-century). Cmaj; c'–g"; 4/4, Allegro con spirito; 4pp.
    b. *Montanus' Sonnet* (Thomas Lodge). Unsettled;

c♯'–f "; 4/4, Andantino con moto; 4pp.
    c. *Fain Would I Have a Pretty Thing* (anon., 16th-century). D-centered; a♯(c♯')–a♯"(f♯"); 4/4, Allegretto con moto e grazia; 5pp.
    d. *To His Lady, of Her Doubtful Answer* (Thomas Howell). Unsettled; c♯'–f "; 4/4, Andante drammatico; 3pp.
    e. *Love Me Little, Love Me Long* (anon., 16th-century). Gmaj; d'–f "; 4/4, Leggero e scorrevole; 4pp.

1824. **FOUR D. H. LAWRENCE SONGS.** General, 1964. cmp1960. Tonal; d'–f♯"; Tess-M; regular meters; varied tempos; 6min; Diff-V/md, P/m-md.
For: baritone; some tenors
Mood: love songs; descriptive; lyrical
Voice: much chromaticism and modulation; many accidentals; skips and leaps
Piano: mostly homophonic with some linear writing; much chromaticism; constant modulation; some "wrong-note" technique; independent of vocal line

    a. *Aware.* Emaj; d♯'–e♯"; 4/4, Sostenuto–slow; 2min.
    b. *Thomas Earp.* Cmaj; d♯'–f "; 2/4, Gaio, alla breve; 1min.
    c. *December Night.* A♭-centered; e♭'–f♯"; 6/8, Andantino; 1+min.
    d. *Quite Forsaken.* Chromatic; d'–f♯"; 4/4, Sostenuto drammatico; 2min.

1825. **TWO SONGS BETWEEN TWO WALTZES** (William Butler Yeats). General, 1964. cmp1954. "To Alice Esty." X; c'–f "; Tess-mL; regular meters with changes; varied tempos; 18pp; Diff-V/md, P/d.
For: baritone
Mood: (a.), like a folksong; (b.), a lyrical love song; (c.) & (d.), philosophical
Voice: stepwise and small skips; somewhat chromatic; triplets and quadruplets; lyrical flowing phrases in the two "songs"; phrases more disjunct in the two "waltzes"; recit.-like introduction to (d.); mostly syllabic; 2-note slurs; occasional melismas
Piano: both chordal and linear; various broken-chord figurations; afterbeat block chords in the "waltzes"; fairly chromatic; incidental doubling of vocal line
Diff: good sense of pitch needed
Uses: interesting program material; must be performed intact for title to make sense

    a. *The Fiddler of Dooney* (A Waltz). X; c'–f "; Tess-mL; 3/4, 2/4, Moderato (♩.=56); 6pp.
    b. *When You Are Old* (A Barcarolle). G-centered; c'–e"; Tess-M; 6/8, 9/8, 2/4, Andantino (♩=66); 5pp.
    c. *Maid Quiet* (A Madrigal). X; d'–f "; Tess-mL; 4/4, 2/4, Andante doloroso (♩=56); 3pp.
    d. *Brown Penny* (Another Waltz). X; c'–e"; Tess-mL, M; 4/4, 3/4, Tempo giusto (♩=88)–Vivace (♩.=80); 4pp.

RILEY, DENNIS
(b. Los Angeles, CA, 1943; d. New York, NY, 1999)

1826. CLOUDS. Five songs for Soprano and Piano. Cycle. American Composers Alliance (Facsimile MS), 1962. cmp1961–1962. Non-traditional tonal organizations; c'–a"; Tess-mH; unmetered and traditional meters; varied tempos; 6+pp; Diff-V/md, P/md.
For: soprano (lyric or light-lyric)
Mood: descriptive
Voice: small skips predominate; largest leap a 9th; whole-tone scale in (a.); (b.) & (d.) have a modal quality; dotted notes; syncopation; some triplets; mostly syllabic; a few 2–4-note slurs; one spoken phrase
Piano: interesting patterns, each different; (a.), arpeggiated non-traditional harmony; (b.), non-tertian block structures; (c.), non-tertian broken-chord and arpeggiated patterning; (d.), a countermelody in 8ves; (e.), linear and chordal approaches; rhythms not difficult, although changing meters in (e.) create some complexity; some staccato; some doubling of vocal line in (e.) only
Diff: a few pitch patterns; possibly ensemble
Uses: as a recital group; lyric voice seems best

   a. *Mist* (poet not indicated). X; c'–f♯"; unmetered, Andantino; 1+pp.
   b. *There Ariseth* (I Kings 18:44). X; e'–f♯"; 6/8, Allegretto non troppo; ½ p.
   c. *When the Clouds Watch Also* (William Wordsworth). X; e'–a"; 2/4, Lento; 2+pp.
   d. *Hooded Clouds* (Henry Wadsworth Longfellow). D-centered; c♯'–e"; unmetered & 4/4, Adagio; ½ p.
   e. *Sometimes* (William Shakespeare). C-centered; c'–g"; 2/4 with many changes, Allegro; 1+pp.

1827. SEVEN SONGS ON POEMS OF EMILY DICKINSON. C. F. Peters, 1987. cmp1981–1982. Atonal; a–b♭"; Tess-cs; changing meters; varied tempos; 15min; Diff-V/d-dd, P/me-d.
For: soprano
Mood: expressionistic bleakness
Voice: typical disjunct lines of atonal expressionism; 8ve displacement; extreme ranges; syllabic
Piano: atonal; chordal; broken-chord patterns
Diff: all the difficulties of atonal expressionism; perfect pitch desirable
Uses: example of the style for 20th-century specialists

   a. *I'm Nobody!* X; b–g"; Tess-cs; 3/4, 2/4, 4/4, ♩= ca.112; 2pp.
   b. *Papa Above.* X; a–g"; Tess-cs; 2/4, 3/8, ♩= 104–108; 2pp.
   c. *New Feet within My Garden Go.* X; c'–a"; Tess-cs; 4/4, 7/8, 9/4, ♩= ca.66; 2pp.
   d. *Of All the Sounds.* X; a–g♯"; Tess-cs; 3/4, 4/4, ♩=144; 7pp.
   e. *The Morns Are Meeker Than They Were.* X; c'–g"; Tess-cs; 4/4, 5/4, Lento (♩= 40); 2pp.
   f. *Heart! We Will Forget Him!* X; b–a"; Tess-cs; 5/16, 3/16, 6/16, 7/16, Agitato (♪= 132); 3pp.
   g. *I Dwell in Possibility.* X; c'–g♭"; Tess-cs; 3/4, 4/4,

Dolce sostenuto (♩= ca.66); 3pp.

1828. TWO SONGS. Baritone Voice and Piano (Theodore Roethke). C. F. Peters, 1988. cmp1986–1987. X; G♯–g♭'; Tess-M, mH, H; compound meters; varied tempos (♪= 66–♩.= 132); 8min; Diff-V/d, P/m.
For: baritone (high)
Mood: descriptive
Voice: mostly conjunct; some large intervals; high tessitura; words relatively uninflected; sustained top tones
Piano: mostly chordal; some moving figures; accidentals; dissonant
Diff: bringing texts alive
Uses: contrast with other Roethke settings

   a. *Idyll.* X; B–f♯'; Tess-mH; 5/8, 6/8, ♪= ca.66; 5+pp.
   b. *Ballad of the Clairvoyant Widow.* X; G♯–g♭'; Tess-H, M; 6/8, 9/8, ♩.= 132; 19+pp.

ROCHBERG, GEORGE
(b. Paterson, NJ, 1918)

1829. BALLAD (from *Tableaux*) (Paul Rochberg). [16]. cmp1968. Atonal, avant-garde techniques; a♭–g♯"; Tess-mL; 3/16, 4/16, ♪= 60; 2pp; Diff-V/dd, P/d.
For: mezzo-soprano
Mood: contemplative; philosophical; not a ballad either in structure or style
Voice: instructions from composer: "Very relaxed, flexible style; like a 'pop' singer. Modulate freely and easily from throat and chest (normal and deep speaking voice range) to head tones"; wide leaps; grace notes; staccato; soft dynamics; abrupt register changes
Piano: many specific instructions for special effects; fragmented style
Diff: avant-garde idiom; perfect pitch desirable
Uses: for the experienced avant-garde singer

1830. ELEVEN SONGS FOR MEZZO-SOPRANO AND PIANO (Paul Rochberg). Theodore Presser, 1973. cmp1969. Atonal (avant-garde techniques); g♯–b♭"; Tess-wide; largely unmetered; 34pp; Diff-V/dd, P/d.
For: mezzo-soprano
Mood: many different moods; highly emotional
Voice: many avant-garde techniques; quarter tones, *Luftpause*, sliding, glissando, quasi-*Sprechstimme*, extreme range, extreme dyanmics, specific articulation of both notes and words; composer indicates voices to be used, e.g., "throat" (meaning dark tone or full voice) and "head" (meaning "white" or "pure" tone); humming, vocalizing, ornaments; vocal noises; highly emotional
Piano: many directions to the pianist to do a certain thing but work out length and details on his own; written-out parts contain repeated tones, chord clusters, some linear writing, trills, etc.; pianist also has to speak once; specific pedalings given, as well as playing "inside" the piano
Diff: all the difficulties of the avant-garde idiom; perfect pitch desirable
Uses: for performers experienced in avant-garde techniques
Rec: D#280

a. *Sunrise, a Morning Sound.* Molto adagio ma liberamente e quasi parlando; 4pp.

b. *We Are like the Mayflies.* 4/8, 5/8, Delicately, intimately, ♪ = ca.76; 1p.

c. *I Am Baffled by This Wall.* [16]. 2/2, agitated; 4pp.

d. *Spectral Butterfly.* 2/4, ♩ = ca.56; 3pp.

e. *All My Life.* 2/2, ♩ = ca.48; 1p.

f. *Le Sacre du Printemps.* Very fast and precise rhythmically; 4pp.

g. *Black Tulips.* Haunting; fantastic; all-pervading sense of stillness; 4pp.

h. *Nightbird Berates.* Precise, mechanical throughout; 4pp.

i. *So Late!* Tempo: "Slow motion"; atmospheric throughout; 2pp.

j. *Angel's Wings (Ballad).* 2/4, 3/4, Very relaxed; loose; rubato; 3pp.

k. *How to Explain (Ballad).* 4/4, Don't drag tempo; 4pp.

1831. FANTASIES For Voice and Piano (Paul Rochberg). Theodore Presser, 1975. cmp1971. X; b♭–a♭"; Tess-M-mH; regular meters and unmetered; mostly fast tempos; 9pp; Diff-V/m, P/md.

For: mezzo-soprano; soprano

Mood: fantastic imaginary moods

Voice: many skips and leaps; some whispering and half-singing; almost like commentary on the piano score

Piano: patterned accomp.; metrical but dissonant; repeated tones; chords; much pedal; cluster harmonies

Diff: perfect pitch desirable

Uses: short set for those wishing to learn a few avant-garde sounds

a. *The Toadstools in a Fairy Ring.* b–f♯"; Tess-M; 2/4, Tempo di marcia; 2+pp.

b. *There Were Frog Prints in the Rime.* b♭–f'; Tess-L; 4/8, 3/8, Molto agitato; like fanfares (sounds of war); 3pp.

c. *The Frogs Hold Court.* b–f♯"; unmetered, Slow, mysterious, nocturnal atmosphere; sensa misura; 2pp.

d. *Five Chessmen on a Board.* d'–a♭"; Tess-mH; 2/4, Giocoso ed ironico; 1+pp.

1832. FOUR SONGS OF SOLOMON. Theodore Presser, 1949. Pub. separately; new ed., 1975 (under one cover). [51]. Traditional keys (with much modulation); c♯'–b♭"(b"); Tess-M, mH, H; regular meters; varied tempos; 13pp; Diff-V/m-d, P/m-md.

For: tenor; soprano

Mood: lyrical; ecstatic love songs

Voice: many skips and leaps; sustained tones; some high phrases; numerous g"s and a"s; final climax on b♭"

Piano: chordal-linear combination; some polymetric structures; broken 8ves and chord figurations; rapid 16th-note passages; somewhat bombastic

Diff: range; tessitura; some pitches; tenor needs secure command of ringing head tones up through b♭"

Uses: should be an exciting group for the right singer; needs a mature sound; program ender

a. *Rise Up, My Love.* Gmaj; d♭'–a"(b"); Tess-cs; 3/4, Joyously ♩ = 100; 30+sec.

b. *Come, My Beloved.* Amaj; c♯'–a"; Tess-M-mH; 4/4, 2/2, With warmth and expression ♩ = 54– Joyously ♩ = 80; 3pp.

c. *Set Me as a Seal.* Gmin-maj; g'–a"; Tess-mH-H; 6/8, With fire ♩. = 116; 3pp.

d. *Behold! Thou Art Fair.* B♭maj; f'–b♭"; Tess-H; 12/8, Fast, with spirit ♩. = 100; 3pp (repeated).

1833. NIGHT PIECE (from *Tableaux*) (Paul Rochberg). [16]. cmp1968. Atonal, avant-garde techniques; a–f"; Tess-M; 5/8, 4/8, 2/8, 3/8, ♪ = 88; 3pp; Diff-V/dd, P/d.

For: mezzo-soprano

Mood: serene; lyrical

Voice: wide leaps; fragmented phrases; soft dynamics; trill (to be continued on one breath as long as is physically comfortable)

Piano: some instructions for special effects, such as thumbnail pizzicato; fragmented style; grace notes requiring large leaps

Diff: avant-garde idiom; perfect pitch desirable; good trill necessary

Uses: for the experienced avant-garde singer

1834. SEVEN EARLY LOVE SONGS. Theodore Presser, 1992. Tonal; b♭–a♭"; Tess-M-mH; common meters; mostly slow tempos; 30min; Diff-V/me-d, P/m-md.

For: soprano; tenor

Mood: aspects of love

Voice: easy pitches, stepwise; chord member skips; easy rhythms except changing meters in (g.); many dynamic markings

Piano: broken chords; block chords; arpeggiation; some linear sections; (g.) features 16th-note pattern over off-beat 8th-note chords; articulation important; some vocal line doubling in each song

Diff: word stress not always well written; if done as a set, keeping the listeners' interest with many slow songs

Uses: apparently intended as a set; individual songs may be excerpted for study and recitals; possible short groups: [a., b., d.]; [a., f., g.]; [a., b., f., g.]

a. *Tell Me Why the Roses Are So Pale* (Heinrich Heine; trans. Francesca Rochberg-Halton). A♭maj; c♭'–f"; Tess-mH; 4/4, Andante; 4pp.

b. *When I Am Dead, My Dearest* (Christina Rossetti). E♭maj; e'–a♭"; Tess-mH; 3/2, 6/4, Andante affetuoso; 4pp.

c. *Girl Whose Mouth Is Red and Laughing* (Heinrich Heine; trans. Louis Untermeyer). Gmaj; b–d♯"; Tess-M; 4/4, Tenderly, with love; 2pp.

d. *You Are like a Flower* (Heinrich Heine; trans. F. Rochberg-Halton). E♭maj; d'–f"; Tess-M; 4/4, Slowly and with deep tenderness; 2pp.

e. *Night Song at Amalfi* (Sara Teasdale). Fmin; f'–f"; Tess-M; 3/4, Con moto; 2pp (repeats).

f. *Sweetest Love* (Arnold Stein). E♭min; e♭'–a♭"; Tess-H; 4/4, With deep tenderness, moderately slow; 4pp.

g. *There Be None of Beauty's Daughters* (Lord Byron). E♭maj; b♭–g♭"; Tess-M; 4/8, 3/8, 2/8,

Tranquil ♪ = 58; 4pp.

1835. SONGS IN PRAISE OF KRISHNA (Jayadeva, 12th-century Bengali poet; ed. Edward C. Dimock, Jr. & Denise Levertov). Cycle for Soprano and Piano. Theodore Presser, 1981. First performed 1971. Written for Neva Pilgrim. No key sigs.; mostly linear writing; non-tertian harmony; a♭–b"; Tess-wide; 35min; Diff-V/dd, P/dd.

For: soprano (dramatic or sizeable lyric voice)

Mood: celebrates several aspects of love between Radha (the Gopi) and Krishna (the God); passionate and emotional Indian mysticism

Voice: pitch patterns chromatic and difficult; predominantly disjunct; many wide leaps; some glissandos; quarter-tones; speech-like, irregular rhythms; many tempo fluctuations; many dynamic markings; various articulations; three speakers–Radha, Krishna, and a messenger (old woman)

Piano: complex; predominantly linear; vertical harmony often built in 2nds or 4ths; reach of 9th required; widely spaced material; specially marked articulations and pedaling; complex rhythms, meters, and tempo changes

Diff: pitch, rhythm, and ensemble difficulties common to avant-garde idiom; excellent vocal control required; dramatic material; long phrases; wide dynamic range within individual songs

Uses: for mature, secure performers and a sophisticated audience

Rec: D#281

a. *Hymn to Krishna (I).* b♭–a♭"; unmetered, recit.-like; 7pp. (*ppp–f*)

b. *Hymn to Krishna (II).* c'–a♭"; 3/2 , 2/2, Molto espress. e rubato, moving (many tempo fluctuations); 3pp. (*pp–ff*)

c. *Her Slender Body* (Krishna speaks). c♯'–a"; unmetered, Recit.: semplice–Quietly ecstatic– At an easy, natural pace; 3pp. (*pp–f*)

d. *As the Mirror to My Hand* (Radha speaks). b–g"; 2/4, Poco allegretto–Happily, lightly–Without a trace of darkness or heaviness; 3pp. (*ppp–f*)

e. *O Madhava, How Shall I Tell You of My Terror?* a–a"; changing meters, Molto agitato, sempre quasi recit.; 7pp. (*pp–ff*)

f. *Lord of My Heart.* c'–b"; changing meters, Joyous, ecstatic (tempo fluctuations); 4pp. (*pp–ff*)

g. *I Brought Honey.* b♭–b♭"; changing meters alternate, Molto espress. e rubato ma semplice–Allegro; 3pp. (*pp–ff*)

h. *My Mind Is Not on Housework.* a♭–b"; unmetered, Recit.–Doloroso–Slow–Generally distracted, erratic, unstable delivery; 6pp. (*pp–ff*)

i. *I Place Beauty Spots* (The messenger speaks). b♭–a"; 3/8, Graceful, yet halting; 2pp. (*pp–ff*)

j. *Shining One* (The messenger speaks). c'–a♭"; 2/4 with changes, Lucid, radiant, lightly, loving; 2pp. (*pp–f*)

k. *My Moon-Faced One* (Krishna speaks). b♯–g♯"; unmetered, Sempre tranquillo–Dolcissimo–Unclouded; 2pp. (*ppp–pp*)

l. *Beloved, What More Shall I Say to You* (Radha

speaks). b♭–b♭"; changing meters, Tenderly, con amore; 5pp. (*ppp–ff*)

m. *Let the Earth of My Body.* c♯'–b♭"; 3/4, Allegro vivace (in one)–Joyously–Ecstatic; 5pp. (*mp–ff*)

n. *O My Friend, My Sorrow Is Unending* (Radha laments). b♭–b♭"; changing meters, Molto espress., broad but not dragging–Doloroso non troppo; 9pp. (*pppp–ff*)

1836. SONGS OF INANNA AND DUMUZI for Contralto and Piano (based on ancient Sumerian texts; Sumerian transliterations and English trans. by Francesca Rochberg-Halton). Theodore Presser, 1983. X; g–g"; Tess-wide; regular and irregular meters with frequent changes; varied tempos; 44pp; Diff-V/d, P/d.

For: contralto specified; mezzo-soprano

Mood: dealing with love between Inanna, the Sumerian goddess of love, and Dumuzi, a shepherd god; quite erotic in nature

Voice: disjunct; large leaps of 7th & 9th; highly chromatic; triplets; frequent meter changes; wide dynamic range; syllabic; 2–4-note slurs; Sumerian and English texts (see note below)

Piano: highly chromatic; chordal-linear 5-voice texture; some rhythmic complexity; much *sfz* and *marcato*; frequently doubles vocal line or supports it strongly; some independence

Diff: frequent meter changes; subject matter and texts require skill in handling; needs a mature voice, a mature person, and secure musicianship; not for most students

Uses: could be highly effective recital material for appropriate singer and situation

a. *Sa Lam-lam-ma* (Luxuriant heart). X; a–f♯"; changing meters, Andante ma un poco sost., sempre espr. e rubato; 6pp.

b. *He Blossoms, He Abounds.* X; g–f"; changing meters, Allegro ma non troppo; 6pp.

c. *She Calls for the Bed of Joy* (Invocation I). X; a–f♯"; Animando, senza misura; 4pp.

d. *He-tum-tum* (May he bring). X, C-centered; a–g"; changing meters, Presto, gioioso;10pp.

e. *Lu-bi-mu Lu-bi-mu* (My lubi, my lubi). X; b–g"; changing meters, Poco allegretto; 6pp.

f. *May the Tigris and the Euphrates* (Invocation II). X, A-centered; b–f♯"; Senza misura; 4pp.

g. *Luxuriant Heart* (sa lam-lam-ma) (same text as 1st song, here sung in English). X; g♯–f♯"; changing meters, Poco allegro, expansive–Con moto espressione e rubato; 8pp.

NOTE: Of the seven songs only (a.) & (d.) are sung entirely in Sumerian; the remainder are sung in English, with interspersed Sumerian phrases. A "glossary of pronunciation" is provided; the pronunciation is largely phonetic and not difficult to learn.

RODRIGUEZ, ROBERT XAVIER
(b. San Antonio, TX, 1946)

1837. PRALINE & FUDGE. Galaxy, 1989. Dmaj (recit.) & Gmaj (aria); D(E)–f♯'(e'); 4/4, Andante con molto anticipazione, & 4/4, Allegro glucoso; 6pp; Diff-V/md,

P/md.

For: bass; bass-baritone
Mood: humorous; two recipes in mock-Handelian style; to be performed as a single song
Voice: recit.: somewhat disjunct; a few accidentals; broken into short phrases; fluctuations in tempo; alternatives provided for low E and D; aria: also somewhat disjunct; intervals of 6th, 7th, 8ve, & 10th; one long melisma and several short ones, in the style of a Handel aria
Piano: recit: block and rolled chords; several brief melodic passages; some accidentals; aria: contrapuntal; some broken-chord passages; few accidentals; trills; several rolled chords; harpsichord suggested as an alternative
Diff: singer will need solid low and high tones, even if alternatives are taken; an opt. *dal segno* is indicated, but it is not clear whether entire "aria" is to be repeated, or only the first section
Uses: a fun song for recital, in the tradition of Hely-Hutchinson's "Old Mother Hubbard," but with a modern flavor

ROGERS, BERNARD
(b. New York, NY, 1893; d. Rochester, NY, 1968)

1838. **IN THE GOLD ROOM** (A Harmony) (Oscar Wilde). Composers' Music Corp., 1924 (Carl Fischer). Gmin; d'–g"; Tess-M; 4/4, Molto delicato; non troppo lento; 6pp; Diff-V/m, P/m.
For: tenor
Mood: lyrical; haunting; evokes colors of red and gold
Voice: conjunct with some skips; speech rhythms
Piano: linear-chordal combination; broken-chord pattern with r.h. countermelody; triplet and quintuplet figures; thin, delicate texture; soft touch needed
Diff: soft legato singing
Uses: haunting, lovely, quiet recital song

ROGERS, CLARA KATHLEEN
(b. Cheltenham, England, 1844; d. Boston, MA, 1931)

1839. **SHE NEVER TOLD HER LOVE** (William Shakespeare). A. P. Schmidt, 1882. A♭maj; d'–e"; Tess-M; 4/4, Adagio ma non troppo; 3pp; Diff-V/m, P/me.
For: soprano; tenor
Mood: lyrical; descriptive; somber
Voice: many skips; dotted rhythms; 2-note slurs
Piano: chordal–block, repeated, afterbeat styles; some syncopation; does not double vocal line
Uses: not so dramatic as the Haydn setting of this text; useful in an American or a Shakespeare group

1840. **SUDDEN LIGHT**, Op. 33, No.1 (Dante Gabriel Rossetti). A. P. Schmidt, 1900. Emaj; d♯'–a"; Tess-mH; 4/4, Andante quasi allegretto; 2+min; Diff-V/md, P/m.
For: tenor; soprano
Mood: love song; feeling of *déjà-vu*
Voice: many chord-member skips; interrupted phrasing; long-ranged phrases; 2–5-note slurs
Piano: block chords; some countermelody; triplets; large

reaches; some doubling of vocal line
Diff: some long phrases; sustained high tones (a", g♯", g")
Uses: effective song for a voice that can handle it; group ender (*subito pp* ending).

ROGERS, JAMES HOTCHKISS
(b. Fair Haven, CT, 1857; d. Pasadena, CA, 1944)

1841. **ABSENCE** (Pai Tai-Shun; trans. Frederick Peterson?). G. Schirmer, 1915. Amin; e'–e"; Tess-M; 4/4, Ben moderato; 3pp; Diff-V/e, P/e.
For: all voices except very low or very heavy
Mood: lyrical; love song
Voice: skips and conjunct; some melismatic passages; simple melody; two strophes
Piano: chordal with some staccato 8th-note figures; open texture
Uses: nice song with Oriental simplicity

1842. **APRIL WEATHER** (Ednah Proctor Clarke). 1899. Reprint: T.I.S. [58]. A♭maj; e♭'–a♭"; Tess-mH; 2/4, Molto animato; 1+min; Diff-V/md, P/md.
For: soprano; tenor
Mood: lyrical; animated love song; reminiscence
Voice: many leaps, esp. 5ths & 6ths; long legato phrases; some recit.-like phrases
Piano: broken-chord pattern; some rolled chords; irregular subdivisions; does not double vocal line
Diff: rapid diction; dynamic and register control; ensemble–duplets vs. piano triplets; sustained a♭" at end
Uses: fairly good song; arching phrases

1843. **AT PARTING** (Frederic Peterson). G. Schirmer, 1906; 1st©1886 by composer. H & L keys: F♯maj & Dmaj; c♯'–f♯' & a–d"; Tess-mH; 6/8, Non troppo vivo, con anima; 3pp; Diff-V/m, P/m.
For: any voice
Mood: lyrical; love song
Voice: some skips of tritone, 5th, 6th; very legato; easy rhythms
Piano: broken-chord pattern in 16ths; a few chords; some doubling of vocal line
Diff: needs expressive dynamics
Uses: nice lyric song of this period

1844. **CLOUD-SHADOWS** (Katharine Pyle). [8, 31]; 1st©1912. H & L keys: Fmaj & E♭maj; c'–e" & b♭–d"; Tess-M; 6/8, Slowly and dreamily; 3pp; Diff-V/e, P/e.
For: any voice
Mood: child-like; tranquil
Voice: stepwise and easy skips; easy rhythms
Piano: chordal in r.h.; rocking bass; no vocal line doubling
Diff: fluctuating tempo; several fermatas
Uses: useful for young beginning student

1845. **FIVE QUATRAINS** from the Rubaiyát of Omar Khayyám (trans. Edward FitzGerald). 1914. Reprint: Classical Vocal Reprints. Traditional keys; c'–g"; Tess-M; regular meters; moderate and slow tempos; 10pp; Diff-V/me-m, P/me-m.
For: tenor; soprano; some high mezzo-sopranos

Mood: love and unkindness, and inevitability of fate; regretful
Voice: stepwise; skips up to 8ve; easy rhythms, many dotted; a few triplets; several tempo fluctuations in each song; mostly syllabic
Piano: broken-, block-, and some repeated-chord patterning; mostly 8th- and quarter-note motion; often doubles vocal line; short preludes and postludes in four songs
Diff: ensemble because of tempo fluctuations; possibly tessitura in (d.)
Uses: an interesting easy, short set for a student recital; illustrates preoccupation with Eastern texts at that time

a. *A Book of Verse underneath the Bough.* A♭maj; e♭'–g"; Tess-M; 4/4, Ben moderato ma con anima; 2pp.
b. *The Moving Finger.* Fmin; c'–f"; Tess-M; 4/4, con moto moderato; 2pp.
c. *Yet Ah, That Spring Should Vanish with the Rose.* Fmaj; d'–f"; Tess-M; 4/4, Lento espressivo; 2pp.
d. *For Some We Loved.* Bmin; d'–g"; Tess-wide; 4/4, Molto lento; 2pp.
e. *So When That Angel of the Darker Drink.* Cmaj; e'–f"; Tess-M; 4/4, 2/4, Lento assai; 2pp.

1846. **IN MEMORIAM.** A Cycle of Songs for Medium Voice (Walt Whitman). Conatus, 1919, 1947. Traditional keys (eclectic romantic harmonic structure with some impressionistic touches); c♯'–g"; Tess-M (tenor), mH (mezzo-soprano); regular meters; varied tempos; 12pp; Diff-V/md, P/m.
For: dramatic tenor; mezzo-soprano
Mood: lyrical and dramatic; ecstatic poems welcoming death
Voice: conjunct melodic line; calls for both gentle and passionate singing
Piano: chordal texture, sometimes thick; arpeggiation; rolled chords; repeated chords; highly romantic but effective sonorous use of piano
Diff: tying the cycle together as a whole and avoiding sentimentality
Uses: dated work stylistically; nevertheless, could be extremely effective if well done; strong poetry set well for the voice; especially useful on an American program

a. *Dark Mother, Always Gliding Near.* A♭maj; e♭'–f"; 4/4, Molto lento; 3pp.
b. *The Last Invocation.* F♯min; c♯'–f♯"; 4/4, Lento e dolce; 3pp.
c. *Joy, Shipmate, Joy.* Dmaj; d'–g"; 4/4, Animato; 2pp.
d. *Sail Forth!* B♭maj; e♭'–g"; 4/4, Spiritoso; 4pp.

1847. **LOVE'S ON THE HIGHROAD** (F. Dana Burnet). G. Schirmer, 1914. H & L keys: Amaj & Fmaj; e'–g♯" & c'–e"; Tess-M; 6/8, Vivace con anima; 3pp; Diff-V/m, P/d.
For: any high or medium light voice
Mood: joyous love song
Voice: somewhat disjunct, but legato; a few accidentals; regular rhythms
Piano: 16ths in broken-chord figuration almost throughout; some accidentals; usually doubles vocal line

Diff: skillful pianist needed
Uses: could be especially effective for a young soprano

1848. **PIERRETTE TRISTE** (Eleanor Clarage). G. Schirmer, 1934. F♯min; f♯'–f♯"; Tess-M; 3/8, Andantino con tristezza; 3pp; Diff-V/me, P/me.
For: soprano
Mood: lyrical; sad; serenade
Voice: opens and closes with humming; skips; characteristic rhythmic motive of two 16ths and two 8ths
Piano: l.h. has characteristic rhythmic motive (above); lute-like figuration; quiet
Diff: humming
Uses: nice song; rare instance of a serenade for female voice

1849. **THE TIME FOR MAKING SONGS HAS COME.** (Hermann Hagedorn). Oliver Ditson, 1919. Classical Vocal Reprints; T.I.S. (M). [53]. H & M keys: E♭maj & D♭maj (orig.); d♯'–g" & c♯'–f"; Tess-mH; 4/4, Ben moderato–Lento e mesto–Agitato–Più animato; 4pp; Diff-V/m, P/md.
For: all voices except very low
Mood: joyous; philosophical; son of nature
Voice: rather dramatic; somewhat fragmented; recit.-like section
Piano: chordal–rolled, arpeggiated, and repeated; triplets; some chromaticism; does not double vocal line
Diff: needs voice with dramatic weight for very powerful climax
Rec: D#48

1850. **WIND AND LYRE** (Edwin Markham). G. Schirmer, 1916. Dmaj; d'–f♯"; Tess-M; 4/4, Con moto, ma non troppo; 4pp; Diff-V/md, P/m.
For: mezzo-soprano; soprano; tenor
Mood: love song
Voice: skips of up to 8ve; speech rhythms; dramatic in parts; many accidentals
Piano: chordal–broken, arpeggiated, and repeated; some doubling of vocal line
Diff: some irregular rhythms
Uses: period piece; effective for a large voice

ROGERS, PATSY
(b. New York, NY, 1938)

1851. **FIVE SONGS from *"Sonja"*** for Soprano and Piano (poems by mother and sisters of Sonja). Cassia Publishing Company, 1992. X; b♭–b♭"; Tess-M, mH, wide; regular changing meters; varied tempos (♩ = 88–144); 15min; Diff-V/md, P/m-md.
For: soprano
Mood: revelations after a death; poems of mother and sisters of Sonja expressing their grief at her early death
Voice: lyrical; sustained; large intervals; long high tones; chromatic; mostly syllabic; some slow melismas
Piano: dissonant; linear; one song chordal; thin textures (mostly 2-voice); motivic
Diff: some pitches; wide intervals
Uses: unusual poetic reactions to the death of a loved one; good for graduate soprano

Rec: D#282

    a. *Sunny* (Karen Lokvam Updike, Elder Sister). X; f'–a♭"; Tess-mH; 2/2, 3/2, 3/4, Very slow, always intense (♩ = 44); 2+min.

    b. *Sounds While Falling into Sleep* (Sonja Lokvan Spallato). Bitonal; c♯'–a"; Tess-M; 3/4, 4/4, 5/8, 6/8, 7/8, Bright but easy (♩ = 120); 2+min.

    c. *Breathing* (Marian Owens Lokvam, Mother). X; d♭'–a♭"; Tess-M; 2/2, 3/2, Very slow (♩ = 40–44); 4+min.

    d. *Healing* (Kirsten Lokvam Chapman, Younger Sister). X; b♭–b♭"; Tess-wide; 3/4, 4/4, Fast, always tense (♩ = 132–144); 1min.

    e. *From the Other Room* (Karen Lokvam Updike). Bitonal; e'–b♭"; Tess-mH; 5/4, 6/4, Gently rocking (♩ = 112–120); 3+min.

ROREM, NED
(b. Richmond, IN, 1923)

[See Appendix for songs with French texts]

[See also D#50; no titles given]

1852. ABSALOM (Paul Goodman). Boosey & Hawkes, 1972. [157]. cmp1947. X; d'–f♯"; Tess-mH; 3/4, 4/4, 6/4, Andantino lamentoso; 2+min; Diff-V/md, P/m.
For: tenor best; dramatic soprano
Mood: dramatic; somber; dirge
Voice: mostly stepwise; small skips; duplets and triplets; syncopation; interrupted phrases
Piano: chordal; some countermelody; large reaches; some syncopation; large dynamic contrasts; many accidentals; does not double vocal line
Diff: dynamic and register control; ensemble
Uses: useful for singer with dramatic flair

1853. ALLELUIA. [159]. cmp1946. "To Jennie Tourel." X, A- & E-centered; b–g"; Tess-M-mH; 7/8 with changing accents, Fast, and somewhat hysterical (♩ = 176); 4pp; Diff-V/d, P/d.
For: mezzo-soprano; soprano
Mood: joyful; ecstatic
Voice: many skips; accidentals; pitches difficult at first; rhythmically complex; short phrases; various stressings of "alleluia"; lyrical middle section; high climax
Piano: chordal with melodic fragments; many accidentals; rhythmically complex; accuracy in wide leaps and rhythmic precision necessary; wide reach helpful
Diff: rhythmic and ensemble difficulties; a hard piece to learn, but once learned, never forgotten
Uses: exciting alleluia for the rhythmically secure singer; wonderful program ender
Rec: D#s 59, 291, 292

1854. AN ANGEL SPEAKS TO THE SHEPHERDS (St. Luke 2:9–15). (Peer)Southern, 1956. cmp1952. G-centered; d'–a♭"; Tess-M; 4/4, Largo e molto sostenuto; 5min; Diff-V/m-md, P/md.
For: soprano best; tenor

Mood: dramatic
Voice: many skips; triplets and duplets; some canon with piano; repetitive; 2–4-note slurs
Piano: broken-chord patterning; some block chords; 8th-note motion; dramatic dynamic contrasts; sectional; some syncopation
Diff: needs good dynamic control (*pp–fff*)
Uses: effective seasonal recital song; quiet ending

1855. ARE YOU THE NEW PERSON? (Walt Whitman). [159]. cmp1989. "to Phyllis Curtin." F♯maj. with modulations; c♯'–a"; Tess-wide; 3/4, Easily (♩ = 72); 4pp; Diff-V/md, P/m.
For: soprano
Mood: questions warning a potential new lover; realism vs. "maya" [illusion]
Voice: mostly conjunct and small skips; several phrases encompass range of 9th to 11th; several melismas; mostly syllabic; chromaticism; easy rhythms
Piano: syncopated l.h. rhythm predominates; r.h. often doubles vocal line; some countermelody and chordal passages; some large reaches; many accidentals; changes in texture and sonority; key sig. changes
Diff: lengthy range of many phrases; dynamic control *pp–ff*
Uses: love song group

1856. AS ADAM EARLY IN THE MORNING (Walt Whitman). [156]. cmp1957. F♯min; c♯'–e"; Tess-M; 3/2, Maestoso; 1+min; Diff-V/m, P/m.
For: baritone
Mood: lyrical; sensuous
Voice: stepwise; easy skips; several afterbeat phrase beginnings; syncopation; 3–7-note slurs
Piano: block chords with 8th-note countermelody; repetitive; 1-meas. prelude; does not double vocal line
Diff: irregular phrase lengths; ensemble
Uses: good song; text may limit usefulness
Rec: D#s 67, 293

1857. CATULLUS: ON THE BURIAL OF HIS BROTHER (trans. Aubrey Beardsley). Boosey & Hawkes, 1969. [158]. cmp1947. "To David Lloyd." X (7♭s); c♭'–a♭"; Tess-H; 4/4, 6/4, Sombre and steady; 2min; Diff-V/md, P/m.
For: tenor
Mood: somber; dirge-like march for the dead
Voice: many skips; some long-ranged phrases; fragmented phrases; one short melisma
Piano: 3–6-voice chordal texture; repeated note in constant 8ths; accidentals; does not double vocal line
Diff: numerous high tones
Uses: good song

1858. A CHILD ASLEEP IN ITS OWN LIFE (Wallace Stevens). (Extracted and re-arr. by composer from "suite *Last Poems of Wallace Stevens*, for voice, cello, & piano") [158]. Cmp 1971. Dmaj; b–f♯"; Tess-M; 3/4, Intense and gentle; 2pp; Diff-V/m, P/m.
For: soprano; mezzo-soprano
Mood: philosophical
Voice: stepwise; small skips; final phrase is long-ranged (b–f♯"); easy rhythms; a few 2-note slurs; final f♯" 6

beats with decresc.
Piano: chordal with countermelody; some imitation but does not double vocal line; a number of accidentals
Diff: one phrase begins on f♯"; a few pitches difficult against piano (M2nd or m2nd away from piano); final note needs to float
Uses: nice recital song
NOTE: Rorem does not mind the practice of excerpting songs from groups or cycle, as in this case; in his preface to *Song Album, Vol. One* (1980) he suggests that the songs may be "treated as a grab bag. Any of these songs may legitimately be sung by any singer, and transposed if need be."

1859. A CHRISTMAS CAROL (about 1500 A.D.). Elkan-Vogel, 1953. D (Dorian flavor); c –f"; Tess-M; 2/2, 3/2, Allegretto; 1+min; Diff-V/m-md, P/m.
For: soprano; mezzo-soprano
Mood: descriptive; lullaby
Voice: stepwise; small skips; melismatic; 13 meas. unaccomp; easy rhythms
Piano: linear; interrupted twice by several meas. of rest; some large reaches; does not double vocal line
Diff: unaccomp. meas.
Uses: effective Christmas song for recital and other situations
Rec: D#s 10, 289, 291

1860. CONVERSATION (Elizabeth Bishop). Boosey & Hawkes, 1969. cmp1957. X; d'–g"; Tess-mL; 4/2, 3/2, Extremely slow; 2pp; Diff-V/m, P/m.
For: soprano; tenor (big voices best)
Mood: dramatic; intense
Voice: skips along chord lines; interrupted phrases; 2–6-meas. phrases on one syllable; quarter-note motion
Piano: chordal texture; block chords with large reaches; many accidentals; large dynamic contrasts
Diff: dynamic contrasts essential (*p–ff*); poem somewhat difficult
Uses: useful for recital group
Rec: D#291

1861. CYCLE OF HOLY SONGS (Psalms 134, 142, 148, & 150). (Peer)Southern, 1955. cmp1951. Traditional keys with many altered chords; each song leads harmonically to the next; b–a"; Tess-cs; regular meters; varied tempos; 10min; Diff-V/md-d, P/md-d.
For: all voices capable of the range and tessitura; most difficult tessitura for baritone; not for bass or contralto
Mood: lyrical; joyful; songs of praise
Voice: many notes; almost constant singing; many skips, some leaps; constant 8th-note motion with a few slower phrases; many 2–3-note slurs; some longer melismas; very rhythmical; much syncopation; high tessitura at climaxes
Piano: chordal-linear combination; many broken-chord figures; 8ves; thick texture in last song; many accidentals; widespread over keyboard; incidental doubling of vocal line
Diff: pitch and rhythm in learning stages; long stretches without adequate breathing time; tessitura could be a problem if cycle is done as a whole by a single singer
Uses: good cycle; useful in many situations; can also excerpt; program ender

Rec: D#289

   a. *Psalm 134.* Amaj; d'–g♯"; 4/4, Allegro moderato maestoso (sempre marcato); 2pp.
   b. *Psalm 142.* Bmin; b–g"; 4/4, 6/4, 5/4, Andante; 3pp.
   c. *Psalm 148.* Cmaj; c'–g"; 4/4, Allegro con brio; 4pp
   d. *Psalm 150.* Gmaj; d'–a"; 3/4, Maestoso; 3pp.

1862. DOLL'S BOY (e. e. cummings). [159]. cmp1944. Amin; d '–g"; Tess-M; 4/4, 3/4, 5/4, 2/4, Adagio; 3pp; Diff-V/d, P/md.
For: soprano; tenor; mezzo-soprano
Mood: dream text
Voice: 16ths predominate; rhythmic complexity; accidentals; some melismas
Piano: 4-meas. prelude; many dotted rhythms; looks like Adagio of an earlier time but sounds modern; many accidentals; supports vocal line, little doubling
Diff: rhythms; irregularity of phrasing and pitch patterns
Uses: with other e. e. cummings poems in a mixed composer group; cf. Bergsma setting of same text

[A DREAM OF NIGHTINGALES. See entry #15 D]

1863. EARLY IN THE MORNING (Robert Hillyer). [14, 156]; 1st©1958. B♭maj; d'–f"; Tess-M; 3/4, Moderato; 1+min; Diff-V/e-me, P/m-me.
For: baritone; tenor
Mood: lyrical; descriptive; nostalgic; lazy
Voice: stepwise; small skips; easy rhythms
Piano: little cabaret piece in waltz style; resembles style of Poulenc; could stand alone; many accidentals; incidental doubling of vocal line
Uses: excellent setting of this text; fun to perform; audiences like it; see also setting by J. Duke.
Rec: D#s 28, 70, 288, 289, 291, 292

1864. ECHO'S SONG ("Slow, slow, fresh fount") (Ben Jonson). Boosey & Hawkes, 1953. [157]. cmp1948. E♭min; e♭'–f"; Tess-M; 4/4, 6/4, 3/4, 5/4, Andantino; 2min; Diff-V/md, P/m.
For: tenor best; soprano; mezzo-soprano
Mood: lyrical; sad
Voice: many skips; interrupted phrases; 2-note slurs; triplets; syncopation
Piano: chordal texture; afterbeat style; brief countermelodies; some large reaches; does not double vocal line
Diff: irregular rhythms and phrase lengths; ensemble
Uses: useful lyric song with quiet ending
Rec: D#289

1865. EPITAPH (on Eleanor Freeman, who died 1650, aged 21) (anon., 15th century). Elkan-Vogel, 1953. cmp1953. X; d'–f"; Tess-M; 3/2, Very slowly; 45sec; Diff-V/me, P/e.
For: any voice
Mood: lyrical; quiet; elegy
Voice: one long-ranged phrase; some long tones; syncopation
Piano: single line except for widely-spaced chords at end; does not double vocal line
Diff: sustained f"; soft dynamics

Uses: useful short song; quiet

1866. EVIDENCE OF THINGS NOT SEEN: 36 Songs for 4 Solo Voices and Piano. Boosey & Hawkes, 1999. [Ed. Note: Although this work does not fit the guidelines of this bibliography, we are including annotation of the solos because it is the most recent work of the most prolific of published living American art song composers. The composer intends this work to be performed in its entirety, without intermission, by four singers, a format which may interest many performers and teachers. There are 18 solos, 8 quartets, 4 trios, and 6 duets in three sections: *Part One: Beginnings*; *Part Two: Middles*; *Part Three: Ends*.] cmp1996–1997 and one song each in 1951 & 1953. Commissioned by the New York Festival of Song, the Leonore & Ira Gershwin Trust, and the Library of Congress; first performed January 1998. Mostly tonal; Sop. c'–c''' / Alto a–a♭'' / Ten. (A♯)B–b♭' / Bar. (F)B–g'; Tess-wide; metered with few changes; various tempos; 165pp (18 solos: Sop. 10pp; Alto 17pp; Ten. 12+pp; Bar. 27pp.); Diff-V/d, P/d.

For: solo quartet specified; soprano, alto (should be mezzo-soprano), tenor, baritone (needs long range)

Mood: varied, but mostly dark, elegiac; themes of life, love, death, and faith

Voice: (in solos) several recitative-like; others wide-ranged with large skips and many melismas; many repeated melodic patterns, some with minor changes; much sequence; many accidentals; various subdivisions of beat; hemiola, syncopation; good text setting; several very short songs

Piano: (in solos) most scoring spare; piano texture of more than 4 voices rare; variety of accomp. styles; several solos have sustained chords under speech-like vocal rhythms with more elaborate piano introductions to each phrase; several fast songs feature perpetual motion in 8ths or 16ths; many accidentals; doubling of vocal line rare but pitches for singer usually in texture; some chord clusters

Diff: tessitura; phrase lengths; endurance, if entire cycle is performed

Uses: for mature, well-trained voices. Although Rorem specifies that the cycle is intended to be performed in its entirety (est. time in score: 100min), some singers will want to excerpt songs. Most could be excerpted, even most of those marked "attacca." "He thinks upon his death" is complete in itself; "How do I love thee" contrasts with other settings of the poem, and could be sung by sopranos or tenors as well as mezzo-sopranos

Rec: D#283

[S., A., T., or B. following # designation indicates the voice type; # is number in the work]

a. *How Do I Love Thee?* (Elizabeth Barrett Browning). [#5.-A.] G♭maj; d♭'–g♯''; Tess-wide; 4/4, Enthusiastic (♩=126); 4pp; V/d, P/md; (love song).

b. *Their Lonely Betters* (W. H. Auden). [#7.-S.] Dmaj; d'–b♭''; Tess-wide; 6/4 (♩=92); 4pp; V/md, P/md; (philosophical).

c. *Boy with a Baseball Glove* (Paul Goodman). [#9.-T.] G♭maj; d♭–f'; Tess-M; 6/8, Hardly moving (♪=100); 2pp; V/m, P/m; (lyrical observation).

d. *A Glimpse* (Walt Whitman). [#10.-B.] D♯min; B–e♭'; Tess-M; 3/4, Casual and plaintive, like "Wasserflut" (♩=60); 3pp; V/md, P/md; (quiet scene).

e. *I Am He* (Walt Whitman). [#11.-T.] Locrian on E; f–a'; Tess-H; 3/4, Strong, free (♩=ca. 63); 1p;V/md, P/e; (longing). *attacca*

f. *Love Cannot Fill* (Edna St. Vincent Millay). [#12.-A.] X; d'–f''; Tess-mH; 4/4, Very very fast (♩=168); 3pp; V/md, P/dd; (limits of love). *attacca*

g. *The More Loving One* (W. H. Auden). [#13.-B.] D-centered; d'–f''; Tess-M; 4/4, Delicate (♩=126); 5pp; V/md, P/d; (cynical).

h. *I Saw a Mass* (John Woolman). [#15.-A.] D♯-centered; c♯'–e''; Tess-M; 3/4, Painfully slow (♩=58); 2pp; V/m, P/m; (surreal). *attacca*

i. *The Comfort of Friends* (William Penn). [#16.-A.] X; b–a♭''; Tess-wide; 7/8, Angry (♩=132); 5pp; V/dd, P/dd; (Quaker values).

j. *A Dead Statesman* (Rudyard Kipling). [#17.-T.] A♭-centered; f–a♭'; Tess-H; 5/4, ♩=112 (a nervous heartbeat); 1+pp; V/md, P/me; (politician's confession). *attacca*

k. *Dear, Though the Night* (W. H. Auden). [#21.-B.] Shifting tonality; c–f♯'; Tess-M; 4/4, 3/2, 5/4, ♩=58, Piano-strict, Voice-free; 3pp; V/md, P/m; (hypnotic).

l. *The Sick Wife* (Jane Kenyon). [#25.-A.] Unsettled–chains of 7th and 9th chords; c'–f''; Tess-wide; 4/4, Paralyzingly slow (♩=50); 3pp; V/m, P/m; (regretful).

m. *Now Is the Dreadful Midnight* (Paul Goodman). [#26.-S.] X; c'–c'''; Tess-H; 4/4, 6/4, ♩=116 & 84, Piano: severe always, Voice: freely pushing; 3pp; V/m, P/m; (love/lust). *attacca*

n. *He Thinks upon His Death* (Julien Green). [#28.-B.] Gmin; d–f'; Tess-mH; 3/4, Molto lento; 3pp; V/md, P/md; (dark).

o. *A Terrible Disaster* (Paul Goodman). [#30.-T.] Modal over piano ostinato; e–a♭'; Tess-mH; 3/4, Cold and sad (♩=80); 3pp; V/m, P/me; (unrequited love).

p. *Come In* (Robert Frost). [#31.-S.] X; c'–b♭''; Tess-wide; 3/2, Smooth and mysterious (♩=63); 3pp; V/d, P/me; (natur).

q. *Faith* (Mark Doty). [#34.-B.] D-center, shifting; B–g'; Tess-wide; 6/8, ♩=132 or faster (sounding out of control, but always rhythmically strict); 13pp; V/dd, P/dd; (dread of another's death; fearful).

r. *Even Now* (Paul Monette). [#35.-T.] X; B–b♭'; Tess-mH; 2/2, 4/4, Overwrought, yet floatingly free; 5pp; V/d, P/md; (bitter; death of a lover). *attacca*

1867. FIVE POEMS OF WALT WHITMAN. Boosey & Hawkes, 1970. cmp1946 & 1957. Tonal, no key sigs.; b♭–f♯'; Tess-M; 4/4 predominates with some changing meters; 8+min for set; Diff-V/m-md, P/m-md. These

-292-

songs probably not intended as a set, but are effective performed as such; moods predominantly intense and dramatic, concerning death, war, and transcendental philosophy; (a.) serves as prologue; mezzo-soprano seems best for the set; each can also be excerpted into other groups; separate entries below.

A.   SOMETIMES WITH ONE I LOVE. [157]. "To Beverly Wolff" X; b–e♭"; Tess-M; 4/4, 3/4, Lento (♩ = 46); 1+min; Diff-V/m, P/m.

For: baritone; mezzo-soprano
Mood: intense
Voice: many repeated tones; stepwise; easy skips
Piano: chordal texture; large reaches; many accidentals; incidental doubling of vocal line
Diff: begins "*ff* intense"; ends *p*; singer needs ample sound
Uses: effective song; use in set or in a group concerning song ("Out of that I have written these songs")
Rec: D#s 67, 291, 292

B.   LOOK DOWN, FAIR MOON. [157]. "To Donald Gramm." E-centered; d'–e"; Tess-M; 4/4, Very slow (♩ = 40); 1+min; Diff-V/m, P/m.

For: baritone; mezzo-soprano
Mood: dramatic; intense; battlefield scene
Voice: many skips; syncopation; afterbeat phrase entrances; 2–5-note slurs
Piano: block chords; large reaches; many accidentals; large dynamic contrasts; does not double vocal line
Diff: some pitches
Uses: can be excerpted; see also settings by Naginski and Hagen
Rec: D#s 67, 290, 292, 293

C.   GLIDING O'ER ALL. "To Phyllis Curtin." E♭maj; b♭–e♭"; Tess-M; 4/4, Allegro; 1+min; Diff-V/m-md, P/m.

For: baritone; mezzo-soprano
Mood: lyrical; transcendental philosophy of the soul
Voice: stepwise; skips along chord lines; plainsong rhythm; melismatic
Piano: linear-chordal combination; middle and high registers of piano; floating quality
Diff: flexibility; dynamic and register control
Uses: effective song; use in set or separately
Rec: D#293

D.   RECONCILIATION. "To Adele Addison." D-centered; d'–f♯"; Tess-M; 4/4, 3/2, 5/4, Quietly; 3pp; Diff-V/md, P/md.

For: baritone; mezzo-soprano; soprano
Mood: quietly intense; war poem; reaction to death of enemy
Voice: disjunct; declamatory; speech rhythms; interrupted phrases; complex
Piano: linear-chordal combination; covers keyboard; many accidentals; does not double vocal line
Diff: pitches; rhythms; ensemble; dramatic intensity in soft passages
Uses: effective song

E.   GODS. "To Patricia Neway." X; c'–f"; Tess-M; 4/4,

3/4, 5/4, 2/4, Declamatory; 4pp; Diff-V/md, P/m.

For: mezzo-soprano; dramatic soprano
Mood: dramatic; intense; transcendental philosophy
Voice: somewhat disjunct; triplets; syncopation; many afterbeat entrances; 2–5-note slurs
Piano: chordal texture; various registers; many accidentals; large dynamic contrasts; incidental vocal line doubling
Diff: opening 5 meas. for voice alone; ensemble
Uses: effective setting in set or separately; not for beginners

1868.   FLIGHT FOR HEAVEN. A Cycle of Robert Herrick Songs for Bass Voice and Piano. Mercury, 1952. cmp1950. Traditional keys with many altered chords; F♯–e♭'; Tess-mH-H; regular meters; varied tempos; 14min; Diff-V/md-d, P/md-d.

For: composer says bass; bass-baritone perhaps better choice
Mood: lyrical; love songs
Voice: conjunct and skips; independent of piano; many accidentals
Piano: linear texture; almost constant 8th-note motion; thick textures; many accidentals; large reach necessary; contrapuntal in places; much solo playing
Diff: pitch perception; some rhythmic groupings; tessitura
Uses: attractive cycle; not for beginners; ends quietly with 10-meas. piano postlude; interior of program

   a.   *To Music, to Becalm His Fever.* E♭min; F♯–e♭'; Tess-mH-H; 3/4, Rather fast, moving; 6pp.
   b.   *Cherry-Ripe.* E♭maj; G–d♭'; Tess-M; 6/8, Allegretto; 2pp.
   c.   *Upon Julia's Clothes.* Dmaj; d–d'; Tess-mH; 2/4, Con spirito; 1p. [**Rec:** D#s 288, 289]
   d.   *To Daisies, Not to Shut So Soon.* Emaj; b–d'; Tess-M; 4/4, Very fast, light; 2pp.
   e.   *Epitaph upon a Child That Died.* Cmin-maj; c–c'; Tess-M; 6/8, Andante; ½ p.
   f.   *Another Epitaph.* Cmaj; c–c'; 4/4, Semplice; ½ p.
   g.   *To the Willow-Tree.* Fmaj; G♯–c'; Tess-cs; 3/4, Moderate; 2pp. [**Rec:** D#s 288, 289]
   h.   *Comfort to a Youth That Had Lost His Love.* Amaj; G♯–d♯'; Tess-M-mH; 4/4, Melancholy, very slow; 2pp.
   i.   (*Piano Interlude*). 2pp; same as introduction to 1st song, but in ♯'s.
   j.   *To Anthea, Who May Command Him Anything.* F♯maj; F♯–e♭'; Tess-mH-H; 4/4, Gentle, passionate; 4pp.

1869.   FOUR POEMS OF TENNYSON. Boosey & Hawkes, 1969. cmp1949 (d.) & 1963 (a.–c.). Tonal centers and traditional keys; b–a"; Tess-covers range; regular and changing meters; varied tempos; 11min together; Diff-V/m-d, P/m-d. (a.–c.) seem to be the set; (d.) is quite different; a soprano could do all four as a set; separate entries below.

A.   ASK ME NO MORE. [158]. "To Ellen Faull." C-centered; b–a"; 3/2, 2/2, 3/2, Passionate, smooth, and supple; 3+min; Diff-V/d, P/m.

For: soprano (dramatic or lyric)
Mood: somber; intense

Voice: many leaps along chord lines; very long-ranged phrases; many melismas and 2–5-note slurs; 11 meas. on a single pitch

Piano: chordal; imitation of the vocal line; 11 meas. of melody; many accidentals

Diff: dynamic and register control; for the mature performer and advanced singer only

Uses: useful song; quiet ending

Rec: D#291

B. **NOW SLEEPS THE CRIMSON PETAL.** [157]. "For Ellen Faull." Bmin–Dmaj; b–a"; Tess-covers range; 4/4, 3/4, Allegretto scherzando–Moderato (3 other changes); 3min; Diff-V/d, P/d.

For: soprano

Mood: lyrical; love song

Voice: many skips; repetitive patterns; sectional construction; triplets; 2–4-note slurs; repetitive patterns

Piano: rapid arpeggios; trills; block chords; various registers; shimmering sound effects; minimal vocal line doubling

Diff: 7 meas. unaccomp.; ensemble; singer needs secure technique and musicianship

Uses: interesting colors; quiet ending

Rec: D#s 291, 292

C. **FAR–FAR–AWAY.** [157]. "For Ellen Faull." Gmin; d'–g"; Tess-covers range; 9/8, 6/8, 8/8, 3/4, Fast and poignant; 1+min; Diff-V/md, P/md.

For: soprano; possibly tenor

Mood: lyrical; lure of the distant and unexplainable

Voice: stepwise; small skips; one downward portamento; irregular rhythmic groupings; many 2-note slurs; one longer melisma

Piano: linear-chordal combination; irregular rhythmic groupings; one r.h. passage in 3rds; some wide spacing; incidental doubling of vocal line

Diff: rhythms; ensemble; many long tones that need to float; little recovery space in this song–singer can become breathless

Uses: very nice song; useful recital material

Rec: D#s 291, 292

D. **THE SLEEPING PALACE.** F-centered; d'–d"; Tess-M; 3/2, Quietly; 3min; Diff-V/m, P/m.

For: mezzo-soprano; baritone; soprano

Mood: lyrical; tranquil

Voice: mostly stepwise; some skips; easy rhythms; many accidentals; many 2–4-note slurs

Piano: chordal-linear combination; many accidentals; some doubling of vocal line

Uses: useful song; possibly not as good as the other three; Rorem calls it "a fitting postlude to the three later songs," although it was composed 14 years earlier and is quite different

1870. **FOUR SONGS** (publisher's group title). E. C. Schirmer, 1968. [155]. cmp1953 & 1963; orig. pub. separately; now together; separate entries below.

A. **FOR POULENC** (Frank O'Hara). cmp1963. Commissioned and first performed by Alice Esty.

Dmin; c'–f#"; Tess-M-mH; 3/4, Like a gymnopédie; 3+min; Diff-V/md, P/md.

For: mezzo-soprano; soprano; high baritone; low tenor

Mood: nostalgic; café-style; flavor of Poulenc

Voice: many skips, incl. aug. 4th and M9th; 2–3-note slurs

Piano: 3–6-voice texture; some countermelody; one linear interlude; many accidentals; occasional doubling of vocal line

Diff: extreme notes of range used often; 9-beat e"

Uses: opener or interior of group

Rec: D#s 290, 292

B. **THE MIDNIGHT SUN** (Paul Goodman). X; d#'–e"; Tess-M; 2/2, Hollow and quite freely; 1+min; Diff-V/me-m, P/e.

For: mezzo-soprano; baritone; soprano; tenor

Mood: surrealistic; dreamworld

Voice: stepwise; small skips; 2 meas. divided into 7 quarter notes, slurred; other 2–3-note slurs

Piano: open 5ths; some 3-part chords; other 5-voice structures; large reaches; does not double vocal line

Diff: some accidentals hard to read and hear; some phrases have tenuous relationship to the piano score; good dynamic control needed

Uses: effective song

C. **THE MILD MOTHER** (anon., 15th century, adapted). Fmaj (modal flavor); c'–f"; Tess-M; 3/4, Restrained and passionate; 1min; Diff-V/e, P/e.

For: mezzo-soprano best; baritone; some sopranos; some tenors (needs a rich sound)

Mood: descriptive; devout

Voice: plainsong flavor; largest skip M6th down; 2–3-note slurs; flowing rhythm

Piano: 2–4-voice linear texture, 6-voice postlude; independent of vocal line

Diff: rhythm, voice part woven into contrapuntal lines of piano score; ends on sustained d'

Uses: within a group, perhaps of religious songs.

D. **THE TULIP TREE** (Paul Goodman). X; c'–a♭"; Tess-mH; 4/4, Moving; 2min; Diff-V/md, P/md.

For: soprano

Mood: somewhat dramatic; intense; surrealistic; foreboding

Voice: skips of 7th & 8ve; long-ranged phrases; 2-note slurs; some syncopation

Piano: quartal harmony; 4–5-voice texture; ostinato; uneasy mood; dramatic climax; fade-away ending

Diff: two characters; control of registration and dynamics (*ppp–ff*)

Uses: very effective song; anywhere in a group

Rec: D#s 290, 292

1871. **FROM AN UNKNOWN PAST** (arr. by the composer from the original version for mixed chorus a cappella). Cycle. (Peer)Southern, 1963. cmp1951. Traditional keys; g#–f#"(g#"); Tess-M, cs; regular meters; varied tempos; 12pp; Diff-V/m-md, P/m.

For: best for baritone; mezzo-soprano

Mood: lyrical; variety of moods

Voice: conjunct; many skips; 2-, 3-, & 4-note slurs;

Piano: linear; 1–5-voice texture; melodic; large reach helpful; frequent doubling of vocal line

Uses: good set for an advanced undergraduate; attractive for any singer; works well as a solo cycle; program ender

Rec: D#284

   a. *The Lover in Winter Plaineth for Spring* (anon., XVI century?). Modal; d'–d"; Tess-M; 2/2, Lonely and smooth; 1+pp.

   b. *Hey Nonny No!* (Christ Church MS). Dmaj; g#–e"; Tess-M; 4/4, Freely; 2+pp.

   c. *My Blood So Red* (The Call) (anon.). Modal; c#'–d#"; Tess-cs; 4/4, Very slowly; 12meas. [Rec: D#289]

   d. *Suspiria* (anon.). Gmaj; d'–e"; Tess-cs; 6/8, Fastish; 9meas.

   e. *The Miracle* (poem ca. 1600). F#min-C#maj; b–f#"; Tess-cs; 3/4, Allegro non troppo; 3pp.

   f. *Tears* (John Dowland). Bmin; b–e"; Tess-M; 6/4, 4/4, 5/4, Melancholy; 2pp.

   g. *Crabbed Age and Youth* (William Shakespeare). b–e"; Tess-cs; 2/2, Allegro con spirito; 2+pp.

1872. FULL OF LIFE NOW (Walt Whitman). [159]. cmp1989. Bmaj-X-Bmaj; c#'–g"; Tess-wide; 3/4, Rambunctious (♩.= 66); 5pp; Diff-V/md, P/md.

For: tenor; possibly soprano

Mood: presence and immortality of the poet in his poetry

Voice: somewhat disjunct; quarter-note motion; some melismas; irregular phrase lengths; many accidentals; 10-meas. final f#"

Piano: dissonant waltz; doubles or supports vocal line; key sig. changes; many accidentals; quarter-note motion; some 8th-note triplets

Diff: irregular phrasing; range of 9th or 8ve in some phrases; ensemble

Uses: group ender; in a group about writing poems or composing music, about age (poet says he is 40 yrs. old), or in a group of various waltzes

1873. HEARING. [Cycle] for medium-low voice (Kenneth Koch, *A Cycle of Poems by Kenneth Koch*). Boosey & Hawkes, 1969. cmp1966. "To Carolyn Reyer." X; f#–a"; Tess-covers range; mostly regular meters, many changes; varied tempos; 26min; Diff-V/dd, P/m-d.

For: mezzo-soprano; high lyric baritone if possible (text better for a man)

Mood: lyrical; descriptions and expressions of being in love

Voice: virtuoso vocal line; skips, leaps, melismas, wide range; fast tempos; various tessituras; speech rhythms; many words

Piano: mostly linear; some chordal sections; ornamental arpeggiations for punctuation; large reach helpful; rhythmic security necessary; does not double vocal line

Diff: endurance; range; diction; length; perfect pitch desirable; poetic images require imagination

Uses: for the virtuoso singer

   a. *In Love with You* (Three Songs in One). g#–g"; 4/4, Large, free, enthusiastic–2/4, Allegretto

semplice–2/2, Straightforward, not too slow; 9pp.

   b. *Down at the Docks.* bb–gb"; 6/8, Moving, like a Barcarole, but more animated; 3pp.

   c. *Poem.* g#–g"; 3/2, Conversationally; 4pp

   d. *Spring.* [157]. a–g"; 2/2, Rather fast strict tempo, yet casual and gracious; 6pp.

   e. *Invitation.* b–g#"; 3/4, Quite slow; 3pp.

   f. *Hearing.* f#–a"; unmetered, Madly Exuberant!; 12pp.

1874. I AM ROSE (Gertrude Stein). [156]. cmp1955. Bmaj; c#'–f#"; Tess-M; 3/4, Allegretto; 20sec; Diff-V/me, P/me.

For: soprano; mezzo-soprano

Mood: lighthearted; whimsical; outgoing

Voice: many small skips; repetitive rhythms

Piano: linear-chordal combination; countermelody imitates but does not double vocal line

Uses: effective very short song; useful for singer of any age or experience level; good encore

Rec: D#s 288, 289, 291, 292

1875. I WILL ALWAYS LOVE YOU (Frank O'Hara). [159]. cmp1957. G#min; c#'–a"; Tess-M; 4/4, 3/4, 2/4, 3/2, ♩= 72; 3pp; Diff-V/m, P/md.

For: soprano; tenor

Mood: first love; nostalgic

Voice: mostly conjunct; mostly syllabic; some repetitive patterning; irregular speech-like accents; well written for the voice

Piano: linear; flowing; several key sig. changes; many accidentals; vertical structures often parallel 2nds, 9ths, 5ths, 4ths

Diff: communicating unusual text; many dynamic markings

Uses: in a group of love songs; good for teaching clear diction in a legato line

Rec: D#292

1876. A JOURNEY (Andrew Glaze). Boosey & Hawkes, 1977. cmp1976. Dmaj; d'–eb"; Tess-M; 4/4, ♩= 104; 3pp; Diff-V/m, P/me.

For: any voice except extremely low or high

Mood: reflective; child-like narrative

Voice: stepwise; some syncopation; some quarter-note triplets against piano duplets

Piano: chordal texture; r.h. often in 3rds; some syncopation; often doubles vocal line

Diff: polyrhythms

Uses: useful for a student

Rec: D#s 291, 292

1877. THE LORDLY HUDSON (Paul Goodman). Mercury, 1947. [16]. cmp1947. "To Janet Fairbank." Fmin; db'–g"; Tess-M-mH; 6/8, ♪= ca.144; 2+min; Diff-V/md, P/md.

For: mezzo-soprano; soprano; tenor

Mood: lyrical; returning home

Voice: stepwise; skips on chord lines; syncopation; accidentals

Piano: 4–5-voice chordal texture; wide reaches; accidentals; block and broken chords

Diff: some pitches; irregular phrase lengths

Uses: one of the best songs of its time; shows off voices to advantage

Rec: D#s 28, 289, 291, 292

1878. THE LORD'S PRAYER. C. F. Peters, 1957. cmp1957. Gmin; c'–g"; Tess-M; 3/4, Moderato; 2min; Diff-V/m-md, P/m.

For: soprano best; tenor; some baritones

Mood: prayer

Voice: skips on chord lines; some syncopation; some melismas

Piano: linear-chordal combination; many accidentals; some large reaches; much doubling of vocal line

Uses: useful setting of this text for church or recital; accomp. for either piano or organ; quiet ending

1879. LOVE (Thomas Lodge). Boosey & Hawkes, 1969. [158]. cmp1953. Emaj; c♯'–g"; Tess-mL; 3/2, Calm and nervous; 3pp; Diff-V/m, P/m.

For: mezzo-soprano; soprano; high baritone

Mood: lyrical; unhappiness of love cannot be eluded

Voice: many skips; repetitive, but unusually melodic; easy rhythms

Piano: block chords; some countermelody; many accidentals; various registers; large reaches; no vocal line doubling

Diff: smooth legato line; dynamic control

Uses: good song for a Rorem or an American group

Rec: D#292

1880. LOVE IN A LIFE (Robert Browning). Boosey & Hawkes, 1972. [157]. cmp1951. E♭-centered; c'–f♯"; Tess-M; 4/4, ♩ = 52; 4min; Diff-V/md, P/m.

For: baritone best

Mood: lyrical; elusive quality of a personality

Voice: many skips, some difficult (dim.8ve); triplets; syncopation; interrupted phrases; 2-note slurs

Piano: chordal texture; some syncopation; dotted rhythms; many accidentals; countermelody; large reaches; does not double vocal line

Diff: ensemble; poem needs explanation

Uses: effective song for the sensitive singer

1881. LULLABY OF THE WOMAN OF THE MOUNTAIN (Padhraic Pearse; trans. Thos. MacDonagh). Boosey & Hawkes, 1956. [158]. cmp1950. C♯min; c♯'–f♯"; Tess-M-mH; 6/8, Easily; 2+min; Diff-V/m, P/m.

For: mezzo-soprano; soprano

Mood: lyrical; quiet

Voice: stepwise; small skips; 2–4-note slurs; syncopation; irregular phrase lengths

Piano: chordal-linear combination; rocking bass pedal tone; countermelody; many accidentals; does not double vocal line

Diff: ensemble

Uses: effective recital song; quiet ending; could group with other lullabies

Rec: D#s 288, 289

1882. MEMORY (Theodore Roethke). [156]. cmp1959. "To Alice Esty." X; d'–e"; Tess-M; 2/2, ♩ = 56; 1min; Diff-V/me, P/me.

For: any voice

Mood: descriptive of a dream; perhaps "ur"-memory

Voice: many skips, esp. 5ths; repetitive; easy rhythms; triplets; 2-note slurs

Piano: chordal-linear combination; tertian, quartal, and quintal structures; some countermelody; no vocal line doubling

Uses: beginner material

1883. MY PAPA'S WALTZ (Theodore Roethke). [156]. cmp1959. "To Alice Esty." Bmin; b–f♯"; Tess-M; 3/4, Very fast but joyless, breathless, crude and free; 1+min; Diff-V/md, P/md.

For: baritone

Mood: nostalgic; descriptive; frightening but exciting

Voice: stepwise; easy skips; chromatic; syncopation; meas. divided into both 2 & 3; irregular rhythm

Piano: waltz-style with countermelody; some fast arpeggios; cumulative texture; syncopation

Diff: ensemble; rhythms; awkward entrances

Uses: an excellent song; group or recital ender

Rec: D#s 288, 289

1884. THE NANTUCKET SONGS. 10 Songs for Voice and Piano. Cycle. Boosey & Hawkes, 1981. cmp1978–1979 (on Nantucket Island, hence the title). First performed by Phyllis Bryn-Julson, 1979. Tonal; b♭–c'''; Tess-wide; traditional meters; varied tempos; 18min; Diff-V/m-d, P/md-d.

For: soprano

Mood: composer intends them to be "popular songs" (i.e., "entertaining"), "emotional rather than intellectual"

Voice: predominantly disjunct, although several songs are mostly conjunct (c. & i.), or have conjunct sections (d.); (c.) & (f.) use only four or five different pitches in the vocal melody; repeated melodic motives used in typical Rorem style; many accidentals; rhythms not complex, although (e.) (a set of questions and answers) features syncopation and speech-like rhythms and (f.), polyrhythms when combined with accomp.; (h.), unaccomp. and rather speech-like in rhythm; flexible voice required for many short and long melismas (b., 15-note melisma b–c'''); (j.), several rapid melismas with difficult pitch patterns; a number of long high notes (g♯", a", b♭"); final song ends on 4-meas. b"; (e.), an 11-beat middle c could be a problem; (a.), voice begins cycle with unaccomp. meas.

Piano: various accomp. styles–block-, broken-, and repeated-chord (or note) patterning, arpeggiation, and contrapuntal style; (b.), "exuberant" fast waltz, primarily a piano solo with vocal obbligato; (j.) features wide piano range and many trills; many accidentals throughout; little piano solo material, except for (b.) (16 meas.) and (j.) (5 meas.); rare vocal line doubling

Diff: endurance; singer has little recovery time; tessitura; range; angularity; leaps of tritones & 9ths in (b.); melody outlines successive major triads in (a.); long high notes that end sections or songs, (d., i., & j.)

Uses: excellent cycle for soprano who has necessary flexibility and "easy" technique in this wide tessitura; audiences like this cycle; songs easily excerpted

Rec: D#285

a. *From Whence Cometh Song?* (Theodore Roethke). X; c♭'–a"; 3/2, Free (alternating ♩ = 48 & 63); 1p.

b. *The Dance* (William Carlos Williams). X; b–c"'; 3/4, Exuberant, ♩ = 160; 4pp.

c. *Nantucket* (William Carlos Williams). F-centered; f'–c"; 3/4, Lilting, nostalgic, austere, ♩ = 69; 1+pp.

d. *Go, Lovely Rose* (Edmund Waller). A♭maj; d♭'–b♭"; 4/4, Allegretto ♩ = 112; 2+pp.

e. *Up-Hill* (Christina Rossetti). F-centered (Aeolian); b♭–c"'; 3/4 with changes, ♩ = 72 (questions)–♩ = 60 (answers); 3pp.

f. *Mother, I Cannot Mind My Wheel* (Walter Savage Landor). X; d'–a♭'; 6/8, Fast, ♩ = 80; 2pp.

g. *Fear of Death* (John Ashbery). F♯min-maj; b–b♭"; 3/4, ♩ = 66; 4pp.

h. *Thoughts of a Young Girl* (John Ashbery). X; d'–b"; 3/4, Freely, effusive, not slow ♩ = c.69; 1p.

i. *Ferry Me Across the Water* (Christina Rossetti). [159]. C♯maj-min (Dorian melody); c♯'–g♯"; 4/4, Very, very languorous, ♩ = 48; 1p. [**Rec:** D#292]

j. *The Dancer* (Edmund Waller). X, ends Emaj; c'–b"; 11/8 with changes, Big and quick and nervous, always strict, ♪ = en sempre = 276 (♩ = 138); 4pp.

1885. NIGHT CROW (Theodore Roethke). [156]. cmp1959. "To Alice Esty." B♭maj; c'–g"; Tess-M; 4/4, Molto lento–Quasi recitativo; 2pp; Diff-V/m-md, P/md.
For: baritone; mezzo-soprano; dramatic soprano
Mood: dramatic; descriptive; theme of regeneration
Voice: many skips; some 2-note slurs; one melisma; triplets
Piano: linear-chordal combination; imitation; rolled chords; large dynamic contrasts; rhythmic divisions of 2, 3, & 4; does not double vocal line
Diff: speech rhythms
Uses: effective song for the right voice; interior of group
Rec: D#290

1886. THE NIGHTINGALE (about 1500 A.D.). Boosey & Hawkes, 1956. [157]. cmp1951. F♯min; c♯'–f♯"; Tess-M; 2/4, Fast and delicate and supple; 1min; Diff-V/m, P/m.
For: lyric tenor best; lyric soprano
Mood: lyrical; love song; secretive; sly
Voice: mostly conjunct; several skips of 6th; easy rhythms; 2–3-note slurs
Piano: thin-textured broken-chord pattern with countermelody; some staccato; 16 meas. solo material; does not double vocal line
Diff: subtle dynamic control
Uses: good lighthearted song
Rec: D#s 63, 289, 291

1887. O DO NOT LOVE TOO LONG (William Butler Yeats). [159]. cmp1951. Cmin; b♭–d"; Tess-M; 4/4, Molto lento; 13meas. (2pp); Diff-V/e, P/e.
For: medium voices; baritone best
Mood: disappointed love
Voice: mostly conjunct; mostly syllabic; 8th-note rhythm with a few triplets; repetitive; no prelude
Piano: begins in 1 voice, gradually increasing to 4-voice texture; some 8ves; little doubling of vocal line

Uses: good student song
Rec: D#292

1888. O YOU WHOM I OFTEN AND SILENTLY COME (Walt Whitman). [156]. cmp1957. Amaj; c♯'–e"; Tess-M; 6/8, Supple ♩. = 92; 20sec; Diff-V/e-me, P/me. (Rorem says the M. M. marking for this song is incorrect; it should be faster).
For: any voice; baritone probably best
Mood: introspective; secretive
Voice: conjunct; 8th-note motion; syllabic
Piano: chordal; tertian, quartal, and quintal structures; some countermelody
Diff: diction at fast tempo
Uses: good very short song for a Rorem group; abrupt ending
Rec: D#s 70, 289, 291, 292, 293

1889. PHILOMEL ("As it fell upon a day . . .") (Richard Barnefield). [159]. cmp1950. Bmin; b–e"; Tess-M; 4/4, Melancholy; 3min; Diff-V/m, P/m.
For: mezzo-soprano
Mood: lyrical; somber; mourning song
Voice: skips; repetitive rhythms; syncopation; grace notes
Piano: mostly chordal; some countermelody; many modulations; accidentals; some large reaches; does not double vocal line
Diff: afterbeat entrances could present problems for the rhythmically insecure
Uses: effective lyric song for the sensitive mezzo-soprano

1890. POEMS OF LOVE AND THE RAIN. A Song Cycle for Mezzo Soprano and Piano. Boosey & Hawkes, 1965. cmp1962–1963. "To Regina Sarfaty." Traditional keys with many altered chords; g–a"; Tess-cs; mostly regular meters (some changes); varied tempos; 28min; Diff-V/dd, P/d-dd.
For: mezzo-soprano with wide range and rich, dark quality
Mood: lyrico-dramatic; many moods of unrequited love
Voice: many skips and wide leaps; several tessituras; rhythmic intricacies; melismatic phrases; many 2–3-note slurs; speech rhythms; long-ranged phrases; (i.), an interlude for voice alone; pitches hard to learn; considerable amount of dramatic singing
Piano: demands flawless technique; many accidentals; wide reach necessary; various ornaments–trills, ornamental arpeggios, etc.; some motor rhythms; incidental doubling of vocal line; big score
Diff: in every area; not for the average singer
Uses: good cycle for the mature virtuoso singer; both performers must be outstanding musicians and expressive interpreters; selections can be made, but the composer prefers this work to remain intact; notice the form of the composition–classical recessed symmetry, or a mirror-image effect
Rec: D#s 286, 287

a. *Prologue: from "The Rain"* (Donald Windham). b–c"; 3/4, Unbearably slow; 2pp.

b. *Stop All the Clocks* (W. H. Auden). g–a♭"; 3/4, Lento appassionata (Rather bluesy); 6pp.

c. *The Air Is the Only* (Howard Moss). b–f♯"; 4/4,

Allegretto grazioso; 2pp.

  d. *Love's Stricken "Why"* (Emily Dickinson).
eb'–eb"; 4/4, Lento; 1p.

  e. *The Apparition* (Theodore Roethke). d'–f"; 4/4,
Allegro agitato; 3pp.

  f. *Do I Love You (Part I)* (Jack Larson). [159]. d'–e";
4/4, Andantino tranquillo; 2pp. [**Rec:** D#292]

  g. *in the rain* (e. e. cummings). b–g"; 4/4, Allegro
(delicate and mutedly); 3pp.

  h. *Song for Lying in Bed During a Night Rain*
(Kenneth Pitchford). bb–g"; 6/8, Marcatissimo;
7pp.

  i. *Interlude* (Theodore Roethke). f♯–g"; unmetered,
Slow and very, very free; almost unmetered; 1p.
voice alone, 1p. piano alone. [**Rec:** D#58]

  j. *Song for Lying in Bed During a Night Rain
(Conclusion)* (Kenneth Pitchford). b–g♯"; 3/4,
Andante; 2pp.

  k. *in the rain* (e. e. cummings). a–f♯"; 3/4, Not slow,
very free; 3pp.

  l. *Do I Love You (Part II)* (Jack Larson). [159]. d'–e";
12/8, Joyous; 2pp.

  m. *The Apparition* (Theodore Roethke). g–f"; 3/4,
Smoothly; 3pp.

  n. *Love's Stricken "Why"* (Emily Dickinson). e'–g";
3/4, Intense; 1p.

  o. *The Air Is the Only* (Howard Moss). a–a"; 6/4,
Calmly; 2pp.

  p. *Stop All the Clocks* (W. H. Auden). g–g"; 7/8 with
changes, Wildly fast and angry; 5pp.

  q. *Epilogue: from "The Rain"* (Donald Windham).
bb–cb"; 3/4, As at the beginning (or even slower);
1p; (same music as Prologue except a half-step
lower).

1891. A PSALM OF PRAISE (Psalm 100). Associated,
1948. cmp1945. D-centered; c'–g"; Tess-M-mH;
changing meters, Rather fast and nervous; 4pp;
Diff-V/md, P/md.

For: soprano seems best; tenor
Mood: joyful; praise to God
Voice: stepwise; small skips; complex rhythms and metric
flow; some triplets; 2–4-note slurs
Piano: linear-chordal combination; 8-meas. prelude; complex
rhythms; does not double vocal line
Diff: rhythms; ensemble
Uses: effective song; forerunner of Rorem's "Alleluia"

1892. RAIN IN SPRING (Paul Goodman). Boosey &
Hawkes, 1956. [157]. cmp1949. Dmaj; a–eb";
Tess-M; 2/2, Very languid; 1min; Diff-V/m, P/m.

For: mezzo-soprano; contralto; baritone
Mood: lyrical; descriptive; arrival of spring; subdued
Voice: many skips; duplets and triplets; 2–4-note slurs
Piano: afterbeat style with countermelody; double-dotted
rhythms; some triplets; many accidentals; does not
double vocal line
Diff: rhythms
Uses: effective song; quiet ending
Rec: D#s 289, 291

1893. REQUIEM (Robert Louis Stevenson). Peer

International, 1950. cmp1948. G♯min; c♯'–f♯";
Tess-M; 3/4, 4/4, 5/4, Very quietly; 2pp; Diff-V/m,
P/m-md.

For: high baritone; tenor
Mood: lyrical; subdued; longing for death
Voice: many small skips; easy rhythms; some syncopation;
2–3-note slurs
Piano: chordal-linear combination; large reaches; many
accidentals; some doubling of vocal line
Diff: ensemble; free-flowing rhythms
Uses: good setting of text; see also setting by Sidney Homer
Rec: D#289

1894. THE RESURRECTION (St. Matthew 27:62–66; 28).
(Peer)Southern, 1956. cmp1952. Tonal/various keys;
bb–ab"; Tess-M; 4/4, 2/2, sectional, tempo changes
several times; 20 pp; Diff-V/md, P/md.

For: soprano
Mood: resembles a solo cantata; narrative
Voice: many small skips; some recit.-like passages; many
2-note phrases; two long-ranged phrases; some long
melismas
Piano: varies sectionally; mostly chordal texture; various
registers; several interludes, one 24 meas.; does not
double vocal line
Diff: wide dynamic variations; mood changes; long tones
Uses: limited usefulness; should stand alone

1895. ROOT CELLAR (Theodore Roethke). [156].
cmp1959. "To Alice Esty." X; bb–g"; Tess-M; 12/8,
Intensely slow, declamatory and strong; 1+min;
Diff-V/m, P/m.

For: baritone; perhaps mezzo-soprano or dramatic soprano
Mood: dramatic; descriptive; dank
Voice: many small skips; long-ranged phrases; 2–4-note slurs;
dramatic dynamic contrasts
Piano: chordal; 9th, 11th, and other structures; two chords per
meas.; wide reaches; wide spacing; dramatic dynamics
Diff: wide dynamic range; needs mature, resonant sound
Uses: effective song; big beginning, quiet ending
Rec: D#s 288, 289, 291

1896. SALLY'S SMILE (Paul Goodman). [156]. cmp1953.
A-centered; e'–f♯"; Tess-mH; 4/4, Fast and delightful;
45sec; Diff-V/md, P/md.

For: tenor; high baritone
Mood: energetic; enthusiastic; love song
Voice: several skips of 7th; almost constant 8th-note motion;
many 2-note slurs; 12-beat final note
Piano: repetitive chordal background with rapid
countermelody; accelerated ending with rapid rolled
chords and rapid motion over the keyboard; some
doubling of vocal line
Diff: some pitches elusive
Uses: good song; group ender
Rec: D#s 289, 291

1897. SEE HOW THEY LOVE ME (Howard Moss). [156].
cmp1956. Dbmaj; eb'–a"; Tess-mH; 6/4, Quietly;
1+min; Diff-V/m, P/m.

For: tenor best; soprano
Mood: nature; transcendental philosophy

Voice: stepwise; easy skips; many accidentals; easy rhythms; 2–3-note slurs; one portamento; some long-ranged phrases

Piano: linear-chordal combination; counterpoint in quarter-note motion; many accidentals

Diff: sustained a" cresc.; register and dynamic control

Uses: good lyric song for recital group; see also setting by William Flanagan

Rec: D#s 70, 289, 291

1898. THE SERPENT (Theodore Roethke). Boosey & Hawkes, 1974. [157]. cmp1970–1972. "For Phyllis Curtin." X; b♭–a"; Tess-mH-H; 4/4 predominates, Very fast; 2min; Diff-V/dd, P/d.

For: soprano (needs flexibility)

Mood: humorous; about a singing serpent

Voice: serpentine; many skips; long-ranged phrases; 2-note slurs; duplets and triplets

Piano: snaky patterns, mostly in 16ths; many accidentals; needs facile technique; does not double vocal line

Diff: some intervals; long-ranged phrases (e.g., g'–b♭"); dynamic control; ends sustained f♯"

Uses: wonderful song for singer with a sense of humor; see also settings by Kubik and Hoiby

Rec: D#s 291, 292

1899. THE SILVER SWAN (Ben Jonson). Peer International, 1949. [65]. cmp1959. Amin; e'–c'''; Tess-mH-H; 6/8, Largo; 3min; Diff-V/md, P/m.

For: soprano best (lyric or coloratura); tenor

Mood: lyrical

Voice: many skips; 8ve leaps; some dotted rhythms; some interrupted phrases; many 2-note slurs; melismas; several high phrases

Piano: linear-chordal combination; syncopation; large reaches; unified by repetitions of the opening motive; counterpoints vocal line but does not double

Diff: legato singing; good register control; flexibility; ensemble; breathing; some difficult entrances; long final phrase

Uses: effective lyric song; excellent recital material; quiet ending

Rec: D#289

1900. SIX IRISH POEMS (George Darley). Cycle. (Peer)Southern, 1971. cmp1950. "To Nell Tangeman." Traditional keys with many altered chords; a–a♭'; Tess-M-mH; regular meters; varied tempos, slow ending; 14min; Diff-V/m-md, P/md-d.

For: mezzo-soprano

Mood: lyrical, somber moods

Voice: lyrical; skips and some leaps; speech rhythms; some melismas; some 2–3-note slurs; accidentals

Piano: linear; 2–5-voice texture; some cluster chords; running 16ths in (d.); widely-spaced sustained chords under melodic line in (f.); wide reach helpful; ear for orchestral color an asset; orchestration indicated in piano score; playable orchestral reduction

Diff: some high phrases; not so difficult as most Rorem cycles

Uses: good cycle; useful with piano; needs warm, full voice quality; graduate level material

a. *Lay of the Forlorn.* F♯min; d'–g♯"; 4/4, Moderate, nostalgic; 5pp.

b. *Robin's Cross.* Emin; d'–f"; 6/8, Plaintive; 2pp.

c. *Chorus of Spirits.* Gmin; d'–g"; 3/4, Waltz–gracefully; 4pp.

d. *The Call of the Morning.* Emaj; a–f♯"; 4/4, Allegro; 3pp.

e. *Runilda's Chant.* Amin; d'–g"; 4/4, Strident; 5pp.

f. *The Sea Ritual.* B♭min; b♭–a♭"; 2/2, 3/2, Sad and mysterious; 7pp.

1901. SIX SONGS FOR HIGH VOICE. C. F. Peters, 1963. cmp1953. Traditional keys; d'–f'''; Tess-HH; regular meters; varied tempos; 11+min; Diff-V/d-dd, P/m-d.

For: coloratura soprano

Mood: spring and themes of young love; (c.), prayerful (sacred text); except for (a.), all refer to earlier times

Voice: many skips and leaps; coloratura techniques; many extremely high phrases (f"–c'''); many words; melodically somewhat repetitive

Piano: chordal and linear; wide-spread over keyboard; trills; many accidentals; wide reach needed

Diff: extremely high tessitura; difficult coloratura of last song; many words on high phrases; endurance for the whole cycle; last song for a true coloratura only; others can be done by high lyric who has good c''', d''' and e'''

Uses: excellent group; can be sung singly or as a cycle

a. *Pippa's Song* ("The year's at the spring") (Robert Browning). Gmaj; d'–d'''; Tess-HH; 2/2, Rustling and unhurried; 2pp. [**Rec:** D#s 3, 288, 289]

b. *Song for a Girl* (John Dryden). Emaj; e'–e'''; Tess-HH; 3/4, Fast, light; 2pp. [**Rec:** D#s 3, 289]

c. *Cradle Song* (16th century). E♭maj-Cmin; f'–c♭'''; Tess-H; 6/8, Andante; 2pp.

d. *Rondelay* (John Dryden). B♭maj; f'–c'''; Tess-H; 3/4, Simply, sadly; 4pp

e. *In a Gondola* (Robert Browning). C♯min; f♯'–c'''; Tess-H; 3/4, Smooth; 2pp. [**Rec:** D#s 3, 289]

f. *Song to a Fair Young Lady, Going Out of Town in the Spring* (John Dryden). Fmaj; c'–f'''; Tess-H-HH; 4/4, Allegro moderato; 7pp.

1902. SNAKE (Theodore Roethke). [156]. cmp1959. "To Alice Esty." Fmin; e'–f"; Tess-M; 4/4, Presto; 1+min; Diff-V/md, P/d.

For: soprano; tenor

Mood: intense; sensuous; compelling; theme of regeneration

Voice: stepwise and chromatic; small skips; direction is snake-like; some dotted notes; repetitive; 2–5-note slurs; two longer melismas

Piano: rapid triplets in serpentine pattern, sometimes in both hands; various registers; dynamic contrasts very important; some doubling of vocal line with 8ve displacement

Diff: needs very smooth legato lines, voice must glide; ensemble difficult; piano may cover voice in low range

Uses: good group or recital ender

Rec: D#s 288, 289, 291

1903. A SONG OF DAVID (Psalm 120). Associated, 1946. [4]. cmp1945. X; d'–g"; Tess-mL; 3/2, 4/4, 3/4, 5/4,

Andantino serioso; 2min; Diff-V/m, P/m.

For: baritone; some tenors
Mood: somber; intense
Voice: skips; interrupted phrases; speech-like rhythms
Piano: chordal–mostly block; some large reaches; does not double vocal line
Diff: rhythms
Uses: direct expression; quiet ending; useful

1904. **SPRING** (Gerard Manley Hopkins). Boosey & Hawkes, 1953. [157]. cmp1947. Amin-Emaj; c'–a"; Tess-M-mH; 4/4, Allegretto con moto; 5pp; Diff-V/md, P/m.

For: soprano; possibly tenor
Mood: lyrical; beauty of spring
Voice: many skips; some leaps; 2-note slurs; speech rhythms; some 3 in voice vs. 4 in piano; high climax
Piano: linear; patterned; built on ostinato figure–4-note bass pattern under single-line melody in r.h.; texture thickens in mid-section; accidentals; modulatory
Diff: pitch perception; some rhythmic irregularities; clear enunciation of highly alliterative poetry; some ensemble problems
Uses: excellent song to open a "spring" group
Rec: D#s 288, 289

1905. **SPRING AND FALL** (Gerard Manley Hopkins). Mercury, 1947. [16]. cmp1946. "For Mme. Eva Gauthier." Emin; d#'–f#"; Tess-mL; 4/4, ♩ = 63; 2min; Diff-V/md, P/m.

For: mezzo-soprano; baritone; soprano; some tenors
Mood: lyrical; philosophical; comforting; seasons compared to life
Voice: stepwise; small skips; some triplets; some syncopations; interrupted phrases
Piano: chordal-linear combination; countermelody; repetitious; many accidentals; vocal and piano phrases interlock; does not double vocal line
Diff: rhythms; interrupted phrases; interlocking phrases; poem requires study–several unusual words and usages
Uses: excellent song for a sensitive singer; interior of group
Rec: D#s 288, 289

1906. **SUCH BEAUTY AS HURTS TO BEHOLD** (Paul Goodman). [156]. cmp1957. B♭min; d'–g♭"; Tess-M; 4/4, 3/4, 5/4, Very slow, very free; 3pp; Diff-V/md, P/m.

For: high baritone; tenor; mezzo-soprano
Mood: philosophical; peace after love's fulfillment
Voice: stepwise; easy skips; 2–4-note slurs; syncopation; some triplets; repetitive; one phrase calls for a "hollow" tone
Piano: chordal-linear combination; many accidentals; some wide reaches; countermelody; no vocal line doubling
Diff: irregular rhythms; dynamic and timbre control
Uses: useful song for teaching and performance
Rec: D#s 289, 291

1907. **THAT SHADOW, MY LIKENESS** (Walt Whitman). [159]. C-centered; c'–c"; Tess-M; 12/8 (voice), 4/4 (piano), Smooth ♩. = 46; 2pp; Diff-V/m, P/me.

For: medium voices

Mood: introspective; true self vs. ego
Voice: melismatic; built on a few repeated melodies; easy rhythms; fairly long phrases
Piano: bass rocks slowly between c and g, providing foundation for singer; embellished by dissonant half-note chords
Diff: dissonant harmonies in piano; requires long breath and legato style; accurate pitches in melismas
Uses: teaches techniques in Diff. above; recital song
Rec: D#67, 292

1908. **THREE CALAMUS POEMS.** For Medium Voice and Piano (Walt Whitman). Boosey & Hawkes, 1982. cmp1982. Tonal; a–g"; Tess-M-mL; traditional meters; varied tempos; 10min; Diff-V/md, P/m-md.

For: baritone
Mood: composer's note: "Calamus . . . was Whitman's symbol for 'the love of comrades'"; about death, life, and love
Voice: stepwise; skips that outline chords; duplet and triplet divisions of beat; dotted rhythms; syncopation; some long-ranged phrases (e.g., a–d"; b–d#"); (a.), somewhat speech-like rhythms; some sections have repetitive patterning
Piano: (a.), alternating sections featuring countermelody, separated by block- and broken-chord patterning; (b.), very fast arpeggiated sections and two slower sections with block chords requiring a wide reach; (c.), repeated-note pattern combined with bass or inner voice countermelody and some block chords; many accidentals; several changes of key sig.; generally independent of vocal line; some doubling in (c.)
Diff: some polyrhythms against the piano; a few pitch patterns
Uses: set for a high baritone

   a. *Of Him I Love Day and Night.* E-centered; b–g"; Tess-M; 3/2, ♩ = 63, Voice: controlled and sad and holding back; Piano: nervous and hard and pushing on; 6pp.
   b. *I Saw in Louisiana a Live-Oak Growing.* Bmaj-G#min; a–e"; Tess-mL; 4/2, Very fast and enthusiastic–3/2, Calmer; 6pp.
   c. *To a Common Prostitute.* Emaj; a–f#"; Tess-M; 3/4, ♩ = 72 (with fluctuations); 4pp.

1909. **THREE POEMS OF DEMETRIOS CAPETANAKIS.** Boosey & Hawkes, 1968. cmp1954. "To Betty Allen." Tonal; c'–a"; Tess-M-mH; traditional and changing meters; slow tempos; 9pp; Diff-V/m, P/me-m.

For: medium voices or sizeable high voices (dramatic soprano; tenor)
Mood: dark; concerns death, guilt, and fear; dramatic
Voice: stepwise motion and small skips predominate in (a.) & (c.); (b.), wide skips and angularity; a number of accidentals throughout; some syncopation; several 2–7-note slurs (fewer in (b.)); several *ff* high notes (g", a♭", and a")
Piano: 4-voice texture predominates; mixture of linear and chordal structure; (b.) features many rests in piano part while voice sounds alone (once for 3 meas.); (b.), built

on a repeated 4-note motif; does not double vocal line
Diff: sustained high notes; dynamic control; intensity of texts
Uses: complete set for a mature and compelling singer; all are slow, dark, heavy, dramatic songs possibly best used as singles in combination with other Rorem songs

    a. *Abel.* Dmaj-Bmin; d'-a"; Tess-mH; 3/4, 4/4, Rigidly calm; 3pp.
    b. *Guilt.* Cmin; c'-g"; Tess-M; 4/4, 6/4, Slow, free, stark; 3pp. [**Rec:** D#10]
    c. *The Land of Fear.* [158]. D-centered; d'-ab"; Tess-M; 2/2, Intense; 3pp.

1910. **THREE POEMS OF PAUL GOODMAN.** Boosey & Hawkes, 1968. cmp1952–1956. Traditional keys; c'-bb"; Tess-M; regular meters; varied tempos; 7min; Diff-V/m-md, P/m.
For: tenor; soprano
Mood: lyrical; intense ending
Voice: stepwise; many skips and repeated tones; 2–5-note slurs; dotted and irregular rhythms; some syncopation; some triplets
Piano: mostly chordal; some linear sections; countermelody; many accidentals; some large reaches; various registers; grace notes; does not double vocal line
Diff: breathing; ensemble; sustained high tones *ff* (g" and bb"); some awkward pitch patterns; legato line
Uses: effective set of songs; as set or separately
Rec: D#s 10, 291 (listed separately by title)

    a. *For Susan.* [157]. Emaj; e'-g"; Tess-M; 6/8, Easily; 3pp. [**Rec:** D#292]
    b. *Clouds.* [158]. Emaj; e'-f♯"; Tess-M; 4/4, Infinitely slow, pale; 2pp. [**Rec:** D#292]
    c. *What Sparks and Wiry Cries.* Gmin; c'-bb"; Tess-M; 4/4, Sharp and intense; 3pp. [**Rec:** D#290]

1911. **TO A YOUNG GIRL** (William Butler Yeats). Boosey & Hawkes, 1972. [157]. cmp1951. Ebmin (Aeolian mode); cb'-eb"; Tess-M; 4/4, 5/4, 6/4, Largo; 1+min; Diff-V/md, P/m.
For: baritone
Mood: dramatic; intense
Voice: many skips; speech rhythms; syncopation; interrupted phrases; large dynamic contrasts
Piano: linear texture; tertian and quartal structures; many accidentals; dramatic dynamic changes; large reaches; does not double vocal line
Diff: rhythms; ensemble; dramatic intensity
Uses: useful for the right singer; quiet ending
Rec: D#292

1912. **TO JANE** (Percy Bysshe Shelley). Boosey & Hawkes, 1976. cmp1974. F♯-centered; b-d"; Tess-mL; 3/4, Smoothly waltzed; 1+min; Diff-V/e, P/me.
For: baritone
Mood: lyrical; descriptive; scene is "Jane" singing to guitar
Voice: stepwise; small skips; repetitious melody; easy rhythms; 2-note slurs
Piano: thin texture; simple waltz style; some parallel descending 4ths & 5ths; large reaches; many

accidentals; partly doubles voice
Uses: good change of pace; much simpler than most Rorem songs; possible beginner song

1913. **TO YOU** (Walt Whitman). Elkan-Vogel, 1965. (bound with "Epitaph" on Eleanor Freeman . . .). cmp1957. Gbmaj; db'-eb"; Tess-M; 4/4, Moderato; 45sec; Diff-V/me, P/m.
For: any voice
Mood: lyrical; questioning
Voice: many skips, esp. 5ths; easy rhythms; some 2-note slurs
Piano: repetitive chordal texture; 8th-note motion; does not double vocal line
Uses: for young and inexperienced singers; recital song
Rec: D#s 288, 289, 293

1914. **TWO POEMS OF EDITH SITWELL.** For Medium-high Voice and Piano. Boosey & Hawkes, 1982. cmp1948. Composer's note states that the 2 songs "need not necessarily be performed as a group."

A. **YOU, THE YOUNG RAINBOW.** [159] Fmin; c'-g"; Tess-M; 3/4, ♩ = ca.66; 3pp; Diff-v/m, P/m.
For: mezzo-soprano; baritone
Mood: austere and bleak
Voice: stepwise motion and small skips predominate; one long-ranged phrase spanning full range of song; duplet and triplet divisions of beat; *ff* climax on g" with quiet ending on 14-beat c"
Piano: countermelody with repeated chords; some syncopation; many accidentals; doubling of vocal line incidental
Diff: making the poem understood (references to mythology)
Uses: pair with other song in this set or use in Rorem group
Rec: D#291

B. **THE YOUTH WITH THE RED-GOLD HAIR.** [3]. Ebmaj; d'-g"; Tess-mH; 4/4, Calm and distant; 3pp; Diff-V/m, P/m.
For: mezzo-soprano; soprano; tenor
Mood: mysterious and wispy; intense
Voice: stepwise motion with small skips; syncopation; some triplets and 2 vs. 3 in piano; several accidentals; dynamics range *p–ff*; high, soft ending on 10-beat f"
Piano: repeated block chords and broken chords in duplets; many accidentals; incidental doubling of vocal line
Diff: some pitch patterns and rhythms; getting the proper mood and suspense
Uses: in American group or pair with other song in this set
Rec: D#291

1915. **TWO POEMS OF THEODORE ROETHKE.** Boosey & Hawkes, 1969. cmp1959. Bound together; not necessarily for the same voice, although dedicated "To Alice Esty."; separate entries below.

A. **ORCHIDS.** [157]. Fmin; c'-e"; Tess-M; 12/8, Sinister, languid and floating; 1+min; Diff-V/m-md, P/m.
For: mezzo-soprano; baritone
Mood: dramatic; dank
Voice: chant-like; repetitive; duplets and triplets; 2–10-note

slurs
Piano: block chords; some countermelody; wide spacing; wide reaches; some doubling of vocal line
Diff: rhythms; tone-color differentiations
Uses: setting is well-mated to the text; effective; could be paired with "I Strolled Across an Open Field" or used separately
Rec: D#s 15, 292

B. I STROLLED ACROSS AN OPEN FIELD. [158]. Amaj; d'–g"; Tess-M; 4/4, Quite fast and exuberant; 1+min; Diff-V/md, P/md.
For: soprano best
Mood: descriptive; overflow of well-being
Voice: stepwise (somewhat chromatic); skips along chord lines; some triplets; 2-note slurs; longer melismas
Piano: repeated chords; chord clusters; rapid scales; many accidentals; doubling of vocal melody
Diff: pitches for melodic sequences; register control; one leap of 9th
Uses: useful song; could be paired with "Orchids" or used separately
Rec: D#s 15, 292

1916. TWO SONGS (Elinor Wylie). Hargail, 1952. [158]. cmp1949. Bound together but rather different; separate entries below.

A. LITTLE ELEGY. [62]. "To Nell Tangeman." E-centered; c♯'–e"; Tess-M; 4/4, Andante; 1min; Diff-V/m, P/me.
For: any voice
Mood: lyrical; quiet
Voice: many skips; easy rhythms; many 2–3-note slurs
Piano: parallel motion triads; 7th, 9th, 11th, & 13th chords; legato; does not double vocal line
Diff: some slurs need careful handling; singer needs secure registration
Uses: excellent quiet song; music well-mated to text; can be paired with "On a Singing Girl"
Rec: D#s 65, 290, 292

B. ON A SINGING GIRL. X; f'–f"; Tess-M; 4/4, 5/4, 2/4, Calm and moderate; 1min; Diff-V/m, P/m.
For: tenor best
Mood: elegy
Voice: small skips; complex speech-like rhythms; interrupted phrases; accidentals
Piano: chordal texture; some large reaches; accidentals; some countermelody; does not double vocal line
Diff: ensemble; irregular rhythms and phrase lengths
Uses: useful recital song; can be paired with "Little Elegy"

1917. VISITS TO ST. ELIZABETH'S (Bedlam) (Elizabeth Bishop). [159]. cmp1957. Emin with many modulations; d'–g"; Tess-mH; 6/8, Allegro (♩. = 132); 10pp; Diff-V/d, P/d.
For: soprano; tenor; mezzo-soprano
Mood: hectic; anxious; describes dementia
Voice: both triple and duple subdivisions of beat and meas.; hemiola; mostly small intervals; a few 8ve skips;

descending 10th at the end; mostly syllabic; a few melismas; many accidentals; several portamentos; dynamics range *p–fff*; one verse calls for "white tone"
Piano: articulations and voicing complex and important; mostly 2–5-voice textures; some arpeggiation and block chords; many accidentals; hemiola; some doubling of vocal line
Diff: hemiola; the amount of text; length and endurance; effective dynamics; effective communication
Uses: can stand alone in recital; dramatic voice needed
Rec: D#s 59, 289, 291

1918. THE WAKING (Theodore Roethke). [156]. cmp1959. "To Alice Esty." C-centered; d'–g"; Tess-M; 4/4, Andante sostenuto; 2+min; Diff-V/m-md, P/m-md.
For: tenor; high baritone; mezzo-soprano; dramatic soprano
Mood: intense; nature and time; transcendental philosophy
Voice: stepwise; small skips; easy rhythms; many accidentals; several long-ranged phrases; all phrases begin low and arch
Piano: repeated chords in l.h.; some broken chords; some countermelody; many accidentals; texture thickens as song progresses; some doubling of vocal line
Diff: dramatic and intense delivery; poem needs study
Uses: perhaps not one of Rorem's best songs, but effective for singer with dramatic abilities

1919. WAR SCENES (Walt Whitman). Cycle. Boosey & Hawkes, 1971. cmp1969. "Designed for Gerard Souzay." Atonal; g–g♭"; Tess-L, M, mH; regular meters; varied tempos; 13min; Diff-V/d-dd, P/d.
For: bass-baritone
Mood: dramatic; somber; anguished description
Voice: disjunct; extreme intervals; extreme dynamics; pitches difficult; some conjunct lines; speech rhythms; pitches derive from 10-tone set first stated by piano; highly declamatory and dramatic
Piano: highly programmatic; chordal sections; some solo playing; ornamental arpeggiated figures; many accidentals; waltz song fast with r.h. duplets and triplets; turns; atonal; large reach helpful; demands great sensitivity to text
Diff: many difficulties in (a., c., & e.); (b.) & (d.) generally easier; perfect pitch desirable; singer must have superior sense of declamatory style
Uses: excellent, starkly dramatic work for the mature singer with advanced technique
Rec: D#293

a. *A Night Battle.* g–g♭"; 2/2, Frantic; 9pp.
b. *Specimen Case.* b♭–f♭"; 4/4, Simply, sad; 2pp.
c. *An Incident.* c'–c"; 2/2, Poignant but vicious, fast; 4pp
d. *Inauguration Ball.* b–f♯"; 3/4, Crude and fast; 5pp.
e. *The Real War Will Never Get in the Books.* g–e♭"; 3/4, Flexible, declamatory, slower than speech, but rich and full, supple and grand; 4pp.

1920. WHAT IF SOME LITTLE PAIN (Edmund Spenser). [158]. cmp1949. B♭min; c'–f"; Tess-mH; 4/4, Lento; 2min; Diff-V/m-md, P/m.

For: baritone; mezzo-soprano; dramatic tenor or soprano
Mood: powerful; concerns relief after pain
Voice: stepwise; small skips; syncopation; afterbeat entrances; some long-ranged phrases
Piano: chordal; countermelody with distinctive repetitive rhythm; does not double vocal line
Diff: several long tones; last four phrases all decresc. from successively quieter starting points
Uses: moving song; one of Rorem's best; quiet ending
Rec: D#289

1921. WHERE WE CAME (Jean Garrigue). Boosey & Hawkes, 1976. cmp1974. X; d'–g#"; Tess-mH; 4/4, Floatingly; 2min; Diff-V/d,P/m.
For: soprano; tenor (flexible voice needed)
Mood: languorous; sensuous world of nature
Voice: winding legato phrases; repetitive patterns; many slurs on single syllables; many triplets
Piano: chordal with non-legato countermelody; large reaches; thin texture; wide, hazy sonorities; repetitive; accidentals; does not double vocal line
Diff: long and long-ranged phrases; opening 6 meas. unaccomp; some difficult pitches; triplets vs. piano duplets
Uses: repetitive and hypnotic; a good nature song

1922. WOMEN'S VOICES. Eleven Songs for Soprano & Piano. Cycle. Boosey & Hawkes, 1979. cmp1975. Commissioned for and dedicated to Joyce Mathis; first performed by her, Alice Tully Hall, 1976. Tonal; bb–b"; Tess-wide; traditional meters; varied tempos; 22min; Diff-V/d, P/me-d.
For: soprano specified; some high mezzo-sopranos
Mood: poetry written by women–philosophical, happy, humorous, complaining, grieving; descriptive of life and death
Voice: some songs predominantly conjunct (a., b., & d.); a few predominantly disjunct (h. & j.); most are a combination; much repetitive melodic patterning; many accidentals; except for asymmetrical meters, rhythms are less complex than pitch patterns; melismas prominent in (a., c., h., i., j., & k.); many 2-note slurs; many long-ranged phrases (e.g., (f.), c#'–a"; (j.), bb–f", bb–gb"); (g.) opens with 9 meas. of voice alone
Piano: some accomps. spare (a. & g.); some elaborate (c., e., j., & k.); (i.), unaccomp; many feature block- and broken-chord patterning; a few are linear; many accidentals; (c., e., f., & j.) use wide keyboard range; wide variety of dynamics; (j.), highly dramatic and features trills; does not double vocal line; little solo piano material except in (c., e., f., j., & k.); not many resting places for singer in such a long work; no prelude to first song; no postlude to final song
Diff: range and wide tessitura; wide dynamic range; loud and soft high notes (e.g., ab"pp, bb"fff); endurance; ensemble
Uses: as a cycle; possible to select an interesting 4- or 5-song group
Rec: D#s 290, 294, 295

   a. *Let No Charitable Hope* (Elinor Wylie). Mostly

Cmaj; e'–a"; 3/4, ♩ = 72, Intense; 3pp.
   b. *A Birthday* (Christina Rossetti). [159]. Dbmaj; b–ab"; 7/8, Allegro grazioso–Brisk; 3pp.
   c. *To My Dear and Loving Husband* (Anne Bradstreet). Db-centered; c'–b"; 3/2, Exuberant; 4pp; *attacca.*
   d. *To the Ladies* (Mary Lee, Lady Chudleigh). F#-centered; d'–ab"; 4/4, Allegretto; 3pp.
   e. *If Ever Hapless Woman Had a Cause* (Mary Sidney Herbert, Countess of Pembroke). X; bb–bb"; 4/4 with changes, Angry; 6pp.
   f. *We Never Said Farewell* (Mary Elizabeth Coleridge). D#min; c#'–a"; 3/4, Smooth; 3pp.
   g. *The Stranger* (Adrienne Rich). C-centered; d'–bb"; 3/4, Stark; 4pp
   h. *What Inn Is This* (Emily Dickinson). X; bb–g"; 3/4, Allegretto; 2pp.
   i. *Defiled Is My Name* (Queen Anne Boleyn). Centers on Ab; d'–a"; 7/8, Supple and sad but firm and not slow; 1/2p; attacca.
   j. *Electrocution* (Lola Ridge). Bb-centered; bb–bb"; 3/4, Brittle and nasty; 4+pp.
   k. *Smile, Death* (Charlotte Mew). Eb- & C-centered; eb'–fb"; 4/4 with changes, ♩ = 88; 3pp.

1923. YOUTH, DAY, OLD AGE, AND NIGHT (Walt Whitman). [156]. cmp1954. Dmin; c'–a"; Tess-M; 3/4, Rather slow; 2pp; Diff-V/m, P/m.
For: mezzo-soprano; soprano; tenor
Mood: lyrico-dramatic; philosophical
Voice: melodic, measured recit.; skips and leaps; modulations; climax on melismatic phrase on word "sun"; ends quietly and low
Piano: chordal with small melodic ornaments; wide-spread rolled chords; large reach helpful
Diff: expressive declamatory style
Uses: excellent song; good for teaching expressive, free treatment of text; mature voice best
Rec: D#289

ROY, KLAUS GEORGE
(b. Vienna, Austria, 1924)

1924. HOLIDAY, Op. 25 (Adrienne Rich). [18]. cmp1953. X, D-centered; c#'–g#"; Tess-M; 6/8, 7/8, 9/8, With quiet motion (♩. = 56); 4pp; Diff-V/md, P/d.
For: soprano; tenor
Mood: lyrical; love song; nature imagery
Voice: somewhat chromatic and disjunct; duplets; other rhythmic complexities; some interrupted phrases
Piano: chromatic; somewhat contrapuntal; independent r.h. melodic line in 3rds
Diff: pitches; rhythms; soft high tones
Uses: good recital song

1925. A SONG FOR MARDI GRAS, Op. 37 (Rolfe Humphries). [19]. cmp1957. E-centered; a–f"; Tess-M-mH; 3/4, 4/4, Very free; 2+min; Diff-V/d, P/d.
For: contralto; bass; mezzo-soprano; baritone
Mood: declamatory; energetic

Voice: disjunct; interrupted phrases; dotted rhythms; syncopation; triplets; long-ranged phrases

Piano: tertian, quartal, and quintal structures; dotted rhythms; beat divided into 2, 3, 4, & 6; syncopation; double 3rds in final variation; some cross-hands; variations separated by repetition or variation of opening figure; does not double vocal line

Diff: complex rhythms and pitch patterns; ensemble challenging

Uses: interesting song for the singer who can handle it; song has refrain–also varied; entire song is set of variations on a Welsh refrain

ROY, WILLIAM
(b. Detriot, MI, 1928)

1926. **THIS LITTLE ROSE** (Emily Dickinson). [24, 31 (L), 59]; 1st©1947. "For Giuseppe DeLuca." H & L keys: Fmaj & Cmaj; e'–f"; & b–c"; Tess-M; 3/4, Moderate, and in a free, gentle manner; 3pp; Diff-V/me, P/me.

For: any voice

Mood: lyrical; philosophical

Voice: triplets; rubato in final stanza; large intervals at climax; conjunct otherwise

Piano: broken-chord figures throughout; rubato; some chromaticism

Uses: good for young students

ROZSA, MIKLOS
(b. Budapest, Hungary, 1907; d. London, England, 1978)

1927. **FIVE SONGS.** Fentone, 1977. Although pub. under one cover, these songs are unrelated; listed separately below.

A. **THE LAND WHERE MY HEART LIES** (Michel Gyarmathy; trans. Christopher Palmer). cmp1972. Dmin; d'–a"; Tess-M-H; 4/4, 3pp; Diff-V/m, P/m.

For: soprano; tenor

Mood: nostalgic; longing for homeland

Voice: stepwise or small skips; dotted rhythms juxtaposed with quarter-note triplets; syncopation; dynamics vary *pp–ff*

Piano: chordal-linear combination; Middle-Eastern flavor in ornamentation; pedal points; repetitions; some arpeggiated 7th chords in l.h.; syncopation

Diff: rhythms

Uses: possibly pair with "My Little Town" (E. of this collection)

B. **INVOCATION** (Lord Vansittart). cmp1940. Cmaj; bb–e"; Tess-L; 4/4, Andante semplice; 4pp; Diff-V/m, P/m.

For: contralto specified; mezzo-soprano; baritone

Mood: sacred song; philosophical

Voice: small skips and stepwise motion; dotted rhythms; some triplets; syncopation; dynamics *pp–ff*

Piano: chordal texture; some arpeggiations; syncopation; prelude; many 8ves, 7ths, & 9ths, both hands

Uses: in group of religious songs; not for church

C. **HIGH FLIGHT** (John Magee). Fmaj; c'–g"(c'''); Tess-M-L; 4/4, Allegro agitato e volatile; 10 pp; Diff-V/m, P/d.

For: tenor specified, but seems low; better for soprano; mezzo-soprano

Mood: excited; soaring flight of spirit

Voice: stepwise; easy skips; dotted rhythms; independent of piano part

Piano: violent arpeggiated groups of 7, 6, 5, 9, 3, & 4 per beat; sometimes 16ths in both hands; prelude and interludes

Diff: too many low c's and d's for tenor

Uses: perhaps useful to end group; not as good as others in collection; piano part seems too much

D. **BEASTS OF BURDEN** (Lord Vansittart). cmp1940. F#maj; b–e"; Tess-M-L; 4/4, Moderato; 5pp; Diff-V/m, P/m.

For: contralto specified; also mezzo-soprano; baritone

Mood: heavy; life as seen by a camel

Voice: stepwise; small skips; dotted rhythms; triplets; some syncopation

Piano: chordal; afterbeat style; Middle-Eastern flavor; grace notes and other ornaments; syncopation

Diff: some unusual modulations and intervals

Uses: "different" type of song subject; could be done by a student

E. **MY LITTLE TOWN** (Michel Gyarmathy; trans. Christopher Palmer). cmp1972. Cmin; c'–eb"; Tess-M-L; 4/4, 5/4; 3pp; Diff-V/me, P/m.

For: tenor specified; seems too low for tenor; better for baritone or mezzo-soprano

Mood: nostalgic; homesickness of an exile

Voice: mostly stepwise; syllabic; repetitive; syncopation

Piano: prelude and interludes sound Middle-Eastern; chordal texture with syncopated afterbeats give hypnotic effect.

Diff: mild dissonances and 5/4 meter good training for young musician

Uses: could be done by a student; possibly pair with "The Land Where My Heart Lies"

RUGGLES, CARL
(b. East Marion, MA, 1876; d. Bennington, VT, 1971)

1928. **TOYS** (Carl Ruggles). Presser, 1920. cmp1919. X; c'–a" (orig. 1 step higher); Tess-M; 7/8 with numerous changes, Anima; 1min; Diff-V/d, P/dd.

For: soprano; mezzo-soprano

Mood: lyrical and descriptive; written for the fourth birthday of the composer's son, but it is difficult to imagine this song appealing to a four-year-old child

Voice: chromatic and disjunct; leaps of aug. 4th, 7th, & 9th; short phrases separated by rests; syllabic

Piano: highly chromatic and disjunct; chordal–block, broken, and rolled; triplet, quadruplet (in 9/8), quintuplet, and septuplet patterns; some 3-stave notation; incidental doubling of vocal line, but not in a helpful manner

Diff: perfect pitch desirable; strong sense of rhythm needed; ends on softly sustained a"

Uses: possible recital material; a very different kind of early

avant-garde song
Rec: D#296
NOTE: This is Ruggles' only song for voice and piano and was regarded by him as "his seminal piece that gave him insights into a style that was subsequently fully realized in the works that followed."

RUSSELL, SYDNEY KING
(b. New York, NY, 1897)

1929. HARBOR NIGHT (Katherine Garrison Chapin). Carl Fischer, 1945. Dmin; d'–f"; Tess-M-mH; 4/4, Andante, calmly; 4pp; Diff-V/m, P/m.
For: baritone; mezzo-soprano; tenor; soprano
Mood: intimate; love song
Voice: conjunct; easy rhythms; phrases somewhat fragmented; sustained; many repeated tones
Piano: chordal texture–block and broken; syncopated repeated tones and chords; arpeggios; some countermelody; does not double vocal line
Diff: sustained f" with cresc. beginning *f*
Uses: useful song; somewhat personal; quiet ending

SACCO, JOHN CHARLES
(b. New York, NY, 1905; d. New York, NY, 1987)

1930. BROTHER WILL, BROTHER JOHN (Elizabeth C. Welborn). [34, 59, 64]; 1st©1947. Fmaj; c'–f"; Tess-M; 4/4, With sly jocularity; 5pp; Diff-V/me, P/d.
For: baritone; tenor
Mood: humorous; "You can't take it with you"
Voice: folksong-like with contrasting parlando sections
Piano: afterbeat style; chromatic grace notes on the beat; large register changes on keyboard; glissando at end
Diff: rapid, semi-spoken section in difficult rhythm; sustained, ringing f" at end
Uses: good for young male students with a flair for comedy
Rec: D#s 11, 47

1931. HAYFOOT, STRAWFOOT (Lalia Mitchell Thornton). Boston Music Co., 1956. Cmaj; c'–e"; Tess-M; 4/4, Moderato (in a relaxed manner); 4pp; Diff-V/m, P/m.
For: baritone
Mood: masculine; strong; rhythmic; energetic
Voice: small skips; syncopation
Piano: chordal; chromaticism; jazzy idiom; some doubling of vocal line
Uses: good light song for final group; encore; mature sound best

1932. HIGH FLIGHT (John G. Magee, Jr.). G. Schirmer, 1943. H & L keys: Dmin & B♭min; e'–g" & c'–e♭"; Tess-M; 4/4, Moderato; 5pp; Diff-V/m, P/md.
For: baritone; tenor
Mood: dramatic; strong expression
Voice: stepwise; easy skips; easy rhythms
Piano: chordal textures; l.h. rocking triplets and quadruplets; block chords; arpeggios; wide-ranged; incidental doubling of vocal line

Diff: final note sustained 4 meas. *ff*; needs ample sound and control of dynamics; many expressive tempo alterations
Uses: group or program ender

1933. LUCK O' THE ROAD (A. G. Barnett). G. Schirmer, 1950. Dmin; (a)c'–d"; Tess-mL; 4/4, Moderate, but with bravado; 6pp; Diff-V/m, P/me.
For: baritone
Mood: narrative; hearty; rough-hewn; strong
Voice: scalar and small skip melody; refrain; triplet rhythms; repetitive; Irish brogue
Piano: block chords and afterbeats in triplet pattern; simple harmonies; incidental doubling of vocal line
Diff: three characters need differentiation; several sustained d"s and c"s
Uses: group ender

1934. METHUSELAH (Don Marquis). G. Schirmer, 1944. Dmin; c♯'–g♭"; Tess-M; 4/4, 2/4, Freely (with mock solemnity)–Moderato, gradually faster and faster, etc.; 9pp; Diff-V/md, P/m.
For: baritone
Mood: dramatic; declamatory; ballad-style narrative; robust; humorous
Voice: speech rhythms; some melismas; sectional; varied declamation
Piano: chordal textures–block, afterbeat, rolled, repeated, tremolo; some doubling of vocal line
Diff: dynamic and register control with robust sound; 7-beat g♭"; much variety of mood; characterization; many dramatic and expressive possibilities
Uses: good group or program ender; colorful and effective for the singer with a dramatic, comic flair

1935. STRICTLY GERM-PROOF (The Antiseptic Baby) (Arthur Guiterman). G. Schirmer, 1941. Dmin; d'–f"; Tess-mH; 4/4, Allegro moderato; 2+min; Diff-V/m, P/m.
For: baritone; mezzo-soprano; soprano
Mood: humorous; satire
Voice: stepwise; easy skips; long melismas; patter-song
Piano: afterbeat pattern; arpeggiated material in 8ves; countermelody in 8ves; trills; glissando; staccato; ornaments; does not double vocal line
Diff: must have a comic flair
Uses: encore; change of pace

1936. THAT'S LIFE (Josephine Royle). [59]; 1st©1934. H & L keys: Gmaj & E♭maj; g'–a" & e♭'–f"; Tess-M; 4/4, Solemn (Agitated–Slower–Faster); 5pp; Diff-V/md, P/m.
For: lyric soprano; tenor
Mood: humorously philosophical; resigned to life
Voice: short phrases; many phrases begin high and descend; dotted rhythms
Piano: chordal; chiefly supports the voice
Diff: phrases beginning high may be difficult for some
Uses: good light song for teaching young singers to begin high tones easily

SALTER, MARY TURNER
(b. Peoria, IL, 1856; d. New York, NY, 1938)

1937. **THE CRY OF RACHEL** (Lisette Woodworth Reese).
G. Schirmer, 1905, 1933. H & L keys: Cmin & Amin;
c'–a" & a–f "; Tess-M; 4/4, Risoluto; 6pp; Diff-V/m,
P/m.

For: mezzo-soprano; dramatic soprano
Mood: dramatic; tragic; mother's lament for her child
Voice: stepwise and chromatic; many skips of 4th, 5th, & 8ve;
dotted rhythms; highly dramatic
Piano: repeated chords in triplets and syncopated pattern; big
dynamic contrasts; chromatic progressions; many
dim.7th chords; some doubling of voice
Diff: dynamic contrast; sustained high tones
Uses: very dramatic song; effective for the right singer

1938. **LYRICS FROM SAPPHO.** Cycle of 8 Songs for
Medium Voice (trans. Bliss Carman). G. Schirmer,
1909. Reprint: Recital Publications, 1985. Traditional
keys with many changes; d'–f "; Tess-M; traditional
meters, varied tempos; 17pp; Diff-V/m, P/m.

For: mezzo-soprano; baritone
Mood: love songs
Voice: predominantly conjunct; many accidentals; duplet and
triplet division of beat; some speech-like rhythms (d.);
syllabic; some 2-note slurs
Piano: block, broken, and repeated chords; some
countermelody; many accidentals; vocal line generally
doubled or outlined; four songs have preludes,
interludes, or postludes
Diff: rhythms; reading the accidentals
Uses: nature of texts require sophisticated performers and
audience

    a. *I. (Hesperus, bringing together).* Emaj; d'–d"; 4/4,
Andante sostenuto; 1+pp.
    b. *II. (Well I found you).* Emaj; d'– e"; 6/8, no tempo
indication; 3+pp.
    c. *III. (There is a medlar tree).* Cmaj; e'–d"; 6/8,
Andantino; 3pp.
    d. *IV. (If death be good).* D♭maj; f '–f "; 4/4, Lento
religioso; 1p.
    e. *V. (It can never be mine).* Dmin-Fmaj; f '–e"; 4/4,
6/8, Allegro; 3+pp
    f. *VI. (I grow weary of the foreign cities).* Cmaj;
f ×'–e"; 4/4, Andante moderato; 2pp.
    g. *VII. (Over the roofs the honey color'd moon).*
Emaj; e'–e"; 6/8, Larghetto; 2pp.
    h. *VIII. (So falls the hour of twilight).* Gmaj-Emaj;
e'–e"; 4/4, Andante sostenuto; 1+pp.

1939. **A NIGHT IN NAISHAPUR** (Nathan Haskell Dole).
Cycle of Six Songs for Low Voice. G. Schirmer, 1906.
Reprint: Recital Publications, 1985. Traditional keys;
b♭–e"; Tess-wide; traditional meters; varied tempos;
12pp; Diff-V/m, P/me.

For: baritone
Mood: pseudo-Middle-Eastern love poetry
Voice: easy stepwise or chord-outlining motion; easy rhythms;
flowing line; mostly syllabic
Piano: mixture of chordal and linear; patterns reflect text

somewhat; accidentals; awkward keys (with changes)
Uses: illustrates Victorian interest in Middle-Eastern poetry

    a. *Long, Long Ago.* F♯min-maj; c♯'–c♯"; 3/4,
Andante con moto; 2pp.
    b. *In the City of Misgar.* D♭maj; b♭–e♭"; 6/8,
Larghetto; 2pp.
    c. *The Song.* E♭maj; b♭–e♭"; 3/4, Allegretto ma non
troppo; 2pp.
    d. *The Moon Has Long Since Wandered.*
A♭min-maj; b♭–e♭"; 4/4, Lento e serioso; 2pp.
    e. *If I Could Prove My Love.* B♭min; c'–e♭"; 3/4,
Allegretto; 2pp.
    f. *The Farewell.* E♭min; c'–e"; 4/4, Lento religioso;
2pp.

1940. **THE PINE-TREE** (Mary Turner Salter). [8];
1st©1904. H & L keys: Emaj & D♭maj; f♯'–f♯" &
e♭'–e♭"; Tess-M; 6/8, Lento; 2pp; Diff-V/me, P/m.
For: any high or medium voice
Mood: lyrical; philosophical; nature imagery
Voice: lyrical; no rests in vocal line; some chromatic notes
Piano: chordal; fairly chromatic; independent melodic lines in
top or inner voice

SAMINSKY, LAZARE
(b. Odessa, Russia, 1882; d. Port Chester, NY, 1959)

1941. **SONGS OF THREE QUEENS,** Op. 25. Carl Fischer,
1937. Pub. separately.

A. **ANNE BOLEYN'S DIRGE,** Op. 25, No, 1
(traditional). Gmin; g'–a"; Tess-M; 3/4, Poco lento,
tragico ma tranquillo; 4pp; Diff-V/me, P/me.
For: lyric or coloratura soprano
Mood: lyrical; quiet; poem about death
Voice: flowing phrases; sustained
Piano: chordal; somewhat independent of voice
Diff: high *pp* at end
Uses: good for teaching legato

B. **MARY STUART'S FAREWELL TO FRANCE,** Op.
25, No. 2 (French traditional text; English version by
Lillian Morgan Saminsky). Emin; d♯'–f♯"; Tess-M;
2/4, Andantino mosso; 4pp; Diff-V/e, P/me.
For: soprano; mezzo-soprano
Mood: sad and lyrical
Voice: lyrical and sustained
Piano: chordal; largely supportive of voice
Diff: high *pp* at end
Uses: good for teaching legato and control of soft tone

C. **QUEEN ESTHERKA'S LAUGH,** Op. 25, No. 3.

    [unavailable for annotation; available from Sibley
Library, Eastman School of Music]

SAMUEL, GERHARD
(b. Bonn, Germany, 1924)

1942. **THIS HEART THAT BROKE SO LONG . . .** Three Songs on Poems of Emily Dickinson. MMB Music, 1991. cmp1991. X; d♯'–a♭"; Tess-H; changing meters; mostly slow tempos; 7pp (MS); Diff-V/md-d, P/m-md.

For: soprano; tenor

Mood: somber; questioning love; anguished death song

Voice: speech-like rhythms; many dotted and speech-inflected pitches; short phrases; many accidentals; one "yelled" line

Piano: thin scoring; (a.), contrapuntal, mostly 2 voices, with polyrhythms; many 7ths & 9ths; (b.), marked "bell-like"; accomp. mostly 8ves in quarter, half, and dotted-half notes; (c.) is 2- & 3-voice linear style with many accidentals; some staccato; little doubling of vocal line

Diff: tessitura; understanding the poems; rhythms; ensemble

Uses: for a high voice; singer must enjoy the challenges

- a. *This Heart That Broke . . .* X; f♯'–a♭"; Tess-H; 4/4, 5/4, 6/4, ♩ = 48; 2pp.
- b. *You Love Me–You Are Sure–.* X; d♯'–a♭"; Tess-H; 5/4, 4/4, 6/4, 7/4, etc., Slow, ♩ = 44; 2pp.
- c. *Dying, Dying in the Night.* X; d♯'–a♭"; Tess-H; 4/4, 5/4, 3/4, 6/4, 7/4, Measured, ♩ = 66; 3pp.

SAPIEYEVSKY, JERZY
(b. Lodz, Poland, 1945)

1943. **LOVE SONGS** for Soprano and Piano (Anne Spencer Lindbergh). Cycle. Merion, 1979. X (usually with a central pitch); a♭(d')–b♭'(d♭'''); Tess-wide; regular meters, chiefly 4/4; varied tempos; 30min; Diff-V/dd, P/dd.

For: soprano

Mood: lyrical and philosophical love songs; nature imagery; some eroticism

Voice: rather disjunct; large leaps (7ths & 10ths); chromatic; triplets; 2 vs. 3 in piano; other rhythmic complexities; melismas on "ah," "might," and "pain"; staccato; humming, whispering, and speaking; glissandos; sforzandos; grace-note figures with special instructions for those beginning on and before the beat; rapid melismas created by grace notes; long, sustained g"s and g♯"s; alternate notes for extremely high and low pitches; syllabic; occasional 2-note slurs

Piano: chordal and linear; block, broken, and rolled chords; rapid 16th-note scalar passages; contrapuntal sections; highly ornamented; grace-note figures with special instructions; 32nd-note figures; much melodic material; chromatic; triplets; 2 vs. 3 and other rhythmic complexities; many articulations specified; large reach helpful; does not double vocal line

Diff: in every area; perfect pitch desirable; absolutely secure sense of rhythm essential; virtuoso pianist required; advanced interpretive skills needed; a *tour de force*

Uses: "A cycle of 12 songs making one piece. The sequence should be preserved even if only a few of the songs are performed." Shorter versions could be created, bearing in mind the composer's wishes; excellent recital material for advanced performers

- a. *I. (You! Standing like a young tree).* E♭-centered; e♭'–a♭"; Tess-mH; 4/4, 3/4, Allegro (♩ = ca.120) (with changes); 4pp.
- b. *II. (Out of troubled symmetry, seven waves).* X; a(c')–b♭"; Tess-L, H; 4/4, Moderato con moto (♩ = 80) (with changes); 3+pp.
- c. *III. (Give me one thing you touched).* X; e♭'–a♭"; Tess-M; 3/4, 4/4, Moderato (♩ = 76) (with changes); 3+pp.
- d. *IV. (In this warm windy night).* A-centered; d'–g♯"; Tess-M; 4/4, Andante con moto (♩ = 80) (with changes); 3+pp.
- e. *V. (Wherever oh my absent love).* A-centered; d'–b"; Tess-mH; 4/4, Allegro molto (♩ = 144) (with changes); 3+pp.
- f. *VI. (Your body was an island in the darkness).* A-centered; b♭(d')–d♭"; Tess-L; 4/4, Moderato (♩ = 60) (with changes); 3pp.
- g. *VII. (As you are in yourself contained).* G-centered; b♭(d')–a"; Tess-M; 4/4, Allegro moderato (♩ = 96) (with changes); 2+pp.
- h. *VIII. (This morning is grey as beeches in a winter wood).* B♭-centered; a♭(e')–g"; Tess-M; 4/4, 3/4, 2/4, Andante con moto (♩ = 72) (with changes); 4+pp.
- i. *IX. (Have you remembered fear).* X; d'–f"; Tess-M; 4/4, 3/4, Moderato (♩ = 80) (with changes); 3+pp.
- j. *X. (You and I in the circle of your arms).* C-centered; g♯'–b♭" (d♭"); Tess-mH; 4/4, 2/4, Allegro moderato e molto espressivo (♩ = 96) (with changes); 3+pp.
- k. *XI. (Comfort me, hold me against you).* B-centered; a'–f"; Tess-M; 3/4, 4/4, Un poco con moto (♩ = 72) (with changes); 1p.
- l. *XII. (Numberless are the mornings we lay together).* X; e'–g"(a♭"); Tess-M; 3/4, 4/4, Un poco con moto (♩ = 72) (with changes); 2+pp.

SARGENT, PAUL
(b. Bangor, ME, 1910; d. 1987)

1944. **MANHATTAN JOY RIDE** (Louise R. Dodd). [59]; 1st©1946. H & L keys: B♭maj & Gmaj; f'–a♭" & d'–f"; Tess-mH; 3/4, 4/4, Fast–with humor; 6pp; Diff-V/m, P/md.

For: any female voice

Mood: humorously sarcastic; description of ride in traffic

Voice: short phrases; declamatory style; rapid enunciation

Piano: much staccato; does not double vocal line

Diff: text; high-lying phrases with repeated tones

Uses: group ender

1945. **STOPPING BY WOODS ON A SNOWY EVENING** (Robert Frost). [20]; 1st©1950. Amin; c'–e"(a'); Tess-M; 4/4, With quiet movement; 6pp; Diff-V/md, P/d.

For: soprano; tenor; mezzo-soprano; baritone (opt. notes)

Mood: lyrical; quiet; descriptive

Voice: flowing phrases; quiet; lyrical

Piano: chordal; rapid chromatic descending arpeggiations in middle section

Diff: chiefly in the accomp.
Uses: fine song for quiet moment in a group or program

1946. XXTH CENTURY (Robert Hillyer). Leeds, 1940. A♭maj; c'–e"; Tess-M; 4/4 predominates, Fast, very rhythmic; 1min; Diff-V/m, P/d.
For: baritone; mezzo-soprano; dramatic soprano
Mood: frantic; animated
Voice: dotted rhythms; recit. section; quick, sharp diction; short legato section
Piano: chords cover keyboard; some broken chords; passages in 6ths in r.h.
Diff: dynamic control; vocal line independent of piano but related
Uses: effective group ender; see also settings by J. Duke and Martin Kalmanoff

SARGON, SIMON
(b. Bombay, India, 1938)

1947. JUMP BACK for High Voice and Piano (Paul Laurence Dunbar). Southern Music Company (San Antonio), 1990. Traditional keys; c'–a"; Tess-M-mH; regular meters; varied tempos ($\quarternote$ = 60–160); 22pp; Diff-V/me-m, P/me-md.
For: tenor
Mood: personal; humorous love song; philosophical; descriptive; prayerful; love song
Voice: tuneful; syncopated; strophic; roots in ragtime; dialect
Piano: repeated patterns structure accomp.; some ragtime formulas; syncopation; rhythmic; repeated chords
Diff: treatment of dialect
Uses: attractive set of songs; singer and pianist need natural feel for quasi-ragtime style

    a. *Jump Back.* Dmaj; d'–g"; Tess-M-mH; 4/4, 6/8, Lightly, with humor $\quarternote$ = 152; 5pp.
    b. *Compensation.* Emin; d'–a"; Tess-M; 4/2, 3/2, Broadly ($\quarternote$ = 40); 2pp.
    c. *A Florida Night.* Fmaj; c'–f"; Tess-M-mH; 12/8, with a lazy, comfortable feeling ($\quarternote.$ = 60); 7pp.
    d. *A Prayer.* Emaj; e'–g♯"; Tess-M; 3/4, Not too slowly ($\quarternote$ = 60); 3+pp.
    e. *Song.* Amaj; e'–a"; Tess-M; 4/4, With spirit ($\quarternote$ = 160); 4pp.

1948. WAVES OF THE SEA. Six Irish Lyrics for Medium Voice and Piano. NATS Vocal Composition Award, 1993. Facsimile ed., n.d. Tonal; b–g"; Tess-M; regular meters, some changes; slow to moderate tempos; 28pp; Diff-V/me-md; P/me-md.
For: mezzo-soprano best; high baritone; some sopranos
Mood: facets of the Irish personality: folklore; lilting lullaby; springtime love; nostalgia; lyrical observation; energetic dance
Voice: mostly stepwise motion or chord member skips; a few leaps exceed 7th; easy rhythms; syncopation; dotted rhythms; several melodies built on repetition and sequence
Piano: patterned accomps. that change during course of most songs; broken chords, some afterbeat style; mildly

dissonant; syncopation; some 2 vs. 3; little doubling of vocal line, but pitches easily found
Diff: some rhythmic complexity in ensemble and tempo changes in (d.); pronunciation of some Irish words; understanding some poetry
Uses: as a group; songs could be excerpted
Rec: D#297

    a. *The Hosting of the Sidhe* (William Butler Yeats). Amin/Emin with modal touches; e'–g"; Tess: mH; 4/4, 12/8, 2/4, Con moto, with an undercurrent of restlessness throughout ($\quarternote$ = 100); 6+pp.
    b. *Lullaby* (Seumas O'Sullivan). Emin with changes; b–f♯"; Tess-M; 6/8, Andante ($\eighthnote$ = 126); 4+pp.
    c. *In May* (John M. Synge). C-centered; e'–f"; Tess-M; 12/8, Lightly, airily ($\quarternote.$ = 104); 2+pp.
    d. *When You Are Old* (William Butler Yeats). Bmaj; c♯'–f♯"; Tess-mL; 4/4, 3/4, 2/4, Andante tranquillo ($\quarternote$ = 40–66 with many tempo changes); 4+pp.
    e. *Sweet Dancer* (William Butler Yeats). Gmin with modal touches; d'–f"; Tess-M; 3/4, Andantino ($\quarternote.$ = 42); 4pp.
    f. *The Fiddler of Dooney* (William Butler Yeats). D-centered; d'–g"(e"); Tess-M; 6/8, 3/8, With rollicking good spirits ($\quarternote.$ = 72); 5pp.

SARONI, HERMAN S.
(b. Germany, 1823; d. Marietta, OH, 1900)

1949. I WANDER'D IN THE WOODLAND (Mrs. Frances S. Osgood, German trans.). Wm. Hall & Son, 1849. Also reprinted in Yerbury, Grace D., *Song in America: From Early Times to About 1850.* Metuchen, NJ: The Scarecrow Press, 1971. A♭maj; c'–e♭"; Tess-M, Andante; 5pp; Diff-V/m, P/m.
For: soprano; mezzo-soprano
Mood: lyrical; narrative
Voice: stepwise; chord-member skips; ornaments; easy rhythms; some 2-note slurs; apparently set to English text, German words (by Herman S. Saroni) also given
Piano: broken-chord patterning; some countermelody; some imitation of voice; ornaments; no vocal line doubling
Diff: long phrases need good breath planning; smooth legato line; good dynamic control
Uses: effective song for American group; rather reminiscent of Mendelssohn

SCHAFMEISTER, HELEN
(b. Ossining, NY, 1900)

1950. THREE SONGS (Stanley Kimmel). Composers Press, 1973. Traditional keys with some impressionistic touches; b–g"; Tess-M; regular meters; varied tempos; 10pp; Diff-V/e-m, P/e-m.
For: mezzo-soprano; some sopranos
Mood: lyrical; prairie scenes and moods
Voice: rather simple vocal line; some sustained tones; some skips; some fast passages
Piano: much parallelism; arpeggiation; strumming effect in last song; repetitious

Uses: attractive group for a young lyric voice

   a. *Prairie.* A-centered; b–d"; 4/4, Lento sostenuto; 3pp

   b. *A Night Myth.* Shifting harmonies; d'–e♭"; 2/2, Driftingly; 3pp.

   c. *Gypsies.* A-centered; d'–g"; 6/8, Andante, ♪ = 124; 4pp

SCHEER, GENE
(b. New York City, 1958)

1951. LEAN AWAY (Gene Scheer). Piano arr. by Andrew Thomas. Classical Vocal Reprints, 1995. Dmaj; a–g"; Tess-mL, mH; 3/4, 4/4, Moderato, gently; 6pp; Diff-V/m, P/md.

For: high baritone; mezzo-soprano
Mood: love song; sailing imagery; somewhat casual
Voice: easy rhythms in quarters, 8ths, & 16ths; mostly conjunct motion; 2- & 3-note slurs; a a' b form; refrain
Piano: mostly 8th- & 16th-note motion; block and broken chords; rocking motion; sea imagery; some counterpoint; wide range in last verse; accidentals; much doubling of vocal line; short prelude, interludes, and postlude
Diff: tessitura; last section requires flexibility
Uses: has a "pop" song flavor; good student song for a light recital group; encore
Rec: D#28

1952. VOICES FROM WORLD WAR II (Gene Scheer). Cycle. Piano arr. by Lee Musiker. Pub. separately and together. Classical Vocal Reprints, 1997, 1998, 1999. Tonal; g–a♭" (G–a♭'); Tess-wide; metered; 36pp; Diff-V/m-md, P/m-md; baritone specified.

A. HOLDING EACH OTHER. Gene Ink Publications, 1997 (Classical Vocal Reprints). Fmin-G♭maj-F♯min-Emin; b♭–g"; Tess-M, wide; 3/4, 4/4, Andante moderato; 6pp; Diff-V/m, P/m.

For: baritone; mezzo-soprano
Mood: nostalgic; scene from the evening when WWII was declared
Voice: many skips within chord structure; stepwise motion in quarters & 8ths; easy rhythms; repetition; sequence; several key changes; long e" at end
Piano: block and broken chords; mostly 8th-note motion; some counterpoint; accidentals; final section a bit overwritten; some doubling of vocal line; short prelude
Diff: tessitura
Uses: in context of cycle or pair with "At Howard Hawks' House"
Rec: D#28

B. THE GERMAN U-BOAT CAPTAIN. Unsettled–ends Gmin; G–f♯'; Tess-wide; 3/8 with many changes, Flowing; 6pp; Diff-V/md, P/md.

For: baritone
Mood: stressful; sinking of a ship; tells story
Voice: fairly conjunct; skips up to 6th; some syncopation; dotted notes; meter and key changes; mostly syllabic
Piano: sectional; 2- & 3-voice 16th-note motion in 3 sections, quarter-note motion in 2 sections; some arpeggiation; some doubling of vocal line; 4-meas. prelude; 5-meas. postlude
Diff: range; tessitura
Uses: in group

C. AT HOWARD HAWKS' HOUSE. Gene Ink Publications, 1998 (Classical Vocal Reprints). C/D♭ with many color chords; A♭–f'; Tess-mL; 4/4, Swing-feel; 7pp; Diff-V/md, P/md.

For: baritone
Mood: narrative; describes WWII soldiers' encounter with Hollywood; lighthearted
Voice: 8th-note motion in duplets, triplets; syncopation; jazzy; stepwise and small skips, but some long-ranged phrases; many accidentals
Piano: block chords, afterbeats; jazz piano style chords and rhythms; many accidentals; articulation changes, rolled chords; some vocal line doubling; 4-meas. prelude, 3-meas. postlude
Diff: pitch patterns; rhythms
Uses: in group; in a 20th-century theme group or with other songs concerning war or soldiers; group ender; encore; best understood by movie buffs
Rec: D#28

D. OMAHA BEACH. Dmin/Fmaj; A–f'; Tess-M; 4/4, 5/4, 3/4, Freely; Slow (steady) [for the refrain]; 6pp; Diff-V/m, P/md.

For: baritone
Mood: intense; tragic; solemn
Voice: mostly conjunct; various speech-like subdivisions of beat; refrain occurs 3 times; syllabic; some long-ranged phrases
Piano: block chords with dissonances; tone clusters; low and middle piano registers predominate; many low pitches; upper registers for color; some wide reaches; long alto-voice trill presents challenge; 16th-note flourishes; some doubling of vocal line
Diff: range; effective communication; word stress
Uses: in this cycle or in a mixed group of songs about war

E. MORRISON SHELTER. Bmin; A–a♭'; Tess-wide; 3/4, 4/4; 11pp; Diff-V/md, P/md.

For: baritone
Mood: scene–taking tea during a London bombing
Voice: stepwise and small skips; one leap of 9th at climax leading to 10-beat f'; key and meter changes
Piano: 8th-note motion in r.h. in 3rds for much of song, long notes in bass; 2 vs. 3 in 8ths; many accidentals; some doubling of vocal line; 4-meas. prelude; 6- & 3-meas. interludes; 9-meas. postlude
Diff: range; leap to f'; long high note
Uses: in group; a strong group together; (a., c. & d.) are strongest separately and could fit into other groups about soldiers or war; more jazzy and folklike in style than Weisgall *Soldier Songs*, Rorem *War Scenes*, or Cumming *We Happy Few* and make their impact in a more casual and middle-class way; mature singer needed

SCHELLE, MICHAEL
(b. Philadelphia, PA, 1950)

1953. THE MISADVENTURES OF STRUWWELPETER
(Heinrich Hoffmann; didactic poems for children,
1850s). Cycle. Norruth Music, Inc., n.d. (MMB Music).
cmp1991. X; B–c" (tenor clef); Tess-M-H; unmetered
and changing meters; mostly fast tempos; 63pp (MS);
Diff-V/m-dd, P/mostly dd.
For: tenor specified
Mood: wry humor; 19th-century poems about naughty children
and the consequences they suffer
Voice: disjunct; wide-ranged phrases; requires acting; special
vocal effects: some humming, *Sprechstimme*, spoken
text, falsetto with British accent; laughter; trills;
glissandos
Piano: covers keyboard, wide reaches; many accidentals;
many notes; forearm clusters; polyrhythms; repeated
pattern accomps. not fully written out; pianist needs to
ad lib rhythms for variety, and to provide "details"
from a chord structure (c.); some controlled
improvisation in unmetered section; last song quotes
Schubert's "Am Feierabend"; also passages in styles of
Liszt, Rachmaninoff, Joplin; pianist part of drama and
speaks once
Diff: requires two excellent musicians; singer must be good
actor and comfortable changing from singing to
Sprechstimme and speech; pianist must be able to do
the "controlled improvisation" and support the singer in
the unmetered passages; will take extra rehearsal time;
endurance could be a problem
Uses: entertaining and unique cycle for two capable
performers; some songs could be excerpted

  a. *Slovenly Peter.* X; f–a'; Tess-mH; free, 4/4, 5/4,
     6/4, ♩ = 164–♩ = 69; 7pp.
  b. *The Story of Flying Robert.* X; f–b'; Tess-mH; free,
     6/8, 5/4, fast; 10pp.
  c. *Cry Baby.* Almost E♭maj; d♭–g'; Tess-mH; 3/4,
     ♩ = c.140+; 10pp.
  d. *Fat Augustus.* X; B–c"; Tess-wide; 4/4, 5/4,
     ♩ = 112; 11pp.
  e. *Cruel Frederick.* X; d–f♯'; Tess-M; free, 4/4, 5/4,
     ♩ = 152; 11pp.
  f. *Little Conrad Suck-a-Thumb.* Tonal–mostly Amin;
     e–g♯'; Tess-mH; 6/8,4/4, free, 9/8, ♩. = 69–72;
     13pp.

SCHICKELE, PETER
(b. Ames, IA, 1935)

1954. DIVERSE AYRES ON SUNDRIE NOTIONS
(S.99-44/100) for Bargain Counter Tenor and
Keyboard. Theodore Presser, 1979. Traditional keys
and harmonies; c'–e''' (modern tenor clef);
Tess-mL-HH; regular meters, 2 Andantes and 1Allegro;
7min; Diff-V/d, P/md.
For: countertenor intended and the only voice type really
successful with this range and tessitura
Mood: humorous; "singing commercials"; typical of the work
of "P. D. Q. Bach (1807–1742)?"
Voice: primarily conjunct motion; easy skips; 8ve leaps;
numerous melismas ranging from short to medium
length; dotted rhythms; scalar passages in 8ths &16ths;
"Baroque" style; most pitches above b♭" touched only
briefly
Piano: like a basso continuo; single-line l.h. (to be doubled by
a bass instrument if harpsichord is used); homophonic
and contrapuntal; a little chromaticism; incidental
doubling of vocal line
Diff: requires true countertenor voice (or accomplished
falsettist); considerable agility required; words must be
projected very clearly; songs might baffle audience
unfamiliar with "P. D. Q. Bach"
Uses: unusual, humorous recital material; also good for
occasional entertainment purposes

  a. *Do You Suffer.* Cmin; c'–d'''; Tess- mL, HH; 4/4,
     Andante (not too slow); 4pp.
  b. *Hear Me Through.* Amaj; c♯'–c♯'''; Tess-M; 6/8,
     Andante; 3pp.
  c. *If You Have Never.* Dmaj; f♯'–e'''; Tess-H; 4/4,
     Allegro; 2pp.

SCHINHAN, JAN PHILIP
(b. Vienna, Austria, 1887; d. Chapel Hill, NC, 1975)

1955. WHITHER SHALL I GO FROM THY SPIRIT
(Psalm 139). Brodt, 1956. cmp1930. Dmaj; c♯'–g';
Tess-mL; 4/4; 4pp; Diff-V/md, P/md.
For: mezzo-soprano; soprano (not light); high baritone
Mood: sacred; omnipresence of God
Voice: mostly stepwise; skips on chord lines; some
long-ranged phrases; syncopation; triplets
Piano: linear-chordal combination; opening vocal phrase used
contrapuntally; large reaches; syncopation; rather
complex texture; some countermelody; many
accidentals
Diff: irregular entrances; ensemble
Uses: good sacred song; recital or service use

SCHONTHAL, RUTH [Schönthal-Seckel]
(b. Hamburg, Germany, 1924)

[See Appendix for songs with German and Spanish texts]

1956. BY THE ROADSIDE. Six Songs to Poems by Walt
Whitman for Soprano and Piano. Oxford Univ. Press,
1979. cmp1975. Tonal, bitonal, and atonal; c'–b♭";
Tess-wide; traditional meters with changes; many
tempo changes; 6min; Diff-V/md-d, P/md.
For: soprano specified
Mood: philosophical and descriptive observations
Voice: many small skips; several long-ranged phrases (e.g.,
d'–f", f♯'–b♭", c'–f", etc.); some accidentals;
fragmented phrases; some rhythmic complexities;
double-dotted rhythms; triplets and duplets juxtaposed;
(b.) & (c.), speech-like rhythms; mostly syllabic; a few
2-note slurs; many dynamic markings
Piano: combination of linear (mostly 2-voice texture), block,
and broken vertical structures, often built in 4ths &

5ths; some harmonics used; special pedal effects; doubling of vocal line rare and incidental

Diff: tessitura and range of some phrases; possibly high, soft dynamics; several occurrences of *messa di voce*; some entrances; ensemble, particularly in (c.)

Uses: nice group to introduce wide tessitura and other advanced vocal and musical techniques to a singer with flexibility and easy technique

   a. *By the Roadside.* Bitonal; e'–g♯"; 6/8 with changes, Moderato–Quasi doppio movimento; 2pp.
   b. *Thought.* Bitonal; d♭'–a"; 2/4 with changes, With energy–Andante con moto; 2pp.
   c. *Visor'd.* X; d'–g♯"; 2/4 with changes, Tempo rubato; 2pp.
   d. *To Old Age.* D-centered; c♯'–b♭"; 6/4, 7/4, Tranquil, but flowing; 1p.
   e. *A Farm Picture.* Cmaj-Amin; c'–a"; 6/8, Gently moving; 1p.
   f. *A Child's Amaze.* Bmaj; f♯'–g♯"; 4/4, 3/2, Like a chorale, Moderato; 2pp.

1957. POOR BIT OF A WENCH (D. H. Lawrence). [11, Vol. 9]. F; c'–f"; Tess-M; 3/8, Mosso, ma molto rubato; 2pp; Diff-V/m, P/m.

For: high baritone; mezzo-soprano
Mood: pitying
Voice: easy rhythms; difficult intervals on first page; some long-ranged phrases (10th)
Piano: some doubling of vocal line; some bitonality; chords; arpeggiation
Diff: intervals on first page; understanding text
Uses: good short song

1958. WILD NIGHTS (Emily Dickinson). [11, Vol. 9]. D; d'–g♯"; Tess-mH; 4/4, 5/4, 3/4, 3/2, Un poco agitato; 2pp; Diff-V/d, P/d.

For: soprano
Mood: passionate
Voice: opens with Lydian mode scale; other stepwise and chromatic passages; a few skips; triplet and duplet subdivisions of beat
Piano: repeated chords; triplet arpeggiation; many accidentals; does not double vocal line
Diff: some intervals hard to sing with little piano help; rhythm; ensemble
Uses: in a group of Dickinson songs or art songs by women composers from this series

SCHOOLEY, JOHN
(b. Nelson, PA, 1943)

1959. FROM A VERY LITTLE SPHINX (Edna St. Vincent Millay). Glouchester Press (Heilman Music), 1982. Cycle. X; a♯–b"; Tess-wide; regular meters with changes; varied tempos; 16pp; Diff-V/d-dd, P/d-dd.

For: soprano
Mood: poetry depicts seven "scenes" in a young girl's life; music characterizes the child in seven contrasting moods–indecisive, playful, lonely, neglected, fickle, puzzled, and carefree [from composer's note]

Voice: predominant melodic interval is the 4th; phrases often long-ranged; pitch patterns more complicated than rhythms; many accidentals; some staccato; (c.), unaccomp; coloratura techniques
Piano: tertian, quartal, and quintal chord structures; patterns mostly broken chords; some afterbeat patterning (g.); some 4-voice chords (d.); some songs have 6–8-meas. prelude and an interlude; doubling of vocal line incidental
Diff: melodic patterns; ensemble; singer must be vocally and musically secure; characterization for some singers
Uses: excellent material for a solid musician with flexible voice and talent for characterizing; see also setting by Bernard Wagenaar

   a. *Come Along In Then, Little Girl!* X; f'–b"; 3/4 with changes, Tempo rubato; 2pp.
   b. *Oh, Burdock!* C-centered; c'–f♯"; 3/4, Bouncing with rhythm; 2+pp.
   c. *Everybody but Just Me.* C-centered; c'–b"; unmetered, Slow with rubato; 1/2 p.
   d. *I Know a Hundred Ways to Die.* X; e'–b♭"; 3/4 with changes, Slow in a whimsical style; 3pp.
   e. *Look, Edwin!* X; c'–f♯"; 4/8, 2 tempos, Flexible rhythm throughout; 2pp.
   f. *All the Grown-Up People Say.* X; d♯'–e♯"; 4/4, Slow with dignity and sonority; 2pp.
   g. *Wonder Where This Horseshoe Went.* X; a♯–b"; 2/4, 2 tempos, In a fast trotting style; 4pp.

1960. I LOVE THEM (John Schooley). Glouchester Press (Heilman Music), 1982. cmp1982. C-centered; a–d"; Tess-M; Andante–Allegro; 5pp; Diff-V/md, P/md.

For: mezzo-soprano or contralto specified
Mood: humorous–describes in informal language the virtues of three men she loves.
Voice: disjunct melody; syncopation; irregular and jazzy rhythms; some spoken lines; two tempos
Piano: mostly linear; some afterbeat-style accomp.; many articulations; no vocal line doubling; two tempos
Diff: two alternating tempos–the second twice as fast as the first; rhythms
Uses: humorous touch for a group about contemporary life, or group of American songs; for the singer who can bring it off

1961. PRAISE OUR GOD (John Schooley). Glouchester Press (Heilman Music), 1982. E-centered using quartal harmony; e'–a"; Tess-mH; 2/4 with changes, Andante espressivo; 1p; Diff-V/me, P/me.

For: soprano; tenor
Mood: sacred; in praise of God
Voice: many small skips; ends on long g♯" *p*; uncomplicated rhythm
Piano: quartal and quintal structures; 4–5-voice texture; doubling of vocal line incidental
Diff: possibly executing the many indicated dynamics
Uses: good short song for sacred recital group or church

1962. VOCALISE for Soprano. Glouchester Press (Heilman Music), 1981. Gmin-Cmin; c'–a♭"; Tess-M; 4/4, Andante cantabile et espressivo; 2pp; Diff-V/m, P/m.

For: soprano specified
Mood: lyric
Voice: vocalise on "ah"; mostly stepwise; some small skips; rhythms of medium difficulty; soft ending; *f* climax at key change
Piano: contrapuntal; does not double vocal line
Diff: length of phrases; endurance
Uses: effective vocalise of moderate range

SCHROEDER, PHILLIP
(b. Sacramento, CA, 1956)

1963. **FIVE WHITMAN SONGS** (Walt Whitman). Soprano and Piano. Recital Publications, 1998. cmp1995. Mostly X; b–b♭"; Tess-mL, M, cs; regular meters; slow to moderate tempos; 23pp; Diff-V/m-md, P/m-md.
For: soprano; tenor
Mood: reflective; dreams of an ideal world; communion with the soul
Voice: lyrical; conjunct and large intervals; flowing phrases; accidentals; sustained high tones; syllabic
Piano: mostly linear; broken-chord patterns; wide spacing; fairly thin textures; tremolo; many accidentals; mildly dissonant
Diff: some pitches; a few high phrases
Uses: good set for a fairly advanced lyric soprano; texts also suitable for tenor; singer must understand and like Whitman

    a. *Memories.* X; c'–f♯"; Tess-mL; 2/4, 3/4, ♩= 52; 4+pp.
    b. *I Dreamed in a Dream.* X on B♭; d'–a"; Tess-M; 6/8, 9/8, ♪= 108; 5pp.
    c. *An Ended Day.* A-centered; d♯'–f♯"; Tess-M; 4/4, ♩= c.44; 3pp.
    d. *This Day, O Soul.* E♭-centered; b–b♭"; Tess-wide; 3/4, ♩= 126; 3+pp.
    e. *A Clear Midnight.* X; c♯'–g♯"; Tess-M; 2/4, 3/4, ♩= 56–58; 5+pp.

SCHULLER, GUNTHER
(b. New York, NY, 1925)

[See Appendix for songs with German texts]

1964. **MEDITATION** (Gertrude Stein). [49]. cmp1960. Atonal; c♯'–f♯"; Tess-M; 4/4, 5/4, 7/8, 5/8, 2/4, 3/4, Slow; 3pp; Diff-V/dd, P/dd.
For: any high or medium voice
Mood: philosophical
Voice: fragmented and disjunct; highly chromatic; difficult rhythms; spoken phrase
Piano: fragmented; highly chromatic; pointillistic; difficult rhythmic patterns
Diff: frequent meter changes; pitches; rhythms; text; ensemble
Uses: for advanced musicians to whom this text appeals

SCHUMAN, WILLIAM H.
(b. New York, NY, 1910; d. New York, NY, 1992)

[See D#50; no titles given]

1965. **GOD'S WORLD** (Edna St. Vincent Millay). Marks, 1933. Fmaj; c'–g"; Tess-mH; 4/4, Andantino, con desiderio; 3pp; Diff-V/md, P/m.
For: soprano (not light); tenor
Mood: fervent; exuberant; beauty of nature in autumn
Voice: many skips; accidentals; fermatas; long phrases; long-ranged phrases
Piano: chordal; some countermelody; some vocal line doubling
Diff: several phrases end on high tones; large dynamic contrasts
Uses: rather romantic; recital use, possibly in seasons of the year group

1966. **ORPHEUS WITH HIS LUTE** (William Shakespeare). [24, 29, 64]; 1st©1944. H & L keys: Dmin & Bmin; c'–f♯" & a–d♯"; Tess-M; 3/4, 4/4, Slowly; 2pp; Diff-V/m, P/e.
For: any medium voice
Mood: lyrical; haunting; in praise of music
Voice: sustained; stepwise descending passages; irregular phrase lengths; some ascending phrases; sustained tone at end
Piano: chordal, 4-voice texture; each chord repeated in quarter-half rhythm; does not double vocal line
Diff: some pitches, esp. c' heard against c♯' in piano; sustained soft final tone on a' (H)
Uses: beautiful song; good for teaching and performance
Rec: D#65

1967. **TIME TO THE OLD.** Three Songs Set on Words of Archibald MacLeish. Cycle. Merion, 1981. cmp1979. "For Rosalind Rees." X; b–g♯"; Tess-M-mH; changing meters; slow tempos; 11+min; Diff-V/d, P/md.
For: mezzo-soprano seems best
Mood: bleak; concerns the "running" of time toward death, as seen by an old person
Voice: often disjunct; leaps of 7th & 9th; speech-like rhythms; many accidentals; slow tempos make long phrases; needs good control of dynamics; portamentos
Piano: mostly block structures, often rolled; some tertian harmony; other types of structures; most chords have several accidentals; many have 7 or 8 notes; no vocal line doubling but most of singer's pitches can be found
Diff: rhythms; dynamics; bleak subject; performed without pause
Uses: as a recital set
Rec: D#298

    a. *The Old Gray Couple.* X; b–g"; changing meters, ♩= ca.44; 3pp.
    b. *Conway Burying Ground.* X (ends A♭); b–g"; changing meters, ♩= ca.60; 3pp.
    c. *Dozing on the Lawn.* X; c'–g♯"; changing meters, ♩= ca.48; 2pp. [**Rec:** D#58]

SCHWANTNER, JOSEPH
(b. Chicago, IL, 1943)

1968. **TWO POEMS OF AGUEDO PIZARRO.** For
Soprano and Piano (trans. Barbara Stoler Miller).
Helicon, 1981. cmp1980. "For Lucy Shelton." X;
b♭–b"; Tess-wide; changing meters; 10 oversized pp.
(very large); Diff-V/dd, P/dd.

For: soprano (lyric or lyric-coloratura probably best)
Mood: dramatic
Voice: angular; long-ranged phrases; rhythms highly complex
but well-marked (grouped); grace notes; many
accidentals; many dynamic markings *pp–fff*; singer
must whistle and hum; part for *crotales* (antique
cymbals) is opt. and can be played by singer; many
melismas; requires flexibility
Piano: linear writing predominates; special instructions for
pianist; many rapid repeated notes; trills; grace notes;
sostenuto pedal; pianist instructed to "whistle with
singer" at one point; tone clusters; polyrhythms; other
difficulties common to contemporary piano scores;
does not double vocal line but sometimes imitates
Diff: tessitura; pitch patterns (perfect pitch desirable);
rhythms; ensemble; tone-color control (*senza vibrato*);
flexibility
Uses: recital material for performers experienced in this style
Rec: D#299

    a. *Shadowinnower.* X; b–b"; unmetered and changing
    meters, Dramatico; 6pp.

    b. *Black Anemones.* X; b♭–b♭"; 3/8 with changes,
    Cantabile con elegante; 4pp. [**Rec:** D#71]

SCOTT, JOHN PRINDLE
(b. Norwich, NY, 1877; d. Syracuse, NY, 1932)

1969. **THE WIND'S IN THE SOUTH** (Song for High
Soprano) (John Prindle Scott). Huntzinger & Dilworth,
1916. Reprint: Willis Music Company. E♭maj; d♭'–c'";
Tess-mH-H; 2/4, Allegro; 6pp; Diff-V/md, P/m.

For: coloratura soprano
Mood: lyrical; spring song
Voice: conjunct with skips; fast; trills and turns; staccato high
tones on "ah"; cadenza with piano; one ascending
syncopated scale from c" to c'"
Piano: chordal–afterbeat patterns; some doubling of vocal line;
some cadenza duetting
Diff: coloratura, staccato accuracy, and trill required
Uses: good teaching song for young coloraturas

SEEGER, CHARLES, JR.
(b. Mexico City, Mexico, 1886, of American parents; d.
Bridgewater, CT, 1979)

1970. **ENDYMION** (Oscar Wilde) (No. 2 of *Seven Songs for
a High Voice*). G. Schirmer, 1911. F♯maj; f'–a♯";
Tess-H; 3/2, 2/2, 2/4, Con moto gentile; 12pp;
Diff-V/d, P/d.

For: soprano
Mood: animated; yearning; love song

Voice: many small skips; 2–4-note slurs; duplets and triplets
Piano: rapid arpeggios and block chords; some countermelody;
some polyrhythms; requires fleet fingers; somewhat
like R. Strauss; orchestral effects
Diff: rhythms; ensemble; register and dynamic control
Uses: effective song; quiet ending; could open a group
Rec: D#300

SEEGER, RUTH CRAWFORD
(b. East Liverpool, OH, 1901; d. Chevy Chase, MD, 1953)

1971. **FIVE SONGS** (Carl Sandburg). Contralto and Piano.
C. F. Peters, 1990. cmp1929; first performance by
Radiana Pazmor. X; g–f♯"; Tess-L-M, wide; changing
meters; varied tempos (♩ = 54–116); 10min; Diff-V/m-
d, P/m-d.

For: contralto
Mood: romantic thoughts: memories, reincarnation, joy,
moonlight, sunsets
Voice: many disjunct phrases; large intervals; some repeated-
note phrases; numerous low phrases; chromatic and
dissonant
Piano: chordal; some linear; broken-chord patterns; dissonant;
many accidentals; some 3-stave scoring; some complex
rhythms
Diff: pitches; some rhythms; dissonant harmonies; perfect
pitch helpful
Uses: good example of atonal composition; probably very
effective for a mature contralto
Rec: D#s 301 (all 5), 302, 303, 304 (3 each)

    a. *Home Thoughts.* X; c'–e"; Tess-M; 3/4, 2/4, 4/4,
    Andante (♩ = 80); 3pp. [**Rec:** D#58]

    b. *White Moon.* X; a–e♭"; Tess-mL; 4/4, 3/4, 5/8, 6/8,
    Tranquillo (♩ = 56); 3pp. [**Rec:** D#s 58, 71]

    c. *Joy.* X; g–f"; Tess-wide; 4/4, 5/4, 3/4, Allegro
    (♩ = 116); 4pp. [**Rec:** D#58]

    d. *Loam.* X; a–f"; Tess-L-M; 4/4, 3/4, 5/4, Grave
    (♩ = 84); 3pp.

    e. *Sunsets.* X; b♭–f♯"; Tess-M, L, cs; 3/4, 2/4, 5/4,
    6/8, 9/8, Lento (♩ = 54); 5pp.

SELBY, WILLIAM (See Special Section)

SERLY, TIBOR
(b. Losonc, Hungary, 1901; d. London, England, 1978)

1972. **THE FLIGHT OF THE LARK** (William
Wordsworth). (Peer)Southern, 1950. Dmaj; e'–a";
Tess-mL; 6/4, 4/4, 5/4, Allegro; 4pp; Diff-V/m,P/d.

For: soprano; mezzo-soprano
Mood: lyrical and philosophical
Voice: stepwise; small skips; largely diatonic; lyrical and
flowing; syllabic
Piano: chordal–block, broken, repeated, rolled; much use of
rustling, arpeggiated chords in septuplet 32nds; some
chromaticism; patterned; triplets and groupings of 5,
17, & 18; programmatic; frequently doubles vocal line
Diff: character and tessitura of vocal line seem somewhat at

odds with nature of text and accomp., making it difficult to interpret; potential for ensemble problems in last section

Uses: recital possibilities

SESSIONS, ROGER
(b. Brooklyn, NY, 1896; d. Princeton, NJ, 1985)

1973. ON THE BEACH AT FONTANA (James Joyce). [22, 49]; 1st©1935. Fmin; c'–ab"; Tess-M; 6/8, 2/4, 3/4, 9/8, Un poco inquieto (♩. = 54); 3pp; Diff-V/d, P/d.

For: soprano
Mood: lyrical; sad; love song
Voice: chromatic vocal line; some large intervals; some pitches difficult
Piano: chromatic; 16th-note movement; 6/8 vs. 2/4 in voice; somewhat re-edited in [49]
Diff: pitches; rhythms; ensemble; poem
Uses: effective song; recital use
Rec: D#s 16, 54

SHAFFER, JEANNE E.
(b. Knoxville, TN, 1925)

1974. CHRISTINA ROSSETTI, MY MOTHER AND ME. A Song Cycle for Mezzo-Soprano or Baritone (Christina Rossetti). Arsis Press, 1997. Tonal; bb–g"; Tess-M, mH, cs; regular and irregular meters with some changes; moderate tempos (♩ = 58–144); 13min; Diff-V/m-md, P/me-md.

For: mezzo-soprano; soprano; baritone
Mood: lyrical; relationship between mother and daughter when mother is near death
Voice: lyrical; melodic; speech rhythms; syllabic; ends on alternating f" and g" sustained
Piano: mostly chordal with various patterns; mildly dissonant; piano sets mood
Uses: useful cycle for lyric mezzo, soprano, or baritone to whom the poems appeal

    a. *Up-Hill.* X on C; bb–g"; Tess-cs; 3/4, 2/4, Maestoso ♩ = 58; 4pp.
    b. *Sleeping at Last.* Cmin-maj; bb–eb"; Tess-cs; 4/4, 5/4, 2/4, 3/4, Larghetto ♩ = 66; 3pp.
    c. *Song.* Gmaj; b–f#"; Tess-M; 5/4, 4/4, 3/4, 6/4, Allegro Moderato ♩ = 82; 3pp.
    d. *Remember.* A-centered; c'–e"; Tess-cs; 4/4, 3/4, Adagio ♩ = 66; 3pp.
    e. *Another Spring.* C-centered; d'–g"; Tess-M-H; 6/8, 7/8, 3/8, Allegro ♩ = 144; 5pp.

1975. ETERNITY (Wiliam Blake). Five Songs to Poems of William Blake for Soprano with Piano Accompaniment. Arsis Press, 1994 (Sisra Publications). cmp1992. Traditional keys; eb'–bb"(db'''); Tess-M-mH-H; mostly regular meters, ♩ = 66–176; 7min; Diff-V/m, P/e-me.

For: soprano
Mood: delicate; lyrical; centers on the fleeting joys of life and the folly of trying to make them permanent

Voice: melodic; good word stress; mostly conjunct; small coda without words floats up to a sustained db''' in last song
Piano: repeated patterns form background mood
Uses: useful short cycle for undergraduate lyric soprano with an easy top; good for teaching legato line; probably attractive to most audiences

    a. *The Wild Flower's Song.* Dbmaj; eb'–g"; Tess-M; 3/4, 4/4, Larghetto ♩ = 72; 2pp.
    b. *Soft Snow.* Fmin; f'–bb"; Tess-mH; 5/4, Andante ♩ = 66; 2pp.
    c. *Infant Joy.* Gmaj; e'–g"; Tess-M; 4/4, 2/4, 5/4, 6/4, Larghetto ♩ = 96; 1p.
    d. *Infant Sorrow.* D minorish; g'–a"; Tess-mH; 4/4, Allegro Moderato ♩ = 144; 2pp.
    e. *Eternity.* Dbmaj; g'–db'''; Tess-H; 3/4, Allegro ♩ = 176; 3pp.

SHAPEY, RALPH
(b. Philadelphia, PA, 1921)

1976. GOETHE SONGS for Soprano and Piano (Wolfgang von Goethe). Theodore Presser, 1999. cmp1995. Atonal (tone row); c#'–f#"; Tess-mL, M, mH, cs; changing meters; slow tempos; 17pp; Diff-V/me-dd, P/e-dd.

For: soprano; mezzo-soprano
Mood: austere; themes of darkness and light
Voice: atonal; tone row construction; some avant-garde techniques; angular lines; repetition of words in different orders; many different rhythmic figures; melismas on tone rows; one song unaccomp.
Piano: atonal; tone row construction; chordal; constant accidentals; many rhythmic groupings
Diff: pitches; rhythms; texts; perfect pitch desirable
Uses: example of tone row construction; for a singer with perfect pitch who specializes in avant-garde music

PART 1

    a. *Spirit.* X; c#'–f"; Tess-M; 3/4, 4/4, 5/4, ♩ = 56 (♪ = 112) Cantabile; 1p.
    b. *The Song.* X; d'–e"; Tess-M; 5/8, 2/4, 3/8, Leggiero (light), Giocoso (playful) ♩ = 84 (♪ = 168); 1p.
    c. *Tree–Life.* X; d'–f#"; Tess-cs; 5/8, 4/8, ♪ = 80 (♩ = 40) Appassionata; 2+pp.
    d. *Peace Gone.* X; f'–g"; Tess-mH; 4/4, 6/4, 5/4, ♩ = 40 (Majestic); ½p.
    e. *Deed–Glory.* X; eb'–f#"; Tess-cs; 5/8, 2/4, ♩ = 45 Solenne (Solemn); 1p.
    f. *Woman.* X; c#'–f"; Tess-M; 3/4, 4/4, 5/4, Cantabile ♩ = 50; 1p.

PART 2

    g. *Master.* X; d'–f"; Tess-M; 3/4, 4/4, 2/4, 5/8, ♩ = 67 Bravura, Spiritoso (spirited), Vibrant; 1+pp.
    h. *Poetry–Life.* X; c#'–eb"; Tess-M; 5/4, 3/4, 4/4, 2/4, Vibrant, vigoroso ♩ = 72; 1+pp.
    i. *Bread–Sorrow.* X; eb'–f#"; Tess-cs; 2/4, 3/4, ♩ = ♩ = 36 (♪ = 72) Solenne; 2pp.
    j. *Light.* X; eb'–eb"; Tess-M; 4/4, 3/4, ♩ = 36 Appassionata, Largamente, Imponent (Imposing,

Impressive); ½p.

k. *Peace.* X; c♯'–c♯"; Tess-M; unmeasured, Dolce, Cantabile ♩ = 31 (♪ = 62); ½p.

l. *Beloved.* X; c♯'–c♯"; Tess-mL-M; 4/4, 3/4, 5/4, 6/4, ♩ = 51 Maestoso, Appassionata, Exaltazione (Exaltation); 4+pp.

SHAPIRO, NORMAN
(b. 1930)

1977. **SONGS FOR SOPRANO SOLO AND PIANO** (Ogden Nash). E. C. Schirmer, 1961. cmp1952, 1954, & 1955. Pub. separately. Tonal; d'–b♭"; Tess-M-mH; regular meters with changes; contrasting tempos; 7pp; Diff-V/e-md, P/m-md.
For: soprano specified
Mood: humorous; whimsical
Voice: stepwise; small skips; some leaps; interrupted phrases; mostly easy rhythms; syncopation; 2–3-note slurs; duplets in compound meter
Piano: linear-chordal combinations; articulations important; much solo material; some doubling of vocal line
Diff: sustained high tones *ff* (g" and a♭"); ensemble
Uses: clever songs; use as set or separately; all good encores

a. *The Fish.* Fmin; d'–b♭"; Tess-mH; 6/8, 3/8, Allegro; 1+min.
b. *The Seagull.* X; f♯'–f♯"; Tess-M; 3/4, 6/8, 2/4, 9/8, Lento; 2pp.
c. *The Termite.* Dmaj; e'–d"; Tess-M; 4/4, 2/4, Allegro ma non troppo; 2pp.

SHAW, CLIFFORD
(b. Little Rock, AR, 1911; d. Louisville, KY, 1976)

1978. **THE LAMB** (William Blake). Ditson, 1950. Fmaj; f'–f"; Tess-M; 4/4, Moderato. With tender devotion and simplicity; 3pp; Diff-V/e, P/m.
For: soprano; tenor
Mood: lyrical; innocent; child-like
Voice: stepwise; small skips; easy rhythms; legato lines
Piano: chordal texture, 5–7 voices; some large reaches; some doubling of vocal line
Uses: useful for a young singer; very good short-ranged, simple-content song
Rec: D#23

1979. **TO YOU** (Walt Whitman). Peer International, 1952. B♭-E♭maj; e♭'–e♭"; Tess-M; 4/4, Moderate tempo; 2pp; Diff-V/me, P/me.
For: baritone; mezzo-soprano; contralto
Mood: lyrical; "as in intimate conversation"
Voice: repetitive melody; speech rhythms; duplets and triplets
Piano: quartal, quintal, and tertian block chords; does not double vocal line
Diff: some pitches
Uses: quiet ending; see also setting by Rorem

SHEPHERD, ARTHUR
(b. Paris, ID, 1880; d. Cleveland, OH, 1958)

1980. **THE FIDDLERS** (Walter de la Mare). Valley, 1948. "To Marie Simmelink Kraft." Emin; d'–g"; Tess-M; 6/8, Allegro alla giga; 4pp; Diff-V/m, P/m-md.
For: soprano; tenor
Mood: lyrical; jaunty; narrative
Voice: many skips; some chromaticism; several key changes; 6/8 rhythms
Piano: linear, 1–4-voice texture; constant 8th-note motion
Diff: a few pitches
Uses: interesting song; different and useful; group ender
Rec: D#305

1981. **FIVE SONGS,** Op. 7, for High Voice and Pianoforte (James Russell Lowell). Wa-Wan Press, 1909. Reprint: Recital Publications, 1986. [66, vol.5]. Traditional keys; d♭'–a"; Tess-mH; traditional meters with changes; varied tempos; 21pp; Diff-V/md, P/md.
For: tenor seems best
Mood: love songs
Voice: predominantly stepwise motion; small skips; some long-ranged phrases (f'–a"); many chromatic progressions, esp. in (a.) & (b.)–also most complex rhythmically; syncopation, triplets, dotted rhythms; speech-like rhythms in (d.) & (e.); (c.), polymetric section (voice, 3/4, piano, 2/4); syllabic setting predominates; some 2-note slurs; wide dynamic range
Piano: block, broken, and repeated chords; arpeggiation; most songs use several accomp. figures; (d.) & (e.), some rolled chords; chromatic harmonies; generally thick textures; many low notes on keyboard; rhythms incl. 2 vs. 3 & groupings of 5; syncopation; polyrhythms with voice; does not double vocal line
Diff: rhythms; ensemble; hearing the unusual harmonic progressions in (a.) & (b.)
Uses: entire group for tenor; soprano could sing (c.) & (d.); attractive to performers who like lush romantic harmonies; singer needs wide dynamic range; poetry somewhat dated

a. *Lift Up the Curtains of Thine Eyes.* A♭maj; e♭'–a♭"; 4/4 with changes, Molto moderato; 4pp.
b. *Nocturn* [sic]. G♭maj; d♭'–f♯"; 4/4, Andante espressivo ed intimo; 4pp.
c. *There Is a Light in Thy Blue Eyes.* Fmaj; f'–a"; 2/4, 3/4, Allegro vivace ma non troppo; 5pp.
d. *The Lost Child.* Dmaj; d'–g"; 4/4, Andante tranquillo; 4pp. [Rec: D#305]
e. *Rhapsody.* G♭maj; e'–g"; 4/4 with changes, Con molto abandono (with fluctuations); 4pp.

1982. **SEVEN SONGS.** Valley, 1961. cmp1930s–1940s. Pub. together but seem to be more a collection than a set; separate entries below; (d.) for voice, piano, and viola omitted.

A. **GOLDEN STOCKINGS** (Oliver St. John Gogarty). cmp1937. Amaj; d'–g"; Tess-M; 3/4, 4/4, 5/4, 6/4, Allegretto giojante; 4pp; Diff-V/d, P/dd.
For: tenor

Mood: joyful; love song; nature imagery
Voice: somewhat disjunct; flowing phrases; some chromaticism
Piano: running 16ths almost throughout; supporting chords
Diff: some pitches and rhythms; requires light, flexible voice
Uses: effective recital song
Rec: D#s 20, 305

B. **MORNING-GLORY** (Siegfried Sassoon). Fmaj; f'–g"; Tess-M; 3/4, 2/4, Andante semplice; 3pp; Diff-V/m, P/md.
For: soprano; tenor
Mood: lyrical; poetic description of the Nativity
Voice: sustained phrases; some chromaticism
Piano: chordal; some counterpoint
Diff: sustained, legato singing
Uses: can be very effective in performance
Rec: D#305

C. **REVERIE** (Walter de la Mare). Cmin; c'–g"; Tess-mL; 4/4, 3/4, 2/4, Allegretto (with firm legato and singing tone); 4pp; Diff-V/m, P/d.
For: tenor; high baritone
Mood: lyrical; descriptive–"When slim Sophia mounts her horse"
Voice: some phrases rather declamatory; staccato in vocal line
Piano: broken-chord figures in l.h.; independent melody in r.h.
Diff: pitches and rhythms somewhat difficult
Uses: effective recital song; see also setting by J. Duke

D. **SOFTLY ALONG THE ROAD OF EVENING** (Walter de la Mare). D♭maj; b♭–g"; Tess-mL; 2/2, 2/4, 3/4, Andante tranquillo; 4pp; Diff-V/md, P/d.
For: mezzo-soprano
Mood: lyrical; nature picture
Voice: broad, flowing phrases; rather chromatic; 2-note slurs
Piano: chromatic; contrapuntal; very sustained
Diff: pitches; requires fine legato and control of soft tone
Uses: effective recital song

E. **TO A TROUT** (Oliver St. John Gogarty). Cmaj-min; c'–f"; Tess-M; 3/4, 2/4, 4/4, [tempo not indicated, but fairly rapid]; 6pp; Diff-V/d, P/dd.
For: baritone
Mood: descriptive; philosophical
Voice: spirited; chromatic; sectional; somewhat declamatory and dramatic in places
Piano: broken-chord figures; chromatic; scale passages; sextuplets; trills; does not double vocal line
Diff: pitches
Uses: effective for the right performer
Rec: D#s 20, 305

F. **VIRGIL** (Oliver St. John Gogarty). Gmaj; c–f♭'; Tess-M; 4/4, 2/4, 3/4, 5/4, Andante espressivo e con ampiezza; 5pp; Diff-V/dd, P/dd.
For: baritone
Mood: dramatic; descriptive
Voice: long phrases; chromatic; recit.-like sections
Piano: highly chromatic; contrapuntal; triplets; irregular groupings; lengthy postlude
Diff: pitches; rhythms; narrative style

Uses: good recital song
Rec: D#20

1983. **THE STARLING LAKE** (Seumas O'Sullivan). Valley, 1948. cmp 1944. "To Marie Simmelink Kraft." Amin-Fmaj; c'–f"; Tess-M; 3/4, 3/2, 3/8, 4/4, Andante tranquillo; 4pp; Diff-V/m, P/m.
For: soprano; tenor
Mood: lyrical; reminiscent; melancholy
Voice: somewhat chromatic; speech rhythms
Piano: patterned in quiet 3rds in high register with counter-melody; linear texture; 3rds broken up into triplet pattern in middle section; quiet and serene
Uses: lovely song; interior of group; quiet throughout
Rec: D#305

SHORE, CLARE
(b. Winston-Salem, NC, 1954)

1984. **FOUR DICKINSON SONGS** for Soprano and Harpsichord (Emily Dickinson). Arsis, 1984. cmp1981–1982. X; c'–c♭'''; Tess-M-H; regular and irregular meters; moderate tempos; 12pp; Diff-V/d, P/dd.
For: high soprano
Mood: lyrical and philosophical; nature imagery
Voice: conjunct and disjunct motion; many leaps of 8ves, 7ths, 9ths, & 10ths; chromatic; triplets; 2 vs. 3 & 3 vs. 2 in piano; speaking and whispering; lyrical and flowing; syllabic with small melismas; longer melismas on "angels" and "laugh"
Piano: although harpsichord is preferred, the accomp. to these songs would seem to be easily adapted to piano; chordal and contrapuntal; prelude to (a.) is fugal; much 2-voice texture; chromatic; triplets and quintuplets; 2 vs. 3 & 3 vs. 4; lengthy interlude in (a.); does not double vocal line; registrations for harpsichord
Diff: singer needs excellent sense of pitch and rhythm and good vocal acting skills; if done with piano, pianist needs to understand harpsichord technique and registration; could be tiring to perform, as tessitura becomes notably higher as cycle progresses
Uses: good recital material

   a. *With a Flower.* X; c♯'–f♯"; Tess-M; 4/4, 6/4, 3/4, Andante espressivo (♩ = ca.56); 4pp.
   b. *I'm Nobody.* G-centered; e♭'–g"; Tess-M; 3/4, ♩ = 76-80; 2pp.
   c. *Summer Shower.* G-centered; d'–c♭'''; Tess-mH; 4/4, 5/4, ♩ = ca.88; 4pp.
   d. *I Shall Know Why . . .* X; c'–b♭"; Tess-H; 3/4, 5/4, 4/4, Andantino tranquillo (♩ = ca.66); 2pp.

SIEGMEISTER, ELIE
(b. New York, NY, 1909; d. Manhasset, NY, 1991)

1985. **AMERICAN LEGENDS.** Six Songs for Voice and Piano. Marks, 1940–1948. Separate entries below.

A. **PAUL BUNYAN** (Leo Paris). Emaj; b–e"; Tess-mL;

2/2, Lively, rambunctious; 5pp (with repeat); Diff-V/m, P/md.

For: baritone
Mood: narrative and descriptive, like a folksong; humorous
Voice: stepwise; easy skips; a little chromaticism; spoken, shouted, and "bellowed" words; glissandos; syllabic
Piano: chordal–block, afterbeat, and rolled; some chromaticism; supports but does not double vocal line
Diff: shouting and "bellowing" without vocal harm; slow glissando; good vocal actor needed
Uses: good for occasional entertainment purposes

B. **NANCY HANKS** (Rosemary Benét). F-centered; e♭'–f"; Tess-M; 2/2, 2/4, Moderately; 3pp; Diff-V/m, P/me.

For: any high or medium voice
Mood: lyrical; questioning; about Abraham Lincoln's mother
Voice: stepwise; small skips; some chromaticism; triplets; lyrical and flowing; syllabic
Piano: chordal; somewhat chromatic; triplets; considerable doubling of vocal line
Uses: good for students; possible recital material; see also setting by Katherine K. Davis
Rec: D#308

C. **JOHN REED** (Lewis Allan). E♭maj; b♭–e♭"; Tess-mL; 4/4, Moderately; 4pp (with repeat); Diff-V/e, P/e.

For: any medium voice
Mood: narrative and descriptive, like a folksong; concern for the poor
Voice: stepwise; small skips; lyrical and flowing; syllabic
Piano: chordal–block, afterbeat, and rolled; little chromaticism; melody in prelude; considerable doubling of vocal line
Diff: good interpretive skills needed
Uses: for young students

D. **JOHNNY APPLESEED** (Rosemary Benét). Emaj; b–e"; Tess-M, mL; 4/4, 2/2, 3/2, Slowly, with a drawl (with changes); 4pp; Diff-V/m, P/m.

For: any medium voice
Mood: narrative and descriptive, like a folksong
Voice: stepwise; small skips; little chromaticism; triplets; 3 vs. 4 in piano; grace notes; syllabic
Piano: chordal–block and afterbeat; rather chromatic; incidental doubling of vocal line
Diff: chromatic chords make vocal line less obvious than it would appear; ends on 8-beat b; good vocal actor needed
Uses: for occasional entertainment purposes
Rec: D#308

E. **LAZY AFTERNOON** (Leo Paris). Dmaj; d'–d"; Tess-M; 4/4, Moderately; 4pp; Diff-V/me, P/me.

For: all voices
Mood: lyrical and philosophical; avoiding work; humorous
Voice: stepwise; easy skips; entirely diatonic; short phrases; soft ending on d"; syllabic
Piano: chordal–block, broken, and afterbeat; top voice doubles vocal line; melodic fragments in interludes;
Diff: good vocal actor needed

Uses: students; occasional entertainment purposes
Rec: D#308

F. **THE LINCOLN PENNY** (Alfred Kreymborg). Emaj; b–e"; Tess-M, mL; 4/4, Moderately; 3pp (with repeat); Diff-V/me, P/e.

For: any medium voice
Mood: narrative and descriptive, like a folksong; philosophical
Voice: stepwise; easy skips; little chromaticism; syllabic
Piano: chordal–block and afterbeat; some chromaticism; strongly supports but does not double vocal line
Uses: for occasional entertainment purposes

1986. **ELEGIES FOR GARCÍA LORCA** (Antonio Machado). Cycle. [160]. cmp1938. Chromatic harmonies; a–f♯"; Tess-mL, M; regular and changing meters; varied tempos; 10pp; Diff-V/me-m, P/e-md.

For: mezzo-soprano; baritone
Mood: philosophical; lyrical and dramatic; sad; abstract and somewhat chilling
Voice: both sweeping and short phrases; some speech rhythms; some low-lying phrases; some static sections
Piano: chordal textures; chromaticism; sustained passages
Diff: dramatic climax on e" and f" in second song perhaps difficult for a low voice
Uses: would work well as small cycle; (a.) might prove low for singer suited to (b.) & (c.)
Rec: D#308

a. *The Crime.* X on B; a–d"; Tess-mL; 4/4, 3/2, 2/4, Moderately; 3pp.
b. *The Poet and Death.* Emin; c'–f"; Tess-M; 2/2, 2/4, 4/4, 3/2, Fiery, with energy; 5pp.
c. *Elegy.* X on E; b–f♯"; Tess-M; 2/2, 3/2, Slowly, with utmost tranquillity; 2pp.

1987. **EVIL** (Richard Eberhart). [160]. cmp1967. X; A♭–e♭'; Tess-M; 3/4, 7/8, 2/4, 4/4, 5/8, 9/8, 6/8, 5/4, Moderately (♩ = 69); 8pp; Diff-V/dd, P/d.

For: baritone; bass
Mood: philosophical; uses irony to make its timeless point about good and evil; reference to Vietnam War; rather chilling
Voice: disjunct; chromatic; dramatic; sweeping phrases; complicated rhythms; staccato
Piano: generally chordal and chromatic; varies in texture to suit the vocal line; some rhythmic complications
Diff: pitches and rhythms; requires large, well-controlled voice and excellent accompanist
Uses: could be effective in recital, perhaps in place of an aria
Rec: D#308

1988. **THE FACE OF WAR.** Five Songs for Low Voice and Piano or Orchestra (Langston Hughes). Cycle. Carl Fischer, 1978; First performed by William Warfield, 1968. X; g–f♭" (H & M voice settings also available); Tess-mL; regular and irregular meters with frequent changes; varied tempos; 8+min; Diff-V/d, P/d; MS.

For: bass-baritone; bass; contralto; any voice with strong low tones if high or med. setting is used
Mood: somber; deals with reactions to war and death; philosophical

-317-

Voice: conjunct with some large leaps of 7th, 8ve, & 9th; highly chromatic; chiefly syllabic; many long sustained tones, frequently low

Piano: good reduction of orchestral score; MS facsimile seems easy to read; chordal; 5–6-voice texture; highly chromatic; independent of vocal line

Diff: pitches and rhythms; singer needs free, strong low voice; cycle ends on long d♭" cresc. to *fff*

Uses: excellent recital material

Rec: D#306

 a. *Official Notice.* X; a–f♭"; Tess-L; 3/4, 5/8, 4/4, Slow (♩ = 69); 1p.
 b. *Listen Here, Joe.* X; g–e♭"; Tess-mL; 6/8 with many changes, Lively, rhythmic (♩ = 80); 4pp.
 c. *Peace.* X; b–d"; Tess-M; 4/4, 2/4, 3/4, Slow (♩ = 55); 2pp.
 d. *The Dove.* X; g♯'–d"; Tess-L; 7/8 with many changes, Moderately, flowing (♩ = 88); 3pp.
 e. *War.* X; b♭–e♭"; Tess-mL; 4/4 with many changes, Quite fast (♩ = 120–126); 5+pp.

1989. FIVE CUMMINGS SONGS (e. e. cummings). [160]. cmp1970. Highly chromatic; a♯–a♭"; regular and irregular changing meters; moderate tempos; 15pp; Diff-V/d-dd, P/d-dd.

For: mezzo-soprano

Mood: lyrical love songs; somewhat abstract; moods range from sad to joyful

Voice: largely disjunct; some flowing phrases; large leaps; highly chromatic; speech rhythms; some dialect; some difficult rhythms

Piano: mostly chordal textures; highly chromatic; some difficult rhythmic structures; lies high on keyboard some of the time

Diff: pitches; rhythms; soft high tones

Uses: excellent recital material for mature professional singer

Rec: D#308

 a. *in spite of everything.* X; c♯'–g♯"; 9/16, 7/8, 2/4, 5/8, etc., Moderately; 2pp.
 b. *the first of all my dreams.* X; c♯'–a♭"; 3/4, 5/4, 4/4, 7/8, etc., Moderately; 4pp.
 c. *raise the shade.* X; a♯–a♭"; 5/8, 3/8, 3/4, 4/4, etc., Fast; 3pp.
 d. *up into silence.* X; c'–a♭"; 9/8, 4/4, 2/4, 3/4, 7/8, etc., Moderately slow; 3pp.
 e. *because it's spring.* X; c♯'–g♯"; 4/4, 9/8, 2/4, 5/8, etc., Flowing, fairly lively; 3pp.

1990. FOR MY DAUGHTERS (Norman Rosten). [160]. cmp1952. Traditional keys; c♯'–g"; Tess-M; regular meters with changes; moderate to lively tempos; 28pp; Diff-V/me-m, P/m-md.

For: soprano; mezzo-soprano; possibly tenor

Mood: lyrical; loving; humorous; subject of various attitudes or incidents in a child's life

Voice: mostly lyrical and flowing; some large leaps; some short, fragmented phrases; some chromaticism

Piano: chordal textures; some polyrhythms; some chromaticism; some long trills in both hands

Diff: set as a whole needs good vocal actor

Uses: could be good for many students; recital possibilities

Rec: D#308

 a. *Have You a Question?* Amaj; e♭'–g"; 4/4, Moderately; 2pp.
 b. *Rain.* Gmaj-Emin; e'–g"; 2/4, 3/4, Lively; 5pp.
 c. *May I Escape?* Amaj; c♯'–f♯"; 2/2, 2/4, Fairly lively; 3pp.
 d. *Good Morning.* Dmaj; d'–g"; 6/8, Lively, brightly; 5pp.
 e. *What Did You Do Today?* Dmaj; e'–f♯"; 4/4, 2/4, Leisurely tempo; 3pp.
 f. *Saying Good Night.* Gmin; c♯'–f"; 6/8, 2/8, 7/8, 2/4, 9/8, Moderately; 4pp.
 g. *Growing.* X; e♭'–f♯"; 2/2, 2/4, 6/8, Moderately lively; 4pp.
 h. *Goodbye, Goodbye.* Gmaj; d'–g"; 2/2, Moderately; 2pp.

1991. LONELY STAR (Elie Siegmeister). (Peer)Southern, 1952. [65]. cmp1950. Gmin; d'–g"; Tess-mH; 4/4, Moderately slow; 3pp; Diff-V/m, P/m.

For: soprano; tenor

Mood: lyrical; the unattainable goal

Voice: syncopation; duplets and triplets; many skips, esp. 5ths & 6ths; folk-like; pseudo-dialect (e.g. "ain't," "lookin'," etc.)

Piano: chordal–syncopated and broken patterns; doubles vocal line

Diff: soft ending; dynamic control (*pp–ff*); soft, sustained high tones (g" and f♯")

Uses: has flavor of a popular song; good for the right singer

Rec: D#62

1992. MADAM TO YOU (Langston Hughes). A Song Cycle. C. F. Peters, 1975. X, very dissonant; a–a♭"; Tess-M; regular and irregular meters with many changes; moderate tempos; 30pp; Diff-V/d, P/d.

For: soprano with medium to large voice

Mood: declamatory; poems humorous–music does not match

Voice: declamatory; speech rhythms; chromatic

Piano: mostly chordal; thick texture; dissonant (constant 2nds & 7ths); somewhat patterned; key sigs. but with many alterations; large reach helpful; harmonic sameness

Diff: lack of harmonic definition and direction may make musical shape difficult to find or create

Rec: D#306

 a. *Madam and the Census Man.* c'–g"; 4/4 with changes, Moderately; 5pp.
 b. *Madam and the Minister.* b♭–f♯"; 7/8 with changes, Lively; 5pp.
 c. *Mama and Daughter.* b♭–a♭"; 3/2, 4/4, Allegretto; 4pp.
 d. *Madam and the Rent Man.* c'–g♯"; 3/2 with changes, Moderately lively; 4pp.
 e. *Madam and the Fortune Teller.* a–g"; 4/4, Moderate blues; 3pp.
 f. *Madam and the Number Runner.* d♯'–f♯"; 4/4 with changes, Moderately fast; 5pp.
 g. *Madam and the Wrong Visitor.* a–f♯"; 6/8 with changes, Broad; 4pp.

1993. SONGS OF EXPERIENCE (William Blake). Carl Fischer, 1978. cmp1966. Dissonant (built mostly of 7ths, 2nds, & tritones); f–e♭"; Tess-LL-M; regular and irregular meters with many changes; varied tempos; 25pp; Diff-V/d, P/d.

For: contralto; bass
Mood: declamatory; dramatic; mostly somber moods
Voice: many leaps of 7ths & 9ths, some larger; very disjunct; rhythmic complexity; syllabic setting of text; numerous tones below c'
Piano: dissonant; spread out on keyboard; many accidentals; rhythmic complexities; some thick scoring, some linear; large reach necessary; needs secure pianist with experience with 20th-century scores
Diff: pitch patterns; register changes frequent; wide intervals; rhythmic complexities
Uses: program material of its type for low voice

   a. *The Voice of the Bard.* f♯–e♭"; 4/4, 7/8, 5/8, 2/4, etc., Fast; 5pp.
   b. *Earth's Answer.* f♯–d♯"; 2/4, 5/4, 3/4, 4/4, Moderately; 4pp.
   c. *The Fly.* a♭–d"; 7/8, 5/8, 6/8, 3/4, 5/4, 2/4, Lightly, lively; 4pp.
   d. *The Garden of Love.* g–d♭"; 4/4, 2/4, 5/4, 7/8, 8/8, Very slow; 3pp.
   e. *The Thief and the Lady.* f♯–d"; 4/4, 5/8, 3/8, 3/4, 2/4, Lively, lightly; 2pp.
   f. *The Tyger.* f–d"; 4/4, 7/8, 5/8, 2/4, Moderately fast; 6+pp.

1994. THE STRANGE FUNERAL IN BRADDOCK (Michael Gold). Presser, 1936. cmp1933. X; g♯–e"; Tess-L; 5/4 with many changes, Andante con moto (♩ = 60 [with many changes]); 11pp; Diff-V/dd, P/dd.

For: bass-baritone
Mood: narrative; descriptive; abstract; somewhat grotesque
Voice: disjunct; difficult intervals; declamatory passages; spoken section
Piano: virtuosic; dissonant; lengthy prelude and interlude; glissandos
Diff: pitches; many changes of meter and tempo; low tessitura; very dramatic; needs great expressive ability
Uses: real *tour-de-force* for the right singer
Rec: D#s 308, 309

1995. TWO SONGS OF THE CITY (Langston Hughes). [160]. cmp1951. Traditional keys; b♭–f♯"; Tess-mL, M; regular meters; contrasting tempos; 8pp; Diff-V/me, P/me-m.

For: mezzo-soprano; baritone
Mood: lyrical, nostalgic, warm; humorous; regarding international and interracial relationships
Voice: generally short phrases; (a.), lyrical and flowing; (b.), disjunct and staccato
Piano: chordal textures; (a.), sustained; (b.), dance-like with dotted rhythms, broken-chord figures, and melodic motives in r.h.
Uses: good for students with limited breath control; excellent recital possibilities, esp. for younger singers
Rec: D#307

   a. *Childhood Memories.* Dmaj-Bmin; d'–f♯"; 4/4, 2/4, Slow; 4pp.
   b. *Chalk Marks on the Sidewalk.* B♭maj; b♭–f"; 4/4, Fast, with humor; 4pp. [**Rec:** D#62]

SINGER, JEANNE
(b. New York, NY, 1924)

1996. ARNO IS DEEP (Along the Arno–Pisa) (Frederika Blankner). [161]; 1st©1976. Cmin–distant modulations–B♭maj; c'–f"; Tess-M; 6/4, 4/4, Larghetto tranquillo, molto legato; 4pp; Diff-V/me, P/m.

For: medium voice specified
Mood: sad
Voice: stepwise; some skips; patterned melody
Piano: l.h. arpeggios with r.h. melody; short chordal section; doubles vocal line
Uses: easy recital song
Rec: D#310

1997. A CYCLE OF LOVE (in memory of R. G. S. [Richard G. Singer]). Four Art Songs for Soprano Voice and Piano. Branch, 1976. Traditional tonal centers; c♯'–a"; Tess-M; regular meters; varied tempos; 13pp; Diff-V/m, P/m.

For: soprano specified; possibly lyric mezzo-soprano
Mood: marriage, life together, death of husband, remembrance
Voice: stepwise; small skips; a few chromatic tones; long flowing phrases; syllabic
Piano: chordal–block and broken; some 2-voice counterpoint; some chromaticism; doubles or supports vocal line
Diff: several long phrases in (a.)
Uses: although these very personal songs might seem to restrict their usefulness, the texts express positive feelings of broader appeal; mildly modern flavor of music might appeal to younger students; recital possibilities
Rec: D#62

   a. *Merging Song* (Anne Marx). Gmaj; c♯'–g"; 3/4, Grazioso, con moto (♩ = 72); 5pp.
   b. *A Decade* (Amy Lowell). F-centered; c'–a"; 4/4, 6/8, Allegro assai (Impetuously); 2pp.
   c. *Lament* (Jeanne Singer). D♭maj; f'–g"; 4/4, Grave (♩ = 54); 3pp.
   d. *All Beauty Brings You Close* (Madeline Mason). E♭maj-Fmaj; d'–a♭"; 4/4, Andante espressivo (Tenderly) (♩ = 92); 3pp.

1998. DOWNING THE BELL TOWER (Suzanne Dale). [161]; 1st©1975. Fmin–B♭min; d♭'–f"; Tess-mH; 2/2, 6/8, 4/4, Largo; 4pp; Diff-V/m, P/me.

For: medium voice specified; also high voice
Mood: somber; uses *Dies irae* theme in piano
Voice: mostly stepwise; some triplets; some phrases end high
Piano: *Dies irae* theme in 2-voice linear and 4–8-voice chordal textures; chordal accomp.
Diff: a few phrases end high
Uses: useful easy recital song

1999. GIFT (Patricia Benton). [161]; 1st©1975. Amaj-Cmaj;

e'–g"; Tess-mH; 4/4; 2pp; Diff-V/m, P/m.

For: soprano; tenor
Mood: philosophical
Voice: many small skips; several accidentals; some dotted rhythms; syllabic
Piano: chordal; many accidentals; some doubling of vocal line
Diff: a few pitch patterns; ends on 6-beat sustained g" *ff*
Uses: pair with "Summons" by Singer (see below)

2000. **MEMENTO** (Cornel Lengyel). [161]; 1st©1981. Emin-Dmin-Dmaj; d♭'–f♯"; Tess-mH; 4/4; 3pp; Diff-V/m, P/m.
For: soprano
Mood: pleased and pleasant
Voice: stepwise; some small skips; some syncopation; several melismas on "ah"
Piano: block chords; broken-chord patterns; accidentals; grace notes; some doubling of vocal line
Diff: possibly the melismas
Uses: in a group about music

2001. **MEMORIA** (Frederika Blankner). [161]; 1st©1978. Begins Amin–Bmin; c'–g"; Tess-M-mH; 4/4, Larghetto espressivo; 5pp; Diff-V/md, P/m.
For: medium or high voice specified
Mood: loneliness
Voice: many skips; rising phrases; rhythmically patterned; syllabic
Piano: broken-chord patterns; rhythmically regular; some accidentals
Diff: meaning of text may be difficult to make clear
Uses: mature text; for older singer
Rec: D#310

2002. **SANGUINARIA** (Bernard Grebanier). [161]; 1st©1975. B♭min-Emin; c♭'–g♭"; Tess-M; 4/4, Lento ma non troppo; 4pp; Diff-V/me, P/me.
For: medium voice specified
Mood: grieving and austere
Voice: stepwise; small skips; somewhat chromatic; rhythmically patterned; easy
Piano: chordal construction; mostly 3–4-voice texture; frequent accidentals; rhythmically regular; easy
Diff: some chromaticism
Uses: mature text; good for older student

2003. **SUMMONS** (Patricia Benton). [161]; 1st©1975. Cmin-maj; b♭–g"; Tess-M; 6/4, 4/4, Allegretto; 3pp; Diff-V/m, P/m.
For: soprano; mezzo-soprano
Mood: philosophical
Voice: stepwise; small skips; accidentals; easy rhythms; some 2-note slurs
Piano: broken-chord and scalar patterning; some block chords; much doubling of vocal line
Uses: song for a student; pair with "Gift" by Singer (see above)

SISKIND, PAUL
(b. East Meadow, NY, 1962)

2004. **POEM** (Langston Hughes). [9]. X-quartal; c'–e♭"; Tess-M; changing simple meters; With subtle expression ♩ = ca. 40; 2min; Diff-V/m, P/e.
For: any voice
Mood: somber and distant; stark and lonely; loss of a loved friend
Voice: all phrases span less than an 8ve; syllabic; chromatic in unexpected ways
Piano: pairs of 4ths a half-step apart create a hesitant, introspective sound and form a repeated pattern with aug.5ths and some m2nds; almost no sense of motion, reflecting emptiness and loss
Diff: some pitch patterns
Uses: interesting song; extremely effective point of stillness in a group of more active songs

SITTON, MICHAEL
(b. Hendersonville, NC, 1958)

2005. **PICTURES OF AUTUMN** (Sara Teasdale). A Song Cycle for Medium Voice and Piano. Voice of the Rockies, 1999. cmp1997. Tonal; c'–f♯"; Tess-M; regular meters, with changes; varied tempos; 13+pp; Diff-V/me-m, P/e-md.
For: mezzo-soprano; soprano
Mood: philosophical impressions of places visited in autumn
Voice: repetitive patterns; stepwise; mostly small skips, some leaps of 7th; many accidentals; duplet and triplet divisions of beat
Piano: block chords, some rolled; some countermelody; final song has chromatic triplet pattern 1 & 2 8ves apart, both hands; often doubles vocal line; short preludes; one 11-meas. interlude
Diff: rhythms; changing meters; whole-tone construction
Uses: cycle for a student, or excerpt single songs

   a. *Autumn (Parc Monceau).* B-centered; d♭'–f♯"; Tess-mH; Unhurried, with flexibility ♩ = 66–72; 3pp.
   b. *September Day (Pont De Neuilly).* E-centered; d'–f♯"; Tess-M; 2/4, 4/4, 5/4, 3/4, Flowing steadily, ♩ = 108; 3pp.
   c. *Fontainebleau.* C-centered; c'–e"; Tess-wide; 3/4, Like a minuet, ♩ = 76; 4pp.
   d. *Late October (Bois de Boulogne).* F♯-centered; d'–d"; Tess-M; 12/8, Swiftly; 3+pp.

SLONIMSKY, NICOLAS
(b. St. Petersburg, Russia, 1894; d. Los Angeles, CA, 1995)

2006. **FRENCH BLUE** (William Alexander Percy). White-Smith, 1928. Fmaj; f'–f"; Tess-M; 4/4, Simply, like a bergerette; 2pp; Diff-V/e, P/e.
For: tenor
Mood: lyrical; reminiscent
Voice: simple melody
Piano: all treble clef; 18th-century style
Uses: small song; useful for young tenors

2007. **I OWE A DEBT TO A MONKEY!** (A Humorous

Encore Song) (Kathleen Lamb). Axelrod, 1945.
cmp1928. Abmaj; eb'–bb"; Tess-mH; 6/8, Lightly and
playfully; 4pp; Diff-V/md, P/d.

For: tenor; soprano
Mood: humorous
Voice: conjunct; some chromaticism; bb" on word "humor"
not sustained
Piano: many 32nd-note passages; some chords; nimble fingers
needed; rather fast
Diff: range; some pitches; not for a beginner
Uses: humorous song; group ender; encore

2008. A VERY GREAT MUSICIAN (T. Marziale).
Axelrod, 1947. cmp1928. Amaj; a–a"; Tess-mH; 3/4,
Tempo di Valse Melancolico (with changes); 4pp;
Diff-V/d, P/d.

For: soprano
Mood: sarcastic; somewhat bitter; difficult to categorize–is it
humorous?
Voice: skips and leaps; two phrases begin low a and rise to a"
Piano: many accidentals; arpeggiation; imitation of violin
playing; 8-meas. solo interlude with long glissando
Diff: pitches; range; ensemble (changing tempos and flexible
waltz meter); interpretive approach
Uses: interesting song; example of interpretation problem that
must be solved

SMIT, LEO
(b. Philadelphia, PA, 1921; d. Encinitas, CA, 1999)

2009. THINNGS [sic] ALL OVER (Carla Rodman, Age 7).
Theodore Presser, 1999. cmp1983. "For Jan
DeGaetani." E-centered; eb'–g"; Tess-wide; 3/4,
Rapturously (♩ = 92); 4pp; Diff-V/md, P/m.

For: soprano
Mood: child's description of the house where she was a guest
Voice: fairly short, but disjunct phrases (m2nds, 4ths, 8ves,
9ths, 10ths); some word repetition
Piano: begins and ends on single note e'; l.h. a single line,
mostly e' and f'; r.h. somewhat melodic; dissonant; thin
texture
Diff: some pitches; wide leaps; childlike presentation
Uses: interesting to program with other songs on texts from a
child's point of view

2010. THE WHITE DIADEM. Seven Songs about Poets
and Poetry for Mezzo-soprano (or Soprano) and Piano
(Emily Dickinson). Theodore Presser, 2000. cmp1989.
Tonal; a♯–g"; Tess-cs; regular meters; varied tempos
(♩ = 58–100); 9+min; Diff-V/m-d, P/e-d.

For: mezzo-soprano; soprano
Mood: praises of poets
Voice: lyrical; melodic; numerous skips and larger intervals;
speech rhythms; one strophic song; some sustained
high tones
Piano: chordal and linear; mostly patterned accomps.; unusual
harmonic progressions
Diff: some pitches in (f.); some large intervals
Uses: interesting songs on Dickinson poems; useful for
undergraduate or graduate singers
Rec: D#311

a. *I Reckon–When I Count at All.* Dmaj; d'–f♯";
Tess-cs; 4/4, Exultant (♩ = 100); 2pp.
b. *I Dwell in Possibility.* Bbmaj; c'–g"; Tess-cs; 4/4,
Reverie (♩ = 58); 1p.
c. *The Martyr Poets–Did Not Tell.* X-F♯; a♯–d";
Tess-mL; 3/4, Aggrieved (♩ = 72); 1p.
d. *The Poets Light But Lamps.* Bbmaj; c'–f"; Tess-
cs; 4/4, Gently (♩ = 66); 1p.
e. *I Would Not Paint–a Picture.* Bb-Amaj; b–f";
Tess-cs; 2/4, Graceful (♩ = 72); 3pp.
f. *To Pile like Thunder to Its Close.* X; c'–g"; Tess-cs;
3/4, 2/4, Stormy (♪ = 92); 3pp.
g. *Me–Come! My Dazzled Face.* X-Fmaj; c'–f♯";
Tess-cs; 3/4, Fervent (♩ = 69); 1p.

SMITH, DAVID STANLEY
(b. Toledo, OH, 1877; d. New Haven, CT, 1949)

2011. ROSE SONG (Charlotte Fiske Bates). [58]; 1st©1899.
H & L keys: Ebmaj & Dbmaj (orig.); (bb)d'–g" &
(ab)c'–f"; Tess-mH, Moderato; 3pp; Diff-V/me, P/m.

For: tenor; soprano; baritone; mezzo-soprano
Mood: immortalizes beauty of the rose in song; transcends
death
Voice: stepwise; easy skips; duplets vs. piano triplets
Piano: repeated chords; 2 vs. 3; duplet and triplet divisions
Diff: duplets vs. piano triplets
Uses: good lyric song

2012. THERE WILL BE STARS, Op. 52, No. 2 (Sara
Teasdale). Church, 1927. Bbmaj; bb–eb"(f");
Tess-mL; 3/4, Quasi adagio; 3min; Diff-V/m, P/md.

For: mezzo-soprano; baritone; contralto; some basses
Mood: lyrical; night-death; timelessness
Voice: stepwise; several skips of 6th; many 2-note slurs;
duplets and triplets
Piano: broken-chord pattern in continuous triplets;
syncopation combined with 2 vs. 3; large reach helpful;
does not double vocal line
Diff: some duplets vs. piano triplets
Uses: very nice song; builds to dramatic climax; quiet ending;
cf. setting by J. Duke

SMITH, HALE
(b. Cleveland, OH, 1925)

2013. BEYOND THE RIM OF DAY (Langston Hughes).
Cycle. Marks, 1970. X; c'–bb"; Tess-M; regular and
irregular changing meters; contrasting tempos; 8min;
Diff-V/d, P/md-d.

For: soprano; tenor
Mood: lyrical; humorous; sad; philosophical
Voice: disjunct, flowing, and fragmented phrases;
chromaticism; some sustained passages
Piano: dissonant; some chordal, some contrapuntal; very
precisely indicated dynamics; tremolo; trills
Diff: pitches; rhythms; soft high tones; ensemble; meter
changes; text
Uses: nice set for good musician with flexible voice

  a. *March Moon.* d'–b♭"; 5/8 with changes, Lively and gracefully; 1+min.
  b. *Troubled Woman.* d♯'–a♭"; 2/2, 3/2, Moderate, somewhat freely; 1+min.
  c. *To a Little Lover-Lass, Dead.* c'–a"; 4/2, 5/2, Slowly; 4+min.

2014. THREE PATTERSON LYRICS for Soprano and Piano (Raymond Patterson). Merion, 1986. X; c'–a♯"; Tess-mL; regular and irregular meters with many changes; varied tempos; 14min; Diff-V/d, P/d.
For: soprano specified; dramatic soprano; mezzo-soprano with easy high voice probably best
Mood: philosophical; filled with unrest and searching for something not attained
Voice: rather disjunct with purposefully awkward skips; highly chromatic; rhythmic complexities; entirely syllabic
Piano: chordal-linear combination; highly chromatic; triplets; rhythmic complexities in (b.); trill figures; independent of vocal line
Diff: excellent sense of pitch and rhythm needed; much of cycle lies low for many sopranos
Uses: excellent recital material

  a. *Night Piece.* X; c'–f♯"; Moderately (♩ = ca.72); 4min.
  b. *To a Weathercock.* X; e♭'–a♯"; (♪ = ca.116–120); 5+min.
  c. *The World Bows Down to Beauty.* X; c♯–g♭"; Slowly (♩ = ca.60); 4+min.

2015. THE VALLEY WIND. Four Songs for Medium Voice and Piano. Cycle. Marks, 1974. Atonal; b–g"; Tess-M-mH; mostly regular meters; 15min; Diff-V/d-dd, P/d-dd.
For: soprano
Mood: lyrical; melancholy; bright; transparent
Voice: pitches difficult; skips and leaps; many accidentals; good vowels for soft head tones
Piano: linear texture; many accidentals; large reach helpful
Diff: melodically and harmonically difficult; no tonal base; perfect pitch desirable; rhythmic irregularities; delicate textures
Uses: very lyrical atonal cycle for advanced musicians; could be quite attractive for a clear, shimmering soprano voice; quiet ending
Rec: D#312

  a. *The Valley Wind* (Lu Yun; trans. Arthur Waley). e♭'–g"; 4/4, Leisurely; 4min.
  b. *Spring* (William Shakespeare). b–g"; 6/8, Bouyantly; 2min.
  c. *Envoy in Autumn* (Tu Fu; trans. Powys Mathers). c'–g♭"; 7/8 with changes, Humidly; 5+min.
  d. *Velvet Shoes* (Elinor Wylie). [6]. d'–f♯"; 6/8, Delicately and very transparent; 3+min.

SMITH, JAMES G.
(b. Raleigh, NC, 1935)

2016. FEARLESS EMILY (Emily Dickinson). Cycle. Music

Espress, Inc., 1996. Tonal; b–b♭"; Tess-M-mH; regular meters; changing tempos (♩ = 40–120); 16pp; Diff-V/md, P/m. Continuous cycle, no separate songs.
For: soprano
Mood: rather gentle treatment of the subject of fear
Voice: syllabic setting; first poem spoken over the piano music; much melodic repetition; vocal line somewhat instrumentally conceived
Piano: continuous throughout; mostly various broken-chord patterns set mood
Uses: useful for a singer who wants something different

  a. *Prologue: Afraid? Of Whom Am I Afraid?*
  b. *Of Life?*
  c. *Not Death*
  d. *Trusting the Morn*

SMITH, JULIA
(b. Denton, TX, 1911; d. New York, NY, 1989)

2017. PRAIRIE KALEIDOSCOPE (Ona Mae Ratcliff). Five Songs for Voice and Piano. Cycle. Mowbray, 1981. Tonal; e♭'–a"; Tess-mH; traditional meters; varied tempos; 11pp; Diff-V/m, P/m.
For: soprano
Mood: describes prairie scenes; mostly lyric
Voice: mostly stepwise motion; small skips; accidentals; rhythms generally uncomplicated; occasional syncopation, triplets, or dotted rhythms; syllabic; a few 2-note slurs
Piano: block chords; arpeggiation and other broken-chord patterning; tremolo; doubles or outlines vocal line
Diff: some intervals involving altered-chord harmonies
Uses: as a group; each song leads into the next song; final song ends in inconclusive tonality (fades into the prairie?); recital material for less experienced singer/musician

  a. *Autumn Orchestra.* Fmaj-Dmin; e♭'–g"; 6/8, 3/8, Allegretto; 2+min.
  b. *Captive.* C minorish; e♭'–e"; 2/4, Lento; 1min.
  c. *Prairie Wind.* F minorish; f♯'–f"; 4/4, Moderato; 2min.
  d. *Answer.* Gmaj; a'–g"; 4/4, Andantino; 1+min.
  e. *Wakening.* D majorish; e'–a"; 4/4, Moderato; 3+min.

2018. THREE LOVE SONGS (Karl Flaster). Theodore Presser, 1954. M & L keys (also H): Traditional keys; c'–g♯" & b♭–f♯"; Tess-mL, M; regular meters; varied tempos; 4min; Diff-V/m, P/me-m.
For: mezzo-soprano; baritone; soprano; tenor
Mood: love songs; tranquil; dramatic; intense
Voice: stepwise; easy skips; some duplets vs. piano triplets; some accidentals; one dramatic climax
Piano: chordal; afterbeat patterns, repeated and broken chords; cross-hands; 2 vs. 3; accidentals; syncopation; does not double vocal line
Diff: dynamic control
Uses: as a set; best for women, possible for men

   a. *I Will Sing the Song.* Emaj & Dmaj; c♯'–g♯" & b–f♯"; Tess-M; 6/8, Moderato; 1+min.

   b. *The Door That I Would Open.* C-centered & B♭-centered; c'–f" & b♭–e♭"; Tess-mL; 3/4, Lento; 2min.

   c. *The Love I Hold.* B♭maj & Amaj; d♭'–g♭" & c'–f"; Tess- M; 9/8, Allegretto moderato; 1+min.

SMITH, MELVILLE
(b. 1898; d. Cambridge, MA, 1962)

2019. **THREE SONGS** (Carl Sandburg). Valley, 1957. X (dissonant); c'–a"; Tess-M-mH; regular and irregular changing meters; 8+pp; Diff-V/d, P/d.

For: tenor

Mood: lyrical; lonely

Voice: mostly conjunct; some large leaps in (c.); some metrical and rhythmical problems; some sustained high phrases

Piano: tertian and quartal structures; some 3-stave notation; generally patterned; (c.) linear with much polymetric structure; accidentals

Diff: pitch perception; irregular meters

Uses: useful for someone interested in the poetry of Sandburg

   a. *Lost.* a'–a"; Tess-mH; 4/4, with changes, Adagio; 2pp.

   b. *A Teamster's Farewell.* d'–g"; Tess- mH; 4/4, 5/4, 2/4, Allegro; 3pp.

   c. *Sketch.* d♭'–a♭"; Tess-M; 6/8, 9/8, Andante espressivo; 3+pp.

SMOLANOFF, MICHAEL
(b. New York, NY, 1942)

2020. **FOUR HAIKU SONGS,** Op. 37. Seesaw, 1973. X; a♭–g♯"; Tess-M; regular meters; moderate to slow tempos; 4+pp; Diff-V/d, P/d.

For: mezzo-soprano

Mood: lyrical poems; Haiku impressions

Voice: disjunct; chromatic; short phrases; widely varying dynamics, very specifically indicated; difficult rhythms; fragmented phrases

Piano: highly chromatic; dissonant; complex rhythms; fragmented by rests

Diff: extended range; perfect pitch desirable

Uses: effective recital group for good musician

   a. *First Dream of the Year* . . . 4/4, Slowly.

   b. *From My Tiny Roof* . . . 3/4, 2/4, 4/4, Moderately.

   c. *Icicles and Water* . . . 4/4, Moderately.

   d. *Ah, Morning Misted Street* . . . 2/4, Slowly.

SOUSA, JOHN PHILIP
(b. Washington, DC, 1854; d. Reading, PA, 1932)

2021. **YOU'LL MISS LOTS OF FUN WHEN YOU'RE MARRIED** (Edward M. Taber). [5]. Gmaj; d '–e"; Tess-mL; 3/4, Valse grazioso; 3pp; Diff-V/me, P/e.

For: any voice; male might be best

Mood: humorous description of the "down side" of marriage; ends on a positive note

Voice: waltz-like; regular phrases; a few intervals larger than 5th; four strophes, same music; spoken word or phrase sets up ending of each strophe

Piano: chordal; afterbeats in waltz style

Diff: good vocal actor needed

Uses: useful humorous song for a variety of situations

SOUTHARD, LUCIEN H.
(b. Sharon, VT, 1827; d. Augusta, GA, 1881)

2022. **THE FOUNTAIN** (James Russell Lowell). Nathan Richardson & J. F. Petrie, 1854. Fmaj; c'–g"(a"); Tess-M; 3/8, Allegretto; 6pp; Diff-V/m, P/m.

For: mezzo-soprano; high baritone

Mood: lyrical; descriptive; sparkling

Voice: scale-wise melody; easy rhythms; many 2-note slurs

Piano: broken chords on scale lines; 14-meas. prelude; does not double vocal line

Diff: sustained f "

Uses: interesting and useful; not just a period piece

SOWERBY, LEO
(b. Grand Rapids, MI, 1895; d. Port Clinton, OH, 1968)

2023. **THE EDGE OF DREAMS.** A Set of Six Songs for Medium Voice and Piano (Mark Turbyfill). Cycle. 1st©1955. The Leo Sowerby Foundation, 1996. Ronald M. Huntington Memorial Edition (Presser). "To Mack Harrell." Traditional keys with many altered chords; b♭–f"; Tess-M; mostly regular meters with some changes; 12min; Diff-V/m, P/m.

For: lyric baritone

Mood: lyrical; reflections on dead love

Voice: stepwise and skips; occasional leaps; some slight chromaticism; easy rhythms; some speech rhythms; some sustained tones

Piano: chordal and linear textures; some arpeggiation; needs delicate touch; wide reach helpful; some syncopation

Diff: 5 of the 6 songs have a sustained, climactic e", usually on open vowels; much soft singing; interpretation

Uses: romantic cycle of great lyricism for singer with warm, lyrical sound and perfect legato line; program with more vigorous groups; very quiet ending

   a. *The Adventurer.* G-centered; b–e"; 4/4, 3/4, 2/4, 7/8, 3/8, Not too slowly; 3pp.

   b. *After-Thought.* Cmin-maj; b♭–f"; 4/4, Slowly and sadly; 3pp.

   c. *Sorrow.* G-centered; d'–e♭"; 4/4, Very quietly; 2pp.

   d. *Pulse of Spring.* Gmaj; d'–e"; 6/8, Merrily; 3pp.

   e. *The Forest of Dead Trees.* B♭maj; b♭–e♭"; 7/4, 6/4, 5/4, Mysteriously and deliberately; 2pp.

   f. *O That Love Has Come at All!* Cmaj; d'–e"; 3/4, Not slowly, but with emotion; 3pp.

2024. **WITH STRAWBERRIES** (William E. Henley). Boston Music Co., 1925. E♭maj; d'–f"; Tess-M; 2/2, Moderately, simple; 4pp; Diff-V/m, P/m.

For:	any high or medium voice
Voice:	long, flowing lines in quarters & 8ths; some chromaticism; considerable rubato
Piano:	chordal; somewhat chromatic; independent but supports vocal line
Uses:	effective recital song
Rec:	D#9

SPALDING, ALBERT
(b. Chicago, IL, 1888; d. New York, NY, 1953)

2025. **THREE SONGS FROM THE HESPERIDES OF ROBERT HERRICK.** G. Schirmer, 1926. Pub. separately. Traditional keys; c♯'–g♯"; Tess-M-mH; regular meters; 9pp; Diff-V/e-m, P/e-m.

For:	lyric baritone; tenor with full low voice; possibly mezzo-soprano best vocally
Mood:	lyrical; love songs to "Julia"
Voice:	skips along chord lines; melody often outlines chords; some chromaticism; straightforward rhythms
Piano:	mostly broken-chord patterns; 8th- & 16th-note motion; large reach helpful
Diff:	tessitura a notch high for baritone and a notch low for tenor; perhaps best for mezzo-soprano, in spite of texts
Uses:	nice songs; good for teaching; set lacks variety for programming

    a. *The Olive Branch.* Amin; d'–e"; 4/4, Con moto; 2pp.

    b. *The Bracelet to Julia.* Amaj; c♯'–f♯"; 4/4, Andantino quasi allegretto; 2pp.

    c. *A Ring Presented to Julia.* Emaj; d♯'–g♯"; 4/4, Cantabile, con moto; 5pp.

SPEAKS, OLEY
(b. Canal Winchester, OH, 1874; d. New York, NY, 1948)

2026. **MORNING** (from the *Atlanta Constitution,* by Frank L. Stanton.). G. Schirmer, 1931. Reprint: T.I.S. (H). [31 (Low)]. B♭min-maj; b♭–f"; Tess-mL; 4/4, Slowly–Animato; 4pp; Diff-V/me, P/m.

For:	mezzo-soprano
Mood:	joyous song of nature; includes a French translation
Voice:	phrases tend to begin low and rise, or begin high and fall; a few large intervals, incl. a descending 8ve; alternatives provided for f" in both cases; a few accidentals
Piano:	chordal; some melodic material in prelude and interlude; triplet repetitions of chords throughout latter part of song; some accidentals; supports strongly or doubles vocal line throughout
Diff:	restraint in accomp. to avoid covering singer
Uses:	if alternative notes are taken, song might work well for a young singer whose high voice is not well developed

2027. **ON THE ROAD TO MANDALAY** (Rudyard Kipling). G. Schirmer, 1907. Reprints: Classical Vocal Reprints (H, M, L); T.I.S. (M & L). [5, 37]. H, M, & L keys: E♭min-maj, Cmin-maj, & B♭min-maj; d♭'–g"(a♭"), b♭–e"(f"), & a♭–d"(e♭"); Tess-M, mL;

4/4, Alla marcia; 6pp (with repeat); Diff-V/me, P/m.

For:	any male voice except very light
Mood:	robust and descriptive; song of adventure
Voice:	stepwise; easy skips; little chromaticism; march-like phrasing; robust; considerable dynamic contrast; syllabic; a few 2-note slurs
Piano:	chordal–block, rolled, and repeated; several chromatic passages; triplets; tremolo; doubles vocal line
Diff:	needs good vocal actor; some phrases lie low
Uses:	well-known, rousing, old-fashioned song; good for occasional entertainment purposes; encore
Rec:	D#s 47, 48

2028. **SYLVIA** (Clinton Scollard). G. Schirmer, 1914, 1941. Reprints: Classical Vocal Reprints; T.I.S. (M). [5]. H, M, mL, & L keys: Gmaj, Fmaj, E♭maj, & D♭maj; d'–g", c'–f", b♭–e♭", & a♭–d♭"; Tess-mL; 4/4, Andantino espressivo; 3pp; Diff-V/e, P/me.

For:	any male voice
Mood:	lyrical; love song; tribute to Sylvia's beauty
Voice:	stepwise; small skips; some phrases encompass an 8ve; easy rhythms
Piano:	afterbeat pattern; cross-hands; doubles vocal line
Uses:	well-known lyric song; very melodic

SPILMAN, JONATHAN E.
(b. Freenville, KY, 1812; d.1896)

2029. **FLOW GENTLY, SWEET AFTON** (Robert Burns). [23]; 1st©1838. A♭maj; e♭'–f"; Tess-M; 3/4, Not too slowly; 2pp (3 strophes); Diff-V/e, P/e.

For:	tenor or other male voices
Mood:	lyrical; descriptive
Voice:	stepwise; skips along chord lines; easy rhythms; 2-note slurs
Piano:	4-voice chordal texture; doubles vocal line
Uses:	well-known song; good to develop flowing line

2030. **THE STAR OF EVE** (Miss Power). George Willig, 1844. Gmaj; d'–f♯"; Tess-M; 2/4, Moderato; 2pp (2 strophes); Diff-V/e, P/e.

For:	tenor
Mood:	lyrical; quiet; praise of beauty
Voice:	some leaps; dotted rhythms; some syncopation
Piano:	simple bass line; broken-chord figure in 8ths; 8-meas. prelude; 6ths; ornaments
Uses:	period piece

SPRATLAN, LEWIS
(b. Miami, FL, 1940)

2031. **IMAGES** for Soprano and Piano (various poets). Cycle. New Valley, 1977. cmp1971. Atonal (some serial techniques); g–d'"(b"); Tess-wide; mostly regular meters with changes; varied tempos; 22pp(MS); Diff-V/dd, P/dd.

For:	soprano (with 2½-8ve range and experience with avant-garde techniques)
Mood:	typical avant-garde approach to expressive content; poems center on a dying love relationship

Voice: large leaps at fast tempo; no melodic cohesion; extreme range (several c'''s); other avant-garde techniques
Piano: typical avant-garde techniques; pointillistic; serial; wide spacing; rhythmic intricacies; demands pianist familiar with this idiom
Diff: extreme range; large leaps; pitch patterns (perfect pitch desirable); text projection; ensemble; rhythmic intricacies; facsimile MS hard to read; demands virtuoso performers
Uses: avant-garde programming

    a. *Prologue* (Robert Frost). bb–ab"; 3/4, 4/4, Andante; 2+ pp.
    b. *Iris* (William Carlos Williams). b–ab"; 4/4 with changes, Vivo; 1+pp.
    c. *November Night* (Adelaide Crapsey). e'–d♯"; 5/8, ♪ = 80; 1p.
    d. *Morning Star* (William Carlos Williams). d♯'–a"; 2/4, Tempo giusto; 1p.
    e. *Nuances* (Wallace Stevens). bb–c'''; 3/4 with changes, Andante; 3+ pp.
    f. *Chameleon* (Marianne Moore). g–d'''; 3/4, 3/8, Lento–Più mosso e ben marcato; 3pp.
    g. *Moth* (Adelaide Crapsey). d'–g"; 3/4, Adagio; 1p.
    h. *Oyster* (Ariake Kambara). ab–c'''; 6/8, Lento, ma con moto quieto; 4pp.
    i. *bells* (e. e. cummings). d'–bb"; 3/8 with changes, Presto–Moderato; 2+pp.
    j. *Epilogue* (T. E. Hulme). db'–eb"; 4/4, 3/4, Andante; 1p.

SPRINGER, PHILIP
(b. New York, NY, 1926)

2032. **COME SLOWLY, EDEN!** (Emily Dickinson). Boston Music Co., 1966. X (serial); a–g"; Tess-M; 3/4 predominates, Adagissimo; 2pp; Diff-V/d, P/m.
For: mezzo-soprano; dramatic soprano
Mood: sensuous poem; intense setting
Voice: many skips; awkward intervals; some help from piano
Piano: thin texture–single line and chordal
Diff: pitches; rhythms; dynamic control (*pp–fff*)
Uses: effective setting; might be used to introduce student to serial techniques

SPROSS, CHARLES GILBERT
(b. Poughkeepsie, NY, 1874; d. Poughkeepsie, NY, 1961)

2033. **WILL O' THE WISP** (Torrence Benjamin). [5]. Fmaj; c'–bb"; Tess-mH; 4/8, Allegro; 4pp; Diff-V/md, P/d.
For: soprano
Mood: ecstatic and lightly dance-like
Voice: most intervals outline F maj. triad; one short low-lying phrase occurs twice; long bb" at climax
Piano: chordal; 32nd-note broken chords; 16th-note afterbeat figures; supports vocal line well
Diff: maintaining light quality without sacrificing tone
Uses: good for a young soprano; possible recital material

ST. PIERRE, DONALD (See entry #15 H)

STARER, ROBERT
(b. Vienna, Austria, 1924; d. 2001)

2034. **ADVICE TO A GIRL** (Sara Teasdale). Leeds, 1951. cmp1950. X; d'–g"; Tess-mH; 3/4 with changes, Allegretto; 3pp; Diff-V/md, P/md.
For: lyric or dramatic soprano; tenor
Mood: advisory
Voice: many skips; speech rhythms; fragmented phrases; many accidentals
Piano: 4–5-voice texture; covers the keyboard; syncopation; articulations important
Diff: fragmented phrases; irregular rhythms; dynamic control; diction; dissonance
Uses: change-of-pace song; would work well with other Starer songs in a group: "Dew," "Silence," and "To Be Superior"

2035. **DEW** (Sara Teasdale). Leeds, 1951. X (bitonal); e'–ab"; Tess-M; 4/4, 2/4, 3/4, Andante; 29meas.; Diff-V/d, P/d.
For: soprano
Mood: love song; introspective
Voice: many skips, some difficult; changing meters
Piano: bitonal; many accidentals
Diff: pitches (highly dissonant); ensemble
Uses: in a group; would work well with other Starer songs (see above)

2036. **EVENING** (Leah Goldberg; English version by Mary Johnson). Israeli, 1953. X; e'–g"; Tess-M; 2/4, 3/4, Andante; 3pp; Diff-V/d, P/d.
For: soprano; mezzo-soprano; tenor
Mood: philosophical; sinister undertones
Voice: rather disjunct; many large leaps; chromatic; many triplets; good English version
Piano: chordal; independent of voice; triplets
Diff: rhythms; frequent meter changes
Uses: could be particularly effective sung in Hebrew

2037. **MY SWEET OLD ETCETERA** (e. e. cummings). Leeds, 1957. cmp1955. First performed by Mack Harrell. X; A–eb"; Tess-M; 4/4, Briskly; 1+min; Diff-V/md, P/m.
For: baritone specified
Mood: narrative; lighthearted song, in a cynical way
Voice: disjointed (*un poco parlando*); some syncopation; some difficult intervals
Piano: bitonal; 3–4-voice texture; bass marches along; articulations important
Diff: parlando style; ensemble
Uses: light song for a group; see also setting by Hugo Weisgall (d. of *Soldier Songs*)

2038. **SILENCE** (D. H. Lawrence). Leeds, 1951. cmp1950. X; bb–eb"; Tess-M; 2/4, 3/4, Non troppo lento; 51meas.; Diff-V/m, P/m.
For: baritone
Mood: dramatic; intense; begins and ends quietly

Voice: some difficult intervals; some triplet rhythms; many accidentals
Piano: slow chords; central section has movement; large reach helpful; bitonality
Diff: pitches (highly dissonant); ensemble; poem
Uses: for contrast in a group; would work well with other Starer songs

2039. **TO BE SUPERIOR** (D. H. Lawrence). Leeds, 1951. cmp1950. X; b–e♭"; Tess-M; 3/4, 2/4, Allegro; 74meas.; Diff-V/md, P/md.
For: baritone; mezzo-soprano
Mood: humorous
Voice: many skips; dotted rhythms; syncopation; some triplets
Piano: bitonal; dotted rhythms; syncopation; jazzy idiom; large reach helpful
Diff: rhythms; dynamic control (*pp–ff*)
Uses: nice humorous song; use within group or to end group softly; would work well with other Starer songs

STEINER, GITTA
(b. Prague, Czechoslovakia, 1932)

2040. **PAGES FROM A SUMMER JOURNAL** (Gitta Steiner). Seesaw, 1969. cmp1963. X; a–a"; Tess-mL; 4/4 with many changes, Andante (♩=c.66)–Più mosso (♪=c.184); 5pp; Diff-V/d, P/d.
For: mezzo-soprano
Mood: lyrical; philosophical; love song
Voice: disjunct; chromatic; large leaps but lyrical and flowing
Piano: highly chromatic; contrapuntal; pointillistic; numerous irregular rhythmic groupings
Diff: pitches; rhythms; meter changes; loud high tones
Uses: very good recital song for singer with wide range

2041. **THREE SONGS FOR MEDIUM VOICE.** Seesaw, 1970. cmp1960. X; b–f"; Tess-mL-M; regular meters; contrasting tempos; 10pp; Diff-V/m, P/m-d.
For: mezzo-soprano; contralto
Mood: lyrical; philosophical; descriptive; joyous
Voice: (a.), flowing 8th-note movement, repeated tones, and 8ve leap upward at end; (b.), somewhat chromatic, quarter-note movement, characteristic phrase begins on f" and descends through the 8ve, and triplets; (c.), declamatory and recit.-like, most phrases intoned on one or two pitches and somewhat chromatic
Piano: chordal; chromatic; some dissonance; some moving voices
Diff: declamatory style; soft dynamics
Uses: good recital songs

　a. *Sleep Now, O Sleep Now* (James Joyce). D♭maj; d♭'–d♭"; Tess-mL; 4/4, 2/4; 2+pp.
　b. *Lean Out of the Window, Goldenhair* (James Joyce). X; e♭'–f"; Tess-M; 4/4, Dolce (♩=104); 2+pp.
　c. *I Envy Seas Whereon He Rides* (Emily Dickinson). X; b–d♭"; Tess-mL; 3/4, Broadly (♩=c.69, 52); 5pp.

2042. **TWO SONGS** (Gitta Steiner). Seesaw, 1966. X

(serial); c'–b"; Tess-H, M, L; changing meters; slow tempos; 6+pp; Diff-V/dd, P/dd.
For: lyric soprano
Mood: lyrical; melancholy; gloomy; nature imagery
Voice: disjunct; large leaps; extremely chromatic; complex rhythmic groupings; short note values
Piano: highly chromatic; dissonant; complex, irregular rhythmic groupings; pointillistic; chord cluster
Diff: requires soprano with clear, easy low tones and great flexibility; perfect pitch desirable; accurate sense of rhythm needed
Uses: effective recital material for the right singer

　a. *Dark Thoughts Bloom like Strange Plants.* c♯'–b"; 4/4 with changes ♩=c.40, ♪=126; 3+pp.
　b. *Branches Struggle against the Wind.* c'–b"; 3/4 with changes ♩=ca.48; 3pp.

STEINERT, ALEXANDER
(b. Boston, MA, 1900; d. 1982)

2043. **FOUR LACQUER PRINTS** (Amy Lowell). Editions Maurice Senart, 1932. "To Eva Gauthier." X; c♯'–e"; Tess-M; mostly regular meters with some changes; varied tempos; 7pp; Diff-V/d, P/d.
For: lyric baritone; mezzo-soprano
Mood: lyrical; shimmering; reflection of delicate images of Japanese lacquer prints
Voice: stepwise; small skips; short ranges; chromatic; rhythmic patterns vary with many different and small divisions of the beat; some 2–3-note slurs
Piano: creates atmosphere and background; mostly patterned; many accidentals; linear textures; 2 vs. 3 vs. 4; light touch needed
Diff: chromaticism; floating vocal lines; singer needs knowledge of and sensitivity to Japanese prints to interpret these songs well
Uses: excellent short set of beautiful songs; could substitute stylistically for French group

　a. *Vicarious.* 2/4, 3/4, Andante sostenuto; 23meas.
　b. *Temple Ceremony.* 2/4, Andante molto; 15meas.
　c. *Storm by the Seashore.* 2/4, 5/8, 3/8, Allegro; 23meas.
　d. *A Burnt Offering.* 4/4, 3/4, Lento; 11meas.

STERNE, COLIN
(b. Wynberg, South Africa, 1921)

2044. **DEAR HEART** (James Joyce). Peer International, 1953. Dmin; c♯'–g"; Tess-mH; 3/4, 4/4, Slowly; 2pp; Diff-V/md, P/m.
For: tenor
Mood: complaining love song; somewhat agitated
Voice: many skips–small and large; some long-ranged phrases; triplets; dotted rhythms; syncopation
Piano: linear texture; spare; many 7ths & 9ths; many accidentals; large reaches; articulations important; does not double vocal line
Diff: rhythms; triplets vs. piano duplets; ensemble

Uses: effective song; groups well with other Sterne/Joyce songs (see below)

2045. **GENTLE LADY** (James Joyce). Peer International, 1953. Fmaj; e'–g"; Tess-mH; 2/2, 3/2, Slowly; 2min; Diff-V/m, P/m.
For: tenor
Mood: lyrical; subdued; concerns passing love
Voice: stepwise; some leaps; some dotted rhythms
Piano: 3rds in r.h.; syncopation; leaps in l.h.; slurrings important; accidentals; does not double vocal line
Diff: rhythms; ensemble
Uses: effective song for interior of group, or quiet ending

2046. **MY LOVE IS IN A LIGHT ATTIRE** (James Joyce). Peer International, 1953. Dmaj; c♯'–g"; Tess-M; 4/4, Moderately fast; 1min; Diff-V/m-md, P/m.
For: tenor
Mood: lyrical; descriptive; sprightly; delicate
Voice: stepwise; chord-member skips; 2-note slurs; cross-accents with piano; some dotted rhythms
Piano: broken chords–staccato-slurred combination; countermelody; accents and articulations important; does not double vocal line
Uses: effective song

STEVENS, HALSEY
(b. Scott, NY, 1908; d. Wilmington, NC, 1989)

2047. **FOUR SONGS FROM *MOTHER GOOSE*** (selected & ed. by Conrad Immel). Edition Helios, 1978. cmp1951–1977. Tonal; c'–g♭"; Tess-M-mL; traditional meters; varied tempos; 10pp; Diff-V/me-m, P/me-m.
For: mezzo-soprano; baritone
Mood: humorous; mock-serious; sometimes nonsensical
Voice: usually easy pitch patterns; sometimes disjunct (a.); accidentals; a few rhythmic complications (c.), syncopation and 3 vs. 4 in piano); syllabic; humorous word repetitions; semi-spoken "quack" at end
Piano: (a.), afterbeat style, melodic fragments, staccato, and bitonal touches; (b.), l.h. arpeggiated, r.h. afterbeat style, and bimodal; (c.), 4-voice chords, broken chords, and some scale passages in 8ths; (d.), afterbeat style and staccato; occasional doubling of vocal line
Diff: attitude and expression of each song; rhythmic ensemble in some places in (c.); needs good vocal actor
Uses: as a short, amusing group; encore songs

   a. ***The Little Man and His Gun*** (Halliwell: *The Nursery Rhymes of England*, 1842). X; c♯'–d♯"; 2/4, Allegretto; 50sec.
   b. ***The Farmer and the Raven*** (Harris: *Original Ditties for the Nursery*, ca.1805). F-centered (bimodal); c'–e"(f♯"); 6/8, Rozzo; 40sec.
   c. ***A Doleful Ditty*** (Halliwell: *The Nursery Rhymes of England*, 1842). Fmaj; c'–g♭"; 4/4, Andante non troppo; 1+min.
   d. ***When I Was a Little Boy*** (Halliwell: *The Nursery Rhymes of England*, 1842). Cmaj (with raised 4th); c'–c"; 2/4, Allegro moderato; 20sec.

2048. **GO, LOVELY ROSE.** For High Voice and Piano (Edmund Waller). Mark Foster, 1954, 1982. A "translation" by the composer of a choral setting of this text. cmp1942. Emin-Gmaj; d'–a"; Tess-M; unmetered, Andante (♩ = 60–72); 1+min; Diff-V/m, P/me.
For: lyric tenor
Mood: lyrical love song; familiar text
Voice: stepwise; easy skips; a few chromatic tones; arching phrases
Piano: chordal; somewhat chromatic; countermelody to voice often doubled in 8ves; reinforces but seldom actually doubles vocal line
Diff: needs fine, lyrical legato and soft high tones
Uses: excellent recital material; a superb setting of this text

STILL, WILLIAM GRANT
(b. Woodville, MS, 1895; d. Los Angeles, CA, 1978)

2049. **THE BREATH OF A ROSE** (Langston Hughes). [48, 51]; 1st©1928. H & L keys: B♭maj & Gmaj; e♭'–f"& c'–d♯"; Tess-mH; 4/4, Slowly; 4pp; Diff-V/md, P/d.
For: all voices
Mood: love poem; nature imagery
Voice: rather disjunct; chromatic; phrases broken by rests; a semi-recit. style
Piano: chordal; chromatic; does not double vocal line
Diff: some pitches
Uses: fine song; good for student with limited ability to sustain long phrases
Rec: D#313

2050. **GRIEF** (Leroy V. Brant). [6, 51]; 1st©1955. X on A; f'–g"; Tess-M; 4/4, Freely (♩ = ca.72); 3pp; Diff-V/m, P/m.
For: all voices except very low
Mood: lyrical; philosophical; sadness with hope
Voice: whole phrases of repeated a'–almost a monotone song; chant-like, but with syncopated rhythms; middle section more melodic and lyrical
Piano: rolled chords; sustained; broken chords and afterbeat figures in middle section
Diff: interpretive skills needed in handling the static sections
Uses: moving recital song for singers with expressive skills
Rec: D#12

2051. **SONGS OF SEPARATION** (various poets). Cycle. Leeds, 1949. Traditional key sigs. (but altered-chord harmonic structures, mostly 6th & 7th chords with some whole-tone structures); d'–a"; Tess-M; regular meters; varied tempos; 11pp; Diff-V/md, P/m.
For: lyric tenor
Mood: lyrical; songs center on broken love relationships
Voice: largely conjunct; some chord outlining; many accidentals; speech rhythms
Piano: chordal texture; many 7th chords; many accidentals
Uses: excellent songs; good cycle for lyric tenor; music shows strong French influence
Rec: D#s 314, 315, 316

   a. ***Idolatry*** (Arna Bontemps). d'–a"; 4/4, 3/4, Moderately slow; 2pp.

b. *Poème* (Philippe Thoby Marcelin). e'–a"; 4/4, Moderately slow; 2pp.

c. *Parted* (Paul Laurence Dunbar). e'–a"; 6/8, Piquantly; 2pp.

d. *If You Should Go* (Countee Cullen). d'–g"; 4/4, Slowly; 2pp.

e. *A Black Pierrot* (Langston Hughes). d'–g"; 4/4, Rapidly; 3pp.

2052. WINTER'S APPROACH (Paul Laurence Dunbar). [51]; 1st©1928. A♭maj; e♭'–a♭"; Tess-mH; 4/4, Animated and humorous-Un poco più lento; 6pp; Diff-V/m, P/m.

For: soprano; tenor
Mood: humorous "tale" about the potential fate of the rabbit
Voice: characterized by syncopated rhythms and a somewhat jazz-like style; frequent downward interval of M6th; comical humming; uses stereotypical African-American dialect
Piano: syncopated, jazz-like bass line with afterbeat chords; dotted rhythms and syncopated rolled chords in last section; supports vocal line without doubling
Diff: rhythms and some pitches
Uses: use of stereotyping subject matter, dialect, and other characteristics may limit the appeal of this song, but could be fun for the singer who is comfortable with it

STILLMAN-KELLEY, EDGAR
(see Kelley, Edgar Stillman)

STRATTON, GEORGE WILLIAM
(b. West Swazey, NH?, 1830?; d. 1901)

2053. MY HEART'S QUEEN (C. L. Wheeler). Tolman, 1852. Cmaj; f♯'–g"; Tess-mH; 4/4, Allegro moderato; 3pp (repeated); Diff-V/m, P/e.
For: tenor
Mood: lyrical love song
Voice: many leaps of 6th & 7th; grace notes; some triplets; many 2-note slurs
Piano: 8-meas. prelude; chordal; afterbeat style; melody in 8ves; concludes with staccato 3rds in solo material
Uses: useful period piece

STRICKLAND, LILY
(b. Anderson, SC, 1887; d. Hendersonville, NC, 1958)

2054. AT EVE I HEARD A FLUTE (poet not indicated). [53]; 1st©1923. H & L keys: Gmin & Fmin (orig.); d'–a" & c'–g"; Tess-mH; 4/4, 3/4, Andante con espressione; 3pp; Diff-V/m, P/m.
For: lyric soprano
Mood: lyrical nature picture
Voice: lyrical; fragmented by rests; very sectional; recit.-like section
Piano: chordal with an independent flute-like melody; enhances the text

STRICKLAND, WILLIAM
(b. Defiance, OH, 1914)

2055. THREE SONGS. Galaxy, 1961. cmp1938–1939. Pub. separately; separate entries below.

A. A FLOWER GIVEN TO MY DAUGHTER (James Joyce). B♭maj; f'–f"; Tess-M; 2/2, Simply; 2pp; Diff-V/m, P/e.
For: tenor; soprano; mezzo-soprano
Mood: quiet, tender, ethereal; compares child to white rose
Voice: stepwise; small skips; some long phrases; sustained; syncopation
Piano: thin texture; wide spacing; repetitive; ethereal
Diff: some long phrases; control of quiet sustained ending
Uses: would be effective in recital group

B. IONE, DEAD THE LONG YEAR (Ezra Pound). Cmaj-Amin; e'–g"; Tess-M; 4/4; 3pp; Diff-V/m, P/e.
For: tenor best; possibly soprano; mezzo-soprano
Mood: lament; doleful; lonely; dramatic
Voice: mostly stepwise; some small skips; some dotted rhythms; two long melismas
Piano: thin texture; wide spacing; no doubling of vocal line
Diff: some awkward text setting
Uses: useful in recital group

C. SHE WEEPS OVER RAHOON (James Joyce). Emin; d'–g"; Tess-M; 4/4, 5/4, 3/4; 1+min; Diff-V/md, P/d.
For: mezzo-soprano; soprano (woman's text)
Mood: lament; somewhat dramatic; bleak
Voice: mostly stepwise; syncopation; irregular phrase lengths
Piano: 2 vs. 3, alternating hands; mostly linear; wide reaches
Diff: rhythms against the accomp. could be difficult for the insecure singer
Uses: nice song if something somber is needed

STRILKO, ANTHONY
(b. Philadelphia, PA, 1931; d. New York, NY, 2000)

2056. THE CANAL BANK (James Stephens). Mercury, 1962. cmp1959. X (C-centered); f'–g"; Tess-M; changing meters, Andantino; 1+min; Diff-V/d, P/m-d.
For: light soprano; light tenor (has "he-she" options)
Mood: lighthearted; exuberant; full of life; young
Voice: stepwise; easy skips; some staccato
Piano: 3–4-voice texture; chords, broken chords; articulations and dynamics important; does not double vocal line
Diff: changing meters; ensemble
Uses: for young singer who has good musical skills; catches spirit of poem, double meaning of sounds

2057. CANTICLE TO APOLLO (Robert Herrick). Mercury, 1963. cmp1960. E-centered; e♭'–f♭"; Tess-M; 5/4, Straightforward; 1+min; Diff-V/m-md, P/m.
For: tenor best; baritone; mezzo-soprano; soprano
Mood: lyrical; the power of nature
Voice: stepwise; small skips; dotted notes; syncopation; 2-note slurs; several melismas; accidentals

Piano: same chord progression throughout; lute-like texture; broken quartal chords with some countermelody; some large reaches; does not double vocal line
Diff: some difficult melodic sequences with little help from piano; meters; rhythms
Uses: in group concerning music

2058. **DAVID'S HARP** (Victor E. Reichert). Mercury, 1968. cmp1965. X; d'–e"; Tess-M; 4/4, 5/4, 3/4, Moderato con moto; 2min; Diff-V/m, P/m.
For: baritone; mezzo-soprano
Mood: somewhat dramatic; narrative; descriptive
Voice: somewhat recit.-like; skips up to 7th; speech rhythms
Piano: harp-like sounds, distorted and out-of-tune; many accidentals; many dynamic markings; does not double vocal line
Diff: rhythms; changing meters; ensemble; dynamic control
Uses: effective, imaginative setting; interior of group; quiet ending

2059. **THE FIDDLER'S COIN** (Patricia Benton). Mercury, 1966. cmp1965. Emin; d♭'–e"; Tess-mL; 3/4, 2/4, 4/4, Moderately, with motion; 3pp; Diff-V/m, P/me.
For: baritone; some basses; mezzo-soprano; contralto
Mood: descriptive; bleak; modern-day "Leiermann"
Voice: stepwise; skips up to 6th; syncopation
Piano: imitates instrument; many 5ths; countermelody; some drone bass; various registers; distortion in harmonies and melodic contours; articulations important; does not double vocal line
Diff: rhythms; changing meters; ensemble; breath control
Uses: very good setting; suits text well; excellent for a modern-living, character, or any American group

2060. **FROM AUTUMN'S THRILLING TOMB** (Edgar Bogardus). Mercury, 1967. cmp1955–1967. C♭-centered; e♭'–a"; Tess-mH; changing meters, Lento; 4pp; Diff-V/md, P/m.
For: tenor best; soprano
Mood: lyrical song about death
Voice: opens with voice alone; disjunct line; complex rhythms; several passages for voice alone.
Piano: chordal-linear combination; wide spacing; large reaches; many accidentals; does not double vocal line
Diff: ensemble; some intervals; some m2nds against piano
Uses: song with quiet ending

2061. **LITTLE ELEGY** (Elinor Wylie). Mercury, 1962. cmp1958. D♭maj; c'–a♭"; Tess-M–mH; 3/4, 2/4, Very slowly; 2pp; Diff-V/m, P/m.
For: tenor; soprano
Mood: lyrical; gentle; elegiac
Voice: skips along chord lines; long tones at phrase ends; dotted notes; irregular phrase lengths; some sequence; word repetition
Piano: simple 3-voice chordal texture; many 3rds & 6ths;
Diff: ensemble
Uses: quiet song; useful for young student with good a♭"; see also settings by Rorem and J. Duke

2062. **OPHELIA** (Elinor Wylie). Mercury, 1965. cmp1963. X; d'–g"; Tess-mL; 4/4, 5/4, 2/4, 3/4, Lento; 3min;

Diff-V/md, P/md.
For: mezzo-soprano best; some sopranos
Mood: dramatic; intense; somber
Voice: many skips; some long-ranged phrases; somewhat fragmented; syncopation
Piano: linear-chordal combination; large reaches; many accidentals; sostenuto pedal; wide spacing; does not double vocal line
Diff: pitches; ensemble; intensity in soft singing
Uses: for secure musician; quiet ending; interior of group

2063. **POINT CHARLES** (Ronald Perry). Mercury, 1967. cmp1957. G-centered; c♯'(d')–g♯"(e"); Tess-M–mH depending on options taken; 2/4, 3/4, Leisurely; 1+min; Diff-V/m, P/m.
For: any voice except extremely low or high
Mood: surrealistic description of scene; naive; cheerful
Voice: many skips, esp. 4ths & 8ves; recit. passages; speech rhythms; syncopation
Piano: spread-out chords; staccato scales; animated chord figuration; moves around keyboard; does not double vocal line
Diff: poem; has many directions to performers
Uses: useful short song for recital group

2064. **SONGS FROM *MARKINGS*, I and II** (Dag Hammarskjöld). Mercury, 1966. cmp1965. Both D-centered; d'–e" & f'–a♭"; Tess-mH; 4/4, 3/4, ♩ = 66 & 3/4, ♩ = 58; 3pp each; Diff-V/d, P/md & V/m, P/m.
For: soprano; tenor
Mood: both philosophical; I: concerns courage; II: sad
Voice: I: disjunct; fragmented; difficult intervals; II: more lyrical with dramatic climax
Piano: I: chordal; dissonant; independent; II: chordal; less dissonant; independent
Diff: meter changes; pitches
Uses: very effective pair of serious short songs for recital

STRONG, GEORGE TEMPLETON
(b. New York, NY, 1856; d. Geneva, Switzerland, 1948)

2065. **HOW FAIR THE NIGHT!** Op. 43, No. 1 (Marguerite Merington). Breitkopf & Härtel, 1893. D♭maj; d♭'–e"; Tess-M; 3/4, Adagio; 3pp; Diff-V/md, P/m-md.
For: mezzo-soprano; soprano; baritone
Mood: lyrical; impressionistic; gentle reminiscence
Voice: stepwise; chord-member skips; some triplets; sustained lines; soft dynamics
Piano: block and broken chords; some countermelody; many accidentals; impressionistic harmonies; incidental doubling of vocal line
Diff: long phrases; needs smooth legato line
Uses: nice subdued song; recital material

STRUKOFF, RUDOLF
(b. Rostov, U.S.S.R., 1935)

2066. **CHILDHOOD SKETCHES** (magazine poetry). Cycle. Hall-Orion, 1973. Pub. separately. Partly traditional keys, partly X; g–g"; Tess-M; mostly regular

meters; varied tempos; 14min; Diff-V/md, P/md.
For: mezzo-soprano; some sopranos
Mood: lyrical; small pictures from birth to out-growing childhood
Voice: appears fairly simple but has some pitch and rhythmic difficulties, esp. with the piano
Piano: quartal harmonies; chord clusters; arpeggiation; much staccato articulation; many accidentals
Diff: pitch perception
Uses: attractive group for a young singer who is an advanced musician; not vocally strenuous

    a. *Pet* (Ethel Jacobson). Gmin; g–d"; Tess-mL; 5/4 with many changes, Moderately and detached; 2min.
    b. *Lullaby* (Kate Barnes). Gmin; d'–e♭"; Tess-M; 6/8, Slowly and gracefully; 4min.
    c. *Mustn't!* (Ethel Jacobson). X; c'–f"; Tess-M; 2/4, Very fast and light; 45sec.
    d. *Locomotion* (Ethel Jacobson). X; b–e"; Tess-M; 2/4, Quickly and with abandon; 1+min.
    e. *Blue* (Mary Joyce Pritchard). X; d♭'–e"; Tess-M; 6/8, Calmly and smoothly; 3min.
    f. *Pianist* (Ethel Jacobson). X; d♭'–g"; Tess-mH; 6/8, With motion but expressive; 2min.
    g. *Gone* (Carol Winters). Ends Emin; b–e"; Tess-M; 4/4, Simply and deliberately; 2min.

SUSA, CONRAD
(b. Springdale, PA, 1935)

2067. HYMNS FOR THE AMUSEMENT OF CHILDREN. For Medium Voice and Piano or Harpsichord (Christopher Smart, 1775). Cycle. E. C. Schirmer, 1980. cmp1972. X; b♭–b♭"; Tess-M-mH; traditional meters with changes; varied tempos; 23pp; Diff-V/dd, P/dd.
For: mezzo-soprano
Mood: texts are hymns and prayers for a child (of 1775), up-dated with contemporary beat and jazzy vocal techniques
Voice: predominantly stepwise motion with small skips; leaps of 7ths, 8ves, & 10ths; much chromatic alteration; complex rhythms, in calypso, jazz, and blues styles; much syncopation; cross-accenting; various divisions of beat juxtaposed; short and long ornaments; several melismas with difficult pitch patterns; some ornaments similar to those of blues or gospel singers
Piano: combination of linear and block- and broken-chord patterning; many accidentals; some 3-stave writing; score hard to read; many notes of small metric value (16th & 32nd) in complex rhythms; thick texture; heavily jazz-influenced; large reach needed; (b.) marked "Boldly (Elton John style)," ending with "Rousing honky-tonk," and 6 meas. of parallel M & m triads in 16ths, first in r.h., then in l.h.; (c.) includes tango rhythm which builds to a frenzy during 12-meas. postlude and moves directly into (d.), which features long trills, with piano part marked "very dancy"
Diff: highly complex rhythms; ensemble; getting the correct mood and musical idiom

Uses: effective for performers familiar with jazz and other musical idioms influencing this cycle
Rec: D#20

    a. *I. For Sunday.* X; c'–g"; 4/4 with a few changes, Gentle calypso; 4pp.
    b. *II. At Dressing in the Morning.* X; b–f♯"; 4/4 with a few changes, Strong-beat blues; 5pp.
    c. *III. Against Despair.* X (begins E♭maj); b♭–g♭"; 7/8 with changes, Quietly flowing; 4pp.
    d. *IV. For Saturday.* Begin in C; c'–e"; 5/4, Intensely rhythmic; 3pp.
    e. *V. At Undressing in the Evening.* X; b♭–b♭"; unmetered & 4/4, Freely, simply, in blues style; 4pp.
    f. *VI. The Conclusion of the Matter.* X; c'–f"; 4/4, Gently rhythmic; 3pp.

SUSKIND, JOYCE HOPE
(b. U. S. A., 20th Century)

2068. SIX SONGS TO POETRY OF YEATS William Butler Yeats). Casia Publishing Company, 1997 (Hildegard). Tonal; b–b"; Tess-M-mH; regular meters with changes; mostly "Andante" but with much motion in piano figurations; 29pp; Diff-V/md-d, P/m-d.
For: lyric soprano
Mood: loving; melancholy; various aspects of old age–both loss and freedom
Voice: wide range; chromatic; syllabic and melismatic; many ascending passages; much tone painting
Piano: uses the full resources of the instrument in various figurations; polyrhythms; much fast passage work; romantic piano technique
Diff: pitch; range; overall musical architecture; piano technique
Uses: excellent cycle for a mature professional level singer

    a. *Those Dancing Days Are Gone.* F♯min; b♯–g♭"; Tess-cs; 3/4, 4/4, Andante; 4pp.
    b. *The Song of Wandering Aengus.* X; b–f♯"; Tess-M; 2/2, Andante ♩ = 42; 6pp.
    c. *The Wild Swans at Coole.* X; d'–b"; Tess-mH-H; 2/4, 4/4, 5/4, Andante ♩ = 54; 7pp.
    d. *After Long Silence.* Gmin; d'–f"; Tess-M; 4/4, 3/2, 2/4, Lento ♩ = 44; 2pp.
    e. *Mad as the Mist and Snow.* Fmin-Cmin; c'–g"; Tess-mH; 4/4, 2/4; 5pp.
    f. *The Lake Isle of Innisfree.* Fmaj; c'–a"; Tess-mH; 2/4, 4/4, Allegro ♩ = 69; 5pp.

SWAN, TIMOTHY (See Special Section)

SWANSON, HOWARD
(b. Atlanta, GA, 1909; d. New York, NY, 1978)

2069. CAHOOTS (Carl Sandburg). Weintraub, 1951. "To William Warfield." X; b–d♭"; Tess-mL; 4/4, Moderately, not too fast; 4pp; Diff-V/d, P/md-d.

For: baritone; bass
Mood: dramatic; strong; lower-class cynicism and conniving; declamatory
Voice: many small skips; interrupted phrasing; speech rhythms; some jazz elements; many accidentals
Piano: many M & m 2nds & 7ths in chords; jarring harmonies; rhythmic subdivisions of 2, 3, 4, & 5 juxtaposed; syncopation; many accidentals; no vocal line doubling
Diff: rhythms; ensemble; singer must have ability to deliver street language convincingly and with dramatic flair
Uses: powerful and colorful song for an American or contemporary living group

2070. A DEATH SONG (Lullaby) (Paul Laurence Dunbar). [6]; 1st©1951. Cmaj; b♭–e♭"; Tess-mL; 4/4, Andante moderato; 4pp; Diff-V/m, P/me.
For: any medium or low voice
Mood: lyrical; philosophical acceptance of death
Voice: folksong-like modal melody; somewhat chromatic
Piano: chordal with contrapuntal 8ths; some chromaticism; supports vocal line well
Diff: originally written in dialect; provided with transcription into standard English with the suggestion that the song "can be sung effectively without using dialect"
Uses: for study and performance
Rec: D#12

2071. FOUR PRELUDES (T. S. Eliot). Weintraub, 1952, 1976. X (wandering harmonies), set ends Fmaj; e♭'–a♭"; Tess-M-mH; regular meters; varied tempos; 12pp; Diff-V/m-md, P/m.
For: tenor probably best
Mood: lyrical; images of city life; tinged with bitterness
Voice: skips; mildly chromatic; harmonic direction uncertain; somewhat repetitious
Piano: linear; generally patterned tonally and rhythmically; accidentals; wandering harmonies
Diff: pitch perception difficult due to lack of predictable harmonic direction; some sustained high tone
Uses: interesting group; useful for a singer interested in Eliot's poetry

    a. *The Winter Evening Settles Down.* e'–g♯"; 4/4, Larghetto; 3pp.
    b. *The Morning Comes to Consciousness.* e♭'–g"; 4/4, Lively and vigorous; 2pp.
    c. *You Tossed a Blanket from the Bed.* f'–g"; 2/2, Allegretto; 3pp.
    d. *His Soul Stretched Tight across the Skies.* f'–a♭"; 4/4, Andantino; 4pp.

2072. IN TIME OF SILVER RAIN (Langston Hughes). Weintraub, 1950. F-centered; d'–a"; Tess-mH; 4/4, Moderato; 3pp; Diff-V/md, P/md.
For: soprano; tenor; light voice probably best
Mood: lyrical; springtime renewed; delicate
Voice: many skips; interrupted phrases; many accidentals; syncopation; somewhat disjointed
Piano: linear texture; many accidentals; syncopation; often doubles vocal line
Diff: singer needs secure register control and easy high tones both *pp* & *f*; ensemble

Uses: see also setting by Jean Berger (in *Four Songs*)

2073. I WILL LIE DOWN IN AUTUMN (May Swenson). Weintraub, 1952. [6]. X; d♭'–c♭"; Tess-M; 4/4, Andante; 3pp; Diff-V/m, P/m.
For: mezzo-soprano or contralto best; baritone; bass
Mood: intense; somber; subdued; poem about death
Voice: conjunct; many accidentals; syncopation; afterbeat phrase beginnings; interrupted phrasing
Piano: block-chord structures, some tertian, some quartal; many 2nds; some dim.8ves; stark; syncopation; dotted rhythms; large reaches; does not double vocal line
Diff: ensemble; intensity of expression in soft dynamic levels; enharmonic spellings
Uses: useful quiet, short-ranged song
Rec: D#12

2074. THE JUNK MAN (Carl Sandburg). Weintraub, 1950. X; e'–g"; Tess-M; 4/4, Moderato; 2+min; Diff-V/md, P/d.
For: tenor; soprano
Mood: declamatory; narrative; song about death
Voice: stepwise; small skips; speech rhythms; some triplets; syncopation; jazz elements; many accidentals
Piano: very high and very low on keyboard; shimmering, soft impressionistic sounds combined with loud, harsh chords and clusters; syncopation; complex rhythms; many accidentals; does not double vocal line
Diff: singer must have superior rhythmic ability; ensemble
Uses: effective song for the secure musician; quiet ending
Rec: D#317

2075. THE NEGRO SPEAKS OF RIVERS (Langston Hughes). Leeds, 1949. [6]. "To Marian Anderson." Gmin; g–d"(e♭"); Tess-mL; 2/2, Moderato (with steady rhythm); 5pp; Diff-V/md-d, P/md-d.
For: contralto; bass; some mezzo-sopranos or bass-baritones
Mood: powerful; narrative; comparison of primal soul of the people to ancient rivers
Voice: stepwise; chord-member skips; dotted rhythms; syncopation; jazz elements; large dynamic contrasts
Piano: jazz elements; syncopation; dotted rhythms; many accidentals; cadenza-like passage; low, somber sounds predominate; large dynamic contrasts; incidental doubling of vocal line
Diff: singer must have rich, mature sound effective *pp–ff*, and sense of drama inherent in the text setting
Uses: excellent song for a powerful singer; fewer unresolved dissonances than in many of Swanson's songs
Rec: D#s 12, 317

2076. PIERROT (Langston Hughes). Weintraub, 1950. Emin; b♭–d"; Tess-mL; 4/4, Allegro–Andante; 6pp; Diff-V/md, P/md.
For: baritone or bass best; possibly mezzo soprano; contralto
Mood: dramatic; narrative; declamatory
Voice: many skips; declamatory; 2-note slurs; many accidentals; some triplets
Piano: recurring theme is accompanied by a 2-meas. ostinato; syncopation; many accidentals; jazz-like elements; covers the keyboard; large reaches; some countermelody; does not double vocal line

Diff: ensemble; differentiation of two characters; dynamic range *pp–fff*; sustained tones on c♯' and d" (*fff*); needs mature, large sound
Uses: good song for a powerful singer

2077. **SAW A GRAVE UPON A HILL** (May Swenson). Weintraub, 1952. X, Bmin-centered; d(a)– b♭'; Tess-L; 3/4, 4/4,5/4, Slow and grave; 3pp; Diff-V/m, P/m.
For: bass
Mood: lyrical; philosophical; somber
Voice: disjunct; chromatic; many dotted rhythms; some triplets
Piano: chordal; some 16th-note repeated tones; many accidentals; rhythmically patterned
Diff: pitch perception
Uses: powerful song for a dark, somber voice with a low D

2078. **SONGS FOR PATRICIA** (Norman Rosten). Cycle. Weintraub, 1952. No key sigs., X (indeterminate harmonies); e'–b♭"; Tess-M-mH; regular meters; varied tempos; 8min; Diff-V/md, P/m.
For: tenor; soprano
Mood: lyrical; songs to an infant
Voice: mostly conjunct with some leaps; chromatic; pitches difficult; most high tones soft; speech rhythms
Piano: linear; indeterminate harmonies and harmonic direction; many accidentals; delicate; tends to group in center of keyboard
Diff: pitch perception difficult due to lack of tonal center and a "wandering" harmonic feeling; soft high tones
Uses: interesting songs; high tones must be floated softly; tenor falsetto effective; interior of program; songs need warmth and affection

    a. *Darling Those Are Birds.* f♯'–g'; Tess-M; 4/4, Moderato; 2pp.
    b. *No Leaf May Fall.* e'–b♭"(g"); Tess-mH; 6/8, Allegretto; 4pp.
    c. *One Day.* g♯'–a"; Tess-H; 3/4, Lento; 1p.
    d. *Goodnight.* g'–b♭"; Tess-H; 4/4, Andante; 4pp.

2079. **STILL LIFE** (Carl Sandburg). Weintraub, 1950. X, C-centered; d♭'–g"; Tess-mH; 4/4, 6/4, 2/4, Moderately fast; 4pp; Diff-V/d, P/md.
For: tenor
Mood: declamatory; descriptive; energetic; American subject
Voice: many skips; jazz elements; syncopation; some triplets vs. quadruplets in piano
Piano: sound effects of a train; disjointed; cross-accents; covers keyboard; many accidentals; 7-meas. prelude; 8th-note motion; does not double vocal line
Diff: singer must have superior rhythmic sense; ensemble
Uses: interesting, colorful song of the American scene; quiet ending
Rec: D#317

2080. **THE VALLEY** (Edwin Markham). Leeds, 1950. B♭maj; b♭–d♭"; Tess-M; 4/4, Andante (quietly); 2pp; Diff-V/m, P/m.
For: baritone; mezzo-soprano
Mood: lyrical; descriptive
Voice: rather static vocal line; many repeated tones; some dissonant intervals

Piano: constant 8th-note motion; accidentals; harmonic emphasis on 2nds; all treble clef; delicate
Diff: a few pitches
Uses: nice song; useful for teaching clear diction and a soft spinning tone
Rec: D#317

SYDEMAN, WILLIAM
(b. New York, 1928)

2081. **FIVE SHORT SONGS.** E. C. Schirmer, 1978. No poet given; songs numbered and untitled. Chromatic harmonies; d'–a♭"; Tess-M; mostly 4/4; 3+min; Diff-V/d, P/d.
For: soprano specified; possibly mezzo-soprano
Mood: lighthearted; whimsical
Voice: many skips and leaps; many accidentals; grace notes; speech-like rhythms; syncopation; one spoken line
Piano: disjunct; linear, spare texture; moves around keyboard; many accidentals; pianist asked to nod and smile at singer in (d.)
Diff: rhythmic and pitch security needed; ensemble
Uses: good short light group for recital; program ender; wonderful for the singer with comic flair

    a. *I.* X; e♭'–a♭"; 4/4, Andante; 1p.
    b. *II.* X; d♯'–g"; 4/4, Allegro; 3pp.
    c. *III.* X; d'–d♯"; 4/4, Andante; 1p.
    d. *IV.* X; e♭'–f"; 4/4; 2pp.
    e. *V.* X; e♭'–e"; 4/4; 2pp.

2082. **A SPIDER** (William Sydeman). E. C. Schirmer, 1970. X; d♭–g'; Tess-mH; 3/4, 4/4, Allegro; 45sec; Diff-V/d, P/d.
For: baritone specified
Mood: descriptive; animated
Voice: several awkward skips on 1-syllable slurs; irregular rhythms; mostly below the accomp. in pitch
Piano: linear; constant rapid motion; many accidentals; articulations important; cluster chords at end
Diff: rhythms awkward against piano; ensemble problems; needs mature singer with perfect command of registers; ends on sustained g'
Uses: good final song for a group

2083. **UPON JULIA'S CLOTHES** (Robert Herrick). E. C. Schirmer, 1970. X; e–g♭'; Tess-HH; 6/8 with many changes, Andante con moto; 4pp; Diff-V/d, P/d.
For: high baritone; tenor
Mood: descriptive; ecstatic love poem
Voice: very high tessitura; chromatic; frequent long tones at ends of phrases
Piano: chromatic; contrapuntal; independent of voice
Diff: tessitura; frequent meter changes; long phrases
Uses: good to teach musicianship and breath control if head voice is operable

TALMA, LOUISE
[See Appendix for songs with French texts]

TATE, TOBY
(b. Washington, D. C., 1933)

2084. **LOVE AND LOSS** (Toby Tate). Five Songs for
Soprano or Tenor. Leyerle Publications, 1993.
Cmp1982. "For Phyllis Bryn-Julson." Mixed
harmonies; c'–b"; Tess-mH, cs; regular meters; varied
tempos (♩ = 66–96); 6+min; Diff-V/md, P/m.
For: soprano; tenor
Mood: melancholy; love is brief; life is long
Voice: wide leaps; disjunct and conjunct lines; some
ornaments; some chromatic lines; mostly syllabic;
numerous high soft passages
Piano: chordal; some thinner texture in (c.) & (d.)
Diff: some pitch patterns
Uses: good short cycle for the mature and advanced
undergraduate or graduate singer

    a. *Morning Glories.* X; c'–b" ; Tess-cs; 3/2, ♩ = 46; 1p.
    (impermanence of love)
    b. *Lightning.* X; e♭'–a♯" ; Tess-M; 4/4, ♩ = 96; 1p.
    (instant of bliss)
    c. *Dawn.* Phrygian on A; d'–a"; Tess-mH; 4/4, ♩ = 88;
    2pp. (shortness of night of love)
    d. *Awake in the Moonlight.* X; c♯'–b♭"; Tess-cs; 3/2,
    ♩ = 72; 1p. (longing at night, alone)
    e. *Memory.* E-centered; c'–g"; Tess-M; 2/2, ♩ = 66;
    2pp. (love is brief; life is long)

TAYLOR, CLIFFORD
(b. Avalon, PA, 1923; d. Philadelphia, PA, 1987)

2085. **FIVE SONGS ON ENGLISH TEXTS,** Op. 4.
Associated, 1954. Pub. separately; can be done as a set
(probably best by a tenor), or separately; separate
entries below.

A. **RONDO, ON A FAVORITE CAT (Drowned in a
Tub of Goldfishes)** (Thomas Gray). E-centered;
d♭'– a♭"; Tess-mH; 6/8, Slowly, but with movement;
4+min; Diff-V/d, P/d.
For: tenor; possibly soprano
Mood: philosophical
Voice: many leaps; one melisma; speech-like, varied rhythms;
accidentals
Piano: chordal-linear combination; five sections with different
patterns; many accidentals; scale-like passages in 8ves;
imitation; some block chords; complex
Diff: ensemble; one high section with many repeated g"s
Uses: perhaps best with others in this set

B. **CHERRY ROBBERS** (D. H. Lawrence). Dorian on F;
f'–a♭"; Tess-mH; 9/4, 6/8, Slowly, but with movement;
3pp; Diff-V/md, P/md.
For: tenor
Mood: lyrical; sensuous poem full of imagery and metaphor
Voice: mostly stepwise and repeated tones; skips along modal
structures; sustained phrases; many accidentals; fairly
high tessitura in some phrases
Piano: open texture with chords and lines moving in 8ves;
linear middle section portrays distant laughter

Diff: catching and sustaining proper mood
Uses: excellent song for a mature tenor

C. **ON A CERTAIN LADY AT COURT** (Alexander
Pope). A-centered; e'–g"; Tess-mH; 2/4, Moderately
fast; 1+min; Diff-V/md, P/md.
For: tenor
Mood: somewhat satirical; compliments a woman
Voice: stepwise; small skips; speech rhythms; phrases
separated by short interludes
Piano: linear; some block chords; scale passages in 8ves;
articulations important; 11-meas. postlude; does not
double vocal line
Diff: ensemble
Uses: good song; could end a group

D. **MERCHANDISE** (Amy Lowell). X; e♭'–g"; Tess-M;
4/4, 5+4/8, Quickly, but well marked rhythmically;
2min; Diff-V/md, P/md.
For: tenor
Mood: narrative; theme is song
Voice: stepwise; small skips, esp. 4ths; speech rhythms;
irregular rhythmic groups; 2-note slurs; one melisma
Piano: chordal block, repeated, and broken; some
countermelody; does not double vocal line
Diff: irregular meters and rhythmic groupings; ensemble
Uses: in a group about song; quiet ending

E. **FIRE AND ICE** (Robert Frost). A♭maj; e♭'–a";
Tess-M; 6/8, Moderately fast; 1+min; Diff-V/m, P/m.
For: tenor; soprano
Mood: philosophical
Voice: stepwise; small skips; dotted rhythms; one phrase
re-barred so that accents are different from piano
Piano: chordal block and broken; some countermelody;
syncopation; introduces vocal melody, but does not
double vocal line
Diff: rhythmic groupings
Uses: quiet ending; see also setting by William T. Ames

TAYLOR, DEEMS
(b. New York, NY, 1885; d. New York, NY, 1966)

2086. **AN EATING SONG** (Deems Taylor). J. Fischer, 1944.
"For John Charles Thomas." Gmaj-Fmaj; b–f";
Tess-M; 4/4, Briskly; 6pp; Diff-V/m, P/m.
For: baritone
Mood: humorous; hearty
Voice: straightforward, march-like vocal line; ends on
sustained f" on "kings"
Piano: chordal; some broken-chord figures; march-like
Diff: sustained f" ending
Uses: good song for teaching clear diction; humorous

2087. **A SONG FOR LOVERS,** Op. 13, No. 2 (James
Stephens). J. Fischer, 1920. H & M keys: E♭maj &
Bmaj; d–f" & a♯–c♯"; Tess-M; 4/4, Smoothly, not too
slowly; 4pp; Diff-V/m, P/m.
For: any voice except extremely high and light
Mood: night scene; the moon and the sea
Voice: many small skips; some dotted rhythms; syncopation;

several 2-note slurs
Piano: repetitive chordal pattern; block chords and broken 8ves; large reaches; needs careful pedaling; impressionistic; does not double vocal line
Uses: useful atmospheric song
Rec: D#318

TAYLOR, RAYNOR (See Special Section)

THOMAS, ALAN
(b. Scranton, PA, 1924)

2088. **FIVE LANDSCAPES** (A Cycle of Songs) (T. S. Eliot). Presser, 1957. Pub. separately. No key sigs., dissonant with some tonal feeling; b–c'''; Tess-L, M, mH; regular meters; varied tempos; 10min; Diff-V/d, P/d.
For: tenor; soprano; texts seem vaguely more suitable for a man
Mood: lyrical; various moods relating to natural scenes described; philosophical
Voice: many skips and leaps; some conjunct motion; many sustained tones; (e.) has irregular rhythmic groupings; entire range used; frequent high and low tones
Piano: rather spare textures, mostly linear; wide reach needed for chords; many accidentals; dynamics and articulations important; rhythmic stability necessary
Diff: some pitches; rhythms of last song; vocally taxing; for the mature singer
Uses: interesting songs; mature, imaginative singer with the required range could make them come alive as cycle or separately

   a. *New Hampshire.* X; gb'–a"; Tess-mH; 2/4, ♩=116; 4pp.
   b. *Virginia.* F♯min; c'–ab"; Tess-L, H; 4/4, ♩=72; 3pp.
   c. *Usk.* Fmaj; c'–ab"; Tess-H, mL; 3/4, ♩=60; 4pp.
   d. *Rannoch, by Glencoe.* X–Bmin; b–g♯"; Tess-M–mL; 4/4, ♩=100; 3pp.
   e. *Cape Ann.* X; eb'–c'''; Tess-M, mH; 8/8, ♩=120; 4pp.

THOMAS, ANDREW
(b. Ithaca, NY, 1939)

2089. **ANOTHER NEW VOICE TEACHER** (Gene Sheer). Classical Vocal Reprints, 1996. Cmaj; b–g"; Tess-cs; 3/4, Moderato; 6pp; Diff-V/md, P/m.
For: soprano
Mood: humorous
Voice: vocal line typical of a waltz song (i.e., J. Strauss); outlines chords, some large leaps, some stepwise motion; one trill; a "la-la-la" passage
Piano: harmonic echoes of J. Strauss, R. Strauss, Poulenc, and a little jazz; accidentals; mostly doubles the vocal line
Diff: keeping a straight face
Uses: hilarious song for an audience of singers, but perhaps, dear singer, not when your teacher is present

THOMAS, RICHARD PEARSON (See entry #15 J)

THOMPSON, RANDALL
(b. New York, NY, 1899; d. Boston, MA, 1984)

2090. **MY MASTER HATH A GARDEN** (anon.). E. C. Schirmer, 1938. E maj; eb'–eb"; Tess-M; 3/4, Allegretto; 47meas.; Diff-V/e, P/m.
For: mezzo-soprano; baritone; also others
Mood: reverent; simple; tranquil
Voice: stepwise; small skips; easy rhythms; some 2-note slurs
Piano: prelude, interlude, and postlude have a melody in triplets; otherwise 3-voice block chords; occasional 8ths; doubles vocal line
Uses: excellent for beginner; useful simple song

2091. **THE PASSENGER** (M. A. DeWolfe Howe). E. C. Schirmer, 1961. cmp1957. "To Gerard Souzay." Cmin-maj; G–f'; Tess-mH; 4/4, Lento tranquillo; 6min; Diff-V/d, P/m.
For: baritone specified
Mood: dramatic; hopeful; song about death
Voice: many leaps, esp. 8ves; various rhythmic subdivisions; syncopation; several short recit.-like sections
Piano: subdued chords, various registers; one 13-meas. interlude (like an "Alleluia"); does not double vocal line
Diff: control of wide dynamic range; needs clear low tones
Uses: effective song for true lyric baritone with good range and beautiful soft tones; quiet ending

2092. **SOLSTICE** (Robert Lee Wolff). E. C. Schirmer, 1986. Fmaj; c–f'; Tess-mL; 4/4, Allegro moderato; 6pp; Diff-V/m, P/m.
For: baritone specified
Mood: cheerful
Voice: patter song; repeated pitches; some 8ve leaps; syllabic
Piano: 2-meas. staccato 16th-note prelude; 4-meas interlude; afterbeat patterning; broken and block chords; doubles vocal line, sometimes in a different 8ve
Diff: possibly diction in 16th-note patter section
Uses: with other songs by same composer, or with other songs about winter, Christmas, or the seasons; good recital material for a mature student

2093. **TAPESTRY** (William Douglas). E. C. Schirmer, 1986. cmp1925. Emaj; b–e"; Tess-M; 4/4, 2/4, 3/2, 6/4, Con moto tranquillo; 6pp; Diff-V/m, P/md.
For: mezzo-soprano specified; possibly baritone
Mood: description of nature; serene
Voice: mostly quarter-note motion; long tones on e" twice; mostly stepwise and small skips
Piano: mostly 16th-note broken chord motion; some simultaneous 16th-note motion in both hands; some accidentals; doubling of vocal line incidental; 5-meas. prelude, 4-meas. postlude
Diff: none for the mature singer; for neophyte, several phrases end on the highest pitch
Uses: nice recital song

2094. **VELVET SHOES** (Elinor Wylie). E. C. Schirmer,

1938. Fmaj; c'–e"; Tess-M; 2/4, 4/4, 3/2, Quasi una marcia in lontananza; 4pp; Diff-V/e, P/md.

For: mezzo-soprano
Mood: lyrical; innocent; serene
Voice: mostly stepwise; some skips; many 2-note slurs; easy rhythms; two meas. hemiola
Piano: 3–4-voice chordal texture; doubles vocal line; lengthy prelude, interludes with tricky accidentals
Diff: abrupt modulation at beginning of last stanza; singer's concentration through the piano solo material
Uses: good for young student
Rec: D#s 69, 319

THOMSON, VIRGIL
(b. Kansas City, MO, 1896; d. New York, NY, 1989)

[See Appendix for songs with French texts]

[See also D#324 for songs not listed below]

2095. AT THE SPRING (Jasper Fisher). H. W. Gray, 1965. cmp1955. Dmaj; d'–g"; Tess-M; 3/4, 4/4, 5/4, Moderate; 4pp; Diff-V/m, P/me.

For: soprano; mezzo-soprano; tenor
Mood: lively; happy salute to springtime
Voice: many small skips; some larger leaps; syncopation; many dotted notes; irregular phrase lengths
Piano: chordal texture; afterbeat and arpeggiated patterns
Diff: rhythms most challenging and interesting aspect of song; sustained g" on word "sing"
Uses: good for students; perhaps to open a group about spring
Rec: D#56

2096. THE BELL DOTH TOLL (Thomas Heywood). (Peer)Southern, 1962. [65]. cmp1955. X; b–e"; Tess-M; 4/4, ♩=72; 1+min; Diff-V/m, P/e.

For: baritone; bass; mezzo-soprano; contralto
Mood: mysterious; nether-worldly; eerie; intense
Voice: many skips; dotted rhythms; syncopation; 2–4-note slurs
Piano: block chords, two per meas.; structures imitate bell sounds; many accidentals; no doubling of vocal line
Diff: pitches; melisma involving skips of 5th, 6th, & 8ve; fragmented phrases; dynamic control; differentiation of legato and detached styles
Uses: recital and teaching material

2097. CONSIDER, LORD (John Donne). (Peer)Southern, 1962. cmp1955. B♭maj; b♭–d"; Tess-M; 2/2, 3/2, Slow and majestic; 1+min; Diff-V/m, P/e.

For: bass; baritone; contralto; mezzo-soprano
Mood: grave; contemplates entering heaven
Voice: mostly stepwise; skips up to a 7th; some syncopation; dotted rhythms; triplets
Piano: wide spacing; parallel 8ves, double 8ves, & 10ths; detached throughout; does not double vocal line
Diff: rhythms; ensemble
Uses: useful recital song; loud ending

2098. THE COURTSHIP OF THE YONGLY BONGLY BO (Edward Lear). G. Schirmer, 1977. cmp1973–1974.
Fmaj-min-Gmin-E♭maj; e♭'–f"; Tess-mH; 4/4, 6/4, ♩=120; 14pp; Diff-V/m, P/md.

For: soprano; tenor
Mood: humorous, nonsensical ballad
Voice: stepwise; small skips; syncopation; some chromaticism; triplets; syllabic with occasional 2-note slurs
Piano: chordal-linear combination; block and broken chords; 2-voice linear section with broken-chord patterns in 10ths; countermelody in r.h. 8ves; somewhat chromatic; frequently doubles vocal line
Diff: may be tiring to sing because of length and tessitura
Uses: good song for recital; group ender; encore
Rec: D#325

2099. THE FEAST OF LOVE (from the *Pervigilium Veneris*, 2nd or 4th century A.D.; trans. by Virgil Thomson). G. Schirmer, 1993. Orig. for baritone and orchestra; first performed, 1964. Bmin (with many changes); d–g'; Tess-H; 12/8, 6/8, Molto ritmico (♩.=60); 8min; Diff-V/d, P/d.

For: baritone specified; tessitura could work well for a dramatic tenor
Mood: ". . . a setting in the composer's free translation of the *Pervigilium Veneris*, a collection of [anonymous] rhymed Latin stanzas . . . celebrating the three day festival of Venus"; many aspects of love and springtime
Voice: conjunct and disjunct motion; intervals up to 8ve; traditional tonal centers; frequent changes; few accidentals; varied compound rhythms; occasional duplets; much of vocal line lies above the bass staff; sustained f', f♯', and g'
Piano: reduction of orchestral score well-planned for the piano; much of the work is chordal; a variety of broken-chord configurations; one section in rolled chords; two sections feature countermelody to the vocal line with l.h. bass line; frequent changes of key sig., with some accidentals in the score; hemiola in 6/8 in middle section; usually supports but does not double vocal line
Diff: vocal stamina needed, as the tessitura could prove quite tiring for a baritone
Uses: an interesting and exciting addition to a recital

2100. FIVE SONGS FROM WILLIAM BLAKE. Cycle. Ricordi, 1953. (Now pub. Peer-Southern). cmp1951. Traditional keys; A♭–g'; Tess-M, mH, H; regular meters; varied tempos; 16min; Diff-V/d, P/e-m.

For: dramatic baritone; bass-baritone
Mood: lyrico-dramatic; mystical; Judeo-Christian themes in poetry; music seems irreverent and ironic
Voice: largely outlines chords; some conjunct motion; modulatory; many ascending intervals, arpeggios, and phrases; many high e's, f's, and a few g's; one f♯' soft and sustained; much *ff*; large dynamic contrasts
Piano: chordal; some arpeggios and broken-chord patterns; motivic passages; parallelism; many accidentals; simplistic harmonies and patterns; much solo material of repetitive nature
Diff: vocal endurance
Uses: songs contain various melodic and harmonic quotations from or allusions to seemingly familiar hymn and/or

folk tunes and from Wagner's *Magic Fire Music*;
modern example of parody technique

Rec: D#s 320, 322, 324

   a. *The Divine Image.* E♭maj; A♭–e♭'; Tess-M; 4/4,
     ♩= ca.80; 4pp.

   b. *Tiger! Tiger!* Emin; A–g'; Tess-mH-H; 4/4, ♩= 96;
     5pp.

   c. *The Land of Dreams.* Cmaj-X; c–f♯'; Tess-H; 3/4,
     4/4, ♩= 72; 6pp.

   d. *The Little Black Boy.* Fmaj; A♭–f'; Tess-mH-H;
     4/4, 3/2, ♩= ca.60; 6pp.

   e. *And Did Those Feet.* Amaj-X; A–g'; Tess-covers
     range; 3/4, ♩= 66; 8pp.

2101. **FOUR SONGS TO POEMS OF THOMAS
CAMPION.** Cycle. Ricordi, 1953. (Now pub.
Peer-Southern). cmp1951. Traditional keys; A♭–a♭";
Tess-M-mH; regular meters; varied tempos; 17pp;
Diff-V/m, P/e.

For: high baritone; medium-range tenor
Mood: lyrical love songs in Elizabethan style
Voice: skips along chord lines; rhythmic awkwardness;
somewhat awkward match of music to words
Piano: elementary keyboard and harmonic technique
Rec: D#s 322, 324, 326

   a. *Follow Your Saint.* Dmin; d'– f"; voice in 6/8,
     ♩. = 84, piano in 2/4, ♩= 84; 5pp.

   b. *There Is a Garden in Her Face.* Gmaj; d'– e"; 3/4,
     ♩= 108; 4pp. [**Rec:** D#51]

   c. *Rose Cheek'd Laura, Come.* D♭maj; d♭'–f"; 4/4,
     5/4, 3/4, ♩= 48; 3pp.

   d. *Follow Thy Fair Sun.* A♭maj; A♭–a♭" (opt. notes
     for both extremes); 4/4, ♩= 56; 5pp.

2102. **HOT DAY AT THE SEASHORE** (Jour de Chaleur
aux Bains de Mer) (Duchesse de Rohan; trans. Sherry
Mangan). Boosey & Hawkes, 1963. cmp1928. Cmaj,
ends B-centered; c'–g"; Tess-mH; 2/4 (piano structured
in 3/4), Tempo commodo; 4pp; Diff-V/me, P/e.

For: soprano; tenor
Mood: descriptive of scene
Voice: scalewise; skips along chord lines; English text causes
syncopations and dotted rhythms
Piano: waltz-style chordal accomp., mis-barred; does not
double vocal line
Diff: ensemble could be difficult due to polymetric effect;
numerous g"s and f♯"s
Uses: fun song for a change of pace; simple setting with
polymeters is expressive of the many things going on at
once in the text; clever setting

2103. **IF THOU A REASON DOST DESIRE TO KNOW**
(Sir Frances Kynaston). (Peer)Southern, 1962.
cmp1955. Cmaj; c'–f"; Tess-M; 2/4, 3/8, 4/8, 3/4,
♩= 60; 4pp; Diff-V/m, P/m.

For: tenor; baritone
Mood: lyrical love song; somewhat erotic; intense; joyous
Voice: stepwise; small skips, esp. 3rds; little chromaticism;
dotted rhythms; repetitive; lyrical and flowing; syllabic
Piano: 2–3-voice simple linear texture; section of 4–6-voice

block chords; 32nd-note trill figure in 3rds & 6ths;
some chromaticism; no vocal line doubling
Diff: irregular rhythms; f" sustained 2½ beats
Uses: good recital material; needs an intense performance
Rec: D#56

2104. **JOHN PEEL** (John Woodcock Graves). (Peer)
Southern, 1962. cmp1955. Emaj-Amaj alternation; b–e';
Tess-M; 4/4, 3/4, ♩= 60; 3+min; Diff-V/d, P/m.

For: baritone
Mood: dramatic; spirited; hunting song
Voice: entirely composed of skips on chord lines in horn-call
patterns; some triplets; syncopation
Piano: broken chords in 8ves in horn-call patterns; duplets and
triplets; some dotted notes; does not double vocal line
Diff: features e'; not a well-constructed song for the baritone
voice, but probably a crowd-pleaser; triplets in voice
vs. duplets in piano and vice versa; ensemble
Uses: group ender
Rec: D#56

2105. **LOOK, HOW THE FLOOR OF HEAVEN** (William
Shakespeare). H. W. Gray, 1963. cmp1955. X;
c♯'– g"(f"); Tess-M; 4/4, 3/4, 2/4, 3/2, ♩= 96; 1+min;
Diff-V/m, P/me.

For: soprano; tenor
Mood: descriptive; "harmony of the spheres"; quiet
Voice: many small skips; dotted rhythms; syncopation;
irregular phrase lengths; interrupted phrases
Piano: chordal; some rolled chords; thin texture; quiet;
medium and high pitches only; no vocal line doubling
Diff: rhythms
Uses: useful subdued song; setting suits text well; quiet
ending

2106. **THE MONKEY AND THE LEOPARD** (Le Singe et
le Leopard) (La Fontaine; trans. Donald Sutherland).
(Peer)Southern, 1973. cmp1930. Gmaj; d'–g"; Tess-M;
4/4, ♩= 96 (with several tempo changes); 8pp;
Diff-V/m, P/me.

For: tenor; soprano
Mood: fable
Voice: stepwise; chord-member skips; easy rhythms; 2-note
slurs; English version creates some different rhythms
Piano: spare texture; linear-chordal combination; some
afterbeat chords; many parallel-motion scales in 8ves
&10ths; does not double vocal line
Diff: differentiation of three characters; ensemble; somewhat
hard to read
Uses: nice song of this type; useful to end a recital group;
refreshingly uncluttered

2107. **MOSTLY ABOUT LOVE** (Kenneth Koch). G.
Schirmer, 1964. cmp1959. Pub. separately. "To Alice
Esty." Traditional keys; c'–g"; Tess-M-mH; regular
meters, varied tempos; 19pp; Diff-V/m, P/me-m.

For: tenor; soprano
Mood: humorous love poems
Voice: many skips; dotted rhythms; somewhat disjunct;
syncopation; duplets and triplets; melismas
Piano: linear-chordal combinations; one waltz-style accomp.;
some scale passages; some doubling of vocal line

Diff: some long phrases; some high tones sustained and crescendoed; interpretive skill needed
Uses: useful set; fairly humorous; see also *Hearing*, by Rorem, for other settings of these texts
Rec: D#s 321, 322

   a. *Love Song.* [51]. Cmaj–Amaj; c'–g"; 4/4, ♩ = ca.120; 5pp.
   b. *Down at the Docks.* Dmaj; d'–g"; 3/4, ♩. = 60; 6pp.
   c. *Let's Take a Walk.* Fmaj; d'–g"; 3/4, ♩. = 72; 4pp. [**Rec:** D#41]
   d. *A Prayer to Saint Catherine.* Emaj–E♭maj; e♭'–f"; 3/4, 4/4, ♩ = 84-96; 4pp. [**Rec:** D#s 51, 56]

2108. PORTRAIT OF F. B. (FRANCES BLOOD) (Gertrude Stein). G. Schirmer, 1971. cmp1929. Dmaj; d'–g"; Tess-M; 4/4, 3/4, 3/2, Tempo commodo–Più lento–Un poco più vivo– Lento–Non troppo vivo; 13pp; Diff-V/d, P/me.
For: soprano; mezzo-soprano
Mood: nonsense text
Voice: many phrases in various rhythms based on Dmaj scale; declamatory sections
Piano: primarily chordal afterbeat style
Diff: rapid enunciation; agility; text
Uses: teaches rapid enunciation; clever recital song

2109. PRAISES AND PRAYERS. Cycle. G. Schirmer, 1963. cmp1963. "Commissioned . . . for Betty Allen." Traditional keys with some modality; d'–g"; Tess-M-mH; regular but changing meters; moderate tempos; 17min; Diff-V/e-md, P/e-m.
For: mezzo-soprano; some sopranos with full middle voice
Mood: lyrical; archaic flavor musically and textually; various religious moods
Voice: many small skips; some conjunct; some leaps; repetitive; various rhythmic groupings; mostly syllabic; many d"s and e"s
Piano: chordal; organum-like parallel harmonies based on 4ths & 5ths or 10ths; archaic sound
Diff: rhythmic groupings; much repetition of same tones
Uses: separate songs good teaching pieces for various levels and techniques
Rec: D#s 321, 323, 326

   a. *From the Canticle of the Sun* (St. Francis of Assisi; trans. Matthew Arnold). Emaj; c♯'– e"(f"); Tess-M; 4/4, ♩ = 84; 8pp.
   b. *My Master Hath a Garden* (anon.). E♭maj; f'–e♭"; Tess-mH; 2/4, 3/4, 4/4, Tempo commodo; 4pp.
   c. *Sung by the Shepherds* (Richard Crashaw). Amin-maj; d'–g"; Tess-M; 3/2 with changes, ♩ = ca.72; 9pp.
   d. *Before Sleeping* (anon.). F-Emaj; d'–d"; Tess-M; 4/4, ♩ = 72; 3pp. [**Rec:** D#41]
   e. *Jerusalem, My Happy Home* (from *The Meditations of Saint Augustine*, Chap. XXV). Dmaj; d'–f♯"; Tess-cs; 4/4, 3/4, Molto ritmico; 7pp.

2110. PRECIOSILLA (Gertrude Stein). [51, 59]; 1st©1948. H & L keys: A♭maj & Fmaj; e♭'–a" & c'–f♯"; Tess-M; 4/4, 3/4, 2/4, Recitative; Aria (Misurato ♩ = 84); 7pp;

Diff-V/d, P/m.
For: soprano
Mood: nonsense poem in mock recit. and aria style
Voice: short phrases; declamatory style in recit.; aria also rather disjunct; many meter changes
Piano: chordal in recit.; somewhat independent in aria
Diff: nonsense text
Uses: recital song for sophisticated singer and audience
Rec: D#s 51, 322, 325

2111. SHAKESPEARE SONGS (William Shakespeare). (Peer)Southern, 1961. Pub. separately. cmp1956–1957. Traditional keys; d'–a"; Tess-mL, M; regular meters; varied tempos; 14pp; Diff-V/me-md, P/e-md.
For: tenor; high and medium voices
Mood: well-known texts; humorous; sad; philosophical; cynical
Voice: rather simple techniques; some humming; some use of repeated tones; short phrases; some syncopation; some half-speaking
Piano: generally chordal with some melodic material; afterbeat patterns; some cross-hands; little doubling of vocal line
Diff: rhythmic flexibility; use of speaking and humming; interpretive skills
Uses: for young singers as a set or separately; set probably best for tenor
Rec: D#s 321, 325

   a. *Was This Fair Face the Cause?* Fmaj; f'–f"; Tess-M; 4/4, Lazy and lackadaisical (♩ = 72–84); 2pp repeated.
   b. *Take, O, Take Those Lips Away.* [65]. Cmaj; e'–f"; Tess-M; 3/4, Very slowly (♩. = 48); 2pp repeated. [**Rec:** D#51]
   c. *Tell Me Where Is Fancy Bred.* E♭maj; f'–g"; Tess-M; 3/4, 4/4, ♩ = 60; 2pp. [**Rec:** D#11]
   d. *Pardon, Goddess of the Night.* B♭maj; d'–e♭"; Tess-mL; 2/2, ♩ = 87, Marcata la melodia–Lento molto espressivo; 2pp.
   e. *Sigh No More, Ladies.* Fmaj; d'–a"(f"); Tess-M; 2/4, 3/4, 3/8, ♩ = 72; 6pp. [**Rec:** D#s 11, 65]

2112. SUSIE ASADO (Gertrude Stein). [22]; 1st©1935. Cmin; e♭'–g"; Tess-M; 5/4, 3/4, 4/4, tempo not indicated; 3pp; Diff-V/md, P/d.
For: soprano; tenor
Mood: nonsense text
Voice: declamatory style, repeated tones; fragmented; triplets
Piano: simple chords, except for rapid Cmin scales in 7ths
Diff: frequent meter changes; rhythms; text
Uses: good rhythm study; program possibilities for the singer who enjoys word play
Rec: D#322

2113. THE TIGER (William Blake). G. Schirmer, 1967. [20, 51]. cmp1926. E- & D-centered; d'–g"; Tess-mH; 5/4 with changes, ♩ = ♩. = 48; 5pp; Diff-V/md, P/m; (this song is different from "Tiger! Tiger!" in *Five Songs from William Blake*).
For: dramatic soprano; tenor; some mezzo-sopranos
Mood: lyric-dramatic; wonder in God's creation
Voice: stepwise; small skips; a few chromatic tones; several

triplets; many phrases in first and last sections lie around e"; syllabic

Piano: chordal in first and last sections; short section of 2-voice counterpoint; somewhat chromatic; rhythm not difficult; only incidental doubling of vocal line

Diff: sustained *f* phrases lying at top of staff; some pitches hard to hear

Uses: not for immature voices; recital material

Rec: D#59

2114. TWO BY MARIANNE MOORE. G. Schirmer, 1966. cmp1963. Pub. in 2 different collections; separate entries below.

A. **ENGLISH USAGE,** Or "Strike till the iron is hot." [20]. Gmaj; d'–e"; Tess-M; 4/4, ♩ = 72; 4pp; Diff-V/d, P/d.

For: any medium voice

Mood: amusing word play

Voice: fragmented; disjunct; rather chromatic

Piano: chordal, broken by frequent rests; 6-voice texture

Diff: demands precise articulation of words; some difficult pitches and rhythms

Uses: clever song for the singer who can deal with this kind of text

Rec: D#s 4, 51, 56, 322, 326

B. **MY CROW PLUTO,** Or "Even when the bird is walking we know that it has wings." (Victor Hugo). [64]. Dmin; d'–f "; Tess-M; 4/4, ♩ = 96; 5pp; Diff-V/md, P/d.

For: any medium or high voice

Mood: nonsense text, using many Italian words and phrases

Voice: disjunct; fragmented

Piano: 2–4-voice texture; arpeggiations, scales, and broken chords in 3rds

Diff: text difficult to learn and memorize

Uses: for mature singer or student with a flair for the unusual

Rec: D#s 4, 56, 322, 326

2115. WHAT IS IT? (Thomas Campion). Presser, 1981. cmp1980. Gmaj-Emaj; e'–e"; Tess-M; 6/8, ♩. = 60–A little slower; 2+min; Diff-V/me, P/m.

For: any medium-range male voice

Mood: lyrical; in praise of women

Voice: stepwise; easy skips; flowing phrases; duplets and one quadruplet

Piano: chordal–block and broken; some scale passages; a "lute-song" flavor; 4–5-voice texture; some chromaticism; duplets and one quadruplet; incidental doubling of vocal line

Uses: recital possibilities

THORNE, FRANCIS
(b. Bayshore, NY, 1922)

2116. NOCTURNES for Voice and Piano on Poems of Robert Fitzgerald. General, 1972. cmp1963. Atonal; b♭–a♭"; Tess-L-M (tenor), M-H (baritone); regular and irregular meters with changes; moderate tempos; 15pp; Diff-V/md-d, P/e-m.

For: tenor (must have b♭); baritone with easy head voice (needs g' and a♭')

Mood: lyrical; hovering quality; night, love, and loneliness

Voice: largely conjunct; chromatic; speech rhythms; climactic high tones; syncopation

Piano: linear; thin texture; many accidentals

Diff: harmonic sameness; good ear for small intervals needed

Uses: (b.) might be interestingly programmed in group of songs on similar theme; lute, night, fantasy, love song at a distance ("Ravished lute–sing to her . . .")

    a. *Night Song.* c'–g"; Tess-M; 4/4 with changes, Andantino; 3pp.
    b. *Song after Campion.* b♭–f "; Tess-M; 3/4, 4/4, Andante; 3pp.
    c. *Horace 1, 25.* b♭–a♭"; Tess-M-mH-H; 4/4 with changes, Allegretto; 5pp.
    d. *Before Harvest.* b♭–f "; Tess-L, M; 4/4, 3/4, Andante calmo; 4pp.

TOLLEFSEN, AUGUSTA
(b. Boise, ID, 1885; d. Brooklyn, NY, 1955)

2117. WINTER (Percy Bysshe Shelley). Composers Press, 1940. D♭maj; e'–g♭"; Tess-M; 4/4, Lento sostenuto; 1+min; Diff-V/m, P/m.

For: soprano; tenor

Mood: lyrical; somber; subdued; impression

Voice: stepwise; easy skips; arching phrases; repetitive rhythms

Piano: constant repeated tone in bass; tied triplet pattern; block chords in r.h.; doubles vocal line

Diff: control of soft dynamics; long phrases

Uses: useful short lyric song for recital

TRAVIS, ROY
(b. New York, NY, 1922)

2118. SONGS AND EPILOGUES. For Bass Voice and Piano (Sappho; trans. Wm. Ellery Leonard, George Lord Byron, Dante Gabriel Rossetti, and Edward Arlington Robinson). Oxford Univ. Press, 1971. Begins and ends Emaj; songs tonal (always ending on a major chord), epilogues atonal; G♯–d♯'; Tess-M-mH; regular, changing meters; varied tempos; 12min; Diff-V/d, P/d.

For: bass

Mood: lyrical

Voice: skips; short snatches, like a mosaic; words divided for singing makes reading difficult; consonants indicated specifically with reference to where they should fall; speech rhythms

Piano: accomp. to songs very much like texture and movement of J. S. Bach 2- and 3-part inventions; piano epilogues and prologues atonal–different tempos from, but same musical material as the songs of the same title; central song, "One Girl," has only an introduction, no separate piano piece; specific articulations and fingerings marked; a somewhat cluttered-looking score

Diff: reading the score, which looks harder than it is

Uses: very interesting songs; should be effective; singer will have to decide whether composer's notation of consonants is meant to indicate merely where to place them or to do something special with them; graduate level material

Rec: D#327

a. *Round about Me.* B–b; 2/4, 3/4, Un poco con moto; 3pp.
b. *Round about Me: Epilogue* (Piano). 2/4, 3/4, 4/4, Adagio; 1p.
c. *Hesperus the Bringer.* G#–b; 2/4, 3/4, Andantino; 2pp.
d. *Hesperus the Bringer: Epilogue* (Piano). 4/8, Allegro leggiero; 1p.
e. *One Girl.* G#–d#'; 4/4, Andantino; 3pp.
f. *The Dust of Timas: Prologue* (Piano). 3/8, 2/8, 2/4, Vivace; 2pp.
g. *The Dust of Timas.* G#–c#'; 4/8, 3/8, Un poco con moto; 2pp.
h. *Full Moon: Prologue* (Piano). 3/8, Allegretto; 2pp.
i. *Full Moon.* A–b; 4/4, 2/4, 3/4, Grave; 2pp.

TUCKER, HENRY L.
(b. U. S. A.?, 1826; d. Brooklyn, NY, 1882)

2119. WEEPING, SAD AND LONELY (or When This Cruel War is Over). [50]; 1st©1863. B♭maj; d'–e♭"; Tess-M; 4/4, Moderato e cantabile; 4 strophes and refrain; Diff-V/e, P/e.

For: soprano; mezzo-soprano
Mood: famous Civil War pacifist song sung by both sides (the Army of the Potomac was forbidden to sing it because it lowered morale); lyrical love song; "distant beloved"
Voice: stepwise; skips along chord lines; some dotted rhythms; 2-note slurs
Piano: broken and some block chords; prelude
Uses: very singable period piece for use in a Civil War group

TURNER, CHARLES
(b. Baltimore, MD, 1921; d. 1999)

2120. HUNTING SONG (Marcia Bradley). G. Schirmer, 1941. Amin; e'–b♭"(a"); Tess-H; 6/8, Allegro, with much excitement; 1+min; Diff-V/md, P/d.

For: soprano; lyric tenor
Mood: animated; excited; "the chase"
Voice: many skips, esp. 4ths & 5ths; many sustained medium and high tones
Piano: hunting-call motives; rapid 8ths; tertian, quartal, and quintal structures; cross-hand passages; big ending; incidental doubling of vocal line
Diff: sustained high tones (b♭", a", a♭", g"); two portamentos; good register and dynamic control needed
Uses: good group ender

TYSON, MILDRED LUND
(b. Moline, IL, 1900; d. 1989)

2121. LIKE BARLEY BENDING (Sara Teasdale). G.

Schirmer, 1932. H & L keys: Cmin-E♭maj & Gmin-B♭maj; f'–a♭"(b♭") & c'–e♭"(f"); Tess-mH; 12/8, Tempo moderato; 3pp; Diff-V/me, P/md.

For: any high or medium voice
Mood: joyful; philosophical; nature imagery
Voice: broad, lyrical phrases; dramatic climax
Piano: arpeggiated l.h. under block chords; melodic motives in solo sections
Diff: needs ringing b♭" (f") for opt. final note

2122. SEA MOODS (Kenneth G. Benham). [37 (L), 59]; 1st©1937. "To Madame Kirsten Flagstad." H & L keys: Cmin-E♭maj & Gmin-B♭maj; f'–a♭"(b♭") & c'–e♭"(f"); Tess-M; 4/4, 3/4, 6/8, Andante molto sostenuto–Molto agitato–Allegretto–Moderato; 6pp; Diff-V/m, P/m.

For: dramatic voices
Mood: dramatic; philosophical; song of sorrow and the sea
Voice: chiefly sustained and legato; high climax at end
Piano: chordal; some arpeggiation; independent
Diff: opt. b♭" (f") sustained *ff* for most effective ending
Uses: possible recital song for dramatic voice; somewhat old-fashioned in style

ULEHLA, LUDMILA
(b. New York, NY, 1923)

2123. THREE SONNETS FROM SHAKESPEARE. General, 1966. X; b–b♭"; Tess-M; irregular and irregular changing meters; contrasting tempos; 23pp; Diff-V/d, P/dd.

For: soprano; tenor
Mood: lyrical; philosophical; love songs
Voice: disjunct; chromatic; fragmented; some lyricism; some recit.
Piano: chromatic; contrapuntal; features 16th-note figures; lengthy preludes and interludes
Diff: pitch; rhythms; easy, powerful high tones; clear low tones
Uses: excellent recital material for an advanced musician

a. *How like a Winter Hath My Absence Been.* c'–b♭"(a"); 5/4, 6/4, 4/4, 3/4, Adagio–Poco più mosso–Meno mosso; 7pp.
b. *O, Never Say That I Was False of Heart.* b–a"; 4/4, 3/4, 6/4, 5/4, 2/4, Allegro–Poco meno mosso; 8pp.
c. *Shall I Compare Thee to a Summer's Day?* c'–b♭"(a♭"); 5/4, 3/4, 4/4, Adagio–Poco più mosso; 8pp.

2124. TIME IS A CUNNING THIEF (James T. Shotwell). General, 1965. A-centered; a'(e♭')–g"(a"); Tess-M; 4/4, 6/4, 2/4; Allegro (♩ = 138); 5pp; Diff-V/md, P/d.

For: mezzo-soprano; soprano
Mood: humorously philosophical
Voice: stepwise; small skips and leaps, incl. 7ths & 8ves; several ascending scalar phrases; somewhat chromatic; staccato; short phrases, some fragmented by rests; syllabic
Piano: primarily linear; some repeated chords; basically 2-voice texture; countermelody, sometimes in 8ves;

chromatic; independent of vocal line
Diff: some pitches hard to hear
Uses: good recital material; group or recital ender

URROWS, DAVID
(b. Honolulu, HI, 1957)

2125. FIVE SONGS FROM A NEW ENGLAND ALMANACK, Op. 54. Boosey and Hawkes, 1989. cmp1985. NATS Vocal Composition Award, 1987. Tonal; (a♭)b–f"; Tess-M; regular meters with some changes; varied tempos; 21pp; Diff-V/md-d, P/m-d.
For: baritone specified
Mood: nature; some religious overtones; (e.), a lumberjack song
Voice: speech-like rhythms resulting in syncopation, hemiola; speech-like melodic inflections, somewhat angular; some melismas; many accidentals
Piano: block chords, some combined with countermelody; broken chords; syncopation; piano triplets vs. voice duplets; chromatic scales in (e.); (d.) features 6ths & 3rds and siciliana rhythms; score has no key sigs.; many accidentals; some doubling of vocal line; preludes in (c., d., & e.); postludes in (b., c., & d.)
Diff: chromaticism; some awkward intervals; enharmonic modulations; singer needs to be secure musician
Uses: a fine recital group for a mature singer/musician; also exists in an edition for baritone and orchestra; individual songs easily excerpted and interesting on their own

   a. *On the Merrimack, 1865* (John Greenleaf Whittier). E-centered; c♯'–e"; Tess-M; 4/4, 3/4, 5/4, 2/4, Lento; 3pp.
   b. *Meditation* (Ann Bradstreet). D-centered; b–e"; Tess-M; 4/2, 3/2, Molto moderato; 4pp.
   c. *October* (Robert Underwood Johnson). G-centered; c♯'–e"; Tess-M; 2/2, 3/2, Allegretto con piacevolezza; 4pp.
   d. *Aftermath* (Henry Wadsworth Longfellow). B-centered; d'–e♭"; Tess-M; 6/8, 9/8, Lento alla Siciliano; 3pp.
   e. *The Lumberman's Alphabet* (Traditional). A-centered; (a♭)b–f"; Tess-M; 2/4, 3/4, Vivo; 7pp.

VAL-SCHMIDT, CAROLYN
(b. Elmhurst, IL, 1944)

2126. OUTWITTED (Edwin Markham). For High Voice and Piano. Voice of the Rockies, 1995. Shifting tonality– F♯maj; d'–a"; Tess-wide; 4/4, 5/4, 2/4, Andante (♩ = 76 & 92); 3pp; Diff-V/md, P/m.
For: soprano (woman's text)
Mood: powerful; turns the tables on a lover
Voice: angular; many dotted rhythms; dramatic beginning; lyrical ending; several melismas; many accidentals
Piano: many dotted rhythms; some syncopation; most motion in 8th and quarter notes; pianist plays 4-meas. passage with maracas
Diff: intervals; finding pitches in first half; long high notes

Uses: recital piece for sizeable voice

VEHAR, PERSIS PARSHALL
(b. New Salem, NY, 1937)

2127. WOMEN, WOMEN. Songs for Soprano (or Mezzo-Soprano) and Piano. Leyerle Publications, 1998. X; c♯'–g♯"(c♯'"); Tess-M; regular and irregular changing meters; moderate tempos; 6min; Diff-V/m-md, P/e-m.
For: soprano; mezzo-soprano
Mood: various aspects of female characters: humorous; desolate; the anticipated privileges of old age stated with mystery and control
Voice: spoken lines; sung lines in both angular phrases and on repeated tones; *Sprechstimme*; wide intervals; final phrase a scale up to c♯'" and an abrupt two-8ve drop; some melismas; theatrical; irregular rhythms
Piano: thin texture; dissonant; repeated patterns
Diff: wide speaking range; rhythms; ensemble
Uses: excellent for a theatrically strong singer who has a wide speaking and singing range and a good ear; interesting to program with other songs with female personae
Rec: D#328

   a. *A Fixture* (May Swenson). X; e♭'–g♭"; Tess-M; 4/4, 5/4, Moderately ♩ = 112–116; 4pp.
   b. *Resisting Each Other* (Anne Waldman). X; d'–f"; Tess-M; 4/4, Slowly; 1p.
   c. *Survival* (Barbara Greenberg). X; c♯'–g♯"(c♯'"); Tess-cs; 5/8, 3/8, 4/8, 6/8, 7/8, 2/8, Moderately ♩ = 112; 7+pp.

VERCOE, ELIZABETH
(b. Washington, DC, 1941)

2128. IRREVERIES FROM SAPPHO. For Soprano with Piano Accompaniment. Arsis, 1983. cmp1981. X; c'–b♭"; Tess-mL-mH; regular meters, varied tempos; 7min; Diff-V/dd, P/dd.
For: soprano
Mood: irreverent or ironic feminine sentiments with Classical allusions
Voice: rather disjunct; much leaping from top of staff to bottom; chromatic; duplets and triplets; syncopation; glissandos and portamentos; *Sprechstimme*; other special effects; syllabic with melisma in (b.) and cadenza-like passage in (c.)
Piano: chordal and linear; (a.) & (b.), essentially 4-voice; (c.), essentially 2–3-voice texture; chromatic; chromatic "boogie-woogie" bass in (c.); syncopation and duplets; grace notes; glissandos; large register changes; considerable doubling of vocal line in (a.) & (c.)
Diff: excellent sense of pitch and rhythm, and secure musicianship needed; excellent vocal actor required; pianist needs agile technique
Uses: good recital material for good musicians and mature, uninhibited singers
Rec: D#329

   a. *Andromeda Rag.* F-centered; d♯'–b♭"; Tess-mH;

2/4, 3/4, Spirited, with a touch of venom (♩ = 56); 4pp.

b. *Older Woman Blues.* X; f '–f "; Tess-M; 12/8, 9/8, Slowly but with movement (♩ = 60); 1+pp.

c. *Boogie for Leda.* X; c'–f♯"; Tess-mH, mL; 4/4 with changes, Flippant (♩ = 144); 5pp.

VON HAGEN, P. A. (See Special Section)

WAGENAAR, BERNARD
(b. Arnhem, Netherlands, 1894; d. York, ME, 1971)

2129. **FROM A VERY LITTLE SPHINX** (Edna St. Vincent Millay). Cycle. G. Schirmer, 1926. Traditional keys; c'–f "; Tess-M; regular meters; varied tempos; 16pp; Diff-V/m, P/m.

For: soprano; mezzo-soprano
Mood: lyrical; "cute" little-girl songs
Voice: skips and leaps; speech rhythms; interrupted phrases; some chromaticism
Piano: chordal-linear combination; broken-chord figures; much staccato articulation; reflects mood well
Diff: pitch perception; rhythms–many follow speech inflections and hesitations of a child
Uses: cute songs; useful for a young student

a. *Come Along Then, Little Girl!* d'–e"; 2/4, ♩ = 56; 2pp.

b. *Oh, Burdock.* d'–e"; 2/4, ♩ = 84; 2pp.

c. *Ev'rybody but Just Me.* c♯'–e"; 3/4, ♩ = 112; 2pp.

d. *I Know a Hundred Ways to Die.* c'–f "; 4/4, ♩ = 112; 2pp.

e. *Look, Edwin!* d'–e"; 2/4, ♩ = 126; 2pp.

f. *All the Grownup People Say.* c'–d"; 3/4, ♩ = 104; 2pp.

g. *Wonder Where This Horseshoe Went.* d'–f "; 2/4, ♩ = 84; 4pp.

2130. **MAY-NIGHT** (Edward B. Koster; English version by Robert A. Simon). G. Schirmer, 1926. D♭maj; c'–g"(e♭"); Tess-mL; 3/4, Slow, with much expression; 3pp; Diff-V/m, P/m.

For: mezzo-soprano; soprano; tenor with good low tones
Mood: descriptive; atmospheric; tranquil
Voice: duplets and triplets; some 2-note slurs; some wide-ranged phrases; English text good for singing
Piano: chordal texture–block and broken; impressionistic effect; many accidentals; wide-spread sonority
Uses: quiet ending; good song

WAGNER, JOSEPH
(b. Springfield, MA, 1900; d. Los Angeles, CA, 1974)

2131. **BEWILDERED BALLADE** (Arthur Kramer). (Peer)Southern, 1951. Emin-maj; d'–e"; Tess-mL; 4/4, 6/8, Slowly, rather pompous–Gaily, folk ballad style (♩. = 104); 6pp; Diff-V/me, P/m.

For: baritone; mezzo-soprano
Mood: humorous; Supreme Court justices "do not always understand the opinions of this court"
Voice: stepwise; small skips; largely diatonic; includes several spoken phrases
Piano: chordal–block, broken, and afterbeat; some chromaticism; several quintuplets; supports but does not double vocal line
Diff: spoken phrases; needs good vocal actor
Uses: could be amusing in group with a political theme

WALKER, GEORGE
(b. Washington, DC, 1922)

2132. **THE BEREAVED MAID** (anon.). [4, 162]; 1st©1971. X-Gmin; d♭'–f "; Tess-M; 3/8, 5/8, 4/8, ♪ = 88, 100, & 104; 4pp; Diff-V/m, P/m.

For: soprano; mezzo-soprano
Mood: lyrical; mystical
Voice: ambivalent tonal center; irregular rhythms and phrasing; unusual words
Piano: 2-note chords both hands; 4ths, 5ths, and other intervals; rather archaic in sound; delicate
Diff: some pitches; changing rhythmic groupings; text
Uses: interesting and haunting song; useful for students with imagination and understanding of symbolism; see also setting by Daniel Pinkham ("The Faucon")
Rec: D#330

2133. **EMILY DICKINSON SONGS.** (Peer)Southern, 1986. X; d'–c'''; Tess-H; changing meters and unmetered; varied tempos; 8pp; Diff-V/md-d, P/md-d.

For: soprano
Mood: love songs; passionate and dramatic with lyrical, quiet ending
Voice: fairly disjunct (d. less so); many accidentals; (b.), (unmetered) difficult rhythms, as well as a semi-sung passage marked "hoarsely"; others have uncomplicated rhythms; predominantly syllabic
Piano: block- and broken-chord patterning; structures built in various intervals, often non-tertian; some linear writing; much chromaticism; some rapid 32nds & 64ths; large reaches; some doubling and imitation of vocal line
Diff: ensemble, esp. in (b.); sustained high tones: 3-beat a♯", 4-beat c''', and 4-beat a", with decresc.
Uses: as a short group
Rec: D#330

a. *Wild Nights.* X; f'–c'''; 4/4, 3/4, Agitated; 3pp.

b. *What If I Say I Shall Not Wait.* D-centered; d'–b"; unmetered, Dramatically; 3pp.

c. *I Have No Life but This.* X; e'–a"; 3/4 with changes, Very slowly; 1p.

d. *Bequest.* X; e'–a"; 3/4, Very slowly; 1p.

2134. **HEY NONNY NO** (Anon.). [162]; 1st©1971. Modal flavor; d'–d"; Tess-M; 3/4, 4/4, ♩ = 126; 3pp; Diff-V/m, P/m.

For: any voice
Mood: happy; enjoying life
Voice: stepwise; some skips of tritone & M7th; syncopated rhythms; hemiola; vocal part often seems to be in 6/8
Piano: repeated double 8th-notes (2nds, 3rds, 4ths, 5ths)

through most of song; syncopation; hemiola; pedal tones

Diff: rhythms; ensemble

Uses: quick, constant-motion song for group

Rec: D#330

2135. I NEVER SAW A MOOR (Emily Dickinson). [163]. X; e'–a"; Tess-mH; 4/4, 3/4, 5/8, 2/4, 7/8, ♩ = 42; 3pp; Diff-V/d, P/d.

For: soprano; tenor

Mood: dramatic; emphatic affirmation of faith

Voice: dotted rhythms; syncopation; dynamics vary *mp–ff*; lines somewhat angular; many accents

Piano: many grace notes; unconventional block and broken chords; features 7ths, 9ths, 4ths in 3-meas. solo passage in 32nd & 64th notes; short dramatic postlude; some doubling of vocal line

Diff: mixed meters; ensemble; angularity of vocal line; wide dynamic range

Uses: pairs well with "In Time of Silver Rain"; in group of other Dickinson poems; cf. setting by Isadore Freed ("Chartless")

2136. IN TIME OF SILVER RAIN (Langston Hughes). [163]. X; d'–b"; Tess-M; 6/8, 4/8, 5/8, 2/8, ♪ = 84; 5pp; Diff-V/d, P/dd.

For: soprano; tenor

Mood: joyous; dramatic

Voice: many small skips; some dotted rhythms; mostly syllabic

Piano: virtuosic writing descriptive of "rain"; 16th-note triplets; syncopation; chromaticism; trills; 9-meas. virtuosic solo passage; large skips; various subdivisions of the beat; wide reaches

Diff: mostly for the pianist, but this also makes the ensemble difficult; very different from the earlier sparely scored songs of this composer

Uses: could be grouped with the other two unrelated songs in this collection; recital song for two good performers

2137. I WENT TO HEAVEN (Emily Dickinson). [4, 162]; 1st©1971. Gmaj; f'–e"; Tess-M; 2/2, Playfully ♩ = 108; 2pp; Diff-V/m, P/m.

For: soprano; mezzo-soprano

Mood: lyrical; whimsical; gentle

Voice: diatonic melody; some interrupted phrases; some melismatic phrasing on "society"

Piano: linear; wide-spread on keyboard; punctuating chords

Diff: rhythms

Uses: interesting delicate miniature; useful for teaching young singer independence from the accomp.

Rec: D#330

2138. LAMENT (Countee Cullen). [6, 162]; 1st©1975. Amin; a–f"; Tess-mL; 5/4, 4/4, ♩ = 96; 5pp; Diff-V/md, P/d.

For: contralto; baritone; bass

Mood: philosophical song about death

Voice: relentless, march-like meter in quarters in irregular rhythm; numerous low-lying phrases; strong accents; some chromaticism

Piano: chordal texture–sustained, then broken-up and more

contrapuntal; strong accents; staccato; triplets

Diff: strong low tones needed; also a powerful climactic f" sustained decresc.

Uses: very effective recital song

Rec: D#12

2139. LEAVING (George Walker). [162]; 1st©1971. X; c'–e"; Tess-M; 4/4, Not too fast; 3pp; Diff-V/m, P/m.

For: baritone; mezzo-soprano; soprano with good low notes

Mood: jazzy farewell song; perhaps mock-serious

Voice: dotted rhythms; a a b a form; syllabic; whole-tone melisma; many small skips; many accidentals

Piano: jazzy rhythms and harmonies; many accidentals; does not double vocal line but provides some pitch clues; beat subdivided into 2s & 3s; 4-meas. bitonal prelude

Diff: not much support from piano; unusual turns in melody; singer needs a good ear

Uses: in group of Walker songs or American group; teaches independence from the piano; attractive to students who enjoy jazz idiom

2140. MOTHER GOOSE (CIRCA 2054) (Irene Sekula). [163]. cmp1992. X; e'–g"; Tess-M; 6/4, 5/4, 3/4, 4/4, 5/8, etc., ♪ = 76; 4pp; Diff-V/dd, P/dd.

For: high or medium voices

Mood: comic; mid-21st-century Humpty Dumpty rhyme

Voice: complex rhythms; fragmented words; two glissandos, one combined with trill; chromaticism

Piano: various subdivisions of beat–many 16ths & 32nds; syncopation and dotted rhythms; somewhat jazzy; chromaticism; many 8ves in l.h.; accents; staccato articulations; 2-meas. prelude; several short virtuosic interludes; does not double vocal line

Diff: rhythms; intervals; ensemble; "shout" at two points

Uses: humorous song; requires two secure performers

2141. NOCTURNE (Donald S. Hayes) [65]. cmp1983. X; c♯'–g♯"; Tess-mH; 3/4 with changes, Quietly (♩ = 48); 3pp; Diff-V/d, P/d.

For: soprano; tenor

Mood: lyrical night scene

Voice: conjunct and disjunct motion; highly chromatic

Piano: contrapuntal; many accidentals

Diff: pitches and rhythms; several high-lying phrases

Uses: excellent recital song

2142. A RED, RED ROSE (Robert Burns). [6]. X; a♯–g"; Tess-mL; 3/4 with many changes, ♩ = 48; 6pp; Diff-V/dd, P/dd.

For: mezzo-soprano

Mood: lyrical love song

Voice: highly chromatic; disjunct; large and difficult leaps; difficult melismas; difficult rhythms

Piano: chromatic; complex rhythms; disjunct 16th- & 32nd-note passages

Diff: perfect pitch desirable; must be comfortable with style

Uses: recital material; cf. other settings of this poem

Rec: D#s 12, 330

2143. RESPONSE (Paul Laurence Dunbar). [162]; 1st©1971. Gmaj; e♭'–e"; Tess-M; 3/4 with changes, ♩ = 52; 2pp; Diff-V/m, P/m.

For: baritone; tenor
Mood: love song; somewhat tense
Voice: some difficult intervals; speech-like rhythms; irregular phrase lengths
Piano: chordal; many accidentals; irregular rhythms; interlude between stanzas; does not double vocal line
Diff: singer needs musical security
Uses: recital material; could pair with "Sweet, Let Me Go," or "With Rue My Heart Is Laden" by Walker
Rec: D#330

2144. **SO WE'LL GO NO MORE A-ROVING** (Lord Byron). [162]. Modal flavor; d'–g"; Tess-M (outer sections low, middle section high); 2/2, Moderately; 3pp; Diff-V/m, P/m.
For: soprano; tenor (comfortable with d ')
Mood: respite from love; dramatic center section framed by serene opening and closing
Voice: easy rhythms; stepwise motion; small skips; syllabic; intense center section
Piano: syncopation; afterbeat pattern; some big chords in center section; many accidentals; does not double vocal line; avoidance of downbeats in many meas.
Diff: lack of doubling and support in piano; syncopation and avoidance of downbeats makes rhythm and entrances challenging; sizeable sound needed in center section to balance piano chords
Uses: nice recital song
Rec: D#330

2145. **SWEET, LET ME GO** (anon.). [4, 162]; 1st©1971. Bmin-X; d'–g♯"; Tess-mH; 3/4, ♩ = 84; 2pp; Diff-V/m, P/m.
For: tenor; soprano
Mood: tense
Voice: some difficult melodic intervals; irregular rhythms; high soft ending
Piano: thin chordal texture; many accidentals
Diff: high soft ending sustained
Uses: possibly pair with "Response" by Walker
Rec: D#330

2146. **WITH RUE MY HEART IS LADEN** (A. E. Housman). [162]; 1st©1972. F♯-centered; c♯'–f♯"; Tess-M; 4/4, Rather slowly; 2pp; Diff-V/m, P/m.
For: tenor; high baritone; soprano; mezzo-soprano
Mood: dirge-like; quiet but tense
Voice: many small skips, some difficult; rhythmic and metric irregularity
Piano: thin texture; irregular rhythms; syncopation; linear; does not double vocal line
Diff: rhythms
Uses: possibly pair with "Response" by same composer
Rec: D#330

WALKER, GWYNETH
(b. New York, NY, 1947)

2147. **MY LOVE WALKS IN VELVET** (Gwyneth Walker). E. C. Schirmer, 1989. Medium-High and Medium-Low editions. Dorian mode; c'–a"(f♯") & b♭–g"(e"); Tess-M;

4/4, 2/4, ♩ = 72, 92; 6pp; Diff-V/m, P/m.
For: medium and high male voices
Mood: fanciful tribute; lyrical
Voice: mostly stepwise; small skips; a few 8ves; some syncopation; legato connections
Piano: patterned; some syncopation and changing accents; mostly 8th-note motion; does not double vocal line but is supportive; 4-meas. prelude
Diff: range, although highest phrase has opt. lower pitches; some entrances, because of irregular phrase lengths
Uses: effective song for a mature voice with control of dynamics, range, and good legato style

2148. **THOUGH LOVE BE A DAY** (e. e. cummings). Five songs for High Voice on Poems by e. e. cummings [4] and Gwyneth Walker [1]. E. C. Schirmer, 1993. cmp1979. Shifting tonalities; b–b"; Tess-M; mostly regular meters with changes; tempos ♩ = 72–88; 17min; Diff-V/m, P/m.
For: soprano; some mezzo-sopranos
Mood: images of love in both intimate and humorous contexts
Voice: speech rhythms; syllabic and melismatic passages; portamentos; much word repetition; fragmented phrases
Piano: 16th- & 8th-note motion; arpeggiation; linear/chordal combination in first song; various divisions of beat; polyrhythms; staccato; rapid repeated notes and chords; some quartal arpeggiations; double 3rds in r.h.; groups of 6–10 16ths used ornamentally; some solo material in each song; piano gives cues for singer's pitches
Diff: ensemble takes two good musicians; requires good dynamic control; (c.) ends with long, soft a"
Uses: very nice group; interesting variety in songs; poetry well set; atmosphere of each very fitting

    a. *thy fingers make early flowers.* Tonal; d'–a"; Tess-wide; 4/4, 3/8, 3/4, 5/4, 6/4, Slowly, quasi recitative–♩ = 72; 3+min.
    b. *lily has a rose.* Tonal; c'–b"; Tess-M; 6/8, 2/4, 5/8, 3/4, ♪ = 160; 2min.
    c. *after all white horses are in bed.* Tonal; d♭'–a"; Tess-M; unmetered, 4/4, 6/4, slowly–♩ = 88; 3+min.
    d. *maggie and milly and molly and may.* Chromatic; (b) e'–a♭"; Tess-M; 12/8, ♩. = 120; 1+min.
    e. *Still* (Gwyneth Walker). Chromatic; c'–g"; Tess-M; unmetered, 2/4, 5/8, ♩ = 72; 5+min.

WALTON, KENNETH
(b. Tulse Hill, England, 1904; deceased)

2149. **SONG OF SLEEP** (Monroe Heath). Leeds, 1937. E♭maj; c'–e"; Tess-M; 4/4, Andante con moto, molto espressivo; 3pp; Diff-V/me, P/m.
For: any voice except extremely low
Mood: lyrical; love song; subdued; serene
Voice: stepwise motion predominates; some chord-member skips; repetitive rhythms
Piano: chordal texture; frequent 3rds in r.h.; 8th-note motion; quiet; doubles vocal line
Uses: useful for an inexperienced singer; quiet ending

2150. **YOU AND I** (Rabindranath Tagore). Sprague-

Coleman, 1937. Dmin; d'–a"; Tess-M; 4/4, Moderato
con moto; 4pp; Diff-V/m, P/md.
For: tenor
Mood: dramatic love song; nature imagery
Voice: stepwise; easy skips; triplets; rather dramatic; phrases
often begin with passage of repeated notes; syllabic;
builds to a big, old-fashioned climax
Piano: chordal-linear combination; broken-chord patterns;
triplets and 2 vs. 3; melody often in 8ves; some
chromaticism; frequently doubles vocal line
Diff: maintaining flow of phrase, esp. in repeated-note
passages
Uses: good for teaching phrasing, building to dramatic climax

WARD, ROBERT
(b. Cleveland, OH, 1917)

**2151. AS I WATCHED THE PLOUGHMAN
PLOUGHING** (Walt Whitman). Peer International,
1951. cmp1940. C-centered; c'–a"; Tess-mH; 4/4, 3/4,
Adagio; 1+min; Diff-V/m, P/m.
For: soprano; tenor
Mood: relationship of life to death
Voice: stepwise; small skips; interrupted phrases; syncopation
Piano: chordal texture; chromaticism; syncopation; large
reaches; 2 vs. 3; some countermelody; does not double
vocal line
Uses: useful in an American group
Rec: D#332

2152. RAIN HAS FALLEN ALL THE DAY (James Joyce).
Peer International, 1951. cmp1940. Cmaj; c'–a";
Tess-mH; 4/4, Moderato; 1+min; Diff-V/m, P/m.
For: tenor; soprano
Mood: love song
Voice: mostly stepwise; some skips; irregular rhythms; several
long high tones
Piano: linear-chordal combination; various registers; many
accidentals; countermelody; does not double vocal line
Diff: rather dramatic song
Uses: effective song; could end a group, probably better in
interior; see also setting by Barber
Rec: D#332

2153. SACRED SONGS FOR PANTHEISTS. For Soprano
with Orchestra or Piano. Cycle. Highgate, 1966.
cmp1951. Traditional keys; c#'–c'''; Tess-H; regular
meters; varied tempos; 15min; Diff-V/md-d, P/d.
For: high lyric soprano
Mood: lyrical; moods of praise and prayer
Voice: many skips; partly conjunct motion; one long ascending
coloratura passage; accidentals; straightforward
rhythms; many high notes, esp. a♭" and a"
Piano: orchestral score reduction (edited for piano) playable
and effective but somewhat difficult; wide reaches;
mostly chordal, some linear; accidentals; sostenuto
pedal used; ear for instrumental colors advantageous
Diff: high tessitura for singer; orchestral reduction for pianist
Uses: good cycle for vibrant, warm lyric soprano with easy
high range; effective performance with piano; best for
advanced singers

Rec: D#331

a. *Pied Beauty* (Gerard Manley Hopkins). Gmaj;
d'–a"; Tess-M-mH; 3/4, Maestoso; 4min.
b. *Little Things* (James Stephens). Bmin; c#'–a";
Tess-M; 6/8, Lento; 2+min.
c. *Intoxication* (Emily Dickinson). Cmaj; d'–b♭";
Tess-M-mH; 4/4, Vivo; 1+min.
d. *Heaven-Haven* (Gerard Manley Hopkins). E♭maj;
e♭'–a♭"; Tess-M; 3/4, Andante tranquillo; 2+min.
e. *God's Grandeur* (Gerard Manley Hopkins). Gmaj;
d'–c'''; Tess-L, mH; 4/4, Moderato; 4min.

2154. SORROW OF MYDATH (John Masefield). Peer
International, 1952. [65]. Emin; e'–a"; Tess-M; 6/4,
Adagio (♩ = 42); 5pp; Diff-V/md, P/d.
For: dramatic soprano; tenor
Mood: dramatic; somber; poet wishes for death
Voice: slow and sustained; primarily stepwise; some large,
difficult leaps
Piano: chordal; much 2 vs. 3; largely independent of voice
Diff: dramatic intensity; legato line; sustained high tones
Uses: excellent recital song for an accomplished singer
Rec: D#s 59, 332

2155. VANISHED (Emily Dickinson). Peer International,
1951. E♭maj; d'–g"; Tess-M; 3/4, 4/4, Andante; 2pp;
Diff-V/me, P/me-m.
For: soprano best; perhaps tenor
Mood: lyrical; quiet; poem about death
Voice: many small skips and stepwise motion; long tones
Piano: chordal texture; much parallel motion in 7ths & 4ths;
some doubling of vocal line
Diff: good dynamic control; rhythms; changing meters
Uses: effective subdued song; quiet ending
Rec: D#332

WARD-STEINMAN, DAVID
(b. Alexandria, LA, 1936)

[See Appendix for songs with French texts]

2156. . . . AND WAKEN GREEN. Seven Poems by Douglas
Worth. A Cycle of Songs for Medium Voice and Piano.
Leyerle Publications, 1984. cmp1983. Tonal; g–g♭";
Tess-M; pulse remains constant; meter sigs. generally
not notated; barlines indicate downbeats or agogic
accents; 12min; Diff-V/md, P/d.
For: medium voice(s)
Mood: happiness shared, then the break-up of a marriage
Voice: stepwise motion; skips along chord-member lines; (f.),
somewhat disjunct; various rhythms; both quarter- &
8th-note triplets; successions of dotted 8ths; many
polyrhythms created between voice and piano; many
accidentals; mostly syllabic; a number of 2–5-note slurs
Piano: often linear (2–3-voice texture); many pedal-tones;
some ostinato; some block- and broken-chord
patterning, often with cross-accents; articulations and
dynamics carefully marked; many accidentals; some
blurred pedal effects; special notation for accel. and rit.;
rare doubling of vocal line; fits hands quite well

Uses: appealing cycle; composer specifies choice of three performance modes: 1. baritone voice throughout, 2. double cycle for baritone and mezzo-soprano (baritone, a., c., e., & g.; mezzo-soprano, b. & f.); (d.) divided between the two; 3. mezzo-soprano or contralto alone (c. & d. omitted, (e.) two specified word changes, and a., b., f., & g. sung as they are)

    a. *When You Come into a Room.* Bmin-Dmaj; d'-e"; unmetered, Tentatively, smoothly flowing (♩ = ca.96); 4pp.

    b. *Marriage.* X; d'-g♭"; unmetered, Musingly (♪= 92) (with changes); 3pp.

    c. *Muse.* A♭maj-Fmin; d'-f"; unmetered, Lively, brightly (♩=152); 3pp.

    d. *Poem on My Thirty-third Birthday.* F-centered; c'-e"; unmetered, Gently rocking (♩ = ca.80); 6pp.

    e. *Affair.* X; b♭-d"; unmetered, Stridently (♩ = ca.88) (with changes); 4pp.

    f. *Divorce.* X; g-f♭"; unmetered, Plangently (with many changes and fluctuations); 5pp.

    g. *Maple.* Fmaj, X; c♯'-e"; unmetered, Smoothly, seamlessly (♩ = ca.100); 3pp.

2157. CHILDREN'S CORNER REVISITED. For Medium Voice & Piano. Leyerle Publications, 1985. cmp1984 (in present form). Various tonal centers; a(b)–a"(g"); Tess-M; regular meters with changes; varied tempos; 7min; Diff-V/m, P/md.

For: mezzo-soprano
Mood: children's songs for grown-ups
Voice: stepwise; skips up to 8ve; somewhat chromatic; triplets; short phrases with much up-and-down motion; syllabic; occasional 2-note slurs
Piano: chordal and linear; block, broken, and rolled chords; countermelodic motives; chromatic; triplets and quintuplets; considerable doubling of vocal line
Diff: much loud singing, esp. in passaggio for medium voices; good vocal actor needed
Uses: good teaching songs and recital material

    a. *I Have a Popliteal* (Susan Lucas). F-centered; c'-c"; Tess-mL; 3/4, Somewhat stiff and mechanical (♩ = ca.120); 35sec.

    b. *Night Flight* (Charles Waller Tucker). X; c'-e"; Tess-M; 6/8, 9/8, 2/4, 2/8, Exuberantly (♩ = ca.104); 1+min.

    c. *Night* (William Blake). A-centered; a(b)–a"(f"); Tess-M; 5/4 with changes, Slow and languorous (♩ = ca.50); 3+min.

    d. *what if a much of a which of a wind* (e. e. cummings). E-centered; e♭'–g"; Tess-M; 6/8, 9/8, Bright and exuberant (♩ = ca.92); 1+min.

2158. SEASON (Robert E. Lee). For High Voice and Fortified Piano. [3]. cmp1970. X; e♭'-b"(g"); Tess-mH; changing meters, Slow–Più mosso–Very slow; 5pp; Diff-V/dd, P/dd.

For: tenor; soprano
Mood: mysterious; ambiguous
Voice: disjunct; staccato; irregular phrase lengths; 4-beat sustained b" on "leaves" (opt. g")

Piano: preparation specified (2 claves, 10 small bolts, etc.); detailed instructions (1p.); many timbre effects called for; fragmented; complex rhythms; 11-meas. prelude, 7-meas. interludes, 6-meas. postlude
Diff: pianist works harder than singer; perfect pitch helpful; difficult ensemble problems
Uses: seems very short for so much piano preparation; dedicated pianist required; would have to stand alone (or prepare a second piano); seems impractical for most recital situations

WARE, HARRIET
(b. Waupun, WI. 1877; d. New York, NY, 1962)

2159. THE LAST DANCE (Frederick H. Martens). Church, 1910. H, M, & L keys: Cmin, B♭min, & Gmin; e♭'–a♭"(c"'), d♭'–g"(b♭"), & b♭–e♭"(g"); Tess-mH; 3/4, Andante; 71meas.; Diff-V/m, P/me.
For: any voice except heavy low voice
Mood: nostalgic; waltz
Voice: many skips, esp. 6ths & 8ves; some vocalizing on "ah"; syncopation
Piano: waltz style; a piece on its own; no vocal line doubling
Diff: opt. ending given for opt. high tones
Uses: good song; interior of a group
Rec: D#57

WARING, TOM
(b. Tyrone, PA, 1902; d. Shawnee, PA, 1960)

2160. THE BANKS OF DOON (Robert Burns). [164]. Cmaj; b–d"; Tess-mL; 6/8, Very fast (♩. = 126); 3pp (with repeat); Diff-V/m, P/m.
For: any medium or low voice
Mood: folksong-like; lament over false lover, nature imagery
Voice: stepwise; skips within chords; a little chromaticism; easy rhythms; syllabic; several short, rapid melismas
Piano: chordal–block, broken, and rolled; 16th-note scale passages in 10ths; a little chromaticism; grace notes; supports but does not double vocal line
Diff: vocal agility needed to handle skips and melismas at rapid tempo; Scottish dialect
Uses: interesting setting of familiar poem; use in group of Robert Burns settings

2161. BLOOMING NELLY (Robert Burns). [164]. D♭maj; c'–e♭"; Tess-M; 2/2, 4/4, Allegro moderato (♩ = 92); 4pp (with repeat); Diff-V/me, P/me.
For: mezzo-soprano; baritone
Mood: narrative and descriptive; nature imagery
Voice: stepwise; small skips; diatonic; easy rhythms; syllabic
Piano: chordal–block, broken, and rolled; melodic material in prelude and interludes; scale passages; grace notes; strongly supports but does not double vocal line
Uses: for students and recital, esp. in group of Robert Burns settings

2162. BONNIE LESLEY (Robert Burns). [164]. D♭maj-Amaj; c'–f"; Tess-M; 4/4, 3/4, Allegro moderato (♩. = 120); 4pp; Diff-V/me, P/m.

For: baritone; tenor
Mood: love song in folksong style
Voice: stepwise and skips within chords; little chromaticism; easy rhythms; lyrical and flowing; syllabic; 2-note slurs
Piano: chordal–block, broken, rolled; some chromaticism; triplets; frequently doubles vocal line
Diff: Scottish dialect
Uses: good for recital, esp. in group of Robert Burns settings

2163. **I CANNOT COME TO YOU** (anon.). [164]. X, F♯-centered; e'–e"; Tess-M; 6/4, Sempre legato, quietly (♩ = 76); 3pp; Diff-V/m, P/d.
For: any high or medium voice
Mood: lyrical and philosophical song about death
Voice: stepwise; small skips, usually 3rds; somewhat chromatic; many phrases descend from e"; syllabic
Piano: chordal–block, broken, and rolled; patterned; chromatic; does not double vocal line
Uses: good as technique piece with phrases that begin high and descend; possible recital material

2164. **I SHALL BE A WANDERER** (anon.). [164]. Emaj; a♯–b'; Tess-L; 2/2, Moderato (♩ = 54); 1p; Diff-V/me, P/me.
For: any low voice
Mood: lyrical and philosophical; life and death
Voice: stepwise; small skips; leaps of aug.2nd, aug.4th, & 8ve; some chromaticism; syllabic
Piano: chordal–block, broken, and rolled; somewhat chromatic; pedal-tone effect at beginning; triplets; strong support and some doubling of vocal line
Diff: some intervals
Uses: for voices of limited range or undeveloped top

2165. **I WILL LIFT UP MINE EYES** (Psalm 121). [164]. A♭maj-E♭maj; a–e♭"; Tess-M; 3/4, 2/2, 4/4, ♩ = 80; 6pp; Diff-V/m, P/d.
For: any medium or low voice
Mood: faith in God; reverent
Voice: conjunct and disjunct; leaps of dim.5th, & 7th, m7th, & 8ve; little chromaticism; triplets and 3 vs. 4 in piano; broadly sweeping phrases; syllabic; 2-note slurs
Piano: chordal–block, broken, rolled, and repeated; melody in prelude and occasionally elsewhere; quite chromatic; supports well and occasionally doubles vocal line
Diff: abrupt large leaps mid-phrase
Uses: useful for religious occasions; possible recital material

2166. **JOHN ANDERSON, MY JO, JOHN** (Robert Burns). [164]. D♭maj; b–d♭"; Tess-mL; 6/8, Allegro moderato; 3pp; Diff-V/me, P/e.
For: mezzo-soprano
Mood: love song in folk-like style
Voice: chiefly stepwise; small skips; leaps of dim.5th & 8ve; a little chromaticism; easy rhythms; syllabic
Piano: chordal–block and rolled; a little chromaticism; supports well but does not double vocal line
Diff: Scottish dialect
Uses: good for recital, esp. in group of Robert Burns settings

2167. **LAZY SONG** (anon.). [164]. Emaj; b–c"; Tess-M; 3/4, Andante cantabile (♩ = 76); 3pp; Diff-V/e, P/m.

For: any medium or low voice
Mood: humorous; a "lazy" song sung by a "lazy" singer
Voice: stepwise; skips along chord lines; a few chromatic tones; easy rhythms; syllabic
Piano: chordal–block, broken, and afterbeat; scalar passages; some chromaticism; triplets; grace notes; strong support and some doubling of vocal line
Uses: younger students might enjoy this song (then again, they might not!); group or program ender; encore

2168. **MY HEART WAS ANCE AS BLITHE AND FREE** (Robert Burns). [164]. B♭maj-Fmaj; c'–f"; Tess-M; 6/8, 2/2, 4/4, Vivace (♩. = 86); 7pp (with repeat); Diff-V/me, P/md.
For: mezzo-soprano
Mood: like a folksong; narrative and descriptive; humorous song about love and its consequences
Voice: stepwise; small skips; little chromaticism; easy rhythms; syllabic; 2-note slurs
Piano: chordal–block, broken, and afterbeat; chromatic scalar passages; quite chromatic; does not double vocal line
Diff: Scottish dialect, incl. meanings of some words
Uses: good for recital, esp. in group of Robert Burns settings

2169. **MY JEAN** (Robert Burns). [164]. D-centered; b–d♯"; Tess-M; 3/4, Moderato; 3pp; Diff-V/me, P/m.
For: baritone
Mood: lyrical love song
Voice: stepwise; small skips; a few chromatic tones; easy rhythms; many phrases begin with a rising motive; lyrical and flowing; syllabic; 2-note slurs
Piano: chordal with melodic material, often in 3rds; rather chromatic; some doubling of vocal line
Uses: good for students and recital, esp. in group of Robert Burns settings

2170. **O, WERE MY LOVE YON LILAC FAIR** (Robert Burns). [164]. Dmaj-Fmaj; b–e"; Tess-M; 3/2, Very dreamily; 3pp; Diff-V/e, P/e.
For: baritone
Mood: lyrical love song; nature imagery
Voice: stepwise; small skips; no chromaticism; easy rhythms; lyrical and flowing; sustained tones in middle range; syllabic
Piano: chordal; a little chromaticism; grace notes; does not double vocal line
Uses: good for students and recital, esp. in group of Robert Burns settings

2171. **A RED, RED ROSE** (Robert Burns). [164]. Gmaj; d'–d"; Tess-mL; 3/4, Andante grazioso (♩. = 50); 3pp; Diff-V/me, P/m.
For: baritone
Mood: lyrical love song; nature imagery
Voice: stepwise; easy skips; some chromaticism; simple rhythms; syllabic; 2-note slurs
Piano: chordal–block and broken; somewhat chromatic; incidental doubling of vocal line
Diff: Scottish dialect
Uses: interesting setting of familiar poem

2172. **SO, WE'LL GO NO MORE A-ROVING** (Lord

Byron). [164]. Gmaj-B♭maj; b♭–d"; Tess-mL; 6/8, Moderato (♩. = 56); 4pp; Diff-V/me, P/m.
For: any medium voice
Mood: lyrical and philosophical love song
Voice: primarily stepwise; a few skips of 3rd; a little chromaticism; characterized by dotted-8th-/16th/8th rhythmic pattern; many phrases begin on b' and descend through lower-middle voice; syllabic; 2-note slurs
Piano: chordal with melodic fragments; rather chromatic; characterized by dotted rhythmic pattern like that of vocal line; 13-note groupings; cross-hands; strongly supports but does not double vocal line
Diff: possibly rhythms
Uses: possible recital material

2173. **YOUNG JESSIE** (Robert Burns). [164]. E♭maj; e♭'–e♭"; Tess-M; 3/4, Moderato (♩ = ca.132); 4pp; Diff-V/me, P/m.
For: baritone
Mood: lyrical love song; nature imagery
Voice: stepwise; small skips; diatonic; easy rhythms; lyrical and flowing; syllabic; a few 2-note slurs
Piano: chordal–block and broken; rather chromatic; fragments of countermelody; considerable doubling of vocal line
Diff: Scottish dialect; some pitches difficult against accomp.
Uses: good for teaching or recital, esp. in group of Robert Burns settings

WARNER, PHILIP
(b. Chicago, IL, 1901)

2174. **HURDY-GURDY** (Frances Frost). Carl Fischer, 1950. Fmaj; c'(d')–a"(f"); Tess-M; 6/8, Allegro; 3pp; Diff-V/m, P/me.
For: soprano; mezzo-soprano; tenor
Mood: descriptive; cheerful
Voice: skips on chord lines; duplets and triplets; some duplets vs. piano triplets
Piano: imitates hurdy-gurdy; waltz-style chordal accomp.; grace notes; does not double vocal line; medium and high registers of keyboard
Diff: polyrhythms; sustained a"s
Uses: good song for interior of a final group

WARREN, ELINOR REMICK
(b. Los Angeles, CA, 1900; d.1991)

[See also D#333 for song not listed below]

2175. **BY A FIRESIDE** (Thomas S. Jones, Jr.). G. Schirmer, 1934. [172]. H & L keys: G♭maj & E♭maj; e♭'–g♭" & c'–e♭"; Tess-M; 4/8, Slowly, dreamily; 2+min; Diff-V/m, P/m.
For: any voice except extremely low
Mood: lyrical; introspective; musing alone
Voice: many small skips; some dotted rhythms; several long tones; accidentals; quiet; does not double vocal line
Diff: sustained g♭" cresc.; soft dynamics
Uses: effective mood song
Rec: D#333

2176. **CHILDREN OF THE MOON** (A Fancy) (Katharine Adams). Flammer, 1923. Dmin; d'–a"; Tess-mH; 4/4, Allegro (Misterioso); 4pp; Diff-V/m, P/md.
For: soprano (not a heavy voice)
Mood: fanciful; child-like (child is the speaker); sprightly and dance-like
Voice: stepwise; small skips; chromatic lines; dotted rhythms
Piano: broken-chord figures; rapid passage work; staccato/legato differentiation; moves around keyboard; word illustration effects; independent of vocal line
Diff: fast articulation of text; descending chromatic scales; 4-beat sustained f♯" and 5 beats on "play"
Uses: group or program ender; for young singer who has developed some technique

2177. **CHRISTMAS CANDLE** (Kate Louise Brown). [165]; 1st©1940. Fmaj; f'–g"(a"); Tess-M; 6/8, Semplice; 5pp; Diff-V/m, P/m.
For: soprano; tenor
Mood: joyful
Voice: mostly stepwise; small skips; easy rhythms; long f" at end
Piano: mostly block chords, some broken; accidentals; little doubling of vocal line
Diff: long f" at end
Uses: nice Christmas song for high voice

2178. **GOD BE IN MY HEART** (Anon., 16th century). Oliver Ditson, 1950. [172]. D♭ major; (c')d♭'–a♭"; Tess-mH; 4/4, Andante con moto; 2pp; Diff-V/m, P/m.
For: any high voice
Mood: dramatic; affirmation of faith
Voice: mixes stepwise motion and skips up to a sixth; 3 non-consecutive unaccomp. meas.; option of starting song unaccomp. (no prelude); easy rhythms, some dotted; many dynamic marks
Piano: mostly block chords, thick and wide-ranged under the last phrase; optional 3-meas. prelude; does not double vocal line, but sometimes imitates at distance of one measure
Diff: dynamic control; nuances of expression of text
Uses: recital and study use; church use in some situations

2179. **IF YOU HAVE FORGOTTEN** (Sara Teasdale). [165]; 1st©1940. B♭maj; g♭'–g♭"; Tess-M; 3/4, Andante, with deep feeling; 4pp; Diff-V/m, P/m.
For: soprano; tenor
Mood: lyrical
Voice: many small skips; accidentals; some syncopation; some dotted rhythms; several alternate lower pitches
Piano: broken-chord patterning; accidentals; predominantly soft dynamics
Uses: for young singers

2180. **LADY LO-FU** (Mona Modini Wood). [165]; 1st©1927. F♯min; d♯'–g♯"; Tess-mH; 4/4, Moderate and even time; 4pp; Diff-V/m, P/m.
For: soprano
Mood: lyrical memory of a Chinese lady
Voice: stepwise; small skips; melismas; accidentals; simple rhythms
Piano: block and broken chords; many accidentals; rare

doubling of vocal line

Diff: a few fairly high, soft, long phrases that need floating quality; some sudden modulations

Uses: for young soprano

Rec: D#333

2181. **MELODY OUT OF MY HEART** (Dorothy Kissling). Carl Fischer, 1937. [172]. B♭min; e♭'–f"; Tess-mH; 9/8, Moderato, not dragging; 4 pp; Diff-V/m, P/md.

For: any high or medium high voice

Mood: love song; longing for love to return

Voice: mostly stepwise motion, skips within harmonic background; easy rhythms, many ties; chromaticism

Piano: wide-ranged block and broken chords; much chromaticism; eighth note motion; does not double vocal line; 2-meas. prelude, two short interludes

Diff: needs good dynamic control for best effect; descending chromatic scale, partial octave

Uses: attractive expressive song for study or recital

2182. **SILENT NOON** (Dante Gabriel Rossetti). Ditson, 1928. [172]. D♭maj; e♭'–a♭"; Tess-M; 4/4, Slowly and tranquilly; 4pp; Diff-V/m, P/m.

For: soprano; tenor

Mood: lyrical

Voice: conjunct; chord-member skips; speech rhythms; different inflections from the familiar Vaughan Williams setting ; some key changes; ends f"(opt. a♭")

Piano: chordal; 2-note chords moving in 8ths over static 8ve bass; triplets; some afterbeat and syncopated figures

Diff: rhythmic divisions

Uses: nice setting; see also setting by Edward T. Cone

Rec: D#333

2183. **SNOW TOWARDS EVENING** (Melville Cane). [59]; 1st©1937. H & L keys: A♭maj & E♭maj; e♭'–a♭" & b♭–e♭"; Tess-mH; 4/4, Andante tranquillo; 3pp; Diff-V/m, P/m.

For: all voices

Mood: lyrical; poetic description of snow

Voice: lyrical and sustained; an important descending phrase begins on highest pitch

Piano: chordal; somewhat chromatic; independent of voice

Diff: soft singing

Uses: good for work on transition to upper register

Rec: D#333

2184. **TIME, YOU OLD GIPSY MAN** (Ralph Hodgson). Enoch, 1926. "To Richard Crooks." H & M keys: Dmin & C♯min; d'–g♭" & c♯'–f"; Tess-M; 4/4, Spiritedly; 4pp; Diff-V/m, P/m.

For: any medium or high voice

Mood: cheerful

Voice: stepwise; easy skips; syncopation; some 2-note slurs; several key sig. changes

Piano: block chords and afterbeat style; some moving lines; often staccato; some triplets; syncopation; does not double vocal line

Diff: many key changes; register control

Uses: useful animated song; group ender; in group with a "time" theme (e.g., with songs like "XXth Century" by Martin Kalmanoff)

2185. **TO A BLUE-EYED BABY** (Richard LeGallienne). Oliver Ditson, 1950, [172]. Emaj; d♯'–g♯"; Tess-mH; 4/4, Tenderly and rhythmically; 3pp; Diff-V/m, P/m.

For: any high or medium high voice

Mood: loving; descriptive

Voice: often stepwise; skips within background harmonies; easy rhythms, some dotted, some syncopated

Piano: block and broken chord figures; some altered chords; 1-meas. prelude; incidental doubling of vocal line

Diff: a few intervals; two phrases have range of octave; controlling soft dynamics

Uses: study and performance situations; nice change of pace in a Warren song group

2186. **WHITE HORSES OF THE SEA** (Hamish Hendry). G. Schirmer, 1932. [165 (H)]. "Dedicated to Richard Crooks." H & L keys: Emin & Cmin; f'–g"(b") & d♭'–e♭"(g♭"); Tess-mH; 4/4, Fast, with abandon; 12pp; Diff-V/md, P/d.

For: tenor; soprano

Mood: agitated and excited; plunging

Voice: stepwise; easy skips; fragmented phrases; vigorous dotted rhythms; a few long high notes; big ending

Piano: arpeggios and other broken chords; subdivisions of 3, 4, 7, 8, & 9 complicate arpeggiation; galloping-horse motive; patterns of 3rds, block triads, and afterbeats

Diff: some chromaticism; endurance; sustained high tones; ensemble

Uses: rouser; group or program ender

Rec: D#333

2187. **WHO LOVES THE RAIN** (Frances Shaw). [165]; 1st©1945. B♭maj; f'–f"; Tess-M; 4/4, Andante, tranquilly; 2pp; Diff-V/me, P/m.

For: soprano

Mood: lyric

Voice: stepwise; small skips; many dotted rhythms; important use of dynamics

Piano: block chords; a few broken chords; syncopated pattern; no doubling of vocal line

Diff: dynamic variations

WATERS, JAMES
(b. Kyoto, Japan, 1930, of American parents)

2188. **WAR IS KIND** (Stephen Crane). [19]. X; g♯–g"; Tess-M; changing meters, several tempo changes–sectional; 11pp; Diff-V/dd, P/dd.

For: mezzo-soprano probably best

Mood: dramatic; intense; powerful setting of a bitter war poem; several mood changes

Voice: fragmentation; complex rhythms and pitch patterns; sudden dynamic changes; wide skips; several long melismas; one two-8ve portamento

Piano: complex harmonies, texture, and rhythms; covers the keyboard; large reach necessary; rapid passages in 16th-note triplets; chord clusters; great dynamic variation; several long interludes; accomp. initiates tempo changes; does not double vocal line

Diff: in all areas; needs mature, powerful voice; singer must be secure in every way; allow much time for ensemble work

Uses: expresses text well; effective song for the right singer; could stand alone

WATSON, WALTER ROBERT
(b. Canton, OH, 1933)

2189. PRAYERS FROM THE ARK (Carmen Bernos de Gasztold, trans. Rumer Godden). Black Squirrel Music, 1995. Tonal (mostly major keys); c'–a"; Tess-M-H; regular meters; varied tempos; 8min; Diff-V/e-m, P/me-m.

For: soprano; possibly tenor
Mood: whimsical, but definitely prayers; naive
Voice: stepwise motion; mostly easy skips; few rhythmic complications; some accidentals; some melismas; ending features leaps of 8ve & 9th
Piano: arpeggiation; broken chord triplets; block chords; last song has register variety; doubling of vocal line in some songs; two songs have 8–12 meas. preludes and interludes
Diff: a few intervals; (d.) most difficult, with modulations and more difficult rhythms; melismas on the word "sing"
Uses: nice group for an undergraduate recital; uncomplicated and refreshing; see also Theron Kirk's set from same source, though most poems chosen are different

    a. *The Prayer of the Cock.* Gmaj; g'–ab"; Tess-mH; 3/4, Moderato; 3+pp.
    b. *The Prayer of the Ox.* Ebmaj; eb'–f"; Tess-M; 2/2, Slow; 2+pp.
    c. *The Prayer of the Little Pig.* C-centered; c'–e"; Tess-M; 5/4, 2/4, 4/4, Freely; 1p.
    d. *The Prayer of the Little Bird.* A-centered; f'–a"; Tess-H; 4/4, Gently; 1+pp.
    e. *The Prayer of the Little Ducks.* Fmaj; f'–f"; Tess-M; 4/4, Lively; 3pp (repeats).
    f. *The Prayer of the Dove.* Gmaj/Emin (ends Amaj); d'–f♯"; Tess-M; 4/4, 2/4, 6/4, Slow; 1+pp.

2190. WORDS FOR SLEEP (Conrad Pendleton). [19]. Gmaj; d'–g"; Tess-M; 3/4, 4/4, Moderato; 3pp; Diff-V/m, P/m.

For: soprano; mezzo-soprano
Mood: cradle-song; soothing
Voice: many small skips; easy rhythms
Piano: linear-chordal combination; broken-chord and scale line in 8th-note motion; some large reaches; moves around keyboard; does not double vocal line
Diff: some intervals against the piano part; changing meters
Uses: interesting colors; quiet song with quiet ending; useful in American group

WATTS, JOHN
(b. Cleveland, TN, 1930; d. New York, NY, 1982)

2191. SIGNALS. Recital Version for Soprano Voice and Piano. Joshua, 1977. X; g♯(a♯)–bb"; Tess-wide; traditional meters; varied tempos; 6min; Diff-V/d, P/d.

For: soprano; mezzo-soprano who can sustain bb"
Mood: wry humor; composer does not explain origin of texts, but they are labels– (a.), warning label on an incinerator; (b.), fabric content on socks; (c.), notice on an envelope containing a brochure offering merchandise "of an adult nature"
Voice: (a.), conjunct; (b.), disjunct; many skips of 4th; long-ranged phrases (e.g., g♯–a", d'–g", and e'–ab"); (c.), fairly disjunct; has spoken phrase, semi-sung phrase, one phrase without vibrato, and speech-like rhythms; all have many accidentals; syllabic
Piano: combination of linear and block vertical structure patterns; mostly non-tertian harmony; tone clusters; pedal effects; trills; staccato; cross-accents; duplets and triplets juxtaposed (b.); many accidentals (often 4 or 5 per chord); does not double vocal line
Diff: pitches and rhythms; 3-beat sustained ab" and 4-meas. sustained bb"; ensemble in (c.)
Uses: clever idea; humorous short group; needs singer who can capitalize on this humor

    a. *I. Warning.* X; b–e"; 4/4, Misterioso, sostenuto; 2pp.
    b. *II. Certification.* X; (g♯)d'–bb"; 6/8, Picaresquely; 6pp.
    c. *III. Notice.* X; a♯–g"; 7/8 with changes, Very introspectively; 2pp.

WATTS, WINTTER
(b. Cincinnati, OH, 1884; d. Brooklyn, NY, 1962)

2192. BARCAROLE (Pai Tai-shun). G. Schirmer, 1918. Fmaj; e'–a"; Tess-mH; 2/4, Tranquilly flowing; 4pp; Diff-V/m, P/m.

For: soprano; tenor
Mood: lyrical; sadness of time and love past
Voice: conjunct; some skips; 2–4-note slurs; delicate; soft ending
Piano: imitates stringed instrument (*biwa*?); measured tremolo; 16th/dotted-8th rhythm imitates plucking; melodic interest
Uses: attractive, bittersweet song on Oriental poetry; useful, esp. in group of Oriental texts

2193. BLUE ARE HER EYES (Mary MacMillan). [13 (2nd year), 53]; 1st©1913. H & L keys: F♯min (orig). & Dmin; f♯'–f♯" & d'–d"; Tess-mH; 2/4, 6/8, Deliberately–Più mosso; 3pp; Diff-V/me, P/me.

For: tenor
Mood: lyrical; love song; nature imagery
Voice: lyrical and flowing; section featuring repeated notes builds in intensity to *ff* climax
Piano: chordal; doubles voice in first section; repeated chords in second section; independent countermelody where voice is static
Uses: useful student recital song

2194. THE LITTLE SHEPHERD'S SONG (13th-century text from Percy's *Reliques*). Ricordi, 1922. H & L keys: Cmaj & Amaj; g'–bb" & e'–g"; Tess-mH; 3/8, Moderato–Allegro; 6pp; Diff-V/m, P/m.

For: soprano; mezzo-soprano (light voices)
Mood: lyrical; lighthearted; cheerful; enjoying nature
Voice: many skips; staccato-legato differentiation important; lilting melody; 2–3-note slurs
Piano: 12-meas. prelude; countermelody over broken chords; arpeggios; some rolled chords; covers the keyboard; incidental doubling of vocal line
Diff: approach to final high tone difficult; needs good register control
Uses: useful for young voices and mature light voices

2195. **THE POET SINGS** (Richard LeGallienne). Ditson, 1919. [16]. "To Mr. John McCormack." H & M keys: D♭maj (orig.) & B♭maj; e♭'–a♭" & c'–f"; Tess-mH; 3/4, Serenely flowing; 3pp; Diff-V/m, P/m.
For: tenor; baritone
Mood: lyrical; quiet; nostalgic
Voice: soaring melody–upward leaps up to 10th; downward motion stepwise; repetitive rhythms
Piano: arpeggiated, rolled, and block chords; accidentals; doubles vocal line
Diff: some rubato; many cresc.–decresc. markings
Uses: good lyric recital song

2196. **TRANSFORMATION** (Jessie B. Rittenhouse). G. Schirmer, 1922. H & L keys: E♭maj & Bmaj; d'–g♭" & a♯'–d"; Tess-mL; 2/4, Lento; 3pp; Diff-V/m, P/m.
For: contralto; mezzo-soprano; soprano
Mood: love song
Voice: stepwise; easy skips; dotted rhythms; long phrases; some wide-ranged phrases
Piano: 4–7-voice block chords, some rolled; many accidentals; some doubling of vocal line
Diff: long phrases; needs mature sound
Uses: quiet ending

2197. **VIGNETTES OF ITALY.** A Cycle of Songs (Sara Teasdale). Oliver Ditson, 1919. Reprint: Classical Vocal Reprints (H). Traditional keys; d'–b♭"; Tess-mH; mostly regular meters; 32pp; Diff-V/md-d, P/md-d.
For: lyric soprano
Mood: lyrical; remembrance of a love relationship in Italy
Voice: many different lyric and romantic techniques; very expressive songs; needs a beautiful, soaring sound and keen understanding of the poetry
Piano: romantic piano techniques required with great sensitivity to the poetry
Uses: fine romantic cycle reflecting in an Italian setting the sadness and pain of a broken love relationship; poems from a woman's viewpoint; music and text of first song return in last song

    a. *Addio.* E♭maj; f'–a♭"; 2/4, Moderato con moto; 5pp.
    b. *Naples.* Gmaj; e'–g"; 2/4, Con brio; 4pp.
    c. *Capri.* [53]. H & M keys: Gmaj & E♭maj; e'–g" & c'–e♭"; 2/2, Well sustained; 3pp.
    d. *Night Song at Amalfi.* B♭maj; f'–g"; 3/4, Rubato; 4pp.
    e. *Ruins of Paestum.* E♭min; e♭'–g♭"; 4/4, Andante sostenuto; 2pp.
    f. *From a Roman Hill.* G♭maj; e♭'–g♭"; 7/4, Con

    moto; 3pp.
    g. *Ponte Vecchio, Florence.* Dmaj; d'–f♯"; 3/4, Andante; 3pp.
    h. *Villa Serbelloni, Bellaggio.* Gmaj; g♯'–g♯"; 4/4, Con moto; 2pp.
    i. *Stresa.* E♭maj; d'–b♭"; 4/8, Andante tranquillo; 6pp.

2198. **WHEN I WAKE** (source not given). Reprint: Tichenor Publishing (T.I.S.), 1998. Dmaj; c♯'–g"; Tess-mH; 2/4, Moderato; 2pp; Diff-V/m, P/m.
For: soprano; tenor
Mood: peaceful, somber love song; dramatic climax
Voice: stepwise and small skips; some accidentals; many dynamic markings; some dotted rhythms
Piano: mostly 8th-note motion; some doubling of vocal line; many accidentals; 3–5-voice chordal texture; countermelodies
Diff: some unexpected melodic and harmonic events; dynamic control; range (ends on d')
Uses: mature subject; recital and study song for an older student; text a bit dated

2199. **WINGS OF NIGHT** (Sara Teasdale). [48]; 1st©1921. H & L keys: Bmaj & A♭maj; c♯'–g" & b♭–f♭"; Tess-M; 6/8, Con moto tranquillo; 4pp; Diff-V/m, P/d.
For: any female voice
Mood: lyrical
Voice: lyrical and flowing, rising phrases; several large intervals
Piano: 3-voice texture; syncopated afterbeats
Rec: D#334

2200. **WOOD SONG** (Eugene Lee Hamilton). Reprint: Tichenor Publishing (T.I.S.), 1998. D♭maj; c'–e"; Tess-M; 2/4, Moderato; 2pp; Diff-V/me, P/m.
For: any medium or medium high voice
Mood: permanence of nature; lyrical
Voice: mostly conjunct; some accidentals color melody; easy rhythms
Piano: 3–4-voice texture, mostly doubling vocal line; many accidentals; 8th-note motion; 4-meas. prelude
Diff: modulations in melody at end of second strophe
Uses: good teaching song for legato connections and dynamic control

WAYNE, HARRY
(b. 1915)

2201. **FOUR POEMS FROM A CHILD'S GARDEN OF VERSES** (Robert Louis Stevenson). Hollow Hills, 1966. Traditional keys; c'–a♭"; Tess-M; regular meters with a few changes; varied tempos; 13+pp; Diff-V/m, P/m.
For: mezzo-soprano; soprano; tenor
Mood: scenes from a child's imagination
Voice: stepwise; skips within chords; a few 8ve leaps; some chromaticism; easy rhythms; flowing phrases; syllabic; occasional 2-note slurs
Piano: chiefly chordal–block and broken; short scale passages; countermelodies; chromatic; grace notes; staccato

marching bass in l.h. 8ves in (d.); strong support and some doubling of vocal line

Diff: some pitches hard to hear, esp. in (d.); needs good vocal actor

Uses: good for students; recital possibilities

a. *The Land of Counterpane.* Fmaj; e♭'–f"; 6/8, Simply, not too fast; 3pp.

b. *Looking-Glass River.* Gmin; c'–g"; 4/4, 2/4, 5/4, 3/4, Simply and wistfully; 3+pp.

c. *The Moon.* Fmin; c'–a♭"; 3/4, Mysteriously; 4pp.

d. *Marching Song.* Modal, E-centered; d'–g♯"; 4/4, In a brisk march tempo; 3+pp.

WEAVER, POWELL
(b. Clearfield, PA, 1890; d. Kansas City, MO, 1951)

2202. MOON-MARKETING (Richard LeGallienne). [64]; 1st©1924. "To Tito Schipa." Dmin; d'–f"; Tess-mL; 4/4, Allegro; 5pp; Diff-V/m, P/d.

For: any voice except very low; text best for young female

Mood: humorous and descriptive

Voice: short phrases separated by rests; occasionally outlines triads

Piano: rapid chords, alternating hands; broken and arpeggiated chords; aug. triads; afterbeats

Diff: requires an accomplished pianist

WEBB, GEORGE J.
(b. Rushmore Lodge, near Salisbury, England, 1803; d. Orange, NJ, 1887)

2203. SONG OVER A CHILD (Barry Cornwald). arr. Oliver Daniel. Carl Fischer, 1951; 1st pub., 18–?. Fmaj; f'–d"; Tess-M; 2/4, Gently; 2pp (3 strophes); Diff-V/e, P/e.

For: mezzo-soprano; soprano

Mood: lullaby

Voice: stepwise motion; one leap of 6th; 2-note slurs

Piano: rocking bass line; 8th-note motion; many 6ths; some doubling of vocal line

Uses: easy song for beginners of any age

2204. 'TIS NOT THE SINGING O' THE BIRD (Charles Sibley Gage, Esq.). Russell, 1868. Fmaj; d'–g"; Tess-M; 2/4, Moderato; 5pp; Diff-V/me, P/me.

For: tenor; high baritone

Mood: folk-like love song

Voice: many skips, not over 6th; dotted rhythms; Scotch snap; some grace notes

Piano: block and broken chords; prelude, interludes, and postlude; does not double vocal line

Uses: useful period piece

WEBER, BEN
(b. St. Louis, MO, 1916; d. New York, NY, 1979)

2205. A BIRD CAME DOWN THE WALK, Op. 57 (Emily Dickinson). American Composers Alliance (Composers Facsimile Edition). cmp1963. Commissioned by Alice Esty; "in memory of Francis Poulenc." X; c'–f"; Tess-M; 3/4 with changes, Animando, rubato; 3min; Diff-V/d, P/d.

For: mezzo-soprano specified; some sopranos

Mood: descriptive with a touch of humor

Voice: rather disjunct; leaps up to dim.8ve; many accidentals; speech-like rhythms; duplet and triplet subdivisions of beat; dotted figures; syncopation; a few staccato notes

Piano: block and broken vertical structures, often non-tertian; staccato bird-like figures; a few rolled chords, tremolos, and trills; graceful and mostly quiet; complicated rhythms include 2 vs. 3 & 5 vs. 6; juxtaposition of groupings of 4, 5, & 6 16th notes per beat; does not double vocal line

Diff: hard to find pitches, perfect pitch helpful; rhythms; ensemble; entrances, from the standpoint of both pitch and rhythms (usually between beats); highly dissonant

Uses: interesting song for two secure musicians

2206. FIVE SONGS, Op. 15. For Soprano and Piano (Adelaide Crapsey). Cycle. American Composers Alliance (Composers Facsimile Edition), 1955. cmp1941. X; b♭(c')–g"; Tess-M; traditional meters; slow and moderate tempos; 5min; Diff-V/d, P/d.

For: soprano; lyric mezzo-soprano

Mood: delicate; sometimes atmospheric; descriptive

Voice: chromatic lines; speech rhythms with many rests; two songs end with downward glissando; several words and phrases "half-sung"; voice used as instrument in chamber ensemble; syllabic with 2–4-note slurs

Piano: highly dissonant, almost atonal, and bristling with accidentals; accomps. not patterned; resemble small piano pieces in texture; some 2 vs. 3; much attention to articulations; many staccatos; a few rolled chords; one long trill; almost exactly half of cycle is piano solo

Diff: hard to find pitches; perfect pitch necessary; ensemble; projecting delicacy of poetry with necessary authority

Uses: interesting short cycle; program material for two experienced and secure musicians; seems to be inspired by George Antheil's *Five Songs,* 1919–1920, although more dissonant

a. *November Night.* X; b♭(d')–g"; 3/4, Slowly; 1+pp.

b. *Susanna and the Elders.* X; e♭'–f♯"; 4/8, Slowly; 1p.

c. *Triad.* X; c♯'–d"; 5/8, 4/8, Allegretto; 1+pp.

d. *Niagara.* X; c'–f♯"; 4/4, Andantino; 1p.

e. *The Warning.* X; e'–e"; 3/4, Nervously animated; 1p.

2207. MOURN! MOURN! (John Dowland). [49]. X; d'–f"; Tess-M; 4/4, 5/4, 3/4, 2/4, Andante mesto, ritardando– Meno mosso–Lento; 3pp; Diff-V/md, P/d.

For: any high or medium voice

Mood: philosophical; gloomy

Voice: features long descending phrases; many triplet quarter notes; somewhat dramatic

Piano: chordal; chromatic; several irregular note groupings

Diff: frequent meter changes; ensemble

Uses: interesting recital song

Rec: D#59

WEESNER, ANNA
(b. Iowa City, IA, 1965)

2208. ALTER? WHEN THE HILLS DO (Emily Dickinson). [9]. X–hovers between 9th-chord consonance and dissonance; f'–a♭"; Tess-M, H; 4/4; Very slow ♩ = 58; 2min; Diff-V/m, P/m.
For: soprano
Mood: ambivalent; questions and answers about faithfulness
Voice: mostly stepwise; three wide leaps; slowly rising line on questions; repeated notes on answers
Piano: 8th-note outlining of harmonic progression rising on questions; imitation of voice and falling line on answers
Diff: some pitch patterns; repeated g"s and a"s
Uses: interesting song for a Dickinson group

WEIL, OSCAR
(b. Columbia County, NY, 1840; d.1921)

2209. SLUMBER SONG ("from the Swedish"). M. Gray, 1874. "To Miss Clara Louise Kellogg." E♭maj; b♭–g"; Tess-mH; 6/8, Allegretto tranquillo; 7pp; Diff-V/m, P/me.
For: soprano; mezzo-soprano
Mood: cradle song; serene; subdued
Voice: stepwise; chord-member skips; easy rhythms; many 2-note slurs
Piano: chordal; rocking bass; rolled chords; some countermelody; some doubling of vocal line
Diff: soft dynamics; sustained tones that decresc.
Uses: good subdued song; useful in American group

2210. STARS OF THE SUMMER NIGHT (Henry Wadsworth Longfellow). M. Gray, 1874. Gmaj; d'–g"(f♯"); Tess-M; 3/4, Andantino, con moto (non troppo lento, ma tranquillo); 5pp; Diff-V/m, P/m.
For: tenor; some high baritones
Mood: lyrical love song; serenade
Voice: stepwise; skips on chord lines; many dotted rhythms; some 2-note slurs
Piano: block and broken chords–some staccato, some rolled; repetitive; guitar-like; cross-hands; does not double vocal line
Diff: soft dynamics; g"s, if taken, are sustained
Uses: effective, charming song; useful for American or serenade group

WEISGALL, HUGO
(b. Ivancice, Czechoslovakia, 1912; d. Baltimore, MD, 1997)

[See also D#50; no titles given]

2211. FOUR SONGS, Op. 1, Nos. 1–4 (Adelaide Crapsey). Axelrod, 1940. Traditional keys with altered chord structures; b♭–g"; Tess-M-mH; regular meters with some changes; slow tempos; 6pp; Diff-V/m, P/m.
For: soprano
Mood: lyrical; grieving
Voice: conjunct; lyrical; minor modes; delicate; soft; some speech rhythms
Piano: linear; some chordal; much treble clef; broken-chord figures; some vocal line doubling; some countermelody
Diff: pitch perception in a few spots; soft, delicate singing
Uses: nice group; good for any lyric soprano capable of a spinning, transparent sound; also possible for a tenor with same qualities
Rec: D#18

   a. *Old Love.* e'–e"; 3/4, 2/4, Very quietly; 1p.
   b. *Song.* Emin; e'–g"; 3/4, Quietly moving; 2pp.
   c. *Oh, Lady, Let the Sad Tears Fall.* E♭min; b♭–g♭"; 4/4, Very slowly; 2pp.
   d. *Dirge.* d'–e"; 4/8, 3/4, Very slowly; 1p.

2212. I LOOKED BACK SUDDENLY (Humbert Wolfe). [16]. cmp1943. B-centered; a–e"; Tess-mL; 3/2, 4/2, 5/2, ♩ = 52; 2pp; Diff-V/md, P/m.
For: mezzo-soprano; contralto; bass-baritone
Mood: lyrical; philosophical
Voice: conjunct motion beginning and end, more disjunct in middle; chromatic; generally quarter-note movement
Piano: chromatic; chordal; follows vocal line, does not double
Diff: pitches; control of lower vocal range
Uses: excellent for the mature low voice

2213. LIEBESLIEDER. Four Songs with Interludes for High Voice and Piano (Deborah Trustman [English texts; no titles]). Cycle. Theodore Presser, 1981. cmp1978–1979. X; c♯'–b♭"; Tess-M; regular and irregular meters with changes; generally fast tempos; 22pp; Diff-V/dd, P/dd.
For: soprano; tenor
Mood: modern "love-songs"; philosophical; ironic; somewhat bitter
Voice: rather disjunct; many skips, sometimes large and/or awkward; phrases fragmented by rests; highly chromatic; rhythmically complex; many dynamic markings; chromatic melismas
Piano: chordal-linear combination; highly chromatic; intricate, complex rhythms; irregular subdivisions of beat; many dynamic markings; articulations important; doubles or supports vocal line only incidentally, except (e.), where doubling is more extensive; solo piano interludes between each song; (a.), 2–3-voice counterpoint; (c.), 4-voice chordal-contrapuntal; (f.), like a Chopin waltz
Diff: perfect pitch desirable; complicated rhythms; much dynamic variation; ensemble; singer and pianist must be superb, secure musicians
Uses: good recital material for sophisticated performers

   a. *I.* X; c♯'–g"; Tess-M; 6/8 with changes, Allegretto con moto (♪ = ca.152); 4pp.
   b. *Interlude I.* X; 6/8, Presto possibile (♩. = 144); 3pp.
   c. *II.* X; d'–a"; Tess-mH, mL; 4/4, 6/4, 5/4, Do not drag (♩ = 72); 3pp.
   d. *Interlude II.* X; unmetered, Flowing eighths (♪ = 104); 1p.
   e. *III.* X; e♭'–b♭"; Tess-M; 3/4, 4/4, Poco agitato (♩ = 112); 3pp.
   f. *Interlude III.* X; 3/4, à la Chopin (♩ = 76); 3pp.
   g. *IV.* X; d♭'–b♭"; Tess-mL, M; 3/4 with changes, Tempo di valse (♩ = 114) (with changes); 5pp.

2214. NO MORE I WILL THY LOVE IMPORTUNE
(*Two Madrigals*) (anon., 17th century). Theodore
Presser, 1958. cmp1945. X-Emaj; a–f "; Tess-M; 3/4,
2/4, Slow and sustained; 40meas.; Diff-V/m, P/me.

For: dramatic baritone
Mood: intense; dramatic; somewhat bitter
Voice: some awkward skips; accidentals; rhythm flows
irregularly; dramatic dynamics
Piano: basic 4-voice texture; some syncopation of chords;
many accidentals
Diff: lowest notes *pp* & *ff*; dramatic intensity throughout
Uses: has a quiet, if intense, ending; interior of group; starts
high and descends

2215. NUPTIAL SONG (*Two Madrigals*) (anon., 17th
century). Theodore Presser, 1958. cmp1955. X
(bitonal); f'–b♭"; Tess-H; 6/8, Fast and light; 6pp;
Diff-V/d, P/md.

For: high soprano
Mood: happy; joyous; dances along
Voice: some difficult intervals; long sustained tones;
articulations important; long melismas
Piano: 3–5-voice linear-chordal combination; many
accidentals; bitonal; moves around keyboard rapidly;
articulations important; some doubling of vocal line
Diff: ensemble; sustained high tones; good register and
dynamic control
Uses: good program ender

2216. SOLDIER SONGS for Baritone. Cycle. Mercury,
1953. cmp1945–1948. Traditional keys with altered
chord structures; a–g♯"; Tess-M, mH, H; regular meters
with some changes; varied tempos; 12min;
Diff-V/d-dd, P/d.

For: baritone (high dramatic with good low notes)
Mood: lyrico-dramatic; war scenes
Voice: many skips and leaps; much high tessitura; speech
rhythms; melismatic phrases; difficult pitch patterns;
wide dynamic range
Piano: many techniques required–repeated notes, tremolo,
3rds, trill; wide reach helpful; fast scale and
broken-chord passages; both forceful and quiet playing
required; quiet ending; accidentals
Diff: many–range and tessitura perhaps the most critical;
mature voice with excellent technique, easy high f's
and g's, advanced musicianship, and great declamatory
skill required
Uses: one of the best cycles in every way; highly effective for
advanced singer

   a. *Lord, I Have Seen Too Much* (Karl Shapiro).
a–g♯"; Tess-cs; 4/4 with changes, Very slow; 4pp.
   b. *Suicide in the Trenches* (Siegfried Sassoon). c'–f ";
Tess-M-mH; 2/2, Tempo giusto; 3pp.
   c. *The Dying Airman* (anon.). a–f♯". Tess-covers
range; 3/4, Tempo di valse; 4pp.
   d. *my sweet old etcetera* (e. e. cummings). a–f♯";
Tess-mH; 2/2, Moderato; 4pp .
   e. *The Dying Soldier* (Isaac Rosenberg). g–f ";
Tess-M-mH; 4/4, Allegro molto e feroce; 3pp.
   f. *Fife Tune* (John Manifold). c'–g♯"; Tess-mH-H;
6/8, Moderato–A la Scottish–gay; 3pp. (See R.

Cumming's *We Happy Few* for another setting)
   g. *Futility* (Wilfred Owen). a–f "; Tess-M-H; 4/8, 3/8,
Very slow; 4pp.
   h. *The Leveller* (Robert Graves). c'–g"; Tess-M-H;
2/2, Alla marcia–Jauntily; 4pp.
   i. *Shiloh. A Requiem. April 1862.* (Herman Melville).
a–e"; Tess-M; 4/8, Very slow; 3pp.

2217. TRANSLATIONS. Seven Songs for Voice and Piano.
Cycle. Theodore Presser, 1977. cmp1971–1972.
Commissioned by and dedicated to Shirley Verrett. X;
a–a♭"(a"); Tess-wide; traditional meters with changes;
varied tempos with many changes; 30pp; Diff-V/dd,
P/dd.

For: mezzo-soprano
Mood: women's texts, beginning with a young girl's thoughts,
progressing to an old woman's reminiscence of youth
Voice: disjunct; many accidentals; complicated rhythms; many
different divisions of beat, made more complex by
combining with other rhythms in piano; several
portamentos; many dynamic markings; mostly syllabic;
often dramatic
Piano: complex, dissonant score; linear style predominates;
use of non-tertian harmony; complicated rhythms;
syncopation, cross-accents; polyrhythms; accidentals
abound; some 3-stave writing; grace notes; many
dynamic markings; does not double vocal line
Diff: in almost all aspects, esp. rhythms and ensemble
Uses: as a set for two excellent musicians
Rec: D#335

   a. *Knoxville, Tennessee* (Nikki Giovanni). X;
e'–g"(f♯"); changing meters, Sognando (with
fluctuations); 4pp.
   b. *Song* (Adrienne Rich). X; c♯'–a♭"; 2/2, Not too
seriously (with fluctuations); 5pp.
   c. *Child Song* (Deborah Trustman). X; b♭–a♭";
changing meters, Molto cantabile, sempre rubato
(with fluctuations); 4pp.
   d. *(1) Poem* (1st version) (Celia Dropkin; trans.
Adrienne Rich). X; c'–g♭"(a"); 5/8 with changes,
Allegro (♪ = 276); 4pp.
   e. *(2) Poem* (2nd version) (Celia Dropkin; trans.
Adrienne Rich). X; a–g"; 5/8 with changes, Allegro
(♪ = 276); 4pp.
   f. *Poem* (Celia Dropkin; trans. Adrienne Rich). X;
b–g♭"; 3/4, With intensity, sustained throughout
(♩ = 56); 2pp.
   g. *The Rebel* (Mari E. Evans). X; c♯'–g"; 3/4 with
changes, Jauntily; 2pp.
   h. *A City by the Sea* (Anna Margolin; trans. Adrienne
Rich). X; b♭–f♯"; 3/4 predominates, Slowly and
languidly (with fluctuations); 5pp.

WELLS, HOWARD
(b. Rockford, IL, 1874; d. Chicago, IL, 1951)

2218. EVERYONE SANG (Siegfried Sassoon). [20];
1st©1967. Dmaj; b–f♯"; Tess-M; 3/2, 4/4, Allegro;
6pp; Diff-V/md, P/dd.

For: mezzo-soprano; lyric baritone

Mood: joyous and ecstatic
Voice: broad and flowing; somewhat dramatic
Piano: chromatic arpeggiations and figurations
Diff: requires some dramatic weight to voice, with solid f♯" at end; some difficult pitches; several phrases begin high and descend
Uses: somewhat overblown, but useful; group/program ender

WETZLER, ROBERT
(b. Minneapolis, MN, 1932)

2219. **THE WILDERNESS** (Henry David Thoreau). Art Masters Studios, 1983. Somewhat modal, various key centers (sectional); d'–a"(c'''); Tess-mH; 4/4, 3/4, 3/2, ♩ = c.63–c.92; 7pp; Diff-V/m, P/m.
For: tenor; soprano
Mood: philosophical; prose text promotes benefits of wilderness areas; nature
Voice: easy rhythms; mostly syllabic; mostly conjunct; choice of high c (over a") and b♭" (over g") at one point; 3-meas. unaccomp. passage
Piano: patterned accomp. figure set up in 2-meas. prelude; varies between sections; hemiola in 3/4 section; mostly 8th & 16th notes; several interludes, 2–4 meas. in length; supports but does not double vocal line
Diff: tessitura varies between sections; rather high in one section, making diction difficult; hemiola cross-accents in piano in one section could cause problems for rhythmically insecure singer
Uses: a nice "message" song, fairly serene; could stand alone or pair with another nature song

WHEELOCK, DONALD (See entry #15 A)

WHELPLY, BENJAMIN
(b. Eastport, ME, 1864; d. Boston, MA, 1946)

2220. **I KNOW A HILL** (Harriet Boyer). Boston Music Co., 1903. C♯min; c♯'–c♯"; Tess-M; 3/4, Andante; 3pp; Diff-V/me, P/m.
For: bass; contralto
Mood: longing for home
Voice: stepwise; easy skips; easy rhythms; mostly syllabic
Piano: broken chords; afterbeat style; some rolled chords; doubles vocal line
Uses: useful song for a low-voiced student

WHITE, DAVID ASHLEY
(b. San Antonio, TX, 1944)

2221. **FOUR ELIZABETHAN IMAGES** for High Voice and Piano. E. C. Schirmer, 2000. cmp1979 & 1989. Tonal; c'–c'''; Tess-M, mH-H, cs; regular meters with changes; slow to quick tempos; 15pp; Diff-V/m-d, P/me-md.
For: soprano; tenor
Mood: romantic; fancy, spring love, adoration, praise
Voice: lyrical; mostly conjunct; melodic; modulating

harmonies; (d.) melismatic; some high phrases
Piano: mostly linear; chords with melody; shifting harmonies; accidentals
Diff: (d.) seems to be for different voice type; singer must have easy high coloratura
Uses: very attractive set for soprano or tenor; good recital material

   a. *O Sleep, Fond Fancy* (Anonymous, ca.1599). Tonal; e♭'–f♯"; Tess-cs; 4/4, 2/4, 3/4, Slowly ♩ = c.58; 3pp.
   b. *This Sweet and Merry Month* (Att. Thomas Watson, ca.1590). G-Cmin; f'–b♭"; Tess-M-mH; 4/4, 3/4, 2/4, 3/8, Fast and Lively (♩ = c.126); 3pp.
   c. *The Curtain Drawn* (Anonymous, ca.1598). Tonal; c'–f♯"; Tess-M; 3/4, 2/4, 4/4, Slowly, dreamily (♩ = c.58); 4pp.
   d. *Long Live Fair Oriana* (Ellis Gibbons, 1573–1603). D-centered; f'–c'''; Tess-mH-H; 3/4, 2/4, Quickly (♩ = c.104); 5pp.

2222. **THREE BYRON SONGS.** Medium Voice and Piano. (Lord Byron) Southern Music Company (San Antonio), 1992. Traditional keys; c♯'–f"; Tess-M; regular meters with some changes; moderate tempos; 11pp; Diff-V/m, P/me-m.
For: any medium voice
Mood: gentle; lyrical; melancholy
Voice: lyrical; mostly conjunct lines; modulating harmonies; syllabic setting; little word inflection; melody governs text; grateful to the voice
Piano: mostly chordal structure; modulating harmonies; accidentals; open texture
Diff: lovely set of relatively easy songs for undergraduates

   a. *She Walks in Beauty.* Dmin; c♯'–e"; Tess-M; 4/4, Moderately (♩ = c.80); 4pp.
   b. *So, We'll Go No More A-Roving.* Cmin; d'–f"; Tess-M; 4/4, 2/4, 3/4, With movement (♩ = c.116); 3pp.
   c. *It Is the Hour.* Gmin; d'–f"; Tess-M; 4/4, 3/4, 3/2, 2/4, Moderately (♩ = ca. 84); 4pp.

WHITE, JOHN DAVID
(b. Rochester, MN, 1931)

2223. **A CRADLE SONG** (William Blake). [18]. X; c♯'–f♯"; Tess-M; 6/8, 2/4, Animato–Poco meno mosso; 4pp; Diff-V/md, P/md.
For: soprano; mezzo-soprano
Mood: lyrical; lullaby
Voice: short phrases; fairly chromatic; syncopation
Piano: contrapuntal; chromatic; independent of voice, but similar in style
Diff: pitches; rhythms
Uses: good introduction to contemporary idiom for students; useful for recital

2224. **THE LAMB** (William Blake). [19]. A-centered; d'–e"; Tess-M; 2/2, 3/2, 6/4, 5/4; 2+min; Diff-V/m, P/m.
For: mezzo-soprano; baritone

Mood: lyrical; naive; child-like
Voice: mostly stepwise; skips up to 6th; irregular rhythms; syncopation; some 2–3-note slurs
Piano: chordal texture–block and broken; repetitive; many accidentals; some large reaches; many vertical 4ths & 6ths; does not double vocal line
Diff: irregular rhythmic patterns; changing meters; ensemble
Uses: useful setting of this well-known poem

WHITHORNE, EMERSON
(b. Cleveland, OH, 1884; d. New York, NY, 1958)

2225. BY THE EASTERN GATE, Op. 16, No. 1 (from Confucius, 500 B.C.; trans. Capt. L. Cranmer-Byng). Carl Fischer, 1918. Emin-maj; f#'–e"; Tess-M; 2/4, Moderato e misterioso; 2pp; Diff-V/e, P/me.
For: baritone
Mood: lyrical; waiting
Voice: conjunct; some small skips; short phrases
Piano: chordal; some odd harmonies; quiet
Uses: period piece of Orientalism; interesting contrast to the "western gate" of J. Duke's "Luke Havergal"

WILDER, ALEC
(b. Rochester, NY, 1907; d. Gainesville, FL, 1980)

2226. CHICK LORIMER (Carl Sandburg). R. D. Row, 1953. Bbmaj; c–gb"; Tess-M; 4/4, Andante; 3min; Diff-V/md, P/m.
For: high baritone
Mood: narrative
Voice: somewhat declamatory; speech rhythms; dramatic
Piano: mostly chords
Diff: ensemble; freedom of tempo
Uses: use in group about people (Richard Cory, etc.)

WILDING-WHITE, RAYMOND
(b. Caterham, Surrey, England, 1922)

2227. FOUR WILLIAM BLAKE SONGS. [19]. cmp1959. No key sigs., but largely tonal; bb–f#'; Tess-M; irregular changing meters; slow tempos; 5pp; Diff-V/m-d, P/m-md.
For: mezzo-soprano; dramatic soprano best for set
Mood: dramatic; intense; some lyricism
Voice: many skips; speech rhythms; dramatic dynamics; interrupted phrases; some long-ranged phrases
Piano: linear-chordal combination; colorful; articulations important; ornaments; trills; some fast passages; wide spacing; no doubling of vocal line
Diff: rhythms; ensemble
Uses: apparently excerpted from a larger set, these cohere as an effective set; program ender

    a. *The Sick Rose.* Fmin; bb–f"; 5/8, Poco adagio cantabile; 1p.
    b. *The Little Boy Lost.* Emin; c'–f#"(e"); 4/4, Andante semplice; 1p.
    c. *Soft Snow.* D-centered; c'–f"; unmetered, Poco adagio; 1p.
    d. *The Wild Flower's Song.* X; d'–f"; changing mixed meters, Allegretto; 2pp.

2228. THREE HOUSMAN POEMS (A. E. Housman). [18]. Tonal; bb–bb"; Tess-M, H & L; regular and irregular changing meters; moderate tempos; 5pp; Diff-V/m-d, P/md-d.
For: lyric soprano; possibly tenor
Mood: lyrical; love songs; nature imagery
Voice: (a.) & (b.) somewhat disjunct with short phrases; (c.), folksong-like in 8th-note motion
Piano: contrapuntal; somewhat chromatic; 8th- & 16th-note motion
Diff: pitch; rhythm; needs light, easy bb"
Uses: good recital material

    a. *The Sloe Was Lost in Flower.* X; d'–b"; Tess-H, L; 2/4, Andante; 1+pp.
    b. *In the Morning.* X; bb–g"; Tess-M; 3/8, 4/8, 5/8, 3/4, Moderato; 1+pp.
    c. *The Halfmoon Westers Low.* Fmaj; c'–bb"; Tess-M; 3/4, 2/4, 6/8, 5/8, Allegretto; 2pp.

WILLIAMS, DAVID H.
(b. Caerphilly, Wales, 1919)

2229. GOOD-BYE, MY FANCY (Walt Whitman). H. W. Gray, 1956. Bbmaj; c'–eb"; Tess-M; 4/4, Moderato; 3pp; Diff-V/me, P/m.
For: baritone
Mood: a farewell
Voice: stepwise; skips along chord lines; syncopation
Piano: 4–5-voice chordal texture; some block-, repeated-, and broken-chord patterns; incidental doubling of vocal line
Uses: attractive song for recital; group ender

WILLIAMS-WIMBERLY, LOU
(b. Amarillo, TX, 1938)

2230. WINTER (William Shakespeare). [12]. Fmaj; c'–d"; Tess-mL; 6/8, 9/8, (♩. = 60); 4pp; Diff-V/me, P/m.
For: any medium or low voice
Mood: humorously descriptive
Voice: mostly conjunct; a few large intervals; dotted rhythms
Piano: chordal; a bit of ornamentation; sometimes doubles vocal line
Diff: a few unfamiliar words
Uses: good song for a young voice

WILLIS, RICHARD STORRS
(b. Boston, MA, 1819; d. Detroit, MI, 1900)

2231. THE FOUNTAIN (Richard Storrs Willis). Ditson, 1849. Amaj; c#'–e"; Tess-M; 4/4, Moderately; 2pp (4 strophes); Diff-V/e, P/e.
For: baritone; mezzo-soprano
Mood: lyrical; philosophical; reflective; an analogy
Voice: many small skips; some dotted rhythms

Piano: broken-chord patterning; 2-meas. prelude, interlude, postlude; does not double vocal line
Uses: useful period piece

2232. **MARCH. APRIL. MAY.** Cycle. 1st pub. in 1859 in consecutive issues of the *Musical World and Times* (New York), 1859–1860. Traditional keys; c'–g "; Tess-M; regular meters; varied tempos; 8pp (with several repeats); Diff-V/me, P/me.
For: high baritone probably best
Mood: describes nature in the months of the titles; lyrical; exuberant; declamatory
Voice: stepwise; chord-member skips; many dotted rhythms; many accidentals in (b.) & (c.)
Piano: broken-chord, afterbeat, block-chord styles; interludes between strophes; does not double vocal line
Uses: when used as a group, piano has opt. modulatory passages to connect the songs; can be done without pause; could be done separately; (b.) & (c.) have interesting harmonic coloring; (c.) probably stands alone best; period pieces

   a. *March.* Cmaj; e'–g "; 3/4, Andantino; 3pp.
   b. *April.* Emaj; c'–g "; 3/8, Allegretto; 2pp (4 strophes).
   c. *May.* Cmaj-Fmaj; c'–f "; 4/4, 3/4, Recit. ad lib–Andantino; 3pp (3 strophes).

2233. **NOVEMBER** (Richard Storrs Willis). 1st pub. in *Musical World*, 1859. Amin; a–f "; Tess-M; 3/4, Andantino; 2pp (with repeat); Diff-V/m, P/me.
For: baritone
Mood: somber; dirge
Voice: mostly stepwise; some leaps of 6th; some dotted rhythms; ornaments; inverted mordent; 2-note slurs; appoggiaturas
Piano: afterbeat broken-chord pattern; 2-meas. prelude, 6-meas. Interlude and postlude; no vocal line doubling
Diff: high portion of song stretches over four consecutive meas.
Uses: useful recital song, esp. as period piece

2234. **A SONG OF REST** (also called Nocturn), No. 3 of *Love in a Cloister* (Richard Storrs Willis). 1st pub. in *The Musical World and Times* (New York), 1849. Fmaj; c'–f "; Tess-M; 3/4, Andantino; 4pp; Diff-V/me, P/e.
For: any voice; could be easily transposed
Mood: introspective; serene; song about death
Voice: stepwise; chord-member skips; features 6ths; some dotted rhythms; some 2-note slurs; graceful
Piano: chordal–afterbeats and pattern in 3rds; 2-meas. prelude, 9-meas. interlude and postlude; no vocal line doubling
Uses: useful for students; effective song for historical group

WILSON, JAMES (or JOSEPH) (See Special Section)

WILSON, RICHARD
(b. Cleveland, OH, 1941)

2235. **FIVE LOVE SONGS ON POEMS OF JOHN**

SKELTON for Voice and Piano. Southern (peermusic), 1995. X; b♯–a♯"; Tess-cs; regular meters; varied tempos (♩ = 60–100–112); 26pp; Diff-V/d, P/d.
For: tenor
Mood: warning; self-pity; worship of beloved's beauty; inebriated love play; music suggests anger and discontent
Voice: highly chromatic lines; syllabic and melismatic; rather instrumentally conceived; 15th-century English texts
Piano: dissonant; many accidentals; difficult rhythmic figures
Diff: rhythmic; harmonic; melodic; poetic; perfect pitch helpful
Uses: good ear training; challenging cycle for an advanced tenor to whom the texts appeal

   a. *Mistress Anne.* X; e♭'–g"; Tess-M; 2/4, In a rustic manner ♩ = 92; 6pp.
   b. *Go, Piteous Heart.* X; c'–g♯"; Tess-cs; 4/4, 5/4, ♩ = 58; 4pp.
   c. *Merry Margaret.* X; e♭'–g"; Tess-cs; 4/4, ♩ = 100; 4pp.
   d. *How Shall I Report?* X; b–g"; Tess-cs; 4/4, ♩ = 60; 3pp.
   e. *Mannerly Margery.* X; b♯–a♯"; Tess-cs; 4/4, 3/4, ♩ = 100–112; 8pp.

[**THE SECOND LAW.** See entry #15 P]

2236. **THREE PAINTERS** (Phyllis McGinley). For High Voice and Piano. [166]. cmp1984; premiered by Paul Sperry. X; c♯'–a♯"; Tess-M, mH, cs; regular meters; slow-slow-fast; 6pp; Diff-V/m-md, P/m.
For: tenor
Mood: sarcastically humorous
Voice: angular; speech rhythms; dissonant; syllabic
Piano: chordal; dissonant; much staccato; chromatic
Uses: humorous short set for singer with good ear
Rec: D#49

   a. *Marc Chagall.* X; c♯'–a"; Tess-cs; 4/4, 3/4, Hesitantly (♩ = 66)–With élan (♩. = 66); 2pp.
   b. *Grandma Moses.* G♭/F♯-centered; f♯'–a"; Tess-M; 4/4, Dolefully (♩ = ca. 52); 2pp.
   c. *Jackson Pollock.* X; e'–a♯"; Tess-mH; 4/4, Jauntily (♩ = 108); 2pp.

2237. **TRIBULATIONS.** [166]. cmp1980; premiered by Dawn Upshaw. X; b–a♭"; Tess-M, cs; changing meters; moderate tempos; 15pp; Diff-V/m-md, P/md-d.
For: soprano
Mood: somewhat macabre humor
Voice: conjunct and disjunct lines; dissonant; syllabic; two songs strophic; some speech rhythms
Piano: dissonant; double 8ves; tremolos; arpeggios; chordal textures; many accidentals
Diff: pitches; some rhythms; perfect pitch helpful
Uses: as a set or excerpt for use in other humorous groups; for advanced performers

   a. *Careless Talk* (Mark Hollis). X; d'–g"; Tess-wide; 5/4, 4/4, (♩ = ca.104); 2pp.
   b. *As into the Garden Elizabeth Ran* (A. E.

Housman). X; c♯'–g"; Tess-cs; 3/4, ♩. = 56–69; 6pp.

c. *Mother Doesn't Want a Dog* (Judith Viorst). X; c'–a♭"; Tess-cs; 4/4, Freely (♩ = 66–88); 2pp.

d. *Henry King* (Hilaire Belloc). X; b–g♭"; Tess-cs; 3/4, 4/4, 5/4, ♩ = 120; 3pp.

e. *The Purist* (Ogden Nash). X; c'–f♯"; Tess-M; 4/4, 5/4, ♩ = 84; 2pp.

WOLF, DANIEL
(b. Baltimore, MD, 1894; d. New York, NY, 1962)

2238.   JACK-IN-THE-BOX (Mabel Livingstone). Carl Fischer, 1951. X; d♯'–c'''(g"); Tess-M; 4/4, Giocoso; 1+min; Diff-V/md, P/md.

For: soprano
Mood: cheerful; jovial; naive; speaker is a child
Voice: many leaps; repetition and sequence; various rhythmic divisions of beat; speech rhythms
Piano: rapid arpeggios and chromatic scale passages; block chords; sound effects; many accidentals; various registers; various subdivisions of beat; syncopation; does not double vocal line
Diff: some pitches; awkward intervals; sustained g" at end
Uses: clever, colorful song; program ender; encore

WOLFE, JACQUES
(b. Botoshan, Rumania, 1896; d. Sarasota, FL, 1973)

2239.   THE NEWS CAME (Eric von der Goltz). Carl Fischer, 1949. Cmaj; e♭'–f"; Tess-M; 4/4, Moderately slow; 5pp; Diff-V/m, P/d.

For: lyric baritone; mezzo-soprano
Mood: lyrical; spring song with a popular flavor
Voice: skips prominent; repeated tones (g'); long tones; ends sustained e" on "spring"; melodically repetitious
Piano: patterned; polyrhythms with syncopation; mild jazz flavor; pianist should have excellent sense of rhythm and a large reach
Diff: mostly for the pianist
Uses: effective song for the right situation; contrasting "spring" song

WOLPE, STEFAN
(b. Berlin, Germany, 1902; d. New York, NY, 1972)

2240.   SIX SONGS FROM THE HEBREW. McGinnis and Marx, 1962. Pub. separately; separate entries below.

NOTE: Except for "Song of Songs," Hebrew texts are given for all songs and can be sung in place of the English texts; four songs in bass clef seem to go together as a set for bass-baritone.

A.   **LILACS** (Noach Stern; trans. Hilda Morley). X; a♭–f♯"; Tess-mL; 12/8, 9/8, Quiet; 1min; Diff-V/d, P/md.

For: mezzo-soprano; contralto; bass-baritone; bass
Mood: remembrance and the present fruition of life
Voice: rather disjunct; 8th-note motion; duplets; many accidentals

Piano: chordal-linear combination; many accidentals; rolled chords; syncopation; some doubling of vocal line
Diff: disjunct melodic line
Uses: rather bleak setting; use with other songs from the set; pair with "Song of Songs" (see below)

B.   **ON A MURAL BY DIEGO RIVERA** (Noach Stern; trans. Hilda Morley). cmp1939. X; G♯–e♭' (𝄢); Tess-M, mH; changing regular and irregular meters; 7pp; Diff-V/d, P/d.

For: bass-baritone
Mood: dramatic; powerful; ironic; barbaric; describes implications of the painting
Voice: chromatic; many skips; some long-ranged phrases
Piano: chordal structure rather brutal, barbaric; complex articulations; 16 meas. solo material
Diff: high tessitura; needs mature singer with dramatic flair
Uses: group opener or ender; dramatic, full ending

C.   **DAVID'S LAMENT OVER JONATHAN** (II Samuel:19–21, 24, 27). X; F–e♭' (𝄢); Tess-wide; changing regular and irregular meters, Quiet; 4pp; Diff-V/d, P/d.

For: bass-baritone
Mood: dramatic; energetic and powerful; lament for fallen warriors
Voice: long-ranged phrases; dotted rhythms; many accidentals and dynamic markings; Middle-Eastern ornamentation
Piano: linear; some work inside piano; complex rhythms; cluster chords; dramatic dynamic changes; blurred pedal effects; does not double vocal line
Diff: secure musicianship needed; voice must be both powerful and flexible
Uses: best with other songs in set

D.   **LINES FROM THE PROPHET MICAH** (Micah 2: 1–2; 7:3–4). X; B–f' (𝄢); Tess-M-H; 5/2, 4/2, 3/2, 1/2, Allegro con brio; 8pp; Diff-V/d, P/d.

For: dramatic baritone
Mood: dramatic; powerful; "Woe to the haughty who work in evil"
Voice: much chromaticism; skips include tritones & aug.2nds; easy rhythms
Piano: linear-chordal combination; chromaticism; many 8ves; 15 meas. solo material
Diff: powerful delivery needed
Uses: fine recital song for mature singer

E.   **ISAIAH** (Isaiah 65:17–22a, 25; English based on King James trans.). X; B♭–e♭' (𝄢); Tess-M; 2/2, 3/8, 3/4, 3/2, Con moto; 11pp; Diff-V/d, P/md-d.

For: baritone; bass
Mood: declamatory; prophecies of life to come
Voice: disjunct; declamatory; many accidentals; easy rhythms; some long-ranged phrases
Piano: linear; many accidentals; complex harmonically and melodically; complex articulations; incidental doubling of vocal line
Diff: perfect pitch desirable; no rest or recovery spots for singer; ensemble
Uses: excellent song for the right voice; big, dramatic ending; group or recital ender

F. **SONG OF SONGS** (Songs of Songs 5:10–12; 2:5; 5: 13–15; 2:5; 5:16; 2:5). X; b–f♯"; Tess-M; 2/4 with many changes, Alive; 10pp; Diff-V/d, P/d.
For: mezzo-soprano; dramatic soprano
Mood: sensuous; total effect is disjunct, almost demented; Eastern flavor
Voice: many skips, often difficult; many accidentals; some difficult rhythms; has refrain (2:5 in text [see above])
Piano: linear; much chromaticism; articulations extensively marked; many color effects (trills, glissando, grace notes, rolled chords); polyrhythms
Diff: musical security and mature voice needed; ensemble will require work
Uses: pair with "Lilacs" (see above).

WOOD, ABRAHAM (See Special Section)

WOOD, JEFFREY
(b. Allentown, PA, 1954)

2241. **THE REAR-GUARD** (Siegfried Sassoon). [9]. E minorish underlying dissonance; e'–a"; Tess-mH; 3/4, March-like ♩= 60; 5min; Diff-V/md, P/md.
For: tenor
Mood: dark and nightmarish; hellish experience of war in WWI
Voice: melodic recitation over relentless repeated motive in piano; conjunct melodic patterns; speech rhythms; wide range of dynamic markings throw emotional tension of text into bold relief
Piano: insistent repeated motive in r.h. over chant-like melody in l.h. 8ves or dissonant chords; many dynamic details
Diff: intensity of dark and frightful mood
Uses: excellent work for graduate or professional level singer; reminiscent of Rorem's *War Scenes*

WOOD, KEVIN
(b. Bronx, NY, 1947)

2242. **ANTS WILL NOT EAT YOUR FINGERS.** Three Songs to African Poems. [3]. X; b–g"; Tess-mL-mH; traditional meters; 5pp; Diff-V/md, P/m.
For: mezzo-soprano; soprano
Mood: simple thoughts–(a.), troubled, (b.), wryly humorous, and (c.), in praise of agriculture
Voice: many small skips; many accidentals (no key sigs.); duplets and triplets juxtaposed; chant-like; dynamics *p–ff*; syllabic
Piano: block structures in 2nds, 3rds, 4ths, 5ths, & 7ths; quarter-note motion in (a.) & (c.), dotted-quarter motion in (b.); does not double vocal line
Diff: getting pitches in (a.) & (b.); rhythms
Uses: possible recital group for singer who has this range

    a. *Girl's Song* (Hlubi; trans. A. C. Jordan). X; e♭'–g"; 4/4, 2/4, Semplice; 2pp.
    b. *Second Song* (Hima; trans. Hugh Tracey). C-centered; c'–c"; 12/8, Jocund; 1p.
    c. *Ants Will Not Eat Your Fingers* (Gurage; trans.

Wolf Leslau). Amin; b–f♯"; 4/4, Maestoso; 2pp.

WOODBURY, ISAAC BAKER
(b. Beverly, MA, 1819; d. Columbia, SC, 1858)

2243. **STARS OF THE SUMMER NIGHT** (Henry Wadsworth Longfellow). [23] and other familiar collections, such as *The Golden Book of Favorite Songs*. 1st pub. in the 1840s or 1850s. E♭maj (available in various keys); e♭'–c"; Tess-M; 4/4, 3 strophes, 13meas. each; Diff-V/e, P/e.
For: any male voice; easily transposed
Mood: lyrical; serenade
Voice: stepwise; skips on chord lines; easy rhythms
Piano: 4-part harmony; simple setting; doubles vocal line
Uses: well-worn song of general appeal; useful in serenade or historical group

2244. **STRIKE THE HARP GENTLY** (Isaac Baker Woodbury). [23]; 1st©1849. A♭maj; e♭'–d♭"; Tess-M; 3/4, Andante affetuoso; 5pp (3 strophes); Diff-V/me, P/me.
For: any voice; easily transposed
Mood: lyrical; quiet; sentimental memorial song
Voice: stepwise; skips on chord lines; some dotted rhythms
Piano: 4-voice block- and broken-chord patterns; staccato chords; little doubling of vocal line
Uses: useful as a period piece

WOODMAN, R. HUNTINGTON
(b. Brooklyn, NY, 1861; d. Brooklyn, NY, 1943)

2245. **I AM THY HARP** (Emily Murray). [48]. H & L keys: Fmaj & D♭maj; c'–g" & a♭–e♭"; Tess-mH; 3/2, Andante sostenuto; 3pp; Diff-V/m, P/me.
For: any voice
Mood: lyrical and serene
Voice: sustained phrases, mostly conjunct motion; one 8ve leap downward from song's climax; several high-lying phrases
Piano: broken and arpeggiated chords throughout, imitative of the harp; some accidentals; supports vocal line clearly
Diff: sustaining high-lying phrases; maintaining musicality in continuously arpeggiated chords for pianist (arpeggiation might well be abandoned in *animato* section, for contrast)
Uses: possibilities for performance in various situations

2246. **MY HEART IS A LUTE** (Lady Lindsay). G. Schirmer, 1913. Dmin; d'–f♯"; Tess-M; 3/4, Andante; 2pp; Diff-V/me, P/e.
For: soprano; tenor
Mood: lyrical; sad; love song
Voice: stepwise; easy skips; several 2-note slurs
Piano: broken- and repeated-chord patterns; afterbeat pattern at climax; little doubling of vocal line
Diff: big climax (not sustained)
Uses: period piece

WORK, JOHN WESLEY
(b. Tullahoma, TN, 1901; d. Nashville, TN, 1968)

2247. **DANCING IN THE SUN** (Howard Weedun). [6].
E♭maj; g'–a♭"; Tess-H; 4/4, 2/4, 3/4, Andantino; 3pp;
Diff-V/m, P/md.
For: soprano; tenor
Mood: humorous; descriptive
Voice: diatonic; regular, dance-like rhythmic patterns
Piano: chordal–broken or afterbeats; supports and occasionally
        doubles vocal line
Diff: high tessitura
Uses: clever recital song; group ender

2248. **DUSK AT SEA** (Thomas S. Jones, Jr.). [47]. E♭min;
e♭'–a"; Tess-mH; 4/4, Lento e vago; 3pp; Diff-V/m,
P/m.
For: tenor; soprano
Mood: atmospheric
Voice: some skips of 5th & 6th; many accidentals; speech-like
        rhythms; fragmented phrases
Piano: broken- and repeated-chord patterns; many accidentals;
        somewhat awkward to play; some vocal line doubling
Diff: several g"s; final note sustained *pp–ppp*
Uses: useful recital song

2249. **A MONA LISA** (A. Grimke). [47]. Ends C♯min;
c♯'–g"; Tess-M; 6/8, 4/8, 4/4, 2/4, Andantino e
tranquillamente; 3pp; Diff-V/m, P/m.
For: tenor
Mood: lyrical; quiet; love song
Voice: phrases range at least one 8ve; sudden key changes;
        some syncopation
Piano: melody in 8ves; block and broken chords; soft tremolo;
        countermelody skillfully combined; some doubling of
        vocal line
Diff: fairly long phrases must arch smoothly; good dynamic
        and register control
Uses: good recital song

2250. **SOLILOQUY** (MyrtleVorst Sheppard). Galaxy, 1946.
[6]. Fmaj–Cmaj; d'–a♭"; Tess-M-mH; 4/2, Lento;
3+min; Diff-V/m, P/e.
For: tenor; soprano
Mood: lyrical; philosophical; sweetness of life, no fear of
        death
Voice: conjunct; some long tones
Piano: chordal–repeated and broken figurations; harmonically
        simple
Uses: nice song; quiet; good for breath control

2251. **THREE GLIMPSES OF NIGHT** (Frank Davis). [17].
"To Louis Nicholas." H & L keys: Cmin & Amin;
f♯'–g" & d♯'–e"; Tess-mH; 4/4, 6/4, Andantino; 5pp;
Diff-V/md, P/d.
For: any high or medium voice
Mood: humorously descriptive
Voice: *quasi recit.* at beginning; fragmented
Piano: rapid afterbeat figures; rapid scale passage work
Diff: rhythm; sustained g"(e") at end
Uses: good recital song

WUORINEN, CHARLES
(b. New York, NY, 1938)

2252. **A SONG TO THE LUTE IN MUSICKE** (ascribed to
Richard Edwards, 16th century). C. F. Peters, 1975.
cmp1969–1970. Atonal; g–a"; Tess-wide; constantly
changing meters, ♪ = 72; 3min; Diff-V/dd, P/dd.
For: soprano
Mood: theme: music soothes the troubled mind
Voice: disjunct; highly complex in pitch and rhythm; wide
        leaps; awkward intervals; independent of piano part
Piano: linear; no patterning; disjunct with wide leaps; many
        accidentals; complex rhythms; some special effects
Diff: requires rhythmic and pitch independence, advanced
        vocal technique, and easily accessible wide range

WYNER, YEHUDI
(b. Calgary, Alberta, Canada, 1929)

2253. **DISILLUSIONMENT OF TEN O'CLOCK** (Wallace
Stevens). For Soprano and Piano. American Composers
Alliance (Composers Facsimile Edition), 1979.
cmp1979. X; c♯'–a♭"; Tess-wide; changing meters,
Animated and flexible (with several changes); 3min;
Diff-V/dd, P/dd.
For: soprano specified
Mood: surreal
Voice: disjunct; complex rhythms involving various
        subdivisions of beat and meas.; polyrhythms against
        accomp.; some words separated by rests; mostly
        syllabic; a few 2-note slurs
Piano: predominantly linear; disjunct; many accidentals;
        highly complex rhythms; many articulation markings;
        considerable staccato; does not double vocal line
Diff: in all areas; perfect pitch desirable; many entrances
        hard to hear; ensemble; making the words understood
Uses: for two excellent musicians; probably more accessible
        than some other pieces of this kind, due to its shorter
        length; music matches surreal quality of poetry well

2254. **PSALMS AND EARLY SONGS.** Associated, 1972.
Four songs printed and bound together, although not
really related; separate entries below.

A.   **EXEUNT** (Richard Wilbur). [4]. cmp1954. D-centered;
a–f"; Tess-M; 4/4 with changes; 2pp; Diff-V/m, P/md.
For: mezzo-soprano; baritone
Mood: descriptive of end of summer
Voice: some skips; syncopation; syllabic
Piano: imitates crickets and other sounds of summer;
        juxtaposes triplets and duplets; many accidentals; some
        wide reaches
Diff: singer's pitches often in 2nds with piano
Uses: nice mood picture for "summer songs" or American
        group

B.   **PSALM 66.** cmp1950; rev.1967. C♯-centered; a–f♯";
Tess-M; 4/4 with changes, Fast, energetic; 4pp;
Diff-V/md, P/md.
For: mezzo-soprano; baritone; contralto
Mood: joyful; praising God

Voice: mostly conjunct; some skips; mostly syllabic; some melismas; syncopation
Piano: constant 8th-note motion; repeated chords; l.h. melody counters vocal line; some large reaches
Diff: rhythms; abrupt pattern changes; needs full sound
Uses: useful for church or recital; exciting setting; program ender; pair with "Psalm 119"

C. PSALM 119. cmp1950; rev.1967. G#-centered (some quartal structures and many vertical 2nds); a–f "; Tess-L; 3/2, 4/2, 5/2; 3pp; Diff-V/m, P/m.
For: mezzo-soprano; contralto; baritone; possibly bass
Mood: somber; resigned; respect for God
Voice: some juxtaposing of duplets and triplets; dotted rhythms; syllabic; speech-like
Piano: climax of song in piano part; some wide reaches; bell-like effects
Diff: mature sound most effective
Uses: for church or recital; pair with "Psalm 66"

D. WHEN YOU ARE OLD (William Butler Yeats). cmp1951. A-centered; a–e "; Tess-M; 9/8, 6/8, 12/8, Slowly; 3pp; Diff-V/md, P/md.
For: baritone; contralto; mezzo-soprano; possibly bass
Mood: somber; contemplative; undying love
Voice: some melismas; abrupt key and pattern changes; wide-ranged phrases; imitation between voice and piano
Piano: 8th-note motion; many accidentals; some staccato; prelude and interludes
Uses: probably intended to be paired with the composer's "Exeunt" (see above); group with other American recital songs

YATES, RONALD
(b. Muskegon, MI, 1947)

2255. MORNING (Luis G. Urbina; trans. Alice Stone Blackwell). [12]. Emin; c'–e "; Tess-M; 4/4, Adagio (♩ = c.80); 3pp.; Diff-V/me, P/me.
For: any medium voice; better for women's voices
Mood: lyrical and tender
Voice: mostly conjunct motion; a few intervals
Piano: melody in r.h. with broken-chord figuration in l.h.; doubles vocal line throughout
Diff: lowered 7th step of scale, although doubled in piano
Uses: useful for a young voice

2256. WINDMILLS (Jose Santos Chocano; trans. Alice Stone Blackwell). [12]. Dmin; d '–e "; Tess-M; 3/8, 4/4, 9/8, Quickly (♪ = c.126)–Slow (♩ = c.60); 3+min; Diff-V/me, P/m.
For: any medium voice
Mood: descriptive, becoming philosophical; reference to Don Quixote
Voice: mostly conjunct; a few small intervals
Piano: almost constantly moving 16ths in melodic and Alberti-bass patterns, suggesting the windmill; clearly supports vocal line
Diff: some meter changes in bridge between strophes
Uses: could be effective for a young singer

YOUNG, GORDON
(b. McPherson, KS, 1919; d. St. Clair Shores, MI, 1998)

2257. REQUIESCAT (Oscar Wilde). Galaxy, 1954. Fmin; c'–f "; Tess-M; 3/4, Andante lamentoso; 3min; Diff-V/m, P/m.
For: high baritone
Mood: lyrical; subdued; dirge
Voice: easy skips; repeated tones; duplets and triplets; somewhat fragmentary
Piano: built over pedal tones; countermelody; 4-voice texture, repeated chords; syncopation; incidental doubling of vocal line
Diff: ensemble
Uses: good song

YOUSE, GLAD ROBINSON
(b. Miami, OK, 1898; d. Baxter Springs, KS, 1985)

2258. THE LITTLE LOST BOY (Grace Noll Crowell). (Peer)Southern, 1950. Cmaj; d#'–f "; Tess-mL; 3/8, Allegretto; 3pp; Diff-V/me, P/m.
For: soprano; mezzo-soprano
Mood: lyrical; philosophical; sentimental
Voice: short phrases; somewhat parlando in style
Piano: afterbeats and arpeggiations; a few independent melodic motives; vocal line doubled in middle section
Uses: useful for young students.

ZAIMONT, JUDITH LANG
(b. Memphis, TN, 1945)

2259. IN THE THEATER OF NIGHT. Six Dream Songs on Poems of Karl Shapiro. For High Voice and Piano. Cycle. Galaxy, 1986. Commissioned for 1st Petit Jean International Art Song Festival, 1983. X; b–d'''(e'''); Tess-wide. H; changing meters; 53pp (MS); Diff-V/dd, P/dd+.
For: soprano (with flexibility)
Mood: dream-like, almost surreal; a series of scenes and ideas held together by interludes with "dream" theme
Voice: complex pitch patterns and rhythms in avant-garde style; some lengthy melismas with difficult patterns; portamentos (one on trilled r); 4-meas. whistled section; cross-accents; many dynamic markings
Piano: uses wide range of keyboard; difficult score (chromaticism, rhythms, rapidity of patterning, etc.) with many special effects (e.g., glissandos, pedal effects, one hand used to damp strings while other plays on keys); in "Flyers" some pitch patterns repeated as fast as possible as many times as necessary; in "Piano" the piano part resembles an etude by Franz Liszt, but in contemporary musical terms
Diff: in all aspects, esp. ensemble; the two performers will need to work closely together, for many hours
Uses: for two excellent musicians attuned to and experienced in this idiom; it could be electric with the right performers; music is continuous, with short pauses between movements

    a. *Introduction.* X; e'–g"; changing meters,
        Rhapsodic–Slow; 2pp.

    b. *Flyers.* X; e♭'–a"; changing meters, Allegretto–
        Presto–Calmly; 5pp.

    c. *Interlude #1.* X; f'–a♭"; changing meters,
        Rhapsodic–Waltz; 1p.

    d. *The Alphabet.* X; c'–a"; changing meters, Stern–
        Majestic–Più mosso; 7pp.

    e. *Interlude #2.* X; f'–g♯"; changing meters,
        Rhapsodic–Waltz; ½ p.

    f. *A Cut Flower.* X; e'–a♯"(d'''); changing meters,
        Fleetly; 8pp.

    g. *Interlude #3.* X; f'–a♭"; changing meters,
        Slowly–Waltz; 1p.

    h. *Calling the Child.* X; b–c'''; changing meters, Fast
        waltz; 8pp.

    i. *Madrigal.* X; e♭'–d'''(e'''); changing meters, Swiftly
        with sly good humor; 5pp.

    j. *Interlude #4.* X; f'–b♭"; changing meters,
        Recitative; 1p.

    k. *Piano.* X; e'–d♭'''; changing meters, Slow–
        Recitative, freely–Più mosso, etc.; 11pp.

    l. *Postlude.* X; e'–b♭"; changing meters, Fluidly–
        Recitative, freely rhapsodic; 3pp.

2260. **SOLILOQUY** (Edna St. Vincent Millay). [3]. X;
d♯'–a"; Tess-mH; 3/4 with many changes, Slow; 5pp;
Diff-V/d, P/d.

For: dramatic soprano (or large lyric voice)

Mood: remembering a lost love; dramatic

Voice: disjunct; many accidentals; complex rhythms; has little
          pitch relationship to piano part; dramatic dynamic
          changes

Piano: difficult to read; written on 3 staves (except for 13
          meas.); many accidentals; thick texture–linear and
          chromatic; r.h. usually moves in 16th-note 3rds

Diff: in all aspects, esp. ensemble

Uses: for two excellent musicians; capability of *ff* singing on
          lowest and highest pitches

ZWILICH, ELLEN TAAFFE

[See Appendix for songs with German text]

Appendix

Compositions with Foreign-Language Texts

French

BARBER, SAMUEL
(b. West Chester, PA, 1910; d. New York, NY, 1981)

A 1. **MÉLODIES PASSAGÈRES**, Op. 27 (Rainer Maria Rilke). Cycle. [79]. cmp1950–51. "To Francis Poulenc and Pierre Bernac." H & L keys: Traditional tonal centers (except (e.)); d'–bb"(g") & b–ab"(f"); Tess-mH; regular meters with a few changes; moderate to slow tempos; 14pp; Diff-V/d, P/d.

For: all voices
Mood: lyrical; fleeting images and hopes
Voice: stepwise; small skips; a few leaps of 7th in (a.) & (b.); some chromaticism; triplets; 2 vs. 3 in piano in (a., b., & e.); greater rhythmic complexity in (b.); syllabic with a few 2-note slurs; French texts only (literal English trans. given)
Piano: chordal–block, broken, and rolled; countermelodies in (a.) & (e.); some chromaticism; triplets; 3 vs. 5 in (b.); 3-stave writing in (d.); impressionistic style; does not double vocal line
Diff: rhythm; some pitches; achieving the delicate, clear, impressionistic French style of the songs
Uses: excellent recital material
Rec: D#s 99, 102

    a. *Puisque tout passe.* H & L keys: Bmin & G♯min; e'–g" & c♯'–e"; 4/4, 3/4, 3/8, Moderato (♩ = 66); 2pp.

    b. *Un cygne.* H & L keys: Emin & C♯min; e'–f♯" & c♯'–d♯"; 4/4, 3/2, Moderato (♩ = 84); 4pp.

    c. *Tombeau dans un parc.* H & L keys: Aeolian on A & Aeolian on F♯; d'–g" & b–e"; 4/4, 3/2, Lento e sereno (♩ = 52); 2pp.

    d. *Le clocher chante.* H & L keys: Gmin & Fmin; d'–bb"(g") & c'–ab"(f"); 4/4, 3/2, 2/4, Non troppo allegro (♩ = 84); 4pp.

    e. *Départ.* H & L keys: X; f'–g" & eb'–f"; 4/4, Molto lento (♩ = 44); 2pp.

BEACH, AMY MARCY CHENEY (MRS. H. H. A.)
(b. Henniker, NH, 1867; d. New York, NY, 1944)

[See also main list: 204 & 218]

A 2. **EXTASE**, Op. 21, No. 2 (Victor Hugo; Eng. trans. given). [11, Vol. 1]. F♯min-maj; b♯–a♯"; Tess-cs; 3/4, Lento con espressione; 5pp; Diff-V/md, P/md.

For: soprano (lyric)
Mood: meditative ecstasy; all nature worships its Creator
Voice: melody moves along chord lines–legato, floating, sustained; dynamics predominantly soft; only two *f* phrases; expressive markings; some *messa di voce*; French text only; some long phrases
Piano: chordal texture–rolled, broken, afterbeat, arpeggiated, softly repeated, contrary motion; shimmering romantic harmonies
Diff: some long phrases; soft dynamics
Uses: luminous song; good recital material
Rec: D#110

A 3. **JE DEMAND À L'OISEAU** (For My Love) (Armand Silvestre; Eng. text by Mme Isidora Martinez). Arthur P. Schmidt, 1903. Reprint: Classical Vocal Reprints. [11, Vol. 1]. Ebmaj; bb–f"; Tess-M; 3/4, Lento con espressione; 3pp; Diff-V/m, P/m.

For: mezzo-soprano; lyric baritone
Mood: a messenger song; love is carried to distant beloved by birds, the breeze, the sun; quiet ecstasy
Voice: conjunct lines; many triplets; *pp* beginning and ending
Piano: block chords provide harmonic motion; some inner-voice triplets
Uses: lovely song for teaching line and soft singing; French or English text usable

A 4. **JUNI (JUNE)**, Op. 51, No. 3 (Erich Jansen). Arthur P. Schmidt, 1903. Reprint: Classical Vocal Reprints. Eng. text given. [81, 82, vol.4]. Fmaj; f'–g"(a"); Tess-mH; 9/8, Allegro assai; 4pp; Diff-V/m, P/m.

For: soprano; tenor
Mood: ecstatic; in praise of the blossoms of June
Voice: mostly stepwise with some skips; a few leaps of 6th, 7th, & 8ve; some tempo fluctuations; syllabic; ends high, *ff*
Piano: repeated-chord style; some tremolo; some melody in l.h.; big ending typical of the romantic style
Diff: ending phrase may be difficult for heavier voices
Uses: could end a group of French romantic songs; English version given also
Rec: D#109

BERG, CHRISTOPHER
(b. Detroit, MI, 1949)

A 5. **HOMMAGE À FRANCIS POULENC** (Robert Desnos). Five Little Songs for Voice and Piano. Tender Tender Music, 2000 (Classical Vocal Reprints). cmp1999. Transitory; bb(b)–g"; Tess-mL-mH; regular meters; varied tempos; 10pp; Diff-V/m-md, P/m-md.

For: mezzo-soprano; high baritone
Mood: humorous in manner of Poulenc's *Le Bestiaire*
Voice: much repetition and sequence; mostly stepwise; small skips; some awkward intervals of aug.2, aug.4th, m7th, m9th; many accidentals; syllabic; some polyrhythms (3 vs. 4); syncopation; otherwise easy rhythms; rhythmic text painting in (a.); French texts
Piano: text painting, scene setting; broken and block chords, various textures; many accidentals; ornamentation; some large reaches; some doubling of vocal line; short preludes in (c.) & (e.); short postludes in (a.) & (c.)
Diff: some rhythms and intervals; a few puns, plays on words; no translations given
Uses: clever songs on clever poetry; a light humorous group for recital; audience appeal

    a. *Le Brochet* [The Pike]. Unsettled, B♭ ending; b♭(e♭')–f"; Tess-M; 2/4, 3/4, 3/8, ♩ = 84; 2pp.
    b. *Le Homard* [The Lobster]. Cmin/B♭maj; b–d"; Tess-mL; 5/4, 6/4, 4/4, Lourd et solennel; 1p.
    c. *Le Ver Luisant* [The Glowworm]. G-centered; c♯'–e" Tess-M; 3/4, Valse lente ♩ = 96; 2+pp.
    d. *Le Blaireau* [The Badger]. Unsettled; d♯'–g"; Tess-mH; 2/4, ♩ = 126, avec enthousiasme; 2pp.
    e. *La Fourmi* [The Ant]. Unsettled/Lydian; c♯'–f"; Tess-mH; 3/2, Andante maestoso; 2pp.

A 6.   **LA MOISSON** (Robert Desnos). Tender Tender Music, 1999 (Classical Vocal Reprints). cmp1999. Tonal, shifting harmonies; c♯'–g♭"; Tess-M; 3/2, Misurato, mesto ♩ = 56; 5pp; Diff-V/md, P/md.
For: lyric baritone seems best
Mood: luminous
Voice: lyrical; sustained; syllabic; floating legato line; French text only
Piano: chordal; shifting harmonies; some arpeggiated chords; soft throughout
Diff: sustaining luminous, floating mood throughout
Uses: a beautiful song; demands beauty of sound and exquisite legato line floating on the breath

BERGER, JEAN
(b. Hamm, Germany, 1909)

A 7.   **QUATRE CHANTS D'AMOUR.** Sheppard, 1975. cmp1937. Traditional keys; d♭'–b"; Tess-H; regular meters; varied tempos; 16pp; Diff-V/m, P/m.
For: soprano; tenor
Mood: lyrical love songs; two songs mourn the torments and loss of love, two celebrate the gifts of love
Voice: many skips, some large; some polyrhythms; many accidentals; syllabic; ends on extended a"
Piano: large reaches; cross-hands; mostly chordal textures; many accidentals
Diff: some awkward declamation–does not always match music well; if performer follows stress of poetry rather than bar-line stress, most problems will be solved
Uses: nice set for high lyric soprano; good undergraduate recital material

    a. *C'est fait, il n'en faut plus parler* (Charles

d'Orleans). G♭maj; d♭'–b♭"(g♭"); Tess-mH; 4/4, 3/4, Infiniment calme; 3pp.
    b. *Qui nombre à* (Joachim de Bellay). Bmin-maj; d♯'–b"; Tess-H; 3/4, 6/4, Assez vite; 6pp.
    c. *Blanche comm' lys* (Guillaume de Machaut). Modal, ends Fmaj; d'–g"; Tess-H; 6/4, Très modéré; 3pp.
    d. *Vivons mignarde* (Jean Antoine de Baïf). Dmaj; f♯'–b"; Tess-H; 2/4, Assez vite; 4pp.

CARPENTER, JOHN ALDEN
(b. Park Ridge, IL, 1876; d. Chicago, IL, 1951)

[See also main list: 422]

A 8.   **FOUR POEMS BY PAUL VERLAINE** (trans. Henry Chapman & Helen Dudley). 1912. Reprints: Classical Vocal Reprints (C. & D., Med.); Masters Music Publications (all); T.I.S. (A., B., & D., Med.). Both French and English texts seem workable; in some cases, the French is better set. All songs do not seem to be for the same voice; separate entries below.

A.   **CHANSON D'AUTOMNE.** B♭min; b–c♯"; Tess- L; 4/4, Lent et grave; Diff-V/me, P/e.
For: bass; contralto
Mood: lyrical; dirge
Voice: slow; sustained; low; dark; repeated tones
Piano: slow chords; ground bass
Diff: soft singing in low tessitura
Uses: excellent song for bass or contralto; good for teaching breath control

B.   **LE CIEL.** Bmaj; c♯'–f♯"; Tess-M; 4/4, Simply and naturally, Lent; 3+min; Diff-V/m, P/m.
For: soprano; mezzo-soprano with easy top
Mood: atmospheric–regretful, nostalgic; final page intense
Voice: stepwise; somewhat chromatic; speech rhythms
Piano: chordal; thin, transparent; bell-like sounds; some block chords; some scales and arpeggios; big climax; quiet ending; does not double vocal line
Diff: big climax on f♯"; dynamic control
Uses: nice song; recital use

C.   **DANSONS LA GIGUE!** Dmaj; b–e"; Tess-M; 3/4, 3/2, Con moto; 2min; Diff-V/me, P/m.
For: baritone
Mood: sprightly; dance-like; remembrance of past love
Voice: stepwise and skips on chord lines; long tones; easy rhythms
Piano: linear; spare texture; Latin flavor; dance-like; ostinato-like bass line varied by articulations; does not double vocal line
Diff: in English trans., word "jig" is on sustained tones–perhaps it could be pronounced "gigue" for a better sustaining vowel
Uses: not as good as other three in this set; could end a group
Rec: D#27

D.   **IL PLEURE DANS MON COEUR.** Dmin; d'–d"; Tess-M; 6/8, Modéré; 1+min; Diff-V/me, P/me.

For: mezzo-soprano; contralto; baritone
Mood: lyrical; somber; hypnotic
Voice: conjunct; rhythms not complicated
Piano: pitch d repeated throughout; block chords; does not double vocal line
Uses: usable song; quite different concept from the setting by Debussy
Rec: D#27

CRESTON, PAUL
(b. New York, NY, 1906; d. San Diego, CA, 1985)

A 9. **LA LETTRE,** Op. 59 (Anon., French). Music Graphics Press, 1978 (Presser). D♭maj; f'–a♭"; Tess-mH; 3/4, Andante; 4pp; Diff-V/md, P/m.
For: soprano
Mood: loving; caressing; a love letter
Voice: long phrases; some enharmonic notation; 2 vs. 3; repeated notes
Piano: lush harmonies; arpeggiated l.h.; accidentals; wide reach helpful; 2 vs. 3
Diff: 2 vs. 3 between voice and piano
Uses: in a group of French songs by American composers

FENNIMORE, JOSEPH
(b. New York, NY, 1940)

A 10. **BERLITZ: INTRODUCTION TO FRENCH** (from Berlitz: *French for Travelers*). Cycle. G. Schirmer, 1974. Reprint: Classical Vocal Reprints. Traditional keys, but many altered chord structures and modulations; a–a"; Tess-M-mH (mezzo), M-L (sop.); regular and irregular meters with changes; varied tempos appropriate to each text; 28pp; Diff-V/d, P/d.
For: mezzo-soprano with good high tones; soprano with full middle and good chest voice
Mood: wildly funny
Voice: many leaps; speech rhythms; some speaking; many expressive markings; fast articulation; French text only
Piano: highly programmatic accomps.; pianist needs secure technique, good rhythmic sense, and ability to project the humor of the scenes with the piano; imagination required and knowledge of the entire French text
Diff: pitch; rhythms; once learned, should present no problems; voice must be flexible
Uses: wonderfully funny cycle for the right singer; singer must know French and must have a flair for comedy; should appeal to most audiences; good program ender
Rec: D#176

    a. *Before You Land.* e'–g♯"; 2/4 with changes, Quickly ♩= 152; 2pp.
    b. *When You Go Sightseeing.* a–a"; 5/8 with changes, Fast ♩= 138; 5pp.
    c. *At Your Hotel.* b–d"; 3/2 with changes, Slow, sadly.
    d. *When You Go Shopping.* b–a♭"; 2/2 with changes, Sprightly ♩= 88; 5pp.
    e. *Is There a Doctor in the House?* a–a"; 3/4, 2/4, Lugubrious ♩= 52; 2pp.
    f. *If You Travel by Car.* b–a"; 6/4 with changes, Fast

    ♩= 208; 5pp.
    g. *And Not to Forget Romance!* a–g"; 4/4 with changes, Tender, freely ♩= 63; 2pp.
    h. *In an Emergency.* a♭–g♯"; 4/4 with changes, ♩= 152; 5pp.

FERKO, FRANK
(b. Barberton, OH, 1950)

A 11. **CHANSON D'AUTOMNE** (Paul Verlaine). E. C. Schirmer, 1999. cmp1978. X; A–e♯' (?); Tess-mL; unmetered, Moderately slow; 3pp; Diff-V/md, P/md.
For: baritone
Mood: melancholy memories
Voice: irregular barring makes rhythms difficult; mostly conjunct; one leap of 9th; many accidentals; e♯" is to be sung *pp*; French text only
Piano: repeated chords (mostly non-tertian), often in both hands, change registers often; 8th-note motion; many accidentals; cross-hands; does not double vocal line; short prelude and interlude
Diff: irregular meas. and phrase lengths; rhythms
Uses: with another Ferko song; or with other Verlaine texts

A 12. **THREE SONGS ON POEMS OF MALLARMÉ** for Soprano and Piano (Stéphane Mallarmé; trans. by Ferko). E. C. Schirmer, 1999. cmp1985. Tonal c'–a"; Tess-M-mH; unmeasured; slow to moderate tempos; 14pp; Diff-V/m-md, P/me-md.
For: soprano
Mood: highly symbolic images of life
Voice: French text and word stress; chant-like; syllabic; one melisma; conjunct; chromatic
Piano: chordal; much harmonic parallelism; many accidentals; some 3-stave scoring
Diff: meaning of text; singer must have a thorough knowledge of French; no metrical structure
Uses: interesting set of highly atmospheric songs on French symbolist poetry; good for graduate level singer if something different is desired

    a. *Salut.* D; e'–f♯"; Tess-M; unmeasured, Rather freely, chantlike (♪= ca.108); 3pp.
    b. *Don du Poëme.* G; c'–g"; Tess-M; unmeasured, Moderately (♪= ca.72–80); 6pp.
    c. *... Mysticis Umbraculis.* D; g'–a"; Tess-mH; unmeasured, Slowly (like a lullaby); 5pp.

A 13. **LE VIERGE, LE VIVACE ET LE BEL AUJOURD'HUI** (The Virginal, lively and lovely today) (Stéphane Mallarmé) for Baritone and Piano. E. C. Schirmer, 1999. cmp1979. X; B–e' (tenor 𝄢); Tess-M; unmetered, Very expressively (♪= ca.120); 4pp; Diff-V/md, P/d.
For: baritone
Mood: cold, subtle, ironic, serious
Voice: chant-like melody; small intervals; syllabic; a few melismas; many accidentals
Piano: variety of spacing; some widely-spaced sonorities; some parallel six-four chords; quartal structures in parallel motion; many chords held with pedal; some

syncopation; does not double vocal line; short prelude; three interludes

Diff: rhythms; irregular bar lines and phrasing; finding pitches; understanding poetry (trans. given; no English singing version)

Uses: pair with "Chanson d'automne" by same composer

HADLEY, HENRY K.
(b. Somerville, MA, 1871; d. New York, NY, 1937)

[See main list: 1055 & 1056]

HARRIS, DONALD
(b. St. Paul, MN, 1931)

A 14. **LES MAINS** (Marguerite Yourcenar). For Mezzo-Soprano & Piano. Theodore Presser, 1986. cmp1983; rev.1984. Dedicated to and premiered by Mignon Dunn, 1983. X; f(g)–g"; Tess-wide; 4/8 with changes, Molto appassionatamente; 5min; Diff-V/dd, P/dd.

For: mezzo-soprano

Mood: questioning nature of death; rather dramatic

Voice: many large leaps and small skips; many accidentals; rhythmic complexities seem to exceed those of pitch; many polyrhythms in ensemble; pitches hard to find; some staccato; many dynamic and tempo variations

Piano: linear; disjunct; "harmonies" are usually 2nds, 7ths, 9ths, or tritones; complex in most ways; many accidentals; much arpeggiation of vertical structures; some 3-stave writing

Diff: perfect pitch desirable; ensemble and most other aspects; both performers must be secure, excellent musicians; singer must have flexibility and an easy technique

Uses: for performers already experienced in contemporary music of this type

Rec: D#213

HOIBY, LEE
(b. Madison, WI, 1926)

A 15. **THREE FRENCH SONGS**, Op. 36 (Arthur Rimbaud). Classical Vocal Reprints, 2000. [118, vol. 3]. cmp1952–1982; rev. 1982. "For Will Parker." X; (a.): c♯'–g"(♮), (b.): B–c♯'(♮), & (c.): c♯–g'(♮); Tess-mH-mL; mostly regular meters; varied tempos; 12pp; Diff-V/d, P/d.

For: baritone; (although two are in bass clef and one in treble, the dedication, as well as the nature of the texts, would suggest a single male voice)

Mood: enigmatic and obscure; (a.), harsh and raw-edged, containing some rather graphic and crude expressions; (b.), lyrical with nature imagery; (c.), lyrical and descriptive

Voice: chromatic; many skips and leaps, incl. 7ths & 9ths; many duplets in 6/8 & 9/8; 2 vs. 3 & 3 vs. 2 in piano; portamentos; lyrical and flowing; sustained passages in low, med., and high range; syllabic; a few small melismas, some on sustained tones

Piano: chordal and linear; block and broken chords; chromatic; chromatic scale passages; duplets, triplets, quadruplets; 2 vs. 3; trills; incidental doubling of vocal line

Diff: good sense of pitch, rhythm, vocal stamina, and solid lower-middle and high registers needed; texts difficult to understand; will require careful study

Uses: possible recital material for mature and advanced performers; first song may offend some audiences

a. *La Coeur Volé.* X; c♯'–g"; Tess-mL; 9/8 with changes, Vivace (♩. = 80); 6pp.

b. *L'Eternité.* X; B–c♯'; Tess-M; 4/4, 5/4, Lento (♩ = ca.56); 1p.

c. *Rêvé pour L'Hiver.* X; c♯–g'; Tess-mH; 9/8, 6/8, 4/4, Allegretto (♩. = 88); 5pp.

JOHNSTON, JACK
(b. Milwaukee, WI, 1935)

A 16. **LA CHANSON DE LA GLU** (Jean Richepin, from the drama *La Glu*). [40]. (also Mintermore Music Co.). X; g♯–e(g♭"); Tess-M; 4/4, 5/4, Lento–Allegretto–Allegro assai; 6pp; Diff-V/md, P/md.

For: medium or low voice

Mood: like a folk-ballad; descriptive and narrative; rather gruesome with a philosophical twist at end

Voice: primarily stepwise except for 8ve leaps; somewhat chromatic; dotted rhythms; triplets; 2 vs. 3 & 3 vs. 2 in piano; portamentos; sectional; text repetitions; syllabic; occasional 2-or 3-note slurs

Piano: chordal–block and broken; r.h. countermelodies; chromatic; dotted rhythms; triplets; incidental doubling of vocal line

Diff: good sense of pitch and excellent vocal actor needed

Uses: possible recital material, where something quite "off-beat" is wanted

LOEFFLER, CHARLES MARTIN
(b. Mulhouse, Alsace, France, 1861; d. Medfield, MA, 1935)

A 17. **FOUR SONGS ON POEMS OF GUSTAV KAHN**, Op. 10. G. Schirmer, 1903. Reprint: Masters Music Publications (MM). Traditional keys; a♭(b♭)–f"; Tess-M-mH; regular meters; mostly slow tempos; 30pp; Diff-V/m-md, P/md-d.

A. **TIMBRES OUBLIÉS** (Forgotten Images), Op. 10, No. 1. A♭maj; a♭(c♭')–f"; Tess-mH; 12/8, 9/8, Andante (Pas trop lent); 7pp; Diff-V/md, P/md.

For: medium voices

Mood: impressionistic reflection on past events and scenes

Voice: mostly stepwise; small skips; many accidentals; some dotted rhythms; graceful; some 2-note slurs

Piano: arpeggiation in 8ths & 16ths (some meas. in triplet groups of 16ths, creating cross-rhythms with the voice); many accidentals; minimal doubling of vocal line; color effects incl. some rolled chords and whole-tone scales; 18-meas. solo, divided among prelude, two interludes, and postlude

Diff: finding pitch at some entrances; polyrhythms in one section; ensemble; no English trans. given

Uses: recital; pair with another from this group, or use in context of set

B.   ADIEU POUR JAMAIS (Adieu then for aye), Op. 10, No. 2 (English version by Marian Judell). [25]. "To Elise Fay." E♭maj; b♭–f"; Tess-M; 4/4, Moderato; 8pp (7 in MM ed.); Diff-V/m, P/m.
For: medium voice
Mood: farewell to a memory
Voice: stepwise motion and small skips predominate; various subdivisions of beat; accidentals
Piano: broken chords; block-chord patterns; some countermelody; accidentals; polyrhythms; two interludes totaling 14 meas.; 6-meas. postlude
Diff: ensemble, particularly in rhythm; no trans. of French text in MM ed. (Eng. Version in [25])
Uses: best sung in French; English trans. rather dated
Rec: D♯253

C.   LES SOIRS D'AUTOMNE (The Evenings of Autumn), Op. 10, No. 3. Emin; b♭–e"; Tess-M; 4/4, 3/4, Andante–Animato ed agitato–Molto animando–Molto agitato ed animato; 6pp; Diff-V/md, P/md.
For: medium voices
Mood: reflection on tragic scene from distant past (a knight and a battle)
Voice: mostly stepwise or small skips; some dotted rhythms; some triplet divisions of the beat; many accidentals
Piano: colorful painting of text; duplet and triplet 8th-note motion predominates; broken chords; arpeggiation; repeated chords; cross-accents; many accidentals; wide reaches; does not double vocal line; 8-meas. prelude; several interludes; 12-meas. postlude in chorale style
Diff: tempo changes; ensemble; finding pitches at some entrances; no trans. of French text
Uses: pair with another song from this set or group with other songs about knights and ladies
Rec: D♯253

D.   LES PAONS (The Peacocks), Op. 10, No. 4 (English version by Marian Judell). [2, 25]. Gmaj; d'–f"; Tess-M; 4/4, Lento; 8pp (7 in MM ed); Diff-V/md, P/d.
For: medium voice
Mood: impressionistic description; languid
Voice: stepwise motion and small skips predominate; various subdivisions of beat; accidentals; subtle dynamics
Piano: describes motions of birds in impressionistic style, using arpeggiation and a Lydian modal tinge to rapid scale passages, rolled chords, etc.; many variations of soft dynamics; one 8-meas. interlude
Diff: ensemble requires care to work out difficulties as well as subtleties; no trans. of French text in MM ed. (Eng. Version in [25])
Uses: very good song; most effective sung in French

ORLAND, HENRY
(b. Saarbrücken, Germany, 1918; d. St. Louis, MO, 1999)

A 18.   COLLOQUE SENTIMENTAL, Op. 8 (Paul Verlaine; English trans.). Seesaw, n.d. X; c'–c'''; Tess-M; 4/4 with changes, Andante sustained (♩ = 58); 4pp; Diff-V/d, P/d.
For: soprano or tenor specified
Mood: lyrical; old lovers meeting
Voice: rather chromatic; some large leaps; 8th-note movement in general; flowing
Piano: highly chromatic; contrapuntal; tremolos and broken-chord figures in 16ths & 32nds
Diff: tenor would need easy high tones and clear low tones; score difficult to read
Uses: possible recital song for the right voice

A 19.   RÊVE, Op. 9 (Georgette Andrien; trans. Henry Orland). Seesaw, 1974. Emin; b–a"; Tess-M; 4/8, Andantino (♪ = 107); 6pp; Diff-V/d, P/d.
For: mezzo-soprano
Mood: lyrical love song
Voice: chromatic; many accidentals (no key signatures); leaps as large as m10th; several mordents, incl. one on an unstressed syllable; generally 8th-note movement; considerable use of extremes of range
Piano: many accidentals; 8th-note movement, increasing to triplet 16ths, then to 32nds; many arpeggiated and broken-chord figures; trills; other rapid passage-work
Diff: requires a wide and usable range with easy, light high tones; excellent pianist needed
Uses: useful recital song

A 20.   SERENADE, Op. 8 (Paul Verlaine; English trans.). Seesaw, 1974. X; b–a"; Tess-M; 6/8, Con moto moderato (♩. = 66); 4pp; Diff-V/d, P/d.
For: mezzo-soprano
Mood: serenade is sung by Death
Voice: chromatic; flowing; dotted rhythms; occasional grace notes; some large, difficult intervals
Piano: chromatic; l.h. sometimes imitates mandolin; independent but related melody in dotted rhythms; rhythmic complexities
Diff: pitches; light, easy high tones and much vocal flexibility needed
Uses: useful recital song

ROREM, NED
(b. Richmond, IN, 1923)

A 21.   JACK L'EVENTREUR (Jack the Ripper) (Marie Laure). [158]. cmp1953. First performed by Chloe Owen. Bmin; a–c♯'''; Tess-wide (composer designed song "for a quite wide-ranging voice"); 4/4, 3/2, Lent et sombre; 3pp; Diff-V/d, P/me.
For: soprano of wide range (dramatic voice seems best)
Mood: dramatic; hypnotic; tense
Voice: rather repetitive; most skips small; accidentals; rhythms not complex; several 2–5-note slurs; portamento; climactic phrase spans entire range of song; c♯''' has fermata and is marked *ffff*; ending is *pp* but intense
Piano: block-chord style; 3–5-voice texture; dramatic background for singer; dynamics range *pppp–ffff*
Diff: range and tessitura; dynamic control; keeping the dramatic intensity; no trans. given
Uses: real spell-binder for soprano with wide pitch and

dynamic range, and dramatic flair

A 22. **POÈMES POUR LA PAIX** (15th- & 16th-century French poets). Boosey & Hawkes, 1970. cmp1953. Key sigs., many altered chords; b–a♭"; Tess-mH, H (many g"s); regular meters; varied tempos; 25pp; Diff-V/md-d, P/m.

For: all voices except very low
Mood: lyrical; reflections on war and peace
Voice: French text only, with trans. given at front; melodies of most songs have an archaic structure reminiscent of 15th and 16th centuries; often repetitive and/or chant-like; wide dynamic range; archaic song forms
Piano: usually block chords in 3–4-voice texture; some countermelodies and imitation of vocal lines; wide dynamic range
Diff: a few rhythms where various subdivisions of beat are juxtaposed; dynamic contrasts; long note at end of last song (d")
Uses: interesting set for singer who is attracted to this combination of old poetry and archaic musical touches; would provide interesting contrast in recital of 20th-century songs

    a. *Lay* (Jehan Regnier). Modal quality (Phrygian); c'–g♭"; 3/4 with changes, Lent et grave, mais sans traîner; 3pp.
    b. *Ode* (Pierre de Ronsard). Modal quality (Mixolydian); e'–g"; 2/2, Allant; 5pp.
    c. *Sonnet (I)* (Olivier de Magny). Modal quality; d'–g"; 4/4, Animé et puissant; 5pp.
    d. *Sonnet (II)* (Olivier de Magny). Cmaj-Fmin; b–g"; 3/4, Pas trop lent; 4pp.
    e. *Sonnet* (Jean Daurat). F♯min; e'–g"; changing meters, Assez vif et triste; 4pp.
    f. *L'hymne de la Paix* (Jean Antoine de Baïf). Gmaj-min; d'–a♭"; 3/2 with changes; 4pp.

TALMA, LOUISE
(b. Arcachon, France, 1906; d. Saratoga Springs, NY, 1996)

A 23. **TERRE DE FRANCE** (The Soil of France). A Cycle of Five Songs for Soprano or Tenor Voice and Piano. Carl Fischer, 1978. cmp1943–1945. Tonal (mostly traditional keys); c'–a"; Tess-M, mH; changing mixed meters, ♩ = 56–132; 26pp; Diff-V/m-d, P/me-d.

For: soprano; tenor
Mood: patriotism in poetry; all but (d.) reflect the connection between the French soldier and the soil of France: (a.) memorial to all the soldiers of France who died to protect her soil; (b.) a soldier's homesickness for his home in France; (c.) soldier at sea who hates war, longs for home, and asks God for peace; (d.) an ode to the rose; poet writes only in praise of roses; (e.) Joan of Arc's farewell to the river Meuse as she leaves for the Crusades–her life will change, but the river remains forever the same
Voice: lyrical; much chord-outlining melody; syllabic; rhythms not distinct but flow with the smoothness of the text; two melismatic passages occur 3 times; some melodic repetition; few high notes

Piano: mostly chordal textures–block and broken; (c.) & (e.), more linear; (e.), some ostinato patterns; some wide spacing in l.h.; numerous accidentals; modulatory
Diff: ensemble in passages with changing mixed meters; some texts in Old French–no trans. given; crowded facsimile score somewhat hard to read
Uses: example of early work of a member of the "Stravinsky School"; Talma studied with Nadia Boulanger
Rec: D♯49

    a. *Mère, voici vos fils . . .* (Charles Péguy). Emin; e♭'–g"; Tess-mH; 4/4, 3/4, ♩ = 56; 2+pp.
    b. *Sonnet* (Joachim Du Bellay). Cmaj; c'–f"; Tess-M; 3/4, 4/4, 2/4, Nonchalant ♩ = 69; 3+pp.
    c. *Ballade* (Charles d'Orléans). Emaj; c♯'–f♯"; Tess-M; 4/4, 3/2, 3/4, 5/4, Andante ♩ = 69–72; 5+pp.
    d. *Ode* (Pierre de Ronsard). Amaj; e'–a"; Tess-mH; 5/8, 4/8, 6/8, 8/8, 3/8, 7/8, Vif ♩♩ = 132; 4+pp.
    e. *Adieux à la Meuse* (Charles Péguy). E♭maj; c'–g"; Tess-M, mH; 4/4, 5/4, 3/2, 9/8, 6/8, 10/8, 5/8, Tranquil ♩ = 56; 10pp.

THOMSON, VIRGIL
(b. Kansas City, MO, 1896; d. New York, NY, 1989)

A 24. **AIR DE PHÈDRE** (Phaedra's Farewell) (Jean Racine; trans. Donald Sutherland). (Peer)Southern, 1974. cmp1930. Fmaj; d'–b♭"; Tess-M; 4/4, 3/4, 5/4, ♩ = ca.72; 13pp; Diff-V/dd, P/md.

For: spinto or dramatic soprano
Mood: dramatic; narrative
Voice: rather disjunct; chromatic; difficult rhythms
Piano: chordal; frequently arpeggiated; independent of voice
Diff: pitches; rhythms; phrases often end high
Uses: good showpiece for soprano

A 25. **LA BELLE EN DORMANT** (Beauty Sleeping) (Georges Huguet; English version by Elaine de Sircay). Cycle. Boosey & Hawkes, 1950. cmp1931. Traditional keys; c'–g"; Tess-M; regular meters; 14pp; Diff-V/e, P/e.

For: baritone; tenor
Mood: lyrical
Voice: simplistic; some polymetric phrases; some melismatic phrases
Piano: simple; patterned; repetitious
Rec: D#322

    a. *Pour chercher sur la carte des mers.* Gmaj; d'–e"; 4/4, Steady (♩ = 72); 2pp.
    b. *La première de toutes.* Fmaj; c'–g"; 3/4, In modo di valzer (♩ = 66); 5pp.
    c. *Mon amour est bon à dire.* Fmaj; c'–f"; 4/4, Tempo di quickstep (♩ = 144); 5pp.
    d. *Partis les vaisseaux.* D-centered; c'–f"; 2/2, With swinging rhythm (♩ = 48); 2pp.

WARD-STEINMAN, DAVID
(b. Alexandria, LA, 1936)

A 26. **LES ODES DE JEUNESSE** (Pierre de Ronsard). [40]. cmp1956; rev.1982. Traditional tonal centers; c'–b♭"(g"); Tess-M; regular meters; varied tempos; 5+min; Diff-V/m-md, P/m-d.
For: tenor
Mood: lyrical love songs; nature imagery; classical allusions
Voice: primarily stepwise and easy skips; leaps of tritone, 7th, & 8ve in (b.); little chromaticism; duplets and triplets; lyrical and flowing; syllabic; occasional 2-note slurs
Piano: chordal and linear; block, rolled, and broken chords; chromatic; duplets, triplets, and groupings of 7 & 8; trills; tremolo; grace notes; articulations important, esp. in (b.); melodic material in interludes in (b.); considerable doubling of vocal line
Diff: rhythms; delicacy of phrasing
Uses: good recital material

    a. *À la Forêt de Gastine.* Amin; e'–e"; 3/4, 4/4, 2/4, Moderately; 2+min.
    b. *À la Fontaine Bellerie.* E♭maj-Amin; c'–b♭"(g"); 12/8 with changes, Fast; 3min.

GERMAN

BACON, ERNST
(b. Chicago, IL, 1898; d. Orinda, CA 1990)

A 27. **DER DU VON DEN HIMMEL BIST** (Wolfgang von Goethe). [77]. cmp1920s. Cmaj; b–e"; Tess-M; 2/2, Sostenuto ♩ = 56–Poco agitato ♩ = 96–Tempo primo; 3pp; Diff-V/m, P/m.
For: mezzo-soprano; baritone
Mood: invocation to the Divine; expansive; quietly exalting; agitated middle section; calm ending
Voice: quietly floating vocal line in mid-range; mostly conjunct; moves slowly; soft dynamics except for middle section
Piano: chordal; long prelude; unexpected harmonies; middle section arpeggiated r.h. with l.h. thumb melody in bass chords; slowly moving chords need good legato
Diff: keeping intensity at slow pace and soft dynamic level
Uses: wonderful song; use in Bacon group, group of German songs by American composers, or settings of same text by different composers

A 28. **GEBET** (Helene Lecher). [77]. cmp1920s. E♭maj; b♭–f♯"; Tess-M; 3/4, 4/4, Andante sostenuto; 5pp; Diff-V/md, P/md.
For: baritone
Mood: prayer asserting the unity of all beings in the Divine; calm-turbulent-majestic-calm
Voice: almost hymn-like melody in outer sections; more dramatic line in middle section; fairly narrow range; some repeated notes in phrases
Piano: chordal prelude; broken-chord 8th-note pattern in r.h. over bass 8ves; 8ve triplets and repeated chords in dotted rhythm in middle section; piano postlude
Diff: balance in dramatic middle section
Uses: interesting to use in group of prayers

A 29. **ICH LIEBE DICH** (Friedrich Rückert). [77]. cmp1920s. D♭maj; c'–g♭"; Tess-cs; 4/4, Lento ♩ = 60; 3pp; Diff-V/md, P/m.
For: soprano; tenor
Mood: romantic; ardent; passionate
Voice: chromatic vocal lines; fairly wide ranged; dramatic, but never louder than *f*
Piano: highly chromatic; wide spacing; some repeated chords with melody
Diff: conveying passionate intensity at all dynamic levels below *f*; chromatic vocal line
Uses: good for a German group where a big song is needed

A 30. **DIE NACHTBLUME** (Joseph von Eichendorff). [77]. cmp1920s. F♯min; b♯–e"; Tess-M; 10/8, Tranquillo; 3pp; Diff-V/md, P/md.
For: mezzo-soprano; baritone
Mood: tender, tranquil night song; water imagery
Voice: many skips; long, floating lines in irregular rhythms; soft dynamics
Piano: built on irregular arpeggio patterns in irregular rhythmic structure; wide reach helpful
Diff: irregular rhythmic structure; ensemble
Uses: beautiful song for rhythmically secure musicians; quiet song in German group

A 31. **SCHILFLIED** (Nicolaus Lenau). [77, 78, 167]. cmp1920s. F♯min; a–g♯"; Tess-cs; 3/4, Andantino ♩ = 88; 4pp; Diff-V/md, P/m.
For: mezzo-soprano; baritone
Mood: nocturnal; shimmering; quiet
Voice: long cantilena; maj-min shifts within single phrase; several phrases span a 10th in arpeggio structure, both ascending and descending; soft throughout
Piano: unexpected harmonies; rhythmic intricacy between hands; wide reach helpful
Diff: rhythmic structure of piano part; long, soft, floating vocal lines; ensemble
Uses: small masterpiece; use in Bacon group or various kinds of German groups

A 32. **WANDERERS NACHTLIED** (Wolfgang von Goethe). [77]. cmp1920s. Bmaj; f♯–f♯"; Tess-cs; 4/4, Adagio ♪ = 46; 1p; Diff-V/md, P/m.
For: mezzo-soprano; baritone
Mood: an uneasy stillness; hushed lament
Voice: wide-ranged phrases ascending softly; floating line; hushed dynamics; last phrase descends to low f♯ at end
Piano: slow, soft syncopated figure in l.h. under countermelody in r.h.; unexpected harmonies
Diff: wide leaps in vocal line at soft dynamic level; extremely slow tempo
Uses: a small masterpiece for German group

A 33. **WAS IST MIR DENN SO WEHE?** (Joseph von Eichendorff). [77]. cmp1920s. Dmaj; c♯'–c♯"; Tess-mL; 3/4, Lento, sempre sotto voce e legato ♩ = 50; 1p; Diff-V/me, P/e.
For: mezzo-soprano; baritone
Mood: grief; dream-like
Voice: slowly moving phrases in low range; numerous repeated notes; soft; ends low

Piano: chordal; little movement; chromatic
Diff: conveying the grief compressed into one page of music at a soft dynamic level
Uses: good for soft singing

BEACH, AMY MARCY CHENEY (MRS. H. H. A.)
(b. Henniker, NH, 1867; d. New York, NY, 1944)

A 34. EIN ALTES GEBET (An Old Prayer). [11, Vol. 1]. Fmaj; e'–f"; Tess-M; 4/4, Andante; 3pp; Diff-V/me, P/e.
For: any voice
Mood: a prayer of faith
Voice: conjunct; many 2-note slurs; modified strophic form
Piano: chordal; quarter-note chords in rocking ostinato pattern
Uses: lovely prayer; use in German or English

A 35. DEINE BLUMEN (Flowers and Fate) (Louis Zacharias; Eng. version by John Bernhoff). [11, Vol. 1]. F♯min-maj; e♯'–a♯"; Tess-M; 6/8, Molto moderato; 4pp; Diff-V/m, P/md.
For: tenor; soprano
Mood: ecstatic love song; gift of flowers represents all of Spring
Voice: phrases build in range and volume to climax; final phrase ascends chromatically c♯"–f♯" *ff*
Piano: arpeggiated figuration in fast harmonic movement; chordal climax and ending
Diff: final phrase for singer
Uses: good group ender; best in German; English text dated

A 36. ICH SAGTE NICHT (Silent Love) (Edward Wissman; Eng. text by Mme. Isidora Martinez). Arthur P. Schmidt, 1903. Reprint: Classical Vocal Reprints. [11, Vol. 1]. Cmaj; f♯'–a♭"; Tess-mH; 4/4, Lento, ma non troppo; 3pp; Diff-V/m, P/m.
For: tenor; soprano
Mood: romantic; unspoken love
Voice: syllabic setting in relatively short phrases; builds to climax on g" and a♭"; last phrase 4-meas. sustained soft floating tone; sudden dynamic changes
Piano: somewhat Straussian in nature; melodic r.h. over chordal l.h.; romantic harmonies
Diff: sustained *pp* last phrase
Uses: good for teaching German late romantic style; best in German; English text dated

A 37. DER TOTENKRANZ, Op. 73, No. 2 (Louis Zacharias). [81]. "Dedicated to Mme. Ernestine Schumann-Heink." Amin-maj; a–f"; Tess-M; 3/8, Non troppo lento, ma sempre espressivo; 4pp; Diff-Vm, P/me.
For: low voice
Mood: mourning; the laying of a wreath on a mother's grave
Voice: stepwise and small skip motion; legato; strophic; syllabic; some 2-note slurs; two phrases end on low a; trans. given
Piano: chordal texture; first strophe in legato afterbeat style; second strophe single voice broken chord pattern; shifting harmonies within key
Uses: hauntingly lovely song; good for a low, rich contralto; teaches legato

FOSS, LUKAS
(b. Berlin, Germany, 1922)

A 38. WANDERERS GEMÜTSRUHE (Johann Wolfgang von Goethe); (Peer)Southern, 1951. F-centered; d'–g"; Tess-H; 4/4, Allegro (♩ = 138); 4pp; Diff-V/d, P/d.
For: soprano; tenor
Mood: plaintive; the strength of evil and the weakness of truth; German original, with usable singing translation
Voice: primarily conjunct and small intervals, with emphasis on the 5th; descending phrases in first section, ascending in second section
Piano: broken-chord patterns in 16ths, in groupings of 4–6 per beat; some triplet 8ths and block chords; does not double vocal line
Diff: singer will need good sense of pitch
Uses: recital possibilities

GRIFFES, CHARLES TOMLINSON
(b. Elmira, NY, 1884; d. New York, NY, 1920)

A 39. DAS IST EIN BRAUSEN UND HEULEN (There Is a Tumult and Howling) (Heinrich Heine; trans. Donna K. Anderson). [113]. cmp between 1903 & 1911. E♭min; b♭–g♭"; Tess-M; 2/4, Molto allegro–Poco più tranquillo; 3pp; Diff-V/m, P/md.
For: baritone best
Mood: stormy; sad
Voice: stepwise; chord-member skips; a few accidentals; some speech-like rhythms; syllabic
Piano: broken-chord, arpeggiated, and syncopated repeated-chord patterns
Diff: a few rhythms
Uses: seems best sung in German; trans. is usable
Rec: D#s 45, 46, 66

A 40. FIVE GERMAN SONGS. G. Schirmer, 1909. Reprints: Classical Vocal Reprints (A. [L], B.[H, M, & L], D.[mH]); Masters Music Publications (all); T.I.S. (B. [M]). [168 (all)]. Separate entries below; all songs have singable English versions.

A. AUF DEM TEICH, DEM REGUNGSLOSEN (O'er the Tarn's Unruffled Mirror) (Nicolaus Lenau; trans. Henry G. Chapman). Emaj; b–g♯"; Tess-M-mL; 4/4, Ruhig und träumerisch; 3pp; Diff-V/m, P/m.
For: mezzo-soprano
Mood: descriptive; somber; lonely
Voice: skips along chord lines; some long-ranged phrases; some dotted rhythms; syncopation
Piano: repeated chords; syncopation; repetitive patterns; many accidentals; does not double vocal line
Diff: *subito pp* g♯"
Uses: very nice atmospheric song; quiet ending
Rec: D#203

B. AUF GEHEIMEM WALDESPFADE (By a Lonely Forest Pathway). (Nicolaus Lenau; trans. Henry G. Chapman). [2, 25, 59]. H & L keys: E♭maj & B♭maj; d'–a♭" & a–e♭"; Tess-M; 2/4, Molto tranquillo; 4pp; Diff-V/m, P/m.

For: any lyric voice
Mood: lyrical; poem of love and nature
Voice: sustained; several large leaps; often sung in English
Piano: broken chords throughout; some 2 vs. 3
Diff: soft high tones; 2 in voice vs. 3 in piano
Uses: good for study of lyrical phrasing, soft singing, extremes of range
Rec: D#s 27, 66, 202, 203 [D#s 10, 69, 198 recorded in English]

C. **NACHT LIEGT AUF DEN FREMDEN WEGEN** (Night on Ways Unknown Has Fallen) (Heinrich Heine; English version by Henry G. Chapman). [46]. C♯min; g♯–f"; Tess-L–mL; 4/4, Adagio; 2min; Diff-V/m, P/m.
For: contralto; possibly mezzo-soprano or baritone
Mood: despair followed by calm
Voice: many skips; smooth legato
Piano: chordal; 4–5-voice texture; syncopated afterbeats; some melodic interest; accidentals
Diff: soft dynamics
Uses: good song for recital; use within a group
Rec: D#203

D. **DER TRÄUMENDE SEE** (The Dreaming Lake) (Julius Mosen; English version by N. H. Dole). F♯maj; b♯–g♯"; Tess-M; 6/4, Tranquillo, ma non troppo; 3pp; Diff-V/m, P/m-md.
For: soprano; mezzo-soprano
Mood: descriptive; peaceful outdoor scene
Voice: stepwise and skips on chord lines; some long-ranged phrases; repetitive rhythms; 2-note slurs
Piano: chordal–block and arpeggiated; grouped in five 16ths in arpeggios; does not double vocal line
Diff: ensemble
Uses: excellent atmospheric song; impressionistic; quiet ending
Rec: D#s 66, 203

E. **WOHL LAG ICH EINST IN GRAM UND SCHMERZ** (Time Was, When I in Anguish Lay) (Emanuel Geibel; trans. Henry G. Chapman). [61]. "To Miss Geraldine Farrar." Bmaj; e'–g♯"; Tess-mH; 4/4, Allegro appassionato; Diff-V/m, P/m.
For: soprano
Mood: joyous
Voice: leaps; fast tempo
Piano: arpeggiated triplets throughout; not thick
Diff: needs soaring voice
Uses: good group or program ender
Rec: D#s 52, 66, 203

A 41. **FOUR GERMAN SONGS.** C. F. Peters, 1970, ed. Donna K. Anderson. cmp1906 (editor's estimate). Never previously pub.; now pub. together; separate entries below.

A. **AM KREUZWEG WIRD BEGRABEN** (They Buried Him at the Crossroads) (Heinrich Heine; trans. Donna K. Anderson). C♯min; c♯'–e♯"; Tess-M; 3/8, Andantino e mesto; 38meas.; Diff-V/e, P/me.
For: mezzo-soprano

Mood: sad; atmospheric
Voice: stepwise and easy skips; accidentals
Piano: 4–7-voice chordal texture; many accidentals; slight doubling of vocal line
Rec: D#s 66, 202

B. **AN DEN WIND** (To the Wind) (Nicolaus Lenau; trans. Donna K. Anderson). Dmin; a–g"; Tess-mH; 12/8, Im Anfang etwas ruhig; 31meas.; Diff-V/md, P/md.
For: high baritone
Mood: dramatic; somber; despair
Voice: many skips; some duplets in compound meter
Piano: linear pattern in 8ves; broken chords; builds in texture toward end; little doubling of vocal line
Diff: awkward range
Rec: D#s 66, 202, 203

C. **MEERES STILLE** (Calm Sea) (Wolfgang von Goethe; trans. Charles T. Griffes). Bmaj; a♯–e"; Tess-M; 4/4, Ruhig; 21meas.; Diff-V/me, P/me.
For: baritone; mezzo-soprano
Mood: peaceful; serene
Voice: conjunct; some 8ve leaps; accidentals; 2-note slurs; dramatic ascending scales
Piano: 6–7-voice chordal texture; mostly sustained; some doubling of vocal line
Uses: effective song; simple but effective harmonic colors
Rec: D#s 66, 202

D. **SO HALT' ICH ENDLICH DICH UMFANGEN** (At Last I Hold You) (Emanuel Geibel; trans. Donna K. Anderson). Bmaj; b♭–g♯"; Tess-mH; 4/4, Nicht zu langsam; 29meas.; Diff-V/d, P/md.
For: soprano
Mood: ecstatic love song
Voice: many phrases cover 7th, 8ve, or more; duplets and triplets
Piano: repeated chords; syncopation; triplets; some arpeggios; some doubling of vocal line
Diff: long-ranged phrases; good register control
Uses: useful song
Rec: D#66
NOTE: Entire set is better material than other composers of the time, but not up to Griffes' own best work.

NOTE: Nos. A42–A47 below are published as *Six Songs* (Medium Voice and Piano. New York: Henmar Press, Inc. [C. F. Peters Corp.] 1986). The editor finds these songs to be "intensely emotional, tonal, but often highly colored harmonically, and abound[ing] with beautiful lyrical melodies." They are probably best sung in German. Although they do not all seem to be for the same voice, and the songs to poems by Emanuel Geibel are all slow, a group could be made from the set.

A 42. **MEIN HERZ IST WIE DIE DUNKLE NACHT** (My Heart Is Like the Gloomy Night) (Emanuel Geibel; trans. Donna K. Anderson). [113]. cmp between 1903 & 1911. Bmaj; b–f♯"; Tess-M; 4/4, Zart aber innig; 3pp; Diff-V/m, P/md.
For: mezzo-soprano seems best; baritone

Mood: quiet; introspective but intense
Voice: stepwise; small skips; some dotted rhythms; irregular phrases
Piano: arpeggiation; repeated block chords; some 2 vs. 3; some accidentals; rare doubling of vocal line
Diff: polyrhythms
Uses: group with some of Griffes' other German-language songs; trans. works but seems best sung in German.
Rec: D#66
NOTE: This song was [re]constructed by the editor from a "rough pencil and ink sketch." It had no text, only an identification of the poet and a page number, and no performance indications.

A 43. MIT SCHWARZEN SEGELN (With Jet Black Sails) (Heinrich Heine; trans. Donna K. Anderson). [113]. cmp between 1903 & 1911. Dmin; a–f"; Tess-M; 6/8, Bewegt und rasch; 3pp; Diff-V/me, P/m.
For: mezzo-soprano; baritone
Mood: faithless love
Voice: mostly stepwise and chord-member skips; some dotted rhythms; mostly syllabic
Piano: r.h. arpeggiation with chords in l.h.; repeated block chords
Diff: possibly range
Uses: when a short song is needed; trans. is workable; probably best sung in German
Rec: D#66

A 44. DAS [DES] MÜDEN ABENDLIED (The Weary One's Evensong) (Emanuel Giebel; trans. Charles T. Griffes). [113]. cmp between 1903 & 1911. B♭maj; b♭–e♭"; Tess-mL; 4/4, Etwas langsam aber nicht schleppend; 4pp; Diff-V/m, P/m.
For: baritone
Mood: despairing; somber
Voice: conjunct; some accidentals; dotted rhythms; some triplets; syllabic
Piano: block- and broken-chord patterns; syncopation; does not double vocal line
Diff: irregular phrases might cause ensemble difficulties
Uses: seems best sung in German; trans. done by Griffes and fits music well, but contains archaic language
Rec: D#s 45, 46, 66

A 45. NACHTLIED (Night Song) (Emanuel Giebel; trans. Donna K. Anderson). Henmar, 1983. cmp1912. A♭maj; d♭'–a"(a♭"); Tess-wide; 3/4, Moderato; 3min; Diff-V/m, P/md.
For: soprano; tenor
Mood: description of night
Voice: stepwise; chord-member skips; accidentals; easy rhythms; mostly soft dynamics; one *f* a♭"
Piano: broken-chord patterning in 8th notes, duplets, and triplets; many accidentals; 8-meas. prelude; 15-meas. postlude; quiet ending; does not double vocal line
Diff: fairly wide tessitura; quiet dynamics
Uses: interesting harmonic coloration; seems best sung in German, although English text is a possibility
Rec: D#s 66, 203

A 46. DAS STERBENDE KIND (The Dying Child)

(Emanuel Geibel; trans. Donna K. Anderson). [113]. cmp between 1903 & 1911. C♯min; b♯–e"; Tess-M; 4/4, Sehr langsam; 2pp; Diff-V/me, P/me.
For: mezzo-soprano; baritone
Mood: quiet and somber
Voice: stepwise; small skips; a few accidentals; easy rhythms; syllabic
Piano: block chords; 6 meas. repeated-chord triplets
Uses: dark subject; English trans. works but probably best sung in German
Rec: D#66
NOTE: This song was [re]constructed by the editor from a rough sketch containing a partial text and no performance indications.

A 47. WO BIN ICH, MICH RINGS UMDUNKELT (Where I Am, the Gloom Surrounds) (Heinrich Heine; trans. Donna K. Anderson). [113]. cmp between 1903 & 1911. Cmin; g–d♭"; Tess-mL; 4/4, Langsam und schwer; 2pp; Diff-V/m, P/m.
For: bass or bass-baritone seems best; contralto
Mood: gloomy; deep despair
Voice: stepwise; small skips along chord lines; some chromatic alterations; syncopation; dotted rhythms
Piano: block chords repeated in syncopated pattern; looks like some Hugo Wolf songs; doubling of vocal line incidental
Diff: possibly a few rhythms
Uses: best sung in German but trans. singable; very dark song
Rec: D#s 45, 46, 66

HOIBY, LEE
(b. Madison, WI, 1926)

A 48. LIED DER LIEBE (Friedrich Hölderlin). Aquarius (Rock Valley Music Company), 1984. cmp1984. E♭maj-X; c♯'–f♯"; Tess-M; 2/2 with changes, Majestic, rhythmic, and light; 4min; Diff-V/md, P/m.
For: medium voice
Mood: lyrical love song
Voice: somewhat disjunct but lyrical; leaps of 7th & 9th; some chromaticism; high-lying, sustained phrases; portamento; syllabic; a few 2-note slurs
Piano: chordal–block and broken; melodic fragments; chromatic; triplets and sextuplets; some doubling of vocal line
Diff: good sense of pitch needed
Uses: recital material

HOWE, MARY
(b. Richmond, VA, 1882; d. Washington, DC, 1964)

A 49. TROCKNET NICHT (WONNE DER WEHMUT) (Wolfgang von Goethe). [11, vol.7]. Amaj; f♯'–a"; Tess-mH; 2/2, Leidenschaftlich mit Gewicht ♩ = 46; 3pp; Diff-V/md, P/md.
For: soprano; tenor
Mood: tears of unhappy love
Voice: quarter-note triplets juxtaposed with dotted-quarter/8th; mostly conjunct; some long phrases; 2 vs. 3 with piano

Piano: block chords; rhythmic complexity; accidentals; supports vocal line, little doubling
Diff: rhythms; ensemble; length of phrases in slow tempo
Uses: German text only; useful in group of Goethe songs

MacDOWELL, EDWARD
(b. New York, NY, 1861; d. New York, NY, 1908)

A 50. FIVE SONGS WITH PIANOFORTE ACCOMPANIMENT, Op. 11 & 12. Breitkopf & Härtel, 1898. cmp1883. Major keys; d#'–g♭"; Tess-M, mH; regular meters; moderate tempos; 37–68meas. Each; Diff-V/me-m, P/m.
For: tenor; baritone
Mood: mostly tranquil; one lighthearted song
Voice: mostly stepwise and easy skips; some sustained phrases; accidentals; legato
Piano: chordal; some countermelody; accidentals
Diff: soft dynamics; some long phrases; some abrupt modulations
Uses: songs have a variety of expressive possibilities; best sung in German; English text dated
Rec: D#258

   a. *Mein Liebchen,* Op. 11, No. 1 (My Love and I Sat Close Together) (Heinrich Heine). E♭maj; e♭'–e"; Tess-mH; 6/8, Allegretto calmato; 68meas.
   b. *Du liebst mich nicht,* Op. 11, No. 2 (You Love Me Not!) (Heinrich Heine). Emaj; d#'–f#"; Tess-M; 4/4, Allegretto giocoso; 39meas.
   c. *Oben, wo die Sterne glühen,* Op. 11, No. 3 (In the Skies, Where Stars Are Glowing) (Heinrich Heine). B♭maj; e♭'–e♭"; Tess-M; 3/4, Andante, ma non troppo; 54meas.
   d. *Nachtlied,* Op. 12, No. 1 (Night-Song) (poet not given). D♭maj-G♭maj; f'–g♭"; Tess-mH; 6/8, Andante; 37meas.
   e. *Das Rosenband,* Op. 12, No. 2 (The Bands of Roses) (poet not given). Emaj; d#'–e"; Tess-M; 6/8, Andantino; 50meas.

MOSS, LAWRENCE
(b. Los Angeles, CA, 1927)

A 51. THREE RILKE SONGS (Rainer Maria Rilke; English trans. Babette Deutsch). For Mezzo-Soprano. Seesaw, 1971. cmp1963; rev.1966–1977. X; a♭–b♭"; Tess-wide; regular and irregular meters with frequent changes; moderate tempos; 8+min; Diff-V/dd, P/dd.
For: mezzo-soprano specified
Mood: lyrical and philosophical; life and death; religious references
Voice: chromatic; disjunct; numerous leaps of 7th, 9th, & 11th; many duplets in 6/8; strong and weak stresses of syllables indicated; many weak syllables on strong beats; triplets; one 5 vs. 6 in piano; phrases fragmented by rests; syllabic; occasional 2-note slurs
Piano: chromatic; disjunct; 1–4-voice texture; leaping, broken-chord-like figures throughout much of cycle; triplets, quintuplets, 5 vs. 4 & 6, 7 vs. 8, and other

rhythmic complexities; large reach helpful; both hands in treble clef throughout much of cycle; numerous pedal markings; does not double vocal line
Diff: in every area; perfect pitch desirable; extremely secure sense of rhythm required; ability to shift from high to low register of voice rapidly and easily; constantly changing meters; for exceptional musicians with experience in the avant-garde idiom
Uses: excellent recital material for superior musicians

   a. *I. (Da neigt sich die Stunde).* X; a♭–g#"; 6/8, 7/8, 9/16, 9/8, Flowing (♩ = 72); 5pp.
   b. *II. (Werkleute sind wir).* X; b♭–b♭"; 2/4+3/4, Decisively (♩ = 84); 4pp.
   c. *III. (Was wirst du tun, Gott).* X; c'–a"; 6/8 with changes, Quietly and very tenderly (♩ = 66); 6+pp.

ORLAND, HENRY
(b. Saarbrücken, Germany, 1918; d. St. Louis, MO, 1999)

A 52. HIRTENGESÄNGE, Op. 3 (Songs of the Shepherd) (Münchhausen). Seesaw, 197-. X; c'–b♭"; Tess-M; changing meters; varied and changing tempos; 15+pp; Diff-V/d, P/d.
For: tenor
Mood: lyrical love songs; serene; sorrowful
Voice: chromatic; lyrical; triplets; several high-lying phrases; sustained a♭"; some vocalizing; some parlando
Piano: chromatic; independent of voice; some melodic interest; tremolo; grace notes; rolled chords; cadenza-like passage work; mostly chordal texture
Diff: numerous low tones
Uses: effective recital material; English trans. usable

   a. *Der Sehnsuchtsgesang* (The Song of Longing). d'–b♭"; 3/8, various tempos; 6pp.
   b. *Der stille Gesang* (The Quiet Song). c'–a♭"; 4/4 with changes, Tranquillo (♩ = 60)–Più mosso (♩ = 90); 3pp.
   c. *Der Trauergesang* (The Song of Grief). c'–a"; 5/4 with changes, various tempos; 6+pp.

A 53. TWO BALLADS BY GOETHE, Op. 1 (Wolfgang von Goethe). Seesaw, 197-. X; E♭–f'; Tess-M; changing meters; changing tempos; 21pp; Diff-V/d-dd, P/d-dd.
For: bass
Mood: descriptive; narrative; macabre (b.)
Voice: disjunct; many large leaps; chromatic; extremes of range; polyrhythms; several high-lying phrases
Piano: independent and descriptive; features rapid passages; chromatic; dissonant; trills; grace notes; rhythmic complexities
Diff: range; skill in declamatory style required
Uses: fine showpieces for a mature singer; probably not a performance pair

   a. *Der Zauberlehrling* (The Sorcerer's Apprentice). E–f'; 12+pp.
   b. *Der Totentanz* (The Dance of the Dead). E♭–e'; 8+pp.

PAINE, JOHN KNOWLES
(b. Portland, ME, 1839; d. Cambridge, MA, 1906)

[See main list: 1666]

PASATIERI, THOMAS
(b. New York, NY, 1945)

A 54.   SIEBEN LEHMANNLIEDER (Lotte Lehmann). Theodore Presser, 1991. cmp1988. Tonal (traditional keys); c♯'–b"; Tess-mH, cs; regular meters with changes; varied tempos; 26min; Diff-V/md-d, P/m-d.
For: soprano (full lyric)
Mood: romantic; evening, silence, solitude, lost love, dreams, Narcissus, peace
Voice: lyrical and dramatic; wide-ranging vocal lines; melismas; syncopation; numerous high phrases; German text (trans. given)
Piano: neo-romantic harmonies; chordal; many 8ves and broken chords; many accidentals
Diff: some unclear harmonic direction; endurance
Uses: neo-romantic cycle on German texts; for advanced singer (orchestral version available from publisher)

   a. *Ich bin allein auf Bergesgipfeln.* E♭min; e♭'–b♭"; Tess-mH; 4/4, Allegro moderato; 3pp.
   b. *Wie lieb' ich diese klare Stunde.* A♭maj; e♭'–a♭"; Tess-mH; 4/4, 6/4, 5/4, Andante lirico; 3pp.
   c. *So hört' ich wieder deiner Stimme.* Emaj; c♯'–a"; Tess-cs; 4/4, 6/4, 5/4, 3/4, Lento Molto; 2pp.
   d. *In Flammen starb dein Bild.* Gmin; e♭'–b♭"; Tess-cs; 4/4, 3/4, 2/4, Allegro violento; 4pp.
   e. *Wie schön ist dieser tiefe Schlummer.* Gmin; d'–f"; Tess-cs; 4/4, 2/4, 3/4, Lento ma non troppo; fluido; 3pp.
   f. *Narzissus* (Auf ein Bild). Emin; e♭'–b♭"; Tess-cs; 4/4, 6/4, Quasi recitativo–Allegro; 6pp.
   g. *Die Welt scheint ganz aus Glut gesponnen.* Emin; c♯'–b"; Tess-cs; 4/4, 5/4, 3/4, Andante serioso; 5pp.

SCHONTHAL, RUTH
(b. Hamburg, Germany, 1924)

A 55.   ARME HEILIGE (Rainer Maria Rilke). [11, vol.11]. E♭min; b♭–g♭"(e♭"); Tess-M; 6/8, Lento, Andante moto; 4pp; Diff-V/md, P/d.
For: mezzo-soprano; possibly baritone
Mood: somewhat bitter outlook on offerings to saints; literal translation given
Voice: mostly stepwise motion; a few large intervals; a few accidentals; several low-lying phrases
Piano: chordal; some melodic material; broken-chord patterns progress 8ths-16ths-32nds; some accidentals; considerable doubling of vocal line
Diff: interpretive insight
Uses: could be effective in recital

A 56.   ERSTE ROSEN (Rainer Maria Rilke). [11, vol.11]. Bmaj; d♯'–e♭"; Tess-M; 3/4, 4/4, Moderato; 3pp; Diff-V/md, P/m.

For: any medium voice
Mood: lyrical nature imagery; literal translation provided
Voice: mostly stepwise motion; several 4ths in final two phrases; mostly quarter- & 8th-note motion, with longer note at end of phrase; some accidentals
Piano: chordal and contrapuntal; continuously-moving 8ths; numerous accidentals; considerable vocal line doubling
Diff: key sig. has 6♯s, but music suggests Bmaj, with excursions into mediant and submediant keys, making pitches somewhat difficult to hear; secure musicianship necessary
Uses: an interesting recital song

A 57.   ICH WILL EIN GARTEN SEIN (Rainer Maria Rilke). [11, vol.11]. X-Emaj; b♭–g♯"; Tess-M; 4/4, Largo, ma rubato; 4pp; Diff-V/md, P/d.
For: mezzo-soprano
Mood: lyrical nature imagery; literal translation provided
Voice: mostly conjunct motion; several 8ves & 9ths; quarter- & 8th-note motion; numerous accidentals in first section
Piano: repeated block chords in 8ths; broken chords in 16ths; many accidentals; little doubling of vocal line
Diff: wide leaps from middle to low and high voice; pitches may be difficult, esp. in first section; skillful pianist needed
Uses: possible recital song

A 58.   IHR MÄDCHEN SEID WIE DIE KÄHNE (Rainer Maria Rilke). [11, vol.11]. Fmaj; b♭–f"; Tess-M; 3/4, Sehr lieblich vorzutragen; 4pp; Diff-V/m, P/me.
For: any medium voice
Mood: lyrical imagery–"You maidens are like small boats"; literal translation provided
Voice: mostly stepwise motion; occasional small intervals; mostly quarter- & 8th-note motion; syllabic; occasional 2-note slurs
Piano: chordal and contrapuntal; broken-chord figures, melodic and countermelodic material in continuously-moving 8ths; some doubling of vocal line
Diff: smooth legato needed by both singer and pianist
Uses: interesting song for recital

A 59.   MEINE FRÜHVERLIEHNEN LIEDER (Rainer Maria Rilke). [11, vol.11]. F♯maj; a♯–f♯"; Tess-mL; 4/4, Sehr zart und innig (rubato); 4pp; Diff-V/m, P/m.
For: baritone; possibly mezzo-soprano
Mood: dreamily abstract poem of unfulfilled love; literal translation provided
Voice: repeated notes and much stepwise motion; only one 4th within a phrase; almost a recit. style; several low-lying phrases; long phrase at end descends through full range of song
Piano: chordal and contrapuntal; broken-chord figures; melodic material; supports clearly but doubles vocal line only incidentally
Diff: voice needs warmth and expressiveness below staff
Uses: effective for recital

A 60.   NOCH AHNST DU NICHTS VOM HERBST DES HAINES (Rainer Maria Rilke). [11, vol.11]. Cmaj; c'–f"; Tess-mL; 3/4, Allegro moderato; 4pp; Diff-V/m,

P/md.

For: any medium voice
Mood: lyrical nature imagery; the passing of summer; literal translation given
Voice: conjunct; small intervals; a few 6ths; quarter- & 8th-note motion
Piano: continuous 16th-note motion; broken chords in l.h.; frequent rubato; few accidentals; considerable doubling of vocal line
Diff: skillful pianist required
Uses: interesting song for recital

A 61. **WEISSE SEELEN** (Rainer Maria Rilke). [11, vol.11]. Cmaj; d'–g"; Tess-M; 4/4, Allegro moderato; 3pp; Diff-V/m, P/m.
For: soprano; tenor
Mood: lyrical poem about death; literal translation provided
Voice: mostly conjunct; a few small intervals; 2 & 3 vs. 6 in piano
Piano: broken-chord figures in sextuplets; melodies in prelude and interlude; supports well, little vocal line doubling
Diff: possibly rhythms for some singers and pianists
Uses: interesting song for recital

A 62. **WIE SOLL ICH MEINE SEELE HALTEN** (Rainer Maria Rilke). [11, vol.11]. Bmaj; b–e"(f♯"); Tess-mL; 2/2, 3/4, Agitato; 5pp; Diff-V/md, P/d.
For: any medium voice
Mood: warm, lyrical love song; musical imagery; literal translation provided
Voice: stepwise motion; a few 4ths & 5ths; much 8th-note motion; many 2-note slurs; some accidentals
Piano: chordal and contrapuntal; 16th-note broken-chord patterns; numerous accidentals; considerable doubling of vocal line
Diff: same difficulties as A56 above
Uses: fine recital song

SCHULLER, GUNTHER
(b. New York, NY, 1925)

A 63. **SIX EARLY SONGS** (Li-Tai-Pe; German paraphrases by Klabund; Eng. trans. not for singing). Margun, 1976. cmp1944–1945. First performance by Eleanor Steber. X; b–b♭"; Tess-M-mH; changing meters, varied tempos; 18min; Diff-V/d, P/d.
For: soprano
Mood: impressionistic; descriptive scenes; picture-like music
Voice: many small skips; speech-like rhythms; trills; portamento; 2 vs. 3 in piano; many accidentals
Piano: 7pp. 3-stave writing; many accidentals; colorful; descriptive of texts; many arpeggiated chords, some rapid; some thick scoring
Diff: singer needs mature command of dynamics, registration, and expressive ability; will take extensive ensemble work
Uses: fine settings of the texts; excellent group; craftsmanship unusually good; in preface composer admits debt to Ravel's *Histoires naturelles*

   a. *Die Kaiserin.* c'–g"; 3/4, 4/4, 5/4, Andante

maestoso; 6pp.
   b. *Im Boot.* f♯'–a♭"; 5/4, 4/4, 3/4, Moderato leggiero; 3pp.
   c. *Die ferne Flöte.* e♭'–b♭"; 6/4 with changes,
   d. *An der Grenze.* b–a♭"; changing meters, Andante; 4pp.
   e. *Der Silberreiher.* f'–g♭"; 3/4, 4/4,2/4, Lento dolce; 2pp.
   f. *Der Fischen im Frühling.* d'–b♭"; 12/8, 4/4, Andante rapsodico; 4pp.

ZWILICH, ELLEN TAAFFE
(b. Miami, FL, 1939)

A 64. **EINSAME NACHT.** A Song Cycle for Baritone and Piano (Hermann Hesse; trans. James Wright [trans. not for performance]). Merion, 1984. cmp1971. X; A–f'; Tess-M-mL; regular and irregular meters with very frequent changes; varied tempos; 14min; Diff-V/dd, P/dd.
For: dramatic baritone; bass-baritone
Mood: in words of composer: "existential loneliness . . . theme of homesickness, alienation and loss are explored," but with "life-affirming sensuousness and immediacy"
Voice: rather disjunct; chromatic leaps of 7th, 8ve, 9th, etc.; highly chromatic; rhythmically complex; syllabic; small chromatic melismas; long sustained b' at end of (c.), decresc.; c♯' at end of (f.), *f*
Piano: chordal and linear; often essentially 2-voice texture; chromatic arpeggiated and broken-chord figures; highly chromatic; rhythmically complex; covers the keyboard; many instructions given for pedaling that composer wants strictly observed; independent of vocal line
Diff: in every area; perfect pitch desirable; extremely secure musicianship required; strong low voice needed if sung by a baritone, as tessitura is a bit low for this voice
Uses: excellent recital material for a mature singer
Rec: D♯336

   a. *Über die Felder.* X; A–d'; Moderato (♪ = ca.104); 2pp.
   b. *Wie sind die Tage schwer.* X; A–e♭'; Andante–Recitativo; 1+pp.
   c. *Schicksal.* X; A–f'; Vivace; 3pp.
   d. *Elisabeth.* X; A–e'; Allegretto non troppo; 3pp.
   e. *Nacht.* X; B–e'; Lento; 2pp.
   f. *Mückenschwarm.* X; B♭–e'; Vivace; 5pp.

HEBREW

[See main list: 2036 & 2240]

ITALIAN

DiGIOVANNI, ROCCO [Rock Johnson]
(b. New York, NY, 1924)

A 65. **ARCO BALENO** (The Rainbow). A Cycle of Seven Songs for Bass (Nicola Rossi-Lemeni). Recital Publications, 1983. X (with some tonal centering); G♭–e♭'; Tess-M; regular and irregular meters; moderate tempos; 14pp; Diff-V/m, P/d.

For: bass; bass-baritone

Mood: lyrical and philosophical; each short song suggests a color of the rainbow ("arco-baleno")

Voice: stepwise; easy skips; leaps of dim.5th, aug.5th, & 8ve; somewhat chromatic; triplets; syncopation; rhythmic irregularities against piano; short, recit.-like phrases with many repeated notes and skips up or down of 4th & 5th; phrases separated by rests; syllabic; a few 2-note slurs; ends softly

Piano: chordal-linear combination; block, broken, repeated, and rolled chords; scale passages; melodic fragments; pedal tones; chromatic; dotted rhythms; triplets and quintuplets; numerous trills; grace notes; glissando; does not double vocal line

Diff: good sense of pitch and rhythm needed

Uses: excellent recital material

    a. *Rosso* (Red). X, A-centered; B♭–c♯'; 5/4, Espressivo (♩ = 72); 2+pp.

    b. *Arancione* (Orange). X; B♭–d'; 3/4, Andante con moto (♩ = 96); 1+pp.

    c. *Giallo* (Yellow). X; c–c♯'; 4/4, 6/4, Molto espressivo (♩ = 84); 1+pp.

    d. *Verde* (Green). X, E♭-centered; d♭–d♭'; 2/4, 3/4, Con vaghezza (♩ = 60); 2pp.

    e. *Azzurro* (Blue). Emin; B–c♯'; 4/4, Andante (♩ = 94); 1+pp.

    f. *Indaco* (Indigo). X; G♭–e♭'; 2/2, 3/2, 4/2, Andante arditamente (♩ = 60); 2pp.

    g. *Violetto* (Purple). X, G-centered; A♭–d'; 5/4, 6/4, Espressivo e sentito (♩ = 92); 2+pp.

HARBISON, JOHN
(b. Orange, NJ, 1938)

A 66. **MOTTETTI DI MONTALE** (Eugenio Montale). Associated Music Publishers, 1981 (Hal Leonard). From *Le Occasioni* (1940); "Honoring the poet on his 85th birthday." X; g♯–a"(b"); Tess-cs; mostly regular meters and varied tempos; 50min; Diff-V/dd, P/dd. [titles below are first lines]

For: mezzo-soprano

Mood: 20 poems (in 4 books) on separation and death, using rather dark imagery; an Italian *Winterreise* for the 21st century(?); English trans. given

Voice: much disjunct motion; intervals up to 10th; frequent tritones; many accidentals; varied rhythmic patterns, irregular groupings; triplets vs. dotted rhythm in piano; grace notes, trills, melismas (usually moderate tempo); many specific dynamic and tempo markings

Piano: chordal and contrapuntal; block, rolled, and broken chords; many accidentals; varied rhythmic patterns in the regular meters; many specific articulation, dynamic and tempo markings

Diff: perfect pitch desirable, secure musicianship and agility required; strength needed throughout vocal range; highly-skilled pianist with thorough grasp of the modern score required

Uses: performance of complete work would consume most, if not all, of a typical recital program; perhaps too much pessimism at once; selections could be made to create a contemporary group, as most songs are quite short

LIBRO 1:

    a. *Lo sai: debbo riperderti e non posso.* a–g"; 5/4, with changes, Moderato (♩ = 60); 5pp.

    b. *Molti anni, e uno più duro sopra il lago straniero.* d'–a"; 4/4, Misurato (♩ = 92); 3pp.

    c. *Brina sui vetri; uniti sempre e sempre in disparte.* e'–a"; 3/2, Largo (♩ = 40); 4pp.

    d. *Lontano, ero con te quando tuo padre entrò nell'ombra.* d'–a"; 4/4, Impetuoso (♩ = 84); 4pp.

    e. *Addii, fischi nel buio, cenni tosse e sportelli abbassati.* b–g"; 3/4, Molto moderato (♩ = 80); 3pp.

    f. *La speranza di pure riverderti m'abbandonava.* a–a♭"; 3/4, Poco lento (♩ = 63); 3pp.

LIBRO 2:

    g. *Il saliscendi bianco e nero dei balestrucci dal palo.* a–e"; 3/4, Allegretto (♩ = 76); 4pp.

    h. *Ecco il segno; s'innerva sul muro che s'ndora.* c'–g"; 6/4, Grazioso (♩ = 90); 2+pp.

    i. *Il ramarro, se scocca sotto la grande fersa dalle stoppie.* g♯–f"; 4/4, Allegro moderato (♩ = 86); 3+pp.

    j. *Perché tardi? Nel pino lo scoiattolo batte la coda.* b–a" 4/4, Allegro fantastico (♩ = 116); 4pp.

    k. *L'anima che dispensa furlana e rigodone.* b♭–f♯"; 4/4, Allegro insistente (♩ = 126); 4pp.

    l. *Ti libero la fronte dai ghiaccioli.* b♭–a♭"; 2/2, Adagio (♩ = 80); 2pp.

LIBRO 3:

    m. *La gondola che scivola in un forte bagliore.* b♭–a"; 6/8, Misterioso (♩. = 50); 4+pp.

    n. *Infuria sale or grandine? Fa strage di campanule.* c♯'–a"; 3/4, Furioso (♩ = 132); 4+pp.

    o. *Al primo chiaro, quando subitaneo un rumore di ferrovia.* b–f"; 4/4, Con moto (♩ = 152); 3pp.

    p. *Il fiore che ripete dall'orlo del burrato.* b♭–f"; 6/4, Largo (♩ = 42); 3pp.

LIBRO 4:

    q. *La rana, prima a ritentar la corda dall stagno.* g♯–g"; 4/4, Tempo giusto (♩ = 120); 6+pp.

    r. *Non recidere, forbice, quel volto, solo nella memoria.* b♭'–g"; 2/2, Lento (♩ = 44); 2+pp.

    s. *La canna che dispiuma mollemente il suo rosso flabello.* b♭–a♭"; 4/4, Poco adagio, affetuoso (♩ = 48); 5pp.

    t. *. . . ma così sia. Un suonno di cornetta dialoga con gli sciami.* c'–a♭"; 4/4, Allegro moderato (♩ = 100); 4pp.

MENOTTI, GIAN CARLO
(b. Cadegliano, Italy, 1911)

A 67. **CANTI DELLA LONTANANZA** (Gian Carlo Menotti). Cycle. G. Schirmer, 1967. Dedicated to and first performed by Elisabeth Schwartzkopf. Tonal with shifting tonality–some bitonal and bimodal; b♯–b♭"; Tess-mL-mH; regular meters with changes; varied tempos; 22pp; Diff-V/m-d, P/m-d.
For: soprano with sizeable sound; some tenors; some mezzo-sopranos
Mood: longing; death; resignation
Voice: conjunct and disjunct mixture; many leaps of 6th & 8ve; speech rhythms; much rubato; many accidentals; big high notes
Piano: broken and block chords; (d.) & (f.) have thick texture and repeated chords; chromaticism; variety of dynamics; several songs have some doubling of vocal line; all have short preludes and postludes; three have short interludes
Diff: requires mature sound and excellent breath control; small voice easily covered by piano; somewhat low tessitura for soprano; trans. in front material; no English singing version
Uses: some cyclic musical procedures suggest performance as a cycle; songs could be excerpted effectively
Rec: D#s 265, 266, 267

  a. *Gli Amanti Impossibili* (Impossible Lovers). Shifting tonality; f♯'–a"; Tess-H; 4/4, 2/4, 3/4, Allegretto–Andante calmo; 3pp.
  b. *Mattinata di Neve* (Snowy Morning). D-centered, bimodal; d'–g♯"; Tess-M; 3/4, 4/4, 2/4, Adagio, ma non troppo–poco più lento e stentato; 3pp.
  c. *Il Settimo Bicchiere di Vino* (The Seventh Glass of Wine). G-centered; d'–g"; Tess-mH; 2/4, 3/4, Allegro molto; 3pp.
  d. *Lo Spettro* (The Specter). Shifting tonality, ends B♭min; c♯'–g♭" Tess-M; 3/4, 2/4, 4/4, Lento; 2pp.
  e. *Dorme Pegaso* (Pegasus Asleep). Fmaj-min; e'–c"; Tess-mL; 4/4, 3/4, 2/4, Andante rubato; 2pp.
  f. *La Lettera* (The Letter). B♭, shifting; b♯–b♭"; Tess-wide; 4/4, 6/4, 5/4, Andante moderato; 5pp.
  g. *Rassegnazione* (Resignation). F♯maj; c♯'–a"; Tess-M; 4/4, 2/4, 3/4, 5/4, Andante calmo; 4pp.

LATIN

PLESKOW, RAOUL
(b. Vienna, Austria, 1931)

A 68. **TWO SONGS ON LATIN FRAGMENTS.** McGinnis and Marx, 1978. cmp1972. X; b♭–a"; Tess-wide; changing meters & tempos; 8pp; Diff-V/dd, P/dd.
For: soprano (score suggests voice or oboe!)
Mood: (a.), praises of God; (b.), lullaby for Child Jesus
Voice: vocal line weaves in and out of piano texture; complex rhythms and pitch relationships; instrumental in concept; melismatic; wide leaps; repetitions and near-repetitions of difficult patterns
Piano: linear texture; some cluster chords; complex rhythms; rapid repeated notes; many accidentals; dynamics,

articulation, and special effects carefully marked; color effects
Diff: perfect pitch desirable; ensemble; singer must be absolutely secure musically and vocally
Uses: effective pair of songs for experienced, mature singer familiar with this idiom

  a. **(no title).** X; b–a"; 4/4 with changes, ♩ = 80.
  b. **(no title).** X; b♭–g♯"; 4/4 with changes, ♩ = 144.

SPANISH

BOWLES, PAUL
(b. Jamaica, NY, 1910; d. Morocco, 1999)

A 69. **CUATRO CANCIONES DE GARCÍA LORCA** (Federico García Lorca). [86]. cmp1944. Fluctuating tonal centers; e♭'–g"; Tess-M-mH; simple meters with changing beats; varied tempos (♩ = 40–104); 13pp; Diff-V/me-m, P/m.
For: tenor; soprano; texts best for a man
Mood: dawn and night scenes; love songs; impressionistic and descriptive
Voice: speech-like rhythms; chromaticism; mostly stepwise; small skips; (d.), sequentially built
Piano: (a.) & (b.), a b a form with broken chords; some doubling of vocal line; (b.), features 11th chords; (c.), short refrain with guitar-like accomp.; (d.), features 7th & 9th chords, some bitonality; short preludes and interludes (one descriptive of trembling water)
Diff: chromaticism against changing key scheme may cause some problems with pitch, esp. at entrances; translations not in score, but (a.) is well known, others easy to translate
Uses: a nice Spanish group with unified poetic theme, though not grouped by the poet
Rec: D#s 27, 124

  a. *Cancioncilla* (Little Song). B♭min/D♭maj; e♭'–f"; Tess-M; 4/4, 3/8, ♩ = 104; 25meas.
  b. *Media Luna* (The Half-Moon). X; g'–e♭"; Tess-M; 4/4 with changes, ♩ = 40; 14meas.
  c. *Balada Amarilla* (Yellow Ballad). C (?); e♭'–g"; Tess-mH; 2/4, ♩ = 76 & 52 (slower refrain); 29meas.
  d. *Murió al Amanecer* (She Died at Dawn). X; f♯'–f♯"; Tess-M; 3/4, 4/4, ♩ = 63; 39meas.

A 70. **MES DE MAYO.** [86]. cmp1944. Gmin; d'–e♭"; Tess-M; 3/4, ♩ = 50; 3pp; Diff-V/me, P/me.
For: all voices
Mood: lyrical; sad spring song; folk-like
Voice: mostly 8th-note motion; stepwise and small skips; strophic
Piano: doubles vocal line; folk-like harmonies; some 7th chords; a distant modulation; 4-meas. solo passage used as prelude, interlude, and postlude
Uses: nice song for student with knowledge of Spanish (no English translation)

CORTÉS, RAMIRO
(b. Dallas, TX, 1933; d. Salt Lake City, UT, 1984)

A 71. **THREE SPANISH SONGS** (Federico García Lorca). Peer International, 1961. cmp1954; rev. 1957. No key sigs.; b♭–a"; Tess-M; regular meters, but with complex rhythms; varied tempos; 14pp; Diff-V/d, P/d.
For: tenor with full low range; mezzo-soprano; texts seem better for a man
Mood: descriptive of the emotional powers of the guitar
Voice: typical Spanish vocal line; many triplet figures and flamenco embellishments; range emphasizes both low tones and tones at top of staff; both Spanish and English texts given; English singable, Spanish better
Piano: guitar figurations; facility and understanding of the style necessary; dissonant
Diff: style; ensemble
Uses: interesting subject; could be very effective for the right singer; program ender

    a. *La Guitarra* (The Guitar). B♭-centered; c♯'–f"; Tess-M; 4/4, 3/4, Lento; 5 pp.
    b. *Las Seis Cuerdas* (The Six Strings). X; f'–f"; Tess-M; 3/4, Andante moderato; 3 pp.
    c. *Adivinanza de la Guitarra* (The Riddle of the Guitar). Dmin-centered; b♭–a"; Tess-M; 2/4, 4/4, 3/4, Tempo agitato; 6pp.

KULP, JONATHAN
(b. Omaha, NE, 1970)

A 72. **CANCIÓN TONTA** (Silly Song) (Federico García Lorca). [9]. cmp1994. Amin-maj; f'–a"; Tess-mH; 6/8; Giocoso ♩. = 126–138; 1min; Diff-V/e, P/m.
For: light soprano
Mood: playful; attempt of child to get his mother's attention
Voice: conjunct, folk-like melodic phrases; one high-lying phrase; two characters (boy & mother); no trans. given
Piano: originally for guitar; figurations are guitar-like and repetitive; harmonies reflect interplay of the two characters
Diff: fast tempo; some cross rhythms
Uses: interesting song for singer with good instincts for being two different characters

SCHONTHAL, RUTH
(b. Hamburg, Germany, 1924)

A 73. **CAZADOR** (Federico García Lorca). [11, Vol. 9]. Bmaj; b–d♯"; Tess-mL; 3/4, Allegro; 3pp; Diff-V/e, P/md.
For: low or medium voices
Mood: nature picture
Voice: both triplet and duplet divisions of the beat; conjunct; syllabic; some long notes at phrase endings; Spanish text; trans. given
Piano: repetitive 1-meas. patterning in the manner of Hugo Wolf in 3 or 4 voices; supports vocal line; some accidentals; 4-meas. prelude; 10-meas. interlude; 5-meas. postlude; almost half of song is solo piano

Uses: pair with "Mi niña se fué a la mar"

A 74. **MI NIÑA SE FUÉ A LA MAR** (Federico García Lorca). [11, Vol. 9]. Fmaj; (g)c'–g"; Tess-M; 4/4, Allegro non troppo; 5pp; Diff-V/m, P/m.
For: medium voices
Mood: light; humorous
Voice: both triplet and duplet divisions and subdivisions of the beat; fairly conjunct; some melismas; long f" at end; Spanish text; trans. given
Piano: dance-like; varied articulations; triplets in one or both hands; short 3/4 section in double time imitates guitar figuration; some doubling of vocal line; 8-meas. prelude; shorter interludes
Diff: long final note; possibly melismas
Uses: pair with "Cazador"

SPECIAL SECTION

ART SONG IN THE UNITED STATES:

1759–1810

by

Gordon Myers

INTRODUCTION

Francis Hopkinson may be the only American-born composer we know about who composed solo or art songs in America before 1800. He furnished only the melodic and bass lines, perhaps because he was skilled in realizing a full keyboard accompaniment when he played them. In general, composers who arrived from England and Europe in the 1790s wrote in the notes of the keyboard part, making sure of how the accompaniment would sound under less skilled hands. Modern editors of our early American song literature tend to create too-full, overly romantic piano accompaniments to these simple and direct singing statements. To my taste, most of them are too heavy and tend to drag down the melodic line into a sea of unneeded notes.

Perhaps the establishment of theater in our cultural life in Philadelphia in the 1790s accounts for the growth of the solo song and its publication in centers such as Boston, New York, Albany, Baltimore, Philadelphia, and Charleston.

In editing and transcribing early American song literature for performance, I prefer to sing or hear them in their original form whenever possible; or, as is the case in my *Six Songs of Early Americans–For Church,* assign the unsung lines of an early hymn or fuguing tune to the keyboard. Only the composer's own notes are used–and the melodies often sound out dramatically in canon form.

I suspect that the early American composer was somewhat more sophisticated than his music, on the surface, suggests. A little probing, a little acquaintance, and a little courage in performing the hymns, the anthems, and the solo songs of America's eighteenth-century composers will reveal something of the power, the solidity, and the spiritual drive that is still a part of our musical life today.

Gordon Myers
Trenton, New Jersey
October 1976

ANTHOLOGIES AND COLLECTIONS

(Numbers given in brackets [ ] in the entries correspond to this key)

ANTHOLOGIES

[MC 1]. **THE FIRST AMERICAN COMPOSER.** Ed. by Harold Milligan. High & Low Voice Editions. Arthur P. Schmidt, 1918.

[MC 2[. **OUR EARLIEST AMERICAN SONGS** (A Series of Individual Publications). Ed. by Philip Weston. Concord Music Publishing Co., 1941. (Hastings-on-Hudson, NY: Henri Elkan Music Publishers).

[MC 3]. **PIONEER AMERICAN COMPOSERS.** Ed. by Harold Milligan. 2 vols. Arthur P. Schmidt, 1921 & 1923. Reprint: Classical Vocal Reprints. High & Medium Vols.

[MC 4]. **SIX SONGS OF EARLY AMERICANS–FOR CHURCH.** Ed. by Gordon Myers. Trenton, NJ: Eastlane Music Corp., 1966.

[MC 5]. **SONGS OF THE FEDERAL PERIOD** With Notes on the Musical Theater of George Washington. Ed. by Angela Talbot. San Diego, CA: Music Graphics Press, 1976.

[MC 6]. **THREE SACRED SONGS FOR SOPRANO.** Ed. by Thor Johnson & Donald McCorkle. New York: Boosey & Hawkes, 1958.

SINGLE COMPOSER COLLECTIONS

[MC 7]. **CARR, Benjamin. SELECTED SECULAR AND SACRED SONGS.** Recent Researches in American Music, vol. XV. Ed. by Eve R. Meyer. Madison, WI: A-R Editions, Inc., 1986.

[MC 8] **HEWITT, James. SELECTED COMPOSITIONS.** Recent Researches in American Music, vol. VII. Ed. by John W. Wagner. Madison, WI: A-R Editions, Inc., 1980.

[MC 9]. **PELISSIER'S COLUMBIAN MELODIES:** Music for the New York and Philadelphia Theaters. Recent Researches in American Music, vols. XIII & XIV. Madison, WI: A-R Editions, 1984.

BELCHER, SUPPLY
(b. Stoughton, MA, 1751; d. Farmington, ME, 1836)

M 1. **WHILE SHEPHERDS WATCH'D** (Nahum Tate). Transcribed & ed. by Gordon Myers. Abingdon, 1964; orig. from *The Harmony of Maine*, 1794. E♭maj (orig. Fmaj); b♭–e♭"; Tess-M; 2/2, ♩ = 66; 4pp (3 strophes); Diff-V/m, P/m.

For: all voices
Mood: Christmas carol; bright; moves along
Voice: varied; legato; melismatic passages
Piano: transcribed vocal parts; tricky; open; stark
Diff: straightforward; legato needed
Uses: practical value; general use
Rec: D#61

BILLINGS, WILLIAM
(b. Boston, MA, 1746; d. Boston, MA, 1800)

M 2. **WHEN JESUS WEPT.** Transcribed & ed. by Gordon Myers. Abingdon, 1965; orig. "A Canon of 4 in 1" in *New England Psalm Singer*, 1770. Emin; b–e"; Tess-M; 3/2, Majestically; 3pp (extra verses by Gordon Myers); Diff-V/m, P/m.

For: all voices
Mood: slow; canonic; religious; "Easterish"
Voice: long, sustained phrases; modal
Piano: transcription of other voices entering
Diff: song starts and ends *a cappella*; lowered 7th gives modal effect
Uses: gem on song program; pure canon has appeal
Rec: D#61

CARR, BENJAMIN
(b. London, England, 1768; d. Philadelphia, PA, 1831)

[See also D#26; no titles given]

M 3. **ALLEN-A-DALE** (Sir Walter Scott). [MC7]; (orig. pub. in *Musical Miscellany in Occasional Numbers*, vol. XI, 1813). Amaj; e'–a"; Tess-mH; 6/8, Allegro moderato; 2pp (5 strophes); Diff-V/m, P/me.

For: high voice
Mood: ballad; narrative
Voice: many skips, some over an 8ve; some dotted rhythms; several ornaments (appoggiaturas, turns)
Piano: staccato broken-chord accomp. in places; one section doubles vocal line
Diff: ornamentation; fitting text of later stanzas to the music
Uses: when a ballad is wanted; period piece for recital (JEC/RMR)

M 4. **AS PANTS THE HART** (Psalm 42). [MC7]; 1st©1832. Cmaj-min; c'–a"; Tess-mH-H; 4/4, Moderato–Largo (Recitative)–Larghetto; 5pp; Diff-V/md, P/m.

For: soprano; tenor
Mood: prayerful
Voice: conjunct with small skips; highly ornamented, esp. at cadences; cadenza-like passages; dotted rhythms;

triplets; more actual musical development than most Carr songs, with a contrasting middle section
Piano: block chords, some in afterbeats; single-voice bass line; r.h. melody in prelude, interlude, and postlude with dotted rhythms; usually doubles vocal line
Diff: ornaments.
Uses: as a period piece; possible church use (JEC/WKG)

M 5. **AVE MARIA** (Hymn to the Virgin) (Sir Walter Scott) (ed. & arr. by Philip Weston). Concord, 1941. [MC7]; (orig. pub. in *Six Ballads from the Lady of the Lake*, 1810). Amaj; d♯'–g"; Tess-H; 4/4, Andante; 6pp; Diff-V/d, P/d.

For: high voice.
Mood: prayerful; calm; slow-moving
Voice: linear; long, sustained notes; legato
Piano: florid, then chordal, then florid again
Diff: sustaining long notes and phrases; maintaining prayerful mood
Uses: one of early America's best songs; "new" setting of "'Ave Maria"; expressive qualities

M 6. **BLANCHE OF DEVAN** (Sir Walter Scott). [MC7]; (orig. pub. in *Six Ballads from the Poem of the Lady of the Lake*, 1810). Gmaj; c'–f"; Tess-M; 3/4, 2/3, Moderato e agitato; 2+pp; Diff-V/m, P/e.

For: mezzo-soprano
Mood: distraught; dramatic
Voice: stepwise and small skips; very spare texture; many dotted rhythms; mostly syllabic; some 2-note slurs
Piano: mixture of block chords (mostly one chord per measure) and 2-voice sections that double vocal line
Diff: dramatic, demented aspects of the song
Uses: as a song from this period that is unusual in mood; could be combined with other songs from *The Lady of the Lake*, such as "Hymn to the Virgin (Ave Maria)" or "Soldier, Rest!" (JEC/RMR)

M 7. **SOLDIER, REST!** (Sir Walter Scott). [MC7]; (orig. pub. in *Six Ballads from the Poem of the Lady of the Lake*, 1810). Gmaj; d'–g"; Tess-M; mixture of siciliana (6/8) & martiale (4/4); 2pp (3 strophes); Diff-V/me, P/m.

For: soprano
Mood: combination of martial and gentle moods
Voice: many small skips; martial sections employ dotted, military rhythms
Piano: *siciliana* sections have harp-like accomp. displaying a characteristic inverted arpeggio figuration in r.h.; some doubling of vocal line; *martiale* sections double vocal line in 8ves
Diff: combining the two moods
Uses: could be combined with other songs from *The Lady of the Lake*, such as "Hymn to the Virgin (Ave Maria)" or "Blanche of Devan" (JEC/RMR)

M 8. **SONG OF THE HEBREW CAPTIVE** (O Sion, O Jerusalem) (Psalm 137). [MC7]; (orig. pub. in *Carr's Sacred Airs*, Op. 16, 1830). E♭maj; d'–b♭"; Tess-H; 3/4, no tempo indication; 8pp; Diff-V/M, P/m.

For: soprano; tenor
Mood: prayerful

Voice: sustained tones giving way to ornamentation in the same phrase; coloratura passages; imitative sections; like Moravian solo compositions of the same period

Piano: repeated block, broken, arpeggiated, rolled, and afterbeat chords; l.h. often in 8ves; accomp. for harp or piano

Diff: tessitura; ornamentation

Uses: for recital or church use (JEC/WKG)

M 9.   TAKE, OH, TAKE THOSE LIPS AWAY (William Shakespeare [2nd strophe attributed to John Fletcher]). [MC7]; (orig. pub. in *Three Ballads from Shakespeare,* 1794). E♭maj; d'–a♭"(b♭"); Tess-H; 2/4, Larghetto amoroso; 2pp (2 strophes); Diff-V/m, P/me.

For: soprano; tenor

Mood: disappointed love song

Voice: stepwise motion; small skips; many ornaments; a few scalar passages in 16ths

Piano: 3–5-voice homophonic texture; doubles vocal line except for 11 meas. that feature afterbeat chordal style; 8-meas. prelude; 4-meas. postlude

Diff: ornamentation (trills; 16th & 32nd notes in other ornaments)

Uses: for a light, flexible voice; group with other Shakespeare songs by Carr (JEC/RMR)

M 10.   TELL ME WHERE IS FANCY BRED (William Shakespeare). [MC7]; (orig. pub. in *Three Ballads from Shakespeare,* 1794). Gmaj; d'–a"; Tess-mH; 6/8, no tempo indication; 2pp; Diff-V/e, P/e.

For: soprano; tenor; easy to transpose for other voices

Mood: questioning

Voice: mostly stepwise or skips outlining the harmony; short phrases

Piano: some harmony in 3rds & 6ths; doubles vocal line; prelude and postlude feature "ding-dong bell" sounds

Uses: group with other Shakespeare songs by Carr (JEC/RMR)

M 11.   THE VI'LET NURS'D IN WOODLAND WILD (poet not given) (from *Lessons and Exercises in Vocal Music, Op. 8*). [MC7]. Fmaj; c'–b♭"; Tess-wide; 3/4, Andantino; 6pp; Diff-V/d, P/m.

For: soprano

Mood: lyrical nature imagery; essentially a vocalise

Voice: sustained tones; much ornamentation, incl. turns, trills, scales, etc.; triplets and dotted-note figures; rather like a Marchesi all-in-one exercise for soprano, but with words

Piano: repeated block and broken chords; scalar passages, sometimes in 3rds; often doubles vocal line

Diff: requires light, flexible technique for coloratura and ornamentation

Uses: as a study to develop flexible technique; could be programmed as a showpiece (JEC/WKG)

M 12.   THE WANDERING HARPER (Sir Walter Scott, text from *Rokeby*). [MC7]; (orig. pub. in *Musical Miscellany in Occasional Numbers,* vol. IX, 1813). E♭maj; d'–g"; Tess-mH; 2/4, Moderato; 3pp (5 strophes); Diff-V/m, P/m.

For: tenor

Mood: minstrel's song; plaintive

Voice: small skips; leaps of a 10th; many dotted rhythms; appoggiaturas and trills; many 2-note slurs

Piano: harp-like, arpeggiated accomp.; no vocal line doubling

Diff: ornamentation

Uses: nice song (JEC/RMR)

M 13.   WHEN ICICLES HANG BY THE WALL (William Shakespeare). [MC7]; (orig. pub. in *Three Ballads from Shakespeare,* 1794). Gmaj; d'–g"; Tess-mH; 6/8, Non troppo allegro; 2pp (2 strophes); Diff-V/md, P/me.

For: soprano; tenor

Mood: descriptive

Voice: mostly conjunct; a few rapid written-out ornaments

Piano: doubles vocal line in r.h.; l.h. has broken chords, single pitches, or 8ves; resembles style of Haydn's German songs

Uses: for a young soprano whose voice works well in this tessitura; group with other Shakespeare songs by Carr (JEC/RMR)

M 14.   WHY, HUNTRESS WHY? (William Dunlap, from *The Archers,* Opera in 3 acts, 1796). [MC2, MC7]. Amaj; e'–a"; Tess-mH; 2/4, Andantino; 4pp (2 stanzas); Diff-V/m, P/m.

For: man's voice

Mood: narrative; descriptive

Voice: rhythmic patterns to express concern

Piano: independent of voice; a little involved; editor has elaborated

Diff: triplets in accomp. fight dotted-8th/16th figure in voice part

Uses: dramatic; programmatic song

M 15.   WILLOW, WILLOW (William Shakespeare). [MC3, vol. I, & MC7 (H)]; 1st© ca.1800. H & L keys: Emin & C♯min; e'–g♯" & c♯'–e"; Tess-M; 6/8, Lento; 4pp; Diff-V/m, P/m.

For: any expressive and dramatic voice

Mood: sad and strong; lament

Voice: strong; full; minor

Piano: chordal; arpeggios

Diff: dramatic song

Uses: classic poem (1794 publication in America)

Rec: D#s 2, 61

NOTE: Following are additional songs by Benjamin Carr found in [MC7]

M 16.   AN AUTUMNAL HYMN (David Paul Brown, Esq.). Dmaj; c♯'–g"; Tess-M–mH; 6/8, Pastorale e moderato; 3pp; Diff-V/md, P/m.

M 17.   THE MINSTREL KNIGHT (poet not given). E♭maj; d'–g"; Tess-M; 2/4, Allegro moderato; 4pp; Diff-V/md, P/md; accomp. for harp or piano.

M 18.   NOAH'S DOVE (poet not given). Fmaj; f'–g"; Tess-mH; 4/4, Moderato; 2pp (3 strophes); Diff-V/m, P/e.

M 19.   A REQUIEM (poet not given). E♭maj; e♭'–f"; Tess-mH; 3/4, Largo; 1+pp (with repeats); Diff-V/m, P/e.

M 20. SEA OF SUSA (poet not given). Gmaj; d'–g"; Tess-mH; 2/4, Andantino espressivo; 2pp (3 strophes); V/m, P/me.

M 21. THY SMILES ARE ALL DECAYING, LOVE (James Gates Percival). Gmaj; d'–f♯"; Tess-M; 6/8, Andante siciliano; 2pp (4 strophes); Diff-V/me, P/e.

M 22. A WEARY LOT IS THINE, SWEET MAID (Sir Walter Scott). B♭maj; d'–g"; Tess-mH; 4/4, Lento; 2pp; Diff-V/md, P/m.

HEWITT, JAMES
(b. Dartmoor, England, 1770; d. Boston, MA, 1827)

M 23. DEEP IN MY SOUL (George Lord Byron, from *The Corsair*). [MC8]. cmp1814–1815. Fmaj; c'–a"; Tess-M; 2/4, Larghetto; 4pp; Diff-V/m, P/m.
For: soprano; tenor
Mood: plea for remembrance by the beloved after death
Voice: "Haydnesque"; appoggiaturas; dotted rhythms
Piano: classical 18th-century accomp.
Diff: style
Uses: lovely song; reminiscent of both "Spirit's Song," by Haydn, and "Abendempfindung," by Mozart (JEC)

M 24. HOPE (Mrs. Wilmot). [MC8]. cmp1807. Amaj; e'–f♯"; Tess-M; 2/4, Andante; 2pp; Diff-V/me, P/e.
For: tenor; soprano
Mood: paean to hope
Voice: classical 18th-century vocal line; stepwise and chordal; many 2-note slurs
Piano: very much like early Mozart
Diff: lightness of style
Uses: lovely song of the period (JEC)

M 25. IN A FAR DISTANT CLIME (R. T. Spence, Esq.). [MC2]. cmp ca.180-. B♭maj; e'–g"; Tess-M; 2/4, Andante moderato; 5pp; Diff-V/e, P/md.
For: any lyric voice
Mood: limpid; lyrical; Mozartean; love song
Voice: very legato and expressive
Piano: sounds like Mozart; editor has "filled in and elaborated"
Diff: style
Uses: excellent example of early art song in America

M 26. KATE OF NEWARK GREEN (Dermoody). [MC5]; 1st©1809. B♭maj; e'–b♭"; Tess-mH; 2/4, Allegretto; 3pp (3 strophes, with repeats); Diff-V/m, P/m.
For: lyric tenor
Mood: lyrical love song; Mozartean
Voice: lyrical and legato; leaps of 8ve & m10th; 2-note slurs; an ascending 16th-note scale
Piano: chordal and linear; r.h. melody supported by broken-chord figures; doubles vocal line
Diff: agility to handle large downward leaps mid-phrase
Uses: good recital song for high, light tenor (WKG)

M 27. KITTY MAGGS AND JOLTER GILES (Charles Dibdin, Jr.). [MC8]. cmp1807. Amin; d♯'–e"; Tess-M; 2/4, tempo not indicated; 2pp; Diff-V/e, P/e.
For: tenor; lyric baritone
Mood: narrative ballad; story of jilted love, suicide, ghosts
Voice: vocal line reminiscent of "The Miller of Dee"
Piano: 18th-century style with bass-line and melody; prelude and postlude
Diff: story-telling
Uses: good 18th-century ballad

M 28. THE TWIN ROSES. [MC3, vol. II]. cmp ca.1811. H & L keys: A♭maj & Fmaj; e♭'–g" & c'–f"; Tess-mH; 3/4, Moderato; 4pp (2 strophes); Diff-V/e, P/e.
For: best for woman's voice
Mood: lyrical; melodramatic; downfall of two roses–symbolic of two women
Voice: long, legato phrases
Piano: mostly chordal; doubles melody
Diff: two 8ve leaps; melody outlines chords
Uses: long expressive phrases; good, fresh, "new," old-fashioned song

HOPKINSON, FRANCIS
(b. Philadelphia, PA, 1737; d. Philadelphia, PA, 1791)

M 29. MY DAYS HAVE BEEN SO WONDROUS FREE (Thomas Parnell). [MC2, MC5, 7]. cmp ca.1759. (also pub. separately and in other collections). Amaj; e'–a"; Tess-M; 2/4; 3pp; Diff-V/e, P/m.
For: any lyric voice
Mood: lyrical; pastoral; legato
Voice: lyrical; sustained phrases
Piano: highly edited and filled in
Diff: straightforward and gracious mood
Uses: good program opener; historical value
Rec: D#s 38, 61

M 30. A WASHINGTON GARLAND (Francis Hopkinson). Orig. title: *Seven Songs for the Harpsichord or Forte Piano* [actually 8 songs]. Ed. & augmented by Harold V. Milligan. A. P. Schmidt, 1918. Reprint: Classical Vocal Reprints, as *Six Songs*. H & L eds. 1st©1788. "To George Washington." Separate entries below. [Rec: D#2]

A. COME, FAIR ROSINA, COME AWAY, No. 1. Amaj (also available in Gmaj); e'–f♯"; Tess-mH; 4/4, Largo (ed. marked *Andante*); 4pp (2 stanzas); Diff-V/e-m, P/e.
For: male voice
Mood: lyrical; limpid; love song
Voice: lyrical line; flowing melody; sustained
Piano: accomp. realized from bass and melody of original
Diff: straightforward; expressive; long phrases
Uses: good opening song in place of the more usual older English song
Rec: D#38

B. MY LOVE IS GONE TO SEA, No. 2. Gmaj (also available in Fmaj); d'–g"; Tess-mL; 2/4, Slow (ed. marked *Andante*); 3pp (3 stanzas); Diff-V/e, P/m.
For: female voice

Mood: melodramatic; one left alone
Voice: simple; diatonic; chord outline
Piano: accomp. realized from bass line and melody of original
Diff: good diction needed; tells a sad story
Uses: historic value; related to early American shipping industry

C.   **BENEATH A WEEPING WILLOW'S SHADE,** No. 3. [14, 27, 32]. Gmaj (also available in Emaj & E♭maj); d'–g"; Tess-M; 6/8, Slow (ed. marked *Andante espressivo*); 4pp (2 stanzas); Diff-V/m, P/m.
For: any lyric voice
Mood: lyrical; descriptive; love song
Voice: linear; smooth; good legato needed
Piano: accomp. realized from bass and melody of original
Diff: sad love–empathetic and lyrical approach needed
Uses: good early program material; old English-style song
Rec: D#38

D.   **ENRAPTURED I GAZE,** No. 4. E♭maj (also available in Cmaj); e♭'–g"; Tess-M; 3/4 (ed. marked *Andante*); 3pp (4 stanzas); Diff-V/md, P/d.
For: male voices
Mood: lyrical; love song
Voice: alternating rhythmic and legato styles
Piano: accomp. realized from bass line and melody of original
Diff: sustaining meaning of word throughout brief melismatic passages
Uses: good for expressing self in love

E.   **SEE, DOWN MARIA'S BLUSHING CHEEK,** No. 5. Cmaj (also available in Amaj); c'–g"; Tess-M; 2/4, Andante (ed. marked *Allegretto*); 6pp (2 stanzas, texts reversed from orig. in edited version); Diff-V/m, P/m.
For: lyric voices
Mood: lyrical; love song
Voice: limpid, clear, and legato (some note changes from original in edited version)
Piano: accomp. realized from bass line and melody of original
Diff: tender, sweet, old-fashioned sentiment; light touch on downward melismatic passages needed
Uses: good recital song

F.   **O'ER THE HILLS,** No. 6. [38]. Dmaj (also available in Cmaj); c♯'–g"; Tess-mH; 4/4, Andante (ed. marked *Allegro spiritoso*); 6pp; Diff-V/m, P/m.
For: any voice
Mood: virile; rhythmic; descriptive of the hunt
Voice: vigorous; rhythmic (melodic line changed in places in edited version)
Piano: accomp. realized from bass line and melodic line of original; tricky in places
Uses: nice ending song for early group; hunting-horn song
Rec: D#61

G.   **MY GENEROUS HEART DISDAINS,** No. 7. Gmaj (also available in Emaj); d'–g"; Tess-M; 2/4, Allegro (ed. marked *Allegretto scherzando*); 10pp; Diff-V/m, P/md.
For: male voice; buffo
Mood: light; comic; pseudo-dramatic; buffo
Voice: legato line; mostly sustained

Piano: accomp. realized from bass line and melody of original
Uses: good for teaching of polite period comedy; forerunner of Gilbert and Sullivan; good ending song; provides insight into theater entertainment of early America

H.   **THE TRAVELLER BENIGHTED,** No. 8. B♭maj (also available in Gmaj); d'–g"; Tess-M; 4/4, Andante (ed. marked *Andante espressivo*); 4pp (3 stanzas); Diff-V/e, P/e-m.
For: any voice
Mood: melodramatic; man lost in the woods
Voice: diatonic; chordal melody
Piano: accomp. realized from bass line and melody of original
Diff: quick change of mood
Uses: period piece; dramatic or melodramatic

INGALLS, JEREMIAH
(b. Andover, MA, 1764; d. Hancock, VT, 1828)

M 31.   **GOD WE SEE ALL AROUND.** [MC4]; orig. pub. in *The Christian Harmony,* 1805. Amin; c'–e"; Tess-mH; 2/2, ♩ = 56; 3pp; Diff-V/m, P/m.
For: all voices
Mood: worship; thanksgiving; majestic
Voice: expressive; legato; long, majestic phrases
Piano: transcribed from vocal parts; independent of melody; some doubling of voice
Diff: long phrases
Uses: general use; worship in a minor key; efficient and expressive melody

M 32.   **TO GRACE A MARRIAGE FEAST.** [MC4]; orig. pub. in *The Christian Harmony,* 1805. Emin (orig. in Amin); d♯'–e"; Tess-M; 4/4, ♩ = 96; 3pp; Diff-V/m, P/m.
For: all voices
Mood: wedding hymn
Voice: long, sweeping phrases
Piano: transcribed from vocal parts; canonic in places; stark; open
Diff: long, expressive minor melody; key change in middle of song
Uses: programmable; practical use; majestic

LYON, JAMES
(b. Newark, NJ, 1735; d. Machias, ME, 1794)

M 33.   **OH, LORD, OUR HEAVENLY KING** (Psalm 8). [MC4]; orig. pub. in *Urania,* 1761. Fmin (orig. in Amin); c'–e"; Tess-L; 3/2, ♩ = 72; 2pp (3 stanzas); Diff-V/m, P/m.
For: all voices
Mood: worship; strong; exuberant
Voice: sustained; legato; ornamented; expressive line; long, slow phrases
Piano: transcribed from vocal parts; open, stark, steady, and rhythmic
Diff: long phrases
Uses: has dignity and majesty; good for capturing and maintaining a mood

Rec: D#61

MEINEKE, CHRISTOPHER
(b. Germany, 1782; d. Baltimore, MD, 1850)

M 34. ABSENCE. Carrs Music Store, 181-? [Library of Congress estimated date]. E♭maj; e♭'–a♭"; Tess-H; 3/4, Andante; 2pp; Diff-V/m,P/e.
For: soprano; tenor
Mood: nostalgic
Voice: melismatic; graceful; skips on chord lines; ornaments
Piano: broken chords; thin texture; some doubling of vocal line

M 35. FORGET ME NOT (Canzonet) (William Frick). Carrs Music Store, ca.1801. E♭maj; e♭'–a♭"; Tess-H; 4/4, Andantino; 2pp (5 strophes); Diff-V/m, P/e.
For: soprano
Mood: lyrical; reminiscent
Voice: melismatic; skips along chord lines
Piano: written-out accomp.; some afterbeats; thin texture; some doubling of vocal line; 8-meas. prelude
NOTE: The above two songs are good period pieces with artistic value.

PELISSIER, VICTOR
(b. France, ca.1745; d. Philadelphia, PA, 1820)

M 36. AH WHY ON QUEBEC'S BLOODY PLAIN (William Dunlap, from Sterne's *Maria,* 1799). [MC9]. Cmin; f'–b♭"; Tess-H; 4/4, Lamentatia con expressione; 2+pp (with repeats); Diff-V/m, P/me.
For: lyric tenor
Mood: sad; wounded soldier left on the battlefield
Voice: stepwise and small skips; leap of dim.7th; appoggiatura; syllabic
Piano: 2-voice linear texture, doubling vocal line in r.h.; 10-meas. prelude and 6-meas. postlude with r.h. in 3rds
Diff: tessitura
Uses: as a period piece (JEC/WKG)

M 37. BELIEVE ME, SIR (Frederick Pilon, from *The Deaf Lover,* 1812). [MC9]. Dmaj; e'–b"; Tess-mH-H; 6/8, Allegretto; 5pp; Diff-V/md, P/me.
For: high soprano
Mood: young lady describes her good character and fine qualities
Voice: mostly conjunct; a few small skips; appoggiaturas; some staccato; syllabic; a few 2-note slurs; two long melismas
Piano: mostly 2-voice linear texture, doubling vocal line in r.h.; some ornaments
Diff: tessitura; long melismatic phrases
Uses: as a period piece (JEC/WKG)

M 38. THE BIRD WHEN SUMMER CHARMS NO MORE (Elihu Hubbard Smith, from *Edwin & Angelina,* 1796). [MC9]. Amaj; e'–c♯'"; Tess-H; 4/4, Moderato; 6+pp; Diff-V/d, P/md.
For: coloratura soprano

Mood: lyrical; nature imagery
Voice: full-blown aria with much coloratura; stepwise with small skips; leaps up to 9th; scalar passages in 16ths; long, sustained b' and e"
Piano: mostly 2-voice linear texture, doubling vocal line in r.h., sometimes in 3rds; 16-meas. prelude; several interludes; postlude; flute obbligato cued in score
Diff: requires extensive, flexible coloratura technique
Uses: could be effectively programmed by a true coloratura soprano; would be even more effective with the flute obbligato (JEC/WKG)

M 39. BRIGHT ORB THAT RULST TH'AETHEREAL WAY (Arthur Murphy, from *Alzuma,* or *The Death of Pizarro,* 1800). [MC9]. E♭maj; e♭'–a♭"; Tess-mH-H; 4/4, Larghetto tempo giusto; 4pp; Diff-V/m, P/m.
For: soprano
Mood: hymn to the sun
Voice: stepwise and small skips; rather stately and hymn-like; 2-part chordal refrain; syllabic
Piano: repeated block and broken chords; single-voice bass line; 32nd-note ornamental figures; often doubles vocal line
Diff: tessitura; probably needs at least a second singer to perform the refrain most effectively
Uses: as a period piece (JEC/WKG)

M 40. DRY THOSE EYES (William Shakespeare). [MC3, vol. II]. cmp ca.1811. H & L keys: Gmaj & Fmaj; d'–g" & c'–f"; Tess-mH; 3/4, Andante; 5pp; Diff-V/md, P/md.
For: best for male voices
Mood: song of comfort; calming love song
Voice: long, sustained, and legato phrases
Piano: mostly chordal; follows melodic line
Diff: some brief, fast scale passages
Uses: for early American or Shakespeare group

M 41. RETURN, O LOVE (Charles Cox). [MC3, vol. I]. cmp ca.1811. H & L keys: Fmaj & Dmaj; f'–a" & d'–f♯"; Tess-M; 3/8, Allegro; 6pp; Diff-V/m, P/m.
For: lyric voices
Mood: love song
Voice: diatonic; chordal outlines
Piano: simple scale passages
Uses: use in place of old English songs; historical value; probably written for the stage; excellent love song

M 42. SONG (Whither Strays My Lover) (William Dimond, from *The Peasant Boy,* 1812). [MC9]. Amaj; e'–b"; Tess-H; 2/4, Andante; 3+pp; Diff-V/md, P/m.
For: soprano
Mood: lyrical love song using nature imagery
Voice: stepwise and small skips; ornaments; sustained e", ending in a cadenza-like figure; syllabic; 2–4-note slurs; small melismas
Piano: 2-voice linear texture, doubling vocal line in r.h.; some chords; 8-meas. prelude; short interludes and postlude
Diff: needs flexible technique and good breath control
Uses: as a period piece (JEC/WKG)

M 43. THE SWEET BLUE-EYE'D MAID (poet not given).

[MC9]. Gmaj; g'–b"; Tess-H; 3/8, tempo not indicated; 5pp; Diff-V/d, P/m.

For: lyric tenor
Mood: lyrical love song
Voice: highly ornamented; lyrical and flowing; short cadenza; 16th-32nd-32nd rest pattern, fragmenting final phrase of each stanza to give a "sighing" effect
Piano: 2–3-voice linear texture, doubling vocal line in r.h.; 14-meas. prelude; 4- & 10-meas. interludes (one featuring dotted rhythms); 8-meas. postlude
Diff: ornaments; fragmented climactic phrases
Uses: as a period piece (JEC/WKG)

REINAGLE, ALEXANDER
(b. Portsmouth, England, 1756; d. Baltimore, MD, 1809)

M 44. I HAVE A SILENT SORROW (R. B. Sheridan). [MC3, vol. I]. cmp ca.1799. H & L keys: Amaj & Gmaj; e'–g♯" & d'–f♯"; Tess-M; 3/4, Slow and plaintive; 3pp; Diff-V/e, P/m.

For: any lyric voice
Mood: sad; broken love; lament
Voice: sustained; expressive
Piano: no difficulties but edited and filled in; perhaps overdone
Diff: long phrases
Uses: good for mood; composer was friend and student of Carl Philipp Emanuel Bach

M 45. JERRY'S SONG. [MC3, vol. II]; from *The Volunteers* (opera), cmp1796. H & L keys: Fmaj & E♭maj; c'–g" & b♭–f"; Tess-M; 6/8, Allegretto giocoso; 4pp (2 stanzas); Diff-V/e, P/m.

For: male voices
Mood: lighthearted
Voice: folk-like melody; fast moving
Piano: realized from original bass line and melody; both chordal and linear
Diff: many words; humorous, complaining mood
Uses: good for putting across point of humor; group ender
Rec: D#61

SELBY, WILLIAM
(b. England, 1738; d. Boston, MA, 1798)

M 46. THE LOVELY LASS (Mr. Brown). [MC2]. cmp1790. Gmaj; d'–g"; Tess-M; 3/4, 4pp; Diff-V/e, P/m.

For: any voice
Mood: pastoral; old English in flavor
Voice: agile; not sustained
Piano: accomp. realized and filled-in considerably by the editor from the bass line and melody of the original
Uses: good and interesting early art song; historical value

SWAN, TIMOTHY
(b. Worcester, MA, 1758; d. Northfield, MA, 1842)

M 47. THE SOLDIER'S FAREWELL. [MC3, vol. I]. cmp ca.1800. H & L keys: Fmaj & Dmaj; c'–g" & a–e";

Tess-L; 2/4, Andante semplice; 3pp; Diff-V/e, P/e.

For: male voices
Mood: soldier's farewell to his bride
Voice: folksong-like
Piano: chordal; follows vocal melody most of the time
Diff: expressing the text
Uses: good example of period piece; melodramatic "tear-jerker"

TAYLOR, RAYNOR
(b. England, ca. 1747; d. Philadelphia, PA, 1825)

M 48. CUPID AND THE SHEPHERD. [MC3, vol. I]. cmp ca.1790 or 1800 (before 1825). H & L keys: Gmaj & E♭maj; f♯'–g" & d'–e♭"; Tess-M; 2/4, Allegretto; 5pp; Diff-V/e, P/e.

For: lyric voices
Mood: bright; happy narration about love
Voice: airy and light melody; mixture of French and English possible
Piano: straightforward; doubles melody some of the time
Diff: practice in dialogue–French or English
Uses: clever, lighthearted song for a French group

M 49. THE LORD MY SHEPHERD IS (Psalm 23, paraphrased). [MC4]; orig. pub. in the *Columbian Repository,* 1805. Cmaj (orig. E♭maj); b–e"; Tess-M; 4/4, ♩ = 84; 3pp (3 stanzas); Diff-V/m, P/m.

For: all voices
Mood: worship; lyrical; somewhat secular in feeling
Voice: legato; moving melodic line
Piano: transcribed from vocal parts; straightforward; doubles vocal line
Diff: long, sustained phrasing; low tones need to match high tones in quality
Uses: classic text; long breaths needed

M 50. THE WOUNDED SOLDIER. [MC3, vol. II]. cmp1794. H & L keys: Fmaj & Dmaj; f'–g"; & d'–e"; Tess-M; 4/4, Marziale; 4pp (3 stanzas); Diff-V/m, P/m.

For: male voices
Mood: dramatic; military; heroic wounded
Voice: dramatic; marching; vigorous; syncopation
Piano: march tempo
Diff: singing words clearly in march tempo
Uses: strong, virile, assertive song; group ender

UNKNOWN

M 51. WHILE SHEPHERDS WATCH'D (Nahum Tate). [MC4]; orig. pub. in James Lyon's *Urania,* 1761. Dmaj (orig. Gmaj); a–e"; Tess-M; 6/8, ♩. = 60; 2pp (3 stanzas); Diff-V/m, P/m.

For: all voices
Mood: happy; Christmas song
Voice: almost a siciliana; rhythmic play against the accomp.
Piano: fashioned from the original melody and bass line; doubles vocal line
Diff: different rhythmic patterns in melody and bass
Uses: good, alive song; some melismas

von HAGEN, P. A.
(b. Charleston, SC, 1781; d. 1837)

M 52. GENTLE ZEPHYR. [MC3, vol. II]. cmp ca.1800. H
& L keys: E♭maj & Bmaj; g'–a♭" & d♯'–e"; Tess-M;
4/4, Allegretto; 3pp (5 strophes); Diff-V/e, P/m.
For: any lyric and beautiful voice
Mood: pastoral; gentle; lyrical
Voice: limpid and graceful; some chromaticism
Piano: comfortable and interesting; 16th-note figures in l.h.
Uses: similar in style to Mozart or Haydn; good song; lovely
relief in a program format

M 53. MAY MORNING. [MC3, vol. II]. cmp ca.1800. H &
L keys: Amaj & Emaj; e'–a" & b–e"; Tess-L; 6/8,
Allegretto; 4pp (3 strophes); Diff-V/m, P/m.
For: light lyric voice
Mood: bright; happy love song
Voice: legato; many words
Piano: chordal in r.h.; arpeggios in l.h.
Diff: excellent melodic section with successive interval leaps
of 4th, 5th, 6th, 5th, 6th, & 7th
Uses: excellent opening song or use in middle of group

M 54. MONODY. [MC3, vol. I]. cmp ca.1810. H & L keys:
Dmin & Bmin; d'–g" & b–e"; Tess-M; 4/4; 5pp; Diff-
V/e, P/e.
For: any voice
Mood: sad; dramatic; somber
Voice: dirge-like; some interrupted phrases
Piano: mostly chordal
Diff: convey message of sadness, yet not drag tempo
Uses: create and hold mood

M 55. THE PRIDE OF OUR PLAINS. [MC3, vol. I]. cmp
ca.1810. H & L keys: Dmaj & B♭maj; d'–g" & b♭–e♭";
Tess-M; 6/8, Siciliana; 4pp; Diff-V/e, P/m.
For: lyrical woman's voice best
Mood: declamatory; narrative; beauty of a rose
Voice: Handelian
Piano: doubles melody part of the time
Diff: poem has double meaning
Uses: good solid program song; light and happy

WILSON, JAMES (or JOSEPH)
(fl. ca. 1780–1820?)

**M 56. I KNEW BY THE SMOKE THAT SO
GRACEFULLY CURLED** (T[homas] Moore). [MC3,
vol. II]. cmp ca.1805–1809. H & L keys: Gmaj &
Fmaj; d'–g" & c'–e"; Tess-M; 6/8, Andante; 5pp; Diff-
V/e, P/m.
For: male voice (light and lyric)
Mood: folk-type; dreamy; wistful; philosophical
Voice: folk-like melody; descriptive
Piano: chordal; melodic; countermelodies
Uses: simple and straightforward; words expressive and
descriptive; general programming

WOOD, ABRAHAM
(b. Northborough, MA, 1752; d. Northborough, MA, 1804)

M 57. ANGELS TELL THE LORD IS RIS'N. [MC4]; orig.
pub. in *The Divine Songs,* 1789. Dmaj (orig. E♭maj);
d'–e"; Tess-mH; 2/2, ♩ = 60; 3pp; Diff-V/e, P/e.
For: all voices
Mood: rejoicing; Easter song
Voice: straightforward; legato; many words
Piano: transcribed from vocal parts; sparse; doubles vocal line
some of the time
Diff: high, soft, joyful singing
Uses: historic value

THE MORAVIANS

The members of the Moravian sect who came to this country at
the end of the 18th century brought their musical practices with
them and continued to compose and perform music in their
churches in Pennsylvania and North Carolina. Some of the
composers immigrated to the United States, settled here, and
became citizens, while others were born here; still others were
here for a time but returned to other countries. At least one listed
in this bibliography, Johann D. Grimm, was never in this country,
but his compositions were widely circulated in the United States.
Christian I. Latrobe was in the United States for a time, but
apparently died in England.

The inclusion of the Moravians in a bibliography of American
song is witness to the great diversity that the culture of the United
States has always embraced. Their music is essentially of the
style of Joseph Haydn and Wolfgang Amadeus Mozart, yet much
of it was composed, and all of it was performed on a regular
basis, in this country. Even though most of the texts were
originally in German, and most of the songs were conceived for
instrumental accompaniment, present-day performers frequently
use these church songs with piano accompaniment in recital.
When one thinks of Moravian music, early America usually
comes to mind; therefore, they are included in this bibliography.

ANTES, JOHN
(b. Frederickstownship, PA, 1740; d. Bristol, England, 1811)

M 58. AND JESUS SAID, IT IS FINISHED (John 19:30).
Ed. & arr. by Donald McCorkle. Boosey & Hawkes,
1958. cmp ca.1790. Gmin; b♭–g"; Tess-M; 4/4, Adagio;
7pp; Diff-V/m, P/e.
For: soprano
Mood: dramatic; somber
Voice: extended phrases; expressive; many half and whole notes
Piano: well-transcribed from string score; style of Mozart and
Haydn; some doubling of voice
Diff: long phrases
Uses: good for sustaining dramatic mood

M 59. GO, CONGREGATION, GO! (Christian Gregor). Ed.
& arr. by Donald McCorkle. Boosey & Hawkes, 1959.
cmp ca.1795. Cmin; b–a♭"; Tess-H; 4/4, Adagio; 3pp;
Diff-V/d, P/md.

For: soprano
Mood: dramatic; somber
Voice: high; expressive; long phrases; extended range
Piano: transcribed from string score; straightforward; some chromatic passages
Diff: range; interrupted phrases
Uses: expressive song for soprano; high tones are the expressive part of the melody

M 60. LOVELIEST IMMANUEL (John Antes?). Ed. & arr. by Donald McCorkle. Boosey & Hawkes, 1958. cmp ca.1800. B♭maj; f'–g"; Tess-mH; 2/4, Andantino; 3pp; Diff-V/e, P/md.
For: soprano; possibly tenor
Mood: song of praise and prayer
Voice: chorale-like; lyric and expressive
Piano: agitated; after-beat figures
Diff: maintaining legato line; long phrases
Uses: invocation; good opening song for group; classical style

GRIMM, JOHANN
(b. Germany, 1719; d. Germany, 1760)

M 61. LAMB OF GOD! THOU SHALT REMAIN FOREVER (Christian R. von Zinzendorf; trans. John Swertner). Adapted by Christian I. Latrobe; ed. by E. V. Nolte. Abingdon, 1966. cmp1750. H & L keys: E♭maj & Cmaj; e♭'–g" & c'–e"; Tess-M; 2/2, Andante; 4pp (with repeat); Diff-V/e, P/e.
For: all voices
Mood: song of praise; bright
Voice: straightforward; uncomplicated
Piano: easy; supportive of voice, but does not double
Uses: general use

HERBST, JOHANNES
(b. Kempton, Swabia, 1735; d. Salem, NC, 1812)

M 62. I WILL GO IN THE STRENGTH OF THE LORD (Psalm 71:16). Ed. & arr. by Donald McCorkle. Boosey & Hawkes, 1958. cmp1773. Fmaj; c'–g"; Tess-M; 3/4, Andante; 5pp; Diff-V/e, P/md.
For: soprano; possibly tenor
Mood: bright; uplifting
Voice: vigorous; assertive
Piano: transcribed from string score; many 3rds and broken-chord passages
Uses: declamatory song with strength, power, and authority
Rec: D#61

LATROBE, CHRISTIAN I.
(b. England, 1758; d. England, 1836)

M 63. HOW SHALL A MORTAL SONG ASPIRE (Ambrose Serle, or Christian I. Latrobe?). Ed. & arr. by Donald McCorkle. Boosey & Hawkes, 1958. cmp ca.1800. Amaj; d'–a"; Tess-H; Recit.: 4/4, Largo–Aria: 3/4, Andante; 9pp; Diff-V/m, P/d.
For: soprano; tenor

Mood: song of praise
Voice: long lines; strong; semi-operatic; sustained; some coloratura; some rhythmic sequence
Piano: needs strong l.h.; florid
Diff: excellent Classical recit. and aria style

MICHAEL, DAVID MORITZ
(b. Künhausen, near Erfurt, Germany, 1751; d. Neuwied am Rhine, Germany, 1825)

M 64. I LOVE TO DWELL IN SPIRIT (Christian R. von Zinzendorf). [MC6]. cmp ca.1800. Fmaj; e'–g"; Tess-mH; 4/4, Andante; 4pp; Diff-V/e, P/m.
For: high voices
Mood: bright; exuberant
Voice: diatonic; outlines chords; a few accidentals
Piano: broken chords; some 3rds
Uses: Classical style; good song

PETER, JOHANN FRIEDRICH
(b. Heerendijk, Netherlands, 1746; d. Bethlehem, PA, 1813)

M 65. THE DAYS OF ALL THY SORROW (Isaiah 60:20). [MC6]. cmp1782. Dmaj (orig. Fmaj); d'–a"; Tess-mH; 2/4, Poco adagio; 3pp; Diff-V/e-m, P/m.
For: soprano
Mood: lyrical; serious
Voice: Classical vocal line; legato; expressive
Piano: straightforward; mostly chordal
Diff: octave leaps in melodic line
Uses: good Classical-style recital material

M 66. I WILL MAKE AN EVERLASTING COVENANT (Isaiah 55:3). [MC6]. cmp1782. B♭maj (orig. Dmaj); d'–f"; Tess-M; 3/8, Andante; 3pp; Diff-V/e-m, P/md.
For: soprano
Mood: uplifting; bright
Voice: lyrical; legato; leaps of 6th, 7th, & 8ve
Piano: transcribed from string score; mostly chordal
Diff: keeping strength of triple meter
Uses: good song

M 67. THE LORD IS IN HIS HOLY TEMPLE (Hebrews 2:20). Ed. & arr. by Thor Johnson & Donald McCorkle. Boosey & Hawkes, 1958. cmp1786. E♭maj; e♭'–f"; Tess-M; 2/4, Poco vivace (editor's marking, should be *Andante*); 5pp; Diff-V/m, P/md.
For: soprano
Mood: quiet; soothing
Voice: long, sustained phrases; expressive soft singing
Piano: transcribed from string score; lacy; 6ths & 3rds
Diff: breath control; sustained phrases
Uses: good song
Rec: D#61

DISCOGRAPHY

The purpose of this Discography is to supplement the Annotated Bibliography by bringing into one place as complete a listing of recorded art songs by American (U.S.) composers as the authors could assemble from readily available sources. Many of the recordings are no longer available commercially and exist only in library or private collections, and CD numbers often change with each reissue. Nevertheless, we believe that this listing will be a valuable tool both for teaching and historical research.

The Discography is divided into two parts: (1) Anthology Recordings, and (2) Single Composer Recordings. The information contained in each entry is as follows: **(1) ANTHOLOGIES: RECORD TITLE;** Performers; Recording (▲) Company and Number; **Composers** and Titles of Individual Songs or *Song Cycles* or *Sets,* where known. (In some instances, only the composers represented were listed.) **(2) SINGLE COMPOSER RECORDINGS: COMPOSER**; *Title* (*Cycle* or *Set* or Individual Song); Performers; Recording (▲) Company and Number; Titles of individual songs where known. (Some entries do not give titles because none were listed in the source. Not all title listings are complete for the same reason. Occasionally there will be song titles that are not in the Bibliography). Note that cycle and set titles are italicized, and single song titles are in Roman type.

The format of the listing is as follows: (1) Every recorded composer who is also in the Annotated Bibliography is listed in one alphabet in the **Single Composer Recordings** section. (2) Each composer who has one or more numbered recording entries (e.g., Barber, with 17, or Bolcom, with 2) may also have an additional numbered entry designated *See also . . .* to cross-reference to songs in Anthology Recordings section. (3) Composers who have no single composer recording entry will simply be cross-referenced to songs in anthologies in an unnumbered *See # . . .* entry. These unnumbered composer entries are included in the alphabetical listing to facilitate use of the Discography without reference to the title entries in the Annotated Bibliography.

The Discography is designed to be used with or without reference to the numbered title entries in the Annotated Bibliography. To use with reference to the Bibliography, find a song title in the numbered entries and go to the **Rec:** line. The number or numbers on this line refer to the numbered entries in the Discography [**D#**(s)]. To use the Discography without reference to the Bibliography, find the composer in the Single Composer Recordings section. The numbers given in the *See . . .* or *See also . . .* entries refer to the anthologies in the first part of the Discography, where you will find songs of the composer of interest listed in one or more multiple-composer recordings. It is also possible to find whether a single song, cycle, or set has been recorded by consulting the Title Index. The ◆ symbol following the Index number indicates that a recording of the song(s) exists, and that the D# can be found on the **Rec:** line of the Bibliography entry of that song.

The ▲ symbol means that the recording is a CD. Recordings that are listed as some form of RCA Victor with 10" or 12" following the company name are pre-LP-technology, 78rpm recordings, many of which have been remastered into CD anthologies. They have been included in their original form for historical perspective. Other recordings are LPs unless identified as cassette tapes.

The Discography was compiled from the following sources:

The American Record Guide (1992–January, 2000).

Cohen, Aaron I. *International Discography of Women Composers.* Discography #10. Westport, CT: Greenwood Press, 1984.

Davis, Elizabeth A. *Index to the New World Recorded Anthology of American Music. A*

User's Guide to the Initial One Hundred Records. New York: W. W. Norton and Company, 1981.

Frasier, Jane. *Women Composers: A Discography.* Detroit Studies in Bibliography, #50. Detroit: Information Coordinators, 1983.

The Gramophone Shop Encyclopedia of Recorded Music. New York: Simon and Schuster, 1942.

Greenfield, Edward, Robert Layton, and Ivan March. *The Penguin Guide to Compact Discs, Cassettes, and LPs.* Harmondsworth, Middlesex, England: Penguin Books, Ltd., 1986.

Lessner, Joanne Sydney. "New from the Studios." *Opera News* 65, no. 4 (October 2000): 27–39.

Schwann Record and Tape Guide. 1974–1990.

Schwann OPUS. 1991–2000. [NOTE: It was not possible to research every issue of the Schwann publications due to lacunae in the library holdings and the practice of keeping only the current issue of OPUS for ordering purposes. However, numerous issues of OPUS that were privately owned were researched, and the Schwann OPUS company kindly supplied some back issues.]

Stahl, Dorothy. *A Selected Discography of Solo Song: Accumulation through 1971.* Detroit: Detroit Studies in American Bibliography, #24, 1972.

———. *A Selected Discography of Solo Song, Supplement, 1971–1974.* Detroit: Detroit Studies in American Bibliography, #34, 1976.

———. *A Selected Discography of Solo Song, Supplement, 1975–1982.* Detroit: Detroit Studies in American Bibliography, #52, 1984.

Villamil, Victoria. *The Singer's Guide to THE AMERICAN ART SONG 1870–1980.* Metuchen, NJ: Scarecrow Press, 1993.

ANTHOLOGY RECORDINGS
(Recordings with more than one composer)

1. THE AIDS QUILT SONGBOOK. Kurt Ollman, William Parker, William Sharp, Sanford Sylvan, baritones. Harmonia Mundi 907602. **Wheelock:** Fury; **Hersch:** blues for an imaginary valentine; **Musto:** Heartbeats; **Rorem:** A Dream of Nightingales; **DeBlasio:** Walt Whitman in 1989; **Krakauer:** The 80's Miracle Diet; **Lockwood:** For Richard; **St. Pierre:** Fairy Book Lines; **Bolcom:** Vaslav's Song; **Thomas:** AIDS Anxiety; **Harbison:** The Flute of Interior Time; **Byron:** The Birds of Sorrow; **Hoiby:** Investiture at Cecconi's; **Brown:** A Certain Light; **Gordon:** I Never Knew.

2. ALBUM OF AMERICAN ART SONGS. Donald Stenberg, baritone; Joann Crossman, piano. Educo Records 4006. **Hopkinson:** The Garland; **Carr:** Willow, Willow; **S. Foster:** Oh, Susanna; **Foote:** The Night Has a Thousand Eyes; **Chadwick:** Thou Art So like a Flower; The Danza; **Homer:** In the Country of the Camisards; In the Meadow; Michael Robartes Bids His Beloved Be at Peace; **Beach:** The Year's at the Spring; **Carpenter:** When I Bring to You Coloured Toys; on the Seashore of Endless Worlds; **Griffes:** An Old Song Resung; **Ives:** Charlie Rutlage; Walking; **Barber:** Sleep Now; I Hear an Army.

3. ALWAYS IT'S SPRING. Erie Mills, soprano; Jeffry Peterson, piano. VAI Audio ▲ VAIA 1151. **Hoiby:** Always It's Spring; What If . . .; The Doe; She Tells Her Love; The Serpent; **Ives:** Two Little Flowers; Ann Street; Memories (Very Pleasant; Rather Sad); **Mollicone:** To Daffodils; The Snowflake; The Snail; If You Were Coming in the Fall; **Bacon:** The Little Stone; This and My Heart; Is There Such a Thing as Day?; Weeping and Sighing; **Farwell:** The Sabbath; Aristocracy; **J. Duke:** The Rose Did Caper on Her Cheek; Bee! I'm Expecting You; Nobody Knows this Little Rose; Good Morning, Midnight; Heart, We Will Forget Him; **Downey:** Remembrance; Swing Set; Reminder; Hungry Squirrel; Reaffirmation; Red Rose; **Rorem:** Song for a Girl; In a Gondola; Pippa's Song.

4. AN AMERICAN ANTHOLOGY. Meriel Dickinson, mezzo-soprano. Unicorn UNI 72017. **Cage:** 5 Songs for Contralto; **E. Carter:** *Three Poems of Robert Frost*; Voyage; **Copland:** Poet's Song; **Thomson:** *Two by Marianne Moore* [and others].

5. AMERICAN DREAMER. Heart Songs. Jean Danton, soprano; Thomas Stumpf, piano. Albany ▲ TROY 319. **Bernstein:** My House; **Carpenter:** The Sleep that Flits on Baby's Eyes; **S. Foster:** Beautiful Dreamer; Ah, May the Red Rose Live Alway; If You've Only Got a Moustache; **Ganz:** A Memory; **Ives:** Memories: A and B; Songs My Mother Taught Me; The Circus Band.

6. AMERICAN SAMPLER. Elizabeth Suderberg, soprano; Robert Suderberg, piano. Washington University Press, OLY 104. **Benshoof:** The Cow; Dinky; The Fox; John Brown's Body; The Waking; **Bond:** I Love You Truly; A

Perfect Day; **Carpenter:** The Player Queen; **S. Foster:** I Cannot Sing Tonight; Some Folks; Summer Longings; Why No One to Love?; **Griffes:** Early Morning in London; Lament of Ian the Proud; **Ives:** Walt Whitman; The White Gulls.

7. AMERICAN SONG RECITAL. Lauren Wagner, soprano; Fred Weldy, piano. Channel 5293 (Allegro). **Bernstein:** Dream with Me; **Bolcom:** Never More Will the Wind; **Bowles:** Secret Words; Sugar in the Cane; Night without Sleep; **Corigliano:** Fort Tryon Park; **J. Duke:** Bee! I'm Expecting You; **Hundley:** Come Ready and See Me; Sweet Suffolk Owl; Waterbird; **Musto:** Recuerdo; Social Note; **Thomas:** I Never Saw a Moor.

8. THE ART OF ARLEEN AUGÉR. Arleen Augér, soprano; Joel Revzen, piano. Koch 3-7248-2 H1. **Larsen:** *Sonnets from the Portuguese.*

9. ART SONG HERITAGE OF THE AMERICAS. Frederick Kennedy, tenor; H. Venazi, piano. CRS Master ▲ CRS 9662. **Paulus:** Archaic Torso of Apollo; The Dance; Moor Swan; **Sowerby:** With Strawberries; A Persian Love Song; Dream Rivers.

10. THE ART SONG IN AMERICA. John Kennedy Hanks, tenor; Ruth Friedberg, piano. Duke University Press 2 ▲ G822320517 (originally on LPs). **MacDowell:** The Sea; Long Ago; Thy Beaming Eyes; **Chadwick:** O, Let Night Speak of Me; **Loeffler:** A Dream within a Dream; **Ives:** Paracelsus; Canon; Charlie Rutlage; **Hageman:** Do Not Go My Love; **Carpenter:** When I Bring to You Colored Toys; **Griffes:** By a Lonely Forest Pathway; Symphony in Yellow; Lament of Ian the Proud; An Old Song Resung; **Josten:** Adoration; **J. Duke:** White in the Moon; Loveliest of Trees; Viennese Waltz; There Will Be Stars; Yellow Hair; In Just Spring; I Carry Your Heart; The Mountains Are Dancing; **Bacon:** It's All I Have to Bring; And This of All My Hopes; **Copland:** When They Come Back; The Chariot; **R. Harris:** Fog; **Dougherty:** Serenader; **Bowles:** Cabin; Heavenly Grass; **Finney:** Wedlock; Drinking Song; **Barber:** Bessie Bobtail; Sure on This Shining Night; Nocturne; I Hear an Army; **Nordoff:** White Nocturne; **Klenz:** Walk the Silver Night Together; Hush; **Dello Joio:** Eyebright; Meeting at Night; **Rorem:** A Christmas Carol; Guilt; For Susan; Clouds; What Sparks and Wiry Cries; **Persichetti:** The Grass; Thou Child So Wise; The Death of a Soldier; The Snow Man; Of the Surface of Things; **Cumming:** Go, Lovely Rose; Memory, Hither Come; The Little Black Boy; **Trimble:** Tell Me Where Is Fancy Bred?; Love Seeketh Not Itself to Please; **Earls:** Entreat Me Not to Leave You; Arise, My Love.

11. ART SONGS BY AMERICAN COMPOSERS. Yolanda Marcoulescou-Stern, soprano. Gasparo ▲ GSCD 287. **Beach:** Empress of Night; The Year's at the Spring; **Bowles:** Once a Lady Was Here (and 2 others?); **Carpenter:** The Sleep That Flits on Baby's Eyes; On the Seashore of Endless Worlds; Serenade; **Creston:** The Bird of the Wilderness; Fountain Song; Lullaby; Psalm XXIII;Serenade; **J. Duke:** Be Still as You Are Beautiful; Bells in the Rain; just-spring; **Griffes:** Evening Song; In a

Myrtle Shade; We'll to the Woods and Gather May; **Hageman:** At the Well; Miranda; **Price:** Song to the Dark Virgin; **Sacco:** Brother Will, Brother John; **Thomson:** Tell Me Where Is Fancy Bred; Sigh No More, Ladies.

12. **ART-SONGS BY BLACK AMERICAN COMPOSERS.** Laura English-Robinson, Hilda Harris, George Shirley, Willis Patterson, Susan Mathews, Cloritha Buggs, and other singers. Book of the Month Club Records, University of Michigan, BOMC 91-6674. **Adams:** For You There Is No Song; **Bonds:** Three Dream Portraits; **Still:** Grief; **Swanson:** A Death Song; The Negro Speaks of Rivers; I Will Lie Down in Autumn; **Walker:** Lament; A Red, Red Rose [and others].

13. **ART SONGS BY WOMEN.** Katherine Eberle, mezzo-soprano; Robin Guy, piano. Vienna Modern Masters 2005 (Albany). **Howe:** Der Einsame; Viennese Waltz; You; Men.

14. **BELOVED THAT PILGRIMAGE.** Sanford Sylvan, baritone; D. Breitman, piano. NON ▲ 79259. **Barber:** *Hermit Songs*; **Chanler:** *Epitaphs*; **Copland:** *Poems (8) of Emily Dickinson.*

15. **BLUE MOODS: American Art Songs.** Theresa Treadway, mezzo-soprano. Orion ORS 84476. **Pasatieri:** *Three Poems of James Agee*; **Rorem:** *Two Poems of Theodore Roethke* [and others].

16. **BUT YESTERDAY IS NOT TODAY: The American Art Song, 1930–1960.** Bethany Beardslee, soprano; Donald Gramm, baritone; Robert Helps and Donald Hassard, pianists. New World Recorded Anthology of American Music: NW 243 (LP). **Barber:** Sure on This Shining Night; **Bowles:** Once a Lady Was Here; Song of an Old Woman; **Copland:** Song; **Chanler:** The Children; Once Upon a Time; The Rose; Moo Is a Cow; Thomas Logge; These, My Ophelia; **Citkowitz:** *Five Songs from "Chamber Music"*; **J. Duke:** Richard Cory; Luke Havergal; Miniver Cheevy; **R. Helps:** *The Running Sun*; **Sessions:** On the Beach at Fontana.

17. **BUT YESTERDAY IS NOT TODAY: The American Art Song, 1927–1972.** NWW ▲ 80243. Same as above except **Citkowitz** listed as Strings in the Earth and Air; When the Shy Star Goes Forth in Heaven; O It Was Out by Donneycarney; Bid Adieu; My Love Is in a Light Attire.

18. **CAROLYN HEAFNER SINGS SONGS BY BEACH, BEESON, WEISGALL, HOIBY, AND BACON.** Carolyn Heafner, soprano; D. R. Neil and Lee Hoiby, pianists. CRI SD 462. **Bacon:** I'm Nobody; Eden; Poor Little Heart; The Little Stone; The Heart; Banks of the Yellow Sea; Simple Days. **Beach:** *Three Browning Songs,Op. 44.*; **Beeson:** Death by Owl-Eyes; The You Should of Done It Blues; Eldorado; **Hoiby:** *Night Songs*; **Weisgall:** *Four Songs on Poems by Adelaide Crapsey.*

19. **A CHARM OF LULLABIES.** Maureen Forrester, contralto; John Newmark, piano. Westminster/abc: WST 17137. **Ives:** Berceuse; **Rich:** American Lullaby.

20. **THE CLOISTERS.** Henry Herford, baritone; R. Bowman, piano. New World: ▲ NW 80327-2 (formerly NW-327). **Corigliano:** *The Cloisters*; **A. Shepherd:** Golden Stockings; To a Trout; Virgil; **Susa:** *Hymns for the Amusement of Children*; **Weber:** *The Way.*

21. **DIVAS IN SONG: A 60TH BIRTHDAY CELEBRATION FOR MARILYN HORNE.** Montserrat Caballé, Helen Donath, Renée Fleming, Ruth Ann Swenson, sopranos; Frederica von Stade, mezzo-soprano; Samuel Ramey, bass; Marilyn Horne, mezzo-soprano; Martin Katz, piano. RCA Victor Red Seal ▲ 62547. **Bolcom:** Amor; **Copland:** At the River; **J. Duke:** The Bird; **S. Foster:** If You've Only Got a Moustache.

22. **DREAMS AND FANCIES: FAVOURITE SONGS.** Sarah Walker, mezzo-soprano; Roger Vignoles, piano. CRD 3473 (Qualitron Imports). **R. Clarke:** The Seal Man; The Aspidistra; **Hoiby:** Jabberwocky.

23. **EILEEN FARRELL IN SONGS AND BALLADS.** Eileen Farrell, soprano; George Trovillo, piano. Angel Records 35608. **Nordoff:** There Shall Be More Joy; **Naginski:** The Pasture; **Sargent:** Hickory Hill; **Homer:** Sing to Me; **Charles:** Let My Song Fill Your Heart; When I Have Sung My Songs; **C. Shaw:** The Lamb; **Taylor:** May-Day Carol.

24. **EV'RY TIME WE SAY GOODBYE.** Samuel Ramey, bass; Warren Jones, piano. Sony Classical ▲ SK 68339. **Barber:** Sea-Snatch; I Hear an Army; Sure on This Shining Night; Bessie Bobtail; **Bowles:** They Cannot Stop Death; *Blue Mountain Ballads*; **S. Foster:** If You've Only Got a Moustache; Gentle Annie; Don't Bet Your Money on the Shanghai; **Griffes:** Evening Song; An Old Song Re-Sung; The Lament of Ian the Proud; Song of the Dagger.

25. **THE FLOWERING OF VOCAL MUSIC IN AMERICA, VOL. I.** Music of the Moravians and Heinrich. Barbara Wallace, Cynthia Clarey, sopranos; Charles Bressler, tenor; H. Wingreen, piano. New World Recorded Anthology of American Music: New World 230. **Herbst:** Abide in Me; See Him; And Thou Shalt Know It; How Gently Doth My Soul Rejoice; Thanks Be to Thee.

26. **THE FLOWERING OF VOCAL MUSIC IN AMERICA, VOL. II.** New World Recorded Anthology of American Music: New World 231. Songs by **Benjamin Carr**, **George Jackson**, and **Oliver Shaw**.

27. **FRENCH, GERMAN, ITALIAN AND SPANISH SONGS BY AMERICAN COMPOSERS.** Yolanda Marcoulescou, soprano; Jeffry Peterson, piano. Orion 685 (tape). **MacDowell:** Bitte; Geistliches Wiegenlied; Idylle; **Carpenter:** Prison; Il pleure dans mon coeur; Dansons la gigue; **Downey:** Qu-en avez vous fait?; **Thomson:** *Le berceaux de Gertrude Stein*; **Griffes:** Auf geheimem Waldespfade; **Menotti:** *Canti della lontananza*; **Bowles:** Cancionilla Sevillana; Media luna; Ballade Amarilla; Murio al amanecer; **Ives:** Feldeinsamkeit.

28. **FROM RAGTIME TO ART SONG: AMERICAN ANTHEM.** Nathan Gunn, baritone; Kevin Murphy, piano.

EMI ▲ 73160. **Barber:** Nocturne; Sure on This Shining Night; **Bolcom:** Black Max; Fur (Murray the Furrier); Over the Piano; **Copland:** At the River; Long Time Ago; **Hoiby:** The Lamb; **Ives:** General William Booth Enters into Heaven; Slugging a Vampire; Two Little Flowers; **Musto:** Recuerdo; **Niles:** I Wonder as I Wander; The Lass from the Low Countree; **Rorem:** Early in the Morning; The Lordly Hudson; **Scheer:** American Anthem; At Howard Hawks' House; Holding Each Other; Lean Away.

29. **HEARTBEATS:** New Songs from Minnesota for the AIDS Quilt Songbook. Innova ▲ 500. **Musto:** Heartbeats; **DeBlasio:** Walt Whitman in 1989; **Bolcom:** Vaslav's Song; **Harbison:** The Flute of Interior Time; **Larsen:** Perineo; **Houtz:** The Enticing Lane [and others].

30. **I CARRY YOUR HEART.** Ruth Ann Swenson, soprano; Warren Jones, piano. EMI Classics ▲CDC 56158. **J. Duke:** Little Elegy; Aubade; The Bird; I Carry Your Heart.

31. **I WILL BREATHE A MOUNTAIN.** Marilyn Horne, mezzo-soprano; Martin Katz, piano. RCA Victor Red Seal ▲ 09026-68771-2. **Barber:** The Daisies; A Nun Takes the Veil; Bessie Bobtail; The Secrets of the Old; Sure on This Shining Night; I Hear an Army; Dover Beach; **Bernstein:** My House; So Pretty; Greeting; Take Care of This House; Rabbit at Top Speed; Sonnet; What Lips My Lips Have Kissed; Dream with Me; **Bolcom:** *I Will Breathe a Mountain.*

32. **JOHN REARDON SINGS CONTEMPORARY ART SONGS.** John Reardon, baritone. Serenus SRE 1019. **Flagello:** *Songs from William Blake's "An Island in the Moon"*: As I Walked Forth; Good English Hospitality; Leave, O Leave Me to My Sorrow; **Hundley:** For Your Delight; Postcard from Spain; **Koch:** Silver; Tame Cat; An Immorality; The Tea Shop; **Owen:** I Saw a Man Pursuing the Horizon; There Were Many Who Went in Huddled Procession; **Reif:** *Five Finger Exercises*; **Rieti:** *Quattro Lyriche Italiane.*

33. **LET MY SONG FILL YOUR HEART (20th CENTURY AMERICAN CONCERT SONGS).** Mary Ann Telese, soprano. PRLP-002. **Charles:** Let My Song Fill Your Heart; **Edwards:** By the Bend of the River; **Hageman:** Miranda; **Homer:** Sing to Me, Sing; **Mana-Zucca:** Nichavo; I Love Life; **Strickland:** I Remember.

34. **THE LISTENERS.** William Parker, baritone; William Huckaby and Dalton Baldwin, pianists. New World 80475. **Bacon:** Billy in the Darbies; **Chanler:** Four Rhymes from Peacock Pie; **Dello Joio:** The Listeners; **Fine:** Four Childhood Fables for Grownups; **Hoiby:** Anatomy Lesson; **Niles:** Evening; Love Winter When the Plant Says Nothing; For My Brother: Reported Missing in Action, 1943; **Rorem:** Mourning Scene; **Ward:** Ballad.

35. **LOVE SONGS.** Arleen Augér, soprano; Dalton Baldwin, piano. Delos ▲ DE 3029. **Copland:** Pastorale; **S. Foster:** Why No One to Love; **Lippé:** How Do I Love Thee.

36. **LOVE'S SECRETS AND OTHER SONGS BY**

AMERICAN COMPOSERS. VoxBox ▲ 5129. See # 59.

37. **MASTERPIECES OF CABARET.** Jody Karin Applebaum, soprano; Marc-André Hamlin, piano. Music & Arts ▲ 729. **Bolcom:** *Cabaret Songs* (12) Vols. 1 & 2.

38. **MUSIC FROM 18th CENTURY PENNSYLVANIA.** Martha Hill, soprano; Darina Tuhy, harpsichord. Department of Music, Bucknell University, LP 623. **Hopkinson:** My Days Have Been So Wondrous Free; Come Fair Rosina; Beneath a Weeping Willow's Shade.

39. **MY NATIVE LAND.** Jennifer Larmore, mezzo-soprano; Antoine Palloc, piano. Teldec ▲ 16069. **Aborn:** Tis Winter Now; Shall I Compare Thee to a Summer's Day; Make Me an Instrument of Thy Peace; **Abramson:** Soldier, Soldier; **Barber:** Bessie Bobtail; I Hear an Army; Sure on This Shining Night; Rain Has Fallen; Sleep Now; **Copland:** The Little Horses; Ching-a-Ring Chaw; At the River; Zion's Walls; **J. Duke:** In the Fields; Twentieth Century; Heart! We Will Forget Him; **Heggie:** He's Gone Away; To Say Before Going to Sleep; White in the Moon; The Leather-Winged Bat; Barb'ry Allen; **Hoiby:** Winter Song; A Letter; **Hundley:** The Astronomers; **Ives:** My Native Land; The Things Our Fathers Loved; Memories (Very Pleasant); **Naginski:** Richard Cory; **Niles:** Fee Simple.

40. **MY SECRET HEART.** Ben Heppner, tenor; Royal Philharmonic, Jonathan Tunick, conductor. RCA ▲ 63508. **Charles:** Let My Song Fill Your Heart; **Giannini:** Sing to My Heart a Song; **Mana-Zucca:** I Love Life.

41. **NANCY TATUM: RECITAL OF AMERICAN SONGS.** Nancy Tatum, soprano. London OS 26053. **Gold:** from *Songs of Love and Parting,* (4); **Guion:** Mary Alone; **Manning:** Shoes; **Thomson:** Let's Take a Walk; Before Sleeping; also songs by **MacDowell, Copland, Barber,** and **Griffes.**

42. **NAUMBERG PRESENTS DAWN UPSHAW, SOPRANO.** Dawn Upshaw, soprano; Margo Garrett, piano. Musicmasters MMD 60128L. **Ives:** Berceuse; The World's Highway.

43. **NEW WORLD RECORDED ANTHOLOGY OF AMERICAN MUSIC.** [213] William Parker, baritone; William Huckaby, piano. NW 213. **Farwell:** *Three Indian Songs, Op. 32* (Song of the Deathless Voice; Inketanga's Thunder Song; The Old Man's Love Song); **Cadman:** *Four American Indian Songs, Op. 45* (From the Land of Sky-Blue Waters; The White Dawn Is Stealing; Far-Off, I Hear a Lover's Flute; The Moon Drops Low).

44. **NEW WORLD RECORDED ANTHOLOGY OF AMERICAN MUSIC.** [300] William Parker, baritone; Dalton Baldwin, piano. NW 300. **Chanler:** *Four Rhymes from "Peacock Pie"*; **Dello Joio:** The Listeners; **Fine:** *Four Songs from "Childhood Fables for Grownups"* (Two Worms; The Duck and the Yak; Lenny the Leopard; Tigeroo); **Ives:** At the River; His Exaltation; Watchman!; The Camp Meeting; Sunrise; Chanson de Florian;

Rosamunde; Qu'il m'irait bien; Elégie; **Ward:** Ballad from Pantaloon–He Who Gets Slapped.

45. **NEW WORLD RECORDED ANTHOLOGY OF AMERICAN MUSIC: American Song Recital. [305]** William Parker, baritone; William Huckaby, piano. NW 305. **Bacon:** Billy in the Darbies; **Griffes:** Das ist ein Brausen und Heulen; Wo ich bin, mich rings umdunkelt; Des müden Abendlied; Zwei Könige; The First Snowfall; An Old Song Resung; **Niles:** Evening; Love Winter When the Plant Says Nothing; For My Brother: Reported Missing in Action, 1943.

46. **AN OLD SONG RESUNG.** William Parker, baritone; William Huckaby and Dalton Baldwin, pianists. New World ▲ 80463 & 80475 compiled from three LPs: NW 213, 300, & 305 (see above). **Cadman:** *Four American Indian Songs*; **Farwell:** *Three Indian Songs*; **Griffes:** Das ist ein Brausen und Heulen; Wo ich bin, mich rings umdunkelt; Des müden Abendlied; Zwei Könige sassen auf Orkadal; The First Snowfall; An Old Song Resung; **Ives:** At the River; His Exaltation; Watchman!; The Camp Meeting; Sunrise; Chanson de Florian; Rosamunde; Qu'il m'irait bien; Elégie.

47. **AN OLD SONG RE-SUNG. AMERICAN CONCERT SONGS.** Thomas Hampson, baritone; Armen Guzelimian, piano. EMI Records ▲ 7 54051 2. **Cadman:** At Dawning; **Charles:** When I Have Sung My Songs; **J. Duke:** Luke Havergal; **S. Foster:** Ah! May the Red Rose Live Alway; **Giannini:** Tell Me, Oh Blue, Blue Sky!; **Griffes:** An Old Song Resung; **Hageman:** Do Not Go, My Love; **Niles:** The Lass from the Low Countree; **Speaks:** On the Road to Mandalay; **Sacco:** Brother Will, Brother John.

48. **ON THE ROAD TO MANDALAY AND OTHER FAVORITE AMERICAN CONCERT SONGS FROM 1900 TO 1950.** Dale Moore, baritone; Betty Ruth Tomfohrde, piano. Cambridge CRS 2715. **Barber:** The Daisies; With Rue My Heart Is Laden; Rain Has Fallen; Sleep Now; I Hear an Army; Sure on This Shining Night; Nocturne; Monks and Raisins; **Charles:** My Lady Walks in Loveliness; **J. Duke:** Luke Havergal; **Griffes:** The Lament of Ian the Proud; **Hageman:** Do Not Go, My Love; **Homer:** The Sick Rose; **J. H. Rogers:** The Time for Making Songs Has Come; **Speaks:** On the Road to Mandalay; **Stillman-Kelley:** El Dorado.

49. **PAUL SPERRY SINGS AMERICAN CYCLES AND SETS.** Paul Sperry, tenor; Irma Vallecillo, piano. ALBA ▲ 58. **Beaser:** *Seven Deadly Sins*; **Ch. Berg:** *Six Poems of Frank O'Hara*; **Gruenberg:** *Animals and Insects*; **L. A. Smith:** *Songs of the Silence*; **Talma:** *Terre de France*; **R. Wilson:** *Three Painters*.

50. **PAUL SPERRY SINGS AN AMERICAN SAMPLER: FROM BILLINGS TO BOLCOM.** Paul Sperry, tenor; Irma Vallecillo, piano. Albany ▲ TROY 081. Songs by **Barber; Beaser; Billings; Bolcom; E. Carter; Cowell; Dougherty; J. Duke; Flanagan; S. Foster; Griffes; Lauridsen; Musto; Rorem; W. Schuman; W. Swenson; Talma; B. Weber; Weill; Weisgall; Yeston.**

51. **PAUL SPERRY SINGS ROMANTIC AMERICAN SONGS.** Paul Sperry, tenor; Irma Vallecillo, piano. Albany ▲ TROY 043-2. **Bowles:** April Fool Baby; Baby, Baby; Letter to Freddy; Once a Lady Was Here; Three; **Chanler:** The Doves; I Rise When You Enter; Memory; O Mistress Mine; These My Ophelia; **Farwell:** Ample Make This Bed; The Grass So Little Has to Do; The Level Bee; Presentiment; Safe in Their Alabaster Chambers; Summer's Armies; Tie the Strings to My Life; **Hundley:** The Astronomers; Ballad on Queen Anne's Death; Bartholomew Green; Come Ready and See Me; On a Wife; I Do; Isaac Greentree; Spring; Sweet Suffolk Owl; **Thomson:** A Prayer to St. Catherine; Preciosilla; Take, O Take Those Lips Away; English Usage; There Is a Garden in Her Face.

52. **PAUL SPERRY SINGS SONGS OF AN INNOCENT AGE: Music from Turn of the Century America.** Paul Sperry, tenor; Irma Vallecillo, piano. Albany ▲ TROY 034-2. **Ayres:** Take, O Take Those Lips Away; Where the Bee Sucks; **Beach:** Ariette; Take, O Take Those Lips Away; O Mistress Mine; **Buck:** The Capture of Bacchus; **Cadman:** From the Land of the Sky-Blue Water; **Chadwick:** La Danza; Euthanasia; **Clough-Leighter:** It Was a Lover and His Lass; **Foote:** Oh Swallow, Swallow; It Was a Lover and His Lass; **Griffes:** Wohl lag ich einst in Gram und Schmerz; **Nevin:** Oh! That We Two Were Maying; Narcissus; and other composers.

53. **PERMIT ME VOYAGE.** Mary Ann Hart, mezzo-soprano; Dennis Helmrich, piano. Albany Troy 118. **Argento:** *From the Diary of Virginia Woolf*; **E. Carter:** Voyage; **Cowell:** How Old Is Song; Firelight and Lamp; St. Agnes Morning; **Flanagan:** Horror Movie; Valentine to Sherwood Anderson; **Gordon:** Once I Was; Afternoon on a Hill; **Hundley:** Arise My Love; Moonlight's Watermelon; Straightway Beauty on Me Waits; Some Sheep Are Loving; **Schocker:** Mama Called.

54. **POMES PENYEACH: SETTINGS OF POETRY BY JAMES JOYCE.** Myron Myers, bass. Musical Heritage Society MHS 9120167. **Antheil:** Night Piece; **Barber:** I Hear an Army; Rain Has Fallen; **Persichetti:** Noise of Waters; **Sessions:** On the Beach at Fontana.

55. **SAMUEL RAMEY IN RECITAL.** Samuel Ramey, bass; Lawrence Skobacs, piano. Legendary Recordings LR 133. **Dougherty:** Shenandoah; Blow Ye Winds.

56. **SONGS FOR BARITONE AND PIANO.** William Sharp, baritone; Steven Blier, piano. New World ▲ NW 369-2. **Bowles:** *Blue Mountain Ballads* (4); Sleeping Song; April Fool Baby; A Little Closer, Please; Three; Letter to Freddy; Secret Words; My Sister's Hand in Mine; **Hoiby:** What If . . .; Jabberwocky; **Hundley:** Sweet Suffolk Owl; **Musto:** *Recuerdo* (cycle); **Thomson:** Prayer to St. Catherine; If Thou a Reason Dost Desire to Know; *Two by Marianne Moore*; John Peel; At the Spring.

57. **SONGS FROM THE HEART.** Jermi Frost, soprano; Julie Frost, piano. Albany 165. **Salter:** A Boat Song; **Strickland:** A Complaint; His Voice; Home They Brought

Her Warrior; My Jeanie; **Ware:** Alone I Wander; How Do I Love Thee?; The Last Dance; April.

58. SONGS OF AMERICA. Jan DeGaetani, mezzo-soprano; Gilbert Kalish, piano. Elektra/Nonesuch 79178-1. **S. Foster:** Beautiful Child of Song; **E. Carter:** Dust of Snow; The Rose Family; **Cadman:** The Moon Drops Low; **Crawford-Seeger:** Home Thoughts; White Moon; Joy; **Babbitt:** The Widow's Lament in Springtime; **Benson:** American Primitive; **Crumb:** The Sleeper; **Fine:** My Father; **Jacobs-Bond:** Nothin' but Love; I Love You Truly; Her Greatest Charm; **Kagen:** The Junk Man; **Davidovsky:** Lost; **Cage:** Little Four Paws; **Wm. Schuman:** Dozing on the Lawn; **R. Clarke:** Lethe; **Ives:** Song (She Is Not Fair); Sunrise; **Rorem:** Interlude; **Adler:** Time, You Old Gypsy Man; **S. Walden:** Grandma; **A. Kernis:** *Stein X Seven*, No. 6; **Bolcom:** Waitin'; **Copland:** There Came a Wind Like a Bugle.

59. SONGS OF AMERICAN COMPOSERS. Eleanor Steber, soprano; Mildred Miller, mezzo-soprano; John McCollum, tenor; Donald Gramm, baritone; Edwin Biltcliffe and Richard Cumming, pianists. Desto DS-6411-6412, LPs. **Now Called:** *Love's Secrets and Other Songs by American Composers.* VoxBox ▲ 5129. (Same performers). STEBER: **Rorem:** Alleluia; **Bacon:** *Four Poems by Emily Dickinson* (It's All I Have to Bring; So Bashful; To Make a Prairie; And This of All My Hopes); **Barber:** Nuvoletta, **D. Moore:** Death Be Not Proud; **Bergsma:** Lullee, Lullay; **Griffes:** Waikiki; **La Montaine:** Stopping by Woods; **Thomson:** The Tiger. McCOLLUM: **MacDowell:** The Sea; **Chanler:** The Rose; I Rise When You Enter; **Copland:** Dirge in the Woods; **Ward:** Sorrow of Mydath; **Gruen:** *Three by e. e. cummings* (lady will you come near with me; now (more near ourselves than we); spring is like a perhaps hand); **Pinkham:** Slow, Slow, Fresh Fount; **B. Weber:** Mourn! Mourn!; **Cowell:** The Donkey. MILLER: **Diamond:** David Mourns for Absalom; Brigid's Song; **Persichetti:** Sonatina to Hans Christian; **Luening:** The Divine Image; Love's Secret; **Fine:** Polaroli; The Frog and the Snake; **Flanagan:** Valentine to Sherwood Anderson; Send Home My Long Strayed Eyes; **Rorem:** Visits to St. Elizabeth's. GRAMM: **Ives:** Gen. William Booth Enters into Heaven; **Beeson:** Calvinistic Evensong; **D. Moore:** Come Away, Death; **Bowles:** *Blue Mountain Ballads* (Lonesome Man; Heavenly Grass; Cabin; Sugar in the Cane); **Edmunds:** The Drummer; The Faucon; **Carpenter:** Looking Glass River; Jazz-Boys.

60. SONGS OF CHARLES IVES AND ERNST BACON. Helen Boatwright, soprano; John Kirkpatrick and Ernst Bacon, pianists. CRI ▲ 675 (formerly Camden 1707 and CRS 1707 Cambridge). See BACON and IVES entries below for titles.

61. SONGS OF EARLY AMERICANS COMPOSED IN AMERICA 1750–1800. Gordon Myers, baritone. Golden Crest Recital Series RE 7020. **Hopkinson:** My Days Have Been So Wondrous Free; O'er the Hills; **Lyon:** Eighth Psalm Tune; **Billings:** When Jesus Wept; Chester; **Belcher:** While Shepherds Watch'd Their Flocks by Night; **T. Swan:** Deep in Our Hearts; O God, My Heart; **O.**

Holden: Columbia's Guardian Sleeps in Dust; **J. Peter:** Der Herr ist in Seinem heiligen Temple; **J. Herbst:** Ich gehe einher in der Kraft; **Van Hagen:** Funeral Dirge on the Death of George Washington; **Selby:** Ode for a New Year, Jan. 1, 1790; **Carr:** Shakespeare's Willow; **Reinagle:** Jerry's Song; **Anon.:** A Net for a Night-Raven.

62. SONGS OF LOVE. Helene Williams, soprano; Leonard Lehrman, piano. Capstone ▲ CPS 8647. **Siegmeister:** Lonely Star; Chalk Marks on the Sidewalk; **J. Singer:** *A Cycle of Love.* (and other composers)

63. SONGS OF THE NIGHTINGALE. Karen Smith Emerson, soprano; Martin Katz, piano. CENT ▲ 2232. **Rorem:** The Nightingale; **Horsman:** The Bird of the Wilderness.

64. SONGS WE FORGOT TO REMEMBER. John Aler, tenor; Grant Gershon, piano. Delos 3181. **Charles:** When I Have Sung My Songs; **Griffes:** Evening Song; **Hageman:** Do Not Go, My Love.

65. SURE ON THIS SHINING NIGHT (THE ROMANTIC SONG IN AMERICA). Robert White, tenor; Samuel Sanders, piano. Hyperion CD A66920. **Barber:** Sure on This Shining Night; **Beach:** The Year's at the Spring; **Bolcom:** Never More Will the Wind; **Chanler:** The Children; These, My Ophelia; **Chadwick:** When Stars Are in the Quiet Skies; **Charles:** When I Have Sung My Songs; **Copland:** Nature, the Gentlest Mother; **Corigliano:** Song to the Witch of the Cloisters; **Ewazen:** The Tiger; **Firestone:** If I Could Tell You; **Griffes:** An Old Song Resung; **Hageman:** Do Not Go, My Love; **Herbert:** Ah! Sweet Mystery of Life; **Hindemith:** Echo; On Hearing 'The Last Rose of Summer'; **Ives:** The Side Show; The Collection; **Korngold:** Come Away, Death; **Malotte:** The Lord's Prayer; **Marder:** To a Stranger; **Musto:** Triolet; **Parker:** June Night; **Rorem:** Little Elegy; **Wm. Schuman:** Orpheus with His Lute; **Thomson:** Sigh No More, Ladies. (Also Friml: Rose Marie; Romberg: One Alone)

66. THOMAS HAMPSON SINGS LIEDER. Thomas Hampson, baritone; Armen Guzelimian, piano. Teldec 72168. **Griffes:** Wohl lag ich einst in Gram; So halt' ich endlich; Mein Herz ist wie die dunkle Nacht; Der träumende See; An den Wind; Auf geheimem Waldespfade; Mit schwarzen Segeln; Das ist ein Brausen; Wo ich bin; Auf ihrem Grab; Am Kreuzweg; Das sterbende Kind; Meeres Stille; Elfe; Zwei Könige; Des müden Abendlied; Nachtlied; **Ives:** Minnelied; Gruss; Frühlingslied; Du bist wie eine Blume; Ballad from Rosamunde; Ein Ton; Widmung; Marie; Rosenzweigs; Wiegenlied; Feldeinsamkeit; Ich grolle nicht; Weil' auf mir; Wanderers Nachtlied; **MacDowell:** Mein Liebchen wir sassen beisammen; Du liebst mich nicht; Oben, wo die Sterne glühen; Nachtlied; Das Rosenband.

67. TO THE SOUL: THOMAS HAMPSON SINGS THE POETRY OF WALT WHITMAN. Thomas Hampson, baritone; Armen Guzelimian, piano. EMI Classics ▲ CDC 55028. **Burleigh:** Ethiopia Saluting the Colors; **Naginski:** Look Down, Fair Moon; **Rorem:** As Adam Early in the

Morning; That Shadow, My Likeness; Sometimes with One I Love; Look Down, Fair Moon; **Bernstein:** To What You Said; **Bacon:** One Thought Ever at the Fore; **Warren:** We Two; **Ives:** Walt Whitman.

68. A TRIBUTE TO SOPRANO BETHANY BEARDSLEE. Bethany Beardslee, soprano; Morey Ritt, Piano. CRI ▲724. **Perle:** *Dickinson Songs* (13).

69. WHEN I HAVE SUNG MY SONGS: THE AMERICAN ART SONG (1900–1940). New World Recorded Anthology of American Music. NW 247. **MacDowell:** Long Ago, Sweetheart Mine; A Maid Sings Light (Alma Gluck, soprano); **Beach:** The Year's at the Spring (Johanna Gadski, soprano); **H. Parker:** Love in May (Emma Eames, soprano); The Lark Now Leaves His Watery Nest (Emilio de Gogorza, baritone); **Kramer:** Swans (John McCormack, tenor); **Dunn:** The Bitterness of Love (John McCormack, tenor); **Damrosch:** Danny Deever (David Bispham, baritone); **Burleigh:** Go Down, Moses (Roland Hayes, tenor); Heav'n, Heav'n (Marian Anderson, contralto); Deep River (Paul Robeson, baritone); **Cadman:** At Dawning (Mary Garden, soprano); **Griffes:** By a Lonely Forest Pathway (Eleanor Steber, soprano); **Hageman:** Do Not Go, My Love (Rose Bampton, contralto); **Carpenter:** When I Bring to You Coloured Toys; Light, My Light (Rose Bampton, contralto); **R. Thompson:** Velvet Shoes (Povla Frijsh, soprano); **Charles:** When I Have Sung My Songs (Kirsten Flagstad, soprano); **J. R. Johnson:** Lit'l Gal (Paul Robeson, baritone); **Ives:** General William Booth Enters into Heaven (Radiana Pazmor, soprano).

70. WHERE THE MUSIC COMES FROM: AMERICAN SONGS. Cynthia Haymon, soprano; Warren Jones, piano. Decca ARGO 436 117-2. **Barber:** O Boundless, Boundless Evening; Sleep Now; **Beck:** Song of Devotion; **Burleigh:** Among the Fuchsias; Till I Wake; Worth While; The Prayer; **Dougherty:** Love in the Dictionary; **Farwell:** Wild Nights! Wild Nights!; **Griffes:** In a Myrtle Shade; **Hoiby:** Where the Music Comes From; Always It's Spring; **Hundley:** Strings in the Earth and Air; Come Ready and See Me; **Lekberg:** The Spring and the Fall; **Logan:** Marrow of My Bone; **Nordoff:** Embroidery for a Faithless Friend; **Rorem:** See How They Love Me; Early in the Morning; O You Whom I Often and Silently Come.

71. WHITE MOON: SONGS TO MORPHEUS. Dawn Upshaw, soprano; Margo Garrett, piano. Nonesuch ▲ 79364. **Crumb:** Night of the Four Moons; **Schwantner:** Black Anemones; **R. C. Seeger:** White Moon

SINGLE COMPOSER RECORDINGS

72. ADLER, SAMUEL. SONGS. F. Herseth, soprano; J. Evans, tenor; R. Karpoff, soprano; C. Lewis, piano. GAS ▲ 322. In Thine Own Image; *Unholy Sonnets*; *Songs About Nature*; *Songs About Love*; *Songs About Time*; *Songs from*

the Portuguese; Wish for a Young Wife.

———. See also # 58.

73. ALEXANDER, JOSEF. *Songs for Eve.* Evelyn Mandac, soprano. Ser. 12038.

74. AMRAM, DAVID. *Three Songs for America.* James Courtney, bass. Newport 85546 (Allegro).

75. ARGENTO, DOMINICK. *The Andrée Expedition.* B. Nordfors, tenor; Barbara Forsberg, piano. MEGD ▲ 73305.

76. ———. *The Andrée Expedition* for Baritone and Piano. William Parker, baritone; William Huckaby, piano. CENT ▲ 2092.

77. ———. *Elizabethan Songs.* Patricia M. Bedi, soprano; Rembrandt Chamber Players. CED ▲ 11.

78. ———. *Elizabethan Songs.* Barbara Bonney, soprano; André Previn, piano. London ▲ CD 289 455511-2.

79. ———. *Elizabethan Songs.* Jean Danton, soprano; with chamber ensemble. ALBA ▲ 264.

80. ———. *Elizabethan Songs.* Frederick Urrey, tenor; R. A. Clark, conductor. NPT ▲ 85602.

81. ———. *From the Diary of Virginia Woolf.* Janet Baker, mezzo-soprano; Martin Isepp, piano. D'Note ▲ DND 1019.

82. ———. *From The Diary of Virginia Woolf.* Virginia Dupuy, mezzo-soprano. GAS ▲ 273.

83. ———. *From The Diary of Virginia Woolf.* Mary Ann Hart, mezzo-soprano; Dennis Helmrich, piano. In *Permit Me Voyage.* Albany Troy 118.

84. ———. *From the Diary of Virginia Woolf.* L. Maxwell, mezzo-soprano; William Huckaby, piano. CENT ▲ 2092.

85. ———. *Six Elizabethan Songs.* Martin; Weisberg. CRI S-380.

86. ———. *Songs about Spring.* Patricia M. Bedi, soprano; E. Buccheri, piano. CED ▲ 29.

87. ———. *Songs about Spring.* Jean Danton, soprano; T. Stumpf, piano. ALBA ▲ 264.

88. AVSHALOMOV, JACOB. *TWENTY-FOUR SONGS.* Alyce Rogers, mezzo-soprano; Linda Barker, piano. Albany ▲ TROY 249. *Songs for Alyce*; *Whimsies*; Threnos; *Wonders*; *Biblical Songs*; *From the Chinese*; Who Is My Shepherd; Fed by my Labors; O Time.

BABBITT, MILTON. See # 58.

89. BACON, ERNST. SONGS. In *Songs of Charles Ives and*

Ernst Bacon [#60 above]. Helen Boatwright, soprano; John Kirkpatrick and Ernst Bacon, pianists. CRI ▲ 675 (formerly Camden 1707 and CRS 1707 Cambridge). *Songs from Emily Dickinson*: It's All I Have to Bring; Eden; I'm Nobody; As Well as Jesus?; A Word; Weeping and Sighing; O Friend; She Went; A Threadless Way; The Imperial Heart; Summer's Lapse; Is There Such a Thing as Day?; To Make a Prairie; A Spider; The Grass So Little Has to Do; The Snake; So Bashful; Alabaster Wool; Eternity; Sunset; The Simple Days; On This Wondrous Sea.

———. See also #s 3, 10, 18, 34, 45, 59, & 67.

90. **BARAB, SEYMOUR.** *A Child's Garden of Verses.* Russell Oberlin, tenor; with orchestra. Counterpoint CPT 539.

91. **BARBER, SAMUEL.** *Despite and Still.* Christopher Trakas. Music Masters ▲ MMD6 0170 M.

92. ———. **[*Dover Beach* and Selected Songs].** Thomas Allen, baritone; Roger Vignoles, piano. Virgin Classsics, Limited CDC 5 450332. *Three Songs, Op. 2*; *Three Songs, Op. 10*; from *Four Songs, Op. 13*: Nocturne; Sure on This Shining Night; *Three Songs, Op. 45*; Solitary Hotel, Op. 41, No. 4.

93. ———. *Hermit Songs, Op. 29.* Barbara Bonney, soprano; André Previn, piano. London ▲ CD 289 455511-2.

94. ———. *Hermit Songs, Op. 29.* P. P. Jones, soprano; P. Martin, piano. ALTA ▲ 9010.

95. ———. *Hermit Songs, Op. 29.* J. Peete, tenor; K. Wyatt, piano. CRS 8633.

96. ———. *Hermit Songs, Op. 29.* Leontyne Price, soprano; Samuel Barber, piano. SNYC (Portrait) ▲ 46727; RCAV (Gold Seal) ▲ 61983; SNYC ▲ 60899.

97. ———. *Hermit Songs, Op. 29.* Sanford Sylvan, baritone; D. Breitman, piano. (In *Beloved that Pilgrimage*, #14)

98. ———. **LEONTYNE PRICE SINGS BARBER.** Leontyne Price, soprano; Samuel Barber, piano. RCAVictor Gold Seal ▲ 09026-61983-2. *Hermit Songs*; Sleep Now; The Daisies; Nocturne; Nuvoletta.

99. ———. *Mélodies Passagères, Op. 27.* Pierre Bernac, baritone; Francis Poulenc, piano. New World 229.

100. ———. *Nuvoletta.* Patricia Neway, soprano. Lyr. 83.

101. ———. *ROBERTA ALEXANDER SINGS SAMUEL BARBER.* Roberta Alexander, soprano; Edo de Waart, Netherlands Philharmonic. Etcetera ▲ KTC 1145. I Hear an Army; Sure on This Shining Night; Nocturne.

102. ———. *SECRETS OF THE OLD: COMPLETE SONGS OF SAMUEL BARBER.* Cheryl Studer, soprano; Thomas Hampson, baritone; John Browning, piano; Emerson String Quartet. Deutsche Grammaphon ▲ 435867-2.

103. ———. SONGS. Roberta Alexander, soprano. Etcetera ▲ KTC1055. Bessie Bobtail; The Daisies; *Despite and Still*; *Hermit Songs*; I Hear An Army; Monks and Raisins; Nocturne; A Nun Takes the Veil; Nuvoletta; The Queen's Face on the Summery Coin; Rain Has Fallen; The Secrets of the Old; Sure on This Shining Night; With Rue My Heart Is Laden.

104. ———. SONGS. D. Fischer-Dieskau, baritone; Charles Wadsworth, piano. Musicm. 20027. *Opus 10,* Nos. 2 & 3; *Opus 13,* Nos. 1–4; *Opus 45,* Nos. 1–3.

105. ———. SONGS. Glenda Maurice, mezzo-soprano; David Garvey, piano. Etc. 1002. Sleep Now; I Hear an Army; A Nun Takes the Veil; The Secrets of the Old; Sure on This Shining Night; Nocturne; Now Have I Fed and Eaten Up the Rose; A Green Lowland of Pianos; O Boundless, Boundless Evening.

106. ———. SONGS. Joan Patenaude. Musical Heritage Society MHS 3770. I Hear An Army; Nocturne; A Nun Takes the Veil; Rain Has Fallen; The Secrets of the Old; Sure on This Shining Night; With Rue My Heart Is Laden; Sleep Now; Solitary Hotel.

107. ———. *Songs for Voice and Piano, Op. 13.* L. Comtois, mezzo-soprano; M. Bourdeau, piano. In *Songs of the Americas.* BRIO ▲ 112. *Opus 13,* Nos. 1–4.

108. ———. *Three Songs, Opus 45.* Sharon Mabry, mezzo-soprano; P. Wade, piano. Owl ▲ 35.

———. See also #s 2, 10, 14, 16, 24, 28, 31, 39, 41, 48, 50, 54, 59, 65, & 70.

109. **BEACH, AMY MARCY CHENEY (MRS. H. H. A.).** SONGS. D'Anna Fortunato, mezzo-soprano. Northeastern Classical Arts NR ▲ 9004-CD (formerly North. 202). Ariette; Ah, Love, but a Day!; Just for This; O Mistress Mine; Dearie; Ye Banks and Braes O' Bonnie Doon; Rendezvous; Chanson d'amour; Juni; Dark Garden; Elle et moi; Ecstasy; Dark Is the Night.

110. ———. SONGS. L. Kolb, soprano; D. McMahon, piano. ALBA ▲ 109. Nachts; Fairy Lullaby; Far Awa'; Extase; Take, O Take Those Lips Away; The Western Wind; Forgotten; Wir Drei.

———. See also #s 2, 11, 18, 52, 65, & 69.

111. **BEASER, ROBERT.** *Seven Deadly Sins.* Jan Opalach, baritone; American Composers Orchestra, D. R. Davies, conductor. Argo 440 337 (Polygram).

———. See also #s 49 & 50.

BECK, JOHN NESS. See # 70.

BEESON, JACK. See #s 18 & 59.

BELCHER, SUPPLY. See # 61.

BENSHOOF, KENNETH. See # 6.

112. **BERG, CHRISTOPHER. SONGS (6).** J. Felty, mezzo-soprano; Christopher Berg, piano. Op. One 49.

———. See also # 49.

BERGSMA, WILLIAM. See # 59.

113. **BERNSTEIN, LEONARD.** *I Hate Music (Cycle of Five Children's Songs).* Harolyn Blackwell, soprano. In *Blackwell Sings Bernstein: A Simple Song.* RCAV ▲ 68321.

114. ———. *I Hate Music.* L. Comtois, mezzo-soprano; M. Bourdeau, piano. In *Songs of the Americas.* BRIO ▲ 112.

115. ———. *I Hate Music.* Caryn Hartglass, soprano; B. Leroy, piano. LIDI ▲ 201033.

116. ———. *I Hate Music.* Blanche Thebom, mezzo-soprano; Leonard Bernstein, piano. In *Bernstein: The Early Years: Vol. IV.* RCAV (Gold Seal) ▲ 68101.

117. ———. *I Hate Music.* J. Vindevogel, soprano; L. Kende, piano. In *The Nursery.* RENE ▲ 92011.

118. ———. **SONGS.** Roberta Alexander, soprano; Crone, piano. ETC 1037. *I Hate Music; La Bonne Cuisine* (in both French and English); Silhouette; *Two Love Songs.*

———. See also #s 5, 7, 31, & 67.

BILLINGS, WILLIAM. See #s 50 & 61.

119. **BISCARDI, CHESTER.** *The Gift of Life* for Soprano and Piano. J. Bettina, soprano; J. Goldsworthy, piano. In *At the Still Point.* CRI ▲ 686.

120. **BLITZSTEIN, MARC. SONGS (21).** K. Holvik, soprano; William Sharp, baritone; Steven Blier, piano. Koch Int. Classics ▲ 3-7050-2. *Four e. e. cummings Songs:* o by the by; until and i heard; open your heart; jimmy's got a goil [and others].

121. **BOLCOM, WILLIAM.** *Black Max–Cabaret Songs of Arnold Weinstein and William Bolcom.* Joan Morris, mezzo-soprano; William Bolcom, piano. REC HRC1-5427. Over the Piano; Fur (Murray the Furrier); He Tipped the Waiter; Waitin'; The Song of Black Max (As Told by the deKooning Boys); Amor; Places to Live; Toothbrush Time; Surprise!; The Actor; Oh Close the Curtain; George.

122. ———. *I Will Breathe a Mountain.* Marilyn Horne, mezzo-soprano. (See # 31.)

———. See also #s 1, 7, 21, 28, 29, 37, 50, 58, & 65.

BONDS, MARGARET. See # 12.

123. **BOWLES, PAUL. SONGS.** Jo Ann Pickens, soprano; Howard Haskin, tenor. In *An American in Paris.* KSCH ▲

315742 (formerly Koch-Schwann 1574). April Fool Baby; My Sister's Hand in Mine. (And nine other songs on texts by Tennessee Williams, Gertrude Stein, Jane Bowles, and William Saroyan)

124. ———. **SONGS.** Brian Staufenbiel, tenor; Irene Hermann, piano. KOCH ▲ 7343. *Canciones de García Lorca* [and others].

———. See also #s 7, 10, 11, 16, 24, 27, 51, 56, & 59.

BROWN, ELIZABETH C. See # 1.

BUCK, DUDLEY. See # 52.

125. **BURLEIGH, HARRY THACKER.** *ART SONGS OF HARRY T. BURLEIGH.* Regina McConnell, soprano; Michael Cordovan, piano. CENT▲ 2252. You Ask Me if I Love You; The Prayer I Make for You; One Day; Elysium; The Prayer; And as the Gulls Soar; Heigh-Ho!; The Man in White; Now Sleeps the Crimson Petal; I Hear His Footsteps; Music Sweet; Just You; He Sent Me You; Were I a Star; O Love of a Day; Adoration; Tide; The Grey Wolf; Oh, My Love!; Why Art Thou Not Near Me?; The Sailor's Wife; Carry Me Back to the Pine Wood; Lovely Dark and Lonely One.

126. ———. *DEEP RIVER: SONGS AND SPIRITUALS.* Oral Moses, bass-baritone; Ann Sears, piano. ALBA ▲ 332. Lovely Dark and Lonely One; Ethiopia Saluting the Colors; The Dove and the Lily; Exile; Little Mother of Mine; The Spring, My Dear, Is No Longer Spring; The Soldier; Mammy's Lil Baby; The Trees Have Grown So; Thy Heart; and arrangements of spirituals.

127. ———. *FROM THE SOUTHLAND.* Hilda Harris, mezzo-soprano; Philip Creech and Steven Cole, tenors; Arthur Woodley, baritone; Joseph Smith, piano. PREM ▲ 1041. Now Sleeps the Crimson Petal; Promis' Lan'; Ethiopia Saluting the Colors; Lovely Dark and Lonely One; Love Watches; Almona; O, Night of Dream and Wonder; His Helmet's Blaze; I Hear His Footsteps, Music Sweet; Thou Art Weary; This is Nirvana; Ahmed's Song of Farewell; Through Moanin' Pines; The Frolic; In de Col' Moonlight; A Jubilee; On Bended Knees; A New Hiding-Place; Worth While; The Jungle Flower; Kashmiri Song; Among the Fuchsias; Till I Wake; By an' By; and arrangements of spirituals.

———. See also #s 67, 69, & 70.

BYRON, CARL. See # 1.

CADMAN, CHARLES WAKEFIELD. See #s 43, 46, 47, 52, 58, & 69.

128. **CAGE, JOHN.** A Flower; and other songs. Cathy Berberian, mezzo-soprano; B. Canino, piano. WER ▲ 60054.

129. ———. A Flower; The Wonderful Widow of Eighteen Springs. Cathy Berberian, mezzo-soprano. ACCO ▲

205722.

130. ———. A Flower for Voice and Prepared Piano; The Wonderful Widow of Eighteen Springs; and other songs. Joan La Barbara, soprano; L. Stein, piano. In *Singing Through*. NALB ▲ 35.

131. ———. SONGS. Adria Firestone, contralto. In *Works for Piano and Prepared Piano, Vol. IV*. WER ▲ 61592.

132. ———. SONGS. A. D. Mare, voice and piano. KOCH ▲ 7104.

133. ———. The Wonderful Widow of Eighteen Springs; A Flower. G. English, tenor; N. Butterly, piano. TP ▲ 025 (Tall Poppies).

——— . See also #s 4 & 58.

134. **CARPENTER, JOHN ALDEN.** *Gitanjali.* Alexandra Hunt, soprano. Orion 7272.

135. ———. Serenade. Gladys Swarthout, mezzo-soprano; Lester Hodges, piano. V-16780.

136. ———. SONGS. Mina Hager, mezzo-soprano; Celius Dougherty, piano. MC-1016 (12"). Berceuse de la Guerre; *Water Colors,* nos. 1 & 2.

137. ———. When I Bring to You Colored Toys. Glenn Darwin, bass; E. Fiedler, piano. V-36224.

138. ———. When I Bring to You Colour'd Toys. Conchita Supervia, soprano. Pearl ▲ 9969.

——— . See also #s 2, 5, 6, 10, 11, 27, 59, & 69.

CARR, BENJAMIN. See #s 2, 26, & 61.

139. **CARTER, ELLIOTT.** *Poems (3) of Robert Frost.* P. Mason, baritone; with chamber ensemble. BRID ▲ 9014.

140. ———. SONGS. Jan DeGaetani, mezzo-soprano; Gilbert Kalish, piano. NON ▲ 79248. *Poems of Robert Frost:* Dust of Snow; The Rose Family.

141. ———. SONGS. Rosalind Rees, soprano; Adirondack Chamber Orchestra. CRI ▲ 648. Warble for Lilac Time; Voyage; *Three Poems of Robert Frost.*

142. ———. SONGS. Lucy Shelton, soprano; John Constable, piano. In *Of Challenge and Of Love*. KOCH ▲ 7425. Of Challenge and Of Love; *Poems of Robert Frost*; Voyage.

——— . See also #s 4, 50, 53, & 58.

CHADWICK, GEORGE WHITEFIELD. See #s 2, 10, 52, & 65.

143. **CHANLER, THEODORE.** *Eight Epitaphs.* Glenda Maurice, mezzo-soprano. Etcetera ▲ KTC 1099.

144. ———. *Nine Epitaphs.* Phyllis Curtin, soprano; F. Ryan Edwards, piano. CSP CMS-6198. Alice Rodd; Susannah Fry; Three Sisters; Thomas Logge; Three Husbands; A Midget; No Voice to Scold; Ann Poverty; Be Very Quiet Now.

——— . See also #s 14, 16, 34, 44, 51, 59, & 65.

145. **CHARLES, ERNEST.** Clouds; Spendthrift. Gladys Swarthout, mezzo-soprano; L. Hodges, piano. V-4318 (10").

146. ———. When I Have Sung My Songs. Kirsten Flagstad, soprano; Edwin McArthur, piano. V-1817 (10").

147. ———. When I Have Sung My Songs. Jeannette MacDonald, soprano; Giuseppe Bamboschek, piano. V-2047 (10").

148. ———. When I Have Sung My Songs. John McCormack, tenor; E. Schneider, piano. G-DA1446 (10").

149. ———. When I Have Sung My Songs. Rosa Ponselle, soprano. In Ponselle, Vol. 2. Nimbus Records ▲ NI 7846.

——— . See also #s 23, 33, 40, 47, 48, 64, 65, & 69.

150. **CHILDS, BARNEY.** SONGS (37). Avant 1008.

CITKOWITZ, ISRAEL. See # 16–17.

CLOUGH-LEIGHTER, HENRY. See # 52.

151. **COPLAND, AARON.** *Dickinson Songs (8).* Dawn Upshaw, soprano; St. Paul Chamber Orchestra, Hugh Wolff conducting. In *Long Time Ago*. TELC ▲ 77310.

152. ———. *Eight Poems of Emily Dickinson.* Marni Nixon, soprano; Keith Clark, conductor. REF ▲ 22. Nature, the Gentlest Mother; There Came a Wind like a Bugle; The World Feels Dusty; Heart, We Will Forget Him; Dear March, Come In; Sleep Is Supposed to Be; Going to Heaven; The Chariot.

153. ———. *Emily Dickinson Songs (8).* Helene Schneiderman, mezzo-soprano; Orchestra of St. Luke's, D. R. Davies, conducting. Music Masters ▲ 67101.

154. ———. *Poems of Emily Dickinson (8).* C. Rovics, soprano; H. Rovics, piano. NSR ▲ 1019.

155. ———. *Poems of Emily Dickinson (12).* Barbara Bonney, soprano; A. Previn, piano. London ▲ CD 289 455511-2.

156. ———. SONGS (complete except for Dirge in the Woods). Roberta Alexander, soprano. Etcetera ▲ KTC 1100. Alone; My Heart Is in the East; Night; Old Poem; Pastorale; Poet's Song; A Summer Vacation; *Twelve Poems of Emily Dickinson.*

157. ———. *Twelve Poems of Emily Dickinson.* Adele Addison, soprano; Aaron Copland, piano. Col. M-30375.

158. ———. *Twelve Poems of Emily Dickinson.* Jan DeGaetani, mezzo-soprano; Leo Smit, piano. In *Aaron Copland: 81st Birthday Concert at the Library of Congress.* Bridge BCD ▲ 9046.

159. ———. *Twelve Poems of Emily Dickinson.* Martha Lipton, mezzo-soprano; Aaron Copland, piano. Columbia ML 5106.

160. ———. Vocalise. Ethel Luening, soprano; Aaron Copland, piano. NMR-1211 (12").

———. See also #s 4, 10, 14, 16, 21, 28, 35, 39, 41, 58, 59, & 65.

CORIGLIANO, JOHN. See #s 7, 20, & 65.

161. **COWELL, HENRY. SONGS.** R. Osborne, bass-baritone; Mary Ann Hart, mezzo-soprano; J. Golan, piano. ALBA ▲ 240. OSBORNE: St. Agnes Morning; April; Music, When Soft Voices Die; Angus Og; Manaunaun's Birthing; *Songs on Mother Goose Rhymes* (Curly Locks; Tommy Trot); *Songs on Poems of Riegger*; Pasture; Daybreak; Mice Lament; Music I Heard; Firelight and Lamp; HART: Dream Bridge; Morning Pool; Song in the Songlese; Where She Lies; How Old Is Song?; Spring Pools; Donkey; Little Black Boy; Because the Cat; Crane; Night Fliers.

———. See also #s 50, 53, & 59.

CRAWFORD-SEEGER, RUTH. See # 58. See also SEEGER, RUTH CRAWFORD

CRESTON, PAUL. See # 11.

162. **CROCKETT, DONALD.** *The Pensive Traveller.* Throngren, singer; Fumston, piano. Orion 84470.

163. **CRUMB, GEORGE.** *Three Early Songs.* Ann Crumb, soprano; George Crumb, piano. Bridge ▲ 9095.

164. ———. *Three Early Songs.* Barbara Ann Martin, soprano; James Freeman, piano. CRI ▲ 803.

———. See also #s 58 & 71.

165. **CUMMING, RICHARD. SONGS.** Carol Bogard, soprano; Donald Gramm, baritone; Richard Cumming, piano. CAM 2778. As Dew in April; The Sick Rose; Memories; London; The Little Black Boy; Heart, We Will Forget Him; Summer Song; Night Song; Love Song; *We Happy Few.*

166. ———. SONGS. Donald Gramm, baritone; John Browning and Richard Cumming, pianists. CRI ▲ 766. Silhouettes; Holidays; The Knight's Page; *We Happy Few.*

———. See also # 10.

167. **DAVIS, SHARON.** *Six Songs on Poems of William Pillin.* Delcina Stevenson, soprano; Sharon Davis, piano. WIMR-23. Love's Wildest Talent; I Dream; The Truth;

Ballade; The Leaf; Poem.

DeBLASIO, CHRIS. See # 1 & 29.

DELLO JOIO, NORMAN. See #s 10, 34, & 44.

DIAMOND, DAVID. See # 59.

168. **DOUGHERTY, CELIUS.** Love in the Dictionary. Blanche Thebom, mezzo-soprano. RCA Victor.

———. See also #s 10, 50, 55, & 70.

169. **DUKE, JOHN.** The Bird. Bidú Sayão, soprano. Columbia ML 4154.

170. ———. *Carole Bogard in a Recital of Songs by John Duke, Accompanied by the Composer.* C. Bogard, soprano; John Duke, piano. CAM 2776. *Five Songs for Soprano* (Teasdale) (All Beauty Calls You to Me; Listen, I Love You; I Am So Weak a Thing; All Things in All the World; O, My Love); Stopping By Woods on a Snowy Evening; *Six Poems by Emily Dickinson* (Good Morning–Midnight; Heart! We Will Forget Him!; Let Down the Bars, Oh Death; An Awful Tempest Mashed the Air; Nobody Knows This Little Rose; Bee, I'm Expecting You!); *Four Poems by Emily Dickinson* (New Feet within My Garden Go; The Rose Did Caper on Her Cheek; Have You Got a Brook in Your Little Heart; I Taste a Liquor Never Brewed); *Four Chinese Love Lyrics* (Waiting; Tucked Up Skirts; Incense–Moonlight; The Fifth Watch of the Night); *Four Poems by e. e. cummings* (just-spring; i carry your heart; hist . . . whist; The Mountains Are Dancing).

171. ———. SONGS. Donald Boothman, baritone; John Duke, piano. Golden Age 1004. Be Still as You Are Beautiful; The End of the World; Loveliest of Trees; I Ride the Great Black Horses; XXTH Century; The White Dress [and others].

172. ———. SONGS. D'Anna Fortunato, mezzo-soprano; G. Lee, piano. In *An American Collage.* ALBA ▲ 98. In the Fields; Acquainted with the Night; To the Thawing Wind.

173. ———. SONGS FOR BARITONE AND PIANO. D. Boothman, baritone; John Duke, piano. AFK-505. Bredon Hill; and 21 other songs.

———. See #s 3, 7, 10, 11, 16, 21, 30, 39, 47, 48, & 50.

174. **EDMUNDS, JOHN. SONGS.** Dorothy Renzi; Jeanine Crader; John Langstaff. Desto 6430. The Isle of Portland; Milkmaids; O Death, Rock Me Asleep; On the Nature of Truth; Why Canst Thou Not [and others].

———. See also # 59.

175. **ELWELL, HERBERT.** *Six Songs.* Maxine Makas, singer. CRI S-270. I Look Back; Wistful; Service of All the Dead; A Child's Grace; This Glittering Grief; The Ouselcock.

FARWELL, ARTHUR. See #s 3, 43, 46, 51, & 70.

176. **FENNIMORE, JOSEPH.** *Music of Joseph Fennimore.* Joyce Castle, mezzo-soprano; Karen Williams, soprano; Joseph Fennimore, piano. ALBA ▲ 23 (formerly TROY 023-2). *Berlitz: Introduction to French* (8 songs) *Inscape* (7 songs); *Six Songs:* Winter Love; Mary Weeps for Her Child; The Snow Grew Out of the Sky Last Night; Infant Joy; Now Death Has Shut Your Eyes; My Heart.

177. **FINE, IRVING.** *Childhood Fables for Grownups,* Sets I & II. Susan Davenny Wyner, mezzo-soprano; Yehudi Wyner, piano. CRI ▲ 574 (formerly CRI S-460).

178. ———. *Mutability.* Eunice Alberts, mezzo-soprano; Irving Fine, piano. CRI ▲630 (formerly CRI 106).

———. See also #s 34, 44, 58, & 59.

179. **FINNEY, ROSS LEE.** *Chamber Music* (36 songs) for Voice and Piano after Joyce. Jeanette Lombard, soprano; Mary Norris, piano. Master Musicians Collective ▲ MMC 2012.

———. See also # 10.

180. **FLAGELLO, NICOLAS.** *An Island in The Moon.* Nancy Tatum, soprano. SER 12005.

———. See also # 32.

181. **FLANAGAN, WILLIAM.** *SONGS AND CYCLES.* Carole Bogard, soprano; Herbert Beattie, bass-baritone; David Del Tredici, piano. Desto 6468. *Time's Long Ago* (Cycle of Songs to Poems of Herman Melville); *The Weeping Pleiads* (A Cycle of Five Songs to Poems of A. E. Housman); If You Can; See How They Love Me; Horror Movie; Plants Cannot Travel; The Upside-Down Man; Good-Bye, My Fancy.

———. See also #s 50, 53, & 59.

182. **FLOYD, CARLISLE.** *The Mystery.* Phyllis Curtin, soprano. London 635.

183. ———. *Pilgrimage: 3 Sacred Songs.* Norman Treigle, bass-baritone. Orion 7268.

FOOTE, ARTHUR. See #s 2 & 52.

184. **FOSTER, STEPHEN COLLINS.** SONGS. Julianne Baird, soprano; Linda Russell, alto; Frederick Urrey, tenor; J. Buskirk, piano. ALBA ▲ 119. Ah! May the Red Rose Live Alway; Beautiful Dreamer; The Moustache Song; I Dream of Jeanie; Some Folks [and others].

185. ———. SONGS. Richard Crooks, tenor; Frank LaForge, piano. RCA AVM 1-1738. Ah! May the Red Rose Live Alway; Beautiful Dreamer; Come Where My Love Lies Dreaming; Jeanie with the Light Brown Hair [and others].

186. ———. SONGS. J. Dooley, countertenor; ensemble. LYR

▲ 8036. Beautiful Dreamer; Ah! May the Red Rose Live Alway; Jeanie with the Light Brown Hair; Summer Longings; Nothing But a Plain Old Soldier [and others].

187. ———. SONGS. Thomas Hampson, baritone; with ensemble, Fiddle Fever. In *American Dreamer: Songs of Stephen Foster.* Angel ▲ CDC 54621. Jeanie with the Light Brown Hair; Open Thy Lattice, Love; Beautiful Dreamer; Gentle Annie [and others].

188. ———. *SONGS BY STEPHEN FOSTER,* VOL. I. Jan DeGaetani, mezzo-soprano; Leslie Guinn, baritone; Gilbert Kalish, piano. NON ▲ 79158. Jeanie with the Light Brown Hair; There's a Good Time Coming; Was My Brother in the Battle?; Sweetly She Sleeps, My Alice Fair; If You've Only Got a Moustache; Gentle Annie; Wilt Thou Be Gone, Love?; That's What's the Matter; Ah! May the Red Rose Live Alway; I'm Nothing But a Plain Old Soldier; Beautiful Dreamer; Mr. & Mrs. Brown; Slumber My Darling; Some Folks.

189. ———. *SONGS BY STEPHEN FOSTER,* VOL. II. Jan DeGaetani, mezzo-soprano; Leslie Guinn, baritone; Gilbert Kalish, piano. NON H-71333. The Voice of By Gone Days; Better Times Are Coming; Linger in Blissful Repose; There Are Plenty of Fish in the Sea; My Old Kentucky Home, Good Night; The Soiree Polka; Larry's Good Bye; Come Where My Love Lies Dreaming; We Are Coming, Father Abraham 300,000 More; Come with Thy Sweet Voice Again; Katy Bell; Hard Times Come Again No More; Village Bells Polka; The Hour for Thee and Me; Summer Longings.

———. See also #s 2, 5, 6, 21, 24, 35, 47, 50, & 58.

190. **GETTY, GORDON.** *The White Election* (song cycle on poetry of Emily Dickinson). Karen Erickson, soprano; A. Guzeliman, piano. DLS ▲ 3057.

191. **GIANNINI, VITTORIO.** *HOPELESSLY ROMANTIC: SONGS ON POEMS OF KARL FLASTER.* Jeffry Price, tenor; Cary Lewis, piano. ACAD ▲ 20011. Little Girl in Blue; Tell Me, Oh Blue, Blue Sky; Heart Cry; Love; Parting; I Shall Think of You; Moonlight; *Three Poems of the Sea*; Far Above the Purple Hills; If I Had Known; It Is a Spring Night; Be Still My Heart; I Only Know; Sing to My Heart a Song; There Were Two Swans; I Did Not Know; Longing; My Love for You Has Grown; The Sun Had Set; *Three Oriental Chants.*

192. ———. Tell Me, O Blue, Blue Sky. Leonard Warren, baritone. RCA ▲ 7807-2-RG.

———. See also #s 40 & 47.

193. **GIDEON, MIRIAM.** *A GIDEON RETROSPECTIVE.* Constantine Cassolas; William Sharp, baritone. New World ▲ 80393-2. *Epitaphs from Robert Burns*; Asturias; *Poet to Poet* (3 songs); To Music.

194. ———. *The Seasons of Time.* Evelyn Mandac, soprano; F. Jehada, piano. Desto 7117.

195. ———. *The Seasons of Time.* Paul Sperry, tenor. Ser. 12078.

196. **GOLD, ERNEST.** *Songs of Love and Parting.* Helen Dilworth, soprano; with guitar. Cambria 1062.

197. ———. *Songs of Love and Parting.* Marni Nixon, soprano; Ernest Gold, conductor. CRYS ▲ 501.

———. See also # 41.

GORDON, RICKY IAN. See #s 1 & 53.

198. **GRIFFES, CHARLES TOMLINSON.** By a Lonely Forest Pathway. Glenn Darwin, bass; E. Fiedler, piano. V-36224 (12").

199. ———. The Lament of Ian the Proud. William Hain, tenor; J. D. Bohm, piano. FRM-5 (12").

200. ———. *Poems of Fiona Macleod* **for Soprano and Orchestra.** L. Toppin, soprano; P. Freeman, conductor. ALBA ▲ 322.

201. ———. SONGS. Alexandra Hunt, soprano. Orion 77272. Waikiki; In a Myrtle Shade; Thy Dark Eyes to Mine; Evening Song.

202. ———. SONGS. Sherrill Milnes, baritone; Olivia Stapp, mezzo-soprano; Phyllis Bryn-Julson, soprano; Jon Spong and D. Richardson, pianists; Seiji Ozawa, conductor. NWW ▲ 273. An den Wind; Am Kreuzweg wird begraben; Meeres Stille; Auf geheimem Waldespfade; *Four Impressions* (Le Jardin; Impression du Matin; La Mer; Le Réveillon); Song of the Dagger; *Three Poems of Fiona MacLeod* (The Lament of Ian the Proud; Thy Dark Eyes to Mine; The Rose of the Night).

203. ———. *THE SONGS OF CHARLES T. GRIFFES.* Faith Esham, soprano; Irene Gubrud, soprano; Jan Opalach, baritone; Lucy Shelton, soprano; Margo Garrett, Thomas Muraco, Jeffrey Goldberg, pianists. Musical Heritage Society ▲ 424678A (2 CDs). Waikiki; Two Birds Flew into the Sunset Glow; The Half-Ring Moon; Pierrot; Les Ballons; Song of the Dagger; The Water-Lily; In the Harem; *Two Rondels* (This Book of Hours; Come, Love, Across the Sunlit Land); Der träumende See; Wohl lag ich einst in Gram und Schmerz; *Three Poems by Fiona Macleod, Op. 11* (The Rose of the Night; Thy Dark Eyes to Mine; The Lament of Ian the Proud); Evening Song; Symphony in Yellow; An Old Song Re-Sung; Auf geheimem Waldespfade; Auf dem Teich, dem Regungslosen; Nachtlied; *Five Poems of Ancient China and Japan, Op. 10*; Phantoms; Sorrow of Mydath; La Fuite de la Lune; Phantoms, Op. 9, No. 3; Könnt' ich mit dir dort oben gehn; Auf ihrem Grab; Elfe; We'll to the Woods and Gather May; The First Snowfall; In a Myrtle Shade; La Mer; An den Wind; Nacht liegt auf den fremden Wegen; *Four Impressions.*

———. See also #s 2, 6, 10, 11, 24, 27, 41, 45, 46, 47, 48, 50, 52, 59, 64, 65, 66, 69, & 70.

GRUENBERG, LOUIS. See #49.

204. **HAGEMAN, RICHARD.** Do Not Go, My Love. Jeannette MacDonald, soprano; with orchestra. V2047 (10").

205. ———. Do Not Go, My Love. Maggie Teyte, soprano. Pearl Gemm ▲ 9326.

206. ———. Music I Heard with You. Lucine Amara, soprano. Cambridge CRM 704.

———. See also #s 10, 11, 33, 47, 48, 64, 65, & 69.

207. **HAGEN, DARON.** *SONG CYCLES.* Susan Crowder, soprano; Bradley Moore, piano. Arsis ▲ ASI 106. *Echo's Songs*; *Love Songs*; *Merrill Songs.*

208. ———. *LOVE IN A LIFE: SONG CYCLES.* Paul Kreider, baritone; D. Hagen, piano. Arsis ▲ 119. *Love in a Life*; *Muldoon Songs.*

209. **HARBISON, JOHN.** *Mirabai Songs.* J. Felty, mezzo-soprano; John Harbison, piano. Northeastern Classical Arts NR▲ 230.

210. ———. *Mirabai Songs.* Dawn Upshaw, soprano; Orchestra of St. Luke's, David Zinman, conductor. NON ▲ 79187.

211. ———. *Simple Daylight.* Karol Bennett, soprano; John McDonald, piano. In ***The Boston Collection.*** ACTR ▲ 60104.

212. ———. *Simple Daylight.* Dawn Upshaw, soprano; Gilbert Kalish, piano. *Words from Paterson.* Sanford Sylvan, baritone; Gilbert Kalish, piano. NON ▲ 79189.

———. See also #s 1 & 29.

213. **HARRIS, DONALD.** *MUSIC OF DONALD HARRIS.* Jane Meyerson, mezzo-soprano; Lucy Shelton, soprano; H. Hinton, piano. CRI ▲ 666. Of Hartford in a Purple Light; Les Mains [and others].

214. **HAYS, DORIS.** *Blues Fragments.* Newman, singer; Thomas, piano. Folk. 37476.

215. **HEGGIE, JAKE.** SONGS. Brian Asawa, Zheng Cao, Kristin Clayton, Renée Fleming, Nicolle Foland, Jennifer Larmore, Sylvia McNair, Frederica von Stade, Carol Vaness, singer; Jake Heggie, piano. In ***The Faces of Love.*** RCA ▲ 63484. from *Eve-Song:* Even; Listen; Snake; *The Faces of Love:* (I Shall Not Live in Vain; As Well as Jesus?; If You Were Coming in the Fall; It Makes No Difference Abroad); from *Natural Selection:* (Animal Passion; Alas! Alack!; Joy Alone); *Paper Wings:* (Bedtime Story; Paper Wings; Mitten Smitten; A Route to the Sky); from *Songs to the Moon:* (Prologue; Fairy-Tales for the Children; The Haughty Snail-King; What the Gray-Winged Fairy Said); *Of Gods and Cats:* (In the Beginning . . .; Once upon a Universe); Sophie's Song; from

Encountertenor: (Countertenor's Conundrum; The Trouble with Trebles in Trousers); My True Love Hath My Heart (duet version).

———. See also # 39.

HELPS, ROBERT. See # 16.

HERBST, JOHANNES. See #s 25 & 61.

HERSCH, FRED. See # 1.

216. **HOIBY, LEE. SONGS.** Kristine Ciesinski, soprano; Lee Hoiby, piano. Leonarda ▲ 120. The Doe; The Serpent; In the Wand of the Wind; Autumn; Winter Song.

217. ———. **SONGS.** D'Anna Fortunato, mezzo-soprano; G. Lee, piano. In *An American Collage.* ALBA ▲ 98. I Was There; Lady of the Harbor; Let This Mind Be in You; Shepherd.

218. ———. *SONGS OF LEE HOIBY.* Peter Stewart, baritone; Lee Hoiby, piano. CRI ▲ 685. *I Was There; Two Songs of Innocence* (The Lamb); *An Immorality; O Florida;* Why Don't You?; Night; What If . . . ; Investiture at Cecconi's; Where the Music Comes From.

———. See also #s 1, 3, 18, 22, 28, 34, 39, 56, & 70.

219. **HOMER, SIDNEY. SONGS.** Louise Homer, contralto; Sidney Homer, piano (?). Pearl Gemm ▲ 9950. Dearest; The House That Jack Built; "How's My Boy?"; Requiem; Sing to Me, Sing; *Mother Goose Rhymes.*

———. See also #s 2, 23, 33, & 48.

HOPKINSON, FRANCIS. See #s 2, 38, & 61.

HORSMAN, EDWARD. See # 63.

220. **HORVIT, MICHAEL.** *MUSIC OF HORVIT.* D. Hayes, soprano; T. Hester, piano. ALBA ▲ 134. *Three Shakespeare Sonnets; Three Faces of Love.*

HOUTZ, STEVEN. See # 29.

221. **HOVHANESS, ALAN. SONGS, Vols. 1 & 3.** Ara Berberian, bass; Alan Hovhaness, piano. POS 1005 & POS S-1009. Vol. 1: Black Pool of Cat; *Love Songs of Hafiz* (8); Lullaby of the Lake. Vol. 3: Pagan Saint [and others].

HOWE, MARY. See # 13.

222. **HUNDLEY, RICHARD.** The Astronomers. D'Anna Fortunato, mezzo-soprano; G. Lee, piano. In *An American Collage.* ALBA ▲ 98.

223. ———. **SONGS.** Paul Sperry, tenor. Ser. 12078. Spring; Wild Plum; Ballad on Queen Anne's Death; Some Sheep Are Loving.

———. See also #s 7, 32, 39, 51, 53, 56, & 70.

224. **IMBRIE, ANDREW.** *Five Roethke Songs.* Susan Narucki, soprano; Anthony Korf, piano. In *Dream Sequence.* NWW ▲ 80441.

225. **IVES, CHARLES.** *AMERICAN SCENES–AMERICAN POETS.* Evelyn Lear, soprano; Thomas Stewart, baritone. Col. M-30229. The Things Our Fathers Loved; Walking; Autumn; Maple Leaves; At the River; Circus Band; The Side Show; Charlie Rutlage; Tom Sails Away; They Are There; In Flanders Fields; Two Little Flowers; The Greatest Man; There Is a Lane; The Last Reader; The Children's Hour; Walt Whitman; The Light that Is Felt; Serenity; Thoreau; Duty; Afterglow; The Housatonic at Stockbridge.

226. ———. *CHARLES IVES: THE 100thANNIVERSARY.* Charles Ives, singer; Helen Boatwright, soprano; Alvin Brahm; Bruch Fifer, baritone; with piano, string quartet, and orchestra. Columbia M4 32504. Ives sings They Are There!; Brahm sings Hymn w/ str. qt.; Fifer sings Naught that Country Needed w/orch.; Boatwright sings Canon; Down East; Feldeinsamkeit; from "The Incantation"; Luck and Work; Mists; The New River; No More; Old Home Day; The One Way; Peaks; Pictures; Requiem; Resolution; On Judge's Walk; A Sea Dirge; September; The Side Show; Slow March; There Is a Certain Garden; There Is a Lane; The Things Our Fathers Loved; The Sea of Sleep (Those Evening Bells); West London; Yellow Leaves.

227. ———. *COMPLETE SONGS, VOLS. I, II, III, & IV.* Dora Ohrenstein, soprano; Mary Ann Hart, mezzo-soprano; Paul Sperry, tenor; William Sharp, baritone; Philip Bush, Dennis Helmrich, Irma Vallecillo, and Steven Blier, pianists. ALBA ▲ 77, 78, 79, & 80.

228. ———. General William Booth Enters into Heaven. Radiana Pazmor, soprano; Bauman, piano. CRI S-390E (see also #69 above). [Villamil cites Philip Miller's assertion that this is the first recording ever made of an Ives song. Pazmor and Ives were friends.]

229. ———. *MELODIES [THE SONGS OF CHARLES IVES].* N. Isherwood, bass; E. Watson, piano. ACCO ▲ 201812. Tom Sails Away; Ann Street; Thoreau; Maple Leaves; The Cage; 1, 2, 3; Evening; Serenity: A Unison Chant; The New River; The White Gulls; Slugging a Vampire; West London; Incantation; Charlie Rutlage; Slow March; The Indians; Walt Whitman; Afterglow; His Exaltation; At the River; In the Mornin'; The Camp Meeting; The Circus Band; Paracelsus; Premonitions; On the Counter; A Sea Dirge; Like a Sick Eagle; Soliloquy; Memories; The One Way; Remembrance; A Farewell to Land.

230. ———. *SELECTED SONGS BY CHARLES IVES.* Peter del Grande, baritone; Vladimir Pleshakov, piano. SCT 106. The New River; Premonitions; The Housatonic at Stockbridge; Thoreau; The Camp Meeting; Watchman; His Exaltation; The Last Reader; The Waiting Soul; Hymn; The Innate; August; December; Rough Wind; The Light That Is Felt; Cradle Song; Those Evening Bells; Elégie; Qu'il m'irait bien; Rosamunde; Weil auf mir; Down East;

Old Home Day.

231. ———. **SONGS, Vol. 1.** Roberta Alexander, soprano; Tan Crone, piano. Etcetera KTC ▲ 1020. Songs My Mother Taught Me; Slow March; Dreams; Memories; Berceuse; Romanza (di Central Park); Slugging a Vampire; Spring Song; The Cage; Autumn; The Things Our Fathers Loved; Tom Sails Away; Down East; Serenity; Maple Leaves; Like a Sick Eagle; On the Counter; The Se'er; Evening; Immortality; The Housatonic at Stockbridge; The Greatest Man; Two Little Flowers; The Side Show; 1, 2, 3; Charlie Rutlage.

232. ———. **SONGS, Vol. 2.** Roberta Alexander, soprano. Tan Crone(?), piano. Etcetera KTC 1068. Ann Street; At Sea; At the River; The Camp Meeting; Chanson de Florian; The Children's Hour; The Circus Band; Elégie; Evidence; A Farewell to Land; Feldeinsamkeit; from "Night of Frost in May"; from "Paracelsus"; Harpalus; His Exaltation; Ich grolle nicht; Ilmenau; Mirage; A Night Song; An Old Flame; The Old Mother; Qu'il m'irait bien; Remembrance; Rosamunde; There Is a Lane; They Are There!; Watchman!; Weil' auf mir.

233. ———. **SONGS.** Mordecai Bauman, bass; Albert Hirsch, piano. CRI SRD 390 [remastering of NMR-1412 (12")]. Ann Street; Charlie Rutlage; Evening; The Greatest Man; Two Little Flowers.

234. ———. **SONGS.** Helen Boatwright, soprano; John Kirkpatrick, piano. CRI ▲ 675 (formerly Overtone 7). Abide with Me; Walking; Where The Eagle; Disclosure; The White Gulls; Two Little Flowers; The Greatest Man; The Children's Hour; Berceuse; Ann Street; General William Booth Enters into Heaven; Autumn; Swimmers; Evening; Harpalus; Tarrant Moss; Serenity; At the River; The See'r; Maple Leaves; 1, 2, 3; Tom Sails Away; He Is There!; In Flanders Fields.

235. ———. **SONGS.** Corinne Curry, soprano; Luise Vosgerchian, piano. Cambridge CRM 804B. 1, 2, 3; Religion; An Election; The Cage; Ich grolle nicht; General Booth; A Farewell to Land; Ann Street.

236. ———. **SONGS.** Jan DeGaetani, mezzo-soprano; Gilbert Kalish, piano. BRID ▲ 2002. Down East; Two Little Flowers; Tom Sails Away; The Se'er; Songs My Mother Taught Me; The Side Show; The White Gulls; West London; Afterglow.

237. ———. **SONGS.** Jan DeGaetani, mezzo-soprano; Gilbert Kalish, piano. NON ▲ 71325. The Housatonic at Stockbridge; Memories; From "Paracelsus"; The Things Our Fathers Loved; Ann Street; The Innate; The Circus Band; In the Mornin'; Serenity; Majority; Thoreau; At the River; The Indians; The Cage; Like a Sick Eagle; A Christmas Carol; A Farewell to Land.

238. ———. **SONGS.** Dietrich Fischer-Dieskau, baritone; Michael Ponti, piano. DG 2530696. Abide with Me; Ann Street; At the River; Autumn; The Children's Hour; A Christmas Carol; Disclosure; Elégie; A Farewell to Land; Feldeinsamkeit; Ich grolle nicht; In Flanders Fields; The Swimmers; Tom Sails Away; Two Little Flowers; Weil' auf mir; West London; Where the Eagle; The White Gulls.

239. ———. **SONGS.** Michael Ingham, singer; H. Brant, piano. AMCA ▲ 10306. Ann Street; His Exaltation; The See'r; The Last Reader; General William Booth Enters into Heaven; The Things Our Fathers Loved; Walking; Luck and Work; An Election; Tom Sails Away; Paracelsus; Walt Whitman; The Camp Meeting; 1, 2, 3; Grantchester; The New River; The Cage; The Housatonic at Stockbridge; Charlie Rutlage; Requiem; Slugging a Vampire; A Sea Dirge; Soliloquy; September; December; Majority; Swimmers; On the Antipodes.

240. ———. **SONGS.** Marni Nixon, soprano; John McCabe, piano. Nonesuch H-71209. The Greatest Man; At the River; Ann Street; A Christmas Carol; From "The Swimmers"; West London; Soliloquy; Evening; Charlie Rutlage; The Side Show; The Cage; A Farewell to Land; Gen. Wm. Booth Enters into Heaven.

241. ———. **SONGS.** Ted Puffer, tenor; James Tenney and Philip Corner, pianists. 2-Folk. 3344/5. Vol. 1: 1894–1915: Gen. Wm. Booth Enters into Heaven; The Indians; The Children's Hour; Canon; Requiem; Mists; from "Paracelsus"; from "Lincoln, the Great Commoner"; Like a Sick Eagle; from "The Swimmers"; The Cage; Walking; A Christmas Carol; West London. Vol. 2: 1915–1929 - Majority; Ann Street; September; Grantchester; Afterglow; Walt Whitman; Tom Sails Away; Maple Leaves; On the Antipodes; Charlie Rutlage; Two Little Flowers; The Side Show; An Election; Serenity; White Gulls; 1, 2, 3; Immortality; A Farewell to Land.

242. ———. **SONGS.** Samuel Ramey, baritone. ARGO ▲ 433 027-2. At the River; Charlie Rutlage; The Children's Hour; The Circus Band; In the Alley; An Old Flame; Romanzo (di Central Park); Slow March; They Are There!

243. ———. **SONGS.** Sheila Schonbrun and Victoria Villamil, sopranos. Musical Heritage Society ▲ 512292Y. Aeschylus and Sophocles; The Housatonic at Stockbridge; On the Antipodes; Remembrance; Soliloquy; Sunrise.

244. ———. **SONGS.** Dawn Upshaw, soprano; Orchestra of St. Luke's, J. Adams, conducting. In *American Elegies*. NON ▲ 79249. Thoreau; Down East; Cradle Song; At the River; Serenity.

245. ———. **SONGS.** Charles van Tassel, baritone; Marien van Nieukerken, piano. RENE ▲ 92010. Disclosure; Kären; From "Paracelsus"; The Camp Meeting; September; Afterglow; The Innate; 1, 2, 3; Serenity; The Side Show; Songs My Mother Taught Me; Like a Sick Eagle; From "The Swimmers"; In Flanders Fields; He Is There; Tom Sails Away; Old Home Day; Ich grolle nicht; Memories; Dirge; Charlie Rutlage; Down East; The Circus Band; La Fède; Berceuse; The Children's Hour; Hymn; At the River; Two Little Flowers; West London; The Cage.

246. ———. **SONGS.** Carolyn Watkinson, singer. Etc. 1007.

Walking; Grantchester; Tom Sails Away; The Cage; The Side Show.

247. ———. *THE SONGS OF CHARLES IVES,* **VOL. I.** Henry Herford, baritone; Robin Bowman, piano. UNIC ▲ 9111. Two Little Flowers; The Children's Hour; Memories, A and B; The Side Show; The Things Our Fathers Loved; The Circus Band; Berceuse; There Is a Certain Garden; In Flanders Field; They Are There; Tom Sails Away; Immortality; The Housatonic at Stockbridge; from "The Swimmers"; The Indians; The New River; Yellow Leaves; from "Paracelsus"; West London; Ann Street; The White Gulls; The Se'er; Pictures; Where the Eagle; Gen. Wm. Booth Enters into Heaven; In the Mornin'.

248. ———. *THE SONGS OF CHARLES IVES,* **VOL. II.** Henry Herford, baritone; Robin Bowman; piano. UNIC ▲ 9112. In the Alley; Religion; Luck and Work; The Cage; Grantchester; Premonitions; Nov. 2, 1920; Duty; from "Lincoln, the Great Commoner"; Thoreau; Walt Whitman; The Greatest Man; So May It Be!; Walking; August; September; December; Autumn; Afterglow; from "The Incantation"; Spring Song; At Sea; Tarrant Moss; Waltz; Romanzo di Central Park; Canon; Mirage; Maple Leaves; Charlie Rutlage; The Camp Tin.

———. See also #s 2, 3, 5, 6, 10, 19, 27, 28, 39, 42, 44, 46, 58, 59, 65, 66, 67, & 69.

KELLEY, EDGAR STILLMAN. See #48.

KOCH, JOHN. See # 32.

KRAKAUER, DAVID. See # 1.

249. LADERMAN, EZRA. *Songs for Eve* and *From the Psalms.* Judith Raskin, soprano; Ryan Edwards, piano. Desto 7105.

250. LaMONTAINE, JOHN. *Songs of The Rose of Sharon.* Eleanor Steber, soprano; Greater Trenton Symphony, N. Harsanyi, conducting. ST/AND Co. Inc. SLP 420.

———. See also # 59.

251. LANE, RICHARD. *Four Songs.* Patricia Berlin, soprano; Howard Hanson, conductor. ERA 1010. Mountain House: December; Dunce's Song; Down Dip the Branches; Will He Come Back?

LARSEN, LIBBY. See #s 8 & 29.

LAURIDSEN, MORTEN. See # 50.

LIPPÉ, EDOUARD. See # 35.

252. LIPTAK, DAVID. *Seven Songs For Baritone And Piano.* William Sharp, baritone; A. Nel, piano. GAS ▲ 286.

LOCKWOOD, ANNEA. See # 1.

253. LOEFFLER, CHARLES MARTIN. SONGS. D'Anna

Fortunato, mezzo-soprano; Eskin, piano. North. 207. Vieille chanson d'amour; To Helen; Les soirs d'automne; Adieu pour jamais; Ton souvenir est comme un livre bien-aimé; The Hosting of the Sidhe; The Host of the Air; The Fiddler of Dooney; *Four Poems, Op. 5.*

254. ———. **SONGS.** Diedra Palmour, mezzo-soprano; Noel Lester, piano. In *Forgotten Songs.* KOCH ▲ 7428.

———. See also # 10.

LYON, JAMES. See #61.

255. MacDOWELL, EDWARD. The Blue Bell, Op. 26, No. 5. Anna Howard, soprano. In *Songs for Children.* V-36032 (12").

256. ———. Long Ago, Sweetheart Mine, Op. 56, No. 1 & A Maid Sings Light, Op. 56, No. 3. Lambert Murphy, tenor. V-4017 (10"). Also: The Sea, Op. 47, No. 7; The Swan Bent Low, Op. 56, No. 2.

257. ———. **SONGS.** Alexandra Hunt, soprano. Orion 77272. To a Wild Rose; The Swan; Midsummer Lullaby; Folksong; Confidence; Fra Nightingale.

258. ———. **SONGS.** S. Tharp, tenor; J. Barbagallo, piano. NIXIN ▲ 8559032. *Two Songs, Op. 34; Drei Lieder, Op. 33; Three Songs, Op. 60; Six Love Songs, Op. 40; Drei Lieder, Op. 11; Zwei Lieder, Op. 12; From an Old Garden, Op. 26; Eight Songs, Op. 47; Two Old Songs, Op. 9; Four Songs, Op. 56; Three Songs, Op. 58.*

259. ———. Thy Beaming Eyes, Op. 40, No. 3. Nelson Eddy, baritone. V-4368 (10").

260. ———. Thy Beaming Eyes, Op. 40, No. 3. Lawrence Tibbett, baritone. V-1172 (10").

261. ———. *TWENTY-FOUR SONGS WITH PIANOFORTE ACCOMPANIMENT.* Suzanne Summerville, mezzo-soprano; Robert McCoy, piano. Von Tejas Records 2040. *Eight Love Songs, Op. 47; From an Old Garden, Op. 26; Four Songs, Op. 56; Three Songs, Op. 58; Three Songs, Op. 60.*

———. See also #s 10, 27, 41, 59, 66, & 69.

262. MAHY, KENNETH. *Four Love Songs, Op. 4.* Allen Henderson, baritone; Anne Glass, piano. Aeolian ▲ ADR60003D.

263. MANA-ZUCCA. I Love Life. John Charles Thomas, baritone. Nimbus ▲ 7838.

———. See also #s 33 & 40.

264. MANNING, KATHLEEN. In The Luxembourg Gardens. Rose Bampton, alto. V-1648 (10").

———. See also # 41.

265. MENOTTI, GIAN CARLO. *Canti Della Lontananza* (7 Songs) for Soprano and Piano. A. V. Banks, mezzo-soprano; S. Costanzo, piano. NUO ▲ 7122.

266. ———. *Canti Della Lontananza.* Yolanda Marcoulescou, soprano; Jeffry Peterson, piano. In *French, German, Italian, and Spanish Songs by American Composers.* Orion 685 (tape). (See #27.)

267. ———. SONGS. Judith Howarth, soprano; Robin Leggate, tenor; Malcom Martineau, piano. CHN ▲ 9605. *Canti Della Lontananza* (7 Songs) for Soprano and Piano; *Five Songs for Tenor and Piano.*

MOORE, DOUGLAS. See # 59.

MUSTO, JOHN. *Recuerdo* & others. See #s 1, 7, 28, 29, 50, 56, & 65.

268. NAGINSKI, CHARLES. The Pasture. Povla Frijsh, soprano; Celius Dougherty, piano. V-2157.

———. See also #s 23, 39, & 67.

269. NEVIN, ETHELBERT. SONGS. Shilkret Salon Group & Orchestra. VM-C5 (10 sides 12"). My Desire; Mighty Lak' a Rose; At Twilight; Oh, That We Two Were Maying; At Rest; Little Boy Blue; The Night Has a Thousand Eyes; The Woodpecker; In Winter I Get Up at Night; Every Night; Best upon Mine; Little Heart; A Life Lesson; Dawn; The Gondoliers; Good Night; A Venetian Love Song.

———. See also # 52.

270. NILES, JOHN JACOB. *Gambling Songs* (4). Mack Harrell, baritone. Remington 199-140.

———. See also #s 28, 34, 39, 45, & 47.

NORDOFF, PAUL. See #s 10, 23 & 70.

OWEN, RICHARD. See #32.

PARKER, HORATIO. See #s 65 & 69.

271. PASATIERI, THOMAS. *Three Poems of James Agee.* Sharon Mabry, mezzo-soprano. Owl 28.

———. See also # 15.

272. PAULUS, STEPHEN. SONG CYCLES. R. Jacobsen, soprano; Paul Sperry, tenor; Håkan Hagegård, baritone; P. Schoenfield, Irma Vallecillo, and Warren Jones, pianists. ALBA ▲ 36. *All My Pretty Ones* for Soprano and Piano; *Artsongs* for Tenor and Piano; *Bittersuite* for Baritone and Piano.

———. See also # 9.

273. PERERA, RONALD. *Apollo Circling.* Gretchen D'Armand, soprano. Opus One 27.

PERLE, GEORGE. See # 68.

PERSICHETTI, VINCENT. See #s 10, 54, & 59.

PETER, JOHANN FRIEDRICH. See # 61.

274. PINKHAM, DANIEL. *MUSIC, THOU SOUL OF HEAVEN.* M. Kennedy, soprano; P. Barnes, piano. ARK ▲ 6153. *Carols and Cries*; Music, Thou Soul of Heaven; Slow, Slow, Fresh Fount; The Hour Glass; Heaven-Haven/World Welter; The Moon Was But a Chin of Gold; To Make a Prairie; A Partridge in a Pear Tree; *Three Canticles from Luke*; For Echo Is the Soul of the Voice; When Love Was Gone; *Three Alleluias.*

———. See also # 59.

275. POWELL, MEL. *Haiku Settings.* Bethany Beardslee, soprano; Robert Helps, piano. None. 78006.

276. PRICE, FLORENCE. SONGS. L. Field, soprano; H. Wingreen, piano. Cambria ▲ 1037. Travel's End; To My Little Son; Night; To the Dark Virgin.

———. See also # 11.

277. READ, GARDNER. SONGS. D'Anna Fortunato, mezzo-soprano; J. McDonald, piano. ALBA ▲ 36. *From a Lute of Jade, Op. 36*; *Nocturnal Visions, Op. 145*; *Nocturnes* (4), Op. 23; *Songs* (3), Op. 68.

278. ———. SONGS. D'Anna Fortunato, mezzo-soprano; J. McDonald, piano. ALBA ▲ 336. *Songs, Op. 23*; *From a Lute of Jade, Op. 36*; *Songs for a Rainy Night, Op. 48*; *Songs to Children, Op. 76.*

REIF, PAUL. See # 32.

REINAGLE, ALEXANDER. See # 61.

279. RHODES, PHILIP. *Mountain Songs.* P. Bryn-Julson, soprano. Orion 77276.

RICH, GLADYS. See # 19.

280. ROCHBERG, GEORGE. *Eleven Songs.* Sharon Mabry, mezzo-soprano. Owl 28.

281. ———. *Songs in Praise of Krishna.* Neva Pilgrim, soprano. CRI▲ 817 (formerly CRI S-360).

ROGERS, JAMES HOTCHKISS. See # 48.

282. ROGERS, PATSY. *Sonja.* L. Field, soprano; H. Wingreen, piano. Cambria ▲ 1037.

283. ROREM, NED. *Evidence of Things Not Seen.* Monique McDonald, soprano; Delores Ziegler, mezzo-soprano; Rufus Müller, tenor; Kurt Ollmann, baritone; Michael Barret & Steven Blier, pianists. New World ▲ 80575 (Albany 2CD). Recorded in concert.

284. ———. *From an Unknown Past.* Solo voices. PHOE ▲ 108 (formerly Desto DC 6480).

285. ———. *Nantucket Songs.* P. Bryn-Julson, soprano; Ned Rorem, piano. CRI ▲ 657 (formerly CRI S-485). (World Premier Performance at the Library of Congress, October 30, 1979)

286. ———. *Poems of Love and the Rain.* Regina Sarfaty, mezzo-soprano; Ned Rorem, piano. CRI 202.

287. ———. *Poems of Love and the Rain.* Beverly Wolff, mezzo-soprano; Ned Rorem, piano. PHOE ▲ 108 (formerly Desto 6480).

288. ———. SONGS. Charles Bressler, tenor; Phyllis Curtin, soprano; Gianna d'Angelo, soprano; Regina Sarfaty, mezzo-soprano; Donald Gramm, baritone; Ned Rorem, piano. New World 229. Early in the Morning; To You; Spring and Fall; Upon Julia's Clothes; To the Willow Tree; Root Cellar; My Papa's Waltz; Spring; Lullaby of the Woman of the Mountain; I Am Rose; Pippa's Song; Snake.

289. ———. SONGS. Charles Bressler, tenor; Phyllis Curtin, soprano; Gianna d'Angelo, soprano; Donald Gramm, bass-baritone; Regina Sarfaty, mezzo-soprano; Ned Rorem, piano. Odyssey 32160274 (formerly MS 6561). Song for a Girl; To the Willow Tree; Echo's Song; Upon Julia's Clothes; The Silver Swan; Three Psalms from *Cycle of Holy Songs*; The Lordly Hudson; Snake; Rain in Spring; Root Cellar; Sally's Smile; Such Beauty as Hurts to Behold; My Papa's Waltz; Early in the Morning; I Am Rose; See How They Love Me; Visits to St. Elizabeth's: *Three Medieval Poems* (A Christmas Carol; The Nightingale; The Call); Spring and Fall; Spring; To You; Youth, Day, Old Age, and Night; O You Whom I Often and Silently Come; Pippa's Song; Lullaby of the Woman of the Mountain; What If Some Little Pain; In a Gondola; Requiem.

290. ———. SONGS. Phyllis Bryn-Julson, soprano; Katherine Ciesinski, mezzo-soprano; Phyllis Curtin, soprano; Beverly Wolff, contralto; Donald Gramm, baritone; Ned Rorem, piano. CRI ▲ 657. *The Nantucket Songs* (cycle); *Some Trees*; Little Elegy; Night Crow; The Tulip Tree; Look Down, Fair Moon; What Sparks and Wiry Cries; For Poulenc; *Women's Voices.*

291. ———. SONGS. Rosalind Rees, soprano; Ned Rorem, piano. GSS 104. Alleluia; The Youth with the Red-Gold Hair; You the Young Rainbow of my Tears; Root Cellar; Snake; The Serpent; Ask Me No More; Now Sleeps the Crimson Petal; Far–Far–Away; Conversation; Visits to St. Elizabeth's; Rain in Spring; For Susan; Such Beauty as Hurts to Behold; Clouds; Sally's Smile; What Sparks and Wiry Cries; The Lordly Hudson; The Nightingale; A Christmas Carol; Sometimes with One I Love; O You Whom I Often and Silently Come; I Am Rose; A Journey; Let's Take a Walk; See How They Love Me; Early in the Morning.

292. ———. *SONGS OF NED ROREM.* Susan Graham, mezzo-soprano; Malcolm Martineau, piano; Ensemble Oriol. Erato ▲ 8573-80222-2. Sonnet; Clouds; Early in the Morning; The Serpent; Now Sleeps the Crimson Petal; Opus 101; I Strolled across an Open Field; To a Young Girl; Jeanie with the Light Brown Hair; Ode; For Poulenc; Little Elegy; Alleluia; Look Down, Fair Moon; O You Whom I Often and Silently Come; I Will Always Love You; The Tulip Tree; The Wintry Mind; I Am Rose; The Lordly Hudson; O Do Not Love Too Long; Far–Far–Away; For Susan; A Journey; Sometimes with One I Love; Love; Orchids; Stopping by Woods on a Snowy Evening; Do I Love You More Than a Day?; Ferry Me across the Water; The Sowers; That Shadow, My Likeness.

293. ———. *War Scenes.* Donald Gramm, bass-baritone; Eugene Istomin, piano. PHOE ▲ 116 (formerly Desto 7101). Also *Five Songs of Walt Whitman* (As Adam Early in the Morning; O You Whom I Often and Silently Come; To You; Look Down, Fair Moon; Gliding O'er All); *Four Dialogues* (A. Darian, soprano; J. Stewart, tenor; N. Rorem and R. Cumming, pianists).

294. ———. *Women's Voices.* Katherine Ciesinski, mezzo-soprano. See #335 above.

295. ———. *Women's Voices.* H. Skok, soprano; M. Hennessy, piano. NPT ▲ 85613.

———. See also #s 1, 3, 10, 15, 28, 34, 50, 58, 59, 63, 65, 67, & 70.

296. RUGGLES, CARL. Toys. J. Litante, soprano; N. Slonimsky, conductor. NMR-1013 (12").

SACCO, JOHN CHARLES. See #11 & 47.

SALTER, MARY TURNER. See # 57.

297. SARGON, SIMON. *Waves of the Sea* (6 Irish Lyrics) for Medium Voice and Piano. Virginia Dupuy, mezzo-soprano; Simon Sargon, piano. In *A Clear Midnight.* GAS ▲ 333.

SCHEER, GENE. See #28.

298. SCHUMAN, WILLIAM. *Time to the Old* (3 Songs). Rosalind Rees, soprano. CRI S-439 (A recording of Schuman's chamber works).

———. See also #s 50, 58, & 65.

299. SCHWANTNER, JOSEPH. *Magabunda (Four Poems of Agueda Pizarro).* Lucy Shelton, soprano; Leonard Slatkin. None. 79072.

———. See also # 71.

300. SEEGER, CHARLES. SONGS. Anna Carol Dudley, soprano; Earle Shenk, piano. Magellan S-1801. Whenas in Silks My Julia Goes; Endymion; The Lady of the South; Alguna Vez; Psalm 138; "to C.R."; The Pride of Youth; To Helen; The Letter; "to R.C.S."; Asleep.

301. SEEGER, RUTH CRAWFORD. *Five Songs* (Sandburg). L. Field, soprano; H. Wingreen, piano. CMB ▲ 1037.

302. ———. *Three Songs* (Sandburg). Patricia Berlin, soprano; P. Hoffman, piano. CRI 658.

303. ———. *Three Songs* (Sandburg). B. Morgan, mezzo-soprano; P. L. Dunkel, conductor. In *Voices from Elysium.* NWW ▲ 80543.

304. ———. *Three Songs* (Sandburg). Lucy Shelton, soprano; R. de Leeuw, piano. In *Portrait.* DG ▲ 449925-2.

———. See also #s 58 (Crawford-Seeger) & 71.

SESSIONS, ROGER. See #s 16 & 54.

SHAW, CLIFFORD. See # 23.

305. SHEPHERD, ARTHUR. SONGS. Marie Simmelink Kraft, mezzo-soprano; M. M. Mastics, piano. CRI ▲ 783. The Starling Lake; The Fiddlers; The Gentle Lady; The Lost Child; Sunday up the River; Golden Stockings; In the Scented Bud of the Morning; Morning Glory; To a Trout; The Charm; Bacchus; Where Loveliness Keeps House.

———. See also # 20.

306. SIEGMEISTER, ELIE. SONG CYCLES. Esther Hinds, soprano; Elizabeth Kirkpatrick, soprano; A. Mandel, piano. CRI ▲ 814. *Madame to You*; *Face of War*; *Ways of Love*.

307. ———. **SONGS.** Elizabeth Kirkpatrick, soprano; C. Ingram, tenor; A. Mandel, piano. GAS ▲ 2008. *City Songs* for Soprano (or Tenor) and Piano; *Songs of Innocence* for Soprano and Piano.

308. ———. **SONGS.** Elizabeth Kirkpatrick, soprano; Herbert Beattie, bass-baritone. Orion 76220. *Elegies for García Lorca*; *Five Cummings Songs*; Johnny Appleseed; Lazy Afternoon; Nancy Hanks; The Strange Funeral at Braddock; Evil; *for My Daughters*.

309. ———. The Strange Funeral in Braddock. Mordecai Bauman, bass; Elie Siegmeister, piano. NMR-1212 (12").

———. See also #62.

310. SINGER, JEANNE. SONGS AND SONG CYCLES. F. Hechtel, soprano; A. Miskell, tenor; Jeanne Singer, piano. CMB ▲ 1051. Arno is Deep; Memoria [and others].

———. See also # 62.

311. SMIT, LEO. *The White Diadem: Songs about Poets & Poetry.* Rosalind Rees, soprano; Leo Smit, piano. BRID ▲ 9080.

312. SMITH, HALE. *Valley Wind.* Harris; Carno. CRI 301.

SOWERBY, LEO. See # 9.

SPEAKS, OLEY. See #s 47 & 48.

313. STILL, WILLIAM GRANT. *MUSIC OF STILL.* L. Toppin, soprano; Robert Honeysucker, baritone; V. Taylor, piano. CMB ▲ 1112. Breath of a Rose; Here's One.

314. ———. **SONGS.** Videmus (Robert Honeysucker, et al.). NWW ▲ 80399-2. *Songs of Separation* (5); Here's One; Song for the Lonely; Citadel; Lift Every Voice and Sing.

315. ———. *Songs of Separation* (5). Bedford; Hughes. Desto 7107.

316. ———. *Songs of Separation.* Claudine Carlson, mezzo-soprano. Bay Cities ▲ 1033.

———. See also # 12.

STILLMAN-KELLEY, EDGAR. See # 48.

ST. PIERRE, DONALD. See # 1.

STRICKLAND, LILY. See #57.

SUSA, CONRAD. See # 20.

317. SWANSON, HOWARD. SEVEN SONGS. Thigpen. Desto 6422E. Ghosts in Love; Joy; The Junk Man; The Negro Speaks of Rivers; Night Song; Still Life; The Valley.

———. See also # 12.

TALMA, LOUISE. See #s 49 & 50.

318. TAYLOR, JOSEPH DEEMS. A Song for Lovers, Op. 13, No. 2. Rose Bampton, alto. V-1648 (10").

———. See also # 23.

THOMAS, RICHARD PEARSON. See # 1.

319. THOMPSON, RANDALL. Velvet Shoes. Povla Frijsh, soprano; Celius Dougherty, piano. V-2157 (now in # 69).

320. THOMSON, VIRGIL. *Four Songs From William Blake.* Mack Harrell, baritone; E. Ormandy. CRI 398E.

321. ———. *MOSTLY ABOUT LOVE AND OTHER SONGS AND VOCAL WORKS.* N. Armstrong, soprano; D'Anna Fortunato, mezzo-soprano; F. Kelley, tenor; P. Kirby, tenor; Sanford Sylvan, baritone; D. Ripley, bass; A. Tommasini, piano. Northeastern ▲ 250 (Koch). *Mostly About Love*; *Shakespeare Songs*; *Praises and Prayers*; Song of Songs; Poems of Gertrude Stein.

322. ———. *NOTHING DIVINE IS MUNDANE.* Dora Ohrenstein, soprano; William Sharp, baritone; Philip Bush, piano. ALBA ▲ 272. Preciosilla; *Mostly About Love*; Susie Asado; *La Belle en Dormant*; *Four Songs to Poems of Thomas Campion*; *Three Estampas de Niñez*; *Five Songs from William Blake*; *Two by Marianne Moore*.

323. ———. *Praises And Prayers.* Betty Allen, mezzo-soprano; Virgil Thomson, piano. CRI 207.

324. ———. SONGS. Phillip Frohnmayer, baritone; M. Tede, mezzo-soprano; E. P. Frohnmayer, soprano; H. J. McCracken, piano. CENT ▲ 2180. *Five Songs* (Blake); *Four Songs* (Campion) [and others].

325. ———. SONGS. Martha Herr. New Albion ▲ 034. The Courtship of Youngly Bongly Bo; Preciosilla; *Shakespeare Songs*; La Valse Grégorienne.

326. ———. SONGS. Ellen Lang, singer. Musical Heritage Society ▲ MHS 512622K. *Praises and Prayers*; *Two by Marianne Moore*; *Four Songs to Poems of Thomas Campion* (w/instruments).

———. See also #s 4, 11, 27, 41, 51, 56, 59, & 65.

327. TRAVIS, ROY. *Songs and Epilogues.* Ennis; Popper. Orion 76219.

328. VEHAR, PERSIS PARSHALL. *Women, Women.* Sharon Mabry, mezzo-soprano; Patsy Wade, piano. Aeolian ▲ ADR60003D.

329. VERCOE, ELIZABETH. *Irreveries from Sappho.* Sharon Mabry, mezzo-soprano; R. Platt, piano. Coro 3127.

330. WALKER, GEORGE. SONGS. Phyllis Bryn-Julson, soprano; George Walker, piano. CRI ▲ 719 (formerly CRI S-488). With Rue My Heart Is Laden; Bequest; I Have No Life But This; What if I Say I Shall Not Wait; A Red, Red Rose; I Went to Heaven; The Bereaved Maid; Sweet Let Me Go; Hey Nonny No; So We'll Go No More A-Roving; Response.

———. See also # 12.

331. WARD, ROBERT. *Sacred Songs for Pantheists.* S. Stahlman, soprano. CRI 206.

332. ———. SONGS. William Stone, singer. Bay Cities ▲ 1029. As I Watched the Ploughman Ploughing; Rain Has Fallen All the Day; Sorrow of Mydath; Vanished.

———. See also #s 34, 44, & 59.

WARE, HARRIET. See #57.

333. WARREN, ELINOR REMICK. SONGS. Marie Gibson, singer. Cambria ▲ 1028. Lady Lo-Fu; Silent Noon; Snow Towards Evening; By a Fireside; White Horses of the Sea [and others].

334. WATTS, WINTTER. The Wings of Night. Eva Gauthier, soprano. Town Hall Records.

WEBER, BEN. See #s 20, 50, & 59.

335. WEISGALL, HUGO. SONGS. Judith Raskin, soprano. CRI SD 417. *The Golden Peacock*; *Translations*:

Knoxville, Tennessee; Song; Child Song; Poem: 1st Version; Poem: 2nd Version; The Rebel; A City by the Sea.

———. See also #s 18 & 50.

WHEELOCK, DONALD. See # 1.

WILSON, RICHARD. See # s 29 & 49.

336. ZWILICH, ELLEN TAAFEE. *Einsame Nacht.* Ostendorf, baritone; Seguin, piano. Leonarda 120.

ADDENDA

337. BOLCOM, WILLIAM. *Briefly It Enters.* Benita Valente, soprano; Cynthia Raim, piano. *Cabaret Songs, Vols. III & IV.* Joan Morris, mezzo-soprano; William Bolcom, piano. Centaur ▲ (TBA-new release).

338. LAITMAN, LORI. *MYSTERY - The Songs of Lori Laitman.* Lauren Wagner, soprano; William Sharp, baritone; Phyllis Bryn-Julson, soprano; Frederick Weldy, Lori Laitman, & Seth Knopp, pianists; Thomas Kraines, cello; Gary Louie, saxophone. Albany ▲ Troy 393. The Metropolitan Tower; The Strong House; The Hour; To a Loose Woman; *Mystery* (5 songs); *The Love Poems of Marichiko* (6 songs); Echo; The Ballad Singer; *I Never Saw Another Butterfly* (6 songs); *Days and Nights* (6 songs).

CHRONOLOGICAL LIST OF COMPOSERS

18th Century

1710s

Grimm, Johann (1719–1760)

1730s

Lyon, James (1735–1794)
Herbst, Johannes (1735–1812)
Hopkinson, Francis (1737–1791)
Selby, William (1738–1798)

1740s

Antes, John (1740–1811)
Pelissier, Victor (1745–1820)
Billings, William (1746–1800)
Peter, Johann Friedrich (1746–1813)
Taylor, Raynor (1747–1825)

1750s

Michael, David Moritz (1751–1825)
Belcher, Supply (1751–1836)
Wood, Abraham (1752–1804)
Reinagle, Alexander (1756–1809)
Latrobe, Christian I. (1758–1836)
Swan, Timothy (1758–1842)

1760s

Ingalls, Jeremiah (1764–1828)
Carr, Benjamin (1768–1831)

1770s

Hewitt, James (1770–1827)

1780s

Von Hagen, P. A. (1781–1837)
Heinrich, Anthony Philip (1781–1861)
Meineke, Christopher (1782–1850)
Horn, Charles Edward (1786–1849)
Wilson, James (Joseph?) (fl. ca.1780–1820?)

19th Century

1800s

Hewitt, John Hill (1801–1890)
Webb, George J. (1803–1887)

1810s

Spilman, Jonathan E. (1812–1896)
Boott, Francis (1813–1904)
Woodbury, Isaac Baker (1819–1858)
Willis, Richard Storrs (1819–1900)

1820s

Browne, Augusta (1820–1882)
Saroni, Herman S. (1823–1900)
Foster, Stephen Collins (1826–1864)
Tucker, Henry L. (1826–1882)
Southard, Lucien H. (1827–1881)
Parker, James Cutler Dunn (1828–1916)
Millard, Harrison (1829–1895)

1830s

Stratton, George William (1830–1901)
Brandeis, Frederick (1832–1899)
Merz, Karl (1836–1890)
Pease, Alfred H. (1838–1882)
Paine, John Knowles (1839–1906)

1840s

Weil, Oscar (1840–1921)
Rogers, Clara Kathleen (1844–1931)
Bartlett, Homer, N. (1845–1920)
Dana, C. Henshaw (1846–1883)
Gleason, Frederick Grant (1848–1903)
McCoy, William J. (1848–1926)

1850s

Jordan, Jules (1850–1927)
Foote, Arthur (1853–1937)
Goetschius, Percy (1853–1943)
Foerster, Adolph M. (1854–1927)
Chadwick, George Whitefield (1854–1931)
Sousa, John Philip (1854–1932)
Salter, Mary Turner (1856–1938)
Strong, George Templeton (1856–1948)
Johns, Clayton (1857–1932)
Kelley, Edgar Stillman (1857–1944)
Pasmore, Henry (1857–1944)
Rogers, James Hotchkiss (1857–1944)
Hawley, Charles Beach (1858–1915)
De Koven, Reginald (1859–1920)

1860s

Barton, Gerard (1861–?)
MacDowell, Edward (1861–1908)
Loeffler, Charles Martin (1861–1935)
Woodman, R. Huntington (1861–1943)
Bond, Carrie Jacobs (1861–1946)
Fisher, William Arms (1861–1948)
Nevin, Ethelbert (1862–1901)
Luckstone, Isidore (1862–1941)
Busch, Carl (1862–1943)
Parker, Horatio (1863–1919)
Bullard, Frederic Field (1864–1904)
Freer, Eleanor Everest (1864–1942)
Whelply, Benjamin (1864–1946)

Homer, Sidney (1864–1953)
Loomis, Harvey Worthington (1865–1930)
Koemmenich, Louis (1866–1922)
Protheroe, Daniel (1866–1934)
Burleigh, Henry Thacker (1866–1949)
Beach, Amy Marcy Cheney (1867–1944)
Lang, Margaret Ruthven (1867–1972)
Gilbert, Henry F. (1868–1928)
Gottschalk, Louis Ferdinand (1868–1934)
Buck, Dudley (1869–1941)
Harris, Victor (1869–1943)

1870s

Hadley, Henry K. (1871–1937)
Converse, Frederic Shepherd (1871–1940)
Huhn, Bruno (1871–1950)
Manney, Charles Fonteyn (1872–1951)
Farwell, Arthur (1872–1952)
Hughes, Rupert (1872–1956)
Horsman, Edward (1873–1918)
Mason, Daniel Gregory (1873–1953)
Hopkins, Harry P. (1873–1954)
Dickinson, Clarence (1873–1969)
Hammond, William G. (1874–1945)
Speaks, Oley (1874–1948)
Wells, Howard (1874–1951)
Ives, Charles (1874–1954)
Clough-Leighter, Henry (1874–1956)
Spross, Charles Gilbert (1874–1961)
Andrews, Mark (1875–1939)
Curran, Pearl G. (1875–1941)
Ayres, Frederic (1876–1926)
Carpenter, John Alden (1876–1951)
Ruggles, Carl (1876–1971)
McGill, Josephine (1877–1919)
Campbell-Tipton, Louis (1877–1921)
Scott, John Prindle (1877–1932)
Fairchild, Blair (1877–1933)
Smith, David Stanley (1877–1949)
Beach, John Parsons (1877–1953)
Ware, Harriet (1877–1962)
Ganz, Rudolf (1877–1972)
Ide, Chester Edward (1878–1944)
La Forge, Frank (1879–1953)

1880s

Andersen, Arthur Olaf (1880–1958)
Shepherd, Arthur (1880–1958)
Cadman, Charles Wakefield (1881–1946)
Branscombe, Gena (1881–1977)
Saminsky, Lazare (1882–1959)
Powell, John (1882–1963)
Howe, Mary (1882–1964)
Hageman, Richard (1882–1966)
O'Hara, Geoffrey (1882–1967)
Engel, Carl (1883–1944)
Deis, Carl (1883–1960)
Crist, Bainbridge (1883–1969)
Griffes, Charles Tomlinson (1884–1920)
Whithorne, Emerson (1884–1958)
Watts, Wintter (1884–1962)
Gruenberg, Louis (1884–1964)

Tollefsen, Augusta (1885–1955)
Riegger, Wallingford (1885–1961)
Taylor, Deems (1885–1966)
Foster, Fay (1886–1960)
Becker, John (1886–1961)
Diton, Carl (1886–1969)
Ballantine, Edward (1886–1971)
Barnett, Alice (1886–1975)
Seeger, Charles, Jr. (1886–1979)
Ilgenfritz, McNair (1887?–1953)
Bauer, Marion (1887–1955)
Harling, W. Franke (1887–1958)
Strickland, Lily (1887–1958)
Golde, Walter (1887–1963)
Edwards, Clara (1887–1974)
Schinhan, Jan Philip (1887–1975)
Mana-Zucca (1887–1981)
Price, Florence B. (1888–1953)
Spalding, Albert (1888–1953)
Loomis, Clarence (1889–1965)

1890s

Dobson, Tom (1890–1918)
Manning, Kathleen Lockhart (1890–1951)
Weaver, Powell (1890–1951)
Clokey, Joseph W. (1890–1960)
Pattison, Lee (1890–1966)
Kramer, A. Walter (1890–1969)
James, Philip (1890–1975)
Jacobi, Frederick (1891–1952)
Donovan, Richard (1891–1970)
Heller, James G. (1891–1971)
Enders, Harvey (1892–1947)
Fiske, Dwight (1892–1959)
Rich, Gladys (1892–1972)
Haubiel, Charles (1892–1978)
Davis, Katherine K. (1892–1980)
Niles, John Jacob (1892–1980)
Guion, David W. (1892–1981)
Blake, Dorothy Gaynor (1893–19?)
Griffis, Elliot (1893–1967)
Rogers, Bernard (1893–1968)
Moore, Douglas (1893–1969)
Wolf, Daniel (1894–1962)
Cohen, Cecil (1894–1967)
Wagenaar, Bernard (1894–1971)
Slonimsky, Nicolas (1894–1995)
Malotte, Albert Hay (1895–1964)
English, Granville (1895–1968)
Sowerby, Leo (1895–1968)
Still, William Grant (1895–1978)
Charles, Ernest (1895–1984)
Wolfe, Jacques (1896–1973)
Hanson, Howard (1896–1981)
Sessions, Roger (1896–1985)
Thomson, Virgil (1896–1989)
Cooper, Esther (1897)
Russell, Sydney King (1897)
Klemm, Gustav (1897–1947)
Cowell, Henry (1897–1965)
Porter, Quincy (1897–1966)
Kerr, Harrison (1897–1978)

Smith, Melville (1898–1962)
Elwell, Herbert (1898–1974)
Harris, Roy (1898–1979)
Youse, Glad Robinson (1898–1985)
Bacon, Ernst (1898–1990)
Rieti, Vittorio (1898–1994)
Harris, Edward C. (1899–19-?)
Chenoweth, Wilbur (1899–1980)
Duke, John (1899–1984)
Lekberg, Sven (1899–1984)
Thompson, Randall (1899–1984)
Pendleton, Edmund (1899–1987)

20th Century

1900s

Schafmeister, Helen (1900)
Antheil, George (1900–1959)
Freed, Isadore (1900–1960)
Wagner, Joseph (1900–1974)
Steinert, Alexander (1900–1982)
Tyson, Mildred Lund (1900–1989)
Copland, Aaron (1900–1990)
Krenek, Ernst (1900–1991)
Warren, Elinor Remick (1900–1991)
Luening, Otto (1900–1996)
Lipsky, Alexander (1901)
Warner, Philip (1901–19-?)
Seeger, Ruth Crawford (1901–1953)
Work, John Wesley (1901–1968)
Serly, Tibor (1901–1978)
Ames, William T. (1901–1987)
Waring, Tom (1902–1960)
Chanler, Theodore (1902–1961)
Wolpe, Stefan (1902–1972)
Dougherty, Celius (1902–1986)
Giannini, Vittorio (1903–1966)
Duke, Vernon (1903–1969)
Walton, Kenneth (1904–19-?)
Friedell, Harold (1905–1958)
Blitzstein, Marc (1905–1964)
Sacco, John Charles (1905–1987)
Moore, Undine Smith (1905–1989)
Bone, Gene (1905–1992) & Fenton, Howard (?)
Fromm, Herbert (1905–1995)
Lockwood, Normand (1906)
Creston, Paul (1906–1985)
Gideon, Miriam (1906–1996)
Talma, Louise (1906–1996)
Finney, Ross Lee (1906–1997)
Kettering, Eunice Lea (1906–2000)
Rózsa, Miklós (1907–1978)
Wilder, Alec (1907–1980)
McArthur, Edwin (1907–1987)
Alexander, Josef (1907–1989)
Clarke, Henry Leland (1907–1992)
Kingsford, Charles (1907–1996)
Carter, Elliott (1908)
Stevens, Halsey (1908–1989)
Heilner, Irwin (1908–1991)
Green, Ray (1908–1997)

Berger, Jean (1909)
Donato, Anthony (1909)
Naginski, Charles (1909–1940)
Kagen, Sergius (1909–1964)
Citkowitz, Israel (1909–1974)
Nordoff, Paul (1909–1977)
Swanson, Howard (1909–1978)
Haussermann, John (1909–1986)
Siegmeister, Elie (1909–1991)

1910s

Brush, Ruth (1910)
Kendrick, Virginia (1910)
Reed, H. Owen (1910)
Reif, Paul (1910–1978)
Goldman, Richard Franko (1910–1980)
Barber, Samuel (1910–1981)
Sargent, Paul (1910–1987)
Raphling, Sam (1910–1988)
Morgenstern, Sam (1910–1989)
Schuman, William H. (1910–1992)
Bowles, Paul (1910–1999)
Agay, Denes (1911)
Menotti, Gian Carlo (1911)
Fax, Mark (1911–1974)
Shaw, Clifford (1911–1976)
Smith, Julia (1911–1989)
Hovhaness, Alan (1911–2000)
Graham, Robert (1912)
Glanville-Hicks, Peggy (1912–1990)
Cage, John (1912–1992)
Weisgall, Hugo (1912–1997)
Dello Joio, Norman (1913)
Read, Gardner (1913)
Bonds, Margaret (1913–1972)
Elmore, Robert (1913–1985)
Edmunds, John (1913–1986)
Meyerowitz, Jan (1913–1998)
Helm, Everett (1913–1999)
Krausz, Susan (1914)
Mopper, Irving (1914)
Strickland, William (1914)
Fine, Irving (1914–1962)
Kubik, Gail (1914–1984)
Cumberworth, Starling (1915)
Diamond, David (1915)
Perle, George (1915)
Wayne, Harry (1915)
Ballou, Esther W. (1915–1973)
Klein, John (1915–1981)
Persichetti, Vincent (1915–1987)
Kerr, Thomas (1915–1989)
Bales, Richard (1915–1998)
Babbitt, Milton (1916)
Binkerd, Gordon (1916)
Nunlist, Juli (1916)
Presser, William (1916)
Bezanson, Philip (1916–1975)
Lubin, Ernest (1916–1977)
Weber, Ben (1916–1979)
Jordan, Alice (1916–1999?)
Birch, Robert Fairfax (1917)

Cone, Edward T. (1917)
Donahue, Bertha Terry (1917)
Hervig, Richard (1917)
Latham, William P. (1917)
Ward, Robert (1917)
Fontrier, Gabriel (1918)
Koepke, Paul (1918)
Rochberg, George (1918)
Bernstein, Leonard (1918–1990)
Boatwright, Howard (1918–1999)
Orland, Henry (1918–1999)
Avshalomov, Jacob (1919)
Kirchner, Leon (1919)
Myers, Gordon (1919)
Williams, David H. (1919)
Nelhybel, Vaclav (1919–1996)
Young, Gordon (1919–1998)
DeVito, Albert (1919–1999)
Kirk, Theron (1919–1999)

1920s

Allen, Robert E. (1920)
Cory, George (1920)
Kalmanoff, Martin (1920)
La Montaine, John (1920)
Lessard, John A. (1920)
Moevs, Robert (1920)
Kim, Earl (1920–1998)
Barab, Seymour (1921)
Beeson, Jack (1921)
Giasson, Paul E. (1921)
Imbrie, Andrew (1921)
Pfautsch, Lloyd (1921)
Shapey, Ralph (1921)
Sterne, Colin (1921)
Bergsma, William (1921–1994)
Gold, Ernest (1921–1999)
Smit, Leo (1921–1999)
Turner, Charles (1921–1999)
Alette, Carl (1922)
Brantley, Royal (1922)
Foss, Lukas (1922)
Owen, Richard (1922)
Thorne, Francis (1922)
Travis, Roy (1922)
Walker, George (1922)
Wilding-White, Raymond (1922)
Kreutz, Robert E. (1922–1996)
Bassett, Leslie (1923)
Bialosky, Marshall (1923)
Ivey, Jean Eichelberger (1923)
Koch, Frederick (1923)
Kurtz, Eugene (1923)
Pinkham, Daniel (1923)
Rorem, Ned (1923)
Ulehla, Ludmila (1923)
Lybbert, Donald (1923–1981)
Taylor, Clifford (1923–1987)
Powell, Mel (1923–1998)
Benson, Warren F. (1924)
Di Giovanni, Rocco (1924)
Frackenpohl, Arthur (1924)

Laderman, Ezra (1924)
Lees, Benjamin (1924)
McKay, Neil (1924)
Marks, James (1924)
Roy, Klaus George (1924)
Samuel, Gerhard (1924)
Schonthal, Ruth (1924)
Singer, Jeanne (1924)
Thomas, Alan (1924)
Starer, Robert (1924–2001)
Beach, Bennie (1925)
Blank, Allan (1925)
Borroff, Edith (1925)
Brook, Claire (1925)
Hamm, Charles (1925)
Hyson, Winifred (1925)
Mechem, Kirke (1925)
Owens, Robert (1925)
Schuller, Gunther (1925)
Shaffer, Jeanne E. (1925)
Smith, Hale (1925)
Calabro, Louis (1926)
Faith, Richard (1926)
Floyd, Carlisle (1926)
Freed, Arnold (1926)
Hoiby, Lee (1926)
Johnson, D. Wayne (1926)
Kupferman, Meyer (1926)
Murray, Bain (1926)
Springer, Philip (1926)
Flanagan, William (1926–1969)
Childs, Barney (1926–2000)
Argento, Dominick (1927)
De Bohun, Lyle (1927)
Diemer, Emma Lou (1927)
Diercks, John (1927)
Freiberger, Katherine (1927)
Garwood, Margaret (1927)
Hartley, Walter S. (1927)
Moss, Lawrence (1927)
Perry, Julia (1927–1979)
Gaburo, Kenneth (1927–1993)
Adler, Samuel (1928)
Cumming, Richard (1928)
Helps, Robert (1928)
Koch, John (1928?)
Korte, Karl (1928)
Roy, William (1928)
Sydeman, William (1928)
Flagello, Nicolas (1928–1994)
King, Betty Jackson (1928–1994)
Crumb, George (1929)
Eversole, James (1929)
Hoffman, Stanley (1929)
London, Edwin (1929)
Parchman, Gen Louis (1929)
Previn, André (1929)
Wyner, Yehudi (1929)
Hancock, Eugene W. (1929–1994)

1930s

Amram, David (1930)

Burge, David (1930)
De Gastyne, Serge (1930)
Gottlieb, Jack (1930)
Peaslee, Richard C. (1930)
Shapiro, Norman (1930)
Waters, James (1930)
Watts, John (1930–1982)
Beck, John Ness (1930–1987)
Baker, David N. (1931)
Daniels, M. L. (1931)
Fornuto, Donato D. (1931)
Harris, Donald (1931)
Heller, Alfred (1931)
Hoag, Charles K. (1931)
Hundley, Richard (1931)
Leyerle, William (1931)
Martino, Donald (1931)
Pleskow, Raoul (1931)
Reed, Phyllis Luidens (1931)
White, John David (1931)
Strilko, Anthony (1931–2000)
Carter, John (1932)
De Pue, Wallace E. (1932)
Glickman, Sylvia (1932)
Horvit, Michael (1932)
Lombardo, Robert (1932)
Mandelbaum, Joel (1932)
Oliveros, Pauline (1932)
Perkinson, Coleridge-Taylor (1932)
Steiner, Gitta (1932)
Wetzler, Robert (1932)
Adams, Leslie (1933)
Benshoof, Kenneth (1933)
Dacosta, Noel (1933)
Getty, Gordon (1933)
Lane, Richard B. (1933)
Tate, Toby (1933)
Watson, Walter Robert (1933)
Cortés, Ramiro (1933–1984)
Brings, Allen (1934)
Foster, Walter Charles (1934)
Holmberg, Patricia T. (1934)
Kennedy, John Brodbin (1934)
Pierce, Alexandra (1934)
Eaton, John (1935)
Johnston, Jack (1935)
Schickele, Peter (1935)
Smith, James (1935)
Strukoff, Rudolf (1935)
Susa, Conrad (1935)
Ward-Steinman, David (1936)
Bricetti, Thomas G. (1936–1999)
Applebaum, Edward (1937)
Davis, Sharon (1937)
Del Tredici, David (1937)
Di Chiera, David (1937)
Edwards, Leo (1937)
Jenni, Donald (1937)
Mahy, Kenneth (1937)
Vehar, Persis Parshall (1937)
Ator, James (1938)
Baksa, Robert (1938)

Bolcom, William (1938)
Corigliano, John (1938)
Engle, David (1938)
Harbison, John (1938)
Rogers, Patsy (1938)
Sargon, Simon A. (1938)
Williams-Wimberly, Lou (1938)
Wuorinen, Charles (1938)
Fink, Michael (1939)
Lockwood, Annea (1939)
Penhorwood, Edwin (1939)
Thomas, Andrew (1939)
Zwilich, Ellen Taaffe (1939)

1940s
Brown, Charles (1940)
Fennimore, Joseph (1940)
Larson, Anna (1940)
Logan, Wendell (1940)
Rhodes, Phillip (1940)
Spratlan, Lewis (1940)
Wheelock, Donald (1940)
Hailstork, Adolphus C. (1941)
Hays, Doris (1941)
Mitchell, Frank (1941)
Perera, Ronald C. (1941)
Vercoe, Elizabeth (1941)
Wilson, Richard (1941)
Albert, Stephen (1941–1992)
Smolanoff, Michael (1942)
Lauridsen, Morten (1943)
McCall, Maurice (1943)
Schooley, John (1943)
Schwantner, Joseph (1943)
Riley, Dennis (1943–1999)
Rahn, Flicka (1944)
Raum, Elizabeth (1944)
White, David Ashley (1944)
Val-Schmidt, Carolyn (1944)
Lindenfeld, Harris (1945)
Pasatieri, Thomas (1945)
Sapieyevski, Jerzy (1945)
Zaimont, Judith Lang (1945)
Kimbell, Michael A. (1946)
Rodriguez, Robert Xavier (1946)
Hess, Benton (1947)
Leichtling, Alan (1947)
Linderman, Ed (1947)
Walker, Gwyneth (1947)
Wood, Kevin (1947)
Yates, Ronald (1947)
Biscardi, Chester (1948)
Lloyd, Charles Jr. (1948)
Berg, Christopher (1949)
Liptak, David (1949)
Paulus, Stephen (1949)
Hogan, David (1949–1996)

1950s
Ferko, Frank (1950)
Larsen, Libby (1950)
Schelle, Michael (1950)

Chronological List of Composers

Bauer, Ross (1951)
Crockett, Donald (1951)
Asia, Daniel (1953)
Munn, Zae (1953)
Beaser, Robert (1954)
Hoekman, Timothy (1954)
Keele, Roger S. (1954)
Musto, John (1954)
Shore, Clare (1954)
Wood, Jeffrey (1954)
Adolphe, Bruce (1955)
Chasalow, Eric (1955)
Conte, David (1955)
Grossman, Deena (1955)
Laitman, Lori (1955)
Gordon, Ricky Ian (1956)
Houtz, Stephen (1956)
Krakauer, David (1956)
Primosch, James (1956)
Schroeder, Phillip (1956)
Biggs, Hayes (1957)
Kohn, Steven Mark (1957)
Thomas, Richard Pearson (1957)
Urrows, David (1957)
Ching, Michael J. (1958)
Rakowski, David (1958)
Scheer, Gene (1958)
Sitton, Michael (1958)
Aikman, James (1959)
DeBlasio, Chris (1959–1993)

1960s

Hagen, Daron (1961)
Heggie, Jake (1961)
Lieberman, Lowell (1961)
Siskind, Paul (1962)
DeWitt, Stan (1963)
Weesner, Anna (1965)

1970s

Kulp, Jonathan (1970)

Birthdates Unknown

Endicott, Samuel (19th Century)
Little, Arthur Reginald (19th Century)

Broutman, Emanuel (20th Century)
Brown, Elizabeth C. (20th Century)
Byron, Carl (20th Century)
Diers, Ann Macdonald (20th Century)
Frost, Anne Klanderman (20th Century)
Grossman, Raphael (20th Century)
Hersch, Fred (20th Century)
Kirkman (Jones), Merle (20th Century)
Lippé, Edouard (fl. 20th Century)
Panetti, Joan (20th Century)
St. Pierre, Donald (20th Century)
Suskind, Joyce Hope (20th Century)
Jones, Marjorie (?–1998)

PUBLISHERS REPRESENTED

The following is an alphabetical listing of all publishers represented in the bibliography. The addresses given are the most recent available. Publishers whose publications are distributed by a separate company are referred to the distributor for an address. Publishers with only a city listed (or no location at all) are older companies, most of them long since defunct. They have been included both for consistency and as an interesting historical note in song publishing activity in the United States since the early nineteenth century.

ABINGDON PRESS
201 Eighth Avenue, South
P.O. Box 801
Nashville, TN 37202
Sales: Theodore Presser Co.

AFFILIATED MUSIC PUBLISHERS
see Edition Musicus, Inc.

AGAPE
see Hope Publishing Company

ALFRED PUBLISHING CO., INC.
P.O. Box 10003
16320 Roscoe Blvd.
Van Nuys, CA 91410

AMBERSON ENTERPRISES, INC.
see Boosey & Hawkes

AMERICAN COMPOSERS ALLIANCE
(Composers Facsimile Edition)
170 West 74th Street
New York, NY 10023

AMERICAN MUSIC EDITION
see Theodore Presser Company

AMSCO MUSIC PUBLISHING CO.
see Music Sales Corporation

A R EDITIONS, INC.
801 Deming Way
Madison, WI 53717

ARNO PRESS and THE NEW YORK TIMES
229 West 43rd Street
New York, NY 10036

ARROW MUSIC PRESS
see Boosey & Hawkes

ARSIS PRESS
1719 Bay Street, S.E.
Washington, DC 20003

ARTMASTERS STUDIOS, INC.
2614 Nicollet Ave.
Minneapolis, MN 55408

ASSOCIATED MUSIC PUBLISHERS
see Hal Leonard Corporation

AVANT MUSIC
see Western International Music

AXELROD PUBLICATIONS
see Shawnee Press, Inc.

BARTLESVILLE PUBLISHING CO.
P. O. Box 265
Bartlesville OK 74005

BELWIN-MILLS PUBLISHING CORP.
see Warner Bros.

C. C. BIRCHARD & COMPANY
see Warner Bros.

SUMMY BIRCHARD, INC.
see Warner Bros.

BIRCH TREE GROUP, LTD.
see Warner Bros.

BLACK SQUIRREL MUSIC, INC.
Box 346
Kent, OH 44240-0006

BOELKE-BOMART PUBLICATIONS
c/o Music Associates of America
224 King St.
Englewood, NJ 07631

BOOSEY & HAWKES, INC.
35 East 21st St.
New York, NY 10010
Sales: Alfred Publishing Company, Inc.

BOSTON MUSIC COMPANY
215 Stuart St.
Boston, MA 02116

BOURNE, INC.
5 West 37th St.
New York, NY 10018

S. BRAINARD & SONS
Cleveland, OH

HAROLD BRANCH PUBLISHING, INC.
42 Cornell Drive
Plainview Long Island, NY 11803

BREITKOPF & HÄRTEL
Postfach 1707
D-6200 Wiesbaden 1
West Germany

BRENTANO'S LITERARY EMPORIUM

BROADCAST MUSIC, INC.
320 W. 57th Street
New York, NY 10019

BRODT MUSIC COMPANY
P. O. Box 9345
1906 Commonwealth Ave.
Charlotte, NC 28299

ALEXANDER BROUDE, INC.

BROUDE BROTHERS, INC.
141 White Oaks Road
Williamstown, MA 01267

WM. C. BROWN COMPANY
2460 Kerper Avenue
Dubuque, IA 52001

BRYANT MUSIC CO.

CARR'S MUSIC STORE

CASIA PUBLISHING COMPANY
see Hildegard Publishing Company Co.

THE CENTER OF BALANCE PRESS
126 E. Fern Avenue
Redlands, CA 92373

CHAPPELL & COMPANY, INC.
see Hal Leonard Corporation

CHAPPLE PUBLISHING CO.
Boston, MA

JOHN CHURCH COMPANY
see Theodore Presser Company

CLASSICAL VOCAL REPRINTS
3253 Cambridge Ave.
Riverdale, NY 10463

FRANCO COLOMBO PUBLICATIONS
see Warner Bros.
Rental: Theodore Presser Co.

COMPOSERS LIBRARY EDITIONS
see Theodore Presser Company

COMPOSERS PRESS
see Opus Music Publishers, Inc.

CONATUS MUSIC PRESS
210 Fifth Avenue
New York, NY 10010

CONCORD MUSIC PUBLISHING CO.
see Henri Elkan Music Pub.

CONSOLIDATED MUSIC PUBLISHERS
see Music Sales Corporation

COS COB PRESS, INC.
see Boosey & Hawkes

DA CAPO PRESS
233 Spring Street
New York, NY 10013

DANTALIAN, INC.
11 Pembroke Street
Newton, MA 02158

DARINGDIVA PRESS
see Classical Vocal Reprints

DAVIS & HORN

ROGER DEAN PUBLISHING CO.
see The Heritage Music Press

OLIVER DITSON COMPANY
see Theodore Presser Company

DOVER PUBLICATIONS, INC.
31 East 2nd Street
Mineola, NY 11501

DRAGON'S TEETH PRESS
see Classical Vocal Reprints

EASTLANE MUSIC CORP.
31 Bayberry Road
Trenton, NJ 08618

ECS PUBLISHING
138 Ipswich St.
Boston, MA 02215-3534

EDITION HELIOS
see Shawnee Press

EDITION MUSICUS, INC.
P. O. Box 1341
Stamford, CT 06904

EDITIONS JOBERT
see Theodore Presser Company

EDITIONS MAURICE SENART (SALABERT)
see Hal Leonard Corporation

EDITIONS SALABERT
see Hal Leonard Corporation

EDITION WILHELM HANSEN
see Shawnee Press

HENRI ELKAN MUSIC PUBLISHERS
P.O. Box 965–Planetarium Station
New York, NY 10024

ELKAN-VOGEL, INC.
see Theodore Presser Company

ENOCH & SONS
See Boosey & Hawkes

EUROPEAN-AMERICAN MUSIC DISTRIBUTION CORPORATION
see Warner Bros.

FEMA MUSIC PUBLICATIONS
P. O. Box 395
Naperville, IL 60566

FENNIMORE HIBBERD PUBLISHING
258 Morton Ave.
Albany, NY 12202-1326
see also Classical Vocal Reprints

FENTONE MUSIC

FILPAT PUBLISHING
277 Pines Lake Drive East
Wayne, NJ 07470-5008

CARL FISCHER, INC.
65 Bleeker St.
New York, NY 10012

J. FISCHER & BROS.
see Warner Bros.

HAROLD FLAMMER, INC.
see Shawnee Press, Inc.

MARK FOSTER MUSIC COMPANY
see Shawnee Press

FOSTER HALL REPRODUCTIONS
Indianapolis, IN

SAM FOX SALES CORP.
see Plymouth Music Company

FRANGIPANI PRESS
see Alfred Publishing Company, Inc.

FREDONIA PRESS
3947 Fredonia Drive
Hollywood, CA 90068

GALAXY MUSIC CORP.
see ECS Publishing

GALLEON PRESS
see Plymouth Music Company

GAMBLE HINGED MUSIC CO.
see Music Publishers Holding Corp.

GENERAL MUSIC PUBLISHING COMPANY, INC.
see Boston Music Company

GLOUCHESTER PRESS (HEILMAN MUSIC)
P. O. Box 1044
Fairmont, WV 26554

H. W. GRAY COMPANY
see Belwin-Mills Publishing Corp.

GUNMAR MUSIC, INC.
see Margun/Gunmar Music

WM. HALL & SON
New York, NY

HALL-ORION MUSIC PRESS
P. O. Box 145
Berrien Springs, MI 49103

HARGAIL
see Warner Bros.

HARMS, INC.
see Warner Bros.

HELICON MUSIC CORP.
see European-American Music Distribution Corporation
Distributed by Warner Bros.

HENMAR PRESS, INC.
see C. F. Peters Corp.

HERITAGE MUSIC PRESS (Lorenz Corp.)
P.O. Box 802
501 E. Third Street
Dayton, OH 45401

HIGHGATE PRESS FACSIMILE EDITION
see Galaxy Music Corp.

HILDEGARD PUBLISHING COMPANY
Box 332
Bryn Mawr, PA 19010

HINSHAW MUSIC CO.
P. O. Box 470
Chapel Hill, NC 27514

HOLLOW HILLS PRESS
7 Landview Drive
Dix Hills, NY 11746

HOPE PUBLISHING COMPANY
380 South Main Place
Carol Stream, IL 60188

HUNTZINGER & DILWORTH

IONE PRESS, INC.
see E. C. Schirmer Music Co.

ISRAELI MUSIC PUB., LTD.
see Theodore Presser Company

JERONA MUSIC CORP.
P.O. Box 671
Englewood, NJ 07631

JOCLEM MUSIC PUBLISHING
see Boosey & Hawkes

JOSHUA CORPORATION
P. O. Box 267
Hastings-on-Hudson, NY 10706

KENDALL/HUNT PUBLISHING COMPANY
4050 Westmark Drive
Dubuque, IA 52002

KENYON PUBLICATIONS
see G. Schirmer

MICHAEL AND EDITH KIMBELL, MUSIC PUBLISHERS
314 Clifton Road
Pacifica, CA 94044

LEEDS MUSIC CORP.
see MCA Music

HAL LEONARD PUBLISHING CORP.
P.O. Box 13819
7777 W. Bluemound Rd.
Milwaukee, WI 53213

LEYERLE PUBLICATIONS
P. O. Box 384
Geneseo, NY 14454

LUDWIG MUSIC PUBLISHING CO.
557-67 East 140th Street
Cleveland, OH 44110

MCA MUSIC
1755 Broadway–8th Floor
New York, NY 10019

MMB MUSIC, INC.
Contemporary Arts Building
3526 Washington Ave.
St. Louis, MO 63103-1019

MAGELLAN MUSIC LTD.
see Warner Bros.

MARGUN/GUNMAR MUSIC
see Music Sales

EDWARD B. MARKS MUSIC CORP.
c/o Carlin America, Inc.
126 E. 38th St.
New York, NY 10016
Sales: Hal Leonard Corporation

MASTERS MUSIC PUBLICATIONS, INC.
P.O. Box 810157
Boca Raton, FL 33481-0157

McGINNIS & MARX
236 W. 26th St., #115
New York, NY 10001-6736

MERCURY MUSIC, INC.
see Theodore Presser Company

MERION MUSIC CORP.
see Theodore Presser Company

MILLS MUSIC
see Warner Bros.

MIRA MUSIC ASSOCIATES
199 Mountain Road
Wilton, CT 06897

JOHN F. MITCHELL
5652 Lemp Avenue
North Hollywood, CA 91601

EDWIN H. MORRIS & COMPANY
see Hal Leonard Pub. Corp.

MOWBRAY MUSIC PUBLISHERS
see Theodore Presser Company

MUSIC ESPRESS [sic], INC.
4014 Nicholas Court
Fairfax, VA 22033

MUSIC GRAPHICS PRESS
117 Washington Street
San Diego, CA

MUSIC PUBLISHERS HOLDING CORP.
488 Madison Avenue
New York, NY 10022

MUSIC SALES CORPORATION
257 Park Ave. South–20th Floor
New York, NY 10010

NEW VALLEY MUSIC PRESS
Sage Hall, Smith College
Northampton, MA 01060

OPUS MUSIC PUBLISHERS, INC.
1880 Holste Road
Northbrook, IL 60062

ORCHESIS PUBLICATIONS

OSBOURNE'S MUSIC SALOON

OXFORD UNIVERSITY PRESS
198 Madison Avenue
New York, NY 10016-4314

JOSEPH PATELSON
see Theodore Presser Company

PEER INTERNATIONAL CORP.
(Peermusic Classical)
see Theodore Presser Company

PEERMUSIC CLASSICAL
see Peer-Southern Music Publishing

PEERMUSIC (SONGS OF PEER, LTD.)
see Theodore Presser Company

PEER-SOUTHERN MUSIC PUBLISHING
Peermusic Classical
810 Seventh Ave.
New York, NY 10019
Sales: Theodore Presser Co.

A. C. PETERS & BRO.
Cincinnati, OH

C. F. PETERS CORPORATION
70-30 80th Street
Glendale, NY 11385

PLYMOUTH MUSIC COMPANY, INC.
170 N.E. 33rd Street
Fort Lauderdale, FL 33334

WM. A. POND
see Carl Fischer, Inc.

PRENTICE-HALL, INC.
Rte. 9W
Upper Saddle River, NJ 07632

THEODORE PRESSER COMPANY
1 Presser Place
Bryn Mawr, PA 19010

RANDOM HOUSE, INC.
201 East 50th Street
New York, NY 10022

RECITAL PUBLICATIONS
738 Robinson Road
Pembroke, NH 03275

NATHAN RICHARDSON (Boston, MA)
& J. F. PETRIE (Baltimore, MD)

G. RICORDI
Sales: Hal Leonard Corporation
Rental and Contemporary Music Sales: Boosey & Hawkes

ROCK VALLEY MUSIC COMPANY
(Formerly AQUARIUS)
P. O. Box 71
Long Eddy, NY 12760
see also Classical Vocal Reprints

RORK MUSIC
see Theodore Presser Company

R. D. ROW MUSIC COMPANY
see Carl Fischer, Inc.

G. D. RUSSELL & CO.
Boston, MA

R. A. SAALFIELD
New York, NY

E. C. SCHIRMER MUSIC COMPANY
ECS Publishing
138 Ipswich Street
Boston, MA 02215

G. SCHIRMER, INC. (Music Sales Corporation)
Distributor: Hal Leonard Corporation

SCHIRMER BOOKS
see Music Sales Corporation

ARTHUR P. SCHMIDT COMPANY
see Warner Bros. and Classical Vocal
Reprints

SCHMITT MUSIC COMPANY
88 South 10th Street
Minneapolis, MN 55403

SCHOTT MUSIC CORPORATION
(Schott and Co., Ltd. and B. Schott's Söhne)
see Warner Bros.

EDWARD SCHUBERTH & CO., INC.
see Music Sales Corporation

SEESAW MUSIC CORPORATION
2067 Broadway
New York, NY 10023

SERENISSIMA MUSIC CO.
see MMB

SHAWNEE PRESS, INC.
49 Waring Drive
Delaware Water Gap, PA 18327-1099

JOHN SHEPPARD MUSIC PRESS
see European-American Music Dist. Corp.
(Warner Bros.)

SMITH PUBLICATIONS
AMERICAN MUSIC
2617 Gwynndale Avenue
Baltimore, MD 21207

SONGFLOWER PRESS
6056 N. 10th St.
Philadelphia, PA 19141
see Hildegard Publishing Company

SOUNDINGS PRESS
Santa Fe, NM

SOUTHERN MUSIC COMPANY
P.O. Box 329
1100 Broadway
San Antonio, TX 78215-1391

SOUTHERN MUSIC PUBLISHING CO., INC.
see Theodore Presser Company

THE LEO SOWERBY FOUNDATION
see Theodore Presser Company

SPRAGUE-COLEMAN
New York, NY

H. G. STEVENS
Boston, MA

CLAYTON F. SUMMY COMPANY
see Summy Birchard

SYRACUSE UNIVERSITY PRESS
1600 Jamesville Avenue
Syracuse, NY 13244

TENDER TENDER MUSIC
see Classical Vocal Reprints

TENUTO PUBLICATIONS
see Theodore Presser Company

THEOPHILOUS MUSIC ENTERPRISES
see Boosey & Hawkes

C. W. THOMPSON
see Boston Music Company

TICHENOR PUBLISHING
Division of T. I. S. Publications
P.O. Box 669
Bloomington, IN 47402

T. I. S. PUBLICATIONS
P.O. Box 669
Bloomington, IN 47402

HENRY TOLMAN
Boston, MA

UNIVERSAL EDITION PUBLISHING, INC.
see Warner Bros.

THE UNIVERSITY SOCIETY
New York, NY

VALLEY MUSIC PRESS
see New Valley Music Press

VOICE OF THE ROCKIES
P.O. Box 1043
Boulder, CO 80306

WARNER BROTHERS PUBLICATIONS
15800 NW 48th Ave.
Miami, FL 33014

WEAVER-LEVANT
see Theodore Presser Company

WEINTRAUB MUSIC COMPANY
see Music Sales Corporation

WESTERN INTERNATIONAL MUSIC, INC.
2859 Holt Avenue
Los Angeles, CA 90034

WHITE-SMITH
Boston, MA

WILLIAMSON MUSIC
see Hal Leonard Corporation

GEORGE WILLIG
Philadelphia, PA

WILLIS MUSIC COMPANY
7380 Industrial Road
Florence, KY 41042

M. WITMARK & SONS
see Warner Bros.

YALE UNIVERSITY PRESS
92A Yale Station
New Haven, CT 06520

REFERENCES

The following list includes selected sources that have been used in the compilation of this bibliography, as well as a few sources that include songs by composers of the United States, included for their usefulness to the person preparing programs. *Our American Music: A Comprehensive History from 1620 to the Present,* by John Tasker Howard, and *Doctoral Dissertations in American Music: A Classified Bibliography,* by Rita H. Mead contain extensive bibliographic entries of articles, dissertations, and books pertaining to various song composers of the United States and their works. References for the Discography are listed in the Discography Introduction.

Anderson, E. Ruth (ed.). *Contemporary American Composers: A Biographical Dictionary.* 2nd ed. Boston: G. K. Hall, 1982.

ASCAP Biographical Dictionary. 4th ed. Compiled for the American Society of Composers, Authors and Publishers by Jaques Cattell Press. New York: R. R. Bowker Company, 1980.

Block, Adrienne Fried, and Neuls-Bates, Carol (eds.). *Women in American Music.* Westport, CT: Greenwood Press, 1979.

Bull, Storm. *Index to Biographies of Contemporary Composers, Vol. II.* Metuchen, NJ: The Scarecrow Press, 1974.

Butterworth, Neil. *A Dictionary of American Composers.* New York: Garland Publishing, Inc., 1984.

Carman, Judith Elaine. 1973. Twentieth-century American song cycles: a study in circle imagery. D.M.A. diss., University of Iowa.

Chase, Gilbert. *America's Music: From the Pilgrims to the Present.* 2nd ed., rev. New York: McGraw-Hill Book Co., 1966.

Claghorn, Charles Eugene. *Biographical Dictionary of American Music.* West Nyack, NY: Parker Publishing Company, 1973.

Claghorn, Gene. *Women Composers and Songwriters. A Concise Biographical Dictionary.* Lanham, MD: The Scarecrow Press, Inc., 1996.

Coffin, Berton. *Singer's Repertoire.* 2nd ed., 4 vols. New York: The Scarecrow Press, 1960.

Cohen, Aaron I. *International Encyclopedia of Women Composers.* New York: R. R. Bowker Company, 1981.

Composium Directory of New Music. Composers Annual Index of Contemporary Composition. Los Angeles: Crystal Record Co., 1974, 1975, 1976, 1977, 1982–83.

De Charms, Desiree, and Breed, Paul F. *Songs in Collections: An Index.* Detroit: Information Service, 1966.

Eagon, Angelo. *Catalog of Published Concert Music by American Composers.* 2nd ed. Metuchen, NJ: The Scarecrow Press, 1969.

———. *Catalog of Published Concert Music by American Composers. Supplement to the Second Edition.* Metuchen, NJ: The Scarecrow Press, 1971.

———. *Catalog of Published Concert Music by American Composers. Second Supplement to the Second Edition.* Metuchen, NJ: The Scarecrow Press, 1974.

Espina, Noni. *Repertoire for the Solo Voice.* A fully annotated guide to works for the solo voice published in modern editions and covering material from the 13th century to the present. 2 vols. Metuchen, NJ: The Scarecrow Press, 1977.

———. *Vocal Solos for Protestant Services.* 2nd ed., rev. New York: Vita d'Arte, 1974.

Ewen, David. *American Composers: A Biographical Dictionary.* New York: G. P. Putnam's Sons, 1982.

Famera, Karen, and Zaimont, Judith Lang (eds.). *Contemporary Concert Music by Women.* A Directory of the Composers and Their Works. Westport, CT: Greenwood Press, 1981.

Finck, Henry T. *Songs and Song Writers.* 5th ed. *The Music Lover's Library.* New York: Charles Scribner's Sons, 1912.

REFERENCES

Friedberg, Ruth C. *American Art Song and American Poetry, Vol. I: America Comes of Age*. Metuchen, NJ: Scarecrow Press, 1981.

———. *American Art Song and American Poetry, Vol. II: Voices of Maturity*. Metuchen, NJ: Scarecrow Press, 1984.

———. *American Art Song and American Poetry, Vol. III: The Century Advances*. Metuchen, NJ: Scarecrow Press, 1987.

Gilbert, Dale. *British and American Art Songs Published Since 1967*. Elmhurst, IL: Chicago Singing Teachers Guild, 1974.

Goleeke, Thomas. *Literature for the Voice: An Index of Songs in Collections and Source Books for Teachers of Singing*. Metuchen, NJ: The Scarecrow Press, 1984. (Contains an extensive bibliography, pp.159–172).

Gray, John. *Blacks in Classical Music*. A Bibliographic Guide to Composers, Performers, and Ensembles. Music Reference Collection #15. New York: Greenwood Press, 1988.

Greene, David Mason. *Greene's Biographical Encyclopedia of Composers*. Garden City, NY: Doubleday & Co., 1985.

Hall, Charles J. *A Chronicle of American Music, 1700–1995*. New York: Schirmer Books, 1996.

Hall, James Husst. *The Art Song*. Norman, OK: University of Oklahoma Press, 1953.

Hitchcock, H. Wiley. *Music in the United States: A Historical Introduction*. Prentice-Hall *History of Music* Series. Englewood Cliffs, NJ: Prentice-Hall, 1969.

Hixon, Don L., and Hennessee, Don. *Women in Music: A Bibliography*. Metuchen, NJ: The Scarecrow Press, 1975.

Hovland, Michael. *Musical Settings of American Poetry: A Bibliography*. Music Reference Collection No. 8. Westport, CT: Greenwood Press, 1986.

Howard, John Tasker. *Our American Music: A Comprehensive History from 1620 to the Present*. 4th ed. New York: Thomas Y. Crowell Co., 1965. (Contains an extensive bibliography, pp. 769-845).

Hughes, Rupert, and Elson, Arthur. *American Composers*. Rev. ed. Boston: The Page Co., 1914.

Huls, Helen Steen, Wilson, Grace, and Sauer, Mabeth. *Repertoire for Young Voices*. Silver Anniversary Publication. New York: National Association of Teachers of Singing, 1969.

International Who's Who in Music and Musicians Directory. 10th ed. Cambridge, England: International Who's Who in Music (Melrose Press), 1985.

International Who's Who in Music and Musicians Directory. 12th ed. Cambridge, England: International Who's Who in Music, 1990.

Kagen, Sergius. *Music for the Voice*. Rev. ed. Bloomington, IN: Indiana University Press, 1968.

Kimball, Carol. *Song: A Guide to Style & Literature*. Seattle: Pst...Inc, 1996.

Lawrence, Vera Brodsky (ed.). *The Wa-Wan Press, 1901–1911*. 5 vols. Reprint: New York: Arno Press and The New York Times, 1970.

Lowens, Irving. *Music and Musicians in Early America*. New York: W. W. Norton & Co., 1964.

Marocco, W. Thomas, and Gleason, Harold. *Music in America, 1620 to 1865: An Anthology*. New York: W. W. Norton & Co., 1964.

Mead, Rita H. *Doctoral Dissertations in American Music: A Classified Bibliography*. Brooklyn, NY: Institute for Studies in American Music, 1974.

Nathan, Hans. "United States of America." *A History of Song*. Ed. by Denis Stevens. New York: W. W. Norton & Co., 1961.

The New Grove Dictionary of American Music. Ed. by H. Wiley Hitchcock and Stanley Sadie. New York: Groves Dictionaries of Music, Inc., 1986.

The New Grove Dictionary of Music and Musicians. 2nd ed. Ed. by Stanley Sadie. 29 vols. London: Macmillan Publishers Limited, 2001.

Pavlakis, Christopher. *The American Music Handbook*. New York: The Free Press, 1974.

Randel, Don Michael. *The Harvard Biographical Dictionary of Music.* Cambridge, MA: Belknap Press of Harvard University Press, 1996.

Rau, Albert G., and David, Hans T. *A Catalog of Music by American Moravians, 1742–1842.* New York: AMS Press, 1970.

Slonimsky, Nicolas, rev. *Baker's Biographical Dictionary of Musicians.* 7th ed. New York: Schirmer Books, 1984.

Slonimsky, Nicolas (ed). *Baker's Biographical Dictionary of Musicians.* 8th ed. New York: Schirmer Books, 1992.

Slonimsky, Nicolas. *Baker's Biographical Dictionary of Twentieth Century Classical Musicians.* Ed. by Laura Kuhn. New York: Schirmer Books, 1997.

Sonneck, Oscar George Theodore. *A Bibliography of Early Secular American Music (18th Century).* 1st pub. in 1905; rev. and enl. by W. T. Upton, 1945. Reprinted, with new preface by Irving Lowens. New York: Da Capo Press, 1964.

Southern, Eileen. *Biographical Dictionary of Afro-American and African Musicians.* The Greenwood Encyclopedia of Black Music. Westport, CT: Greenwood Press, 1982.

Stewart-Green, Miriam. *Women Composers: A Checklist of Works for the Solo Voice.* A Reference Publication in Women's Studies. Ed. by Barbara Haber. Boston: G. K. Hall Co., 1980.

U. S. Library of Congress. *A Catalog of Books Represented by Library of Congress Printed Cards, Issued to July 31, 1942.* 167 vols. Ann Arbor, MI: J. W. Edwards, 1942–1946.

———. *Supplement: Cards Issued August 1, 1942 to December 31, 1947.* 42 vols. U. S. Library of Congress. Library of Congress: Music and Phonorecords, 1963–1971. Ann Arbor, MI: J. W. Edwards.

———. *The National Union Catalog Pre-1956 Imprints.* Cumulative Author List. Chicago: American Library Association, 1968– .

Upton, William Treat. *Art-Song in America.* Boston: Oliver Ditson Co., 1930; A Supplement to Art-Song in America, 1930–1938. Boston: Oliver Ditson Co., 1930. Series in American Studies. Ed. by Joseph J. Kwiat (bound together). New York: Johnson Reprint Corp., 1969.

Villamil, Victoria Etnier. *A Singer's Guide to The American Art Song 1870–1980.* Metuchen, NJ: The Scarecrow Press, 1993.

Vinton, John (ed.). *Dictionary of Contemporary Music.* New York: E. P. Dutton and Co., 1974.

Who's Who in American Music: Classical. 1st & 2nd eds. Ed. by Jaques Cattell Press. New York: R. R. Bowker Co., 1983, 1985.

Yerbury, Grace D. *Song in America: From Early Times to About 1850.* Metuchen, NJ: The Scarecrow Press, 1971.

COMPOSER INDEX

NOTE: Reference numbers are to page numbers

POET INDEX
(AUTHOR, OR SOURCE OF TEXT)

NOTE: Reference numbers are to entry numbers, not page numbers

A

Adamo, Mark, 511
Adams, Franklin P., 1075
Adams, Katharine, 2176
Adams, Leonie, 1601f
Adams, Robert, 517d
Æ, see Russell, George William
Agee, James, 180, 414, 548, 1598d, 1699
Aïdé, Hamilton, 435
Aiken, Conrad, 518, 531, 536, 538, 540, 697, 1070, 1643, 1649, 1651
Albeck, Joseph H., 1135
Albee, Edward, 901
Aldis, Dorothy, 1406
Aldrich, Thomas Bailey, 562, 582, 1298, 1351B
Allan, Lewis, 1985C
Allingham, William, 842
Alsadir, Nuar, 1081c
Ames, Evelyn, 1794
Andersen, Hans Christian, 1532d
Anderson, Maxwell, 525
Andrée, S. A., 39c, f, h, j, m
Andrien, Georgette, A19
Angell, Barbara, 1404
Anglo-Saxon riddles, 488
Antipater, 707A,b
Arens, Egmont H., 186, 1821
Armour, Richard, 1789
Arnold, Sir Edwin, 199
Arnold, Matthew, 845, 906,1339
Ashbery, John, 1884g, h
Auden, W. H., 249b, d, 1758, 1866b, g, k, 1890b, p
Augustine, Saint, 2109e
Avshalomov, Doris, 47

B

Baïf, Jean Antoine de, A7d, A22f
Bailey, Anne Howard, 1683
Ballet, William, 1744
Banning, Kendall, 350
Barber, Charles, 15H
Barbour, John, 491a
Barnefield, Richard, 1889
Barnes, Kate, 2066b
Barnett, A. G., 1933
Baro, Gene, 521
Basho, 45d, 1418d, g, m, n, r, w,
1719b, c, d, g, k, m, 1740c, j, n
Bass, George Houston, 561
Bates, Arlo, 430, 432, 434, 440, 444
Bates, Charlotte Fiske, 2011
Batres, José, 1570
Beach, H. H. A., 207, 225
Beaumont, Francis, 661b
Beddoes, Thomas L., 285, 300
Beers, Robert, 1168
Bellamann, Henry, 1311, 1343
Bellay, Joachim de, A7b, A23b
Belloc, Hilaire, 1069, 1545, 1738, 2237d
Benét, Rosemary, 566, 1985B, D
Benét, Stephen Vincent, 323, 1582
Benét, William Rose, 27
Benham, Kenneth G., 2122
Benjamin, Torrence, 2033
Benton, Patricia, 1999, 2003, 2059
Bergman, David, 15D
Berlitz: French for Travelers, A10
Bernard, April, 1785c
Bernstein, Leonard, 1013
Bertrand, Aloysius, 512c
Besseguier, Le Comte Jules de, 218
Betjeman, John, 244, 251
Beye, Holly, 1453
Beyers, Irene, 1797
Biblical texts (chiefly from the
Psalms), 4, 5, 46, 239, 240, 395, 528, 557j, 612, 724, 799, 808, 823, 905, 960, 1041, 1089, 1090, 1200, 1436, 1451, 1477, 1614–1616, 1618, 1655C, 1753, 1762, 1826b, 1832, 1854, 1861, 1878, 1891, 1894, 1903, 1955, 2165, 2240C, D, E, F, 2254B, C, M4, M8, M33, M49, M58, M62, M65–M67
Bickel, Mary, 1433c
Bierbaum, Otto Julius, 1420
Bierce, Ambrose, 138
Billings, William, 197c
Birney, Earle, 256a
Bishop, Elizabeth, 318k, 485, 1162, 1860, 1917
Blake, William, 58, 93, 355A-B, 401, 410, 450, 455, 457, 520, 522, 553, 554, 653, 685, 733, 774, 791, 801, 838, 860, 865, 867, 892, 927, 1006, 1030A, 1080a, 1082c, 1102, 1165, 1179, 1364, 1367, 1473c, 1512, 1515, 1517, 1518b, c, 1576, 1580,
1646, 1668d, 1804, 1975, 1978, 1993, 2100, 2113, 2157c, 2223, 2224, 2227
Blanden, C. G., 925
Blankner, Frederika, 1996, 2001
Bloch, Chana, 598
Bly, Robert, 1352a
Bogan, Louise, 318i, 1602c
Bogardus, Edgar, 2060
Boleyn, Anne, 807, 1922i
Bomen, Lord, 1668e
Bonelli, Mona, 482
Bontemps, Arna, 2051a
The Book of the Thousand and One Nights, 683
Booth, Philip, 56b
Bourdillon, Francis William, 1072, 1723
Bovet, Félix, 204
Bowles, Fred G., 373
Bowles, Jane, 336
Bowman, H., 1458
Bowring, John, 1338
Boyer, Harriet, 2220
Bradley, Marcia, 2120
Bradstreet, Anne, 51, 195c, 1922c, 2125b
Brandt, Carolyn, 19a
Brant, Leroy V., 2050
Brass, Perry, 15E
Breck, John Leslie, 436
Breid, Minnie K., 969
Bridges, Robert, 1136a, 1183
Brinnin, John Malcolm, 57
Brontë, Emily, 84, 762, 855, 1572, 1579
Brooke, Rupert, 1030B, 1282
Brooks, Gwendolyn, 318c, 1352c
Brown, Abbie Farwell, 217
Brown, David Paul, M16
Brown, Kate Louise, 2177
Brown, Mr., M46
Browne, Michael Dennis, 1708, 1709g
Browning, Elizabeth Barrett, 40, 116, 229, 351, 593f, 1047, 1390, 1467, 1492, 1701, 1866a
Browning, Robert, 224, 236, 353f, 593c, 678, 1054, 1060, 1081a, 1277, 1510, 1783, 1880, 1901a, e
Bruno, William, 467
Bryant, Edward W., 1513
Bunyan, John, 643

-433-

COMPOSERS WHO SET THEIR OWN TEXTS

SPECIAL CHARACTERISTICS INDEX

Note: Reference numbers are to entry numbers—not page numbers.

This index is intended as a useful tool for choosing music to teach and to perform. Included are Cycles by voice type, Easy/Moderately Easy Songs, Encore Songs, [Songs] Especially Suitable for Elementary School Audiences, Extended Songs, Group/Program Enders, Humorous Songs, Oriental Poetry in English Translation, Special Vocal Effects/Techniques (coloratura techniques, high-tessitura songs, special vocal effects [glissando, humming, scat singing, straight tone, vocal noises, vocalized consonants, vocalizing, etc.]), Physical Movement Required, Prepared Piano and Other Special Piano Techniques, Speaking, Sprechstimme, or Whistling, Special Voice Types (bass, bass-baritone, coloratura voices, contralto and countertenor), and Vocalises.

CYCLES:

All Voices: 161, 162, 298, 434, 1575, 1861, A1

Baritone: 15, 39, 139, 238, 259, 312, 595, 620, 771, 793, 965, 1090, 1155, 1353, 1384, 1471, 1494, 1577, 1873, 1939, 1986, 2023, 2100, 2101, 2216, 2232, A64

Bass/Bass-Baritone: 15, 557, 632, 905, 1397, 1868, 1919, 1988, 2100, 2118, A64

Coloratura Soprano: 926, 950, 1901

Contralto: 391, 764, 877

Countertenor: 1083

Mezzo-Soprano: 40, 41, 156, 312, 318, 362, 391, 404, 451, 508, 510, 551, 598, 629, 648, 649, 659, 764, 877, 927, 974, 1114, 1154, 1353, 1474, 1681, 1699, 1701, 1741, 1764, 1873, 1890, 1900, 1938, 1967, 1986, 2005, 2067, 2109, 2129, 2206, A10, A66

Soprano: 20, 38, 42, 43, 197, 200, 241, 249, 272, 293, 308, 315, 362, 373, 404, 426, 451, 508, 597, 659, 715, 717, 794, 829, 843, 881, 885, 904, 926, 950, 963, 970, 971, 974, 989, 1003, 1008, 1092, 1109,1112, 1125, 1192, 1250, 1254, 1385, 1397 1436, 1437, 1451, 1472, 1519, 1579, 1594, 1668, 1731, 1734, 1737, 1740, 1745, 1811, 1813–1815, 1818, 1826, 1835, 1884, 1922, 1943, 1959, 1992, 1997, 2013, 2017, 2031, 2067, 2078, 2088, 2129, 2148, 2153, 2189, 2197, 2206, 2259, A10

Tenor: 11, 12, 42, 44, 138, 155, 197, 238, 241, 248, 265, 276, 373, 394, 426, 489, 546, 593, 595, 829, 843, 881, 882, 884, 885, 970, 989, 1003, 1093, 1154, 1397, 1436, 1527, 1579, 1580, 1668, 1709, 1729, 1791, 1813–1816, 1846, 1953, 2013, 2051, 2078, 2088, A71

EASY/MODERATELY-EASY SONGS: 13, 23, 36,
59, 81, 126, 147, 148, 156, 178, 179, 190, 194, 201, 203, 206, 217, 262, 263, 274, 284, 295, 298, 303, 309, 319, 329, 330, 331, 335–337, 342, 344–346, 349, 355A, 360, 361, 370, 376, 380, 382–384, 387, 400, 419, 423A, 427, 428, 435, 442, 446, 455, 462B, 467, 469, 470, 473, 492, 516, 531–534, 537, 538,

551, 554, 556, 559, 560, 564, 574, 582, 602, 603, 609, 617, 645, 650a–d, 654, 655, 664–666, 673, 685, 716, 731, 743, 751, 754, 795, 804, 807, 816, 820, 821, 824, 837A, 842, 849, 862, 864B,a, c–e, g, l, C, 866, 878b, 883, 888, 907, 909, 912, 913, 915, 918, 921, 925, 929–945, 957, 969, 993, 998, 1006, 1022a–c, 1025, 1027, 1031C, 1032, 1034A, 1043, 1062, 1088, 1095, 1098, 1102, 1106, 1122, 1128, 1172, 1177, 1178g, o, 1182–1185, 1197, 1207, 1210, 1215, 1216, 1219, 1220, 1222, 1224, 1229, 1236, 1276, 1292, 1323, 1327, 1329, 1332, 1342, 1344, 1349, 1350, 1351B–F, H, I, 1354, 1356, 1363, 1368, 1378, 1383, 1391–1393, 1395, 1396, 1399, 1401, 1403, 1407, 1410, 1420, 1421, 1424, 1440, 1456C–E, 1458, 1459, 1462, 1478, 1479, 1485, 1500, 1507, 1514, 1517, 1520, 1521A–C, E, H, 1522B, 1523, 1525, 1527b, f, 1530, 1531, 1532d, 1538, 1540–1543, 1552, 1555–1557, 1566, 1568, 1569, 1571, 1573, 1585, 1590, 1606, 1619, 1621–1625, 1627–1629, 1632, 1635, 1637, 1672, 1677, 1687, 1714, 1732, 1736, 1738A, 1741, 1744, 1746, 1750, 1772, 1773, 1779– 1781, 1788a, c, 1797, 1804, 1819, 1834e, 1841, 1844, 1848, 1863, 1865, 1870B, 1874, 1882, 1887, 1888, 1912, 1913, 1926, 1927E, 1940, 1941, 1950, 1961, 1978, 1979, 1985E, 1986, 1990, 1995, 1996, 2002, 2006, 2011, 2021, 2028–2030, 2047, 2090, 2094, 2102, 2111b, d, 2115, 2119, 2121, 2149, 2155, 2161, 2162, 2164, 2166, 2170–2173, 2187, 2189, 2193, 2200, 2203, 2204, 2220, 2225, 2230–2232, 2234, 2243, 2244, 2246, 2255, 2256, 2258, A25, A41A, C, A43, A46, A70, A73, M10, M21, M24, M25, M27–M29, M30A, B, H, M44–M48, M52, M54–M57, M60–M62, M64–66

ENCORE SONGS: 69, 122, 149, 154a, f, 296c, f, 316a, e,
370, 381, 454, 463, 474, 499, 556, 660, 663, 670, 681, 712a–e, 729, 798, 806, 831, 837B, 871, 931, 934, 935, 939, 943, 994, 1000, 1052, 1062, 1067, 1075, 1113a, b, 1116, 1140, 1168, 1174, 1244, 1252, 1309, 1322, 1374, 1402, 1441, 1442, 1486, 1492, 1506, 1507, 1533–1535, 1549, 1590, 1606, 1738B, 1768, 1789, 1819, 1874, 1931, 1935, 1951C, 1977c, 2007, 2021, 2027, 2098, 2140, 2167, 2218, 2238

ESPECIALLY SUITABLE FOR ELEMENTARY
SCHOOL AUDIENCES: 50, 89, 90, 93, 97, 141g, 147,
148, 162h, 167, 182B, 217, 254, 255, 272, 324, 449, 453, 455, 469, 508c, 523, 534, 537, 544, 545, 566, 653, 663, 664, 681,

TITLE INDEX

NOTE: Reference numbers are to entry numbers, not page numbers.
(◆ following a number indicates that the song is recorded)

My Love Is Gone to Sea, M30B

My Love Is in a Light Attire, 489e◆, 881g◆, 2046

My Love Is like the Red, Red Rose, 348 (see also 106, 213, 1002, 1003c, 1412, 2142, & 2171)

My Love Walks in Velvet, 2147

My Lovely Rose, 387

My Lover Is a Farmer Lad, 1634

My Luve Is like a Red, Red, Rose, 213 (see also 106, 348, 1002, 1003c, 1412, 2142, & 2171)

My Master Hath a Garden, 1242, 2090, 2109b◆

My Mind Is Not on Housework, 1835h◆

My Moon-Faced One, 1835k◆

My Mother Says That Babies Come in Bottles, 272a◆

My Name, 1109a

My Native Land, 1302◆

My Own Beloved, 351f

My Papa's Waltz, 637, 1883◆

My People, 1008i

My Phoenix, 1250f

My Phyllis, 1721a

My River Runs to Thee, 99

My Shadow, 148s, 1052

My Silks and Fine Array, 1576c

My Song, 1745b

My Soul Is an Enchanted Boat, 738

My Soul Is Dark, 620a

My Spirit Will Not Haunt the Mound, 638

My Sweet Old Etcetera, 2037, 2216d

My True Love, 1351D

My True Love (Hath/Has My Heart), 909, 1053, 1111◆, 1136c (see also 6b)

My Wars Are Laid Away in Books, 974aa◆

My Wife Is a Most Knowing Woman, 936

The Myrtle, 1523b◆

The Mysterious Cat, 1042e◆

The Mystery, 904◆

Mysticis Umbraculis, A11c

N

Nacht, A64e◆

Nacht liegt auf den fremden Wegen, A40C◆

Die Nachtblume, A30

Nachtlied, A45◆, A50d◆

Names, 1252

Nancy Hanks, 566, 1985B◆

Nantucket, 1884c◆

The Nantucket Songs, 1884◆

Naples, 2197b

Narzissus (auf ein Bild), A54f

The Nash Menagerie, 1133

Natural Selection, 1112◆

Nature, the Gentlest Mother, 508a◆

Nature's Holiday, 1071

Nature's Way, 1303◆

Near This Stone, 1763f

The Negro Speaks of Rivers, 320, 2075◆

A Net of Fireflies, 1740

Never More Will the Wind, 318e◆

Never Pain to Tell Thy Love, 1080a◆

Never Seek to Tell Thy Love, 355B

Nevertheless, 966a

New Born, 591

New Corn, 843g

New England Pastoral, 675

New Feet Within My Garden Go, 713a◆, 974e◆, 1730a, 1827c

New Hampshire, 2088a

The New Love and the Old, 1469

The New River, 1304◆

New Songs of Old Mother Goose, 1411

New Songs on 4 Romantic Poems, 1790

The News Came, 2239

Niagara, 2206d

Night, 196c, 214◆, 357, 478, 504A◆, 547a◆, 843c, 1154a◆, 1459, 1551, 1723, 1778◆, 2157c

A Night Battle, 1919a◆

Night Bird, 1708g◆

Night Coming Out of a Garden, 739

Night Crow, 1885◆

Night Flight, 2157b

The Night Has a Thousand Eyes, 1072

A Night in Naishapur, 1939

Night is my sister, 991b, 1574a

The Night Is of the Color, 356a

The Night Is Still, 967

A Night Myth, 1950b

Night of All Nights, 1802a◆

A Night of Love, 1698a

Night on Ways Unknown Has Fallen, 879C

Night Piece, 1833, 2014a

Night Practice, 318j◆

Night Scene, 276c

Night Song, 555b◆, 2116a

Night Song (Silent, Silent Night), 838

Night Song at Amalfi, 1834e, 2197d

Night Songs, 1154◆

A Night Thought, 1305◆

Night Wanderers, 168◆

The Night Was Wide, 974o◆

The Night Wind, 1579h

Nightbird Berates, 1830h◆

Night-Fall, 1673

(The) Nightingale, 196d, 1886◆

Nightingale Lane, 187

The Nightingale Unheard, 990b

Nine Songs, 1351

Nirvana, 188

No Coward Soul Is Mine, 1572o

No Dew upon the Grass, 100

No Leaf May Fall, 2078b

No Longer Mourn for Me When I Am Dead, 648g

No Matter–Now–Sweet, 140f

No More, 1306◆

No More I Will Thy Love Importune, 2214

No More Than Dust, 391d

No Voice to Scold, 451f◆

No Wonder Today All the Men Need Naps, 45c

No Worst, There Is None, 868g◆

Noah's Dove, M18

Noah's Prayer, 1397m

Nobody Knows This Little Rose, 761e◆ (see also 1926)

Noch ahnst du nichts vom Herbst des Haines, A60

Nocturn, 1981b

Nocturnal Visions, 1802◆

(A) Nocturne, 169◆, 559, 834, 1423, 1803◆, 2141

Nocturnes, 2116

Nod, 1100

Noise of Waters, 1739c◆

Non recidere, forbice, quel volto, solo nella memoria, A66r

Nonsense Rhymes and Pictures by Edward Lear, 1460

Noon, 1740f

Noon and Night, 1106

Noonday, 770a

Norah Acushla!, 1569

A Northern Romance, 1706

Not All the Knives of the Lamp Posts, 356d

Not Death, 2016c

Note Left on a Door-Step, 592

Nothing but a Plain Old Soldier, 937◆

Nothing Gold Can Stay, 28, 1605a

Notice, 2191c

November, 959, 2233

November Night, 37a, 1354b, 2031c, 2206a

Now, o now, in this brown land, 881gg◆

Now all the hungry broken men, 1813b

Now and Then, 319j

Now at Liberty, 156b

Now Close the Windows, 1595

Now for Cherry Bloom!, 298G

Now God Be Thanked for Mutability, 877f◆

Now Have I Fed and Eaten up the Rose, 182A◆

Now Hollow Fires, 793f

Now Is the Dreadful Midnight, 1866m◆

Now it is high time to awake out of sleep, 1753f

Now It Is Spring, 989a◆

Now Sleeps the Crimson Petal,

ABOUT THE AUTHORS

Judith E. Carman, mezzo-soprano, a native of Kentucky, holds B.M. and M.M. degrees in vocal performance from George Peabody College (Nashville, Tennessee) and a D.M.A. degree in vocal performance and pedagogy from the University of Iowa, where she studied voice with Herald I. Stark. Her doctoral dissertation in American music (*Twentieth-Century American Song Cycles: A Study in Circle Imagery*) led to the initial research for the first edition of *Art Song in the United States: An Annotated Bibliography,* of which she was editor. Dr. Carman has taught studio voice and related subjects at Shenandoah Conservatory of Music (Winchester, Virginia), Central Michigan University (Mt. Pleasant), Houston Baptist University (Houston, Texas), and Texas Southern University (Houston) and has maintained a private voice studio in Houston since 1979. She is a member of the National Association of Teachers of Singing and is the current Music Reviewer for the *NATS Journal of Singing.*

William K. Gaeddert, baritone, a native of Kansas, holds a B.M. degree from Bethany College (Kansas), an M.M. degree from Illinois Wesleyan University, and M.F.A. and Ph.D. degrees from the University of Iowa, where he studied voice with Herald I. Stark. He taught public school music in Kansas and Illinois and voice at Northwestern State University of Louisiana. Dr. Gaeddert has taught voice and related courses at Baker University in Kansas since 1974, retiring as professor of music in 2001. He did doctoral research on the songs of Robert Franz and has contributed numerous annotations to all three editions of *Art Song in the United States: An Annotated Bibliography,* serving as editor of the second edition (1987). He has appeared in recital and opera, as a soloist in major choral works, and has directed opera and musical theater productions. He is a member of the National Association of Teachers of Singing, and is active as a vocal adjudicator and clinician.

Gordon Myers, baritone, a student of Francis German, received the B.M. degree at Cornell College (Mt. Vernon, Iowa). He also holds an M.A. degree and an Ed.D. degree in music from Teachers College, Columbia University. After completing a fellowship in singing at the Juilliard Graduate School, he was baritone soloist with the New York Pro Musica, where he became interested in researching early American music. While completing his Ed.D. degree, Dr. Myers researched and prepared a lecture-recital called "Songs of Early Americans," which came under professional management and was subsequently recorded for Golden Crest. The recipient of two Rockefeller Foundation grants for further research in American music, he added about 500 titles to the catalog of eighteenth-century American vocal compositions. Dr. Myers is retired from the music faculty of Trenton State University in Trenton, New Jersey. Also a composer, his songs and choral works have been published by Bourne, Inc., Carl Fischer, Inc., Abingdon Press, Leyerle Publications, and Eastlane Music Corp. His recent book, *I Sing, Therefore I Am,* was published in 1997.

Rita M. Resch, soprano, was born in North Dakota and earned a B.S.Ed. degree in music education from Minot State University. She also holds an M.M. degree in music literature from the Eastman School of Music, an M.A. degree in English literature from the University of North Dakota, an M.F.A. degree in vocal performance (Herald I. Stark, major professor) and a D.M.A. degree in piano chamber music and accompanying (Kenneth Amada and John Sims, major professors) from the University of Iowa. She has taught at Fontbonne College (St. Louis), University of Wisconsin–Stevens Point, and is currently professor of music at Central Missouri State University (Warrensburg). Dr. Resch has been active as a recitalist, oratorio soloist, and accompanist. She is a member of the National Association of Teachers of Singing, Music Teachers National Association, and Sigma Alpha Iota. Dr. Resch is a contributing author to all three editions of *Art Song in the United States: An Annotated Bibliography.*